SHAKESPEARE
IN THE THEATRE
1701–1800

LONDON
1751–1800

SHAKESPEARE IN THE THEATRE
1701-1800

A RECORD OF PERFORMANCES
IN LONDON
1751–1800

By
Charles Beecher Hogan

OXFORD
AT THE CLARENDON PRESS
1957

Oxford University Press, Amen House, London E.C.4

GLASGOW NEW YORK TORONTO MELBOURNE WELLINGTON
BOMBAY CALCUTTA MADRAS KARACHI
CAPE TOWN IBADAN NAIROBI ACCRA SINGAPORE

PRINTED IN GREAT BRITAIN

PREFACE

THIS book completes the recording of the performances in London—somewhat over 7,000 in number—of Shakespeare's plays from 1701 to 1800.

For the last fifty years of the eighteenth century the history of the London stage is almost completely documented. For the first fifty years the same thing cannot be said; scarcely any of the actual playhouse bills for that period are now in existence. In tabulating the performances from 1701 to 1750 I was therefore obliged to turn to the advertisements printed in various newspapers. But the material in the present volume (the arrangement of which follows throughout that of its predecessor) is based not only on newspapers but on a virtually complete, day-by-day run of the playbills used in the theatres themselves.

C. B. H.

Jonathan Edwards College
Yale University

ACKNOWLEDGEMENTS

ENCOURAGEMENT and assistance from many sources have been offered me in extraordinary measure. May I in particular extend my thanks to Miss K. M. D. Barker, Mr A. Stuart Brown, Mr D. M. Davin, Mr and Mrs Ifan Kyrle Fletcher, Mr R. Nash, Mr Charles Nolte, Mr C. V. Pilkington, Miss S. Rosenfeld, Dr G. W. Stone, Dr William VanLennep, Mr C. B. Young. In my first volume I acknowledged my great indebtedness to the libraries in which I have pursued the better part of my research: the Birmingham Public Library, the Boston Public Library, the British Museum, the Folger Shakespeare Library, Harvard, the Huntington Library, the Victoria and Albert Museum, and Yale. This acknowledgement I am now happy to repeat. I am once again profoundly grateful to Mr and Mrs Arthur Cook for their loyal and reliable help in solving many difficulties. I wish especially to thank Sir St. Vincent Troubridge for offering me the freedom of the Garrick Club and its library, Miss Helen Thacker for her painstaking researches on my behalf in the Public Record Office and at Somerset House, and Mr Arthur Hudd, of the staff of the British Museum, who with infinite skill and patience has investigated and re-checked for me details by, literally, the hundreds.

My first volume was, I observed therein, as much my wife's as it was my own. This volume, many times over, is equally hers. I do not know why, save for her affectionate modesty, her name does not appear on the title-page.

CONTENTS

CUE-TITLES AND ABBREVIATIONS	xi
PART I. CALENDAR OF PERFORMANCES	1
PART II. THE PLAYS	109
APPENDIX A. SOURCES	690
APPENDIX B. SHAKESPEARE'S POPULARITY IN THE THEATRE, 1751–1800 [AND 1701–1800]	715
APPENDIX C. ORDER OF POPULARITY OF SHAKESPEARE'S PLAYS, 1751–1800 [AND 1701–1800]	716
APPENDIX D. LONDON THEATRES IN USE BETWEEN 1751 AND 1800	720
INDEX I. ACTORS	725
INDEX II. CHARACTERS	773

CUE-TITLES AND ABBREVIATIONS

BM	British Museum
BPL	Boston (Massachusetts) Public Library
BT	Benefit, *or* for the benefit of
CG	Covent Garden Theatre
CH	China Hall Theatre, Rotherhithe
C–H	Manuscript diary kept by Richard Cross and William Hopkins, successively prompters at Drury Lane (in Folger Shakespeare Library)
DA	*The Daily Advertiser* (newspaper)
DAB	*Dictionary of American Biography*
Dibdin	James C. Dibdin, *The Annals of the Edinburgh Stage*, Edinburgh, 1888
DL	Drury Lane Theatre
DL Account-Book	Manuscript account-books of Drury Lane, 1766–7, 1771–1800 (in Folger Shakespeare Library)
DNB	*Dictionary of National Biography*
DWR	*The Diary, or Woodfall's Register* (newspaper)
Dyce	Dyce Collection, Victoria and Albert Museum
Egerton	MSS 2273–99 (in British Museum)
EM	*The European Magazine*
FSL	Folger Shakespeare Library, Washington
GA	*The General Advertiser* (newspaper)
Gaz	*The Gazetteer* (newspaper)
GEC	Gabrielle Enthoven Collection, Victoria and Albert Museum
Genest	John Genest, *Some Account of the English Stage*, Bath, 1832
Gilliland	Thomas Gilliland, *The Dramatic Mirror*, London, 1808
GM	*The Gentleman's Magazine*
Grove	*Grove's Dictionary of Music and Musicians*, New York, 1935
Harris	Harris Collection (in British Museum)
Hay	Haymarket Theatre
H–B	Beaufoy Collection of Haymarket playbills, 1778–1800 (in Harvard Theatre Collection)
HTC	Harvard Theatre Collection (in Houghton Library, Harvard University)
JPK	Playbills collected by John Philip Kemble (Drury Lane, 1751–6, 1758–82 in Huntington Library, 1782–1800 in Harvard Theatre Collection; Covent Garden, 1758–1800 in Huntington Library)
Kemble Mem.	John Philip Kemble, *Memoranda* (Add. MSS 31,972–5, in British Museum)
LC	*The London Chronicle* (newspaper)
Lysons Coll.	Daniel Lysons, *Theatrical Collectanea* (Scrapbooks, 5 vols., in Folger Shakespeare Library)
MacMillan	Dougald MacMillan, *Drury Lane Calendar 1747–1776*, Oxford, 1938

CUE-TITLES AND ABBREVIATIONS

MC	*The Morning Chronicle* (newspaper)
MM	*The Monthly Mirror* (magazine)
MP	*The Morning Post* (newspaper)
Not. Dram.	Joseph Reed, *Notitia Dramatica* (Add. MSS 25,391–2, in British Museum)
O	*The Oracle* (newspaper)
Odell	George C. D. Odell, *Shakespeare from Betterton to Irving*, New York, 1920
PA	*The Public Advertiser* (newspaper)
Pb	The playbill for the performance in question. The most comprehensive collection of Drury Lane and Covent Garden playbills is JPK, q.v.; of Haymarket playbills H–B, q.v.
Powell	MS annotations by William Powell, Drury Lane prompter, in Vols. 4 and 5 of Drury Lane playbills, in British Museum
Reed	Joseph Reed, *Diaries 1762–1804*, ed. Claude E. Jones, Berkeley (California), 1946
TB	*The True Briton* (newspaper)
TM	*The Thespian Magazine*
W	*The World* (newspaper)
WEP	*The Whitehall Evening Post* (newspaper)

PART I

CALENDAR OF PERFORMANCES

THE following tabulation is arranged in the same fashion as in my first volume: by the calendar year rather than by the theatrical season. The only change is the addition to each date of the day of the week. I have, as before, also listed the benefits allowed to actors and others,[1] and, in so far as they are available, the receipts of each performance.

In the second half of the eighteenth century three Theatres Royal were in use. They were Drury Lane and Covent Garden, whose seasons extended from September to, generally, May; and the Haymarket, which was open from May to September and, by permission of the Lord Chamberlain, on occasional nights (usually benefits) in the winter. All three enjoyed the protection of a patent from the Crown. They gave six performances a week, except on Christmas Eve, Christmas Day, January 30 (the anniversary of the martyrdom of Charles I), Wednesdays and Fridays in Lent,[2] Holy Week, and Whitsun Eve. The theatres were also closed during periods of mourning for members of the royal family, and on fast days and thanksgiving days. The average number of acting nights a season was, for Drury Lane and Covent Garden, about 190, and for the Haymarket, about 100. A few unlicensed theatres were, in addition, opened from time to time, but as commercial ventures they were seldom profitable.

Each theatre had its own company of actors, who used a repertory system of performing, in principle, a different play each night, the play proper being followed (and occasionally preceded) by a farce or pantomime.[3] New plays or revivals were sometimes acted on consecutive nights, but long runs, because of the size of the theatre-going public, were not practicable.

[1] In the Calendar the word 'same' applies only to a performance of the same play, not to a repetition of a benefit. That is, 'Apr. 10 Hamlet BT. Smith; Apr. 13 same', means that Hamlet was performed twice, but that Smith had only one benefit, on Apr. 10.

[2] These Wednesdays and Fridays were customarily utilized for the performance of oratorios and sacred music.

[3] It was usual, on the first few nights of performing a new play, to omit the after-piece. Several of Shakespeare's plays were altered into after-pieces of one, two, or three acts. They are as follows: *Catharine and Petruchio* and *The Cobler of Preston* (both from *The Taming of the Shrew*), *A Fairy Tale* and *Pyramus and Thisbe* (both from *A Midsummer-Night's Dream*), *Florizel and Perdita*, by Morgan, and *The Sheep Shearing*, by Colman (both from *The Winter's Tale*), and *The Humourists* (from *Henry IV, Part II*).

1751

1751 DRURY LANE

			£	s.	d.
Th Jan. 3	As You Like It		140	0	0
M 7	Twelfth Night		120	0	0
F 11	same		120	0	0
Th 31	Romeo and Juliet		200	0	0
W Feb. 13	same		180	0	0
S 16	Richard III *BT. Garrick*		190	0	0

    The recipient of the BT. is named in C-H, but not in GA.

| Th Mar. 7 | Othello | receipts omitted |

    A private play, acted by amateurs. See p. 498.

S 16	Romeo and Juliet *BT. Woodward*	300	0	0
Th Apr. 11	Much Ado about Nothing *BT. Mad. Auretti*	230	0	0
Tu 23	Hamlet *BT. Lee*	130	0	0
Th 25	Much Ado about Nothing *BT. Cross, prompter, and Mrs Cross*	164	0	0
Tu May 7	Richard III	220	0	0
F 17	Hamlet	200	0	0
Tu Sept. 10	The Merchant of Venice	120	0	0
W 18	Hamlet	210	0	0
F 20	Romeo and Juliet	190	0	0
Th 26	Richard III	210	0	0
F 27	same	100	0	0
S 28	Romeo and Juliet	180	0	0
Tu Oct. 1	Richard III	180	0	0
S 5	same	100	0	0
F 11	Much Ado about Nothing	120	0	0
S 19	Romeo and Juliet	140	0	0
M 21	Hamlet	130	0	0
F Nov. 1	Much Ado about Nothing	150	0	0
S 2	King Lear	200	0	0
M 18	Romeo and Juliet	160	0	0
Tu 26	Richard III	210	0	0
W 27	Much Ado about Nothing	200	0	0
M Dec. 16	Romeo and Juliet	170	0	0

COVENT GARDEN

W Jan. 2	The Merchant of Venice
F 11	Henry IV, Part I
Tu 15	Macbeth *BT. Monet*
Th 17	Romeo and Juliet
F 18	Henry IV, Part II
F 25	The Merry Wives of Windsor
S 26	Romeo and Juliet
F Feb. 8	Henry IV, Part I
S 9	Othello
M 11	Romeo and Juliet

1751

1751 COVENT GARDEN (*cont.*)

Tu	Feb. 19	Julius Caesar
Th	21	Henry IV, Part I
S	23	King John
M	25	same
Th	28	same
S	Mar. 2	same
M	4	same
Th	7	Julius Caesar
S	9	Henry IV, Part I
M	11	Othello *BT. Quin*
Tu	12	Henry IV, Part II
M	18	Romeo and Juliet *BT. Barry*
Tu	Apr. 16	Henry VIII *BT. Arthur and Mrs Vincent*
F	19	Othello *BT. Ridout and Barrington*
S	20	Hamlet *BT. Lowe*
Th	25	King John *BT. Bencraft and Miss Haughton*
Tu	30	Romeo and Juliet
W	May 1	Julius Caesar *BT. Lalauze*
M	6	The Merchant of Venice *BT. Anderson, Miles, and Madam Gondou*
F	17	Romeo and Juliet
Tu	21	same
M	Oct. 7	same
W	9	Othello
F	11	Hamlet
Tu	15	Romeo and Juliet
W	23	same
S	Nov. 2	same
Tu	12	same
S	16	The Merchant of Venice
W	20	same
F	22	Richard III
S	23	The Merchant of Venice
Tu	Dec. 3	same
M	9	Pyramus and Thisbe
S	21	Romeo and Juliet
Th	26	Richard III
M	30	The Merchant of Venice
Tu	31	Romeo and Juliet

HAYMARKET

?   Henry IV, Part I

The actual date of this performance has not as yet come to light. According to DA, Dec. 10, *Othello* was to be performed on Dec. 28, q.v., by the same gentlemen who acted *Henry IV, Part I* at the Haymarket 'last winter'.

S   Dec. 28   Othello *BT. a brother [Mason] under misfortunes*

1751–1752

1751 NEW WELLS, GOODMAN'S FIELDS

Tu Aug. 6   Richard III *BT. Goodfellow*
W   7   same *BT. Goodfellow*
Th Sept. 5   Othello *BT. Mrs Hallam*

BOWLING GREEN, SOUTHWARK

W Sept. 18   Hamlet *BT. Phillips*

1752 DRURY LANE

		£	s.	d.
M Jan. 6	Twelfth Night	110	0	0
W 8	Much Ado about Nothing	180	0	0
W 15	Richard III	150	0	0
F 17	King Lear	180	0	0
Tu 21	The Merchant of Venice *BT. Worsdale*	230	0	0
W 22	Twelfth Night	110	0	0
Th 23	Much Ado about Nothing	160	0	0
M 27	Romeo and Juliet	190	0	0
Tu 28	Macbeth	150	0	0
W 29	same	110	0	0
M Feb. 3	Richard III *BT. Garrick*	210	0	0

The recipient of the BT. is named in C-H, but not in Pb or GA.

S 8	Macbeth	200	0	0
Tu 11	[Richard III]			

Bill in GA, and listed by Genest (iv. 345), but not acted. JPK has, '*Richard* the Third (*On Account of the Indisposition of a* Principal Performer) Is oblig'd to be Chang'd to The Conscious Lovers.'

S 29	Romeo and Juliet	receipts omitted		
Tu Mar. 3	King Lear	190	0	0
Th 12	Othello *BT. Mossop*	150	0	0
Th 19	Much Ado about Nothing *BT. Mrs Ward*	130	0	0
M 30	Macbeth	110	0	0
Tu 31	Romeo and Juliet *BT. Ross*	200	0	0
W Apr. 1	Richard III *BT. Blakes*	110	0	0
M 6	King Lear *BT. Lee*	180	0	0
Tu 7	Hamlet	200	0	0
Th 9	Much Ado about Nothing *BT. Mrs Mills*	128	0	0
F 10	Henry VIII *BT. Sowdon*	230	0	0
Tu 14	Othello *BT. Winstone and Burton*	89	0	0
Tu 21	As You Like It *BT. Scrase, Costollo, and Wilder*	160	0	0
F 24	Henry VIII *BT. Simson and Raftor*	173	0	0
W 29	same *BT. Jones*	120	0	0
S May 2	The Merchant of Venice *BT. Foley, Tomlinson, and Burk*	170	0	0
Th 7	Romeo and Juliet	180	0	0

1752 DRURY LANE (cont.)

			£	s.	d.
Tu Sept. 19	The Merchant of Venice		55	0	0
Tu 26	Henry VIII		140	0	0
S 30	Richard III		70	0	0
M Oct. 9	Henry VIII		110	0	0
F 13	Romeo and Juliet		160	0	0
M 16	Macbeth		100	0	0
Th 19	Much Ado about Nothing		140	0	0
F 20	Romeo and Juliet		170	0	0
M 23	Hamlet		160	0	0
Tu 24	Henry VIII		100	0	0
W 25	Romeo and Juliet		150	0	0
M 30	Macbeth		150	0	0
F Nov. 3	King Lear		170	0	0
Th 9	The Merchant of Venice		100	0	0
F 10	Romeo and Juliet		140	0	0
M 13	Much Ado about Nothing		receipts omitted		
F 17	Hamlet		170	0	0
S 18	Macbeth		100	0	0
M 20	King Lear		180	0	0
F 24	Richard III		200	0	0
S 25	As You Like It		100	0	0
S Dec. 2	Henry VIII		150	0	0
M 4	Macbeth		140	0	0
Th 14	As You Like It		120	0	0
W 20	Hamlet *BT. Goodfellow*		140	0	0
Tu 26	As You Like It		200	0	0

COVENT GARDEN

S Jan. 4 Hamlet
Tu 7 Othello
W 15 Romeo and Juliet
Th 23 same
F 31 same
S Feb. 1 Othello
F 7 The Merchant of Venice
S 8 Romeo and Juliet
M 10 same
M Mar. 16 Henry IV, Part I *BT. Ryan*
Tu 17 Macbeth *BT. Mrs Cibber*
M 30 Henry V *BT. Bencraft and Mrs Vincent*
F Apr. 10 Hamlet *BT. Ridout*
F 17 Othello *BT. Arne*
S 18 Richard III *BT. Howard*

    A clipping from an unnamed newspaper dated Apr. 17, in the Garrick Club, states that this performance would be for the benefit of Mme Camargo. No such notice appears anywhere in Pb or in PA.

5

1752–1753

1752 COVENT GARDEN (cont.)

M Apr. 20	Hamlet *BT. the widow of the late Mr Lampe, and Miss [Esther] Young*	
W 29	The Merchant of Venice *BT. Marten and Stoppelaer*	
Tu May 5	Richard III *BT. Collins, Paddick, Ricard, and Miss Ferguson*	
M 11	Romeo and Juliet	
F Sept. 22	Richard III	
F Oct. 6	The Merchant of Venice	
M 16	King Lear	
Tu 17	same	
S 21	Romeo and Juliet	
Tu 24	Othello	
W 25	Romeo and Juliet	
M 30	Macbeth	
M Nov. 13	Romeo and Juliet	
S 18	same	
Tu 21	The Merchant of Venice	
F 24	Romeo and Juliet	
Tu 28	Hamlet	
F Dec. 1	Othello	
W 6	Romeo and Juliet	
M 18	same	

NEW WELLS, GOODMAN'S FIELDS

Th Nov. 16 Othello *BT. [W.] Hallam*
Th 23 Richard III *BT. [W.] Hallam*

1753 DRURY LANE

		£	s.	d.
Th Jan. 4	Much Ado about Nothing	200	0	0
M 8	Twelfth Night	170	0	0
Th 11	The Merchant of Venice	160	0	0
W 17	Much Ado about Nothing	200	0	0
Th 18	Richard III	130	0	0
W 24	Romeo and Juliet	200	0	0
S 27	Twelfth Night	160	0	0
M Feb. 5	Henry VIII	180	0	0
F 23	Richard III	50	0	0
W 28	Henry VIII	140	0	0
Tu Mar. 13	As You Like It	130	0	0
M 26	Much Ado about Nothing *BT. Devisse and Mme Auguste*	200	0	0
Th 29	Romeo and Juliet *BT. Havard*	230	0	0
M Apr. 2	Othello *BT. Mossop*	200	0	0
S 7	Richard III	220	0	0
M 23	As You Like It	180	0	0
Tu May 1	Hamlet *BT. Lacey and Wilder*	170	0	0
W 2	Henry VIII *BT. Winstone and Burton*	180	0	0

1753

1753 DRURY LANE (cont.)

				£	s.	d.
M	May	7	Macbeth *BT. Mr, Mrs, and Master Simson*	170	0	0
	Tu	8	Romeo and Juliet	110	0	0
	W	9	Richard III *BT. Ackman, W. Vaughan, and Dickinson*	230	0	0
	F	18	The Merry Wives of Windsor *BT. Varney, house-keeper*	210	0	0
	W	23	[King Lear]			

Bill in PA, and in MacMillan (34), but not acted. C-H has, 'King Lear . . . given out for Wed. 23 & bills put up, but not play'd on Account of Mr Havard's illness.' No substitute play is mentioned; the theatre was, presumably, dark.

				£	s.	d.
	Th Sept.	13	As You Like It	60	0	0
	Tu	25	Richard III	120	0	0
	Th	27	Much Ado about Nothing	150	0	0
W	Oct.	3	Macbeth	60	0	0
	Th	4	Romeo and Juliet	190	0	0
	F	5	same	150	0	0
	S	6	Henry VIII	120	0	0
	Th	11	same	50	0	0
	Tu	16	Hamlet	190	0	0
	F	19	Romeo and Juliet	120	0	0
	F	26	Richard III	80	0	0
F	Nov.	9	Henry VIII	120	0	0
	Tu	13	Macbeth	170	0	0
	Th	15	King Lear	200	0	0
	Tu	20	As You Like It	80	0	0
	W	21	Much Ado about Nothing	receipts omitted		
	Th	22	King Lear	200	0	0
	W	28	Richard III	210	0	0
M	Dec.	17	Henry VIII	70	0	0
	Tu	18	Richard III	150	0	0

COVENT GARDEN

M	Jan.	1	Romeo and Juliet
	Th	4	The Merchant of Venice
	S	6	Richard III *BT. Joseph Lowe, citizen of London, under misfortunes*
	F	26	The Merchant of Venice
M	Feb.	5	Romeo and Juliet
M	Mar.	19	Henry IV, Part I *BT. Ryan*
M	Apr.	2	Hamlet *BT. Arthur*
	Th	5	Othello *BT. [T.] Lowe*
	M	23	The Merchant of Venice *BT. Mr and Mrs Barrington*
F	May	4	Romeo and Juliet
	M	7	Julius Caesar *BT. White, treasurer*

Genest (iv. 374) erroneously has May 6, a Sunday.

| | M | 14 | same *BT. Cushing, Redman, and Madem. De Henny* |

1753–1754

1753 COVENT GARDEN (cont.)

F May 18   Richard III *BT. Lawrence, [M.] Vaughan, and Plummer, box-keepers*
    S 19   Romeo and Juliet
    S 26   same

> Genest (iv. 374) also lists a performance of *Romeo and Juliet* on May 24, on which night the theatre was dark.

F Sept. 21   Richard III
W Oct. 10   Romeo and Juliet
    Th 11   same
    F 12   same
    S 13   same
    M 15   same
    Th 18   same
    M 22   As You Like It
    Tu 23   Romeo and Juliet
    Th 25   same
    S 27   Othello
    Tu 30   Hamlet
S Nov. 3   Romeo and Juliet
    S 24   same
M Dec. 3   same
    S 8   same
    Tu 18   same

PHILLIPS'S BOOTH, BOWLING GREEN, SOUTHWARK

Th Sept. 27   Richard III *BT. a gentlewoman in distress*

1754 DRURY LANE

				£	s.	d.
M	Jan. 7	Twelfth Night		110	0	0
W	9	Richard III		130	0	0
S	12	Much Ado about Nothing		190	0	0
M	14	Macbeth		120	0	0
Tu	15	Romeo and Juliet		180	0	0
Th	17	Hamlet		200	0	0
W	23	King John		180	0	0
Th	24	Twelfth Night		100	0	0
S	26	King John		200	0	0
M	28	same		200	0	0
Th	31	same		200	0	0
S	Feb. 2	same		180	0	0
W	6	same		180	0	0
F	8	same		150	0	0
M	11	Romeo and Juliet		170	0	0
Tu	12	Twelfth Night		80	0	0
M	18	King Lear *BT. Garrick*		230	0	0

> The recipient of the BT. is named in C-H, but not in Pb or PA.

1754

1754 DRURY LANE (cont.)

			£	s.	d.
W	Feb. 20	The Merry Wives of Windsor	140	0	0
S	Mar. 16	King John *BT. Mrs Cibber*	240	0	0
	M 18	Catharine and Petruchio *BT. Mrs Pritchard*	298	0	0
	S 30	Much Ado about Nothing *BT. Yates*	260	0	0
M	Apr. 15	Henry VIII	180	0	0
	Tu 16	The Merchant of Venice *BT. Blakes*	170	0	0
	Tu 30	Much Ado about Nothing *BT. Pritchard, treasurer*	160	0	0
Th	May 2	Richard III *BT. Burton and Miss Minors*	160	0	0
	M 6	Macbeth *BT. Lacey and Miss Thomas*	130	0	0
	Th 9	Henry VIII *BT. Scrase, [H.] Vaughan, and the sub-treasurer [Wood]*	202	0	0
	F 10	The Merry Wives of Windsor *BT. Mr, Mrs, and Master Simson*	206	0	0
	W 15	The Merchant of Venice *BT. Roger, Shawford, and the widow Reinhold*	130	0	0
Tu	July 2	The Humourists *BT. Cibber*	206	0	0
Tu	Sept. 24	Macbeth	110	0	0
Tu	Oct. 1	Richard III	100	0	0
	Th 10	Henry VIII	120	0	0
	F 11	Romeo and Juliet	170	0	0
	W 16	Hamlet	180	0	0
	Th 24	Richard III	200	0	0
	S 26	Romeo and Juliet	180	0	0
F	Nov. 1	Henry VIII	80	0	0
	S 2	Macbeth	200	0	0
	M 11	Coriolanus	70	0	0
	W 13	same	50	0	0
	F 15	same	70	0	0
	M 18	same	120	0	0
	W 20	same	120	0	0
	F 22	Much Ado about Nothing *BT. Mrs James*	200	0	0

The recipient of the BT. is named in C-H, but not in Pb or PA.

S 23	Coriolanus	160	0	0
W 27	same	90	0	0
F 29	same	80	0	0
W Dec. 11	Much Ado about Nothing	180	0	0
F 13	The Merry Wives of Windsor	120	0	0
S 28	Richard III	100	0	0

COVENT GARDEN

S	Jan. 5	Romeo and Juliet
	Tu 8	Othello
Tu	Mar. 5	Hamlet
	S 9	Julius Caesar

1754

1754 COVENT GARDEN (cont.)

Tu Mar. 12 Julius Caesar
S 16 same
M 18 Romeo and Juliet *BT. Miss Nossiter*
M 25 Florizel and Perdita *BT. Barry*
    Announced as *The Sheep-Shearing.*

M Apr. 1 Othello *BT. Ryan*
Tu 2 Richard III *BT. Dyer*
S 6 The Merchant of Venice *BT. Arthur*
M 15 Romeo and Juliet
W 17 Henry V *BT. Shuter*
F 19 Hamlet *BT. Bencraft and Miss Kennedy*
W 24 Florizel and Perdita *BT. Mrs Elmy*
    Announced as *The Sheep-Shearing.*

Th May 2 Pyramus and Thisbe *BT. Howard*
Tu 7 The Merry Wives of Windsor *BT. Mr and Mrs Dunstall*
W 8 Henry V *BT. Stevens, Mrs Chambers, and Mrs Pitt*
Th 9 The Merchant of Venice *BT. Marten, Stoppelaer, and Mrs Gondou*
Tu 21 As You Like It *BT. Lawrence and [M.] Vaughan, box-keepers*
W 22 Romeo and Juliet
F Sept. 20 Richard III
M 23 The Merchant of Venice
W 25 As You Like It
F Oct. 18 Othello
S 19 same
M 21 same
Th 24 Hamlet
S 26 Richard III
W 30 The Merchant of Venice
S Nov. 2 Hamlet
Th 14 Richard III
F 15 Othello
S 16 Macbeth
W 20 Romeo and Juliet
Th Dec. 5 Othello
Tu 10 Coriolanus
W 11 same
Th 12 same
S 14 same
W 18 same
S 21 same
Th 26 Romeo and Juliet
F 27 same
S 28 Richard III

1754-1755

1754 PHILLIPS'S BOOTH, BOWLING GREEN, SOUTHWARK

- W Sept. 18 The Jew of Venice
- Th 19 same
- F 20 same
- S 21 same
- M 23 same
- Tu 24 same

1755 DRURY LANE

			£	s.	d.
M Jan. 6	Twelfth Night		180	0	0
Th 9	Much Ado about Nothing		200	0	0
F 10	The Merry Wives of Windsor		170	0	0
F 24	Much Ado about Nothing		170	0	0
M Feb. 3	The Fairies		200	0	0
W 5	Twelfth Night		100	0	0
Th 6	The Fairies		140	0	0
F 7	Romeo and Juliet		140	0	0
M 10	The Fairies *BT. the composer* [*John Christopher Smith*]		170	0	0
Th 13	same		180	0	0
M 17	same		160	0	0
Tu 18	As You Like It		130	0	0
Th 20	The Fairies *BT. the composer*		170	0	0
S 22	Measure for Measure		150	0	0
M 24	The Fairies		160	0	0
Th 27	Measure for Measure		160	0	0
M Mar. 3	The Fairies		140	0	0
Tu 4	King Lear *BT. Garrick*		220	0	0

The recipient of the BT. is named in C-H, but not in Pb or PA.

Th 6	Macbeth	210	0	0
M 10	The Fairies *BT. the composer*	160	0	0

The recipient of the BT. is named in C-H, but not in Pb or PA.

Tu 11	King Lear	200	0	0
Th 20	Hamlet *BT. Woodward*	300	0	0
M 31	Henry VIII	170	0	0
W Apr. 9	Measure for Measure	110	0	0
S 12	Much Ado about Nothing *BT. Miss Haughton*	100	0	0
S 19	Henry VIII *BT. Raftor and Miss [I.] Young*	80	0	0

PA lists Raftor as one of the recipients of the BT.; Pb lists only Miss Young.

Tu 22	Coriolanus *BT. Leviez, ballet-master*	120	0	0
S 26	Richard III *BT. Scrase and Miss Thomas*	130	0	0
Th May 1	Macbeth *BT. Saunderson*	140	0	0
F 2	The Merry Wives of Windsor *BT. Ackman and Dickinson*	receipts omitted		

11

1755

1755 DRURY LANE (*cont.*)

		£	s.	d.
Tu May 13	As You Like It *BT. Foley and Veal*	220	0	0
M 19	Henry VIII	40	0	0
F 23	King Lear	180	0	0
Th Sept. 18	As You Like It	80	0	0
S Oct. 4	Hamlet	180	0	0
W 8	Romeo and Juliet	180	0	0
F 10	Macbeth	150	0	0
Th 23	Richard III	180	0	0
W 29	The Fairies	140	0	0
S Nov. 1	Much Ado about Nothing	180	0	0
F 7	The Fairies	100	0	0
Tu 11	Romeo and Juliet	200	0	0
F 14	As You Like It	140	0	0
S 15	Much Ado about Nothing	receipts omitted		
Tu Dec. 2	Hamlet	180	0	0
Th 4	King Lear	210	0	0
M 8	Richard III	120	0	0
Tu 9	King Lear	200	0	0
Th 18	Henry VIII	120	0	0
F 26	same	150	0	0

COVENT GARDEN

Th Jan. 16 Hamlet
F 24 Othello
M 27 Coriolanus
Tu 28 Julius Caesar
Tu Feb. 18 Henry V
M Mar. 3 Hamlet
M 31 Coriolanus
Th Apr. 3 Romeo and Juliet

    Genest (iv. 422) says that this was probably Smith's BT.; it was, however, nobody's. This season Smith took no BT. at all.

F 4 Hamlet *BT. Murphy*
Th 10 Henry IV, Part I *BT. Shuter*
F 11 Romeo and Juliet *BT. Dyer*
S 12 Henry IV, Part I
Th 17 Richard III *BT. Mrs Elmy*
F 25 Hamlet *BT. Bencraft and Mrs Baker*
F May 2 The Merchant of Venice *BT. Miles and Mrs Pitt*
S 3 Henry IV, Part I *BT. Mr and Mrs Dunstall*
M 5 Macbeth *BT. White, treasurer*
Th 8 Othello *BT. Legg and Crudge, house-keeper*
W 14 Romeo and Juliet
Th 15 The Merry Wives of Windsor *BT. Evans, box-keeper*
W Oct. 8 The Merchant of Venice
Tu 14 Henry IV, Part I
M 20 Romeo and Juliet

1755–1756

1755 COVENT GARDEN (*cont.*)

- W Oct. 22 The Merry Wives of Windsor
- W 29 Romeo and Juliet
- W Nov. 5 same
- Th 6 Henry IV, Part I
- Tu 11 The Merry Wives of Windsor
- W 12 Hamlet
- M 17 Macbeth
- M Dec. 1 Henry IV, Part I
- Tu 2 The Merchant of Venice
- W 3 Henry V
- S 6 Romeo and Juliet
- M 8 Macbeth
- W 17 The Merry Wives of Windsor
- F 26 Macbeth
- S 27 Romeo and Juliet
- M 29 same
- Tu 30 same
- W 31 The Merry Wives of Windsor

HAYMARKET

- M Sept. 1 Othello
- W 3 same
- S 6 same *BT. Hackett*

BOWLING GREEN, SOUTHWARK

- M Jan. 13 Romeo and Juliet
- Th 16 same
- M 20 Hamlet *BT. Phillips*

1756 DRURY LANE

			£	s.	d.
M	Jan. 5	Much Ado about Nothing	220	0	0
	Tu 6	Henry VIII	70	0	0
	W 21	The Winter's Tale and *Catharine and Petruchio*	180	0	0
	F 23	same and same	160	0	0
	S 24	same and same	170	0	0
	M 26	same and same	180	0	0
	Tu 27	same and same	180	0	0
	W 28	same and same	170	0	0
	Th 29	same and same	200	0	0

1756 DRURY LANE (cont.)

			£	s.	d.
S Jan. 31	The Winter's Tale *and* Catharine and Petruchio		180	0	0
Tu Feb. 3	same *and* same		150	0	0
W 4	same *and* same		140	0	0
W 11	The Tempest		180	0	0
Th 12	King Lear		210	0	0

Genest (iv. 452) erroneously has Feb. 13.

F 13	The Tempest		140	0	0
S 14	Hamlet *BT. Garrick*		212	0	0

The recipient of the BT. is named in C-H, but not in Pb or PA.

W 18	The Tempest		100	0	0
F 20	same		90	0	0
M 23	Much Ado about Nothing *and* Catharine and Petruchio		130	0	0
Tu 24	All's Well that Ends Well		130	0	0
W 25	Richard III		210	0	0
Th 26	The Tempest		100	0	0
Tu Mar. 2	All's Well that Ends Well		120	0	0
M 8	same		120	0	0
S 13	The Winter's Tale *and* Catharine and Petruchio		170	0	0
Tu 16	The Tempest		130	0	0
S 20	The Winter's Tale		190	0	0
Th Apr. 1	Romeo and Juliet *BT. Havard*		265	0	0
Tu 6	Catharine and Petruchio *BT. Ross*		180	0	0
S 10	Much Ado about Nothing *BT. Yates*		220	0	0
Tu 20	Hamlet *BT. Holland*		270	0	0
W 28	The Winter's Tale *and* Catharine and Petruchio *BT. Pritchard, treasurer*		190	0	0
Tu May 4	Henry VIII *BT. Wood, sub-treasurer*		210	0	0
M 10	The Merry Wives of Windsor *BT. Berrisford, [R.] Palmer [Sr.], Broad, and Master Moore*		260	0	0
Tu 11	Henry VIII *BT. Saunderson, machinist*		140	0	0
W 19	King Lear		190	0	0
Th 20	Hamlet *BT. Raftor, Morris, Lebrun, and Goodwin*		140	0	0
Th 27	same		190	0	0
F 28	Much Ado about Nothing		180	0	0
Tu Sept. 21	Richard III		120	0	0
S 25	Henry VIII		140	0	0
Th 30	Hamlet		210	0	0
S Oct. 9	Romeo and Juliet		226	0	0
M 11	same		200	0	0

1756

1756 DRURY LANE (cont.)   £   s.   d.

Tu	Oct. 12	Romeo and Juliet	170	0	0
F	15	same	180	0	0
S	16	Macbeth	100	0	0
Tu	19	Much Ado about Nothing	100	0	0
W	20	Romeo and Juliet	170	0	0
F	22	Richard III	140	0	0
Tu	26	Romeo and Juliet	170	0	0
Th	28	King Lear	200	0	0
S	30	same	200	0	0
W	Nov. 3	Hamlet	170	0	0
Tu	9	Henry VIII	130	0	0
Tu	16	Romeo and Juliet	180	0	0
F	19	Measure for Measure	120	0	0
M	29	Much Ado about Nothing	200	0	0
Tu	30	same	170	0	0
S	Dec. 4	same	200	0	0
M	13	Hamlet	190	0	0
S	18	Much Ado about Nothing *BT. the General Lying-in Hospital for married and unmarried women, in Duke-street, Grosvenor-square*	266	0	0
Th	30	Measure for Measure	200	0	0

COVENT GARDEN

Th Jan. 1   Romeo and Juliet
   M   5   Henry IV, Part I
F   Feb. 13 The Merry Wives of Windsor
   S   14   Romeo and Juliet
   Tu 24   same
   Th 26   King Lear
   S   28   same
Tu Mar. 2   same
   S   6   same
   M   8   Hamlet *BT. Foote*
   Tu   9   King Lear
   S   13   same
   Th 18   Othello
   S   20   Romeo and Juliet
M   Apr. 5   Hamlet *BT. Arthur*
   Th   8   Macbeth *BT. Dyer*
   W   21   Romeo and Juliet
   Th 22   The Merchant of Venice *BT. Mons. Guerin and Madem. Capdeville*
   M   26   Othello *BT. Mrs Elmy*
W   May 5   The Merry Wives of Windsor *BT. Holtom, Miss [Esther] Young, Miss Ferguson, Mrs Stephens, Miss Helme, and Jona*
   F   7   Henry V *BT. Dunstall and Costollo*

15

1756–1757

1756 COVENT GARDEN (cont.)

M	May 10	Henry IV, Part I *BT. White, treasurer*
W	12	Romeo and Juliet
	M 17	As You Like It *BT. Anderson, Wignell, and Mrs Gondou*
M	Sept. 20	The Merry Wives of Windsor
M	Oct. 4	Romeo and Juliet
W	6	Macbeth
F	8	Henry IV, Part I
M	11	Othello
F	15	King Lear
S	16	Romeo and Juliet
Tu	26	The Merchant of Venice
F	29	The Merry Wives of Windsor
W	Nov. 10	Macbeth
Th	18	Othello
S	20	same
M	22	As You Like It
W	24	Henry IV, Part I
Th	25	The Merry Wives of Windsor
F	26	Othello
Th	Dec. 23	The Merchant of Venice *BT. William Cole, citizen of London, and family, under misfortunes, who has been a Free-Mason these thirty years, and master of several lodges*
Tu	28	Macbeth
Th	30	Romeo and Juliet

HAYMARKET

?   King Lear

The actual date of this performance has not come to light. The year is indicated in an obituary of William Parsons in EM, Mar. 1795, 147. See p. 338.

1757 DRURY LANE

			£	s.	d.
Tu	Jan. 4	Richard III	170	0	0
M	10	Measure for Measure	160	0	0
W	19	same	120	0	0
Th	Feb. 17	Henry VIII	160	0	0
Th	24	Macbeth	180	0	0

Genest (iv. 481) erroneously has Feb. 25, a Friday in Lent.

Tu	Mar. 1	Measure for Measure	180	0	0
S	5	Richard III	160	0	0
S	19	Much Ado about Nothing	190	0	0
Th	24	The Winter's Tale *BT. Woodward*	320	0	0
S	Apr. 16	Macbeth	120	0	0
M	18	Catharine and Petruchio *BT. Miss Pritchard*	340	0	0
W	20	The Merchant of Venice	130	0	0

1757

1757 DRURY LANE (cont.)

			£	s.	d.
Th Apr. 21	Catharine and Petruchio BT. *the French dancers*		140	0	0
	The recipients of the BT. are named in C-H, but not in PA. [No Pb for this performance has come to light.]				
S 23	Much Ado about Nothing		160	0	0
Th 28	Romeo and Juliet BT. *Cross, prompter, and Mrs Cross*		256	0	0
Tu May 3	Hamlet BT. *Wood, sub-treasurer*		140	0	0
M 9	Richard III BT. *Scrase, Ackman, Sturt, and Mrs Cooke*		180	0	0
Tu 10	Henry VIII BT. *Raftor, Clough, Roger, and Bullbrick*		180	0	0
F 20	Measure for Measure BT. *Veal, Tomlinson, and Humphreys*		210	0	0
Tu 24	The Winter's Tale		200	0	0
Tu Sept. 13	Richard III		90	0	0
S 17	Romeo and Juliet		150	0	0
Th 22	Measure for Measure		100	0	0
S 24	Hamlet		200	0	0
Tu 27	Henry VIII		120	0	0
S Oct. 1	Romeo and Juliet		150	0	0
Tu 4	Macbeth		90	0	0
Th 20	The Tempest		150	0	0
F 21	same		140	0	0
M 24	same		170	0	0
Th 27	same		130	0	0
F 28	Richard III		210	0	0
M 31	Measure for Measure		80	0	0
M Nov. 7	The Tempest		140	0	0
Tu 8	Much Ado about Nothing		170	0	0
W 9	The Tempest		140	0	0
Th 10	King Lear		210	0	0
F 11	The Tempest		110	0	0
S 12	King Lear		200	0	0
M 14	The Tempest		130	0	0
W 16	same		130	0	0
Th 17	King Lear		180	0	0
S 19	As You Like It		100	0	0
M 21	The Tempest		120	0	0
Tu 22	All's Well that Ends Well		120	0	0
W 23	The Tempest		220	0	0
Th 24	Romeo and Juliet		200	0	0
M 28	Henry VIII		120	0	0
Tu 29	Hamlet		160	0	0
W 30	All's Well that Ends Well		100	0	0
M Dec. 5	The Tempest		160	0	0

1757

1757 DRURY LANE (cont.)

			£	s.	d.
F Dec. 16	Henry VIII		120	0	0
S 17	Macbeth		200	0	0
M 19	The Tempest		140	0	0
W 21	Much Ado about Nothing BT. the Middlesex Hospital for sick and lame, and for lying-in married women		280	0	0
M 26	The Tempest		130	0	0

COVENT GARDEN

			£	s.	d.
S Jan. 1	Romeo and Juliet				
Th 6	The Merry Wives of Windsor				
Tu 11	Othello BT. *a gentleman under misfortunes*				
Tu 25	Henry IV, Part I				
Th 27	Richard III				
S 29	same				
Tu Feb. 1	same				
Tu 8	same				
Th 10	same				
S 12	Romeo and Juliet				
W 16	Hamlet				
Tu Mar. 1	King Lear				
M 7	Othello				
M 21	King Lear BT. *Barry*				
Tu 22	Hamlet BT. *Smith*				
S 26	Macbeth *and* Catharine and Petruchio BT. *Mrs Gregory*				
F Apr. 15	Catharine and Petruchio BT. *Mrs Hamilton*				
Tu 19	The Merry Wives of Windsor BT. *Lowe*				
Th 21	Catharine and Petruchio BT. *Mrs Elmy*				
S 23	Henry IV, Part I BT. *Poitier Jr. and Mrs Vincent*				
Tu May 3	As You Like It BT. *Howard and Collins*				
W 4	Hamlet BT. *Costollo and Ballard, treasurer*				
Th 5	Romeo and Juliet				
S 7	Othello				
Th 12	Catharine and Petruchio BT. *Cushing, Desse, and Stede*				
F 13	same BT. *Bennet, [E]. White, and Legg*				
Tu 17	same BT. *[M.] Vaughan, Condell, and Green, box-keepers*				
M 23	Romeo and Juliet				
F Sept. 23	The Merry Wives of Windsor	65	19	6
F 30	The Merchant of Venice	124	4	6
W Oct. 5	Henry IV, Part I	123	15	6
S 8	Hamlet	70	7	0
M 10	As You Like It	114	14	6
S 29	Hamlet	71	0	0
S Nov. 5	Henry V *and* Catharine and Petruchio	171	13	0
Tu 8	The Merry Wives of Windsor	55	8	0

1757–1758

1757 COVENT GARDEN (*cont.*)

				£	s.	d.
F	Nov. 11	Richard III		111	18	6
	W 16	Othello		51	18	6
	Th 17	Henry IV, Part I		97	18	0
	Th 24	Henry V		107	17	0
	M 28	same		74	15	0
M	Dec. 5	King Lear		203	8	6
	Tu 6	The Merchant of Venice		56	1	6
	W 7	Romeo and Juliet		155	6	0
	S 10	Macbeth		106	11	0
	M 12	Othello		98	3	6
	F 16	Romeo and Juliet		87	10	6
	Tu 27	same		122	7	6
	W 28	Henry V		92	17	0

1758 DRURY LANE

			£	s.	d.
S	Jan. 14	All's Well that Ends Well	190	0	0
	S 21	The Tempest	150	0	0
M	Feb. 13	same	80	0	0
S	Mar. 11	The Winter's Tale *BT. Mrs Pritchard*	280	0	0
	M 13	Henry IV, Part II *BT. Woodward*	300	0	0
	M 27	The Tempest	200	0	0
	W 29	Catharine and Petruchio *BT. Beard*	280	0	0
	Th 30	Hamlet *BT. Mossop*	280	0	0
	F 31	Romeo and Juliet *BT. Havard*	200	0	0
S	Apr. 1	Henry IV, Part II	180	0	0
	Tu 4	same	170	0	0
	W 5	Much Ado about Nothing *BT. the British Lying-in Hospital, in Brownlow-Street*	140	0	0
	S 8	Hamlet	100	0	0
	F 21	Henry IV, Part II *BT. Blakes*	170	0	0
	M 24	The Tempest *BT. Leviez, ballet-master*	180	0	0
	W 26	The Winter's Tale *BT. Cross, prompter, and Mrs Cross*	236	0	0
	F 28	Henry VIII *BT. Pritchard, treasurer*	150	0	0
	S 29	Measure for Measure *BT. Mozeen, Miss Minors, Miss Barton, Mrs Miller, and Mrs Bradshaw*	180	0	0
W	May 3	Macbeth *BT. Rooker and Champnes*	180	0	0
	F 5	All's Well that Ends Well *BT. Dickinson, first gallery office-keeper*	200	0	0
	Tu 9	Henry VIII *BT. Morris, Marr, Berrisford, and Gray*	170	0	0
	F 12	As You Like It *BT. Varney, house-keeper*	270	0	0
	M 29	Hamlet	120	0	0
S	Sept. 16	As You Like It	128	15	0
	Th 21	Henry VIII	99	0	6
	S 23	Much Ado about Nothing	174	0	6

1758

1758 DRURY LANE (cont.)

			£	s.	d.
Tu Sept. 26	Hamlet		202	3	6
Th 28	Romeo and Juliet		210	19	0
S 30	same		163	13	6
F Oct. 6	same		112	9	6
Tu 10	Measure for Measure		167	2	0
Th 12	Richard III		154	12	0
F 13	Romeo and Juliet		153	6	0
Tu 17	Measure for Measure		183	3	0
Tu 24	The Tempest		105	4	6
W 25	King Lear		207	13	6
S 28	Romeo and Juliet		119	17	0
M 30	Macbeth		160	10	6
Th Nov. 9	Henry VIII		142	18	0
M 20	The Tempest		137	0	6
F Dec. 1	Measure for Measure		91	8	0
F 8	Romeo and Juliet		132	3	6
M 18	The Merchant of Venice *BT. Foote*		receipts omitted		
S 23	Much Ado about Nothing		133	10	0
Tu 26	Romeo and Juliet		125	0	0
W 27	The Tempest		123	16	0

COVENT GARDEN

		£	s.	d.
S Jan. 7	The Merry Wives of Windsor	88	4	0
Tu 10	King Lear	109	9	6
Th 12	Henry IV, Part I	106	3	0
F 20	Hamlet	110	6	6
S 21	As You Like It	37	15	0
Th 26	Catharine and Petruchio	69	1	0
Tu Feb. 7	same	115	8	6
Tu 14	Romeo and Juliet	185	1	6
S 18	King Lear	112	13	6
Tu 21	Othello	139	7	6
Tu 28	Hamlet	140	17	0
Tu Mar. 7	Macbeth	124	7	6
M 13	Richard III and Florizel and Perdita *BT. Barry*	296	17	6
Tu 14	Coriolanus and same *BT. Smith*	282	17	6
	Both performances of *Florizel and Perdita* announced as *The Sheep-Shearing*.			
M 27	Romeo and Juliet	224	10	6
Tu Apr. 4	Othello *BT. the Marine Society, towards cloathing men and boys for the sea*	137	2	6
F 7	King Lear *BT. Dyer*	217	16	0
Tu 11	Henry IV, Part I *BT. Poitier*	172	4	6
Th 13	Henry V *BT. Barrington and Mrs Lampe*	181	4	0
F 14	Julius Caesar *BT. Mrs Elmy*	127	2	0

1758-1759

1758 COVENT GARDEN (*cont.*)

			£	s.	d.
M Apr. 17	King John *and* Catharine and Petruchio *BT. Bencraft and Mrs Vincent*		167	19	0
Th 20	Coriolanus *BT. Miss Hilliard*		152	6	0
S 22	The Merry Wives of Windsor *BT. Holtom, Mrs Stephens, Miss Helme, and Carmichael, prompter*		119	12	0
M 24	Hamlet *BT. Mattocks, Mrs Pitt, and Mrs Chambers*		183	5	6
S 29	Catharine and Petruchio *BT. [E.] Roberts*		149	6	6
M May 1	Macbeth *BT. Ballard, treasurer*		246	18	6
Tu 16	Henry IV, Part I		23	9	6
Th 18	Hamlet		31	6	6
M Sept. 25	The Merry Wives of Windsor				
W Oct. 4	Henry IV, Part I				
S 14	Catharine and Petruchio				
S 21	Henry IV, Part I				
M 23	Othello				
F 27	Catharine and Petruchio				
M 30	Hamlet				
Tu 31	The Merry Wives of Windsor				
W Nov. 1	Romeo and Juliet				
Th 2	Coriolanus				
F 3	same				
W 8	Romeo and Juliet				
F 10	Catharine and Petruchio				
Tu 21	As You Like It				
W 29	Henry IV, Part I				
Th 30	Romeo and Juliet				
Th Dec. 14	Catharine and Petruchio				
Tu 26	Romeo and Juliet				

1759 DRURY LANE

W Jan. 3	Antony and Cleopatra	193	14	0
F 5	same	174	12	0
Tu 9	same	194	10	6
F 12	same	190	15	6
S 13	The Merchant of Venice	185	15	0

PA announces *The Provoked Wife*, which 'was in the Bills for this Night, but Mr. Garrick finding himself ill in the Morning fresh bills for the Merchant were posted at one o'Clock' (C-H, Jan. 13). JPK has the bills for both plays; that for *The Provoked Wife* is deleted, and has a MS note, 'The Play this night was The Merchant of Venice.'

Th 18	Antony and Cleopatra	184	9	0
F 19	The Merchant of Venice	174	18	6
M 29	Measure for Measure	152	3	6

1759

1759 DRURY LANE (cont.) £ s. d.

Tu Feb. 6	As You Like It	186	4	0
M 26	Much Ado about Nothing	197	12	6
Tu 27	Richard III	191	1	6
M Mar. 5	The Tempest	149	16	0
Th 8	Richard III	200	4	6
M 12	Macbeth	147	0	0
Tu 27	Much Ado about Nothing *BT. Miss Macklin*	180	0	0
Th Apr. 5	Romeo and Juliet *BT. Havard*	240	0	0
M 16	The Tempest *BT. Berry*	104	8	6
Tu 17	Hamlet *BT. Fleetwood*	160	0	0
Th May 10	Romeo and Juliet *BT. Pritchard, treasurer*	140	0	0
M 14	Othello *BT. Wilkinson*	130	0	0
F 18	Antony and Cleopatra	150	0	0
Tu 22	Henry VIII *BT. Clough, Raftor, Shawford, and Walker*	180	0	0
W 23	Hamlet *BT. the widow Simson and her three children*	140	0	0
Tu Sept. 25	Romeo and Juliet	100	0	0
S 29	Hamlet	210	0	0
F Oct. 12	Macbeth	190	0	0
F 19	Richard III	200	0	0
M 22	Henry VIII	200	0	0
Tu 23	Much Ado about Nothing	170	0	0
W 24	Romeo and Juliet	150	0	0
S Nov. 10	King Lear	receipts omitted		
Th 15	same	190	0	0
Tu 27	Hamlet	100	0	0
W 28	King Lear	120	0	0
W Dec. 12	The Merchant of Venice	190	0	0
Th 13	same	90	0	0
S 15	Much Ado about Nothing	180	0	0
W 26	Romeo and Juliet	170	0	0

COVENT GARDEN

Tu Jan. 2 Hamlet
  F 5 Henry IV, Part I
  S 6 Romeo and Juliet
  Tu 16 The Merry Wives of Windsor *BT. the Middlesex Hospital for sick and lame, and lying-in married women*
  W 17 Othello
Th Feb. 1 Henry V
  S 3 Coriolanus
    and Catharine and Petruchio
  Th 15 Cymbeline
  S 17 same
  M 19 same *BT. the author [of the alteration—William Hawkins]*
  Tu 20 same

1759 COVENT GARDEN (cont.)

W	Feb. 21	Cymbeline			
	Th 22	same *BT. the author [of the alteration]*			
	M 26	Romeo and Juliet			
	Tu 27	Hamlet			
S	Mar. 24	Florizel and Perdita *BT. Mrs Bellamy*			
	Tu 27	same *BT. Smith*			
S	Apr. 7	same			
	Tu 17	Romeo and Juliet			
		and Catharine and Petruchio *BT. Bencraft and Mrs Vincent*			
	Th 19	Cymbeline			
	Tu 24	Florizel and Perdita *BT. Mrs Elmy*			
	W 25	Henry V *BT. Lalauze*			
	Th 26	The Merry Wives of Windsor			
	M 30	Hamlet *BT. Miles, Mrs Baker, and Miss [Esther] Young*			
Tu	May 1	Henry IV, Part I *BT. Mattocks, Stede, and Mrs Pitt*			
	W 2	Florizel and Perdita *BT. Collins and Mrs Green*			
	Th 3	The Merchant of Venice *BT. Dunstall*			
	F 11	Richard III *BT. Marten, Anderson, and R. Smith*			
	Th 17	Othello *BT. Wignell, Stoppelaer, and Davis*			
	Tu 22	Romeo and Juliet			
	W 23	The Cobler of Preston *BT. Evans and Condell, box-keepers*			
			£	s.	d.
W	Sept. 26	The Merry Wives of Windsor	65	3	6
S	Oct. 13	Catharine and Petruchio	109	15	6
	F 19	same	144	6	0
	S 27	same	95	19	0
Tu	Nov. 6	same	180	14	6
	Th 15	same	146	4	6
	W 28	Henry IV, Part I	116	1	0
M	Dec. 3	Catharine and Petruchio	154	12	6
	M 10	The Merry Wives of Windsor	203	7	0
	Tu 11	As You Like It	158	7	6
	W 19	Othello	114	2	0
	F 28	Henry V	132	1	0
	S 29	The Merry Wives of Windsor	127	0	0

1760 DRURY LANE

S	Jan. 5	King Lear	200	0	0[1]
Th	Feb. 7	Romeo and Juliet			
S	Mar. 22	same *BT. Palmer*			
	S 29	Catharine and Petruchio *BT. King*			
M	Apr. 7	Romeo and Juliet			
	Tu 8	Henry VIII			
	M 21	Hamlet *BT. Blakes*			
	Tu 22	The Merry Wives of Windsor *BT. Rooker*			
	M 28	Henry IV, Part I *BT. Burton*			

[1] No receipts appear in C-H (see p. 713) after Jan. 22. Cross died on Feb. 20.

1760

1760 DRURY LANE (cont.)

Th	May 1	Richard III *BT. Austin and Wood, sub-treasurer*
	Tu 6	Romeo and Juliet
		and Catharine and Petruchio *BT. Clough, Raftor, Walker, and Watkins*
	W 7	As You Like It *BT. Mrs and Miss Simson*
	S 10	Hamlet
	S 17	The Merchant of Venice
	Th 22	Richard III
	F 23	Much Ado about Nothing
	M 26	Henry VIII
	S 31	Richard III
S	Sept. 20	Romeo and Juliet
	Tu 30	Much Ado about Nothing
Tu	Oct. 7	As You Like It
	Th 9	Richard III
	M 13	same
	M 20	Romeo and Juliet
W	Nov. 19	Richard III
	F 21	same
	Th 27	Hamlet
W	Dec. 10	same
	Th 11	The Tempest
	Tu 16	Much Ado about Nothing
	W 17	King John
	S 20	same
	Tu 23	same
	F 26	Romeo and Juliet
	S 27	The Tempest

COVENT GARDEN

			£	s.	d.
M	Jan. 7	Henry IV, Part I	130	18	0
	Tu 8	Catharine and Petruchio	184	18	0
	F 11	The Merry Wives of Windsor	119	11	0
F	Feb. 1	Catharine and Petruchio	150	13	6
	S 9	Henry IV, Part I	124	17	0
Tu	Mar. 18	Hamlet *BT. Smith*	269	6	6
	F 21	[Othello]			

    Listed by Genest (iv. 593). No play was acted on this night; it was a Friday in Lent.

			£	s.	d.
	Tu 25	Catharine and Petruchio *BT. Ross*	183	1	0
Tu	Apr. 8	Romeo and Juliet *BT. Dyer*	218	8	0
	W 9	Henry IV, Part I *BT. Clarke*	158	4	6
	Th 10	Catharine and Petruchio *BT. Lowe*	266	0	0
	Th 17	Macbeth *BT. Poitier Jr.*	86	7	0
	F 18	Coriolanus *BT. Barrington and Mrs Lampe*	113	5	6
	Tu 22	Othello *BT. Miss Hilliard*	104	4	6
	W 30	Romeo and Juliet *BT. Miss Mowat*	143	16	0

1760-1761

1760 COVENT GARDEN (*cont.*)

			£	s.	d.
F May 2	Catharine and Petruchio *BT. Ballard, treasurer*		242	15	6
M 5	Henry V *BT. Marten, Anderson, and R. Smith*		226	15	6
W 7	The Merchant of Venice *BT. Bennet and Legg*		205	4	0
F 16	Henry IV, Part I *BT.* [M.] *Vaughan, Condell, and Green, box-keepers*		238	9	0
Tu 20	Romeo and Juliet		50	12	0
M Sept. 29	same		206	4	6

Genest (iv. 620) erroneously has Sept. 27, on which night the theatre was dark.

W Oct. 1	Hamlet	141	0	0
F 3	Romeo and Juliet	91	0	6
F 10	Henry IV, Part I	71	11	0
F 17	The Merry Wives of Windsor	55	15	0
S 18	Othello	94	15	0
Tu Nov. 18	Henry V	101	0	6
Th 20	Romeo and Juliet	113	0	0
Tu 25	Catharine and Petruchio	123	14	0
Tu Dec. 2	Henry V	210	0	0

Pb, PA, and Genest (iv. 623) all give *Tancred and Sigismunda* for this night. But by royal command it was changed to *Henry V* (PA, Dec. 3). On Dec. 4 *Tancred and Sigismunda* was performed, and the bills have, 'Not acted this Season'.

F 5	Henry IV, Part I	98	4	0
S 6	Romeo and Juliet	134	17	0
Tu 9	King John	128	19	0
W 10	same	97	14	0
S 13	Catharine and Petruchio	122	9	6
W 17	King John	135	7	6
F 19	Henry IV, Part I	242	0	0
M 22	Hamlet and Florizel and Perdita *BT. the composer to the theatre* [*Thomas Augustine Arne*]	194	1	6
Tu 23	King John	191	15	0

1761 DRURY LANE

- M Feb. 2   The Tempest
- M 9   Much Ado about Nothing
- M Mar. 9   Hamlet
- Tu 24   The Tempest
- S 28   Othello
- Th Apr. 2   King John *BT. Mrs Yates*
- M 6   Romeo and Juliet *BT. Holland*
- Th 9   Hamlet *BT. Mrs Vincent* [*Jr.*]
- M 13   Romeo and Juliet *BT. Mr and Mrs Kennedy*
- M 20   same *BT. Blakes*
- Tu 21   Richard III *BT. Philips and Bransby*

1761

1761 DRURY LANE (*cont.*)

W	Apr. 29	Macbeth *BT. Pritchard, treasurer*
	Th 30	Othello *BT. Miss Mowat*
F	May 1	Henry VIII
	Tu 5	Romeo and Juliet *BT. Ackman and Settree*
	F 8	The Tempest *BT. Clough, et al.*

The other recipients of the BT. are nowhere named.

    S 23 [Henry VIII]

MacMillan (84) queries this performance. It is, however, clear that the theatre was dark. There is no JPK bill for this night, and PA carries only the announcement that *Jane Shore*, originally intended for performance, was 'obliged to be deferred'. It also states that *Henry VIII* would be acted 'on Tuesday next', i.e. May 26, q.v.

	Tu 26	Henry VIII
	Th 28	King Lear
	F 29	Richard III *BT. Scrase, Courtney, and Miss Read*
W	June 3	Hamlet
	Th 4	Henry VIII *BT. decay'd actors who formerly belong'd to the Theatres Royal*
Tu Sept. 8		Romeo and Juliet
	Tu 15	Hamlet
	S 26	Richard III
	M 28	As You Like It
	W 30	Henry VIII
Th Oct. 1		Much Ado about Nothing
	F 2	Henry VIII
	S 3	same
	M 5	same
	Tu 6	same
	Th 8	same
	F 9	same
	Tu 13	Hamlet
	S 17	Othello
	M 19	same

Genest (iv. 634) erroneously has Oct. 18, a Sunday.

	W 21	Richard III
	F 23	Henry VIII
	S 31	Macbeth
M Nov. 2		Henry VIII
	S 7	Romeo and Juliet
	Th 12	Macbeth
	Tu 24	Hamlet
	S 28	Cymbeline
	M 30	same
Tu Dec. 1		same
	W 2	same

1761

1761 DRURY LANE (cont.)

Th	Dec. 3	Cymbeline
S	5	same
M	7	same
Tu	8	same
Th	10	same
W	16	same
W	23	King Lear
S	26	Romeo and Juliet

COVENT GARDEN

			£	s.	d.
Th	Jan. 1	Henry V	162	4	0
S	3	King John	114	1	6
F	9	Catharine and Petruchio	129	14	6
S	10	The Merchant of Venice	216	14	0
Tu	13	Romeo and Juliet *and* Florizel and Perdita	175	7	0
Th	15	Henry IV, Part I	175	17	0
S	17	Othello	114	4	6
Th	Feb. 12	The Merry Wives of Windsor	182	8	0
Th	26	The Merchant of Venice	240	5	6
S	Mar. 7	Catharine and Petruchio	180	3	6
Th	12	The Merchant of Venice	191	13	0
Tu	24	Romeo and Juliet *and* Florizel and Perdita *BT. Ross*	143	17	6
S	28	Henry IV, Part I	91	1	6
M	30	Richard III *BT. Smith*	257	11	6
Th	Apr. 2	Macbeth *BT. Clarke*	153	9	6
S	4	The Merchant of Venice	55	9	6
F	10	Romeo and Juliet *BT. Barrington and Mrs Lampe*	188	13	0
Th	16	Florizel and Perdita *BT. Mrs Vincent*	139	11	0
F	24	Hamlet *BT. Collins and Younger, prompter*	145	8	0
F	May 1	Henry V *BT. Legg and Bennet*	202	2	6
M	4	The Merchant of Venice *BT. Ballard, treasurer*	250	14	6
Tu	5	Richard III *BT. Holtom, Davis, Buck, and Perry*	234	18	6
W	20	Romeo and Juliet	96	2	6
Th	21	Richard III	41	9	0
F	22	Henry V	26	12	6
M	25	Macbeth	43	7	6
Tu	June 23	Othello *BT. Cooke*	79	15	6
M	Sept. 14	Henry IV, Part I	receipts omitted		
M	21	The Merchant of Venice	,,	,,	
W	23	The Merry Wives of Windsor	,,	,,	
F	25	Romeo and Juliet	89	8	0
S	Oct. 10	Hamlet	72	18	0

1761

1761 COVENT GARDEN (*cont.*)

			£	s.	d.
Tu Oct. 13	Othello		131	0	6
Th 15	The Merry Wives of Windsor		137	15	6
W 28	Romeo and Juliet		110	9	6
F Nov. 13	Henry V		244	7	0
S 14	same		213	18	0
M 16	same		238	16	0
Tu 17	same		207	0	0
W 18	same		217	17	0
Th 19	same		231	6	6
F 20	same		191	1	0
S 21	same		219	3	0
M 23	same		229	2	0
Tu 24	same		230	9	0
W 25	same		225	0	0
Th 26	same		230	18	0
F 27	same				
S 28	same				
M 30	same				
Tu Dec. 1	same				
W 2	same				
Th 3	same				
F 4	same				
S 5	same				
M 7	same				
Tu 8	same				
W 9	same				

This run of 23 successive nights is the longest accorded to any play by Shakespeare in the eighteenth century. It was acted at this time and later in the season (as were several of the other Histories) in connexion with an elaborate replica of the coronation of George III, which took place on Sept. 22, 1761.

F 11	Henry IV, Part II
S 12	same
M 14	same
Tu 15	same
Th 17	same
F 18	same
S 19	same
M 21	same
Tu 22	Hamlet *BT. the General Lying-in Hospital, in Duke-Street, Grosvenor Square*
W 23	Henry IV, Part II
S 26	same
M 28	Richard III
Tu 29	Henry V
W 30	King John
Th 31	Henry IV, Part II

1762 DRURY LANE

S	Jan. 2	Richard III
Tu	5	Much Ado about Nothing
W	6	Cymbeline
S	9	Macbeth
Tu	12	Cymbeline
Tu	19	Hamlet
M	25	Romeo and Juliet
W	27	The Winter's Tale
		and Catharine and Petruchio
Th	28	same
		and same
Tu Feb.	2	The Winter's Tale
Th	4	same
		and Catharine and Petruchio
S	6	same
		and same

All performances of *The Winter's Tale* announced as *Florizel and Perdita, or, The Winter's Tale, a Dramatic Pastoral in Three Acts.*

M	8	Cymbeline
Th	25	same
M Mar.	1	The Tempest
Th	25	Cymbeline BT. *Holland*
M	29	The Winter's Tale
		and Catharine and Petruchio BT. *Havard*

The Winter's Tale announced as noted under Feb. 6.

M Apr.	12	The Tempest
S	17	King Lear
Tu	27	Much Ado about Nothing BT. *Miss Pope*
W	28	Cymbeline BT. *Noverre and Miss Bride*
F	30	Henry IV, Part I
Tu May	4	Hamlet
		and Catharine and Petruchio
Th	6	Richard III

Genest (iv. 644) has, 'This was doubtless a benefit—probably Moody's'. It was nobody's BT., nor did Moody have a BT. this season.

Th	13	Romeo and Juliet BT. *Scrase, Fawcett, and Miss Read*
M	17	The Merry Wives of Windsor BT. *Stevens, Weston, and Courtney*
S Sept.	25	Henry IV, Part I
Tu	28	Romeo and Juliet
S Oct.	2	Henry IV, Part I
Tu	5	Richard III
W	6	Hamlet
S	23	All's Well that Ends Well

1762 DRURY LANE (cont.)

W	Oct.	27	Romeo and Juliet
	F	29	Cymbeline
	S	30	The Tempest
W	Nov.	3	Henry IV, Part II
	F	5	same
	S	6	Hamlet
	M	8	Cymbeline
	Tu	9	The Tempest
	Th	11	Henry IV, Part II
	M	15	same
	F	19	King Lear
	Th	25	All's Well that Ends Well
F	Dec.	3	Henry IV, Part II
	S	4	Romeo and Juliet
	W	8	Cymbeline
	S	18	Richard III
	W	22	The Two Gentlemen of Verona
	Th	23	Richard III
	Tu	28	The Two Gentlemen of Verona
	Th	30	same
	F	31	King Lear

COVENT GARDEN

F	Jan.	1	Henry V
	S	2	King John
	M	4	Henry IV, Part II
	Tu	5	Richard III
	W	6	King John
	Th	7	The Merry Wives of Windsor
	F	8	Richard III
	S	9	Henry IV, Part II
	M	11	Richard III
	Th	14	same
	S	16	same
	M	18	Henry IV, Part II
	Tu	19	Richard III
	W	20	King John
	Th	21	Henry IV, Part II
	S	23	Richard III
	Tu	26	Henry IV, Part II
	W	27	King John
M	Feb.	8	Richard III
	W	10	Henry IV, Part II
	S	13	King John
	S	20	Richard III
	Th	25	Romeo and Juliet
	S	27	Henry IV, Part II

1762-1763

1762 COVENT GARDEN (cont.)

- S Mar. 6 Richard III
- Th 11 Henry IV, Part II
- S 13 Romeo and Juliet
- Tu 16 Richard III
- Th 18 Henry IV, Part II
- S 20 Florizel and Perdita *BT. Ross*
- M 22 Catharine and Petruchio *BT. Smith*
- Tu 23 Florizel and Perdita *BT. Mrs Hamilton*
- S Apr. 3 The Merry Wives of Windsor *BT. Sparks*
- M 12 Henry V
- Tu 13 Catharine and Petruchio *BT. Clarke*
- Th 22 Romeo and Juliet *BT. Mr and Mrs Barrington*
- S 24 The Twins *BT. Hull*
- M May 3 Florizel and Perdita *BT. Ballard, treasurer*
- Tu 4 Henry IV, Part I *BT. [E.] Roberts, the widow of the late Mr Lampe, and Miss [Esther] Young*
- F 7 Hamlet *BT. Davis, Perry, and Madame Jansolin*
- S 8 The Merry Wives of Windsor *BT. Stoppelaer, Chapman, Jarvis, and Miss Fielding*
- M 10 Richard III
- Tu 11 Macbeth *BT. Wignell and Mrs Abegg*
- Tu 18 Richard III
- M 24 Henry IV, Part II
- S Sept. 22 Romeo and Juliet
- F 24 Henry IV, Part I
- M 27 Hamlet
- S Oct. 2 Henry IV, Part II
- S 9 Richard III
- Tu 12 Othello
- S 16 Henry V
- M 18 Romeo and Juliet
- W 20 The Merry Wives of Windsor
- S 23 Henry IV, Part II
- W Nov. 3 As You Like It
- Th 18 The Merry Wives of Windsor
- F 26 Richard III
- M 29 All's Well that Ends Well
- Th Dec. 2 same
- M 6 same
- F 31 Henry IV, Part II

1763 DRURY LANE

- S Jan. 1 Romeo and Juliet
- Tu 4 The Two Gentlemen of Verona
- Th 6 same
- M 10 Henry IV, Part II
- Tu 11 Richard III

1763

1763 DRURY LANE (cont.)

   F   Jan. 14   As You Like It
           S 15   Cymbeline
          M 17   Macbeth
           S 22   Catharine and Petruchio
          Tu 25   [The Two Gentlemen of Verona *BT. the author of the alteration—Benjamin Victor*]

                     Not acted because of a riot instituted by the opposers of the abolition of the half-price, i.e. the privilege of coming into the theatre, at the conclusion of the third act, for half the usual price of admission. For an account of this riot see Genest, v. 14–16, and MacMillan, xiv.

          W 26   Catharine and Petruchio *BT. the author* [*of Elvira, also acted this night—David Mallet*]
W Feb. 2   The Two Gentlemen of Verona
Tu Mar. 1   Much Ado about Nothing
           Th 3   Catharine and Petruchio
            S 5   Romeo and Juliet
          Th 10   Cymbeline
          Tu 15   Catharine and Petruchio *BT. Mrs Cibber*
          Th 17   Macbeth
M Apr. 4   Hamlet *BT. Palmer*
           W 6   Cymbeline *BT. Havard*
           Th 7   The Tempest
          W 13   Macbeth *BT. Mr and Master Burton*
           F 15   Henry IV, Part II *BT. Love*
           S 16   Much Ado about Nothing *BT. Mrs Palmer*
          W 20   Catharine and Petruchio *BT. Jackson*
           F 22   Romeo and Juliet *BT. Bransby and Philips*
          Th 28   Cymbeline
           F 29   Hamlet *BT. Rooker and Saunderson, machinist*
M May 2   Macbeth *BT. Lee*
           Tu 3   The Tempest *BT. Ackman and Moody*
           Th 5   [King Lear]

                     Listed by MacMillan (96). This was a general thanksgiving day; the theatre was therefore dark (C-H, May 5; PA, May 6).

			£	s.	d.
	Th 12	King Lear			
	F 20	Macbeth			
Tu	Sept. 20	Hamlet	194	17	6
W	Oct. 19	Twelfth Night	99	3	0
	M 24	Richard III	154	12	0
	W 26	Hamlet	103	1	0
	F 28	Twelfth Night	81	7	6
	M 31	Romeo and Juliet	125	5	6
Tu	Nov. 1	Catharine and Petruchio	100	17	6
	W 9	Henry IV, Part I	147	0	0
	Tu 15	The Tempest	174	17	6
	W 16	Henry IV, Part I	110	13	6

1763–1764

1763 DRURY LANE (*cont.*)

			£	s.	d.
F	Nov. 18	Richard III	138	1	6
W	23	A Midsummer-Night's Dream	98	7	0
F	25	Romeo and Juliet	123	18	0
S	26	A Fairy Tale	115	5	0
M	28	same	124	0	6
Tu	29	Macbeth *and* A Fairy Tale	146	9	6
Th	Dec. 1	Cymbeline	252	9	6
S	3	same	233	9	0
Tu	6	same *and* A Fairy Tale	175	3	6
Th	8	Cymbeline	195	9	6
F	9	The Tempest *BT. the author of the farce* [The Mayor of Garratt, *also acted this night—Samuel Foote*]	108	7	6
F	16	A Fairy Tale	165	6	6
M	19	Cymbeline *and* A Fairy Tale	195	8	0
Th	22	A Fairy Tale	152	14	0
F	23	Cymbeline *and* A Fairy Tale	138	7	6

COVENT GARDEN

Tu	Jan. 4	All's Well that Ends Well
M	24	Romeo and Juliet
S	Feb. 5	All's Well that Ends Well
S	Mar. 5	same
F	Apr. 29	same *BT. Lalauze*
S	30	Catharine and Petruchio *BT. Costollo, Mrs Pitt, and Stede*
W	May 18	Hamlet *BT. Wignell, Stoppelaer, and Young*
Th	26	Romeo and Juliet *BT. Wilford and Clingo, pit door-keepers, Abbot, stage-door-keeper, and Trott, lobby door-keeper*
W	Sept. 21	same
M	26	Henry IV, Part I
F	Oct. 7	All's Well that Ends Well
Th	Nov. 10	The Merry Wives of Windsor
M	Dec. 26	Richard III
Th	29	Romeo and Juliet

1764 DRURY LANE

W	Jan. 4	The Merry Wives of Windsor	201	7	0
F	6	Twelfth Night	141	2	0
W	18	Henry IV, Part II	142	3	0
S	21	same	191	18	0
Tu	24	Cymbeline	180	12	0
F	27	Much Ado about Nothing	130	9	0
S	Feb. 4	Richard III	150	8	0

1764

1764 DRURY LANE (*cont.*)

				£	s.	d.
M	Feb.	6	Cymbeline	180	7	0
	Tu	7	Much Ado about Nothing	97	2	0
	Th	9	A Fairy Tale	146	15	6
	F	10	Henry IV, Part II and A Fairy Tale	104	18	6
	S	11	Hamlet	181	8	0
	M	13	A Fairy Tale	159	18	6
	W	15	same	118	16	6
	Tu	28	Macbeth	158	10	6
S	Mar.	3	A Fairy Tale	231	19	0
	Tu	6	same	167	2	0
	M	26	Cymbeline *BT. Yates*	217	0	0

Genest (v. 46) erroneously states that this was Mrs Yates's BT.

	S	31	Othello *BT. Powell*	268	11	0
S	Apr.	14	same *BT. Vernon*	receipts omitted		
	F	27	Cymbeline *BT. Mrs Vincent [Jr.]*	,,	,,	
	S	28	Othello *BT. Miss Wright*	,,	,,	
S	May	5	A Fairy Tale *BT. Jackson*	47	4	6
	Tu	8	same *BT. Philips and Mrs Lee*			
	W	9	Catharine and Petruchio *BT. Lee and Evans, sub-treasurer*			
	Th	10	Richard III *BT. Baddeley and Ackman*			
	F	11	Cymbeline *BT. Moody and Weston*			
	Tu	15	A Fairy Tale *BT. Mrs Simson; and removing a public nuisance, by opening the way at the end of Great Queen-Street*			
	W	16	Hamlet *BT. Dickinson, first gallery office-keeper*			
	Th	17	A Fairy Tale *BT. Watkins, Mortimer, Tomlinson, and West*			
	M	21	Romeo and Juliet *BT. [R.] Palmer [Sr.], pit door-keeper, and Roberts, box-lobby door-keeper*			
	W	23	A Fairy Tale *BT. the Fairies, who perform in the* Fairy Tale			
	Th	24	Othello *BT. Hopkins, prompter, and Mrs Hopkins*			
	Th	Sept. 20	Richard III			
	S	22	Romeo and Juliet and A Fairy Tale			
	Th	27	Hamlet and same			
S	Oct.	6	A Fairy Tale			
	Tu	9	Cymbeline			
	Th	11	A Fairy Tale			
	M	15	same			
	W	17	Henry IV, Part I and A Fairy Tale			
	S	27	A Fairy Tale			
	M	29	Romeo and Juliet			
F	Nov.	9	Henry IV, Part II			
	Tu	13	Richard III			

1764 DRURY LANE (cont.)

- W Nov. 14 Cymbeline
  and A Fairy Tale
- Th 22 Hamlet
- Tu 27 Macbeth
- W Dec. 12 Hamlet *BT. the British Lying-in Hospital, in Brownlow-Street, Long-Acre*
- F 14 Cymbeline
- F 21 Henry IV, Part II

COVENT GARDEN

- M Jan. 16 As You Like It
- S 21 The Merry Wives of Windsor
- W 25 Henry IV, Part I
- W Feb. 15 Henry V
- M 20 Richard III
- Th Mar. 8 The Merry Wives of Windsor
- Th 15 All's Well that Ends Well
- Th 29 Hamlet *BT. Walker*
- M Apr. 2 Romeo and Juliet *BT. Mrs Ward*
- Tu 10 The Merchant of Venice *BT. Miss Macklin*
- M May 7 King Lear *BT. Younger*
- S 12 Romeo and Juliet *BT. Weller, [P.] Lewis, and Gardner*
- Tu 15 Richard III *BT. Hallam, Davis, and Perry*
- F 18 All's Well that Ends Well *BT. Wignell and Stoppelaer*
- M 21 Macbeth *BT. Holtom, Buck, Dibdin, and Miss Sledge*
- W Sept. 19 Hamlet
- F 21 Romeo and Juliet
- W 26 Henry IV, Part I
- M Oct. 8 Richard III
- W 17 The Merry Wives of Windsor
- S 27 Romeo and Juliet
- M 29 King Lear
- Tu Nov. 6 All's Well that Ends Well
- M 12 Richard III
- Tu 13 Hamlet
- Tu 27 King Lear
- W 28 The Merry Wives of Windsor
- M Dec. 3 King Lear
- F 21 King John
- M 31 King Lear

1765 DRURY LANE

- W Jan. 2 King Lear
- F 4 Richard III
- S 5 King Lear
- M 7 Romeo and Juliet
- W 9 King Lear

1765

1765 DRURY LANE (cont.)

S   Jan. 12 King Lear
    S 26 A Fairy Tale *BT. the author* [*of* The Platonic Wife, *also acted this night—Elizabeth Griffith*]
    M 28 same
    Th 31 same *BT. the author* [*of* The Platonic Wife]
F Feb. 1 King Lear
    F 8 Cymbeline
    S 16 Hamlet
    Tu 26 Macbeth
M Mar. 11 Richard III
    Tu 19 Othello *BT. Holland*
    Th 21 A Fairy Tale
    M 25 King Lear *BT. Powell*
    Tu 26 The Winter's Tale *BT. Yates*
    S 30 Cymbeline *BT. King*
W Apr. 10 Othello *BT. Palmer*
    W 17 King Lear
        and A Fairy Tale
    M 22 Macbeth *BT. Miss* [*I.*] *Young*
    F 26 The Winter's Tale *BT. Lee and Miss Slack*
    S 27 Hamlet *BT. Slingsby*
W May 1 The Tempest *BT. Grimaldi, ballet master, and Aldridge*
    F 3 Cymbeline *BT. Burton and Miss Plym*
    W 8 Richard III *BT. Philips and Mrs Lee*
    F 10 Othello *BT. Evans, sub-treasurer*
    Th 16 Romeo and Juliet *BT. Granger, Adcock, Preston, and Keen*
    Tu 21 Henry IV, Part I *BT. Foley, Robinson, and Kaygill*
    Th 23 King Lear
Tu Sept. 17 Romeo and Juliet
M Oct. 14 Richard III
    Tu 22 King Lear
    M 28 Macbeth
Th Nov. 14 Much Ado about Nothing
    W 20 Cymbeline
    F 22 Much Ado about Nothing
    S 23 King Lear
S Dec. 14 A Fairy Tale
    W 18 same *BT. the General Lying-in Hospital*
    F 20 Macbeth *BT. a public charity*
    M 23 Romeo and Juliet

COVENT GARDEN

Tu Jan. 1 Richard III
    M 7 King Lear
    Th 10 Catharine and Petruchio
    M 14 Othello
        and Catharine and Petruchio

1765 COVENT GARDEN (cont.)

- M Jan. 21 Romeo and Juliet
- W 23 The Merry Wives of Windsor
- S 26 Catharine and Petruchio
- M Feb. 18 Coriolanus
- Tu Mar. 19 King Lear *BT. Ross*
- M 25 Romeo and Juliet *BT. Mrs Bellamy*
- Tu Apr. 9 The Merchant of Venice *BT. Miss Macklin*
- Th 18 Catharine and Petruchio *BT. Mons. Duquesney and Signora Manesière*
- M 29 Romeo and Juliet *BT. Miles, Mrs Green, and Mrs [T.] Baker*
- Th May 2 King Lear *BT. Hull*
- F 3 Richard III *BT. Younger*
- S 11 Macbeth *BT. Tindal and Charles Sarjant, book- and housekeeper*
- M 13 Othello *BT. Perry and Dibdin*
- W 22 Catharine and Petruchio *BT. Hussey, Curtet, Mrs Viviez, and Miss Daw*
- W Sept. 18 Hamlet
- M 23 King Lear
- W 25 Catharine and Petruchio
- M 30 Richard III
- M Oct. 7 Romeo and Juliet

  Genest (v. 103) erroneously has Oct. 6, a Sunday.

- M 14 Macbeth
- M 28 Othello
- W 30 The Merry Wives of Windsor
- M Nov. 11 Hamlet
- M 18 Richard III
- M 25 Romeo and Juliet
- W 27 Henry IV, Part I
- Th Dec. 19 King Lear
- M 23 Romeo and Juliet

1766 DRURY LANE

- W Jan. 8 Cymbeline
- Th 9 Henry IV, Part I
- S 11 King Lear
- M 13 Hamlet
- F 24 The Merry Wives of Windsor *BT. Love and Saunderson*

  The recipients of the BT. are named in a MS note on JPK. Their names are not printed in the bill, or in PA.

- M Feb. 3 The Tempest
- W 5 Cymbeline
- Tu 11 Much Ado about Nothing *and* A Fairy Tale
- Th 13 Othello

1766

1766 DRURY LANE (cont.)

Tu	Feb. 18	A Fairy Tale *BT. the author [of Almena, also acted this night—Richard Rolt] and composers [Michael Arne and Jonathan Battishill]*			
Th	Mar. 20	King John *BT. Holland*			
Tu	Apr. 1	Othello *BT. King*			
W	2	Macbeth *BT. Palmer*			
S	5	King Lear *BT. Vernon*			
W	9	A Fairy Tale *BT. Mrs. Fitzhenry*			
F	11	King John *BT. Havard*			
S	12	A Fairy Tale *BT. Love*			
Tu	22	Cymbeline *BT. Hopkins, prompter, and Mrs Hopkins*			
M	28	Hamlet *BT. Grimaldi and Aldridge*			
Tu	29	King Lear *BT. Mr and Mrs Baddeley*			
W	30	The Tempest *BT. Rooker*			
F	May 2	Romeo and Juliet *and* Catharine and Petruchio *BT. Mr and Master Burton*			
S	3	Catharine and Petruchio *BT. Moody, Hurst, and Mrs Dorman*			
M	5	Henry IV, Part II *BT. Evans, sub-treasurer, Giorgi, and Miss Rogers*			
Tu	6	Cymbeline *BT. Ackman and Mrs Bradshaw*			
W	14	The Tempest *and* A Fairy Tale *BT. Mortimer, Tomlinson, and West*			
M	19	A Fairy Tale *BT. Watson, Roberts, and [R.] Palmer [Sr.]*	£	s.	d.
Tu	Sept. 23	Hamlet	112	19	0
Tu	30	Romeo and Juliet	145	16	6
S	Oct. 4	same	145	11	6
Tu	21	Cymbeline	130	15	0
Th	23	Much Ado about Nothing	234	12	6
Tu	28	A Fairy Tale	85	7	0
W	29	King Lear	157	1	0
F	31	A Fairy Tale	259	13	0
F	Nov. 7	Hamlet	261	10	6
W	12	Cymbeline	154	10	0
S	29	same	115	16	0
S	Dec. 6	Othello *BT. the author of the farce [Neck or Nothing, also acted this night—David Garrick]*	116	15	6
Th	11	Cymbeline	141	16	6
F	26	Romeo and Juliet	164	8	6

COVENT GARDEN

M	Jan. 6	Richard III
Th	16	Catharine and Petruchio
F	31	Julius Caesar
M	Feb. 3	same

1766 COVENT GARDEN (cont.)

F	Feb. 7	Julius Caesar *and* Catharine and Petruchio			
	Th 20	Romeo and Juliet			
	M 24	Julius Caesar			
Tu	Mar. 4	King Lear			
	M 10	Richard III			
Tu	Apr. 8	Romeo and Juliet *BT. Mrs Ward*			
	M 21	Richard III *BT. Miles, Mrs Green, and Mrs Pitt*			
	W 23	King Lear *BT. Morris, Anderson, and Stede*			
	F 25	Catharine and Petruchio *BT. Younger*			
	M 28	Romeo and Juliet *BT. Mrs [T.] Baker*			
Tu	May 6	King John *and* Catharine and Petruchio *BT. Wignell*			
	M 12	Hamlet *BT. [P.] Lewis, Banks, and Mrs Schuchart*			
	F 16	Catharine and Petruchio *BT. Green and Ansell, box-keepers*			
	M 19	Romeo and Juliet	£	s.	d.
M	Sept. 22	Henry V	271	18	6
	W 24	same	224	3	0
	F 26	Richard III	177	14	6
	M 29	Henry V	206	3	0
W	Oct. 1	same	169	8	6
	F 3	same	144	9	6
	M 6	Henry IV, Part II	222	0	0

Genest (v. 129) erroneously has Oct. 5, a Sunday.

	Tu 7	same	107	8	0
	Th 9	same	144	11	0
	S 11	same	114	12	6
	M 13	same	142	18	0
	F 17	Henry V	153	8	6
	M 20	Richard III	189	19	6
	Tu 21	Romeo and Juliet	85	1	6
	F 24	Richard III	146	1	6
	M 27	same	160	3	6
	Th 30	Hamlet	85	0	0
	F 31	King John	146	10	6
S	Nov. 1	Catharine and Petruchio	147	5	0
	M 3	King John	125	17	6
	W 5	same	110	9	6
	S 8	The Merry Wives of Windsor	82	19	6
	M 10	Richard III	177	9	0
	M 17	Henry V	200	8	6
	W 19	King Lear	177	11	0
	M 24	same	185	19	0
F	Dec. 12	Catharine and Petruchio	193	5	0
	F 26	Richard III	189	3	0
	S 27	Henry V	149	3	0
	M 29	Henry IV, Part II	170	8	6

1766–1767

1766 KING'S, HAYMARKET

F	Aug.	8	Othello
	M	11	same
	M	18	Romeo and Juliet
	W	20	same
	M	25	King Lear
	F	29	same
W	Sept.	3	Othello
	S	13	As You Like It
	W	17	Othello *BT. Barry*

1767 DRURY LANE

				£	s.	d.
S	Jan.	24	Cymbeline	171	18	0
S	Feb.	7	King John	138	7	6
	F	20	same	97	5	0
S	Mar.	21	Macbeth *BT. Mrs Pritchard*	261	3	0
S	Apr.	4	The Tempest *BT. Mrs Arne*	219	14	0
	M	6	Cymbeline *BT. King* cash:[1]	67	2	0
	S	11	Richard III *BT. Palmer*	201	19	0
	Th	23	King Lear *BT. Rooker and Miss [I.] Young* cash:[1]	65	1	0
	M	27	Cymbeline *BT. Dodd*	178	14	0
	Tu	28	A Fairy Tale *BT. Bensley* cash:[1]	66	2	6
Tu	May	5	The Tempest *BT. Champnes*	149	11	6
	F	8	Henry IV, Part II *BT. [F.] Aickin and Mrs Lee* cash:[1]	64	19	6

Genest (v. 126) has, 'bt. of Rooker and Aickin'. This is erroneous: Rooker had his BT. on Apr. 23, q.v.

				£	s.	d.
	S	9	Othello *BT. Mr and Mrs Baddeley*	135	15	0
	M	11	Richard III *BT. Bransby and Burton*	115	18	6
	W	13	Macbeth *BT. Hurst, Tassoni, and Mrs Dorman*	131	11	6
	M	18	Romeo and Juliet *BT. Duquesney* cash:[1]	68	8	0
	W	20	King Lear *BT. Dickinson, first gallery office-keeper*	113	6	0
	Tu	26	Cymbeline *BT. J. Palmer, Kear, and Keen*	96	13	0
	Th	28	Hamlet	262	7	6
	S	30	Romeo and Juliet *BT. Cridland, box-keeper, Foley, lobby door-keeper, and Robinson, upper gallery door-keeper*	101	6	0
Tu	Sept.	15	Hamlet			
	Th	17	Richard III			
	M	21	Romeo and Juliet			
S	Oct.	10	Cymbeline			
	Tu	13	same			

[1] i.e. the so-called 'house-charges'. The recipients of a BT. were obliged to pay to the treasurer a stipulated sum to cover the expenses, the 'charges', of the theatre on the night of the BT. On this night the actual box-office receipts are not entered in the Account-Book.

1767 DRURY LANE (cont.)

- M Oct. 19 Cymbeline
- W 21 King Lear
- Th 22 As You Like It
- S 24 King Lear
- Tu 27 As You Like It
- W 28 Much Ado about Nothing
- Th 29 Othello
- S 31 same
- M Nov. 9 Hamlet
- Tu 10 As You Like It
- Tu 17 Cymbeline
- Tu Dec. 22 Romeo and Juliet

COVENT GARDEN

			£	s.	d.
M Jan. 19	King Lear		221	3	6
F 23	All's Well that Ends Well		116	9	6
S 24	Catharine and Petruchio		167	7	0
M 26	Hamlet		213	2	0
M Feb. 16	Romeo and Juliet		230	18	6
M Mar. 9	King Lear		187	8	6

Genest (v. 134) erroneously has Mar. 8, a Sunday.

			£	s.	d.
Tu 17	Romeo and Juliet		183	0	0
M Apr. 6	The Merchant of Venice *BT. Miss Macklin*		154	4	0
M 20	Romeo and Juliet *BT. Dyer*		240	2	0
Th 23	Henry V		230	1	0
S 25	Julius Caesar *BT. Walker*		130	11	0
W May 13	King Lear *and* Catharine and Petruchio *BT. Perry and Holtom*		183	10	0
W 20	Romeo and Juliet *BT. Redman, Dumai, Mrs Viviez, and Mrs Naylor*		265	12	0
W 27	Richard III		127	14	6
Th 28	King John		85	11	0
Tu Sept. 22	Henry V		189	4	6
W 23	King John		91	8	0
Th 24	Henry V		77	1	6
F 25	Romeo and Juliet		109	19	0
M 28	[same]				

Announced by both Pb and PA, but not acted, on account of the death of the Duke of York, the King's brother.

			£	s.	d.
Tu Oct. 6	The Merchant of Venice		227	15	6
S 10	same		227	2	6
M 12	Romeo and Juliet		190	3	6
W 14	The Merchant of Venice		233	19	0
W 21	same		224	19	0

1767–1768

1767 COVENT GARDEN (*cont.*) £ s. d.

W	Oct. 28	The Merchant of Venice	204	13	6
S	Nov. 7	Richard III	192	7	0
	M 16	Romeo and Juliet	200	13	6
	S 21	The Merchant of Venice	237	5	0
	M 30	Richard III	170	10	6
S	Dec. 5	Othello	205	1	0
	Th 10	The Merchant of Venice	225	15	0
	Tu 22	King John *BT. a public charity* [*the Lock Hospital*]	121	0	0

The Lock Hospital is identified in PA, Dec. 14.

M 28	Cymbeline	247	4	0
Tu 29	Richard III	170	19	6
Th 31	Cymbeline	193	10	0

HAYMARKET

M	June 22	Romeo and Juliet
	Tu 30	Othello
W	July 15	King Lear
	F 24	Othello
W	Sept. 2	same
	M 21	same *BT. Barry*

1768 DRURY LANE

S	Jan. 9	The Merry Wives of Windsor
	W 13	Hamlet
	Th 14	Macbeth
	M 18	Cymbeline
	F 29	same
Th	Feb. 4	Macbeth
	M 8	same
	M 29	Hamlet
Tu	Mar. 15	Florizel and Perdita *BT. Mrs Dancer*
	S 19	Catharine and Petruchio
	Th 24	The Merchant of Venice *BT. King*
	S 26	As You Like It *BT. Vernon*
M	Apr. 4	Hamlet *BT. Palmer*
	F 8	King Lear *BT. Havard*
	M 11	Romeo and Juliet *BT. Dodd*
	Tu 12	Richard III *BT. Reddish*
	W 13	As You Like It *BT. Mrs* [*W.*] *Barry*
	S 16	The Merchant of Venice *BT. Mrs King*
	F 22	The Tempest *BT. Champnes and Miss* [*I.*] *Young*
	M 25	Macbeth *BT. Mrs Pritchard*

Genest (v. 170) erroneously has Apr. 24, a Sunday.

Tu 26	Cymbeline *BT. Grimaldi and Moody*

1768

1768 DRURY LANE (cont.)

Th May 5   Othello *BT. Barry*
F 13   [Catharine and Petruchio]
      Bill in PA, but not acted, on account of the death of Princess Louisa, the King's sister. There is no JPK bill for this night.
M 23   Catharine and Petruchio *BT. Mortimer, Tomlinson, and Lings*
M 30   Romeo and Juliet *BT. Watson, Roberts, Kaygill, and [R.] Palmer [Sr.]*
Tu 31   Hamlet *BT. a fund, for the relief of those who from their age or infirmities, shall be obliged to retire from the stage*
S Sept. 17   same
Th 22   Macbeth
Th 29   Richard III
F 30   The Merchant of Venice
M Oct. 10   Cymbeline
Th 13   As You Like It
M 17   Hamlet
Th 20   Much Ado about Nothing
S 22   Cymbeline
M 24   same
Th 27   same
S 29   same
M 31   Othello
Th Nov. 3   Cymbeline
S 5   The Merchant of Venice
Tu Dec. 20   same *BT. the City of London Lying-in Hospital, in Aldersgate-Street*

COVENT GARDEN

			£	s.	d.
F	Jan. 1	The Merchant of Venice	163	4	6
M	4	Romeo and Juliet	176	4	0
F	8	Cymbeline	226	19	0
W	20	Macbeth	244	17	6
F	22	The Merchant of Venice	215	4	6
M	25	same	234	11	0
W	27	Macbeth	234	19	6
Tu	Feb. 16	same	225	2	0
S	20	King Lear	237	14	0
M	29	The Merchant of Venice *BT. Macklin*	258	13	0
M	Mar. 7	King Lear *BT. Powell*	280	4	0
S	12	Catharine and Petruchio	178	6	0
S	19	Cymbeline *BT. Smith*	268	10	6
Th	24	Catharine and Petruchio *BT. Mrs Bellamy*	237	18	0
Tu	Apr. 5	Macbeth *BT. Mrs Mattocks*	193	2	0
W	6	The Merchant of Venice *BT. Miss Macklin*	210	3	6
S	9	Cymbeline *BT. Mrs Bulkley*	232	15	0
M	11	Richard III *BT. Mrs Thompson*	160	7	6

43

1768-1769

1768 COVENT GARDEN (cont.)

				£	s.	d.
Tu	Apr.	12	The Merchant of Venice *BT.* Dyer	235	5	0
	M	18	Cymbeline *BT.* Clarke	243	19	0
	W	20	Coriolanus *BT.* Mrs Lessingham	164	4	6
	M	25	Hamlet *BT.* Bensley	241	3	0
	Th	28	King Lear	109	7	0
	F	29	Romeo and Juliet *BT.* Hull	127	7	0
M	May	9	Cymbeline *BT.* Garton, *treasurer*	165	3	0
	Tu	31	Richard III *BT.* Redman, Casey, Dumai, and [R.] Bates	152	13	6
S	June	4	Cymbeline	115	15	6
Tu	Sept.	20	same	244	7	6
	Th	22	Richard III	238	13	0
	M	26	Romeo and Juliet	133	8	0
Tu	Oct.	4	The Merry Wives of Windsor	116	9	6
	S	8	same	127	4	6
	Th	13	same	209	1	6
	M	17	Macbeth	196	4	6
	W	19	Richard III	175	11	0
	F	21	Cymbeline	114	13	0
Th	Nov.	3	Catharine and Petruchio	163	9	0
	F	4	Henry V	157	12	6
	S	5	Richard III	115	15	0
	Th	10	Macbeth	190	19	6
	Th	17	King Lear	198	17	6
	M	21	Cymbeline	145	13	0
	Tu	22	Henry V	159	7	0
	S	26	Romeo and Juliet	227	19	6
	M	28	same	221	3	6
	Tu	29	same	165	17	6
	W	30	same	181	18	0
Th	Dec.	1	same	187	2	6
	F	2	same	125	16	0
	W	14	The Merry Wives of Windsor	75	18	6
	Tu	20	King Lear *BT. a fund (established by the performers of this theatre) for the support of such actors, and their families, who from age or infirmities, shall be obliged to quit the stage*	184	18	0
	F	23	Macbeth	198	17	6

1769 DRURY LANE

S	Jan.	7	The Merchant of Venice
	Th	12	Richard III
	M	23	Cymbeline
	Tu	24	Macbeth
	Th	26	The Merchant of Venice
	S	28	Othello
F	Feb.	3	Hamlet

1769 DRURY LANE (cont.)

 Th Mar. 16 The Tempest BT. Mrs Arne
  M 27 same BT. Vernon
  Th 30 The Merchant of Venice
F Apr. 7 Cymbeline
   and Florizel and Perdita BT. Miss Younge
  Tu 18 Catharine and Petruchio BT. J. Aickin and Mrs Jefferies
  F 21 Hamlet BT. Rooker and Parsons
M May 1 Romeo and Juliet BT. Ackman and Mrs Bradshaw
  Tu 2 The Tempest BT. Miss Radley and Miss Rogers
  W 3 The Merchant of Venice BT. Hartry and Strange
  F 5 The Tempest BT. Hurst and Evans, sub-treasurer
  S 6 As You Like It BT. Fawcett and Mr and Mrs Johnston
  Tu 16 Richard III BT. Raftor, Walker, and Mrs Simson
  F 19 The Merchant of Venice BT. Watson, Roberts, Kaygill, and [R.] Palmer [Sr.]
  M 22 Catharine and Petruchio BT. Cridland, Foley, and Robinson
Tu Sept. 19 Hamlet
  S 23 Cymbeline
M Oct. 2 Romeo and Juliet
   Genest (v. 255) erroneously has Oct. 1, a Sunday.
  Th 5 The Merchant of Venice
  S 7 King Lear
  M 9 The Tempest
  F 13 As You Like It
  M 23 Henry IV, Part I
  Th 26 The Merchant of Venice
  S 28 Hamlet
M Nov. 13 Richard III
  Tu 14 Much Ado about Nothing
  F 17 Cymbeline
  S 18 Othello
  M 20 The Tempest
S Dec. 2 The Merchant of Venice
  Tu 12 Cymbeline
  S 16 The Merry Wives of Windsor
  W 20 Othello BT. the General Lying-in Hospital
   An advance bill in PA, Dec. 19, notes that this hospital was situated in Oxford Road.
  W 27 The Tempest
  Th 28 Cymbeline
  F 29 The Merry Wives of Windsor

COVENT GARDEN

			£	s.	d.
M	Jan. 2	Hamlet	217	19	6
	F 6	Romeo and Juliet	197	16	6
	W 11	King Lear	227	14	0

1769

1769 COVENT GARDEN (cont.)

			£	s.	d.
F	Jan. 20	[Catharine and Petruchio]			
		Announced by both Pb and PA, but not acted. *The Musical Lady* was performed in its stead (Egerton 2274).			
S 21		King Lear	241	6	0
Th Feb. 16		Hamlet *BT. Powell*	283	8	0
M 27		same	221	0	6
M Mar. 6		Macbeth	230	13	6
S 11		Cymbeline *BT. Woodward*	220	11	0
M 13		Catharine and Petruchio *BT. Mrs Yates*	284	18	6
M 27		Richard III	231	5	0
F 31		Hamlet *BT. Mrs Mattocks*	178	4	0
M Apr. 3		Macbeth *BT. Mattocks*	191	5	0
W 12		King Lear *BT. Clarke*	244	12	6
S 15		Romeo and Juliet *BT. Miss Morris*	221	13	6
Tu 25		Cymbeline *BT. Hull*	180	15	6
W 26		Catharine and Petruchio *BT. Mrs Green*	102	11	6
M May 1		King Lear *BT. Garton, treasurer*	186	6	6
Tu 2		Catharine and Petruchio *BT. Mr and Mrs Du-Bellamy*	182	13	6
W 3		King John *BT. Morris and [Lee] Lewes*	210	10	0
M 8		Cymbeline *BT. Gardner and R. Smith*	158	4	0
Tu 9		Romeo and Juliet *BT. Legg, Mrs Lampe, and Mrs Jones*	160	18	0
Tu 16		Cymbeline *BT. Condell, Potter, box-keepers, and Eddis*	253	4	6
Th 18		Richard III *BT. Green and Ansell, box-keepers*	301	4	0
Tu 23		Macbeth	53	9	6
F Sept. 22		Henry V	226	14	6
W Oct. 4		Richard III	163	1	0
F 6		Romeo and Juliet	82	2	0
S 28		Richard III	127	11	6
M Nov. 27		Hamlet	166	5	0
Tu Dec. 19		Macbeth *BT. the Theatrical Fund, instituted by the performers of this theatre*	187	19	6
Th 28		Richard III	161	6	0
F 29		Henry IV, Part I	149	17	6

HAYMARKET

Tu Feb. 28		Othello *BT. Phillips*
M Aug. 7		Hamlet
M 14		Richard III
W 30		Othello
F Sept. 1		Hamlet *BT. Sheridan*
W 6		Richard III
M 11		Julius Caesar
Tu 19		Richard III *BT. Weston and Miss Ogilvie*

1770

1770 DRURY LANE

	Th	Jan. 4	Macbeth
	Tu	9	Henry IV, Part I
	M	15	King Lear
	Th	18	Cymbeline
	F	19	Henry IV, Part II
	F	26	same
F	Feb.	2	same
	W	21	King Lear
	S	24	Henry IV, Part I
Th	Mar.	8	King Lear
	M	12	Cymbeline
	Tu	13	King Lear
	S	17	Othello
Tu	Apr.	17	The Tempest *BT. Jefferson*
	F	20	Richard III *BT. Mrs King*
	Tu	24	Othello
W	May	2	Hamlet *BT. Grimaldi, Messink, and Giorgi*
	Tu	8	Romeo and Juliet *BT. Brereton*
	W	9	As You Like It *BT. Ackman*
	Tu	15	Cymbeline *BT. Hartry and Miss Burton*
	W	16	Richard III *BT. Wright and Keen*
	W	23	The Tempest *BT. Raftor, Walker, and Mrs Simson*
	Tu	29	The Merchant of Venice
F	June	1	Cymbeline *BT. Cridland, Foley, Robinson, and Carleton Jr.*
S	Sept.	22	same
W	Oct.	3	Hamlet
	Tu	9	As You Like It
	M	22	The Merchant of Venice

Genest (v. 292) erroneously has Oct. 21, a Sunday.

	M	29	Romeo and Juliet
	W	31	King Lear
Th	Nov.	1	Romeo and Juliet
	S	10	Othello
	Tu	13	Much Ado about Nothing
	W	14	Macbeth
	M	19	The Tempest
	Th	22	As You Like It
S	Dec.	1	Cymbeline
	S	8	same
	F	21	The Merchant of Venice *BT. the Westminster New Lying-in Hospital, near Westminster-Bridge*

COVENT GARDEN

				£	s.	d.
M	Jan.	1	Romeo and Juliet	180	10	0
	W	3	Macbeth	210	12	0
	M	8	Hamlet	176	0	0

1770

1770 COVENT GARDEN (cont.)

		£	s.	d.
Th Jan. 11	Macbeth *BT. the composer* [*of* The Court of Alexander, *also acted this night—John Abraham Fisher*]	166	5	0
F 19	Cymbeline	250	0	6
M 22	same	197	6	6

Genest (v. 283) erroneously has Jan. 21, a Sunday.

F 26	Richard III	124	0	6
M Feb. 5	Hamlet	212	6	0
M 12	Measure for Measure *BT. Woodward*	226	0	0
W 14	Macbeth	187	14	0
Th 15	Measure for Measure	188	13	0
Th 22	same	150	12	0
Tu Mar. 27	The Merchant of Venice *BT. Yates*	207	5	6
Th Apr. 5	same *BT. Miss Macklin*	290	8	0
W 18	Cymbeline *BT. Mrs Thompson*	73	0	0
M 23	Macbeth *BT. Gibson*	129	15	6
S 28	Romeo and Juliet *BT. Mrs Lessingham*	186	13	6
S May 12	Measure for Measure *BT. Davis, Holtom, and Merrifield*	178	7	6
M 14	Richard III *BT. [Lee] Lewes and Morris*	274	2	0
W 16	Henry V *BT. Legg, Mrs Lampe, and Mrs Jones*	143	12	0
Tu 22	Hamlet *and* Catharine and Petruchio *BT. Quick, Fox, Hamilton, and [R.] Bates*	199	19	0

W Sept. 26	Richard III
M Oct. 8	Macbeth
Tu 16	Cymbeline
Th 25	Henry V
F 26	Richard III
M 29	King Lear
W Nov. 21	Cymbeline
M 26	Henry V
M Dec. 3	Hamlet
F 14	Macbeth
F 28	Henry V
M 31	Richard III

HAYMARKET

W May 23	Hamlet
M June 18	King Lear
W Aug. 8	[King John]

Announced by PA, but not acted. No mention is made of what play, if any, was substituted. The performance of *King John* on Aug. 13, q.v., is advertised as 'Never Acted Here', with Mrs. Burton as Constance for 'the first time'. Her 'second appearance on any stage' was as Constance on Aug. 30, q.v.

| M 13 | King John |

1770-1771

1770 HAYMARKET (cont.)

Th Aug. 30   King John *BT. Mrs Burton*
Tu Sept. 11   King Lear
M   Oct. 1   Othello *BT. Davis and Griffiths*

1771 DRURY LANE

W   Jan. 2   Catharine and Petruchio
S   5   Cymbeline
M   Mar. 4   same
M   Apr. 1   As You Like It *BT. Love*
Tu   2   Richard III *BT. Dodd*
Tu   9   Florizel and Perdita *BT. Cautherley*
M   15   The Tempest *BT. Baddeley*
W   24   The Merchant of Venice *BT. Sig. Grimaldi, Sig. Giorgi, and Messink*
S   27   Cymbeline *BT. Champnes and Mrs Scott*
W   May 8   As You Like It *BT. Mrs Wrighten and Miss Rogers*
F   24   Much Ado about Nothing *BT. a fund for the relief of those who from their infirmities shall be obliged to retire from the stage*
S   25   Romeo and Juliet *BT. Mortimer, Tomlinson, and Lings*
M   27   The Merry Wives of Windsor *BT. Kear, [J.] Booth, and Jacobs*
Tu   28   The Tempest *BT. Watson, Roberts, Kaygill, and [R.] Palmer [Sr.]*
Th   30   Hamlet *BT. Cridland, box-keeper, Carleton Jr., Robinson, and Percey*

		£	s.	d.
Th Sept. 26	Cymbeline	164	5	0
Tu Oct. 1	As You Like It	249	11	6
Th 3	The Merchant of Venice	185	17	0
Th 10	Romeo and Juliet	203	1	6
Th 17	Much Ado about Nothing	244	8	0
W 23	As You Like It	131	9	6
S Nov. 9	Hamlet	183	7	0
S 23	King Lear	142	13	6
M Dec. 2	The Tempest	162	0	0
W 4	Timon of Athens	243	1	0
Th 5	Cymbeline	133	2	0
M 9	Timon of Athens	153	10	0
Tu 10	Twelfth Night	162	2	0
W 11	Timon of Athens	136	18	0
Th 12	same	162	12	6
F 13	Twelfth Night	211	17	0
S 14	Timon of Athens	128	17	0
Tu 17	As You Like It *BT. the new building of the City of London Lying-in Hospital, in the City-Road, Old-Street*	228	18	6
W 18	Twelfth Night	161	9	0

1771

1771 DRURY LANE (*cont.*)

			£	s.	d.
Th Dec. 19	Timon of Athens		172	6	6
F 20	Twelfth Night		221	4	6
S 21	The Tempest *BT. the British Lying-in Hospital for married women, in Brownlow Street, Longacre*		180	10	6
M 23	Hamlet		289	10	6
F 27	Twelfth Night		203	19	6
S 28	Timon of Athens		202	5	0

COVENT GARDEN

			£	s.	d.
S Jan. 12	Measure for Measure				
M 14	King Lear				
W 23	Cymbeline				
M 28	Othello				
S Feb. 2	Measure for Measure				
W Apr. 3	The Merchant of Venice *BT. Miss Macklin*				
F 5	As You Like It *BT. Mrs Bulkley*				
Th 11	Henry V				
F 12	Catharine and Petruchio *BT. Fishar, ballet-master, and Signora Manesière*				
M 15	Macbeth *BT. Miss Ward, (daughter, of the late Mrs Ward)*				
Tu 16	Cymbeline *BT. Miss D'Arcy*				
W 24	The Winter's Tale *BT. Hull*				
F 26	Cymbeline *BT. the widow of the late Mr Miles*				
M 29	Hamlet *BT. Garton, treasurer*				
Tu 30	Romeo and Juliet *BT. Miss Miller*				
S May 4	Richard III *BT. Morris and Perry*				
Tu 7	The Merchant of Venice *BT. Mrs Pitt and Mrs Vincent*				
M 13	Measure for Measure *BT. Sarjant, box-book and housekeeper*				
M 20	Macbeth				
Tu 28	Romeo and Juliet *BT. Redman, Wild, Roffe, and Mrs Naylor*				
W Sept. 25	Hamlet		205	0	6
F Oct. 4	Catharine and Petruchio		134	5	6
W 9	Measure for Measure		192	3	0
Tu 15	Richard III		193	14	0
Tu 22	The Merchant of Venice		244	19	6
W 23	Measure for Measure		101	16	0
Th 24	The Merchant of Venice		240	9	6
F 25	Romeo and Juliet		146	12	6
S 26	The Merchant of Venice		209	1	0
Tu 29	same		195	3	6
Th 31	same		203	10	6
M Nov. 25	Richard III		220	9	6
M Dec. 16	same		148	10	0

1771-1772

1771 COVENT GARDEN (*cont.*)   £   s.   d.
 Tu Dec. 17   Romeo and Juliet
       and Catharine and Petruchio BT. *the increase
       of a fund, for the support of such actors and
       their families, who through age or infirmity
       are obliged to retire from the stage*   138   14   0
    S 21   Othello BT. *the Westminster New Lying-in
       Hospital, near Westminster-Bridge*   185   16   0
    M 30   King Lear   200   8   0

HAYMARKET
 F   May 31   Catharine and Petruchio
 F   June 14   same
 F   Sept. 20   The Merchant of Venice BT. *Mrs Gardner*

1772 DRURY LANE
 W   Jan. 1   Twelfth Night   195   5   0
   Th   2   Timon of Athens   202   11   6
   M   6   Twelfth Night   162   8   6
   Tu   7   Othello   220   0   0
   W   8   Hamlet   287   12   0
   F   10   Timon of Athens   193   10   0
   S   11   The Merchant of Venice   245   11   0
   M   13   Twelfth Night   234   3   0
   W   15   The Merry Wives of Windsor   158   6   0
   S   18   Timon of Athens   210   2   6
 M Feb. 3   Twelfth Night   212   9   0
   W   5   Hamlet   288   1   6
   Th   6   Timon of Athens   123   0   6
   W   19   Twelfth Night   169   14   0
   F   28   Much Ado about Nothing   258   13   6
 Tu Mar. 3   Twelfth Night   181   15   6
 Th Apr. 9   As You Like It BT. *[F.] Aickin*   162   2   0
   F   24   Twelfth Night BT. *D'Egville and Signora
       Vidini*   151   4   0
     In the bill D'Egville's name is spelled 'Daigville'.
   S   25   Macbeth BT. *Baddeley*   135   1   6
 F   May 1   Twelfth Night BT. *Dibdin*   134   2   0
   S   2   The Merchant of Venice BT. *[C.] Bannister*   140   9   6
   Th   7   Cymbeline BT. *Croft*   179   5   6
   Tu   26   The Tempest BT. *Keen and Wright*   197   8   6
   F   29   Twelfth Night BT. *Johnston, box-book and
       house-keeper*   292   19   6
   S   30   Richard III   268   8   6
 Tu June 2   same BT. *a fund, for the relief of those who from
       their infirmities shall be obliged to retire from
       the stage*   313   4   3

1772

1772 DRURY LANE (cont.)

			£	s.	d.
F	June 5	As You Like It *BT. Watson, [R.] Palmer [Sr.], Kaygill, and Roberts*	240	3	0
	Tu 9	Macbeth *BT. Cridland, Percey, Carleton Jr., and Robinson*	258	15	0
S	Sept. 19	Cymbeline	156	15	6
Th	Oct. 1	Romeo and Juliet	208	13	0
	S 3	same	162	13	6
	Th 8	Twelfth Night	221	11	0
	S 10	Romeo and Juliet	199	5	0
	S 31	Othello	167	12	6
Tu	Nov. 3	Much Ado about Nothing	224	11	0
	Tu 17	As You Like It	152	4	6
F	Dec. 18	Hamlet	284	5	6
	M 21	same	272	10	0
	W 23	same	264	13	0
	Th 31	Twelfth Night	181	14	0

COVENT GARDEN

			£	s.	d.
W	Jan. 1	Cymbeline	144	6	6
	S 25	Othello	198	16	6
	M 27	Macbeth	209	15	6
M	Feb. 3	Richard III	205	6	0
	W 19	Measure for Measure	142	7	6
	M 24	Romeo and Juliet	236	15	6
M	Mar. 2	Macbeth	221	16	6
	Th 5	Richard III	218	12	0

Both Pb and PA announce the first night of *A Wife in the Right*, but it was changed to *Richard III* (Egerton 2276; Reed, 74). 'Mr. Shuter . . . was taken so ill Yesterday Morning as to be obliged to leave the Theatre, where he was attending on Business, and the New Comedy of A Wife in the Right, in which he has a very capital Part, was . . . obliged to be postponed' (PA, Mar. 6). [It was first acted on Mar. 9.]

			£	s.	d.
	M 16	Romeo and Juliet	201	4	0
	Tu 31	Twelfth Night *BT. Mrs Mattocks*	210	18	6
M	Apr. 6	Macbeth *BT. Clarke*	254	0	0
	S 11	Cymbeline *BT. Bensley*	212	17	6
	Tu 21	Hamlet *BT. Mrs Lessingham*	233	12	6
	Tu 28	Macbeth *BT. Dunstall*	247	4	6
F	May 1	Catharine and Petruchio	133	12	0
	S 2	Romeo and Juliet *BT. Mrs [T.] Baker*	151	16	6
	M 4	The Winter's Tale *BT. Hull*	129	6	0
	Tu 5	Twelfth Night *BT. Mrs Green*	138	12	6
	F 8	All's Well that Ends Well *BT. [Lee] Lewes*	214	15	6
	S 9	Cymbeline *BT. Morris and Perry*	155	0	6
	Tu 12	Richard III *BT. Quick*	154	6	6

1772-1773

1772 COVENT GARDEN (*cont.*)   £   s.   d.

W	May 13	The Merchant of Venice and Catharine and Petruchio *BT. Gardner and R. Smith*	159	17	0
	Th 21	King Lear *BT. Legg, Mrs Lampe, Mrs Jones, and Miss Besford*	203	8	0
M	June 1	Macbeth	85	3	6
M	Sept. 28	Richard III	226	7	6
M	Oct. 19	same	164	11	6
	M 26	Hamlet	149	10	0
M	Nov. 2	Romeo and Juliet	163	18	0
F	6	Henry VIII	223	13	6
S	7	same	205	10	0
M	9	same	234	16	0
W	11	same	215	10	0
F	13	same	140	3	0
M	16	same	183	3	0
W	18	same	235	1	0
F	20	same	136	5	6
Th	Dec. 3	All's Well that Ends Well	133	18	0
	Tu 8	same	154	8	6
	M 21	Henry VIII *BT. the establishment of a fund for the relief of performers retiring from the stage*	218	8	0
	W 30	Richard III	177	5	6
	Th 31	All's Well that Ends Well	118	13	6

HAYMARKET

Th Sept. 17   Richard III

1773 DRURY LANE

M	Jan. 4	The Merchant of Venice	199	19	0
W	6	Twelfth Night	134	8	0
Tu	Feb. 2	King Lear	218	16	0
F	5	The Merchant of Venice	138	15	0
M	8	Cymbeline *BT. the author of* The Wedding Ring [*also acted this night—Charles Dibdin*]	176	10	6
W	10	Hamlet	268	13	6
Tu	16	Twelfth Night	161	9	0
W	17	King Lear	286	8	0
F	19	same	284	12	6
Th	Apr. 1	Twelfth Night and Catharine and Petruchio *BT. Dodd*	237	5	6
	M 19	As You Like It *BT. Hopkins, prompter, and Mrs Hopkins*	241	17	6
	Th 29	Othello *BT. Barry*	255	17	0
M	May 10	Macbeth *BT. Champnes and Mrs Scott*	197	18	6
W	12	The Tempest *BT. Ackman*	296	11	6
S	15	Twelfth Night *BT. Hartry and Fawcett*	298	10	6

1773

1773 DRURY LANE (cont.)   £   s. d.

W May 26 King Lear *BT. a fund, for the relief of those, who from their infirmities, shall be obliged to retire from the stage* 304 11 6

    M 31 Cymbeline *BT. Watson, Roberts, and* [R.] *Palmer* [Sr.] 330 5 6

Tu Sept. 21 same 166 14 0

M Oct. 11 Catharine and Petruchio 176 6 6

    Th 28 Much Ado about Nothing 251 15 6

Tu Nov. 2 As You Like It 183 18 6

    S 20 Othello 160 8 6

S Dec. 4 [Twelfth Night]

    Announced by both Pb and PA, but not acted. Mrs Abington was ill, and the play was changed to *The Fair Quaker* (MacMillan, 174).

    F 10 Twelfth Night 122 0 6

COVENT GARDEN

F Jan. 1 Romeo and Juliet 172 10 0

    M 4 Hamlet 179 17 6

    W 6 Henry V 126 2 6

    S 16 Cymbeline 183 17 0

    M 18 Henry VIII 180 18 6

    M 25 King Lear 189 0 0

    Genest (v. 364) erroneously has Jan. 24, a Sunday.

    F 29 Henry VIII 168 16 6

M Feb. 1 Hamlet 218 15 6

    W 10 Henry VIII 190 2 0

    F 12 Cymbeline 160 8 6

    M 15 Henry VIII 174 3 0

M Mar. 22 Macbeth *BT. Mrs Hartley* 249 9 0

    Tu 23 Henry VIII *BT. Shuter* 220 15 0

S Apr. 17 The Merchant of Venice *BT. Miss Macklin* 283 0 6

    Tu 20 Macbeth *BT. Reinhold* 198 13 6

    Tu 27 Henry IV, Part II *BT. Mrs Lessingham* 185 9 6

Tu May 4 Julius Caesar *BT. Wroughton* 123 18 0

    S 8 King Lear *BT. Quick* 153 6 6

    M 10 Macbeth *BT. Miss Barsanti* 217 17 0

    M 17 Romeo and Juliet *BT. Sarjant, box-book and house-keeper* 234 10 6

    Genest (v. 373) erroneously has May 11, on which night the play was *The Rival Queens*.

    W 19 Hamlet *BT. Branson, Mrs Lampe, Mrs Jones, and Miss Besford* 199 16 6

    Th 20 Richard III *BT. Wignell and Davis* 209 19 0

    M 24 The Merchant of Venice *BT. Wild, Holtom,* [R.] *Bates, and Hamilton* 179 9 0

1773-1774

1773 COVENT GARDEN (*cont.*)

			£	s.	d.
W	Sept. 22	Henry VIII	190	18	0
M	Oct. 4	Richard III	207	1	0
	Tu 5	The Merchant of Venice	206	15	6
	F 8	Henry VIII	81	2	6
	Th 14	The Merchant of Venice	182	14	0
	M 18	Hamlet	146	18	0
	S 23	Macbeth	200	7	6
	M 25	Romeo and Juliet	140	11	6
	S 30	Macbeth	152	11	6
S	Nov. 6	same	237	19	6
	Tu 9	Henry VIII	145	12	0
	F 12	Cymbeline	160	8	6
	S 13	Macbeth	201	16	0
	M 15	Cymbeline	125	4	6
	Tu 16	Catharine and Petruchio	114	8	0
	W 17	Cymbeline	186	3	0
	Th 18	[The Merchant of Venice]			

Announced by both Pb and PA, but not acted (Egerton 2278). A cabal had been formed against Macklin because of displeasure occasioned by his performance of Macbeth. On this night a riot took place that resulted in his dismissal from the CG company (J. T. Kirkman, *Memoirs . . . of Macklin*, 1799, ii. 188-95).

			£	s.	d.
	M 22	Hamlet	124	3	6
	Th 25	Cymbeline	122	0	6
	S 27	Othello *and* Catharine and Petruchio	188	1	0
	M 29	Othello	137	1	0
M	Dec. 6	Cymbeline	139	11	0
	Th 9	Richard III	148	10	6
	M 13	Romeo and Juliet	106	4	0
	W 15	Cymbeline	151	14	0
	M 20	Richard III	161	13	6
	W 22	Henry VIII	131	6	0

1774 DRURY LANE

			£	s.	d.
S	Jan. 1	Catharine and Petruchio	213	4	0
	M 17	same	159	15	0
	F 28	Cymbeline	125	12	0
W	Feb. 2	King John	162	18	6
	F 4	same	167	13	0
	Tu 8	Hamlet	287	12	0
	W 9	King John	205	10	0
	F 11	same	139	1	6
S	Mar. 12	King Lear *BT. Barry*	271	0	0
	Th 17	As You Like It *BT. Vernon*	213	9	0
M	Apr. 4	The Tempest *BT.* [*F.*] *Aickin*	123	14	6

1774

1774 DRURY LANE (cont.)

			£	s.	d.
Tu Apr. 5	Cymbeline *BT. Dibdin*		184	9	0
Tu 12	Othello *and* Florizel and Perdita *BT. [J.] Palmer*		199	16	0
M 18	Much Ado about Nothing		245	8	6
M 25	King Lear *BT. Baddeley*		203	7	0
S 30	Twelfth Night *BT. Rooker, Messink, and Giorgi*		232	7	0
F May 6	Hamlet		261	11	6
S 7	Florizel and Perdita *BT. [F.] Waldron and Dimond*		188	11	6
S 14	The Merchant of Venice *BT. Wright and Keen*		133	12	0
Tu 17	King Lear *BT. a fund for the relief of those, who from their infirmities, shall be obliged to retire from the stage*		300	3	6
M 23	Cymbeline *BT. Dickinson, first gallery office-keeper*		287	2	0
Th Sept. 22	Richard III		239	8	6
Tu 27	Cymbeline		240	15	6
S Oct. 1	As You Like It		226	3	0
Tu 4	Hamlet		135	5	0
Tu 18	Cymbeline		132	6	0
W 19	As You Like It		137	15	0
F 28	Much Ado about Nothing		242	11	6
S 29	Richard III		104	1	6
W Nov. 30	Catharine and Petruchio		199	3	6
F Dec. 2	Hamlet		264	1	6
M 12	same		259	5	6
Tu 13	As You Like It		156	17	6
S 17	Cymbeline *BT. persons imprisoned for small debts*		122	17	0
M 26	The Tempest		157	16	6

COVENT GARDEN

			£	s.	d.
S Jan. 1	Richard III		133	13	6
W 26	same		174	16	0
S Feb. 5	Cymbeline		138	9	0
W 9	Romeo and Juliet		166	12	0
M 14	Henry VIII		186	6	0
S Mar. 12	The Winter's Tale *BT. Woodward*		259	14	0
Tu 15	Henry IV, Part I *BT. Shuter*		267	2	0
M 21	Henry VIII *BT. Clarke*		227	2	0
F Apr. 8	Henry IV, Part I *BT. Reinhold*		244	0	0
W 13	Macbeth *BT. Mrs Hartley*		189	2	6
M 18	Catharine and Petruchio *BT. Lewis*		155	13	0
M 25	Henry VIII *BT. Mrs Green*		116	7	0
F 29	Macbeth *BT. Miss Wilde*		119	11	6
S 30	Henry IV, Part I *BT. Gardner and Davis*		187	0	0
Tu May 3	Hamlet *BT. Mr and Mrs Kniveton*		179	8	0

1774-1775

1774 COVENT GARDEN (cont.)   £   s.   d.

   S May   7   Henry IV, Part I *BT. Miss Stede and T. Ansell* 229 15   6
        Tu 10 Richard III *BT. R. Smith and Branson*   150 17   6
   M Sept. 19   All's Well that Ends Well
   Th Oct. 13   Romeo and Juliet
       S 15   Henry VIII
       S 22   Richard III
       S 29   same
   M Nov. 7   same
       Tu 8   Much Ado about Nothing
       M 14   Henry VIII
       W 16   Much Ado about Nothing
       S 19   The Winter's Tale
       M 21   same
       Th 24   King Lear
       S 26   same
   M Dec. 5   Richard III
       S 10   Much Ado about Nothing
       Th 15   Othello
       Tu 20   As You Like It
       Th 29   Henry VIII
       S 31   Richard III

HAYMARKET

   Tu Apr. 12   Catharine and Petruchio *BT. Stewart, Jefferson, and Hutton*
   M June 13   same
   M July 4   same
       F 22   same
   F Aug. 5   same
   F Sept. 30   Richard III *BT. Mrs Williams and Mrs Weston*

1775 DRURY LANE

   Tu Jan. 10   Much Ado about Nothing   253 16   0
       W 11   Twelfth Night   255 16   0
   S Feb. 4   Catharine and Petruchio   194   7   6
       S 18   same   226 10   0
   S Mar. 18   Measure for Measure *BT. King*   291   2   6
       Th 23   Macbeth *BT. Smith*   281   9   6
   Tu Apr. 4   Twelfth Night *BT. Dodd*   281 11   0
       Th 20   Measure for Measure *BT. [J.] Palmer*   203 12   0
       W 26   Twelfth Night *BT. Mrs Wrighten*   142 16   0
       F 28   Richard III *BT. Mrs Sutton*   156   8   6
       S 29   Cymbeline   88 13   0
   Tu May   2   [same]

               Listed by Genest (v. 452), for Mrs Smith's BT. Advance notices (PA, Apr. 20, &c.) advertise *Cymbeline*, but subsequently the play was changed to *Love in a Village*, which is announced by both Pb and PA on May 2.

1775 DRURY LANE (cont.)   £   s.   d.

M	May 15	Richard III *BT. Giorgi, Keen, and Legg*	180	0	0
Th	18	The Tempest *and* Catharine and Petruchio *BT. Percey, Wood, and Robinson*	189	12	6
S	20	As You Like It *BT. Johnston, box-book and house-keeper*	276	4	6
Tu	23	Twelfth Night *BT. Tomlinson, Mortimer, Walton, and Carleton Sr.*	239	16	0
F	26	same *BT. Carleton Jr., Berrisford, and Kaygill*	211	16	0
Tu Sept.	26	As You Like It	243	16	0
Tu Oct.	3	Richard III	263	6	0
F	13	As You Like It	132	16	6
Tu	17	Othello	220	4	0
W	18	As You Like It	260	12	0
Th	19	Othello	114	19	6
M	23	Hamlet	183	3	0
W Nov.	1	Cymbeline	142	14	0
M	6	Much Ado about Nothing	264	9	6
Tu	7	Richard III	136	17	0
W	8	Much Ado about Nothing	278	1	0
F	10	same	272	1	6
Th	16	same	267	7	6
S	18	Measure for Measure	133	12	6
W	22	Much Ado about Nothing	280	1	0
W	29	Hamlet	286	14	6
Th Dec.	7	Macbeth	188	9	6
F	8	Hamlet	276	0	6
Tu	12	Richard III	143	1	6
Th	28	Othello	217	0	6
F	29	The Merchant of Venice	197	0	0

COVENT GARDEN

Tu Jan.	3	Hamlet
Tu	24	As You Like It
W Feb.	1	same
Th	9	Othello
M	20	Hamlet
Tu Mar.	28	As You Like It *BT. Shuter*
S Apr.	18	Richard III *BT. Mr and Mrs Melmoth*
S	29	As You Like It *BT. Aldridge*
S May	13	same *BT. Miss Wilde*
W	17	Henry IV, Part I *BT. Whitfield and Mrs Pitt*
Th	18	The Merchant of Venice *BT. Miss Macklin*
S	20	Cymbeline *BT. Branson and Booth*
Th	25	Richard III
M	29	The Merchant of Venice
Th June	1	Richard III *BT. Macklin*

1775–1776

1775 COVENT GARDEN (cont.)

   M Sept. 25 Romeo and Juliet
       F 29 Much Ado about Nothing
   M Oct. 2 Romeo and Juliet
       F 6 The Merchant of Venice
       M 9 Romeo and Juliet
      Th 19 Macbeth
       F 27 The Merchant of Venice
  Tu Nov. 7 Romeo and Juliet
      Th 9 Henry VIII
  F Dec. 1 King John
       F 15 same
      Th 21 Catharine and Petruchio
      W 27 Romeo and Juliet
       F 29 Hamlet

HAYMARKET

  Th Mar. 23 The Merchant of Venice *BT.* [*S.*] *Johnson*
  F July 14 Catharine and Petruchio *BT. the author* [*of Eldred, also acted this night—John Jackson*]
          Genest (v. 471) erroneously has July 13.

1776 DRURY LANE   £ s. d.

M	Jan. 1	Macbeth	219	12	6
Tu	2	The Merchant of Venice	243	8	6
W	10	Measure for Measure	288	5	0
F	19	Macbeth	167	2	0
M	Feb. 12	Much Ado about Nothing	276	5	6
W	Apr. 10	Twelfth Night *BT.* [*J.*] *Palmer*	183	15	0
F	12	As You Like It *BT.* [*C.*] *Bannister*	149	1	6
Tu	16	Much Ado about Nothing	269	6	6
S	27	Hamlet	297	6	6
M	29	Cymbeline *BT. Whitfield and Miss Sharpe*	137	19	0
Th	May 9	Much Ado about Nothing	270	10	6
F	10	As You Like It *BT. Fawcett, Legg, and Kear*	98	4	6
M	13	King Lear	308	1	0
Tu	14	Measure for Measure *BT. Fosbrook, box-bookkeeper*	106	9	6
S	18	The Tempest *BT. Mortimer, Tomlinson, Carleton Sr., and Walton*	127	14	6
Tu	21	King Lear	309	13	6
W	22	Romeo and Juliet *BT. Berrisford, Carleton Jr., Kaygill, and Edelston*	113	9	0
M	27	Richard III	307	3	6
Th	30	Hamlet *BT. a fund, for the relief of those who from their infirmities shall be obliged to retire from the stage* cash:[1]	85	3	0

[1] See note, p. 40.

1776 DRURY LANE (cont.)

			£	s.	d.
M June 3	Richard III		284	10	0
W 5	same		293	5	0
S 8	King Lear		305	13	6
S Sept. 21	Twelfth Night		269	19	6
W Oct. 9	As You Like It		267	6	0
S 12	Richard III		186	18	6

The Hypocrite was originally intended for performance, but both Pb and PA, in the bill for this night, state that it was 'obliged to be deferred'. The DL Account-Book deletes it, and erroneously substitutes *Hamlet*. But the bill for *Hamlet* on Oct. 23, q.v., has 'Not acted this season'.

S 19	Measure for Measure		208	16	6
W 23	Hamlet		243	13	6
Th 24	Twelfth Night		150	12	6
S 26	Cymbeline		164	15	6
Tu Nov. 12	same		124	3	6
M 25	Macbeth		191	1	6
S 30	Hamlet		106	11	0
F Dec. 6	Richard III		167	8	0
Tu 10	Romeo and Juliet		170	8	0
Th 12	same		141	15	0
S 21	same		127	6	0
Th 26	Macbeth		209	0	6
F 27	Romeo and Juliet		131	2	0
M 30	Macbeth		133	3	0

COVENT GARDEN

M Jan. 1   Richard III
   W 3   Catharine and Petruchio
M Feb. 5   As You Like It
   Tu 13   Catharine and Petruchio
   S 17   same
   Th 22   King Lear
   Tu 27   [same]

     Listed by Genest (v. 518), for Webster's BT., but not acted. It was announced (PA, Feb. 26), but changed to *Douglas*; Pb carries the notice, 'Mr. Barry being taken ill, the Tragedy of *King Lear* is obliged to be deferred'.

Th Mar. 14   Catharine and Petruchio
   Tu 19   As You Like It BT. *Woodward*
   S 23   King Lear
       and Catharine and Petruchio BT. *Lee*
S Apr. 13   The Merchant of Venice BT. *Miss Macklin*
   F 19   Catharine and Petruchio BT. *Dunstall*
Tu May 7   As You Like It BT. *Du-Bellamy*

1776–1777

1776 COVENT GARDEN (*cont.*)

			£	s.	d.
F	May 10	Henry IV, Part I *BT. Shuter*			
	Th 30	Catharine and Petruchio			
M	Oct. 7	Romeo and Juliet	302	17	6
	F 11	Catharine and Petruchio	212	12	0
	M 14	Romeo and Juliet	281	15	0
	Th 17	Hamlet	233	10	0
	M 21	Romeo and Juliet	257	2	0
	Tu 29	The Merchant of Venice	196	9	0
F	Nov. 8	Romeo and Juliet	87	18	0
	M 11	Richard III	172	16	6
	Tu 12	As You Like It	125	15	6
	F 22	The Merchant of Venice	179	7	6
	M 25	Henry VIII *BT. Dibdin* [*composer of* The Seraglio, *also acted this night*]	receipts omitted		
M	Dec. 2	Macbeth	158	0	6
	Th 12	Catharine and Petruchio	120	9	6
	Th 19	The Merchant of Venice	170	12	6
	F 27	The Tempest	245	18	0
	M 30	same	224	13	0
	Th 31	same	159	8	6

HAYMARKET

M Apr. 22   Catharine and Petruchio *BT. Mrs Fisher*
W   July 24   same
W   Aug. 21   same
Tu Sept. 17   Henry IV, Part I *BT.* [*J.*] *Palmer*

CHINA HALL, ROTHERHITHE

M   July 15   Romeo and Juliet
F   Aug. 2   The Merchant of Venice
    F 9   As You Like It
    W 14   Hamlet
    F 16   As You Like It
M Sept. 9   Cymbeline *BT. Mrs Massey*
    M 16   King Lear *BT. Mrs Marklew*
    W 25   Henry VIII *BT. Miss Reynolds*
F   Oct. 4   Richard III *BT. Harrison and Thompson*

1777 DRURY LANE

			£	s.	d.
W	Jan. 1	Hamlet	172	12	0
	S 4	The Tempest	231	10	0
	M 6	same	203	12	6
	F 10	same	243	19	6
	M 13	same	247	5	6
	S 18	same	229	6	6
	Th 23	same	212	15	6

1777

1777 DRURY LANE (cont.)   £   s.   d.

S	Jan. 25	The Tempest	186	19	6
F	31	same	243	12	0
M	Feb. 3	Hamlet	157	11	6
	Tu 4	The Tempest	189	17	6
	S 8	Hamlet	105	10	6
	Tu 18	The Tempest	158	1	0
M	Mar. 3	same	171	17	0
	S 15	same *BT. Vernon*	200	8	6
	M 17	Twelfth Night *BT. Dodd*	197	16	6
F	Apr. 4	The Tempest	211	18	0
	F 11	Othello	99	7	0
	M 14	The Tempest	157	8	6
	Tu 22	Macbeth *BT. Miss Sherry and Signora Crespi*	185	12	0
	F 25	The Tempest *BT. Wright, Carpenter, and Butler*	117	15	0
	M 28	Twelfth Night *BT. a fund, for the relief of those who from their infirmities shall be obliged to retire from the stage* cash:[1]	100	9	6
F	May 2	The Tempest	58	2	0
	S 3	As You Like It *BT. Fosbrook, box-book-keeper*	163	8	0
	M 5	Hamlet	59	12	6
	W 7	The Tempest	219	13	0
	F 30	same *BT. Mortimer, Tomlinson, Carleton Sr., and Walton*	107	19	0
S	Sept. 20	same	183	4	0
	Tu 30	Hamlet	225	8	0
S	Oct. 4	same	235	18	6
	Tu 7	Richard III	260	7	0
	S 11	same	250	9	6
	Tu 14	The Merchant of Venice	234	6	6
	Th 16	same	136	5	0
	F 17	Henry IV, Part I	207	10	6
	S 18	Twelfth Night	204	0	6
	Tu 21	Henry IV, Part I	183	0	0
	Th 23	Hamlet	208	2	6
	F 31	Cymbeline	104	3	6
M	Nov. 3	Hamlet	173	17	0
	W 5	Henry IV, Part I	161	7	6
	F 7	The Merchant of Venice	92	8	0
	M 10	Henry IV, Part I	177	7	0
	Th 13	Measure for Measure	90	0	0
	F 14	The Tempest	116	13	6
	Th 20	Henry IV, Part I	159	3	0
	M 24	Henry IV, Part II	186	19	0
	Th 27	same	125	18	0
	S 29	King John	144	12	6

[1] See note, p. 40.

1777

1777 DRURY LANE (*cont.*)

			£	s.	d.
Tu Dec. 2	King John		127	15	0
W 3	As You Like It		92	7	0
S 6	Hamlet		144	6	0
W 10	Henry IV, Part I		108	16	0
M 15	Henry IV, Part II		190	15	6
F 26	The Tempest		185	19	0
M 29	Hamlet		175	4	6
Tu 30	Henry IV, Part I *BT. the Dispensary for the Infant Poor, in Soho-Square*		212	0	0

COVENT GARDEN

		£	s.	d.
W Jan. 8	Measure for Measure	191	15	6
M 13	The Tempest	224	16	0
W 15	The Merchant of Venice	208	2	6
Th Feb. 13	The Tempest	167	6	0
S 15	The Merchant of Venice	210	15	0
M Mar. 17	Twelfth Night *BT. Mrs [S.] Barry*	271	15	6
S 22	The Merchant of Venice *BT. Macklin*	273	16	0
W Apr. 16	Othello *BT. Mrs Lessingham*	224	1	6
S 19	The Merchant of Venice *BT. Miss Macklin*	191	16	0
M May 19	The Tempest *BT. Sarjant, box-book-keeper*	253	17	0
M Sept. 29	Romeo and Juliet	174	5	6
M Oct. 6	King Lear	203	9	6
M 13	same	212	14	6
W 15	Much Ado about Nothing	178	12	0
Th 16	The Merchant of Venice	205	8	6
Tu 28	same	149	1	6
S Nov. 1	Othello	160	3	0
F 7	Richard III	132	11	6
M 10	King Lear	167	2	6
F 14	Othello	101	13	0
W 19	Catharine and Petruchio	153	1	0
M 24	same	123	9	0
M Dec. 29	King Lear	183	2	0

HAYMARKET

Tu Feb. 11 Henry IV, Part I *BT. West and [S.] Johnson*
Th May 1   Catharine and Petruchio *BT. a gentleman*
W June 11 The Merchant of Venice
Th 12   same
M 16   same
W 18   same
Th 26   Hamlet
F 27   same
Th July 3 same
F 4   same
Tu 8   The Merchant of Venice

1777–1778

1777 HAYMARKET (cont.)

- Th July 10   Hamlet
- F 18   The Sheep Shearing *and* A Fairy Tale
- M 21   Hamlet *and* same
- Tu 22   A Fairy Tale
- W 23   The Merchant of Venice *and* A Fairy Tale
- Th 24   Henry IV, Part I
- M 28   same
- Tu 29   A Fairy Tale
- Th 31   Henry IV, Part I
- S Aug. 2   same
- M 4   Hamlet
- Th 7   Richard III
- F 8   same
- M 11   same
- W 13   Henry IV, Part I
- F 15   The Merchant of Venice
- Th 21   Henry IV, Part I
- M 25   A Fairy Tale *BT. Henderson*
- F 29   Henry VIII
- W Sept. 3   The Merry Wives of Windsor *BT. Jewell, treasurer*
- F 5   Henry VIII *and* A Fairy Tale
- S 6   Hamlet
- Tu 9   The Merry Wives of Windsor
- S 13   Henry IV, Part I
- M 15   Hamlet

CHINA HALL, ROTHERHITHE

- M July 21   Othello

HAMMERSMITH

- Tu Oct. 28   Henry IV, Part I

1778 DRURY LANE

		£	s.	d.
Th Jan. 1	King John	163	13	6
S 3	Twelfth Night	139	6	0
M 5	Macbeth	212	15	6
Tu 6	The Tempest	108	18	0
M 12	Macbeth	151	7	6
W 21	Henry IV, Part I	278	19	6
Tu Feb. 10	Much Ado about Nothing	243	8	6
W 11	same	255	17	0
Tu 17	same	90	0	6

64

1778

1778 DRURY LANE (*cont.*)

			£	s.	d.
Th Feb. 19	Cymbeline		180	0	6
Tu 24	The Merry Wives of Windsor		231	15	6
W 25	same		273	10	0
S 28	same		210	18	0
M Mar. 9	same		209	13	0
Tu 17	Hamlet		160	1	0
S 21	Henry IV, Part I		146	17	6
Tu 24	Twelfth Night *BT. the author of* Belphegor [*also acted this night—Miles Peter Andrews*]		99	18	6

Genest (vi. 9) erroneously has Mar. 25.

Tu 31	Macbeth *BT. Henderson*	275	18	0
Th Apr. 2	The Merry Wives of Windsor *BT. Vernon*	222	19	0
Th 30	Macbeth *BT. Mrs Robinson*	153	17	6
W May 6	Much Ado about Nothing	168	12	0
F 8	Richard III *BT. Lamash, Legg, and Blurton*	225	5	6
Th 14	As You Like It *BT. Mrs Bradshaw, Mrs Love, and Mrs Johnston*	132	16	0
F 15	The Tempest *BT. Gaudry, Griffith, Norris, and Miss Armstrong*	211	12	0
S 23	Romeo and Juliet *BT. Watson, Wilson, Devoto, Kaygill, and Burroughs*	182	18	6
Tu 26	Richard III *BT. Wood, Percey, Cameron, and the widow Robinson*	288	13	0
Th Sept. 17	The Merry Wives of Windsor	226	8	6
S 19	Hamlet	157	14	6
Tu 22	Henry IV, Part I	170	3	0
Th 24	Macbeth	153	11	6
S 26	As You Like It	148	2	6
Tu 29	Henry IV, Part II	157	4	6
F Oct. 16	Hamlet	224	7	6
S 17	The Merchant of Venice	225	12	0
Tu 20	Measure for Measure	226	18	6
S 24	Henry IV, Part II	209	16	6

PA incorrectly has, 'Not acted this season'. But the performance of this play on Sept. 29 was reviewed in detail in MC on Sept. 30 and again on Oct. 1.

M 26	Richard III	224	6	6
F 30	Henry IV, Part I	195	9	0
M Nov. 2	The Tempest	213	2	0
W 4	Much Ado about Nothing	156	15	0
F 6	The Merry Wives of Windsor	137	16	6
Tu 10	Twelfth Night	190	8	6
M 23	Richard III	153	17	6
Th 26	Macbeth	158	17	6
F 27	The Tempest	127	1	0
Tu Dec. 15	Hamlet	149	3	0

1778 DRURY LANE (cont.)

			£	s.	d.
M Dec. 28	Henry IV, Part I		186	14	6
Tu 29	Macbeth		146	17	0

COVENT GARDEN

M Jan. 12	Romeo and Juliet	174	19	0
W 28	The Merchant of Venice	282	9	0
Th Feb. 5	King Lear	201	3	6
M 23	Romeo and Juliet	199	10	0
Tu 24	As You Like It	164	12	6
Tu Mar. 24	The Merchant of Venice *BT. Macklin*	212	8	0
F Apr. 24	same *BT. Mrs Lessingham*	160	7	0
W May 6	Macbeth	161	10	0
M 11	Henry V *BT. Wild, prompter*	224	18	0
M 18	same *BT. Sarjant, box-book and house-keeper*	243	1	0

M Sept. 21 same
M 28 King Lear
M Oct. 5 Richard III
M 12 Hamlet
F 16 Henry VIII
M 19 King Lear
S 24 Cymbeline
M 26 Romeo and Juliet
M Nov. 9 King Lear
Tu Dec. 1 Catharine and Petruchio
M 7 Richard III
M 28 Romeo and Juliet

HAYMARKET

M Mar. 23 Catharine and Petruchio *BT. a lady in distress*
Tu 24 Richard III *BT. West*
F June 19 Henry VIII
Th 25 same
Th July 2 same
W 8 same
F Aug. 14 same *BT. the author of the farce* [Tony Lumpkin in Town, also acted this night—John O'Keeffe]
Tu 25 same *BT. Miss Harper*
M Sept. 7 Macbeth
    Genest (vi. 36) erroneously says that this was Digges's BT. See Sept. 17.
W 9 same
Th 17 King Lear *BT. Digges*

CHINA HALL, ROTHERHITHE

F May 29 Catharine and Petruchio
W June 10 Romeo and Juliet
F 26 Richard III

1778-1779

1778 TEMPORARY BOOTH, CHINA HALL, ROTHERHITHE

Th Aug. 6   The Merchant of Venice
Aug.   King Lear
> Acted three times (E. C. Everard, *Memoirs of an Unfortunate Son of Thespis*, 1818, 78). The actual dates I have been unable to ascertain.

1779 DRURY LANE

			£	s.	d.
Tu Jan. 5	Much Ado about Nothing		74	11	6
W 6	Twelfth Night		58	18	6
S 9	Richard III		209	9	0
M 11	As You Like It		285	5	0
Tu 12	Hamlet		222	15	0
Tu 19	The Merchant of Venice		187	13	0
W 20	[Henry IV, Part I]				

> Announced by both Pb and PA, but 'Not perform'd on Acct. of Mr. Garrick's Death (at 8 o'Clo' Morng)' (MS annotation on JPK). See also PA, Jan. 21: 'Drury Lane Theatre was shut up last night on [this] melancholy occasion.'

			£	s.	d.
F 22	Henry IV, Part I		171	13	8
Tu 26	The Merry Wives of Windsor		208	11	0
S Feb. 6	Hamlet		151	6	0
M Mar. 22	King Lear *BT. Henderson*		259	9	0
W Apr. 7	Macbeth *BT. Brereton*		188	10	6
W 14	King Lear *BT. Mrs Robinson*		210	14	0
M May 3	The Merry Wives of Windsor *BT. Mrs Sharp and Mrs Brereton*		133	9	6
Tu 4	King Lear *BT. Hurst and [J.] Burton*		194	13	0
W 5	Much Ado about Nothing *BT. Grimaldi (ballet-master), and Lamash*		175	5	6
S 8	The Tempest *BT. [F.] Waldron and Miss Abrams*		138	5	0
F 14	The Merchant of Venice		215	14	6
Tu 18	Richard III *BT. Chaplin, Griffith, Holcroft, and Miss Field*		253	8	0
W 19	Henry IV, Part I *BT. Mrs Colles, the widow Legg, and Miss Kirby*		225	15	0
S 29	Much Ado about Nothing *BT. Mortimer, Tomlinson, Carleton Sr., and Woollams*		243	3	0
Tu June 1	Henry IV, Part II *BT. Wood, Percey, [T.] Shade, and Cameron*		301	6	6
S Sept. 18	Hamlet		173	19	4
S 25	Richard III		158	0	6
S Oct. 16	Othello		109	2	6
S 23	Twelfth Night		98	5	6
S 30	Hamlet		241	19	6
M Nov. 1	Othello		229	16	6

1779

1779 DRURY LANE (cont.)

			£	s.	d.
W Nov. 3	The Tempest		185	2	6
W 10	Othello		168	8	6
F 12	The Tempest		115	8	6
S 20	The Winter's Tale		188	8	0
Tu 23	same		194	15	6
F 26	same		184	2	0
M 29	same		172	11	6
W Dec. 1	same		151	13	6
F 3	same		251	11	0
S 11	same		126	14	6
M 20	Henry IV, Part I		106	16	0
Tu 21	Twelfth Night *BT. the Middlesex Hospital*		205	8	0
M 27	Romeo and Juliet		162	2	0
Th 30	The Tempest		96	19	0
F 31	Twelfth Night		92	13	6

COVENT GARDEN

			£	s.	d.
F Jan. 1	Henry V				
F 22	The Comedy of Errors				
W 27	same				
M Feb. 1	same				
S 6	same				
Tu 9	same				
Tu 16	Catharine and Petruchio				
S 20	The Comedy of Errors				
Th Mar. 4	Othello				
M Apr. 19	Romeo and Juliet *BT. Mattocks*				
Tu 20	Cymbeline *BT. Daly*				
S 24	Henry IV, Part I *BT. [J.] Bannister*				
M 26	Hamlet *BT. Quick*				
Tu May 4	The Comedy of Errors *BT. Whitfield and Mrs Morton*				
W 5	Cymbeline *BT. Reddish*				
Th 13	The Tempest *BT. Condell, Evans, and Curteen, box-keepers*				
F 21	The Comedy of Errors				
M Sept. 20	Henry V		132	14	6
F 24	As You Like It		142	19	6
M Oct. 18	Macbeth		249	10	6
S 23	Henry IV, Part I		133	15	0
M 25	Macbeth		190	10	0
F 29	The Comedy of Errors		154	17	6
M Nov. 1	Richard III		124	8	6
M 8	Romeo and Juliet		111	8	0
Th 11	The Merchant of Venice		188	8	6
S 13	The Merry Wives of Windsor *and* Catharine and Petruchio		111	9	0

1779–1780

1779 COVENT GARDEN (cont.)

			£	s.	d.
F	Nov. 19	King Lear	124	4	0
	S 20	The Merchant of Venice	154	8	0
	M 22	Hamlet	117	16	6
	W 24	Henry IV, Part I	106	15	6
	M 29	Macbeth	113	14	0
S	Dec. 4	The Merchant of Venice	175	4	0
	M 6	Richard III	187	15	0
	Tu 7	The Merry Wives of Windsor	160	7	0
	Tu 14	The Comedy of Errors	123	1	0
	F 17	As You Like It	111	18	0
	Tu 21	Henry IV, Part I *BT. the establishment of a fund for the relief of performers and others retiring from the stage*	receipts omitted		
	W 22	The Merry Wives of Windsor *BT. the Dispensary for the Infant Poor in Soho-Square*	193	18	0
	Tu 28	Macbeth	196	1	0
	F 31	Much Ado about Nothing	171	12	0

HAYMARKET

Tu Aug. 24 Henry VIII *BT. Digges*

1780 DRURY LANE

			£	s.	d.
S	Jan. 1	The Winter's Tale	153	2	0
	S 8	Othello	198	5	6
	Tu 11	The Winter's Tale	196	18	0
	F 14	Henry IV, Part I	203	8	6
	S 22	The Winter's Tale	203	14	6
	M 24	Julius Caesar	238	4	0
	Tu 25	same	211	9	6
	F 28	As You Like It	173	5	6
Th	Feb. 10	The Winter's Tale	208	18	0
	S 12	Henry IV, Part I	171	2	6
	Tu 15	Julius Caesar	192	9	0
	S 19	same	161	7	0
S	Mar. 11	same	104	13	6
	M 13	The Tempest	271	14	0
	Th 30	The Winter's Tale	90	0	6
F	Apr. 7	As You Like It *BT. Mrs Robinson*	201	12	0
	M 10	Richard III	195	3	0
	W 12	The Winter's Tale	107	5	6
	Tu 18	Cymbeline *BT. Henry*	147	15	6
	F 21	Hamlet *BT. [J.] Bannister*	280	8	6
	M 24	The Tempest	151	2	0
	W 26	Macbeth *BT. Miss Sherry and Miss Wright*	257	15	0
	Th 27	Julius Caesar	51	19	0
	S 29	Twelfth Night *BT. Lamash, Holcroft, and Norris*	190	14	6

69

1780

1780 DRURY LANE (cont.)

		£	s.	d.
Tu May 2	As You Like It *BT. Delpini and Signora Crespi*	163	11	0
W 3	Macbeth *BT. the author of* The Artifice [*also acted this night—William Augustus Miles*]	50	8	6
Th 11	Othello	82	4	6
F 12	Richard III *BT. Fawcett, Spencer, and Chaplin*	273	2	0
Th 18	The Winter's Tale	56	17	6
S 20	Twelfth Night *BT. Watson, Carleton Jr., Wilson, and Hicks*	256	14	0
Tu 23	Henry IV, Part I *BT. Mortimer, Tomlinson, Carleton Sr., Woollams, and Bayne*	24	3	6
W 24	The Winter's Tale	143	19	0
S Sept. 16	Hamlet	161	12	0
S 23	The Tempest	144	9	6
M Oct. 2	Henry IV, Part I	91	8	0
Th 5	As You Like It *BT. R. B. Sheridan* [*author of* The Critic, *also acted this night*]	236	3	6

The recipient of the BT. is named in the DL Account-Book, but not in Pb or PA.

		£	s.	d.
Th 19	The Winter's Tale	114	7	6
F 20	As You Like It	90	12	0
M 23	Richard III	110	7	0
W Nov. 1	Catharine and Petruchio	157	18	0
W 15	same	93	0	0
W 29	Othello	94	11	6
W Dec. 6	Macbeth	133	17	6
Tu 12	The Tempest	184	11	6
Tu 26	Macbeth	214	18	6

COVENT GARDEN

		£	s.	d.
M Jan. 3	King Lear	189	2	0
Th 6	The Comedy of Errors	79	17	0
S 8	The Merchant of Venice	192	6	0
M 10	Richard III	195	2	0
Tu 11	Much Ado about Nothing	116	2	0
W 19	Catharine and Petruchio	113	10	6
F 21	The Merry Wives of Windsor	148	18	6
F 28	The Merchant of Venice	190	19	6
Th Feb. 17	Much Ado about Nothing	223	15	6
M 21	King Lear	230	13	0
W Apr. 5	The Merchant of Venice *BT. Macklin*	268	0	0
S 22	Much Ado about Nothing *BT. Edwin* [*Sr.*]	107	10	6
Tu 25	Hamlet	168	5	0
Th 27	Macbeth *BT. Mattocks*	193	5	6
F 28	The Merry Wives of Windsor *BT. Peile*	190	4	6
S 29	The Merchant of Venice	119	0	6

1780–1781

1780 COVENT GARDEN (*cont.*)   £   s.   d.
- F May 12   The Merchant of Venice *BT. Booth, Egan, and Fearon*   177   3   0
- Tu 16   The Comedy of Errors *BT. Dumai, Harris, and Holloway*   277   18   0
- M Oct. 2   Henry IV, Part I   133   13   0
- M 9   Richard III   188   14   0
- W 11   Measure for Measure   131   10   0
- Th 19   Much Ado about Nothing   118   12   6
- M 23   Macbeth   216   12   6
- Th 26   Hamlet   152   5   0
- M 30   Henry VIII   180   6   6
- W Nov. 1   The Merry Wives of Windsor   167   4   6
- Th 2   The Merchant of Venice   246   4   0
- M 6   same   287   0   0
- Th 9   same   282   15   0
- F 10   Othello   149   18   0
- Th 16   The Merchant of Venice   265   0   0
- M 20   Macbeth   182   8   0
- Th 23   The Merchant of Venice   230   8   0
- Th 30   same   254   1   6
- Th Dec. 7   same *BT. the proprietors*   253   11   0
- Th 14   same *BT. Macklin*   receipts omitted
- F 15   Catharine and Petruchio   101   12   0
- Tu 26   Richard III   146   7   6
- W 27   King Lear   171   19   0
- S 30   Much Ado about Nothing   212   3   0

HAYMARKET
- S July 1   Richard III
- M 24   Othello *BT. Mrs Crawford*
- M 31   [same]

   H-B for this night is lacking. PA gives *Othello*, and so does the advance notice on the H-B bill of July 29. But MP, July 31, announces that 'Mrs Crawford not being well enough to act the part of Desdemona ... The Suicide ... will be performed This Evening'. Both MP and the Haymarket bill in BM give *The Suicide*.

- F Aug. 4   same
- Th 17   Hamlet *BT. [J.] Bannister*
- Th 24   The Merchant of Venice *BT. Edwin [Sr.]*

CROWN INN, ISLINGTON
- M Mar. 6   Richard III
- M 13   Romeo and Juliet

1781 DRURY LANE
- W Jan. 3   The Tempest *and* Catharine and Petruchio   86   18   0

1781

1781 DRURY LANE (cont.)   £   s.   d.

Tu Jan. 23	The Winter's Tale		81	16	0
M 29	same		257	19	0
Tu Feb. 20	Catharine and Petruchio BT. the author [of The Royal Suppliants, also acted this night— John Delap]		142	8	6
Th Mar. 1	Hamlet		159	4	0

Both Pb and PA announce *The Royal Suppliants*, 'The Seventh Night'. In the DL Account-Book it is deleted, and *Hamlet* substituted. The next performance of *The Royal Suppliants* was on Mar. 17, when it is correctly billed as 'The Seventh Night'.

Th 8	Richard III		162	3	6
Tu Apr. 3	Catharine and Petruchio BT. Dodd		195	5	6
Tu May 1	Romeo and Juliet		92	19	0
F 18	Richard III		183	5	0
S 19	Catharine and Petruchio BT. Crawford		113	3	0
Th 24	Hamlet BT. Watson, Carleton Jr., Wilson, Hicks, and [R.] Palmer [Sr.]		289	16	6
Tu Sept. 18	Richard III		130	0	0
Tu 25	Hamlet		170	8	0
W Oct. 24	Catharine and Petruchio		95	18	0
F Nov. 2	Hamlet		147	8	6
M 5	Macbeth		158	13	6
Tu 13	The Tempest		135	8	0
Tu Dec. 11	Catharine and Petruchio		104	0	0

COVENT GARDEN

M Jan. 1	Hamlet		235	19	0
M 15	Macbeth		283	13	0
W 17	Measure for Measure		195	0	0
Th 18	The Comedy of Errors		202	5	0
M 22	King Lear		261	13	0
W 24	The Merry Wives of Windsor		222	13	0
F 26	same		278	4	0
Th Feb. 8	The Comedy of Errors		252	1	0
Tu 13	The Merchant of Venice		171	0	0
Tu 20	same		230	15	0
S Mar. 3	The Merry Wives of Windsor		171	8	6
M 5	Macbeth		194	13	0
Th 15	Much Ado about Nothing		139	1	0
M 19	Hamlet		167	18	0
Tu 20	The Comedy of Errors		87	0	6
Th 22	The Merry Wives of Windsor		166	17	0
M 26	King Lear		112	19	0
M Apr. 16	Henry VIII		158	18	0
F 20	The Merchant of Venice BT. Lee Lewes		223	13	6

1781

1781 COVENT GARDEN (cont.)

			£	s.	d.
W Apr. 25	The Merry Wives of Windsor *BT. Reinhold*		194	2	6
Th May 3	Much Ado about Nothing		144	12	6
W 9	Macbeth *BT. Peile*		181	10	6
Th 22	The Comedy of Errors *BT. Green and Ansell, box-keepers*		292	11	0
M Sept. 24	Romeo and Juliet		208	8	0
M Oct. 1	same		224	0	6
M 8	same		220	1	6
M 15	same		150	10	6
W 31	King Lear		164	6	0
Th Nov. 8	The Merchant of Venice		217	6	0
M 12	Romeo and Juliet		112	5	6
W 14	King Lear		109	16	6
Th 15	The Merchant of Venice		166	5	6
Tu Dec. 4	same		140	14	6
W 5	Much Ado about Nothing		158	9	6
S 8	The Merry Wives of Windsor		155	1	0
Tu 11	Henry IV, Part I		170	15	6
M 17	Macbeth		165	3	0
M 31	Hamlet		277	0	0

HAYMARKET

Tu Aug. 7   The School of Shakespeare *BT. Digges*

This entertainment consisted of excerpts from five of Shakespeare's plays. Each Act was given its own title, as follows:
1. VANITY: *Henry IV, Part I* (II. parts of i and iv)
2. PARENTAL TENDERNESS: *Henry IV, Part II* (parts of IV. iv and v, and parts of V. ii)
3. CRUELTY: *The Merchant of Venice* (IV. i)
4. FILIAL PIETY: *Hamlet* (III. iii and iv)
5. AMBITION: *Henry VIII* (III. ii)

F 17   same *BT. [J.] Bannister*

On this night only four excerpts were selected, as follows:
1. FILIAL PIETY (as 4 above)
2. PARENTAL TENDERNESS (as 2 above)
3. AMBITION (as 5 above)
4. LOVE: *Romeo and Juliet* (parts of V. i and iii)

W 22   The Feast of Thalia *BT. [R.] Wilson*

A potpourri similar to the above. The only excerpt from Shakespeare was FILIAL PIETY; the other 'courses', as Wilson called them, were new one-act plays, and scenes from stock comedies.

F 24   The Merry Wives of Windsor *BT. Edwin [Sr.]*

CROWN INN, ISLINGTON

F Mar. 30   Richard III

1782 DRURY LANE

			£	s.	d.
Th Jan. 17	Hamlet		122	18	6
Tu Feb. 5	Macbeth		115	10	6
Tu 12	The Tempest		102	12	6
S Apr. 6	same		104	9	6
Th 11	As You Like It		103	12	0
Tu 23	Othello				
	and Catharine and Petruchio BT. *Farren*		208	4	6
Th 25	Romeo and Juliet		123	19	6
S 27	As You Like It		66	6	0
W May 15	Macbeth BT. *Norris, Chaplin, Walker, and Mrs Booth*		246	2	0
F 24	Catharine and Petruchio		68	4	6
S June 1	As You Like It BT. *Miss Blower*		118	9	0
W Sept. 18	Catharine and Petruchio		98	16	0
S 21	Twelfth Night		144	11	0
Tu 24	Hamlet		189	14	6
S 28	As You Like It		167	19	6
Tu Oct. 1	Othello		152	0	6
Th 17	As You Like It		85	17	0
S 19	Twelfth Night		79	2	0
F 25	Catharine and Petruchio		174	0	0
Tu Nov. 5	As You Like It		84	17	0
W Dec. 11	Hamlet		109	13	0

COVENT GARDEN

S Jan. 5	Measure for Measure	209	17	0
M 7	Richard III	208	19	0

Genest (vi. 223) erroneously has Jan. 6, a Sunday.

M 14	Macbeth	232	7	0
Tu 22	As You Like It	194	17	0
F 25	The Merry Wives of Windsor	181	5	0
Tu 29	Henry IV, Part I	201	14	0
Th 31	The Merchant of Venice	243	17	0

Both Pb and PA announce *The Man of the World*, in which Miss Younge was to have acted. But '*The Merchant of Venice* . . . was performed last night (on account of Miss Younge's sudden indisposition)' (PA, Feb. 1).

M Feb. 4	Hamlet	203	4	0
Th 7	Measure for Measure	142	12	0
Th Mar. 21	Macbeth	153	5	6
M Apr. 8	The Merchant of Venice	191	8	6
S 27	The Merry Wives of Windsor BT. *Aldridge, ballet-master*	238	6	6
W May 1	Henry IV, Part I BT. *Mrs Martyr*	209	10	6

1782-1783

1782 COVENT GARDEN (*cont.*)

M May 13 [Henry VIII]
    Announced by both Pb and PA, but not acted. The JPK bill is deleted, but the substitute play is not given. Egerton 2283 has, 'Alter'd to the Count of Narbonne'. On Dec. 30, q.v., *Henry VIII* is advertised as 'Not Acted these two years'.

			£	s.	d.
M	20	Henry V	141	7	0
Tu	21	The Merry Wives of Windsor *BT. Fearon, L'Estrange, Thompson, and Guard*	251	2	6
M	27	Macbeth	126	18	0
M Oct.	7	Romeo and Juliet	223	8	6
M	14	Richard III	241	19	0
Th	17	The Merry Wives of Windsor	191	3	0
Tu	29	The Merchant of Venice	205	15	0
F Nov.	1	Hamlet	174	0	0
M	18	Macbeth	189	13	0
S	30	Henry IV, Part I	209	16	0
Tu Dec.	3	The Merchant of Venice	181	0	6
M	9	Hamlet	214	2	6
Th	12	Measure for Measure	111	1	0
M	16	Richard III	165	18	0
M	23	Macbeth	181	8	6
Th	26	Romeo and Juliet	185	11	6
M	30	Henry VIII	207	2	0

HAYMARKET

M Mar. 4 Richard III *BT. Mrs Lefevre*
F Aug. 9 Cymbeline *BT. [J.] Bannister*
Th 15 Twelfth Night *BT. Mrs Bulkley*
F 30 same *BT. Miss Harper*
M Dec. 30 The Merchant of Venice [IV. i only] *BT. Gardner*

1783 DRURY LANE

W Jan.	1	Twelfth Night	154	16	0
Th Feb.	6	Hamlet	135	9	5
Tu	18	Cymbeline	174	11	6
S	22	The Merchant of Venice	126	15	6
Tu	25	Cymbeline	74	8	0
S Mar.	1	The Merchant of Venice	113	5	6
M	3	Much Ado about Nothing	97	16	0
M	10	Richard III	148	16	0
M	24	Hamlet	166	7	0
S Apr.	26	The Merchant of Venice *BT. Suett and Chapman*	160	15	0
Tu Sept.	23	Richard III	209	19	6
Tu	30	Hamlet	285	16	0
Th Oct.	2	same	232	4	6

1783 DRURY LANE (cont.)

				£	s.	d.
S	Oct.	4	Hamlet	242	16	0
M		6	same	198	7	0
S		11	Catharine and Petruchio	285	5	0
M		13	Hamlet	187	0	0
Th		16	As You Like It	97	2	6
Tu		28	Hamlet	160	0	0
M	Nov.	3	Measure for Measure	281	2	0
W		5	same	291	16	0
Th		6	Richard III	130	10	6
F		7	Measure for Measure	212	4	0
M		10	Richard III	210	7	6
Tu		11	Measure for Measure	218	9	6
S		15	Hamlet	149	11	6
Tu		25	same	128	14	0
W	Dec.	10	King John	300	9	0
S		13	same	257	4	0
M		15	Richard III	118	13	6
Tu		16	King John	161	10	6
W		17	Catharine and Petruchio	86	11	0
S		27	Hamlet	123	8	6

COVENT GARDEN

				£	s.	d.
W	Jan.	1	King Lear	201	8	0
S		4	Henry IV, Part I	150	12	6
M		6	Henry VIII	190	4	6
S		18	The Merry Wives of Windsor	236	4	6
Th	Feb.	13	The Merchant of Venice	264	15	6
F		14	The Merry Wives of Windsor BT. Signora Sestini	256	5	6
W		19	Much Ado about Nothing	244	12	6
S		22	The Merry Wives of Windsor	148	9	0
M		24	King Lear	227	8	6
S	Mar.	29	King John	receipts omitted		
F	Apr.	25	Much Ado about Nothing	262	1	6
W		30	The Merchant of Venice BT. Macklin	208	3	0
M	May	5	Much Ado about Nothing	193	18	0
W		7	Twelfth Night BT. Edwin [Sr.]	304	0	6
M		12	[same]			

Listed by Genest (vi. 274). The play on this night was *The Castle of Andalusia*.

				£	s.	d.
W		14	same BT. Mrs [S.] Wilson	86	6	6
S		17	As You Like It BT. Miss Satchell	163	12	0
M		19	The Winter's Tale BT. Wild	304	1	6
W		21	The Merry Wives of Windsor BT. Booth, Egan, Stevens, and the widow of the late Mr Branson	204	2	0

1783–1784

1783 COVENT GARDEN (*cont.*)   £   s. d.

M	May 26	Henry VIII *BT. Brandon, box-book and house-keeper*	319 17 0
	Th 29	Henry IV, Part I	181 3 6
Tu	June 3	Hamlet *BT. Curteen, Condell [Jr.], and Colborne, box-keepers*	227 14 6
M	Sept. 22	Romeo and Juliet	261 9 6
	W 24	Othello	288 12 6
	M 29	same	239 8 6
F	Oct. 3	Hamlet	199 4 6
	M 6	Macbeth	206 13 6
	Th 9	The Winter's Tale	158 19 0
	S 11	The Merry Wives of Windsor	150 4 6
	M 13	Richard III	189 14 6
	F 17	Henry IV, Part I	177 14 6
	M 20	King Lear	153 11 0
	Th 23	Hamlet	221 10 6
	M 27	Romeo and Juliet	173 4 6
	W 29	Hamlet	126 13 6
M	Nov. 3	Richard III	165 0 0
	M 10	Henry VIII	198 8 6
	M 17	Henry IV, Part I	157 18 0
F	Dec. 5	The Merchant of Venice	257 12 6
	Tu 16	same	126 3 0
	Th 18	Macbeth	129 8 0
	Tu 23	The Winter's Tale	288 1 0
	S 27	Othello	198 2 0
	M 29	Richard III	226 1 0
	Tu 30	The Merry Wives of Windsor	221 11 0

HAYMARKET

F	June 6	Hamlet
F	July 4	As You Like It
	W 9	same
	S 12	same
W	Aug. 20	The Sheep Shearing *BT. Mrs Bannister*
	W 27	same *BT. [C.] Bannister*
M	Dec. 15	Richard III *BT. Harricks and Williams*

1784 DRURY LANE

S	Jan. 3	Cymbeline	110 5 6
	Tu 6	Hamlet	102 3 6
	S 10	The Merry Wives of Windsor	274 2 0
	M 12	Richard III	240 7 0
	Tu 13	The Merry Wives of Windsor	219 16 0
	M 19	Hamlet	256 7 6
	Th 22	The Merchant of Venice	167 19 6
	S 24	same	149 10 6

1784

1784 DRURY LANE (cont.)

			£	s.	d.
Tu Jan. 27	The Merry Wives of Windsor		139	8	0
W Feb. 4	Measure for Measure		171	0	6
M Mar. 8	Hamlet		167	2	6
M 22	The Merchant of Venice		139	13	0
M May 3	Twelfth Night *BT. Suett and R. Palmer*		227	18	0
F 14	The Merry Wives of Windsor *BT. Phillimore, Thompson, and Nix*		222	13	0
F 21	Othello *BT. Chaplin, Wilson, Walker, and Mrs Booth*		176	6	0
Tu Sept. 21	Hamlet		97	12	6
M Oct. 11	The Merry Wives of Windsor		104	0	6
S 23	Catharine and Petruchio		280	5	0
Tu 26	As You Like It		129	10	0
M Nov. 1	Hamlet		101	18	6
F 5	Richard III		80	10	6
Tu 9	The Tempest		161	11	0
Th 18	same		80	8	6
F 19	Cymbeline		127	9	6

COVENT GARDEN

			£	s.	d.
M Jan. 5	King Lear		209	6	0
F 9	Much Ado about Nothing		149	14	0
M 12	Henry IV, Part I		150	16	0
F 16	King John		168	19	6
M 19	Romeo and Juliet		174	10	6
M Feb. 9	Macbeth		156	11	0
Th Mar. 18	The Merchant of Venice		222	11	0
Tu 23	The Merry Wives of Windsor *BT. Henderson*		292	2	6
M Apr. 12	Romeo and Juliet		186	18	6
Tu 13	The Two Gentlemen of Verona *BT. Quick*		316	5	0
Tu May 4	The Merry Wives of Windsor *BT. Mrs [S.] Wilson*		177	4	6
M 10	The Winter's Tale *BT. Mrs Martyr*		181	15	0
Tu 25	Henry IV, Part I *BT. Brandon, box-book and house-keeper*		291	16	6
Th June 10	The Merchant of Venice *BT. Wild*		receipts omitted		

The bill for this performance is in BM, but not in JPK. On the BM bill is written 'Extra night'. The season this year had officially closed on June 2.

F Sept. 17	As You Like It	
M 20	Hamlet	
M 27	Othello	
Tu 28	Catharine and Petruchio *BT. the widow and children of the unfortunate Mr Linton, late of this theatre*	

Linton, a musician belonging to the CG band, had been attacked and killed by footpads on July 8.

W 29	Henry IV, Part I	

1784-1785

1784 COVENT GARDEN (*cont.*)

- M   Oct. 4   Macbeth
- M 11   Richard III
- M 18   Cymbeline
- M 25   Romeo and Juliet
- Tu 26   same
- F 29   Henry IV, Part I
- S 30   Henry IV, Part II
- M   Nov. 1   Romeo and Juliet
- F 5   same
- M 8   same
- W 10   The Merchant of Venice
- F 12   Macbeth
- S 13   The Merry Wives of Windsor
- M 15   Macbeth
- F 19   Romeo and Juliet
- M 22   Macbeth
- F 26   Romeo and Juliet
- M   Dec. 6   same
- S 11   The Merry Wives of Windsor
- W 29   Romeo and Juliet
- Th 30   Macbeth

Bill in JPK. The play was changed from *Douglas*, which had originally been announced for this night. PA has the bill for *Douglas*.

HAYMARKET

- M Sept. 13   Hamlet
- F 17   Richard III

1785 DRURY LANE

			£	s.	d.
M	Jan. 10	The Tempest	173	5	0
Tu	11	Hamlet	146	11	6
Tu	18	The Tempest	120	5	0
W	Feb. 2	Macbeth *BT. Mrs Siddons*	345	16	0
F	4	same	275	1	6
M	7	same	283	1	6
S	12	same	273	18	6
Tu	15	same	273	9	6
S	19	same	279	6	6
Tu	22	same	206	18	6
S	26	same	230	18	0
S	Mar. 5	same	268	7	0
Tu	8	Othello	259	14	0
S	12	same	291	0	0
Tu	15	Macbeth *BT. Smith*	287	17	6
M	28	The Tempest *BT.* [C.] *Bannister*	321	9	0
Tu	29	Othello	262	13	6

1785

1785 DRURY LANE (cont.)

				£	s.	d.
	Th Mar. 31	Macbeth *BT. Kemble*		293	3	0
	Tu Apr. 5	Othello		225	10	0
	M 18	The Winter's Tale *BT. [J.] Bannister*		276	16	0
	Tu 19	Macbeth		168	10	0
	Th 21	Othello		170	4	6
	Th 28	The Tempest		86	8	0
	S 30	As You Like It *BT. Mrs Siddons*		333	8	6
S	May 7	same		233	16	6
	Tu 10	Macbeth *BT. a fund for the relief of those who from their infirmities shall be obliged to retire from the stage*		241	10	0
	S 14	As You Like It		241	9	6
	W 18	same		295	14	0
S	Sept. 17	Othello		280	16	6
S	Oct. 1	Macbeth		280	5	6
	M 10	Othello		163	5	6
	M 17	The Tempest		183	8	6
	S 22	Measure for Measure		172	15	6
	S 29	Macbeth		205	10	6
W	Nov. 2	Measure for Measure		262	13	6
	M 7	Richard III		91	15	0
	Th 10	The Tempest		83	14	0
	F 11	Twelfth Night		108	12	0
	W 16	same		142	11	6
	Th 17	Hamlet		93	19	6
	F 18	The Winter's Tale		241	9	0
	S 19	Macbeth		210	12	0
	M 21	Cymbeline		174	6	0
	Tu 22	King John		147	1	6
	W 23	Twelfth Night		279	13	0
	Th 24	The Tempest		108	11	6
	M 28	Twelfth Night		164	2	0
Tu	Dec. 6	same		159	19	6
	F 16	same		213	16	6
	W 28	Hamlet		172	7	0
	Th 29	The Winter's Tale		167	7	0

COVENT GARDEN

W Jan. 12	Richard III
M 17	same
F 21	Much Ado about Nothing
W 26	same
Th 27	same
M 31	Romeo and Juliet
M Feb. 14	The Merchant of Venice
Tu 15	Hamlet *BT. Holman*
M Mar. 28	Romeo and Juliet

80

1785–1786

1785 COVENT GARDEN (cont.)

F	Apr. 8	Henry VIII BT. *Clarke*				
	M 18	Romeo and Juliet BT. *Booth*				
	F 22	Hamlet BT. *Hull*				
	S 23	Othello BT. *Pope*				
	S 30	The Merry Wives of Windsor				
Tu	May 3	Macbeth BT. *Mrs Webb*				
	S 7	The Winter's Tale BT. *[R.] Wilson*				
	M 16	Othello BT. *Brandon, box-book and house-keeper*				
	Tu 24	The Merry Wives of Windsor		£	s.	d.
W	Sept. 21	Richard III		188	17	6
	F 23	Hamlet		150	13	6
	M 26	Henry IV, Part I		231	13	6
M	Oct. 17	Catharine and Petruchio		337	18	0
	S 22	Henry IV, Part I		207	2	0
Tu	Nov. 1	The Merry Wives of Windsor		139	6	0
	W 2	Much Ado about Nothing		151	5	0
	M 14	Romeo and Juliet		326	9	6
	Th 17	same		289	18	6
	M 21	same		247	12	6
	F 25	same		239	13	0
	M 28	same		204	11	0
M	Dec. 5	Richard III		147	1	6
	M 19	Romeo and Juliet		234	16	0
	F 30	The Comedy of Errors		247	3	0

HAYMARKET

F	June 24	Hamlet
W	July 13	same
	Tu 26	All's Well that Ends Well BT. *[J.] Bannister*
	Th 28	same
F	Sept. 9	Othello

1786 DRURY LANE

Tu	Jan. 3	Twelfth Night		194	17	0

Both Pb and PA announce for this night *The Country Girl*, in which King was to perform. But 'In consequence of poor King and his gout . . . *The Country Girl* . . . [was] changed [to] . . . *Twelfth Night*' (MC, Jan. 5).

S	Feb. 18	As You Like It		222	8	6
Th	Mar. 2	Macbeth		213	0	6
	M 6	Twelfth Night		175	14	0
	Tu 7	The Tempest		99	14	0
Th	Apr. 6	The Merchant of Venice and Catharine and Petruchio BT. *Kemble*		284	2	6
	M 17	Twelfth Night BT. *Dodd*		302	15	6
	Th 20	The Merchant of Venice		219	4	0

81

1786

1786 DRURY LANE (cont.)

				£	s.	d.
S	Apr. 22	Macbeth *BT. Bensley*		267	19	6
	S 29	The Merchant of Venice		203	3	6
M	May 1	Twelfth Night *BT. Suett and R. Palmer*		307	5	0
	Tu 9	same *BT. Chapman and Williames*		283	6	0
	S 13	The Merchant of Venice		154	11	6
	M 15	Hamlet *BT. Mrs Siddons*		326	14	6
F	June 2	Catharine and Petruchio *BT. Carleton [Jr.], Wilson, Newton, and J. Shade*		231	18	6
	W 7	As You Like It		219	16	6
Tu Sept. 19		Hamlet		191	4	0
Tu Oct. 3		Catharine and Petruchio		302	12	0
	M 9	Macbeth		206	16	6
	S 21	Twelfth Night		163	12	6
	Tu 24	The Winter's Tale		226	0	0
Th Nov. 23		Twelfth Night		157	7	6
S	Dec. 2	Macbeth		223	5	0
	Tu 5	The Tempest *and* Catharine and Petruchio		91	19	0
	W 27	The Tempest		173	6	6

COVENT GARDEN

				£	s.	d.
F	Jan. 6	Cymbeline		145	9	0
	Th 12	The Comedy of Errors		222	18	0
	W 18	Macbeth		261	3	0
	M 23	Romeo and Juliet		228	17	0
	Tu 24	Much Ado about Nothing		196	19	0
	W 25	The Comedy of Errors		293	4	0
Tu Feb. 7		As You Like It		171	3	0
	S 18	The Merchant of Venice		222	7	6
	M 20	Romeo and Juliet		206	9	0
	F 24	The Comedy of Errors *BT. Delpini*		185	13	0

The recipient of the BT. is named in Egerton 2286, but not in Pb or PA.

				£	s.	d.
	M 27	The Merchant of Venice		264	1	0
M Mar. 6		King Lear		170	7	0
M Apr. 17		Romeo and Juliet		207	5	0
S	May 13	Timon of Athens *BT. Hull* cash:[1]		80	10	0
	W 24	The Comedy of Errors *BT. [Wm.] Palmer and Meadows*		208	10	0
	M 29	Macbeth		63	14	6
W Sept. 20		Richard III		172	17	0
Th Oct. 12		The Merchant of Venice		250	16	6
	M 23	Romeo and Juliet		200	17	6
W Nov. 22		Henry IV, Part I		215	16	0
	W 29	The Merry Wives of Windsor		192	11	0

[1] See note, p. 40.

1786–1787

1786 COVENT GARDEN (*cont.*)

			£	s.	d.
M Dec. 11	Romeo and Juliet		172	16	6
M 18	Henry IV, Part I		117	0	6

    Both Pb and PA announce *Fontainbleau*. A note on the BM bill states that 'Edwin was taken ill and the performance [was] changed to Henry 4th'. See also PA, Dec. 19.

| Tu 19 | The Merchant of Venice | 194 | 2 | 6 |

HAYMARKET

F July 14   Othello *BT. Miss Woollery*
F 21   Henry IV, Part I *BT. Mrs Webb*

HAMMERSMITH

F June 9   The Merchant of Venice
W July 12   Romeo and Juliet

1787 DRURY LANE

Tu Jan. 9	The Tempest	150	9	0
Th 11	Hamlet	203	3	6
M 15	The Winter's Tale	192	18	0
Tu 16	Twelfth Night	204	1	6
Tu 23	Othello	253	11	6
M 29	Cymbeline *BT. Mrs Siddons*	344	17	6
Th Feb. 1	same	264	18	0
S 3	[same]			

    Announced in the advance bills of this week, but not acted. On this night the theatre was dark: 'It is apprehended that ... on Account of the Fire ... in Bridge's-St., that the Avenues to the Theatre will be ... impassable, for which Reason there will Not be any Performance' (PA, Feb. 3).

M 5	same	318	8	0
Th 8	same	266	9	6
Tu Mar. 20	same *BT. Smith*	313	0	0
F Apr. 13	As You Like It *BT. Mrs Jordan*	304	2	0
Th 19	Macbeth	197	5	0
Th May 3	The Winter's Tale	137	9	0

    Both Pb and PA announce *Isabella*, in which Mrs Siddons was to appear. But she was ill, and 'the play was changed into *The Winter's Tale*' (W, May 4). A similar report is in MH, May 4. The DL Account-Book says that *Isabella* was acted.

W 9	Twelfth Night *BT. Mrs [J.] Wilson*	196	4	6
Th 24	Cymbeline *BT. a fund for the relief of those who from their infirmities shall be obliged to retire from the stage*	263	7	0
Tu 29	As You Like It	198	5	0

1787

1787 DRURY LANE (cont.)

			£	s.	d.
S	June 2	Macbeth	249	9	0
	M 4	The Tempest	284	4	6
Tu	Sept. 18	Hamlet	186	5	6
S	Oct. 27	Othello	117	16	0
	M 29	Hamlet	118	19	6
S	Nov. 3	Macbeth	210	0	0
	M 5	Cymbeline	94	2	0
	Tu 6	As You Like It	174	5	6
	S 24	The Merchant of Venice	236	16	6
M	Dec. 3	Hamlet	105	19	6
	M 10	Richard III	145	8	6
	M 17	same	128	17	6
	M 31	Hamlet	138	12	0

COVENT GARDEN

			£	s.	d.
Th	Jan. 18	The Merry Wives of Windsor	191	7	0
	M 29	Romeo and Juliet	243	14	6
S	Feb. 3	The Merry Wives of Windsor	191	0	0
	Th 8	The Merchant of Venice	222	10	6
M	Mar. 26	Henry VIII *BT. Mrs Pope*	289	8	0
W	Apr. 11	Much Ado about Nothing *BT. Miss Brunton*	197	17	6
	F 13	The Merry Wives of Windsor *BT. O'Keeffe* [*author of* Love and War, *also acted this night*]	120	1	6

The recipient of the BT. is named in Egerton 2287, but not in Pb or PA.

			£	s.	d.
	F 27	Cymbeline *BT. Pope*	207	4	6
M	May 14	Henry VIII *BT. Booth*	262	10	0
	M 21	The Winter's Tale *BT. Wild*	222	16	6
S	June 2	The Merry Wives of Windsor	152	6	0
M	Sept. 17	same	213	6	6
	M 24	Romeo and Juliet	220	8	6
M	Oct. 1	Macbeth	225	0	0
	F 12	Othello	196	7	0
	M 15	same	262	4	0
M	Nov. 5	Henry IV, Part I	199	0	6
	W 7	Much Ado about Nothing	196	17	6
	M 12	Romeo and Juliet	154	3	0
	F 16	Macbeth *BT. Cambray*	189	1	6
	M 19	Henry VIII	145	13	6
	M 26	The Merry Wives of Windsor	158	18	6

Both Pb and PA announce *The Tender Husband*, in which Mrs Abington was to appear. But she was ill, and the play was changed to *The Merry Wives of Windsor* (PA, Nov. 27). The bill for *The Tender Husband* on Dec. 5 has, 'Never Acted at this Theatre'.

			£	s.	d.
M	Dec. 31	Henry IV, Part I	204	5	0

1787-1788

1787 HAYMARKET
F May 18 Hamlet
  M 21 same
  F 25 Much Ado about Nothing
F July 27 The Merchant of Venice BT. [J.] Williamson
F Aug. 17 Much Ado about Nothing BT. Miss Farren

ROYALTY
W June 20 As You Like It BT. the London Hospital

RED LION INN, STOKE NEWINGTON
S Mar. 31 Romeo and Juliet

1788 DRURY LANE

		£	s.	d.
S Jan. 5	The Merchant of Venice	211	8	6
Th 10	[Cymbeline]			

Announced by both Pb and PA, but not acted. A printed slip attached to the BM bill states that because 'of the Indisposition of Mrs. Taylor *Cymbeline* is obliged to be postponed'. *The Beggar's Opera* was performed in its stead.

		£	s.	d.
S 12	The Merchant of Venice	218	12	6
W 16	Richard III	189	0	6
M 21	King Lear BT. Mrs Siddons	343	12	6
Th 24	same	233	7	0
Tu 29	same	220	10	0
F Feb. 1	The Merchant of Venice	238	6	6
M 18	Richard III	158	15	0
S Mar. 1	King Lear	248	6	6
S 8	same	195	17	0
M 10	Macbeth BT. Smith	363	19	6
Th 13	Catharine and Petruchio BT. Kemble	324	12	0
Tu Apr. 8	Twelfth Night	189	18	6
Th 17	Richard III	112	7	6
F 25	Twelfth Night	249	14	6
W 30	Much Ado about Nothing BT. Mrs [J.] Kemble	92	14	0

The recipient of the BT. is named in the DL Account-Book, but not in Pb or PA.

		£	s.	d.
Th May 1	The Winter's Tale BT. Mrs [J.] Wilson	169	19	0
M 5	Catharine and Petruchio BT. Mrs Siddons	327	3	0
Th 15	King Lear BT. *a fund, for the relief of those who from their infirmities shall be obliged to retire from the stage*	258	2	6
W 21	The Merry Wives of Windsor BT. Fosbrook, box-book and house-keeper	297	12	6
Tu 27	Twelfth Night	47	15	0

1788

1788 DRURY LANE (cont.)

			£	s.	d.
Th May 29	Macbeth		199	17	6
W June 4	Hamlet		55	14	6
W 11	The Winter's Tale BT. Wood, Cameron, and Percey		250	9	6
Tu Sept. 16	same		109	18	6
S 27	The Merry Wives of Windsor		176	9	6
Tu 30	Hamlet		182	8	0
Th Oct. 2	As You Like It		174	6	6
S 4	Twelfth Night		236	16	0
Tu 7	As You Like It		129	3	6
Tu 14	Richard III		201	12	0
Th 16	Macbeth		267	13	6
S 18	Twelfth Night		219	0	6
Tu 21	Macbeth		202	4	0
F 24	Twelfth Night		158	5	0
M Nov. 10	Richard III		173	16	0
Th 13	As You Like It		81	0	6
M 17	Romeo and Juliet		157	19	6
Tu 18	same		111	11	0
S 22	Macbeth		244	8	6
Tu 25	Henry VIII		260	11	0
S 29	same		219	1	0
Tu Dec. 2	same		221	10	6
S 6	same		212	8	6
Th 11	The Merry Wives of Windsor		110	16	6
F 12	The Winter's Tale		60	10	6
S 13	Henry VIII		244	6	6
W 17	As You Like It BT. Mrs Jordan		282	6	0
S 20	Henry VIII		240	8	0
Tu 23	Macbeth		211	3	6
S 27	Henry VIII		201	9	0
M 29	Richard III		179	7	0

COVENT GARDEN

			£	s.	d.
F Jan. 4	The Comedy of Errors		199	12	0
M 7	Romeo and Juliet		152	15	0
Th 10	The Merchant of Venice		309	2	6
Th 24	same		265	18	6
F 25	Much Ado about Nothing		218	15	0
S Feb. 16	The Merchant of Venice		223	4	6
Th Apr. 3	same		185	5	0
F 11	The Winter's Tale BT. Mrs Martyr		260	17	0
M 14	Much Ado about Nothing BT. Mrs Abington		296	19	6
F 18	Othello BT. Pope		184	9	6
S May 3	The Winter's Tale BT. Mrs Mountain		201	7	0
M Sept. 22	Romeo and Juliet		304	13	0
M 29	same		291	18	6

1788-1789

1788 COVENT GARDEN (*cont.*)

				£	s.	d.
M	Oct.	6	Romeo and Juliet	238	13	6
	W	8	Henry IV, Part I	175	14	0
	M	13	Romeo and Juliet	251	12	6
	S	18	The Merchant of Venice	208	16	0
	M	20	Romeo and Juliet	197	14	6
M	Nov.	3	same	191	12	6
	W	12	The Merry Wives of Windsor	191	13	0
	S	22	Catharine and Petruchio	200	0	0
M	Dec.	15	same	145	8	6
	M	22	Romeo and Juliet	140	19	0

1789 DRURY LANE

S	Jan.	3	Henry VIII	197	19	6
	S	10	same			
			and Catharine and Petruchio	194	6	6
	M	12	Richard III	142	16	6
	S	17	The Merchant of Venice	156	5	6
	S	24	Henry VIII	238	14	0
	S	31	Macbeth	253	1	6
Tu	Feb.	3	Henry VIII	226	10	6
	S	7	Coriolanus	196	13	6
	Tu	10	same	201	11	6
	S	14	same	214	19	0
	F	20	As You Like It	103	4	6
	S	21	Coriolanus	230	6	0
Tu	Mar.	3	same	173	10	6
	S	7	same	172	6	0
	Tu	10	As You Like It	25	19	6
	S	14	Coriolanus	217	11	6
	Th	19	Twelfth Night	173	12	6
	M	30	Macbeth			
			and Catharine and Petruchio BT. Kemble	284	0	6
Tu	Apr.	28	same			
			and same BT. Bensley	260	2	0
	W	29	Henry VIII BT. *a fund for the relief of those who from their infirmities shall be obliged to retire from the stage*	181	17	6
M	May	11	Romeo and Juliet BT. Mrs Siddons	320	6	6
	W	13	Twelfth Night BT. Mrs Goodall	160	5	0
	Th	21	same	84	17	0
S	June	6	As You Like It BT. *Alfred,* [T.] *Shade, Hicks, and Portal*	269	14	0
	Tu	9	The Winter's Tale	257	2	6
	S	13	As You Like It BT. [J.] *Palmer*	131	11	6
S	Sept.	12	Richard III	159	6	6
	Tu	22	As You Like It	220	4	6
Th	Oct.	1	Henry V	167	18	6

1789

1789 DRURY LANE (cont.)

			£	s.	d.
M Oct. 5	Henry V		176	2	0
M 12	same		228	3	6
Tu 13	The Tempest		156	11	6
S 17	same		244	5	0
M 19	Henry V		145	7	6
Tu 20	The Tempest		191	8	6
M 26	Henry V		200	2	6
Tu 27	The Tempest		185	5	0
M Nov. 2	Henry V		144	11	6
Tu 3	The Tempest		155	19	6
M 9	Henry V		165	17	6
Tu 10	The Tempest		166	2	0
Th 12	Richard III		100	12	6
M 16	Henry V		197	1	0
Tu 17	The Tempest		210	5	0
M 23	Henry V		166	11	6
F 27	Much Ado about Nothing		146	13	6
M 30	Othello		139	15	0
M Dec. 7	[Henry V]				

Announced by both Pb and PA, but not acted. The play was changed to *George Barnwell* (MS annotation on JPK), 'on account of the indisposition of Mr. Kemble' (PA, Dec. 8). Kemble Mem. notes the same change.

W 9	Much Ado about Nothing	161	17	0
F 18	same	182	12	6
M 21	The Tempest	206	5	6
S 26	Much Ado about Nothing	217	4	6
M 28	Henry V	171	5	0
W 30	The Tempest	171	19	0

COVENT GARDEN

F Jan. 2	The Comedy of Errors	178	14	6
M 12	Henry IV, Part I	205	18	0
Tu 20	Much Ado about Nothing	248	7	0
W Feb. 11	As You Like It BT. *Miss Wallis*	297	10	0
W 18	[The Merchant of Venice]			

Announced by both Pb and PA, but not acted. 'On account of Mr. Macklin's sudden indisposition, the Play of The Merchant of Venice, Cannot be performed; And This Evening will be presented ... The Nunnery' (printed notice attached to the BM bill). See also PA, Feb. 19.

M Mar. 16	The Comedy of Errors	257	16	6
M 23	same	238	19	6
Th May 7	The Merchant of Venice BT. *Macklin*	278	13	6
F 22	The Winter's Tale BT. *Mr and Mrs Bernard*	189	15	0
F 29	The Comedy of Errors BT. *Wewitzer*	182	8	6

1789–1790

1789 COVENT GARDEN (*cont.*)

			£	s.	d.
M	Sept. 14	Romeo and Juliet	255	6	0
M	21	same	289	19	6
F	25	Richard III	262	10	6
M	28	same	254	4	6
M	Oct. 5	same	175	1	0
F	9	The Merry Wives of Windsor	201	1	6
M	12	Macbeth	219	1	6
F	16	Othello	242	16	6
M	19	Macbeth	163	4	6
F	23	Richard III	197	1	0
M	26	Othello	216	7	0
M	Nov. 2	Henry IV, Part I	168	1	6
F	6	The Merchant of Venice	147	7	0
M	9	Romeo and Juliet	225	3	6
M	16	Hamlet	226	9	6
F	20	As You Like It	241	19	6
M	23	King Lear	215	8	6
Tu	Dec. 1	As You Like It	187	1	0
F	4	The Merry Wives of Windsor	126	18	0

    Both Pb and PA announce *The Beggar's Opera*. But 'Mrs. Billington was taken ill & The Merry Wives of Windsor . . . [was] substituted' (MS annotation on BM bill). See also DWR, Dec. 5.

M	7	Romeo and Juliet	167	6	0
Tu	8	Richard III	126	15	6
M	28	Romeo and Juliet	256	4	0

HAYMARKET

M June 1 Hamlet

1790 DRURY LANE

M	Jan. 4	Richard III	163	1	6
W	6	Much Ado about Nothing	137	8	0
M	11	The Tempest	208	2	0
F	15	The Two Gentlemen of Verona	169	7	6
M	18	The Tempest	207	0	0
W	20	The Two Gentlemen of Verona	136	5	0
M	25	The Tempest	201	17	6
W	Feb. 3	Much Ado about Nothing	126	17	6
W	10	Twelfth Night	218	16	0
M	22	The Tempest	202	5	0
S	27	As You Like It	232	10	6
S	Mar. 6	same	203	19	0
F	Apr. 9	Twelfth Night *BT. Bensley*	204	2	0
W	21	same *BT. Morris* [*author of* The Adventurers, *also acted this night*]	187	3	6

    The recipient of the BT. is named in Kemble Mem., but not in Pb or PA.

89

1790

1790 DRURY LANE (*cont.*)

			£	s.	d.
S Apr. 24	The Tempest		192	0	0
M 26	Twelfth Night		191	15	6

    Both Pb and PA announce *The Rivals*. But 'Mr [J.] Bannister ill prevented The Rivals' (Kemble Mem.). 'At Drury Lane. Saw Twelfth Night' (Reed, 176).

W 28	As You Like It	126	0	6
Tu May 11	Henry V *BT. Mrs* [*J.*] *Wilson and Williames*	225	5	0

    Williames as a recipient of the BT. is named in the DL Account-Book, but not in Pb. (PA does not advertise this performance.)

W 12	Much Ado about Nothing *BT. Whitfield*	220	5	6
Th June 3	The Two Gentlemen of Verona *BT. Portal,* [*T.*] *Shade, Hicks, and W. Purser*	343	10	0
Th Oct. 7	Henry V	227	16	0
M 11	The Tempest	199	18	6
Th 21	Richard III	266	14	0
W 27	As You Like It	265	14	0
Th 28	Richard III	240	12	6
W Nov. 3	Twelfth Night	166	7	0
W 24	The Tempest	199	3	0
W Dec. 8	Twelfth Night	122	5	0

    Both Pb and PA announce the 6th night of *Better Late than Never*. The DL Account-Book deletes this, and enters *Twelfth Night*. On Dec. 29 the bill for *Better Late than Never* has, '6th time'; on Jan. 6, 1791, '7th time'.

COVENT GARDEN

M Jan. 4	King Lear	269	8	6
M 11	same	247	5	6
M 18	same	224	13	6
M Feb. 1	same	235	5	6
M 8	Macbeth	211	6	6
Th 11	Florizel and Perdita *BT. King*	321	2	6

    Announced as *The Sheep-Shearing*.

M 15	King Lear	182	0	6
M 22	Henry IV, Part I	174	5	6
M Mar. 1	Richard III	185	7	6
S 13	Catharine and Petruchio *BT. O'Keeffe* [*author of* The Czar, *also acted this night*]	185	12	6

    The recipient of the BT. is named in Egerton 2290, but not in Pb or PA.

Tu Apr. 6	Richard III *and* Catharine and Petruchio *BT. Quick*	430	17	6
W 7	The Comedy of Errors *BT. Edwin* [*Sr.*]	366	8	0

1790–1791

1790 COVENT GARDEN (*cont.*)

				£	s.	d.
M	Apr. 19	King Lear		182	6	6
F	30	Henry IV, Part I *BT*. [*F*.] *Aickin*		209	0	0
S	May 1	The Merchant of Venice		147	19	6
M	3	Macbeth *BT*. *Harley*		360	12	0
Th	13	Catharine and Petruchio *BT*. *Mrs Mountain*		251	11	6
S	15	Othello *BT*. *Fennell*		200	6	0
F	28	Florizel and Perdita		177	11	0
Tu	June 1	The Comedy of Errors *BT*. *Mrs Warrell and Darley*		216	12	0
W	2	Hamlet *BT*. *Mrs Billington*		351	9	6
M	7	same		139	11	6
Th	10	The Comedy of Errors *BT*. *Cubitt, Macready, Thompson, and Boyce*		258	13	0
M	Sept. 13	Romeo and Juliet		216	9	6
W	Oct. 6	Macbeth		240	1	0
M	11	King Lear		218	4	0
W	13	The Merry Wives of Windsor		165	4	0
M	18	Richard III		184	1	6

Genest (vii. 22) erroneously has Oct. 10, a Sunday.

				£	s.	d.
W	20	As You Like It		182	14	6
M	25	Romeo and Juliet		200	7	6
M	Nov. 8	Othello		144	14	6
Tu	9	As You Like It		223	10	0
M	15	same		193	7	0
M	22	King Lear		209	7	6
F	26	Macbeth		149	8	0
S	27	Florizel and Perdita		171	2	6
F	Dec. 3	As You Like It		146	3	6
M	6	Hamlet		222	5	6
M	13	same		151	12	6

HAYMARKET

Tu	June 22	The Merchant of Venice
Th	Aug. 12	Catharine and Petruchio
F	20	same *BT*. [*C*.] *Bannister*
Th	26	same
W	Sept. 8	same

1791 DRURY LANE

				£	s.	d.
Th	Jan. 27	Twelfth Night		188	1	6
W	Feb. 16	same		204	0	6
F	25	same		146	15	0
Th	Mar. 17	As You Like It		217	16	6
M	28	Othello		329	13	6
F	Apr. 29	As You Like It *BT*. *Wrighten, prompter*		328	18	0
Th	May 5	The Tempest *BT*. *Mrs Goodall*		262	15	0

1791 DRURY LANE (cont.)

			£	s.	d.
S	May 28	As You Like It BT. Wood, Percey, Cameron, Wilson, George, and Woollams	363	4	6
M	30	The Tempest	123	13	6

DRURY LANE (company at KING'S, HAYMARKET)[1]

			£	s.	d.
M	Oct. 3	As You Like It	251	4	6
M	17	[Henry V]			

Announced by both Pb and PA, but not acted. 'On Account of the Sudden Indisposition of a Principal Performer, *The Siege of Belgrade* . . . [was] substituted' (MS annotation on JPK). See also MP, Oct. 18.

			£	s.	d.
M	31	Henry V	223	5	6
F	Nov. 4	Twelfth Night	198	12	6
M	7	Henry IV, Part I	195	14	0
W	9	The Tempest	225	11	6
M	14	Richard III	189	2	0
Tu	15	As You Like It	196	13	6
F	25	The Tempest	151	5	6
M	28	Henry V	156	9	0
W	30	Catharine and Petruchio	110	9	6
M	Dec. 5	Henry IV, Part I	159	13	6
Tu	13	As You Like It	244	16	6
W	14	The Tempest	154	14	6
Tu	27	same	182	15	0

COVENT GARDEN

			£	s.	d.
M	Jan. 3	Henry IV, Part I	239	0	6
S	8	As You Like It	248	3	0
M	10	King Lear	213	12	6
Tu	18	As You Like It	158	3	0
Th	Feb. 3	same	172	9	0
M	7	same	371	18	0
F	May 20	Catharine and Petruchio BT. Incledon	278	0	6
Tu	31	The Comedy of Errors BT. Hull	186	2	6
M	Sept. 26	Romeo and Juliet	212	2	6
Th	Oct. 6	As You Like It	85	17	6
M	10	Macbeth	180	5	0
M	17	Hamlet	217	6	6
M	24	Richard III	243	13	6
F	Nov. 4	King Lear	138	17	6
Th	24	Henry IV, Part I	155	12	0
M	28	Romeo and Juliet	189	15	6

[1] See p. 720.

1791-1792

1791 HAYMARKET

- M June 6   Catharine and Petruchio
- Tu 14   same
- M 20   Henry IV, Part I
- W 29   same
- W Aug. 24   Richard III *BT. [C.] Bannister*
- Th Sept. 1   Catharine and Petruchio
- W 14   same
- F 16   same *BT. R. Palmer*

1792 DRURY LANE (company at KING'S, HAYMARKET)[1]

M Jan. 23   [Catharine and Petruchio]
Announced by both Pb and PA, but not acted, because of Mrs Goodall's indisposition. *The Apprentice* was substituted (MS annotation on JPK). This change of play is also indicated in the DL Account-Book.

		£	s.	d.
Tu 31	Catharine and Petruchio	447	11	0
Tu Feb. 7	Richard III	371	9	6
Tu 14	Othello	398	6	6
S 18	Macbeth	425	6	0
M 20	Twelfth Night	292	2	0
Th Mar. 1	King John	278	10	6
Tu 6	King Lear	350	9	6
S 10	The Merchant of Venice	317	7	0
Tu 20	Macbeth	351	15	0
M 26	Henry VIII *BT. Mrs Siddons*	493	16	0
S 31	Coriolanus *BT. Kemble*	377	13	0

The recipient of the BT. is named in DWR, Apr. 2, but not in Pb or PA.

		£	s.	d.
M Apr. 9	As You Like It *BT. Dodd*	418	11	6
Th 12	The Tempest *BT. Baddeley*	356	12	0
Tu 17	Henry VIII	221	17	0
S 21	Coriolanus	269	11	0
Tu 24	Catharine and Petruchio	264	1	0
W 25	Othello *BT. a fund for the relief of those whose infirmities oblige them to retire from the stage*	372	1	0
Tu May 1	Twelfth Night *BT. Suett*	406	9	6
Tu 8	The Tempest *BT. Mrs Bland and Mrs Powell*	369	9	0
W 9	Catharine and Petruchio	294	8	0
M 28	same	231	14	6
Th 31	Twelfth Night *BT. [J.] Burton, Fawcett [Sr.], Phillimore, Miss Tidswell, and Miss Hagley*	516	6	6
Th June 7	As You Like It *BT. the young D'Egvilles, Johnston, Nix, and Dale*	518	6	0
S 9	Catharine and Petruchio	208	10	6

[1] See p. 720.

1792

1792 DRURY LANE (company at KING'S, HAYMARKET)[1] (cont.)

			£	s.	d.
Tu Sept. 18	Catharine and Petruchio		232	9	0
Tu 25	Henry V		169	9	6
M Oct. 29	same		178	0	0
F Nov. 2	Much Ado about Nothing		125	11	6
M 5	Richard III		183	16	0
M 12	same		173	10	6
Th 15	Catharine and Petruchio		104	5	0
W 21	same		359	10	6
S Dec. 1	same		252	18	0
Th 13	The Tempest		120	9	6
W 26	Macbeth		315	4	6
Th 27	Much Ado about Nothing		217	19	0
F 28	Othello		201	8	0

COVENT GARDEN

F Jan. 6 [Macbeth]

    Announced by both Pb and PA, but not acted, because of Harley's indisposition. The play was changed to *The Farmer* (MS annotation on the BM bill). See also MC, Jan. 7.

		£	s.	d.
M 16	Romeo and Juliet	197	13	0
M 23	Macbeth	247	2	0
F May 11	The Winter's Tale BT. *Mrs Mountain*	119	9	6
Tu 15	Catharine and Petruchio BT. *Miss Chapman*	244	18	0
F 18	The Comedy of Errors BT. *Harley*	308	14	6
S 19	Cymbeline BT. *Marshall and Mrs Harlowe*	256	7	0
M Oct. 1	Othello	336	4	0
M 8	Romeo and Juliet	340	9	6
W 10	As You Like It	254	19	6
M 15	Richard III	268	7	6
M 22	Romeo and Juliet	364	14	6
M 29	Macbeth	277	14	6
M Nov. 5	Hamlet	319	2	0
F 9	Macbeth	349	11	0
M 26	Romeo and Juliet	264	11	0
W Dec. 26	Richard III	244	18	6
Th 27	Hamlet	302	11	6

HAYMARKET

M Feb. 6   Othello BT. *Mrs Churton*
    M 20   The Merchant of Venice BT. *Wilkinson*
M Apr. 16   Richard III BT. *the Literary Fund*
M Aug. 6   Henry IV, Part I
    F 10   same
    F 17   Catharine and Petruchio

[1] See p. 720.

1792–1793

1792 HAYMARKET (cont.)

  Th Aug. 30 Henry IV, Part I
  Tu Sept. 4 Catharine and Petruchio
     W 12 Henry IV, Part I

1793 DRURY LANE (company at KING'S, HAYMARKET)[1]

		£	s.	d.
W Jan. 2	The Tempest	229	2	0
Th 10	Much Ado about Nothing	237	6	6
Tu 22	Catharine and Petruchio	245	15	6

DL (company at HAYMARKET)[1]

Tu Feb. 12	King John	195	15	0
S 16	King Lear	183	13	0
S 23	Coriolanus	149	19	0

DL (company at KING'S, HAYMARKET)

M Mar. 4	As You Like It	255	18	0

DL (company at HAYMARKET)

Tu Mar. 5	The Merchant of Venice	139	11	0
S 9	Henry VIII	164	18	0
Tu Apr. 16	Macbeth	204	12	0
S 20	Othello	164	1	0

DL (company at KING'S, HAYMARKET)

F May 3	As You Like It	204	1	0

DL (company at HAYMARKET)

Tu May 7	The Tempest BT. [C.] *Bannister*	227	8	0

DL (company at KING'S, HAYMARKET)

W May 8	Macbeth	349	1	0

DL (company at HAYMARKET)

Tu May 14	Henry VIII	115	10	0
Tu 21	Coriolanus	128	13	0

DL (company at KING'S, HAYMARKET)

F May 24	Twelfth Night BT. *Dignum and Mrs Powell*	510	1	0

COVENT GARDEN

M Jan. 7	Romeo and Juliet	220	17	0
M Apr. 15	The Comedy of Errors	345	5	0
F May 10	Catharine and Petruchio BT. *Incledon*	469	16	0
Th 23	same BT. *Harley*	341	5	6

[1] See p. 720.

1793 COVENT GARDEN (cont.)   £   s. d.

F	May 24	Henry VIII *BT. Hull and Macready*	282	14	0
	Th 30	As You Like It	233	11	3
M	June 3	The Comedy of Errors *BT. Brandon, box-book and house-keeper*	456	4	0
	W 5	same	295	18	0
W	Sept. 18	Much Ado about Nothing	203	12	0
	M 23	Othello	281	12	0
	M 30	Macbeth	260	16	0
M	Oct. 7	Romeo and Juliet	251	2	6
	Tu 8	The Comedy of Errors	232	6	0
	W 9	Hamlet	332	4	0
	M 14	Richard III	197	19	0
	W 16	Hamlet	324	13	0
	M 21	same	304	10	0
	S 26	The Comedy of Errors	173	8	0

PA announces *Love in a Village*, which was not acted 'in consequence of the sudden indisposition of Miss Poole' (MP, Oct. 28). Pb for this night refers to the postponement of *Love in a Village*.

	M 28	Macbeth	269	19	0
	W 30	Hamlet	263	4	6
M	Nov. 4	same	231	16	6
	M 11	Romeo and Juliet	249	16	6
	F 15	Hamlet	224	2	0
	M 18	Cymbeline	291	11	6
	F 22	same	191	17	6
M	Dec. 9	Macbeth	263	9	6
	M 16	Hamlet	245	8	0
	F 27	Macbeth	330	10	0

HAYMARKET

F	July 5	Catharine and Petruchio
Tu	Aug. 6	Richard III *BT. Mrs [S.] Kemble*
Tu	Sept. 24	Henry V
	M 30	Richard III
M	Oct. 21	Othello
Tu	Nov. 19	The Tempest
Th	Dec. 5	same
	M 23	Richard III
	Th 26	The Tempest

1794 DRURY LANE

M	Apr. 21	Macbeth	658	18	0
	Tu 22	same	459	0	0
	W 23	same	408	2	0
	Th 24	same	418	7	6
	F 25	As You Like It	386	11	0

96

1794

1794 DRURY LANE (cont.)   £   s.   d.

M	Apr. 28	Macbeth	540	6	0
W	30	same	396	8	6
Th	May 1	Henry VIII	450	7	6
F	2	Macbeth	461	6	6
M	5	same	417	7	6
W	7	same	567	15	0
M	12	same	480	7	6
W	14	Henry VIII	368	0	0
M	19	Macbeth	366	5	0
M	26	same	356	12	6
F	30	Catharine and Petruchio	281	5	6
M	June 2	Macbeth	315	8	6
W	11	As You Like It	178	17	6
W	18	same	205	11	6
F	20	same	208	8	0

         Pb announces *Much Ado about Nothing*. But a principal performer was ill, and the play was changed to *As You Like It* (Kemble Mem.; DL Account-Book).

Tu	Sept. 23	Henry V	323	12	0
M	Oct. 6	same	235	0	6
Tu	7	Macbeth	253	19	6
S	18	Henry VIII	307	6	0
W	29	As You Like It	251	13	0
Tu	Nov. 11	Macbeth	249	14	6
F	14	Twelfth Night	232	2	6
Tu	18	Othello	157	13	0
S	Dec. 6	Macbeth	201	3	0
Tu	9	Henry VIII	194	3	0
F	12	All's Well that Ends Well	282	1	0
Tu	30	Measure for Measure	248	8	6
W	31	same	474	0	6

COVENT GARDEN

M	Jan. 6	King Lear	297	16	0
Tu	7	The Comedy of Errors	340	8	6
Th	9	Hamlet	325	8	6
W	15	Much Ado about Nothing	371	19	6
Th	16	The Comedy of Errors	466	9	0
M	20	King Lear	383	8	0
Tu	28	Hamlet	240	11	0
F	31	King Lear	242	2	6
M	Feb. 3	Macbeth	306	1	0
F	21	Hamlet	195	7	6
W	26	Catharine and Petruchio	328	0	6
M	Apr. 21	King Lear	316	5	6
W	30	Romeo and Juliet *BT. Mrs Twistleton*	262	10	6

1794-1795

1794 COVENT GARDEN (*cont.*)

			£	s.	d.
S May 10	Hamlet *BT. Pope*		231	17	0
M 12	King Lear		141	10	0
S 17	The Comedy of Errors		82	5	0
W 21	Othello *BT. Harley*		339	19	0
W Sept. 17	same		230	12	6
M 22	Macbeth		312	7	0
M 29	Hamlet		320	17	0
Tu Oct. 7	Cymbeline		228	1	6
F 10	same		292	13	0
M 13	Hamlet		204	1	0
W 15	Richard III		227	10	6
M 20	Romeo and Juliet		299	13	0
W 22	same		132	1	0
M 27	same		160	0	6
Th Nov. 6	Macbeth		80	9	0
M 10	Cymbeline		210	16	0
W 12	Much Ado about Nothing		159	18	0
W 19	The Comedy of Errors		265	0	0
M Dec. 29	Hamlet		298	7	0

HAYMARKET

S Jan. 4 The Tempest
Tu Feb. 25 Richard III
Th July 10 Catharine and Petruchio
W Aug. 27 Richard III *BT.* [*C.*] *Bannister*

1795 DRURY LANE

			£	s.	d.
Tu Jan. 13	Measure for Measure		284	2	0
W 21	As You Like It		149	12	0
S Feb. 7	same		103	7	6
Th 26	Measure for Measure		406	19	0
S Mar. 7	same		348	14	6
Tu 10	The Merchant of Venice		285	7	6
S 14	King John		255	3	0
Tu 17	Measure for Measure		261	1	6
Tu Apr. 7	Macbeth		337	16	6
S 18	Measure for Measure		212	9	6
W 22	Twelfth Night *BT. Dodd*		386	7	6
S 25	Macbeth		246	7	6
S May 30	Twelfth Night *BT. Portal, Gibson, Percey, George, Bowley, Stevenson, Hicks, and J. Shade*		565	19	6
Tu Sept. 29	Macbeth		340	7	6
F Nov. 6	Henry VIII		211	1	6
M 9	Macbeth		371	18	6
Th 12	As You Like It		212	6	6
Th 19	Twelfth Night		252	9	6

1795

1795 DRURY LANE (*cont.*)

			£	s.	d.
F	Nov. 20	King Lear	214	19	6
F	Dec. 11	Measure for Measure	199	17	6
	F 18	King John	257	19	6
	W 23	Macbeth	218	11	6

COVENT GARDEN

			£	s.	d.
Th	Jan. 1	Cymbeline	182	13	6
	M 5	Romeo and Juliet	235	7	0
	S 10	The Comedy of Errors	220	2	0

Pb announces *The Dramatist*. But 'In consequence of the indisposition of Mr. Lewis, The Dramatist was obliged to be postponed ... The Comedy of Errors was the substitute' (MP, Jan. 12).

			£	s.	d.
	M 12	Hamlet	216	14	0
	M 19	King Lear	176	3	6
	M 26	Romeo and Juliet	130	6	0
Tu	Feb. 17	King Lear	108	14	6
M	Mar. 9	Macbeth	124	16	6
	M 16	Catharine and Petruchio *BT. Mrs Pope*	293	18	0
	Tu 17	The Comedy of Errors	194	12	0
W	Apr. 8	same *BT. Quick*	409	11	0
	Tu 28	Catharine and Petruchio *BT. Incledon*	467	12	6
M	May 18	Macbeth	121	13	6
W	June 10	same	218	14	0
	F 12	Catharine and Petruchio *BT. Powel, Rock, Sloper, and Farley*	354	5	6
M	Sept. 14	Macbeth	267	3	0
	M 21	Romeo and Juliet	279	16	0
	M 28	King Lear	271	17	6
M	Oct. 12	Romeo and Juliet	267	7	6
	F 16	Richard III	195	18	0
	M 19	Hamlet	221	9	6
	M 26	same	221	12	6
M	Nov. 2	same	196	2	0
	M 23	Romeo and Juliet	158	3	0
	M 30	Macbeth	137	0	0
W	Dec. 9	Henry IV, Part I	170	12	0
	M 14	same	234	5	0
	W 16	same	168	5	0
	Tu 22	The Winter's Tale	253	9	6
	Th 31	The Comedy of Errors	225	0	0

HAYMARKET

| M | Aug. 3 | The Merchant of Venice *BT. Mrs Gibbs* |
| Tu | 18 | Hamlet *BT.* [C.] *Bannister* |

1796

1796 DRURY LANE

				£	s.	d.
F	Jan.	1	Henry VIII	211	8	6
	Tu	5	As You Like It	236	6	0
	Tu	12	Twelfth Night	222	19	0
	F	15	Henry VIII	298	3	6
M	Apr.	11	Macbeth	360	5	6
	M	18	Coriolanus BT. *Kemble*	475	5	0
	M	25	Romeo and Juliet BT. *Mrs Jordan*	658	19	6
	Th	28	same	231	8	0
	F	29	Hamlet BT. *King*	498	17	6
Th	May	12	same BT. *Mrs Powell*	466	11	6
	F	20	Romeo and Juliet BT. *Barrymore*	372	14	0
	F	27	Hamlet BT. *Sedgwick*	370	0	0
Th	June	2	same BT. *R. Palmer and Russell*	370	1	0
	W	8	The Merry Wives of Windsor BT. *[J.] Burton, Misses Heard and Tidswell, and Mrs Bramwell*	337	6	6
	M	13	Catharine and Petruchio BT. *[T.] Shade, Cameron, Woollams, Wood, Wilson, Dangerfield, Irish, Edwards, Griffiths, Nix, Wooldridge, Panchaud, and Cole*	580	17	6
M	Oct.	3	Coriolanus	390	17	6
	M	10	Macbeth	283	13	6
	M	24	Hamlet	427	19	0
	M	31	same	400	11	0
S	Nov.	5	Measure for Measure	320	4	0
	M	7	Hamlet	290	9	6
	W	9	Richard III	318	4	6
	M	21	Hamlet	275	19	0
M	Dec.	5	same	201	10	0
	Tu	13	Macbeth	240	7	6
	F	16	The Merchant of Venice	205	1	0
			Genest (vii. 288) erroneously has Dec. 15.			
	W	28	Macbeth	210	16	0
	F	30	Romeo and Juliet	155	4	0

COVENT GARDEN

				£	s.	d.
M	Jan.	11	Henry IV, Part I	264	14	6
	M	18	same	276	5	0
M	Mar.	14	The Merry Wives of Windsor BT. *Mrs Pope*	498	5	0
	S	19	Catharine and Petruchio BT. *Lewis*	384	18	0
	M	28	The Merry Wives of Windsor	318	8	0
F	Apr.	1	Henry IV, Part I BT. *Holman*	318	19	0
	M	4	The Merry Wives of Windsor	246	10	0
	S	16	same	193	7	6
	M	18	Henry IV, Part I	201	12	6
	F	22	The Comedy of Errors BT. *Munden*	454	11	6
	M	25	King Lear	234	4	0

1796–1797

1796 COVENT GARDEN (*cont.*)   £   s.   d.
- W Apr. 27 The Merry Wives of Windsor   163   1   6
- Tu May 3 Catharine and Petruchio *BT. Mrs Serres*   288   2   6
- M   9 Henry IV, Part I   156 15   6
- Th   12 The Merchant of Venice *BT. Harley*   219 12   6
- Tu   17 Romeo and Juliet *BT. Middleton*   287 12   0
- M Sept. 12 Hamlet   281   1   6
- M   19 Romeo and Juliet   230 14   0
- M   26 Macbeth   285   2   0
- F   30 The Merchant of Venice   281 17   0
- F Oct. 7 same   220 19   6
- M   10 King Lear   158   1   0
- Th   20 Henry IV, Part I   107   1   6
- M   24 Othello   210 14   6
- Th   27 Romeo and Juliet   172   7   0
- S Nov. 5 Richard III   191   2   6
- M   7 The Merry Wives of Windsor   254   7   6
- M   14 Macbeth   140   5   6
- M   21 Catharine and Petruchio   175 12   6
- W Dec. 7 same   161 12   0
- M   12 Othello   102 18   0
- W   28 The Merry Wives of Windsor   216 15   6

HAYMARKET

- Th June 16 The Merchant of Venice
- Tu   21 same
- W   29 Catharine and Petruchio
- Th July 14 same
- Tu   26 same
- S Aug. 6 The Merchant of Venice
- Th   11 Hamlet *BT.* [C.] *Bannister*
- Th   18 Henry IV, Part I *BT. Fawcett* [*Jr.*]
- Tu   30 The School of Shakespeare *BT.* [*J.*] *Palmer*

    This entertainment consisted of excerpts from five of Shakespeare's plays. Each Act was given its own title, as follows:
1. CRUELTY: *The Merchant of Venice* (IV. i)
2. VANITY: *Henry IV, Part I* (parts of II. iv)
3. AMBITION: *Henry VIII* (parts of III. ii)
4. RUSTICITY: *As You Like It* (III. iii)
5. TYRANNY: Cibber's *Richard III* (parts of I. ii; II. ii and V)

- W Sept. 7 Romeo and Juliet *BT. Elliston*

1797 DRURY LANE
- W Jan. 11 Measure for Measure   213   0   6
- Th   12 Much Ado about Nothing   115 14   0
- S Feb. 11 The Merchant of Venice   258   1   0
- M   20 Macbeth   253 15   0
- W   22 The Tempest   212   2   6

1797

1797 DRURY LANE (cont.)

				£	s.	d.
M	Feb.	27	Coriolanus	175	15	6
	Tu	28	The Tempest	180	3	6
M	Mar.	6	Cymbeline	253	9	0
	Tu	14	Macbeth	173	18	6
	S	18	The Tempest	181	4	6
	M	20	Othello	219	6	6
	Th	23	Much Ado about Nothing	189	6	0
	Tu	28	Measure for Measure	191	3	0
M	Apr.	24	Catharine and Petruchio	283	17	0
Tu	May	2	same	186	18	6
	W	3	Hamlet	250	2	6
	F	12	As You Like It *BT. Miss Pope*	386	18	0
	W	17	Twelfth Night *BT. Suett*	320	4	0
	Th	25	Hamlet *BT. Mrs Powell*	288	3	6
Th	Oct.	5	same	543	8	0
	S	7	As You Like It	368	14	6
	M	9	Hamlet	366	10	0
	M	16	same	369	3	6
	M	23	same	220	9	6
Tu	Nov.	7	Macbeth	258	7	0
	M	13	Hamlet	351	14	0
	F	17	Measure for Measure	237	9	6
	Th	23	Othello	237	7	6
	S	25	Henry IV, Part I	140	18	0
	M	27	Hamlet	251	6	0
S	Dec.	2	The Merchant of Venice	169	6	6
	S	9	The Tempest	142	7	6
	M	11	Macbeth	237	9	6
	W	13	The Merchant of Venice	134	15	0
	Th	21	Catharine and Petruchio	318	1	6
	S	23	The Tempest	154	3	0

COVENT GARDEN

				£	s.	d.
M	Jan.	2	Henry IV, Part I	244	15	6
	S	7	The Comedy of Errors	236	15	6
M	Feb.	13	The Merry Wives of Windsor	471	9	6
W	Apr.	26	The Comedy of Errors *BT. Miss Wallis*	376	9	6
F	June	2	Richard III	152	0	0
M	Sept.	18	Henry IV, Part I	270	18	0
	M	25	Hamlet	248	18	0
	W	27	The Merry Wives of Windsor	236	0	0
M	Oct.	2	Richard III	286	17	0
	F	6	Much Ado about Nothing	348	2	0
	M	9	same	270	12	0
W	Nov.	1	Henry IV, Part I	162	16	6
	Th	2	Romeo and Juliet	197	3	6
	F	3	The Merchant of Venice	413	17	0

1797–1798

1797 COVENT GARDEN (*cont.*)

			£	s.	d.
M Nov. 6	Romeo and Juliet		235	12	0
Th 9	The Merry Wives of Windsor		193	6	6
M 13	Romeo and Juliet		268	4	0
W 15	Catharine and Petruchio		244	8	0
M 20	King Lear		192	16	0
Th Dec. 14	Much Ado about Nothing		150	19	0
Tu 19	Romeo and Juliet		289	17	0

HAYMARKET

Tu June 13	Catharine and Petruchio
Tu 20	same
M Aug. 28	The Merchant of Venice
Tu 29	same
M Sept. 4	Othello *BT. Elliston*

1798 DRURY LANE

W Jan. 24	Hamlet	461	11	6
Th Feb. 8	same	417	18	0
F 9	As You Like It	271	19	6
Tu 13	Twelfth Night	279	9	6
Th 15	Hamlet	244	6	6
S 24	The Tempest	278	13	0
Th Mar. 1	Hamlet	466	11	0
S 3	Measure for Measure	406	2	6
Tu 6	Macbeth	413	8	6
Tu 20	Hamlet	371	2	0
Tu Apr. 24	same	245	9	6
M May 14	same	264	7	6
Th 24	Much Ado about Nothing *BT. Miss Leak*	505	1	6
M June 4	Macbeth	207	1	6
Tu 5	The Tempest *BT. [C.] Bannister*	318	6	0
Tu Sept. 18	Macbeth	319	4	0
Tu 25	Richard III	327	8	0
Th Oct. 4	Hamlet	270	3	6
Th 11	Much Ado about Nothing	219	14	0
Tu 16	Hamlet	258	5	6
M 22	Richard III	302	0	6
S 27	Measure for Measure	264	2	6
Tu Nov. 13	The Merchant of Venice	156	14	0
M 19	Richard III	159	0	0

COVENT GARDEN

M Jan. 1	Romeo and Juliet	285	11	6
M 8	same	298	4	6
M 22	same	277	14	0

1798–1799

1798 COVENT GARDEN (*cont.*)   £   s.   d.

M	Jan. 29	Romeo and Juliet	188	13	6
M	Feb. 5	Henry IV, Part I	158	16	0
M	Mar. 12	Romeo and Juliet	167	3	6
	Th 15	Much Ado about Nothing	372	1	6
Tu	Apr. 10	The Comedy of Errors	141	5	0
	S 21	Catharine and Petruchio *BT. Incledon*	528	10	6
	S 28	Hamlet *BT. [H.] Johnston*	230	19	6
F	May 4	Richard III	90	6	0
	M 7	Romeo and Juliet	100	17	0
	S 12	Florizel and Perdita *BT. Murray*	198	17	0
	M 14	Much Ado about Nothing	114	6	6
	F 18	The Merchant of Venice	237	18	3
S	June 2	The Comedy of Errors *BT. Simpson, Powel, Rees, and Mrs Henley*	267	19	6
M	Sept. 17	Hamlet	242	5	6
	M 24	same	215	16	0
M	Oct. 8	Romeo and Juliet	179	0	6
	M 15	Othello	294	15	6
M	Nov. 19	Catharine and Petruchio	226	13	0
S	Dec. 15	Macbeth	299	15	6

HAYMARKET

S   Apr. 21   Richard III
       and Catharine and Petruchio *BT. a distressed family*
Tu   Aug. 21   Much Ado about Nothing *BT. Miss De Camp*
   W 29   The Merchant of Venice
M   Sept. 3   Hamlet
   W 5   The Merchant of Venice

1799 DRURY LANE

	Th Jan. 17	Measure for Measure	190	5	6
	S Feb. 2	Much Ado about Nothing	156	15	0
	M 11	Hamlet	266	14	0
	Th 14	As You Like It	301	15	6
	M 18	Hamlet	312	13	6
	Th 21	As You Like It	352	3	6
	S 23	Twelfth Night	296	19	0
	Th 28	As You Like It	323	4	0
Tu	Apr. 2	Macbeth	352	16	6
	Th 4	As You Like It	200	11	0
	Tu 9	Measure for Measure	201	6	0
	M 15	As You Like It *BT. Mrs Crouch*	673	6	6
	Th 18	Hamlet *BT. Barrymore and Wathen*	640	5	6
	Th 25	As You Like It *BT. R. Palmer and Russell*	534	15	6
F	May 3	Catharine and Petruchio *BT. Miss De Camp*	447	8	0

104

1799

1799 DRURY LANE (cont.)

			£	s.	d.
S May 4	The Tempest BT. Sedgwick		390	8	6
	Genest (vii. 419) erroneously has, 'Powell's bt.'				
F 17	As You Like It BT. *Dignum*		713	9	0
M 20	Catharine and Petruchio		201	14	0
Th June 13	same		516	14	6
F 21	same		310	11	6
F 28	same		470	0	0
Th July 4	Much Ado about Nothing BT. Portal, Stevenson, Percey, George, Bowley, Woollams, Massingham [Sr.], Edwards, and Chumbley cash:[1]		61	3	0
Th Sept. 19	Hamlet		331	17	0
Tu Oct. 1	As You Like It		274	17	0
M 7	Richard III		225	16	6
Th 10	Hamlet		229	17	0
S 12	Much Ado about Nothing		252	16	0
Tu 15	As You Like It		301	18	0
M 28	Hamlet		409	12	6
M Nov. 4	same		303	13	0
Tu 5	Much Ado about Nothing		137	2	6
W 6	Catharine and Petruchio		178	17	0
F 8	The Merchant of Venice		173	14	6
M 11	Hamlet		257	3	6
Th 14	The Tempest		186	7	0
M 18	Richard III		281	4	0
Th 21	As You Like It		122	8	6
Th 28	The Tempest		176	10	0
F 29	Measure for Measure		192	12	6

COVENT GARDEN

			£	s.	d.
S Mar. 16	Catharine and Petruchio BT. *Lewis*		542	0	6
M May 6	Richard III		176	13	6
F 10	Romeo and Juliet BT. *Murray*		263	0	6
Tu 14	Macbeth BT. *Mr and Miss Betterton*		267	1	6
W 15	Henry VIII BT. *Mrs [M.A.] Pope*		391	0	6
S 18	Catharine and Petruchio BT. *Townsend and Mrs Johnson*		443	0	6
F June 7	The Merchant of Venice BT. *Hill, Rees, and Miss Sims*		287	7	0
M Sept. 23	Richard III		336	14	6
F 27	Catharine and Petruchio		226	3	0
M 30	Macbeth		334	17	0
F Oct. 4	Othello		245	16	0
M 7	Romeo and Juliet		284	10	6
M 28	Macbeth		177	13	6

[1] See note, p. 40.

1799 COVENT GARDEN (cont.)

			£	s.	d.
Tu	Oct. 29	King Lear	161	7	0
M	Nov. 18	Romeo and Juliet	293	9	0
M	Dec. 9	same	180	11	6
M	30	Henry IV, Part I	350	7	0

HAYMARKET

| W | Apr. 17 | The Merchant of Venice *BT. an infant orphan family* |

1800 DRURY LANE

M	Jan. 13	Hamlet	365	14	0
M	Feb. 24	As You Like It	173	16	6
W	Apr. 16	same	285	15	6
	M 21	The Merchant of Venice	245	19	0
M	May 19	same *BT. Mrs Powell*	353	10	6
W	June 18	Othello *BT. Lacy*	receipts omitted
Th	Sept. 16	Hamlet	304	7	6
	Tu 23	Richard III	390	19	6
S	Oct. 18	The Merchant of Venice	433	2	6
	M 20	Hamlet	504	9	0
	M 27	Richard III	353	16	6
W	Nov. 5	The Merchant of Venice	294	3	0
	S 15	Hamlet	216	6	6
	Th 20	King John	261	6	6
	F 21	As You Like It	221	11	0
	S 29	King John	314	13	6
Th	Dec. 4	same	218	11	6
	Th 11	same	205	10	0
	S 20	same	250	15	6
	M 29	Hamlet	239	8	0
	Tu 30	King John	253	7	6

COVENT GARDEN

Tu	May 13	Cymbeline *BT. Mrs [M. A.] Pope*	272	4	6
M	Sept. 29	Hamlet	331	19	6
F	Oct. 3	same	243	1	0
	M 6	Romeo and Juliet	232	12	0
	M 13	same	241	3	6
	F 31	Richard III	196	5	6
W	Nov. 5	same	243	7	6
	M 10	The Merchant of Venice	301	16	0
	Th 13	same	267	1	6
	M 17	Richard III	327	6	0
	Th 20	The Merchant of Venice	262	2	6
	M 24	Richard III	259	3	0
W	26	The Merchant of Venice	402	4	0

1800

1800 COVENT GARDEN (*cont.*)

				£	s.	d.
F	Nov.	28	Othello	295	14	6
M	Dec.	1	Richard III	296	9	0
	W	3	Othello	283	15	6
	F	5	Macbeth	290	17	6
	M	8	Richard III	281	12	0
	Th	11	Othello	271	15	0
	S	13	Macbeth	257	8	6
	M	15	Richard III	300	14	0
	Th	18	Macbeth	223	15	0
	S	20	Othello	334	16	6
	M	29	Richard III	347	19	6

PART II

THE PLAYS

In the following pages appear in alphabetical order the twenty-nine plays of Shakespeare that were acted in London between 1751 and 1800.[1] Many of these plays were performed in altered versions, either under the original title or under a new title. The new titles (*The Twins, A Fairy Tale*, &c.) are noted in the general alphabetical listing. As in my first volume, I include short summaries both of the acting versions of the plays and of the alterations. The act, scene, and line references are to the one-volume 'Oxford' Shakespeare, edited by W. J. Craig, edition of 1943. When denoting the play as Shakespeare wrote it, these references appear in italics. The letter 'a' indicates the first half of a line; 'b' the second half.

In the left-hand column is given the full cast of characters for the earliest performance in each calendar year. The exact order in which the characters are listed on the playbill is reproduced: the male characters first, followed by the female characters. In the right-hand column, in small type, are listed the changes in the casting that occurred throughout the year. Each performance in this column, or each set of performances that were identical, is numbered. The corresponding number or numbers against the name of a character in the left-hand column indicates the change in casting, thus:

Jan. 24
   ROSALIND (1, 2)   Mrs Barry

(1) *Mar. 13*
   ROSALIND   Mrs Bulkley
(2) *Apr. 9, 14; May 7*
   ROSALIND   Miss Younge

The numbers on the right are not cumulative; each refers independently to the corresponding number on the left.

On the right I have also noted additions to and omissions from the casting. The fact that certain characters were 'omitted' can be misleading. In order to save room for other information, or perhaps by inadvertence, or for other reasons, the playbills occasionally omitted the names of actors (usually those of secondary importance) who clearly must have appeared in the actual performance.

I have, again as in Volume I, spelt the names of the characters in accordance with modern usage: 'Rosencrantz' instead of the eighteenth-century 'Rosencraus', &c. Occasional variants in the spelling of the names of the actors have been regularized, as has the name 'Shakespeare'.

[1] Seven plays (or alterations of them), acted in the first half of the century, were not acted in the second half: *Henry VI, Parts I, II, and III*; *Pericles*; *Richard II*; *Titus Andronicus*; and *Troilus and Cressida*. Two plays not acted in the first half were revived in the second: *Antony and Cleopatra*; and *The Two Gentlemen of Verona*. The only play by Shakespeare never to be acted in the eighteenth century was *Love's Labour's Lost*. See p. 719.

ALL'S WELL THAT ENDS WELL

(1) 'As Performed at the Theatre-Royal, Drury-Lane. Regulated from the Prompt-Book.'

1773   John Bell.

Following are the principal omissions:

Act I. i. 96–104a ('bright particular star'), 235–end (Helena's second soliloquy); *iii.* 162–77a (the quibble on daughter-mother).

Act II. i. 1–26 (the King's farewell to the Lords), 122b–55 ('the weakest minister'); *ii.* 31–68 (the Clown as a courtier); *iii.* 71–108 (Helena's rejection of the three Lords).

Act III. i entire (the Duke undertaking war); *iii* entire (Bertram as general of the horse); *v.* 14–29 (Mariana's advice to Diana).

Act IV. iii. 1–44a (the Lords' reprobation of Bertram).

Act V. i entire (Helena and the Astringer).

Throughout there are minor omissions.

See also Odell, ii. 21.

(2) 'As it is Acted at the Theatres-Royal in Drury-Lane and Covent-Garden.'

1778   J. Harrison.

This is identical with (1).

(3) Altered by Frederick Pilon. In three acts.

1785   Not published.

WEP, July 27, 1785: 'Pilon ... has extracted from the two first acts what was worth preserving, and judiciously blended them in the three acts which are retained.' MP, July 27, 1785: 'The two first acts are lopped off ... and the recovery of the ring contained in them given afterwards by Helena in relation ... The old Lord Lafeu also is taken with Bertram to Florence, and the character enriched by blending it with one of the Lords who assist in the stratagem practiced on Parolles.'

(4) 'With Alterations by J. P. Kemble. As it is Performed [at] ... the Theatre-Royal, Drury-Lane.'

1793   J. Debrett.

Act I consists of *Act I. i*, omitting 116b–204 (Parolles and Helena on the subject of virginity), 235–end (Helena's second soliloquy, for which is substituted 96–110a); and of *I. iii*, omitting 29–68 (the Clown's discussion of marriage).

Act II consists of *Act I. ii*, omitting 24–69a (the King's praise of Bertram's father), and of *II. i.* 5b–10a, 24–47, 61–2, 77–end.

Act III begins with *Act II. iii*, omitting 82b–108 (Helena's rejection of the three Lords), followed by *II. iv* and *v*, and *III. ii*.

Act IV begins with *Act III. iv*, omitting 3b–18 (Helena's sonnet-letter), followed by *III. v*, omitting 14–29 (Mariana's advice to Diana), *vi*, *vii*, and *IV. i–iii*.

Act V begins with *Act IV. v*, followed by *IV. iv.* 1–30a, and by *V*.

Throughout there are minor omissions and transpositions. In *I. ii* Lafeu has the 1st Lord's speeches.

ALL'S WELL THAT ENDS WELL

1756 DRURY LANE
Feb. 24

PAROLLES	Woodward	(1) *Mar. 2, 8*
BERTRAM	Palmer	omitted
LAFEU	Berry	DUKE
KING	Davies	
CLOWN	Yates	
DUKE (1)	Burton	
STEWARD	Simson	
1ST LORD	Bransby	
2ND LORD	Walker	
SOLDIER		
[INTERPRETER]	Blakes	
COUNTESS	Mrs Pritchard	
DIANA	Mrs Davies	
WIDOW	Mrs Cross	
HELENA	Miss Macklin	

1757 DRURY LANE
Nov. 22, 30

PAROLLES	Woodward
BERTRAM	Palmer
LAFEU	Berry
KING	Davies
CLOWN	Yates
STEWARD	Burton
1ST LORD	Bransby
2ND LORD	Walker
SOLDIER	
[INTERPRETER]	Blakes
COUNTESS	Mrs Pritchard
DIANA	Mrs Davies
WIDOW	Mrs Cross
HELENA	Miss Macklin

1758 DRURY LANE
Jan. 14; May 5

PAROLLES	Woodward
BERTRAM	Palmer
LAFEU	Berry
KING	Davies
CLOWN	Yates
STEWARD	Burton
1ST LORD	Bransby
2ND LORD	Walker
SOLDIER	
[INTERPRETER]	Blakes
COUNTESS	Mrs Pritchard

ALL'S WELL THAT ENDS WELL

1758 DRURY LANE (cont.)
Jan. 14; May 5 (cont.)
DIANA	Mrs Davies
WIDOW	Mrs Cross
HELENA	Miss Macklin

1762 DRURY LANE
Oct. 23
PAROLLES	King
BERTRAM	Palmer
LAFEU	Burton
KING	Havard
1ST LORD	Bransby
2ND LORD (1)	Mozeen
CLOWN	Yates
COUNTESS	Mrs Pritchard
DIANA	Mrs Davies
WIDOW	Mrs Cross
HELENA	Mrs Palmer

(1) Nov. 25
2ND LORD	Fox
added	
SOLDIER	
[INTERPRETER]	Blakes
GENTLEMAN	Ackman

[In the acting version published by Bell in 1773 the cast is the same as that of this performance, with the following changes:

SOLDIER	
[INTERPRETER]	Baddeley
WIDOW	Mrs Simson

and the following additions:
STEWARD	Castle
MARIANA	Mrs [S.] Smith]

COVENT GARDEN
Nov. 29; Dec. 2, 6
PAROLLES	Woodward
BERTRAM	Ross
LAFEU	Gibson
KING	Walker
CLOWN	Shuter
1ST LORD	White
2ND LORD	Davis
SOLDIER	
[INTERPRETER]	Bennet
WIDOW	Mrs Stephens
COUNTESS	Mrs Ward
DIANA	Miss Hallam
HELENA	Miss Macklin

1763 COVENT GARDEN
Jan. 4; Feb. 5
PAROLLES	Woodward
BERTRAM	Ross
LAFEU	Gibson
KING	Walker
CLOWN	Shuter
1ST LORD (1)	White
2ND LORD (1)	Davis

(1) Mar. 5; Apr. 29; Oct. 7
COUNTESS	Mrs [D.] Baker (on *Apr. 29* only)

added
MARIANA	Mrs Ferguson

omitted on *Apr. 29, Oct. 7* only
  LORDS, SOLDIER

112

ALL'S WELL THAT ENDS WELL

1763 COVENT GARDEN (cont.)
Jan. 4; Feb. 5 (cont.)

SOLDIER	
[INTERPRETER] (1)	Bennet
WIDOW	Mrs Stephens
COUNTESS (1)	Mrs Ward
DIANA	Miss Hallam
HELENA	Miss Macklin

1764 COVENT GARDEN
Mar. 15; Nov. 6

PAROLLES	Woodward
BERTRAM	Ross
LAFEU	Gibson
KING	Walker
CLOWN	Shuter
COUNTESS	Mrs Ward
MARIANA	Mrs Ferguson
WIDOW	Mrs Stephens
DIANA	Miss Hallam
HELENA	Miss Macklin

(1) *May 18*
added

DUKE	Anderson
1ST LORD	White
2ND LORD	Davis
SOLDIER	
[INTERPRETER]	Bennet
STEWARD	Wignell

1767 COVENT GARDEN
Jan. 23

PAROLLES	Woodward
BERTRAM	Ross
LAFEU	Gibson
KING	Walker
CLOWN	Shuter
DUKE	Anderson
SOLDIER	
[INTERPRETER]	Bennet
COUNTESS	Mrs Du-Bellamy
MARIANA	Mrs Ferguson
WIDOW	Mrs Stephens
DIANA	Mrs Mattocks
HELENA	Miss Macklin

1772 COVENT GARDEN
May 8

PAROLLES	Woodward
KING	Hull
LAFEU	Clarke
BERTRAM	[Lee] Lewes
CLOWN (1)	Quick
DUKE	Owenson

(1) *Dec. 3, 8, 31*

CLOWN	Shuter
COUNTESS	Miss Miller

added on *Dec. 8, 31* only

SOLDIER	
[INTERPRETER]	Thompson

[In the acting version published by Bell in 1773 the cast is the same as

5365.2   113   I

ALL'S WELL THAT ENDS WELL

1772 COVENT GARDEN (cont.)

May 8 (cont.)

STEWARD	Wignell
1ST LORD	Davis
2ND LORD	Gardner
DIANA	Mrs Mattocks
COUNTESS (1)	Mrs Du-Bellamy
HELENA	Miss Macklin

(1) *Dec. 3, 8, 31 (cont.)*

that of these performances, with the following additions:

WIDOW	Mrs Barrington
MARIANA	Mrs Ferguson]

1774 COVENT GARDEN

Sept. 19

PAROLLES	Woodward
KING	Hull
LAFEU	Clarke
BERTRAM	[Lee] Lewes
CLOWN	Shuter
DUKE	Du-Bellamy
STEWARD	Fearon
1ST LORD	Cushing
2ND LORD	Davis
SOLDIER [INTERPRETER]	Thompson
DIANA	Mrs Mattocks
WIDOW	Miss Pearce
COUNTESS	Mrs Hull
HELENA	Miss Macklin

[*as altered by* PILON]

1785 HAYMARKET

July 26

CLOWN (1)	Edwin
LAFEU	Baddeley
BERTRAM	[J.] Williamson
DUKE	[J.] Burton
KING	Gardner
SOLDIER [INTERPRETER]	R. Palmer
PAROLLES	[J.] Bannister
COUNTESS	Mrs Inchbald
DIANA	Mrs Cuyler
WIDOW	Mrs Poussin
HELENA	Miss Farren

(1) *July 28*

CLOWN	Swords

[The part is not assigned, but Swords' name appears in place of Edwin's.]

[Pb and PA give the actors' names only. The assignments of Edwin, Baddeley, Williamson, Bannister, Mrs Inchbald, and Miss Farren are taken from Genest (vi. 368). The other five assignments are my own conjecture.]

114

ALL'S WELL THAT ENDS WELL

[*as altered by* KEMBLE]

1794 DRURY LANE
Dec. 12

BERTRAM	Kemble
PAROLLES	King
KING	Bensley
LAFEU	[J.] Aickin
CLOWN	[J.] Bannister
DUMAIN	Whitfield
LEWIS	C. Kemble
BIRON	Benson
TOURVILLE	Bland
SOLDIER	
[INTERPRETER]	R. Palmer
JAQUEZ	Caulfield
STEWARD	Packer
SOLDIER	Phillimore
HELENA	Mrs Jordan
COUNTESS	Mrs Powell
WIDOW	Mrs Booth
DIANA	Miss Miller
MARIANA	Miss Tidswell

[Pb and PA give the actors' names only. The above assignment is taken from Genest (vii. 183), who conflated the printed text of this version (published in 1793) with the playbill. Two names—those of Phillimore and Miss Tidswell—appear in the playbill, but are not assigned by Genest. The text assigns Phillimore to the SOLDIER, as indicated above, but makes no mention of Miss Tidswell. The reason for Genest's conflation, as he himself observes, is that between the date of publication of this version and the date of its performance several changes occurred in the casting: in the 1793 text LEWIS is assigned to Barrymore, HELENA to Mrs Siddons, the COUNTESS to Mrs Ward, and DIANA to Mrs Powell. Contemporary reviews of the performance are surprisingly few in number, and those few are not always in agreement with Genest. O, Dec. 13, 1794 gives only one assignment: the CLOWN to King. EM, Jan. 1795, 48, also assigns the CLOWN to King, and PAROLLES to Bannister. But Genest appears to be reliable.]

ANTONY AND CLEOPATRA

(1) 'Fitted for the stage [by David Garrick and Edward Capell] by abridging only; and now acted, at the Theatre-Royal in Drury-Lane.'

1758   J. and R. Tonson.

In *Act I. i* Philo's speeches are given to Thyreus, and Demetrius's to Dollabella. Following *I. i. 55* is inserted *II. ii. 192–253* (Cleopatra on her barge). Thyreus here has Enobarbus's speeches, and Dollabella those of Mecaenas and Agrippa.

Act II begins with *II. i* and ends with *III. vi.* Following are the principal omissions from *Act II*: *i entire* (Pompey's disdain of Antony); *iii entire* (Antony and the Soothsayer); *iv entire* (Lepidus's departure for Misenum); *vi. 1–83a* (Pompey and the triumvirs); *vii. 1–19* (the Servants discuss their masters' drunkenness).

ANTONY AND CLEOPATRA

Act III begins with *III. vii*. The principal omissions from *Act III* are: *i entire* (Ventidius's victory); *ii entire* (the parting between Octavius and Octavia); *iv entire* (Octavia leaves Antony); *v entire* (the news of Pompey's murder). Diomedes has the Soldier's speeches in *III. vii*, and Scarus's speeches in *III. viii*. The Soothsayer has Euphronius's speeches in *III. x*.

Following are the principal omissions from *Act IV*: *i entire* (Octavius's scorn of Antony); *ii entire* (Antony's wish for a final feast); *iii entire* (the sentinels hear the aerial music). In *IV. vii* Scarus's speeches are given to Diomedes.

Act V is verbatim.

Throughout the play there are numerous minor excisions.

See also Odell, i. 367.

1759 DRURY LANE
Jan. 3, 5, 9, 18

ANTONY	Garrick
ENOBARBUS (2)	Berry
POMPEY	Havard
EROS	Davies
DIOMEDES	Bransby
AGRIPPA	Packer
CANIDIUS	Austin
ALEXAS	Ackman
MENAS (2)	Burton
DERCETAS (2)	Reinhold
OFFICER	Scrase
OCTAVIUS	Fleetwood
LEPIDUS	Blakes
THYREUS (1)	Holland
DOLLABELLA	Mozeen
[MECAENAS	Atkins]
[PROCULEIUS	Austin]
[SOOTHSAYER	Burton]
[MARDIAN	Perry]
[SELEUCUS	Burton]
OCTAVIA	Mrs Glen
CHARMIAN	Miss Hippisley
IRAS	Miss Mills
CLEOPATRA	Mrs Yates

(1) *Jan. 12*

THYREUS	Moody [first appearance in London]

[Both Pb and PA retain Holland as THYREUS. A MS annotation on the JPK bill has, 'Though King Henry the Eighth is advertised as Mr. Moody's first appearance [on May 22, 1759 at this theatre, q.v.], he himself told me, that his first Appearance was really this Night, in the Part of Thyreus, Mr. Holland finding himself suddenly so ill as not to be able to act.']

(2) *May 18*

ENOBARBUS	Burton
MENAS	Clough
DERCETAS	Perry

[The printed text of this acting version was ready two months in advance of the performance: the printer gives, on p. 99, the date 'Oct. 23, 1758'. Between this date and the date of the performance certain changes in the casting took place. The acting version assigns POMPEY to Austin, CANIDIUS to Wilkinson, and DERCETAS to Blakes. It omits the OFFICER, but includes the five characters that appear above in brackets; that they were actually thus performed is not unlikely. Neither Pb nor PA lists these five characters.]

AS YOU LIKE IT

(1) 'As Performed at the Theatre-Royal, Drury-Lane. Regulated from the Prompt-Book.'
    1773   John Bell.

Following are the principal omissions:
Act II. v. *14–60* (Jaques and Amiens, 'ducdame'); *vii. 35–87* (Jaques's motley coat).
Act III. ii. *50b–77* (Touchstone and Corin discussing courtiers); *iii* (all of Jaques's asides), and *64b–end* (Martext).
Act IV. i. *1–31* (Jaques's definition of his melancholy); *ii entire* (Jaques and the deer).
Act V. ii. *96–119* ('And so am I . . . And so am I . . .'); *iii entire* ('It was a lover and his lass'); *iv* (Hymen: only his first song is retained, but the singer of it is not specified).

In *Act II. i* Jaques has the 1st Lord's speeches. Following *IV. i. 185* Rosalind sings the 'Cuckoo Song', i.e. the two stanzas entitled 'Spring' from the last scene of *Love's Labour's Lost*. Throughout there are minor omissions.

See also Odell, ii. 21–23.

(2) 'As Performed at the Theatre-Royal, Drury-Lane.'
    1775   J. Rivington [&c.].
This is identical with (1).

(3) 'As it is Acted at the Theatres-Royal in Drury-Lane and Covent-Garden.'
    1777   J. Wenman.
(4) 'As it is Acted at the Theatres-Royal in Drury-Lane and Covent-Garden.'
    1777   W. Oxlade.
These are both reading editions, verbatim throughout.

(5) 'Taken from the Manager's Book, at the Theatre Royal in Drury-Lane.'
    n. d. [c. 1785]   R. Butters.
(6) 'Marked with the Variations in the Manager's Book, at the Theatre-Royal in Covent-Garden.'
    1786   C. Bathurst [&c.].
(7) 'As Performed at the Theatres Royal. Regulated from the Prompt-Book.'
    1794   J. Barker.

All these are identical with (1), except that in *Act II. i* the 1st Lord has his own speeches.

1751 DRURY LANE
Jan. 3

DUKE SENIOR	Blakes
DUKE FREDERICK	Winstone
JAQUES	Berry
ORLANDO	Palmer
OLIVER	Burton
AMIENS	Beard
ADAM	Shuter

AS YOU LIKE IT

1751 DRURY LANE (cont.)
Jan. 3 (cont.)

SILVIUS	Mozeen
CORIN	Taswell
LE BEAU	Scrase
CHARLES	Layfield
TOUCHSTONE	Woodward
JAQUES DE BOIS	Simson
WILLIAM	[H.] Vaughan
PHEBE	Mrs Bennet
AUDREY	Mrs James
CELIA	Mrs Clive
ROSALIND	Mrs Pritchard

1752 DRURY LANE
Apr. 21

TOUCHSTONE	Woodward
DUKE SENIOR	Blakes
DUKE FREDERICK (1)	Simson
JAQUES	Berry
ORLANDO	Palmer
OLIVER (1)	Scrase
CORIN	Taswell
AMIENS (1)	Wilder
ADAM (1)	Havard
WILLIAM (1)	Costollo
CELIA	Mrs Clive
AUDREY	Mrs James
ROSALIND	Mrs Pritchard

(1) *Nov. 25; Dec. 14, 26*

DUKE FREDERICK	Winstone
OLIVER	Burton
AMIENS	Beard
ADAM	Lacey
WILLIAM	[H.] Vaughan
added	
SILVIUS	Mozeen
LE BEAU	Ackman
CHARLES	Wilder
PHEBE	Mrs Bennet

1753 DRURY LANE
Mar. 13

TOUCHSTONE (2)	Woodward
ORLANDO	Palmer
JAQUES	Berry
DUKE SENIOR	Blakes
DUKE FREDERICK (2)	Winstone
AMIENS	Beard
ADAM (2)	Lacey
CELIA	Mrs Clive
ROSALIND	Mrs Pritchard

(1) *Apr. 23*

added

OLIVER	Burton
AUDREY	Mrs James

(2) *Sept. 13; Nov. 20*

TOUCHSTONE	Yates (on *Sept. 13* only)
DUKE FREDERICK	Bransby
ADAM	Havard
added	
OLIVER	Burton
CORIN	Taswell
SILVIUS	Mozeen
LE BEAU	Ackman
WILLIAM	[H.] Vaughan
CHARLES	Wilder
AUDREY	Mrs James
PHEBE	Mrs Bennet

AS YOU LIKE IT

1753 COVENT GARDEN
Oct. 22

ORLANDO	Smith
JAQUES	Sparks
DUKE SENIOR	Ridout
OLIVER	Anderson
DUKE FREDERICK	Gibson
SILVIUS	Bennet
TOUCHSTONE	Shuter
CORIN	Dunstall
LE BEAU	White
CHARLES	Bencraft
WILLIAM	Collins
ADAM	Bridgwater
AMIENS	Lowe
AUDREY	Mrs Pitt
PHEBE	Miss Cokayne
CELIA	Mrs Vincent
ROSALIND	Mrs Bland

1754 COVENT GARDEN
May 21

ORLANDO	Smith
JAQUES	Sparks
DUKE SENIOR	Ridout
OLIVER	Anderson
DUKE FREDERICK	Redman
SILVIUS (1)	Bennet
TOUCHSTONE	Shuter
CORIN	Dunstall
LE BEAU	White
CHARLES (1)	Stevens
WILLIAM	Collins
ADAM	Gibson
AMIENS	Lowe
AUDREY	Mrs Pitt
PHEBE	Miss Cokayne
CELIA (1)	Mrs Vincent
ROSALIND (1)	Mrs Bland

(1) *Sept. 25*

SILVIUS	R. Smith
CELIA	Mrs Barrington
ROSALIND	Mrs Vincent
added	
JAQUES DE BOIS	Holtom
omitted	
CHARLES	

1755 DRURY LANE
Feb. 18

TOUCHSTONE	Woodward
ORLANDO	Palmer
JAQUES	Berry
DUKE SENIOR	Blakes
DUKE FREDERICK	Bransby

(1) *May 13*

ADAM	Davies
omitted	
LE BEAU, WILLIAM, CHARLES, AUDREY	

(2) *Sept. 18; Nov. 14*

PHEBE	Miss Hippisley

1755 DRURY LANE (cont.)

Feb. 18 (cont.)

OLIVER	Burton
AMIENS	Beard
ADAM (1)	Havard
CORIN	Taswell
SILVIUS	Jefferson
LE BEAU (1, 2)	Ackman
WILLIAM (1, 2)	[H.] Vaughan
CHARLES (1, 2)	Wilder
AUDREY (1, 2)	Mrs Bradshaw
CELIA	Mrs Clive
PHEBE (2)	Mrs Bennet
ROSALIND	Miss Macklin

(2) Sept. 18; Nov. 14 (cont.)

omitted
SAME as *May 13*

1756 COVENT GARDEN

May 17

JAQUES	Sparks
DUKE SENIOR	Ridout
DUKE FREDERICK (1)	Wignell
JAQUES DE BOIS	Holtom
LE BEAU	White
SILVIUS	Bennet
CORIN	Dunstall
CHARLES	Buck
WILLIAM (1)	Collins
ORLANDO	Smith
OLIVER	Anderson
ADAM	Gibson
AMIENS	Lowe
TOUCHSTONE	Shuter
CELIA	Mrs Vincent
PHEBE	Miss Mullart
AUDREY	Mrs Pitt
ROSALIND	Mrs Woffington

(1) Nov. 22

DUKE FREDERICK	Redman
WILLIAM	Costollo

1757 DRURY LANE

Nov. 19

TOUCHSTONE	Woodward
ORLANDO	Palmer
JAQUES	Berry
DUKE SENIOR	Blakes
DUKE FREDERICK	Bransby
OLIVER	Burton
AMIENS	Beard
ADAM	Havard

AS YOU LIKE IT

1757 DRURY LANE (*cont.*)
Nov. 19 (cont.)
CORIN	Taswell
SILVIUS	Jefferson
CELIA	Mrs Clive
PHEBE	Miss Hippisley
ROSALIND	Miss Macklin

COVENT GARDEN
May 3
JAQUES	Sparks
ORLANDO	Smith
DUKE FREDERICK	Redman
OLIVER	Anderson
SILVIUS	Bennet
CHARLES	Buck
DUKE SENIOR	Ridout
TOUCHSTONE (1)	Collins
CORIN	Dunstall
LE BEAU	White
JAQUES DE BOIS	Holtom
WILLIAM (1)	Costollo
AMIENS	Lowe
ADAM	Gibson
PHEBE (1)	Miss Mullart
AUDREY	Mrs Pitt
CELIA	Mrs Vincent
ROSALIND (1)	Mrs Woffington

(1) *Oct. 10*
TOUCHSTONE	Shuter
WILLIAM	Collins
PHEBE	Miss Cokayne
ROSALIND	Mrs Hamilton

1758 DRURY LANE
May 12
TOUCHSTONE (1)	Woodward
ORLANDO	Palmer
JAQUES	Berry
DUKE SENIOR	Blakes
DUKE FREDERICK (1)	Mozeen
OLIVER	Burton
AMIENS (1)	Vernon
ADAM	Havard
CORIN (1)	Philips
SILVIUS (1)	Jefferson
CELIA	Mrs Clive
PHEBE	Miss Hippisley
AUDREY	Mrs Bradshaw
ROSALIND	Miss Macklin

(1) *Sept. 16*
TOUCHSTONE	Yates
DUKE FREDERICK	Bransby
AMIENS	Beard
CORIN	Taswell
SILVIUS	Austin

AS YOU LIKE IT

1758 COVENT GARDEN
Jan. 21   (1) *Nov. 21*

JAQUES	Sparks	LE BEAU	Davis
ORLANDO	Smith	PHEBE	Miss Mullart
DUKE FREDERICK	Redman		
OLIVER	Anderson		
SILVIUS	Bennet		
CHARLES	Buck		
DUKE SENIOR	Ridout		
TOUCHSTONE	Shuter		
CORIN	Dunstall		
LE BEAU (1)	White		
JAQUES DE BOIS	Holtom		
WILLIAM	Collins		
AMIENS	Lowe		
ADAM	Gibson		
PHEBE (1)	Miss Cokayne		
AUDREY	Mrs Pitt		
CELIA	Mrs Vincent		
ROSALIND	Mrs Hamilton		

1759 DRURY LANE
Feb. 6

TOUCHSTONE	Yates
ORLANDO	Palmer
JAQUES	Berry
DUKE SENIOR	Blakes
DUKE FREDERICK	Bransby
OLIVER	Burton
AMIENS	Beard
ADAM	Havard
CORIN	Philips
SILVIUS	Austin
CELIA	Mrs Clive
PHEBE	Miss Hippisley
AUDREY	Mrs Bradshaw
ROSALIND	Miss Macklin

COVENT GARDEN
Dec. 11

JAQUES	Sparks
ORLANDO	Smith
TOUCHSTONE	Shuter
AMIENS	Lowe
ROSALIND	Mrs Hamilton

No other parts assigned

[Both Pb and PA have, 'The other Parts as Usual'.]

AS YOU LIKE IT

1760 DRURY LANE
May 7

TOUCHSTONE	Yates
ORLANDO	Palmer
JAQUES	Burton
DUKE SENIOR	Blakes
DUKE FREDERICK	Bransby
OLIVER	Packer
AMIENS (1)	Atkins
ADAM	Havard
CORIN (1)	Philips
SILVIUS (1)	Austin
CELIA	Mrs Clive
PHEBE (1)	Mrs Hippisley
AUDREY (1)	Mrs Bradshaw
ROSALIND (1)	Miss Macklin

(1) *Oct. 7*

AMIENS	Lowe
ROSALIND	Mrs Yates

omitted
   CORIN, SILVIUS, PHEBE, AUDREY

1761 DRURY LANE
Sept. 28

TOUCHSTONE	Yates
ORLANDO	Holland
JAQUES	Burton
DUKE SENIOR	Blakes
DUKE FREDERICK	Bransby
OLIVER	Packer
AMIENS	Lowe
ADAM	Havard
CELIA	Mrs Clive
ROSALIND	Mrs Yates

1762 COVENT GARDEN
Nov. 3

ORLANDO	Smith
JAQUES	Sparks
TOUCHSTONE	Shuter
DUKE SENIOR	Walker
OLIVER	White
DUKE FREDERICK	Tindal
SILVIUS	R. Smith
CHARLES	Buck
CORIN	Dunstall
WILLIAM	Costollo
LE BEAU	Davis
DENNIS	Gardner
JAQUES DE BOIS	Perry
AMIENS	Mattocks
ADAM	Gibson
CELIA	Mrs Vincent
ROSALIND	Miss Macklin

AS YOU LIKE IT

1763 DRURY LANE
Jan. 14

TOUCHSTONE	Yates
ORLANDO	Palmer
JAQUES	Burton
DUKE SENIOR	Blakes
DUKE FREDERICK	Bransby
OLIVER	Packer
AMIENS	Vernon
ADAM	Havard
CELIA	Mrs Clive
AUDREY	Mrs Bradshaw
ROSALIND	Mrs Yates

[AUDREY is listed by Genest (v. 12). The part does not appear either in Pb or in PA.]

1764 COVENT GARDEN
Jan. 16

ORLANDO	Smith
JAQUES	Sparks
TOUCHSTONE	Shuter
DUKE SENIOR	Walker
OLIVER	White
AMIENS	Mattocks
ADAM	Gibson
CELIA	Mrs Vincent
ROSALIND	Miss Macklin

1766 KING'S, HAYMARKET
Sept. 13

ORLANDO	Davis
DUKE SENIOR	[F.] Aickin
DUKE FREDERICK	[J.] Palmer
JAQUES	Lee
OLIVER	Johnston
LE BEAU	McGeorge
AMIENS	The Gentleman who sung in the Conscious Lovers [at this theatre, Sept. 9: Du-Bellamy (PA, Sept. 20)]
CHARLES	Keen
CORIN	Castle
ADAM	Hurst
DENNIS	Mahon
WILLIAM	Hamilton
SILVIUS	Quick
TOUCHSTONE	Shuter
CELIA	Mrs McGeorge
PHEBE	Miss Madden
AUDREY	Mrs Worley
ROSALIND	Mrs Dancer

1767 DRURY LANE

Oct. 22

TOUCHSTONE	King
ORLANDO (1, 2)	Palmer
JAQUES	Love
DUKE SENIOR	Hurst
DUKE FREDERICK	Bransby
OLIVER	Packer
LE BEAU	Ackman
CORIN	Hartry
JAQUES DE BOIS	Fox
CHARLES	Moody
SILVIUS	Strange
WILLIAM	Messink
AMIENS	Vernon
ADAM	Havard
CELIA	Mrs Baddeley
PHEBE (2)	Miss Simson
AUDREY	Mrs Bradshaw
ROSALIND	Mrs Dancer

(1) *Oct. 27*

ORLANDO	Reddish

(2) *Nov. 10*

ORLANDO	Reddish
PHEBE	Miss Reynolds

1768 DRURY LANE

Mar. 26; Apr. 13

TOUCHSTONE	King
ORLANDO	Reddish
JAQUES	Love
DUKE SENIOR	Hurst
DUKE FREDERICK	Bransby
OLIVER	Packer
AMIENS	Vernon
LE BEAU	Ackman
CORIN	Hartry
JAQUES DE BOIS (1)	Fox
CHARLES	Keen
SILVIUS	Strange
WILLIAM	Messink
ADAM	Moody
CELIA	Mrs Baddeley
PHEBE (1)	Miss Simson
AUDREY	Mrs Bradshaw
ROSALIND (1)	Mrs Dancer

(1) *Oct. 13*

JAQUES DE BOIS	Fawcett
PHEBE	Mrs W. Palmer
ROSALIND	Mrs [S.] Barry [i.e. formerly Mrs Dancer]

1769 DRURY LANE

May 6

TOUCHSTONE	King
ORLANDO	Reddish
JAQUES	Love
DUKE SENIOR	Hurst

(1) *Oct. 13*

AMIENS	Vernon
SILVIUS	Wheeler
AUDREY	Mrs Bradshaw
omitted	
JAQUES DE BOIS, WILLIAM	

125

1769 DRURY LANE (cont.)

May 6 (cont.)

DUKE FREDERICK	Bransby
OLIVER	Packer
AMIENS (1)	Fawcett
ADAM	Moody
LE BEAU	Ackman
CORIN	Hartry
JAQUES DE BOIS (1)	Fawcett
CHARLES	Keen
SILVIUS (1)	Strange
WILLIAM (1)	Messink
CELIA	Mrs Baddeley
AUDREY (1)	Mrs Johnston
PHEBE	Mrs W. Palmer
ROSALIND	Mrs [S.] Barry

[Fawcett doubled AMIENS and JAQUES DE BOIS.]

1770 DRURY LANE

May 9

TOUCHSTONE	King
ORLANDO	Reddish
JAQUES	Love
DUKE SENIOR (1, 2)	Ackman
DUKE FREDERICK (1, 2)	J. Aickin
OLIVER	Packer
AMIENS (1)	Vernon
ADAM	Moody
LE BEAU (1, 2)	Wright
CORIN	Hartry
CHARLES	Keen
SILVIUS	Wheeler
CELIA (1, 2)	Mrs W. Barry
AUDREY (2)	Mrs Bradshaw
PHEBE (2)	Miss Platt
ROSALIND	Mrs [S.] Barry

(1) *Oct. 9*

DUKE SENIOR	Hurst
DUKE FREDERICK	Bransby
AMIENS	Davies
LE BEAU	Ackman
CELIA	Mrs Baddeley

[PA assigns PHEBE to Mrs Davies.]

(2) *Nov. 22*

DUKE SENIOR	Hurst
DUKE FREDERICK	Bransby
LE BEAU	Ackman
CELIA	Mrs Baddeley
AUDREY	Mrs Love
PHEBE	Mrs Davies

1771 DRURY LANE

Apr. 1

TOUCHSTONE (1)	Love
ORLANDO (1)	Reddish
JAQUES (1)	[F.] Aickin
DUKE SENIOR (1)	Hurst
DUKE FREDERICK (1)	Bransby
OLIVER	Packer
AMIENS	Vernon

(1) *May 8; Oct. 1, 23; Dec. 17*

TOUCHSTONE	King
ORLANDO	Brereton
JAQUES	Love
DUKE SENIOR	Wrighten (on *May 8* only)
CELIA	Miss Rogers
PHEBE	Miss Ambrose (on *Dec. 17* only)

1771 DRURY LANE (cont.)

Apr. 1 (cont.)

ADAM	Moody
LE BEAU	Ackman
SILVIUS	Wheeler
CHARLES	Keen
JAQUES DE BOIS (1)	Fawcett
CORIN	Hartry
WILLIAM (1)	Messink
CELIA (1)	Mrs Baddeley
AUDREY	Mrs Bradshaw
PHEBE (1)	Mrs Davies
ROSALIND	Mrs [S.] Barry

(1) *May 8; Oct. 1, 23; Dec. 17 (cont.)*
omitted
    DUKE FREDERICK (on *Oct. 1, 23* only)
    JAQUES DE BOIS and WILLIAM (on *May 8* only)
[In the acting version published by Bell in 1773 the cast is the same as that of these performances, with the following addition:

DENNIS	Watkins]

COVENT GARDEN

Apr. 5

ORLANDO	Smith
JAQUES	Clarke
ADAM	Gibson
DUKE SENIOR	Hull
OLIVER	Perry
AMIENS	Mattocks
TOUCHSTONE	Geo. Alex. Stevens
CELIA	Mrs [T.] Baker
ROSALIND	Mrs Bulkley

[In the acting version published by Bell in 1773 the cast is the same as that of this performance, with the following changes:

TOUCHSTONE	Shuter
ROSALIND	Miss Macklin

and the following additions:

DUKE FREDERICK	Gardner
LE BEAU	Davis
DENNIS	Holtom
CHARLES	Morris
CORIN	Dunstall
SILVIUS	R. Smith
WILLIAM	Quick
PHEBE	Miss Pearce
AUDREY	Mrs Pitt]

1772 DRURY LANE

Apr. 9

TOUCHSTONE	King
ORLANDO	Brereton
JAQUES (1, 2)	[F.] Aickin
DUKE SENIOR	Hurst
DUKE FREDERICK	Bransby

(1) *June 5*

JAQUES	Love
ROSALIND	Miss Younge

(2) *Nov. 17*

JAQUES	Love
CELIA	Miss Ambrose

AS YOU LIKE IT

1772 DRURY LANE (cont.)
Apr. 9 (cont.)

OLIVER	Packer
AMIENS	Vernon
ADAM	Moody
LE BEAU	Ackman
SILVIUS	Wheeler
CHARLES	Keen
JAQUES DE BOIS	Fawcett
CORIN	Hartry
WILLIAM	Messink
CELIA (2)	Miss Rogers
AUDREY	Mrs Bradshaw
PHEBE	Mrs Davies
ROSALIND (1)	Mrs [S.] Barry

1773 DRURY LANE
Apr. 19   (1) *Nov. 2*

TOUCHSTONE	King		JAQUES	Love
ORLANDO	Brereton		CORIN	[F.] Waldron
JAQUES (1)	[F.] Aickin		CELIA	Miss Jarratt
DUKE SENIOR	Hurst			
DUKE FREDERICK	Bransby			
OLIVER	Packer			
AMIENS	Vernon			
ADAM	Moody			
LE BEAU	Ackman			
SILVIUS	Wheeler			
CHARLES	Keen			
JAQUES DE BOIS	Fawcett			
CORIN (1)	Hartry			
WILLIAM	Messink			
CELIA (1)	Miss [E.] Hopkins [first appearance on the stage, i.e. according to Genest (v. 355), 'as a woman']			
PHEBE	Mrs Davies			
AUDREY	Mrs Bradshaw			
ROSALIND	Mrs [S.] Barry			

1774 DRURY LANE
Mar. 17   (1) *Oct. 1, 19; Dec. 13*

TOUCHSTONE	King		ORLANDO	Reddish
ORLANDO (1)	Brereton		JAQUES	Jefferson
JAQUES (1)	[F.] Aickin		LE BEAU	Everard (on *Oct. 19, Dec. 13* only)
DUKE SENIOR	Hurst			
DUKE FREDERICK	Bransby		CORIN	[F.] Waldron (on *Oct. 19, Dec. 13* only)
OLIVER	Packer		CELIA	Mrs Baddeley
AMIENS	Vernon		ROSALIND	Miss Younge

1774 DRURY LANE (cont.)

Mar. 17 (cont.)

ADAM	Moody
LE BEAU (1)	Ackman
SILVIUS	Wheeler
CHARLES	Keen
JAQUES DE BOIS	Fawcett
CORIN (1)	Hartry
WILLIAM	Messink
CELIA (1)	Miss Jarratt
SHEPHERDESS (1)	Mrs Hunt
PHEBE	Mrs Davies
AUDREY	Mrs Bradshaw
ROSALIND (1)	Mrs [S.] Barry

(1) *Oct. 1, 19; Dec. 13 (cont.)*

omitted
   SHEPHERDESS

[On *Oct. 1* Genest (v. 440) erroneously retains Brereton as ORLANDO.]

COVENT GARDEN

Dec. 20

JAQUES	Barry
ORLANDO	Lewis
ADAM	Lee
DUKE SENIOR	Hull
AMIENS	Mattocks
OLIVER	Wroughton
DUKE FREDERICK	Fearon
LE BEAU	Booth
SILVIUS	Whitfield
CORIN	Thompson
TOUCHSTONE	Shuter
CHARLES	Fox
WILLIAM	Wewitzer
CELIA	Mrs Mattocks
PHEBE	Miss Dayes
AUDREY	Mrs Pitt
ROSALIND	Mrs [S.] Barry

1775 DRURY LANE

May 20

TOUCHSTONE	King
ORLANDO (1, 2)	Brereton
JAQUES	Jefferson
DUKE SENIOR	Hurst
DUKE FREDERICK	Bransby
OLIVER (1, 2)	Packer
AMIENS	Vernon
ADAM	Moody
LE BEAU (2)	Everard
SILVIUS (1, 2)	Wheeler

(1) *Sept. 26*

ORLANDO	Reddish
OLIVER	Davies
SILVIUS	Whitfield
CHARLES	Wrighten
WILLIAM	Messink
CELIA	Miss Jarratt

(2) *Oct. 13, 18*

ORLANDO	Reddish
OLIVER	Davies
SILVIUS	Whitfield
CELIA	Miss Jarratt

AS YOU LIKE IT

1775 DRURY LANE (cont.)
May 20 (cont.)

CHARLES (1, 2)	Keen
JAQUES DE BOIS (2)	Fawcett
CORIN (2)	[F.] Waldron
WILLIAM (1, 2)	[J.] Burton
CELIA (1, 2)	Mrs Baddeley
PHEBE	Mrs Davies
AUDREY	Mrs Bradshaw
ROSALIND (2)	Miss Younge

(2) Oct. 13, 18 (cont.)

ROSALIND   Mrs King [first appearance, Oct. 13, in London]
omitted
    LE BEAU, CHARLES, JAQUES DE BOIS, CORIN, WILLIAM

COVENT GARDEN
Jan. 24; Feb. 1

JAQUES	Barry
ORLANDO	Lewis
ADAM	Lee
DUKE SENIOR	Hull
AMIENS	Mattocks
OLIVER (1)	Wroughton
DUKE FREDERICK	Fearon
LE BEAU (1, 2, 3)	Booth
SILVIUS (1, 2, 3)	Whitfield
CORIN (1, 2, 3)	Thompson
TOUCHSTONE	Shuter
CHARLES (1, 2, 3)	Fox
WILLIAM (1, 2, 3)	Wewitzer
CELIA	Mrs Mattocks
PHEBE (1)	Miss Dayes
AUDREY (1)	Mrs Pitt
ROSALIND (3)	Mrs [S.] Barry

(1) Mar. 28

OLIVER   L'Estrange
omitted
    LE BEAU, SILVIUS, CORIN, CHARLES, WILLIAM, PHEBE, AUDREY

(2) Apr. 29

omitted
    LE BEAU, SILVIUS, CORIN, CHARLES, WILLIAM

(3) May 13

ROSALIND   Mrs Bulkley
omitted
    SAME as *Apr. 29*

1776 DRURY LANE
Apr. 12

TOUCHSTONE	King
ORLANDO	Reddish
JAQUES (1, 2)	[C.] Bannister
DUKE SENIOR	Hurst
DUKE FREDERICK	Bransby
OLIVER	Packer
AMIENS (1)	Vernon
JAQUES DE BOIS (1, 2)	Fawcett
LE BEAU	Everard
SILVIUS (2)	Whitfield
CORIN	[F.] Waldron
WILLIAM	Messink
ADAM	Moody

(1) May 10

JAQUES	Jefferson
AMIENS	Fawcett

omitted
    JAQUES DE BOIS

(2) Oct. 9

JAQUES	Jefferson
SILVIUS	R. Palmer
CELIA	Mrs Baddeley

omitted
    JAQUES DE BOIS

AS YOU LIKE IT

1776 DRURY LANE (cont.)
Apr. 12 (cont.)

CELIA (2)	Miss Jarratt
PHEBE	Mrs Davies
AUDREY	Mrs Bradshaw
ROSALIND	Miss Younge

COVENT GARDEN
Feb. 5; Mar. 19

JAQUES (2)	Barry
ORLANDO	Lewis
ADAM	Lee
DUKE SENIOR	Hull
AMIENS (1)	Mattocks
OLIVER (1, 2)	Wroughton
DUKE FREDERICK	Fearon
TOUCHSTONE	Woodward
CELIA	Mrs Mattocks
PHEBE (2)	Miss Dayes
AUDREY	Mrs Pitt
ROSALIND	Mrs [S.] Barry

(1) May 7

AMIENS	Du-Bellamy
OLIVER	L'Estrange

(2) Nov. 12

JAQUES	Clarke
OLIVER	L'Estrange
omitted	
PHEBE	

CHINA HALL, ROTHERHITHE
Aug. 9

TOUCHSTONE (1)	Shuter
DUKE SENIOR	[P.] Lewis
DUKE FREDERICK	Massey
ORLANDO	Stokes
SILVIUS	Dancer
ADAM (1)	Comerford
CORIN	[S.] Johnson
OLIVER	[J.] Smith
AMIENS	Kenny
WILLIAM (1)	Russell
JAQUES	West
ROSALIND	Miss Reynolds
PHEBE	Mrs Smith
AUDREY	Mrs Russell
CELIA	Mrs Wilks

(1) Aug. 16

TOUCHSTONE	Comerford
ADAM	Newton
omitted	
WILLIAM	

1777 DRURY LANE
May 3

TOUCHSTONE	King
ORLANDO (1)	Reddish
JAQUES (1)	Jefferson
DUKE SENIOR	Hurst
DUKE FREDERICK (1)	Bransby

(1) Dec. 3

ORLANDO	Brereton
JAQUES	[J.] Palmer
DUKE FREDERICK	Chaplin
AMIENS	Vernon
LE BEAU	Farren
WILLIAM	[J.] Burton

AS YOU LIKE IT

1777 DRURY LANE (cont.)

May 3 (cont.)

OLIVER	Packer
AMIENS (1)	Davies
CORIN	[F.] Waldron
LE BEAU (1)	Everard
SILVIUS	R. Palmer
WILLIAM (1)	Messink
ADAM	Moody
CELIA	Miss [E.] Hopkins
PHEBE	Mrs Davies
AUDREY	Mrs Bradshaw
ROSALIND	Miss Younge

(1) Dec. 3 (cont.)

added
JAQUES DE BOIS   Lamash

1778 DRURY LANE

May 14

TOUCHSTONE	King
ORLANDO	Brereton
DUKE SENIOR	Hurst
DUKE FREDERICK	Chaplin
OLIVER	Packer
AMIENS (1)	Vernon
CORIN	[F.] Waldron
JAQUES DE BOIS	Lamash
SILVIUS	R. Palmer
WILLIAM	[J.] Burton
LE BEAU	Phillimore
ADAM	Moody
JAQUES	[J.] Palmer
CELIA (1)	Miss [E.] Hopkins
PHEBE (1)	Mrs Davies
AUDREY	Mrs Bradshaw
ROSALIND	Miss Younge

(1) Sept. 26

AMIENS	Davies
CELIA	Mrs Sharp [i.e. formerly Miss Hopkins]
PHEBE	Miss Kirby

added
CHARLES   Wrighten

COVENT GARDEN

Feb. 24

JAQUES	[F.] Aickin
ORLANDO	Lewis
ADAM	Hull
DUKE SENIOR	L'Estrange
AMIENS	Mattocks
OLIVER	Whitfield
DUKE FREDERICK	Fearon
TOUCHSTONE	Quick
CELIA	Mrs Mattocks
PHEBE	Miss Dayes
AUDREY	Mrs Pitt
ROSALIND	Mrs [S.] Barry

AS YOU LIKE IT

1779 DRURY LANE
Jan. 11

TOUCHSTONE	King
ORLANDO	Brereton
DUKE SENIOR	Hurst
DUKE FREDERICK	Chaplin
OLIVER	Packer
LE BEAU	Phillimore
AMIENS	Vernon
CORIN	[F.] Waldron
JAQUES DE BOIS	Lamash
SILVIUS	R. Palmer
WILLIAM	[J.] Burton
ADAM	Moody
CHARLES	Wrighten
JAQUES	[J.] Palmer
CELIA	Mrs Sharp
PHEBE	Miss Kirby
AUDREY	Mrs Bradshaw
ROSALIND	Miss Younge

COVENT GARDEN
Sept. 24

JAQUES (1)	Clarke
ORLANDO	Lewis
ADAM	Hull
DUKE SENIOR	L'Estrange
AMIENS (1)	Mattocks
OLIVER	Whitfield
CORIN	Thompson
SILVIUS	Robson
DUKE FREDERICK	Fearon
CHARLES	Wrighten
TOUCHSTONE (1)	Edwin
CELIA	Mrs Morton
AUDREY	Mrs Pitt
PHEBE	Mrs Whitfield
ROSALIND (1)	Mrs Bulkley

(1) *Dec. 17*

JAQUES	Henderson
AMIENS	Davies
TOUCHSTONE	Quick
ROSALIND	Miss Younge
added	
WILLIAM	W. Bates
LE BEAU	Booth

1780 DRURY LANE
Jan. 28

TOUCHSTONE	King
ORLANDO	Brereton
AMIENS	Vernon
OLIVER	Packer
ADAM (1)	Henry
DUKE SENIOR	Hurst
DUKE FREDERICK	Chaplin

(1) *Apr. 7*

ADAM	Moody
JAQUES	Henderson
added	
JAQUES DE BOIS	Lamash
SILVIUS	R. Palmer
LE BEAU	Phillimore
CHARLES	Wrighten

133

1780 DRURY LANE (*cont.*)

Jan. 28 (cont.)
JAQUES (1)	[J.] Palmer
CELIA	Mrs Sharp
PHEBE	Miss Kirby
AUDREY	Mrs Bradshaw
ROSALIND	Mrs Robinson

May 2
TOUCHSTONE	King
ORLANDO	Brereton
AMIENS	Vernon
OLIVER	Packer
ADAM	Moody
DUKE SENIOR (1)	Hurst
DUKE FREDERICK	Chaplin
WILLIAM	[J.] Burton
CORIN	[F.] Waldron
JAQUES DE BOIS	Lamash
SILVIUS	R. Palmer
LE BEAU	Phillimore
CHARLES	Wrighten
JAQUES	[J.] Palmer
CELIA (1)	Mrs Sharp
PHEBE	Miss Kirby
AUDREY (1)	Mrs Bradshaw
ROSALIND (1)	Mrs Robinson

(1) *Oct. 5, 20*
DUKE SENIOR	[J.] Aickin
CELIA	Mrs Baddeley
AUDREY	Mrs Wrighten
ROSALIND	Mrs Crawford

1782 DRURY LANE

Apr. 11
TOUCHSTONE	King
ORLANDO	Brereton
AMIENS	Du-Bellamy
DUKE SENIOR	[J.] Aickin
ADAM	Moody
OLIVER	Packer
DUKE FREDERICK	Chaplin
JAQUES	[J.] Palmer
CELIA	Miss Wheeler
AUDREY	Mrs Wrighten
ROSALIND	A Young Lady [Miss Glassington (MS annotation on JPK); first appearance in London]

Apr. 27
TOUCHSTONE	King
ORLANDO	Brereton
AMIENS (1, 2)	Du-Bellamy
DUKE SENIOR	[J.] Aickin

(1) *June 1*
AMIENS	Williames
AUDREY	Mrs Davenett

(2) *Sept. 28; Oct. 17; Nov. 5*
AMIENS	Williames

1782 DRURY LANE (cont.)

Apr. 27 (cont.)

ADAM	Moody
OLIVER	Packer
DUKE FREDERICK	Chaplin
CORIN	[F.] Waldron
CHARLES	Wrighten
SILVIUS	R. Palmer
JAQUES DE BOIS (2)	Lamash
WILLIAM	[J.] Burton
LE BEAU	Phillimore
LORD (2)	Norris
JAQUES	[J.] Palmer
CELIA	Miss Wheeler
PHEBE (2)	Miss Barnes
AUDREY (1)	Mrs Wrighten
ROSALIND (2)	A Young Lady [Miss Blower (MS annotation on JPK); first appearance on the stage]

(2) Sept. 28; Oct. 17; Nov. 5 (cont.)

JAQUES DE BOIS	Fawcett (on *Nov.* 5 only)
PHEBE	Miss Wright
ROSALIND	Mrs Bulkley
omitted	
LORD	

COVENT GARDEN

Jan. 22

JAQUES	Henderson
ORLANDO	Lewis
ADAM	Hull
DUKE SENIOR	Clarke
CORIN	Thompson
WILLIAM	W. Bates
LE BEAU	Booth
SILVIUS	J. Bates
AMIENS	Mattocks
OLIVER	Whitfield
DUKE FREDERICK	Fearon
CHARLES	Webb
TOUCHSTONE	Quick
CELIA	Miss Satchell
AUDREY	Mrs Davenett
PHEBE	Miss Stuart
ROSALIND	Miss Younge

1783 DRURY LANE

Oct. 16

TOUCHSTONE	[Lee] Lewes
ORLANDO	Brereton
AMIENS	Williames
DUKE SENIOR	[J.] Aickin
ADAM	Moody
OLIVER	Packer

1783 DRURY LANE (cont.)
Oct. 16 (cont.)

JAQUES	[J.] Palmer
CELIA	Miss Wheeler
AUDREY	Mrs Wells
ROSALIND	Miss E. Kemble

COVENT GARDEN
May 17

JAQUES	Henderson
ORLANDO	A Gentleman [unidentified]
ADAM	Hull
DUKE SENIOR	Booth
CORIN	Thompson
SILVIUS	Helme
AMIENS	Mattocks
OLIVER	Whitfield
DUKE FREDERICK	Fearon
CHARLES	Webb
WILLIAM	Wewitzer
TOUCHSTONE	Quick
CELIA	Miss Satchell
AUDREY	Mrs Davenett
PHEBE	Miss Stuart
ROSALIND	Miss Younge

HAYMARKET
July 4, 9, 12

JAQUES	Bensley
ORLANDO	[J.] Bannister
ADAM	[J.] Aickin
DUKE SENIOR	Usher
CORIN	Massey
SILVIUS	R. Palmer
AMIENS	Brett
OLIVER	[J.] Williamson
DUKE FREDERICK	Gardner
LE BEAU	Reily
CHARLES	Egan
WILLIAM	Barrett
TOUCHSTONE	Edwin
CELIA	Miss Hooke
AUDREY	Mrs Brett
PHEBE	Miss [C.] Morris
ROSALIND	Miss Frodsham [first appearance, July 4, in London]

1784 DRURY LANE
Oct. 26

TOUCHSTONE	King
ORLANDO	Brereton
AMIENS	Williams
DUKE SENIOR	[J.] Aickin
ADAM	Moody
OLIVER	Packer
DUKE FREDERICK	Chaplin
SILVIUS	R. Palmer
JAQUES DE BOIS	Fawcett
CORIN	[F.] Waldron
CHARLES	Wrighten
WILLIAM	[J.] Burton
LE BEAU	Phillimore
JAQUES	[J.] Palmer
CELIA	Mrs [J.] Wilson
AUDREY	Mrs Wrighten
PHEBE	Miss Barnes
ROSALIND	Miss E. Kemble

COVENT GARDEN
Sept. 17

JAQUES	Henderson
ORLANDO	Lewis
AMIENS	Johnstone
DUKE SENIOR	Clarke
ADAM	Hull
OLIVER	Davies
DUKE FREDERICK	Fearon
LE BEAU	Booth
SILVIUS	Chalmers
WILLIAM	Wewitzer
CORIN	Thompson
CHARLES	Darley
TOUCHSTONE	Quick
CELIA	Mrs Inchbald
AUDREY	Mrs [S.] Wilson
PHEBE	Miss Stuart
ROSALIND	Miss Younge

1785 DRURY LANE
Apr. 30; May 14, 18

TOUCHSTONE	King
ORLANDO	Brereton
AMIENS	Williams
DUKE SENIOR (1)	[J.] Aickin
ADAM	Moody

(1) *May 7*
DUKE SENIOR Staunton
[Both Pb and PA retain Aickin as DUKE SENIOR. In JPK his name is deleted, and that of Staunton (partially cut by the binder) substituted.]

1785 DRURY LANE (cont.)
Apr. 30; May 14, 18 (cont.)

OLIVER	Packer
DUKE FREDERICK	Chaplin
SILVIUS	R. Palmer
JAQUES DE BOIS	Fawcett
CORIN	[F.] Waldron
CHARLES	Wrighten
WILLIAM	[J.] Burton
LE BEAU	Phillimore
JAQUES	[J.] Palmer
CELIA	Mrs [J.] Wilson
AUDREY	Mrs Wrighten
PHEBE	Miss Barnes
ROSALIND	Mrs Siddons

1786 DRURY LANE
Feb. 18

TOUCHSTONE	King
ORLANDO	Kemble
AMIENS	Williames
DUKE SENIOR	[J.] Aickin
ADAM	Moody
OLIVER	Packer
DUKE FREDERICK	Chaplin
SILVIUS	R. Palmer
JAQUES DE BOIS	Fawcett
CORIN	[F.] Waldron
CHARLES	Wrighten
WILLIAM	[J.] Burton
LE BEAU	Phillimore
JAQUES	[J.] Palmer
CELIA	Mrs [J.] Wilson
AUDREY (1)	Mrs Wrighten
PHEBE	Miss Barnes
ROSALIND	Mrs Siddons

(1) June 7

AUDREY	Mrs Davenett

COVENT GARDEN
Feb. 7

JAQUES	[F.] Aickin
ORLANDO	Lewis
AMIENS	Johnstone
ADAM	Hull
OLIVER	Davies
DUKE FREDERICK	Fearon
DUKE SENIOR	Gardner

1786 COVENT GARDEN (*cont.*)
Feb. 7 (cont.)

LE BEAU	[Wm.] Palmer
SILVIUS	Helme
WILLIAM	Wewitzer
CORIN	Thompson
CHARLES	Darley
TOUCHSTONE	Quick
AUDREY	Mrs Brown
CELIA	Mrs Inchbald
PHEBE	Miss Stuart
ROSALIND	Mrs Wells

1787 DRURY LANE
Apr. 13

TOUCHSTONE	King
ORLANDO	Kemble
AMIENS	Williams
DUKE SENIOR	[J.] Aickin
ADAM	Moody
OLIVER	Packer
DUKE FREDERICK	Chaplin
SILVIUS	Benson
JAQUES DE BOIS	Fawcett
CORIN	[F.] Waldron
CHARLES	Phillimore
WILLIAM	[J.] Burton
LE BEAU	[W.] Bates
JAQUES (2)	[J.] Palmer
CELIA	Mrs [J.] Wilson
AUDREY	Mrs Booth
PHEBE	Miss Barnes
ROSALIND (1, 2)	Mrs Jordan

(1) *May 29*

ROSALIND	Mrs Siddons

(2) *Nov. 6*

JAQUES	Wroughton
ROSALIND	Mrs Siddons

ROYALTY
June 20

JAQUES	[J.] Palmer
ORLANDO	Herrington
OLIVER	Shatford
TOUCHSTONE	Kipling
DUKE SENIOR	L'Estrange
DUKE FREDERICK	Hudson
AMIENS	Wm. Palmer
ADAM	Swendall
SILVIUS	Marriot
ROSALIND	Mrs Belfille
CELIA	Mrs Fox

AS YOU LIKE IT

1787 ROYALTY (cont.)
June 20 (cont.)

AUDREY	Miss Hale
PHEBE	Miss Burnet

[The newspaper bills for this performance do not give the cast, and no play-house bill appears to have survived. The above assignment is taken from the article on John Palmer in the *Thespian Dictionary*, 1805. Shatford's name is there misspelt 'Shetfield'. For the fact that he acted OLIVER, see Henry Lee, *Memoirs of a Manager*, 1830, i. 92.]

1788 DRURY LANE
Oct. 2, 7; Nov. 13

TOUCHSTONE	[J.] Palmer
ORLANDO (1)	Kemble
AMIENS	Williames
DUKE SENIOR	[J.] Aickin
ADAM	Moody
OLIVER	Packer
DUKE FREDERICK	Chaplin
WILLIAM (1)	[J.] Burton
LE BEAU	Lamash
SILVIUS (1)	Benson
JAQUES DE BOIS (1)	Fawcett
CORIN (1)	[F.] Waldron
CHARLES (1)	Phillimore
JAQUES	Wroughton
CELIA (1)	Mrs [J.] Wilson
AUDREY (1)	Mrs Booth
PHEBE (1)	Miss Barnes
ROSALIND (1)	Mrs Goodall [first appearance, Oct. 2, in London]

(1) *Dec. 17*

ORLANDO	Barrymore
WILLIAM	Benson
CELIA	Miss Collins
ROSALIND	Mrs Jordan
omitted	
SILVIUS, JAQUES DE BOIS, CORIN, CHARLES, AUDREY, PHEBE	

1789 DRURY LANE
Feb. 20; Mar. 10

TOUCHSTONE (2)	[J.] Bannister
ORLANDO	Barrymore
AMIENS	Williames
DUKE SENIOR	[J.] Aickin
ADAM	Moody
OLIVER	Packer
DUKE FREDERICK (2)	Chaplin
WILLIAM	[J.] Burton
LE BEAU	Lamash
JAQUES	Wroughton
CELIA	Mrs [J.] Wilson
AUDREY	Mrs Booth
PHEBE	Miss Barnes
ROSALIND	Mrs Goodall

(1) *June 6*
added

JAQUES DE BOIS	Fawcett
CHARLES	Alfred

(2) *Sept. 22*

TOUCHSTONE	Suett
DUKE FREDERICK	Maddocks

added

CORIN	[F.] Waldron
JAQUES DE BOIS	Fawcett
CHARLES	Phillimore

140

1789 DRURY LANE
June 13

TOUCHSTONE	[J.] Palmer
ORLANDO	Whitfield
AMIENS	Johnstone
DUKE SENIOR	[J.] Aickin
ADAM	Moody
OLIVER	Benson
DUKE FREDERICK	Chaplin
WILLIAM	[J.] Burton
LE BEAU	R. Palmer
JAQUES DE BOIS	Lyons
CHARLES	Alfred
JAQUES	Wroughton
CELIA	Miss Collins
AUDREY	Mrs Love
PHEBE	Miss Barnes
ROSALIND	Mrs Jordan

COVENT GARDEN
Feb. 11

JAQUES (1)	[F.] Aickin
ORLANDO (1)	Lewis
AMIENS	Johnstone
ADAM	Hull
DUKE SENIOR (1)	Booth
CORIN	Thompson
WILLIAM (1)	Wewitzer
LE BEAU	Macready
SILVIUS	Evatt
OLIVER	Davies
DUKE FREDERICK (1)	Fearon
CHARLES (1)	Gardner
TOUCHSTONE (1)	Quick
CELIA (1)	Mrs Inchbald
AUDREY	Mrs Rock
PHEBE	Miss Stuart
ROSALIND (1)	Miss Wallis

(1) *Nov. 20; Dec. 1*

JAQUES	Harley
ORLANDO	Holman
DUKE SENIOR	Powel
WILLIAM	C. Powell
DUKE FREDERICK	Gardner
CHARLES	Cubitt
TOUCHSTONE	King
CELIA	Miss Chapman
ROSALIND	Mrs Pope

1790 DRURY LANE
Feb. 27

DUKE SENIOR	[J.] Aickin
DUKE FREDERICK	Maddocks
AMIENS	Williames
JAQUES	Wroughton
LE BEAU	Banks
OLIVER	Packer

(1) *Mar. 6*

AUDREY	Mrs Edwards

(2) *Apr. 28*

TOUCHSTONE	Suett

1790 DRURY LANE (cont.)

Feb. 27 (cont.)

JAQUES DE BOIS	Fawcett
ORLANDO	Barrymore
ADAM	Moody
TOUCHSTONE (2)	[J.] Bannister
CORIN	[F.] Waldron
SILVIUS	Benson
WILLIAM	[J.] Burton
CHARLES	Phillimore
DENNIS	Alfred
ROSALIND	Mrs Jordan
CELIA	Mrs [J.] Wilson
PHEBE	Miss Barnes
AUDREY (1)	Mrs Booth

Oct. 27

DUKE SENIOR	[J.] Aickin
DUKE FREDERICK	Fox
AMIENS	Dignum
JAQUES	[J.] Palmer
LE BEAU	R. Palmer
OLIVER	Whitfield
JAQUES DE BOIS	Benson
ORLANDO	Kemble
ADAM	Moody
TOUCHSTONE	King
ROSALIND	Mrs Jordan
CELIA	Mrs [J.] Kemble
PHEBE	Miss Collins
AUDREY	Mrs Williames

COVENT GARDEN

Oct. 20; Nov. 9, 15; Dec. 3

TOUCHSTONE	Quick
ORLANDO	Holman
AMIENS	Johnstone
ADAM	Hull
DUKE SENIOR	Powel
CORIN	Cross
WILLIAM	C. Powell
LE BEAU	Macready
SILVIUS	Evatt
OLIVER	Davies
DUKE FREDERICK	Thompson
CHARLES	Cubitt
JAQUES	[F.] Aickin
CELIA	Mrs Mountain

AS YOU LIKE IT

1790 COVENT GARDEN (cont.)
Oct. 20; Nov. 9, 15; Dec. 3 (cont.)

AUDREY	Mrs Rock
PHEBE	Miss Stuart
ROSALIND	Mrs Esten [first appearance, Oct. 20, in London]

1791 DRURY LANE
Mar. 17

DUKE SENIOR	[J.] Aickin
DUKE FREDERICK (2)	Fox
AMIENS	Dignum
JAQUES	[J.] Palmer
LE BEAU	R. Palmer
OLIVER	Whitfield
JAQUES DE BOIS	Benson
ORLANDO (1, 2)	Kemble
ADAM	Moody
TOUCHSTONE (1)	King
ROSALIND	Mrs Jordan
CELIA (2)	Mrs [J.] Kemble
PHEBE (1, 2)	Miss Barnes
AUDREY (2)	Mrs Williames

(1) *Apr. 29; May 28*

ORLANDO	Barrymore
TOUCHSTONE	[J.] Bannister
PHEBE	Miss Collins

added

CORIN	[F.] Waldron
SILVIUS	Bland
WILLIAM	[J.] Burton
CHARLES	Phillimore
DENNIS	Webb (on *May 28* only)

[On *Apr. 29* both Pb and PA assign ORLANDO to Kemble, but in Kemble Mem. he states, 'I had fallen from the Ladder in my Book-room, and bruised my Leg. Mr. Barrymore acted Orlando for me'. On *May 28* Barrymore's name is in the bill.]

(2) *Oct. 3; Nov. 15; Dec. 13* (DL company at KING'S, HAYMARKET)

DUKE FREDERICK	Packer
ORLANDO	Barrymore
CELIA	Miss Collins (on *Nov. 15* only)
PHEBE	Miss Heard (on *Nov. 15* only)
AUDREY	Mrs Edwards

added

CORIN	[F.] Waldron
SILVIUS	Bland
WILLIAM	[J.] Burton
CHARLES	Phillimore (on *Nov. 15, Dec. 13* only)

[On *Oct. 3* both Pb and PA assign ORLANDO to Kemble, but he was indisposed, and Barrymore again substituted for him (O, Oct. 4). On *Nov. 15, Dec. 13* Barrymore's name is in the bills. On *Dec. 13* PA assigns CELIA to Miss Collins, and PHEBE to Miss Heard.]

COVENT GARDEN
Jan. 8, 18; Feb. 3, 7

TOUCHSTONE	Quick
ORLANDO	Holman

(1) *Oct. 6*

CHARLES	[D.] Williamson

AS YOU LIKE IT

1791 COVENT GARDEN (cont.)
Jan. 8, 18; Feb. 3, 7 (cont.)

AMIENS	Johnstone
ADAM	Hull
DUKE SENIOR	Powel
CORIN	Cross
WILLIAM	C. Powell
LE BEAU	Macready
SILVIUS	Evatt
OLIVER	Davies
DUKE FREDERICK	Thompson
CHARLES (1)	Cubitt
JAQUES	[F.] Aickin
CELIA	Mrs Mountain
AUDREY	Mrs Rock
PHEBE	Miss Stuart
ROSALIND	Mrs Esten

1792 DRURY LANE (company at KING'S, HAYMARKET)
Apr. 9 (1) *June 7*

DUKE SENIOR	[J.] Aickin	TOUCHSTONE	King
DUKE FREDERICK	Packer	omitted	
AMIENS	Dignum	CORIN, SILVIUS, WILLIAM, CHARLES	
JAQUES	[J.] Palmer		
LE BEAU	R. Palmer		
OLIVER	Whitfield		
JAQUES DE BOIS	Benson		
ORLANDO	Barrymore		
ADAM	Moody		
TOUCHSTONE (1)	Dodd		
CORIN (1)	[F.] Waldron		
SILVIUS (1)	Bland		
WILLIAM (1)	[J.] Burton		
CHARLES (1)	Phillimore		
ROSALIND	Mrs Jordan		
CELIA	Mrs [J.] Kemble		
PHEBE	Miss Collins		
AUDREY	Mrs Edwards		

COVENT GARDEN
Oct. 10

TOUCHSTONE	Quick
ORLANDO	Holman
AMIENS	Johnstone
ADAM	Hull
DUKE SENIOR	Powel
OLIVER	Davies
WILLIAM	Farley

AS YOU LIKE IT

1792 COVENT GARDEN (cont.)

Oct. 10 (cont.)

LE BEAU	Macready
SILVIUS	Evatt
CORIN	Cross
DUKE FREDERICK	Thompson
CHARLES	Rowson
JAQUES	[F.] Aickin
CELIA	Miss Chapman
AUDREY	Mrs Rock
PHEBE	Miss Stuart
ROSALIND	Mrs Esten

[PA assigns WILLIAM to C. Powell. This is erroneous; he was no longer in the CG company.]

1793 DRURY LANE (company at KING'S, HAYMARKET)

Mar. 4

DUKE SENIOR	[J.] Aickin			
DUKE FREDERICK	Packer			
AMIENS	Dignum			
JAQUES (1)	[J.] Palmer			
LE BEAU (1)	R. Palmer			
OLIVER	Whitfield			
JAQUES DE BOIS	Benson			
ORLANDO	Barrymore			
ADAM	Moody			
TOUCHSTONE	King			
CORIN	[F.] Waldron			
SILVIUS	Bland			
WILLIAM	[J.] Burton			
ROSALIND	Mrs Jordan			
CELIA (1)	Mrs [J.] Kemble			
PHEBE (1)	Miss Collins			
AUDREY	Mrs Edwards			

(1) *May 3*

JAQUES	Wroughton
LE BEAU	Banks
CELIA	Miss Collins
PHEBE	Miss Heard

COVENT GARDEN

May 30

TOUCHSTONE	Quick
ORLANDO	Holman
AMIENS	Johnstone
ADAM	Hull
DUKE SENIOR	Powel
OLIVER	Davies
WILLIAM	Farley
CORIN	Rees
LE BEAU	Macready
SILVIUS	Evatt

AS YOU LIKE IT

1793 COVENT GARDEN (cont.)
May 30 (cont.)

DUKE FREDERICK	Thompson
CHARLES	Rowson
JAQUES	Harley
CELIA	Miss Chapman
AUDREY	Mrs Rock
PHEBE	Miss Stuart
ROSALIND	Mrs Esten

1794 DRURY LANE
Apr. 25; June 11

DUKE SENIOR	[J.] Aickin
DUKE FREDERICK	Packer
AMIENS	Dignum
JAQUES	[J.] Palmer
LE BEAU (3)	Benson
OLIVER	Whitfield
JAQUES DE BOIS	C. Kemble
ORLANDO	Barrymore
ADAM	Moody
TOUCHSTONE	King
CORIN (1)	[F.] Waldron
SILVIUS (1)	Bland
WILLIAM (1, 3)	[J.] Burton
CHARLES (1, 3)	Phillimore
ROSALIND (3)	Mrs Goodall
CELIA (2)	Mrs [J.] Kemble
PHEBE (1, 2)	Miss Collins
AUDREY	Miss Pope

(1) *June 18*
 omitted
  CORIN, SILVIUS, WILLIAM, CHARLES, PHEBE

(2) *June 20*

CELIA	Miss Collins
PHEBE	Miss Heard

[Bill not in JPK; see p. 97. 'Mrs Kemble being ill, Miss Collins played Celia for Mrs Kemble and Miss Heard Phebe for Miss Collins' (Powell). Since Powell mentions no other changes, it may be assumed that the cast was otherwise the same as on Apr. 25.]

(3) *Oct. 29*

LE BEAU	R. Palmer
ROSALIND	Mrs Jordan

omitted
  WILLIAM, CHARLES

1795 DRURY LANE
Jan. 21

DUKE SENIOR	[J.] Aickin
DUKE FREDERICK	Packer
AMIENS	Dignum
JAQUES (1, 2)	Wroughton
LE BEAU (2)	R. Palmer
OLIVER	Whitfield
JAQUES DE BOIS (1, 2)	Benson
ORLANDO (1, 2)	C. Kemble
ADAM	Moody
TOUCHSTONE	King
CORIN (1, 2)	[F.] Waldron
SILVIUS (1, 2)	Bland
ROSALIND (2)	Mrs Goodall

(1) *Feb. 7*

JAQUES	[J.] Palmer
JAQUES DE BOIS	C. Kemble
ORLANDO	Barrymore

omitted
  CORIN, SILVIUS, PHEBE

(2) *Nov. 12*

JAQUES	[J.] Palmer
LE BEAU	Benson
JAQUES DE BOIS	C. Kemble
ORLANDO	Barrymore
ROSALIND	Mrs Jordan
PHEBE	Miss DeCamp

omitted
  CORIN, SILVIUS

AS YOU LIKE IT

1795 DRURY LANE (*cont.*)
Jan. 21 (cont.)
CELIA	Mrs [J.] Kemble
PHEBE (1, 2)	Miss Collins
AUDREY	Miss Pope

[In the bill JAQUES DE BOIS is assigned to C. Kemble, and ORLANDO to Barrymore. 'Orlando Mr. C. Kemble, Mr. Barrymore ill; Jaques de Bois Mr. Benson for C. Kemble' (Powell).]

1796 DRURY LANE
Jan. 5
DUKE SENIOR	[J.] Aickin
DUKE FREDERICK	Packer
AMIENS	Dignum
JAQUES	Wroughton
LE BEAU	R. Palmer
OLIVER	Whitfield
JAQUES DE BOIS	C. Kemble
ORLANDO	Barrymore
ADAM	Moody
TOUCHSTONE	[J.] Palmer
ROSALIND	Mrs Jordan
CELIA	Mrs [J.] Kemble
PHEBE	Miss Heard
AUDREY	Miss Pope

HAYMARKET
Aug. 30
TOUCHSTONE	[J.] Bannister
AUDREY	Mrs Harlowe

[The above consisted of III. iii only. The entertainment on this evening was called *The School of Shakespeare*, for a description of which see p. 101.]

1797 DRURY LANE
May 12
DUKE SENIOR	[J.] Aickin
DUKE FREDERICK (1)	Caulfield
AMIENS	Dignum
JAQUES	[J.] Palmer
LE BEAU	R. Palmer
OLIVER (1)	Whitfield
JAQUES DE BOIS	Holland
ORLANDO	Barrymore
ADAM	Packer
TOUCHSTONE (1)	[J.] Bannister
CORIN	Hollingsworth

(1) *Oct. 7*
DUKE FREDERICK	Maddocks
OLIVER	Caulfield
TOUCHSTONE	King

147

1797 DRURY LANE (cont.)

May 12 (cont.)

SILVIUS	Trueman
ROSALIND	Mrs Jordan
CELIA	Miss Mellon
PHEBE	Miss Heard
AUDREY	Miss Pope

1798 DRURY LANE

Feb. 9

DUKE SENIOR	[J.] Aickin
DUKE FREDERICK	Maddocks
AMIENS	Dignum
JAQUES	Wroughton
LE BEAU	Russell
OLIVER	Caulfield
JAQUES DE BOIS	Holland
ORLANDO	Barrymore
ADAM	Packer
TOUCHSTONE	[J.] Palmer
CORIN	Hollingsworth
SILVIUS	Trueman
ROSALIND	Mrs Jordan
CELIA	Miss Mellon
PHEBE	Miss Heard
AUDREY	Miss Pope

1799 DRURY LANE

Feb. 14, 21

DUKE SENIOR	[J.] Aickin
DUKE FREDERICK	Maddocks
AMIENS	Dignum
JAQUES	Kemble
OLIVER (3)	Caulfield
JAQUES DE BOIS	Holland
ORLANDO (1)	Barrymore
ADAM	Packer
TOUCHSTONE (3)	King
CORIN (2)	Hollingsworth
SILVIUS (2)	Trueman
ROSALIND (3)	Mrs Jordan
CELIA	Miss Mellon
PHEBE	Miss Heard
AUDREY	Miss Pope

(1) *Feb. 28; Apr. 4, 15*

ORLANDO	C. Kemble (on *Feb. 28* only)

added
LE BEAU	Surmont

(2) *Apr. 25; May 17*

added
LE BEAU	Surmont (on *May 17* only)

omitted
    CORIN, SILVIUS

(3) *Oct. 1, 15; Nov. 21*

OLIVER	Clarke (on *Oct. 1* only)
TOUCHSTONE	[J.] Bannister (on *Oct. 1, Nov. 21* only)
ROSALIND	Miss Biggs

added
LE BEAU	Surmont

AS YOU LIKE IT

1800 DRURY LANE

Feb. 24

DUKE SENIOR	[J.] Powell
DUKE FREDERICK	Maddocks
AMIENS	Dignum
JAQUES	Kemble
LE BEAU	Surmont
OLIVER	Caulfield
JAQUES DE BOIS	Holland
ORLANDO	Barrymore
ADAM (2)	Packer
TOUCHSTONE	King
CORIN (2)	Hollingsworth
SILVIUS	Trueman
ROSALIND (1)	Miss Biggs
CELIA	Miss Mellon
PHEBE (2)	Miss Heard
AUDREY	Miss Pope

(1) *Apr. 16*

ROSALIND	Mrs Jordan

(2) *Nov. 21*

ADAM	Dowton
CORIN	[F.] Waldron
PHEBE	Miss Arne

added

WILLIAM	Chippendale
CHARLES	[J.] Cooke
1ST LORD	Evans
2ND LORD	Webb
3RD LORD	Sparks

CATHARINE AND PETRUCHIO

David Garrick's alteration of THE TAMING OF THE SHREW, q.v.

THE COBLER OF PRESTON

Christopher Bullock's alteration of THE TAMING OF THE SHREW, q.v.

THE COMEDY OF ERRORS

(1) Altered as THE TWINS, by Thomas Hull. In five acts.

1762   Not published.

This version was privately printed in 1770. See (2).

(2) 'With Alterations from Shakespeare [by Thomas Hull]. As it is performed at the Theatre-Royal in Covent-Garden.'

1770   Printed for the Editor. Sold by J. Bell. [A MS. note in the Garrick Club copy reads, 'Once performed in Year 1761 [*recte* 1762] but never publish'd tho' thus printed'.]

In *Act I. i* Aegeon's account of his life is briefly interrupted by the Duke at 62.

From *Act II* are omitted *ii. 61–112* (Dromio of Syracuse's jests on baldness), and *192–206* (his 'transformation'). The act ends with 16 new lines: his reflections on the confusion of everybody's affairs.

From *Act III* are omitted *i. 13–29* (Balthazar's lack of gaiety), *i. 65–84* (the quibbles on 'breaking'), and *ii. 102–44* (the kitchen-wench's 'geography'). Instead of Balthazar, Angelo speaks *i. 94–106*.

From *Act V. i* is omitted *214–54* (Antipholus of Ephesus's dispute with

THE COMEDY OF ERRORS

Pinch). Following *347* are 18 new lines: Aegeon and the Abbess rejoice at being reunited. The play ends at *409*.

Throughout there are minor omissions and brief additions, frequently pieced together with a few lines of the original.

(3) 'And now Acted at the Theatre Royal in Covent-Garden.'

1770   J. Rivington.

A reading edition, verbatim throughout.

(4) 'As it is Acted at the Theatres-Royal in Drury-Lane and Covent-Garden.'

1779   Harrison and Co.

A reading edition, presumably reprinted from (3). The title-page is misleading: the play was never acted at DL. The playbills for the performances in 1779 at CG have, 'With Alterations'. MC, Jan. 23, 1779 notes that the play was 'altered by Mr. Hull'. See (5).

(5) 'Adapted for Theatrical Representation by Thomas Hull. As Performed at the Theatre-Royal, Covent-Garden. A New Edition.'

1793   John Bell.

This is identical with (2), except for the following changes (to which the words, 'A New Edition', seem to refer): *Act III. ii* begins with about 30 new lines: Antipholus of Syracuse prefers Luciana to Adriana. This is followed by a song, 'Stray not', composed by Michael Arne. Then Adriana speaks a rewritten version of her defence of her chastity (*II. ii. 134–50*). Then come *III. ii. 1–70*, rearranged as blank verse, and *71–162*, omitting *102–44* (the kitchen-wench's 'geography'). In *IV. iii* the dialogue in the Courtezan's scene (*44–end*) has been almost completely rewritten.

See also Odell, ii. 45–48.

[*as* THE TWINS]

1762 COVENT GARDEN
Apr. 24

DROMIO OF EPHESUS	Shuter
DROMIO OF SYRACUSE	Dunstall
AEGEON	Gibson
ANTIPHOLUS OF SYRACUSE	Hull
ANTIPHOLUS OF EPHESUS	Davis
DUKE	Anderson
OFFICER	Wignell
BALTHAZAR	Tindal
ANGELO	Perry
1ST MERCHANT	R. Smith
2ND MERCHANT	Holtom
PINCH	Buck

THE COMEDY OF ERRORS [*as* THE TWINS]

1762 COVENT GARDEN (*cont.*)
Apr. 24 (*cont.*)

ADRIANA	Mrs Vincent
LUCIANA	Mrs Lessingham
LESBIA	Mrs Stephens
BRIDGET	Mrs Copin
ABBESS	Mrs Ward

[The bill gives the actors' names only. In 1770 Hull, who altered the play, privately printed his version of it. From this version the following assignments, as given above, are taken: Shuter, Dunstall, Gibson, Hull, Perry, R. Smith, Mrs Vincent, Mrs Lessingham, Mrs Copin (whose name is not listed on the playbill), and Mrs Ward. The other assignments are my own conjecture, i.e. the printed text of 1770 assigns ANTIPHOLUS OF EPHESUS, DUKE, OFFICER, BALTHAZAR, 2ND MERCHANT, PINCH, LESBIA to other actors, some of whom were not on the stage in 1762 (e.g. Wroughton, who first appeared in 1768, is assigned to ANTIPHOLUS OF EPHESUS, and Quick, who first appeared in 1766, is assigned to PINCH). It seems likely that a revival was contemplated in 1770, and duly cast. This revival, however, was deferred (see below) until 1779.]

[*The original*]

[*as altered by* HULL]

1779 COVENT GARDEN
Jan. 22, 27; Feb. 1, 6, 9, 20;
May 4, 21

ANTIPHOLUS OF SYRACUSE	Lewis
ANTIPHOLUS OF EPHESUS	Whitfield
DUKE	L'Estrange
ANGELO (1)	Fearon
BALTHAZAR (1)	Egan
AEGEON	Hull
PINCH (1)	Wewitzer
OFFICER (1)	Jones
1ST MERCHANT (1)	Robson
2ND MERCHANT (1)	Thompson
DROMIO OF SYRACUSE	Brunsdon
DROMIO OF EPHESUS	Quick
ADRIANA	Mrs Jackson
LUCIANA	Mrs Lessingham
LESBIA (1)	Miss Platt
ABBESS	Mrs Hartley

(1) *Oct. 29; Dec. 14*
omitted
ANGELO, BALTHAZAR, PINCH,
OFFICER, MERCHANTS, LESBIA

1780 COVENT GARDEN
Jan. 6

ANTIPHOLUS OF SYRACUSE	Lewis

(1) *May 16*

LUCIANA	Mrs Whitfield

151

THE COMEDY OF ERRORS [as altered by HULL]

1780 COVENT GARDEN (cont.)
Jan. 6 (cont.)

ANTIPHOLUS OF EPHESUS	Whitfield
DUKE	L'Estrange
AEGEON	Hull
DROMIO OF SYRACUSE	Brunsdon
DROMIO OF EPHESUS	Quick
ADRIANA	Mrs Jackson
LUCIANA (1)	Mrs Lessingham
ABBESS	Mrs Hartley

1781 COVENT GARDEN
Jan. 18

ANTIPHOLUS OF SYRACUSE	Lewis
ANTIPHOLUS OF EPHESUS	Whitfield
DUKE	L'Estrange
AEGEON	Hull
PINCH	Wewitzer
DROMIO OF SYRACUSE	Edwin
DROMIO OF EPHESUS	Quick
ADRIANA	Mrs Green
LUCIANA (1)	Mrs Lessingham
LESBIA (1)	Miss Platt
ABBESS	Mrs Inchbald

(1) *Feb. 8; Mar. 20; May 22*
LUCIANA Mrs Whitfield (on *May 22* only)
LESBIA omitted

1785 COVENT GARDEN
Dec. 30

ANTIPHOLUS OF SYRACUSE	Lewis
ANTIPHOLUS OF EPHESUS	[Wm.] Palmer
DUKE	Gardner
AEGEON	Hull
DROMIO OF SYRACUSE	Edwin
DROMIO OF EPHESUS	Quick
ABBESS	Mrs Inchbald
LUCIANA	Mrs T. Kennedy
ADRIANA	Mrs Bates

THE COMEDY OF ERRORS [as altered by HULL]

1786 COVENT GARDEN
Jan. 12, 25; Feb. 24

ANTIPHOLUS OF SYRACUSE	Lewis
ANTIPHOLUS OF EPHESUS	[Wm.] Palmer
DUKE	Gardner
AEGEON	Hull
DROMIO OF SYRACUSE	Edwin
DROMIO OF EPHESUS	Quick
ABBESS	Mrs Inchbald
LUCIANA (1)	Mrs T. Kennedy
ADRIANA	Mrs Bates

(1) *May 24*

LUCIANA	Miss Rowson

1788 COVENT GARDEN
Jan. 4

ANTIPHOLUS OF SYRACUSE	Lewis
ANTIPHOLUS OF EPHESUS	Bernard
DUKE	Gardner
AEGEON	Hull
DROMIO OF SYRACUSE	Edwin
DROMIO OF EPHESUS	Quick
ABBESS	Mrs Inchbald
LUCIANA	Mrs Mountain
ADRIANA	Mrs Bernard

1789 COVENT GARDEN
Jan. 2

ANTIPHOLUS OF SYRACUSE	Lewis
ANTIPHOLUS OF EPHESUS	Bernard
DUKE	Gardner
ANGELO	Fearon
PINCH (1, 2)	Booth
AEGEON	Hull
DROMIO OF SYRACUSE	Edwin
DROMIO OF EPHESUS	Quick
ABBESS	Mrs Inchbald
LUCIANA	Mrs Mountain
ADRIANA	Mrs Bernard

(1) *Mar. 16, 23*

PINCH	Wewitzer

(2) *May 29*

PINCH added	Wewitzer
LESBIA	Mrs Platt

153

THE COMEDY OF ERRORS [as altered by HULL]

1790 COVENT GARDEN
Apr. 7

DROMIO OF SYRACUSE	Edwin
ANTIPHOLUS OF SYRACUSE	Macready
ANTIPHOLUS OF EPHESUS	Bernard
DROMIO OF EPHESUS	Quick
ABBESS	Miss Chapman
LUCIANA	Mrs Mountain
ADRIANA	Mrs Bernard

(1) *June 1, 10*
added
AEGEON Hull

1791 COVENT GARDEN
May 31

DROMIO OF EPHESUS	Quick
ANTIPHOLUS OF SYRACUSE	Macready
ANTIPHOLUS OF EPHESUS	Bernard
AEGEON	Hull
DUKE	Davies
DROMIO OF SYRACUSE	Blanchard
ABBESS	Miss Chapman
LUCIANA	Mrs Mountain
ADRIANA	Mrs Bernard

1792 COVENT GARDEN
May 18

DROMIO OF EPHESUS	Quick
ANTIPHOLUS OF SYRACUSE	A Young Gentleman [unidentified; first appearance on the stage]
ANTIPHOLUS OF EPHESUS	Harley
DUKE	Davies
ANGELO	Powel
PINCH	Cubitt
AEGEON	Hull
DROMIO OF SYRACUSE	Blanchard
ABBESS	Miss Chapman
LUCIANA	Mrs Mountain
ADRIANA	Mrs Fawcett

[The assignment of PINCH is taken from an advance bill in PA, May 17.]

THE COMEDY OF ERRORS [*as altered by* HULL]

1793 COVENT GARDEN
Apr. 15; June 3, 5; Oct. 8, 26

ANTIPHOLUS OF SYRACUSE	Pope
ANTIPHOLUS OF EPHESUS	Holman
DUKE	Davies
ANGELO	Powel
PINCH	Cubitt
AEGEON	Hull
DROMIO OF SYRACUSE	Munden
DROMIO OF EPHESUS	Quick
LUCIANA	Mrs Esten
ABBESS	Miss Chapman
ADRIANA	Mrs Mattocks

[On Oct. 26 the bill in PA is *Love in a Village*. 'In consequence of the sudden indisposition of Miss Poole . . . the Opera was changed, and the Comedy of Errors was substituted' (MP, Oct. 28). JPK has the correct bill. In the acting version published by Bell in 1793 LUCIANA is assigned to Mrs Kennedy. The cast is otherwise the same as that of these performances, with the following additions:

1ST MERCHANT	Thompson
2ND MERCHANT	Evatt
LESBIA	Mrs Platt]

1794 COVENT GARDEN
Jan. 7, 16

ANTIPHOLUS OF SYRACUSE	Pope
ANTIPHOLUS OF EPHESUS	Holman
DUKE (2)	Davies
ANGELO (2)	Powel
PINCH (2)	Cubitt
AEGEON (2)	Hull
DROMIO OF SYRACUSE	Munden
DROMIO OF EPHESUS	Quick
LUCIANA (1, 2)	Mrs Esten
ABBESS	Miss Chapman
ADRIANA	Mrs Mattocks

(1) *May 17*

LUCIANA	Mrs Mountain

(2) *Nov. 19*

LUCIANA	Mrs Mountain
omitted	
DUKE, ANGELO, PINCH, AEGEON	

1795 COVENT GARDEN
Jan. 10. No parts assigned

[See p. 99. The cast was probably the same as that of the following performance, on Mar. 17. MP, Jan. 12, reporting the change of play, refers to 'the acting of Pope, Holman, Quick, Munden, &c.'.]

155

THE COMEDY OF ERRORS [as altered by HULL]

1795 COVENT GARDEN (cont.)
Mar. 17

ANTIPHOLUS OF SYRACUSE	Pope
ANTIPHOLUS OF EPHESUS	Holman
DUKE (2)	Davies
ANGELO	Powel
AEGEON	Hull
DROMIO OF SYRACUSE	Munden
DROMIO OF EPHESUS	Quick
LUCIANA (1, 2)	Mrs Fawcett
ABBESS	Miss Chapman
ADRIANA	Mrs Mattocks

(1) *Apr. 8*

LUCIANA added	Mrs Mountain
LESBIA	Miss Morris

(2) *Dec. 31*

DUKE	Richardson
LUCIANA	Mrs Mountain

1796 COVENT GARDEN
Apr. 22

ANTIPHOLUS OF SYRACUSE	Pope
ANTIPHOLUS OF EPHESUS	Holman
DUKE	Richardson
ANGELO	Powel
AEGEON	Hull
DROMIO OF SYRACUSE	Munden
DROMIO OF EPHESUS	Quick
LUCIANA	Mrs Mountain
ABBESS	Miss Chapman
LESBIA	Miss Morris
ADRIANA	Mrs Mattocks

1797 COVENT GARDEN
Jan. 7

ANTIPHOLUS OF SYRACUSE	Pope
ANTIPHOLUS OF EPHESUS	Holman
DUKE	Haymes
ANGELO	Powel
AEGEON	Hull
DROMIO OF SYRACUSE	Munden
DROMIO OF EPHESUS	Quick

(1) *Apr. 26*

ADRIANA	Miss Wallis

THE COMEDY OF ERRORS [as altered by HULL]

1797 COVENT GARDEN (cont.)
Jan. 7 (cont.)

LUCIANA	Mrs Mountain
ABBESS	Miss Chapman
LESBIA	Miss Morris
ADRIANA (1)	Mrs Mattocks

1798 COVENT GARDEN
Apr. 10 (1) June 2

ANTIPHOLUS OF SYRACUSE	Pope	DROMIO OF EPHESUS	Rees added
ANTIPHOLUS OF EPHESUS	Holman	PINCH	Wilde
DUKE	Clarke		
ANGELO	Powel		
AEGEON	Hull		
DROMIO OF SYRACUSE	Munden		
DROMIO OF EPHESUS (1)	Quick		
LUCIANA	Mrs Mountain		
ABBESS	Miss Chapman		
LESBIA	Miss Leserve		
ADRIANA	Mrs Mattocks		

[The bill states that Rees's performance would be 'In Imitation of Mr. Munden's Voice, Manner &c.'.]

CORIOLANUS

(1) 'Taken from Shakespeare and Thomson [by Thomas Sheridan]. As it is Acted at the Theatre-Royal in Covent-Garden.'
    1755 A. Millar.

    Act I is entirely omitted, with the exception of *iii*. *1–51*, which opens the play. The remainder of the act consists of *Act II*, the following being the most important omissions: *ii*. *1–41* (the Officers discuss Coriolanus's pride), *ii*. *54–86* (Coriolanus is reluctant to hear Cominius praise him), *iii*. *15–43, 90–131* (the Citizens' acceptance of Coriolanus as consul), *iii*. *184b–207a, 228b–61a* (the Tribunes discredit Coriolanus).
    Act II is *Act III*, omitting *i*. *40b–154a* (Coriolanus's altercation with the Tribunes regarding the distribution of corn), *i*. *183–222a* (the Tribunes incite the Citizens against Coriolanus). The act ends with *iii*. *133* ('There is a world elsewhere').
    Act III consists of Act I and of Act II, scenes iii–vi, of James Thomson's *Coriolanus* (1749). *Act IV. v. 107b–19a* is retained.
    Act IV begins with Thomson, III. i and ii. Then come *IV. vi. 81–148a*, *V. i. 8–end*, and *V. iv. 1–33*. This is followed by about 30 new lines: the Citizens' belief that only Coriolanus can save Rome from invasion. The act ends with Thomson, IV. i and iv.

Act V is Thomson's Act V, in which are introduced *V. v. 92–104, 114–17a*. See also Genest, iv. 417–18; Odell, i. 355.

(2) 'Taken from Shakespeare and Thomson. As it is Acted at the Theatre-Royal in Smock-Alley.'

1757   Dublin: M. Williamson.

This is the same as (1). But it is somewhat more abridged, and Act V here consists of the following: *V. iii. 22–50a*, followed by Thomson, V. i. 3–8, and by *V. iii. 94–168*. The rest is Thomson: the last half of his V. i and all of his V. ii, iii, and iv.

(3) 'As it is now Performed at the Theatres in London and Dublin.'

1762   Dublin: R. Watts and W. Whitestone.

A reading edition, verbatim throughout.

(4) 'As Performed at the Theatre-Royal, Drury-Lane. Regulated from the Prompt-Book.'

1773   John Bell.

Of *Act I* only scenes *i, iii*, and *ix* are retained. In *i* the 1st Senator's speeches are spoken by Lartius, Cominius, and Menenius.

From the remaining acts the following are the most important omissions: *Act II. ii. 1–41* (the Officers discuss Coriolanus's pride), and *iii. 184b–207a, 243b–59a* (the Tribunes discredit Coriolanus).

Act III. i. 90–111a, 118b–60 (the quarrel about the corn), *ii. 138–end* ('The word is "mildly"'), *iii. 1–24* (the Tribunes instruct the Aedile). The act ends with *iii. 133* ('There is a world elsewhere').

Act IV. iii entire and *iv. 154–end* (Aufidius's servants).

See also Odell, i. 356.

(5) 'As it is Acted at the Theatres-Royal in Drury-Lane and Covent-Garden.'

1780   Harrison and Co.

(6) 'Marked with the Variations in the Manager's Book, at the Theatre-Royal in Drury-Lane.'

1786   C. Bathurst [&c.].

These are both identical with (4).

(7) 'Altered from Shakespeare and Thompson [sic], by Mr. J. P. Kemble; and Printed conformably to the Representation, at the Theatre Royal, Drury-Lane.'

1789   J. Christie.

From *Act I* are omitted *i. 53–170a* (Menenius's parable of the belly), scenes *ii, iv, v, vii, viii, x entire*.

From *Act II* is omitted *ii. 1–41* (the Officers discuss Coriolanus's pride).

Act III ends at *iii. 133* ('There is a world elsewhere').

Act IV consists of Thomson, I. i–iii, drastically reduced, followed by *IV. v. 59–153* and by *IV. vi. 1–74*. Then comes Thomson, III. i and ii, reduced, followed by *IV. vi. 81–149a, V. i. 8–74*, and *V. iv. 1–33*.

Acts V begins with *V. iii. 22–140a*, followed by an abridgement of Thomson, V. i and ii, and by *V. v. 87–end*.

Throughout there are minor omissions, and, on three occasions, brief new speeches written, presumably, by Kemble.

See also Genest, vi. 531–4; Odell, ii. 56–58.

(8) 'Altered from Shakespeare, by Mr. T. Sheridan. With the Variations in the Manager's Book, at the Theatre Royal Drury-Lane.'

1789   J. F. and C. Rivington [&c.].

(9) 'Altered from Shakespeare, by Mr. T. Sheridan. Taken from the Manager's Book, at the Theatre Royal in Drury-Lane.'

n.d. [*c.* 1789]   R. Butters.

Neither of these is Sheridan's alteration; both are Kemble's, of which they are reprints, probably unauthorized.

1754 DRURY LANE

Nov. 11   (1) *Nov. 13, 15, 18, 20, 23, 27, 29*

CORIOLANUS	Mossop	added	
MENENIUS	Berry	LARTIUS	Simson
AUFIDIUS	Havard		
COMINIUS	Davies		
SICINIUS	Bransby		
BRUTUS	Burton		
1ST CITIZEN	Yates		
2ND CITIZEN	Blakes		
3RD CITIZEN	Mozeen		
4TH CITIZEN	[H.] Vaughan		
5TH CITIZEN	Clough		
6TH CITIZEN	W. Vaughan		
SENATOR	Walker		
AEDILE	Jefferson		
ROMAN	Ackman		
LIEUTENANT	Scrase		
1ST SERVANT	Taswell		
2ND SERVANT	Philips		
3RD SERVANT	Vernon		
VIRGILIA	Mrs Davies		
VALERIA	Mrs Bennet		
VOLUMNIA	Mrs Pritchard		

[*as altered by* SHERIDAN]

COVENT GARDEN

Dec. 10, 11, 12, 14, 18, 21

CORIOLANUS	Sheridan
COMINIUS	Ridout
MENENIUS	Shuter

CORIOLANUS [as altered by SHERIDAN]

1754 COVENT GARDEN (cont.)
Dec. 10, 11, 12, 14, 18, 21 (cont.)

SICINIUS	Bennet
BRUTUS	Stevens
1ST CITIZEN	Dunstall
2ND CITIZEN	Barrington
3RD CITIZEN	Collins
4TH CITIZEN	Costollo
5TH CITIZEN	Stoppelaer
AUFIDIUS	Ryan
VOLUSIUS	Sparks
GALESUS	Gibson
VOLUMNIA	Mrs Bellamy
VETURIA	Mrs Woffington

[The bills have, 'Partly taken from Shakespeare, partly from Thomson'. This version was first acted at the Smock Alley Theatre, Dublin, on Feb. 29, 1752 (Dublin Gazette). In the acting version published by Millar in 1755 the cast is the same as that of these performances, with the following additions:

MINUCIUS	Anderson
1ST SENATOR	Redman
2ND SENATOR	Wignell
AEDILE	Hurst
OFFICER	Holtom
TITUS	Cushing
HERALD	White
GENTLEWOMAN	Miss Helme]

[*The original*]

1755 DRURY LANE
Apr. 22

CORIOLANUS	Mossop
MENENIUS	Berry
AUFIDIUS	Havard
COMINIUS	Davies
SICINIUS	Bransby
BRUTUS	Burton
LARTIUS	Simson
1ST CITIZEN	Yates
2ND CITIZEN	Blakes
3RD CITIZEN	Mozeen
4TH CITIZEN	[H.] Vaughan
5TH CITIZEN	Clough
6TH CITIZEN	W. Vaughan
SENATOR	Walker
AEDILE	Jefferson
ROMAN	Ackman
LIEUTENANT	Scrase
1ST SERVANT	Taswell

160

CORIOLANUS

1755 DRURY LANE (*cont.*)
Apr. 22 (*cont.*)
2ND SERVANT	Philips
3RD SERVANT	Vernon
VIRGILIA	Mrs Davies
VALERIA	Mrs Bennet
VOLUMNIA	Mrs Pritchard

[In the acting version published by Bell in 1773 the cast is the same as that of this performance except for several omissions and the following addition:
YOUNG MARCIUS	Master J. Simson]

[*as altered by* SHERIDAN]

COVENT GARDEN
Jan. 27
CORIOLANUS	Sheridan
COMINIUS	Ridout
MENENIUS	Shuter
SICINIUS	Bennet
BRUTUS	Stevens
1ST CITIZEN	Dunstall
2ND CITIZEN	Barrington
3RD CITIZEN	Collins
4TH CITIZEN	Costollo
5TH CITIZEN	Stoppelaer
AUFIDIUS	Ryan
VOLUSIUS	Sparks
GALESUS	Gibson
VOLUMNIA (1)	Mrs Bellamy
VETURIA	Mrs Woffington

(1) *Mar. 31*
VOLUMNIA	Mrs Vincent

1758 COVENT GARDEN
Mar. 14
CORIOLANUS	Smith
AUFIDIUS	Ryan
VOLUSIUS	Sparks
MENENIUS	Shuter
COMINIUS	Ridout
GALESUS	Gibson
BRUTUS (1, 2)	White
SICINIUS (1)	Bennet
1ST CITIZEN	Dunstall
2ND CITIZEN	Barrington
3RD CITIZEN	Collins
4TH CITIZEN	Costollo
VOLUMNIA (1, 2)	Miss Condill
VETURIA	Mrs Hamilton

(1) *Apr. 20*
VOLUMNIA	Mrs Vincent
omitted	
BRUTUS, SICINIUS	

(2) *Nov. 2, 3*
BRUTUS	Davis
VOLUMNIA	Mrs Vincent
added on *Nov. 3* only	
5TH CITIZEN	Stoppelaer

CORIOLANUS [as altered by SHERIDAN]

1759 COVENT GARDEN
Feb. 3

CORIOLANUS	Smith
AUFIDIUS	Ryan
VOLUSIUS	Sparks
MENENIUS	Shuter
COMINIUS	Ridout
GALESUS	Gibson
BRUTUS	Davis
SICINIUS	Bennet
1ST CITIZEN	Dunstall
2ND CITIZEN	Barrington
3RD CITIZEN	Collins
4TH CITIZEN	Costollo
5TH CITIZEN	Stoppelaer
VOLUMNIA	Mrs Vincent
VETURIA	Mrs Hamilton

1760 COVENT GARDEN
Apr. 18

CORIOLANUS	Smith
AUFIDIUS	Clarke
VOLUSIUS	Sparks
MENENIUS	Shuter
COMINIUS	Ridout
GALESUS	Gibson
BRUTUS	Davis
SICINIUS	Bennet
1ST CITIZEN	Dunstall
2ND CITIZEN	Barrington
3RD CITIZEN	Collins
4TH CITIZEN	Costollo
5TH CITIZEN	Stoppelaer
VOLUMNIA	Mrs Vincent
VETURIA	Mrs Hamilton

1765 COVENT GARDEN
Feb. 18

CORIOLANUS	Smith
MENENIUS	Shuter
COMINIUS	Gibson
MINUCIUS	Anderson
SICINIUS	Bennet
BRUTUS	Davis
1ST CITIZEN	Barrington
2ND CITIZEN	Dunstall
3RD CITIZEN	Cushing

CORIOLANUS [*as altered by* SHERIDAN]

1765 COVENT GARDEN (*cont.*)
Feb. 18 (cont.)

4TH CITIZEN	Costollo
5TH CITIZEN	[P.] Lewis
AUFIDIUS	Clarke
VOLUSIUS	Walker
GALESUS	Hull
TITUS	White
VOLUMNIA	Miss Macklin
VETURIA	Mrs Bellamy

1768 COVENT GARDEN
Apr. 20

CORIOLANUS	Smith
MENENIUS	Shuter
COMINIUS	Gibson
BRUTUS	Davis
SICINIUS	Casey
MINUCIUS	Perry
TITUS	Du-Bellamy
AUFIDIUS	Younger
GALESUS	Hull
VOLUSIUS	Gardner
1ST CITIZEN	Barrington
2ND CITIZEN	Cushing
3RD CITIZEN	Dunstall
4TH CITIZEN	Stoppelaer
5TH CITIZEN	Quick
VOLUMNIA	Miss Macklin
VETURIA	Mrs Bellamy

[Both Pb and PA assign AUFIDIUS to Clarke, but he was indisposed, and Younger substituted for him (PA, Apr. 21).]

[*as altered by* KEMBLE]

1789 DRURY LANE
Feb. 7, 10, 21; Mar. 3, 7, 14

CORIOLANUS	Kemble
MENENIUS	Baddeley
COMINIUS	[J.] Aickin
SICINIUS (1)	Barrymore
BRUTUS	Whitfield
1ST CITIZEN	Suett
2ND CITIZEN	[J.] Burton
3RD CITIZEN	Fawcett
4TH CITIZEN	Jones
ROMAN OFFICER	Phillimore

(1) *Feb. 14*

SICINIUS Benson
omitted
VOLSCIAN OFFICER

[PA retains Barrymore as SICINIUS, and does not omit the VOLSCIAN OFFICER. MP, Feb. 16, reviewing this performance: 'Barrymore's illness continuing, his character of one of the Tribunes was given to Benson'.]

163

CORIOLANUS [*as altered by* KEMBLE]

1789 DRURY LANE (cont.)
Feb. 7, &c. (cont.)

VOLSCIAN OFFICER (1)	Benson
VOLUSIUS	Williames
AUFIDIUS	Wroughton
VIRGILIA	Mrs Farmer
VALERIA	Mrs Ward
VOLUMNIA	Mrs Siddons

[SICINIUS, BRUTUS, the ROMAN and VOLSCIAN OFFICERS are so specified in the acting version; in the bills they are called respectively the 1ST and 2ND TRIBUNES, and the 1ST and 2ND OFFICERS. In this version the cast is the same as that of these performances, with the following additions:

YOUNG MARCIUS	Master Grimaldi
GENTLEWOMAN	Miss Tidswell]

1792 DRURY LANE (company at KING'S, HAYMARKET)
Mar. 31   (1) *Apr. 21*

CORIOLANUS	Kemble		3RD CITIZEN	Webb
AUFIDIUS	Wroughton			
MENENIUS	Baddeley			
COMINIUS	[J.] Aickin			
SICINIUS	Barrymore			
BRUTUS	Whitfield			
VOLUSIUS	Benson			
YOUNG MARCIUS	Master Chatterley			
ROMAN OFFICER	Caulfield			
VOLSCIAN OFFICER	Alfred			
1ST CITIZEN	Suett			
2ND CITIZEN	Maddocks			
3RD CITIZEN (1)	Fawcett			
4TH CITIZEN	Jones			
VOLUMNIA	Mrs Siddons			
VIRGILIA	Mrs Powell			
VALERIA	Mrs Ward			
GENTLEWOMAN	Miss Tidswell			

1793 DRURY LANE (company at HAYMARKET)
Feb. 23   (1) *May 21*

CORIOLANUS	Kemble		VOLSCIAN OFFICER	Webb
AUFIDIUS	Wroughton		4TH CITIZEN	Jones
MENENIUS	Baddeley			
COMINIUS	[J.] Aickin			
SICINIUS	Barrymore			
BRUTUS	Whitfield			
VOLUSIUS	Benson			

CORIOLANUS [*as altered by* KEMBLE]

1793 DRURY LANE (company at HAYMARKET) (*cont.*)

Feb. 23 (cont.)

YOUNG MARCIUS	Master Chatterley
ROMAN OFFICER	Caulfield
VOLSCIAN OFFICER (1)	Phillimore
1ST CITIZEN	Suett
2ND CITIZEN	[J.] Burton
3RD CITIZEN	Fawcett
4TH CITIZEN (1)	Maddocks
VOLUMNIA	Mrs Siddons
VIRGILIA	Mrs Powell
VALERIA	Mrs Ward
GENTLEWOMAN	Miss Tidswell

[PA assigns the VOLSCIAN OFFICER to Alfred.]

1796 DRURY LANE

Apr. 18

CORIOLANUS	Kemble
AUFIDIUS	Wroughton
MENENIUS (1)	Benson
COMINIUS	[J.] Aickin
SICINIUS	Barrymore
BRUTUS	Whitfield
VOLUSIUS	Caulfield
YOUNG MARCIUS (1)	Master Chatterley
1ST OFFICER (1)	Wentworth
2ND OFFICER (1)	Phillimore
1ST CITIZEN	Suett
2ND CITIZEN (1)	[J.] Burton
3RD CITIZEN	Maddocks
4TH CITIZEN (1)	Jones
VOLUMNIA	Mrs Siddons
VIRGILIA	Mrs Powell
VALERIA	Miss Heard
GENTLEWOMAN	Miss Tidswell

(1) *Oct. 3*

MENENIUS	R. Palmer
YOUNG MARCIUS	Master Wells
1ST OFFICER	Trueman
2ND OFFICER	Webb
2ND CITIZEN	Wathen
4TH CITIZEN	Hollingsworth

1797 DRURY LANE

Feb. 27

CORIOLANUS	Kemble
AUFIDIUS	Wroughton
MENENIUS	R. Palmer
COMINIUS	[J.] Aickin
SICINIUS	Barrymore

CORIOLANUS [*as altered by* KEMBLE]

1797 DRURY LANE (*cont.*)
Feb. 27 (*cont.*)

BRUTUS	Whitfield
VOLUSIUS	Caulfield
YOUNG MARCIUS	Master Wells
1ST OFFICER	Trueman
2ND OFFICER	Webb
1ST CITIZEN	Suett
2ND CITIZEN	Wathen
3RD CITIZEN	Maddocks
4TH CITIZEN	Hollingsworth
VOLUMNIA	Mrs Siddons
VIRGILIA	Mrs Powell
VALERIA	Miss Heard
GENTLEWOMAN	Miss Tidswell

CYMBELINE

(1) 'Altered from Shakespeare. As it is perform'd at the Theatre-Royal in Covent-Garden. By William Hawkins.' In five acts.

1759   James Rivington and James Fletcher.

Act I. i begins with about 70 new lines reciting the same story as in *I. i. 1–69*, followed by a rewriting of *III. i*. The rest of the scene is new: Cymbeline, who has made Cloten his heir, tells him to kill Leonatus [i.e. Posthumus] should he return from Italy to England. Pisanio [i.e. Iachimo] has already been in Rome and told Leonatus that Imogen is false. This he has done at Cloten's order, since Cloten desires Imogen for himself. A few lines from *II. ii* are incorporated here. Scene ii is *III. ii*, expanded.

Act II. i is the discovery, from *III. v*, of Imogen's flight. Scene ii is *III. iii* almost verbatim. Scene iii is *III. iv*, much reduced. Scene iv is chiefly new: the introduction of Imogen to Belarius.

Act III begins with a new scene: Philario [i.e. Pisanio] tests Imogen's fidelity by accusing her of adultery. Her wish to die satisfies him that she is innocent. A few speeches from *II. v* ('mutability', &c.) are utilized here. This is followed by *IV. ii. 62–281*, considerably reduced and rewritten.

Act IV is entirely new: Cymbeline accepts Belarius, Palador [i.e. Arviragus], Cadwal [i.e. Guiderius], and Philario into his army. In the battle Leonatus rescues Cymbeline, and Palador kills Pisanio, who gives him a missive written by Cloten that reveals his guilt. Leonatus is given the missive, and grieves for his mistrust in Imogen. Cymbeline honours Leonatus and the others for their valour.

Act V is also new: Imogen forgives Philario, and is reunited to Leonatus. Cloten's perfidy is revealed to Cymbeline, and Belarius is pardoned. Occasional lines from *V. v* are retained.

See also Genest, iv. 561–4; Odell, i. 367–71.

CYMBELINE

(2) 'With Alterations [by David Garrick].'
    1762   J. and R. Tonson.

Act I is arranged in the following order: *I. i. 1–159a, I. iii. 4–39, I. v. 4–end, II. i. 64–end*, which is spoken by Pisanio instead of by the 2nd Lord, and all of *I. iv. I. ii* (Cloten and the Lords) is omitted.

Act II begins with *I. vi* and ends with *II. iii. II. iii. 40–68* is inserted after *II. i. 36*.

Act III begins with *II. iv* and ends with *III. iv*. Omitted are *III. i. 14b–46* (the defiance of Rome by Cloten and the Queen), *III. iii. 45–73a* (Belarius on the 'art o' the court'), and *III. vii* (Lucius made general of the Roman army). *III. v. 1–65* is inserted after *III. iii*.

Act IV begins with *III. v. 70* and ends with *IV. ii*. Omitted are *IV. ii. 264–90* (the three last verses of 'Fear no more'). *IV. iii* is inserted after *IV. ii. 263*.

Act V begins with *IV. iv*. Omitted are *V. iii. 84–end* (the capture of Posthumus), *V. iv entire* (Posthumus in prison), *V. v. 236b–61* (Cornelius confesses to having made the potion), *V. v. 381–402a* (Cymbeline interrogates Imogen), and *V. v. 422b–76a* (the Soothsayer). In *V. iii* Pisanio has Posthumus's speeches.

Throughout there are minor omissions, and occasional new lines, chiefly intended to facilitate the transition from one omitted or transposed passage to the next.

On the first night of the play's revival (Nov. 28, 1761) the account of the Queen's perfidy and death (*V. v. 23–68*) was retained, but was thereafter omitted.

See also Odell, i. 371–2.

(3) 'With Alterations, by David Garrick, Esq.'
    1770   J. Rivington [&c.].

(4) 'As Performed at the Theatre-Royal, Drury-Lane. Regulated from the Prompt-Book.'
    1773   John Bell.

These are both identical with (2), omitting *V. v. 23–68*.

(5) 'As it is Acted at the Theatres-Royal in Drury-Lane and Covent-Garden.'
    1777   W. Oxlade.

This is identical with (2), omitting *V. v. 23–68*, as well as a few other brief passages.

(6) 'As it is Acted at the Theatres-Royal in Drury-Lane and Covent-Garden.'
    1777   J. Wenman.

(7) 'Altered . . . by David Garrick, Esq. Marked with the Variations in the Manager's Book, at the Theatre-Royal in Drury-Lane.'
    1784   C. Bathurst [&c.].

(8) 'Taken from the Manager's Book, at the Theatre-Royal, Drury-Lane.'
    1788   For the Proprietors.

(9) 'As Performed at the Theatres Royal.'
    1795   J. Barker.

All these are identical with (5).

CYMBELINE

[as altered by HAWKINS]

1759 COVENT GARDEN

Feb. 15, 17, 19, 20, 21, 22; Apr. 19

CYMBELINE	Ryan
CLOTEN	Clarke
LEONATUS	Ross
BELARIUS	Sparks
PALADOR	Smith
CADWAL	Lowe
PHILARIO	Ridout
LUCIUS	Gibson
PISANIO	Dyer
IMOGEN	Mrs Vincent

[The bills give the actors' names only. The above assignment is taken from the printed text.]

[The original]

1761 DRURY LANE

Nov. 28, 30; Dec. 1, 2, 3, 5, 7, 8, 10, 16

POSTHUMUS	Garrick
CYMBELINE	Davies
IACHIMO	Holland
PISANIO	Packer
CLOTEN	King
BELARIUS	Havard
GUIDERIUS	Obrien
ARVIRAGUS	Palmer
LUCIUS	Bransby
CORNELIUS	Burton
PHILARIO	Kennedy
FRENCH GENTLE-MAN	Scrase
CAPTAIN	Castle
1ST GENTLEMAN	Fox
2ND GENTLEMAN	Ackman
IMOGEN	Miss Bride
QUEEN	Mrs Bennet
HELEN	Mrs Hippisley

[The bills give the actors' names only. The above assignment is taken from the printed text (Tonson, 1762). Castle's name appears in the bills, but not in the text, in which the only unassigned part is that of the CAPTAIN. Genest (iv. 635) erroneously assigns BELARIUS to Burton.]

1762 DRURY LANE

Jan. 6, 12

POSTHUMUS	Garrick
CYMBELINE	Davies
IACHIMO	Holland
PISANIO	Packer

(1) *Feb. 8, 25*

FRENCH GENTLEMAN Blakes

[The part is not assigned, but Blakes's name is given in place of Scrase's.]

168

CYMBELINE

1762 DRURY LANE (*cont.*)

Jan. 6, 12 (*cont.*)

CLOTEN	King
BELARIUS	Havard
GUIDERIUS	Obrien
ARVIRAGUS	Palmer
LUCIUS	Bransby
CORNELIUS	Burton
PHILARIO	Kennedy
FRENCH GENTLE-MAN (1)	Scrase
CAPTAIN	Castle
1ST GENTLEMAN	Fox
2ND GENTLEMAN	Ackman
IMOGEN	Miss Bride
QUEEN	Mrs Bennet
HELEN	Mrs Hippisley

[The bills give the actors' names only. The above assignment is taken from the printed text. For Castle, see above, 1761.]

Mar. 25

POSTHUMUS	Garrick
IACHIMO	Holland
CYMBELINE (2)	Davies
CLOTEN	King
BELARIUS	Havard
ARVIRAGUS	Palmer
GUIDERIUS	Obrien
PISANIO	Packer
FRENCH GENTLE-MAN	Blakes
PHILARIO (2)	Kennedy
QUEEN (2)	Mrs Bennet
IMOGEN	Miss Bride

[The parts are assigned in this, and in all subsequent bills.]

(1) *Apr. 28*

added
    CORNELIUS   Stevens

(2) *Oct. 29; Nov. 8; Dec. 8*

CYMBELINE	Love
PHILARIO	Parsons

added
    LUCIUS   Bransby
omitted on *Oct. 29* only
    QUEEN

1763 DRURY LANE

Jan 15; Mar. 10; Apr. 6, 28

POSTHUMUS (1)	Garrick
IACHIMO	Holland
CYMBELINE	Love
CLOTEN	King
BELARIUS	Havard
ARVIRAGUS	Palmer
GUIDERIUS (1)	Obrien
PISANIO	Packer
FRENCH GENTLE-MAN (1)	Blakes

(1) *Dec. 1, 3, 6, 8, 19, 23*

POSTHUMUS	Powell
GUIDERIUS	Jackson

omitted
    FRENCH GENTLEMAN, PHILARIO, LUCIUS

169

CYMBELINE

1763 DRURY LANE (cont.)
Jan. 15; Mar. 10; Apr. 6, 28 (cont.)
PHILARIO (1)	Parsons
LUCIUS (1)	Bransby
QUEEN	Mrs Bennet
IMOGEN	Miss Bride

1764 DRURY LANE
Jan. 24; Feb. 6
POSTHUMUS	Powell
IACHIMO	Holland
CYMBELINE	Love
CLOTEN	King
BELARIUS (2)	Havard
ARVIRAGUS	Palmer
GUIDERIUS	Jackson
PISANIO	Packer
QUEEN	Mrs Bennet
IMOGEN (1, 2)	Miss Bride

(1) *Mar. 26; Nov. 14; Dec. 14*
IMOGEN   Mrs Yates

(2) *Apr. 27; May 11; Oct. 9*
BELARIUS   Lee (on *Apr. 27* only)
IMOGEN   Mrs Palmer

[On *Apr. 27* both Pb and PA assign BELARIUS to Havard, but 'Mrs. Havard died this Morning, on which Account Mr. Lee read Bellarius [*sic*], and introduced two long Speeches that were never spoke before' (C-H).]

1765 DRURY LANE
Feb. 8; Mar. 30
POSTHUMUS	Powell
IACHIMO	Holland
CYMBELINE	Love
CLOTEN	King
BELARIUS (1)	Havard
ARVIRAGUS	Palmer
GUIDERIUS (2)	Jackson
PISANIO	Packer
QUEEN	Mrs Bennet
IMOGEN (1)	Mrs Yates

(1) *May 3*
BELARIUS   Burton
IMOGEN   Miss Plym

(2) *Nov. 20*
GUIDERIUS   [F.] Aickin

1766 DRURY LANE
Jan. 8; Apr. 22
POSTHUMUS	Powell
IACHIMO	Holland
CYMBELINE	Love
CLOTEN (3)	King
BELARIUS	Havard
ARVIRAGUS	Palmer
GUIDERIUS	[F.] Aickin
PISANIO (1)	Packer
QUEEN	Mrs Bennet
IMOGEN (2)	Mrs Yates

(1) *Feb. 5*
PISANIO   Hurst

(2) *May 6*
IMOGEN   Miss Plym
added
GENTLEMAN Ackman
[In the bill the GENTLEMAN is called CLAUDIO.]

(3) *Oct. 21; Nov. 12, 29; Dec. 11*
CLOTEN   Dodd

CYMBELINE

1767 DRURY LANE
Jan. 24

POSTHUMUS	Powell
IACHIMO	Holland
CYMBELINE	Love
CLOTEN (2)	King
BELARIUS	Havard
ARVIRAGUS (2, 3)	Palmer
GUIDERIUS (3)	[F.] Aickin
PISANIO	Packer
QUEEN (2)	Mrs Bennet
IMOGEN (1, 2, 3)	Miss Plym

Oct. 10

POSTHUMUS	Reddish
IACHIMO	Holland
CYMBELINE	Hurst
CLOTEN	King
BELARIUS	Havard
ARVIRAGUS	J. Palmer
GUIDERIUS	[F.] Aickin
LUCIUS	Bransby
CORNELIUS	Burton
PISANIO	Packer
QUEEN (1)	Mrs Johnston
IMOGEN	Mrs Baddeley

COVENT GARDEN
Dec. 28

POSTHUMUS	Powell
IACHIMO	Smith
PISANIO	Hull
PHILARIO	Morris
CYMBELINE	Gibson
CLOTEN	Yates
BELARIUS	Clarke
GUIDERIUS	Bensley
ARVIRAGUS	Perry
QUEEN	Mrs Vincent
IMOGEN	Mrs Yates

1768 DRURY LANE
Jan. 18

POSTHUMUS	Reddish
IACHIMO	Holland
CYMBELINE	Hurst
CLOTEN (3)	King
BELARIUS (2, 3)	Havard

(1) *Apr. 6*

IMOGEN	Mrs Yates

(2) *Apr. 27*

CLOTEN	Dodd
ARVIRAGUS	J. Palmer
IMOGEN	Mrs Yates
QUEEN	omitted

(3) *May 26*

ARVIRAGUS	J. Palmer
GUIDERIUS	Keen
IMOGEN	Mrs Lessingham

(1) *Oct. 13, 19; Nov. 17*

QUEEN	Mrs Hopkins

(1) *Dec. 31*

added

LUCIUS	Gardner
HELEN	Miss Mills

(1) *Jan. 29*

QUEEN	Mrs Reddish

(2) *Apr. 26*

BELARIUS	Burton

[PA assigns Burton both to BELARIUS and to CORNELIUS—

1768 DRURY LANE (cont.)

Jan. 18 (cont.)
ARVIRAGUS (3)	J. Palmer
GUIDERIUS	[F.] Aickin
LUCIUS (3)	Bransby
CORNELIUS (3)	Burton
PISANIO	Packer
QUEEN (1, 3)	Mrs Hopkins
IMOGEN (3)	Mrs Baddeley

(2) Apr. 26 (cont.)
clearly a misprint. Pb omits CORNELIUS.]

(3) Oct. 10, 22, 24, 27, 29; Nov. 3
CLOTEN	Dodd
BELARIUS	Burton
ARVIRAGUS	Palmer [i.e. J. Palmer]
QUEEN	Mrs Reddish (on *Nov. 3* only)
IMOGEN	A Young Gentlewoman [Miss Younge (Genest, v. 217); first appearance, Oct. 22, on the stage] (on *Oct. 22, 24, 27, 29, Nov. 3* only)

omitted
LUCIUS, CORNELIUS
[On *Nov. 3* Miss Younge's name is in the bill.]

COVENT GARDEN

Jan. 8
POSTHUMUS	Powell
IACHIMO	Smith
PISANIO	Hull
CYMBELINE	Gibson
CLOTEN	Yates
PHILARIO (2)	Morris
LUCIUS	Gardner
BELARIUS	Clarke
GUIDERIUS	Bensley
ARVIRAGUS	Perry
QUEEN	Mrs Vincent
HELEN (1, 2)	Miss Mills
IMOGEN	Mrs Yates

(1) Mar. 19; Apr. 9, 18; May 9; June 4; Sept. 20; Oct. 21
omitted
HELEN
[On *Apr. 9* Genest (v. 204) erroneously assigns IMOGEN to Mrs Bulkley.]

(2) Nov. 21
PHILARIO   [P.] Lewis
omitted
HELEN

1769 DRURY LANE

Jan. 23; Apr. 7; Sept. 23
POSTHUMUS	Reddish
IACHIMO	Holland
CLOTEN	Dodd
CYMBELINE	Hurst
BELARIUS	Burton
ARVIRAGUS	[J.] Palmer
GUIDERIUS	[F.] Aickin
PISANIO	Packer
QUEEN	Mrs Hopkins
IMOGEN	Miss Younge

CYMBELINE

1769 DRURY LANE (cont.)

Nov. 17

POSTHUMUS	Reddish
IACHIMO (1)	Holland
CYMBELINE	Hurst
CLOTEN (1)	Jefferson
BELARIUS	Burton
ARVIRAGUS (1)	[J.] Palmer
GUIDERIUS (1)	[F.] Aickin
LUCIUS	Bransby
PHILARIO	Parsons
CAPTAIN (1)	Keen
FRENCH GENTLE- MAN (1)	Fawcett
1ST GENTLE- MAN (1)	Ackman
2ND GENTLEMAN(1)	Wright
PISANIO	Packer
QUEEN	Mrs Reddish
IMOGEN (1)	Miss Younge

(1) *Dec. 12, 28*

IACHIMO	[J.] Palmer
CLOTEN	Dodd (on *Dec. 28* only)
ARVIRAGUS	Brereton
GUIDERIUS	Cautherley
CAPTAIN	Ackman
FRENCH GENTLEMAN	Keen
IMOGEN	Mrs Baddeley (on *Dec. 28* only)

omitted
   GENTLEMEN

COVENT GARDEN

Mar. 11

POSTHUMUS	Powell
IACHIMO	Smith
PISANIO (3)	Hull
CYMBELINE	Gibson
CLOTEN	Yates
PHILARIO (2, 3)	[P.] Lewis
LUCIUS (1, 2)	Gardner
BELARIUS (3)	Clarke
GUIDERIUS	Bensley
ARVIRAGUS (2, 3)	Perry
QUEEN	Mrs Vincent
IMOGEN (2, 3)	Mrs Yates

(1) *Apr. 25*

LUCIUS	Mahon

(2) *May 8*

PHILARIO	Morris
LUCIUS	Mahon
ARVIRAGUS	R. Smith
IMOGEN	Mrs Bulkley

[PA retains Lewis as PHILARIO.]

(3) *May 16*

PISANIO	Perry
PHILARIO	Morris
BELARIUS	Hull
ARVIRAGUS	R. Smith
IMOGEN	Mrs Bulkley

1770 DRURY LANE

Jan. 18; Mar. 12

POSTHUMUS	Reddish
IACHIMO	[J.] Palmer
CYMBELINE	Hurst
CLOTEN	Dodd
BELARIUS	Burton
LUCIUS	Bransby
PHILARIO	Parsons
FRENCH GENTLE- MAN	Keen

173

CYMBELINE

1770 DRURY LANE (cont.)

Jan. 18; Mar. 12 (cont.)

CAPTAIN	Ackman
PISANIO	Packer
GUIDERIUS	Cautherley
ARVIRAGUS	Brereton
QUEEN	Mrs Reddish
IMOGEN	Miss Younge

May 15

POSTHUMUS	Reddish
IACHIMO	[J.] Palmer
CYMBELINE	Hurst
CLOTEN	Dodd
BELARIUS (2)	J. Aickin
PISANIO	Packer
LUCIUS (2, 3)	Wrighten
PHILARIO	Parsons
FRENCH GENTLE-MAN	Fawcett
1ST GENTLE-MAN (2, 3)	Ackman
GUIDERIUS	Cautherley
ARVIRAGUS	Brereton
QUEEN	Mrs Reddish
IMOGEN (3)	Miss Younge

(1) *June 1*

added

CAPTAIN	Keen
2ND GENTLEMAN	Wright

(2) *Sept. 22*

BELARIUS	Burton
LUCIUS	Bransby

omitted
  1ST GENTLEMAN

(3) *Dec. 1, 8*

LUCIUS	Bransby
IMOGEN	Mrs [S.] Barry (on *Dec. 1* only)
	Mrs Baddeley (on *Dec. 8* only)

omitted
  1ST GENTLEMAN

COVENT GARDEN

Jan. 19, 22

POSTHUMUS (1, 2)	A Young Gentleman [Warboys (WEP, Jan. 20); first appearance, Jan. 19, on the stage]
IACHIMO	Smith
PISANIO	Hull
CYMBELINE	Gibson
CLOTEN	Yates
PHILARIO (2)	Morris
LUCIUS (2)	Gardner
BELARIUS	Clarke
GUIDERIUS (1, 2)	Bensley
ARVIRAGUS (1)	Perry
QUEEN	Mrs Vincent
IMOGEN (1, 2)	Mrs Yates

(1) *Apr. 18*

POSTHUMUS	Bensley
GUIDERIUS	Wroughton
ARVIRAGUS	R. Smith
IMOGEN	Mrs Bulkley

(2) *Oct. 16; Nov. 21*

POSTHUMUS	Bensley
GUIDERIUS	Du-Bellamy
IMOGEN	Mrs Bulkley (on *Nov. 21* only)

omitted
  PHILARIO, LUCIUS

1771 DRURY LANE
Jan. 5

POSTHUMUS	Reddish
IACHIMO	[J.] Palmer
CLOTEN	Dodd
CYMBELINE	Hurst
BELARIUS	Burton
PISANIO	Packer
GUIDERIUS	Cautherley
ARVIRAGUS	Brereton
PHILARIO (2, 3)	Parsons
FRENCH GENTLE-	
MAN	Fawcett
LUCIUS	Bransby
1ST GENTLEMAN	Ackman
CAPTAIN	Keen
QUEEN	Mrs Reddish
IMOGEN (1, 2, 3)	Mrs [S.] Barry

(1) *Mar. 4*

IMOGEN	Mrs Baddeley

(2) *Apr. 27*

PHILARIO	Wright
IMOGEN	Mrs Baddeley

(3) *Sept. 26; Dec. 5*

PHILARIO	Wright
IMOGEN	Miss Younge
added	
2ND GENTLEMAN	Wheeler

COVENT GARDEN
Jan. 23

POSTHUMUS	Bensley
IACHIMO	Smith
PISANIO (1)	Wroughton
CLOTEN (1)	Yates
CYMBELINE (1)	Gibson
BELARIUS	Clarke
GUIDERIUS (1)	Du-Bellamy
ARVIRAGUS	Perry
QUEEN	Mrs Vincent
IMOGEN (1)	Mrs Bulkley

(1) *Apr. 16, 26*

PISANIO	Hull
CLOTEN	[Lee] Lewes
CYMBELINE	Morris
GUIDERIUS	Wroughton
IMOGEN	Miss D'Arcy (on *Apr. 16* only)

1772 DRURY LANE
May 7

POSTHUMUS (1)	Croft
IACHIMO	[J.] Palmer
CLOTEN	Dodd
CYMBELINE	Hurst
BELARIUS	J. Aickin
PISANIO	Packer
GUIDERIUS	Cautherley
ARVIRAGUS	Brereton
PHILARIO	Wright
FRENCH GENTLE-	
MAN	Fawcett
LUCIUS	Bransby

(1) *Sept. 19*

POSTHUMUS	Reddish
QUEEN	Mrs Hopkins
added	
CAPTAIN	Keen

1772 DRURY LANE (cont.)
May 7 (cont.)
GENTLEMAN	Ackman
QUEEN (1)	Mrs Reddish
IMOGEN	Miss Younge

[In the bill the GENTLEMAN is called CLAUDIO.]

COVENT GARDEN
Jan. 1
POSTHUMUS	Bensley
IACHIMO	Smith
BELARIUS	Clarke
CLOTEN	Yates
CYMBELINE	Morris
PISANIO	Hull
GUIDERIUS	Wroughton
ARVIRAGUS (1, 2)	R. Smith
QUEEN	Mrs Vincent
IMOGEN (1)	Mrs Bulkley

(1) *Apr. 11*
ARVIRAGUS	Perry
IMOGEN	Mrs Yates

(2) *May 9*
ARVIRAGUS	Perry

1773 DRURY LANE
Feb. 8
POSTHUMUS	Reddish
IACHIMO (1, 2)	Jefferson
CLOTEN	Dodd
CYMBELINE	Hurst
BELARIUS	J. Aickin
PISANIO	Packer
GUIDERIUS	Cautherley
ARVIRAGUS	Brereton
PHILARIO	Wright
FRENCH GENTLE- MAN	Fawcett
LUCIUS	Bransby
CAPTAIN (2)	Keen
1ST GENTLE- MAN (1)	Ackman
2ND GENTLE- MAN (2)	Wheeler
QUEEN (1)	Mrs Hopkins
IMOGEN	Miss Younge

(1) *May 31*
IACHIMO	[J.] Palmer
1ST GENTLEMAN	Griffith
QUEEN	Mrs Johnston

(2) *Sept. 21*
IACHIMO	[J.] Palmer
omitted	
CAPTAIN, 2ND GENTLEMAN	

[In these two bills the 1ST GENTLE- MAN is called CLAUDIO.]

[In the bill the GENTLEMEN are called BRITISH GENTLEMEN. In the acting version published by Bell in 1773 the cast is the same as that of this performance (save for the assignment of IACHIMO to Palmer), with the following additions:

CORNELIUS	Wrighten
HELEN	Mrs [T.] Smith]

1773 COVENT GARDEN
Jan. 16; Feb. 12

POSTHUMUS (1)	Bensley
IACHIMO	Smith
PISANIO	Hull
CLOTEN	[Lee] Lewes
CYMBELINE (1)	Morris
BELARIUS	Clarke
GUIDERIUS	Wroughton
ARVIRAGUS (1)	Perry
QUEEN (1)	Mrs Vincent
IMOGEN (1)	Mrs Bulkley

(1) *Nov. 12, 15, 17, 25; Dec. 6, 15*

POSTHUMUS	Lewis
CYMBELINE	Gardner
ARVIRAGUS	R. Smith
QUEEN	Mrs P. Green
IMOGEN	Mrs Lessingham

[In the acting version published by Bell in 1773 the cast is the same as that of these performances (save for the assignment of ARVIRAGUS to R. Smith), with the following additions:

PHILARIO	[R.] Bates
LUCIUS	Gardner
FRENCH GENTLE-MAN	Davis
CORNELIUS	Redman
HELEN	Miss Pearce]

1774 DRURY LANE
Jan. 28; May 23

POSTHUMUS	Reddish
IACHIMO (2)	[J.] Palmer
CLOTEN	Dodd
CYMBELINE	Hurst
BELARIUS (2)	J. Aickin
PISANIO	Packer
GUIDERIUS	Cautherley
ARVIRAGUS	Brereton
LUCIUS (2)	Bransby
FRENCH GENTLE-MAN	Fawcett
PHILARIO	Wright
GENTLEMAN (2)	Ackman
QUEEN	Miss Sherry
IMOGEN (1)	Miss Younge

[In the bills the GENTLEMAN is called CLAUDIO.]

(1) *Apr. 5*

IMOGEN	Mrs Lessingham

(2) *Sept. 27; Oct. 18; Dec. 17*

IACHIMO	Smith
BELARIUS	Aickin [i.e. J. Aickin]
LUCIUS	Usher (on *Dec. 17* only)
GENTLEMAN	Griffiths (on *Oct. 18, Dec. 17* only)

[In these three bills the GENTLEMAN is called CLAUDIO.]

COVENT GARDEN
Feb. 5

POSTHUMUS	Lewis
IACHIMO	Smith
PISANIO	Hull
CLOTEN	[Lee] Lewes

1774 COVENT GARDEN (cont.)
Feb. 5 (cont.)

CYMBELINE	Gardner
BELARIUS	Clarke
GUIDERIUS	Wroughton
ARVIRAGUS	R. Smith
QUEEN	Mrs P. Green
IMOGEN	Mrs Lessingham

1775 DRURY LANE
Apr. 29

IACHIMO	Smith
POSTHUMUS (1)	Brereton
CLOTEN	Dodd
CYMBELINE (1)	Hurst
PISANIO	Packer
BELARIUS	[J.] Aickin
GUIDERIUS (1)	Cautherley
ARVIRAGUS	Davies
LUCIUS	Bransby
FRENCH GENTLE-MAN	Fawcett
PHILARIO	Wright
GENTLEMAN	Griffiths
CORNELIUS (1)	Wrighten
CAPTAIN (1)	Keen
QUEEN	Miss Sherry
IMOGEN	Miss Younge

(1) Nov. 1

POSTHUMUS	Reddish
CYMBELINE	Wrighten
GUIDERIUS	Brereton
CORNELIUS	Cubitt
CAPTAIN	Norris

[In the bill the GENTLEMAN is called CLAUDIO.]

COVENT GARDEN
May 20

POSTHUMUS	Lewis
IACHIMO	Bensley
CLOTEN	Booth
CYMBELINE	L'Estrange
PISANIO	Wroughton
BELARIUS	Clarke
GUIDERIUS	Du-Bellamy
ARVIRAGUS	Whitfield
LUCIUS	Fearon
FRENCH GENTLE-MAN	Davis
PHILARIO	Chaplin
CORNELIUS	Thompson
QUEEN	Mrs Hull
IMOGEN	Mrs Lessingham

[PA assigns CORNELIUS to Fox.]

CYMBELINE

1776 DRURY LANE
Apr. 29

POSTHUMUS (1)	Reddish
CLOTEN	Dodd
CYMBELINE	Hurst
PISANIO	Packer
BELARIUS	[J.] Aickin
GUIDERIUS (1, 2)	Whitfield
ARVIRAGUS	Davies
LUCIUS	Bransby
FRENCH GENTLE-MAN	Fawcett
PHILARIO	Wright
IACHIMO	Smith
QUEEN	Miss Sherry
IMOGEN	Miss Younge

(1) *Oct. 26*

POSTHUMUS	Brereton
GUIDERIUS	Farren

(2) *Nov. 12*

GUIDERIUS	Brereton

CHINA HALL, ROTHERHITHE
Sept. 9

POSTHUMUS	Stokes
CYMBELINE	Massey
GUIDERIUS	Garland
ARVIRAGUS	A Gentleman [unidentified; first appearance on the stage]
CLOTEN	Russell
PISANIO	Comerford
BELARIUS	Newton
FRENCH GENTLE-MAN	[S.] Johnson
LUCIUS	[P.] Lewis
1ST LORD	Dancer
2ND LORD	[J.] Smith
PHILARIO	W. Smith
IACHIMO	A Young Gentleman [unidentified; second appearance on the stage]
QUEEN	Mrs Smith
HELEN	Mrs West
IMOGEN	Mrs Massey

[In the bill the title of the play is spelled *Cymberline*.]

1777 DRURY LANE
Oct. 31

POSTHUMUS	Brereton
CLOTEN	Dodd

1777 DRURY LANE (cont.)

Oct. 31 (cont.)

CYMBELINE	Hurst
PISANIO	Packer
BELARIUS	[J.] Aickin
GUIDERIUS	Farren
ARVIRAGUS	Davies
LUCIUS	Wrighten
FRENCH GENTLE-MAN	Chaplin
PHILARIO	Wright
IACHIMO	Smith
QUEEN	Miss Sherry
IMOGEN	Miss Younge

1778 DRURY LANE

Feb. 19

POSTHUMUS	Brereton
CLOTEN	Dodd
CYMBELINE	Hurst
PISANIO	Packer
BELARIUS	[J.] Aickin
GUIDERIUS	Farren
ARVIRAGUS	Davies
LUCIUS	Wrighten
FRENCH GENTLE-MAN	Chaplin
PHILARIO	Wright
IACHIMO	Smith
QUEEN	Miss Sherry
IMOGEN	Miss Younge

COVENT GARDEN

Oct. 24

POSTHUMUS	Brereton
CLOTEN	Lee Lewes
CYMBELINE	L'Estrange
PISANIO	Hull
BELARIUS	Clarke
GUIDERIUS	Wroughton
ARVIRAGUS	Whitfield
LUCIUS	Fearon
PHILARIO	Booth
IACHIMO	Smith
QUEEN	Mrs Jackson
IMOGEN	Mrs Crawford

[Both Pb and PA assign POSTHUMUS to Reddish. He was indisposed, and the part was acted by Brereton (PA, Oct. 26).]

CYMBELINE

1779 COVENT GARDEN
Apr. 20

POSTHUMUS (1)	Crawford
CLOTEN	Lee Lewes
CYMBELINE	L'Estrange
PISANIO	Hull
BELARIUS	Clarke
GUIDERIUS	Wroughton
ARVIRAGUS	Whitfield
LUCIUS	Fearon
PHILARIO	Booth
IACHIMO (1)	Daly
QUEEN	Mrs Jackson
IMOGEN (1)	Mrs Crawford

(1) *May 5*

POSTHUMUS	Reddish
IACHIMO	Smith
IMOGEN	Mrs Bulkley

1780 DRURY LANE
Apr. 18

POSTHUMUS	Henry
CLOTEN	Dodd
CYMBELINE	Hurst
PISANIO	Packer
BELARIUS	[J.] Aickin
GUIDERIUS	R. Palmer
ARVIRAGUS	Davies
LUCIUS	Wrighten
FRENCH GENTLE-MAN	Chaplin
PHILARIO	Wright
IACHIMO	Smith
QUEEN	Miss Sherry
IMOGEN	Mrs Robinson

1782 HAYMARKET
Aug. 9

POSTHUMUS	[J.] Bannister
PISANIO	Staunton
BELARIUS	[J.] Aickin
ARVIRAGUS	Wood
GUIDERIUS	R. Palmer
LUCIUS	Usher
PHILARIO	Webb
CLOTEN	Edwin
CYMBELINE	Gardner
1ST LORD	Ledger
2ND LORD	Stevens
FRENCH GENTLE-MAN	Davis
CORNELIUS	Swords

1782 HAYMARKET (cont.)
Aug. 9 (cont.)

IACHIMO	[J.] Palmer
QUEEN	Miss Sherry
HELEN	Mrs Poussin
IMOGEN	Mrs Bulkley

1783 DRURY LANE
Feb. 18   (1) *Feb. 25*

POSTHUMUS	Brereton	omitted
BELARIUS	[J.] Aickin	PHILARIO, CORNELIUS
GUIDERIUS	Farren	
ARVIRAGUS	Barrymore	
CYMBELINE	Wrighten	
PISANIO	Packer	
LUCIUS	Phillimore	
FRENCH GENTLE-MAN	Fawcett	
PHILARIO (1)	Wright	
CORNELIUS (1)	Chaplin	
CLOTEN	R. Palmer	
IACHIMO	Smith	
QUEEN	Mrs Hopkins	
IMOGEN	Mrs [J.] Mills [first appearance in London]	

1784 DRURY LANE
Jan. 3   (1) *Nov. 19*

POSTHUMUS	Brereton	GUIDERIUS	Barrymore
CLOTEN	Dodd	IMOGEN	Mrs Wells
BELARIUS	[J.] Aickin		
GUIDERIUS (1)	Farren		
ARVIRAGUS	R. Palmer		
CYMBELINE	Wrighten		
PISANIO	Packer		
LUCIUS	Phillimore		
FRENCH GENTLE-MAN	Fawcett		
PHILARIO	Wright		
CORNELIUS	Chaplin		
IACHIMO	Smith		
QUEEN	Mrs Hopkins		
IMOGEN (1)	Miss E. Kemble		

COVENT GARDEN
Oct. 18

POSTHUMUS	Henderson
CLOTEN	Quick

1784 COVENT GARDEN (cont.)
Oct. 18 (cont.)

CYMBELINE	Fearon
PISANIO	Hull
BELARIUS	Clarke
GUIDERIUS	Farren
ARVIRAGUS	Davies
LUCIUS	Cubitt
PHILARIO	Thompson
IACHIMO	Wroughton
QUEEN	Miss Platt
HELEN	Mrs Poussin
IMOGEN	Miss Younge

1785 DRURY LANE
Nov. 21

POSTHUMUS	Kemble
BELARIUS	[J.] Aickin
GUIDERIUS	Barrymore
ARVIRAGUS	R. Palmer
CYMBELINE	Wrighten
PISANIO	Packer
LUCIUS	Phillimore
FRENCH GENTLE-MAN	Fawcett
PHILARIO	Wright
CORNELIUS	Chaplin
CLOTEN	Dodd
IACHIMO	Smith
QUEEN	Mrs Hopkins
IMOGEN	Mrs Jordan

1786 COVENT GARDEN
Jan. 6

POSTHUMUS	Holman
CLOTEN	Quick
CYMBELINE	Fearon
PISANIO	Hull
GUIDERIUS	Farren
ARVIRAGUS	Davies
IACHIMO	Wroughton
IMOGEN	Mrs Wells

1787 DRURY LANE
Jan. 29; Feb. 1, 5, 8; Mar. 20

POSTHUMUS (1)	Kemble	(1) *May 24*	
BELARIUS	[J.] Aickin	POSTHUMUS	Bensley
GUIDERIUS	Barrymore	(2) *Nov. 5*	
		ARVIRAGUS	Benson

1787 DRURY LANE (cont.)

Jan. 29; Feb. 1, 5, 8; Mar. 20 (cont.)　　(2) *Nov. 5 (cont.)*

ARVIRAGUS (2)	R. Palmer	CLOTEN	R. Palmer
CYMBELINE	Staunton	QUEEN	Mrs Ward
PISANIO	Packer	IMOGEN	Mrs [W.] Taylor
LUCIUS	Phillimore		
FRENCH GENTLE-MAN	Fawcett		
PHILARIO	Chaplin		
CORNELIUS	Alfred		
CLOTEN (2)	Dodd		
IACHIMO	Smith		
QUEEN (2)	Mrs Hopkins		
IMOGEN (2)	Mrs Siddons		

[On Feb. 8 PA assigns the QUEEN to Mrs Ward.]

COVENT GARDEN

Apr. 27

POSTHUMUS	Holman
BELARIUS	[F.] Aickin
GUIDERIUS	Farren
ARVIRAGUS	Davies
CYMBELINE	Gardner
PISANIO	Hull
FRENCH GENTLE-MAN	Macready
PHILARIO	Fearon
LUCIUS	Cubitt
CORNELIUS	Thompson
CLOTEN	Quick
IACHIMO	Pope
QUEEN	Miss Platt
HELEN	Miss Stuart
IMOGEN	Mrs Pope

1792 COVENT GARDEN

May 19

POSTHUMUS	Holman
BELARIUS	[F.] Aickin
GUIDERIUS	Harley
ARVIRAGUS	Davies
CYMBELINE	Powel
PISANIO	Hull
CLOTEN	Marshall
IACHIMO	Farren
QUEEN	Mrs Platt
HELEN	Mrs Watts
IMOGEN	Mrs Pope

1793 COVENT GARDEN
Nov. 18

POSTHUMUS	Holman
CYMBELINE	Powel
CLOTEN	Bernard
BELARIUS	Farren
ARVIRAGUS	Townsend
GUIDERIUS	Macready
PISANIO	Harley
LUCIUS	Davies
1ST LORD	Campbell
2ND LORD	Evatt
FRENCH GENTLE-MAN	Claremont
PHILARIO	Rock
IACHIMO	Pope
HELEN	Mrs Watts
IMOGEN	A Young Lady [Miss Jones (TM, Dec. 1793, 359); first appearance in London]

(1) *Nov. 22*
added

CORNELIUS	Thompson
QUEEN	Mrs Fawcett

1794 COVENT GARDEN
Oct. 7, 10; Nov. 10

POSTHUMUS	Holman
CYMBELINE	Richardson
CLOTEN	Bernard
BELARIUS	Farren
ARVIRAGUS	Middleton
GUIDERIUS	Macready
PISANIO	Harley
LUCIUS	Davies
1ST LORD	Claremont
2ND LORD	Davenport
PHILARIO	Powel
FRENCH GENTLE-MAN	Farley
IACHIMO	Pope
QUEEN	Mrs Fawcett
HELEN	Miss Leserve
IMOGEN	Miss Wallis

1795 COVENT GARDEN
Jan. 1

POSTHUMUS	Holman
CYMBELINE	Richardson
CLOTEN	Bernard
BELARIUS	Farren
ARVIRAGUS	Middleton
PISANIO	Harley

1795 COVENT GARDEN (cont.)
Jan. 1 (cont.)

IACHIMO	Pope
QUEEN	Mrs Fawcett
IMOGEN	Miss Wallis

1797 DRURY LANE
Mar. 6

CYMBELINE	Packer
CLOTEN	R. Palmer
POSTHUMUS	Kemble
ARVIRAGUS	Holland
GUIDERIUS	C. Kemble
BELARIUS	[J.] Aickin
PHILARIO	Maddocks
IACHIMO	[J.] Palmer
LUCIUS	Denman
PISANIO	Caulfield
QUEEN	Mrs Cuyler
IMOGEN	A Young Lady [Mrs Worthington (O, Mar. 7); first appearance on the stage]
HELEN	Mrs Crossman

1800 COVENT GARDEN
May 13

POSTHUMUS	Holman
CYMBELINE	Waddy
BELARIUS	Murray
CLOTEN	Betterton
ARVIRAGUS	Claremont
GUIDERIUS	H. Johnston
PISANIO	Whitfield
LUCIUS	Mansel
CORNELIUS	Thompson
1ST LORD	Curties
2ND LORD	Abbot
FRENCH GENTLE-MAN	Klanert
PHILARIO	Atkins
IACHIMO	Pope
QUEEN	Mrs Dibdin
HELEN	Miss Mills
IMOGEN	Mrs [M. A.] Pope

THE FAIRIES

David Garrick's alteration, as an opera libretto, of A MIDSUMMER-NIGHT'S DREAM, q.v.

A FAIRY TALE
George Colman, the elder's, alteration of A MIDSUMMER-NIGHT'S DREAM, q.v.

FLORIZEL AND PERDITA
McNamara Morgan's alteration of THE WINTER'S TALE, q.v.
[This was originally published and acted under the title of THE SHEEP-SHEARING —which title was used, after 1758, on only a few occasions.]

FLORIZEL AND PERDITA
The title used for six performances at Drury Lane in 1762 of Garrick's three-act alteration of THE WINTER'S TALE, q.v.

HAMLET
(1) 'As it is now Acted by His Majesty's Servants.'
1751   J. and P. Knapton [&c.].

Following are the more important omissions:
Act I. i. *109–25* (Horatio's description of the portents in Rome), *155b–65* ('our Saviour's birth'); ii. *16b–41* (the King's message to Norway); iii. *11–18, 22–28, 38–44* (Laertes' advice to Ophelia), *57b–81* (Polonius's advice to Laertes); iv. *17–38a* ('the vicious mole of nature'); v. *150–63* ('hic et ubique'). I. v. *80* ('O, horrible!') is spoken by Hamlet.

Act II. i. *1–74a* (Polonius and Reynaldo); ii. *51–85* (the return of Voltimand and Cornelius), *248b–82a* ('king of infinite space'), *360–87* (the child actors), *485–94* (the description of Pyrrhus), *601–12* ('John-a-dreams').

Act III. ii. *121–9* (Hamlet's bawdry preceding the play), *the dumbshow, 208–25* (the Player King discussing will and fate); iii. *3–24* (Rosencrantz and Guildenstern flatter the King), *73–end* (Hamlet's refusal to kill the King as he prays) [a note in Bell's version, 1773, states that this scene is 'commendably thrown aside', because it tends to 'degrade' Hamlet's character]; iv. *71b–81* (the 'hoodman-blind'), *161–70a* (Hamlet begging his mother to abstain from the King's bed), *180–end* (the King's 'reechy kisses', and the journey to England).

Act IV. i. *14–23a* (the King's misgivings as to Hamlet's liberty); iii. *22b–34* (Hamlet's discussion of worms), *62–end* (the King's wish to have Hamlet killed in England, for which one new line is substituted: 'Let it be testified in Hamlet's death'); *iv entire* (Hamlet and the Norwegian captain, and 'How all occasions do inform against me') [Bell, 1773, calls this soliloquy 'unworthy of the closet or the stage . . . quite superfluous']; v. *3–13* (the Gentleman's description of Ophelia's madness), *59–66* ('By Gis and by Saint Charity'), *77b–98a* (the King's troubles coming 'in battalions'); vii. *176b–84a* (Ophelia's garments 'heavy with their drink').

Act V. i. *110b–25a* ('the great buyer of land'); ii. *4–80* (the King's scheme to have Hamlet killed, and Hamlet's scheme to have Rosencrantz and Guildenstern killed), *118–33* (Hamlet's bombast, 'the verity of extolment'), *375–414, 417* (Fortinbras). Horatio speaks the two penultimate lines.

187

There are numerous minor excisions, and occasional verbal changes, among which may be noted: *I. ii. 190*, Saw! who? (*for* Saw who?); *II. ii. 584*, O! what a wretch (*for* O! what a rogue); *III. i. 72*, The pangs of despis'd love (*for* The pangs of dispriz'd love); *V. i. 201*, Alas! poor Yorick. I knew him well, Horatio (*for* ... I knew him, Horatio); *V. ii. 374*, And choirs of angels (*for* And flights of angels).

(2) 'As it is now Acted by His Majesty's Servants.'

    1754   J. and P. Knapton. Reprinted 1756.

(3) 'As it is now Acted By His Majesty's Servants.'

    1758   [Publisher not specified].

(4) 'As it is now Acted By His Majesty's Servants.'

    1759   C. Hitch [&c.]. Reprinted 1760, 1761.

(5) 'As it is now acted At the Theatres-Royal in Drury-Lane, and Covent-Garden.'

    1763   Hawes and Co. [&c.].

(6) 'As it is now acted At the Theatres Royal in Drury-Lane, and Covent-Garden.'

    1755 [but *recte* 1765]   T. Witford.

(7) 'As it is now acted At the Theatres-Royal in Drury-Lane, and Covent-Garden.'

    1768   H. Woodfall [&c.].

All these are, save for minor omissions or restorations, identical with (1).

See also Odell, ii. 31–33.

(8) Altered by David Garrick. In five acts.

    1772   Not published.

The first four acts of the original, except for the omissions noted below, are retained almost verbatim. Act I consists of *I. i* and *ii*; Act II of *I. iii, iv,* and *v*; Act III of *II*; Act IV of *III*; Act V of *IV* and a few lines of *V*.

Following are the principal omissions:

I. iv. 17–38a ('the vicious mole of nature'); *II. ii. 248b–82a* ('king of infinite space'); *II. ii. 360–87* (the child actors); *II. ii. 601–12* ('John-a-dreams'); *III. ii* (the dumbshow); *IV. iii. 22b–34* (the king and the beggar); *IV. iv. 1–8* (Fortinbras); *IV. vi entire* (the sailors); *IV. vii entire* (the King suborns Laertes; the Queen reports Ophelia's death); *V. i. 1–268a* (the Gravediggers); *V. ii entire* (Hamlet and Osric; the fencing).

In *IV. iv* the Norwegian captain's speeches are given to Guildenstern. *IV. vi. 203b–19* are transposed to precede *151b*. The concluding scene of the play is, except for three or four lines of the original, entirely new. It is 33 lines in length: Hamlet kills the King, the Queen preserves her life by running away, and Hamlet 'runs on Laertes's sword and falls'. As he dies he asks Horatio and Laertes to 'calm this troubled land'. 'Good-night, sweet prince' is retained.

The above account is extracted from 'Garrick's Long Lost Alteration of *Hamlet*', by G. W. Stone, Jr., in *PMLA*, xlix (1934), 890–921. Dr Stone reprints

HAMLET

Garrick's Act V in its entirety. [In 1773 Bell printed the play as it was ordinarily acted, but included the cast of Garrick's alteration.]

(9) 'As Performed at the Theatre-Royal, Covent-Garden. Regulated from the Prompt-Book.'

1773   John Bell.

(10) 'As it is now acted at the Theatres-Royal in Drury-Lane and Covent-Garden.'

1776   W. Oxlade.

(11) 'As it is Acted at the Theatres-Royal in Drury-Lane and Covent-Garden.'

1779   Harrison and Co.

(12) 'Marked with the Variations in the Manager's Book, at the Theatre-Royal in Drury-Lane.'

1782   C. Bathurst [&c.].

(13) 'Taken from the Manager's Book, at the Theatre-Royal, Drury-Lane.'

1787   For the Proprietors.

(14) 'With the Variations in the Manager's Book, at the Theatre-Royal in Drury-Lane.'

1789   J. F. and C. Rivington [&c.].

All these, save for minor omissions or restorations, are identical with (1).

(15) Altered, probably by Joseph George Holman.

1793   Not published.

On July 29, 1794 Holman acted Hamlet at the Crow Street Theatre, Dublin. The playbill reads, 'Dressed in the Habits of the Times, and with other Alterations, adopted in its Representation 19 Nights last Winter, at the Theatre Royal, Covent Garden'. It further states that the part of Ophelia would be performed 'without the Airs, and with a considerable Restoration of the Text'.

During the season of 1793-4 *Hamlet* had been acted at CG 11, not 19 times. Holman had appeared in all but two of these performances. What his alterations consisted of I have not been able to ascertain.

(16) 'Altered ... by I [sic]. P. Kemble, Esq., and Represented by Their Majesties Servants, at the Theatre Royal, Drury-Lane.'

1796   C. Lowndes. Reprinted 1797.

This is virtually the same as (1). Further omissions include *I. i. 70-108* (Horatio describes the quarrel between Denmark and Norway); *V. ii. 243-54* ('madness is poor Hamlet's enemy'). *IV. iii. 22b-34* and *V. ii. 118-33* are retained.

(17) 'As Performed at the Theatres Royal. Regulated from the Prompt-Books.'

n.d. [*c.* 1798]   J. Barker.

Save for minor omissions or restorations this is identical with (1).

HAMLET

(18) 'Revised by J. P. Kemble... As it is acted by Their Majesties Servants of the Theatre Royal, Drury Lane. September 16th. 1800.'

n.d. [c. 1800] C. Lowndes.

This is the same as (16), but with still further omissions, notably *II. ii. 578b–625a* (the first third of 'O! what a rogue and peasant slave am I'), and *III. iii. 36–72* (the King's soliloquy preceding his prayer).

1751 DRURY LANE
Apr. 23

HAMLET (1)	Lee
KING (1)	Bridges
GHOST	Berry
HORATIO (1)	Palmer
POLONIUS	Taswell
LAERTES	Blakes
OSRIC (1)	Shuter
1ST GRAVEDIGGER	Yates
2ND GRAVE-DIGGER (1)	Ray
OPHELIA	Mrs Clive
QUEEN	Mrs Pritchard

(1) *May 17; Sept. 18; Oct. 21*

HAMLET	Garrick
KING	Winstone
HORATIO	Havard (on Sept. 18, Oct. 21 only)
OSRIC	Woodward
2ND GRAVEDIGGER	W. Vaughan (on *May 17* only)
added	
LUCIANUS	James (on *May 17* only) / Shuter (on *Sept. 18, Oct. 21* only)
ROSENCRANTZ	Simson
GUILDENSTERN	Scrase
BERNARDO	Marr
PLAYER KING	Burton
PLAYER QUEEN	Mrs Yates

COVENT GARDEN
Apr. 20

HAMLET	Barry
KING	Sparks
HORATIO	Ridout
GHOST	Ryan
ROSENCRANTZ	Usher
GUILDENSTERN	Bransby
MARCELLUS	Anderson
BERNARDO (1)	Elrington
LAERTES	Gibson
OSRIC	Dyer
PLAYER KING	Redman
1ST GRAVEDIGGER	Dunstall
2ND GRAVE-DIGGER (1)	Stoppelaer
POLONIUS	Macklin
QUEEN (1)	Mrs Woffington
PLAYER QUEEN	Mrs Bambridge
OPHELIA (1)	Mrs Vincent

(1) *Oct. 11*

BERNARDO	Bencraft
2ND GRAVEDIGGER	Collins
QUEEN	Mrs Elmy
OPHELIA	Mrs Cibber
added	
FRANCISCO	Holtom

BOWLING GREEN, SOUTHWARK
Sept. 18. No parts assigned

HAMLET

1752 DRURY LANE
Apr. 7; Oct. 23

HAMLET (2)	Garrick
KING	Winstone
GHOST	Berry
HORATIO (2)	Havard
POLONIUS	Taswell
LAERTES	Blakes
OSRIC (2)	Woodward
LUCIANUS (2)	Shuter
ROSENCRANTZ	Simson
GUILDENSTERN	Scrase
BERNARDO	Marr
PLAYER KING	Burton
1ST GRAVEDIGGER	Yates
2ND GRAVEDIGGER	[H.] Vaughan
PLAYER QUEEN (1, 2)	Mrs Yates
OPHELIA	Mrs Clive
QUEEN	Mrs Pritchard

(1) *Nov. 17*

PLAYER QUEEN	Mrs Cross

(2) *Dec. 20*

HAMLET	Goodfellow
HORATIO	Palmer
OSRIC	Shuter
PLAYER QUEEN	Mrs Cross
added	
FRANCISCO	Raftor
omitted	
LUCIANUS	

COVENT GARDEN
Jan. 4

HAMLET	Barry
KING	Sparks
HORATIO	Ridout
GHOST	Ryan
ROSENCRANTZ	Usher
GUILDENSTERN	Bransby
MARCELLUS	Anderson
BERNARDO	Bencraft
LAERTES (2)	Gibson
OSRIC (1, 2)	Dyer
FRANCISCO	Holtom
PLAYER KING	Redman
1ST GRAVEDIGGER	Dunstall
2ND GRAVE-DIGGER (2)	Collins
POLONIUS	Macklin
QUEEN	Mrs Elmy
PLAYER QUEEN	Mrs Bambridge
OPHELIA	Mrs Cibber

(1) *Apr. 10, 20*

OSRIC	Cushing

(2) *Nov. 28*

LAERTES	Dyer
OSRIC	Cushing
2ND GRAVEDIGGER	Stoppelaer

1753 DRURY LANE
May 1

HAMLET (1)	Lacey
KING (1)	Winstone
GHOST	Berry

(1) *Oct. 16*

HAMLET	Garrick
KING	Davies
OSRIC	Woodward

HAMLET

1753 DRURY LANE (cont.)

May 1 (cont.)

HORATIO	Havard
POLONIUS	Taswell
LAERTES	Blakes
OSRIC (1)	Shuter
ROSENCRANTZ	Simson
GUILDENSTERN (1)	Ackman
PLAYER KING	Burton
1ST GRAVEDIGGER	Yates
2ND GRAVEDIGGER	[H.] Vaughan
PLAYER QUEEN	Mrs Bennet
OPHELIA (1)	Mrs Clive
QUEEN	Mrs Pritchard

(1) Oct. 16 (cont.)

GUILDENSTERN	Scrase
OPHELIA	Mrs Cibber

COVENT GARDEN

Apr. 2

HAMLET	Barry
KING	Sparks
HORATIO	Ridout
GHOST	Ryan
ROSENCRANTZ	Usher
GUILDENSTERN (1)	Bransby
MARCELLUS	Anderson
BERNARDO	Bencraft
OSRIC	Cushing
FRANCISCO	Holtom
PLAYER KING	Redman
LAERTES	Dyer
1ST GRAVE-DIGGER (1)	Dunstall
2ND GRAVEDIGGER	Stoppelaer
POLONIUS	Arthur
QUEEN	Mrs Elmy
PLAYER QUEEN	Mrs Bambridge
OPHELIA (1)	Mrs Cibber

(1) Oct. 30

GUILDENSTERN	White
1ST GRAVEDIGGER	Shuter
OPHELIA	Mrs Vincent

1754 DRURY LANE

Jan. 17

HAMLET	Garrick
KING	Davies
GHOST	Berry
HORATIO	Havard
POLONIUS	Taswell
LAERTES	Blakes
OSRIC	Woodward
ROSENCRANTZ	Simson

(1) Oct. 16

PLAYER KING added	Bransby
BERNARDO	Vernon
FRANCISCO	Raftor

HAMLET

1754 DRURY LANE (cont.)
Jan. 17 (cont.)

GUILDENSTERN	Scrase
PLAYER KING (1)	Burton
1ST GRAVEDIGGER	Yates
2ND GRAVEDIGGER	[H.] Vaughan
PLAYER QUEEN	Mrs Bennet
OPHELIA	Mrs Cibber
QUEEN	Mrs Pritchard

COVENT GARDEN
Mar. 5

HAMLET (2, 3)	Barry
KING	Sparks
HORATIO	Ridout
GHOST	Ryan
ROSENCRANTZ (2, 3)	Usher
GUILDENSTERN	White
MARCELLUS	Anderson
BERNARDO (1)	Bencraft
OSRIC (3)	Cushing
FRANCISCO (3)	Holtom
PLAYER KING	Redman
LAERTES	Dyer
1ST GRAVEDIGGER	Shuter
2ND GRAVEDIGGER	Stoppelaer
POLONIUS	Arthur
QUEEN	Mrs Elmy
PLAYER QUEEN	Mrs Bambridge
OPHELIA (1, 3)	Mrs Vincent

(1) *Apr. 19*

BERNARDO	Wignell
OPHELIA	Miss Kennedy

(2) *Oct. 24*

HAMLET	Sheridan
ROSENCRANTZ	Wignell

(3) *Nov. 2*

HAMLET	Sheridan
ROSENCRANTZ	Wignell
OSRIC	Cibber
OPHELIA	Mrs Chambers
FRANCISCO omitted	

1755 DRURY LANE
Mar. 20

HAMLET	Garrick
POLONIUS	Woodward
QUEEN	Mrs Pritchard
OPHELIA	Mrs Cibber

No other parts assigned

Oct. 4

HAMLET	Garrick
KING	Davies
GHOST	Berry
HORATIO	Havard
POLONIUS	Taswell
LAERTES	Blakes
OSRIC	Woodward
ROSENCRANTZ	Simson

(1) *Dec. 2*

OPHELIA	Miss Macklin

HAMLET

1755 DRURY LANE (cont.)
Oct. 4 (cont.)

GUILDENSTERN	Scrase
BERNARDO	Marr
MARCELLUS	Bransby
PLAYER KING	Burton
1ST GRAVEDIGGER	Yates
2ND GRAVEDIGGER	[H.] Vaughan
PLAYER QUEEN	Mrs Bennet
OPHELIA (1)	Mrs Cibber
QUEEN	Mrs Pritchard

COVENT GARDEN
Jan. 16; Mar. 3

HAMLET (1, 2, 3)	Sheridan
KING	Sparks
HORATIO	Ridout
GHOST	Ryan
ROSENCRANTZ (1, 3)	Wignell
GUILDENSTERN (1)	White
MARCELLUS (1)	Anderson
BERNARDO (1, 2)	Bencraft
LUCIANUS (1)	Collins
FRANCISCO (1)	Holtom
PLAYER KING (1)	Redman
LAERTES	Dyer
OSRIC (3)	Cibber
1ST GRAVEDIGGER	Shuter
2ND GRAVEDIGGER	Stoppelaer
POLONIUS	Arthur
QUEEN (1, 2, 3)	Mrs Elmy
PLAYER QUEEN (1)	Miss Ferguson
OPHELIA (2)	Mrs Chambers

(1) *Apr. 4*

| HAMLET | Murphy |
| QUEEN | Mrs Woffington |

omitted ROSENCRANTZ, GUILDENSTERN, MARCELLUS, BERNARDO, LUCIANUS, FRANCISCO, PLAYER KING, PLAYER QUEEN

(2) *Apr. 25*

HAMLET	Murphy
BERNARDO	R. Smith
QUEEN	Mrs Woffington
OPHELIA	Mrs Baker

(3) *Nov. 12*

HAMLET	Barry
ROSENCRANTZ	Bennet
OSRIC	Cushing
QUEEN	Mrs Woffington

[Genest (iv. 463) erroneously implies that Mrs Vincent acted OPHELIA.]

BOWLING GREEN, SOUTHWARK
Jan. 20. No parts assigned

1756 DRURY LANE
Feb. 14

HAMLET (1)	Garrick
KING	Davies
GHOST	Berry
HORATIO	Havard
POLONIUS (1, 3)	Taswell
LAERTES	Blakes
OSRIC (1, 2, 3)	Woodward
ROSENCRANTZ (1, 3)	Simson

(1) *Apr. 20; May 20*

HAMLET	Holland
POLONIUS	Woodward (on *Apr. 20* only)
OSRIC	Palmer
OPHELIA	Miss Macklin

omitted ROSENCRANTZ, GUILDENSTERN, BERNARDO, MARCELLUS, PLAYER KING, PLAYER QUEEN

194

HAMLET

1756 DRURY LANE (cont.)

Feb. 14 (cont.)

GUILDENSTERN (1, 2, 3)	Usher
BERNARDO (1)	Marr
MARCELLUS (1)	Bransby
PLAYER KING (1)	Burton
1ST GRAVEDIGGER	Yates
2ND GRAVEDIGGER	[H.] Vaughan
PLAYER QUEEN (1)	Mrs Bennet
OPHELIA (1, 2, 3)	Mrs Cibber
QUEEN	Mrs Pritchard

(2) May 27

OSRIC	Palmer
GUILDENSTERN	Scrase
OPHELIA	Miss Macklin

(3) Sept. 30; Nov. 3; Dec. 13

POLONIUS	Philips (on *Dec. 13* only)
OSRIC	Palmer
ROSENCRANTZ	Usher
GUILDENSTERN	Jefferson
OPHELIA	Miss Macklin

COVENT GARDEN

Mar. 8; Apr. 5

HAMLET	Barry
KING	Sparks
HORATIO	Ridout
ROSENCRANTZ	Bennet
GUILDENSTERN	White
MARCELLUS	Anderson
BERNARDO	Bencraft
LAERTES	Dyer
OSRIC	Cushing
LUCIANUS	Collins
FRANCISCO	Holtom
PLAYER KING	Redman
POLONIUS	Arthur
1ST GRAVEDIGGER	Shuter
2ND GRAVEDIGGER	Stoppelaer
GHOST	Ryan
PLAYER QUEEN	Miss Ferguson
OPHELIA	Mrs Chambers
QUEEN	Mrs Woffington

1757 DRURY LANE

May 3

HAMLET (1, 2)	Holland
KING	Davies
GHOST	Berry
HORATIO	Havard
POLONIUS	Taswell
LAERTES	Blakes
OSRIC	Palmer
ROSENCRANTZ	Usher
GUILDENSTERN	Jefferson
BERNARDO	Marr
MARCELLUS	Bransby

(1) Sept. 24

HAMLET	Garrick

(2) Nov. 29

HAMLET	Garrick
OPHELIA	Miss Macklin

195

1757 DRURY LANE (cont.)

May 3 (cont.)

PLAYER KING	Burton
1ST GRAVEDIGGER	Yates
2ND GRAVEDIGGER	[H.] Vaughan
PLAYER QUEEN	Mrs Bennet
OPHELIA (2)	Mrs Cibber
QUEEN	Mrs Pritchard

COVENT GARDEN

Feb. 16

HAMLET (1, 3)	Barry
KING	Sparks
HORATIO	Ridout
ROSENCRANTZ	Bennet
GUILDENSTERN	White
MARCELLUS	Anderson
BERNARDO (2, 3)	Bencraft
LAERTES	Dyer
OSRIC	Cushing
LUCIANUS	Collins
FRANCISCO	Holtom
PLAYER KING	Redman
POLONIUS (2)	Arthur
1ST GRAVEDIGGER	Shuter
2ND GRAVEDIGGER	Stoppelaer
GHOST	Ryan
PLAYER QUEEN	Miss Ferguson
OPHELIA	Mrs Chambers
QUEEN (3)	Mrs Woffington

(1) *Mar. 22*

HAMLET	Smith

(2) *May 4*

BERNARDO	R. Smith
POLONIUS	Costollo

[Mrs Woffington's name is in the bill as the QUEEN, but it is almost certain that she did not appear. Genest (iv. 495, 501) quotes Wilkinson's detailed account (in his *Memoirs*, i. 117–19) of her performance in *As You Like It* on May 3, at the conclusion of which she was seized with what proved to be her final illness.]

(3) *Oct. 8, 29*

HAMLET	Ross
BERNARDO	R. Smith
QUEEN	Mrs Elmy

1758 DRURY LANE

Mar. 30

HAMLET	Mossop
KING	Davies
HORATIO	Havard
GHOST	Berry
1ST GRAVEDIGGER	Yates
2ND GRAVEDIGGER	[H.] Vaughan
OPHELIA	Mrs Cibber
QUEEN	Mrs Pritchard

Apr. 8

HAMLET (1, 2)	Mossop
KING	Davies
GHOST	Berry
HORATIO	Havard
POLONIUS	Taswell
LAERTES	Blakes

(1) *May 29*

HAMLET	Garrick

(2) *Sept. 26*

HAMLET	Garrick
ROSENCRANTZ	Packer
GUILDENSTERN	Austin
OPHELIA	Miss Macklin

HAMLET

1758 DRURY LANE (cont.)
Apr. 8 (cont.)

OSRIC	Palmer
ROSENCRANTZ (2)	Usher
GUILDENSTERN (2)	Jefferson
BERNARDO	Marr
MARCELLUS	Bransby
PLAYER KING	Burton
1ST GRAVEDIGGER	Yates
2ND GRAVEDIGGER	[H.] Vaughan
PLAYER QUEEN	Mrs Bennet
OPHELIA (2)	Mrs Cibber
QUEEN	Mrs Pritchard

COVENT GARDEN
Jan. 20; Feb. 28

HAMLET (2, 3)	Barry
KING	Sparks
HORATIO	Ridout
ROSENCRANTZ	Bennet
GUILDENSTERN (3)	White
MARCELLUS	Anderson
BERNARDO	Bencraft
LAERTES	Dyer
OSRIC	Cushing
LUCIANUS (3)	Collins
FRANCISCO	Holtom
PLAYER KING	Redman
POLONIUS (3)	Arthur
1ST GRAVEDIGGER	Shuter
2ND GRAVE-DIGGER (1)	Stoppelaer
GHOST	Ryan
PLAYER QUEEN	Miss Ferguson
OPHELIA (3)	Mrs Chambers
QUEEN	Mrs Elmy

(1) *Apr. 24*

2ND GRAVEDIGGER	Costollo

(2) *May 18*

HAMLET	Ross

(3) *Oct. 30*

HAMLET	Ross
GUILDENSTERN	Wignell
LUCIANUS	Dunstall
POLONIUS	Collins
OPHELIA	Mrs Vincent

1759 DRURY LANE
Apr. 17

HAMLET (1)	Fleetwood
KING	Davies
GHOST	Bransby
HORATIO	Havard
LAERTES (1, 2)	Obrien
OSRIC (2)	Palmer
POLONIUS	Blakes
ROSENCRANTZ	Packer

(1) *May 23; Sept. 29*

HAMLET	Mossop (on *May 23* only) / Garrick (on *Sept. 29* only)
LAERTES	Austin
GUILDENSTERN	Scrase
OPHELIA	Miss Macklin

added on *Sept. 29* only

BERNARDO	Marr
MARCELLUS	Ackman

197

HAMLET

1759 DRURY LANE (cont.)

Apr. 17 (cont.)

GUILDENSTERN (1,2)	Austin
PLAYER KING	Burton
1ST GRAVEDIGGER	Yates
2ND GRAVEDIGGER	[H.] Vaughan
PLAYER QUEEN	Mrs Bennet
OPHELIA (1)	Mrs Cibber
QUEEN	Mrs Pritchard

(2) Nov. 27

LAERTES	Austin
OSRIC	Perry
GUILDENSTERN added	Scrase

   SAME as *Sept. 29*

COVENT GARDEN

Jan. 2

HAMLET	Ross
KING	Sparks
HORATIO	Ridout
ROSENCRANTZ	Bennet
GUILDENSTERN	Wignell
MARCELLUS	Anderson
BERNARDO	Bencraft
LAERTES	Dyer
OSRIC (1, 2)	Cushing
LUCIANUS	Dunstall
FRANCISCO	Holtom
PLAYER KING	Redman
POLONIUS	Collins
1ST GRAVEDIGGER	Shuter
2ND GRAVEDIGGER	Stoppelaer
GHOST	Ryan
PLAYER QUEEN	Miss Ferguson
OPHELIA (2)	Mrs Vincent
QUEEN	Mrs Elmy

(1) Feb. 27

OSRIC	Creswick

(2) Apr. 30

OSRIC	Creswick
OPHELIA	Mrs Baker

1760 DRURY LANE

Apr. 21

HAMLET (1, 2)	Fleetwood
KING	Davies
GHOST	Bransby
HORATIO	Havard
POLONIUS	Blakes
LAERTES	Austin
OSRIC	Palmer
ROSENCRANTZ	Packer
GUILDENSTERN	Scrase
BERNARDO	Marr
MARCELLUS	Ackman
PLAYER KING	Burton
1ST GRAVEDIGGER	Yates
2ND GRAVEDIGGER	[H.] Vaughan

(1) May 10

HAMLET	Garrick
OPHELIA	Mrs Cibber

(2) Nov. 27; Dec. 10

HAMLET	Sheridan
OPHELIA	Mrs Davies

1760 DRURY LANE (*cont.*)

Apr. 21 (cont.)

PLAYER QUEEN	Mrs Bennet
OPHELIA (1, 2)	Miss Macklin
QUEEN	Mrs Pritchard

COVENT GARDEN

Mar. 18

HAMLET (1)	Smith
KING	Sparks
HORATIO	Ridout
ROSENCRANTZ	Bennet
GUILDENSTERN	Wignell
MARCELLUS	Anderson
BERNARDO (1)	Weller
LAERTES	Dyer
OSRIC	Creswick
LUCIANUS	Dunstall
FRANCISCO	Holtom
PLAYER KING	Redman
POLONIUS	Collins
1ST GRAVEDIGGER	Shuter
2ND GRAVEDIGGER	Stoppelaer
GHOST (1)	Ryan
PLAYER QUEEN	Mrs Ferguson
OPHELIA (1)	Mrs Vincent
QUEEN	Mrs Elmy

(1) *Oct. 1; Dec. 22*

HAMLET	Ross
BERNARDO	Bencraft
GHOST	Gibson
OPHELIA	{ Miss Macklin (on *Oct. 1* only) Miss Brent (on *Dec. 22* only) }

1761 DRURY LANE

Mar. 9

HAMLET (1, 2, 3, 4)	Sheridan
KING	Davies
GHOST	Bransby
HORATIO	Havard
POLONIUS (3)	Blakes
LAERTES (3, 4)	Austin
OSRIC (3)	Palmer
ROSENCRANTZ	Packer
GUILDENSTERN (2)	Scrase
BERNARDO	Marr
MARCELLUS	Ackman
PLAYER KING	Burton
1ST GRAVEDIGGER	Yates
2ND GRAVEDIGGER	[H.] Vaughan
PLAYER QUEEN	Mrs Bennet
OPHELIA (1)	Mrs Cibber
QUEEN	Mrs Pritchard

(1) *Apr. 9*

HAMLET	Holland
OPHELIA	Mrs Vincent [Jr.]

(2) *June 3*

HAMLET	Garrick
GUILDENSTERN	Castle

(3) *Sept. 15*

HAMLET	Holland
POLONIUS	Weston
LAERTES	Blakes
OSRIC	King

(4) *Oct. 13; Nov. 24*

HAMLET	Garrick
LAERTES	Kennedy

[On *Oct. 13* Genest (iv. 633) erroneously assigns LAERTES to Blakes, POLONIUS to Weston, and OSRIC to King.]

1761 COVENT GARDEN
Apr. 24

HAMLET (2)	Ross
KING	Sparks
HORATIO	Hull
ROSENCRANTZ (1, 2)	Bennet
GUILDENSTERN (1, 2)	Wignell
MARCELLUS (1, 2)	Anderson
BERNARDO (1, 2)	Bencraft
LAERTES (2)	Dyer
OSRIC (2)	Creswick
LUCIANUS (1, 2)	Dunstall
FRANCISCO (1, 2)	Holtom
PLAYER KING (1, 2)	Redman
POLONIUS	Collins
1ST GRAVEDIGGER	Shuter
2ND GRAVEDIGGER (1, 2)	Stoppelaer
GHOST	Gibson
PLAYER QUEEN (1, 2)	Mrs Ferguson
QUEEN	Mrs Elmy
OPHELIA	Mrs Vincent

(1) *Oct. 10*

2ND GRAVEDIGGER Costollo omitted
ROSENCRANTZ, GUILDENSTERN, MARCELLUS, BERNARDO, LUCIANUS, FRANCISCO, PLAYER KING, PLAYER QUEEN

(2) *Dec. 22*

HAMLET	Sheridan
LAERTES	Davis
OSRIC	Dyer
2ND GRAVEDIGGER	Costollo omitted

SAME as *Oct. 10*

1762 DRURY LANE
Jan. 19

HAMLET (2)	Holland
KING (2)	Davies
GHOST	Bransby
HORATIO (1)	Havard
POLONIUS	Blakes
LAERTES (2)	Kennedy
OSRIC (1)	Palmer
ROSENCRANTZ (1, 2)	Packer
GUILDENSTERN (2)	Scrase
BERNARDO	Marr
MARCELLUS	Ackman
PLAYER KING	Burton
1ST GRAVEDIGGER	Yates
2ND GRAVEDIGGER (1)	[H.] Vaughan
PLAYER QUEEN	Mrs Bennet
OPHELIA	Mrs Cibber
QUEEN	Mrs Pritchard

(1) *May 4*

HORATIO	Packer
OSRIC	King
ROSENCRANTZ	Castle
2ND GRAVEDIGGER	Philips

(2) *Oct. 6; Nov. 6*

HAMLET	Garrick
KING	Packer
LAERTES	Lee
ROSENCRANTZ	Parsons
GUILDENSTERN	Castle

COVENT GARDEN
May 7

HAMLET	Ross
KING (1)	Anderson

(1) *Sept. 27*

KING	Sparks
ROSENCRANTZ	White

HAMLET

1762 COVENT GARDEN (*cont.*)

May 7 (*cont.*)

HORATIO	Hull
ROSENCRANTZ (1)	Bennet
GUILDENSTERN (1)	Wignell
MARCELLUS	Gardner
BERNARDO	Weller
OSRIC (1)	Perry
LAERTES	Davis
LUCIANUS (1)	Weller
FRANCISCO	Holtom
PLAYER KING	Redman
POLONIUS	Collins
1ST GRAVEDIGGER	Shuter
2ND GRAVEDIGGER	Costollo
GHOST	Gibson
PLAYER QUEEN	Mrs Ferguson
QUEEN (1)	Mrs Elmy
OPHELIA (1)	Mrs Vincent

[Weller doubled BERNARDO and LUCIANUS.]

(1) *Sept. 27* (*cont.*)

GUILDENSTERN	Perry
OSRIC	Dyer
QUEEN	Mrs Lewis [first appearance in London]
OPHELIA	Miss Macklin

added
    OFFICER   R. Smith
omitted
    LUCIANUS

1763 DRURY LANE

Apr. 4

HAMLET	Holland
KING	Packer
HORATIO	Havard
POLONIUS (1, 2)	Blakes
LAERTES	Lee
OSRIC	Palmer
ROSENCRANTZ (1, 2)	Parsons
GUILDENSTERN	Castle
BERNARDO	Marr
MARCELLUS	Ackman
PLAYER KING	Burton
1ST GRAVEDIGGER	Yates
2ND GRAVEDIGGER	[H.] Vaughan
GHOST (1, 2)	Garrick
PLAYER QUEEN	Mrs Bennet
OPHELIA (2)	Mrs Cibber
QUEEN	Mrs Pritchard

(1) *Apr. 29*

POLONIUS	Parsons
ROSENCRANTZ	Fox
GHOST	Bransby

(2) *Sept. 20; Oct. 26*

POLONIUS	Baddeley
ROSENCRANTZ	Fox
GHOST	Bransby
OPHELIA	Mrs Hopkins

[On *Sept.* 20 Genest (v. 35) erroneously assigns the KING to Love.]

COVENT GARDEN

May 18

HAMLET	Ross
KING	Walker
HORATIO	Hull
ROSENCRANTZ	White

HAMLET

1763 COVENT GARDEN (cont.)
May 18 (cont.)

GUILDENSTERN	Perry
POLONIUS	Stamper
LAERTES	Young
PLAYER KING	Wignell
GHOST	Gibson
OSRIC	Dyer
1ST GRAVEDIGGER	Shuter
2ND GRAVEDIGGER	Stoppelaer
QUEEN	Mrs Lewis
PLAYER QUEEN	Miss Helme
OPHELIA	Miss Macklin

1764 DRURY LANE
Feb. 11

HAMLET	Holland
KING	Love
GHOST (1)	Bransby
HORATIO (2, 3)	Havard
POLONIUS	Baddeley
LAERTES	Lee
OSRIC	Palmer
ROSENCRANTZ (1, 2, 3)	Strange
GUILDENSTERN (2, 3)	Castle
BERNARDO (1)	Marr
MARCELLUS	Ackman
PLAYER KING (3)	Burton
1ST GRAVEDIGGER	Yates
2ND GRAVEDIGGER	[H.] Vaughan
PLAYER QUEEN (2)	Mrs Bennet
OPHELIA (2, 3)	Mrs Hopkins
QUEEN	Mrs Pritchard

[PA assigns POLONIUS to Parsons.]

(1) *May 16*

GHOST	Powell
ROSENCRANTZ	Fox
BERNARDO	Strange

(2) *Sept. 27; Nov. 22*

HORATIO	Packer
ROSENCRANTZ	Fox
GUILDENSTERN	Strange (on *Nov. 22* only)
PLAYER QUEEN	Mrs Hippisley (on *Nov. 22* only)
OPHELIA	A Young Gentlewoman [Mrs Baddeley (MacMillan, 255); first appearance, Sept. 27, on the stage]

(3) *Dec. 12*

HORATIO	Packer
ROSENCRANTZ	Fox
GUILDENSTERN	Strange
PLAYER KING	Moody
OPHELIA	Mrs Cibber

COVENT GARDEN
Mar. 29

HAMLET	Ross
KING	Sparks
HORATIO	Hull
POLONIUS	Shuter
LAERTES	Davis
ROSENCRANTZ	White
GUILDENSTERN	Perry
MARCELLUS	Gardner

(1) *Sept. 19; Nov. 13*

GHOST	Gibson

[On *Sept. 19* PA assigns MARCELLUS to Anderson.]

HAMLET

1764 COVENT GARDEN (cont.)
Mar. 29 (cont.)

LUCIANUS	Weller
PLAYER KING	Redman
GHOST (1)	Walker
OSRIC	Dyer
1ST GRAVEDIGGER	Dunstall
2ND GRAVEDIGGER	Costollo
PLAYER QUEEN	Mrs Ferguson
OPHELIA	Miss Macklin
QUEEN	Mrs Ward

[PA assigns MARCELLUS to Anderson.]

1765 DRURY LANE
Feb. 16

HAMLET	Holland
KING	Love
GHOST (1)	A Young Gentleman [unidentified; first appearance on the stage]
HORATIO	Packer
POLONIUS	Baddeley
LAERTES	Lee
OSRIC	Palmer
ROSENCRANTZ	Fox
GUILDENSTERN	Strange
BERNARDO	Marr
MARCELLUS	Ackman
PLAYER KING	Burton
1ST GRAVEDIGGER	Yates
2ND GRAVEDIGGER	[H.] Vaughan
PLAYER QUEEN (1)	Mrs Hippisley
QUEEN (1)	Mrs Pritchard
OPHELIA (1)	Mrs Cibber

(1) Apr. 27

GHOST	Bransby
PLAYER QUEEN	Mrs Bennet
QUEEN	Mrs Hopkins
OPHELIA	Mrs Baddeley

COVENT GARDEN
Sept. 18

HAMLET	Ross
KING	Walker
HORATIO (1)	Gardner
POLONIUS	Shuter
LAERTES	Davis
ROSENCRANTZ	White
GUILDENSTERN	Perry
MARCELLUS (1)	Anderson

(1) Nov. 11

HORATIO	Hull
MARCELLUS	Gardner
BERNARDO	Weller

203

1765 COVENT GARDEN (cont.)

Sept. 18 (cont.)

BERNARDO (1)	R. Smith
PLAYER KING	Redman
GHOST	Gibson
OSRIC	Dyer
1ST GRAVEDIGGER	Dunstall
2ND GRAVEDIGGER	Costollo
PLAYER QUEEN	Mrs Ferguson
OPHELIA	Miss Macklin
QUEEN	Mrs Ward

1766 DRURY LANE

Jan. 13

HAMLET (2)	Holland
KING	Love
GHOST	Bransby
HORATIO (1, 2)	Havard
POLONIUS	Baddeley
LAERTES (2)	Lee
OSRIC	Dodd
ROSENCRANTZ (2)	[F.] Aickin
GUILDENSTERN (2)	Strange
BERNARDO	Marr
MARCELLUS	Ackman
PLAYER KING	Burton
1ST GRAVEDIGGER	Yates
2ND GRAVE-DIGGER (2)	[H.] Vaughan
PLAYER QUEEN	Mrs Bennet
OPHELIA	Mrs Baddeley
QUEEN (1)	Mrs Pritchard

(1) Apr. 28

HORATIO	Packer
QUEEN	Mrs Hopkins

(2) Sept. 23; Nov. 7

HAMLET	Cautherley (on Sept. 23 only) / Garrick (on Nov. 7 only)
HORATIO	Packer
LAERTES	[F.] Aickin
ROSENCRANTZ	Strange
GUILDENSTERN	Fawcett
2ND GRAVEDIGGER	Castle

COVENT GARDEN

May 12

HAMLET	Ross
KING	Walker
HORATIO	Hull
POLONIUS	Shuter
LAERTES (1)	Davis
GHOST	Gibson
OSRIC	Dyer
ROSENCRANTZ	Bennet
GUILDENSTERN (1)	Perry
PLAYER KING (1)	[P.] Lewis
1ST GRAVEDIGGER	Dunstall
2ND GRAVE-DIGGER (1)	Costollo

(1) Oct. 30

LAERTES	Perry
GUILDENSTERN	Wignell
PLAYER KING	Redman
2ND GRAVEDIGGER	[P.] Lewis

HAMLET

1766 COVENT GARDEN (cont.)
May 12 (cont.)
PLAYER QUEEN	Mrs Ferguson
OPHELIA	Miss Macklin
QUEEN	Mrs Ward

1767 DRURY LANE
May 28

HAMLET (1)	Garrick
KING	Love
GHOST	Bransby
HORATIO	Packer
POLONIUS	Baddeley
LAERTES	[F.] Aickin
OSRIC	Dodd
ROSENCRANTZ	Strange
GUILDENSTERN	Fawcett
BERNARDO	Marr
MARCELLUS	Ackman
PLAYER KING	Burton
1ST GRAVE-DIGGER (1)	Yates
2ND GRAVEDIGGER	Castle
PLAYER QUEEN (1)	Mrs Bennet
OPHELIA	Mrs Baddeley
QUEEN	Mrs Pritchard

(1) *Sept. 15; Nov. 9*
HAMLET	Holland
1ST GRAVEDIGGER	Parsons
PLAYER QUEEN	Mrs Johnston
added	
LUCIANUS	Weston

COVENT GARDEN
Jan. 26

HAMLET	Ross
KING	Walker
HORATIO	Hull
POLONIUS	Shuter
LAERTES	Davis
ROSENCRANTZ	Bennet
GUILDENSTERN	Perry
PLAYER KING	Redman
GHOST	Gibson
OSRIC	Dyer
1ST GRAVEDIGGER	Dunstall
2ND GRAVEDIGGER	Buck
PLAYER QUEEN	Mrs Ferguson
OPHELIA	Miss Macklin
QUEEN	Mrs Du-Bellamy

1768 DRURY LANE
Jan. 13

HAMLET (2, 4)	Garrick
KING	Love

(1) *Feb. 29*
LUCIANUS	Hartry
2ND GRAVEDIGGER	Messink

205

HAMLET

1768 DRURY LANE (cont.)

Jan. 13 (cont.)

GHOST	Bransby
HORATIO	Packer
POLONIUS	Baddeley
LAERTES	[F.] Aickin
OSRIC	Dodd
ROSENCRANTZ	Strange
GUILDENSTERN	Fawcett
BERNARDO	Marr
MARCELLUS	Ackman
PLAYER KING	Burton
LUCIANUS (1, 2, 3, 4)	Weston
1ST GRAVEDIGGER	Parsons
2ND GRAVE- DIGGER (1)	Castle
PLAYER QUEEN	Mrs Johnston
OPHELIA	Mrs Baddeley
QUEEN (3, 4)	Mrs Pritchard

(2) *Apr. 4*

HAMLET	Holland
LUCIANUS	Hartry

[PA retains Weston as LUCIANUS.]

(3) *May 31*

LUCIANUS	Hartry
QUEEN	Mrs Hopkins

(4) *Sept. 17; Oct. 17*

HAMLET	Holland
LUCIANUS	Hartry
QUEEN	Mrs Hopkins

COVENT GARDEN

Apr. 25

HAMLET	Powell
GHOST	Bensley
HORATIO	Hull
LAERTES	Davis
KING	Gibson
POLONIUS	Shuter
ROSENCRANTZ	R. Smith
GUILDENSTERN	Perry
PLAYER KING	Redman
LUCIANUS	Morgan
OSRIC	Dyer
1ST GRAVEDIGGER	Dunstall
2ND GRAVEDIGGER	Stoppelaer
OPHELIA	Miss Macklin
QUEEN	Mrs Yates

[PA assigns LUCIANUS to Cushing.]

1769 DRURY LANE

Feb. 3

HAMLET (1)	Garrick
KING (1)	Love
GHOST	Bransby
HORATIO	Packer
POLONIUS	Baddeley

(1) *Apr. 21; Sept. 19; Oct. 28*

HAMLET	Holland
KING	Jefferson
OSRIC	[J.] Palmer (on *Oct. 28* only)
ROSENCRANTZ	J. Aickin (on *Sept. 19, Oct. 28* only)

HAMLET

1769 DRURY LANE (cont.)

Feb. 3 (cont.)

LAERTES	[F.] Aickin
OSRIC (1)	Dodd
ROSENCRANTZ (1)	Strange
GUILDENSTERN	Fawcett
BERNARDO	Marr
MARCELLUS	Ackman
PLAYER KING	Burton
LUCIANUS	Hartry
1ST GRAVEDIGGER	Parsons
2ND GRAVEDIGGER	Castle
PLAYER QUEEN	Mrs Johnston
OPHELIA	Mrs Baddeley
QUEEN	Mrs Hopkins

COVENT GARDEN

Jan. 2

HAMLET (1)	Smith
KING	Gibson
GHOST	Bensley
LAERTES	Davis
HORATIO	Hull
POLONIUS	Shuter
ROSENCRANTZ (1, 2)	R. Smith
GUILDENSTERN (1, 2)	Perry
PLAYER KING (1, 2)	Redman
LUCIANUS (1, 2)	Cushing
OSRIC	Dyer
1ST GRAVEDIGGER	Dunstall
2ND GRAVEDIGGER	Stoppelaer
OPHELIA (1)	Miss Macklin
QUEEN	Mrs Ward

(1) *Feb. 16, 27; Mar. 31*

HAMLET	Powell
OPHELIA	Mrs Mattocks (on *Mar. 31* only)

omitted
   ROSENCRANTZ, GUILDENSTERN, PLAYER KING, LUCIANUS

(2) *Nov. 27*

omitted
   SAME as *Feb. 16*

HAYMARKET

Aug. 7

HAMLET	Sheridan
KING	[C.] Bannister
LAERTES	[J.] Aickin
HORATIO	Du-Bellamy
ROSENCRANTZ (1)	Strange
MARCELLUS (1)	Wheeler
BERNARDO (1)	Jacobs
GHOST	Sowdon
1ST GRAVEDIGGER	[I.] Sparks
2ND GRAVEDIGGER	Castle

(1) *Sept. 1*

ROSENCRANTZ	Wheeler
BERNARDO	Lings
POLONIUS	Vandermere
PLAYER KING	Farrell

omitted
   MARCELLUS

HAMLET

1769 HAYMARKET (cont.)
Aug. 7 (cont.)

POLONIUS (1)	Arthur
OSRIC	Hamilton
GUILDENSTERN	Kearny
PLAYER KING (1)	Vandermere
PRIEST	Sharpless
LUCIANUS	Summers
QUEEN	Mrs Du-Bellamy
PLAYER QUEEN	Mrs White
OPHELIA	Mrs Jewell

1770 DRURY LANE
May 2

HAMLET	Cautherley
KING	Jefferson
GHOST	Bransby
HORATIO	Packer
POLONIUS (1)	Love
LAERTES	Brereton
OSRIC	Dodd
ROSENCRANTZ	J. Aickin
PLAYER KING	Burton
GUILDENSTERN	Fawcett
BERNARDO	Marr
MARCELLUS	Ackman
LUCIANUS	Hartry
1ST GRAVE-DIGGER (1)	Parsons
2ND GRAVE-DIGGER (1)	Messink
PLAYER QUEEN	Mrs Johnston
OPHELIA (1)	Miss Radley
QUEEN	Mrs Hopkins

(1) Oct. 3

POLONIUS	Baddeley
1ST GRAVEDIGGER	[F.] Waldron
2ND GRAVEDIGGER	Castle
OPHELIA	Mrs Baddeley

COVENT GARDEN
Jan. 8

HAMLET	Smith
KING	Gibson
GHOST (2)	Bensley
HORATIO	Hull
OSRIC (2)	Dyer
LAERTES (1)	Davis
POLONIUS	Shuter
1ST GRAVE-DIGGER (1, 2)	Saunders
2ND GRAVE-DIGGER (2)	Stoppelaer

(1) Feb. 5; Dec. 3

LAERTES	Perry
1ST GRAVEDIGGER	Dunstall

(2) May 22

GHOST	Clarke
OSRIC	Hamilton
1ST GRAVEDIGGER	Quick
2ND GRAVEDIGGER	[R.] Bates
added	
LUCIANUS	Fox

HAMLET

1770 COVENT GARDEN (*cont.*)
Jan. 8 (cont.)

OPHELIA	Miss Macklin
QUEEN	Mrs Ward

HAYMARKET
May 23

HAMLET	Sheridan
KING	Gardner
LAERTES	[J.] Aickin
HORATIO	Du-Bellamy
OSRIC	Hamilton
ROSENCRANTZ	Smyth
GUILDENSTERN	Dancer
POLONIUS	Weston
PLAYER KING	Farrell
MARCELLUS	Wheeler
BERNARDO	Lings
FRANCISCO	Griffith
LUCIANUS	Jacobs
1ST GRAVEDIGGER	Vandermere
2ND GRAVEDIGGER	Castle
GHOST	Sowdon
QUEEN	Mrs Jefferies
PLAYER QUEEN	Mrs White
OPHELIA	Mrs Jewell

1771 DRURY LANE
May 30

HAMLET (2)	Cautherley
KING	Jefferson
GHOST	Bransby
HORATIO	Packer
POLONIUS	Baddeley
LAERTES (2)	Brereton
OSRIC	Dodd
ROSENCRANTZ	J. Aickin
GUILDENSTERN	Fawcett
BERNARDO (1, 2)	Wright
MARCELLUS	Ackman
PLAYER KING (1)	Burton
LUCIANUS (2)	Hartry
1ST GRAVEDIGGER	Parsons
2ND GRAVE-DIGGER (1, 2)	Castle
OPHELIA (1, 2)	Mrs Baddeley
PLAYER QUEEN	Mrs Johnston
QUEEN (2)	Mrs Hopkins

(1) *Nov. 9*

PLAYER KING	Keen
2ND GRAVEDIGGER	[F.] Waldron
OPHELIA	Mrs Morland
omitted	
BERNARDO	

(2) *Dec. 23*

HAMLET	Garrick
LAERTES	[F.] Aickin
2ND GRAVEDIGGER	[F.] Waldron
OPHELIA	Mrs Abington
QUEEN	Mrs Egerton
omitted	
BERNARDO, LUCIANUS	

HAMLET

1771 COVENT GARDEN
Apr. 29

HAMLET	Smith
KING	Younger
GHOST	Bensley
HORATIO	Hull
OSRIC	Dyer
LAERTES	Perry
POLONIUS (1)	Shuter
1ST GRAVEDIGGER	Dunstall
2ND GRAVEDIGGER	Stoppelaer
OPHELIA (1)	Miss Macklin
QUEEN	Miss Miller

(1) *Sept. 25*

POLONIUS	Baddeley
OPHELIA	Mrs Mattocks
added	
ROSENCRANTZ	R. Smith
GUILDENSTERN	Thompson

[In both Pb and PA POLONIUS is assigned to Shuter. A handbill dated 'Covent Garden Theatre, Sept. 25, 1771' in the Burney collection (BM, 938. e. 2) has, 'Mr. Shuter having this day sprained his ankle . . . Mr. Baddeley of Drury Lane Theatre has . . . kindly undertaken to supply the part of Polonius'.]

1772 DRURY LANE
Jan. 8

HAMLET	Garrick
KING	Jefferson
GHOST	Bransby
HORATIO	Packer
POLONIUS	Baddeley
LAERTES (1, 2)	[F.] Aickin
OSRIC (2)	Dodd
ROSENCRANTZ (1, 2)	J. Aickin
GUILDENSTERN	Fawcett
MARCELLUS	Ackman
PLAYER KING	Keen
1ST GRAVE-DIGGER (2)	Parsons
2ND GRAVE-DIGGER (2)	[F.] Waldron
QUEEN (2)	Mrs Egerton
PLAYER QUEEN (1)	Mrs Johnston
OPHELIA (2)	Mrs Abington

(1) *Feb. 5*

LAERTES	J. Aickin
ROSENCRANTZ	Davies
PLAYER QUEEN	Mrs Reddish

[*as altered by* GARRICK]

(2) *Dec. 18, 21, 23*

LAERTES	J. Aickin
ROSENCRANTZ	Davies
QUEEN	Mrs Hopkins
OPHELIA	Mrs [T.] Smith
omitted	
OSRIC, GRAVEDIGGERS	

[In the acting version published by Bell in 1773 the cast is the same as that of these performances (OSRIC and the GRAVEDIGGERS being retained), with the following additions:

BERNARDO	Wrighten
FRANCISCO	Griffith][1]

[*The original*]
COVENT GARDEN
Apr. 21

HAMLET	Smith
KING (1)	Clarke
GHOST	Bensley
HORATIO	Hull
OSRIC	Dyer
LAERTES	Davis
POLONIUS (1)	Baddeley

(1) *Oct. 26*

KING	Gardner
POLONIUS	Shuter
1ST GRAVEDIGGER	Quick
OPHELIA	Mrs Mattocks

[1] Bell prints the cast of Garrick's alteration (OSRIC and the GRAVEDIGGERS excepted), but not the text. See pp. 188–9.

210

HAMLET

1772 COVENT GARDEN (*cont.*)
Apr. 21 (*cont.*)

1ST GRAVE-DIGGER (1)	Dunstall
2ND GRAVEDIGGER	Stoppelaer
OPHELIA (1)	Mrs Lessingham
QUEEN	Miss Miller

[*as altered by* GARRICK]

1773 DRURY LANE
Feb. 10

HAMLET	Garrick
KING	Jefferson
GHOST	Bransby
HORATIO	Packer
POLONIUS	Baddeley
LAERTES	J. Aickin
ROSENCRANTZ	Davies
GUILDENSTERN	Fawcett
MARCELLUS	Ackman
PLAYER KING	Keen
QUEEN	Mrs Hopkins
PLAYER QUEEN	Mrs Johnston
OPHELIA	Mrs [T.] Smith

[*The original*]

COVENT GARDEN
Jan. 4; May 19   (1) *Feb. 1*

HAMLET	Smith		OSRIC	[Lee] Lewes
KING	Gardner	(2) *Oct. 18; Nov. 22*		
GHOST	Bensley		OPHELIA	Miss Macklin
HORATIO	Hull			
OSRIC (1)	Dyer			
LAERTES	Davis			
POLONIUS	Shuter			
1ST GRAVEDIGGER	Dunstall			
2ND GRAVEDIGGER	Stoppelaer			
OPHELIA (2)	Mrs Mattocks			
QUEEN	Miss Miller			

[In the acting version published by Bell in 1773 the cast is the same as that of these performances, with the following additions:

ROSENCRANTZ	R. Smith
GUILDENSTERN	[Lee] Lewes
MARCELLUS	Thompson
BERNARDO	[R.] Bates
FRANCISCO	Holtom
PLAYER KING	Wignell
PLAYER QUEEN	Miss Pearce]

HAMLET

[*as altered by* GARRICK]

1774 DRURY LANE
Feb. 8; May 6

HAMLET (1)	Garrick
KING	Jefferson
GHOST	Bransby
HORATIO	Packer
POLONIUS	Baddeley
LAERTES (1)	J. Aickin
ROSENCRANTZ	Davies
GUILDENSTERN	Fawcett
MARCELLUS (1)	Ackman
PLAYER KING	Keen
LUCIANUS	Parsons
MESSENGER	Wright
BERNARDO (1)	Wrighten
FRANCISCO (1)	Griffith
QUEEN	Mrs Hopkins
PLAYER QUEEN	Mrs Johnston
OPHELIA	Mrs [T.] Smith

(1) *Oct. 4; Dec. 2, 12*

HAMLET	Smith (on *Oct.* 4 only)
LAERTES	Aickin [i.e. J. Aickin]
MARCELLUS	Wrighten
BERNARDO	Griffiths
FRANCISCO	Norris

[Referring to *Dec.* 2, *12* Genest (v. 444) erroneously has, 'Hamlet—probably by Smith'.]

[*The original*]

COVENT GARDEN
May 3

HAMLET	The Young Gentleman who performed Cyrus [in *Cyrus*, at this theatre, Apr. 11: Brunton (MS annotation on JPK)]
KING	Gardner
GHOST	Kniveton
HORATIO	Hull
OSRIC	[Lee] Lewes
LAERTES	Davis
POLONIUS	Shuter
1ST GRAVEDIGGER	Dunstall
2ND GRAVEDIGGER	Stoppelaer
OPHELIA	Mrs Mattocks
QUEEN	Miss Miller

[*as altered by* GARRICK]

1775 DRURY LANE
Oct. 23

HAMLET (1)	Smith
KING	Jefferson
GHOST	Bransby
HORATIO	Packer
POLONIUS	Baddeley
LAERTES	[J.] Aickin

(1) *Nov. 29; Dec. 8*

HAMLET	Garrick

HAMLET [as altered by GARRICK]

1775 DRURY LANE (cont.)
Oct. 23 (cont.)

ROSENCRANTZ	Davies
GUILDENSTERN	Fawcett
MARCELLUS	Wrighten
PLAYER KING	Usher
LUCIANUS	Parsons
MESSENGER	Wright
BERNARDO	Griffiths
FRANCISCO	Norris
QUEEN	Mrs Hopkins
PLAYER QUEEN	Mrs Johnston
OPHELIA	Mrs [T.] Smith

[*The original*]

COVENT GARDEN

Jan. 3

HAMLET (1, 2)	A Gentleman [L. Hallam Jr. (LC, Jan. 5); first appearance in London]
KING	Clarke
GHOST (2)	Bensley
HORATIO	Hull
LAERTES	Wroughton
OSRIC (2)	Lee Lewes
POLONIUS (2)	Shuter
1ST GRAVEDIGGER	Dunstall
2ND GRAVEDIGGER (2)	Hollingsworth
OPHELIA	Mrs Mattocks
QUEEN (1, 2)	Mrs Hull

(1) Feb. 20

HAMLET	Melmoth
QUEEN	Mrs Melmoth

(2) Dec. 29

HAMLET	Sheridan
GHOST	[F.] Aickin
OSRIC	Booth
POLONIUS	Quick
2ND GRAVEDIGGER	Jones
QUEEN	Mrs Hunter

[*as altered by* GARRICK]

1776 DRURY LANE

Apr. 27; May 30

HAMLET (1)	Garrick
KING	Jefferson
GHOST (1)	Bransby
HORATIO	Packer
POLONIUS	Baddeley
LAERTES	[J.] Aickin
ROSENCRANTZ	Davies
GUILDENSTERN	Fawcett

(1) Oct. 23; Nov. 30

HAMLET	Smith
GHOST	Farren (on *Nov. 30* only)
PLAYER KING	Hurst
LUCIANUS	[F.] Waldron
OPHELIA	Mrs Baddeley

[On *Nov. 30* PA retains Parsons as LUCIANUS.]

213

HAMLET [as altered by GARRICK]

1776 DRURY LANE (cont.)
Apr. 27; May 30 (cont.)

MARCELLUS	Wrighten
PLAYER KING (1)	Usher
LUCIANUS (1)	Parsons
MESSENGER	Wright
BERNARDO	Griffiths
FRANCISCO	Norris
QUEEN	Mrs Hopkins
PLAYER QUEEN	Mrs Johnston
OPHELIA (1)	Mrs [T.] Smith

[*The original*]
COVENT GARDEN
Oct. 17

HAMLET	Lewis
KING	Clarke
GHOST	[F.] Aickin
HORATIO	Hull
LAERTES	Whitfield
OSRIC	Lee Lewes
POLONIUS	Quick
PLAYER KING	L'Estrange
MARCELLUS	Fearon
BERNARDO	Booth
FRANCISCO	Wewitzer
ROSENCRANTZ	Robson
GUILDENSTERN	Thompson
1ST GRAVEDIGGER	Dunstall
2ND GRAVEDIGGER	Jones
OPHELIA	Mrs Mattocks
PLAYER QUEEN	Mrs Poussin
QUEEN	Mrs Jackson

CHINA HALL, ROTHERHITHE
Aug. 14

HAMLET	West
KING	Stokes
POLONIUS	Massey
ROSENCRANTZ	[S.] Johnson
GUILDENSTERN	Kenny
HORATIO	[J.] Smith
LAERTES	Russell
1ST GRAVEDIGGER	Newton
2ND GRAVEDIGGER	[P.] Lewis
GHOST	Comerford

HAMLET

1776 CHINA HALL, ROTHERHITHE (cont.)
Aug. 14 (cont.)

QUEEN	Mrs Smith
PLAYER QUEEN	Mrs Wilks
OPHELIA	Miss Taylor

[*as altered by* GARRICK]

1777 DRURY LANE
Jan. 1

HAMLET (1, 2)	Smith
KING (2)	Jefferson
GHOST (1, 2)	Bransby
HORATIO (1, 2)	Packer
POLONIUS	Baddeley
LAERTES	[J.] Aickin
ROSENCRANTZ	Davies
GUILDENSTERN (2)	Fawcett
MARCELLUS	Wrighten
PLAYER KING	Hurst
LUCIANUS	[F.] Waldron
MESSENGER	Wright
BERNARDO (1)	Griffiths
FRANCISCO (2)	Norris
QUEEN	Mrs Hopkins
PLAYER QUEEN (2)	Mrs Johnston
OPHELIA (1, 2)	Mrs Baddeley

[PA assigns the GHOST to Farren.]

(1) *Feb. 3, 8; May 5*

HAMLET	Lacy
GHOST	Reddish
HORATIO	Barrett
BERNARDO	Chaplin (on *Feb. 8* only)
OPHELIA	Mrs Mattocks (on *May 5* only)

(2) *Sept. 30; Oct. 4, 23; Nov. 3; Dec. 6, 29*

HAMLET	Henderson
KING	Packer
GHOST	[J.] Palmer
HORATIO	Farren
GUILDENSTERN	Lamash
FRANCISCO	Phillimore (on *Dec 6* only)
PLAYER QUEEN	Mrs Colles (on *Dec. 29* only)
OPHELIA	Mrs Robinson

[*The original*]

HAYMARKET
June 26, 27; July 3, 4, 10, 21; Aug. 4; Sept. 6

HAMLET	Henderson
KING (1)	Fearon
HORATIO	Davies
ROSENCRANTZ	Stevens
GUILDENSTERN (1)	Egan
POLONIUS	Edwin
LAERTES	[J.] Aickin
PLAYER KING	Griffiths
LUCIANUS	Blissett
OSRIC	R. Palmer
1ST GRAVEDIGGER	Parsons
2ND GRAVEDIGGER	Massey
GHOST	[J.] Palmer
OPHELIA	Mrs Hitchcock
PLAYER QUEEN	Mrs Poussin
QUEEN	Mrs Hunter

(1) *Sept. 15*

KING	Younger
GUILDENSTERN added	T. Davis
BERNARDO	Kenny

[PA retains Egan as GUILDENSTERN.]

HAMLET
[as altered by GARRICK]

1778 DRURY LANE
Mar. 17

HAMLET	Henderson
KING	Packer
HORATIO (2)	Farren
POLONIUS	Baddeley
LAERTES	[J.] Aickin
ROSENCRANTZ (2, 3)	Davies
GUILDENSTERN	Lamash
MARCELLUS	Wrighten
PLAYER KING (1)	Hurst
LUCIANUS	[F.] Waldron
MESSENGER	Wright
BERNARDO (2, 3)	Griffiths
FRANCISCO	Norris
GHOST	[J.] Palmer
QUEEN	Mrs Hopkins
PLAYER QUEEN	Mrs Johnston
OPHELIA (3)	Mrs Robinson

[PA assigns the PLAYER QUEEN to Mrs Colles.]

(1) *Sept. 19*

PLAYER KING	Chambers

(2) *Oct. 16*

HORATIO	Davies
ROSENCRANTZ	R. Palmer
BERNARDO	Phillimore

(3) *Dec. 15*

ROSENCRANTZ	R. Palmer
BERNARDO	Phillimore
OPHELIA	Mrs Baddeley

[The original]

COVENT GARDEN
Oct. 12

HAMLET	Reddish
KING	Clarke
GHOST	[F.] Aickin
HORATIO	Hull
LAERTES	Whitfield
OSRIC	Lee Lewes
POLONIUS	Quick
1ST GRAVEDIGGER	Dunstall
2ND GRAVEDIGGER	Jones
QUEEN	Mrs Jackson
OPHELIA	Mrs Mattocks

[as altered by GARRICK]

1779 DRURY LANE
Jan. 12

HAMLET (2, 3)	Henderson
KING (3)	Packer
HORATIO (1, 2, 3)	Davies
POLONIUS	Baddeley
LAERTES	[J.] Aickin

(1) *Feb. 6*

HORATIO	Farren

(2) *Sept. 18*

HAMLET	Smith
HORATIO	Farren
GUILDENSTERN	Fawcett

HAMLET [as altered by GARRICK]

1779 DRURY LANE (cont.)
Jan. 12 (cont.)

ROSENCRANTZ	R. Palmer
GUILDENSTERN (2)	Lamash
MARCELLUS	Wrighten
PLAYER KING (2, 3)	Hurst
LUCIANUS	[F.] Waldron
MESSENGER	Wright
BERNARDO	Phillimore
FRANCISCO	Norris
GHOST	[J.] Palmer
QUEEN	Mrs Hopkins
PLAYER QUEEN (2, 3)	Mrs Johnston
OPHELIA (3)	Mrs Robinson

(2) Sept. 18 (cont.)

PLAYER KING	Chaplin
PLAYER QUEEN	Mrs Colles

(3) Oct. 30

HAMLET	Smith
KING	Hurst
HORATIO	Farren
PLAYER QUEEN	Mrs Colles
OPHELIA	Mrs Baddeley
omitted	
PLAYER KING	

[The original]
COVENT GARDEN
Apr. 26

HAMLET	Henderson
KING (1)	Fearon
GHOST	[F.] Aickin
POLONIUS	[R.] Wilson
1ST GRAVEDIGGER	Quick
2ND GRAVEDIGGER	Jones
HORATIO	Hull
LAERTES	Whitfield
MARCELLUS (1)	Thompson
BERNARDO	Booth
OSRIC	Lee Lewes
PLAYER KING	L'Estrange
QUEEN	Mrs Jackson
OPHELIA	Mrs Mattocks

(1) Nov. 22

KING	Clarke
MARCELLUS	Fearon
added	
FRANCISCO	[R.] Smith
ROSENCRANTZ	Robson
GUILDENSTERN	Thompson
PLAYER QUEEN	Mrs Poussin

1780 DRURY LANE
Apr. 21

HAMLET	[J.] Bannister
KING (1)	Hurst
HORATIO (1)	Davies
POLONIUS	Baddeley
LAERTES	[J.] Aickin
OSRIC	Lamash
ROSENCRANTZ	R. Palmer
GUILDENSTERN	Williams
PLAYER KING	Chaplin
MARCELLUS	Wrighten
1ST GRAVEDIGGER	Parsons
2ND GRAVEDIGGER	[J.] Burton

(1) Sept. 16

KING	Packer
HORATIO	Farren
GHOST	[J.] Palmer
added	
LUCIANUS	[F.] Waldron
MESSENGER	Wright
FRANCISCO	Norris
BERNARDO	Phillimore

217

1780 DRURY LANE (cont.)
Apr. 21 (cont.)

GHOST (1)	Henry
QUEEN	Mrs Hopkins
OPHELIA	Mrs Baddeley

[The bill has, 'As originally written by Shakespeare'. Genest's remark (vi. 133), 'Garrick's alteration seems never to have been acted after this night', is correct.]

COVENT GARDEN
Apr. 25

HAMLET	Henderson
KING (1)	Fearon
GHOST	[F.] Aickin
HORATIO	Hull
LAERTES	Whitfield
MARCELLUS (1)	W. Bates
BERNARDO	Booth
OSRIC (1)	Lee Lewes
PLAYER KING	L'Estrange
ROSENCRANTZ	Robson
GUILDENSTERN	Thompson
POLONIUS	[R.] Wilson
1ST GRAVEDIGGER	Quick
2ND GRAVEDIGGER	Jones
QUEEN (1)	Mrs Jackson
PLAYER QUEEN	Mrs Poussin
OPHELIA (1)	Mrs Mattocks

(1) Oct. 26

KING	Clarke
MARCELLUS	Fearon
OSRIC	Berry
QUEEN	Mrs Webb
OPHELIA	The Young Lady Who performed Polly [in *The Beggar's Opera*, at this theatre, Sept. 21: Miss Satchell (Genest, vi. 188)]

added

FRANCISCO	[R.] Smith

HAYMARKET
Aug. 17

HAMLET	[J.] Bannister
KING	Gardner
HORATIO	Wood
ROSENCRANTZ	Stevens
GUILDENSTERN	Egan
POLONIUS	[R.] Wilson
LAERTES	[J.] Aickin
PLAYER KING	Blissett
LUCIANUS	Barrett
OSRIC	R. Palmer
MARCELLUS	Davis
1ST GRAVEDIGGER	Edwin
2ND GRAVEDIGGER	Massey
GHOST	Bensley
OPHELIA	Miss Harper
PLAYER QUEEN	Mrs Poussin
QUEEN	Miss Sherry

HAMLET

1781 DRURY LANE

Mar. 1. No parts assigned
  [See p. 72.]

May 24

HAMLET (1)	[J.] Bannister
KING	Packer
HORATIO	Farren
POLONIUS	Baddeley
LAERTES	[J.] Aickin
OSRIC	Lamash
ROSENCRANTZ	R. Palmer
GUILDENSTERN	Williames
PLAYER KING	Chaplin
MARCELLUS	Wrighten
LUCIANUS	[F.] Waldron
MESSENGER	Wright
FRANCISCO	Norris
BERNARDO	Phillimore
1ST GRAVEDIGGER	Parsons
2ND GRAVEDIGGER	[J.] Burton
GHOST	[J.] Palmer
OPHELIA	Miss Field
QUEEN	Mrs Hopkins

(1) *Sept. 25; Nov. 2*

HAMLET added	Smith
PRIEST	Griffiths

COVENT GARDEN

Jan. 1

HAMLET	Henderson
KING	Fearon
GHOST	[F.] Aickin
HORATIO	Hull
LAERTES	Whitfield
OSRIC (2)	Berry
POLONIUS (2)	[R.] Wilson
PLAYER KING	L'Estrange
MARCELLUS (1, 2)	Fearon
BERNARDO (1, 2)	Booth
FRANCISCO (1, 2)	[R.] Smith
ROSENCRANTZ	Robson
GUILDENSTERN	Thompson
1ST GRAVEDIGGER	Quick
2ND GRAVEDIGGER	Jones
QUEEN (2)	Mrs Green
PLAYER QUEEN	Mrs Poussin
OPHELIA (2)	Mrs Mattocks

(1) *Mar. 19*

MARCELLUS omitted
BERNARDO, FRANCISCO Booth

(2) *Dec. 31*

OSRIC	W. Bates
POLONIUS	Quick
MARCELLUS	Booth
BERNARDO	J. Wilson
FRANCISCO	J. Bates
QUEEN	Mrs Inchbald
OPHELIA	Miss Satchell

[Quick doubled POLONIUS and the 1ST GRAVEDIGGER.]

[The assignment of Fearon to MARCELLUS appears to be a misprint. Doubling this part with that of the KING is unlikely.]

HAMLET

1781 HAYMARKET
Aug. 7, 17, 22

HAMLET	[J.] Bannister
KING	Gardner
POLONIUS	[R.] Wilson
GHOST	Staunton
QUEEN	Miss Sherry

[The above consisted of III. iii and iv only. The entertainment on *Aug.* 7 and 17 was called *The School of Shakespeare*, and on *Aug.* 22 *The Feast of Thalia*, for descriptions of which see p. 73. In the bills Staunton's name is misprinted 'Stanton'.]

1782 DRURY LANE
Jan. 17

HAMLET	Smith
KING	Packer
HORATIO	Farren
POLONIUS	Baddeley
LAERTES	[J.] Aickin
OSRIC (2)	Lamash
ROSENCRANTZ	R. Palmer
GUILDENSTERN (2)	Williams
PLAYER KING	Chaplin
MARCELLUS	Wrighten
LUCIANUS	[F.] Waldron
MESSENGER (2)	Wright
FRANCISCO (2)	Norris
BERNARDO (2)	Phillimore
PRIEST (1, 2)	Griffiths
1ST GRAVEDIGGER	Parsons
2ND GRAVEDIGGER	[J.] Burton
GHOST (1, 2)	[J.] Palmer
OPHELIA (2)	Miss Field
QUEEN	Mrs Hopkins

(1) *Sept. 24*

GHOST added	Bensley
SAILOR omitted	Wright
PRIEST	

[Wright doubled the MESSENGER and the SAILOR.]

(2) *Dec. 11*

OSRIC	Barrymore
GUILDENSTERN	Phillimore
GHOST	Bensley
OPHELIA omitted	Miss Wheeler
MESSENGER, FRANCISCO, BERNARDO, PRIEST	

[In the acting version published by Bathurst in 1782 the cast is the same as that of this performance, with the following addition:

PLAYER QUEEN	Mrs Booth]

COVENT GARDEN
Feb. 4

HAMLET	Henderson
KING	Clarke
GHOST (1)	[F.] Aickin
HORATIO (1)	Hull
LAERTES	Whitfield
OSRIC (1, 2)	W. Bates
POLONIUS (1, 2)	Edwin
PLAYER KING (1, 2)	L'Estrange

(1) *Nov. 1*

GHOST	Hull
HORATIO	Davies
OSRIC	Wewitzer
POLONIUS	[R.] Wilson
PLAYER KING	Mahon
FRANCISCO	Helme
ROSENCRANTZ	Booth
QUEEN omitted	Mrs Hunter
BERNARDO	

220

HAMLET

1782 COVENT GARDEN (cont.)

Feb. 4 (cont.)

MARCELLUS	Fearon
BERNARDO (1, 2)	Booth
FRANCISCO (1, 2)	J. Bates
ROSENCRANTZ (1, 2)	Robson
GUILDENSTERN	Thompson
1ST GRAVEDIGGER	Quick
2ND GRAVEDIGGER	Jones
QUEEN (1, 2)	Mrs Inchbald
PLAYER QUEEN	Mrs Poussin
OPHELIA	Miss Satchell

(2) Dec. 9

OSRIC	Wewitzer
POLONIUS	[R.] Wilson
PLAYER KING	Mahon
BERNARDO	Egan
FRANCISCO	Helme
ROSENCRANTZ	Booth
QUEEN	Mrs Hunter

1783 DRURY LANE

Feb. 6; Mar. 24

HAMLET	Smith
KING	Packer
HORATIO	Farren
POLONIUS	Baddeley
LAERTES	[J.] Aickin
OSRIC	Barrymore
ROSENCRANTZ	R. Palmer
GUILDENSTERN	Williams
PLAYER KING	Chaplin
MARCELLUS	Wrighten
BERNARDO	Phillimore
LUCIANUS	[F.] Waldron
1ST GRAVEDIGGER	Parsons
2ND GRAVEDIGGER	[J.] Burton
GHOST	Bensley
OPHELIA	Miss Field
QUEEN	Mrs Hopkins

Sept. 30; Oct. 2; Nov. 15, 25

HAMLET	Kemble [first appearance, Sept. 30, in London]
KING	Packer
HORATIO	Farren
POLONIUS	Baddeley
LAERTES	Barrymore
OSRIC	R. Palmer
ROSENCRANTZ	Phillimore
GUILDENSTERN	Williams
PLAYER KING	Chaplin
MARCELLUS	Wrighten
LUCIANUS (1)	[F.] Waldron

(1) Oct. 4, 6, 13

LUCIANUS	[J.] Wilson

[On *Oct. 4* PA retains Waldron as LUCIANUS.]

(2) Oct. 28

1ST GRAVEDIGGER	Parsons

[PA assigns LUCIANUS to Wilson.]

(3) Dec. 27

1ST GRAVEDIGGER	Parsons
OPHELIA	Miss Wheeler

HAMLET

1783 DRURY LANE (*cont.*)
Sept. 30; Oct. 2; Nov. 15, 25 (cont.)

1ST GRAVE-DIGGER (2, 3)	Suett
2ND GRAVEDIGGER	[J.] Burton
GHOST	Bensley
OPHELIA (3)	Miss Field
PLAYER QUEEN	Mrs Hedges
QUEEN	Mrs Hopkins

[On *Sept. 30* both Pb and PA assign the 1ST GRAVEDIGGER to Parsons. He was ill, and Suett took his place (MS annotation on JPK; PA, Oct. 2). On *Oct. 2, 4, 6, 13, Nov. 15, 25* Suett's name is in the bills.]

COVENT GARDEN
June 3

HAMLET	Henderson
KING	Clarke
GHOST	[F.] Aickin
HORATIO (1)	Hull
LAERTES (1)	Whitfield
OSRIC (1)	Wewitzer
POLONIUS (1)	Quick
PLAYER KING (1)	Mahon
MARCELLUS	Fearon
ROSENCRANTZ (1)	Booth
GUILDENSTERN	Thompson
1ST GRAVE-DIGGER (1)	Booth
2ND GRAVEDIGGER	Jones
QUEEN (1)	Mrs Hunter
PLAYER QUEEN (1)	Mrs Poussin
OPHELIA	Miss Satchell

(1) *Oct. 3, 23, 29*

HORATIO	Whitfield
LAERTES	Davies
OSRIC	Bonnor
POLONIUS	[R.] Wilson
PLAYER KING	Booth (on *Oct. 23* only)
ROSENCRANTZ	J. Bates (on *Oct. 23* only)
1ST GRAVEDIGGER	Quick
QUEEN	Mrs Inchbald
PLAYER QUEEN	Miss Stuart

[Booth doubled ROSENCRANTZ and the 1ST GRAVEDIGGER.]

HAYMARKET
June 6

HAMLET	[J.] Williamson
KING	Gardner
HORATIO	[J.] Aickin
ROSENCRANTZ	Stevens
GUILDENSTERN	Egan
POLONIUS	Edwin
LAERTES	R. Palmer
OSRIC	Reily [first appearance in London]
MARCELLUS	Booth
1ST GRAVEDIGGER	Parsons
2ND GRAVEDIGGER	Massey
GHOST	Bensley

HAMLET

1783 HAYMARKET (cont.)
June 6 (cont.)

OPHELIA	Mrs Bannister
PLAYER QUEEN	Mrs Poussin
QUEEN	Mrs Wheatly

[This was Williamson's first appearance at this theatre. He had acted at CG in 1773. See p. 510.]

1784 DRURY LANE
Jan. 6

HAMLET	Kemble
KING	Packer
HORATIO (2)	Farren
POLONIUS	Baddeley
LAERTES	Barrymore
OSRIC	R. Palmer
ROSENCRANTZ	Phillimore
GUILDENSTERN	Williams
PLAYER KING	Chaplin
MARCELLUS	Wrighten
LUCIANUS	[F.] Waldron
1ST GRAVEDIGGER	Parsons
2ND GRAVEDIGGER	[J.] Burton
GHOST	Bensley
OPHELIA (1, 2)	Miss Wheeler
PLAYER QUEEN	Mrs Hedges
QUEEN	Mrs Hopkins

(1) Jan. 19; Mar. 8

OPHELIA	Miss Field

(2) Sept. 21; Nov. 1

HORATIO	Staunton
OPHELIA	Miss Field

COVENT GARDEN
Sept. 20

HAMLET	Henderson
KING	Clarke
GHOST	[F.] Aickin
HORATIO	Hull
LAERTES	Davies
POLONIUS	[R.] Wilson
OSRIC	Bonnor
PLAYER KING	Booth
MARCELLUS	Fearon
ROSENCRANTZ	Cubitt
GUILDENSTERN	Thompson
1ST GRAVEDIGGER	Quick
2ND GRAVEDIGGER	Jones
QUEEN	Mrs Bates
PLAYER QUEEN	Miss Stuart
OPHELIA	Mrs Bannister

[Pb erroneously assigns the 1ST GRAVEDIGGER to Jones, and the 2ND GRAVEDIGGER to Quick.]

223

1784 HAYMARKET
Sept. 13

HAMLET	Lacy
KING	Gardner
HORATIO	[J.] Aickin
ROSENCRANTZ	Stevens
GUILDENSTERN	Egan
POLONIUS	[R.] Wilson
LAERTES	Davies
PLAYER KING	Usher
MARCELLUS	Reily
OSRIC	R. Palmer
1ST GRAVEDIGGER	Parsons
2ND GRAVEDIGGER	Wewitzer
GHOST	Bensley
OPHELIA	Mrs Bannister
PLAYER QUEEN	Mrs Poussin
QUEEN	Mrs Bates

1785 DRURY LANE
Jan. 11

HAMLET	Kemble
KING	Packer
HORATIO	Staunton
POLONIUS	Baddeley
LAERTES	Barrymore
OSRIC	R. Palmer
ROSENCRANTZ	Phillimore
GUILDENSTERN	Williames
PLAYER KING	Chaplin
MARCELLUS	Wrighten
LUCIANUS	[F.] Waldron
1ST GRAVEDIGGER (1, 2)	Suett
2ND GRAVEDIGGER (2)	[J.] Burton
GHOST	Bensley
OPHELIA	Miss Field
PLAYER QUEEN	Mrs Hedges
QUEEN	Mrs Hopkins

(1) *Nov. 17*

1ST GRAVEDIGGER	Parsons

(2) *Dec. 28*

1ST GRAVEDIGGER	Parsons
2ND GRAVEDIGGER	Jones

COVENT GARDEN
Feb. 15

HAMLET	Holman
KING (1, 2)	Fearon
GHOST (1)	[F.] Aickin
HORATIO	Farren

(1) *Apr. 22*

KING	Clarke
GHOST	Hull
QUEEN added	Mrs Bates
MARCELLUS	Fearon

HAMLET

1785 COVENT GARDEN (cont.)

Feb. 15 (cont.)

LAERTES	Davies
POLONIUS (2)	Edwin
OSRIC (2)	Bonnor
PLAYER KING (2)	Booth
ROSENCRANTZ	Cubitt
GUILDENSTERN	Thompson
1ST GRAVEDIGGER	Quick
2ND GRAVE-DIGGER (2)	Jones
QUEEN (1, 2)	Mrs Inchbald
PLAYER QUEEN	Miss Stuart
OPHELIA	Mrs Bannister

(2) Sept. 23

KING	Clarke
POLONIUS	[R.] Wilson
OSRIC	[Wm.] Palmer
PLAYER KING	Gardner
2ND GRAVEDIGGER	Booth
QUEEN	Mrs Bates
added	
MARCELLUS	Fearon
BERNARDO	[T.] Kennedy
LUCIANUS	Stevens

[Both Pb and PA erroneously assign the 1ST GRAVEDIGGER to Jones, and the 2ND GRAVEDIGGER to Quick.]

HAYMARKET

June 24; July 13

HAMLET	Lacy
KING	Gardner
HORATIO	[J.] Aickin
ROSENCRANTZ	[J.] Burton
GUILDENSTERN	Booth
POLONIUS	Baddeley
LAERTES	Davies
PLAYER KING	Usher
MARCELLUS	Swords
LUCIANUS	Barrett
OSRIC	R. Palmer
1ST GRAVEDIGGER	Parsons
2ND GRAVEDIGGER	Wewitzer
GHOST	Bensley
OPHELIA	Mrs Bannister
PLAYER QUEEN	Mrs Poussin
QUEEN	Mrs Bates

1786 DRURY LANE

May 15

HAMLET	Kemble
KING (1)	Packer
HORATIO	Staunton
POLONIUS	Baddeley
LAERTES	Barrymore
OSRIC	R. Palmer
ROSENCRANTZ	Phillimore
GUILDENSTERN	Williames
PLAYER KING	Chaplin

(1) Sept. 19

KING	Gardner
2ND GRAVEDIGGER	Jones
PLAYER QUEEN	Miss Tidswell
OPHELIA	Mrs Forster
added	
BERNARDO	[J.] Wilson

1786 DRURY LANE *(cont.)*

May 15 (cont.)

MARCELLUS	Wrighten
LUCIANUS	[F.] Waldron
1ST GRAVEDIGGER	Parsons
2ND GRAVE-	
DIGGER (1)	[J.] Burton
GHOST	Bensley
QUEEN	Mrs Hopkins
PLAYER QUEEN (1)	Mrs Hedges
OPHELIA (1)	Mrs Siddons

1787 DRURY LANE

Jan. 11

HAMLET (2)	Kemble
KING	Packer
HORATIO (2, 3)	Staunton
POLONIUS	Baddeley
LAERTES	Barrymore
OSRIC	R. Palmer
ROSENCRANTZ	Phillimore
GUILDENSTERN	Williames
PLAYER KING	Chaplin
MARCELLUS (1, 2, 3)	Wrighten
LUCIANUS	[F.] Waldron
1ST GRAVEDIGGER	Suett
2ND GRAVEDIGGER	[J.] Burton
GHOST	Bensley
OPHELIA	Mrs Forster
PLAYER QUEEN	Miss Tidswell
QUEEN (1, 2)	Mrs Ward

(1) *Sept. 18*

MARCELLUS	Benson
QUEEN	Mrs Hopkins
added	
BERNARDO	[J.] Wilson
GENTLEMAN	Fawcett
FRANCISCO	Spencer
MESSENGER	Alfred
SAILOR	Jones

(2) *Oct. 29; Dec. 3*

HAMLET	Wroughton (on *Dec. 3* only)
HORATIO	Whitfield
MARCELLUS	[J.] Wilson
QUEEN	Mrs Hopkins

[On *Dec. 3* both Pb and PA assign HAMLET to Kemble. But he was ill, and Wroughton substituted for him (W, Dec. 4).]

(3) *Dec. 31*

HORATIO	Whitfield
MARCELLUS	[J.] Wilson

HAYMARKET

May 18

HAMLET	Browne [first appearance in London]
KING	[S.] Kemble
POLONIUS	Moss
GRAVEDIGGER	Moss
LAERTES	Baker
HORATIO	[J.] Johnson
OSRIC (1)	Meadows
GHOST	[J.] Williamson

(1) *May 21*

omitted
OSRIC

HAMLET

1787 HAYMARKET (cont.)
May 18 (cont.)
QUEEN	Mrs Bulkley
OPHELIA	Mrs [S.] Kemble

[Moss doubled POLONIUS and the GRAVEDIGGER.]

1788 DRURY LANE
June 4

HAMLET (1)	A Gentleman [Seymour (MS annotation on JPK)]
KING	Packer
HORATIO	Whitfield
POLONIUS	Baddeley
LAERTES	Barrymore
OSRIC	R. Palmer
ROSENCRANTZ	Phillimore
GUILDENSTERN	Williams
PLAYER KING	Chaplin
MARCELLUS (1)	[J.] Wilson
LUCIANUS (1)	[F.] Waldron
1ST GRAVE-DIGGER (1)	Suett
2ND GRAVEDIGGER	[J.] Burton
GHOST	Bensley
OPHELIA	Mrs Forster
PLAYER QUEEN	Miss Tidswell
QUEEN	Mrs Hopkins

(1) Sept. 30

HAMLET	Kemble
MARCELLUS	Benson
LUCIANUS	Hollingsworth
1ST GRAVEDIGGER added	Parsons
BERNARDO	[J.] Wilson

1789 COVENT GARDEN
Nov. 16

HAMLET	Holman
KING	Gardner
GHOST	[F.] Aickin
HORATIO	Farren
LAERTES	Davies
POLONIUS	Edwin
OSRIC	Bernard
PLAYER KING	Thompson
MARCELLUS	Powel
BERNARDO	Evatt
LUCIANUS	Cubitt
ROSENCRANTZ	Egan [Jr.]
GUILDENSTERN	Macready
1ST GRAVEDIGGER	Quick
2ND GRAVEDIGGER	Milburne

1789 COVENT GARDEN (cont.)

Nov. 16 (cont.)

OPHELIA	Mrs Achmet
PLAYER QUEEN	Mrs Lefevre
QUEEN	Mrs Pope

HAYMARKET

June 1

HAMLET	A Gentleman [Lloyd (EM, June 1789, 488); first appearance in London]
KING	[S.] Kemble
POLONIUS	Moss
LAERTES	Iliff
HORATIO	[J.] Johnson
OSRIC	Edwin [Jr.]
ROSENCRANTZ	Chapman
GUILDENSTERN	Chambers
FRANCISCO	Abbot
MARCELLUS	Reeve
PLAYER KING	Usher
1ST GRAVEDIGGER	Powel
2ND GRAVEDIGGER	Barrett
GHOST	[J.] Williamson
QUEEN	Mrs Barresford
PLAYER QUEEN	Mrs Lefevre
OPHELIA	Mrs [S.] Kemble

1790 COVENT GARDEN

June 2, 7

HAMLET	Holman
KING	Hull
GHOST	[F.] Aickin
HORATIO	Farren
LAERTES (1)	Davies
POLONIUS (1)	Edwin
OSRIC	Bernard
PLAYER KING	Thompson
MARCELLUS	Powel
BERNARDO	Evatt
LUCIANUS	Cubitt
ROSENCRANTZ (1)	Egan [Jr.]
GUILDENSTERN (1)	Macready
1ST GRAVEDIGGER	Quick
2ND GRAVEDIGGER	Milburne
QUEEN (1)	Mrs Pope
PLAYER QUEEN	Mrs Lefevre
OPHELIA (1)	Mrs Billington

(1) *Dec. 6, 13*

LAERTES	Fennell
POLONIUS	[R.] Wilson
ROSENCRANTZ	Macready
GUILDENSTERN	Davies
QUEEN	Mrs Bernard
OPHELIA	Mrs Esten

HAMLET

1791 COVENT GARDEN
Oct. 17

HAMLET	Holman
KING	Hull
GHOST	[F.] Aickin
HORATIO	Farren
LAERTES	Harley
POLONIUS	[R.] Wilson
OSRIC	Marshall
PLAYER KING	Thompson
MARCELLUS	Powel
BERNARDO	Evatt
LUCIANUS	Cubitt
ROSENCRANTZ	Macready
GUILDENSTERN	Davies
1ST GRAVEDIGGER	Quick
2ND GRAVEDIGGER	Milburne
QUEEN	Mrs Fawcett
PLAYER QUEEN	Mrs Platt
OPHELIA	Mrs Esten

1792 COVENT GARDEN
Nov. 5   (1) *Dec. 27*

HAMLET	Holman
KING	Hull
GHOST (1)	[F.] Aickin
HORATIO	Farren
LAERTES (1)	Harley
POLONIUS	Munden
OSRIC	Marshall
PLAYER KING	Thompson
MARCELLUS	Powel
BERNARDO	Evatt
LUCIANUS	Cubitt
ROSENCRANTZ (1)	Macready
GUILDENSTERN	Davies
1ST GRAVEDIGGER	Quick
2ND GRAVEDIGGER	Rees
QUEEN	Mrs Fawcett
PLAYER QUEEN	Mrs Platt
OPHELIA	Mrs Esten

GHOST	Harley
LAERTES	Macready
ROSENCRANTZ	Evatt

[PA indicates none of these changes. Evatt doubled BERNARDO and ROSENCRANTZ. Munden's name is in the bill as POLONIUS.]

[Both Pb and PA assign POLONIUS to Wilson. But he was indisposed, and Munden substituted for him (PA, Nov. 6; TM, Dec. 1792, 153).]

1793 COVENT GARDEN
Oct. 9, 16, 21; Nov. 4, 15; Dec. 16   (1) *Oct. 30*

HAMLET (1)	Holman
GHOST	Farren

HAMLET	Pope

229

HAMLET

1793 COVENT GARDEN (*cont.*)
Oct. 9, 16, 21; Nov. 4, 15; Dec. 16 (*cont.*)

HORATIO	Harley
LAERTES	Middleton
KING	Powel
POLONIUS	Munden
OSRIC	Bernard
ROSENCRANTZ	Macready
GUILDENSTERN	Davies
PLAYER KING	Thompson
MARCELLUS	Evatt
1ST GRAVEDIGGER	Quick
2ND GRAVEDIGGER	Rees
OPHELIA	Miss Poole [first appearance, Oct. 9, on the stage]
PLAYER QUEEN	Mrs Platt
QUEEN	Mrs Pope

1794 COVENT GARDEN
Jan. 9, 28

HAMLET (2)	Holman
GHOST	Farren
HORATIO	Harley
LAERTES	Middleton
KING	Powel
OSRIC	Bernard
POLONIUS	Munden
ROSENCRANTZ (2)	Macready
GUILDENSTERN (2)	Davies
MARCELLUS (2, 3, 4)	Evatt
1ST GRAVEDIGGER	Quick
2ND GRAVEDIGGER	Rees
OPHELIA (4)	Miss Poole
QUEEN (4)	Mrs Pope

(1) *Feb. 21*
added
PLAYER KING	Thompson
PLAYER QUEEN	Mrs Platt

(2) *May 10*
HAMLET	Pope
omitted	
ROSENCRANTZ, GUILDENSTERN, MARCELLUS	

(3) *Sept. 29; Oct. 13*
MARCELLUS	Claremont

(4) *Dec. 29*
MARCELLUS	Claremont
OPHELIA	Mrs Mountain
QUEEN	Miss Morris

1795 COVENT GARDEN
Jan. 12

HAMLET	Holman
GHOST	Farren
HORATIO	Harley
LAERTES	Middleton
KING	Powel
OSRIC	Bernard
POLONIUS	Munden
ROSENCRANTZ	Macready

230

1795 COVENT GARDEN (cont.)
Jan. 12 (cont.)

GUILDENSTERN	Davies
MARCELLUS	Claremont
1ST GRAVEDIGGER	Quick
2ND GRAVEDIGGER	Rees
OPHELIA	Mrs Mountain
QUEEN	Mrs Pope

Oct. 19   (1) Oct. 26; Nov. 2

HAMLET	A Young Gentleman [Cooper (Genest, vii. 263); first appearance in London]		omitted SAILOR, GENTLEMAN [On *Nov.* 2 Cooper's name is in the bill.]
GHOST	Toms		
HORATIO	Harley		
LAERTES	Middleton		
KING	Richardson		
OSRIC	Bernard		
POLONIUS	Munden		
ROSENCRANTZ	Macready		
GUILDENSTERN	Claremont		
MARCELLUS	[D.] Williamson		
FRANCISCO	Farley		
BERNARDO	Cross		
PRIEST	Powel		
PLAYER KING	Thompson		
LUCIANUS	Davenport		
SAILOR (1)	Ledger		
GENTLEMAN (1)	Abbot		
1ST GRAVEDIGGER	Quick		
2ND GRAVEDIGGER	Rees		
OPHELIA	Mrs Mountain		
PLAYER QUEEN	Mrs Platt		
QUEEN	Mrs Pope		

HAYMARKET
Aug. 18

HAMLET	[J.] Bannister
GHOST	Bensley
KING	Benson
POLONIUS	Suett
LAERTES	C. Kemble
HORATIO	Davies
OSRIC	Wathen
1ST GRAVEDIGGER	Fawcett [Jr]

HAMLET

1795 HAYMARKET (cont.)
Aug. 18 (cont.)

2ND GRAVEDIGGER	[G.] Waldron
QUEEN	Mrs Harlowe
PLAYER QUEEN	Miss Tidswell
OPHELIA	Mrs [S.] Kemble

[MP, Aug. 17, and O, Aug. 18, both assign HORATIO to Barrymore.]

1796 DRURY LANE
Apr. 29

KING	Packer
HAMLET (1, 2, 3)	Wroughton
POLONIUS	Dodd
HORATIO	Whitfield
LAERTES	C. Kemble
ROSENCRANTZ	Caulfield
GUILDENSTERN	Trueman
OSRIC (1, 2, 3)	[J.] Bannister
MARCELLUS (2, 3)	Benson
BERNARDO	Phillimore
GHOST (1, 2, 3)	Bensley
PLAYER KING (2, 3)	Maddocks
LUCIANUS (2, 3)	Hollingsworth
1ST GRAVEDIGGER	King
2ND GRAVEDIGGER	[J.] Burton
QUEEN (1, 2, 3)	Mrs Siddons
OPHELIA	Mrs Jordan
PLAYER QUEEN (2, 3)	Miss Tidswell

(1) May 12

HAMLET	Mrs Powell
OSRIC	R. Palmer
GHOST	[J.] Palmer
QUEEN	Miss Morris

(2) May 27

HAMLET	Holman
OSRIC	R. Palmer
GHOST	[J.] Palmer
QUEEN	Mrs Powell
omitted	
MARCELLUS, PLAYER KING,	
LUCIANUS, PLAYER QUEEN	

(3) June 2

HAMLET	[J.] Palmer
OSRIC	R. Palmer
GHOST	[J.] Aickin
QUEEN	Mrs Powell
omitted	
SAME as May 27	

Oct. 24

KING	Packer
HAMLET	Kemble
POLONIUS	Suett
HORATIO	Whitfield
LAERTES	Barrymore
ROSENCRANTZ	Caulfield
GUILDENSTERN	Trueman
OSRIC	R. Palmer
GENTLEMAN	Evans
MARCELLUS (1, 2, 3)	Dignum
BERNARDO	Webb
FRANCISCO	[J.] Cooke
GHOST	Wroughton
PLAYER KING	Maddocks
LUCIANUS	Wewitzer
1ST GRAVE-DIGGER (3)	King
2ND GRAVEDIGGER	Hollingsworth

(1) Oct. 31

MARCELLUS	Holland
omitted	
PLAYER QUEEN	

(2) Nov. 7

MARCELLUS	Holland

(3) Nov. 21; Dec. 5

MARCELLUS	Holland
1ST GRAVEDIGGER	Dowton

1796 DRURY LANE (cont.)
Oct. 24 (cont.)

QUEEN	Mrs Powell
OPHELIA	Mrs Jordan
PLAYER QUEEN (1)	Miss Tidswell

COVENT GARDEN
Sept. 12

HAMLET	Holman
KING	Powel
GHOST	Toms
POLONIUS	Munden
HORATIO	Macready
LAERTES	Middleton
OSRIC	Farley
ROSENCRANTZ	Haymes
MARCELLUS	Davenport
GUILDENSTERN	Claremont
PLAYER KING	Thompson
LUCIANUS	Wilde
1ST GRAVEDIGGER	Quick
2ND GRAVEDIGGER	Rees
OPHELIA	Mrs Mountain
PLAYER QUEEN	Mrs Platt
QUEEN	Mrs Pope

HAYMARKET
Aug. 11

HAMLET	[J.] Bannister
GHOST	[J.] Aickin
KING	Caulfield
POLONIUS	Suett
LAERTES	C. Kemble
HORATIO	Davies
ROSENCRANTZ	Trueman
GUILDENSTERN	[J.] Palmer Jr.
PLAYER KING	Usher
LUCIANUS	[F.] Waldron
BERNARDO	Abbot
MARCELLUS	Lyons
OSRIC	R. Palmer
1ST GRAVEDIGGER	Fawcett [Jr.]
2ND GRAVEDIGGER	[G.] Waldron
QUEEN	Mrs Harlowe
PLAYER QUEEN	Miss Tidswell
OPHELIA	Mrs [S.] Kemble

HAMLET

1797 DRURY LANE

May 3

KING (1)	Caulfield
HAMLET (1)	Kemble
POLONIUS (1)	Suett
HORATIO	Whitfield
LAERTES	Barrymore
ROSENCRANTZ (1)	Phillimore
GUILDENSTERN	Trueman
OSRIC	R. Palmer
GENTLEMAN	Evans
MARCELLUS	Holland
BERNARDO (1)	Webb
FRANCISCO (1)	[J.] Cooke
GHOST	Wroughton
PLAYER KING	Maddocks
LUCIANUS	Wewitzer
1ST GRAVE-DIGGER (1)	Dowton
2ND GRAVEDIGGER	Hollingsworth
QUEEN (1)	Mrs Powell
OPHELIA	Mrs Jordan
PLAYER QUEEN (1)	Miss Tidswell

Oct. 5

KING	Packer
HAMLET	Kemble
POLONIUS	Suett
HORATIO (2, 3, 4)	Barrymore
LAERTES	C. Kemble
ROSENCRANTZ	Caulfield
GUILDENSTERN	Trueman
OSRIC (2, 3, 4)	R. Palmer
GENTLEMAN (1, 2, 3)	Evans
PRIEST (1, 2)	Webb
MARCELLUS (2, 3, 4)	Holland
BERNARDO (2, 3)	Wentworth
GHOST	Wroughton
PLAYER KING (2)	Maddocks
LUCIANUS (2, 3)	Wewitzer
1ST GRAVE-DIGGER (3)	King
2ND GRAVEDIGGER	Hollingsworth
FRANCISCO (1, 2, 3, 4)	[J.] Cooke
1ST SAILOR (1, 2)	Simpson
2ND SAILOR (1, 2)	Fisher
QUEEN	Mrs Powell
OPHELIA	Mrs Jordan
PLAYER QUEEN (2, 3)	Miss Tidswell

(1) May 25

KING	Packer
HAMLET	Mrs Powell
POLONIUS	Dowton
ROSENCRANTZ	Caulfield
1ST GRAVEDIGGER	King
QUEEN	Miss Morris

omitted
    BERNARDO, FRANCISCO, PLAYER QUEEN

(1) Oct. 9

omitted
    GENTLEMAN, PRIEST, FRANCISCO, SAILORS

(2) Oct. 16, 23

HORATIO	Holland
OSRIC	Russell (on *Oct. 23* only)

omitted
    GENTLEMAN, PRIEST, MARCELLUS, BERNARDO, PLAYER KING, LUCIANUS, FRANCISCO, SAILORS, PLAYER QUEEN

(3) Nov. 13

HORATIO	Holland
OSRIC	Russell
LUCIANUS	Wathen
1ST GRAVEDIGGER	Dowton

omitted
    GENTLEMAN, MARCELLUS, BERNARDO, FRANCISCO, PLAYER QUEEN

(4) Nov. 27

HORATIO	Holland
OSRIC	Russell
MARCELLUS	Dignum

omitted
    FRANCISCO

234

HAMLET

1797 COVENT GARDEN
Sept. 25

HAMLET	Holman
GHOST	Murray
POLONIUS	Munden
KING	Waddy
HORATIO	Toms
LAERTES	A Young Gentleman [Wheatley (EM, Oct. 1797, 262); first appearance on the stage]
OSRIC	Farley
ROSENCRANTZ	Clarke
MARCELLUS	Davenport
GUILDENSTERN	Claremont
PLAYER KING	Thompson
LUCIANUS	Wilde
1ST GRAVEDIGGER	Powel
2ND GRAVEDIGGER	Rees
OPHELIA	Mrs Mountain
PLAYER QUEEN	Mrs Platt
QUEEN	Miss Chapman

1798 DRURY LANE
Jan. 24; Feb. 8, 15; Mar. 1, 20; (1) *Oct. 4, 16*
Apr. 24; May 14

KING	Packer	HORATIO	Holland
HAMLET	Kemble	GHOST	Barrymore
POLONIUS	Dowton	1ST GRAVEDIGGER added	King
HORATIO (1)	Barrymore	PRIEST	Webb
LAERTES	C. Kemble	MARCELLUS	Surmont
ROSENCRANTZ	Caulfield	BERNARDO	Wentworth
GUILDENSTERN	Trueman	FRANCISCO	Evans
OSRIC	R. Palmer		
GHOST (1)	Wroughton		
1ST GRAVE-DIGGER (1)	Wewitzer		
2ND GRAVEDIGGER	Hollingsworth		
QUEEN	Mrs Powell		
OPHELIA	Mrs Jordan		

COVENT GARDEN
Apr. 28   (1) *Sept. 17, 24*

HAMLET (1)	[H.] Johnston	HAMLET	Holman
GHOST	Murray	HORATIO	Betterton
POLONIUS	Munden	1ST GRAVEDIGGER	Powel
KING	Waddy	OPHELIA	Mrs [H.] Johnston
HORATIO (1)	Egerton	added	
LAERTES	Whitfield	MARCELLUS	Davenport

HAMLET

1798 COVENT GARDEN (cont.)

Apr. 28 (cont.)

OSRIC	Farley
ROSENCRANTZ	Clarke
1ST GRAVE-DIGGER (1)	Quick
2ND GRAVEDIGGER	Rees
OPHELIA (1)	Mrs Mountain
QUEEN	Miss Chapman

(1) Sept. 17, 24 (cont.)

GUILDENSTERN	Claremont
PLAYER KING	Thompson
LUCIANUS	Wilde
PLAYER QUEEN	Mrs Platt

HAYMARKET

Sept. 3

HAMLET	[H.] Johnston
GHOST	Barrymore
KING	Caulfield
POLONIUS	Munden
LAERTES	C. Kemble
HORATIO	Davies
ROSENCRANTZ	Trueman
GUILDENSTERN	[J.] Palmer Jr.
PLAYER KING	Davenport
BERNARDO	Abbot
MARCELLUS	Lyons
MESSENGER	Chippendale
PRIEST	Usher
SAILOR	Ledger
OSRIC	R. Palmer
1ST GRAVEDIGGER	Suett
2ND GRAVEDIGGER	[G.] Waldron
QUEEN	Mrs Harlowe
PLAYER QUEEN	Mrs Edward
OPHELIA	Mrs [H.] Johnston [first appearance in London]

1799 DRURY LANE

Feb. 11, 18

KING	Packer
HAMLET	Kemble
POLONIUS	Dowton
HORATIO	Holland
LAERTES	C. Kemble
ROSENCRANTZ (2)	Caulfield
GUILDENSTERN	Trueman
OSRIC (2, 3)	R. Palmer
PRIEST	Webb
MARCELLUS	Surmont
BERNARDO	Wentworth
FRANCISCO	Evans

(1) Apr. 18

1ST GRAVEDIGGER	Wathen

[LUCIANUS is not listed in the bill; presumably Wewitzer acted it.]

(2) Sept. 19

ROSENCRANTZ	Clarke
OSRIC	Palmer [i.e. R. Palmer]
2ND GRAVEDIGGER	Sparks
LUCIANUS	Ryder
OPHELIA added	Miss Biggs
PLAYER KING	Maddocks
PLAYER QUEEN	Miss Tidswell

HAMLET

1799 DRURY LANE (cont.)

Feb. 11, 18 (cont.)

GHOST	Barrymore
1ST GRAVEDIGGER (1, 3)	King
2ND GRAVEDIGGER (2)	Hollingsworth
LUCIANUS (2, 3)	[R.] Chatterley
QUEEN	Mrs Powell
OPHELIA (2, 3)	Mrs Jordan

(3) Oct. 10, 28; Nov. 4, 11

OSRIC	Palmer [i.e. R. Palmer]
1ST GRAVEDIGGER	Wewitzer
LUCIANUS	Sparks
OPHELIA	Miss Biggs

added on *Oct. 10, Nov. 4* only
SAME as *Sept. 19*

[LUCIANUS is listed in neither of these two bills. Kemble Mem., Feb. 11: 'Mr. Wewitzer never came to act Lucianus, so the Prompter's Call-boy [identified as Chatterley in Kemble's listing, at the beginning of the season, of the theatre's servants] acted it'—as did Wewitzer, presumably, on *Feb. 18*.]

1800 DRURY LANE

Jan. 13

KING	Packer
HAMLET	Kemble
POLONIUS	Dowton
HORATIO	Holland
LAERTES	C. Kemble
ROSENCRANTZ	Caulfield
GUILDENSTERN	Trueman
OSRIC	[R.] Palmer
PRIEST	Webb
MARCELLUS	Surmont
BERNARDO	Wentworth
FRANCISCO	Evans
GHOST	Barrymore
1ST GRAVEDIGGER	Wewitzer
2ND GRAVEDIGGER	Hollingsworth
QUEEN	Mrs Powell
OPHELIA	Miss Biggs
PLAYER QUEEN	Miss Tidswell

Sept. 16

KING	Packer
HAMLET	Kemble
POLONIUS	Dowton
HORATIO	Holland
LAERTES (1)	J. Palmer [Jr.]
ROSENCRANTZ	Caulfield
GUILDENSTERN	Trueman
OSRIC	[R.] Palmer
PRIEST	Webb
MARCELLUS	Surmont
BERNARDO (1)	Wentworth
FRANCISCO	Evans

(1) Oct. 20; Nov. 15; Dec. 29

LAERTES	C. Kemble
BERNARDO	Chippendale
GHOST	Wroughton
1ST GRAVEDIGGER	Suett (on *Dec. 29* only)
2ND GRAVEDIGGER	Grimaldi
OPHELIA	Mrs Stephen Kemble (on *Oct. 20* only)

omitted
    SAILORS (on *Dec. 29* only), MESSENGER

237

1800 DRURY LANE (cont.)

Sept. 16 (cont.)

GHOST (I)	Cory
1ST GRAVE-DIGGER (I)	King
2ND GRAVE-DIGGER (I)	Chippendale
PLAYER KING	Maddocks
LUCIANUS	Sparks
1ST SAILOR (I)	Fisher
2ND SAILOR (I)	Johnson
MESSENGER (I)	Evans
QUEEN	Mrs Powell
OPHELIA (I)	Miss Biggs
PLAYER QUEEN	Miss Tidswell

[The bill assigns BERNARDO to Archer. But on this night he was acting at Brighton, and Wentworth substituted for him (*Dramatic Censor*, Nov. 1800, 226). Evans doubled FRANCISCO and the MESSENGER.]

COVENT GARDEN

Sept. 29; Oct. 3

HAMLET	Brunton [Jr.]
GHOST	Murray
POLONIUS	Munden
KING	Waddy
HORATIO	Whitfield
LAERTES	Betterton
OSRIC	Farley
MARCELLUS	Davenport
GUILDENSTERN	Claremont
ROSENCRANTZ	Klanert
PLAYER KING	Thompson
LUCIANUS	Wilde
1ST GRAVEDIGGER	Emery
2ND GRAVEDIGGER	Simmons
OPHELIA	Mrs H. Johnston
PLAYER QUEEN	Miss Leserve
QUEEN	Miss Chapman

HENRY IV, PART I

(1) 'With Alterations, as perform'd at the Theatres.'

1763   C. Hitch [&c.].

Following are the principal omissions:

Act I. i. 18b–30a (Henry's resolution to visit the Holy Land).

Act II. i. 52–end (Gadshill and the Chamberlain); *iii. 49–67a* (Hotspur's dreams of 'iron wars'); *iv. 418–540* (the play extempore). Preceding *iv. 299* is inserted a new line: 'Ha! ha! ha! d'ye think I did not know you?'.

HENRY IV, PART I

Act III. i entire (Glendower and Mortimer); *ii. 50–87a* (Henry's scorn of Richard II's mingling 'his royalty with capering fools').
Act IV. iv entire (the Archbishop of York).
Act V. ii. 6–23 (Worcester's reasons for refusing the King's offer to arbitrate); *iv. 1–58* (the Prince of Wales saves his father's life); *v. 16–33* (Henry pardons Douglas).

It may be noted that *III. i* was restored at CG in 1751 and 1769, and at DL from 1762 to 1765, and in 1770.

(2) 'With Alterations, As performed at the Theatres-Royal in Drury-Lane and Covent-Garden.'

    1770   J. Rivington [&c.].

(3) 'As Performed at the Theatre-Royal, Drury-Lane. Regulated from the Prompt-Book.'

    1773   John Bell.

(4) 'Marked with the Variations in the Manager's Book, at the Theatre-Royal in Drury-Lane.'

    1785   C. Bathurst [&c.].

(5) 'Taken from the Manager's Book, at the Theatre Royal, Covent-Garden.'

    n.d. [*c.* 1788]   R. Butters.

All these are identical with (1).
See also Odell, ii. 40–41.

1751 COVENT GARDEN

Jan. 11

FALSTAFF	Quin	
HENRY	Sparks	
PRINCE OF WALES	Ryan	
WORCESTER	Bransby	
NORTHUMBERLAND	Redman	
MORTIMER (1)	Dyer	
BLUNT (1)	Cushing	
DOUGLAS	Anderson	
PRINCE JOHN (1)	Miss Hippisley	
VERNON	Gibson	
GLENDOWER (1)	Ridout	
WESTMORLAND	Usher	
1ST CARRIER	Arthur	
2ND CARRIER	Dunstall	
FRANCIS	Collins	
GADSHILL	Bencraft	
BARDOLPH	Marten	
HOTSPUR	Barry	
HOSTESS	Mrs Macklin	
LADY PERCY	Mrs Vincent	

(1) Feb. 8, 21; Mar. 9

BLUNT Elrington omitted
MORTIMER, GLENDOWER, and on Feb. 21, Mar. 9 also omitted PRINCE JOHN

1751 HAYMARKET
?

[The actual date of this performance I have been unable to trace. Referring on Dec. 10, 1751 to a forthcoming performance of *Othello* at this theatre on Dec. 28, DA notes that it was to be undertaken by the same company that had acted *Henry IV, Part I* at the Haymarket 'last winter', the part of OTHELLO 'by the Gentleman who play'd Hotspur'.]

1752 COVENT GARDEN
Mar. 16

FALSTAFF	Quin
HENRY	Sparks
PRINCE OF WALES	Ryan
VERNON	Gibson
WORCESTER	Bransby
NORTHUMBERLAND	Redman
WESTMORLAND	Usher
DOUGLAS	Anderson
BLUNT	Cushing
1ST CARRIER	Arthur
2ND CARRIER	Dunstall
FRANCIS	Collins
GADSHILL	Holtom
BARDOLPH	Marten
HOTSPUR	Barry
HOSTESS	Mrs Macklin
LADY PERCY	Mrs Vincent

1753 COVENT GARDEN
Mar. 19

FALSTAFF	Quin
HENRY	Sparks
PRINCE OF WALES	Ryan
VERNON	Usher
WORCESTER	Bransby
NORTHUMBERLAND	Redman
WESTMORLAND	Ricard
DOUGLAS	Anderson
BLUNT	Cushing
1ST CARRIER	Arthur
2ND CARRIER	Dunstall
FRANCIS	Collins
GADSHILL	Bencraft
BARDOLPH	Marten
HOTSPUR	Barry
HOSTESS	Mrs Macklin
LADY PERCY	Mrs Vincent

HENRY IV, PART I

1755 COVENT GARDEN
Apr. 10, 12; Nov. 6

FALSTAFF (1)	Shuter
HENRY	Sparks
PRINCE OF WALES	Ryan
VERNON	Gibson
WORCESTER	Ridout
1ST CARRIER	Arthur
2ND CARRIER (1)	Dunstall
HOTSPUR (3)	Smith
LADY PERCY	Mrs Bellamy
HOSTESS	Mrs Pitt

(1) *May 3*

FALSTAFF	Dunstall
2ND CARRIER	Costollo

(2) *Oct. 14*
added

FRANCIS	Collins

(3) *Dec. 1*

HOTSPUR	Barry

1756 COVENT GARDEN
Jan. 5; May 10

FALSTAFF	Shuter
HENRY	Sparks
PRINCE OF WALES	Ryan
VERNON	Gibson
WORCESTER	Ridout
1ST CARRIER	Arthur
2ND CARRIER	Dunstall
HOTSPUR	Barry
LADY PERCY (1)	Mrs Bellamy
HOSTESS	Mrs Pitt

(1) *Oct. 8; Nov. 24*

LADY PERCY	Mrs Dyer

added on *Nov. 24* only

PRINCE JOHN	Miss Mullart
NORTHUMBERLAND	Redman
WESTMORLAND	Holtom
DOUGLAS	Anderson
BLUNT	Cushing
PETO	R. Smith
GADSHILL	Bencraft
FRANCIS	Bennet
BARDOLPH	Stoppelaer
SHERIFF	Wignell

1757 COVENT GARDEN
Jan. 25

FALSTAFF	Shuter
HENRY	Sparks
PRINCE JOHN	Miss Mullart
NORTHUMBERLAND	Redman
WESTMORLAND	Holtom
DOUGLAS	Anderson
PRINCE OF WALES	Ryan
WORCESTER	Ridout
BLUNT	Cushing
PETO	R. Smith
GADSHILL	Bencraft
FRANCIS	Collins
VERNON	Gibson
1ST CARRIER	Arthur
2ND CARRIER	Dunstall
BARDOLPH	Stoppelaer
SHERIFF	Wignell
HOTSPUR (1)	Smith
HOSTESS	Mrs Pitt
LADY PERCY (1, 2)	Mrs Dyer

(1) *Apr. 23*

HOTSPUR	Barry
LADY PERCY	Mrs Vincent

(2) *Oct. 5; Nov. 17*

LADY PERCY	Mrs Vincent

5365.2   241   R

1758 COVENT GARDEN

Jan. 12; May 16

FALSTAFF	Shuter
HENRY	Sparks
PRINCE JOHN	Miss Mullart
NORTHUMBERLAND	Redman
WESTMORLAND	Holtom
DOUGLAS	Anderson
PRINCE OF WALES (2)	Ryan
WORCESTER	Ridout
BLUNT	Cushing
PETO	R. Smith
GADSHILL	Bencraft
FRANCIS	Collins
VERNON	Gibson
1ST CARRIER (2)	Arthur
2ND CARRIER	Dunstall
BARDOLPH	Stoppelaer
SHERIFF	Wignell
HOTSPUR (1, 2)	Smith
HOSTESS	Mrs Pitt
LADY PERCY	Mrs Vincent

(1) *Apr. 11*

FALSTAFF	Shuter
HENRY	Sparks
HOTSPUR	Barry

No other parts assigned

(2) *Oct. 4, 21; Nov. 29*

PRINCE OF WALES	Ross
1ST CARRIER	Bennet
HOTSPUR	Clarke

1759 COVENT GARDEN

Jan. 5

FALSTAFF	Shuter
HENRY	Sparks
PRINCE OF WALES	Ross
PRINCE JOHN	Miss Mullart
NORTHUMBERLAND	Redman
WESTMORLAND	Holtom
DOUGLAS	Anderson
WORCESTER	Ridout
BLUNT (1, 2)	Cushing
PETO	R. Smith
GADSHILL	Bencraft
FRANCIS	Collins
VERNON	Gibson
1ST CARRIER	Bennet
2ND CARRIER (1, 2)	Barrington
BARDOLPH (2)	Stoppelaer
SHERIFF (2)	Wignell
HOTSPUR	Clarke
HOSTESS	Mrs Pitt
LADY PERCY (1)	Mrs Vincent

(1) *May 1*

BLUNT	Perry
2ND CARRIER	Dunstall
LADY PERCY	Mrs Stephens

(2) *Nov. 28*

BLUNT	Perry
2ND CARRIER	Dunstall
BARDOLPH	Wignell
SHERIFF	Buck

1760 DRURY LANE

Apr. 28

FALSTAFF	Burton
HENRY	Havard
PRINCE OF WALES	Palmer
PRINCE JOHN	Miss Bride
WESTMORLAND	Ackman
NORTHUMBERLAND	Scrase
BLUNT	Mozeen
HOTSPUR	Holland
WORCESTER	Bransby
VERNON	Blakes
DOUGLAS	Austin
POINS	Packer
BARDOLPH	Clough
GADSHILL	Marr
PETO	Atkins
1ST CARRIER	Yates
2ND CARRIER	Philips
FRANCIS	[H.] Vaughan
HOSTESS	Mrs Bradshaw
LADY PERCY	Miss Pritchard

COVENT GARDEN

Jan. 7

FALSTAFF	Shuter
HENRY	Sparks
PRINCE OF WALES	Ross
WORCESTER	Ridout
VERNON	Gibson
NORTHUMBERLAND	Redman
DOUGLAS	Anderson
WESTMORLAND	Holtom
BLUNT	Perry
PETO	R. Smith
GADSHILL (1, 2)	Bencraft
FRANCIS	Collins
BARDOLPH	Stoppelaer
1ST CARRIER	Bennet
2ND CARRIER	Dunstall
SHERIFF	Wignell
HOTSPUR	Clarke
HOSTESS	Mrs Pitt
LADY PERCY	Mrs Vincent

(1) *Feb. 9*

GADSHILL	Buck

(2) *Apr. 9; May 16; Dec. 5, 19*

GADSHILL	Buck
added	
PRINCE JOHN	Miss Mullart

(3) *Oct. 10*

added
PRINCE JOHN   Miss Mullart

1761 COVENT GARDEN

Jan. 15

FALSTAFF	Shuter
HENRY	Sparks
PRINCE OF WALES	Ross
PRINCE JOHN (2)	Miss Mullart
NORTHUMBERLAND	Redman
WESTMORLAND	Holtom
DOUGLAS	Anderson
WORCESTER (1, 2)	Ridout
BLUNT	Perry
PETO	R. Smith
GADSHILL	Buck
FRANCIS	Collins
VERNON	Gibson
1ST CARRIER	Bennet
2ND CARRIER	Dunstall
BARDOLPH (2)	Stoppelaer
SHERIFF (2)	Wignell
HOTSPUR	Clarke
HOSTESS	Mrs Pitt
LADY PERCY	Mrs Vincent

(1) *Mar. 28*

WORCESTER	Hull

(2) *Sept. 14*

WORCESTER	Hull
BARDOLPH	Wignell
SHERIFF	Davis

omitted
    PRINCE JOHN

1762 DRURY LANE

Apr. 30

FALSTAFF (1)	Yates
HENRY (1)	Davies
PRINCE OF WALES	Palmer
GLENDOWER (1)	King
VERNON	Blakes
WORCESTER	Bransby
DOUGLAS (1)	Kennedy
MORTIMER	Castle
POINS	Packer
HOTSPUR	Holland
NORTHUMBER- LAND (1)	Scrase
WESTMORLAND	Ackman
SHERIFF	Fox
BARDOLPH	Clough
1ST CARRIER	Moody
2ND CARRIER (1)	Weston
FRANCIS	[H.] Vaughan
HOSTESS	Mrs Bradshaw
LADY PERCY	Mrs Palmer

(1) *Sept. 25; Oct. 2*

FALSTAFF	Love
HENRY	Havard
GLENDOWER	Stevens (on *Sept. 25* only) / Lee (on *Oct. 2* only)
DOUGLAS	Parsons
2ND CARRIER	[H.] Vaughan (on *Sept. 25* only)

added
    BLUNT   Mozeen

omitted on *Oct. 2* only
    NORTHUMBERLAND, 2ND CARRIER

[On *Sept. 25* Vaughan doubled the 2ND CARRIER and FRANCIS. In the acting version published by Hitch in 1763 the cast is the same as that on *Sept. 25*, with the following addition:
    PRINCE JOHN   Master Burton]

244

1762 COVENT GARDEN
May 4   (1) *Sept. 24*

FALSTAFF	Shuter	HENRY	Sparks
HENRY (I)	Gibson	WESTMORLAND	Davis
PRINCE OF WALES	Ross	BARDOLPH	[P.] Lewis
WORCESTER	Hull	SHERIFF	Wignell
NORTHUMBERLAND	Redman	added	
WESTMORLAND (I)	Holtom	PRINCE JOHN	Young
DOUGLAS	Anderson	POINS	White
VERNON	Gibson		
BLUNT	Perry		
PETO	R. Smith		
GADSHILL	Buck		
FRANCIS	Collins		
1ST CARRIER	Bennet		
2ND CARRIER	Dunstall		
BARDOLPH (I)	Wignell		
SHERIFF (I)	Davis		
HOTSPUR	Smith		
HOSTESS	Mrs Pitt		
LADY PERCY	Mrs Vincent		

[PA erroneously retains Davis as the SHERIFF.]

[That Gibson acted both HENRY and VERNON is unlikely. Pb omits VERNON; the assignment to Gibson in PA seems to be a misprint.]

1763 DRURY LANE
Nov. 9, 16

FALSTAFF	Love
HENRY	Havard
PRINCE OF WALES	Obrien
GLENDOWER	Lee
VERNON	Jackson
WORCESTER	Bransby
MORTIMER	Castle
POINS	Packer
DOUGLAS	Parsons
BLUNT	J. Palmer
NORTHUMBERLAND	Burton
WESTMORLAND	Ackman
SHERIFF	Stevens
BARDOLPH	Clough
1ST CARRIER	Moody
2ND CARRIER	Weston
FRANCIS	[H.] Vaughan
HOTSPUR	Holland
HOSTESS	Mrs Bradshaw
LADY PERCY	Mrs Palmer

HENRY IV, PART I

1763 COVENT GARDEN
Sept. 26

FALSTAFF	Shuter
HENRY	Sparks
PRINCE JOHN	Miss Valois
NORTHUMBERLAND	Redman
WESTMORLAND	Davis
DOUGLAS	Anderson
PRINCE OF WALES	Ross
WORCESTER	Hull
BLUNT	Perry
PETO	R. Smith
GADSHILL	Buck
FRANCIS	Stamper
VERNON	Gibson
POINS	White
1ST CARRIER	Dunstall
2ND CARRIER	Bennet
BARDOLPH	[P.] Lewis
SHERIFF	Wignell
HOTSPUR	Smith
LADY PERCY	Mrs Vincent
HOSTESS	Mrs Pitt

[Genest (v. 52) erroneously assigns BARDOLPH to Lee Lewes, who first appeared at this theatre in 1767.]

1764 DRURY LANE
Oct. 17

FALSTAFF	Love
HENRY	Havard
PRINCE OF WALES	Palmer
GLENDOWER	Lee
VERNON	Jackson
WORCESTER	Bransby
MORTIMER	Castle
POINS	Packer
DOUGLAS	Parsons
NORTHUMBERLAND	Burton
WESTMORLAND	Ackman
MESSENGER	Fox
BARDOLPH	Clough
1ST CARRIER	Moody
2ND CARRIER	Granger
FRANCIS	[H.] Vaughan
BLUNT	Strange
HOTSPUR	Holland
HOSTESS	Mrs Bradshaw
LADY PERCY	Mrs Palmer

[PA assigns MORTIMER to Baddeley.]

1764 COVENT GARDEN
Jan. 25

FALSTAFF	Shuter
HENRY	Sparks
PRINCE JOHN (1)	Miss Valois
NORTHUMBERLAND (1)	Redman
WESTMORLAND	Davis
DOUGLAS	Anderson
PRINCE OF WALES	Ross
WORCESTER	Hull
BLUNT	Perry
PETO (1)	R. Smith
GADSHILL (1)	Buck
FRANCIS	Cushing
VERNON	Gibson
POINS	White
1ST CARRIER	Bennet
2ND CARRIER	Dunstall
BARDOLPH (1)	[P.] Lewis
SHERIFF (1)	Wignell
HOTSPUR	Smith
LADY PERCY (1)	Mrs Vincent
HOSTESS	Mrs Pitt

(1) *Sept. 26*

LADY PERCY   Mrs Godwin [first appearance in London]
omitted
PRINCE JOHN, NORTHUMBERLAND, PETO, GADSHILL, BARDOLPH, SHERIFF

1765 DRURY LANE
May 21

FALSTAFF	Love
HENRY	Havard
PRINCE OF WALES	Palmer
GLENDOWER	Lee
VERNON	Jackson
WORCESTER	Bransby
MORTIMER	Adcock
POINS	Packer
DOUGLAS	Parsons
NORTHUMBERLAND	Burton
WESTMORLAND	Ackman
BARDOLPH	Clough
BLUNT	Strange
1ST CARRIER	Moody
2ND CARRIER	Granger
FRANCIS	[H.] Vaughan
SHERIFF	Fox
HOTSPUR	Holland
HOSTESS	Mrs Bradshaw
LADY PERCY	Mrs Palmer

1765 COVENT GARDEN
Nov. 27

FALSTAFF	Shuter
HENRY	Gibson
WESTMORLAND	Gardner
DOUGLAS	Anderson
PRINCE OF WALES	Ross
WORCESTER	Hull
BLUNT	Perry
FRANCIS	Morgan
VERNON	Davis
POINS	Cushing
1ST CARRIER	Dunstall
2ND CARRIER	Bennet
HOTSPUR	Smith
LADY PERCY	Mrs Vincent
HOSTESS	Mrs Pitt

1766 DRURY LANE
Jan. 9

FALSTAFF	Love
HENRY	Havard
PRINCE OF WALES	Palmer
VERNON	Lee
WORCESTER	Bransby
BLUNT	Strange
POINS	Packer
DOUGLAS	[F.] Aickin
NORTHUMBERLAND	Burton
WESTMORLAND	Ackman
BARDOLPH	Clough
1ST CARRIER	Moody
2ND CARRIER	Parsons
FRANCIS	[H.] Vaughan
HOTSPUR	Holland
HOSTESS	Mrs Bradshaw
LADY PERCY	Mrs Palmer

1769 DRURY LANE
Oct. 23

FALSTAFF	Love
HENRY	[C.] Bannister
PRINCE OF WALES	Cautherley
VERNON	Hurst
POINS	Packer
WORCESTER	Bransby

HENRY IV, PART I

1769 DRURY LANE (*cont.*)

Oct. 23 (*cont.*)

BLUNT	[J.] Palmer
DOUGLAS	Fawcett
NORTHUMBERLAND	Burton
WESTMORLAND	Ackman
BARDOLPH	Clough
1ST CARRIER	Moody
2ND CARRIER	Parsons
FRANCIS	[F.] Waldron
HOTSPUR	Holland
HOSTESS	Mrs Bradshaw
LADY PERCY	Mrs Stephens

COVENT GARDEN

Dec. 29

HOTSPUR	Smith
HENRY	Gibson
WORCESTER	Hull
PRINCE OF WALES	Wroughton
VERNON	Davis
DOUGLAS	Gardner
FALSTAFF	Shuter
POINS	Perry
WESTMORLAND	Cushing
BARDOLPH	Wignell
BLUNT	R. Smith
FRANCIS	Hamilton
1ST CARRIER	Dunstall
2ND CARRIER	Quick
HOSTESS	Mrs Pitt
LADY PERCY	Mrs Bulkley

[In the acting version published by Rivington in 1770 the cast is the same as that of this performance, with the following additions:

MORTIMER	[Lee] Lewes
GLENDOWER	Morris
PRINCE JOHN	Miss Cokayne
NORTHUMBERLAND	Redman
GADSHILL	T. Smith
PETO	Wild]

1770 DRURY LANE

Jan. 9

HOTSPUR	Barry
HENRY	[C.] Bannister
PRINCE OF WALES	Cautherley

(1) *Feb. 24*

POINS	J. Aickin
LADY PERCY	Mrs Stephens
omitted	
BLUNT	

249

1770 DRURY LANE (cont.)

Jan. 9 (cont.)

VERNON	Hurst
POINS (1)	Packer
WORCESTER	Bransby
BLUNT (1)	[J.] Palmer
DOUGLAS	Fawcett
NORTHUMBERLAND	Burton
WESTMORLAND	Ackman
BARDOLPH	Clough
1ST CARRIER	Moody
2ND CARRIER	Parsons
FRANCIS	[F.] Waldron
FALSTAFF	Love
HOSTESS	Mrs Bradshaw
LADY PERCY (1)	Mrs [S.] Barry

[In the acting version published by Rivington in 1770 the cast is the same as that of this performance, with the following additions:

MORTIMER	Castle
GLENDOWER	Keen
PRINCE JOHN	J. Burton
GADSHILL	Wrighten
PETO	Watkins]

1774 COVENT GARDEN

Mar. 15; May 7

HOTSPUR	Smith
HENRY	Clarke
PRINCE OF WALES	Lewis
PRINCE JOHN (1)	Harris
DOUGLAS (1)	Owenson
WESTMORLAND (1)	Thompson
BLUNT (1)	R. Smith
VERNON (2)	Hull
WORCESTER	Gardner
POINS	[Lee] Lewes
BARDOLPH (1, 2)	Davis
FRANCIS (1)	Cushing
1ST CARRIER	Dunstall
2ND CARRIER	Quick
FALSTAFF	Shuter
HOSTESS	Mrs Pitt
LADY PERCY	Mrs Hartley

(1) *Apr. 8*

omitted
   PRINCE JOHN, DOUGLAS, WEST-
   MORLAND, BLUNT, BARDOLPH,
   FRANCIS

(2) *Apr. 30*

VERNON	Davis
BARDOLPH	Baker

[The bills have, 'With . . . the Restoration of a Capital Scene from the Original'. This was probably the play extempore in II. iv, which was (Genest, ii. 220) usually omitted. On *Mar. 15* PA assigns HENRY to Younger.]

250

1775 COVENT GARDEN
May 17

HOTSPUR	Whitfield
HENRY	Clarke
PRINCE OF WALES	Lewis
WESTMORLAND	Thompson
BLUNT	Booth
VERNON	Hull
WORCESTER	Fearon
POINS	Lee Lewes
BARDOLPH	Baker
FRANCIS	Cushing
1ST CARRIER	Dunstall
2ND CARRIER	Quick
FALSTAFF	Shuter
HOSTESS	Mrs Pitt
LADY PERCY	Mrs Hartley

1776 COVENT GARDEN
May 10

HOTSPUR	Wroughton
HENRY	Clarke
PRINCE OF WALES	Lewis
WESTMORLAND	Thompson
BLUNT	Booth
VERNON	Hull
WORCESTER	Fearon
POINS	Lee Lewes
BARDOLPH	Davis
FRANCIS	Cushing
1ST CARRIER	Dunstall
2ND CARRIER	Quick
FALSTAFF	Shuter
HOSTESS	Mrs Pitt
LADY PERCY	Mrs Hartley

HAYMARKET
Sept. 17

FALSTAFF	Shuter
HOTSPUR	[J.] Aickin
HENRY	L'Estrange
WORCESTER	Fearon
POINS	Davies
NORTHUMBERLAND	[S.] Johnson
WESTMORLAND	Griffiths
VERNON	R. Palmer
BLUNT	Wright

HENRY IV, PART I

1776 HAYMARKET (cont.)
Sept. 17 (cont.)

BARDOLPH	Lloyd
GADSHILL	Stephens
1ST CARRIER	Parsons
2ND CARRIER	[F.] Waldron
PRINCE OF WALES	[J.] Palmer
HOSTESS	Mrs Love
LADY PERCY	Miss [E.] Hopkins

1777 DRURY LANE
Oct. 17, 21; Nov. 5, 10, 20; Dec. 10, 30

HOTSPUR	Smith
HENRY	Bensley
WORCESTER	[J.] Aickin
VERNON	Farren
NORTHUMBERLAND	Packer
BLUNT	Hurst
PRINCE JOHN	Lamash
WESTMORLAND	Wrighten
DOUGLAS	Chaplin
POINS	R. Palmer
1ST CARRIER	Moody
2ND CARRIER	Parsons
FRANCIS	[F.] Waldron
BARDOLPH	Wright
SHERIFF	Griffiths
GADSHILL	Holcroft
PETO	Nash
PRINCE OF WALES	[J.] Palmer
FALSTAFF	Henderson
HOSTESS	Mrs Bradshaw
LADY PERCY	Mrs Cuyler

HAYMARKET
Feb. 11

FALSTAFF	[S.] Johnson
HENRY	A Gentleman [unidentified; first appearance on the stage]
PRINCE OF WALES	Frodsham
WORCESTER	Comerford
NORTHUMBERLAND	Kenny
HOTSPUR	West
HOSTESS	Mrs Fowler
LADY PERCY	Mrs West

[The bill states that this was Mrs West's first appearance in London. In 1776 she had acted at CHINA HALL, ROTHERHITHE.]

1777 HAYMARKET (cont.)

July 24, 28, 31; Aug. 2, 13, 21

FALSTAFF	Henderson
HOTSPUR (1)	[J.] Aickin
HENRY	Younger
WESTMORLAND	Egan
BLUNT	T. Davis
VERNON	Davies
WORCESTER	Fearon
POINS	R. Palmer
BARDOLPH	Massey
PETO	Kenny
GADSHILL	Besford
FRANCIS	Edwin
1ST CARRIER	[T.] Jackson
2ND CARRIER	Blissett
PRINCE OF WALES	[J.] Palmer
HOSTESS	Mrs Love
LADY PERCY	Mrs Colles

(1) Sept. 13

HOTSPUR	[W.] Smith

[On *July 24* PA misprints Mrs Colles's name as 'Collins'.]

HAMMERSMITH

Oct. 28. No parts assigned

1778 DRURY LANE

Jan. 21; Mar. 21

HOTSPUR	Smith
HENRY	Bensley
WORCESTER	[J.] Aickin
VERNON	Farren
NORTHUMBERLAND	Packer
BLUNT (1)	Hurst
PRINCE JOHN	Lamash
WESTMORLAND	Wrighten
DOUGLAS	Chaplin
POINS	R. Palmer
1ST CARRIER	Moody
2ND CARRIER	Parsons
FRANCIS	[F.] Waldron
SHERIFF (1)	Griffiths
GADSHILL (1)	Holcroft
PETO (1)	Nash
BARDOLPH	Wright
PRINCE OF WALES	[J.] Palmer
FALSTAFF	Henderson
HOSTESS	Mrs Bradshaw
LADY PERCY	Mrs Cuyler

(1) Sept. 22; Oct. 30; Dec. 28

BLUNT	Fawcett (on *Sept. 22* only)
omitted	
SHERIFF, GADSHILL, PETO	

HENRY IV, PART I

1779 DRURY LANE
Jan. 22

HOTSPUR	Smith
HENRY	Bensley
WORCESTER	[J.] Aickin
VERNON	Farren
NORTHUMBERLAND	Packer
BLUNT	Hurst
PRINCE JOHN (2)	Lamash
WESTMORLAND	Wrighten
DOUGLAS	Chaplin
POINS	R. Palmer
1ST CARRIER	Moody
2ND CARRIER	Parsons
FRANCIS	[F.] Waldron
BARDOLPH	Wright
PRINCE OF WALES (2)	[J.] Palmer
FALSTAFF (2)	Henderson
HOSTESS	Mrs Bradshaw
LADY PERCY (1)	Mrs Cuyler

(1) *May 19*

LADY PERCY	Mrs Colles

(2) *Dec. 20*

PRINCE JOHN	Master Benson
PRINCE OF WALES	Brereton
FALSTAFF	[J.] Palmer

COVENT GARDEN
Apr. 24

HOTSPUR (1)	Wroughton
HENRY (1)	Bensley
PRINCE OF WALES (1)	[J.] Bannister
WESTMORLAND	Thompson
BLUNT (1)	Booth
VERNON	Hull
WORCESTER	Fearon
POINS	Robson
BARDOLPH (1)	Egan
FRANCIS (1)	Cushing
1ST CARRIER (1)	Wewitzer
2ND CARRIER	Messink
FALSTAFF	Henderson
HOSTESS	Mrs Pitt
LADY PERCY	Mrs Hartley

(1) *Oct. 23; Nov. 24; Dec. 21*

HOTSPUR	Peile (on *Oct. 23* only)
HENRY	Clarke
PRINCE OF WALES	Lewis (on *Oct. 23, Nov. 24* only)
BLUNT	Whitfield
BARDOLPH	Booth
FRANCIS	Edwin
1ST CARRIER	Jones (on *Dec. 21* only)

added
DOUGLAS	L'Estrange

[On *Nov. 24* PA assigns the 1ST CARRIER to Jones.]

1780 DRURY LANE
Jan. 14; Feb. 12

HOTSPUR (2)	Smith
HENRY	Bensley
PRINCE OF WALES	Brereton
WORCESTER	[J.] Aickin
VERNON (2)	Farren
NORTHUMBERLAND	Packer

(1) *May 23*

2ND CARRIER	[J.] Burton

(2) *Oct. 2*

HOTSPUR	Farren
VERNON	Williams
BLUNT	Fawcett
HOSTESS	Mrs Love

1780 DRURY LANE (cont.)

Jan. 14; Feb. 12 (cont.)

BLUNT (2)	Hurst
PRINCE JOHN	Master Benson
WESTMORLAND	Wrighten
DOUGLAS (2)	Chaplin
POINS	R. Palmer
1ST CARRIER	Moody
2ND CARRIER (1)	Parsons
FRANCIS	[F.] Waldron
BARDOLPH (2)	Wright
FALSTAFF	[J.] Palmer
HOSTESS (2)	Mrs Bradshaw
LADY PERCY	Mrs Cuyler

(2) Oct. 2 (cont.)

omitted
DOUGLAS, BARDOLPH

COVENT GARDEN

Oct. 2

FALSTAFF	Henderson
HENRY	Clarke
PRINCE OF WALES	Lewis
WESTMORLAND	Thompson
BLUNT	W. Bates
VERNON	Whitfield
WORCESTER	Fearon
NORTHUMBERLAND	Webb
SHERIFF	Egan
POINS	Robson
FRANCIS	Edwin
BARDOLPH	Booth
DOUGLAS	L'Estrange
1ST CARRIER	Jones
2ND CARRIER	Messink
HOTSPUR	Wroughton
HOSTESS	Mrs Pitt
LADY PERCY	Mrs Lewis

1781 COVENT GARDEN

Dec. 11

FALSTAFF	Henderson
HENRY	Clarke
PRINCE OF WALES	Lewis
BLUNT	W. Bates
VERNON	Whitfield
WORCESTER	Fearon
NORTHUMBERLAND	Webb
SHERIFF	J. Wilson

HENRY IV, PART I

1781 COVENT GARDEN (cont.)
Dec. 11 (cont.)

POINS	Robson
FRANCIS	Edwin
BARDOLPH	Booth
DOUGLAS	L'Estrange
WESTMORLAND	Thompson
1ST CARRIER	Jones
2ND CARRIER	Egan
HOTSPUR	Wroughton
HOSTESS	Mrs Pitt
LADY PERCY	Mrs Inchbald

HAYMARKET
Aug. 7

FALSTAFF	Digges
FRANCIS	Edwin
POINS	R. Palmer
PETO	Painter
BARDOLPH	Massey
GADSHILL	Ledger
1ST CARRIER	Stevens
2ND CARRIER	Barrett
PRINCE OF WALES	[J.] Palmer
HOSTESS	Mrs Love

[The above consisted of parts of scenes i and iv from Act II. The entertainment on this evening was called *The School of Shakespeare*, for a description of which see p. 73. PA assigns GADSHILL to Kenny.]

1782 COVENT GARDEN
Jan. 29

FALSTAFF	Henderson
HENRY (1)	Clarke
PRINCE OF WALES	Lewis
VERNON	Whitfield
WORCESTER	Fearon
BLUNT (2)	J. Bates
NORTHUMBER- LAND (2)	Webb
SHERIFF (2)	J. Wilson
POINS (2)	Robson
FRANCIS (2)	Edwin
BARDOLPH (2)	Booth
DOUGLAS (2)	L'Estrange
WESTMORLAND (2)	Thompson
1ST CARRIER (2)	Egan

(1) *May 1*

HENRY	Hull
LADY PERCY	Mrs Lewis

(2) *Nov. 30*

BLUNT	Booth
POINS	Davies
FRANCIS	W. Bates
BARDOLPH	Jones
DOUGLAS	Mahon
LADY PERCY	Mrs Lewis

added
    GADSHILL   Ledger
    PETO   Stevens
omitted
    NORTHUMBERLAND, SHERIFF, WESTMORLAND, CARRIERS

256

1782 COVENT GARDEN (cont.)
Jan. 29 (cont.)

2ND CARRIER (2)	Jones
HOTSPUR	Wroughton
HOSTESS	Mrs Pitt
LADY PERCY (1, 2)	Mrs Inchbald

[PA assigns BLUNT to W. Bates.]

1783 COVENT GARDEN
Jan. 4

FALSTAFF	Henderson
HENRY	Clarke
PRINCE OF WALES (1, 2)	Mahon
VERNON	Whitfield
WORCESTER	Fearon
POINS	Davies
FRANCIS	Edwin
BLUNT	Booth
BARDOLPH	Jones
DOUGLAS (1, 2)	W. Bates
GADSHILL	Ledger
PETO	Stevens
HOTSPUR	Wroughton
HOSTESS	Mrs Pitt
LADY PERCY (1)	Mrs Lewis

(1) *May 29*

PRINCE OF WALES	Lewis
DOUGLAS	Mahon
LADY PERCY	Mrs Whitfield

(2) *Oct. 17; Nov. 17*

PRINCE OF WALES	Lewis
DOUGLAS added	Mahon
1ST CARRIER	[R.] Wilson (on *Oct. 17* only) / [R.] Bates (on *Nov. 17* only)
2ND CARRIER	Wewitzer

1784 COVENT GARDEN
Jan. 12

FALSTAFF	Henderson
HENRY (1, 2)	Hull
PRINCE OF WALES	Lewis
VERNON (2)	Whitfield
WORCESTER	Fearon
POINS (2)	Davies
FRANCIS	Edwin
BLUNT (1)	Booth
1ST CARRIER	[R.] Bates
2ND CARRIER (1)	Wewitzer
BARDOLPH (1)	Jones
DOUGLAS (1, 2)	Mahon
GADSHILL (1)	Ledger
PETO (1)	Stevens
HOTSPUR	Wroughton
HOSTESS	Mrs Pitt
LADY PERCY (1, 2)	Mrs Inchbald

(1) *May 25*

HENRY	Clarke
BLUNT	Chalmers
2ND CARRIER	Booth
LADY PERCY omitted	Mrs Lewis
BARDOLPH, DOUGLAS, GADSHILL, PETO	

(2) *Sept. 29; Oct. 29*

HENRY	Clarke
VERNON	Davies
POINS	Chalmers (on *Sept. 29* only) / [T.] Kennedy (on *Oct. 29* only)
DOUGLAS	Cubitt
LADY PERCY	Mrs Lewis (on *Oct. 29* only)

HENRY IV, PART I

1785 COVENT GARDEN
Sept. 26; Oct. 22

FALSTAFF	Henderson
PRINCE OF WALES	Lewis
HENRY	Clarke
VERNON	Farren
WORCESTER	Fearon
WESTMORLAND	Thompson
NORTHUMBERLAND	Gardner
POINS	Davies
FRANCIS	Wewitzer
BLUNT	[Wm.] Palmer
BARDOLPH	[R.] Bates
DOUGLAS	Cubitt
1ST CARRIER	Booth
2ND CARRIER	[T.] Kennedy
GADSHILL	Ledger
PETO	Stevens
HOTSPUR	Holman
HOSTESS	Mrs Pitt
LADY PERCY	Mrs Lewis

1786 COVENT GARDEN
Nov. 22

FALSTAFF	Ryder
HENRY	Hull
PRINCE OF WALES	Lewis
VERNON	Farren
WORCESTER	Fearon
POINS	Davies
FRANCIS	Edwin
BLUNT	Macready
BARDOLPH	Swords
DOUGLAS	Cubitt
1ST CARRIER	Wewitzer
2ND CARRIER	Booth
GADSHILL	Ledger
PETO	Stevens
HOTSPUR	Holman
HOSTESS	Mrs Pitt
LADY PERCY	Mrs Wells

(1) *Dec. 18*. No parts assigned [See p. 83.]

HAYMARKET
July 21

FALSTAFF	Mrs Webb
HOTSPUR	A Gentleman [unidentified; first appearance on the stage]
HENRY	Bensley

1786 HAYMARKET (cont.)
July 21 (cont.)

WESTMORLAND	Usher
BLUNT	Reily
PRINCE JOHN	Master Farley
WORCESTER	Gardner
POINS	R. Palmer
VERNON	Davies
BARDOLPH	Wewitzer
FRANCIS	Barrett
1ST CARRIER	Parsons
2ND CARRIER	[J.] Burton
PRINCE OF WALES	[J.] Palmer
HOSTESS	Mrs Love
LADY PERCY	Mrs Cuyler

1787 COVENT GARDEN
Nov. 5; Dec. 31

FALSTAFF	Ryder
HENRY	[F.] Aickin
PRINCE OF WALES	Lewis
VERNON	Farren
WORCESTER	Fearon
POINS	Davies
FRANCIS	Edwin
BLUNT	Macready
BARDOLPH	Rock
DOUGLAS	Cubitt
1ST CARRIER	Wewitzer
2ND CARRIER	Booth
GADSHILL	Ledger
PETO	Stevens
HOTSPUR	Pope
HOSTESS	Mrs Pitt
LADY PERCY	Mrs Inchbald

1788 COVENT GARDEN
Oct. 8

FALSTAFF	Ryder
HENRY	[F.] Aickin
PRINCE OF WALES	Lewis
VERNON	Farren
WORCESTER	Fearon
POINS	Davies
FRANCIS	Edwin
BLUNT	Macready
BARDOLPH	Rock

HENRY IV, PART I

1788 COVENT GARDEN (cont.)
Oct. 8 (cont.)

DOUGLAS	Cubitt
1ST CARRIER	Wewitzer
2ND CARRIER	Booth
GADSHILL	Ledger
PETO	Stevens
HOTSPUR	Pope
HOSTESS	Mrs Pitt
LADY PERCY	Mrs Inchbald

1789 COVENT GARDEN
Jan. 12

FALSTAFF	Ryder
HENRY	[F.] Aickin
PRINCE OF WALES	Lewis
VERNON	Farren
WORCESTER (1)	Fearon
POINS	Davies
FRANCIS	Edwin
BLUNT	Macready
BARDOLPH	Rock
DOUGLAS (1)	Cubitt
1ST CARRIER (1)	Wewitzer
2ND CARRIER (1)	Booth
GADSHILL (1)	Ledger
PETO (1)	Stevens
HOTSPUR (1)	Pope
HOSTESS	Mrs Pitt
LADY PERCY (1)	Mrs Inchbald

(1) *Nov. 2*

WORCESTER	Powel
DOUGLAS	Egan [Jr.]
1ST CARRIER	Bernard
2ND CARRIER	Blanchard
HOTSPUR	Fennell
LADY PERCY	Miss Chapman

omitted
  GADSHILL, PETO

1790 COVENT GARDEN
Feb. 22

FALSTAFF (1)	Ryder
HENRY (1)	[F.] Aickin
PRINCE OF WALES	Lewis
VERNON	Farren
WORCESTER	Powel
POINS	Davies
FRANCIS	Edwin
BLUNT	Macready
BARDOLPH	Rock
DOUGLAS	Egan [Jr.]
1ST CARRIER	Bernard
2ND CARRIER	Blanchard
HOTSPUR	Holman
HOSTESS	Mrs Pitt
LADY PERCY	Miss Chapman

(1) *Apr. 30*

FALSTAFF	[F.] Aickin
HENRY	Hull

HENRY IV, PART I

1791 DRURY LANE (company at KING'S, HAYMARKET)
Nov. 7

HENRY	Bensley		
PRINCE OF WALES	Wroughton		
PRINCE JOHN	Bland		
WORCESTER	[J.] Aickin		
NORTHUMBERLAND	Packer		
HOTSPUR	Kemble		
DOUGLAS	Caulfield		
VERNON	Barrymore		
WESTMORLAND	Fawcett		
BLUNT	Whitfield		
FALSTAFF	[J.] Palmer		
POINS	R. Palmer		
GADSHILL	[J.] Cooke		
PETO	Benson		
BARDOLPH	Alfred		
FRANCIS (1)	[J.] Bannister		
1ST CARRIER	Moody		
2ND CARRIER	[J.] Burton		
SHERIFF	Maddocks		
TRAVELLER	Lyons		
MESSENGER	Banks		
LADY PERCY	Mrs Powell		
HOSTESS	Mrs Hopkins		

(1) *Dec. 5*

FRANCIS	Suett

COVENT GARDEN
Jan. 3

FALSTAFF	[R.] Wilson
HENRY	[F.] Aickin
PRINCE OF WALES	Lewis
VERNON	Farren
WORCESTER	Powel
POINS	Davies
FRANCIS	Blanchard
BLUNT	Macready
BARDOLPH	Rock
DOUGLAS	Marshall
1ST CARRIER (1)	Bernard
2ND CARRIER	Cross
HOTSPUR	Holman
HOSTESS	Mrs Pitt
LADY PERCY	Miss Chapman

(1) *Nov. 24*

1ST CARRIER	Munden

HAYMARKET
June 20, 29

HENRY	[J.] Williamson
PRINCE OF WALES	[J.] Palmer Jr. [first appearance, June 20, on the stage]

261

HENRY IV, PART I

1791 HAYMARKET (cont.)
June 20, 29 (cont.)

PRINCE JOHN	Bland
WORCESTER	[J.] Aickin
NORTHUMBERLAND	Chapman
HOTSPUR	Bensley
DOUGLAS	Evatt
VERNON	Davies
WESTMORLAND	Usher
BLUNT	Iliff
FALSTAFF	[J.] Palmer
POINS	R. Palmer
GADSHILL	Ledger
PETO	Farley
BARDOLPH	Rock
1ST CARRIER	Wewitzer
2ND CARRIER	[J.] Burton
FRANCIS	Barrett
LADY PERCY	Mrs Cuyler
HOSTESS	Mrs Webb

1792 HAYMARKET
Aug. 6, 10

HENRY	[J.] Aickin			
PRINCE OF WALES	[J.] Williamson			
PRINCE JOHN	Miss DeCamp			
WORCESTER	Davies			
NORTHUMBERLAND	[J.] Johnson			
HOTSPUR	Bensley			
DOUGLAS	Evatt			
VERNON	Bland			
WESTMORLAND	Usher			
BLUNT (1)	Cleveland			
FALSTAFF	King			
POINS	R. Palmer			
GADSHILL	Ledger			
PETO (1)	Farley			
BARDOLPH	Cubitt			
1ST CARRIER	Wewitzer			
2ND CARRIER	Parsons			
FRANCIS	Barrett			
LADY PERCY	Mrs Cuyler			
HOSTESS	Mrs Webb			

(1) *Aug. 30; Sept. 12*

BLUNT	Farley
PETO	Abbot

[PA retains Cleveland as BLUNT.]

1795 COVENT GARDEN
Dec. 9

FALSTAFF	Fawcett [Jr.]
HENRY	Harley

(1) *Dec. 14, 16*

1ST CARRIER	Powel

262

HENRY IV, PART I

1795 COVENT GARDEN (cont.)

Dec. 9 (cont.)

PRINCE OF WALES	Lewis
VERNON	Middleton
WORCESTER	Hull
POINS	Macready
FRANCIS	Knight
BLUNT	Richardson
BARDOLPH	Thompson
DOUGLAS	Farley
NORTHUMBERLAND	Davenport
WESTMORLAND	Claremont
SHERIFF	Haymes
PETO	Rees
GADSHILL	[D.] Williamson
PRINCE JOHN	Holland
MESSENGER	Abbot
HOTSPUR'S SERVANT	Master Curties
1ST TRAVELLER	Blurton
2ND TRAVELLER	Coombs
3RD TRAVELLER	Wilde
1ST CARRIER (1)	Quick
2ND CARRIER	Munden
HOTSPUR	Holman
HOSTESS	Mrs Davenport
LADY PERCY	Miss Chapman

1796 COVENT GARDEN

Jan. 11

FALSTAFF	Fawcett [Jr.]
HENRY (4)	Harley
PRINCE OF WALES	Lewis
VERNON	Middleton
WORCESTER	Hull
POINS	Macready
FRANCIS	Knight
BARDOLPH	Thompson
BLUNT (4)	Richardson
DOUGLAS	Farley
PRINCE JOHN (2, 3)	Holland
1ST CARRIER	Munden
2ND CARRIER (1, 3, 4)	Powel
HOTSPUR	Holman

(1) *Jan. 18*

2ND CARRIER	Quick

(2) *Apr. 1*

HOSTESS added	Mrs Davenport
NORTHUMBERLAND	Davenport
omitted PRINCE JOHN	

(3) *Apr. 18; May 9*

2ND CARRIER	Quick
HOSTESS added	Mrs Davenport
NORTHUMBERLAND	Davenport
WESTMORLAND	Claremont
SHERIFF	Haymes
PETO	Rees
omitted PRINCE JOHN	

HENRY IV, PART I

1796 COVENT GARDEN (cont.)

Jan. 11 (cont.)

HOSTESS (2, 3, 4)	Mrs Platt
LADY PERCY	Miss Chapman

(4) *Oct. 20*

HENRY	Murray
BLUNT	Toms
2ND CARRIER	Quick
HOSTESS	Mrs Davenport

added

NORTHUMBERLAND	Davenport
WESTMORLAND	Claremont
SHERIFF	Haymes

HAYMARKET

Aug. 18

FALSTAFF	Fawcett [Jr.]
HOTSPUR	C. Kemble
HENRY	[J.] Aickin
PRINCE JOHN	Miss Granger
WORCESTER	Davies
DOUGLAS	Caulfield
VERNON	[J.] Palmer Jr.
BLUNT	Trueman
WESTMORLAND	Usher
NORTHUMBERLAND	Abbot
POINS	R. Palmer
BARDOLPH	Ledger
PETO	Lyons
GADSHILL	Chippendale
FRANCIS	[G.] Waldron
1ST CARRIER	Suett
2ND CARRIER	Wathen
PRINCE OF WALES	[J.] Bannister
HOSTESS	Mrs Hopkins
LADY PERCY	Miss Logan

Aug. 30

FALSTAFF	Fawcett [Jr.]
PRINCE OF WALES	[J.] Palmer Jr.
FRANCIS	[J.] Bannister

[The above consisted of parts of II. iv only. The entertainment on this evening was called *The School of Shakespeare*, for a description of which see p. 101.]

1797 DRURY LANE

Nov. 25

HENRY	Wroughton
PRINCE OF WALES	C. Kemble
PRINCE JOHN	Gregson
WORCESTER	[J.] Aickin
NORTHUMBERLAND	Packer
HOTSPUR	Kemble

HENRY IV, PART I

1797 DRURY LANE (*cont.*)

Nov. 25 (*cont.*)

DOUGLAS	Caulfield
VERNON	Barrymore
WESTMORLAND	Trueman
BLUNT	Holland
FALSTAFF	A Gentleman [Longley (EM, Dec. 1797, 410); first appearance on the stage]
POINS	Russell
GADSHILL	Gibbon
PETO	Simpson
BARDOLPH	Webb
FRANCIS	Suett
1ST CARRIER	Dowton
2ND CARRIER	Hollingsworth
SHERIFF	Maddocks
TRAVELLER	Fisher
MESSENGER	Evans
LADY PERCY	Mrs Powell
HOSTESS	Mrs Walcot

COVENT GARDEN

Jan. 2

FALSTAFF	Fawcett [Jr.]
HENRY	Murray
PRINCE OF WALES	Lewis
VERNON	Waddy
WORCESTER	Hull
POINS (1)	Claremont
FRANCIS	Knight
WESTMORLAND (1)	Townsend
1ST CARRIER (1)	Quick
2ND CARRIER	Munden
HOTSPUR	Holman
HOSTESS	Mrs Davenport
LADY PERCY	Miss Chapman

(1) *Sept. 18; Nov. 1*

POINS	Whitfield (on *Nov. 1* only)
WESTMORLAND	Clarke
1ST CARRIER	Rees
added	
BLUNT	Toms
BARDOLPH	Thompson
DOUGLAS	Farley (on *Sept. 18* only)
NORTHUMBERLAND	Davenport
SHERIFF	Abbot
PETO	Street
GADSHILL	Wilde
PRINCE JOHN	Curties (on *Sept. 18* only)
MESSENGER	Dyke (on *Sept. 18* only)

1798 COVENT GARDEN

Feb. 5

FALSTAFF	Fawcett [Jr.]
HENRY	Murray
PRINCE OF WALES	Lewis
VERNON	Waddy
WORCESTER	Hull
POINS	Whitfield
FRANCIS	Simmons

265

1798 COVENT GARDEN (cont.)
Feb. 5 (cont.)

BLUNT	Toms
BARDOLPH	Thompson
NORTHUMBERLAND	Davenport
WESTMORLAND	Clarke
SHERIFF	Abbot
PETO	Street
GADSHILL	Wilde
1ST CARRIER	Powel
2ND CARRIER	Rees
HOTSPUR	Holman
HOSTESS	Mrs Davenport
LADY PERCY	Miss Chapman

1799 COVENT GARDEN
Dec. 30

FALSTAFF	Fawcett [Jr.]
HENRY	Murray
PRINCE OF WALES	Lewis
VERNON	Waddy
WORCESTER	Hull
POINS	Whitfield
FRANCIS	Knight
BLUNT	Mansel
BARDOLPH	Thompson
DOUGLAS	Farley
NORTHUMBERLAND	Davenport
WESTMORLAND	Claremont
GADSHILL	Wilde
PETO	Street
1ST CARRIER	Emery
2ND CARRIER	Rees
HOTSPUR	Holman
HOSTESS	Mrs Davenport
LADY PERCY	Miss Chapman

HENRY IV, PART II

(1) Altered, probably by Theophilus Cibber, as THE HUMOURISTS. In two acts.
   1754 Not published.
   The dramatis personae indicates that the play almost certainly consisted of *II. iv* and *III. ii*.

(2) 'As it is Acted at the Theatres of London and Dublin.'
   1761 Dublin: Hulton Bradley.
   A reading edition, verbatim throughout.

HENRY IV, PART II

(3) 'As Performed at the Theatre-Royal, Drury-Lane. Regulated from the Prompt-Book.'

1773   John Bell.

Following are the principal omissions:
The *Induction*.
Act I. i entire (Northumberland learns of Hotspur's death, and vows revenge); *iii*. *41b–62* (Lord Bardolph's simile of 'the model of a house').
Act II. ii. 7b–31 (Poins's linen); *iii* entire (Lady Percy mourns for Hotspur); *iv. 1–23* (the apple-johns), *218–45a* (Doll praises Falstaff's valour), *364–85* ('mutton in Lent').
Act III. i. 32–end (Henry perceives the truth of Richard II's forebodings).
Act IV. i. 1–26 (Northumberland's defection), *90–139* (Mowbray's hatred of Henry); *iv. 1–12a*, for which is substituted *III. i. 1–31* (Henry's soliloquy on sleep).
The scenes of *Act V* are transposed as follows: *i, iv, iii, ii, v*.
The *Epilogue* is omitted.
See also Odell, ii. 41–42.

1751 COVENT GARDEN

Jan. 18

FALSTAFF	Quin
HENRY	Gibson
PRINCE OF WALES	Ryan
ARCHBISHOP OF YORK	Bridgwater
MOWBRAY	Redman
HASTINGS	Anderson
WESTMORLAND	Usher
PRINCE JOHN	Ridout
PRINCE HUMPHREY	Baker
CLARENCE	Miss Hippisley
POINS	Bransby
COLEVILE (1)	Holtom
LORD CHIEF JUSTICE	Sparks
SILENCE	Stoppelaer
BARDOLPH	Marten
PETO	Atkins
SHALLOW	Arthur
BULLCALF	Dunstall
FEEBLE	Collins
MOULDY	Bencraft
SHADOW	Hacket
PISTOL	Cushing
DOLL TEARSHEET (1)	Miss Haughton
HOSTESS (1)	Mrs Macklin

(1) *Mar. 12*

COLEVILE	Elrington
DOLL TEARSHEET	Mrs Dunstall
HOSTESS	Mrs Bambridge

HENRY IV, PART II

[*as* THE HUMOURISTS]

1754 DRURY LANE
July 2

PISTOL	Cibber
SHALLOW	Shuter
FALSTAFF	Phillips
SILENCE	Stoppelaer
BARDOLPH	Clough
MOULDY	W. Vaughan
FEEBLE	Blakey
SHADOW	Slim
PRINCE OF WALES	Cross
POINS	Master Cross
DAVY	H. Vaughan
WART	Johnston
HOSTESS	Mrs Cross
DOLL TEARSHEET	Mrs Bradshaw

[Announced as 'a Dramatic Entertainment of two Acts'. C-H refers to it as 'a farce from ye 2^d p^t of Henry 4th'.]

[*The original*]

1758 DRURY LANE
Mar. 13; Apr. 1, 4, 21

HENRY	Garrick
PRINCE OF WALES	Palmer
PRINCE JOHN	Usher
ARCHBISHOP OF YORK	Havard
LORD CHIEF JUSTICE	Bransby
SHALLOW	Yates
SILENCE	Rooker
PISTOL	Blakes
FALSTAFF	Woodward
HOSTESS	Mrs Macklin
DOLL TEARSHEET	Miss Minors

1761 COVENT GARDEN
Dec. 11, 12, 14, 15, 17, 18, 19, 21, 23, 26, 31

HENRY	Sparks
PRINCE OF WALES	Ross
PRINCE JOHN	Davis
PRINCE HUMPHREY	Perry
CLARENCE	Young
MOWBRAY	Tindal
HASTINGS	Anderson

HENRY IV, PART II

1761 COVENT GARDEN (*cont.*)
Dec. 11, 12, 14, 15, 17, 18, 19, 21, 23, 26, 31 (cont.)

ARCHBISHOP OF YORK	Clarke
LORD BARDOLPH	Wignell
WESTMORLAND	Storer
COLEVILE	R. Smith
GOWER	Buck
FALSTAFF	Shuter
LORD CHIEF JUSTICE	Gibson
POINS	Maguire
BARDOLPH	[P.] Lewis
PISTOL	Dyer
SHALLOW	Collins
SILENCE	Costollo
MOULDY	Gardner
FEEBLE	Holtom
BULLCALF	Dunstall
HOSTESS	Mrs Pitt
DOLL TEARSHEET	Mrs Green

1762 DRURY LANE
Nov. 3

HENRY	Garrick
PRINCE JOHN	Lee
PRINCE HUMPHREY	Master Cautherley
CLARENCE	Master Burton
PRINCE OF WALES	Holland
ARCHBISHOP OF YORK	Havard
LORD CHIEF JUSTICE	Bransby
WESTMORLAND	Burton
HASTINGS	Ackman
LORD BARDOLPH	Mozeen
MOWBRAY	Stevens
GOWER	Castle
SHALLOW	Yates
SILENCE	Blakes
POINS	Packer
COLEVILE	Fox
BARDOLPH	Clough
FEEBLE	[H.] Vaughan
MOULDY	Moody
PISTOL	King
SHADOW (1, 2)	Parsons
BULLCALF	Philips

(1) *Nov. 5*

DAVY added	Parsons
SERVANT omitted	Marr
SHADOW	

(2) *Nov. 11, 15; Dec. 3*

omitted
SHADOW

269

HENRY IV, PART II

1762 DRURY LANE (cont.)

Nov. 3 (cont.)

DAVY (1)	Marr
FANG	Watkins
FALSTAFF'S PAGE	Miss Rogers
FALSTAFF	Love
HOSTESS	Mrs Bradshaw
DOLL TEARSHEET	Mrs Lee

COVENT GARDEN

Jan. 4, 9

HENRY (1)	Sparks
PRINCE OF WALES	Ross
PRINCE JOHN	Davis
PRINCE HUMPHREY	Perry
CLARENCE (2)	Young
MOWBRAY	Tindal
HASTINGS (1)	Anderson
ARCHBISHOP OF YORK	Clarke
LORD BARDOLPH	Wignell
WESTMORLAND (1, 2)	Storer
COLEVILE (2)	R. Smith
GOWER (2)	Buck
FALSTAFF	Shuter
LORD CHIEF JUSTICE (1)	Gibson
POINS (2)	Maguire
BARDOLPH	[P.] Lewis
PISTOL	Dyer
SHALLOW	Collins
SILENCE	Costollo
MOULDY (2)	Gardner
FEEBLE	Holtom
BULLCALF	Dunstall
HOSTESS	Mrs Pitt
DOLL TEARSHEET (2)	Mrs Green

(1) *Jan. 18, 21, 26; Feb. 10, 27; Mar. 11, 18; May 24*

HENRY	Gibson
WESTMORLAND	Hull
LORD CHIEF JUSTICE	Anderson
omitted	
HASTINGS	

(2) *Oct. 2, 23; Dec. 31*

WESTMORLAND	Hull (on Oct. 2, 23 only)
POINS	White
MOULDY	Buck
DOLL TEARSHEET	Mrs Stephens (on Oct. 2 only)
added	
WARWICK	Gardner
omitted	
CLARENCE, WESTMORLAND (on *Dec. 31* only), COLEVILE, GOWER	

1763 DRURY LANE

Jan. 10

HENRY	Garrick
PRINCE OF WALES	Holland
PRINCE JOHN	Lee
PRINCE HUMPHREY (1)	Master Cautherley

(1) *Apr. 15*

omitted
PRINCE HUMPHREY, CLARENCE, HASTINGS, LORD BARDOLPH, MOWBRAY, GOWER, COLEVILE, BARDOLPH, FEEBLE, MOULDY, BULLCALF, DAVY, FANG, FALSTAFF'S PAGE

HENRY IV, PART II

1763 DRURY LANE (cont.)
Jan. 10 (cont.)

CLARENCE (1)	Master Burton
ARCHBISHOP OF YORK	Havard
LORD CHIEF JUSTICE	Bransby
WESTMORLAND	Burton
HASTINGS (1)	Ackman
LORD BARDOLPH (1)	Mozeen
MOWBRAY (1)	Stevens
GOWER (1)	Castle
SHALLOW	Yates
SILENCE	Blakes
POINS	Packer
COLEVILE (1)	Fox
BARDOLPH (1)	Clough
FEEBLE (1)	[H.] Vaughan
MOULDY (1)	Moody
PISTOL	King
BULLCALF (1)	Philips
DAVY (1)	Marr
FANG (1)	Watkins
FALSTAFF'S PAGE (1)	Miss Rogers
FALSTAFF	Love
HOSTESS	Mrs Bradshaw
DOLL TEARSHEET	Mrs Lee

1764 DRURY LANE
Jan. 18, 21; Feb. 10

HENRY	Powell
PRINCE OF WALES	Holland
PRINCE JOHN	Lee
PRINCE HUMPHREY	Miss Plym
CLARENCE	Master Burton
ARCHBISHOP OF YORK	Havard
LORD CHIEF JUSTICE	Bransby
WESTMORLAND	Burton
SHALLOW	Yates
SILENCE	Rooker
POINS (1)	Jackson
PISTOL	King
HASTINGS (1)	Ackman
MOWBRAY (1)	Stevens
FEEBLE (1)	[H.] Vaughan
DAVY (1)	Weston
SHADOW (1)	Parsons
MOULDY	Moody

(1) *Nov. 9; Dec. 21*

POINS	Packer
DAVY	Granger

added
GOWER — Strange
LORD BARDOLPH — Parsons
omitted
HASTINGS, MOWBRAY, FEEBLE, SHADOW

1764 DRURY LANE (cont.)

Jan. 18, 21; Feb. 10 (cont.)

FALSTAFF'S PAGE	Miss Rogers
FALSTAFF	Love
HOSTESS	Mrs Bradshaw
DOLL TEARSHEET	Mrs Lee

1766 DRURY LANE

May 5

HENRY	Powell
PRINCE OF WALES	Holland
PRINCE JOHN	Lee
PRINCE HUMPHREY	Miss Plym
ARCHBISHOP OF YORK	Havard
LORD CHIEF JUSTICE	Bransby
WESTMORLAND	Burton
SHALLOW	Yates
SILENCE	Rooker
POINS	Packer
PISTOL	King
FALSTAFF'S PAGE	Miss Rogers
FALSTAFF	Love
HOSTESS	Mrs Bradshaw
DOLL TEARSHEET	Mrs Lee

COVENT GARDEN

Oct. 6, 7

HENRY	Gibson
PRINCE OF WALES	Ross
PRINCE JOHN	Davis
MOWBRAY	Morris
HASTINGS	Bennet
ARCHBISHOP OF YORK	Clarke
LORD BARDOLPH (2)	Mozeen
COLEVILE	R. Smith
GOWER	Cushing
WESTMORLAND	Hull
LORD CHIEF JUSTICE	Anderson
CLARENCE	Murden
WARWICK	Gardner
POINS	Perry
FALSTAFF	Shuter
PISTOL	Dyer
SHALLOW	Woodward
SILENCE (2)	[P.] Lewis

(1) *Oct. 9, 11, 13*

added

SHADOW	Besford
FALSTAFF'S PAGE	Master Besford

(2) *Dec. 29*

LORD BARDOLPH	Baker
SILENCE	Dibdin

added

SAME as *Oct. 9*

1766 COVENT GARDEN (cont.)
Oct. 6, 7 (cont.)

BARDOLPH	Wignell
FANG	Redman
MOULDY	Buck
FEEBLE	Holtom
BULLCALF	Dunstall
HOSTESS	Mrs Pitt
DOLL TEARSHEET	Mrs Gardner

1767 DRURY LANE
May 8

HENRY	Powell
PRINCE OF WALES	[F.] Aickin
PRINCE JOHN	J. Palmer
PRINCE HUMPHREY	J. Burton
CLARENCE	Master Cape
ARCHBISHOP OF YORK	Havard
LORD CHIEF JUSTICE	Bransby
WESTMORLAND	Burton
SHALLOW	Yates
SILENCE	Rooker
POINS	Packer
MOWBRAY	Hurst
HASTINGS	Ackman
LORD BARDOLPH	Fawcett
FEEBLE	Weston
MOULDY	Moody
PISTOL	King
FALSTAFF'S PAGE	Miss Rogers
FALSTAFF	Love
HOSTESS	Mrs Bradshaw
DOLL TEARSHEET	Mrs Lee

[PA assigns PISTOL to Baddeley.]

1770 DRURY LANE
Jan. 19

HENRY	Garrick
PRINCE OF WALES	Cautherley
PRINCE JOHN	Brereton
PRINCE HUMPHREY	Miss Rogers
CLARENCE	Master Cape
ARCHBISHOP OF YORK	Jefferson
LORD CHIEF JUSTICE	Bransby

(1) *Jan. 26*
added
   PISTOL   Baddeley
omitted
   LORD BARDOLPH

(2) *Feb. 2*
   SHALLOW   Weston
added
   PISTOL   Baddeley

HENRY IV, PART II

1770 DRURY LANE (cont.)
Jan. 19 (cont.)

SHALLOW (2)	Parsons
HASTINGS	Ackman
MOWBRAY	Hurst
LORD BARDOLPH (1)	Fawcett
GOWER	Wright
SILENCE	Hartry
POINS	Packer
BARDOLPH	Clough
FALSTAFF'S PAGE	Miss Collett
FALSTAFF	Love
DOLL TEARSHEET	Miss Platt
HOSTESS	Mrs Bradshaw

(2) *Feb. 2 (cont.)*
[In the acting version published by Bell in 1773 there are the following additions to the cast:

COLEVILE	Keen
WESTMORLAND	Burton
PETO	Wrighten
DAVY	Jacobs
MOULDY	Moody
SHADOW	J. Burton
FEEBLE	[F.] Waldron
BULLCALF	Messink]

1773 COVENT GARDEN
Apr. 27

HENRY	A Gentleman [Carey (LC, Apr. 29, 1773, in which the name is misspelled 'Casey'; but see MC, Nov. 13, 1773); first appearance on the stage]
PRINCE OF WALES	Mrs Lessingham
ARCHBISHOP OF YORK	Clarke
PRINCE JOHN	Davis
WESTMORLAND	Hull
LORD CHIEF JUSTICE	Younger
SHALLOW	Woodward
PISTOL	Hamilton
POINS	Wroughton
BULLCALF	Dunstall
FALSTAFF	Shuter
HOSTESS	Mrs Pitt
DOLL TEARSHEET	Mrs Gardner

[In the acting version published by Bell in 1773 there are the following additions to the cast:

PRINCE HUMPHREY	Miss Besford
COLEVILE	Gardner
BARDOLPH	Wignell
FALSTAFF'S PAGE	Master Bates
SILENCE	Stoppelaer]

1777 DRURY LANE
Nov. 24

FALSTAFF	Henderson
HENRY	Bensley
PRINCE OF WALES	[J.] Palmer
LORD CHIEF JUSTICE	[J.] Aickin

(1) *Nov. 27; Dec. 15*
added
WESTMORLAND	Farren

1777 DRURY LANE (*cont.*)

Nov. 24 (cont.)

ARCHBISHOP OF YORK	Packer
PRINCE JOHN	Lamash
PRINCE HUMPHREY	Mrs Colles
CLARENCE	Miss Collett
MOWBRAY	Hurst
HASTINGS	Barrett
SILENCE	Parsons
PISTOL	Baddeley
POINS	R. Palmer
BARDOLPH	Wright
DAVY	[F.] Waldron
FALSTAFF'S PAGE	Master Pulley
SHALLOW	Yates
HOSTESS	Mrs Bradshaw
DOLL TEARSHEET	Mrs Davies

1778 DRURY LANE

Sept. 29; Oct. 24

FALSTAFF	Henderson
HENRY	Bensley
PRINCE OF WALES	[J.] Palmer
LORD CHIEF JUSTICE	[J.] Aickin
ARCHBISHOP OF YORK	Packer
PRINCE JOHN	Lamash
PRINCE HUMPHREY	Mrs Colles
CLARENCE	Miss Collett
WESTMORLAND	Farren
MOWBRAY	Hurst
HASTINGS	Wrighten
SILENCE	Parsons
PISTOL	Baddeley
POINS	R. Palmer
BARDOLPH	Wright
DAVY	[F.] Waldron
FALSTAFF'S PAGE	Master Pulley
SHALLOW	Yates
HOSTESS	Mrs Bradshaw
DOLL TEARSHEET	Mrs Davies

[On *Oct. 24* the PA bill incorrectly has, 'Not acted this season'. See p. 65.]

1779 DRURY LANE

June 1

FALSTAFF	Henderson
HENRY	Bensley

HENRY IV, PART II

1779 DRURY LANE (cont.)
June 1 (cont.)

PRINCE OF WALES	[J.] Palmer
LORD CHIEF JUSTICE	[J.] Aickin
ARCHBISHOP OF YORK	Packer
PRINCE JOHN	Lamash
WESTMORLAND	Farren
PRINCE HUMPHREY	Master Benson
CLARENCE	Miss Collett
MOWBRAY	Hurst
HASTINGS	Wrighten
SILENCE	Parsons
PISTOL	Baddeley
POINS	R. Palmer
BARDOLPH	Wright
DAVY	[F.] Waldron
FALSTAFF'S PAGE	Master Pulley
SHALLOW	Yates
HOSTESS	Mrs Bradshaw
DOLL TEARSHEET	Mrs Davies

1781 HAYMARKET
Aug. 7

HENRY	Bensley
CLARENCE	Miss Wood
PRINCE JOHN	Miss Francis
PRINCE HUMPHREY (1)	Miss Painter
LORD CHIEF JUSTICE	Gardner
WESTMORLAND	Davis
ATTENDANT	Painter
PRINCE OF WALES	[J.] Palmer

(1) *Aug. 17*

PRINCE HUMPHREY Miss M. Francis
[Both Pb and PA print this name without the initial; the identification is made clear in the bill in MC.]

[The above consisted of parts of IV. iv and v, and parts of V. ii only. The entertainment on this evening was called *The School of Shakespeare*, for a description of which see p. 73.]

1784 COVENT GARDEN
Oct. 30

HENRY	[F.] Aickin
PRINCE OF WALES	Wroughton
PRINCE JOHN	Farren
ARCHBISHOP OF YORK	Clarke
LORD CHIEF JUSTICE	Hull
MOWBRAY	Davies
WESTMORLAND	Fearon

276

HENRY IV, PART II

1784 COVENT GARDEN (cont.)
Oct. 30 (cont.)

SHALLOW	[R.] Wilson
SILENCE	Quick
POINS	Bonnor
PISTOL	[T.] Kennedy
FALSTAFF	Henderson
DOLL TEARSHEET	Miss Platt
HOSTESS	Mrs Pitt

HENRY V

(1) 'As it is acted at the Theatre Royal in Drury-Lane, and Covent Garden.'

1769   H. Woodfall [&c.].

A reading edition, verbatim throughout.

(2) 'As performed at the Theatre-Royal, Covent-Garden. Regulated from the Prompt-Book.'

1773   John Bell.

Following are the principal omissions:
All the *Choruses*.
Act I. ii. *66–88* (the list of French kings who broke the Salic law), *166–78*, *183b–213a* (the simile of the honey-bees).
Act II. ii. *105–42* (Henry's anger at the three traitors); *iii* (the phrase, 'a' babbled of green fields').
Act III. i. *7–17a, 21–30* ('Stiffen the sinews,' &c.); ii. *24–59* (the Boy's opinion of his masters); *iv entire* (Katharine and Alice); *vii. 1–139* (the Dauphin and his horse).
Act IV. i. *169b–88* (kings not responsible for evil soldiers).
Act V. ii. *38–67* (Burgundy's lament for France), *144b–55a, 186–204a, 238b–65, 272–81* (parts of Henry's wooing of Katharine), *316–50* (the discussion of love's blindness).

(3) 'As it is Acted at the Theatres-Royal in Drury-Lane and Covent-Garden.'

1780   Harrison and Co.

This is identical with (2).

(4) 'Printed exactly conformable to the Representation, on Its Revival at the Theatre Royal, Drury Lane, October 1, 1789.'

1789   J. Debrett.

This alteration was made by J. P. Kemble. It follows (2), with the following differences:
Also omitted are *I. i. 24–69a* (Henry's reformation on becoming king); *III. ii. 72–152* (the dispute between Flucllen and Macmorris); *III. iii. 10–41* (Henry threatens the citizens of Harfleur); *III. vii. 140–end* (the French leaders' disdain of the English); *IV. iv entire* (the Boy and the French soldier).
Henry's exhortation in *III. i* is reduced to four lines: *1–2* of the original, one

HENRY V

new line, and line *28* from *Henry VI, Part I, I. v.* Lines *17a–34* are preserved, and appear at the end of *IV. iii. IV. ii* has been entirely rewritten into prose.

(5) 'Taken from the Manager's Book, at the Theatre Royal, Drury-Lane.' n.d. [*c.* 1789] R. Butters.

This is identical with (4).

1752 COVENT GARDEN
Mar. 30

HENRY	Barry
EXETER	Ridout
ARCHBISHOP OF CANTERBURY	Sparks
SALISBURY	Bencraft
WESTMORLAND	Ricard
WILLIAMS	Bransby
GOWER	Anderson
SCROOP	Paddick
GREY	Redman
KING OF FRANCE	Gibson
DAUPHIN	Usher
BURGUNDY	Cushing
MONTJOY	Baker
CONSTABLE	Bridgwater
FLUELLEN	Macklin
MACMORRIS	Barrington
JAMY	Dunstall
BARDOLPH	Marten
NYM	Stoppelaer
BOY	Miss Morrison
PISTOL	Dyer
CHORUS	Ryan
ISABEL	Mrs Bambridge
HOSTESS	Mrs Macklin
KATHARINE	Mrs Vincent

1754 COVENT GARDEN
Apr. 17   (1) *May 8*

HENRY	Barry	FLUELLEN added	Arthur
EXETER	Ridout	DAUPHIN	Usher
ARCHBISHOP OF CANTERBURY	Sparks	HOSTESS omitted	Mrs Pitt
KING OF FRANCE	Gibson	CONSTABLE	
CONSTABLE (1)	Bridgwater		
PISTOL	Dyer		
CHORUS	Ryan		
FLUELLEN (1)	Shuter		
KATHARINE	Mrs Dyer		

278

1755 COVENT GARDEN
Feb. 18

HENRY (I)	Smith
EXETER	Ridout
ARCHBISHOP OF CANTERBURY	Sparks
KING OF FRANCE	Gibson
DAUPHIN	White
FLUELLEN	Arthur
PISTOL	Dyer
CHORUS	Ryan
HOSTESS	Mrs Pitt
KATHARINE	Mrs Dyer

(1) Dec. 3

HENRY	Barry
added	
GLOUCESTER	Bennet
BEDFORD	Holtom
SALISBURY	Bencraft
WESTMORLAND	Buck
BISHOP OF ELY	Wignell
SCROOP	R. Smith
GOWER	Anderson
BARDOLPH	Marten
MACMORRIS	Barrington
ERPINGHAM	Redman
JAMY	Dunstall
NYM	Stoppelaer
BOY	Miss Mullart
BURGUNDY	Cushing
MONTJOY	Baker
ISABEL	Mrs Stephens

1756 COVENT GARDEN
May 7

HENRY	Smith
EXETER	Ridout
GLOUCESTER	Bennet
BEDFORD	Holtom
SALISBURY	Bencraft
WESTMORLAND	Buck
ARCHBISHOP OF CANTERBURY	Sparks
FLUELLEN	Arthur
BISHOP OF ELY	Wignell
SCROOP	R. Smith
GOWER	Anderson
BARDOLPH	Marten
PISTOL	Dyer
WILLIAMS	Dunstall
ERPINGHAM	Redman
MACMORRIS	Barrington
NYM	Stoppelaer
BOY	Miss Mullart
KING OF FRANCE	Gibson
BURGUNDY	Cushing
DAUPHIN	White
MONTJOY	Baker
CHORUS	Ryan
ISABEL	Mrs Stephens
KATHARINE	Mrs Dyer
HOSTESS	Mrs Pitt

1757 COVENT GARDEN
Nov. 5

HENRY	Smith	
EXETER	Ridout	
GLOUCESTER	Bennet	
BEDFORD	Holtom	
SALISBURY	Bencraft	
WESTMORLAND	Buck	
ARCHBISHOP OF CANTERBURY	Sparks	
FLUELLEN	Arthur	
BISHOP OF ELY	Wignell	
SCROOP	R. Smith	
GOWER	Anderson	
BARDOLPH	Marten	
PISTOL	Dyer	
ERPINGHAM	Redman	
MACMORRIS (1)	Barrington	
NYM	Stoppelaer	
BOY	Miss Mullart	
KING OF FRANCE	Gibson	
BURGUNDY	Cushing	
DAUPHIN	White	
MONTJOY	Baker	
WILLIAMS (1)	Dunstall	
CHORUS	Ryan	
ISABEL	Mrs Stephens	
HOSTESS	Mrs Pitt	
KATHARINE	Mrs Hamilton	

(1) *Nov. 24, 28; Dec. 28*

WILLIAMS added — Barrington
JAMY omitted — Dunstall
MACMORRIS

1758 COVENT GARDEN
Apr. 13

HENRY	Barry
EXETER	Ridout
GLOUCESTER	Bennet
BEDFORD	Holtom
SALISBURY	Bencraft
WESTMORLAND	Buck
ARCHBISHOP OF CANTERBURY	Sparks
FLUELLEN	Arthur
BISHOP OF ELY	Wignell
SCROOP	R. Smith
GOWER	Anderson
BARDOLPH	Marten
PISTOL	Dyer

1758 COVENT GARDEN (cont.)

Apr. 13 (cont.)

ERPINGHAM	Redman
JAMY	Dunstall
NYM	Costollo
BOY	Miss Hallam
KING OF FRANCE	Gibson
BURGUNDY	Cushing
DAUPHIN	White
MONTJOY	Baker
WILLIAMS	Barrington
CHORUS	Ryan
ISABEL	Mrs Stephens
HOSTESS	Mrs Pitt
KATHARINE	Mrs Dyer

1759 COVENT GARDEN

Feb. 1

HENRY	Smith
EXETER	Ridout
GLOUCESTER (1)	Bennet
BEDFORD (1)	Holtom
SALISBURY (1)	Bencraft
WESTMORLAND (1)	Buck
ARCHBISHOP OF CANTERBURY	Sparks
FLUELLEN	Shuter
BISHOP OF ELY (1)	Wignell
SCROOP (1)	R. Smith
GOWER (1)	Anderson
BARDOLPH (1)	Marten
PISTOL	Dyer
WILLIAMS (1)	Barrington
ERPINGHAM (1)	Redman
JAMY (1)	Dunstall
NYM (1)	Stoppelaer
BOY (1)	Miss Mullart
KING OF FRANCE	Gibson
CONSTABLE	Clarke
BURGUNDY (1)	Cushing
DAUPHIN (1)	Davis
MONTJOY (1)	Baker
CHORUS	Ryan
ISABEL (1)	Mrs Stephens
HOSTESS	Mrs Pitt
KATHARINE	Mrs Dyer

(1) *Apr. 25; Dec. 28*

BURGUNDY Bennet (on *Apr. 25* only)

omitted GLOUCESTER, BEDFORD, SALISBURY, WESTMORLAND, BISHOP OF ELY, SCROOP, GOWER, BARDOLPH, WILLIAMS (on *Dec. 28* only), ERPINGHAM, JAMY, NYM, BOY, BURGUNDY (on *Dec. 28* only), DAUPHIN (on *Dec. 28* only), MONTJOY, ISABEL

1760 COVENT GARDEN

May 5

HENRY	Smith
EXETER	Ridout
ARCHBISHOP OF CANTERBURY	Sparks
FLUELLEN	Shuter
GOWER	Anderson
SCROOP	R. Smith
PISTOL	Dyer
WILLIAMS	Barrington
KING OF FRANCE	Gibson
BURGUNDY	Bennet
CONSTABLE	Clarke
DAUPHIN	Davis
BARDOLPH	Marten
CAMBRIDGE (1)	Wignell
GREY (1)	Redman
JAMY (1)	Dunstall
NYM (1)	Costollo
HOSTESS	Mrs Pitt
ISABEL	Mrs Stephens
KATHARINE	Mrs Dyer

(1) *Nov. 18*
added

BISHOP OF ELY	Wignell
BEDFORD	Holtom
WESTMORLAND	Buck
MONTJOY	Baker

omitted
CAMBRIDGE, GREY, JAMY, NYM

(2) *Dec. 2.* No parts assigned
[For this night both Pb and PA announce *Tancred and Sigismunda*. See p. 25.]

1761 COVENT GARDEN

Jan. 1

HENRY	Smith
EXETER (1, 2)	Ridout
ARCHBISHOP OF CANTERBURY	Sparks
FLUELLEN	Shuter
GOWER	Anderson
SCROOP (2)	R. Smith
BISHOP OF ELY (2)	Wignell
BEDFORD (2)	Holtom
WESTMORLAND (2)	Buck
PISTOL	Dyer
WILLIAMS (2)	Barrington
KING OF FRANCE	Gibson
BURGUNDY (2)	Bennet
CONSTABLE	Clarke
DAUPHIN	Davis
MONTJOY (2)	Baker
BARDOLPH (2)	Marten
HOSTESS	Mrs Pitt
ISABEL	Mrs Stephens
KATHARINE (2)	Mrs Dyer

(1) *May 1, 22*

EXETER	Hull

(2) *Nov. 13, 14, 16*

EXETER	Tindal
WILLIAMS	Buck
BURGUNDY	Hull
KATHARINE	Mrs Bellamy

omitted
SCROOP, BISHOP OF ELY, BEDFORD, WESTMORLAND, MONTJOY, BARDOLPH

HENRY V

1761 COVENT GARDEN (cont.)

Nov. 17, 18, 19, 20, 21, 23

HENRY (1)	Smith
EXETER	Tindal
ARCHBISHOP OF CANTERBURY	Sparks
FLUELLEN	Shuter
GOWER	Anderson
MACMORRIS	Barrington
JAMY	Dunstall
PISTOL	Dyer
BARDOLPH	Marten
WILLIAMS	Buck
KING OF FRANCE	Gibson
BURGUNDY (1, 2, 3)	Hull
DAUPHIN	Davis
CONSTABLE	Clarke
HOSTESS	Mrs Pitt
ISABEL	Mrs Stephens
KATHARINE	Mrs Bellamy

(1) Nov. 24, 25, 26

HENRY	Hull
BURGUNDY	Bennet

(2) Nov. 27, 28, 30; Dec. 1, 2, 3, 4, 5, 7, 8, 9

BURGUNDY	Bennet

(3) Dec. 29

BURGUNDY	Bennet
added	
FRENCH SOLDIER	Holtom

1762 COVENT GARDEN

Jan. 1

HENRY (1)	Smith
EXETER	Tindal
ARCHBISHOP OF CANTERBURY (1)	Sparks
FLUELLEN	Shuter
GOWER	Anderson
MACMORRIS	Barrington
FRENCH SOLDIER	Holtom
JAMY	Dunstall
PISTOL	Dyer
BARDOLPH	Marten
WILLIAMS	Buck
KING OF FRANCE	Gibson
BURGUNDY	Bennet
DAUPHIN	Davis
CONSTABLE	Clarke
HOSTESS	Mrs Pitt
ISABEL	Mrs Stephens
KATHARINE (1, 2)	Mrs Bellamy

(1) Apr. 12

HENRY	Hull
KATHARINE	A Young Gentlewoman [Miss Hallam (MS annotation on JPK)]
omitted	
ARCHBISHOP OF CANTERBURY	

(?) Oct. 16

KATHARINE	Miss Hallam
added	
FRENCH AMBASSADOR	White
MONTJOY	Baker

1764 COVENT GARDEN

Feb. 15

HENRY	Smith
EXETER	Tindal

283

1764 COVENT GARDEN (cont.)

Feb. 15 (cont.)

WESTMORLAND	White
ARCHBISHOP OF CANTERBURY	Sparks
FLUELLEN	Shuter
GOWER	Anderson
PISTOL	Dyer
BARDOLPH	Marten
MACMORRIS	Barrington
JAMY	Dunstall
FRENCH AMBASSADOR	White
WILLIAMS	Buck
KING OF FRANCE	Gibson
BURGUNDY	Bennet
DAUPHIN	Davis
CONSTABLE	Clarke
HOSTESS	Mrs Pitt
ISABEL	Mrs Stephens
KATHARINE	Miss Hallam

[The assignment of both WESTMORLAND and the FRENCH AMBASSADOR to White appears to be a misprint. Doubling these parts is not possible.]

1766 COVENT GARDEN

Sept. 22

HENRY (1, 2)	Smith
ARCHBISHOP OF CANTERBURY	Walker
SALISBURY (2, 4)	Cushing
WESTMORLAND	Morris
EXETER (1, 2)	Hull
MACMORRIS	Barrington
JAMY	Dunstall
GOWER	Anderson
FLUELLEN	Shuter
NYM	Hallam
BOY	Miss Valois
BARDOLPH (4)	[P.] Lewis
FRENCH SOLDIER	Holtom
PISTOL	Dyer
WILLIAMS	Buck
ENGLISH HERALD (1, 2, 3, 4)	Hallam
KING OF FRANCE	Gibson
DAUPHIN	Davis
CONSTABLE (2)	Clarke

(1) *Sept. 24, 29; Oct. 1, 3*

HENRY	Hull
EXETER	Younger
ENGLISH HERALD	Weller (on *Oct. 3* only)

added on *Oct. 1, 3* only

BEDFORD	R. Smith
GLOUCESTER	Murden
CAMBRIDGE	Wignell
SCROOP	Perry
GREY	Redman

(2) *Oct. 17*

HENRY	Hull
SALISBURY	Gardner
EXETER	Younger
ENGLISH HERALD	Weller
CONSTABLE	Cushing
GOVERNOR OF HARFLEUR	Redman

added

BEDFORD	R. Smith
GLOUCESTER	Murden
CAMBRIDGE	Wignell
SCROOP	Perry

HENRY V

1766 COVENT GARDEN (cont.)

Sept. 22 (cont.)

GOVERNOR OF HARFLEUR (2, 4)	Gardner
MONTJOY	Baker
BURGUNDY	Bennet
ISABEL	Mrs Stephens
HOSTESS	Mrs Pitt
KATHARINE	Mrs Mattocks

[Hallam doubled NYM and the ENGLISH HERALD.]

(3) *Nov. 17*

ENGLISH HERALD Weller
added
   SAME as *Oct. 1*
[PA assigns SALISBURY to Gardner; CONSTABLE to Cushing; GOVERNOR OF HARFLEUR to Redman.]

(4) *Dec. 27*

SALISBURY	Gardner
BARDOLPH	Cushing
ENGLISH HERALD added	Weller

   SAME as *Oct. 1*
omitted
   GOVERNOR OF HARFLEUR

1767 COVENT GARDEN

Apr. 23

HENRY	Smith
ARCHBISHOP OF CANTERBURY (1)	Walker
BEDFORD (1)	R. Smith
SALISBURY (1)	Gardner
GLOUCESTER (1)	Murden
WESTMORLAND (1)	Morris
EXETER	Hull
CAMBRIDGE (1)	Wignell
SCROOP (1)	Perry
GREY (1)	Redman
MACMORRIS	Barrington
JAMY	Dunstall
GOWER (1)	Du-Bellamy
FLUELLEN	Shuter
NYM (1)	Hallam
BOY (1)	Miss Valois
BARDOLPH (1)	Cushing
FRENCH SOLDIER (1)	Holtom
PISTOL	Dyer
WILLIAMS (1)	Buck
KING OF FRANCE	Gibson
DAUPHIN	Davis
CONSTABLE	Clarke
BURGUNDY (1)	Bennet
MONTJOY (1)	Baker
ISABEL	Mrs Stephens
HOSTESS	Mrs Pitt
KATHARINE	Mrs Mattocks

(1) *Sept. 22, 24*

ARCHBISHOP OF CANTERBURY	Gardner
WILLIAMS	Morris
BURGUNDY added	Perry
CHORUS	Powell

omitted
   BEDFORD, SALISBURY, GLOUCESTER, WESTMORLAND, CAMBRIDGE, SCROOP, GREY, GOWER, NYM, BOY, BARDOLPH, FRENCH SOLDIER, MONTJOY

[The bills note that the CHORUS would be 'restored'. It had last been performed on Dec. 28, 1759.]

285

1768 COVENT GARDEN

Nov. 4   (1) *Nov. 22*

HENRY	Smith	MACMORRIS	Fox
ARCHBISHOP OF		WILLIAMS	Barrington
CANTERBURY	Gardner		
EXETER	Hull		
GOWER	Du-Bellamy		
MACMORRIS (1)	Barrington		
BARDOLPH	Morgan		
BOY	Miss Valois		
FRENCH SOLDIER	Holtom		
WESTMORLAND	[P.] Lewis		
GLOUCESTER	[Lee] Lewes		
BEDFORD	R. Smith		
FLUELLEN	Shuter		
PISTOL	Hamilton		
WILLIAMS (1)	Morris		
JAMY	Dunstall		
KING OF FRANCE	Gibson		
DAUPHIN	Davis		
CONSTABLE	Clarke		
BURGUNDY	Perry		
ISABEL	Mrs Vincent		
HOSTESS	Mrs Pitt		
KATHARINE	Mrs Mattocks		

[PA assigns ISABEL to Mrs Stephens.]

1769 COVENT GARDEN

Sept. 22

HENRY	Smith
ARCHBISHOP OF	
CANTERBURY	Gardner
EXETER	Hull
GOWER	Du-Bellamy
MACMORRIS	Barrington
BARDOLPH	Barnshaw
FLUELLEN	Shuter
PISTOL	Dyer
WILLIAMS	Morris
JAMY	Dunstall
KING OF FRANCE	Gibson
DAUPHIN	Davis
CONSTABLE	Clarke
BURGUNDY	Perry
ISABEL	Mrs Vincent
HOSTESS	Mrs Pitt
KATHARINE	Mrs Mattocks

HENRY V

1770 COVENT GARDEN
May 16

HENRY	Smith
ARCHBISHOP OF CANTERBURY	Gardner
EXETER	Hull
GOWER	Du-Bellamy
FLUELLEN	Shuter
PISTOL	Dyer
JAMY	Dunstall
KING OF FRANCE	Gibson
DAUPHIN (1)	Davis
CONSTABLE	Clarke
KATHARINE	Mrs Mattocks

(1) *Oct. 25; Nov. 26; Dec. 28*

DAUPHIN added	[Lee] Lewes
WESTMORLAND	R. Smith
MACMORRIS	Barrington (on *Oct. 25* only)
BARDOLPH	Barnshaw (on *Oct. 25* only)
WILLIAMS	Morris
FRENCH SOLDIER	Holtom (on *Dec. 28* only)
BURGUNDY	Perry
ISABEL	Mrs Vincent
HOSTESS	Mrs Pitt

1771 COVENT GARDEN
Apr. 11

HENRY	Smith
ARCHBISHOP OF CANTERBURY	Gardner
EXETER	Younger
GOWER	Du-Bellamy
WESTMORLAND	R. Smith
FLUELLEN	Shuter
PISTOL	Dyer
WILLIAMS	Morris
JAMY	Dunstall
KING OF FRANCE	Hull
DAUPHIN	[Lee] Lewes
BURGUNDY	Perry
CONSTABLE	Clarke
ISABEL	Mrs Vincent
HOSTESS	Mrs Pitt
KATHARINE	Mrs Mattocks

1773 COVENT GARDEN
Jan. 6

HENRY	Smith
ARCHBISHOP OF CANTERBURY	Gardner
EXETER	Hull
FLUELLEN	Shuter
PISTOL	Dyer
JAMY	Dunstall
DAUPHIN	[Lee] Lewes
GOWER	Du-Bellamy
WILLIAMS	Morris
KING OF FRANCE	Kniveton

1773 COVENT GARDEN (cont.)
Jan. 6 (cont.)

CONSTABLE	Clarke
KATHARINE	Mrs Mattocks

[In the acting version published by Bell in 1773 the cast is the same as that of this performance (except for the assignment of the DAUPHIN to Davis), with the following additions:

GLOUCESTER	Harris
BEDFORD	Wild
SALISBURY	Cushing
WESTMORLAND	R. Smith
CAMBRIDGE	Wignell
SCROOP	Fox
GREY	Redman
NYM	Stoppelaer
BARDOLPH	Wignell
BOY	Miss Valois
BURGUNDY	Perry
GOVERNOR OF HARFLEUR	[R.] Bates
MONTJOY	Baker
ISABEL	Mrs Vincent
HOSTESS	Mrs Pitt]

[Wignell is assigned to both CAMBRIDGE and BARDOLPH.]

1778 COVENT GARDEN
May 11, 18

HENRY (1)	Wroughton
ARCHBISHOP OF CANTERBURY	Hull
EXETER	L'Estrange
GOWER (1)	Bowles
WILLIAMS (1)	Booth
FLUELLEN	[R.] Wilson
BURGUNDY (1)	Robson
FRENCH SOLDIER (1)	Wewitzer
JAMY	Dunstall
BISHOP OF ELY (1)	Thompson
SALISBURY (1)	Cushing
MACMORRIS (1)	Mahon
BARDOLPH (1)	Fox
NYM (1)	Jones
PISTOL	Quick
KING OF FRANCE	Fearon
DAUPHIN	Whitfield
BOY (1)	Miss Francis
MONTJOY (1)	Baker
CONSTABLE	Clarke

(1) *Sept. 21*

HENRY omitted — Smith

GOWER, WILLIAMS, BURGUNDY, FRENCH SOLDIER, BISHOP OF ELY, SALISBURY, MACMORRIS, BARDOLPH, NYM, BOY, MONTJOY, WESTMORLAND, CHORUS

1778 COVENT GARDEN (cont.)

May 11, 18 (cont.)

WESTMORLAND (1)	[R.] Smith
CHORUS (1)	Hull
ISABEL	Mrs Poussin
HOSTESS	Mrs Pitt
KATHARINE	Mrs Mattocks

[Hull doubled the ARCHBISHOP OF CANTERBURY and the CHORUS.]

1779 COVENT GARDEN

Jan. 1

HENRY (1)	Smith
ARCHBISHOP OF CANTERBURY	Hull
EXETER	L'Estrange
FLUELLEN	[R.] Wilson
JAMY (1)	Egan
MACMORRIS (1)	Mahon
PISTOL	Quick
KING OF FRANCE	Fearon
DAUPHIN	Whitfield
CONSTABLE (1)	Peile
CHORUS (1)	Henderson
ISABEL	Mrs Poussin
HOSTESS	Mrs Pitt
KATHARINE	Mrs Whitfield

(1) *Sept. 20*

HENRY	Wroughton
MACMORRIS	Egan
CONSTABLE	Clarke
CHORUS	Hull
added	
BEDFORD	Phillimore
BISHOP OF ELY	Thompson
BURGUNDY	Robson
WILLIAMS	Booth
GOWER	Norris
FRENCH SOLDIER	Wewitzer
MONTJOY	Baker
BOY	Miss Francis
omitted	
JAMY	

[Hull doubled the ARCHBISHOP OF CANTERBURY and the CHORUS.]

1782 COVENT GARDEN

May 20

HENRY	Wroughton
ARCHBISHOP OF CANTERBURY	Hull
BISHOP OF ELY	Thompson
MACMORRIS	Egan
GOWER	Norris
EXETER	L'Estrange
BURGUNDY	Robson
FRENCH SOLDIER	Joules
BOY	Miss Francis
FLUELLEN	Booth
PISTOL	Quick
KING OF FRANCE	Fearon
DAUPHIN	Whitfield
CONSTABLE	Clarke
ISABEL	Mrs Poussin
HOSTESS	Mrs Pitt
KATHARINE	Mrs Whitfield

HENRY V

1789 DRURY LANE
Oct. 1, 5, 12, 19, 26; Nov. 2, 9, 16, 23

HENRY	Kemble
EXETER	[J.] Aickin
WESTMORLAND	R. Palmer
BEDFORD	Dignum
GLOUCESTER (1)	Benson
PISTOL	Suett
ERPINGHAM	[F.] Waldron
BARDOLPH	Alfred
WILLIAMS	Whitfield
NYM	[J.] Burton
GOWER	Williames
ARCHBISHOP OF CANTERBURY	Maddocks
BISHOP OF ELY	Jones
GREY	Lamash
SCROOP	[J.] Wilson
CAMBRIDGE	Webb
BATES	Banks
BOY	Master Gregson
FLUELLEN	Baddeley
KING OF FRANCE	Packer
BURGUNDY	Phillimore
CONSTABLE	Fawcett
MONTJOY	Haymes
GOVERNOR OF HARFLEUR	Hollingsworth
DAUPHIN (1)	Barrymore
HOSTESS	Mrs Booth
KATHARINE	Miss Collins
ISABEL	Mrs Ward

(1) *Dec. 28*

DAUPHIN   Benson
omitted
  GLOUCESTER
[PA retains Barrymore as the DAUPHIN; does not omit GLOUCESTER; and assigns the HOSTESS to Mrs Heard.]

1790 DRURY LANE
May 11

HENRY	Kemble
BEDFORD	Dignum
EXETER	[J.] Aickin
WESTMORLAND	R. Palmer
CAMBRIDGE	Webb
BISHOP OF ELY	Jones
ARCHBISHOP OF CANTERBURY	Maddocks
SCROOP (1)	Lyons
ERPINGHAM	[F.] Waldron
GOWER (1)	Benson
FLUELLEN (1)	Williames

(1) *Oct. 7*

SCROOP	Chapman
GOWER	Williames
FLUELLEN	Baddeley
added	
GLOUCESTER	Benson
GREY	Bland
BATES	Banks
GOVERNOR OF HARFLEUR	Hollingsworth
MONTJOY	Haymes

290

HENRY V

1790 DRURY LANE (cont.)

May 11 (cont.)

NYM	[J.] Burton
BARDOLPH	Alfred
PISTOL	Suett
BOY	Master Gregson
WILLIAMS	Whitfield
KING OF FRANCE	Packer
DAUPHIN	Barrymore
BURGUNDY	Phillimore
CONSTABLE	Fawcett
ISABEL	Mrs Ward
KATHARINE	Miss Collins
HOSTESS	Mrs Booth

1791 DRURY LANE (company at KING'S, HAYMARKET)

Oct. 31   (1) **Nov. 28**

HENRY	Kemble		SCROOP	[J.] Cooke
GLOUCESTER	Benson
BEDFORD	Dignum
EXETER	[J.] Aickin
WESTMORLAND	Sedgwick
ARCHBISHOP OF CANTERBURY	Maddocks
BISHOP OF ELY	Jones
CAMBRIDGE	Webb
SCROOP (1)	Chapman
GREY	Bland
ERPINGHAM	[F.] Waldron
GOWER	R. Palmer
NYM	[J.] Burton
BARDOLPH	Alfred
FLUELLEN	Baddeley
PISTOL	Suett
BOY	Master Gregson
WILLIAMS	Whitfield
BATES	Banks
KING OF FRANCE	Packer
DAUPHIN	Barrymore
BURGUNDY	Phillimore
CONSTABLE	Fawcett
GOVERNOR OF HARFLEUR	Hollingsworth
MONTJOY	Caulfield
ISABEL	Mrs Ward
KATHARINE	Miss Collins
HOSTESS	Mrs Booth

HENRY V

1792 DRURY LANE (company at KING'S, HAYMARKET)
Sept. 25   (1) *Oct. 29*

HENRY	Kemble	DAUPHIN	Barrymore
GLOUCESTER	Benson		
BEDFORD	Dignum		
EXETER	[J.] Aickin		
WESTMORLAND	Sedgwick		
ARCHBISHOP OF CANTERBURY	Maddocks		
BISHOP OF ELY	Jones		
CAMBRIDGE	Webb		
SCROOP	[J.] Cooke		
GREY	Bland		
ERPINGHAM	[F.] Waldron		
GOWER	R. Palmer		
NYM	[J.] Burton		
FLUELLEN	Baddeley		
BARDOLPH	Alfred		
BOY	Master Gregson		
PISTOL	Suett		
WILLIAMS	Whitfield		
BATES	Banks		
KING OF FRANCE	Packer		
DAUPHIN (1)	Benson		
BURGUNDY	Phillimore		
CONSTABLE	Fawcett		
GOVERNOR OF HARFLEUR	Hollingsworth		
MONTJOY	Caulfield		
ISABEL	Mrs Ward		
KATHARINE	Miss Collins		
HOSTESS	Mrs Booth		

[Both Pb and PA assign the DAUPHIN to Barrymore. But 'Benson performed the Dauphin instead of Barrymore' (TM, Nov. 1792, 125). It is not stated who acted GLOUCESTER; doubling these two parts is not likely.]

1793 HAYMARKET
Sept. 24

HENRY	Kemble
GLOUCESTER	[J.] Palmer Jr.
EXETER	[J.] Aickin
ARCHBISHOP OF CANTERBURY	Hull
BISHOP OF ELY	Jones
CAMBRIDGE	Lyons
SCROOP	[J.] Cooke
GREY	Bland
ERPINGHAM	[F.] Waldron

HENRY V

1793 HAYMARKET (*cont.*)

Sept. 24 (cont.)

GOWER	Dignum
NYM	[J.] Burton
FLUELLEN	Baddeley
PISTOL	Suett
BARDOLPH	Barrett
BOY	Master DeCamp
WILLIAMS	Benson
BATES	[G.] Waldron
KING OF FRANCE	Usher
DAUPHIN	Barrymore
GOVERNOR OF HARFLEUR	Hollingsworth
MONTJOY	Caulfield
ISABEL	Mrs Hopkins
KATHARINE	Mrs Goodall
HOSTESS	Mrs Booth

1794 DRURY LANE

Sept. 23

HENRY	Kemble
GLOUCESTER	C. Kemble
BEDFORD	Dignum
EXETER	[J.] Aickin
WESTMORLAND	Sedgwick
ARCHBISHOP OF CANTERBURY (1)	Maddocks
BISHOP OF ELY (1)	Jones
CAMBRIDGE (1)	Webb
SCROOP (1)	[J.] Cooke
GREY (1)	Bland
ERPINGHAM (1)	[F.] Waldron
GOWER	R. Palmer
FLUELLEN	Baddeley
NYM	[J.] Burton
BARDOLPH	Phillimore
PISTOL	Suett
BOY	Master Chatterley
WILLIAMS	Whitfield
BATES	Banks
KING OF FRANCE	Packer
DAUPHIN	Barrymore
BURGUNDY	Trueman
CONSTABLE	Benson
GOVERNOR OF HARFLEUR (1)	Hollingsworth

(1) *Oct. 6*

omitted ARCHBISHOP OF CANTERBURY, BISHOP OF ELY, CAMBRIDGE, SCROOP, GREY, ERPINGHAM, GOVERNOR OF HARFLEUR, MONTJOY

HENRY V

1794 DRURY LANE (*cont.*)

Sept. 23 (*cont.*)

MONTJOY (1)	Caulfield
ISABEL	Mrs Powell
KATHARINE	Miss DeCamp
HOSTESS	Mrs Booth

HENRY VIII

(1) 'With Alterations. As it is Performed at the Theatre-Royal in Drury-Lane.'

    1762   C. Hitch [&c.].

Following are the principal omissions:

The Prologue.

Act I. i. *54b–72a* (Wolsey compared to a spider), *174b–90a* (the secret pact between Wolsey and the Emperor Charles).

Act II. i. *1–55* (the Gentleman's report of Buckingham's trial), *137–end* (rumours of the King's divorce); ii. *24–44* (Wolsey's machinations in securing the divorce).

Act III. i. *119b–41a* (Katharine defends her virtuous love).

Act IV. i entire (the Gentlemen's account of the coronation [the *Order of the Coronation* is retained]); ii. *The Vision.*

Act V. i. *1–55* (Gardiner's mistrust of Cromwell); iv. *35b–72* (the Porter's description of the mob); v. *33b–55a* (the prophesy regarding James I).

The Epilogue.

For *II.* i. *136* are substituted the words, 'Remember Buckingham!'. In this scene Vaux's speech is given to Lovell. *III.* ii ends with three new lines: Wolsey submits to heaven's chastisement. In *IV.* ii Griffith's speeches are given to Cromwell.

(2) 'As it is Performed at the Theatre-Royal in Drury-Lane.'

    1762   Dublin: T. and J. Whitehouse.

This is identical with (1).

(3) 'As Performed at the Theatre-Royal, Covent-Garden. Regulated from the Prompt-Book.'

    1773   John Bell.

This is identical with (1), but somewhat more abridged.

See also Odell, ii. 43–44.

(4) 'As it is Acted at the Theatres-Royal in Drury-Lane and Covent-Garden.'

    1778   J. Wenman.

(5) 'Marked with the Variations in the Manager's Book at the Theatre-Royal in Covent-Garden.'

    1786   C. Bathurst [&c.].

HENRY VIII

(6) 'Taken from the Manager's Book, at the Theatre Royal, Covent-Garden.'
n.d. [*c*. 1787] R. Butters.

(7) 'As performed at the Theatres Royal. Regulated from the Prompt-Book.'
n.d. [*c*. 1794] J. Barker.

All these are identical with (3).

1751 COVENT GARDEN
Apr. 16

HENRY	Quin
WOLSEY	Ryan
BUCKINGHAM	[T.] Lacy
NORFOLK	Sparks
CROMWELL	Ridout
SUFFOLK	Usher
CAPUCIUS	Bransby
ABERGAVENNY	Elrington
GUILDFORD	Cushing
LORD CHANCELLOR	Marten
CAMPEIUS	Dunstall
SANDS	Collins
LOVELL	Holtom
LORD CHAMBER-LAIN	Anderson
BUTTS	Redman
CRANMER	Bridgwater
GARDINER	Arthur
OLD LADY	Mrs Bambridge
PATIENCE	Miss Allen
ANNE BULLEN	Mrs Vincent
QUEEN KATHARINE	Mrs Woffington

1752 DRURY LANE
Apr. 10

HENRY (2)	Sowdon
WOLSEY	Mossop
BUCKINGHAM	Ross
NORFOLK	Palmer
SUFFOLK	Blakes
SURREY (1, 2)	Lee
CRANMER (2)	Havard
GARDINER	Taswell
SANDS	Shuter
LORD CHAMBER-LAIN	Winstone
CROMWELL	Mozeen
ANNE BULLEN	Mrs Mills

(1) *Apr. 24, 29*

SURREY	Simson

omitted on *Apr. 29* only
PATIENCE

(2) *Sept. 26; Oct. 9, 24; Dec. 2*

HENRY	Berry
SURREY	Lacey
CRANMER	Dexter (on *Dec.* 2 only)

added
SURVEYOR   Simson
omitted on *Dec. 2* only
PATIENCE
[On *Sept. 26* Genest (iv. 356) erroneously assigns NORFOLK to Blakes.]

HENRY VIII

1752 DRURY LANE (cont.)
Apr. 10 (cont.)

    PATIENCE (1, 2)   Miss Norris
    QUEEN KATHARINE   Mrs Pritchard

[Pb assigns GARDINER to Yates, and ANNE BULLEN to Mrs Ward.]

1753 DRURY LANE
Feb. 5

HENRY	Berry
WOLSEY	Mossop
BUCKINGHAM	Ross
NORFOLK (1)	Palmer
SURREY (1)	Lacey
SANDS (1, 2, 3)	Shuter
CRANMER (1, 2, 3)	Dexter
GARDINER	Taswell
ANNE BULLEN (2, 3)	Mrs Mills
QUEEN KATHARINE	Mrs Pritchard

(1) *Feb. 28; May 2*

CRANMER	Havard

added on *May 2* only

SUFFOLK	Blakes
CAMPEIUS	Burton
LORD CHAMBERLAIN	Winstone
CROMWELL	Mozeen

omitted on *Feb. 28* only
    NORFOLK, SURREY, SANDS

(2) *Oct. 6, 11*

SANDS	Philips
CRANMER	Havard
ANNE BULLEN	Mrs Jefferson [first appearance on the stage]

added

SUFFOLK	Blakes
LORD CHAMBERLAIN	Davies
SURVEYOR	Simson
CROMWELL	Mozeen

(3) *Nov. 9; Dec. 17*

CRANMER	Havard
ANNE BULLEN	Mrs Jefferson

added

LORD CHAMBERLAIN	Davies

omitted
    SANDS

1754 DRURY LANE
Apr. 15

HENRY	Berry
WOLSEY	Mossop
BUCKINGHAM	Ross
NORFOLK	Palmer
SURREY (2)	Lacey
LORD CHAMBERLAIN (2)	Davies
CRANMER	Havard
GARDINER	Taswell
SUFFOLK (1)	Blakes

(1) *May 9*

added

CROMWELL	Scrase
SANDS	Vernon

omitted
    SUFFOLK

(2) *Oct. 10; Nov. 1*

SURREY	Davies
LORD CHAMBERLAIN	Bransby

added

SANDS	Philips
CROMWELL	Mozeen

1754 DRURY LANE (cont.)
Apr. 15 (cont.)

ANNE BULLEN	Mrs Jefferson
QUEEN KATHARINE	Mrs Pritchard

(2) Oct. 10; Nov. 1 (cont.)
also added on *Oct. 10* only

SURVEYOR	Simson
LOVELL	Ackman
GUILDFORD	Marr
BRANDON	Wilder
CAPUCIUS	Scrase
BUTTS	[H.] Vaughan
DENNY	Vernon
OLD LADY	Mrs James

1755 DRURY LANE
Mar. 31; Apr. 19

HENRY	Berry
WOLSEY (2)	Mossop
BUCKINGHAM	Ross
NORFOLK	Palmer
SURREY	Davies
LORD CHAMBERLAIN	Bransby
CRANMER (1, 2)	Havard
GARDINER	Taswell
ANNE BULLEN	Mrs Jefferson
QUEEN KATHARINE	Mrs Pritchard

(1) May 19

CRANMER	Burton

(2) Dec. 18, 26

WOLSEY	Havard
CRANMER	Burton

added

CROMWELL	Usher (on *Dec. 18* only) / Mozeen (on *Dec. 26* only)
PATIENCE	Miss [I.] Young

1756 DRURY LANE
Jan. 6

HENRY	Berry
WOLSEY (2)	Havard
BUCKINGHAM	Ross
NORFOLK	Palmer
SURREY	Davies
LORD CHAMBERLAIN	Bransby
CRANMER (2)	Burton
GARDINER	Taswell
CROMWELL (1)	Mozeen
ANNE BULLEN	Mrs Jefferson
PATIENCE	Miss [I.] Young
QUEEN KATHARINE	Mrs Pritchard

(1) May 4, 11
omitted
   CROMWELL

(2) Sept. 25; Nov. 9

WOLSEY	Mossop
CRANMER	Havard

added

SUFFOLK	Blakes
SANDS	Philips
SURVEYOR	Simson
LOVELL	Ackman
GUILDFORD	Marr
CAPUCIUS	Scrase
BUTTS	[H.] Vaughan
BRANDON	Jefferson
CAMPEIUS	Burton
OLD LADY	Mrs Bradshaw

1757 DRURY LANE
Feb. 17

HENRY	Berry
WOLSEY	Mossop
BUCKINGHAM (2)	Ross
NORFOLK (1)	Palmer
SURREY	Davies
LORD CHAMBERLAIN	Bransby

(1) May 10

NORFOLK	Usher
SANDS	Clough
CROMWELL	Mozeen

omitted
   SURVEYOR, LOVELL, GUILDFORD, CAPUCIUS, BUTTS, BRANDON, CAMPEIUS, OLD LADY

HENRY VIII

1757 DRURY LANE (cont.)
Feb. 17 (cont.)

SUFFOLK	Blakes
SANDS (1)	Philips
CROMWELL (1, 2)	Usher
SURVEYOR (1, 2)	Simson
LOVELL (1, 2)	Ackman
GUILDFORD (1, 2)	Marr
CAPUCIUS (1, 2)	Scrase
BUTTS (1, 2)	[H.] Vaughan
BRANDON (1, 2)	Jefferson
CAMPEIUS (1, 2)	Burton
CRANMER	Havard
GARDINER	Taswell
OLD LADY (1, 2)	Mrs Bradshaw
ANNE BULLEN	Mrs Jefferson
PATIENCE	Miss [I.] Young
QUEEN KATHARINE	Mrs Pritchard

(2) Sept. 27; Nov. 28; Dec. 16

BUCKINGHAM	Austin
CROMWELL	Mozeen
omitted	
SAME as *May 10*	

1758 DRURY LANE
Apr. 28

HENRY	Berry
WOLSEY	Mossop
BUCKINGHAM	Austin
NORFOLK	Palmer
SURREY	Davies
LORD CHAMBERLAIN	Bransby
SUFFOLK	Blakes
CROMWELL	Mozeen
CRANMER	Havard
GARDINER	Taswell
SANDS	Philips
ANNE BULLEN (2)	Mrs Jefferson
PATIENCE (1)	Miss [I.] Young
QUEEN KATHARINE	Mrs Pritchard

(1) May 9

PATIENCE	Mrs Vernon

(2) Sept. 21; Nov. 9

ANNE BULLEN	Mrs Glen

1759 DRURY LANE
May 22

HENRY	A Gentleman [Moody (MacMillan, 66, 259)]
WOLSEY (1)	Mossop
BUCKINGHAM	Austin
NORFOLK	Palmer
SURREY	Davies
LORD CHAMBERLAIN	Bransby

(1) Oct. 22

WOLSEY	Havard
CRANMER	Burton
ANNE BULLEN	Mrs Bennet

[Moody's name is in the bill.]

HENRY VIII

1759 DRURY LANE (cont.)
May 22 (cont.)

SUFFOLK	Blakes
SANDS	Philips
CROMWELL	Mozeen
CRANMER (1)	Havard
GARDINER	Clough
ANNE BULLEN (1)	Mrs Glen
PATIENCE	Miss [I.] Young
QUEEN KATHARINE	Mrs Pritchard

[This was Moody's official debut. His actual first appearance, however, had taken place at this theatre on Jan. 12, 1759 as THYREUS in *Antony and Cleopatra*. See p. 116.

1760 DRURY LANE
Apr. 8; May 26

HENRY	Moody
WOLSEY	Havard
BUCKINGHAM	Austin
NORFOLK	Palmer
SURREY	Davies
LORD CHAMBERLAIN	Bransby
SUFFOLK	Blakes
SANDS	Philips
CROMWELL	Mozeen
CRANMER	Burton
GARDINER	Clough
ANNE BULLEN	Mrs Bennet
PATIENCE	Miss [I.] Young
QUEEN KATHARINE	Mrs Pritchard

1761 DRURY LANE
May 1   (1) *May 26; June 4*

HENRY	Bransby
WOLSEY	Havard
BUCKINGHAM	Austin
NORFOLK	Palmer
SURREY	Davies
LORD CHAMBER- LAIN (1)	Kennedy
SUFFOLK	Blakes
CRANMER	Burton
GARDINER	Clough
ANNE BULLEN	Mrs Bennet
PATIENCE	Miss [I.] Young
QUEEN KATHARINE	Mrs Pritchard

LORD CHAMBERLAIN Baddeley

Sept. 30   (1) *Oct. 2*

HENRY	Bransby
WOLSEY	Havard

added
CROMWELL   Mozeen

HENRY VIII

1761 DRURY LANE (cont.)
Sept. 30 (cont.)

BUCKINGHAM	Holland
NORFOLK	Palmer
SURREY	Davies
LORD CHAMBERLAIN	Kennedy
SUFFOLK	Blakes
CRANMER	Burton
GARDINER	Yates
ANNE BULLEN (2)	Mrs Yates
PATIENCE	Miss [I.] Young
QUEEN KATHARINE	Mrs Pritchard

(2) *Oct. 3, 5, 6, 8, 9, 23; Nov. 2*

ANNE BULLEN	Mrs Davies (on Oct. 6, 8, 9, 23 only) Miss Haughton (on Nov. 2 only)

added

SANDS	Philips
CROMWELL	Mozeen

[In the acting version published by Hitch in 1762 the cast is the same as that of the performances on *Oct. 3, 5*, with the following additions:

CAMPEIUS	Packer
CAPUCIUS	Scrase
ABERGAVENNY	Raftor
GUILDFORD	Marr
LOVELL	Ackman
DENNY	Castle
BUTTS	Fox
SURVEYOR	Packer
PORTER	Weston
OLD LADY	Mrs Bradshaw]

[Packer doubled CAMPEIUS and the SURVEYOR.]

1772 COVENT GARDEN
Nov. 6, 7, 9, 11, 13, 16, 18, 20; Dec. 21

HENRY	Clarke
WOLSEY	Bensley
NORFOLK	Perry
SUFFOLK	Owenson
SURREY	Dyer
LORD CHAMBERLAIN	[Lee] Lewes
BUCKINGHAM	Wroughton
CRANMER	Gardner
CROMWELL	Hull
SANDS	Kniveton
GUILDFORD	R. Smith
LOVELL	Davis
CAMPEIUS	Morris
GARDINER	Shuter
CAPUCIUS	Du-Bellamy
BUTTS	Stoppelaer
SURVEYOR	Thompson
BRANDON	Fox
OLD LADY	Mrs Pitt
ANNE BULLEN	Miss Ogilvie
PATIENCE	Mrs [T.] Baker
QUEEN KATHARINE	Mrs Hartley

300

HENRY VIII

1773 COVENT GARDEN

Jan. 18

HENRY	Clarke
WOLSEY	Bensley
NORFOLK	Perry
SUFFOLK	Owenson
SURREY (1)	Dyer
LORD CHAMBER- LAIN	[Lee] Lewes
BUCKINGHAM	Wroughton
CRANMER	Gardner
CROMWELL	Hull
SANDS (2)	Kniveton
GUILDFORD	R. Smith
LOVELL (1, 2)	Davis
CAMPEIUS	Morris
GARDINER	Shuter
CAPUCIUS	Du-Bellamy
BUTTS	Stoppelaer
SURVEYOR	Thompson
BRANDON	Fox
ANNE BULLEN (1)	Miss Ogilvie
PATIENCE	Mrs [T.] Baker
OLD LADY	Mrs Pitt
QUEEN KATHARINE	Mrs Hartley

[In the acting version published by Bell in 1773 there are the following additions to the cast:

ABERGAVENNY	Harris
PORTER	Saunders]

(1) *Jan. 29*

SURREY	Davis
ANNE BULLEN omitted	Mrs Bulkley
LOVELL	

(2) *Feb. 10, 15; Mar. 23*

SANDS omitted	Quick
LOVELL	

Sept. 22

HENRY (1)	Moody
WOLSEY	Bensley
NORFOLK (1)	Davis
SUFFOLK (1)	Owenson
SURREY (1)	Dyer
LORD CHAMBER- LAIN (1)	[Lee] Lewes
BUCKINGHAM	Wroughton
CRANMER	Gardner
CROMWELL	Hull
CAMPEIUS (1)	Du-Bellamy
SANDS (1)	Kniveton
GARDINER	Shuter
ANNE BULLEN (1)	Mrs [T.] Baker
PATIENCE	Miss [S.] Twist
QUEEN KATHARINE	Mrs Hartley

(1) *Oct. 8; Nov. 9; Dec. 22*

HENRY	Clarke
ANNE BULLEN omitted	Miss Ogilvie (on Dec. 22 only)

CAMPEIUS, SANDS, and on *Oct. 8* only, NORFOLK, SUFFOLK, SURREY, LORD CHAMBERLAIN

HENRY VIII

1774 COVENT GARDEN
Feb. 14

HENRY (2)	Clarke
WOLSEY	Bensley
NORFOLK (1, 2)	Davis
SUFFOLK (1, 2)	Owenson
SURREY (1, 2)	Dyer
LORD CHAMBER- LAIN (1, 2)	[Lee] Lewes
BUCKINGHAM	Wroughton
CRANMER (2)	Gardner
CROMWELL (2)	Hull
GARDINER	Shuter
ANNE BULLEN	Miss Ogilvie
PATIENCE (2)	Miss [S.] Twist
QUEEN KATHARINE	Mrs Hartley

(1) *Mar. 21; Apr. 25*
omitted
   NORFOLK, SUFFOLK, SURREY, LORD CHAMBERLAIN

(2) *Oct. 15; Nov. 14; Dec. 29*

HENRY	Moody (on *Oct. 15* only)
CRANMER	Hull
CROMWELL	Whitfield
PATIENCE	Miss Dayes

added
   SANDS   Quick
omitted
   SAME as *Mar. 21*

1775 COVENT GARDEN
Nov. 9

HENRY	Clarke
WOLSEY	Lee
BUCKINGHAM	Wroughton
CRANMER	Hull
CROMWELL	Young
GARDINER	[R.] Wilson
SANDS	Quick
ANNE BULLEN	Miss Ambrose
PATIENCE	Miss Brown
QUEEN KATHARINE	Mrs Jackson

1776 COVENT GARDEN
Nov. 25

HENRY	Clarke
WOLSEY	Lee
BUCKINGHAM	Wroughton
CRANMER	Hull
SURREY	Ward
CROMWELL	Whitfield
GARDINER	[R.] Wilson
SANDS	Wewitzer
LORD CHAMBERLAIN	Lee Lewes
NORFOLK	Davis
SUFFOLK	Booth
LORD CHANCELLOR	Fearon
ANNE BULLEN	Miss Ambrose
PATIENCE	Miss Dayes
QUEEN KATHARINE	Mrs Hartley

HENRY VIII

1776 CHINA HALL, ROTHERHITHE
Sept. 25

HENRY	A Gentleman [unidentified]
BUCKINGHAM	Stacy
NORFOLK	Comerford
SUFFOLK	Kenny
SURREY	Garland
CRANMER	[P.] Lewis
GARDINER	Massey
SANDS	Ware
LORD CHAMBERLAIN	[S.] Johnson
CAMPEIUS	Sparrow
CROMWELL	W. Smith
BUTTS	Ward
WOLSEY	Stokes
QUEEN KATHARINE	Miss Reynolds
ANNE BULLEN	Mrs West
PATIENCE	Mrs Davies
OLD LADY	Mrs Ross
LADY OF THE BEDCHAMBER	Miss C. Reynolds

[In the bill the OLD LADY is called DAME PRATTLE.]

1777 HAYMARKET
Aug. 29; Sept. 5

WOLSEY	Digges
BUCKINGHAM	[J.] Palmer
CRANMER	Younger
SURREY	Davies
CROMWELL	R. Palmer
GARDINER	Parsons
SANDS	[T.] Jackson
LORD CHAMBERLAIN	Egan
NORFOLK	T. Davis
SUFFOLK	Fearon
HENRY	A Gentleman [Fotteral (LC, Aug. 30, in which the name is misspelled 'Fotheril'); first appearance, Aug. 29, in London]
ANNE BULLEN	Mrs Colles
PATIENCE	Miss Twist
QUEEN KATHARINE	Mrs Massey

1778 COVENT GARDEN
Oct. 16

HENRY	Clarke
BUCKINGHAM	Wroughton

HENRY VIII

1778 COVENT GARDEN (cont.)
Oct. 16 (cont.)

CRANMER	Hull
LORD CHAMBERLAIN	Lee Lewes
CROMWELL	Farren
GARDINER	[R.] Wilson
SANDS	Quick
NORFOLK	Peile
SUFFOLK	Booth
ABERGAVENNY	R. Smith
WOLSEY	Digges
ANNE BULLEN	Mrs Morton
PATIENCE	Mrs Farrell
QUEEN KATHARINE	Miss Younge

[ABERGAVENNY appears neither in Pb nor in PA. The fact that R. Smith acted it is referred to by MC on Oct. 28.]

HAYMARKET
June 19, 25; July 2, 8; Aug. 14, 25

WOLSEY	Digges
BUCKINGHAM	[J.] Palmer
CRANMER	Gardner
SURREY	[J.] Aickin
CROMWELL	R. Palmer
GARDINER	Parsons
SANDS	Massey
LORD CHAMBERLAIN	Egan
LORD CHANCELLOR	Blissett
LOVELL	Stevens
NORFOLK	Davis
SUFFOLK	Lamash
HENRY	Usher
ANNE BULLEN	Miss Hale
PATIENCE	Miss Twist
QUEEN KATHARINE	Mrs Massey

1779 HAYMARKET
Aug. 24

WOLSEY	Digges
BUCKINGHAM	[J.] Palmer
CRANMER	Gardner
SURREY	[J.] Aickin
CROMWELL	R. Palmer
GARDINER	Parsons
SANDS	Massey

1779 HAYMARKET (cont.)

Aug. 24 (cont.)

LORD CHAMBERLAIN	Egan
LORD CHANCELLOR	Blissett
LOVELL	Stevens
NORFOLK	Davis
SUFFOLK	Lamash
CAPUCIUS	Kenny
CAMPEIUS	Painter
HENRY	Usher
ANNE BULLEN	Mrs Cuyler
PATIENCE	Miss Twist
QUEEN KATHARINE	Mrs Massey

1780 COVENT GARDEN

Oct. 30

HENRY	Clarke
BUCKINGHAM	Wroughton
CRANMER	Hull
SURREY	Whitfield
LORD CHAMBERLAIN	Robson
GARDINER	[R.] Wilson
CROMWELL	Davies
SANDS	Jones
NORFOLK	Peile
SUFFOLK	Booth
WOLSEY	Henderson
ANNE BULLEN	Mrs Inchbald
QUEEN KATHARINE	Miss Younge

1781 COVENT GARDEN

Apr. 16

HENRY	Clarke
BUCKINGHAM	Wroughton
CRANMER	Hull
SURREY	Whitfield
LORD CHAMBERLAIN	Robson
GARDINER	[R.] Wilson
CROMWELL	Davies
SANDS	Jones
NORFOLK	Peile
SUFFOLK	Booth
WOLSEY	Henderson
ANNE BULLEN	Mrs Inchbald
QUEEN KATHARINE	Miss Younge

HENRY VIII

1781 HAYMARKET
Aug. 7, 17

WOLSEY	Digges
SURREY	[J.] Aickin
SUFFOLK	Lamash
LORD CHAMBERLAIN	Egan
NORFOLK	Davis
CROMWELL	R. Palmer
HENRY	Usher

[The above consisted of III. ii only. The entertainment on these evenings was called *The School of Shakespeare*, for a description of which see p. 73.]

1782 COVENT GARDEN
Dec. 30

HENRY	Clarke
BUCKINGHAM	Wroughton
CRANMER	Hull
SURREY	Whitfield
LORD CHAMBERLAIN	Wewitzer
GARDINER	[R.] Wilson
CROMWELL	Davies
SANDS	Jones
NORFOLK	Fearon
SUFFOLK	Booth
WOLSEY	Henderson
ANNE BULLEN	Miss Cleland
OLD LADY	Mrs Pitt
QUEEN KATHARINE	Miss Younge

1783 COVENT GARDEN
Jan. 6

HENRY	Clarke
BUCKINGHAM	Wroughton
CRANMER	Hull
SURREY	Whitfield
LORD CHAMBERLAIN (2)	Wewitzer
GARDINER (1)	[R.] Wilson
CROMWELL	Davies
SANDS	Jones
NORFOLK	Fearon
SUFFOLK	Booth
WOLSEY	Henderson
ANNE BULLEN (2)	Miss Cleland
OLD LADY	Mrs Pitt
QUEEN KATHARINE	Miss Younge

(1) *May 26*

GARDINER	Edwin

(2) *Nov. 10*

LORD CHAMBERLAIN	Bonnor
ANNE BULLEN	Mrs Inchbald
added	
LOVELL	Chalmers

306

1785 COVENT GARDEN
Apr. 8

HENRY	Clarke
BUCKINGHAM	Wroughton
CRANMER	Hull
SURREY	Farren
LORD CHAMBERLAIN	Bonnor
CROMWELL	Davies
GARDINER	Wewitzer
SANDS	T. Kennedy
NORFOLK	Fearon
SUFFOLK	Booth
LOVELL	Chalmers
WOLSEY	Henderson
ANNE BULLEN	Mrs Inchbald
OLD LADY	Mrs Pitt
QUEEN KATHARINE	Miss Younge

1787 COVENT GARDEN
Mar. 26

HENRY (1)	[F.] Aickin	(1) *May 14*		
BUCKINGHAM	Farren	HENRY	Booth
CRANMER	Hull	SANDS	Wewitzer
GARDINER	Edwin	(2) *Nov. 19*		
CROMWELL	Davies	SANDS	Wewitzer
SANDS (1, 2)	Booth		
SURREY	Macready		
LORD CHAMBERLAIN	Cubitt		
NORFOLK	Fearon		
SUFFOLK	Gardner		
WOLSEY	Pope		
ANNE BULLEN	Mrs Inchbald		
QUEEN KATHARINE	Mrs Pope		

1788 DRURY LANE
Nov. 25, 29; Dec. 2, 6, 13, 20, 27

HENRY	[J.] Palmer
BUCKINGHAM	Wroughton
CRANMER	[J.] Aickin
NORFOLK	Whitfield
SUFFOLK	Williams
SURREY	Barrymore
LORD CHAMBERLAIN	R. Palmer
CROMWELL	Kemble
SANDS	Baddeley
GARDINER	Suett
CAMPEIUS	Packer

HENRY VIII

1788 DRURY LANE (cont.)
Nov. 25, 29; Dec. 2, 6, 13, 20, 27 (cont.)

GUILDFORD	Lamash
LOVELL	Fawcett
BUTTS	[F.] Waldron
SURVEYOR	Benson
WOLSEY	Bensley
ANNE BULLEN	Mrs Farmer
OLD LADY	Mrs Love
QUEEN KATHARINE	Mrs Siddons

1789 DRURY LANE
Jan. 3, 10, 24

HENRY	[J.] Palmer
BUCKINGHAM	Wroughton
CRANMER	[J.] Aickin
NORFOLK	Whitfield
SUFFOLK	Williames
SURREY	Barrymore
LORD CHAMBER-LAIN (1)	R. Palmer
CROMWELL (1)	Kemble
SANDS	Baddeley
GARDINER	Suett
CAMPEIUS	Packer
GUILDFORD	Lamash
LOVELL	Fawcett
BUTTS	[F.] Waldron
SURVEYOR (1)	Benson
WOLSEY (1)	Bensley
ANNE BULLEN	Mrs Farmer
OLD LADY	Mrs Love
QUEEN KATHARINE	Mrs Siddons

(1) Feb. 3; Apr. 29

LORD CHAMBERLAIN	Benson
CROMWELL	R. Palmer
WOLSEY	Kemble
omitted	
SURVEYOR	

1792 DRURY LANE (company at KING'S, HAYMARKET)
Mar. 26

HENRY	[J.] Palmer
WOLSEY	Bensley
CAMPEIUS	Packer
CAPUCIUS	Phillimore
BUCKINGHAM	Wroughton
SURREY	Barrymore
LORD CHAMBER-LAIN (1)	R. Palmer
GARDINER	Suett
SANDS	Baddeley
LOVELL	Fawcett

(1) Apr. 17

LORD CHAMBERLAIN	Benson
SURVEYOR	Webb
added	
SUFFOLK	Caulfield

308

HENRY VIII

1792 DRURY LANE (company at KING'S, HAYMARKET) (*cont.*)

Mar. 26 (*cont.*)

CROMWELL	Kemble
BUTTS	[F.] Waldron
SURVEYOR (1)	Benson
BRANDON	Banks
SERGEANT	Lyons
DOOR-KEEPER	Jones
CRIER	Alfred
CRANMER	[J.] Aickin
NORFOLK	Whitfield
QUEEN KATHARINE	Mrs Siddons
ANNE BULLEN	Mrs Powell
OLD LADY	Mrs Booth
PATIENCE	Mrs Bland
AGATHA	Miss Collins

1793 DRURY LANE (company at HAYMARKET)

Mar. 9

HENRY	[J.] Palmer
WOLSEY	Bensley
CAMPEIUS	Packer
CAPUCIUS	Phillimore
CRANMER	[J.] Aickin
NORFOLK	Whitfield
BUCKINGHAM	Wroughton
SUFFOLK	Caulfield
SURREY	Barrymore
LORD CHANCELLOR	Maddocks
LORD CHAMBER-LAIN (1)	R. Palmer
GARDINER	Suett
SANDS	Baddeley
GUILDFORD	Bland
LOVELL	Fawcett
CROMWELL	Kemble
BUTTS	[F.] Waldron
SURVEYOR (1)	Benson
BRANDON	Banks
SERGEANT	Lyons
DOOR-KEEPER (1)	Jones
CRIER (1)	Alfred
QUEEN KATHARINE	Mrs Siddons
ANNE BULLEN	Mrs Powell
OLD LADY	Mrs Booth
PATIENCE (1)	Mrs Bland
AGATHA	Miss Collins

(1) May 14

LORD CHAMBERLAIN	Benson
SURVEYOR	Webb
CRIER	Jones
PATIENCE	Mrs Jones
omitted	
DOOR-KEEPER	

HENRY VIII

1793 COVENT GARDEN
May 24

HENRY	Holman
BUCKINGHAM	Farren
CRANMER	Hull
CROMWELL	Davies
LORD CHAMBERLAIN	Cubitt
GARDINER	Quick
SURREY	Macready
NORFOLK	Harley
SUFFOLK	Marshall
WOLSEY	Pope
ANNE BULLEN	Miss Chapman
QUEEN KATHARINE	Mrs Pope

1794 DRURY LANE
May 1, 14

HENRY	[J.] Palmer
WOLSEY	Bensley
CAMPEIUS (1)	Packer
CAPUCIUS (1)	Phillimore
CRANMER	[J.] Aickin
NORFOLK	Whitfield
BUCKINGHAM	Wroughton
SUFFOLK (1)	Caulfield
SURREY	Barrymore
LORD CHANCELLOR (1)	Maddocks
LORD CHAMBERLAIN (1)	Trueman
GARDINER	Suett
SANDS (1, 2)	Baddeley
GUILDFORD (1)	Bland
LOVELL (1)	Dignum
CROMWELL	C. Kemble
BUTTS (1)	[F.] Waldron
SURVEYOR (1)	Benson
BRANDON (1)	Banks
SERGEANT (1)	Lyons
CRIER (1)	Evans
DOOR-KEEPER (1)	Jones
QUEEN KATHARINE	Mrs Siddons
ANNE BULLEN (1)	Mrs Powell
OLD LADY (1)	Mrs Booth
PATIENCE	Mrs Bland
AGATHA (1)	Miss Collins

(1) *Oct. 18*

SANDS	Hollingsworth
ANNE BULLEN	Miss DeCamp

omitted
CAMPEIUS, CAPUCIUS, SUFFOLK, LORD CHANCELLOR, LORD CHAMBERLAIN, SANDS [see note], GUILDFORD, LOVELL, BUTTS, SURVEYOR, BRANDON, SERGEANT, CRIER, DOORKEEPER, OLD LADY, AGATHA

[SANDS is omitted from the bill, but Powell has, 'Sands Mr. Hollingsworth, Mr. Baddeley ill'.]

(2) *Dec. 9*

SANDS	Hollingsworth

HENRY VIII

1795 DRURY LANE
Nov. 6

HENRY	[J.] Palmer
WOLSEY	Bensley
CAMPEIUS	Packer
CAPUCIUS	Phillimore
CRANMER	[J.] Aickin
NORFOLK	Whitfield
BUCKINGHAM	Wroughton
SUFFOLK	Caulfield
SURREY	Barrymore
LORD CHANCELLOR	Maddocks
LORD CHAMBERLAIN	Trueman
GARDINER	Suett
SANDS	Hollingsworth
GUILDFORD	Russell
LOVELL	Dignum
CROMWELL	C. Kemble
BUTTS	[J.] Burton
SURVEYOR	Benson
BRANDON	Banks
SERGEANT	[J.] Cooke
CRIER	Evans
DOOR-KEEPER	Jones
QUEEN KATHARINE	Mrs Siddons
ANNE BULLEN	Mrs Powell
OLD LADY	Mrs Booth
PATIENCE	Mrs Bland
AGATHA	Miss Heard

1796 DRURY LANE
Jan. 1

HENRY	[J.] Palmer
WOLSEY	Bensley
CAMPEIUS	Packer
CAPUCIUS	Phillimore
CRANMER (1)	[J.] Aickin
NORFOLK	Whitfield
BUCKINGHAM	Wroughton
SUFFOLK	Caulfield
SURREY	Barrymore
LORD CHANCELLOR	Maddocks
LORD CHAMBERLAIN	Trueman
GARDINER	Suett
SANDS (1)	[F.] Waldron
GUILDFORD	Russell
LOVELL	Dignum
CROMWELL	C. Kemble

(1) *Jan. 15*

CRANMER	Benson
SANDS	Hollingsworth
BUTTS	[F.] Waldron
SURVEYOR	Webb

HENRY VIII

1796 DRURY LANE (cont.)
Jan. 1 (cont.)

BUTTS (I)	[J.] Burton
SURVEYOR (I)	Benson
QUEEN KATHARINE	Mrs Siddons
ANNE BULLEN	Miss DeCamp
OLD LADY	Mrs Booth
PATIENCE	Mrs Bland
AGATHA	Miss Heard

HAYMARKET
Aug. 30

WOLSEY	[J.] Palmer
HENRY	R. Palmer

[The above consisted of parts of III. ii only. The entertainment on this evening was called *The School of Shakespeare*, for a description of which see p. 101.]

1799 COVENT GARDEN
May 15

HENRY	Holman
CROMWELL	Lewis
GARDINER	Munden
SANDS	Fawcett [Jr.]
BUCKINGHAM	H. Johnston
SURREY	Knight
CRANMER	Murray
BUTTS	Emery
NORFOLK	Whitfield
SUFFOLK	Waddy
CAMPEIUS	Davenport
BRANDON	Claremont
DOOR-KEEPER	Claremont
LORD CHAMBERLAIN	Clarke
LOVELL	Farley
SURVEYOR	Thompson
LORD CHANCELLOR	Whitmore
PORTER	Rees
CAPUCIUS	Abbot
PORTER'S MAN	Wilde
CRIER	Street
SERGEANT	[J. N.] Lee
ABERGAVENNY	Curties
WOLSEY	Pope
ANNE BULLEN	Miss Chapman
PATIENCE	Mrs Atkins
QUEEN KATHARINE	Mrs [M.A.] Pope

[Claremont doubled BRANDON and the DOOR-KEEPER.]

THE HUMOURISTS

An alteration, probably by Theophilus Cibber, of HENRY IV, PART II, q.v.

THE JEW OF VENICE

George Granville, Baron Lansdowne's alteration of
THE MERCHANT OF VENICE, q.v.

JULIUS CAESAR

(1) 'As it is Acted at the Theatre Royal in Drury-Lane.'
1751   J. and R. Tonson.
A reading edition, verbatim throughout.

(2) 'As Performed at the Theatre-Royal, Covent-Garden. Regulated from the Prompt-Book.'
1773   John Bell.
In *Act I. i* the speeches of Flavius and Marullus are given to Casca, except for *59–end*, which is made into one speech and spoken by Decius. In *iii* Cicero's speeches are given to Trebonius.
Act II. i. 307–end (Ligarius decides to join the conspiracy) is omitted. In *iv* the Soothsayer's speeches are given to Artemidorus.
Act III. i. 1–24 (Artemidorus and Popilius make suit to Caesar) and *iii* entire (Cinna the Poet) are omitted.
In *Act IV. ii* Lucilius's speeches are given to Trebonius, as are Messala's speeches in *iii*. Omitted is *iii. 123–38a* (the Poet).
Act V. i. 69–93a (Cassius's forebodings) is omitted. In *iii* Messala's speeches are given to Trebonius, and Titinius's speeches to Casca. From *iv* is omitted *1–17a* (young Cato's death). In *v* Clitus's speeches are given to Decius, and Volumnius's speeches to Metellus.
Throughout there are minor omissions.
See also Odell, ii. 35–38.

(3) 'As it is Acted at the Theatres-Royal in Drury-Lane and Covent-Garden.'
1780   Harrison and Co.
This is identical with (2).

(4) 'Marked with the Variations in the Manager's Book, at the Theatre-Royal in Drury-Lane.'
1786   C. Bathurst [&c.].
This shows a few variations from (2), with which it is otherwise identical. The most important change is the substitution of five new lines for Brutus's last speeches before his suicide (*V. v. 37–50a*).

(5) 'Taken from the Manager's Book, at the Theatre Royal, Drury-Lane.'
n.d. [*c.* 1788]   R. Butters.
This is identical with (4).

1751 COVENT GARDEN

Feb. 19

BRUTUS	Quin
CASSIUS	Ryan
CAESAR	Sparks
CASCA	Ridout
TREBONIUS (2)	Anderson
METELLUS (2)	Bransby
DECIUS (1, 2)	Elrington
LEPIDUS (2)	Bencraft
ANTONY	Barry
OCTAVIUS	Gibson
LIGARIUS (1, 2)	Usher
CINNA (2)	Redman
PUBLIUS (2)	Roberts
1ST CITIZEN (2)	Collins
2ND CITIZEN (2)	Dunstall
3RD CITIZEN (2)	Stoppelaer
4TH CITIZEN (2)	Barrington
5TH CITIZEN (2)	Arthur
CALPHURNIA (2)	Mrs Bambridge
PORTIA	Mrs Woffington

(1) Mar. 7

DECIUS	Usher
LIGARIUS	Holtom

(2) May 1
omitted
TREBONIUS, METELLUS, DECIUS, LEPIDUS, LIGARIUS, CINNA, PUBLIUS, CITIZENS, CALPHURNIA

1753 COVENT GARDEN

May 7

ANTONY	Barry
CAESAR	Bridgwater
TREBONIUS	Anderson
METELLUS	Bransby
CINNA	Redman
LEPIDUS	Bencraft
BRUTUS	Sparks
CASSIUS	Ryan
LIGARIUS	Holtom
PINDARUS	Ricard
ANTONY'S SERVANT	Cushing
LUCIUS	Miss Mullart
CASCA	Ridout
OCTAVIUS	Usher
1ST CITIZEN	Arthur
2ND CITIZEN	Collins
3RD CITIZEN	Barrington
4TH CITIZEN	Dunstall
5TH CITIZEN	Stoppelaer
CALPHURNIA	Mrs Bambridge
PORTIA	Mrs Bland

(1) May 14
added

DECIUS	White
PUBLIUS	R Smith

1754 COVENT GARDEN
Mar. 9, 12, 16

ANTONY	Barry
CAESAR	Bridgwater
TREBONIUS	Anderson
METELLUS	Stevens
DECIUS	White
CINNA	Redman
LEPIDUS	Bencraft
SOOTHSAYER	Marten
BRUTUS	Sparks
CASSIUS	Ryan
LIGARIUS	Holtom
PINDARUS	R. Smith
ANTONY'S SERVANT	Cushing
LUCIUS	Miss Mullart
CASCA	Ridout
OCTAVIUS	Usher
1ST CITIZEN	Arthur
2ND CITIZEN	Collins
3RD CITIZEN	Barrington
4TH CITIZEN	Dunstall
5TH CITIZEN	Stoppelaer
CALPHURNIA	Mrs Vincent
PORTIA	Mrs Bland

1755 COVENT GARDEN
Jan. 28

BRUTUS	Sheridan
CAESAR	Sparks
TREBONIUS	Anderson
METELLUS	Stevens
CINNA	Redman
LEPIDUS	Bencraft
ANTONY	Smith
CASSIUS	Ryan
DECIUS	White
PINDARUS	R. Smith
SOOTHSAYER	Marten
ANTONY'S SERVANT	Cushing
CASCA	Ridout
OCTAVIUS	Gibson
1ST CITIZEN	Arthur
2ND CITIZEN	Collins
3RD CITIZEN	Barrington
4TH CITIZEN	Dunstall
5TH CITIZEN	Stoppelaer

1755 COVENT GARDEN (cont.)
Jan. 28 (cont.)
- CALPHURNIA — Mrs Vincent
- PORTIA — Mrs Hamilton

1758 COVENT GARDEN
Apr. 14
- ANTONY — Barry
- BRUTUS — Sparks
- CAESAR — Clarke
- TREBONIUS — Anderson
- LUCILIUS — Buck
- CINNA — Redman
- LEPIDUS — Bencraft
- CASSIUS — Ryan
- DECIUS — White
- PINDARUS — R. Smith
- SOOTHSAYER — Marten
- ANTONY'S SERVANT — Cushing
- CASCA — Ridout
- OCTAVIUS — Gibson
- 1ST CITIZEN — Arthur
- 2ND CITIZEN — Collins
- 3RD CITIZEN — Barrington
- 4TH CITIZEN — Dunstall
- 5TH CITIZEN — Costollo
- 6TH CITIZEN — Stoppelaer
- CALPHURNIA — Mrs Vincent
- PORTIA — Mrs Elmy

1766 COVENT GARDEN
Jan. 31; Feb. 3, 7, 24
- BRUTUS — Walker
- CASSIUS — Smith
- ANTONY — Ross
- CAESAR — Clarke
- CASCA — Gibson
- CINNA — Gardner
- METELLUS — Cushing
- LEPIDUS — Morris
- LIGARIUS — Holtom
- OCTAVIUS — Hull
- PINDARUS — R. Smith
- SOOTHSAYER — Redman
- VOLUMNIUS — Weller
- POPILIUS — Hallam
- LUCILIUS — Murden

1766 COVENT GARDEN (cont.)

Jan. 31; Feb. 3, 7, 24 (cont.)

PUBLIUS	Wignell
LUCIUS	Master Besford
ANTONY'S SERVANT	Perry
TREBONIUS	Anderson
DECIUS	Davis
1ST CITIZEN	Barrington
2ND CITIZEN	Dunstall
3RD CITIZEN	Costollo
4TH CITIZEN	[P.] Lewis
CALPHURNIA	Mrs Vincent
PORTIA	Mrs Bellamy

1767 COVENT GARDEN

Apr. 25

BRUTUS	Walker
CASSIUS	Smith
ANTONY	Hull
CAESAR	Clarke
CASCA	Gibson
CINNA	Gardner
METELLUS	Cushing
LEPIDUS	Buck
LIGARIUS	Holtom
OCTAVIUS	Du-Bellamy
TREBONIUS	Perry
DECIUS	Davis
1ST CITIZEN	Barrington
2ND CITIZEN	Dunstall
3RD CITIZEN	Morgan
CALPHURNIA	Mrs Vincent
PORTIA	Mrs Bellamy

[Genest (v. 136) erroneously assigns ANTONY to Ross.]

1769 HAYMARKET

Sept. 11

BRUTUS	Sheridan
OCTAVIUS	Du-Bellamy
LEPIDUS	Lings
DECIUS	Jacobs
CINNA	Summers
CASCA	[C.] Bannister
ANTONY	A Young Gentleman [Miller (WEP, May 12, 1770); first appearance on the stage]
PINDARUS	Vandermere
TREBONIUS	Wheeler

1769 HAYMARKET (cont.)

Sept. 11 (cont.)

METELLUS	Kearny
CAESAR	[J.] Aickin
ARTEMIDORUS	Sharpless
POPILIUS	Farrell
1ST CITIZEN	[I.] Sparks
2ND CITIZEN	Castle
3RD CITIZEN	Hamilton
CASSIUS	Sowdon
CALPHURNIA	Mrs Du-Bellamy
PORTIA	Mrs Dyer

1773 COVENT GARDEN

May 4

ANTONY	Smith
BRUTUS	Bensley
CASSIUS	Hull
CAESAR	Clarke
CASCA	Gardner
OCTAVIUS	Wroughton
TREBONIUS	Perry
DECIUS	Davis
PUBLIUS	Wignell
METELLUS	Cushing
1ST CITIZEN	Dunstall
2ND CITIZEN	Quick
3RD CITIZEN	Saunders
4TH CITIZEN	Hamilton
CALPHURNIA	Mrs Vincent
PORTIA	Mrs Hartley

[In the acting version published by Bell in 1773 the cast is the same as that of this performance, with the following additions:

LIGARIUS	Holtom
CINNA	[R.] Bates
PINDARUS	R. Smith]

1780 DRURY LANE

Jan. 24, 25

ANTONY	Smith
CASSIUS (1)	Henry
CASCA (1)	Gardner
CAESAR	Packer
OCTAVIUS	Farren
TREBONIUS	Chaplin
DECIUS	Wrighten
METELLUS	Williams

(1) *Feb. 15, 19; Mar. 11; Apr. 27*

CASSIUS	Bensley
CASCA	[J.] Aickin

1780 DRURY LANE (cont.)

Jan. 24, 25 (cont.)

CINNA	Norris
PINDARUS	R. Palmer
SOOTHSAYER	Fawcett
ANTONY'S SERVANT	Phillimore
LUCIUS	Master Pulley
1ST CITIZEN	Baddeley
2ND CITIZEN	[F.] Waldron
3RD CITIZEN	[J.] Burton
4TH CITIZEN	Holcroft
BRUTUS	[J.] Palmer
CALPHURNIA	Miss Sherry
PORTIA	Mrs Baddeley

[On *Jan. 24* both Pb and PA assign CASCA to [J.] Aickin. But 'Mr. Gardner ... read Casca, at a short notice, on Mr. Aickin's being taken ill' (Gaz, Jan. 25). On *Jan. 25* Gardner's name is in the bill.]

KING JOHN

(1) 'As Performed at the Theatre-Royal, Drury-Lane. Regulated from the Prompt-Book.'

1773   John Bell.

Following are the principal omissions:

Act II. i. *159b–97* (Constance and Elinor quarrel).

Act III. i. *204–23* (Pandulph's demands perplex King Philip), *268–94a* (Pandulph decries King Philip's oaths); iv. *140–59* (Pandulph incites the Dauphin against John).

Act IV. ii. *17–39* (the courtiers question John's 'double coronation'), *147–59a* (Peter of Pomfret).

Act V. v entire (the loss of the French army's supply on Goodwin sands); vii. *74–98* (the Dauphin's capitulation).

Following *III. i. 133* are inserted 12 lines from *The Troublesome Raigne of King John, Part I*, 1591, Act I. ii. IV. ii. *251a* ('Young Arthur is alive') is transposed to follow *259*. In IV. iii Bigot's speeches are given to Essex. In V. iv Melun's speeches are given to Chatillon.

See also Odell, ii. 39–40.

(2) 'Marked with the Variations of the Manager's Book, at the Theatre-Royal in Drury-Lane.'

1784   C. Bathurst [&c.].

This is identical with (1).

(3) 'Revised by J. P. Kemble. . . . As it is acted [at] the Theatre Royal, Drury Lane. November 15 [*recte* 20], 1800.'

n.d. [1800]   C. Lowndes.

This is the same as (1), except that the following are also omitted: *I. i. 188–216*

KING JOHN

(the Bastard's 'mounting spirit'), and *V. ii. 9–64* (Salisbury's dismay at the 'infection of the time'). The following, omitted in (1), are retained: *II. i. 163b–73*, which is substituted for *122–33*, and *V. v.*

1751 COVENT GARDEN

Feb. 23, 25   (1) *Feb. 28; Mar. 2, 4; Apr. 25*

JOHN	Quin	ESSEX	Redman
HUBERT	Bridgwater	CONSTANCE	Mrs Woffington
PRINCE HENRY	Miss Morrison		
SALISBURY	Ridout		
PEMBROKE	Gibson		
ESSEX (1)	Elrington		
BASTARD	Barry		
KING PHILIP	Ryan		
DAUPHIN	[T.] Lacy		
ARTHUR	Miss Mullart		
AUSTRIA	Bransby		
CHATILLON	Dyer		
PANDULPH	Sparks		
ELINOR	Mrs Elmy		
BLANCH	Mrs Vincent		
CONSTANCE (1)	Mrs Cibber		

1754 DRURY LANE

Jan. 23, 26, 28, 31; Feb. 2, 6, 8   (1) *Mar. 16*

JOHN	Mossop	omitted
SALISBURY	Palmer	PRINCE HENRY, ESSEX, CITIZEN OF ANGERS, ENGLISH HERALD, R. FALCONBRIDGE, GURNEY, AUSTRIA, CHATILLON, FRENCH HERALD, LADY FALCONBRIDGE
PEMBROKE	Blakes	
HUBERT	Berry	
PRINCE HENRY (1)	Mrs Toogood	
ESSEX (1)	Jefferson	
CITIZEN OF ANGERS (1)	Burton	
ENGLISH HERALD (1)	Scrase	
R. FALCONBRIDGE (1)	Simson	
GURNEY (1)	W. Vaughan	
BASTARD	Garrick	
KING PHILIP	Davies	
DAUPHIN	Lacey	
PANDULPH	Havard	
AUSTRIA (1)	Mozeen	
CHATILLON (1)	Vernon	
FRENCH HERALD (1)	Ackman	
ARTHUR	Master Simson	
LADY FALCONBRIDGE (1)	Mrs Bennet	

320

KING JOHN

1754 DRURY LANE (cont.)
Jan. 23, 26, 28, 31; Feb. 2, 6, 8 (cont.)

ELINOR	Mrs Mills
BLANCH	Miss Minors
CONSTANCE	Mrs Cibber

1758 COVENT GARDEN
Apr. 17

JOHN	Sparks
HUBERT	Ridout
PRINCE HENRY	R. Smith
SALISBURY	Anderson
PEMBROKE	Cushing
ESSEX	Redman
BASTARD	Barry
KING PHILIP	Ryan
PANDULPH	Gibson
AUSTRIA	Marten
CHATILLON	White
DAUPHIN	Dyer
ARTHUR	Miss Mullart
ELINOR	Mrs Elmy
BLANCH	Mrs Vincent
CONSTANCE	Mrs Bellamy

1760 DRURY LANE
Dec. 17, 20, 23

JOHN	Sheridan
SALISBURY	Packer
PEMBROKE	Blakes
HUBERT	Havard
PRINCE HENRY	Master Cautherley
ESSEX	Fox
CITIZEN OF ANGERS	Burton
ENGLISH HERALD	Moody
R. FALCONBRIDGE	Johnston
GURNEY	Watkins
BASTARD	Garrick
KING PHILIP	Davies
DAUPHIN	Austin
PANDULPH	Bransby
AUSTRIA	Mozeen
CHATILLON	Scrase
FRENCH HERALD	Ackman
ARTHUR	Master Kennedy

1760 DRURY LANE (*cont.*)

Dec. 17, 20, 23 (cont.)

LADY FALCON-BRIDGE	Mrs Johnston
ELINOR	Mrs Bennet
BLANCH	Miss Read
CONSTANCE	Mrs Yates

COVENT GARDEN

Dec. 9, 10, 17, 23

JOHN	Sparks
BASTARD	Smith
PRINCE HENRY	R. Smith
SALISBURY	Anderson
PEMBROKE	Hull
ESSEX	Redman
HUBERT	Ridout
KING PHILIP	Clarke
PANDULPH	Gibson
AUSTRIA	Buck
CHATILLON	Davis
DAUPHIN	Dyer
ARTHUR	Miss Mullart
ELINOR	Mrs Elmy
BLANCH	Mrs Vincent
CONSTANCE	Mrs Ward

1761 DRURY LANE

Apr. 2

JOHN	Sheridan
SALISBURY	Packer
PEMBROKE	Blakes
HUBERT	Havard
PRINCE HENRY	Master Cautherley
ESSEX	Fox
CITIZEN OF ANGERS	Burton
ENGLISH HERALD	Moody
R. FALCONBRIDGE	Johnston
GURNEY	Watkins
BASTARD	Garrick
KING PHILIP	Davies
DAUPHIN	Austin
PANDULPH	Bransby
AUSTRIA	Mozeen
CHATILLON	Scrase
FRENCH HERALD	Ackman

KING JOHN

1761 DRURY LANE (cont.)
Apr. 2 (cont.)

ARTHUR	Master Kennedy
LADY FALCON- BRIDGE	Mrs Johnston
ELINOR	Mrs Bennet
BLANCH	Miss Read
CONSTANCE	Mrs Yates

COVENT GARDEN
Jan. 3

JOHN (1)	Sparks
BASTARD	Smith
PRINCE HENRY	R. Smith
SALISBURY (1)	Anderson
PEMBROKE (1)	Hull
ESSEX (1)	Redman
HUBERT (1)	Ridout
KING PHILIP	Clarke
PANDULPH	Gibson
AUSTRIA (1)	Buck
CHATILLON (1)	Davis
DAUPHIN	Dyer
ARTHUR (1)	Miss Mullart
ELINOR	Mrs Elmy
BLANCH	Mrs Vincent
CONSTANCE	Mrs Ward

(1) Dec. 30

JOHN	Ross
SALISBURY	Hull
PEMBROKE	Anderson
ESSEX	Gardner
HUBERT	Sparks
ARTHUR	Mrs Evans [i.e. formerly Miss Mullart]

omitted
AUSTRIA, CHATILLON

[PA retains Anderson as SALISBURY, and Hull as PEMBROKE. This is probably correct.]

1762 COVENT GARDEN
Jan. 2, 6

JOHN	Ross
PRINCE HENRY	R. Smith
SALISBURY	Anderson
PEMBROKE	Hull
ESSEX	Gardner
BASTARD	Smith
HUBERT (1)	Sparks
KING PHILIP	Clarke
PANDULPH (1)	Gibson
DAUPHIN	Dyer
CHATILLON	Davis
AUSTRIA	Buck
ARTHUR	Mrs Evans
ELINOR	Mrs Elmy
BLANCH	Mrs Vincent
CONSTANCE	Mrs Ward

(1) Jan. 20, 27; Feb. 13

HUBERT	Gibson
PANDULPH	Tindal

KING JOHN

1764 COVENT GARDEN
Dec. 21

JOHN	Ross
PEMBROKE	Hull
PRINCE HENRY	R. Smith
ESSEX	Gardner
SALISBURY	Anderson
BASTARD	Smith
HUBERT	Sparks
KING PHILIP	Clarke
DAUPHIN	White
PANDULPH	Tindal
CHATILLON	Davis
AUSTRIA	Buck
ARTHUR	Miss Valois
ELINOR	Mrs [D.] Baker
BLANCH	Miss Vincent
CONSTANCE	Mrs Bellamy

1766 DRURY LANE
Mar. 20; Apr. 11

JOHN	Powell
HUBERT	Havard
SALISBURY	Packer
PEMBROKE	[F.] Aickin
BASTARD	Holland
KING PHILIP	Lee
ARTHUR	Miss Rogers
PANDULPH	Bransby
DAUPHIN	Cautherley
CHATILLON	Vernon
ENGLISH HERALD	Moody
ELINOR	Mrs Bennet
BLANCH	Miss Plym
LADY FALCON- BRIDGE	Mrs Hopkins
CONSTANCE	Mrs Yates

[The ENGLISH HERALD is not given in the bills, but is listed by Genest (v. 94) The assignment appears to be correct; Moody acted the part regularly from 1760 to 1767.]

COVENT GARDEN
May 6

JOHN	Ross
PRINCE HENRY	R. Smith
PEMBROKE	Gardner
ESSEX	Redman

(1) *Oct. 31; Nov. 3, 5*

CONSTANCE	Mrs Ward

KING JOHN

1766 COVENT GARDEN (cont.)

May 6 (cont.)

SALISBURY	Anderson
BASTARD	Smith
HUBERT	Gibson
ARTHUR	Master Wignell [first appearance on the stage]
R. FALCONBRIDGE	Holtom
AUSTRIA	Buck
KING PHILIP	Clarke
DAUPHIN	Hull
CHATILLON	Davis
CITIZEN OF ANGERS	Wignell
PANDULPH	Walker
BLANCH	Miss Vincent
LADY FALCON-BRIDGE	Mrs Ferguson
ELINOR	Mrs Vincent
CONSTANCE (I)	Mrs Bellamy

1767 DRURY LANE

Feb. 7, 20

JOHN	Powell
HUBERT	Havard
SALISBURY	Packer
PEMBROKE	Fawcett
PRINCE HENRY	Master Burton
ESSEX	Strange
CITIZEN OF ANGERS	Hurst
BASTARD	Holland
KING PHILIP	Bensley
ARTHUR	Miss Rogers
PANDULPH	Bransby
DAUPHIN	[F.] Aickin
AUSTRIA	Keen
FRENCH HERALD	Ackman
ENGLISH HERALD	Moody
CHATILLON	Vernon
ELINOR	Mrs Bennet
BLANCH	Miss Plym
LADY FALCON-BRIDGE	Mrs Lee
CONSTANCE	Mrs Yates

[In the acting version published by Bell in 1773 the cast is the same as that of these performances (save for the assignment of Burton to the CITIZEN OF ANGERS). There are the following additions:

R. FALCONBRIDGE	Castle
GURNEY	Watkins]

325

1767 COVENT GARDEN
May 28

JOHN (1)	Ross
PEMBROKE (1)	Gardner
PRINCE HENRY (1)	R. Smith
ESSEX (1)	Redman
SALISBURY (1)	Du-Bellamy
BASTARD	Smith
R. FALCON-BRIDGE (1)	Holtom
AUSTRIA (1)	Buck
HUBERT (1)	Gibson
KING PHILIP	Clarke
DAUPHIN (1)	Hull
CHATILLON (1)	Davis
CITIZEN OF ANGERS	Wignell
PANDULPH (1)	Walker
ARTHUR (1)	Master Wignell
ELINOR	Mrs Vincent
BLANCH (1)	Miss Vincent
LADY FALCON-BRIDGE	Mrs Ferguson
CONSTANCE	Mrs Bellamy

(1) *Sept. 23; Dec. 22*

JOHN	Powell
PEMBROKE	Davis
PRINCE HENRY	[Lee] Lewes
ESSEX	Gardner
SALISBURY	Perry
R. FALCONBRIDGE	Weller (on *Sept. 23* only)
AUSTRIA	Morris
HUBERT	Bensley
DAUPHIN	Dyer
CHATILLON	Hull
PANDULPH	Gibson
ARTHUR	Miss Ford
BLANCH	Mrs Du-Bellamy

1769 COVENT GARDEN
May 3

JOHN	Powell
PEMBROKE	Davis
PRINCE HENRY	[Lee] Lewes
ESSEX	Mahon
SALISBURY	Perry
BASTARD	Smith
AUSTRIA	Morris
HUBERT	Bensley
KING PHILIP	Clarke
CHATILLON	Hull
DAUPHIN	Dyer
PANDULPH	Gibson
ARTHUR	Master Bates
CONSTANCE	Mrs Bellamy

1770 HAYMARKET
Aug. 13

JOHN	Sheridan
PRINCE HENRY	Knowles
PEMBROKE	Dancer
HUBERT	[F.] Gentleman
SALISBURY	Du-Bellamy

(1) *Aug. 30*

omitted
ARTHUR

1770 HAYMARKET (cont.)

Aug. 13 (cont.)

R. FALCONBRIDGE	Hamilton
ENGLISH HERALD	Farrell
BASTARD	[J.] Fleetwood
KING PHILIP	Gardner
DAUPHIN	Robson
AUSTRIA	Griffith
PANDULPH	Wheeler
CHATILLON	Smyth
FRENCH HERALD	Saunders
ARTHUR (1)	Master Saunders
ELINOR	Mrs Dyer
LADY FALCON-BRIDGE	Mrs White
BLANCH	Miss Trowell
CONSTANCE	Mrs Burton

1774 DRURY LANE

Feb. 2, 4, 9, 11

JOHN	Reddish
HUBERT	[F.] Aickin
SALISBURY	Packer
PEMBROKE	Brereton
ESSEX	J[ames] Bannister
PRINCE HENRY	Everard
R. FALCONBRIDGE	W. Palmer
BASTARD	[J.] Palmer
KING PHILIP	J. Aickin
DAUPHIN	Dimond
ARTHUR	Master Blanchard
PANDULPH	Bransby
CHATILLON	Davies
AUSTRIA	Keen
CITIZEN OF ANGERS	Hurst
FRENCH HERALD	Ackman
ENGLISH HERALD	Wright
ELINOR	Miss Sherry
BLANCH	Miss Jarratt
LADY FALCON-BRIDGE	Mrs Johnston
CONSTANCE	Mrs [S.] Barry

[The bills have HERALDS—Ackman and Wright. They are differentiated in the acting version published by Bell in 1774 [the 2nd edition], in which the cast is the same as that of these performances, with the following addition:

GURNEY	Watkins]

KING JOHN

1775 COVENT GARDEN
Dec. 1

JOHN	Sheridan
PRINCE HENRY (1)	Young
SALISBURY	Clinch
HUBERT	Hull
PEMBROKE	Booth
ESSEX	Davis
KING PHILIP	Clarke
DAUPHIN	Wroughton
AUSTRIA	Mahon
PANDULPH	Fearon
CHATILLON	L'Estrange
CITIZEN OF ANGERS	Thompson
ARTHUR	A Young Lady [unidentified]
BASTARD	Lewis
ELINOR	Mrs Booth
LADY FALCON-BRIDGE	Mrs Poussin
BLANCH	Miss Dayes
CONSTANCE	Mrs [S.] Barry

(1) *Dec. 15*

PRINCE HENRY	Miss Besford

1777 DRURY LANE
Nov. 29; Dec. 2

JOHN	Henderson
HUBERT	Bensley
SALISBURY	Packer
PEMBROKE	Farren
ESSEX	Lamash
PRINCE HENRY	R. Palmer
R. FALCONBRIDGE	[F.] Waldron
MESSENGER	Norris
BASTARD	Smith
KING PHILIP	[J.] Aickin
DAUPHIN	Brereton
ARTHUR	Miss Field
PANDULPH	Chambers [first appearance in London]
CHATILLON	Davies
AUSTRIA	Wrighten
CITIZEN OF ANGERS	Hurst
FRENCH HERALD	Chaplin
ENGLISH HERALD	Wright
ELINOR	Miss Sherry
BLANCH	Mrs Colles
LADY FALCON-BRIDGE	Mrs Johnston
CONSTANCE	Mrs Yates

1778 DRURY LANE

Jan. 1

JOHN	Henderson
HUBERT	Bensley
SALISBURY	Packer
PEMBROKE	Farren
ESSEX	Lamash
PRINCE HENRY	R. Palmer
R. FALCONBRIDGE	[F.] Waldron
MESSENGER	Norris
BASTARD	Smith
KING PHILIP	[J.] Aickin
DAUPHIN	Brereton
ARTHUR	Master Pulley
PANDULPH	Chambers
CHATILLON	Davies
AUSTRIA	Wrighten
CITIZEN OF ANGERS	Hurst
FRENCH HERALD	Chaplin
ENGLISH HERALD	Wright
ELINOR	Miss Sherry
BLANCH	Mrs Colles
LADY FALCON-BRIDGE	Mrs Johnston
CONSTANCE	Mrs Yates

1783 DRURY LANE

Dec. 10, 13, 16

JOHN	Kemble
HUBERT	Bensley
SALISBURY	Staunton
PEMBROKE	Williames
ESSEX	Chaplin
BASTARD	Smith
KING PHILIP	[J.] Aickin
DAUPHIN	Barrymore
ARTHUR	Miss Field
PANDULPH	Packer
CHATILLON	Farren
AUSTRIA	Wrighten
CITIZEN OF ANGERS	Fawcett
ELINOR	Mrs Hopkins
BLANCH	Miss Palmer
LADY FALCON-BRIDGE	Mrs Hedges
CONSTANCE	Mrs Siddons

1783 COVENT GARDEN
Mar. 29

JOHN	Henderson
PRINCE HENRY	W. Bates
ESSEX	Egan
HUBERT	[F.] Aickin
PEMBROKE	Booth
SALISBURY	Davies
KING PHILIP	Clarke
DAUPHIN	Whitfield
AUSTRIA	Mahon
PANDULPH	Fearon
CHATILLON	Hull
CITIZEN OF ANGERS	Thompson
ARTHUR	Miss Heard
BASTARD	Wroughton
ELINOR	Miss Platt
LADY FALCON-BRIDGE	Mrs Poussin
BLANCH	Mrs Whitfield
CONSTANCE	Mrs Yates

1784 COVENT GARDEN
Jan. 16

JOHN	Henderson
HUBERT	[F.] Aickin
ARTHUR	Miss Heard
SALISBURY	Davies
PEMBROKE	[S.] Kemble
KING PHILIP	Clarke
DAUPHIN	Whitfield
AUSTRIA	Mahon
PANDULPH	Fearon
PRINCE HENRY	Miss Francis
ESSEX	Helme
CHATILLON	Booth
CITIZEN OF ANGERS	Thompson
BASTARD	Wroughton
ELINOR	Miss Platt
LADY FALCON-BRIDGE	Mrs Poussin
BLANCH	Mrs Inchbald
CONSTANCE	Mrs Crawford

1785 DRURY LANE
Nov. 22

JOHN	Kemble
HUBERT	Bensley

1785 DRURY LANE (cont.)
Nov. 22 (cont.)

SALISBURY	Staunton
PEMBROKE	Williames
ESSEX	Chaplin
BASTARD	Smith
KING PHILIP	[J.] Aickin
DAUPHIN	Barrymore
ARTHUR	Miss Field
PANDULPH	Packer
AUSTRIA	Wrighten
CITIZEN OF ANGERS	Fawcett
CHATILLON	[J.] Bannister
ELINOR	Mrs Hopkins
BLANCH	Miss Palmer
LADY FALCON-BRIDGE	Mrs Hedges
CONSTANCE	Mrs Siddons

1792 DRURY LANE (company at KING'S, HAYMARKET)
Mar. 1

JOHN	Kemble
ARTHUR	Miss DeCamp
PEMBROKE	Dignum
ESSEX	Caulfield
SALISBURY	Whitfield
HUBERT	Bensley
BASTARD	[J.] Palmer
R. FALCONBRIDGE	[F.] Waldron
GURNEY	Lyons
KING PHILIP	[J.] Aickin
DAUPHIN	Barrymore
AUSTRIA	Phillimore
PANDULPH	Packer
CHATILLON	Benson
ELINOR	Mrs Hopkins
CONSTANCE	Mrs Siddons
BLANCH	Miss Collins
LADY FALCON-BRIDGE	Mrs Cuyler

1793 DRURY LANE (company at HAYMARKET)
Feb. 12

JOHN	Kemble
ARTHUR	Master DeCamp
PEMBROKE	Dignum
ESSEX	Caulfield

KING JOHN

1793 DRURY LANE (company at HAYMARKET) (cont.)
Feb. 12 (cont.)

SALISBURY	Whitfield
HUBERT	Bensley
BASTARD	[J.] Palmer
R. FALCONBRIDGE	[F.] Waldron
GURNEY	Lyons
KING PHILIP	[J.] Aickin
DAUPHIN	Barrymore
AUSTRIA	Phillimore
PANDULPH	Packer
CHATILLON	Benson
ELINOR	Mrs Ward
CONSTANCE	Mrs Siddons
BLANCH	Miss Collins
LADY FALCON-BRIDGE	Mrs Cuyler

[PA assigns ELINOR to Mrs Hopkins.]

1795 DRURY LANE
Mar. 14

JOHN	Kemble
PRINCE HENRY (1)	Bland
ARTHUR	Master Welsh
PEMBROKE	Dignum
ESSEX	Caulfield
SALISBURY	Whitfield
HUBERT	Bensley
BASTARD	[J.] Palmer
R. FALCONBRIDGE	[F.] Waldron
ENGLISH HERALD	Trueman
KING PHILIP	[J.] Aickin
DAUPHIN	Barrymore
AUSTRIA	Phillimore
PANDULPH	Packer
ELINOR	Mrs Hopkins
CONSTANCE	Mrs Siddons
BLANCH (1)	Miss Collins

(1) *Dec. 18*

PRINCE HENRY	C. Kemble
BLANCH added	Miss Mellon
GURNEY	Welsh
SHERIFF	[J.] Cooke
EXECUTIONER	Evans

[Trueman is listed as the ENGLISH HERALD.]

[Pb does not list the ENGLISH HERALD. 'English Herald Mr Trueman; Mr Cooke Ill' (Powell).]

1800 DRURY LANE
Nov. 20

JOHN	Kemble
PRINCE HENRY	DeCamp
PEMBROKE	Caulfield
ESSEX	Dignum

(1) *Nov. 29*

CONSTANCE	Mrs Siddons

(2) *Dec. 4, 11, 20, 30*

ENGLISH HERALD	Webb (on *Dec. 20* only)

332

KING JOHN

1800 DRURY LANE (cont.)
Nov. 20 (cont.)

SALISBURY	Raymond
HUBERT	Barrymore
BASTARD	C. Kemble
R. FALCONBRIDGE	[F.] Waldron
ENGLISH HERALD (2)	Surmont
GURNEY (2)	Chippendale
1ST EXECU- TIONER (2)	Evans
2ND EXECU- TIONER (2)	Fisher
KING PHILIP	Wroughton
DAUPHIN	Holland
ARTHUR	Miss Kelly
AUSTRIA	Cory
PANDULPH (2)	[J.] Powell
CHATILLON	Trueman
FRENCH HERALD (2)	[J.] Cooke
CITIZEN OF ANGERS (2)	Maddocks
ELINOR (2)	Miss Tidswell
CONSTANCE (1, 2)	Mrs Powell
BLANCH	Miss B. Menage
LADY FALCON- BRIDGE	Mrs Humphries

(2) *Dec. 4, 11, 20, 30* (cont.)

PANDULPH	Packer
ELINOR	Mrs Sparks (on *Dec. 11, 20* only)
CONSTANCE	Mrs Siddons

omitted on *Dec. 30* only
ENGLISH HERALD, GURNEY, EXECU- TIONERS, FRENCH HERALD, CITIZEN OF ANGERS

KING LEAR

(1) 'As it is now acted at the King's Theatres.'

    1756   C. Hitch [&c.]. Reprinted in 1759 (two issues), 1760, 1763.

(2) 'As it is now acted at the King's Theatres.'

    1757   The Proprietors.

(3) 'As it is now acted at the Theatres Royal, in Drury-Lane and Covent-Garden.'

    1767   F. and J. Noble [&c.]. Reprinted in 1771.

All these are Nahum Tate's alteration, for a description of which see my Volume I, 244.

(4) 'As it is performed at The Theatre Royal in Covent Garden.'

    1768   R. Baldwin and T. Becket.

This alteration was made by George Colman, the elder. The first four acts are left virtually as Shakespeare wrote them, except for the omission of the Fool. The love-story of Edgar and Cordelia, invented by Tate, is eliminated.

KING LEAR

In *Act I. iv* Lear's curse on Goneril is transposed to follow *334a*, and ends the act. *I. v entire* ('Let me not be mad') is omitted.

Act II. i. 1–15 (Edmund and Curan) is omitted. *II. i. 88–end* is inserted following *ii. 47*. *II. iv. 290–end* (the sisters refuse to give Lear shelter from the storm) is omitted.

Act III. i entire (Kent and the Gentleman discuss Lear's plight) is omitted. III. iii consists of *III. iv. 1–143* (omitting *113–31*), followed by *III. vi. 8–18, 63–86*, *III. iv. 118–29, 146–68a*, *III. vi. 80–91*. *III. v entire* (Cornwall and Edmund discredit Edgar) is omitted. *III. iv* is *III. vii*, opening with 13 lines from Tate's III. iv. At *72a* Gloucester is led away, and returns, blinded, at *85*. The last seven lines (the Servants decide to help Gloucester) are omitted.

In *Act IV. iv* a few lines from Tate (III. ii) are included. Omitted are *IV. v entire* (Regan's mistrust of Goneril), and *IV. vi. 42–83* (Gloucester supposes that he has fallen over the cliff). Following *IV. vi. 138* is inserted *III. vi. 49–62* (the arraignment of Goneril and Regan).

Act V begins with *IV. vii. 14–84*; this is followed by about 35 lines from Tate's IV. v and V. i (Edmund prepares for battle). The rest of the Act is Tate's Act V, omitting (see above) the Edgar–Cordelia love-story.

Throughout there are minor omissions and transpositions.

See also Genest, v. 191–200; Odell, i. 379–81.

(5) 'As Performed at the Theatre-Royal, Drury-Lane. Regulated from the Prompt-Book.'

1773   John Bell.

This alteration was made by David Garrick, and was first acted in 1756 (but not then printed). It retains the first three acts of the original almost verbatim, except for the omission of the Fool. Also retained is the Edgar–Cordelia love-story written by Tate.

Act I. i. 211b–end (France's acceptance of Cordelia, and the discussion between Regan and Goneril of Lear's 'unconstant starts') is omitted, as are *I. iii entire* (Goneril's instructions to Oswald), and *I. iv. 61–81* (the 'abatement of kindness'). In *I. iv. 281–334* the speeches are slightly rearranged, and end with the curse on Goneril (*298b–313*). The rest of the scene (Goneril's disdain of Albany) is omitted, as is all of *I. v* ('Let me not be mad').

Following *Act II. ii. 47* is inserted *II. i. 88–end*. *II. iv. 254–73a, 290–end* ('Tis a wild night') is omitted.

From *Act III* are omitted *i entire* (Kent and the Gentleman discuss Lear's plight), *v entire* (Cornwall and Edmund discredit Edgar), and the better part of *vi* (the hovel). A few speeches from *vi* are inserted in *iv*. *III. vii* is given in Tate's version (his III. iv).

In *Act IV. i* are inserted about 50 lines of Tate's IV. ii (Gloucester, Kent, and Cordelia conspire to aid the King). *IV. ii* is Tate's IV. iii. *IV. iv entire* (Cordelia and the Doctor) and *v entire* (Regan's instructions to Oswald) are omitted.

Act V is Tate's IV. v and V, except that *V. iii. 164–76, 245–58* are retained.

Throughout there are minor omissions and transpositions.

See also Genest, v. 202; Odell, i. 377–8.

334

KING LEAR

(6) 'As it is now acted at the Theatres Royal, in Drury-Lane and Covent-Garden.'
1775   W. Oxlade.

(7) 'As it is Acted at the Theatres-Royal in Drury-Lane and Covent-Garden.'
1779   Harrison and Co.
These are both Tate's alteration. See my Volume I, 244.

(8) 'As it is acted at the Theatres Royal, in Drury Lane and Covent Garden.'
n.d. [c. 1779]   T. Sabine.
This is Garrick's alteration, identical with (5).

(9) 'Marked with the Variations in the Manager's Book, at the Theatre-Royal in Drury-Lane.'
1786   C. Bathurst [&c.].

(10) 'Taken from the Manager's Book, at the Theatre Royal in Drury-Lane.'
n.d. [c. 1788]   R. Butters.
These are both Garrick's alteration. But several of Tate's lines have been eliminated, and II. iv. 254-66 restored.

(11) 'As Performed at the Theatres Royal.'
1794   J. Barker.
This is identical with (8).

(12) 'As altered by N. Tate, Newly Revised by J. P. Kemble, and acted ... at the Theatre Royal, Drury Lane.'
n.d. [1795]   C. Lowndes.
Kemble adopts Tate throughout, omitting Gloucester's soliloquy at the end of III. iv, and that part of IV. iv in which Gloucester supposes that he had fallen over the cliff. The only important restorations are I. iv. 28-42 (Kent's age); II. i. 39-58 (Edmund's pretence that Edgar has wounded him); and V. iii. 245-58 (Edmund's wish to rescue Lear and Cordelia).

[as altered by TATE]

1751 DRURY LANE
Nov. 2

LEAR	Garrick
GLOUCESTER	Berry
EDGAR	Havard
EDMUND	Lee
KENT	Winstone
ALBANY	Mozeen
CORNWALL	Blakes
GENTLEMAN USHER	Shuter
BURGUNDY	Marr
GONERIL	Mrs Bennet
REGAN	Mrs Cross
CORDELIA	Miss Bellamy

KING LEAR [as altered by TATE]

1752 DRURY LANE
Jan. 17; Mar. 3

LEAR (1)	Garrick
GLOUCESTER	Berry
EDGAR	Havard
EDMUND (1, 2)	Lee
KENT	Winstone
ALBANY	Mozeen
CORNWALL	Blakes
GENTLEMAN USHER	Shuter
BURGUNDY	Marr
GONERIL	Mrs Bennet
REGAN	Mrs Cross
CORDELIA (1)	Miss Bellamy

(1) *Apr. 6*

LEAR	Lee
EDMUND	Sowdon
CORDELIA	Mrs Ward
added	
DOCTOR	Simson

(2) *Nov. 3, 20*

EDMUND	Palmer

COVENT GARDEN
Oct. 16, 17

LEAR	Giffard
EDGAR	Ryan
GLOUCESTER	Sparks
KENT	Bransby
EDMUND	Ridout
CORNWALL	Usher
ALBANY	Anderson
BURGUNDY	Bencraft
GENTLEMAN USHER	Dyer
GONERIL	Miss Haughton
REGAN	Mrs Ridout
CORDELIA	Mrs Vincent

1753 DRURY LANE
Nov. 15, 22

LEAR	Garrick
GLOUCESTER	Berry
EDGAR	Havard
EDMUND	Palmer
KENT	Bransby
ALBANY	Mozeen
CORNWALL	Blakes
GENTLEMAN USHER	Lacey
BURGUNDY	Jefferson
GONERIL	Mrs Bennet
REGAN	Mrs Cowper
CORDELIA	Mrs Cibber

KING LEAR [*as altered by* TATE]

1754 DRURY LANE
Feb. 18

LEAR	Garrick
GLOUCESTER	Berry
EDGAR	Havard
EDMUND	Palmer
KENT	Burton
ALBANY	Mozeen
CORNWALL	Blakes
GENTLEMAN USHER	Lacey
BURGUNDY	Jefferson
GONERIL	Mrs Bennet
REGAN	Mrs Cowper
CORDELIA	Mrs Cibber

1755 DRURY LANE
Mar. 4, 11

LEAR	Garrick
GLOUCESTER	Berry
EDGAR (1)	Havard
EDMUND	Palmer
KENT	Bransby
ALBANY (2)	Mozeen
CORNWALL	Blakes
GENTLEMAN USHER (2)	Vernon
BURGUNDY	Jefferson
GONERIL	Mrs Bennet
REGAN (2)	Miss Haughton
CORDELIA (1)	Mrs Davies

(1) *May 23*

EDGAR	Ross
CORDELIA	Mrs Cibber

(2) *Dec. 4, 9*

ALBANY	Usher
REGAN	Mrs Cowper
added	
ARANTE	Miss Minors
omitted	
GENTLEMAN USHER	

1756 DRURY LANE
Feb. 12

LEAR	Garrick
GLOUCESTER	Berry
EDGAR	Havard
EDMUND	Palmer
KENT	Bransby
GENTLEMAN USHER (1)	Yates
ALBANY	Usher
CORNWALL	Blakes
BURGUNDY	Jefferson
ARANTE	Miss Minors
GONERIL	Mrs Bennet
REGAN	Mrs Cowper
CORDELIA (1, 2)	Mrs Cibber

(1) *May 19*

CORDELIA Mrs Davies
omitted
GENTLEMAN USHER

[Genest (iv. 458) erroneously assigns CORDELIA to Mrs Cibber.]

[*as altered by* GARRICK]

(2) *Oct. 28, 30*

CORDELIA Mrs Davies

[The bills have, 'With Restorations from Shakespeare'.]

KING LEAR [as altered by TATE]

1756 COVENT GARDEN
Feb. 26, 28; Mar. 2, 6, 9, 13; Oct. 15

LEAR	Barry
EDGAR	Ryan
GLOUCESTER	Ridout
KENT	Sparks
EDMUND	Smith
CORNWALL	Anderson
ALBANY	White
BURGUNDY	Bennet
GENTLEMAN USHER	Shuter
GONERIL	Mrs Stephens
REGAN	Mrs Hamilton
CORDELIA	Miss Nossiter

HAYMARKET
?

KENT	Parsons [first appearance on the stage]
EDMUND	Powell

[The actual date of this performance has not as yet come to light. The above assignment (which includes the year and the theatre) appears in an obituary of Parsons in EM, Mar. 1795, 147.]

[as altered by GARRICK]

1757 DRURY LANE
Nov. 10, 12

LEAR	Garrick
GLOUCESTER	Berry
EDGAR	Havard
EDMUND	Palmer
KENT	Bransby
ALBANY	Usher
CORNWALL	Blakes
BURGUNDY	Austin
ARANTE	Miss Minors
GONERIL	Mrs Bennet
REGAN	Miss Haughton
CORDELIA	Mrs Cibber

(1) Nov. 17
added
GENTLEMAN USHER Vernon

[as altered by TATE]

COVENT GARDEN
Mar. 1, 21

LEAR	Barry
EDGAR	Ryan

(1) Dec. 5

REGAN	Mrs Elmy
CORDELIA	Mrs Bellamy

KING LEAR [as altered by TATE]

1757 COVENT GARDEN (cont.)
Mar. 1, 21 (cont.)

GLOUCESTER	Ridout
KENT	Sparks
EDMUND	Smith
CORNWALL	Anderson
ALBANY	White
BURGUNDY	Bennet
GENTLEMAN USHER	Shuter
GONERIL	Mrs Stephens
REGAN (1)	Mrs Hamilton
CORDELIA (1)	Miss Nossiter

[as altered by GARRICK]

1758 DRURY LANE
Oct. 25

LEAR	Garrick
GLOUCESTER	Berry
EDGAR	Havard
EDMUND	Palmer
KENT	Bransby
GENTLEMAN USHER	Yates
ALBANY	Packer
CORNWALL	Blakes
BURGUNDY	Austin
ARANTE	Miss Hippisley
GONERIL	Mrs Bennet
REGAN	Miss Haughton
CORDELIA	Mrs Cibber

[as altered by TATE]

COVENT GARDEN
Jan. 10; Feb. 18 (1) *Apr. 7*

LEAR	Barry	EDGAR	Dyer
EDGAR (1)	Ryan		
GLOUCESTER	Ridout		
KENT	Sparks		
EDMUND	Smith		
CORNWALL	Anderson		
ALBANY	White		
BURGUNDY	Bennet		
GENTLEMAN USHER	Shuter		
GONERIL	Mrs Stephens		
REGAN	Mrs Elmy		
CORDELIA	Mrs Bellamy		

KING LEAR
[as altered by GARRICK]

1759 DRURY LANE
Nov. 10, 15, 28

LEAR	Garrick
GLOUCESTER	Davies
EDGAR	Havard
EDMUND	Palmer
KENT	Bransby
GENTLEMAN USHER	Perry
ALBANY	Packer
CORNWALL	Blakes
BURGUNDY	Austin
ARANTE	Mrs Hippisley
GONERIL	Mrs Bennet
REGAN	Miss Haughton
CORDELIA	Mrs Cibber

1760 DRURY LANE
Jan. 5

LEAR	Garrick
GLOUCESTER	Davies
EDGAR	Havard
EDMUND	Palmer
KENT	Bransby
ALBANY	Packer
CORNWALL	Blakes
BURGUNDY	Austin
ARANTE	Mrs Hippisley
GONERIL	Mrs Bennet
REGAN	Miss Haughton
CORDELIA	Mrs Cibber

1761 DRURY LANE
May 28

LEAR	Garrick
GLOUCESTER	Davies
EDGAR	Havard
EDMUND	Palmer
KENT	Bransby
GENTLEMAN USHER (1)	King
ALBANY	Packer
CORNWALL	Blakes
BURGUNDY (1)	Austin
ARANTE (1)	Mrs Johnston
GONERIL	Mrs Bennet
REGAN	Miss Haughton
CORDELIA	Mrs Cibber

(1) *Dec. 23*

GENTLEMAN USHER	Castle
ARANTE	Mrs Hippisley
omitted	
BURGUNDY	

[In the bill Mrs Johnston's name is misspelled 'Johnson'.]

340

KING LEAR [as altered by GARRICK]

1762 DRURY LANE
Apr. 17

LEAR	Garrick
GLOUCESTER (1, 2)	Davies
EDGAR	Havard
EDMUND (2)	Palmer
KENT	Bransby
GENTLEMAN USHER	Castle
ALBANY	Packer
CORNWALL	Blakes
ARANTE	Mrs Hippisley
GONERIL	Mrs Bennet
REGAN	Miss Haughton
CORDELIA	Mrs Cibber

(1) *Nov. 19*

GLOUCESTER added	Burton
BURGUNDY	Fox

(2) *Dec. 31*

GLOUCESTER	Burton
EDMUND	Lee

1763 DRURY LANE
May 12

LEAR	Garrick
GLOUCESTER	Burton
EDGAR	Havard
EDMUND	Lee
KENT	Bransby
GENTLEMAN USHER	Castle
ALBANY	Packer
CORNWALL	Jackson
ARANTE	Mrs Hippisley
GONERIL	Mrs Bennet
REGAN	Miss Haughton
CORDELIA	Mrs Cibber

[as altered by TATE]
1764 COVENT GARDEN
May 7

LEAR	Ross
EDGAR	Smith
EDMUND	Clarke
GLOUCESTER	Gibson
KENT	Sparks
ALBANY (1)	White
BURGUNDY (1, 2, 3)	Bennet
CORNWALL (1)	Anderson
OFFICER (1, 2, 3)	Wignell
GENTLEMAN USHER (2, 3)	Shuter
GONERIL	Mrs Stephens
REGAN	Mrs Vincent
ARANTE (1, 2, 3)	Mrs Evans
CORDELIA (1, 2, 3)	Miss Ward

(1) *Oct. 29*

CORDELIA omitted
ALBANY, BURGUNDY, CORNWALL, OFFICER, ARANTE

(2) *Nov. 27; Dec. 3*

GENTLEMAN USHER	Cushing
CORDELIA omitted	Miss Hallam

BURGUNDY, OFFICER, ARANTE

(3) *Dec. 31*

GENTLEMAN USHER	Cushing
CORDELIA omitted	Mrs Bellamy

SAME as *Nov. 27*

KING LEAR

[*as altered by* GARRICK]

1765 DRURY LANE

Jan. 2
- LEAR — Powell
- GLOUCESTER — Burton
- EDGAR — Havard
- EDMUND — Lee
- KENT — Bransby
- ALBANY — Packer
- CORNWALL (2) — Jackson
- BURGUNDY — Adcock
- OLD MAN — Baddeley
- ARANTE — Mrs Hippisley
- GONERIL — Mrs Lee
- REGAN — Mrs Hopkins
- CORDELIA (3) — Mrs Cibber

Oct. 22
- LEAR — Powell
- GLOUCESTER — Burton
- EDGAR — Havard
- EDMUND — Lee
- KENT — Bransby
- GENTLEMAN USHER — Dodd
- ALBANY — Packer
- CORNWALL — Hurst
- OLD MAN (1) — Baddeley
- ARANTE — Mrs Hippisley
- GONERIL — Mrs Bennet
- REGAN (1) — Mrs Hopkins
- CORDELIA (1) — Mrs Yates

(1) *Jan. 5, 9, 12*
 added
  GENTLEMAN USHER [R.] Griffith

(2) *Feb. 1*
  CORNWALL — Parsons
 added
  GENTLEMAN USHER [R.] Griffith

(3) *Mar. 25; Apr. 17; May 23*
  CORDELIA — Mrs Yates
 added
  GENTLEMAN USHER [R.] Griffith
 [On *Apr. 17* PA assigns CORNWALL to Parsons.]

(1) *Nov. 23*
  REGAN — Mrs Lee
  CORDELIA — Mrs Palmer
 omitted
  OLD MAN

[*as altered by* TATE]

COVENT GARDEN

Jan. 7; Mar. 19; Sept. 23
- LEAR — Ross
- EDGAR (1) — Smith
- EDMUND (2) — Clarke
- GLOUCESTER — Gibson
- KENT — Walker
- GENTLEMAN USHER — Cushing
- ALBANY (2) — White
- CORNWALL — Anderson
- GONERIL — Mrs Stephens
- REGAN — Mrs Vincent
- CORDELIA — Mrs Bellamy

(1) *May 2*
  EDGAR — Hull

(2) *Dec. 19*
  EDMUND — Gardner
  ALBANY — Davis

KING LEAR

[*as altered by* GARRICK]

1766 DRURY LANE

Jan. 11
LEAR	Powell
GLOUCESTER	Burton
EDGAR	Havard
EDMUND (3)	Lee
KENT	Bransby
GENTLEMAN USHER (2)	Dodd
ALBANY	Packer
CORNWALL	Hurst
ARANTE (1, 2, 3)	Mrs Hippisley
GONERIL	Mrs Bennet
REGAN (1)	Mrs Lee
CORDELIA (2)	Mrs Yates

(1) *Apr. 5*
REGAN	Mrs Hopkins
omitted ARANTE	

(2) *Apr. 29*
GENTLEMAN USHER	Baddeley
CORDELIA	Mrs Baddeley
omitted ARANTE	

(3) *Oct. 29*
EDMUND	Bensley
omitted ARANTE	

[*as altered by* TATE]

COVENT GARDEN

Mar. 4
LEAR	Ross
EDGAR	Smith
EDMUND (1)	Clarke
GLOUCESTER	Gibson
KENT (1)	Walker
GENTLEMAN USHER	Cushing
ALBANY	Davis
CORNWALL	Anderson
GONERIL	Mrs Stephens
REGAN	Mrs Vincent
CORDELIA (2)	Mrs Bellamy

(1) *Apr. 23*
EDMUND	Gardner
KENT	Morris

(2) *Nov. 19, 24*
CORDELIA	Miss Wilford

KING'S, HAYMARKET

Aug. 25
LEAR	Barry
GLOUCESTER	Johnston
KENT	[F.] Aickin
EDGAR	Davis
CORNWALL	Hurst
ALBANY	[J.] Palmer
BURGUNDY (1)	Murden
EDMUND	Lee
OFFICER	McGeorge
DOCTOR	Castle
CORNWALL'S SERVANT	Keen
OLD MAN	[P.] Lewis

(1) *Aug. 29*
BURGUNDY	Quick
GONERIL	Mrs Johnston

KING LEAR [as altered by TATE]

1766 KING'S, HAYMARKET (cont.)
Aug. 25 (cont.)

1ST RUFFIAN	Mathews
2ND RUFFIAN	[T.] Powell
GENTLEMAN USHER	Hamilton
GONERIL (1)	Mrs Worley
REGAN	Mrs McGeorge
ARANTE	Miss Madden
CORDELIA	Mrs Dancer

[as altered by GARRICK]

1767 DRURY LANE
Apr. 23

LEAR (2)	Powell
GLOUCESTER	Burton
EDGAR (2)	Havard
EDMUND (2)	Bensley
KENT	Bransby
GENTLEMAN USHER	Dodd
ALBANY	Packer
CORNWALL	Hurst
GONERIL (2)	Mrs Bennet
REGAN (2)	Mrs Lee
CORDELIA (1, 2)	Mrs Baddeley

(1) *May 20*

CORDELIA	Mrs Palmer
added	
BURGUNDY	J. Palmer
ARANTE	Mrs Hippisley

(2) *Oct. 21, 24*

LEAR	Barry
EDGAR	Reddish
EDMUND	J. Palmer
GONERIL	Mrs [W.] Barry
REGAN	Mrs Hopkins
CORDELIA	Mrs Dancer
added	
BURGUNDY	Fox
ARANTE	Mrs Hippisley

[as altered by TATE]

COVENT GARDEN
Jan. 19

LEAR	Ross
EDGAR	Smith
EDMUND (2)	Clarke
GLOUCESTER	Gibson
KENT	Walker
GENTLEMAN USHER (2)	Cushing
ALBANY	Davis
CORNWALL (2)	Anderson
BURGUNDY (1)	Bennet
GONERIL	Mrs Stephens
REGAN	Mrs Vincent
CORDELIA	Mrs Bellamy

(1) *Mar. 9*

omitted	
BURGUNDY	

(2) *May 13*

EDMUND	Perry
GENTLEMAN USHER	Holtom
CORNWALL	Gardner

[Pb assigns CORDELIA as above; Genest (v. 132), following PA, assigns the part to Miss Wilford. This seems to be the performance referred to by Mrs Bellamy in her *Apology*, 1785, iv. 145–7 (she does not give the actual date). She relates that she was originally announced as CORDELIA by the prompter, but that the manager gave the part to Miss Wilford. Mrs Bellamy refused to surrender it, and although Miss Wilford made her entrance the audience forced her to withdraw, and Mrs Bellamy acted the entire part.]

KING LEAR [as altered by TATE]

1767 HAYMARKET
July 15

LEAR	Barry
EDGAR	T. Barry
GLOUCESTER	Thompson
CORNWALL	Gardner
ALBANY	Ellard
BURGUNDY	Keen
KENT	[J.] Palmer
DOCTOR	Castle
EDMUND	Sowdon
GENTLEMAN USHER	Weston
GONERIL	Mrs Burden
REGAN	Mrs Gardner
ARANTE	Miss Ogilvie
CORDELIA	Mrs Dancer

[as altered by GARRICK]

1768 DRURY LANE
Apr. 8

LEAR	Barry
GLOUCESTER	Burton
EDGAR	Reddish
EDMUND	J. Palmer
KENT	Bransby
GENTLEMAN USHER	Dodd
ALBANY	Packer
CORNWALL	Hurst
BURGUNDY	Fox
GONERIL	Mrs [W.] Barry
REGAN	Mrs Hopkins
ARANTE	Mrs Hippisley
CORDELIA	Mrs Dancer

[as altered by COLMAN]

COVENT GARDEN
Feb. 20; Mar. 7; Apr. 28

LEAR	Powell
EDGAR	Smith
GLOUCESTER	Gibson
ALBANY	Hull
EDMUND	Bensley
KENT	Clarke
GENTLEMAN USHER	Cushing
CORNWALL	Gardner

(1) *Nov. 17; Dec. 20*

GONERIL	Mrs Vincent

KING LEAR [as altered by COLMAN]

1768 COVENT GARDEN (cont.)
Feb. 20; Mar. 7; Apr. 28 (cont.)

FRANCE	Davis
BURGUNDY	[Lee] Lewes
GONERIL (1)	Mrs Stephens
REGAN	Mrs Du-Bellamy
CORDELIA	Mrs Yates

[In the acting version published by Baldwin and Becket in 1768 the cast is the same as that of these performances, with the following additions:

DOCTOR	Redman
CAPTAIN	Wignell
OLD MAN	Hallam
HERALD	Holtom
CORNWALL'S SERVANT	T. Smith]

[as altered by GARRICK]

1769 DRURY LANE
Oct. 7

LEAR	Barry
GLOUCESTER	Burton
EDGAR	Reddish
EDMUND	[J.] Palmer
KENT	Bransby
GENTLEMAN USHER	Dodd
ALBANY	Packer
CORNWALL	Hurst
CAPTAIN	Ackman
1ST OFFICER	Keen
2ND OFFICER	Fawcett
OLD MAN	Hartry
REGAN	Mrs W. Barry
GONERIL	Mrs Stephens
CORDELIA	Mrs [S.] Barry

[as altered by COLMAN]

COVENT GARDEN
Jan. 11, 21

LEAR	Powell
EDGAR	Smith
ALBANY	Hull
CORNWALL (2)	Gardner
GLOUCESTER	Gibson
EDMUND	Bensley
FRANCE	Davis

(1) *Apr. 12*

CORDELIA	Mrs Yates

(2) *May 1*

CORNWALL	Mahon
CORDELIA	Mrs Bulkley

KING LEAR [as altered by COLMAN]

1769 COVENT GARDEN (cont.)

Jan. 11, 21 (cont.)

BURGUNDY	[Lee] Lewes
KENT	Clarke
GENTLEMAN USHER	Cushing
GONERIL	Mrs Vincent
REGAN	Mrs Du-Bellamy
CORDELIA (1, 2)	Miss Morris

[as altered by GARRICK]

1770 DRURY LANE

Jan. 15

LEAR (1)	Barry
EDGAR	Reddish
GLOUCESTER	Burton
EDMUND	[J.] Palmer
KENT	Bransby
GENTLEMAN USHER	Dodd
ALBANY (1)	Packer
CORNWALL	Hurst
CAPTAIN	Ackman
OFFICER	Keen
MESSENGER (2)	Fawcett
OLD MAN	Hartry
REGAN (1, 2)	Mrs Reddish
ARANTE	Miss Platt
GONERIL (2)	Mrs Stephens
CORDELIA	Mrs [S.] Barry

(1) *Feb. 21; Mar. 8, 13*

LEAR	Garrick
ALBANY	J. Aickin (on *Feb. 21* only)
REGAN added	Mrs W. Barry
BURGUNDY	Wrighten

(2) *Oct. 31*

REGAN	Mrs W. Barry
GONERIL added	Mrs Reddish
CURAN omitted	Fawcett
MESSENGER	

[as altered by COLMAN]

COVENT GARDEN

Oct. 29

LEAR	Ross
EDGAR	Smith
GLOUCESTER	Gibson
EDMUND	Bensley
FRANCE	Du-Bellamy
BURGUNDY	[Lee] Lewes
CORNWALL	Gardner
ALBANY	Hull
KENT	Clarke
GENTLEMAN USHER	Cushing
GONERIL	Mrs Vincent
REGAN	Mrs Du-Bellamy
CORDELIA	Miss Miller

KING LEAR
[as altered by TATE]

1770 HAYMARKET
June 18; Sept. 11

LEAR	Ross
EDGAR	[J.] Aickin
GLOUCESTER	[F.] Gentleman
KENT	Gardner
EDMUND	Robson
ALBANY	Smyth
CORNWALL	Dancer
BURGUNDY	Knowles
GENTLEMAN USHER	Hamilton
CAPTAIN	McGeorge
DOCTOR	Griffith
OLD MAN	Farrell
1ST SERVANT	Lings
2ND SERVANT	Pearce
ARANTE	Miss Trowell
CORDELIA	Mrs Jefferies

[as altered by GARRICK]

1771 DRURY LANE
Nov. 23

LEAR	Barry
EDGAR	Reddish
GLOUCESTER	J. Aickin
KENT	Bransby
EDMUND	[J.] Palmer
GENTLEMAN USHER	Dodd
ALBANY	Packer
CORNWALL	Hurst
CAPTAIN	Ackman
CURAN	Fawcett
OLD MAN	Hartry
GONERIL	Mrs Reddish
REGAN	Mrs Egerton
CORDELIA	Mrs [S.] Barry

[as altered by COLMAN]

COVENT GARDEN

Jan. 14   (1) *Dec. 30*

LEAR	Ross	GLOUCESTER	Hull
EDGAR	Smith	ALBANY	Owenson
GLOUCESTER (1)	Gibson	REGAN	Miss Pearce

348

KING LEAR [*as altered by* COLMAN]
1771 COVENT GARDEN (*cont.*)
Jan. 14 (*cont.*)

EDMUND	Bensley
ALBANY (1)	Hull
CORNWALL	Gardner
KENT	Clarke
GENTLEMAN USHER	Cushing
GONERIL	Mrs Vincent
REGAN (1)	Mrs Du-Bellamy
CORDELIA	Miss Miller

1772 COVENT GARDEN
May 21

LEAR	Ross
EDGAR	Smith
GLOUCESTER	Hull
EDMUND	Bensley
ALBANY	Owenson
CORNWALL	Gardner
KENT	Clarke
GENTLEMAN USHER	Cushing
GONERIL	Mrs Vincent
REGAN	Miss Pearce
CORDELIA	Miss Miller

[*as altered by* GARRICK]

1773 DRURY LANE
Feb. 2

LEAR (1, 2)	Barry
EDGAR	Reddish
GLOUCESTER	J. Aickin
KENT	Bransby
EDMUND	[J.] Palmer
GENTLEMAN USHER (1, 2)	Dodd
ALBANY	Packer
CORNWALL	Hurst
BURGUNDY	Yates
CAPTAIN (2)	Ackman
CURAN	Fawcett
GONERIL	Miss Sherry
REGAN	Mrs Egerton
CORDELIA (2)	Mrs [S.] Barry

(1) *Feb. 17, 19*

LEAR	Garrick
GENTLEMAN USHER	[J.] Burton

[In the acting version published by Bell in 1773 the cast is the same as that of these performances, with the following additions:

DOCTOR	Wright
OLD MAN	Hartry
CORNWALL'S SERVANT	Keen
ARANTE	Miss Platt]

(2) *May 26*

LEAR	Garrick
GENTLEMAN USHER	[J.] Burton
CAPTAIN	Griffith
CORDELIA	Miss Younge

349

KING LEAR

[as altered by COLMAN]

1773 COVENT GARDEN
Jan. 25

LEAR	Ross	(1) *May 8*	
EDGAR	Smith	GENTLEMAN USHER	Quick
GLOUCESTER	Hull		
EDMUND	Bensley		
ALBANY	Owenson		
CORNWALL	Gardner		
KENT	Clarke		
GENTLEMAN USHER (1)	Cushing		
GONERIL	Mrs Vincent		
REGAN	Miss Pearce		
CORDELIA	Miss Miller		

[as altered by GARRICK]

1774 DRURY LANE
Mar. 12; Apr. 25

LEAR (1)	Barry	(1) *May 17*	
EDGAR	Reddish	LEAR	Garrick
GLOUCESTER	J. Aickin	BURGUNDY	J[ames] Bannister
KENT	Bransby	REGAN	Mrs Hopkins
EDMUND	[J.] Palmer	CORDELIA	Miss Younge
GENTLEMAN USHER	[J.] Burton		
ALBANY	Packer		
CORNWALL	Hurst		
BURGUNDY (1)	Norris		
CAPTAIN	Ackman		
CURAN	Fawcett		
GONERIL	Miss Sherry		
REGAN (1)	Mrs Jefferson		
ARANTE	Miss Platt		
CORDELIA (1)	Mrs [S.] Barry		

[as altered by TATE]

COVENT GARDEN
Nov. 24, 26

LEAR	Barry
EDGAR	Lewis
GLOUCESTER	Hull
EDMUND	Bensley
KENT	Clarke
ALBANY	Whitfield
CORNWALL	Davis

KING LEAR [as altered by TATE]

1774 COVENT GARDEN (cont.)
Nov. 24, 26 (cont.)

GENTLEMAN USHER	Quick
BURGUNDY	Thompson
GONERIL	Miss Pearce
REGAN	Mrs Whitfield
ARANTE	Miss Dayes
CORDELIA	Mrs [S.] Barry

[as altered by GARRICK]

1776 DRURY LANE
May 13

LEAR	Garrick
GLOUCESTER	[J.] Aickin
KENT	Bransby
EDMUND	[J.] Palmer
GENTLEMAN USHER	[J.] Burton
ALBANY	Packer
CORNWALL	Hurst
BURGUNDY	Norris
CAPTAIN (1)	Whitfield
CURAN	Fawcett
EDGAR	Reddish
GONERIL	Miss Sherry
REGAN	Mrs Hopkins
ARANTE	Miss Platt
CORDELIA	Miss Younge

(1) May 21; June 8
added
   OLD MAN [F.] Waldron
omitted
   CAPTAIN

[as altered by TATE]

COVENT GARDEN
Feb. 22

LEAR (1)	Barry
GLOUCESTER	Hull
EDMUND	[F.] Aickin
KENT	Clarke
ALBANY	L'Estrange
CORNWALL	Thompson
GENTLEMAN USHER	Quick
BURGUNDY (1)	Young
EDGAR (1)	Webster
GONERIL	Mrs Hunter
REGAN	Miss Ambrose
ARANTE (1)	Miss Dayes
CORDELIA (1)	Mrs [S.] Barry

(1) Mar. 23

LEAR	Lee
BURGUNDY	Booth
EDGAR	Lewis
ARANTE	Mrs Masters
CORDELIA	A Young Gentlewoman [Miss Lee (MC, Mar. 22); first appearance on the stage]

[Genest (v. 518) erroneously assigns CORDELIA to Mrs Bulkley.]

351

KING LEAR [as altered by TATE]

1776 CHINA HALL, ROTHERHITHE
Sept. 16

LEAR	A Gentleman [unidentified; first appearance on the stage]
GLOUCESTER	[P.] Lewis
EDMUND	[J.] Smith
KENT	Massey
ALBANY	[S.] Johnson
CORNWALL	W. Smith
BURGUNDY	Kenny
GENTLEMAN USHER	Russell
EDGAR	Comerford
GONERIL	Mrs Wilks
REGAN	Mrs Smith
ARANTE	Miss Taylor
CORDELIA	A Young Lady [unidentified; first appearance on the stage]

1777 COVENT GARDEN
Oct. 6

LEAR	Ross
EDGAR	Lewis
GLOUCESTER	Hull
EDMUND	[F.] Aickin
KENT (2)	Clarke
ALBANY	L'Estrange
CORNWALL	Thompson
GENTLEMAN USHER (1, 2)	Quick
BURGUNDY	Booth
GONERIL	Mrs Poussin
REGAN	Miss Ambrose
ARANTE	Miss Green
CORDELIA (2)	Mrs Hartley

(1) *Oct. 13; Nov. 10*

GENTLEMAN USHER	Death

(2) *Dec. 29*

KENT	Fearon
GENTLEMAN USHER	Death
CORDELIA	Mrs Jackson

1778 COVENT GARDEN
Feb. 5

LEAR (1, 2)	Ross
EDGAR	Lewis
EDMUND	[F.] Aickin
GLOUCESTER	Hull
KENT	Clarke
ALBANY	L'Estrange
CORNWALL	Thompson
GENTLEMAN USHER (1, 2)	Death
BURGUNDY (1, 2)	Booth
GONERIL (1, 2)	Mrs Poussin
REGAN	Miss Ambrose
ARANTE	Miss Green
CORDELIA (1)	Mrs Jackson

(1) *Sept. 28; Oct. 19*

LEAR	Digges
GENTLEMAN USHER	Brundson
BURGUNDY	Robson
GONERIL	Miss Platt
CORDELIA	Miss Younge

(2) *Nov. 9*

LEAR	A Gentleman [Rundell (MS annotation on BM bill)]
GENTLEMAN USHER	Brunsdon
BURGUNDY	Robson
GONERIL	Miss Platt

KING LEAR [as altered by TATE]

1778 HAYMARKET
Sept. 17

LEAR	Digges
EDMUND	West
KENT	Gardner
GLOUCESTER	Mitchell
GENTLEMAN USHER	Blissett
ALBANY	Taylor
BURGUNDY	Turner
CORNWALL	Davis
EDGAR	Dimond
GONERIL	Mrs Lefevre
REGAN	Mrs West
CORDELIA	Mrs Massey

BOOTH, CHINA HALL, ROTHERHITHE
Aug.

LEAR	Everard
EDGAR	Cooke

[The above assignment is given in E. C. Everard's *Memoirs of an Unfortunate Son of Thespis*, 1818, 78. See p. 67.]

[as altered by GARRICK]

1779 DRURY LANE
Mar. 22

LEAR	Henderson
GLOUCESTER	[J.] Aickin
EDMUND	[J.] Palmer
KENT	Hurst
ALBANY	Packer
CORNWALL	Wrighten
BURGUNDY	Norris
GENTLEMAN USHER	[J.] Burton
DOCTOR	Wright
OLD MAN	[F.] Waldron
CORNWALL'S SERVANT	R. Palmer
CURAN	Fawcett
CAPTAIN	Chaplin
EDGAR	Webster
GONERIL	Miss Sherry
REGAN	Mrs Colles
ARANTE	Miss Kirby
CORDELIA (1)	Miss Younge

(1) *Apr. 14; May 4*

CORDELIA	Mrs Robinson

KING LEAR
[as altered by TATE]

1779 COVENT GARDEN
Nov. 19

LEAR	Henderson
GLOUCESTER	Hull
EDMUND	[F.] Aickin
KENT	Clarke
ALBANY	L'Estrange
CORNWALL	Thompson
GENTLEMAN USHER	Brunsdon
BURGUNDY	Robson
EDGAR	Lewis
GONERIL	Miss Platt
REGAN	Miss Ambrose
ARANTE	Miss Green
CORDELIA	Miss Younge

1780 COVENT GARDEN
Jan. 3

LEAR (1)	Henderson
GLOUCESTER	Hull
EDMUND	[F.] Aickin
KENT	Clarke
ALBANY	L'Estrange
CORNWALL	Thompson
GENTLEMAN USHER (2)	Brunsdon
BURGUNDY	Robson
EDGAR	Lewis
GONERIL	Miss Platt
REGAN	Miss Ambrose
ARANTE (2)	Miss Green
CORDELIA (1)	Miss Younge

(1) *Feb. 21*

LEAR	A Gentleman [Bludrick(MS annotation on JPK); first appearance on the stage]
CORDELIA	Mrs Jackson

(2) *Dec. 27*

GENTLEMAN USHER	Berry
ARANTE added	Miss Stuart
DOCTOR	Baker

1781 COVENT GARDEN
Jan. 22; Mar. 26

LEAR (1)	Henderson
GLOUCESTER	Hull
EDMUND	[F.] Aickin
KENT	Clarke
ALBANY	L'Estrange
CORNWALL	Thompson
BURGUNDY	Robson
DOCTOR	Baker
GENTLEMAN USHER (1)	Berry

(1) *Oct. 31; Nov. 14*

LEAR	Wroughton (on *Nov. 14* only)
GENTLEMAN USHER	W. Bates
CORDELIA	A Lady [Mrs Roope (MS annotation on JPK); first appearance, Oct. 31, on the stage]

KING LEAR [as altered by TATE]

1781 COVENT GARDEN (cont.)
Jan. 22; Mar. 26 (cont.)

EDGAR	Lewis
GONERIL	Miss Platt
REGAN	Miss Ambrose
ARANTE	Miss Stuart
CORDELIA (1)	Miss Younge

1783 COVENT GARDEN
Jan. 1

LEAR	Henderson
GLOUCESTER	Hull
EDMUND	[F.] Aickin
KENT	Clarke
ALBANY	Davies
CORNWALL	Thompson
BURGUNDY (2)	Helme
DOCTOR (2)	[R.] Bates
GENTLEMAN USHER	Wewitzer
EDGAR	Lewis
GONERIL	Miss Platt
REGAN (1, 2)	Miss Cleland
ARANTE	Miss Stuart
CORDELIA (1, 2)	Miss Younge

(1) *Feb. 24*

REGAN	Mrs Whitfield
CORDELIA	Mrs [H.] Robinson

(2) *Oct. 20*

BURGUNDY	J. Bates
DOCTOR	Booth
REGAN	Mrs Whitfield
CORDELIA	Miss Satchell

1784 COVENT GARDEN
Jan. 5

LEAR	Henderson
GLOUCESTER	Hull
EDMUND	[F.] Aickin
KENT	Clarke
ALBANY	Davies
CORNWALL	Thompson
BURGUNDY	J. Bates
DOCTOR	Booth
GENTLEMAN USHER	Wewitzer
EDGAR	Lewis
GONERIL	Miss Platt
REGAN	Mrs Davenett
ARANTE	Miss Stuart
CORDELIA	Mrs [S.] Kemble

1786 COVENT GARDEN
Mar. 6

LEAR	Farren
GLOUCESTER	Hull

KING LEAR [as altered by TATE]

1786 COVENT GARDEN (cont.)
Mar. 6 (cont.)

KENT	[F.] Aickin
EDMUND	[Wm.] Palmer
ALBANY	Davies
GENTLEMAN USHER	Wewitzer
CORNWALL	Thompson
BURGUNDY	Cubitt
EDGAR	Holman
REGAN	Mrs Inchbald
GONERIL	Miss Platt
ARANTE	Miss Stuart
CORDELIA	Miss Brunton

[as altered by GARRICK]

1788 DRURY LANE
Jan. 21, 24, 29

LEAR	Kemble
GLOUCESTER	Packer
KENT	[J.] Aickin
EDMUND	Barrymore
GENTLEMAN USHER	Lamash
ALBANY	Whitfield
CORNWALL (1)	Staunton
BURGUNDY (1)	Benson
CAPTAIN	Phillimore
OLD MAN	[J.] Burton
DOCTOR	Chaplin
GENTLEMAN	Fawcett
OFFICER (1)	[W.] Bates
EDGAR	Wroughton
REGAN	Mrs Ward
GONERIL	Mrs Cuyler
ARANTE	Miss Tidswell
CORDELIA	Mrs Siddons

(1) Mar. 1, 8; May 15

CORNWALL	Benson
BURGUNDY	[W.] Bates

omitted on *Mar. 8, May 15* only

OFFICER

[On *Mar. 1* PA retains Staunton as CORNWALL, and Benson as BURGUNDY.]

[as altered by TATE]

1789 COVENT GARDEN
Nov. 23

LEAR	Harley
EDMUND	Fennell
GLOUCESTER	Hull
KENT	[F.] Aickin
ALBANY	Davies

356

KING LEAR [as altered by TATE]

1789 COVENT GARDEN (cont.)
Nov. 23 (cont.)

CORNWALL	Macready
BURGUNDY	Blurton
DOCTOR	Gardner
GENTLEMAN USHER	Bernard
EDGAR	Holman
REGAN	Mrs Bernard
GONERIL	Mrs Platt
ARANTE	Miss Rowson
CORDELIA	Miss Brunton

1790 COVENT GARDEN
Jan. 4, 11

LEAR	Harley
EDMUND (3)	Macready
GLOUCESTER	Hull
KENT	[F.] Aickin
ALBANY	Davies
CORNWALL (3)	Evatt
BURGUNDY (2, 3)	Blurton
DOCTOR (1, 2, 3)	Gardner
GENTLEMAN USHER	Bernard
EDGAR	Holman
REGAN	Mrs Bernard
GONERIL	Mrs Platt
ARANTE (3)	Miss Rowson
CORDELIA	Miss Brunton

(1) *Jan. 18; Feb. 1, 15; Apr. 19*

DOCTOR	Rock

(2) *Oct. 11*

DOCTOR	Rock
omitted	
BURGUNDY	
[PA assigns the DOCTOR to Powel.]	

(3) *Nov. 22*

EDMUND	Fennell
CORNWALL	Macready
DOCTOR	Rock
ARANTE	Miss Brangin
omitted	
BURGUNDY	

1791 COVENT GARDEN
Jan. 10

LEAR	Harley
EDMUND (1)	Fennell
GLOUCESTER	Hull
KENT	[F.] Aickin
ALBANY	Davies
CORNWALL (1)	Macready
DOCTOR	Rock
GENTLEMAN USHER (1)	Bernard
EDGAR	Holman
REGAN (1)	Mrs Bernard
GONERIL	Mrs Platt
ARANTE (1)	Miss Brangin
CORDELIA (1)	Miss Brunton

(1) *Nov. 4*

EDMUND	Macready
CORNWALL	Bloomfield
GENTLEMAN USHER	Munden
REGAN	Mrs Fawcett
ARANTE	Miss Leserve
CORDELIA	Mrs Merry [i.e. formerly Miss Brunton]

KING LEAR

[*as altered by* KEMBLE]

1792 DRURY LANE (company at KING'S, HAYMARKET)
Mar. 6

LEAR	Kemble
BURGUNDY	Caulfield
CORNWALL	Benson
ALBANY	Whitfield
GLOUCESTER	Packer
KENT	[J.] Aickin
EDGAR	Wroughton
EDMUND	Barrymore
GENTLEMAN USHER	R. Palmer
ESQUIRE	Dignum
DOCTOR	Jones
ATTENDANT	Fawcett
CAPTAIN	Maddocks
HERALD	[J.] Cooke
OLD MAN	Hollingsworth
GENTLEMAN	Phillimore
GONERIL	Mrs Cuyler
REGAN	Mrs Ward
CORDELIA	Mrs Siddons

1793 DRURY LANE (company at HAYMARKET)
Feb. 16

LEAR	Kemble
BURGUNDY	Caulfield
CORNWALL	Benson
ALBANY	Whitfield
GLOUCESTER	Packer
KENT	[J.] Aickin
EDGAR	Wroughton
EDMUND	Barrymore
GENTLEMAN USHER	R. Palmer
ESQUIRE	Dignum
DOCTOR	Jones
ATTENDANT	Fawcett
CAPTAIN	Maddocks
HERALD	[J.] Cooke
OLD MAN	[J.] Burton
GENTLEMAN	Phillimore
GONERIL	Mrs Cuyler
REGAN	Mrs Ward
CORDELIA	Mrs Siddons

[PA assigns the OLD MAN to Hollingsworth.]

KING LEAR

[*as altered by* TATE]

1794 COVENT GARDEN

Jan. 6, 31

LEAR	Pope
EDMUND	Middleton
GLOUCESTER	Hull
KENT	Harley
ALBANY	Davies
CORNWALL (3)	Macready
GENTLEMAN USHER	Bernard
EDGAR	Holman
REGAN	Mrs Fawcett
GONERIL	Mrs Platt
ARANTE	Miss Leserve
CORDELIA (2, 3)	Mrs Esten

(1) *Jan. 20*
  added
  DOCTOR   Evatt

(2) *Apr. 21*
  CORDELIA   Mrs Twistleton

(3) *May 12*
  CORNWALL   Campbell
  CORDELIA   Mrs Twistleton

[*as altered by* KEMBLE]

1795 DRURY LANE

Nov. 20

LEAR	Kemble
BURGUNDY	Dignum
CORNWALL	C. Kemble
ALBANY	Whitfield
KENT	[J.] Aickin
GLOUCESTER	Packer
EDGAR	Wroughton
EDMUND	Barrymore
1ST KNIGHT	Caulfield
2ND KNIGHT	Phillimore
3RD KNIGHT	Maddocks
4TH KNIGHT	Welsh
DOCTOR	Jones
CAPTAIN	Trueman
OFFICER	[J.] Cooke
GENTLEMAN USHER	Russell
HERALD	Banks
GONERIL'S PAGE	Master Chatterley
REGAN'S PAGE	Master Gell
OLD MAN	[J.] Burton
CORNWALL'S SERVANT	Benson
1ST RUFFIAN	Webb
2ND RUFFIAN	Evans
GONERIL	Mrs Cuyler
REGAN	Mrs Maddocks

KING LEAR [as altered by KEMBLE]
1795 DRURY LANE (cont.)
Nov. 20 (cont.)

CORDELIA	Mrs Siddons
ARANTE	Miss Tidswell

[In the bill the GENTLEMAN USHER is called OSWALD, and CORNWALL'S SERVANT is called EDWARD. See the acting version, Lowndes [1795].]

[as altered by TATE]
COVENT GARDEN
Jan. 19

LEAR	Pope
EDMUND	Middleton
GLOUCESTER	Hull
KENT	Harley
CORNWALL	Macready
GENTLEMAN USHER	Bernard
EDGAR	Holman
REGAN	Mrs Fawcett
GONERIL	Miss Morris
CORDELIA	Miss Wallis

(1) *Feb. 17*
added
    ALBANY   Davies

(2) *Sept. 28*
added
    ALBANY   Richardson
    ARANTE   Miss Leserve

1796 COVENT GARDEN
Apr. 25

LEAR	Pope
EDMUND	Middleton
GLOUCESTER	Hull
KENT (1)	Harley
CORNWALL	Macready
ALBANY (1)	Richardson
GENTLEMAN USHER	Farley
EDGAR	Holman
REGAN	Mrs Fawcett
GONERIL	Miss Morris
ARANTE (1)	Miss Leserve
CORDELIA	Miss Wallis

(1) *Oct. 10*

KENT	Waddy
ALBANY	Toms

added
    BURGUNDY   Philipps
    CORNWALL'S
    SERVANT   Thompson
omitted
    ARANTE

1797 COVENT GARDEN
Nov. 20

LEAR	Murray
EDMUND	Whitfield
GLOUCESTER	Hull
KENT	Waddy
CORNWALL	Clarke
ALBANY	Toms
GENTLEMAN USHER	Simmons
DOCTOR	Davenport

KING LEAR [as altered by TATE]

1797 COVENT GARDEN (cont.)
Nov. 20 (cont.)

CORNWALL'S SERVANT	Thompson
EDGAR	Holman
REGAN	Mrs Litchfield
GONERIL	Miss Mansel
ARANTE	Miss Leserve
CORDELIA	Mrs Spencer

1799 COVENT GARDEN
Oct. 29

LEAR	Pope
EDMUND	Whitfield
GLOUCESTER	Hull
KENT	Waddy
CORNWALL	Macartney
ALBANY	Claremont
GENTLEMAN USHER	Farley
BURGUNDY	Mills
DOCTOR	Davenport
CORNWALL'S SERVANT	Thompson
GENTLEMAN	Klanert
OLD MAN	Rees
EDGAR	Holman
REGAN	Mrs Litchfield
GONERIL	Mrs Dibdin
ARANTE	Miss Leserve
CORDELIA	Mrs [M. A.] Pope

MACBETH

(1) Altered by Sir William Davenant. In five acts.
   1674 P. Chetwin.
For a description of this see my Volume I, 267–8.

(2) 'As it is Acted at the Theatre-Royal in Drury-Lane.'
   1755 Glasgow: William Duncan.
This is a reading edition, verbatim throughout.

(3) 'As performed at the Theatres in London and Dublin.'
   1761 Dublin: W. Whitestone.
This is an alteration made by John Lee, first acted at Edinburgh on Jan. 1, 1754. It was never performed in London.

MACBETH

(4) 'As Performed at the Theatre-Royal, Drury-Lane. Regulated from the Prompt-Book.'

1773   John Bell.

From *Act II. iii* is omitted *1–47* (the Porter). In this scene Lennox's speech, *60–67a*, is inserted before *48*. Lady Macbeth does not appear.

Act III. vi entire (Lennox and the Lord hope for speedy assistance from England) is omitted.

Act IV. ii. 30b–62, 77b–end (Lady Macduff and her son) is omitted. In this scene the Messenger's speech is given to Angus. From *IV. iii* are omitted *61b–97a* (Malcolm's description of his intemperance), and *140–59a* (the cure called the King's evil).

Act V. ii entire (the revolted nobles' hatred of Macbeth) is omitted.

Added are two scenes of the 'Singing Witches', written by Davenant. They are the last scene of his Act II, inserted between *II. iii* and *iv*, and an abridgement of the last scene of his Act III, which follows *III. v. 33*. Following *V. vii. 63* are 15 lines written by Garrick: Macbeth dies on the stage with the observation that his 'soul is clogged with blood'. For *V. vii. 83–84* are substituted six new lines, also written by Garrick, in which Macduff presents Macbeth's sword to Malcolm.

Throughout there are minor omissions, and a few verbal changes, for example: *I. vii. 59b*, 'How fail!' (*for* 'We fail!'); *IV. i. 107–9*, 'Appear!' (*for* 'Show!'). *V. v. 18–19* is pointed, 'There would have been a time for such a word | To-morrow.—To-morrow, and to-morrow'.

A note on p. 65 of this text says that at CG 'the characters of Ross and Angus have been blended into those of Macduff and Lennox'.

(5) 'As it is Acted at the Theatres-Royal in Drury-Lane and Covent-Garden.'

1780   Harrison and Co.

This is identical with (4).

(6) 'Taken from the Manager's Books, at the Theatres Drury-Lane and Covent-Garden.'

1785   For the Proprietors.

(7) 'Marked with the Variations in the Manager's Book, at the Theatre-Royal in Drury-Lane.'

1785   C. Bathurst [&c.].

(8) 'Taken from the Manager's Book, at the Theatre Royal, Drury-Lane.'

n.d. [1785]   R. Butters.

All these are identical with (4), except that Lennox's speech, *II. iii. 60–67a*, is in its proper place; in *IV. i. 107–9* 'Show!' has been restored; and in *IV. ii* the Messenger has been restored.

(9) 'As it is Performed at the Theatres Royal.'

1788   G. Lister.

(10) 'As Performed at the Theatres Royal. Regulated from the Prompt-Book.'

1794   J. Barker.

Both of these are identical with (4).

MACBETH

(11) 'With . . . the Variations in the Manager's Book at the Theatre-Royal Drury-Lane.'
    1794   T. Longman [&c.].
    This is identical with (6).

(12) 'As Represented . . . on opening the Theatre Royal Drury Lane, On Monday, April 21st, 1794.'
    n.d. [1794]   C. Lowndes.

This alteration is by J. P. Kemble. He adopts the text of (4), with all its omissions and additions, and makes the following further changes:

In *Act I. ii* line *46b* reads, 'The worthy Thane of Fife'; it is spoken by Ross. Macduff then enters, and has Ross's speeches. In *I. iii* Ross's speeches are given to Macduff, and Angus's to Lennox. In *I. v* the Messenger's speeches are given to Seyton.

From *Act II* are omitted *ii. 37–42* ('the ravell'd sleave of care'); *ii. 142–end* (Malcolm and Donalbain decide to which countries to flee); and *iv. 1–20* (the Old Man's superstitious beliefs). In *iii. 60–67a* Lennox's speech is in its proper place. In *iv* Lennox has Ross's speeches.

From *Act III* are omitted *i. 91b–107* (the simile of the dogs), and *v. 22–end* (the moon's 'vaporous drop'). In *III. i* Lady Macbeth does not appear; her speech is given to Macbeth. The 3rd Murderer is omitted from *III. iii*.

Following *Act IV. i. 43* the Singing Witches are again introduced, from the 1st scene of Davenant's Act IV. In *IV. i* Seyton has Lennox's speeches, and 'Show!', *107–9*, is restored. *IV. ii* (Lady Macduff, her son, and Ross) is entirely omitted.

From *Act V* is omitted *vii. 64–82* (Siward is told of his son's death). *V. v. 18–19* is pointed in the conventional manner.

Throughout there are minor omissions, and occasional new readings, for example: *I. vii. 1–2*, 'If it were done, when 'tis done, then 'twere well. | It were done quickly, if the assassination|'; *I. vii. 59b*, 'If we should fail,— | We fail.—|'; *II. ii. 64*, 'Making the green—one red.'

(13) 'As performed at the Theatre Royal, Drury-Lane.'
    n.d. [1798]   C. Lowndes.
    This is identical with (12).

[*as altered by* DAVENANT]

1751 COVENT GARDEN
Jan. 15

MACBETH	Quin
MACDUFF	Ryan
DUNCAN	Gibson
BANQUO	Sparks
MALCOLM	Anderson
DONALBAIN	Bennet
FLEANCE	Miss Morrison
SIWARD	Bransby

MACBETH [as altered by DAVENANT]

1751 COVENT GARDEN (cont.)
Jan. 15 (cont.)

LENNOX	Ridout
SEYTON	Usher
HECATE	Arthur
1ST MURDERER	Bencraft
2ND MURDERER	Marten
1ST WITCH	Dunstall
2ND WITCH	Collins
3RD WITCH	Cushing
LADY MACDUFF	Mrs Barrington
LADY MACBETH	Mrs Woffington

[The original]

1752 DRURY LANE
Jan. 28, 29

MACBETH (1, 3)	Mossop
DUNCAN	Burton
MACDUFF (3)	Havard
ROSS (3)	Lee
MALCOLM	Blakes
BANQUO (3)	Sowdon
ANGUS	Simson
LENNOX	Scrase
SIWARD (1, 2, 3)	Winstone
DONALBAIN (3)	Mattocks
1ST WITCH	W. Vaughan
2ND WITCH	Yates
3RD WITCH	Shuter
HECATE (1, 3)	Berry
LADY MACDUFF	Mrs Mills
LADY MACBETH	Mrs Pritchard

(1) Feb. 8

MACBETH	Garrick
HECATE	Winstone

added
YOUNG SIWARD Palmer
omitted
SIWARD

(2) Mar. 30

added
YOUNG SIWARD Marr
omitted
SIWARD

(3) Oct. 16, 30; Nov. 18; Dec. 4

MACBETH	Garrick (on Oct. 30, Dec. 4 only)
MACDUFF	Lacey (on Dec. 4 only)
ROSS	Davies
BANQUO	Ross
DONALBAIN	Master Cross
HECATE	Beard

added on Oct. 16 only
YOUNG SIWARD Marr
omitted on Oct. 16 only
SIWARD

COVENT GARDEN
Mar. 17

MACBETH	Barry
MACDUFF	Ryan
DUNCAN (1)	Gibson
MALCOLM	Usher
DONALBAIN	Miss Morrison
FLEANCE (1)	Miss Mullart
ANGUS	Bennet

(1) Oct. 30

DUNCAN	Bransby
YOUNG SIWARD	Ricard
3RD WITCH	Bencraft

omitted
FLEANCE

1752 COVENT GARDEN (cont.)

Mar. 17 (cont.)

SIWARD	Anderson
YOUNG SIWARD (1)	Bransby
LENNOX	Redman
SEYTON	Paddick
BANQUO	Sparks
ROSS	Ridout
1ST MURDERER	Stoppelaer
2ND MURDERER	Marten
HECATE	Arthur
1ST WITCH	Dunstall
2ND WITCH	Collins
3RD WITCH (1)	Cushing
LADY MACDUFF	Mrs Barrington
LADY MACBETH	Mrs Cibber

1753 DRURY LANE

May 7

MACBETH (1)	Mossop
DUNCAN (1)	Burton
MACDUFF	Havard
MALCOLM (1)	Blakes
BANQUO	Ross
ROSS (1)	Simson
HECATE (1)	Winstone
1ST WITCH (1)	W. Vaughan
2ND WITCH (1)	Shuter
3RD WITCH (1)	Yates
LADY MACDUFF	Mrs Mills
GENTLEWOMAN (1)	Mrs Simson
LADY MACBETH	Mrs Pritchard

(1) Oct. 3; Nov. 13

MACBETH	Garrick (on *Nov. 13* only)
DUNCAN	Berry
MALCOLM	Lacey
ROSS	Davies
HECATE	Beard
1ST WITCH	Burton
2ND WITCH	Yates
3RD WITCH	Blakes
added	
ANGUS	Simson
LENNOX	Scrase
SIWARD	Bransby
DONALBAIN	Vernon
omitted	
GENTLEWOMAN	

1754 DRURY LANE

Jan. 14

MACBETH (2)	Mossop
DUNCAN	Berry
MACDUFF (1)	Havard
ROSS	Davies
MALCOLM (1, 2)	Lacey
BANQUO	Ross
HECATE	Beard
1ST WITCH	Burton
2ND WITCH	Yates
3RD WITCH	Blakes
LADY MACDUFF	Mrs Mills
LADY MACBETH	Mrs Pritchard

(1) May 6

MACDUFF	Lacey
MALCOLM	Scrase
added	
LENNOX	Ackman

(2) Sept. 24; Nov. 2

MACBETH	Garrick (on *Nov. 2* only)
MALCOLM	Usher
added	
ANGUS	Simson
LENNOX	Scrase
SIWARD	Bransby
DONALBAIN	Vernon

MACBETH

1754 COVENT GARDEN
Nov. 16

MACBETH	Sheridan
MACDUFF	Ryan
DUNCAN	Gibson
BANQUO	Sparks
MALCOLM	Anderson
DONALBAIN	Bennet
SIWARD	White
LENNOX	Ridout
HECATE	Arthur
1ST MURDERER	Bencraft
2ND MURDERER	Marten
1ST WITCH	Dunstall
2ND WITCH	Collins
3RD WITCH	Cushing
LADY MACDUFF	Mrs Barrington
LADY MACBETH	Mrs Woffington

1755 DRURY LANE
Mar. 6

MACBETH (1)	Garrick
DUNCAN	Berry
MACDUFF (1)	Havard
ROSS	Davies
MALCOLM	Usher
BANQUO (1)	Ross
ANGUS	Simson
LENNOX	Scrase
SIWARD	Bransby
DONALBAIN (2)	Vernon
HECATE	Beard
1ST WITCH	Burton
2ND WITCH	Yates
3RD WITCH	Blakes
LADY MACDUFF (2)	Mrs Mills
LADY MACBETH	Mrs Pritchard

(1) *May 1*

MACBETH	Mossop
MACDUFF	Ross
BANQUO	Palmer

(2) *Oct. 10*

DONALBAIN	Master Simson
LADY MACDUFF	Mrs Cowper

[PA assigns MACBETH to Mossop. C-H: 'This day ye newspaper thro some carelessness of the servants put in Mr Mossop's Name instead of Mr Garrick's for Macbeth, the Master printer discovered it about eight in the Morning, & had the paper reprinted & sent & chang'd it all over the Town—it was all he could do, but I believe it hurt the House.' In the BM file of PA Mossop's name is deleted, and Garrick's substituted in a contemporary hand.]

COVENT GARDEN
May 5

MACBETH (1)	Murphy
MACDUFF	Ryan
DUNCAN	Gibson
BANQUO	Sparks
MALCOLM	Anderson
DONALBAIN	Bennet

(1) *Nov. 17; Dec. 8, 26*

MACBETH	Barry
added	
SEYTON	Redman
DOCTOR	Wignell
FLEANCE	Miss Mullart

MACBETH

1755 COVENT GARDEN (cont.)
May 5 (cont.)

LENNOX	Ridout
SIWARD	White
HECATE	Arthur
1ST MURDERER	Bencraft
2ND MURDERER	Marten
1ST WITCH	Collins
2ND WITCH	Dunstall
3RD WITCH	Cushing
LADY MACDUFF	Mrs Barrington
LADY MACBETH	Mrs Woffington

1756 DRURY LANE
Oct. 16

MACBETH	Mossop
DUNCAN	Berry
MACDUFF	Havard
ROSS	Davies
MALCOLM	Usher
BANQUO	Ross
ANGUS	Simson
LENNOX	Scrase
SIWARD	Bransby
DONALBAIN	Master Simson
HECATE	Beard
1ST WITCH	Burton
2ND WITCH	Yates
3RD WITCH	Blakes
LADY MACDUFF	Mrs Cowper
LADY MACBETH	Mrs Pritchard

COVENT GARDEN
Apr. 8

MACBETH	Barry
MACDUFF (1, 2)	Dyer
DUNCAN	Gibson
MALCOLM	Anderson
DONALBAIN	Bennet
SEYTON	Redman
SIWARD	White
DOCTOR	Wignell
FLEANCE	Miss Mullart
BANQUO	Sparks
LENNOX	Ridout
HECATE	Arthur
1ST MURDERER	Bencraft

(1) *Oct. 6; Dec. 28*

MACDUFF	Ryan

(2) *Nov. 10*

MACDUFF	Ryan
1ST WITCH	Costollo

367

MACBETH

1756 COVENT GARDEN (*cont.*)
Apr. 8 (cont.)

2ND MURDERER	Marten
1ST WITCH (2)	Collins
2ND WITCH	Dunstall
3RD WITCH	Cushing
LADY MACDUFF	Mrs Barrington
LADY MACBETH	Mrs Woffington

1757 DRURY LANE
Feb. 24

MACBETH (3)	Mossop
DUNCAN	Berry
MACDUFF	Havard
ROSS	Davies
MALCOLM	Usher
BANQUO (2, 3)	Ross
ANGUS (1)	Walker
LENNOX (1)	Scrase
SIWARD (1)	Bransby
DONALBAIN (1)	Master Simson
HECATE	Beard
1ST WITCH	Burton
2ND WITCH	Yates
3RD WITCH	Blakes
LADY MACDUFF (2, 3)	Mrs Cowper
LADY MACBETH	Mrs Pritchard

(1) *Apr. 16*
omitted ANGUS, LENNOX, SIWARD, DONALBAIN

(2) *Oct. 4*

BANQUO	Palmer
LADY MACDUFF	Mrs Bennet

(3) *Dec. 17*

MACBETH	Garrick
BANQUO	Palmer
LADY MACDUFF	Mrs Jefferson

COVENT GARDEN
Mar. 26

MACBETH	Barry
MACDUFF	Ryan
DUNCAN	Gibson
MALCOLM	Anderson
DONALBAIN	Bennet
SEYTON	Redman
SIWARD	White
DOCTOR	Wignell
FLEANCE	Miss Mullart
BANQUO	Sparks
LENNOX	Ridout
HECATE	Arthur
1ST MURDERER	Bencraft
2ND MURDERER	Marten
1ST WITCH	Collins

(1) *Dec. 10*

LADY MACBETH	Mrs Bellamy

MACBETH

1757 COVENT GARDEN (cont.)
Mar. 26 (cont.)

2ND WITCH	Dunstall
3RD WITCH	Cushing
LADY MACDUFF	Mrs Barrington
LADY MACBETH (1)	Mrs Gregory

1758 DRURY LANE
May 3

MACBETH	Mossop			
DUNCAN	Berry			
MACDUFF	Havard			
ROSS	Davies			
MALCOLM (1)	Usher			
BANQUO	Palmer			
ANGUS (1)	Walker			
LENNOX	Scrase			
SIWARD	Bransby			
DONALBAIN	Master Simson			
HECATE	Champnes			
1ST WITCH	Burton			
2ND WITCH	Yates			
3RD WITCH	Blakes			
LADY MACBETH	Mrs Pritchard			

(1) Oct. 30

MALCOLM	Austin
ANGUS	Perry
added	
LADY MACDUFF	Mrs Glen

COVENT GARDEN
Mar. 7; May 1

MACBETH	Barry
MACDUFF	Ryan
DUNCAN	Gibson
MALCOLM	Anderson
DONALBAIN	Bennet
SEYTON	Redman
SIWARD	White
DOCTOR	Wignell
FLEANCE	Miss Mullart
BANQUO	Sparks
LENNOX	Ridout
HECATE	Arthur
1ST MURDERER	Bencraft
2ND MURDERER	Marten
1ST WITCH	Collins
2ND WITCH	Dunstall
3RD WITCH	Cushing
LADY MACDUFF	Mrs Barrington
LADY MACBETH	Mrs Bellamy

MACBETH

1759 DRURY LANE
Mar. 12

MACBETH (1)	Mossop
MACDUFF	Havard
ROSS	Davies
MALCOLM	Austin
BANQUO	Palmer
ANGUS	Perry
LENNOX	Scrase
SIWARD (1)	Bransby
DONALBAIN	Master Simson
HECATE	Champnes
1ST WITCH	Burton
2ND WITCH	Yates
3RD WITCH	Blakes
LADY MACDUFF (1)	Mrs Glen
LADY MACBETH	Mrs Pritchard

(1) *Oct. 12*

MACBETH	Garrick
SIWARD	Moody
LADY MACDUFF	Mrs Bennet
added	
DUNCAN	Bransby

1760 COVENT GARDEN
Apr. 17

MACBETH	Ross
MACDUFF	Dyer
DUNCAN	Gibson
BANQUO	Sparks
LENNOX	Ridout
HECATE	Wignell
1ST WITCH	Collins
2ND WITCH	Dunstall
3RD WITCH	Costollo
LADY MACDUFF	Mrs Barrington
LADY MACBETH	Mrs Hamilton

1761 DRURY LANE
Apr. 29

MACBETH (1)	Sheridan
DUNCAN	Bransby
MACDUFF	Havard
ROSS	Davies
MALCOLM (1)	Austin
BANQUO	Palmer
ANGUS	Fox
LENNOX	Scrase
SIWARD	Moody
DONALBAIN	Master Cautherley

(1) *Oct. 31; Nov. 12*

MACBETH	Garrick
MALCOLM	Packer
added	
DOCTOR	Stevens

[On *Nov. 12* PA assigns ANGUS to Scrase, and LENNOX to Fox.]

370

1761 DRURY LANE (cont.)

Apr. 29 (cont.)

HECATE	Champnes
1ST WITCH	Burton
2ND WITCH	Yates
3RD WITCH	Blakes
LADY MACDUFF	Mrs Bennet
LADY MACBETH	Mrs Pritchard

COVENT GARDEN

Apr. 2; May 25

MACBETH	Ross
MACDUFF	Clarke
DUNCAN	Gibson
MALCOLM	Anderson
DONALBAIN	Bennet
SEYTON	Redman
SIWARD	R. Smith
MACBETH'S SERVANT	Holtom
FLEANCE	Mrs Evans
BANQUO	Sparks
LENNOX	Hull
HECATE	Wignell
1ST MURDERER	Bencraft
2ND MURDERER	Marten
1ST WITCH	Collins
2ND WITCH	Dunstall
3RD WITCH	Costollo
LADY MACDUFF	Mrs Barrington
LADY MACBETH	Mrs Hamilton

1762 DRURY LANE

Jan. 9

MACBETH	Garrick
DUNCAN	Bransby
MACDUFF	Havard
ROSS	Davies
MALCOLM	Packer
BANQUO	Palmer
ANGUS	Fox
LENNOX	Scrase
SIWARD	Moody
DONALBAIN	Master Cautherley
DOCTOR	Stevens

MACBETH

1762 DRURY LANE (cont.)
Jan. 9 (cont.)

HECATE	Champnes
1ST WITCH	Burton
2ND WITCH	Yates
3RD WITCH	Blakes
LADY MACDUFF	Mrs Bennet
LADY MACBETH	Mrs Pritchard

[PA assigns ANGUS to Scrase, and LENNOX to Fox.]

COVENT GARDEN
May 11

MACBETH	Ross
MACDUFF	Dyer
BANQUO	Gibson
HECATE	Wignell
1ST WITCH	Collins
2ND WITCH	Dunstall
3RD WITCH	Costollo
LADY MACDUFF	Mrs Barrington
LADY MACBETH	Mrs Hamilton

1763 DRURY LANE
Jan. 17

MACBETH (1, 2, 3, 5)	Garrick
DUNCAN	Bransby
MACDUFF	Havard
ROSS	Lee
MALCOLM	Packer
BANQUO	Palmer
ANGUS	Fox
LENNOX	Parsons
SIWARD	Moody
DONALBAIN (5)	Master Cautherley
FLEANCE (5)	Master Burton
DOCTOR	Stevens
HECATE (2)	Champnes
1ST WITCH	Burton
2ND WITCH	Yates
3RD WITCH (3, 4, 5)	Blakes
LADY MACDUFF (1)	Mrs Bennet
LADY MACBETH	Mrs Pritchard

(1) *Mar. 17*

MACBETH	Holland
LADY MACDUFF	Mrs Hopkins

(2) *Apr. 13*

MACBETH	Holland
HECATE	Vernon

(3) *May 2*

MACBETH	Holland
3RD WITCH	Love

(4) *May 20*

3RD WITCH	Love

(5) *Nov. 29*

MACBETH	Holland
DONALBAIN	Master Burton
FLEANCE	Miss Rogers
3RD WITCH	Love
added	
SERGEANT	Jackson

[PA assigns ANGUS to Scrase.]

MACBETH

1764 DRURY LANE
Feb. 28

MACBETH	Holland
DUNCAN	Bransby
MACDUFF	Havard
ROSS	Lee
MALCOLM (1)	Jackson
BANQUO	Palmer
ANGUS	Fox
LENNOX	Parsons
SIWARD	Moody
DONALBAIN	Master Burton
FLEANCE	Miss Rogers
DOCTOR (1)	Stevens
HECATE	Champnes
1ST WITCH (1)	Burton
2ND WITCH	Yates
3RD WITCH	Love
LADY MACDUFF	Mrs Bennet
LADY MACBETH	Mrs Pritchard

(1) *Nov. 27*

MALCOLM	Packer
1ST WITCH	Granger
added	
SERGEANT	Jackson
SEYTON	Ackman
omitted	
DOCTOR	

COVENT GARDEN
May 21

MACBETH	Ross
MACDUFF	Clarke
DUNCAN	Gibson
MALCOLM	Anderson
DONALBAIN	Bennet
SEYTON	Gardner
SIWARD	R. Smith
FLEANCE	Master Morgan
BANQUO	Sparks
LENNOX	Hull
HECATE	Wignell
1ST MURDERER	Buck
2ND MURDERER	Holtom
1ST WITCH	Dunstall
2ND WITCH	Costollo
LADY MACDUFF	Mrs Barrington
LADY MACBETH	Mrs Ward

1765 DRURY LANE
Feb. 26

MACBETH	Holland
DUNCAN	Bransby
MACDUFF	Havard
ROSS	Lee

(1) *Apr. 22*

LENNOX	Adcock
1ST WITCH	Parsons
LADY MACBETH	Mrs Palmer
added	
SERGEANT	Jackson

MACBETH

1765 DRURY LANE (cont.)
Feb. 26 (cont.)

MALCOLM	Packer
BANQUO	Palmer
ANGUS (2, 3)	Fox
LENNOX (1)	Parsons
SIWARD (2)	Moody
SEYTON	Ackman
DONALBAIN (2, 3)	Master Burton
FLEANCE (2, 3)	Miss Rogers
HECATE	Champnes
1ST WITCH (1, 3)	Yates
2ND WITCH	Love
3RD WITCH	Burton
LADY MACDUFF	Mrs Bennet
LADY MACBETH (1)	Mrs Pritchard

(2) *Oct. 28*
added
  DOCTOR   Hurst
  SERGEANT [F.] Aickin
omitted
  ANGUS, SIWARD, DONALBAIN, FLEANCE

(3) *Dec. 20*
  1ST WITCH Baddeley
added
SAME as *Oct. 28*
omitted
  ANGUS, DONALBAIN, FLEANCE

COVENT GARDEN
May 11

MACBETH	Ross
MACDUFF (1)	Tindal
DUNCAN	Gibson
MALCOLM	Davis
DONALBAIN	Murden
SEYTON	Gardner
BANQUO (1)	Sparks
LENNOX	Hull
HECATE	Wignell
1ST MURDERER	Buck
2ND MURDERER (1)	Holtom
1ST WITCH	Dunstall
2ND WITCH	Costollo
3RD WITCH	[P.] Lewis
LADY MACDUFF (1)	Mrs Barrington
LADY MACBETH	Mrs Ward

(1) *Oct. 14*

MACDUFF	Clarke
BANQUO	Walker
2ND MURDERER	Redman
LADY MACDUFF	Mrs Burden

1766 DRURY LANE
Apr. 2

MACBETH	Holland
DUNCAN	Bransby
MACDUFF	Havard
ROSS	Lee
MALCOLM	Packer
BANQUO	Palmer
SERGEANT	[F.] Aickin
DOCTOR	Hurst
LENNOX	Parsons
SEYTON	Ackman

1766 DRURY LANE (cont.)
Apr. 2 (cont.)

SIWARD	Moody
HECATE	Champnes
1ST WITCH	Burton
2ND WITCH	Love
3RD WITCH	Baddeley
LADY MACDUFF	Mrs Bennet
LADY MACBETH	Mrs Pritchard

1767 DRURY LANE
Mar. 21

MACBETH	Holland
DUNCAN	Bransby
MACDUFF (1)	Havard
ROSS	[F.] Aickin
MALCOLM	Packer
BANQUO	Palmer
SEYTON	Ackman
SIWARD (1)	Moody
HECATE	Champnes
1ST WITCH	Burton
2ND WITCH	Love
3RD WITCH	Baddeley
LADY MACDUFF	Mrs Bennet
LADY MACBETH	Mrs Pritchard

(1) *May 13*

MACDUFF added	Hurst
ANGUS	Keen
omitted SIWARD	

1768 DRURY LANE
Jan. 14

MACBETH (1, 2)	Barry
DUNCAN	Bransby
MACDUFF (2)	Havard
ROSS	[F.] Aickin
MALCOLM (2)	Packer
BANQUO (2)	Palmer
SEYTON (2)	Ackman
ANGUS (2)	Keen
HECATE	Champnes
LENNOX (2)	Fawcett
SERGEANT (2)	Hurst
1ST WITCH	Burton
2ND WITCH	Love
3RD WITCH	Baddeley
FLEANCE (1, 2)	Miss Rogers
LADY MACDUFF	Mrs Reddish
LADY MACBETH (1, 2)	Mrs Dancer

(1) *Feb. 4, 8*

MACBETH	Garrick
LADY MACBETH	Mrs Pritchard
omitted FLEANCE	

(2) *Apr. 25; Sept. 22*

MACBETH	Garrick
MACDUFF	Reddish
MALCOLM	Cautherley
BANQUO	Packer
LADY MACBETH	Mrs Pritchard (on *Apr. 25* only) / Mrs [S.] Barry [i.e. formerly Mrs Dancer] (on *Sept. 22* only)

omitted FLEANCE, and on *Sept. 22* also omitted SEYTON, ANGUS, LENNOX, SERGEANT

1768 COVENT GARDEN
Jan. 20

MACBETH	Powell
MACDUFF	Clarke
LENNOX	Hull
MALCOLM (1, 2, 3)	Casey
BANQUO	Bensley
DUNCAN	Gibson
SEYTON	Gardner
HECATE	Legg
1ST WITCH (2, 3)	Shuter
2ND WITCH (3)	Dunstall
3RD WITCH	Morgan
LADY MACBETH	Mrs Yates

(1) *Jan. 27; Feb. 16; Apr. 5*

MALCOLM	Perry

(2) *Oct. 17; Nov. 10*

MALCOLM	Perry
1ST WITCH	[P.] Lewis

(3) *Dec. 23*

MALCOLM	Perry
1ST WITCH	[P.] Lewis
2ND WITCH	Quick

1769 DRURY LANE
Jan. 24

MACBETH	Barry
DUNCAN	Bransby
MACDUFF	Reddish
ROSS	[F.] Aickin
MALCOLM	Cautherley
BANQUO	Packer
LENNOX	Fawcett
SERGEANT	J. Aickin
HECATE	Champnes
1ST WITCH	Burton
2ND WITCH	Moody
3RD WITCH	Baddeley
LADY MACDUFF	Mrs Reddish
LADY MACBETH	Mrs [S.] Barry

COVENT GARDEN
Mar. 6; Apr. 3

MACBETH (2)	Powell
MACDUFF (1)	Clarke
LENNOX (1)	Hull
MALCOLM (1)	Perry
BANQUO	Bensley
DUNCAN	Gibson
SEYTON	Gardner
HECATE (1, 2)	Legg
1ST WITCH (2)	Dunstall
2ND WITCH (1, 2)	Morgan
3RD WITCH (1, 2)	[P.] Lewis
LADY MACBETH	Mrs Yates

(1) *May 23*

MACDUFF	Hull
LENNOX	Perry
MALCOLM	Wroughton
HECATE	Barnshaw
2ND WITCH	Quick
3RD WITCH	Mrs Pitt

(2) *Dec. 19*

MACBETH	Smith
HECATE	Reinhold
1ST WITCH	Quick
2ND WITCH	Mrs Pitt
3RD WITCH	Cushing

1770 DRURY LANE
Jan. 4

MACBETH	Barry
DUNCAN	Bransby
MACDUFF	Reddish
ROSS	[F.] Aickin
MALCOLM	Cautherley
BANQUO	Packer
ANGUS	Keen
LENNOX	Fawcett
SEYTON	Ackman
SERGEANT	J. Aickin
HECATE	Champnes
1ST WITCH (1)	Burton
2ND WITCH	Moody
3RD WITCH	Baddeley
LADY MACDUFF	Mrs Reddish
LADY MACBETH	Mrs [S.] Barry

(1) *Nov. 14*

1ST WITCH added	Parsons
DOCTOR	Wright

COVENT GARDEN
Jan. 3

MACBETH	Smith
MACDUFF (1)	Hull
LENNOX (1)	Perry
MALCOLM (1)	Wroughton
BANQUO	Bensley
DUNCAN	Gibson
SEYTON	Gardner
HECATE	Reinhold
1ST WITCH	Dunstall
2ND WITCH	Mrs Pitt
3RD WITCH	Quick
LADY MACBETH	Mrs Yates

(1) *Jan. 11; Feb. 14; Apr. 23; Oct. 8; Dec. 14*

MACDUFF	Clarke
LENNOX	Hull
MALCOLM	Perry

1771 COVENT GARDEN
Apr. 15; May 20

MACBETH	Smith
MACDUFF	Clarke
LENNOX	Hull
MALCOLM	Perry
BANQUO	Bensley
DUNCAN	Younger
SEYTON	Gardner
HECATE	Reinhold
1ST WITCH	Dunstall
2ND WITCH	Mrs Pitt
3RD WITCH	Quick
LADY MACBETH	Mrs Yates

1772 DRURY LANE
Apr. 25; June 9

MACBETH	Reddish
MACDUFF	[F.] Aickin
DUNCAN	Bransby
ROSS	J. Aickin
MALCOLM	Cautherley
BANQUO	Packer
DONALBAIN	Master Cape
SEYTON	Ackman
LENNOX	Fawcett
SERGEANT	Davies
ANGUS	Keen
HECATE	Champnes
1ST WITCH	Parsons
2ND WITCH	Moody
3RD WITCH	Baddeley
LADY MACDUFF	Mrs Reddish
LADY MACBETH	A Gentlewoman [Miss Sherry (MacMillan, 161); first appearance, Apr. 25, on the stage]

COVENT GARDEN
Jan. 27; June 1

MACBETH	Smith
MACDUFF	Clarke
LENNOX	Hull
MALCOLM (1, 2)	Wroughton
BANQUO	Bensley
DUNCAN	Gardner
SEYTON	Thompson
HECATE	Reinhold
1ST WITCH	Dunstall
2ND WITCH (2)	Mrs Pitt
3RD WITCH	Quick
LADY MACBETH	Mrs Yates

(1) *Mar. 2; Apr. 6*

MALCOLM	Perry

(2) *Apr. 28*

MALCOLM	Perry
2ND WITCH	Saunders

1773 DRURY LANE
May 10

MACBETH	Reddish
MACDUFF	[F.] Aickin
DUNCAN	Bransby
ROSS	J. Aickin
MALCOLM	Cautherley
BANQUO	Packer
LENNOX	Fawcett

1773 DRURY LANE (cont.)

May 10 (cont.)

DONALBAIN	Master Cape
ANGUS	Keen
SEYTON	Ackman
SIWARD	Hurst
DOCTOR	Wright
SERGEANT	Davies
FLEANCE	Miss Collett
HECATE	Champnes
1ST WITCH	Parsons
2ND WITCH	Moody
3RD WITCH	Baddeley
LADY MACDUFF	Miss Ambrose
LADY MACBETH	Miss Younge

COVENT GARDEN

Mar. 22; Apr. 20

MACBETH (2)	Smith
MACDUFF (1)	Clarke
LENNOX (1)	Hull
MALCOLM (1, 2)	Perry
BANQUO	Bensley
DUNCAN	Gardner
SEYTON	Thompson
HECATE	Reinhold
1ST WITCH	Dunstall
2ND WITCH	Mrs Pitt
3RD WITCH	Quick
LADY MACBETH	Mrs Hartley

(1) *May 10*

MACDUFF	Hull
LENNOX	Perry
MALCOLM	Owenson

(2) *Oct. 23, 30; Nov. 6, 13*

MACBETH	Macklin
MALCOLM	Wroughton

1774 COVENT GARDEN

Apr. 13, 29

MACBETH	Smith
MACDUFF	Clarke
LENNOX	Hull
MALCOLM	Wroughton
BANQUO	Bensley
DUNCAN	Gardner
SEYTON	Thompson
HECATE	Reinhold
1ST WITCH	Dunstall
2ND WITCH	Mrs Pitt
3RD WITCH	Quick
LADY MACBETH	Mrs Hartley

1775 DRURY LANE
Mar. 23

MACBETH	Smith
MACDUFF	Reddish
DUNCAN (1)	Usher
ROSS	[J.] Aickin
MALCOLM (1)	Cautherley
BANQUO	Packer
LENNOX	Fawcett
DONALBAIN	Everard
ANGUS (1)	Keen
SIWARD	Hurst
DOCTOR	Wright
SERGEANT (1)	Davies
FLEANCE	Master Pulley
SEYTON	Griffiths
HECATE	Legg
1ST WITCH	Parsons
2ND WITCH	Moody
3RD WITCH	Baddeley
LADY MACDUFF	Miss Sherry
LADY MACBETH	Mrs Yates

(1) *Dec. 7*

DUNCAN	Bransby
MALCOLM	Davies
ANGUS	Whitfield
SERGEANT	Usher

COVENT GARDEN
Oct. 19

MACBETH	Macklin
MACDUFF	Clarke
DUNCAN	Hull
MALCOLM	Wroughton
BANQUO	[F.] Aickin
LENNOX	L'Estrange
SEYTON	Thompson
HECATE	Reinhold
1ST WITCH	Dunstall
2ND WITCH	Mrs Pitt
3RD WITCH	Quick
LADY MACBETH	Mrs Hartley

1776 DRURY LANE
Jan. 1

MACBETH	Smith
MACDUFF (1)	Reddish
DUNCAN	Bransby
ROSS	[J.] Aickin
MALCOLM	Davies
BANQUO	Packer
LENNOX (2)	Fawcett

(1) *Jan. 19*

MACDUFF	Farren
LADY MACBETH	Mrs King

(2) *Nov. 25; Dec. 26, 30*

LENNOX	Grist
DONALBAIN	R. Palmer
ANGUS	Chaplin
SERGEANT	Farren

MACBETH

1776 DRURY LANE (cont.)

Jan. 1 (cont.)

DONALBAIN (2)	Everard
ANGUS (2)	Whitfield
SIWARD	Hurst
DOCTOR	Wright
SERGEANT (2)	Usher
FLEANCE	Master Pulley
SEYTON	Griffiths
HECATE (2)	Legg
1ST WITCH	Parsons
2ND WITCH	Moody
3RD WITCH	Baddeley
LADY MACDUFF	Miss Sherry
LADY MACBETH (1, 2)	Mrs Yates

(2) *Nov. 25; Dec. 26, 30 (cont.)*

HECATE	[C.] Bannister
LADY MACBETH	Mrs Melmoth

[On *Nov. 25* PA assigns DUNCAN to Hurst, and SIWARD to Wrighten.]

COVENT GARDEN

Dec. 2

MACBETH	Macklin
MACDUFF	Clarke
DUNCAN	Hull
MALCOLM	Ward
BANQUO	[F.] Aickin
LENNOX	L'Estrange
SEYTON	Thompson
SIWARD	Davis
DOCTOR	Fearon
HECATE	Reinhold
1ST WITCH	Dunstall
2ND WITCH	Mrs Pitt
3RD WITCH	Quick
LADY MACBETH	Mrs Hartley

1777 DRURY LANE

Apr. 22

MACBETH	Smith
MACDUFF	Reddish
DUNCAN	Bransby
ROSS	[J.] Aickin
MALCOLM	Davies
BANQUO	Packer
LENNOX	Grist
DONALBAIN	R. Palmer
ANGUS	Chaplin
SIWARD	Hurst
DOCTOR	Wright

1777 DRURY LANE (cont.)

Apr. 22 (cont.)

SERGEANT	Farren
FLEANCE	Master Pulley
SEYTON	Griffiths
HECATE	[C.] Bannister
1ST WITCH	Parsons
2ND WITCH	Moody
3RD WITCH	Baddeley
LADY MACDUFF	Miss Platt
LADY MACBETH	Miss Sherry

1778 DRURY LANE

Jan. 5, 12

MACBETH (1)	Smith
MACDUFF (1)	Brereton
DUNCAN	Chambers
ROSS	[J.] Aickin
MALCOLM	Davies
BANQUO	Packer
LENNOX	Norris
DONALBAIN	R. Palmer
ANGUS	Chaplin
SIWARD	Hurst
DOCTOR	Wright
SERGEANT (1, 3)	Farren
HECATE	[C.] Bannister
1ST WITCH	Parsons
2ND WITCH	Moody
3RD WITCH	Baddeley
LADY MACDUFF	Miss Sherry
LADY MACBETH (2)	Miss Younge

(1) *Mar. 31*

MACBETH	Henderson
MACDUFF	Farren
omitted	
SERGEANT	

(2) *Apr. 30*

LADY MACBETH	Mrs Robinson

(3) *Sept. 24; Nov. 26; Dec. 29*

SERGEANT added	Wrighten
SEYTON	Griffiths

COVENT GARDEN

May 6

MACBETH	[F.] Aickin
MACDUFF	Clarke
DUNCAN	Hull
MALCOLM	Whitfield
BANQUO	Wroughton
LENNOX	L'Estrange
SEYTON	Thompson
HECATE	Reinhold
1ST WITCH	Dunstall
2ND WITCH	Stevens
3RD WITCH	Quick
LADY MACBETH	Mrs Jackson

1778 HAYMARKET
Sept. 7, 9

MACBETH	Digges
MACDUFF	[J.] Aickin
DUNCAN	Gardner
MALCOLM	R. Palmer
LENNOX	Egan
SEYTON	Webb
DOCTOR	Massey
BANQUO	[J.] Palmer
HECATE	[C.] Bannister
1ST WITCH	Parsons
2ND WITCH	Edwin
3RD WITCH	Baddeley
GENTLEWOMAN	Mrs Poussin
LADY MACBETH	Mrs Massey

1779 DRURY LANE
Apr. 7

MACBETH	Smith
MACDUFF	Brereton
DUNCAN	Chambers
ROSS	[J.] Aickin
MALCOLM	Davies
DONALBAIN	Master Benson
BANQUO	Packer
LENNOX	Norris
ANGUS	Chaplin
SIWARD	Hurst
DOCTOR	Wright
SERGEANT	Wrighten
SEYTON	Griffiths
HECATE	[C.] Bannister
1ST WITCH	Parsons
2ND WITCH	Moody
3RD WITCH	Baddeley
LADY MACDUFF	Miss Sherry
LADY MACBETH	Mrs Yates

COVENT GARDEN
Oct. 18, 25

MACBETH	Henderson
MACDUFF	Clarke
DUNCAN	Hull
BANQUO	Wroughton
MALCOLM	Whitfield
LENNOX	L'Estrange

(1) *Nov. 29; Dec. 28*

LADY MACBETH	Mrs Jackson

1779 COVENT GARDEN (cont.)
Oct. 18, 25 (cont.)

SEYTON	Thompson
HECATE	Reinhold
1ST WITCH	Quick
2ND WITCH	Mrs Pitt
3RD WITCH	Brunsdon
LADY MACBETH (1)	Mrs Hartley

1780 DRURY LANE
Apr. 26

MACBETH	Smith
MACDUFF	Brereton
DUNCAN (1, 2)	Hurst
ROSS	[J.] Aickin
MALCOLM (2)	Davies
DONALBAIN (2)	Master Benson
BANQUO (2)	Packer
HECATE	[C.] Bannister
1ST WITCH	Parsons
2ND WITCH	Moody
3RD WITCH	Baddeley
LADY MACDUFF (2)	Mrs Sharp
LADY MACBETH (2)	Miss Sherry

(1) *May 3*

omitted	
DUNCAN	

(2) *Dec. 6, 26*

DUNCAN	Packer
MALCOLM	R. Palmer
DONALBAIN	Master Pulley
BANQUO	Farren
LADY MACDUFF	Miss Sherry (on *Dec. 26* only)
LADY MACBETH	Mrs Crawford

COVENT GARDEN
Apr. 27

MACBETH	Henderson
MACDUFF	Clarke
DUNCAN	Hull
BANQUO (1)	Wroughton
MALCOLM	Whitfield
LENNOX	L'Estrange
SEYTON	Thompson
HECATE	Reinhold
1ST WITCH (1)	Quick
2ND WITCH	Mrs Pitt
3RD WITCH (1)	Brunsdon
LADY MACBETH (1)	A Lady [Mrs Sage (MC, *Apr. 27*); second appearance on the stage]

(1) *Oct. 23; Nov. 20*

BANQUO	Peile
1ST WITCH	Booth (on *Nov. 20* only)
3RD WITCH	Webb
LADY MACBETH	Mrs Yates
added	
SIWARD	Robson
DOCTOR	Fearon
GENTLEWOMAN	Mrs Poussin

1781 DRURY LANE
Nov. 5

MACBETH	Smith
MACDUFF	Brereton
DUNCAN	Packer

MACBETH

1781 DRURY LANE (cont.)
Nov. 5 (cont.)

ROSS	[J.] Aickin
MALCOLM	R. Palmer
DONALBAIN	Master Pulley
BANQUO	Farren
HECATE	[C.] Bannister
1ST WITCH	Parsons
2ND WITCH	Moody
3RD WITCH	Baddeley
LADY MACDUFF	Mrs Sharp
LADY MACBETH	Miss Sherry

COVENT GARDEN

Jan. 15

MACBETH	Henderson
MACDUFF (1, 2, 3)	Hull
DUNCAN (1, 2, 3)	Thompson
BANQUO (2, 3)	Peile
MALCOLM (3)	Whitfield
LENNOX	L'Estrange
SEYTON (1, 2, 3)	W. Bates
SIWARD	Robson
DOCTOR	Fearon
HECATE	Reinhold
1ST WITCH	Booth
2ND WITCH	Mrs Pitt
3RD WITCH	Webb
GENTLEWOMAN	Mrs Poussin
LADY MACBETH	Mrs Yates

(1) *Mar. 5*

MACDUFF	Clarke
DUNCAN	Hull
SEYTON	Thompson

(2) *May 9*

MACDUFF	Peile
DUNCAN	Hull
BANQUO	Davies
SEYTON	Thompson

(3) *Dec. 17*

MACDUFF	Clarke
DUNCAN	Hull
BANQUO	Whitfield
MALCOLM	J. Bates
SEYTON	Thompson

1782 DRURY LANE
Feb. 5

MACBETH (1)	Smith
MACDUFF	Brereton
BANQUO	Farren
DUNCAN	Packer
ROSS	[J.] Aickin
MALCOLM	R. Palmer
DONALBAIN	Master Pulley
HECATE	[C.] Bannister
1ST WITCH	Parsons
2ND WITCH	Moody
3RD WITCH	Baddeley
LADY MACDUFF	Mrs Sharp
LADY MACBETH	Miss Sherry

(1) *May 15*

MACBETH added	Henderson
LENNOX	Norris
ANGUS	Chaplin

1782 COVENT GARDEN

Jan. 14

MACBETH	Henderson
MACDUFF (1)	Clarke
DUNCAN	Hull
BANQUO (1)	Whitfield
MALCOLM (3)	J. Bates
LENNOX (3)	L'Estrange
SEYTON	Thompson
SIWARD (3)	Robson
DOCTOR	Fearon
HECATE (2)	Reinhold
1ST WITCH	Booth
2ND WITCH	Mrs Pitt
3RD WITCH (2)	Webb
GENTLEWOMAN	Mrs Poussin
LADY MACBETH	Mrs Yates

(1) *Mar. 21*

MACDUFF	Whitfield
BANQUO	Davies

(2) *May 27*

HECATE	Davies
3RD WITCH	Stevens

(3) *Nov. 18; Dec. 23*

MALCOLM	Davies
LENNOX	Mahon
SIWARD	Helme

1783 COVENT GARDEN

Oct. 6; Dec. 18

MACBETH	Henderson
MACDUFF	Clarke
DUNCAN	Hull
BANQUO	Whitfield
LENNOX	Davies
MALCOLM	J. Bates
SEYTON	Thompson
SIWARD	Helme
DOCTOR	Fearon
HECATE	Reinhold
1ST WITCH	Booth
2ND WITCH	Mrs Pitt
3RD WITCH	Stevens
GENTLEWOMAN	Mrs Poussin
LADY MACBETH	Mrs Bates

1784 COVENT GARDEN

Feb. 9

MACBETH (2)	Henderson
MACDUFF	Clarke
DUNCAN	Hull
BANQUO (1, 2)	Whitfield
LENNOX (1, 2)	Mahon
MALCOLM	Davies
SEYTON	Thompson
SIWARD (1, 2)	Helme
DOCTOR	Fearon

(1) *Oct. 4*

BANQUO	Farren
LENNOX	Cubitt
HECATE	Darley
3RD WITCH	[T.] Kennedy
LADY MACBETH	A Lady [Mrs Gordon (MS annotation on JPK)]

omitted
SIWARD

386

MACBETH

1784 COVENT GARDEN (cont.)
Feb. 9 (cont.)

HECATE (1, 2)	Reinhold
1ST WITCH	Booth
2ND WITCH	Mrs Pitt
3RD WITCH (1, 2)	Jones
GENTLEWOMAN	Mrs Poussin
LADY MACBETH (1, 2)	Mrs Bates

[PA assigns the 3RD WITCH to Stevens.]

(2) Nov. 12, 15, 22; Dec. 30

MACBETH	Holman
BANQUO	Farren
LENNOX	Cubitt
HECATE	Darley
3RD WITCH	[T.] Kennedy
LADY MACBETH	Miss Younge (on Nov. 12, 15, 22 only)

omitted
SIWARD

[On *Dec. 30* the only parts assigned by Pb are MACBETH to Holman, and LADY MACBETH to Mrs Bates, with 'The rest of the Characters... as usual'. PA announces *Douglas* for this night. See p. 79.]

1785 DRURY LANE
Feb. 2

MACBETH (3)	Smith
BANQUO (1, 2, 3, 4)	Hull
DUNCAN	Packer
ROSS	[J.] Aickin
MALCOLM (3)	R. Palmer
MACDUFF (4)	Brereton
HECATE	[C.] Bannister
1ST WITCH	Parsons
2ND WITCH	Moody
3RD WITCH	Baddeley
LADY MACBETH	Mrs Siddons

[Both Pb and PA assign BANQUO to Bensley. But he was indisposed, and Hull took his place (James Boaden, *Life of John Philip Kemble*, 1825, i. 247; PA, Feb. 4).]

(1) Feb. 4

BANQUO	Barrymore

(2) Feb. 7, 12, 15, 19, 22, 26; Mar. 5, 15; Apr. 19; May 10; Oct. 29

BANQUO	Bensley

(3) Mar. 31

MACBETH	Kemble
BANQUO	Bensley
MALCOLM	read by Barrymore

[Both Pb and PA retain R. Palmer as MALCOLM. In JPK his name is deleted, but the substitute name, with the exception of the initial letter 'B', has been cut by the binder. The part was read by Barrymore (MC, Apr. 1). The reason for Palmer's absence was the death, on this day, of his mother (General Evening Post, Apr. 4).]

(4) Oct. 1; Nov. 19

BANQUO	Bensley
MACDUFF	Kemble

COVENT GARDEN
May 3

MACBETH	Henderson
MACDUFF	Clarke
BANQUO	Farren
DUNCAN	Hull
MALCOLM	Davies

1785 COVENT GARDEN (cont.)
May 3 (cont.)

HECATE	Mrs Webb
LENNOX	Cubitt
SEYTON	Thompson
DOCTOR	Fearon
1ST WITCH	Booth
2ND WITCH	Mrs Pitt
3RD WITCH	[T.] Kennedy
GENTLEWOMAN	Mrs Poussin
LADY MACBETH	Mrs Bates

1786 DRURY LANE
Mar. 2; Apr. 22; Oct. 9

MACBETH	Smith
BANQUO	Bensley
DUNCAN	Packer
ROSS (1)	[J.] Aickin
MALCOLM	R. Palmer
MACDUFF	Kemble
HECATE	[C.] Bannister
1ST WITCH (1)	Parsons
2ND WITCH	Moody
3RD WITCH	Baddeley
LADY MACBETH	Mrs Siddons

(1) *Dec. 2*

ROSS	Williams
1ST WITCH	[J.] Aickin

COVENT GARDEN
Jan. 18

MACBETH	Holman
MACDUFF	[F.] Aickin
BANQUO	Farren
DUNCAN	Hull
MALCOLM	Davies
HECATE	Darley
LENNOX	Cubitt
SEYTON	Thompson
DOCTOR	Fearon
GENTLEWOMAN (1)	Mrs Poussin
LADY MACBETH	Mrs Bates

(1) *May 29*

GENTLEWOMAN added	Miss Platt
1ST WITCH	Booth
2ND WITCH	Mrs Pitt
3RD WITCH	[T.] Kennedy

1787 DRURY LANE
Apr. 19

MACBETH	Smith
BANQUO	Bensley
DUNCAN	Packer
ROSS (2)	Williams

(1) *June 2*

MACDUFF	Kemble

(2) *Nov. 3*

ROSS	Benson
MACDUFF	Kemble

MACBETH

1787 DRURY LANE (cont.)

Apr. 19 (cont.)

MALCOLM	R. Palmer
MACDUFF (1, 2)	Whitfield
HECATE (2)	[C.] Bannister
1ST WITCH	[J.] Aickin
2ND WITCH	Moody
3RD WITCH (2)	Baddeley
LADY MACBETH	Mrs Siddons

(2) Nov. 3 (cont.)

HECATE	Williames
3RD WITCH added	[J.] Burton
LENNOX	Phillimore

COVENT GARDEN

Oct. 1

MACBETH (1)	A Young Gentleman [Seymour (EM, Oct. 1787, 315); first appearance on the stage]
MACDUFF	[F.] Aickin
BANQUO	Farren
DUNCAN	Hull
MALCOLM	Macready
LENNOX	Davies
SEYTON	Thompson
DOCTOR	Fearon
HECATE	Darley
1ST WITCH	Booth
2ND WITCH	Mrs Pitt
3RD WITCH	Brown
GENTLEWOMAN	Mrs Platt
LADY MACBETH	Mrs Pope

(1) Nov. 16

MACBETH	Cambray

1788 DRURY LANE

Mar. 10; May 29

MACBETH (1)	Smith
BANQUO	Bensley
DUNCAN	Packer
MALCOLM (1)	R. Palmer
ROSS (1)	Benson
LENNOX (1)	Phillimore
MACDUFF (1)	Kemble
HECATE	Williames
1ST WITCH	[J.] Aickin
2ND WITCH	Moody
3RD WITCH	[J.] Burton
LADY MACBETH	Mrs Siddons

(1) Oct. 16, 21; Nov. 22; Dec. 23

MACBETH	Kemble
MALCOLM	Seymour (on *Oct. 16, 21* only) / Whitfield (on *Nov. 22, Dec. 23* only)
ROSS	Barrymore
LENNOX	Benson
MACDUFF	Wroughton

389

1789 DRURY LANE
Jan. 31; Mar. 30; Apr. 28

MACBETH	Kemble
BANQUO	Packer
DUNCAN	Chaplin
MALCOLM	Whitfield
ROSS	Barrymore
LENNOX	Benson
MACDUFF	Wroughton
HECATE	Williames
1ST WITCH	[J.] Aickin
2ND WITCH	Moody
3RD WITCH	[J.] Burton
LADY MACBETH	Mrs Siddons

COVENT GARDEN
Oct. 12, 19

MACBETH	Holman
MACDUFF	[F.] Aickin
BANQUO	Farren
DUNCAN	Hull
MALCOLM	Macready
ROSS	Davies
DONALBAIN	Egan [Jr.]
SIWARD	Gardner
SEYTON	Thompson
DOCTOR	Powel
HECATE	[C.] Bannister
1ST WITCH	Blanchard
2ND WITCH	Bernard
3RD WITCH	Reeve
LADY MACBETH	Mrs Pope

1790 COVENT GARDEN
Feb. 8

MACBETH (1)	Holman
MACDUFF	[F.] Aickin
BANQUO	Farren
DUNCAN	Hull
MALCOLM	Macready
ROSS	Davies
DONALBAIN (2)	Egan [Jr.]
SIWARD	Cubitt
SEYTON	Thompson
DOCTOR	Powel
HECATE	[C.] Bannister
1ST WITCH	Blanchard

(1) *May 3*

MACBETH	Harley

(2) *Oct. 6; Nov. 26*

DONALBAIN	Cross

1790 COVENT GARDEN (cont.)

Feb. 8 (cont.)

2ND WITCH	Bernard
3RD WITCH	Reeve
LADY MACBETH	Mrs Pope

1791 COVENT GARDEN

Oct. 10

MACBETH	Holman
MACDUFF	[F.] Aickin
BANQUO	Farren
DUNCAN	Hull
MALCOLM	Macready
ROSS	Davies
DONALBAIN	Cross
SEYTON	Thompson
DOCTOR	Powel
HECATE	Darley
1ST WITCH	Blanchard
2ND WITCH	Munden
3RD WITCH	Cubitt
LADY MACBETH	Mrs Pope

1792 DRURY LANE (company at KING'S, HAYMARKET)

Feb. 18

DUNCAN	Packer
MALCOLM (2)	[J.] Palmer Jr.
DONALBAIN (2)	Bland
MACBETH	Kemble
BANQUO	Bensley
LENNOX	Whitfield
MACDUFF	Wroughton
ROSS	Barrymore
FLEANCE (2)	Master Gregson
SIWARD	Fawcett
SEYTON	Phillimore
DOCTOR	Jones
SERGEANT	Benson
HECATE	[C.] Bannister
1ST WITCH	[J.] Aickin
2ND WITCH	Moody
3RD WITCH (1)	[J.] Burton
MESSENGER	Banks
MURDERER	Webb
LADY MACBETH	Mrs Siddons
GENTLEWOMAN	Miss Tidswell

(1) *Mar. 20*

3RD WITCH	Suett

(2) *Dec. 26*

MALCOLM	Bland
DONALBAIN	Master DeCamp
FLEANCE	Miss [M.] Menage

1792 COVENT GARDEN
Jan. 23; Oct. 29; Nov. 9

MACBETH	Holman
MACDUFF	[F.] Aickin
BANQUO	Farren
DUNCAN	Hull
MALCOLM	Macready
ROSS	Davies
DONALBAIN	Cross
SEYTON	Thompson
DOCTOR	Powel
HECATE	Darley
1ST WITCH	Blanchard
2ND WITCH	Munden
3RD WITCH	Cubitt
LADY MACBETH	Mrs Pope

1793 DRURY LANE (company at HAYMARKET)
Apr. 16

DUNCAN	Packer
MALCOLM	Bland
DONALBAIN	Master DeCamp
MACBETH	Kemble
BANQUO	Bensley
LENNOX (1)	Whitfield
MACDUFF	Wroughton
ROSS	Barrymore
FLEANCE	Miss [M.] Menage
SIWARD	Fawcett
SEYTON (1)	Caulfield
DOCTOR (1)	Maddocks
SERGEANT (1)	Benson
MESSENGER	Banks
MURDERER	Webb
HECATE	[C.] Bannister
1ST WITCH	[J.] Aickin
2ND WITCH	Moody
3RD WITCH	[J.] Burton
LADY MACBETH	Mrs Siddons
GENTLEWOMAN	Miss Tidswell

(1) *May 8* (company at KING'S, HAYMARKET)

LENNOX	Benson
SEYTON	Phillimore
DOCTOR	Jones
omitted	
SERGEANT	

[PA retains Maddocks as the DOCTOR.]

COVENT GARDEN
Sept. 30

MACBETH	Holman
MACDUFF	Pope

(1) *Oct. 28*
added

FLEANCE	Miss Standen

1793 COVENT GARDEN (*cont.*)

Sept. 30 (cont.)

BANQUO	Farren
DUNCAN	Hull
MALCOLM	Macready
ROSS	Davies
DONALBAIN	Simmons
SEYTON	Thompson
DOCTOR (3)	Powel
HECATE	Cubitt
1ST WITCH (2, 3)	Blanchard
2ND WITCH	Munden
3RD WITCH	Fawcett [Jr.]
GENTLEWOMAN (3)	Mrs Platt
LADY MACBETH	Mrs Pope

(2) *Dec. 9*

1ST WITCH	Bernard

added

FLEANCE	Miss Standen

(3) *Dec. 27*

1ST WITCH	Bernard

omitted
    DOCTOR, GENTLEWOMAN

1794 DRURY LANE

Apr. 21

DUNCAN	Bensley
MALCOLM	C. Kemble [first appearance in London]
DONALBAIN	Master DeCamp
MACBETH (4, 6)	Kemble
BANQUO (4, 6)	Wroughton
MACDUFF (4, 6)	[J.] Palmer
LENNOX	Whitfield
ROSS	Barrymore
FLEANCE	Master Gregson
SIWARD	[J.] Aickin
SEYTON	Benson
DOCTOR (3, 4, 6)	Packer
OFFICER (2, 3, 4)	Banks
SERGEANT (2, 3, 4)	Caulfield
1ST MURDERER (2, 3, 4, 5, 6)	Phillimore
2ND MURDERER (2, 3, 4, 5, 6)	Webb
ARMED HEAD (1, 2, 3, 4, 5, 6)	Jones
BLOODY CHILD (1, 2, 3, 4, 5, 6)	Master Harlowe
CROWNED CHILD (1, 2, 3, 4, 5, 6)	Master Chatterley
HECATE	[C.] Bannister
1ST WITCH	Moody

(1) *Apr. 22, 23, 24*

omitted
    ARMED HEAD, BLOODY CHILD, CROWNED CHILD

(2) *Apr. 28, 30*

omitted
    OFFICER, SERGEANT, MURDERERS, ARMED HEAD, BLOODY CHILD, CROWNED CHILD

(3) *May 2, 5, 7, 12*

DOCTOR	Jones

omitted
    SAME as *Apr. 28*

[On *May 2* both Pb and PA assign the DOCTOR to Packer. But 'Mr Jones the Doctor . . . Mr Packer ill' (Powell). On *May 5, 7, 12* Jones's name is in the bills.]

(4) *May 19, 26; June 2*

MACBETH	[J.] Palmer
BANQUO	Packer
MACDUFF	Wroughton
DOCTOR	Jones

omitted
    SAME as *Apr. 28*

(5) *Oct. 7*

omitted
    MURDERERS, ARMED HEAD, BLOODY CHILD, CROWNED CHILD

(6) *Nov. 11; Dec. 6*

MACBETH	[J.] Palmer (on *Dec. 6* only)

1794 DRURY LANE (cont.)

Apr. 21 (cont.)

2ND WITCH	Dodd
3RD WITCH	Suett
LADY MACBETH	Mrs Siddons
GENTLEWOMAN	Miss Tidswell

(6) *Nov. 11; Dec. 6 (cont.)*

BANQUO	Packer
MACDUFF	Wroughton
DOCTOR	Jones
omitted	
SAME as *Oct. 7*	

[On *Dec. 6* Pb assigns MACBETH to Kemble, BANQUO to Wroughton, MACDUFF to Palmer, the DOCTOR to Packer. A printed slip attached to the JPK bill reads, 'Mr Kemble being confined with a complaint in his Throat ... prevents his ... appearing', and assigns the parts as above, with the exception of the DOCTOR. Powell also notes these changes, and adds, 'Mr Jones [acted] the Physician'.]

COVENT GARDEN

Feb. 3

MACBETH	Holman
MACDUFF	Pope
BANQUO	Farren
DUNCAN	Hull
MALCOLM	Macready
ROSS	Davies
DONALBAIN	Simmons
SEYTON	Thompson
HECATE (1)	Cubitt
1ST WITCH	Munden
2ND WITCH	Fawcett [Jr.]
3RD WITCH	Bernard
LADY MACBETH	Mrs Pope

(1) *Sept. 22; Nov. 6*

HECATE	Richardson
added	
DOCTOR	Powel

also added on *Nov. 6* only

SIWARD	Davenport
FLEANCE	Master Curties

1795 DRURY LANE

Apr. 7, 25

DUNCAN	Bensley
MALCOLM	C. Kemble
DONALBAIN	Master DeCamp
MACBETH (2)	Kemble
BANQUO (2)	Wroughton
MACDUFF (2)	[J.] Palmer
LENNOX (2)	Whitfield
ROSS (1)	Barrymore
FLEANCE	Master Gregson
SIWARD	[J.] Aickin
SEYTON	Benson
DOCTOR (2)	Packer

(1) *Sept. 29; Nov. 9*

ROSS	Caulfield
SERGEANT	Trueman

(2) *Dec. 23*

MACBETH	[J.] Palmer
BANQUO	Packer
MACDUFF	Wroughton
LENNOX	Trueman
DOCTOR	Jones

[In the bill MACBETH, BANQUO, and MACDUFF are assigned respectively to Kemble, Wroughton, and Palmer. But a printed slip attached to the JPK bill states that because

MACBETH

1795 DRURY LANE (*cont.*)
Apr. 7, 25 (*cont.*)

OFFICER	Banks
SERGEANT (1)	Caulfield
HECATE	[C.] Bannister
1ST WITCH	Moody
2ND WITCH	Dodd
3RD WITCH	Suett
LADY MACBETH	Mrs Siddons
GENTLEWOMAN	Miss Tidswell

(2) *Dec. 23* (*cont.*)

of Kemble's indisposition these three parts would be acted as indicated above. No mention is made of the DOCTOR, but Jones was Packer's usual substitute in this part.]

COVENT GARDEN
Mar. 9

MACBETH (2)	Holman
MACDUFF (1, 2)	Middleton
BANQUO (1, 2)	Farren
DUNCAN	Hull
MALCOLM (2)	Macready
ROSS (2)	Davies
DONALBAIN (1)	Simmons
SEYTON (1)	Thompson
DOCTOR	Powel
HECATE (2)	Richardson
SIWARD	Davenport
FLEANCE	Master Curties
1ST WITCH	Munden
2ND WITCH (2)	Fawcett [Jr.]
3RD WITCH (2)	Bernard
LADY MACBETH	Mrs Pope

(1) *May 18; June 10*

MACDUFF	Pope
BANQUO	Harley
omitted	
DONALBAIN, SEYTON	

(2) *Sept. 14; Nov. 30*

MACBETH	Cooper (on *Nov. 30* only)
MACDUFF	Pope
BANQUO	Harley
MALCOLM	Middleton
ROSS	Macready
HECATE	Bowden (on *Nov. 30* only)
2ND WITCH	Townsend
3RD WITCH	Fawcett [Jr.] (on *Nov. 30* only)

added

MACBETH'S SERVANT	Ledger
SERGEANT	Farley
1ST MURDERER	Claremont
2ND MURDERER	Abbot
3RD MURDERER	Rees
GENTLEWOMAN	Mrs Platt

1796 DRURY LANE
Apr. 11

DUNCAN (1)	Bensley
MALCOLM	C. Kemble
DONALBAIN (1)	Master DeCamp
MACBETH	Kemble
BANQUO (1)	Packer
MACDUFF (1)	Wroughton
LENNOX	Whitfield
ROSS (1)	Caulfield
FLEANCE (1)	Master Gregson
SIWARD (1)	[J.] Aickin
SEYTON (1)	Benson

(1) *Oct. 10; Dec. 13, 28*

DUNCAN	[J.] Aickin
DONALBAIN	Master Gregson
BANQUO	Wroughton
MACDUFF	[J.] Palmer
ROSS	Barrymore
FLEANCE	Master Menage
SIWARD	Packer
SEYTON	Trueman
DOCTOR	Maddocks
SERGEANT	Caulfield (on *Oct. 10* only)
1ST WITCH	R. Palmer
2ND WITCH	Wewitzer

395

1796 DRURY LANE (cont.)

Apr. 11 (cont.)

DOCTOR (1)	Jones
SERGEANT (1)	Trueman
MESSENGER (1)	Banks
HECATE	[C.] Bannister
1ST WITCH (1)	Moody
2ND WITCH (1)	Dodd
3RD WITCH	Suett
LADY MACBETH	Mrs Siddons
GENTLEWOMAN (1)	Miss Tidswell

(1) *Oct. 10; Dec. 13, 28 (cont.)*
omitted on *Dec. 28* only
FLEANCE, SEYTON, DOCTOR, SERGEANT, MESSENGER, GENTLEWOMAN
[On *Dec. 13* Trueman doubled SEYTON and the SERGEANT.]

COVENT GARDEN

Sept. 26

MACBETH	Holman
MACDUFF	Pope
DUNCAN	Hull
MALCOLM	Middleton
BANQUO	Macready
DONALBAIN	Simmons
DOCTOR	Powel
SIWARD	Davenport
SEYTON	Thompson
FLEANCE	Curties
MACBETH'S SERVANT (1)	Ledger
SERGEANT	Farley
1ST MURDERER	Claremont
2ND MURDERER	Abbot
3RD MURDERER	J. [N.] Lee
1ST WITCH	Munden
2ND WITCH	Townsend
3RD WITCH	[H.] Lee
HECATE	Bowden
GENTLEWOMAN	Mrs Platt
LADY MACBETH	Mrs Pope

(1) *Nov. 14*
added
ROSS   Toms
omitted
MACBETH'S SERVANT

1797 DRURY LANE

Feb. 20

DUNCAN	[J.] Aickin
MALCOLM	C. Kemble
DONALBAIN	Master Gregson
MACBETH	[J.] Palmer
MACDUFF	Wroughton
BANQUO	Packer
LENNOX	Whitfield
ROSS	Barrymore

396

1797 DRURY LANE (cont.)

Feb. 20 (cont.)

HECATE	[C.] Bannister
1ST WITCH	R. Palmer
2ND WITCH	Wewitzer
3RD WITCH	Suett
LADY MACBETH	Mrs Siddons

Mar. 14

DUNCAN	[J.] Aickin
MALCOLM	C. Kemble
DONALBAIN	Master Gregson
MACBETH	Kemble
BANQUO (1)	Barrymore
MACDUFF	[J.] Palmer
LENNOX (1)	Campbell
ROSS	Holland
FLEANCE	Master Menage
SIWARD	Packer
SEYTON	Trueman
DOCTOR	Maddocks
SERGEANT	Caulfield
MESSENGER (1)	Banks
HECATE	[C.] Bannister
1ST WITCH (1)	R. Palmer
2ND WITCH	Wewitzer
3RD WITCH	Suett
LADY MACBETH (1)	Mrs Powell

(1) *Nov. 7; Dec. 11*

BANQUO	Wroughton (on Nov. 7 only)
LENNOX	Gibbon
MESSENGER	Evans
1ST WITCH	Dowton
LADY MACBETH	Mrs Siddons
added	
GENTLEWOMAN	Miss Tidswell

[The bill assigns LADY MACBETH to Mrs Siddons. A printed slip attached to the BM bill reads, 'The Publick is most respectfully informed that Mrs. Siddons, being suddenly taken ill . . . The Character of LADY MACBETH will be performed by Mrs. Powell'.]

1798 DRURY LANE

Mar. 6

DUNCAN	[J.] Aickin
MALCOLM	C. Kemble
DONALBAIN (2)	Master Palmer
MACBETH (1)	Kemble
BANQUO (2)	Barrymore
MACDUFF (1, 2)	[J.] Palmer
LENNOX (2)	Gibbon
ROSS	Holland
FLEANCE (2)	Master Menage
SIWARD (2)	Packer
SEYTON	Trueman
DOCTOR	Maddocks
HECATE (2)	[C.] Bannister

(1) *June 4*

MACBETH	[J.] Palmer
MACDUFF	Wroughton
1ST WITCH	Dowton

(2) *Sept. 18*

DONALBAIN	Fisher
BANQUO	Packer
MACDUFF	Barrymore
FLEANCE	Master Chatterley
SIWARD	Sparks
HECATE	Sedgwick
added	
SERGEANT	Caulfield
MESSENGER	Evans
1ST MURDERER	Wentworth
2ND MURDERER	Webb

1798 DRURY LANE (cont.)

Mar. 6 (cont.)   (2) *Sept. 18 (cont.)*

1ST WITCH (1)	R. Palmer	omitted
2ND WITCH	Wewitzer	LENNOX
3RD WITCH	Suett	
LADY MACBETH	Mrs Siddons	
GENTLEWOMAN	Miss Tidswell	

[In the acting version published by Lowndes in 1798 the cast is the same as that of this performance, with the following additions:

OFFICER	Evans
SERGEANT	Caulfield
1ST MURDERER	Wentworth
2ND MURDERER	Webb
BLOODY CHILD	Master Gell
CROWNED CHILD	Master Chatterley]

COVENT GARDEN

Dec. 15

MACBETH	Turner [first appearance on the stage]
MACDUFF	Pope
DUNCAN	Hull
BANQUO	Murray
MALCOLM	Clarke
LENNOX	Whitfield
DONALBAIN	Simmons
DOCTOR	Waddy
SIWARD	Davenport
SEYTON	Thompson
FLEANCE	Master Rees
SERGEANT	Klanert
1ST MURDERER	Claremont
2ND MURDERER	Abbot
1ST WITCH	Munden
2ND WITCH	Emery
3RD WITCH	Rees
HECATE	Townsend
GENTLEWOMAN	Mrs Platt
LADY MACBETH	Mrs Johnson [first appearance in London]

1799 DRURY LANE

Apr. 2

DUNCAN	[J.] Aickin
MALCOLM	C. Kemble
DONALBAIN	Fisher
MACBETH	Kemble
MACDUFF	Barrymore

MACBETH

1799 DRURY LANE (cont.)
Apr. 2 (cont.)

BANQUO	Packer
ROSS	Holland
LENNOX	Surmont
SIWARD	Sparks
SEYTON	Trueman
DOCTOR	Maddocks
SERGEANT	Caulfield
MESSENGER	Evans
1ST MURDERER	Wentworth
2ND MURDERER	Webb
HECATE	Sedgwick
1ST WITCH	R. Palmer
2ND WITCH	Wewitzer
3RD WITCH	Suett
LADY MACBETH	Mrs Siddons
GENTLEWOMAN	Miss Tidswell

COVENT GARDEN
May 14

MACBETH (1)	Betterton
MACDUFF	Pope
DUNCAN	Hull
BANQUO	Murray
MALCOLM (1)	Clarke
LENNOX	Whitfield
DONALBAIN (1)	Simmons
DOCTOR	Waddy
SIWARD	Davenport
SEYTON	Thompson
FLEANCE (1)	Master Rees
1ST WITCH (1)	Munden
2ND WITCH	Emery
3RD WITCH	Rees
HECATE	Townsend
GENTLEWOMAN	Mrs Platt
LADY MACBETH	Miss Betterton

(1) *Sept. 30; Oct. 28*

MACBETH	Holman
MALCOLM	Mansel
DONALBAIN	Mills
FLEANCE	Curties
1ST WITCH	Gardner (on *Oct. 28* only)

added

SERGEANT	Klanert

1800 COVENT GARDEN
Dec. 5, 18

MACBETH	Cooke
MACDUFF	Pope
DUNCAN	Hull
BANQUO	Murray
MALCOLM	Claremont
DONALBAIN	Curties

(1) *Dec. 13*

omitted
    FLEANCE, SERGEANT

399

1800 COVENT GARDEN (*cont.*)
Dec. 5, 18 (*cont.*)

LENNOX	Whitfield
DOCTOR	Waddy
SIWARD	Davenport
SEYTON	Thompson
FLEANCE (1)	Mrs Findlay
SERGEANT (1)	Klanert
1ST WITCH	[W.] Blanchard
2ND WITCH	Emery
3RD WITCH	Simmons
HECATE	Townsend
GENTLEWOMAN	Miss Leserve
LADY MACBETH	Mrs Litchfield

MEASURE FOR MEASURE

(1) 'As it is Acted at the Theatres in London and Dublin.'
    1761   Dublin: Hulton Bradley.

(2) 'As it is Acted at the Theatres of London and Dublin.'
    1761   Dublin: Sarah Cotter.
    These are both reading editions, verbatim throughout.

(3) 'As Performed at the Theatre-Royal, Covent-Garden. Revised by Mr. Younger, Prompter of that Theatre.'
    1773   John Bell.
    The principal omissions are:
    Act I. ii. *1–124* (Lucio's quibbles on 'list', and Mrs Overdone and the Clown).
    Act II. i. *41–end* (the dispute between Elbow and the Clown).
    Act III. ii. *205–23* (Mrs Overdone sent to prison).
    Act IV. i. *1–27* (Mariana and the Duke); iii. *1–21* (the Clown's list of prisoners); v *entire* (the Duke's instructions to Friar Peter); vi *entire* (Isabella's misgivings as to the Duke's clemency).
    Throughout there are minor omissions. For the last four lines of the play are substituted five new lines, in praise of good rulers.
    See also Odell, ii. 23–25.

(4) 'As it is Acted at the Theatres-Royal in Drury-Lane and Covent-Garden.'
    1779   J. Harrison.
    This is identical with (3).

(5) 'Marked with the Variations in the Manager's Book, at the Theatre-Royal in Drury-Lane.'
    1784   C. Bathurst [&c.].
    This is identical with (3), except that it has a few more omissions, the principal

one being *Act IV. i entire* (Mariana's consent to the deception of Angelo). Occasional lines of the original are restored. The last four lines of the play consist of *V. i. 538–9*, followed by *V. i. 411–12*.

(6) 'As altered by J. P. Kemble, and acted by their Majesties Servants, at the Theatre Royal, Drury Lane.'
    n.d. [1795]   C. Lowndes.

The principal omissions are:
Act I. i. 29b–42 (the Duke moralizes on virtue); *ii. 22–61* (Lucio's quibbles on 'list'); *iv. 30–45a* ('a thing ensky'd and sainted').
Act II. i. 232–65a (the Clown's trade); *iii entire* (Juliet's confession).
Act III. ii. 205–23 (Mrs Overdone sent to prison).
Act IV. i entire (Mariana's consent to the deception of Angelo); *ii. 33–54* (Abhorson's occupation); *iii. 4b–21* (the Clown's list of prisoners); *v entire* (the Duke's instructions to Friar Peter); *vi entire* (Isabella's misgivings as to the Duke's clemency).

Throughout there are minor omissions, and two transpositions: *I. iii* comes before *I. ii*, and *II. ii. 18–187* is inserted following *II. i. 37*. The last four lines of the play are the same as in (3).

This is the edition referred to on the DL bill of Jan. 13, 1795, which has, 'A new edition of Measure for Measure to be had in the theatre'.

1755 DRURY LANE
Feb. 22, 27; Apr. 9

DUKE	Mossop
ANGELO	Havard
ESCALUS	Bransby
CLAUDIO	Davies
PROVOST	Blakes
LUCIO	Woodward
ELBOW	Taswell
BARNARDINE	Clough
ABHORSON	[H.] Vaughan
FRIAR PETER	Walker
CLOWN	Yates
MARIANA	Mrs Bennet
ISABELLA	Mrs Cibber

1756 DRURY LANE
Nov. 19   (1) *Dec. 30*

DUKE	Mossop	ELBOW	Philips
ANGELO	Havard	ISABELLA	Mrs Pritchard
ESCALUS	Bransby		
CLAUDIO	Davies		
PROVOST	Blakes		
LUCIO	Woodward		
ELBOW (1)	Taswell		
BARNARDINE	Clough		

MEASURE FOR MEASURE

1756 DRURY LANE *(cont.)*
Nov. 19 (cont.)
ABHORSON	[H.] Vaughan
FRIAR PETER	Walker
CLOWN	Yates
MARIANA	Mrs Bennet
ISABELLA (1)	Mrs Cibber

1757 DRURY LANE
Jan. 10

DUKE	Mossop
ANGELO	Havard
ESCALUS	Bransby
CLAUDIO	Davies
PROVOST	Blakes
LUCIO (4)	Woodward
ELBOW (2, 3, 4)	Philips
BARNARDINE (3, 4)	Clough
ABHORSON (3, 4)	[H.] Vaughan
FRIAR PETER (3, 4)	Walker
CLOWN	Yates
MARIANA	Mrs Bennet
ISABELLA (1, 3, 4)	Miss Pritchard

(1) *Jan. 19; Mar. 1*
ISABELLA   Mrs Cibber

(2) *May 20*
ELBOW   Taswell

(3) *Sept. 22*
ISABELLA   Mrs Cibber
omitted
   ELBOW, BARNARDINE, ABHORSON, FRIAR PETER

(4) *Oct. 31*
LUCIO   Yates
ISABELLA   Mrs Cibber
omitted
SAME as *Sept. 22*
[Woodward's name is in the bill as LUCIO, but he 'was taken ill, & Mr. Yates [acted] . . . Lucio' (C-H). It is not stated who substituted for Yates as the CLOWN.]

1758 DRURY LANE
Apr. 29

DUKE	Mossop
ANGELO	Havard
ESCALUS	Bransby
CLAUDIO	Davies
PROVOST	Blakes
LUCIO (1)	Woodward
CLOWN	Yates
MARIANA	Mrs Bennet
ISABELLA	Mrs Cibber

(1) *Oct. 10, 17; Dec. 1*
LUCIO   Obrien

1759 DRURY LANE
Jan. 29

DUKE	Mossop
ANGELO	Havard
ESCALUS	Bransby
CLAUDIO	Davies
PROVOST	Blakes

1759 DRURY LANE (cont.)
Jan. 29 (cont.)

LUCIO	Obrien
CLOWN	Yates
MARIANA	Mrs Bennet
ISABELLA	Miss Pritchard

1770 COVENT GARDEN
Feb. 12, 15

DUKE	Bensley
ANGELO	Clarke
ESCALUS (2)	Hull
CLAUDIO (1)	Wroughton
CLOWN	Dunstall
FRIAR THOMAS (1, 2)	Redman
PROVOST	Gardner
ELBOW (2)	Quick
LUCIO	Woodward
BARNARDINE	Stoppelaer
FRIAR PETER	R. Smith
MARIANA (2)	Mrs Bulkley
JULIET (2)	Miss Ogilvie
FRANCISCA	Miss Mills
ISABELLA	Mrs Bellamy

(1) *Feb. 22*

CLAUDIO	Perry
omitted	
FRIAR THOMAS	

(2) *May 12*

ESCALUS	Davis
ELBOW	Holtom
MARIANA	Miss Ogilvie
JULIET	Miss Garman
omitted	
FRIAR THOMAS	

1771 COVENT GARDEN
Jan. 12

DUKE	Bensley
ANGELO	Clarke
ESCALUS (1)	Hull
CLAUDIO	Wroughton
CLOWN	Dunstall
LUCIO	Yates
MARIANA (1)	Mrs Bulkley
ISABELLA	Mrs Yates

(1) *Feb. 2; May 13; Oct. 9, 23*

ESCALUS	Perry (on *Feb. 2* only)
MARIANA	Mrs Kniveton (on *Oct. 9, 23* only)
added	
PROVOST	Gardner

[In the acting version published by Bell in 1773 the cast is the same as that of this performance (except that LUCIO is assigned to Woodward), with the following additions:

PROVOST	Gardner
FRIAR THOMAS	Redman
FRIAR PETER	R. Smith
ELBOW	Quick
ABHORSON	[R.] Bates
BARNARDINE	Stoppelaer
JULIET	Miss Ogilvie
FRANCISCA	Miss Pearce
MRS OVERDONE	Mrs White]

MEASURE FOR MEASURE

1772 COVENT GARDEN
Feb. 19

DUKE	Bensley
ANGELO	Clarke
ESCALUS	Hull
CLAUDIO	Wroughton
CLOWN	Dunstall
PROVOST	Gardner
LUCIO	Yates
MARIANA	Mrs Kniveton
ISABELLA	Mrs Yates

1775 DRURY LANE
Mar. 18; Apr. 20   (1) *Nov. 18*

DUKE	Smith	BARNARDINE	Wrighten
CLAUDIO	Reddish		
ANGELO	[J.] Palmer		
ESCALUS	[J.] Aickin		
CLOWN	Parsons		
PROVOST	Davies		
FRIAR PETER	Usher		
ELBOW	Wright		
BARNARDINE (1)	Keen		
ABHORSON	Carpenter		
LUCIO	King		
MARIANA	Miss [E.] Hopkins		
JULIET	Miss Platt		
MRS OVERDONE	Mrs Bradshaw		
FRANCISCA	Mrs Johnston		
ISABELLA	Mrs Yates		

1776 DRURY LANE
Jan. 10; May 14   (1) *Oct. 19*

DUKE	Smith	CLAUDIO	Farren
ANGELO	[J.] Palmer	omitted	
CLAUDIO (1)	Reddish	FRIAR PETER	
ESCALUS	[J.] Aickin		
CLOWN	Parsons		
PROVOST	Davies		
FRIAR PETER (1)	Usher		
ELBOW	Wright		
BARNARDINE	Wrighten		
ABHORSON	Carpenter		
LUCIO	King		

1776 DRURY LANE (cont.)

Jan. 10; May 14 (cont.)

MARIANA	Miss [E.] Hopkins
JULIET	Miss Platt
MRS OVERDONE	Mrs Bradshaw
FRANCISCA	Mrs Johnston
ISABELLA	Mrs Yates

1777 DRURY LANE

Nov. 13

DUKE	Smith
ANGELO	[J.] Palmer
CLAUDIO	Brereton
ESCALUS	[J.] Aickin
CLOWN	Parsons
PROVOST	Davies
ELBOW	Wright
BARNARDINE	Wrighten
ABHORSON	Carpenter
LUCIO	King
MARIANA	Miss [E.] Hopkins
JULIET	Mrs Colles
MRS OVERDONE	Mrs Bradshaw
FRANCISCA	Mrs Johnston
ISABELLA	Mrs Yates

COVENT GARDEN

Jan. 8

DUKE	Lee
ANGELO	Hull
ESCALUS	Fearon
CLAUDIO	Wroughton
PROVOST	L'Estrange
FRIAR PETER	Davis
FRIAR THOMAS	Booth
ELBOW	Wewitzer
CLOWN	Dunstall
ABHORSON	[R.] Bates
BARNARDINE	Jones
LUCIO	Woodward
MARIANA	Miss Leeson
JULIET	Mrs Whitfield
FRANCISCA	Miss Green
ISABELLA	Mrs Jackson

1778 DRURY LANE
Oct. 20

DUKE	Smith
ANGELO	[J.] Palmer
CLAUDIO	Brereton
ESCALUS	[J.] Aickin
CLOWN	Parsons
PROVOST	Davies
ELBOW	Wright
FRIAR PETER	Chambers
BARNARDINE	Wrighten
ABHORSON	Carpenter
LUCIO	King
MARIANA	Mrs Sharp
JULIET	Mrs Colles
FRANCISCA	Mrs Johnston
MRS OVERDONE	Mrs Bradshaw
ISABELLA	Mrs Yates

1780 COVENT GARDEN
Oct. 11

DUKE	Henderson
ANGELO	Clarke
ESCALUS	Fearon
CLAUDIO	Wroughton
PROVOST	L'Estrange
FRIAR PETER	Thompson
ELBOW	W. Bates
ABHORSON	[R.] Bates
BARNARDINE	Jones
CLOWN	Booth
LUCIO	Lee Lewes
MARIANA	Mrs Inchbald
JULIET	Mrs Whitfield
FRANCISCA	Mrs Poussin
ISABELLA	Mrs Yates

1781 COVENT GARDEN
Jan. 17

DUKE	Henderson
ANGELO	Hull
ESCALUS	Fearon
CLAUDIO	Wroughton
PROVOST	L'Estrange
FRIAR PETER	Thompson
ELBOW	W. Bates
ABHORSON	[R.] Bates
BARNARDINE	Jones

1781 COVENT GARDEN (cont.)

Jan. 17 (cont.)

CLOWN	Booth
LUCIO	Lee Lewes
MARIANA	Mrs Inchbald
JULIET	Miss Stuart
FRANCISCA	Mrs Poussin
ISABELLA	Mrs Yates

[PA assigns JULIET to Mrs Whitfield.]

1782 COVENT GARDEN

Jan. 5; Feb. 7   (1) *Dec. 12*

DUKE	Henderson		ANGELO	Clarke
ANGELO (1)	Hull		PROVOST	Davies
ESCALUS	Fearon		MARIANA	Mrs Lewis
CLAUDIO	Wroughton			
PROVOST (1)	L'Estrange			
FRIAR PETER	Thompson			
ELBOW	W. Bates			
ABHORSON	[R.] Bates			
BARNARDINE	Jones			
CLOWN	Booth			
LUCIO	Lee Lewes			
MARIANA (1)	Mrs Inchbald			
JULIET	Miss Stuart			
FRANCISCA	Mrs Poussin			
ISABELLA	Mrs Yates			

1783 DRURY LANE

Nov. 3, 5, 7, 11

DUKE	Smith
ANGELO	[J.] Palmer
CLAUDIO	Brereton
ESCALUS	[J.] Aickin
CLOWN	Parsons
PROVOST	Wrighten
ELBOW	Wright
FRIAR PETER	Chaplin
BARNARDINE	Fawcett
ABHORSON	Alfred
LUCIO	[Lee] Lewes
MARIANA	Mrs Ward
JULIET	Miss Barnes
ISABELLA	Mrs Siddons

[In the acting version published by Bathurst in 1784 the cast is the same as that of these performances, with the following addition:

FRANCISCA	Miss Simson]

1784 DRURY LANE
Feb. 4

DUKE	Smith
ANGELO	[J.] Palmer
CLAUDIO	Brereton
ESCALUS	[J.] Aickin
CLOWN	Parsons
PROVOST	Wrighten
ELBOW	Wright
FRIAR PETER	Chaplin
BARNARDINE	Fawcett
ABHORSON	Alfred
LUCIO	[Lee] Lewes
MARIANA	Mrs Ward
JULIET	Miss Barnes
ISABELLA	Mrs Siddons

1785 DRURY LANE
Oct. 22   (1) *Nov. 2*

DUKE	Smith	CLAUDIO	Brereton
ANGELO	[J.] Palmer		
CLAUDIO (1)	Barrymore		
ESCALUS	[J.] Aickin		
CLOWN	Parsons		
PROVOST	Wrighten		
ELBOW	Wright		
FRIAR PETER	Chaplin		
BARNARDINE	Fawcett		
ABHORSON	Alfred		
LUCIO	[J.] Bannister		
MARIANA	Mrs Ward		
JULIET	Miss Barnes		
ISABELLA	Mrs Siddons		

1794 DRURY LANE
Dec. 30, 31

DUKE	Kemble
ANGELO	[J.] Palmer
ESCALUS	[J.] Aickin
CLAUDIO	Wroughton
LUCIO	[J.] Bannister
1ST GENTLEMAN	Dignum
2ND GENTLEMAN	Trueman
PROVOST	Caulfield
FRIAR PETER	Packer
ELBOW	Parsons
FROTH	Bland

1794 DRURY LANE (cont.)
Dec. 30, 31 (cont.)

CLOWN	Suett
ABHORSON	Phillimore
BARNARDINE	R. Palmer
FRIAR THOMAS	Maddocks
ISABELLA	Mrs Siddons
MARIANA	Mrs Powell
FRANCISCA	Miss Tidswell
MRS OVERDONE	Mrs Booth

1795 DRURY LANE
Jan. 13

DUKE	Kemble
ANGELO	[J.] Palmer
ESCALUS	[J.] Aickin
CLAUDIO	Wroughton
LUCIO	[J.] Bannister
1ST GENTLEMAN (1, 2)	Dignum
2ND GENTLEMAN (1, 2)	Trueman
PROVOST	Caulfield
FRIAR PETER	Packer
ELBOW (1, 2, 3)	Parsons
FROTH (1, 3)	Bland
CLOWN	Suett
ABHORSON (1)	Phillimore
BARNARDINE (1, 2)	R. Palmer
FRIAR THOMAS (1, 2)	Maddocks
ISABELLA	Mrs Siddons
MARIANA (1, 2, 3)	Miss Heard
FRANCISCA	Miss Tidswell
MRS OVERDONE (1)	Mrs Booth

(1) Feb. 26; Mar. 7, 17

ELBOW	[F.] Waldron
MARIANA	Mrs Powell
MRS OVERDONE	Mrs Maddocks

omitted GENTLEMEN, and on Mar. 17 also omitted FROTH, ABHORSON, BARNARDINE, FRIAR THOMAS

[On Feb. 26 Pb assigns MRS OVERDONE to Mrs Booth. But 'Mrs Overdone Mrs Maddocks—Mrs Booth ill' (Powell). On Mar. 7, 17 Mrs Maddocks's name is in the bills.]

(2) Apr. 18

ELBOW	[F.] Waldron
MARIANA	Mrs Powell

omitted GENTLEMEN, BARNARDINE, FRIAR THOMAS

(3) Dec. 11

ELBOW	Dodd
FROTH	Benson
MARIANA	Mrs Goodall

1796 DRURY LANE
Nov. 5

DUKE	Kemble
ANGELO	[J.] Palmer
ESCALUS	[J.] Aickin
CLAUDIO	Wroughton
LUCIO	[J.] Bannister
1ST GENTLEMAN	Dignum
2ND GENTLEMAN	Trueman
PROVOST	Caulfield
FRIAR PETER	Packer
ELBOW	Wewitzer

1796 DRURY LANE (cont.)

Nov. 5 (cont.)

FROTH	Russell
CLOWN	Suett
ABHORSON	Phillimore
BARNARDINE	R. Palmer
FRIAR THOMAS	Maddocks
ISABELLA	Mrs Siddons
MARIANA	Mrs Powell
FRANCISCA	Miss Tidswell
MRS OVERDONE	Mrs Booth

1797 DRURY LANE

Jan. 11; Mar. 28

DUKE	Kemble
ANGELO	[J.] Palmer
ESCALUS	[J.] Aickin
CLAUDIO	Wroughton
LUCIO	[J.] Bannister
1ST GENTLEMAN	Dignum
2ND GENTLEMAN	Trueman
PROVOST	Caulfield
FRIAR PETER	Packer
ELBOW (1)	Wewitzer
FROTH	Russell
CLOWN	Suett
ABHORSON (1)	Phillimore
BARNARDINE (1)	R. Palmer
FRIAR THOMAS	Maddocks
ISABELLA	Mrs Siddons
MARIANA	Mrs Powell
FRANCISCA	Miss Tidswell
MRS OVERDONE (1)	Mrs Booth

(1) Nov. 17

ELBOW	Hollingsworth
ABHORSON	Davis
BARNARDINE	Dowton
MRS OVERDONE	Mrs Maddocks

1798 DRURY LANE

Mar. 3

DUKE	Kemble
ANGELO (1)	[J.] Palmer
ESCALUS	[J.] Aickin
CLAUDIO (1)	Wroughton
LUCIO	R. Palmer
1ST GENTLEMAN (1)	Gibbon
2ND GENTLEMAN	Trueman
PROVOST	Caulfield
FRIAR PETER	Packer
ELBOW	Wewitzer
FROTH (1)	Russell

(1) Oct. 27

ANGELO	Barrymore
CLAUDIO	C. Kemble
1ST GENTLEMAN	Surmont
FROTH	Fisher
ABHORSON	Wentworth
BARNARDINE	Hollingsworth

1798 DRURY LANE (cont.)
Mar. 3 (cont.)

CLOWN	Suett
ABHORSON (1)	Davis
BARNARDINE (1)	Dowton
FRIAR THOMAS	Maddocks
ISABELLA	Mrs Siddons
MARIANA	Mrs Powell
FRANCISCA	Miss Tidswell
MRS OVERDONE	Mrs Maddocks

1799 DRURY LANE
Jan. 17; Apr. 9   (1) *Nov. 29*

DUKE	Kemble		
ANGELO	Barrymore		
ESCALUS	[J.] Aickin		
CLAUDIO	C. Kemble		
LUCIO (1)	R. Palmer	LUCIO	Palmer [i.e. R. Palmer]
1ST GENTLEMAN	Surmont		
2ND GENTLEMAN	Trueman		
PROVOST	Caulfield		
FRIAR PETER	Packer		
ELBOW	Wewitzer		
FROTH	Fisher		
CLOWN	Suett		
ABHORSON	Wentworth		
BARNARDINE	Hollingsworth		
FRIAR THOMAS	Maddocks		
ISABELLA	Mrs Siddons		
MARIANA	Mrs Powell		
FRANCISCA	Miss Tidswell		
MRS OVERDONE	Mrs Maddocks		

THE MERCHANT OF VENICE

(1) Altered as THE JEW OF VENICE, by George Granville, Baron Lansdowne. In five acts.

    1701 Ber. Lintott.

For a description of this see my Volume I, 309.

(2) 'Now Acting with Universal Applause at the Theatres in London and Dublin.'

    1762 Dublin: T. Dyton.
    1766 Dublin: B. Corcoran.

These are reading editions, verbatim throughout.

(3) 'As Performed at the Theatre-Royal, Drury-Lane. Regulated from the Prompt-Book.'

    1773   John Bell.

Following are the principal omissions:

Act I. ii. 60b–88 (Portia's English and Scottish suitors).

Act II. i entire (Morocco); *vii entire* (Morocco) [According to the playbills these scenes continued to be performed until 1757. In the bills the name is usually given as 'Morochius']; *ix entire* (Arragon).

Act III. ii. 14b–24a, 26–38, 45b–72, 87–101a (parts of the scene in which Bassanio chooses the casket).

Throughout there are minor omissions. Jessica has a song at the end of *II. iii*, and Lorenzo has two songs, following *II. vi. 25*, and *V. i. 68*.

See also Odell, ii. 25–27.

(4) 'As it is Acted at the Theatres-Royal in Drury-Lane and Covent-Garden.'

    1777   W. Oxlade.

(5) 'As it is Acted at the Theatres-Royal in Drury-Lane and Covent-Garden.'

    1777   J. Wenman.

(6) 'Marked with the Variations in the Manager's Book, at the Theatre-Royal in Drury-Lane.'

    1783   C. Bathurst [&c.].

(7) 'Taken from the Manager's Book, at the Theatre-Royal, Covent-Garden.'

    1787   For the Proprietors.

(8) 'As it is performed at the Theatres Royal.'

    1788   M. Lister.

All these are identical with (3).

1751 DRURY LANE

Sept. 10

SHYLOCK	Yates
ANTONIO	Berry
BASSANIO	Havard
GRATIANO	Palmer
LAUNCELOT	Shuter
MOROCCO	Burton
SALARINO	Blakes
SOLANIO	Scrase
GOBBO	Ray
TUBAL	Taswell
BALTHAZAR	Simson
DUKE	Winstone
LORENZO	Beard
JESSICA	Miss Minors
NERISSA	Mrs Bennet
PORTIA	Mrs Clive

1751 COVENT GARDEN
Jan. 2

SHYLOCK	Macklin
ANTONIO	Sparks
BASSANIO	Ryan
GRATIANO	Dyer
LORENZO	Lowe
LAUNCELOT	Arthur
SALARINO	Ridout
SOLANIO	Gibson
DUKE (2)	Anderson
TUBAL	Cushing
JESSICA (2)	Mrs Ridout
NERISSA (2)	Mrs Vincent
PORTIA (2)	Mrs Woffington

(1) *May 6*
    added
      GOBBO   Collins

(2) *Nov. 16, 20, 23; Dec. 3, 30*

JESSICA	Mrs Chambers
NERISSA	Mrs Barrington
PORTIA	Mrs Vincent

added
    GOBBO   Collins
omitted
    DUKE

1752 DRURY LANE
Jan. 21

SHYLOCK	Yates
ANTONIO	Berry
BASSANIO	Havard
GRATIANO (1)	Palmer
LAUNCELOT	Shuter
MOROCCO	Burton
SALARINO	Blakes
SOLANIO	Scrase
GOBBO	W. Vaughan
TUBAL (1, 2)	Costollo
BALTHAZAR	Simson
DUKE	Winstone
LORENZO	Beard
JESSICA	Miss Minors
NERISSA	Mrs Bennet
PORTIA	Mrs Clive

(1) *May 2*

GRATIANO	Mozeen
TUBAL	Taswell

    [GA retains Costollo as TUBAL.]

(2) *Sept. 19; Nov. 9*

TUBAL	Taswell

COVENT GARDEN
Feb. 7

SHYLOCK	Macklin
ANTONIO	Sparks
BASSANIO	Ryan
GRATIANO	Dyer
LORENZO	Lowe
LAUNCELOT	Arthur
SALARINO	Ridout
SOLANIO (2)	Gibson
GOBBO	Collins

(1) *Apr. 29*

TUBAL	Stoppelaer

added
    DUKE   Marten

(2) *Oct. 6; Nov. 21*

SOLANIO	Bransby
TUBAL	Stoppelaer
PORTIA	Mrs Bland
NERISSA	Mrs Vincent

added
    DUKE   Anderson

1752 COVENT GARDEN (cont.)

Feb. 7 (cont.)

TUBAL (1, 2)	Cushing
PORTIA (2)	Mrs Vincent
NERISSA (2)	Mrs Barrington
JESSICA	Mrs Chambers

1753 DRURY LANE

Jan. 11

SHYLOCK	Yates
ANTONIO	Berry
BASSANIO	Davies
GRATIANO	Palmer
LAUNCELOT	Shuter
MOROCCO	Burton
SALARINO	Blakes
SOLANIO	Scrase
GOBBO	W. Vaughan
TUBAL	Taswell
BALTHAZAR	Simson
DUKE	Winstone
LORENZO	Beard
JESSICA	Miss Minors
NERISSA	Mrs Bennet
PORTIA	Mrs Clive

COVENT GARDEN

Jan. 4, 26

SHYLOCK	Macklin
ANTONIO	Sparks
BASSANIO	Ryan
DUKE	Anderson
GRATIANO	Dyer
LORENZO	Lowe
LAUNCELOT (1)	Arthur
SALARINO	Usher
SOLANIO	Bransby
GOBBO	Collins
TUBAL	Stoppelaer
NERISSA (1)	Mrs Vincent
JESSICA	Mrs Chambers
PORTIA	Mrs Bland

(1) *Apr. 23*

LAUNCELOT	Barrington
NERISSA	Mrs Barrington

[PA assigns SALARINO to Ridout.]

[The BM copy of PA for *Jan. 4* is missing. That there were any important changes in the cast seems unlikely.]

THE MERCHANT OF VENICE

1754 DRURY LANE
Apr. 16

SHYLOCK	Yates
ANTONIO	Berry
BASSANIO	Havard
GRATIANO (1)	Blakes
LAUNCELOT (1)	Woodward
DUKE	Bransby
LORENZO	Beard
JESSICA	Miss Minors
NERISSA	Mrs Bennet
PORTIA	Mrs Clive

(1) *May 15*

GRATIANO	Palmer
LAUNCELOT added	Vernon
MOROCCO	Burton

COVENT GARDEN
Apr. 6

SHYLOCK (3)	Arthur
ANTONIO	Sparks
BASSANIO	Ryan
DUKE (1)	Anderson
GRATIANO	Dyer
LORENZO	Lowe
SALARINO	Ridout
SOLANIO	Gibson
GOBBO (1)	Collins
TUBAL	Stoppelaer
LAUNCELOT (1)	Shuter
JESSICA	Mrs Chambers
NERISSA (2)	Mrs Vincent
PORTIA (2, 3)	Mrs Bland

(1) *May 9*

DUKE	Marten
GOBBO	Bennet
LAUNCELOT	Collins

(2) *Sept. 23*

NERISSA	Mrs Barrington
PORTIA	Mrs Vincent

(3) *Oct. 30*

SHYLOCK	Sheridan
PORTIA	Mrs Woffington

[*as* THE JEW OF VENICE]

PHILLIPS'S BOOTH, BOWLING GREEN, SOUTHWARK
Sept. 18, 19, 20, 21, 23, 24. No parts assigned

[The bills entitle the play, 'An excellent Droll, called, *The Distressed Merchant; or, The Jew of Venice*'.]

[*The original*]

1755 COVENT GARDEN
May 2; Dec. 2

SHYLOCK	Arthur
ANTONIO	Sparks
BASSANIO	Ryan
DUKE	Anderson
GRATIANO	Dyer
LORENZO	Lowe

(1) *Oct. 8*

JESSICA	Mrs Baker

415

1755 COVENT GARDEN (cont.)
May 2; Dec. 2 (cont.)

SALARINO	Ridout
SOLANIO	Gibson
GOBBO	Collins
TUBAL	Stoppelaer
LAUNCELOT	Shuter
JESSICA (1)	Mrs Chambers
NERISSA	Mrs Vincent
PORTIA	Mrs Woffington

1756 COVENT GARDEN
Apr. 22; Oct. 26; Dec. 23

SHYLOCK	Arthur
ANTONIO	Sparks
BASSANIO	Ryan
DUKE	Anderson
GRATIANO	Dyer
LORENZO	Lowe
SALARINO	Ridout
SOLANIO	Gibson
GOBBO	Collins
TUBAL	Stoppelaer
LAUNCELOT	Shuter
JESSICA	Mrs Chambers
NERISSA	Mrs Vincent
PORTIA	Mrs Woffington

1757 DRURY LANE
Apr. 20

SHYLOCK	Yates
ANTONIO	Berry
BASSANIO	Havard
GRATIANO	Palmer
DUKE	Bransby
LORENZO	Beard
MOROCCO	Burton
JESSICA	Miss Minors
NERISSA	Mrs Bennet
PORTIA	Mrs Clive

COVENT GARDEN
Sept. 30 (1) *Dec. 6*

SHYLOCK	Arthur
ANTONIO	Sparks
BASSANIO	Ryan

SALARINO   White

THE MERCHANT OF VENICE

1757 COVENT GARDEN (cont.)
Sept. 30 (cont.)

DUKE	Anderson
GRATIANO	Dyer
LORENZO	Lowe
SALARINO (1)	Ridout
SOLANIO	Gibson
GOBBO	Collins
TUBAL	Stoppelaer
LAUNCELOT	Shuter
JESSICA	Mrs Chambers
NERISSA	Mrs Vincent
PORTIA	Mrs Hamilton

1758 DRURY LANE
Dec. 18

SHYLOCK	Foote
ANTONIO	Davies
BASSANIO	Havard
GRATIANO	Palmer
LAUNCELOT	[H.] Vaughan
DUKE	Bransby
LORENZO	Beard
JESSICA	Miss Hippisley
NERISSA	Mrs Bennet
PORTIA	Mrs Clive

1759 DRURY LANE
Jan. 13, 19   (1) *Dec. 12, 13*

SHYLOCK (1)	Yates		SHYLOCK	Macklin
ANTONIO	Davies		LORENZO	Moody
BASSANIO	Havard			
GRATIANO	Palmer			
LAUNCELOT	[H.] Vaughan			
DUKE	Bransby			
LORENZO (1)	Beard			
JESSICA	Miss Hippisley			
NERISSA	Mrs Bennet			
PORTIA	Mrs Clive			

[On *Jan. 13* the play was changed from *The Provoked Wife* to *The Merchant of Venice*. See p. 21.]

COVENT GARDEN
May 3

SHYLOCK	Shuter
ANTONIO	Sparks

1759 COVENT GARDEN (cont.)

May 3 (cont.)

BASSANIO	Ryan
DUKE	Anderson
GRATIANO	Dyer
LORENZO	Lowe
SALARINO	Davis
SOLANIO	Gibson
GOBBO	Collins
TUBAL	Stoppelaer
LAUNCELOT	Dunstall
JESSICA	Mrs Baker
NERISSA	Mrs Vincent
PORTIA	Mrs Hamilton

1760 DRURY LANE

May 17

SHYLOCK	Macklin
ANTONIO	Davies
BASSANIO	Havard
GRATIANO	Palmer
LAUNCELOT	[H.] Vaughan
DUKE	Bransby
LORENZO	Moody
JESSICA	Mrs Hippisley
NERISSA	Mrs Bennet
PORTIA	Mrs Clive

COVENT GARDEN

May 7

BASSANIO	Clarke
ANTONIO	Sparks
DUKE	Anderson
GRATIANO	Dyer
LORENZO	Lowe
SALARINO	Davis
SOLANIO	Gibson
GOBBO	Collins
TUBAL	Stoppelaer
SHYLOCK	Shuter
LAUNCELOT	Bennet
JESSICA	Miss Mullart
NERISSA	Mrs Vincent
PORTIA	Mrs Hamilton

1761 COVENT GARDEN

Jan. 10; Feb. 26; Mar. 12; Apr. 4

SHYLOCK (2)	Macklin
ANTONIO	Sparks
BASSANIO	Clarke
DUKE	Anderson
GRATIANO	Dyer
LORENZO	Mattocks
SALARINO	Davis
SOLANIO	Gibson
GOBBO	Collins
TUBAL	Stoppelaer
LAUNCELOT	Shuter
JESSICA (2)	Mrs Burden
NERISSA	Mrs Vincent
PORTIA (1, 2)	Miss Macklin

(1) *May 4*

PORTIA	Mrs Hamilton

(2) *Sept. 21*

SHYLOCK	Storer [first appearance in London]
JESSICA	Mrs Abegg
PORTIA	Mrs Ward

1764 COVENT GARDEN

Apr. 10

SHYLOCK	Macklin
ANTONIO	Sparks
BASSANIO	Clarke
DUKE	Anderson
GRATIANO	Dyer
LORENZO	Mattocks
LAUNCELOT	Shuter
JESSICA	Miss [E.] Miller
NERISSA	Mrs Vincent
PORTIA	Miss Macklin

1765 COVENT GARDEN

Apr. 9

SHYLOCK	Macklin
ANTONIO	Sparks
BASSANIO	Clarke
DUKE	Anderson
GRATIANO	Dyer
LORENZO	Mattocks
LAUNCELOT	Shuter
JESSICA	Mrs [T.] Baker
NERISSA	Mrs Vincent
PORTIA	Miss Macklin

THE MERCHANT OF VENICE

1767 COVENT GARDEN
Apr. 6
SHYLOCK	Macklin
ANTONIO (1)	Ross
BASSANIO (1)	Clarke
DUKE (1)	Anderson
GRATIANO	Dyer
LORENZO (1)	Mattocks
LAUNCELOT	Shuter
JESSICA (1)	Mrs [T.] Baker
NERISSA (1)	Mrs Vincent
PORTIA	Miss Macklin

(1) *Oct. 6, 10, 14, 21, 28; Nov. 21; Dec. 10*
ANTONIO	Clarke
BASSANIO	Bensley
DUKE	Morris
LORENZO	Du-Bellamy (on *Oct. 14, 21, 28, Nov. 21, Dec. 10* only)
JESSICA	Mrs Mattocks (on *Oct. 28* only)
NERISSA	Mrs Lessingham

[On *Dec. 10* Pb retains Mattocks as LORENZO.]

1768 DRURY LANE
Mar. 24
ANTONIO (1)	Barry
BASSANIO	Holland
GRATIANO	Palmer
LAUNCELOT	Wingfield
GOBBO	Parsons
LORENZO (1)	Vernon
SHYLOCK	King
JESSICA	Mrs Baddeley
NERISSA	Mrs Jefferies
PORTIA	Mrs Dancer

(1) *Apr. 16*
ANTONIO	Reddish
LORENZO	Dodd

Sept. 30
ANTONIO	Reddish
BASSANIO	Cautherley
GRATIANO	Dodd
LAUNCELOT	W. Palmer
LORENZO	Vernon
SHYLOCK	King
JESSICA	Mrs Baddeley
NERISSA	Mrs Jefferies
PORTIA (1)	Mrs [S.] Barry

(1) *Nov. 5; Dec. 20*
PORTIA	Mrs Abington
added	
GOBBO	Parsons
SALARINO	Hurst
SOLANIO	Fawcett
DUKE	Bransby
BALTHAZAR	Ackman
TUBAL	Messink

COVENT GARDEN
Jan. 1
SHYLOCK	Macklin
ANTONIO (1)	Clarke
BASSANIO	Bensley
DUKE	Morris
GRATIANO	Dyer
LORENZO	Mattocks
LAUNCELOT	Shuter
JESSICA	Mrs [T.] Baker
NERISSA (2)	Mrs Lessingham
PORTIA (1, 2)	Mrs Bulkley

(1) *Jan. 22, 25*
ANTONIO	Hull (on *Jan. 22* only)
PORTIA	Miss Macklin

(2) *Feb. 29; Apr. 6, 12*
NERISSA	Mrs Vincent
PORTIA	Miss Macklin
added on *Feb. 29* only	
SOLANIO	Gardner
SALARINO	Davis

[On *Feb. 29* PA retains Mrs Lessingham as NERISSA.]

420

THE MERCHANT OF VENICE

1769 DRURY LANE
Jan. 7

SHYLOCK	King
BASSANIO	Cautherley
ANTONIO	Reddish
GRATIANO (3)	Dodd
LORENZO	Vernon
LAUNCELOT (2)	W. Palmer
GOBBO	Parsons
DUKE (3)	Bransby
SALARINO (1, 2, 3)	Hurst
SOLANIO	Fawcett
BALTHAZAR	Ackman
TUBAL	Messink
JESSICA	Mrs Baddeley
NERISSA	Mrs Jefferies
PORTIA (2)	Mrs Abington

(1) *Jan. 26; Mar. 30; May 19*

SALARINO	J. Aickin

(2) *May 3*

LAUNCELOT	Hartry
SALARINO	J. Aickin
PORTIA	Miss Macklin

[Pb retains Hurst as SALARINO.]

(3) *Oct. 5, 26; Dec. 2*

GRATIANO	Jefferson (on *Oct. 26, Dec. 2* only)
DUKE	Wright (on *Oct. 5* only)
SALARINO	J. Aickin

1770 DRURY LANE
May 29

SHYLOCK	King
LAUNCELOT	W. Palmer
LORENZO	Vernon
GOBBO	Parsons
SALARINO	J. Aickin
SOLANIO	Fawcett
DUKE (1)	Wright
BALTHAZAR (1)	Ackman
TUBAL (1)	Messink
ANTONIO	Reddish
BASSANIO	Cautherley
GRATIANO	Dodd
JESSICA (1)	Miss Radley
NERISSA	Mrs Jefferies
PORTIA	Mrs Abington

(1) *Oct. 22; Dec. 21*

DUKE	Bransby
JESSICA	Mrs Baddeley (on *Oct. 22* only)

omitted BALTHAZAR, TUBAL

COVENT GARDEN
Mar. 27

SHYLOCK (1)	Yates
ANTONIO	Clarke
BASSANIO	Bensley
DUKE	Morris
GRATIANO	Dyer
LORENZO	Mattocks
LAUNCELOT	Shuter
JESSICA	Mrs [T.] Baker
NERISSA (1)	Mrs Vincent
PORTIA (1)	Mrs Yates

(1) *Apr. 5*

SHYLOCK	Macklin
NERISSA	Mrs Lessingham
PORTIA	Miss Macklin

THE MERCHANT OF VENICE

1771 DRURY LANE
Apr. 24

SHYLOCK	King
BASSANIO	Cautherley
ANTONIO	Reddish
GRATIANO	Dodd
LORENZO	Vernon
LAUNCELOT	W. Palmer
TUBAL	Messink
GOBBO	Parsons
SOLANIO	Fawcett
SALARINO (1)	Hurst
DUKE (1)	Bransby
JESSICA (1)	Mrs Baddeley
NERISSA (1)	Mrs Jefferies
PORTIA	Mrs Abington

(1) *Oct. 3*

SALARINO	J. Aickin
DUKE	Wright
JESSICA	Miss Rogers
NERISSA	Miss Ambrose

COVENT GARDEN
Apr. 3; Oct. 22, 24, 31

SHYLOCK (1)	Macklin
ANTONIO	Clarke
BASSANIO (2)	Bensley
DUKE	Morris
GRATIANO	Dyer
LORENZO	Mattocks
LAUNCELOT	Shuter
JESSICA	Mrs [T.] Baker
NERISSA	Mrs Lessingham
PORTIA	Miss Macklin

(1) *May 7*

SHYLOCK	Yates

(2) *Oct. 26, 29*

BASSANIO	Wroughton

HAYMARKET
Sept. 20

SHYLOCK	Gardner
BASSANIO	Fearon
GRATIANO	Vandermere
LORENZO	Dancer
ANTONIO	[F.] Gentleman
GOBBO	Wooller
SOLANIO	Vowell
SALARINO	Griffith
LAUNCELOT	Graham
DUKE	Lloyd
PORTIA	Mrs Gardner
NERISSA	Mrs Collet
JESSICA	Mrs Granger

THE MERCHANT OF VENICE

1772 DRURY LANE
Jan. 11

SHYLOCK	King
BASSANIO	Cautherley
ANTONIO (1)	Reddish
GRATIANO	Dodd
LORENZO	Vernon
LAUNCELOT	W. Palmer
GOBBO	Parsons
SOLANIO	Fawcett
SALARINO	J. Aickin
DUKE	Bransby
TUBAL	Messink
JESSICA	Miss Rogers
NERISSA	Miss Ambrose
PORTIA	Mrs Abington

(1) *May 2*

ANTONIO	[C.] Bannister

COVENT GARDEN
May 13

SHYLOCK	Gardner
ANTONIO	Clarke
BASSANIO	Bensley
DUKE	Thompson
GRATIANO	Dyer
LORENZO	Mattocks
SALARINO	R. Smith
SOLANIO	Owenson
LAUNCELOT	Quick
JESSICA	Mrs [T.] Baker
NERISSA	Mrs Lessingham
PORTIA	Miss Macklin

[Genest (v. 335) erroneously assigns SHYLOCK to Yates.]

1773 DRURY LANE
Jan. 4

SHYLOCK	King
BASSANIO	Cautherley
ANTONIO	Reddish
GRATIANO	Dodd
LORENZO	Vernon
LAUNCELOT	W. Palmer
GOBBO	Parsons
SOLANIO	Fawcett
SALARINO	J. Aickin
DUKE	Bransby
JESSICA	Miss Jarratt
NERISSA	Miss Ambrose
PORTIA	Mrs Abington

(1) *Feb. 5*

added

TUBAL	Messink

423

1773 COVENT GARDEN
Apr. 17

SHYLOCK (1)	Macklin
ANTONIO	Clarke
BASSANIO (2)	Bensley
GRATIANO (1, 2)	[Lee] Lewes
LORENZO	Mattocks
LAUNCELOT (1)	Shuter
JESSICA (2)	Mrs [T.] Baker
NERISSA (1, 2)	Mrs Lessingham
PORTIA	Miss Macklin

[In the acting version published by Bell in 1773 the cast is the same as that of this performance (except for the assignment of GRATIANO to Dyer), with the following additions:

DUKE	Morris
SALARINO	Davis
SOLANIO	Gardner
TUBAL	[R.] Bates
GOBBO	Saunders]

(1) *May 24*

SHYLOCK	Shuter
GRATIANO	Dyer
LAUNCELOT	Hamilton
NERISSA	Mrs Vincent

added

DUKE	Morris
SOLANIO	Owenson
SALARINO	Thompson
TUBAL	[R.] Bates
BALTHAZAR	Holtom
GOBBO	Saunders

(2) *Oct. 5, 14*

BASSANIO	Wroughton
GRATIANO	Dyer
JESSICA	Miss Valois
NERISSA	Mrs [T.] Baker

added

DUKE	Thompson

1774 DRURY LANE
May 14

SHYLOCK	King
BASSANIO	Cautherley
ANTONIO	Reddish
GRATIANO	Dodd
LORENZO	Vernon
GOBBO	Parsons
LAUNCELOT	W. Palmer
SALARINO	Keen
DUKE	Wright
SOLANIO	Fawcett
TUBAL	Messink
JESSICA	Miss Jarratt
NERISSA	Mrs Davies
PORTIA	Mrs Abington

1775 DRURY LANE
Dec. 29

SHYLOCK	King
ANTONIO	Reddish
GRATIANO	Dodd
LORENZO	Vernon
DUKE	Bransby
LAUNCELOT	Parsons
GOBBO	[F.] Waldron

THE MERCHANT OF VENICE

1775 DRURY LANE (cont.)
Dec. 29 (cont.)

SOLANIO	Fawcett
SALARINO	Farren
TUBAL	Messink
BASSANIO	Bensley
JESSICA	Miss Jarratt
NERISSA	Mrs Davies
PORTIA	A Young Lady [Mrs Siddons (Genest, v. 484); first appearance in London]

COVENT GARDEN

May 18

SHYLOCK	Macklin
ANTONIO	Clarke
BASSANIO (2)	Bensley
GRATIANO	Lee Lewes
LORENZO (1)	Mattocks
DUKE	Fearon
LAUNCELOT (2)	Shuter
TUBAL	Thompson
JESSICA (2)	Mrs [T.] Baker
NERISSA	Mrs Lessingham
PORTIA	Miss Macklin

(1) *May 29*

LORENZO	Du-Bellamy

(2) *Oct. 6, 27*

BASSANIO	Wroughton
LAUNCELOT	Quick
JESSICA	Miss Dayes

HAYMARKET
Mar. 23

SHYLOCK	[S.] Johnson
ANTONIO	[P.] Lewis
GRATIANO	Russell
LORENZO	Bradney
DUKE	Saul
LAUNCELOT	Jacobs
GOBBO	Lucas
TUBAL	Errington
BASSANIO	West
NERISSA	Mrs Simmons
JESSICA	Mrs Moore
PORTIA	A Young Lady [unidentified; first appearance in London]

[The bill states that Johnson would act SHYLOCK 'in the Jewish Dialect'.]

1776 DRURY LANE
Jan. 2

SHYLOCK	King
ANTONIO	Reddish
GRATIANO	Dodd
LORENZO	Vernon

1776 DRURY LANE (cont.)
Jan. 2 (cont.)

DUKE	Bransby
LAUNCELOT	Parsons
GOBBO	[F.] Waldron
SOLANIO	Fawcett
SALARINO	Farren
TUBAL	Messink
BASSANIO	Bensley
JESSICA	Miss Jarratt
NERISSA	Mrs Davies
PORTIA	A Young Lady [Mrs Siddons (Genest, v. 484)]

COVENT GARDEN
Apr. 13; Oct. 29; Nov. 22   (1) *Dec. 19*

SHYLOCK	Macklin	NERISSA added	Miss Ambrose
ANTONIO	Clarke		
BASSANIO	Wroughton	SOLANIO	Booth
GRATIANO	Lee Lewes	SALARINO	Davis
LORENZO	Mattocks		
DUKE	Fearon		
LAUNCELOT	Quick		
TUBAL	Thompson		
JESSICA	Miss Dayes		
NERISSA (1)	Mrs Lessingham		
PORTIA	Miss Macklin		

CHINA HALL, ROTHERHITHE
Aug. 2

LAUNCELOT	Shuter
SHYLOCK	Comerford
ANTONIO	[P.] Lewis
GRATIANO	Russell
LORENZO	Kenny
DUKE	Massey
GOBBO	Newton
SOLANIO	[S.] Johnson
SALARINO	[J.] Smith
BASSANIO	West
PORTIA	Mrs Fisher
NERISSA	Miss Taylor
JESSICA	Mrs Wilks

1777 DRURY LANE
Oct. 14, 16; Nov. 7

SHYLOCK	Henderson
ANTONIO	Bensley

THE MERCHANT OF VENICE

1777 DRURY LANE (cont.)
Oct. 14, 16; Nov. 7 (cont.)

GRATIANO	Dodd
LORENZO	Vernon
DUKE	Packer
LAUNCELOT	Parsons
GOBBO	Wrighten
SOLANIO	Farren
SALARINO	Lamash
TUBAL	[F.] Waldron
BASSANIO	[J.] Palmer
JESSICA	Miss Walpole
NERISSA	Mrs Davies
PORTIA	Miss Younge

COVENT GARDEN
Jan. 15; Feb. 15; Mar. 22; Apr. 19

SHYLOCK	Macklin
ANTONIO	Clarke
BASSANIO	Wroughton
GRATIANO	Lee Lewes
LORENZO	Mattocks
DUKE	Fearon
LAUNCELOT	Quick
TUBAL	Thompson
SOLANIO	Booth
SALARINO (1)	Davis
JESSICA	Miss Dayes
NERISSA	Mrs Lessingham
PORTIA (1)	Miss Macklin

(1) *Oct. 16, 28*

SALARINO	L'Estrange
PORTIA	Mrs [S.] Barry

[In both these performances PA retains Davis as SALARINO.]

[On *Feb. 15* PA assigns NERISSA to Miss Ambrose.]

HAYMARKET
June 11, 12; July 8, 23; Aug. 15

SHYLOCK	Henderson [first appearance, June 11, in London]
ANTONIO (1)	Younger
BASSANIO	Davies
SOLANIO	Egan
SALARINO	T. Davis
LORENZO	Du-Bellamy
GOBBO	Blissett
TUBAL	Massey
LAUNCELOT	Edwin

(1) *June 16, 18*

ANTONIO	Hull

427

THE MERCHANT OF VENICE

1777 HAYMARKET (*cont.*)
June 11, 12; July 8, 23; Aug. 15 (cont.)

DUKE	Fearon
GRATIANO	[J.] Palmer
NERISSA	Mrs Hunter
JESSICA	Mrs Hitchcock
PORTIA	Miss Barsanti

1778 DRURY LANE
Oct. 17

SHYLOCK	Henderson
ANTONIO	Bensley
GRATIANO	Dodd
LORENZO	Vernon
LAUNCELOT	Parsons
DUKE	Packer
BASSANIO	[J.] Palmer
JESSICA	Mrs Morton
NERISSA	Mrs Davies
PORTIA	Miss Younge

COVENT GARDEN
Jan. 28

SHYLOCK	Macklin
ANTONIO	Clarke
BASSANIO	Wroughton
GRATIANO	Lee Lewes
LORENZO	Mattocks
DUKE	Fearon
TUBAL	Thompson
SOLANIO	Booth
SALARINO	Davis
LAUNCELOT	Quick
JESSICA (2)	Miss Dayes
NERISSA (2)	Mrs Lessingham
PORTIA (1, 2)	Mrs [S.] Barry

(1) *Mar. 24*

PORTIA	Mrs Bulkley

(2) *Apr. 24*

JESSICA	Mrs Morton [i.e. formerly Miss Dayes]
NERISSA	Miss Ambrose
PORTIA	Mrs Lessingham

BOOTH, CHINA HALL, ROTHERHITHE
Aug. 6

SHYLOCK	Machin
LAUNCELOT	Everard
JESSICA	Mrs Nost
PORTIA	Miss Taylor

No other parts assigned

THE MERCHANT OF VENICE

1779 DRURY LANE

Jan. 19

SHYLOCK	Henderson
ANTONIO	Bensley
GRATIANO	Dodd
LORENZO	Vernon
LAUNCELOT (1)	[J.] Burton
DUKE	Packer
BASSANIO	[J.] Palmer
JESSICA (1)	Miss Walpole
NERISSA	Mrs Davies
PORTIA (1)	Miss Younge

(1) *May 14*

LAUNCELOT	Parsons
JESSICA	Mrs Morton
PORTIA	Mrs Bulkley

COVENT GARDEN

Nov. 11, 20; Dec. 4

SHYLOCK	Macklin
ANTONIO	Clarke
BASSANIO	Wroughton
GRATIANO	Lee Lewes
LORENZO	Mattocks
DUKE	Fearon
LAUNCELOT	Quick
TUBAL	Thompson
SOLANIO	Booth
SALARINO	L'Estrange
JESSICA	Mrs Morton
NERISSA	Miss Ambrose
PORTIA	Mrs Bulkley

1780 COVENT GARDEN

Jan. 8

SHYLOCK (1)	Macklin
ANTONIO	Clarke
BASSANIO	Wroughton
GRATIANO	Lee Lewes
LORENZO (1, 2)	Vernon
DUKE (2)	Fearon
LAUNCELOT	Quick
TUBAL (2)	Thompson
SOLANIO (1, 2)	Booth
SALARINO (2)	L'Estrange
JESSICA (1, 2)	Mrs [S.] Wilson
NERISSA (2)	Miss Ambrose
PORTIA (2)	Mrs Bulkley

(1) *Jan. 28; Apr. 5, 29; May 12*

SHYLOCK	Henderson (on *May 12* only)
LORENZO	Mattocks
SOLANIO	W. Bates (on *May 12* only)
JESSICA	Mrs Morton

(2) *Nov. 2, 6, 9, 16, 23, 30; Dec. 7, 14*

LORENZO	Mattocks
JESSICA	Mrs Morton
NERISSA	Mrs Lessingham
PORTIA	Mrs Yates

omitted on *Nov. 2* only
DUKE, TUBAL, SOLANIO, SALARINO

1780 HAYMARKET
Aug. 24

SHYLOCK	Digges
ANTONIO	Bensley
GRATIANO	Lamash
GOBBO	Blissett
TUBAL	Stevens
LORENZO	Du-Bellamy
LAUNCELOT	Edwin
DUKE	Usher
SALARINO	Davis
SOLANIO	Egan
BASSANIO	[J.] Palmer
JESSICA	Mrs Hitchcock
NERISSA	Mrs [S.] Wilson
PORTIA	Miss Farren

1781 COVENT GARDEN
Feb. 13

SHYLOCK (2)	Macklin
ANTONIO	Clarke
BASSANIO (1)	Wroughton
GRATIANO	Lee Lewes
LORENZO	Mattocks
LAUNCELOT	Quick
SOLANIO	Booth
SALARINO	L'Estrange
DUKE	Fearon
TUBAL	Thompson
GOBBO (3, 4)	Baker
JESSICA	Mrs Morton
NERISSA	Mrs Lessingham
PORTIA (3)	Mrs Yates

(1) *Feb. 20*

BASSANIO	Whitfield

(2) *Apr. 20*

SHYLOCK	Henderson

(3) *Nov. 8, 15*

PORTIA	Miss Younge
omitted GOBBO	

(4) *Dec. 4*

omitted GOBBO	

HAYMARKET
Aug. 7

SHYLOCK	Digges
ANTONIO	Gardner
BASSANIO	Staunton
DUKE	Usher
GRATIANO	Lamash
SOLANIO	Davis
NERISSA	Mrs [S.] Wilson
PORTIA	Mrs Massey

[The above consisted of IV. i only. The entertainment on this evening was called *The School of Shakespeare*, for a description of which see p. 73. In the bill Staunton's name is misprinted 'Stanton'.]

THE MERCHANT OF VENICE

1782 COVENT GARDEN
Jan. 31. No parts assigned
[See p. 74.]

Apr. 8

SHYLOCK	Macklin
ANTONIO	Clarke
BASSANIO	Wroughton
GRATIANO	Lee Lewes
LORENZO	Mattocks
LAUNCELOT	Quick
SOLANIO	Booth
SALARINO (1)	L'Estrange
DUKE	Fearon
TUBAL	Thompson
JESSICA	Mrs Morton
NERISSA (1)	Mrs Lessingham
PORTIA (1)	Mrs Yates

(1) Oct. 29; Dec. 3

SALARINO	Davies
NERISSA	Mrs [S.] Wilson (on Dec. 3 only)
PORTIA	Miss Younge

[In the acting version published by Bathurst in 1783 the cast is the same as that of the performance on Dec. 3, with the following additions:

GOBBO	Jones
BATHAZAR	Ledger
ANTONIO'S SERVANT	Helme
LEONARDO	Painter]

HAYMARKET
Dec. 30

ANTONIO	Usher
BASSANIO	The Gentleman who plays Lothario [in *The Fair Penitent*—unidentified; first appearance on the stage]
DUKE	Roberts
GRATIANO	Wetherhead
SHYLOCK	Gardner
NERISSA	Miss Painter
PORTIA	The Lady who plays Calista [in *The Fair Penitent*—Mrs Mills (MC, Jan. 1, 1783); first appearance on the stage]

[The above consisted of IV. i only, and was performed as an after-piece to *The Fair Penitent*. MC assigns NERISSA to Miss Thompson.]

1783 DRURY LANE
Feb. 22; Mar. 1

SHYLOCK	King
GRATIANO	[J.] Palmer
BASSANIO	Farren
LAUNCELOT (1)	Parsons
DUKE	Packer
LORENZO (1)	Williames
ANTONIO	Bensley
JESSICA	Miss Wheeler
NERISSA	Miss Collett
PORTIA (1)	Miss E. Kemble [first appearance, Feb. 22, in London]

(1) Apr. 26

LAUNCELOT	Suett
LORENZO	Chapman
PORTIA	Mrs Bulkley
added	
GOBBO	Wrighten
TUBAL	[F.] Waldron
SOLANIO	Fawcett
SALARINO	Phillimore

[In the acting version published by

431

THE MERCHANT OF VENICE

1783 DRURY LANE (cont.)
Feb. 22; Mar. 1 (cont.)

Bathurst in 1783 the cast is the same as that of these performances, with the following additions:

SOLANIO	Fawcett
SALARINO	Phillimore
TUBAL	[F.] Waldron
GOBBO	Wrighten
BALTHAZAR	Norris
ANTONIO'S SERVANT	Spencer
LEONARDO	Alfred]

COVENT GARDEN

Feb. 13

SHYLOCK	Macklin
ANTONIO	Clarke
BASSANIO	Wroughton
GRATIANO (1, 2)	Lee Lewes
LORENZO	Mattocks
LAUNCELOT	Quick
SOLANIO	Booth
SALARINO	Davies
DUKE	Fearon
TUBAL	Thompson
JESSICA	Mrs Morton
NERISSA	Mrs [S.] Wilson
PORTIA (1, 2)	Mrs Bulkley

(1) *Apr. 30*

GRATIANO	Whitfield
PORTIA	Miss Younge

(2) *Dec. 5, 16*

GRATIANO	Bonnor
PORTIA	A Young Lady [Miss Ranoe (MS annotation on JPK); first appearance, Dec. 5, on the stage]

1784 DRURY LANE

Jan. 22

SHYLOCK	Kemble
GRATIANO (2)	[J.] Palmer
BASSANIO	Farren
LAUNCELOT	Parsons
DUKE	Packer
LORENZO	Williams
ANTONIO (1, 2)	Clarke
JESSICA	Miss Wheeler
NERISSA	Mrs [J.] Wilson
PORTIA	Miss E. Kemble

(1) *Jan. 24*

ANTONIO	[J.] Aickin

(2) *Mar. 22*

GRATIANO	Dodd
ANTONIO	Bensley

[Both Pb and PA assign ANTONIO to Bensley. In the JPK bill his name is deleted, but the substitute name has been cut by the binder. 'Mr. Clarke played Antonio in the room of Mr. Bensley, who was taken ill' (MC, Jan. 23).]

THE MERCHANT OF VENICE

1784 COVENT GARDEN
Mar. 18

SHYLOCK	Macklin
ANTONIO	Clarke
BASSANIO	Wroughton
GRATIANO (1)	Whitfield
LORENZO (1)	Mattocks
LAUNCELOT	Quick
SOLANIO	Booth
SALARINO	Davies
DUKE	Fearon
TUBAL	Thompson
JESSICA (1)	Miss Wheeler
NERISSA (1)	Mrs [S.] Wilson
PORTIA	Miss Younge

(1) *Nov. 10*

GRATIANO	Bonnor
LORENZO	Johnstone
JESSICA	Mrs Morton
NERISSA	Mrs Inchbald

June 10

SHYLOCK	Macklin
BASSANIO	Wroughton
GRATIANO	Bonnor
LAUNCELOT	Edwin
LORENZO	Davies
DUKE	Fearon
SOLANIO	Gardner
SALARINO	L'Estrange
ANTONIO	Bensley
NERISSA	Mrs Bates
JESSICA	Mrs Morton
PORTIA	Miss Younge

[Bill not in JPK. See p. 78.]

1785 COVENT GARDEN
Feb. 14

SHYLOCK	Macklin
ANTONIO	Hull
BASSANIO	Wroughton
GRATIANO	Bonnor
LORENZO	Johnstone
LAUNCELOT	Quick
SOLANIO	Booth
SALARINO	Davies
DUKE	Fearon
TUBAL	Thompson
JESSICA	Mrs Morton
NERISSA	Mrs Inchbald
PORTIA	Miss Younge

[Both Pb and PA assign ANTONIO to Clarke. In the JPK bill his name is deleted, and that of Hull substituted.]

THE MERCHANT OF VENICE

1786 DRURY LANE
Apr. 6

SHYLOCK	King
GRATIANO	Dodd
BASSANIO	Kemble
LAUNCELOT	Parsons
DUKE	Packer
LORENZO	Williames
ANTONIO	Bensley
JESSICA	Mrs Forster
NERISSA	Mrs [J.] Wilson
PORTIA	Mrs Siddons

(1) *Apr. 20, 29; May 13*
added

SOLANIO	Fawcett
SALARINO	Phillimore
TUBAL	[F.] Waldron
GOBBO	Wrighten

COVENT GARDEN
Feb. 18, 27

SHYLOCK	Macklin
ANTONIO (1)	Farren
BASSANIO (1)	Wroughton
GRATIANO (1)	[Wm.] Palmer
LORENZO	Johnstone
LAUNCELOT	Quick
SOLANIO	Booth
SALARINO	Davies
DUKE	Fearon
TUBAL	Thompson
JESSICA	Mrs Morton
NERISSA (1)	Mrs [S.] Wilson
PORTIA (1)	Mrs Wells

(1) *Oct. 12; Dec. 19*

ANTONIO	Hull (on *Dec. 19* only)
BASSANIO	Pope
GRATIANO	Macready
NERISSA	Mrs Inchbald
PORTIA	Mrs Pope

added

GOBBO	Swords

HAMMERSMITH
June 9

SHYLOCK	[F.] Waldron
LAUNCELOT	Wright

No other parts assigned

1787 DRURY LANE
Nov. 24

SHYLOCK	King
GRATIANO	R. Palmer
BASSANIO	Kemble
LAUNCELOT	Suett
DUKE	Packer
LORENZO	Williames
SOLANIO	Fawcett
SALARINO	Phillimore
TUBAL	[F.] Waldron

THE MERCHANT OF VENICE

1787 DRURY LANE (cont.)
Nov. 24 (cont.)

GOBBO	Jones
ANTONIO	Bensley
JESSICA	Mrs Forster
NERISSA	Miss Collins
PORTIA	Mrs Siddons

COVENT GARDEN
Feb. 8

SHYLOCK	Macklin
ANTONIO	Farren
BASSANIO	Pope
GRATIANO	Macready
LORENZO	Johnstone
LAUNCELOT	Quick
SOLANIO	Booth
SALARINO	Davies
DUKE	Fearon
GOBBO	Swords
TUBAL	Thompson
JESSICA	Mrs Morton
NERISSA	Mrs Inchbald
PORTIA	Mrs Pope

HAYMARKET
July 27

SHYLOCK	[J.] Williamson
ANTONIO	[J.] Aickin
GRATIANO	[J.] Bannister
GOBBO	Barrett
TUBAL	Chapman
LORENZO	[J.] Johnson
LAUNCELOT	Edwin
DUKE	Usher
SOLANIO	Lawrance
SALARINO	Swords
BASSANIO	Bensley
JESSICA	Mrs Forster
NERISSA	Mrs Inchbald
PORTIA	Mrs Bulkley

1788 DRURY LANE
Jan. 5

SHYLOCK	King
GRATIANO (1)	Dodd
BASSANIO (2)	Wroughton

(1) *Jan. 12*

GRATIANO	R. Palmer

(2) *Feb. 1*

BASSANIO	Kemble

435

THE MERCHANT OF VENICE

1788 DRURY LANE (cont.)
Jan. 5 (cont.)

LAUNCELOT	Suett
DUKE	Packer
LORENZO	Williames
SOLANIO	Fawcett
SALARINO	Phillimore
TUBAL	[F.] Waldron
GOBBO	Hollingsworth
ANTONIO	Bensley
JESSICA	Mrs Forster
NERISSA	Mrs [J.] Wilson
PORTIA	Mrs Siddons

COVENT GARDEN
Jan. 10, 24; Feb. 16; Apr. 3   (1) *Oct. 18*

SHYLOCK	Macklin	JESSICA	Mrs Mountain
ANTONIO	Farren		
BASSANIO	Pope		
GRATIANO	Bernard		
LORENZO	Johnstone		
LAUNCELOT	Quick		
SOLANIO	Booth		
SALARINO	Davies		
DUKE	Fearon		
GOBBO	Wewitzer		
TUBAL	Thompson		
JESSICA (1)	Mrs Morton		
NERISSA	Mrs Inchbald		
PORTIA	Mrs Pope		

1789 DRURY LANE
Jan. 17

SHYLOCK	Kemble
GRATIANO	R. Palmer
BASSANIO	Wroughton
LAUNCELOT	Suett
DUKE	Packer
LORENZO	Williames
SOLANIO	Fawcett
SALARINO	Phillimore
TUBAL	[F.] Waldron
GOBBO	Jones
ANTONIO	Bensley
JESSICA	Mrs Forster
NERISSA	Mrs [J.] Wilson
PORTIA	Mrs Siddons

THE MERCHANT OF VENICE

1789 COVENT GARDEN
May 7

SHYLOCK (1)	Macklin [beginning of Shylock's first scene]; Ryder [remainder of play]		
ANTONIO (1)	Farren		
BASSANIO (1)	Pope		
GRATIANO	Bernard		
LORENZO	Johnstone		
LAUNCELOT	Quick		
SOLANIO	Gardner		
SALARINO (1)	Davies		
GOBBO (1)	Wewitzer		
DUKE (1)	Fearon		
TUBAL	Thompson		
JESSICA	Mrs Mountain		
NERISSA (1)	Mrs Inchbald		
PORTIA	Mrs Pope		

(1) *Nov. 6*

SHYLOCK	Harley
ANTONIO	[F.] Aickin
BASSANIO	Farren
SALARINO	Egan [Jr.]
GOBBO	Cubitt
DUKE	Powel
NERISSA	Miss Chapman

[In the middle of his first scene Macklin's memory failed him.[1] He apologized to the audience, and Ryder, who had been asked by the manager to be prepared for this eventuality, finished the part (PA, May 9; J. T. Kirkman, *Memoirs of . . . Macklin*, 1799, ii. 327).]

1790 COVENT GARDEN
May 1

SHYLOCK	King
ANTONIO	[F.] Aickin
BASSANIO	Farren
GRATIANO	Bernard
LORENZO	Davies
LAUNCELOT	Quick
SOLANIO	Evatt
SALARINO	Egan [Jr.]
GOBBO	Cubitt
DUKE	Powel
TUBAL	Thompson
JESSICA	Mrs Mountain
NERISSA	Miss Chapman
PORTIA	Mrs Pope

HAYMARKET
June 22

SHYLOCK	Ryder
ANTONIO	[J.] Aickin

[1] Macklin was at this time nearly ninety; he had first appeared as Shylock forty-eight years earlier.

THE MERCHANT OF VENICE

1790 HAYMARKET (cont.)

June 22 (cont.)

GRATIANO	R. Palmer
GOBBO	Barrett
TUBAL	Chapman
LORENZO	Davies
LAUNCELOT	Moss
DUKE	Usher
SOLANIO	Evatt
SALARINO	Iliff
BASSANIO	Bensley
JESSICA	Mrs [M.] Taylor
NERISSA	Miss Fontenelle
PORTIA	Miss Ryder

1792 DRURY LANE (company at KING'S, HAYMARKET)

Mar. 10

DUKE	Packer
ANTONIO	Bensley
BASSANIO	Wroughton
SOLANIO	Whitfield
SALARINO	Barrymore
GRATIANO	R. Palmer
LORENZO	Dignum
SHYLOCK	Kemble
TUBAL	[F.] Waldron
LAUNCELOT	Suett
GOBBO	Jones
LEONARDO	[J.] Cooke
BALTHAZAR	Maddocks
PORTIA	Mrs Siddons
NERISSA	Mrs Goodall
JESSICA	Mrs Bland

HAYMARKET

Feb. 20

BASSANIO	Baker
ANTONIO	A Gentleman [unidentified]
GRATIANO	[Lee] Lewes
LAUNCELOT	Gull
LORENZO	Tanner
SHYLOCK	Wilkinson
NERISSA	Miss Chatterley
PORTIA	A Young Lady [probably Miss Thompson (DNB, under Mary Anne Clarke)]

THE MERCHANT OF VENICE

1793 DRURY LANE (company at HAYMARKET)
Mar. 5

DUKE	Packer
ANTONIO	Bensley
BASSANIO	Wroughton
SOLANIO	Whitfield
SALARINO	Barrymore
GRATIANO	Dodd
LORENZO	Dignum
SHYLOCK	Kemble
TUBAL	[F.] Waldron
LAUNCELOT	[J.] Bannister
GOBBO	Suett
LEONARDO	[J.] Cooke
BALTHAZAR	Maddocks
PORTIA	Mrs Siddons
NERISSA	Miss Collins
JESSICA	Miss Heard

[Both Pb and PA assign JESSICA to Mrs Bland. But she was indisposed, and Miss Heard substituted for her (TM, Apr. 1793, 243).]

1795 DRURY LANE
Mar. 10

DUKE	Packer
ANTONIO	Bensley
BASSANIO	Wroughton
SOLANIO	Whitfield
SALARINO	Barrymore
GRATIANO	Dodd
LORENZO	Dignum
SHYLOCK	Kemble
TUBAL	[F.] Waldron
LAUNCELOT	[J.] Bannister
GOBBO	Suett
LEONARDO	Evans
PORTIA	Mrs Siddons
NERISSA	Mrs Goodall
JESSICA	Miss Collins

[In the bill LEONARDO is omitted, and JESSICA is assigned to Mrs Bland. 'Leonardo Mr. Evans, Mr. Cooke Ill; Jessica Miss Collins, Mrs. Bland Ill' (Powell).]

HAYMARKET
Aug. 3

SHYLOCK	[J.] Bannister
ANTONIO	Bensley
GRATIANO	Fawcett [Jr.]
GOBBO	Wathen
TUBAL	[F.] Waldron

THE MERCHANT OF VENICE

1795 HAYMARKET (cont.)
Aug. 3 (cont.)

LORENZO	Davies
LAUNCELOT	Suett
DUKE	Benson
SOLANIO	Caulfield
SALARINO	C. Kemble
LEONARDO	Lyons
BALTHAZAR	Ledger
BASSANIO	Barrymore
JESSICA	Mrs Bland
NERISSA	A Young Gentlewoman [Miss Logan (H–B MS index to 1795 season); first appearance on the stage]
PORTIA	Mrs [S.] Kemble

1796 DRURY LANE
Dec. 16

DUKE	Packer
ANTONIO	Wroughton
BASSANIO	Barrymore
SOLANIO	Whitfield
SALARINO	Campbell
GRATIANO	R. Palmer
LORENZO	Dignum
SHYLOCK	Kemble
TUBAL	Maddocks
LAUNCELOT	Suett
GOBBO	Hollingsworth
LEONARDO	[J.] Cooke
BALTHAZAR	Trueman
PIETRO	Webb
STEPHANO	Evans
PORTIA	Mrs Siddons
NERISSA	Miss DeCamp
JESSICA	Mrs Bland

COVENT GARDEN

May 12

SHYLOCK (1)	Harley
ANTONIO	Macready
BASSANIO	Pope
GRATIANO (1)	Knight
LORENZO (1)	Johnstone
LAUNCELOT	Quick
SOLANIO (1)	Claremont
SALARINO (1)	[D.] Williamson
GOBBO	Powel

(1) Sept. 30; Oct. 7

SHYLOCK	Murray [first appearance, *Sept. 30*, in London]
GRATIANO	Farley (on *Oct. 7* only)
LORENZO	Townsend
SOLANIO	Haymes
SALARINO	Claremont
NERISSA added	Miss Mansel
TUBAL	Thompson
BALTHAZAR	Ledger

440

THE MERCHANT OF VENICE

1796 COVENT GARDEN (cont.)
May 12 (cont.)

DUKE	Davenport
JESSICA	Mrs Mountain
NERISSA (1)	Mrs Townsend
PORTIA	Mrs Pope

HAYMARKET
June 16, 21; Aug. 6

SHYLOCK	[J.] Palmer
ANTONIO	[J.] Aickin
GRATIANO	R. Palmer
GOBBO	Wathen
TUBAL	[F.] Waldron
LORENZO	Davies
LAUNCELOT	Suett
DUKE	Usher
SOLANIO	Caulfield
SALARINO	Trueman
LEONARDO	Lyons
BALTHAZAR	Ledger
BASSANIO	C. Kemble
JESSICA	Mrs Bland
NERISSA	Miss Logan
PORTIA	Mrs [S.] Kemble

Aug. 30

SHYLOCK	[J.] Palmer
ANTONIO	[J.] Aickin
BASSANIO	C. Kemble
GRATIANO	R. Palmer
PORTIA	Mrs [S.] Kemble

[The above consisted of IV. i only. The entertainment on this evening was called *The School of Shakespeare*, for a description of which see p. 101.]

1797 DRURY LANE
Feb. 11

DUKE	Packer
ANTONIO	Wroughton
BASSANIO	Barrymore
SOLANIO (1)	Whitfield
SALARINO (1)	Campbell
GRATIANO (1)	R. Palmer
LORENZO	Dignum
SHYLOCK (1)	Kemble
TUBAL	Maddocks
LAUNCELOT	Suett
PORTIA	Mrs Siddons

(1) Dec. 2, 13

SOLANIO	Trueman
SALARINO	Holland
GRATIANO	Russell (on *Dec. 2* only)
SHYLOCK	Archer (on *Dec. 13* only; first appearance in London)
NERISSA added	Mrs Goodall
GOBBO	Hollingsworth
LEONARDO	Evans

441

THE MERCHANT OF VENICE

1797 DRURY LANE (*cont.*)
Feb. 11 (cont.)
    NERISSA (1)   Miss DeCamp
    JESSICA   Mrs Bland

COVENT GARDEN
Nov. 3
    SHYLOCK   Murray
    BASSANIO   Whitfield
    GRATIANO   Knight
    LORENZO   Clarke
    LAUNCELOT   Quick
    SALARINO   Claremont
    SOLANIO   Toms
    GOBBO   Powel
    DUKE   Davenport
    TUBAL   Thompson
    BALTHAZAR   Ledger
    ANTONIO   Holman
    JESSICA   Mrs Mountain
    NERISSA   Miss Mansel
    PORTIA   Miss Betterton

HAYMARKET
Aug. 28, 29
    SHYLOCK   Elliston
    ANTONIO   [J.] Aickin
    GRATIANO   R. Palmer
    LORENZO   Davies
    TUBAL   [F.] Waldron
    GOBBO   [G.] Waldron
    LAUNCELOT   Suett
    DUKE   Davenport
    SOLANIO   Caulfield
    SALARINO   Trueman
    LEONARDO   Lyons
    BALTHAZAR   Ledger
    BASSANIO   C. Kemble
    JESSICA   Mrs Bland
    NERISSA   Mrs Harlowe
    PORTIA   Miss DeCamp

1798 DRURY LANE
Nov. 13
    DUKE   Packer
    ANTONIO   Archer
    BASSANIO   Barrymore

THE MERCHANT OF VENICE

1798 DRURY LANE (cont.)
Nov. 13 (cont.)

SOLANIO	Trueman
SALARINO	Holland
GRATIANO	R. Palmer
LORENZO	Dignum
SHYLOCK	Kemble
TUBAL	Maddocks
LAUNCELOT	Suett
GOBBO	Hollingsworth
LEONARDO	Evans
PORTIA	Mrs Siddons
NERISSA	Miss DeCamp
JESSICA	Mrs Bland

COVENT GARDEN
May 18

SHYLOCK	Murray
BASSANIO	Pope
LAUNCELOT	Munden
GRATIANO	Knight
LORENZO	Townsend
SALARINO	Claremont
SOLANIO	Toms
GOBBO	Powel
DUKE	Davenport
TUBAL	Thompson
BALTHAZAR	Ledger
ANTONIO	Holman
JESSICA	Mrs Mountain
NERISSA	Miss Mansel
PORTIA	Miss Betterton

HAYMARKET
Aug. 29; Sept. 5

SHYLOCK	C. Kemble
ANTONIO	[J.] Aickin
GRATIANO	R. Palmer
LORENZO	Davies
TUBAL	[F.] Waldron
GOBBO	[G.] Waldron
LAUNCELOT	Suett
DUKE	Davenport
SOLANIO	Caulfield
SALARINO	Trueman
LEONARDO	Lyons
BALTHAZAR	Ledger
BASSANIO	Barrymore

1798 HAYMARKET (cont.)
Aug. 29; Sept. 5 (cont.)

JESSICA	Mrs Bland
NERISSA	Mrs Harlowe
PORTIA	Miss DeCamp

1799 DRURY LANE
Nov. 8

DUKE	Packer
ANTONIO	Archer
BASSANIO	Barrymore
SOLANIO	Caulfield
SALARINO	Holland
GRATIANO	[R.] Palmer
LORENZO	Trueman
SHYLOCK	Kemble
TUBAL	Maddocks
LAUNCELOT	Suett
GOBBO	Hollingsworth
LEONARDO	Evans
PORTIA	Mrs Powell
NERISSA	Miss DeCamp
JESSICA	Mrs Bland

COVENT GARDEN
June 7

SHYLOCK	Rees
BASSANIO	Pope
LAUNCELOT	Munden
GRATIANO	Knight
LORENZO	Hill
SALARINO	Claremont
SOLANIO	Klanert
GOBBO	Wilde
DUKE	Davenport
TUBAL	Thompson
BALTHAZAR	Curties
ANTONIO	Holman
JESSICA	Mrs Atkins
NERISSA	Miss Sims
PORTIA	Miss Betterton

HAYMARKET
Apr. 17

PORTIA	Mrs Sumbel
NERISSA	A Young Lady [unidentified; first appearance on the stage].

No other parts assigned

THE MERCHANT OF VENICE

1800 DRURY LANE
Apr. 21

DUKE	Packer
ANTONIO (2)	Archer
BASSANIO	Barrymore
SOLANIO	Trueman
SALARINO	Holland
GRATIANO	[R.] Palmer
LORENZO	Dignum
SHYLOCK	Kemble
TUBAL (2)	Maddocks
LAUNCELOT	Suett
GOBBO (2)	Hollingsworth
LEONARDO	Evans
PORTIA (1, 2)	Mrs Siddons
NERISSA (2)	Miss DeCamp
JESSICA (2)	Miss Heard

(1) *May 19*

PORTIA	Mrs Powell

(2) *Oct. 18; Nov. 5*

ANTONIO	Wroughton
TUBAL	[F.] Waldron (on Nov. 5 only)
GOBBO	Wewitzer
PORTIA	Mrs Powell (on Oct. 18 only)
NERISSA	Miss Heard (on Nov. 5 only)
JESSICA added	Mrs Mountain
BALTHAZAR	Surmont
STEPHANO	Fisher
PIETRO	Webb
JAILER	Sparks

COVENT GARDEN
Nov. 10, 13, 20

SHYLOCK	Cooke
BASSANIO	Pope
GRATIANO	Knight
LAUNCELOT	Munden
GOBBO	Emery
LORENZO	Hill
DUKE	Davenport
SALARINO	Claremont
TUBAL	Thompson
SOLANIO	Klanert
BALTHAZAR	Curties
ANTONIO	Murray
JESSICA	Miss Dixon
NERISSA	Mrs Litchfield
PORTIA (1)	Miss Murray

(1) *Nov. 26*

PORTIA	Mrs Hamilton

THE MERRY WIVES OF WINDSOR

(1) 'As it is acted at the Theatres.'
    1753   Dublin: James Dalton.
    This is a reading edition, verbatim throughout.

(2) 'As Performed at the Theatre-Royal, Drury-Lane. Regulated from the Prompt-Book.'
    1773   John Bell.
    Following are the principal omissions:
      Act I. i. *88–100* ('the fallow greyhound'); iii. *1–36* (Falstaff's being 'out at heels').

Act II. i. *111–72* (Ford is told that Falstaff loves Mrs Ford).
Act IV. *i entire* (William Page's Latin lesson); *iv. 49–81, 84–end* (the arrangements for the plot at Herne's oak); *v. 64–97a* (the Germans commandeer the horses); *vi entire* (Fenton tells the Host about Herne's oak).
Act V. v. *39–108* (Anne Page and the others as fairies).
Throughout there are minor omissions.

(3) 'As it is Acted at the Theatres-Royal in Drury-Lane and Covent-Garden.'
1778   J. Wenman.
This is identical with (2).

(4) 'Marked with the Variations of the Manager's Book, at the Theatre-Royal in Drury-Lane.'
1782   C. Bathurst [&c.].
This is the same as (2), with a few restorations from the original, and a few further omissions, the most important being *I. iv. 136–end* (Mrs Quickly promises to help Fenton), and *V. i. 10–end* (Falstaff describes being cudgelled by Ford).

(5) 'Taken from the Manager's Book at the Theatre-Royal, Covent-Garden.'
1787   For the Proprietors.
This is identical with (4).

(6) 'Revised by J. P. Kemble, Esq.'
1797   C. Lowndes.
Kemble adopts the text of (2), but makes a few restorations from the original, for example: *I. iii. 1–14; II. i. 111–50;* and *IV. vi. 1–10, 48–end*, and a few further omissions, notably: *IV. iii entire* (the Germans need the Host's horses), and *V. i entire* (Falstaff describes being cudgelled by Ford). *IV. vi* is transposed to follow *IV. i*.

1751 COVENT GARDEN

Jan. 25

FALSTAFF	Quin
FORD	Ryan
PAGE	Ridout
FENTON	Gibson
SHALLOW	Collins
CAIUS	[T.] Lacy
EVANS	Arthur
SLENDER	Bennet
ROBIN	Miss Mullart
PISTOL	Cushing
NYM	Holtom
BARDOLPH	Marten
HOST	Dunstall
MRS PAGE	Mrs Barrington

THE MERRY WIVES OF WINDSOR

1751 COVENT GARDEN (cont.)
Jan. 25 (cont.)

ANNE PAGE	Miss Haughton
MRS QUICKLY	Mrs Macklin
MRS FORD	Mrs Woffington

1753 DRURY LANE
May 18

FALSTAFF	Berry
FORD	Havard
EVANS	Yates
SHALLOW	Taswell
PAGE	Winstone
CAIUS	Blakes
SLENDER	Woodward
RUGBY	Marr
HOST	W. Vaughan
BARDOLPH	Clough
PISTOL	Ackman
NYM	Allen
SIMPLE	H. Vaughan
FENTON	Scrase
ROBIN	Master Simson
MRS PAGE	Mrs Mills
ANNE PAGE	Miss Minors
MRS QUICKLY	Mrs James
MRS FORD	Mrs Pritchard

[PA assigns EVANS to Clough, and BARDOLPH to Johnston.]

1754 DRURY LANE
Feb. 20

FALSTAFF	Berry
FORD	Havard
EVANS (2)	Yates
SHALLOW	Taswell
PAGE	Burton
CAIUS	Blakes
SLENDER	Woodward
RUGBY (1, 2)	Marr
HOST	W. Vaughan
FENTON (1)	Scrase
ROBIN (1)	Master Simson
MRS PAGE	Mrs Mills
ANNE PAGE	Miss Minors
MRS QUICKLY (1, 2)	Mrs James
MRS FORD (1, 2)	Miss Haughton

(1) *May 10*

FENTON	Simson
MRS QUICKLY	Mrs Simson
MRS FORD	Mrs Pritchard
added	
WILLIAM PAGE	Master Simson
omitted	
RUGBY, ROBIN	

[The bill states that WILLIAM PAGE would 'be restored by' Master Simson.]

(2) *Dec. 13*

EVANS	Clough
MRS QUICKLY	Mrs Macklin
MRS FORD	Mrs Pritchard
omitted	
RUGBY	

THE MERRY WIVES OF WINDSOR

1754 COVENT GARDEN
May 7

FALSTAFF	Dunstall
FORD	Ryan
PAGE	Ridout
FENTON	Gibson
SLENDER	Bennet
SHALLOW	Collins
CAIUS	Stoppelaer
RUGBY	C. Smith
EVANS	Arthur
SIMPLE	Bencraft
ROBIN	Miss Mullart
PISTOL	Cushing
NYM	Holtom
BARDOLPH	Wignell
HOST	Marten
MRS PAGE	Mrs Barrington
ANNE PAGE	Mrs Baker
MRS QUICKLY	Mrs Pitt
MRS FORD	Mrs Bland

[Genest (iv. 401) assigns SLENDER to Shuter, '1st time'. This is erroneous; there is **no** evidence that Shuter ever acted this part in London.]

1755 DRURY LANE
Jan. 10

FALSTAFF	Berry
FORD (1)	Havard
EVANS	Yates
SHALLOW	Taswell
CAIUS	Blakes
PAGE	Burton
FENTON	Scrase
HOST	W. Vaughan
SLENDER	Woodward
ROBIN	Master Simson
MRS PAGE	Mrs Mills
ANNE PAGE	Miss Minors
MRS QUICKLY	Mrs Macklin
MRS FORD	Mrs Pritchard

(1) *May 2*

FORD	Davies
added	
PISTOL	Ackman

COVENT GARDEN
May 15; Oct. 22; Nov. 11; Dec. 17, 31

FALSTAFF	Shuter
FORD	Ryan
PAGE	Ridout
FENTON	Gibson

448

THE MERRY WIVES OF WINDSOR

1755 COVENT GARDEN (cont.)
May 15; Oct. 22; Nov. 11; Dec. 17, 31 (cont.)

SHALLOW	Collins
CAIUS	Stoppelaer
SLENDER	Bennet
RUGBY	C. Smith
EVANS	Arthur
SIMPLE	Bencraft
ROBIN	Miss Mullart
PISTOL	Cushing
NYM	Holtom
BARDOLPH	Wignell
HOST	Dunstall
MRS PAGE	Mrs Barrington
ANNE PAGE	Mrs Baker
MRS QUICKLY	Mrs Pitt
MRS FORD	Mrs Woffington

1756 DRURY LANE
May 10

FALSTAFF	Berry
FORD	Havard
EVANS	Yates
SHALLOW	Taswell
CAIUS	Blakes
PAGE	Burton
FENTON	Scrase
HOST	W. Vaughan
SLENDER	H. Vaughan
ROBIN	Master Simson
MRS PAGE	Mrs Cowper
ANNE PAGE	Miss Minors
MRS QUICKLY	Mrs Macklin
MRS FORD	Mrs Pritchard

COVENT GARDEN
Feb. 13

FALSTAFF	Shuter
FORD	Ryan
PAGE	Ridout
FENTON	Gibson
SLENDER	Bennet
CAIUS (1)	Stoppelaer
RUGBY (1)	C. Smith
EVANS	Arthur
SHALLOW (3)	Collins

(1) May 5

CAIUS	Holtom
RUGBY	R. Smith
NYM	Hackett

(2) Sept. 20

HOST	Marten

(3) Oct. 29; Nov. 25

SHALLOW	Costollo
SIMPLE	Bencraft
HOST	Marten

THE MERRY WIVES OF WINDSOR

1756 COVENT GARDEN (cont.)
Feb. 13 (cont.)

SIMPLE (3)	Costollo
ROBIN	Miss Mullart
PISTOL	Cushing
NYM (1)	Holtom
BARDOLPH	Wignell
HOST (2, 3)	Dunstall
MRS PAGE	Mrs Barrington
ANNE PAGE	Mrs Baker
MRS QUICKLY	Mrs Pitt
MRS FORD	Mrs Woffington

1757 COVENT GARDEN
Jan. 6; Apr. 19

FALSTAFF	Shuter
FORD	Ryan
PAGE	Ridout
FENTON	Gibson
SLENDER	Bennet
CAIUS	Stoppelaer
RUGBY	C. Smith
EVANS	Arthur
SHALLOW	Collins
SIMPLE	Costollo
ROBIN	Miss Mullart
PISTOL	Cushing
NYM	Holtom
BARDOLPH	Wignell
HOST	Marten
MRS PAGE	Mrs Barrington
ANNE PAGE	Mrs Baker
MRS QUICKLY	Mrs Pitt
MRS FORD (1)	Mrs Woffington

(1) Sept. 23; Nov. 8

MRS FORD	Mrs Hamilton

1758 COVENT GARDEN
Jan. 7

FALSTAFF	Shuter
FORD	Ryan
PAGE	Ridout
FENTON (1, 2)	Gibson
SLENDER	Bennet
CAIUS	Stoppelaer
RUGBY	C. Smith
EVANS (2)	Arthur
SHALLOW (2)	Collins
SIMPLE (2)	Costollo

(1) Apr. 22

FENTON	White

(2) Sept. 25; Oct. 31

FENTON	Fox (on *Sept. 25* only) / Davis (on *Oct. 31* only)
EVANS	Collins
SHALLOW	Costollo
SIMPLE	Holtom
ROBIN	Miss Valois
NYM	Buck

THE MERRY WIVES OF WINDSOR

1758 COVENT GARDEN (cont.)
Jan. 7 (cont.)
ROBIN (2)	Miss Hallam
PISTOL	Cushing
NYM (2)	Holtom
BARDOLPH	Wignell
HOST	Marten
MRS PAGE	Mrs Barrington
ANNE PAGE	Mrs Baker
MRS QUICKLY	Mrs Pitt
MRS FORD	Mrs Hamilton

1759 COVENT GARDEN
Jan. 16
FALSTAFF	Shuter
FORD	Ryan
PAGE	Ridout
FENTON	Davis
SLENDER	Bennet
CAIUS	Stoppelaer
RUGBY (3)	C. Smith
EVANS	Collins
SHALLOW	Costollo
SIMPLE	Holtom
ROBIN	Miss Valois
PISTOL (1, 2, 3)	Cushing
NYM	Buck
BARDOLPH	Wignell
HOST	Marten
MRS PAGE (1)	Mrs Barrington
ANNE PAGE	Mrs Baker
MRS QUICKLY (2)	Mrs Pitt
MRS FORD	Mrs Hamilton

(1) *Apr. 26*
PISTOL	R. Smith
MRS PAGE	Miss Ferguson

(2) *Sept. 26*
PISTOL	R. Smith'
MRS QUICKLY	Mrs Copin

(3) *Dec. 29*
RUGBY	Blakey
PISTOL	R. Smith

Dec. 10
FALSTAFF	Shuter
FORD	Ryan
MRS FORD	Mrs Hamilton

No other parts assigned

[The bill has, 'The other Parts as Usual'.]

1760 DRURY LANE
Apr. 22
FALSTAFF	H. Howard [first appearance on the stage]
FORD	Havard
EVANS	Yates
SHALLOW	Clough

451

1760 DRURY LANE (cont.)
Apr. 22 (cont.)

CAIUS	Blakes
PAGE	Packer
FENTON	Scrase
HOST	Philips
SLENDER	Obrien
SIMPLE	[H.] Vaughan
PISTOL	Ackman
MRS PAGE	Miss Haughton
ANNE PAGE	Mrs Hippisley
MRS QUICKLY	Mrs Bradshaw
MRS FORD	Mrs Pritchard

COVENT GARDEN
Jan. 11

FALSTAFF	Shuter
FORD (1)	Ryan
PAGE	Ridout
FENTON	Davis
SLENDER	Bennet
CAIUS (1)	Holtom
RUGBY (1)	Blakey
EVANS	Collins
SHALLOW	Costollo
SIMPLE (1)	Miss Mullart
ROBIN	Miss Valois
PISTOL	R. Smith
NYM	Buck
BARDOLPH	Wignell
HOST	Marten
MRS PAGE	Mrs Barrington
ANNE PAGE (1)	Mrs Baker
MRS QUICKLY	Mrs Pitt
MRS FORD	Mrs Hamilton

(1) Oct. 17

FORD	Ross
CAIUS	Stoppelaer
RUGBY	C. Smith
SIMPLE	Holtom
ANNE PAGE	Mrs Burden

1761 COVENT GARDEN
Feb. 12

FALSTAFF	Shuter
FORD	Ross
PAGE (1, 2)	Ridout
FENTON	Davis
SLENDER	Bennet
CAIUS (1, 2)	Stoppelaer
RUGBY	C. Smith
EVANS (1)	Collins
SHALLOW	Costollo

(1) Sept. 23

PAGE	Hull
CAIUS	Holtom
EVANS	[P.] Lewis
SIMPLE	Master Younger
ANNE PAGE	Miss Cokayne
MRS FORD	Mrs Ward

omitted PISTOL, NYM, BARDOLPH, HOST

(2) Oct. 15

PAGE	Hull

1761 COVENT GARDEN (cont.)

Feb. 12 (cont.)

SIMPLE (1, 2)	Holtom
ROBIN	Miss Valois
PISTOL (1, 2)	R. Smith
NYM (1, 2)	Buck
BARDOLPH (1, 2)	Wignell
HOST (1, 2)	Marten
MRS PAGE	Mrs Barrington
ANNE PAGE (1)	Mrs Burden
MRS QUICKLY	Mrs Pitt
MRS FORD (1)	Mrs Hamilton

(2) Oct. 15 (cont.)

CAIUS	Holtom
SIMPLE	Master Younger

omitted
SAME as *Sept. 23*

1762 DRURY LANE

May 17

FALSTAFF	Stevens
EVANS	Williams
FORD	Havard
SHALLOW	Weston
CAIUS	Blakes
PAGE	Packer
FENTON	Scrase
SLENDER	Obrien
HOST	Philips
SIMPLE	[H.] Vaughan
PISTOL	Ackman
BARDOLPH	Clough
NYM	Watkins
RUGBY	Marr
MRS PAGE	Miss Haughton
ANNE PAGE	Mrs Hippisley
MRS QUICKLY	Mrs Bradshaw
MRS FORD	Mrs Pritchard

COVENT GARDEN

Jan. 7

FALSTAFF	Shuter
FORD	Ross
PAGE	Hull
FENTON	Davis
SLENDER	Bennet
CAIUS (2)	Holtom
RUGBY (3)	C. Smith
EVANS	Collins
SHALLOW	Costollo
PISTOL	R. Smith

(1) Apr. 3

HOST	Marten
SIMPLE	Master Younger

(2) May 8

CAIUS	Stoppelaer
SIMPLE	Master Younger
ANNE PAGE	Miss Fielding

(3) Oct. 20; Nov. 18

HOST	Marten
SIMPLE	Master Morgan
ANNE PAGE	Miss [E.] Miller

1762 COVENT GARDEN (*cont*).

Jan. 7 (cont.)
  HOST (1, 3) — Dunstall
  NYM (3) — Buck
  BARDOLPH (3) — Wignell
  SIMPLE (1, 2, 3) — Mrs Evans
  ROBIN (3) — Miss Valois
  MRS PAGE — Mrs Barrington
  ANNE PAGE (2, 3) — Mrs Burden
  MRS QUICKLY — Mrs Pitt
  MRS FORD (3) — Mrs Hamilton

(3) *Oct. 20; Nov. 18 (cont.)*
  MRS FORD { Mrs Lewis (on *Oct. 20* only)
            Mrs Ward (on *Nov. 18* only) }
omitted
  RUGBY, NYM, BARDOLPH, ROBIN

1763 COVENT GARDEN
Nov. 10
  FALSTAFF — Shuter
  FORD — Ross
  PAGE — Hull
  CAIUS — Holtom
  EVANS — [P.] Lewis
  SHALLOW — Costollo
  SLENDER — Bennet
  PISTOL — R. Smith
  HOST — Marten
  FENTON — Davis
  SIMPLE — Master Morgan
  MRS PAGE — Mrs Barrington
  ANNE PAGE — Miss [E.] Miller
  MRS QUICKLY — Mrs Pitt
  MRS FORD — Mrs Ward

1764 DRURY LANE
Jan. 4
  FALSTAFF — Love
  EVANS — Yates
  FORD — Havard
  SHALLOW — Weston
  CAIUS — Baddeley
  PAGE — Packer
  FENTON — Jackson
  SLENDER — Obrien
  ROBIN — Miss Rogers
  HOST — Bransby
  SIMPLE — [H.] Vaughan
  PISTOL — Ackman
  BARDOLPH — Clough
  NYM — Watkins

THE MERRY WIVES OF WINDSOR

1764 DRURY LANE (*cont.*)

Jan. 4 (cont.)

RUGBY	Marr
MRS PAGE	Miss Haughton
ANNE PAGE	Mrs Hippisley
MRS QUICKLY	Mrs Bradshaw
MRS FORD	Mrs Pritchard

COVENT GARDEN

Jan. 21

FALSTAFF	Shuter
FORD	Ross
PAGE	Hull
CAIUS	Holtom
EVANS (1)	Hayes
SHALLOW	Costollo
HOST (1)	Dunstall
SLENDER	Bennet
MRS PAGE	Mrs Barrington
ANNE PAGE (1)	Mrs Stephens
MRS QUICKLY	Mrs Pitt
MRS FORD	Mrs Ward

[Genest (v. 55) erroneously assigns EVANS to Lewis.]

(1) *Mar. 8; Oct. 17; Nov. 28*

EVANS	[P.] Lewis
HOST	Marten (on *Mar. 8* only) / Anderson (on *Oct. 17, Nov. 28* only)
ANNE PAGE added	Miss Vincent
FENTON	Davis
PISTOL	R. Smith
NYM	Buck
BARDOLPH	Wignell
SIMPLE	Master Morgan
RUGBY	Cushing (on *Mar. 8* only) / C. Smith (on *Oct. 17, Nov. 28* only)

1765 COVENT GARDEN

Jan. 23

FALSTAFF	Shuter
FORD	Ross
PAGE	Hull
CAIUS	Holtom
EVANS	[P.] Lewis
SHALLOW	Costollo
SLENDER	Bennet
FENTON	Davis
HOST	Anderson
BARDOLPH	Wignell
NYM	Buck
PISTOL (1)	R. Smith
RUGBY	C. Smith
SIMPLE	Master Morgan
MRS PAGE	Mrs Barrington
ANNE PAGE	Miss Vincent
MRS QUICKLY	Mrs Pitt
MRS FORD	Mrs Ward

(1) *Oct. 30*

PISTOL	Cushing

1766 DRURY LANE
Jan. 24

FALSTAFF	Love
EVANS	Yates
FORD	Havard
SHALLOW	Parsons
CAIUS	Baddeley
PAGE	Hurst
FENTON	Strange
SLENDER	Dodd
ROBIN	Miss Rogers
HOST	Bransby
SIMPLE	[H.] Vaughan
PISTOL	Ackman
BARDOLPH	Clough
NYM	Watkins
RUGBY	Marr
MRS PAGE	Mrs Bennet
ANNE PAGE	Mrs Hippisley
MRS QUICKLY	Mrs Bradshaw
MRS FORD	Mrs Pritchard

COVENT GARDEN
Nov. 8

FALSTAFF	Shuter
FORD	Ross
PAGE	Hull
CAIUS	Holtom
EVANS	[P.] Lewis
SHALLOW	Cushing
SLENDER	Bennet
FENTON	Davis
HOST	Anderson
BARDOLPH	Wignell
NYM	Buck
PISTOL	R. Smith
RUGBY	C. Smith
SIMPLE	Morgan
MRS PAGE	Mrs Barrington
ANNE PAGE	Miss Vincent
MRS QUICKLY	Mrs Pitt
MRS FORD	Mrs Ward

1768 DRURY LANE
Jan. 9

FALSTAFF	Love
FORD	Havard
EVANS	Parsons

1768 DRURY LANE (cont.)

Jan. 9 (cont.)

SHALLOW	Hartry
CAIUS	Baddeley
HOST	Bransby
FENTON	Strange
PAGE	Packer
SLENDER	Dodd
SIMPLE	Wingfield
PISTOL	Ackman
BARDOLPH	Fox
ROBIN	Miss Collett
MRS PAGE	Mrs Hopkins
MRS QUICKLY	Mrs Bradshaw
ANNE PAGE	Mrs Hippisley
MRS FORD	Mrs Pritchard

COVENT GARDEN

Oct. 4

FORD	Powell
SLENDER	Woodward
EVANS	Yates
SHALLOW	[P.] Lewis
PISTOL	Cushing
HOST	Dunstall
BARDOLPH	Wignell
PAGE	Hull
FALSTAFF	Shuter
CAIUS	Quick
FENTON	[Lee] Lewes
SIMPLE	Morgan
NYM	Stoppelaer
ROBIN	Master Harris
MRS PAGE	Mrs [T.] Baker
ANNE PAGE	Miss Ward
MRS FORD	Mrs Bulkley

(1) *Oct. 8, 13; Dec. 14*

added
   MRS QUICKLY   Mrs Pitt
[In the acting version published by Bell in 1773 there is the following addition to the cast:
   RUGBY   C. Smith]

1769 DRURY LANE

Dec. 16, 29

FALSTAFF	Love
FORD	[F.] Aickin
EVANS	Parsons
SHALLOW	Hartry
CAIUS	Baddeley
PAGE	Packer
HOST	Bransby
FENTON	Wheeler
SLENDER	Cautherley

THE MERRY WIVES OF WINDSOR

1769 DRURY LANE (cont.)
Dec. 16, 29 (cont.)

SIMPLE	W. Palmer
PISTOL	Ackman
BARDOLPH	Clough
ROBIN	Miss Collett
MRS PAGE	Mrs Stephens
MRS QUICKLY	Mrs Bradshaw
ANNE PAGE	Miss Platt
MRS FORD	Mrs Abington

[In the acting version published by Bell in 1773 there are the following additions to the cast:

NYM	Watkins
RUGBY	Marr]

1771 DRURY LANE
May 27

FALSTAFF	Love
FORD	Davies
EVANS	Parsons
SHALLOW	Hartry
CAIUS	Baddeley
PAGE	Packer
HOST	Bransby
FENTON	Wheeler
SLENDER	Cautherley
SIMPLE	Jacobs
PISTOL	[J.] Booth
BARDOLPH	Kear
NYM	Watkins
ROBIN	Miss Collett
MRS PAGE	Mrs Jefferies
MRS QUICKLY	Mrs Bradshaw
ANNE PAGE	Miss Hayward
MRS FORD	Mrs Abington

1772 DRURY LANE
Jan. 15

FALSTAFF	Love
FORD	[F.] Aickin
EVANS	Parsons
SHALLOW	Hartry
CAIUS	Baddeley
PAGE	Packer
HOST	Bransby
FENTON	Wheeler
SLENDER	Dodd

1772 DRURY LANE (cont.)

Jan. 15 (cont.)

SIMPLE	W. Palmer
PISTOL	Ackman
BARDOLPH	Wright
NYM	Watkins
MRS PAGE	Miss Ambrose
MRS QUICKLY	Mrs Bradshaw
ANNE PAGE	Miss Platt
MRS FORD	Mrs Abington

1777 HAYMARKET

Sept. 3

FALSTAFF	Henderson
SHALLOW	Blissett
EVANS	Parsons
CAIUS	[T.] Jackson
PAGE	Fearon
SLENDER (1)	[R.] Bates
FENTON (1)	R. Palmer
HOST	Massey
BARDOLPH	Kenny
PISTOL	Stevens
ROBIN	Master Hitchcock
SIMPLE	Master Pulley
FORD	[J.] Palmer
MRS PAGE	Mrs Davies
ANNE PAGE	Mrs Colles
MRS QUICKLY	Mrs Love
MRS FORD	Mrs Lisley

(1) *Sept. 9*

SLENDER	R. Palmer
FENTON	Egan

[PA retains Bates as SLENDER, and R. Palmer as FENTON.]

1778 DRURY LANE

Feb. 24, 25, 28; Mar. 9; Apr. 2

FORD	Smith
EVANS	Parsons
CAIUS	Baddeley
PAGE	Packer
HOST	Moody
SHALLOW	[F.] Waldron
FENTON (2)	Farren
SIMPLE	[J.] Burton
BARDOLPH	Wright
PISTOL	Holcroft
NYM (1, 2)	Nash
RUGBY	Carpenter
ROBIN	Master Pulley

(1) *Sept. 17*

omitted
   NYM

(2) *Nov. 6*

FENTON	Lamash
ANNE PAGE	Miss Collett

omitted
   NYM

[PA retains Farren as FENTON, and Mrs Colles as ANNE PAGE.]

1778 DRURY LANE (*cont.*)

Feb. 24, 25, 28; Mar. 9; Apr. 2 (cont.)

SLENDER	Dodd
FALSTAFF	Henderson
MRS PAGE	Miss Pope
ANNE PAGE (2)	Mrs Colles
MRS QUICKLY	Mrs Bradshaw
MRS FORD	Miss Younge

1779 DRURY LANE

Jan. 26

FORD	Smith
EVANS	Parsons
CAIUS	Baddeley
PAGE	Packer
HOST	Moody
SHALLOW	[F.] Waldron
FENTON	Lamash
SIMPLE	[J.] Burton
BARDOLPH	Wright
PISTOL	Holcroft
RUGBY	Carpenter
ROBIN	Master Pulley
SLENDER	Dodd
FALSTAFF	Henderson
MRS PAGE	Miss Pope
ANNE PAGE	Mrs Colles
MRS QUICKLY	Mrs Bradshaw
MRS FORD (1)	Miss Younge

(1) *May 3*

MRS FORD	Mrs Brereton

COVENT GARDEN

Nov. 13

FORD	Wroughton
EVANS	Edwin
CAIUS (1)	Wewitzer
PAGE	Hull
HOST	Booth
FENTON (1)	Whitfield
SHALLOW	[R.] Wilson
SIMPLE	W. Bates
BARDOLPH	Baker
PISTOL	Cushing
SLENDER	Quick
FALSTAFF	Henderson
MRS PAGE (1)	Mrs Bulkley
ANNE PAGE	Mrs Lewis
MRS QUICKLY	Mrs Pitt
MRS FORD	Miss Younge

(1) *Dec. 7, 22*

CAIUS	Whitfield
FENTON	Robson
MRS PAGE	Mrs [S.] Wilson (on Dec. 7 only)

added

ROBIN	Miss Langrish

THE MERRY WIVES OF WINDSOR

1780 COVENT GARDEN
Jan. 21

FORD (1)	Wroughton
EVANS	Edwin
CAIUS (1)	Whitfield
PAGE	Hull
HOST	Booth
FENTON	Robson
SHALLOW	[R.] Wilson
SIMPLE (1)	W. Bates
BARDOLPH (1)	Baker
PISTOL (1)	Cushing
SLENDER	Quick
FALSTAFF	Henderson
MRS PAGE (2)	Mrs Bulkley
ANNE PAGE (2)	Mrs Lewis
MRS QUICKLY	Mrs Pitt
MRS FORD	Miss Younge

(1) *Apr. 28*

FORD	Peile
CAIUS	Wewitzer
omitted	
SIMPLE, BARDOLPH, PISTOL	

(2) *Nov. 1*

MRS PAGE	Mrs [S.] Wilson
ANNE PAGE	Miss [C.] Morris

1781 COVENT GARDEN
Jan. 24, 26

FORD	Wroughton
EVANS	Edwin
CAIUS (3)	Wewitzer
PAGE	Hull
HOST	Booth
FENTON	Robson
SHALLOW	[R.] Wilson
SIMPLE (1, 2, 3)	W. Bates
BARDOLPH	Baker
PISTOL	Cushing
FAIRY (3)	Miss Langrish
SLENDER	Quick
FALSTAFF	Henderson
MRS PAGE (3)	Mrs [S.] Wilson
ANNE PAGE (3)	Mrs Lewis
MRS QUICKLY	Mrs Pitt
MRS FORD (2, 3)	Miss Younge

(1) *Mar. 3; Apr. 25*

SIMPLE	Joules

(2) *Mar. 22*

SIMPLE	Joules
MRS FORD	Mrs Mattocks

(3) *Dec. 8*

CAIUS	Whitfield
SIMPLE	Joules
MRS PAGE	Mrs Whitfield
ANNE PAGE	Miss [C.] Morris
MRS FORD	Mrs Mattocks
omitted	
FAIRY	

[Both Pb and PA assign MRS PAGE to Mrs Wilson, and MRS FORD to Miss Younge. In the JPK bill both these names are deleted. Mrs Whitfield's is written above Mrs Wilson's, but the name of Miss Younge's substitute has been cut by the binder. But she was almost certainly Mrs Mattocks.]

HAYMARKET
Aug. 24

FALSTAFF	Henderson
EVANS	Edwin
SHALLOW	[R.] Wilson
CAIUS	Baddeley
HOST	[C.] Bannister

461

THE MERRY WIVES OF WINDSOR

1781 HAYMARKET (*cont.*)
Aug. 24 (*cont.*)

PAGE	Staunton
SLENDER	R. Palmer
FENTON	Wood
BARDOLPH	Massey
PISTOL	Egan
SIMPLE	Blissett
ROBIN	Master Edwin
FORD	[J.] Palmer
MRS QUICKLY	Mrs Edwin
MRS PAGE	Mrs Hitchcock
ANNE PAGE	Miss Wewitzer
MRS FORD	Miss Farren

[In the bill Staunton's name is misprinted 'Stanton'.]

1782 COVENT GARDEN
Jan. 25

FORD	Wroughton
EVANS	Edwin
CAIUS (3)	Whitfield
PAGE	Hull
HOST (1)	Booth
FENTON (1, 3)	Robson
SHALLOW (2)	Fearon
SIMPLE (1)	Joules
BARDOLPH (1, 3)	Baker
PISTOL (1, 3)	Cushing
SLENDER (3)	Quick
FALSTAFF	Henderson
MRS PAGE	Mrs [S.] Wilson
ANNE PAGE (1, 2)	Miss [C.] Morris
MRS QUICKLY	Mrs Pitt
MRS FORD (1)	Mrs Mattocks

(1) *Apr. 27*

ANNE PAGE	Mrs Lewis
MRS FORD	Miss Younge

omitted
   HOST, FENTON, SIMPLE, BARDOLPH, PISTOL

(2) *May 21*

SHALLOW	[F.] Waldron
ANNE PAGE	Mrs Lewis

added
   FAIRY   Miss Langrish

[Both Pb and PA retain Fearon as SHALLOW. In the JPK bill his name is deleted, and that of Waldron substituted. PA assigns MRS FORD to Miss Younge.]

(3) *Oct. 17*

CAIUS	Wewitzer
FENTON	Davies
BARDOLPH	[R.] Bates
PISTOL	Egan
SLENDER	W. Bates

1783 COVENT GARDEN
Jan. 18

FORD	Wroughton
EVANS	Edwin
CAIUS	Wewitzer
PAGE	Hull
SHALLOW	[R.] Wilson
FALSTAFF	Henderson
MRS PAGE	Mrs [S.] Wilson
MRS FORD	Mrs Mattocks

462

THE MERRY WIVES OF WINDSOR

1783 COVENT GARDEN (*cont.*)

Feb. 14, 22

FORD	Wroughton
EVANS	Edwin
CAIUS	Wewitzer
PAGE	Hull
HOST	Booth
FENTON (2)	Davies
SHALLOW (1)	[R.] Wilson
SIMPLE (1, 2)	Joules
BARDOLPH (1)	[R.] Bates
PISTOL (2)	Egan
SLENDER (1, 2)	W. Bates
FALSTAFF	Henderson
MRS PAGE (1, 2)	Mrs [S.] Wilson
ANNE PAGE (2)	Miss [C.] Morris
MRS QUICKLY	Mrs Pitt
MRS FORD	Mrs Mattocks

(1) *May 21*

SHALLOW	Fearon
SLENDER	Stevens
MRS PAGE	Mrs Whitfield
omitted	
SIMPLE, BARDOLPH	

(2) *Oct. 11; Dec. 30*

FENTON	J. Bates
PISTOL	Thompson
SLENDER	Quick
MRS PAGE	Mrs Whitfield (on *Oct. 11* only)
ANNE PAGE	Mrs Chalmers
omitted	
SIMPLE	

[On *Feb. 22* Pb assigns SHALLOW to Fearon. PA retains Wilson, which appears to be correct: a review of this performance in PA, Feb. 24, mentions Wilson as SHALLOW.]

1784 DRURY LANE

Jan. 10, 13

FORD	Smith
EVANS	Parsons
CAIUS	Baddeley
PAGE	Packer
HOST	Moody
SHALLOW	[F.] Waldron
FENTON	Phillimore
SIMPLE	[J.] Burton
BARDOLPH	Wright
PISTOL	Alfred
NYM	[J.] Wilson
SLENDER (1)	Dodd
FALSTAFF	[Lee] Lewes
MRS PAGE	Miss Pope
ANNE PAGE (1, 2)	Miss Wheeler
MRS QUICKLY	Mrs Hopkins
MRS FORD	Miss Farren

(1) *Jan. 27*

SLENDER	Ward
ANNE PAGE	Miss Field

(2) *May 14; Oct. 11*

ANNE PAGE	Miss Field

COVENT GARDEN

Mar. 23

FORD	Wroughton
EVANS	Edwin
CAIUS	Wewitzer

(1) *May 4*

SHALLOW	Fearon
omitted	
PISTOL, BARDOLPH	

463

THE MERRY WIVES OF WINDSOR

1784 COVENT GARDEN (cont.)

Mar. 23 (cont.)

PAGE	Hull
HOST	Booth
FENTON (2)	Chalmers
PISTOL (1)	Thompson
BARDOLPH (1)	[R.] Bates
SHALLOW (1, 2)	[R.] Wilson
SLENDER	Quick
FALSTAFF	Henderson
MRS PAGE (2)	Mrs [S.] Wilson
ANNE PAGE (2)	Mrs Chalmers
MRS QUICKLY	Mrs Pitt
MRS FORD (2)	Mrs Mattocks

(2) *Nov. 13; Dec. 11*

FENTON	Cubitt
SHALLOW	Fearon (on *Dec.* 11 only)
MRS PAGE	Mrs Inchbald
ANNE PAGE	Mrs Lewis
MRS FORD	Mrs Bates

1785 COVENT GARDEN

Apr. 30

FORD	Wroughton
EVANS	Edwin
SHALLOW	Fearon
PAGE	Hull
SLENDER	Quick
CAIUS	Wewitzer
HOST	Booth
FENTON	Cubitt
PISTOL	Thompson
BARDOLPH	[R.] Bates
FALSTAFF	Henderson
MRS PAGE	Mrs [S.] Wilson
ANNE PAGE	Mrs Lewis
MRS QUICKLY	Mrs Pitt
MRS FORD	Mrs Bates

(1) *May 24; Nov. 1*

added

| SIMPLE | [T.] Kennedy |
| RUGBY | Stevens |

[On *Nov. 1* both Pb and PA assign SHALLOW to Wilson. In the JPK bill his name is deleted, but the substitute name has been cut by the binder. In a review of this performance in PA, Nov. 2, Wilson is referred to as having acted SHALLOW. In the *General Advertiser*, Nov. 3, the accuracy of this review is questioned, and the statement made that Wilson was confined to his home with gout. His substitute is not named, but he was almost certainly Fearon.]

1786 COVENT GARDEN

Nov. 29

FORD	Farren
EVANS	Edwin
SHALLOW	Fearon
PAGE	Hull
SLENDER	[T.] Kennedy
CAIUS	Wewitzer
HOST	Thompson
PISTOL	Cubitt
FENTON	Macready
BARDOLPH	Swords
FALSTAFF	Ryder

THE MERRY WIVES OF WINDSOR

1786 COVENT GARDEN (cont.)
Nov. 29 (cont.)

MRS PAGE	Mrs Bates
ANNE PAGE	Mrs Lewis
MRS QUICKLY	Mrs Pitt
MRS FORD	Mrs Pope

1787 COVENT GARDEN
Jan. 18; Feb. 3

FORD	Farren
EVANS	Edwin
SHALLOW	Fearon
PAGE	Hull
SLENDER (3)	[T.] Kennedy
CAIUS (1)	Wewitzer
HOST (3)	Thompson
PISTOL (1, 2, 3)	Cubitt
FENTON	Macready
BARDOLPH (3)	Swords
FALSTAFF	Ryder
MRS PAGE (2, 3, 4)	Mrs Bates
ANNE PAGE (3)	Mrs Lewis
MRS QUICKLY	Mrs Pitt
MRS FORD	Mrs Pope

(1) *Apr. 13*

CAIUS	Cubitt
PISTOL	Gaudry

(2) *June 2*

PISTOL	Helme
MRS PAGE added	Mrs Inchbald
NYM	Gaudry
RUGBY	Stevens

(3) *Sept. 17*

SLENDER	Cubitt
HOST	Booth
PISTOL	Thompson
BARDOLPH	Helme
MRS PAGE	Mrs Wells
ANNE PAGE added	Miss Rowson
SIMPLE	Rock
RUGBY	Stevens

(4) *Nov. 26.* No parts assigned

[See p. 84. The BM bill for this night gives *The Tender Husband*. It is deleted, and has a MS annotation stating that in the substitute play Mrs Bernard acted MRS PAGE.]

1788 DRURY LANE
May 21

FORD (1, 2)	Smith
EVANS (1)	Hollingsworth
CAIUS	Baddeley
PAGE	Packer
HOST	Moody
SHALLOW	[F.] Waldron
SIMPLE	[J.] Burton
FENTON	Phillimore
BARDOLPH (1, 2)	[W.] Bates
PISTOL	Alfred
NYM	[J.] Wilson
RUGBY	Spencer

(1) *Sept. 27*

FORD	Wroughton
EVANS	Parsons
BARDOLPH	Hollingsworth

(2) *Dec. 11*

FORD	Wroughton
BARDOLPH	Benson
SLENDER	Suett
MRS QUICKLY	Mrs Booth

THE MERRY WIVES OF WINDSOR

1788 DRURY LANE (cont.)
May 21 (cont.)

SLENDER (2)	Dodd
FALSTAFF	[J.] Palmer
MRS PAGE	Miss Pope
ANNE PAGE	Miss Collins
MRS QUICKLY (2)	Mrs Hopkins
MRS FORD	Miss Farren

COVENT GARDEN
Nov. 12

FORD	Farren
EVANS	Edwin
PAGE	Hull
CAIUS	Wewitzer
HOST	Booth
FENTON	Macready
SHALLOW	Fearon
SIMPLE	Rock
RUGBY	Stevens
BARDOLPH	Helme
PISTOL	Thompson
SLENDER	Cubitt
FALSTAFF	Ryder
MRS PAGE	Mrs Bernard
ANNE PAGE	Mrs Lewis
MRS QUICKLY	Mrs Pitt
MRS FORD	Mrs Pope

1789 COVENT GARDEN
Oct. 9

FORD	Farren
EVANS	Edwin
PAGE	Hull
CAIUS	C. Powell
HOST	Thompson
FENTON	Macready
SHALLOW	Powel
SIMPLE	Milburne
BARDOLPH	Rock
PISTOL	Evatt
SLENDER	Cubitt
FALSTAFF	Ryder
MRS PAGE	Mrs Bernard
ANNE PAGE	Mrs Lewis
MRS QUICKLY	Mrs Pitt
MRS FORD	Mrs Pope

(1) *Dec. 4.* No parts assigned
[For this night both Pb and PA give *The Beggar's Opera*. See p. 89.]

THE MERRY WIVES OF WINDSOR

1790 COVENT GARDEN
Oct. 13

FORD	Farren
EVANS	[R.] Wilson
PAGE	Hull
CAIUS	Marshall
HOST	Thompson
FENTON	Macready
SHALLOW	Powel
SIMPLE	Milburne
BARDOLPH	Rock
PISTOL	Evatt
SLENDER	Cubitt
FALSTAFF	Ryder
MRS PAGE	Mrs Bernard
ANNE PAGE	Mrs Lewis
MRS QUICKLY	Mrs Pitt
MRS FORD	Mrs Pope

1796 DRURY LANE
June 8

FALSTAFF	[J.] Palmer
FENTON	Trueman
SHALLOW	[F.] Waldron
SLENDER	Russell
PAGE	Packer
FORD	Wroughton
EVANS	Dodd
CAIUS	Wewitzer
HOST	Moody
BARDOLPH	Hollingsworth
PISTOL	R. Palmer
NYM	Webb
ROBIN	Master Kean
SIMPLE	[J.] Burton
MRS PAGE	Miss Pope
MRS FORD	Mrs Goodall
ANNE PAGE	Miss Heard
MRS QUICKLY	Mrs Hopkins

COVENT GARDEN
Mar. 14

FORD	Pope
CAIUS (3, 5)	Quick
PAGE	Macready
EVANS	Townsend
SLENDER	Knight
FENTON	Toms

(1) *Mar. 28; Apr. 4*
omitted
   HOST, RUGBY

(2) *Apr. 16*
added
SIMPLE	Simmons
PISTOL	[D.] Williamson
BARDOLPH	Rees

467

1796 COVENT GARDEN (cont.)

Mar. 14 (cont.)
- SHALLOW (5) — Powel
- HOST (1, 5) — Thompson
- RUGBY (1, 5) — Farley
- FALSTAFF — Fawcett [Jr.]
- MRS PAGE — Mrs Mattocks
- ANNE PAGE — Miss Mansel
- MRS QUICKLY — Mrs Davenport
- MRS FORD (4) — Mrs Pope

(3) Apr. 27
- CAIUS — Wilde
- added
- SAME as Apr. 16

(4) Nov. 7
- MRS FORD — Miss Chapman
- added
- SIMPLE — Simmons

(5) Dec. 28
- CAIUS — Murray
- added
- SIMPLE — Simmons
- omitted
- SHALLOW, HOST, RUGBY

1797 COVENT GARDEN

Feb. 13
- FORD (2) — Pope
- CAIUS — Murray
- PAGE (1, 2) — Macready
- EVANS — Townsend
- SLENDER — Knight
- FENTON — Toms
- SHALLOW — Powel
- HOST — Thompson
- RUGBY (2) — Farley
- SIMPLE — Simmons
- BARDOLPH (1, 2) — Street
- FALSTAFF — Fawcett [Jr.]
- MRS PAGE — Mrs Mattocks
- ANNE PAGE — Miss Mansel
- MRS QUICKLY — Mrs Davenport
- MRS FORD — Miss Chapman

(1) Sept. 27
- PAGE — Clarke
- omitted
- BARDOLPH

(2) Nov. 9
- FORD — Whitfield
- PAGE — Clarke
- added
- PISTOL — Davenport
- omitted
- RUGBY, BARDOLPH

A MIDSUMMER-NIGHT'S DREAM

(1) Altered as PYRAMUS AND THISBE, by John Frederick Lampe. In one act.
 1745 H. Woodfall.
For a description of this see my Volume I, 339.

(2) Altered as THE FAIRIES, by David Garrick. In three acts. 'As it is Perform'd at the Theatre-Royal in Drury-Lane.'
 1755 J. and R. Tonson.
Act I consists of *Act I. i* and *II. i. 1–185*. Act II consists of *Act II. i. 186–end* and *ii*. Act III consists of *Act III. ii* and *IV. i. 82–194*. Everything is considerably curtailed. The clowns are entirely omitted.

A MIDSUMMER-NIGHT'S DREAM

The bills announce this as 'A new English opera'. Twenty-eight songs are introduced, set to music by John Christopher Smith.

See also Genest, iv. 407; Odell, i. 358-9.

(3) 'With Alterations and Additions [by George Colman, the elder, and David Garrick], and Several New Songs. As it is Performed at the Theatre-Royal In Drury-Lane.'

1763   J. and R. Tonson. Reprinted Dublin: P. Wilson [&c.], 1764.

Act I consists of *Act I*; Act II of *Act II. i*; Act III of *Act II. ii* and *III. i*; Act IV of *Act III. ii*; and Act V of *Act IV. i. 1-192*, with Bottom's speech on awakening, *206-26*, inserted following *108*. There is considerable curtailment throughout.

Thirty-three songs are introduced, set to music by Michael Arne, J. C. Smith, Dr Charles Burney, Jonathan Battishill, G. F. Handel and Theodore Aylward.

See also Genest, v. 40-41; Odell, i. 376.

(4) Altered as A FAIRY TALE, by George Colman, the elder. In two acts. 'As it is Performed at the Theatre-Royal in Drury-Lane.'

1763   J. and R. Tonson.

Act I consists of *Act I. ii*; *II. i. 1-185*; *II. ii. 1-34*. Act II consists of *Act III. i*; *III. ii. 1-6, 35, 375-7, 394-5*; *IV. i. 1-108*. Everything has been somewhat curtailed, and there are a few short new speeches.

Thirteen songs, with music by Michael Arne and Charles Dibdin, are introduced. This version was prepared from the text of (3).

See also Genest, v. 41; Odell, i. 376.

(5) 'As it is Performed at the Theatre-Royal in the Hay-Market.'

1777   G. Kearsly.

This is identical with (4), but is somewhat shorter. Eleven songs are introduced, the composers being Michael Arne, Charles Dibdin, Dr Burney, James Hook, Theodore Smith and Dr Samuel Arnold.

(6) 'As it is Acted at the Theatres-Royal in Drury-Lane and Covent-Garden.'

1778   J. Wenman.

This is a reading edition, verbatim throughout.

[*as* PYRAMUS AND THISBE]

1751 COVENT GARDEN

Dec. 9

PYRAMUS	Lowe
LION	Howard
WALL	Baker
MOONSHINE	[E.] Roberts
THISBE	Mrs Lampe

A MIDSUMMER-NIGHT'S DREAM [*as* PYRAMUS AND THISBE]

1754 COVENT GARDEN
May 2

PYRAMUS	Lowe
LION	Howard
WALL	Baker
MOONSHINE	[E.] Roberts
THISBE	Mrs Lampe

[*as* THE FAIRIES]

1755 DRURY LANE
Feb. 3, 6, 10, 13, 17, 20, 24;
Mar. 3, 10

THESEUS	Beard
EGEUS	Wilder
LYSANDER	Guadagni
DEMETRIUS	Vernon
OBERON	Master Reinhold [first appearance on the stage (Grove, iv. 361)]
PUCK	Master Moore
FAIRY	Master Evans
HIPPOLYTA	Mrs Jefferson
HERMIA	Sig. Passerini
HELENA (1)	Miss Poitier
TITANIA	Miss [I.] Young

(1) *Oct. 29; Nov. 7*

HELENA Mrs Vernon [i.e. formerly Miss Poitier]
[The bills give neither the parts nor the actors' names. But Miss Poitier married Vernon on June 27 of this year. It is possible that the assignments in Genest (see note under Feb. 3) apply to the two performances listed here.]

[The bills give neither the parts nor the actors' names. The above assignment is taken from the printed text. Genest (iv. 407), on what authority I have been unable to discover, assigns EGEUS to Chamnys [i.e. Champnes], LYSANDER to Sig. Curioni [a 'seconda donna' who occasionally appeared in male parts], DEMETRIUS to Atkins, and HELENA to Mrs Vernon. But see note under Oct. 29.]

[*The original*]

1763 DRURY LANE
Nov. 23

THESEUS	Bransby
EGEUS	Burton
LYSANDER	Vernon
DEMETRIUS	W. Palmer
QUINCE	Love
SNUG	Clough
BOTTOM	Yates
FLUTE	Baddeley
SNOUT	Ackman
STARVELING	Parsons
OBERON	Miss Rogers
PUCK	Master Cape

470

A MIDSUMMER-NIGHT'S DREAM

1763 DRURY LANE (cont.)
Nov. 23 (cont.)

1ST FAIRY	Miss Wright
2ND FAIRY	Master Raworth
MUSTARDSEED	R. Palmer [first appearance on the stage]
HIPPOLYTA	Mrs Hopkins
HERMIA	Miss [I.] Young
HELENA	Mrs Vincent [Jr.]
TITANIA	Miss Ford

[The bill gives the actors' names only. The above assignment is taken from the printed text. R. Palmer appears neither in the bill nor in the text; the assignment is taken from Gilliland (ii. 890).]

[as A FAIRY TALE]
DRURY LANE
Nov. 26

QUINCE	Love
BOTTOM (1)	Yates
SNUG	Clough
FLUTE (1)	Baddeley
SNOUT	Ackman
STARVELING	Parsons
OBERON	Miss Rogers
PUCK	Master Cape
1ST FAIRY	Miss Wright
2ND FAIRY	Master Raworth
TITANIA	Miss Ford

(1) *Nov. 28, 29; Dec. 6, 16, 19, 22, 23*

BOTTOM	Baddeley
FLUTE	Castle

[C-H, Nov. 28: 'Mr. Yates sent me the Part of Bottom, and said I must give it to Somebody else ... Mr. Baddeley played it.' The bills give both Baddeley's and Castle's names.]

[All the bills for this year give the actors' names only.[1] The above assignment is taken from the printed text, which, as on *Nov. 28*, &c., assigns BOTTOM to Baddeley, and FLUTE to Castle.]

1764 DRURY LANE
Feb. 9, 10, 13

QUINCE (1, 2)	Love
BOTTOM	Baddeley
SNUG (2)	Clough
FLUTE (2)	Castle
SNOUT	Ackman
STARVELING	Parsons
OBERON	Miss Rogers
PUCK	Master Cape
1ST FAIRY	Miss Wright
2ND FAIRY	Master Raworth
TITANIA	Miss Ford

[All the bills for this year give the actors' names only. On *Feb. 13* PA gives Moody's name in place of Love's (i.e. as QUINCE).]

(1) *Feb. 15; Mar. 3, 6; May 5, 8, 15, 17, 23; Sept. 22, 27*

QUINCE	Moody

[On *May 23* the bill has only, 'The Characters as Usual'. On *Sept. 22* Genest (v. 61) has, 'Moody seems to have played Bottom instead of Yates'. This is incorrect: Baddeley succeeded Yates as BOTTOM, and Moody succeeded Love as QUINCE.]

(2) *Oct. 6, 11, 15, 17, 27; Nov. 14*

QUINCE	Moody
SNUG	Strange
FLUTE	Watkins (on *Oct. 17, 27, Nov. 14* only)

[On *Oct. 17, 27, Nov. 14* PA retains Castle's name (i.e. as FLUTE).]

---

[1] No bill of *A Fairy Tale*, from Nov. 26, 1763 to Apr. 28, 1767, assigns the parts. The changes in the cast are, therefore, deduced from the substitution of one actor's name for another's.

A MIDSUMMER-NIGHT'S DREAM [as A FAIRY TALE]

1765 DRURY LANE
Jan. 26, 28, 31; Mar. 21; Apr. 17   (1) *Dec. 14, 18*

QUINCE	Moody	STARVELING	Castle
BOTTOM	Baddeley	omitted	
SNUG	Strange	2ND FAIRY	
FLUTE	Watkins		
SNOUT	Ackman		
STARVELING (1)	Parsons		
OBERON	Miss Rogers		
PUCK	Master Cape		
1ST FAIRY	Miss Wright		
2ND FAIRY (1)	Master Raworth		
TITANIA	Miss Ford		

[All the bills for this year give the actors' names only, except on *Jan. 28*, when all the names are omitted.]

1766 DRURY LANE
Feb. 11, 18; Apr. 9   (1) *Apr. 12; May 14, 19; Oct. 28, 31*

QUINCE	Moody	SNOUT	Ackman
BOTTOM	Baddeley	[Castle's name (i.e. as SNOUT) is	
SNUG	Strange	retained on *May 19* by Pb, and on	
FLUTE	Watkins	*Oct. 28, 31* by PA.]	
SNOUT (1)	Castle		
STARVELING	Parsons		
OBERON	Miss Rogers		
PUCK	Master Cape		
FAIRY	Miss Wright		
TITANIA	Miss Ford		

[All the bills for this year give the actors' names only.]

1767 DRURY LANE
Apr. 28

QUINCE	Moody
BOTTOM	Baddeley
SNUG	Strange
FLUTE	Watkins
SNOUT	Ackman
STARVELING	Parsons
OBERON	Miss Rogers
PUCK	Master Cape
FAIRY	Mrs Arne
TITANIA	Miss Ford

[The bill gives the actors' names only.]

A MIDSUMMER-NIGHT'S DREAM [*as* A FAIRY TALE]

1777 HAYMARKET

July 18, 21, 22, 23, 29; Aug. 25; Sept. 5

QUINCE	Edwin
BOTTOM	Parsons
SNUG	[C.] Bannister
FLUTE	Blissett
SNOUT	Kenny
STARVELING	Peirce
OBERON	Miss [C.] Morris
PUCK	The Admiral of Lilliput [Master Edwin]
1ST FAIRY	Master Harrison
2ND FAIRY	Miss Twist
TITANIA	Miss P[eggy] Farren

[The bills omit FLUTE, OBERON and TITANIA. The assignment of these parts is taken from the printed text, which also identifies Master Edwin.]

MUCH ADO ABOUT NOTHING

(1) 'As Performed at the Theatre-Royal, Drury-Lane. Regulated from the Prompt-Book.'

1773   John Bell.

Following are the principal omissions:
Act II. i. 118–31 (Ursula and Antonio at the masquerade); *iii.* 141–65 ('Benedick and Beatrice between the sheet'), 200–19 (Benedick ironically praised by his friends).
Act III. iv. 55–71a ('I cannot smell').
Act IV. i. 225–45 (the Friar's assurance that Claudio will grieve for Hero).
Act V. i. 11–26 (the patient man), 164–86 (Don Pedro recounts Beatrice's praise of Benedick's wit); *iii entire* (Claudio at Hero's supposed tomb).
    Throughout there are minor omissions. I. *ii* is the first scene of *II*. In IV. *ii* a new character, the Town Clerk, is introduced; he has most of Dogberry's speeches in this scene, except for the concluding one.

(2) 'As it is Acted at the Theatres-Royal in Drury-Lane and Covent-Garden.'

1778   J. Wenman.

This is identical with (1).

(3) 'Taken from the Manager's Book at the Theatre Royal, Drury-Lane.'

n.d. [*c.* 1788]   R. Butters.

This is identical with (1), except for a few further omissions.

(4) 'Revised by J. P. Kemble, and acted ... at the Theatre Royal, Drury-Lane.'

1797   C. Lowndes.

This is identical with (1), except for further omissions, the most important

MUCH ADO ABOUT NOTHING

being *II. i. 45-53* (Beatrice's arrival in heaven), *105-17* (Balthazar and Margaret at the masquerade); and *III. iv. 5-38a* (Hero's wardrobe), *79b-94* (Margaret is confident that Benedick loves Beatrice).

1751 DRURY LANE

Apr. 11

BENEDICK	Garrick
DON PEDRO	Mozeen
LEONATO	Berry
CLAUDIO	Palmer
BALTHAZAR (1)	Beard
HERO	Mrs Willoughby
BEATRICE	Mrs Pritchard

(1) *Apr. 25*

BALTHAZAR	Wilder
added	
DON JOHN	Winstone
DOGBERRY	Taswell
VERGES	Shuter
CONRADE	Mozeen
TOWN CLERK	James
SEXTON	Ray
MARGARET	Mrs Pitt
URSULA	Miss Minors

[Both DON PEDRO and CONRADE are assigned to Mozeen. This is almost certainly a misprint; doubling these parts is not likely.]

Oct. 11; Nov. 1

BENEDICK	Garrick
DON PEDRO	Havard
LEONATO	Berry
DON JOHN	Winstone
CLAUDIO	Palmer
ANTONIO	Simson
FRIAR	Burton
BORACHIO	Blakes
DOGBERRY	Taswell
BALTHAZAR	Beard
VERGES	Shuter
CONRADE	Mozeen
TOWN CLERK	R. Vaughan
SEXTON	Ray
HERO	Mrs Willoughby
MARGARET (1)	Mrs Havard
URSULA	Miss Minors
BEATRICE	Mrs Pritchard

(1) *Nov. 27*

MARGARET	Mrs Yates

1752 DRURY LANE

Jan. 8, 23

BENEDICK	Garrick
DON PEDRO	Havard
LEONATO	Berry
DON JOHN	Winstone
CLAUDIO	Palmer
ANTONIO (1, 2)	Simson
FRIAR (1, 2)	Burton
BORACHIO (1, 2)	Blakes

(1) *Mar. 19*

HERO	Mrs Ward
omitted	

ANTONIO, FRIAR, BORACHIO, VERGES, CONRADE, TOWN CLERK, SEXTON

(2) *Apr. 9*

HERO	Mrs Mills
MARGARET	Mrs Yates
omitted	

SAME as *Mar. 19*

474

MUCH ADO ABOUT NOTHING

1752 DRURY LANE (cont.)

Jan. 8, 23 (cont.)

DOGBERRY	Taswell
BALTHAZAR	Beard
VERGES (1, 2)	Shuter
CONRADE (1, 2)	Mozeen
TOWN CLERK (1, 2, 3)	R. Vaughan
SEXTON (1, 2, 3)	Ray
HERO (1, 2, 3)	Mrs Willoughby
MARGARET (2)	Mrs Havard
URSULA	Miss Minors
BEATRICE	Mrs Pritchard

(3) Oct. 19; Nov. 13

TOWN CLERK	W. Vaughan
SEXTON	Clough
HERO	Mrs Davies

[On *Jan. 23* Pb assigns the TOWN CLERK to W. Vaughan, and the SEXTON to Costollo.]

1753 DRURY LANE

Jan. 4, 17

BENEDICK	Garrick
DON PEDRO (1, 2)	Mozeen
LEONATO	Berry
CLAUDIO	Palmer
BALTHAZAR	Beard
HERO	Mrs Davies
BEATRICE	Mrs Pritchard

(1) Mar. 26

DON PEDRO added	Havard
DON JOHN	Winstone
DOGBERRY	Taswell

(2) Sept. 27; Nov. 21

DON PEDRO added	Havard
DON JOHN	Bransby
FRIAR	Burton
DOGBERRY	Taswell
ANTONIO	Simson
VERGES	Philips
BORACHIO	Blakes
CONRADE	Mozeen
MARGARET	Mrs Havard
URSULA	Miss Minors

1754 DRURY LANE

Jan. 12

BENEDICK	Garrick
DON PEDRO	Havard
LEONATO	Berry
CLAUDIO	Palmer
DON JOHN (1, 2, 3)	Davies
DOGBERRY (1)	Taswell
ANTONIO (2)	Simson
VERGES (1, 2)	Philips
BORACHIO	Blakes
BALTHAZAR	Beard
HERO	Mrs Davies
BEATRICE	Mrs Pritchard

(1) Mar. 30

DON JOHN	Bransby
DOGBERRY	Yates
VERGES	Vernon

[PA retains Davies as DON JOHN.]

(2) Apr. 30

DON JOHN Bransby
omitted
 ANTONIO, VERGES

(3) Nov. 22; Dec. 11

DON JOHN added	Bransby
CONRADE	Mozeen
FRIAR	Burton
TOWN CLERK	W. Vaughan
SEXTON	Clough
MARGARET	Mrs Havard
URSULA	Miss Minors

MUCH ADO ABOUT NOTHING

1755 DRURY LANE
Jan. 9, 24

BENEDICK	Garrick
DON PEDRO	Havard
LEONATO	Berry
DON JOHN	Bransby
CLAUDIO	Palmer
DOGBERRY	Taswell
ANTONIO	Simson
VERGES	Philips
BORACHIO	Blakes
CONRADE (2)	Mozeen
FRIAR (2)	Burton
TOWN CLERK (2)	W. Vaughan
SEXTON (2)	Clough
BALTHAZAR	Beard
HERO	Mrs Davies
MARGARET	Mrs Havard
URSULA	Miss Minors
BEATRICE (1)	Mrs Pritchard

(1) *Apr. 12*

BEATRICE	Miss Haughton

(2) *Nov. 1, 15*
omitted
    CONRADE, FRIAR, TOWN CLERK, SEXTON

1756 DRURY LANE
Jan. 5; Feb. 23

BENEDICK	Garrick
DON PEDRO	Havard
LEONATO	Berry
DON JOHN	Bransby
CLAUDIO	Palmer
DOGBERRY (1, 2)	Taswell
ANTONIO	Simson
VERGES	Philips
BORACHIO	Blakes
BALTHAZAR	Beard
HERO	Mrs Davies
MARGARET (1, 2)	Mrs Havard
URSULA (1, 2)	Miss Minors
BEATRICE (2)	Mrs Pritchard

(1) *Apr. 10; May 28; Oct. 19*

DOGBERRY	Yates (on *Apr. 10* only)

omitted
    MARGARET, URSULA

(2) *Nov. 29, 30; Dec. 4, 18*

DOGBERRY	Yates (on *Dec. 4, 18* only)
BEATRICE	Miss Pritchard

omitted
    MARGARET, URSULA

1757 DRURY LANE
Mar. 19

BENEDICK	Garrick
DON PEDRO	Havard
LEONATO (1)	Davies
CLAUDIO	Palmer
DON JOHN	Bransby
DOGBERRY	Taswell
ANTONIO	Walker
VERGES	Philips

(1) *Apr. 23; Nov. 8; Dec. 21*

LEONATO	Berry

476

1757 DRURY LANE (*cont.*)
Mar. 19 (*cont.*)

BORACHIO	Blakes
BALTHAZAR	Beard
HERO	Mrs Davies
BEATRICE	Miss Pritchard

1758 DRURY LANE
Apr. 5; Sept. 23

BENEDICK	Garrick
DON PEDRO	Havard
LEONATO (1)	Berry
CLAUDIO	Palmer
DON JOHN	Bransby
DOGBERRY (1)	Taswell
FRIAR	Burton
VERGES	Philips
BORACHIO	Blakes
BALTHAZAR	Beard
HERO	Mrs Davies
BEATRICE	Miss Pritchard

(1) *Dec. 23*

LEONATO	Davies
DOGBERRY	Yates

[On *Sept. 23* Genest (iv. 536) erroneously assigns DOGBERRY to Yates.]

1759 DRURY LANE
Feb. 26

BENEDICK	Garrick
DON PEDRO	Havard
LEONATO	Davies
CLAUDIO	Palmer
FRIAR	Burton
DON JOHN	Bransby
DOGBERRY	Yates
VERGES	Philips
BORACHIO	Blakes
BALTHAZAR (2)	Beard
HERO	Mrs Davies
BEATRICE (1)	Miss Pritchard

(1) *Mar. 27*

BEATRICE added	Miss Macklin
MARGARET	Mrs Havard

(2) *Oct. 23; Dec. 15*

BALTHAZAR	Atkins

1760 DRURY LANE
May 23

BENEDICK	Garrick
DON PEDRO	Havard
LEONATO	Davies
CLAUDIO	Palmer
FRIAR	Burton
DON JOHN	Bransby
DOGBERRY	Yates

(1) *Sept. 30; Dec. 16*

BALTHAZAR	Fawcett

1760 DRURY LANE (cont.)

May 23 (cont.)

VERGES	Philips
BORACHIO	Blakes
BALTHAZAR (1)	Atkins
HERO	Mrs Davies
MARGARET	Mrs Havard
BEATRICE	Miss Pritchard

1761 DRURY LANE

Feb. 9

BENEDICK	Garrick
DON PEDRO	Havard
LEONATO	Davies
CLAUDIO	Palmer
FRIAR	Burton
DON JOHN	Bransby
BALTHAZAR	Fawcett
DOGBERRY	Yates
VERGES	Philips
BORACHIO	Blakes
HERO	Mrs Davies
MARGARET	Mrs Havard
BEATRICE (1)	Miss Pritchard

(1) *Oct. 1*

BEATRICE	Mrs Palmer [i.e. formerly Miss Pritchard]

1762 DRURY LANE

Jan. 5

BENEDICK	Garrick
DON PEDRO	Havard
LEONATO	Davies
CLAUDIO	Palmer
FRIAR	Burton
DON JOHN	Bransby
BALTHAZAR	Lowe
DOGBERRY	Yates
VERGES	Philips
BORACHIO	Blakes
HERO	Mrs Davies
MARGARET	Mrs Bradshaw
BEATRICE (1)	Mrs Palmer

(1) *Apr. 27*

BEATRICE	Miss Pope

[PA assigns MARGARET to Mrs Havard.]

1763 DRURY LANE

Mar. 1

BENEDICK	Garrick
DON PEDRO	Packer
LEONATO	Havard

(1) *Apr. 16*

VERGES	Philips

MUCH ADO ABOUT NOTHING

1763 DRURY LANE (*cont.*)
Mar. 1 (cont.)

CLAUDIO	Palmer
FRIAR	Burton
DON JOHN	Bransby
DOGBERRY	Yates
VERGES (1)	Parsons
BORACHIO	Blakes
BALTHAZAR	Vernon
HERO	Mrs Davies
MARGARET	Mrs Bradshaw
URSULA	Mrs Hippisley
BEATRICE	Mrs Palmer

1764 DRURY LANE
Jan. 27; Feb. 7

BENEDICK	Obrien
DON PEDRO	Packer
LEONATO	Havard
CLAUDIO	Palmer
FRIAR	Burton
DON JOHN	Bransby
DOGBERRY	Yates
VERGES	Philips
BORACHIO	Parsons
TOWN CLERK	Baddeley
SEXTON	Clough
BALTHAZAR	Vernon
HERO	Mrs Davies
MARGARET	Mrs Bradshaw
URSULA	Mrs Hippisley
BEATRICE	Miss Pope

1765 DRURY LANE
Nov. 14

BENEDICK	Garrick
DON PEDRO	Packer
LEONATO	Havard
CLAUDIO	Palmer
DOGBERRY	Yates
BALTHAZAR	Vernon
HERO	Miss Plym
BEATRICE	Miss Pope

(1) *Nov. 22*
added
DON JOHN — Lee

1766 DRURY LANE
Feb. 11

BENEDICK	Garrick
DON PEDRO (1)	Havard

(1) *Oct. 23*

DON PEDRO	Packer
LEONATO	Havard

1766 DRURY LANE (cont.)

Feb. 11 (cont.)

LEONATO (1)	Hurst
CLAUDIO	Palmer
DOGBERRY	Yates
BALTHAZAR (1)	Vernon
DON JOHN (1)	Lee
ANTONIO (1)	Ackman
HERO	Miss Plym
BEATRICE	Miss Pope

(1) Oct. 23 (cont.)

BALTHAZAR	Dodd
DON JOHN	[F.] Aickin
ANTONIO	Hurst
added	
SEXTON	Weston
TOWN CLERK	Baddeley
BORACHIO	Ackman

1767 DRURY LANE

Oct. 28

BENEDICK	Garrick
DON PEDRO	Packer
LEONATO	Havard
CLAUDIO	Palmer
DOGBERRY	Parsons
BALTHAZAR	Vernon
DON JOHN	[F.] Aickin
ANTONIO	Hurst
BORACHIO	Ackman
TOWN CLERK	Baddeley
SEXTON	Weston
HERO	Mrs Baddeley
BEATRICE	Miss Pope

1768 DRURY LANE

Oct. 20

BENEDICK	Garrick
DON PEDRO	Packer
LEONATO	[F.] Aickin
CLAUDIO	Cautherley
DON JOHN	Bransby
BALTHAZAR	Vernon
ANTONIO	Hurst
DOGBERRY	Parsons
VERGES	Hartry
CONRADE	Strange
BORACHIO	Ackman
TOWN CLERK	Baddeley
SEXTON	Clough
HERO	Mrs Baddeley
MARGARET	Mrs Bradshaw
URSULA	Mrs Hippisley
BEATRICE	Miss Pope

MUCH ADO ABOUT NOTHING

1769 DRURY LANE
Nov. 14

BENEDICK	Garrick
LEONATO	[F.] Aickin
DON PEDRO	Packer
CLAUDIO	Cautherley
DON JOHN	J. Aickin
BALTHAZAR	Vernon
ANTONIO	Hurst
DOGBERRY	Parsons
VERGES	Hartry
CONRADE	Strange
BORACHIO	Ackman
TOWN CLERK	Baddeley
SEXTON	Clough
HERO	Mrs Baddeley
BEATRICE	Miss Pope

1770 DRURY LANE
Nov. 13

BENEDICK	Garrick
LEONATO	[F.] Aickin
DON PEDRO	Packer
CLAUDIO	Cautherley
BALTHAZAR	Vernon
DON JOHN	J. Aickin
ANTONIO	Hurst
DOGBERRY	Parsons
VERGES	Hartry
BORACHIO	Ackman
TOWN CLERK	Baddeley
SEXTON	[F.] Waldron
HERO	Mrs Morland
MARGARET	Mrs Bradshaw
URSULA	Mrs Millidge
BEATRICE	Miss Pope

1771 DRURY LANE
May 24

BENEDICK	Garrick			(1) *Oct. 17*
LEONATO	[F.] Aickin		HERO added	Mrs Morland
DON PEDRO	Packer		FRIAR	Burton
CLAUDIO	Cautherley			
BALTHAZAR	Vernon			
DON JOHN	J. Aickin			
ANTONIO	Hurst			
DOGBERRY	Parsons			

1771 DRURY LANE (cont.)
May 24 (cont.)

VERGES	Hartry
BORACHIO	Ackman
TOWN CLERK	Baddeley
HERO (1)	Mrs Baddeley
MARGARET	Mrs Bradshaw
URSULA	Mrs Millidge
BEATRICE	Miss Pope

1772 DRURY LANE
Feb. 28

BENEDICK	Garrick			
LEONATO	[F.] Aickin			
DON PEDRO	Packer			
CLAUDIO	Cautherley			
BALTHAZAR	Vernon			
DON JOHN	J. Aickin			
ANTONIO	Hurst			
DOGBERRY	Parsons			
VERGES	Hartry			
BORACHIO	Ackman			
TOWN CLERK	Baddeley			
FRIAR (1)	Inchbald			
HERO (1)	Miss Hayward			
MARGARET	Mrs Bradshaw			
URSULA	Mrs Millidge			
BEATRICE	Miss Pope			

(1) Nov. 3

FRIAR	Wright
HERO	Miss Mansell

1773 DRURY LANE
Oct. 28

BENEDICK	Garrick
LEONATO	[F.] Aickin
DON PEDRO	Packer
CLAUDIO	Cautherley
BALTHAZAR	Vernon
DON JOHN	J. Aickin
ANTONIO	Hurst
DOGBERRY	Parsons
VERGES	Jones
BORACHIO	Ackman
TOWN CLERK	Baddeley
FRIAR	Wright
HERO	Miss [E.] Hopkins
MARGARET	Mrs Bradshaw
URSULA	Mrs Millidge

MUCH ADO ABOUT NOTHING

1773 DRURY LANE (cont.)
Oct. 28 (cont.)

    BEATRICE   Miss Pope

[In the acting version published by Bell in 1773 the cast is the same as that of this performance (except for the assignment of VERGES to Hartry), with the following additions:

CONRADE	Griffith
SEXTON	[F.] Waldron]

1774 DRURY LANE
Apr. 18   (1) *Oct. 28*

BENEDICK	Garrick		LEONATO	Jefferson
LEONATO (1)	[F.] Aickin		DON JOHN	Aickin [i.e. J. Aickin]
DON PEDRO	Packer		VERGES	Carpenter
CLAUDIO	Cautherley		BORACHIO	Usher
BALTHAZAR	Vernon		HERO	Mrs Baddeley
DON JOHN (1)	J. Aickin		added	
ANTONIO	Hurst		CONRADE	Griffith
DOGBERRY	Parsons			
VERGES (1)	Hartry			
BORACHIO (1)	Ackman			
TOWN CLERK	Baddeley			
FRIAR	Wright			
HERO (1)	Mrs Canning			
MARGARET	Mrs Bradshaw			
URSULA	Mrs Millidge			
BEATRICE	Miss Pope			

COVENT GARDEN
Nov. 8, 16; Dec. 10

BENEDICK	Lee
LEONATO	Hull
DON PEDRO	Wroughton
CLAUDIO	Lewis
BALTHAZAR	Du-Bellamy
DON JOHN	Booth
ANTONIO	Thompson
DOGBERRY	Shuter
BORACHIO	Whitfield
VERGES	Cushing
CONRADE	Davis
TOWN CLERK	Quick
FRIAR	Fearon
HERO	Mrs Lessingham
MARGARET	Miss Valois
URSULA	Mrs Whitfield
BEATRICE	Mrs [S.] Barry

1775 DRURY LANE
Jan. 10

BENEDICK	Garrick
LEONATO	Jefferson
DON PEDRO	Packer
CLAUDIO (1)	Cautherley
BALTHAZAR	Vernon
DON JOHN	[J.] Aickin
ANTONIO	Hurst
DOGBERRY (1)	Parsons
BORACHIO	Usher
VERGES (1)	Wrighten
CONRADE (1)	Lamash
TOWN CLERK	Baddeley
FRIAR	Wright
HERO (1)	Mrs Baddeley
MARGARET	Mrs Bradshaw
URSULA	Mrs Millidge
BEATRICE (1)	Miss Pope

(1) *Nov. 6, 8, 10, 16, 22*

CLAUDIO	Brereton
DOGBERRY	[F.] Waldron (on *Nov. 6, 8, 10* only)
VERGES	Carpenter (on *Nov. 6, 10, 16, 22* only)
	[J.] Burton (on *Nov. 8* only)
CONRADE	Griffiths
HERO	Miss [E.] Hopkins
BEATRICE	Mrs Abington
added	
SEXTON	Wrighten
MESSENGER	Lamash

[On *Nov. 10, 16, 22* PA assigns VERGES to Burton.]

COVENT GARDEN
Sept. 29

BENEDICK	Lee
LEONATO	Hull
DON PEDRO	Wroughton
CLAUDIO	Lewis
BALTHAZAR	Du-Bellamy
DON JOHN	Booth
ANTONIO	Thompson
DOGBERRY	Shuter
BORACHIO	Young
VERGES	Cushing
CONRADE	Davis
TOWN CLERK	Quick
FRIAR	Fearon
HERO	Mrs Lessingham
MARGARET	Miss Valois
URSULA	Mrs Williams
BEATRICE	Mrs Bulkley

1776 DRURY LANE
Feb. 12; Apr. 16; May 9

BENEDICK	Garrick
LEONATO	Jefferson
DON PEDRO	Packer
CLAUDIO	Brereton
BALTHAZAR	Vernon

1776 DRURY LANE (cont.)

Feb. 12; Apr. 16; May 9 (cont.)

DON JOHN	[J.] Aickin
DOGBERRY	Parsons
ANTONIO	Hurst
BORACHIO	Usher
VERGES	Carpenter
CONRADE	Griffiths
TOWN CLERK	Baddeley
MESSENGER	Lamash
SEXTON	Wrighten
FRIAR	Wright
HERO	Miss [E.] Hopkins
MARGARET	Mrs Bradshaw
URSULA	Mrs Millidge
BEATRICE	Mrs Abington

1777 COVENT GARDEN

Oct. 15

BENEDICK	Lewis
LEONATO	Hull
DON PEDRO	Wroughton
CLAUDIO	Whitfield
BALTHAZAR	Mattocks
DON JOHN	Booth
ANTONIO	Thompson
DOGBERRY	Quick
BORACHIO	L'Estrange
VERGES	Cushing
CONRADE	Robson
TOWN CLERK	Wewitzer
FRIAR	Fearon
HERO	Mrs Lessingham
BEATRICE	Mrs Bulkley

1778 DRURY LANE

Feb. 10, 11, 17; May 6

BENEDICK	Henderson
DON PEDRO	Packer
CLAUDIO	Brereton
BALTHAZAR	Vernon
DON JOHN	[J.] Aickin
ANTONIO	Hurst
BORACHIO (1)	Farren
FRIAR	Wright
MESSENGER (1)	Lamash
DOGBERRY	Parsons

(1) *Nov. 4*

BORACHIO	Lamash
HERO	Mrs Sharp [i.e. formerly Miss Hopkins]

omitted
MESSENGER

MUCH ADO ABOUT NOTHING

1778 DRURY LANE (cont.)
Feb. 10, 11, 17; May 6 (cont.)

TOWN CLERK	Baddeley
CONRADE	Griffiths
SEXTON	Wrighten
VERGES	Carpenter
1ST WATCHMAN	[J.] Burton
2ND WATCHMAN	Holcroft
LEONATO	Bensley
HERO (1)	Miss [E.] Hopkins
MARGARET	Mrs Bradshaw
URSULA	Mrs Colles
BEATRICE	Miss Pope

1779 DRURY LANE
Jan. 5

BENEDICK (1)	Lewis
CLAUDIO	Brereton
DON PEDRO	Packer
DON JOHN	[J.] Aickin
BALTHAZAR (1)	Mattocks
ANTONIO	Hurst
BORACHIO (1)	Wrighten
DOGBERRY (1)	Moody
TOWN CLERK	Baddeley
VERGES	Carpenter
CONRADE	Griffiths
SEXTON	Wrighten
FRIAR	Wright
1ST WATCHMAN	[J.] Burton
2ND WATCHMAN	Holcroft
LEONATO	Bensley
HERO (1)	Mrs Sharp
MARGARET	Mrs Bradshaw
URSULA	Mrs Colles
BEATRICE	Miss Pope

(1) May 5, 29

BENEDICK	Henderson
BALTHAZAR	Vernon
BORACHIO	Lamash
DOGBERRY	Parsons
HERO	Mrs Lessingham (on *May 5* only)

[Both Pb and PA assign BENEDICK to Henderson, BALTHAZAR to Vernon, BORACHIO to Lamash, and DOGBERRY to Parsons. Late in the afternoon Henderson, Vernon and Parsons sent word that they were indisposed, and the substitutions noted above were made, two by actors borrowed from CG. Lamash never came to the theatre at all; his scenes in the first two acts were omitted, and for the remainder of the play were acted by Wrighten. It is not stated who took Wrighten's place as the SEXTON, i.e. this part cannot be doubled with that of BORACHIO. For these, and other difficulties attending this performance, see Garrick, *Private Correspondence*, 1831–3, ii. 328–9.]

COVENT GARDEN
Dec. 31

BENEDICK	Henderson
LEONATO	Hull

1779 COVENT GARDEN (cont.)
Dec. 31 (cont.)

DON PEDRO	Wroughton
CLAUDIO	Whitfield
BALTHAZAR	Reinhold
DON JOHN	Booth
ANTONIO	Thompson
DOGBERRY	Quick
VERGES	Cushing
CONRADE	Robson
TOWN CLERK	Edwin
BORACHIO	L'Estrange
FRIAR	Fearon
HERO	Mrs Lessingham
MARGARET	Mrs Whitfield
URSULA	Mrs Poussin
BEATRICE	Miss Younge

1780 COVENT GARDEN
Jan. 11

BENEDICK	Henderson
LEONATO	Hull
DON PEDRO (3)	Wroughton
CLAUDIO	Whitfield
BALTHAZAR (1, 2, 3)	Reinhold
DON JOHN (2)	Booth
ANTONIO (2)	Thompson
DOGBERRY (2)	Quick
BORACHIO (2)	L'Estrange
VERGES (2)	Cushing
CONRADE (2)	Robson
TOWN CLERK (2)	Edwin
FRIAR (2)	Fearon
HERO	Mrs Lessingham
MARGARET	Mrs Whitfield
URSULA	Mrs Poussin
BEATRICE (2)	Miss Younge

(1) *Feb. 17*

BALTHAZAR	Mattocks

(2) *Apr. 22*

BALTHAZAR	Mattocks
DOGBERRY	Edwin
TOWN CLERK	Wewitzer
BEATRICE	Mrs [S.] Wilson

omitted DON JOHN, ANTONIO, BORACHIO, VERGES, CONRADE, FRIAR

(3) *Oct. 19; Dec. 30*

DON PEDRO	Peile
BALTHAZAR	Mattocks

1781 COVENT GARDEN
Mar. 15; May 3

BENEDICK	Henderson
LEONATO	Hull
DON PEDRO (1)	Peile
CLAUDIO	Whitfield
BALTHAZAR	Mattocks
DON JOHN	Booth
ANTONIO	Thompson

(1) *Dec. 5*

DON PEDRO	Davies
MARGARET	Miss Platt

1781 COVENT GARDEN (*cont.*)
Mar. 15; May 3 (cont.)

BORACHIO	L'Estrange
CONRADE	Robson
FRIAR	Fearon
VERGES	Cushing
DOGBERRY	Quick
TOWN CLERK	Edwin
HERO	Mrs Lessingham
MARGARET (1)	Mrs Whitfield
URSULA	Mrs Poussin
BEATRICE	Miss Younge

1783 DRURY LANE
Mar. 3

BENEDICK	King
CLAUDIO	Brereton
DON PEDRO	Packer
DON JOHN	[J.] Aickin
BALTHAZAR	Williames
ANTONIO	Wrighten
DOGBERRY	Parsons
TOWN CLERK	Baddeley
VERGES	[J.] Burton
LEONATO	Bensley
HERO	Mrs Brereton
BEATRICE	Miss [F.] Kemble

COVENT GARDEN
Feb. 19; Apr. 25; May 5

BENEDICK	Henderson
LEONATO	Hull
DON PEDRO	Davies
CLAUDIO	Whitfield
BALTHAZAR	Mattocks
DON JOHN	Booth
ANTONIO	Thompson
BORACHIO	W. Bates
CONRADE	Mahon
FRIAR	Fearon
VERGES	Mills
DOGBERRY	Quick
TOWN CLERK	Edwin
HERO	Miss Cleland
MARGARET	Mrs Whitfield
URSULA	Mrs Poussin
BEATRICE	Mrs Abington

1784 COVENT GARDEN
Jan. 9

BENEDICK	Henderson
LEONATO	Hull
DON PEDRO	Davies
CLAUDIO	Whitfield
BALTHAZAR	Mattocks
DON JOHN	Booth
ANTONIO	Thompson
BORACHIO	J. Bates
CONRADE	Mahon
FRIAR	Fearon
VERGES	Wewitzer
DOGBERRY	Quick
TOWN CLERK	Edwin
HERO	Mrs [S.] Kemble
MARGARET	Mrs Davenett
URSULA	Mrs Poussin
BEATRICE	Miss Younge

[PA assigns BORACHIO to W. Bates.]

1785 COVENT GARDEN
Jan. 21, 26

BENEDICK	Henderson
LEONATO	Hull
DON PEDRO	Davies
CLAUDIO	Farren
BALTHAZAR	Brett
DON JOHN	Booth
ANTONIO	Thompson
BORACHIO (2)	Egan
CONRADE	Cubitt
FRIAR	Fearon
VERGES (1)	Wewitzer
DOGBERRY	Quick
TOWN CLERK (1)	Edwin
HERO	Mrs Inchbald
MARGARET	Mrs Davenett
URSULA (2)	Mrs Poussin
BEATRICE	Mrs Abington

(1) *Jan. 27*

VERGES	[T.] Kennedy
TOWN CLERK	Wewitzer

(2) *Nov. 2*

BORACHIO	[Wm.] Palmer
URSULA	Miss Platt

1786 COVENT GARDEN
Jan. 24

BENEDICK	Holman
LEONATO	Hull
DON PEDRO	Davies
CLAUDIO	Farren

1786 COVENT GARDEN (*cont.*)

Jan. 24 (cont.)

BALTHAZAR	Brett
DON JOHN	Booth
ANTONIO	Thompson
BORACHIO	[Wm.] Palmer
CONRADE	Cubitt
FRIAR	Fearon
VERGES	Wewitzer
DOGBERRY	Quick
TOWN CLERK	Edwin
HERO	Mrs Inchbald
MARGARET	Mrs Davenett
URSULA	Miss Platt
BEATRICE	Mrs Abington

1787 COVENT GARDEN

Apr. 11

BENEDICK (1)	Holman
LEONATO	Hull
DON PEDRO	Davies
CLAUDIO	Farren
BALTHAZAR (1)	[G.] King
DON JOHN	Booth
ANTONIO	Thompson
BORACHIO	Macready
CONRADE	Cubitt
FRIAR	Fearon
VERGES (1)	[T.] Kennedy
DOGBERRY	Quick
TOWN CLERK	Edwin
HERO	Mrs Inchbald
MARGARET (1)	Mrs Davenett
URSULA (1)	Miss Platt
BEATRICE (1)	Miss Brunton

(1) *Nov. 7*

BENEDICK	Lewis
BALTHAZAR	Darley
VERGES	Wewitzer
BEATRICE	Mrs Abington
omitted	
MARGARET, URSULA	

HAYMARKET

May 25

BENEDICK (1)	Browne
CLAUDIO	[J.] Williamson
DON PEDRO (1)	[J.] Johnson
DON JOHN	Usher
BALTHAZAR	Meadows
ANTONIO	Chapman
DOGBERRY	Moss
BORACHIO (1)	Baker
CONRADE	Lyons

(1) *Aug. 17*

BENEDICK	King
DON PEDRO	Davies
BORACHIO	[J.] Johnson
MARGARET	Miss Brangin
BEATRICE	Miss Farren
added	
TOWN CLERK	Baddeley
FRIAR	Gardner

490

1787 HAYMARKET (cont.)

May 25 (cont.)

VERGES	Barrett
LEONATO	[S.] Kemble
HERO	Miss Woollery
URSULA	Mrs Poussin
MARGARET (1)	Mrs Gaudry
BEATRICE (1)	Mrs Bulkley

1788 DRURY LANE

Apr. 30

BENEDICK	Kemble
CLAUDIO	Barrymore
DON PEDRO	Whitfield
DON JOHN	[J.] Aickin
BALTHAZAR	Williams
ANTONIO	Packer
DOGBERRY	Parsons
TOWN CLERK	Baddeley
VERGES	[J.] Burton
LEONATO	Bensley
HERO	Mrs [J.] Kemble
BEATRICE	Miss Farren

COVENT GARDEN

Jan. 25

BENEDICK	Lewis
LEONATO	Hull
DON PEDRO	Davies
CLAUDIO	Farren
BALTHAZAR	Darley
DON JOHN	Booth
ANTONIO	Thompson
BORACHIO	Macready
CONRADE	Cubitt
FRIAR	Fearon
VERGES	Wewitzer
DOGBERRY	Quick
TOWN CLERK	Edwin
HERO	Mrs Inchbald
BEATRICE (1)	A Young Lady [Mrs Henry (EM, Feb. 1788, 106); first appearance on the stage]

(1) Apr. 14

BEATRICE	Mrs Abington

1789 DRURY LANE

Nov. 27; Dec. 9, 18, 26

BENEDICK	Kemble
CLAUDIO	Barrymore

1789 DRURY LANE (cont.)
Nov. 27; Dec. 9, 18, 26 (cont.)

DON PEDRO	Whitfield
DON JOHN	[J.] Aickin
BALTHAZAR	Williames
ANTONIO	Packer
DOGBERRY	Moody
TOWN CLERK	Baddeley
VERGES	[J.] Burton
LEONATO	Bensley
HERO	Mrs [J.] Kemble
BEATRICE	Miss Farren

COVENT GARDEN
Jan. 20

BENEDICK	Lewis
LEONATO	Hull
DON PEDRO	Davies
CLAUDIO	Farren
BALTHAZAR	Darley
DON JOHN	Booth
ANTONIO	Thompson
BORACHIO	Macready
CONRADE	Cubitt
FRIAR	Fearon
VERGES	Wewitzer
DOGBERRY	Quick
TOWN CLERK	Edwin
HERO	Mrs Inchbald
BEATRICE	Mrs Abington

1790 DRURY LANE
Jan. 6

BENEDICK	Kemble
CLAUDIO	Barrymore
DON PEDRO	Whitfield
DON JOHN	[J.] Aickin
BALTHAZAR	Williames
TOWN CLERK	Baddeley
ANTONIO	Packer
DOGBERRY	Moody
VERGES	[J.] Burton
LEONATO	Bensley
HERO	Mrs [J.] Kemble
BEATRICE	Miss Farren

(1) *Feb. 3; May 12*
added

BORACHIO	Phillimore
CONRADE	Haymes
MARGARET	Miss Tidswell
URSULA	Miss Barnes

MUCH ADO ABOUT NOTHING

1792 DRURY LANE (company at KING'S, HAYMARKET)
Nov. 2   (1) *Dec. 27*

DON PEDRO	Whitfield	MARGARET	Mrs Shaw
LEONATO	Bensley		
DON JOHN	[J.] Aickin		
CLAUDIO	Barrymore		
BENEDICK	Kemble		
BALTHAZAR	Dignum		
ANTONIO	Packer		
BORACHIO	Phillimore		
CONRADE	Caulfield		
DOGBERRY	Moody		
VERGES	[J.] Burton		
HERO	Mrs [J.] Kemble		
BEATRICE	Miss Farren		
MARGARET (1)	Miss Tidswell		
URSULA	Miss Heard		

1793 DRURY LANE (company at KING'S, HAYMARKET)
Jan. 10

DON PEDRO	Whitfield
LEONATO	Bensley
DON JOHN	[J.] Aickin
CLAUDIO	Barrymore
BENEDICK	Kemble
BALTHAZAR	Dignum
ANTONIO	Packer
BORACHIO	Phillimore
CONRADE	Caulfield
DOGBERRY	Moody
VERGES	[J.] Burton
HERO	Mrs [J.] Kemble
BEATRICE	Miss Farren
MARGARET	Miss Tidswell
URSULA	Miss Heard

[PA assigns MARGARET to Mrs Shaw.]

COVENT GARDEN
Sept. 18

BENEDICK	Lewis
LEONATO	Hull
DON PEDRO	Davies
CLAUDIO	Farren
BALTHAZAR	[D.] Williamson
DON JOHN	Cubitt
ANTONIO	Thompson
BORACHIO	Macready
CONRADE	Claremont

1793 COVENT GARDEN (cont.)
Sept. 18 (cont.)

FRIAR	Powel
VERGES	Fawcett [Jr.]
DOGBERRY	Quick
TOWN CLERK	Munden
HERO	Miss Chapman
BEATRICE	Mrs Esten

1794 COVENT GARDEN
Jan. 15

BENEDICK	Lewis
LEONATO	Hull
DON PEDRO	Davies
CLAUDIO	Farren
BALTHAZAR	Townsend
DON JOHN (1)	Cubitt
ANTONIO	Thompson
BORACHIO	Macready
CONRADE	Claremont
FRIAR	Powel
VERGES	Fawcett [Jr.]
DOGBERRY	Quick
TOWN CLERK	Munden
HERO	Miss Chapman
BEATRICE (1)	Mrs Esten

(1) *Nov. 12*

DON JOHN	Richardson
BEATRICE	Miss Wallis

1797 DRURY LANE
Jan. 12

DON PEDRO	Whitfield
LEONATO	[J.] Aickin
ANTONIO	Packer
DON JOHN	Campbell
CLAUDIO	Barrymore
BENEDICK	Kemble
BORACHIO (1)	Phillimore
CONRADE (1)	Caulfield
FRIAR (1)	Maddocks
BALTHAZAR	Dignum
DOGBERRY	Suett
VERGES	Dowton
SEXTON (1)	Hollingsworth
OATCAKE (1)	Wewitzer
SEACOAL (1)	Denman
HERO	Miss Mellon
BEATRICE	Miss Farren
MARGARET	Miss Tidswell
URSULA	Miss Heard

(1) *Mar. 23*

SEACOAL	Hollingsworth
omitted	
BORACHIO, CONRADE, FRIAR, SEXTON, OATCAKE	

1797 COVENT GARDEN
Oct. 6; Dec. 14

BENEDICK	Lewis
LEONATO	Hull
DON PEDRO	Clarke
CLAUDIO	Toms
BALTHAZAR	Townsend
DON JOHN	Waddy
ANTONIO	Thompson
BORACHIO	Farley
CONRADE	Claremont
FRIAR (1)	Davenport
VERGES	Simmons
DOGBERRY	Munden
TOWN CLERK	Powel
HERO	Mrs Mountain
MARGARET	Miss Leserve
URSULA	Mrs Platt
BEATRICE	Mrs Abington

(1) Oct. 9

FRIAR	omitted

1798 DRURY LANE
May 24

DON PEDRO	Holland
LEONATO	[J.] Aickin
DON JOHN	Caulfield
CLAUDIO	Barrymore
BENEDICK	Kemble
BALTHAZAR	Dignum
ANTONIO	Packer
BORACHIO	Trueman
CONRADE (1)	Gibbon
DOGBERRY	Suett
VERGES	Dowton
SEACOAL (1)	Wewitzer
HERO (1)	Miss Leak
BEATRICE	Mrs Jordan
MARGARET	Miss Tidswell
URSULA	Miss Heard

(1) Oct. 11

CONRADE	Surmont
SEACOAL	Sparks
HERO	Miss Mellon
added	
FRIAR	Maddocks
SEXTON	Hollingsworth

COVENT GARDEN
Mar. 15

BENEDICK	Lewis
LEONATO	Hull
DON PEDRO	Clarke
CLAUDIO	Toms
DON JOHN	Waddy
BALTHAZAR (1)	Gray

(1) May 14

BALTHAZAR	Townsend

495

1798 COVENT GARDEN (*cont.*)
Mar. 15 (cont.)

ANTONIO	Thompson
BORACHIO	Farley
CONRADE	Claremont
FRIAR	Davenport
VERGES	Simmons
DOGBERRY	Munden
TOWN CLERK	Powel
HERO	Mrs Mountain
MARGARET	Miss Leserve
URSULA	Mrs Platt
BEATRICE	Mrs Abington

HAYMARKET
Aug. 21

BENEDICK	Barrymore
CLAUDIO	C. Kemble
DON PEDRO	Davies
LEONATO	[J.] Aickin
ANTONIO	Usher
DON JOHN	Caulfield
BORACHIO	Trueman
CONRADE	[G.] Waldron
FRIAR	Davenport
BALTHAZAR	D'Arcy
DOGBERRY	Suett
VERGES	[F.] Waldron
SEXTON	Abbot
OATCAKE	Chippendale
SEACOAL	Ledger
BEATRICE	Mrs Jordan
MARGARET	Miss Leserve
URSULA	Miss Heard
HERO	Miss DeCamp

1799 DRURY LANE
Feb. 2

DON PEDRO	Holland
LEONATO	[J.] Aickin
DON JOHN	Caulfield
CLAUDIO	Barrymore
BENEDICK (1)	Kemble
BALTHAZAR (1)	Dignum
ANTONIO	Packer
BORACHIO (1)	Trueman
CONRADE (1)	Surmont

(1) *July 4*

BENEDICK	[J.] Powell
BALTHAZAR	Fisher
VERGES	Banks
HERO	Miss Heard
URSULA	Miss Wentworth

omitted BORACHIO, CONRADE, SEXTON, SEACOAL

(2) *Oct. 12; Nov. 5*

VERGES	Banks (on *Nov. 5* only)

MUCH ADO ABOUT NOTHING

1799 DRURY LANE (cont.)

Feb. 2 (cont.)

DOGBERRY	Suett
VERGES (1, 2)	Dowton
FRIAR	Maddocks
SEXTON (1, 2)	Hollingsworth
SEACOAL (1, 2)	Sparks
HERO (1)	Miss Mellon
BEATRICE (2)	Mrs Jordan
MARGARET	Miss Tidswell
URSULA (1, 2)	Miss Heard

(2) Oct. 12; Nov. 5 (cont.)

SEXTON	Webb (on *Nov. 5* only)
BEATRICE	Miss Biggs
URSULA	Miss Wentworth
omitted SEACOAL	

OTHELLO

(1) 'As it is now acted at the Theatre Royal in Covent-Garden.'

1755 T. Witford.

Following are the principal omissions:

Act I. i. *43–60* (the two kinds of knaves), *121b–38a* (the details of Desdemona's elopement); iii. *19b–30* (the importance of Cyprus to the Turks), *195b–220* (the Duke and Brabantio moralizing on Fortune), *324b–40a* ('our bodies are our gardens').

Act II. i. *1–42* (the storm at sea and the destruction of the Turkish fleet), *124–44a* (Iago's paradoxes), *230b–55* (Desdemona compelled 'to some second choice'); ii entire (the proclamation to hold revelry).

Act III. i entire (the Clown and the musicians); ii entire (Iago as Othello's secretary); iv. *1–23* (the Clown ordered to find Cassio), *109b–21a* (Cassio's wish to be restored to favour), *140b–53* (Desdemona the 'unhandsome warrior'), *168–end* (Bianca is given the handkerchief).

Act IV. i. *37b–209* (the trance, Othello's eavesdropping, and Bianca's returning the handkerchief); iii. *19–end* (the willow song, and the discussion of women's infidelity).

Act V. i. *28–36* (Othello sees Cassio wounded), *73–88a* (Bianca assists Cassio), *91–110* (Iago imputes the quarrel to Bianca), *115–25* (Emilia upbraids Bianca).

Throughout there are minor omissions.

(2) 'As it is now Acted by His Majesty's Servants.'

1756 C. Hitch [&c.].

This is a reading edition, verbatim throughout.

(3) 'As it is now acted at the Theatre Royal in Covent Garden.'

1761 C. Hitch [&c.].

This is identical with (1).

(4) 'Printed Exactly agreeable to the Representation [at Drury Lane].'

n.d. [1764] H. Garland. Reprinted Dublin: John Exshaw, 1764.

This is identical with (1), except for occasional restorations of the original, the most important being IV. i. *186–209*, and IV. iii. *19a, 61b–64, 107–8*.

OTHELLO

(5) 'As it is now acted at the Theatres Royal in Drury-Lane and Covent-Garden.'

1771   Hawes [&c.].

(6) 'As Performed at the Theatre-Royal, Drury-Lane. Regulated from the Prompt-Book.'

1773   John Bell.

(7) 'As it is Acted at the Theatres-Royal in Drury-Lane and Covent-Garden.'

1777   J. Wenman.

(8) 'As it is Acted at the Theatres-Royal in Drury-Lane and Covent-Garden.'

1780   Harrison.

(9) 'Taken from the Manager's Book, at the Theatre-Royal, Covent-Garden.'

n.d. [c. 1780]   Sabine and Son.

(10) 'Marked with the Variations in the Manager's Book, at the Theatre-Royal in Drury-Lane.'

1784   C. Bathurst [&c.].

(11) 'Taken from the Manager's Book, at the Theatre-Royal, Covent-Garden.'

n.d. [c. 1788]   R. Butters.

Except for occasional minor restorations, all these are identical with (1). See also Odell, ii. 33–35.

1751 DRURY LANE
Mar. 7

OTHELLO	F. Delaval
IAGO	J. Delaval
CASSIO	E. Delaval
BRABANTIO	S. Pine
LODOVICO	S. Pine
RODERIGO	Capt. Stevens
DESDEMONA	Mrs Quarme
EMILIA	Mrs Stevens

[Bill not in GA. The actors in this performance were amateurs; their names are listed by Genest (iv. 325). He says that 'Lady Mexborough acted Desdemona—this is certainly right—she was sister to Sir Francis Delaval, but at the time when the play was acted she might be Mrs. Quon [Genest's misspelling of "Quarme"]'. This statement is certainly not right: one of Sir Francis's sisters later married Lord Mexborough, but in 1751 she was only nine years old, and neither of his other two sisters became Mrs Quarme. DA, Mar. 8, *Reed's Weekly Journal*, Mar. 9, and the *Penny London Post*, Mar. 11 all refer to Mrs 'Qualm' as DESDEMONA, and assign EMILIA to Miss Roche. Miss Roche (later Lady Echlin) was Sir Francis's mistress, and Mrs Quarme was her sister. WEP, Sept. 5, 1771, in an obituary of Sir Francis, gives the correct spelling of Mrs Quarme's name. Genest also gives 'Stephens'; all the contemporary sources 'Stevens'. In the above performance Pine doubled BRABANTIO and LODOVICO.]

COVENT GARDEN

Feb. 9

OTHELLO (1, 2)	Quin
IAGO (1, 2)	Ryan

(1) *Mar. 11*

OTHELLO	Barry
IAGO	Quin

OTHELLO

1751 COVENT GARDEN (cont.)

Feb. 9 (cont.)

BRABANTIO	Sparks
CASSIO	Ridout
RODERIGO	Dyer
LODOVICO	Anderson
GRATIANO	Redman
MONTANO	Bransby
EMILIA	Mrs Macklin
DESDEMONA (2)	Mrs Cibber

(2) Apr. 19; Oct. 9

OTHELLO	Barry
IAGO	Macklin
DESDEMONA	Mrs Elmy (on *Apr. 19* only)

added

DUKE	Marten

HAYMARKET
Dec. 28. No parts assigned

NEW WELLS, GOODMAN'S FIELDS
Sept. 5

OTHELLO	Goodfellow
RODERIGO	L. Hallam
DESDEMONA	Mrs Hallam

No other parts assigned

1752 DRURY LANE
Mar. 12

OTHELLO	Mossop
BRABANTIO (1)	Berry
CASSIO	Palmer
RODERIGO	Yates
LODOVICO	Blakes
IAGO (1)	Montgomery [first appearance in London]
DESDEMONA	Miss Bellamy
EMILIA	Mrs Pritchard

(1) Apr. 14

BRABANTIO	Burton
IAGO	Havard

added

DUKE	Winstone
MONTANO	Mozeen
GRATIANO	Simson

COVENT GARDEN
Jan. 7; Feb. 1; Apr. 17; Oct. 24; Dec. 1

OTHELLO	Barry
IAGO	Macklin
BRABANTIO	Sparks
CASSIO	Ridout
RODERIGO	Dyer
LODOVICO	Anderson
GRATIANO	Redman
DUKE	Marten
MONTANO	Bransby
EMILIA	Mrs Macklin
DESDEMONA	Mrs Cibber

OTHELLO

1752 NEW WELLS, GOODMAN'S FIELDS
Nov. 16
- OTHELLO — Goodfellow
- IAGO — Wignell
- EMILIA — Mrs Bradshaw
- DESDEMONA — Mrs Fisher

No other parts assigned

1753 DRURY LANE
Apr. 2
- OTHELLO — Mossop
- BRABANTIO — Berry
- CASSIO — Palmer
- IAGO — Garrick
- RODERIGO — Yates
- LODOVICO — Blakes
- EMILIA — Mrs Pritchard
- DESDEMONA — Miss Bellamy

COVENT GARDEN
Apr. 5
- OTHELLO — Barry
- IAGO (1) — Macklin
- BRABANTIO — Sparks
- CASSIO — Ridout
- RODERIGO — Dyer
- EMILIA (1) — Mrs Macklin
- DESDEMONA (1) — Mrs Cibber

(1) *Oct. 27*
- IAGO — Ryan
- EMILIA — Mrs Bland
- DESDEMONA — Mrs Elmy
added
- LODOVICO — Anderson
- GRATIANO — Redman
- DUKE — Wignell
- MONTANO — White

1754 COVENT GARDEN
Jan. 8
- OTHELLO (2) — Barry
- IAGO — Ryan
- BRABANTIO — Sparks
- CASSIO — Ridout
- RODERIGO — Dyer
- LODOVICO — Anderson
- GRATIANO — Redman
- DUKE (1, 2) — Wignell
- MONTANO — White
- EMILIA (2) — Mrs Bland
- DESDEMONA — Miss Bellamy

(1) *Apr. 1*
- DUKE — Marten

(2) *Oct. 18, 19, 21; Nov. 15; Dec. 5*
- OTHELLO — A Gentleman [Murphy (Genest, iv. 413); first appearance, Oct. 18, on the stage]
- DUKE — Marten
- EMILIA — Mrs Hamilton [i.e. formerly Mrs Bland] (on *Oct. 18, 19, 21, Nov. 15* only) Mrs Green (on *Dec. 5* only)

[Beginning with *Nov. 15* Murphy's name is in the bills.]

OTHELLO

1755 COVENT GARDEN
Jan. 24

OTHELLO	Murphy
IAGO	Ryan
BRABANTIO (1)	Gibson
CASSIO	Ridout
RODERIGO	Dyer
LODOVICO	Anderson
GRATIANO	Redman
DUKE	Marten
MONTANO	White
EMILIA	Mrs Hamilton
DESDEMONA	Mrs Bellamy

(1) *May 8*

BRABANTIO	Sparks

HAYMARKET
Sept. 1, 3, 6

OTHELLO	Hackett [first appearance, Sept. 1, on the stage]
CASSIO	Quelch
BRABANTIO	Marshall
RODERIGO	Charles
IAGO	Cibber
DUKE	Carr
MONTANO	Parker
LODOVICO	Metteer
EMILIA	Mrs Price
DESDEMONA	Miss Barton

1756 COVENT GARDEN
Mar. 18; Oct. 11

OTHELLO	Barry
IAGO	Ryan
BRABANTIO (2)	Sparks
CASSIO	Ridout
RODERIGO	Dyer
LODOVICO	Anderson
GRATIANO	Redman
DUKE	Marten
MONTANO	White
EMILIA	Mrs Hamilton
DESDEMONA (1, 2)	Miss Nossiter

(1) *Apr. 26*

DESDEMONA	Mrs Elmy

(2) *Nov. 18, 20, 26*

BRABANTIO	Gibson
DESDEMONA	A Young Gentlewoman [Mrs Stott (Genest, iv. 496); first appearance, Nov. 18, on the stage]

1757 COVENT GARDEN
Jan. 11; Mar. 7; May 7

OTHELLO (1)	Barry
IAGO	Ryan
BRABANTIO	Sparks
CASSIO	Ridout

(1) *Nov. 16*

OTHELLO	Ross
DESDEMONA	Mrs Elmy

(2) *Dec. 12*

DESDEMONA	Mrs Bellamy

OTHELLO

1757 COVENT GARDEN (cont.)
Jan. 11; Mar. 7; May 7 (cont.)

RODERIGO	Dyer
LODOVICO	Anderson
GRATIANO	Redman
DUKE	Marten
MONTANO	White
EMILIA	Mrs Hamilton
DESDEMONA (1, 2)	Miss Nossiter

1758 COVENT GARDEN
Feb. 21

OTHELLO (2)	Barry
IAGO	Ryan
BRABANTIO	Sparks
CASSIO	Ridout
ROGERIGO (1, 2)	Bennet
LODOVICO	Anderson
GRATIANO	Redman
DUKE	Marten
MONTANO (2)	White
EMILIA	Mrs Hamilton
DESDEMONA	Mrs Bellamy

(1) *Apr. 4*

RODERIGO	Dyer

(2) *Oct. 23*

OTHELLO	Ross
RODERIGO	Dyer
MONTANO	Davis

1759 DRURY LANE
May 14

OTHELLO	Wilkinson
DUKE	Bransby
BRABANTIO	Burton
RODERIGO	Yates
CASSIO	Palmer
LODOVICO	Blakes
IAGO	Havard
EMILIA	Mrs Bennet
DESDEMONA	Mrs Davies

COVENT GARDEN
Jan. 17

OTHELLO	Ross
IAGO	Ryan
BRABANTIO	Sparks
CASSIO	Ridout
RODERIGO	Dyer
LODOVICO (1, 2)	Anderson
GRATIANO (1, 2)	Redman
DUKE (1, 2)	Marten

(1) *May 17*

LODOVICO	Wignell
DUKE	Stoppelaer
EMILIA	Mrs Hamilton
omitted	
GRATIANO	

(2) *Dec. 19*

EMILIA	Mrs Hamilton
DESDEMONA	Mrs Ward

OTHELLO

1759 COVENT GARDEN (cont.)

Jan. 17 (cont.)
MONTANO (2)	Davis
EMILIA (1, 2)	Mrs Green
DESDEMONA (2)	Mrs Bellamy

(2) Dec. 19 (cont.)
omitted
  LODOVICO, GRATIANO, DUKE, MONTANO

1760 COVENT GARDEN

Apr. 22
OTHELLO	Ross
IAGO	Sparks
CASSIO	Ridout
BRABANTIO	Gibson
RODERIGO	Dyer
EMILIA	Mrs Hamilton
DESDEMONA	Mrs Ward

(1) Oct. 18
added
LODOVICO	Anderson
GRATIANO	Redman
DUKE	Marten
MONTANO	Davis

1761 DRURY LANE

Mar. 28
OTHELLO (2)	Sheridan
IAGO	Havard
BRABANTIO	Burton
CASSIO	Palmer
RODERIGO	Yates
EMILIA (2)	Mrs Pritchard
DESDEMONA (1)	Mrs Cibber

(1) Apr. 30
DESDEMONA	Miss Mowat

(2) Oct. 17, 19
OTHELLO	A Young Gentleman [Bridges (Genest, iv. 634)]
EMILIA	Mrs Kennedy

COVENT GARDEN

Jan. 17
OTHELLO	Ross
IAGO	Sparks
CASSIO (1)	Ridout
BRABANTIO	Gibson
RODERIGO	Dyer
LODOVICO	Anderson
GRATIANO	Redman
DUKE	Marten
MONTANO	Davis
EMILIA (1)	Mrs Green
DESDEMONA (1)	Mrs Ward

(1) Oct. 13
CASSIO	Hull
EMILIA	Mrs Hamilton
DESDEMONA	Mrs Bellamy

June 23
OTHELLO	A Gentleman (who hath not appeared on the Stage for several Years) [unidentified]
IAGO	Storer
BRABANTIO	Wignell
RODERIGO	[H.] Vaughan
CASSIO	Cooke

1761 COVENT GARDEN (cont.)
June 23 (cont.)

DUKE	Stoppelaer
MONTANO	Turner
EMILIA	Mrs [S.] Smith
DESDEMONA	Mrs Osborne

1762 COVENT GARDEN
Oct. 12

OTHELLO	Ross
IAGO	Sparks
BRABANTIO	Gibson
CASSIO	Hull
RODERIGO	Dyer
LODOVICO	Tindal
MONTANO	Davis
DUKE	Anderson
GRATIANO	Redman
EMILIA	Mrs Ward
DESDEMONA	Miss Macklin

1764 DRURY LANE
Mar. 31

OTHELLO	Powell
IAGO (1)	Havard
RODERIGO (1)	King
CASSIO	Palmer
BRABANTIO	Burton
DUKE	Bransby
LODOVICO	Packer
MONTANO (1, 2)	Mozeen
GRATIANO	Parsons
MESSENGER	Ackman
EMILIA	Mrs Hopkins
DESDEMONA (1)	Mrs Yates

(1) *Apr. 14, 28*

IAGO	King (on *Apr. 28* only)
RODERIGO	Vernon
MONTANO	Fox
DESDEMONA	Mrs Davies

[C-H, *Apr. 14*: 'Mr. King Iago. Mr. Havard could not play Mrs Havard being dead'. MacMillan, 107, quotes this, and appends a note by Kemble: 'This is a Mistake in the Diary. Mrs. Havard died Friday 27th [April]'. Kemble is right. On *Apr. 14* both Pb and PA correctly retain Havard as IAGO. On *Apr. 28* the bill assigns IAGO to King, and adds, 'Being his First Appearance in that Character'. See also *Cymbeline* at this theatre, Apr. 27, 1764.]

(2) *May 24*

MONTANO	Fox

1765 DRURY LANE
Mar. 19

OTHELLO	Powell
RODERIGO	King
CASSIO	Palmer

(1) *Apr. 10; May 10*

BRABANTIO	Burton
DESDEMONA	Mrs Palmer

1765 DRURY LANE (cont.)

Mar. 19 (cont.)

BRABANTIO (1)	Love
DUKE	Bransby
LODOVICO	Packer
IAGO	Holland
MONTANO	Fox
GRATIANO	Parsons
MESSENGER	Ackman
EMILIA	Mrs Hopkins
DESDEMONA (1)	Mrs Yates

COVENT GARDEN

Jan. 14

OTHELLO	Ross
IAGO	Smith
BRABANTIO	Gibson
CASSIO (1)	Hull
RODERIGO	Dyer
LODOVICO (2)	Tindal
MONTANO	Davis
DUKE	Anderson
GRATIANO	Redman
EMILIA	Mrs Ward
DESDEMONA	Mrs Bellamy

(1) May 13

CASSIO	Perry

(2) Oct. 28

LODOVICO	Morris

1766 DRURY LANE

Feb. 13

OTHELLO	Powell
RODERIGO (1)	Dodd
CASSIO	Palmer
BRABANTIO	Burton
DUKE	Bransby
LODOVICO (1, 2)	Hurst
IAGO	Holland
MONTANO	[F.] Aickin
GRATIANO (2)	Parsons
MESSENGER	Strange
EMILIA (1)	Mrs Lee
DESDEMONA	Mrs Yates

(1) Apr. 1

RODERIGO	King
LODOVICO	Packer
EMILIA	Mrs Hopkins

(2) Dec. 6

LODOVICO	Packer
GRATIANO	Hurst

KING'S, HAYMARKET

Aug. 8, 11; Sept. 3

OTHELLO	Barry
IAGO	Lee
CASSIO	Davis

(1) Sept. 17

EMILIA	Mrs Johnston

1766 KING'S, HAYMARKET (cont.)
Aug. 8, 11; Sept. 3 (cont.)

RODERIGO	Hamilton
BRABANTIO	[F.] Aickin
LODOVICO	Hurst
MONTANO	[J.] Palmer
GRATIANO	Murden
DUKE	Keen
MESSENGER	McGeorge
EMILIA (1)	Mrs Burden
DESDEMONA	Mrs Dancer

1767 DRURY LANE
May 9

OTHELLO (1)	Powell
RODERIGO (1)	Baddeley
CASSIO	Palmer
BRABANTIO	Burton
DUKE	Bransby
LODOVICO	Packer
IAGO	Holland
MONTANO	[F.] Aickin
GRATIANO	Hurst
EMILIA	Mrs Hopkins
DESDEMONA (1)	Mrs Baddeley

(1) Oct. 29, 31

OTHELLO	Barry
RODERIGO	Dodd
DESDEMONA	Mrs Dancer

COVENT GARDEN
Dec. 5

OTHELLO	Powell
IAGO	Macklin
RODERIGO	Dyer
DUKE	Morris
BRABANTIO	Gibson
LODOVICO	Gardner
CASSIO	Clarke
MONTANO	Davis
GRATIANO	Mozeen
EMILIA	Mrs Ward
DESDEMONA	Mrs Yates

HAYMARKET
June 30

OTHELLO	Barry
IAGO	Sowdon
DUKE	Keen
BRABANTIO (2)	Gardner

(1) July 24; Sept. 2

DESDEMONA	Mrs Jefferies (on *Sept.* 2 only)
added	
GRATIANO	Ellard

OTHELLO

1767 HAYMARKET (cont.)
June 30 (cont.)

CASSIO (2)	Davis
LODOVICO	Strange
MONTANO	[J.] Palmer
RODERIGO (2)	Weston
EMILIA	Mrs Burden
DESDEMONA (1)	Mrs Dancer

(2) Sept. 21

BRABANTIO	Hurst
RODERIGO	Hamilton
omitted	
CASSIO	

1768 DRURY LANE
May 5

OTHELLO	Barry
RODERIGO	Dodd
CASSIO (1)	J. Palmer
BRABANTIO	Burton
DUKE	Bransby
LODOVICO	Packer
IAGO	Holland
MONTANO	[F.] Aickin
GRATIANO	Hurst
EMILIA	Mrs Hopkins
DESDEMONA (1)	Mrs Dancer

(1) Oct. 31

CASSIO	Palmer [i.e. J. Palmer]
DESDEMONA	Mrs [S.] Barry [i.e. formerly Mrs Dancer]

1769 DRURY LANE
Jan. 28

OTHELLO	Barry
RODERIGO (1)	Dodd
CASSIO	[J.] Palmer
BRABANTIO	Burton
DUKE	Bransby
LODOVICO	Packer
IAGO (2)	Holland
MONTANO (1, 2)	[F.] Aickin
GRATIANO	Hurst
EMILIA (2)	Mrs Hopkins
DESDEMONA	Mrs [S.] Barry

(1) Nov. 18

RODERIGO	Vernon
MONTANO	J. Aickin

(2) Dec. 20

IAGO	Reddish
MONTANO	J. Aickin
EMILIA	Mrs Stephens

HAYMARKET
Feb. 28

OTHELLO	Phillips
IAGO	Henry
DUKE	Foster
BRABANTIO	Martial
CASSIO	[W.] Palmer
GRATIANO	Smith
LODOVICO	Wooller

1769 HAYMARKET (cont.)
Feb. 28 (cont.)

MONTANO	Moss
RODERIGO	Vandermere
EMILIA	Miss Thomson
DESDEMONA	Mrs Smith

Aug. 30

OTHELLO	Sheridan
CASSIO	[J.] Aickin
BRABANTIO	Gardner
MONTANO	Wheeler
GRATIANO	Kearny
RODERIGO	Hamilton
DUKE	Du-Bellamy
LODOVICO	Vandermere
OFFICER	Lings
1ST SENATOR	Sharpless
2ND SENATOR	Summers
IAGO	Sowdon
EMILIA	Mrs Jefferies
DESDEMONA	A Young Lady [Miss Hamilton (Reed, 61); first appearance on the stage]

[PA erroneously assigns the 2ND SENATOR to Lings.]

1770 DRURY LANE
Mar. 17; Apr. 24

OTHELLO	Barry
RODERIGO	Dodd
CASSIO	[J.] Palmer
BRABANTIO (1)	Burton
DUKE	Bransby
LODOVICO	Packer
IAGO	Reddish
MONTANO	J. Aickin
GRATIANO (1)	Hurst
EMILIA	Mrs Hopkins
DESDEMONA	Mrs [S.] Barry

(1) *Nov. 10*

BRABANTIO	Hurst
omitted	
GRATIANO	

HAYMARKET
Oct. 1

OTHELLO	Davis
IAGO	[J.] Palmer
CASSIO	Dancer
RODERIGO	Vandermere
BRABANTIO	Lloyd
MONTANO	Collins

OTHELLO

1770 HAYMARKET (cont.)
Oct. 1 (cont.)

GRATIANO	Farrell
DUKE	Parker
LODOVICO	Griffith
DESDEMONA	A Young Gentlewoman [unidentified]
EMILIA	Miss Roberts

[The above assignment is taken from the playhouse bill in JPK. The PA bill disagrees to such an extent that I reproduce it in full:

OTHELLO	Davis
IAGO	Lloyd
CASSIO	Dancer
RODERIGO	Vandermere
BRABANTIO	Rogers
MONTANO	Freeman
GRATIANO	Farrell
DUKE	Parker
LODOVICO	Griffith
DESDEMONA	Mrs Dyer
EMILIA	Mrs Read]

1771 COVENT GARDEN
Jan. 28

OTHELLO	Ross
IAGO	Bensley
BRABANTIO (1)	Gibson
CASSIO	Clarke
LODOVICO (1)	Gardner
RODERIGO	Dyer
MONTANO	[Lee] Lewes
DUKE	Morris
EMILIA	Mrs Green
DESDEMONA	Miss Miller

(1) Dec. 21

BRABANTIO	Gardner
LODOVICO	Owenson

1772 DRURY LANE
Jan. 7

OTHELLO	Barry
RODERIGO	Dodd
CASSIO	[J.] Palmer
BRABANTIO (1)	Burton
DUKE	Bransby
LODOVICO	Packer
IAGO	Reddish
MONTANO	J. Aickin
EMILIA (1)	Mrs Egerton
DESDEMONA (1)	Mrs [S.] Barry

(1) Oct. 31

BRABANTIO	Hurst
EMILIA	Mrs Hopkins
DESDEMONA	Miss Younge

OTHELLO

1772 COVENT GARDEN
Jan. 25

OTHELLO	Ross
IAGO	Bensley
BRABANTIO	Gardner
CASSIO	Clarke
LODOVICO	Owenson
DUKE	Morris
MONTANO	Davis
RODERIGO	Dyer
EMILIA	Mrs Green
DESDEMONA	Miss Miller

[In the acting version published by Bell in 1773 the cast is the same as that of this performance (except that MONTANO is assigned to Perry), with the following additions:

GRATIANO	Redman
MESSENGER	Holtom]

1773 DRURY LANE
Apr. 29

OTHELLO	Barry
RODERIGO	Dodd
CASSIO (1)	Cautherley
BRABANTIO	Hurst
DUKE	Bransby
LODOVICO	Packer
IAGO (1)	[J.] Palmer
MONTANO	J. Aickin
EMILIA	Mrs Hopkins
DESDEMONA	Mrs [S.] Barry

(1) *Nov. 20*

CASSIO	[J.] Palmer
IAGO	Reddish
added	
GRATIANO	Wrighten
MESSENGER	Wheeler

COVENT GARDEN
Nov. 27, 29

OTHELLO	A Gentleman [Williamson (Not. Dram., Nov. 27, 1773; June 6, 1783); first appearance, Nov. 27, on the stage]
IAGO	Bensley
CASSIO	Clarke
BRABANTIO	Gardner
RODERIGO	[Lee] Lewes
LODOVICO	Owenson
MONTANO	Davis
DUKE	Thompson
GRATIANO	Redman
EMILIA	Mrs Green
DESDEMONA	Miss Miller

[James Brown Williamson used this season the stage name of Brown. It is so given in a MS annotation on the JPK bill, Nov. 27. And see Genest, v. 422–3.]

1774 DRURY LANE
Apr. 12

OTHELLO	Barry
RODERIGO	Dodd
CASSIO	Cautherley
BRABANTIO	Hurst
DUKE	Bransby
LODOVICO	Packer
IAGO	[J.] Palmer
MONTANO	J. Aickin
GRATIANO	Wrighten
MESSENGER	Wheeler
EMILIA	Mrs Hopkins
DESDEMONA	Miss Younge

COVENT GARDEN
Dec. 15

OTHELLO	Barry
IAGO	Bensley
RODERIGO	Woodward
CASSIO	Lewis
BRABANTIO	Hull
LODOVICO	Whitfield
MONTANO	Davis
DUKE	L'Estrange
GRATIANO	Fearon
EMILIA	Mrs Mattocks
DESDEMONA	Mrs [S.] Barry

1775 DRURY LANE
Oct. 17, 19; Dec. 28

OTHELLO	A Young Gentleman [Grist (Genest, v. 479); first appearance, Oct. 17, on the stage]
RODERIGO	Dodd
CASSIO	[J.] Palmer
BRABANTIO	[J.] Aickin
DUKE	Bransby
LODOVICO	Packer
IAGO	Bensley
MONTANO	Davies
GRATIANO	Wrighten
MESSENGER	Whitfield
EMILIA	Mrs Hopkins
DESDEMONA	Miss Younge

1775 COVENT GARDEN
Feb. 9

OTHELLO	Barry
IAGO	Bensley
CASSIO	Lewis
BRABANTIO	Hull
RODERIGO	Lee Lewes
LODOVICO	Whitfield
MONTANO	Davis
DUKE	L'Estrange
GRATIANO	Fearon
EMILIA	Mrs Mattocks
DESDEMONA	Mrs [S.] Barry

1777 DRURY LANE
Apr. 11

OTHELLO	Lacy
RODERIGO	Dodd
CASSIO	[J.] Palmer
BRABANTIO	[J.] Aickin
DUKE	Bransby
LODOVICO	Packer
IAGO	Reddish
MONTANO	Davies
GRATIANO	Wrighten
MESSENGER	Chaplin
EMILIA	Mrs Hopkins
DESDEMONA	Miss Younge

COVENT GARDEN
Apr. 16

OTHELLO (1)	Peile
RODERIGO	Lee Lewes
CASSIO (1)	Lewis
BRABANTIO	Hull
LODOVICO (1)	Whitfield
MONTANO (1)	Davis
DUKE	L'Estrange
GRATIANO	Fearon
IAGO	Macklin
EMILIA	Mrs Mattocks
DESDEMONA (1)	Mrs Lessingham

(1) *Nov. 1, 14*

OTHELLO	Ross
CASSIO	Whitfield
LODOVICO	Booth
MONTANO	Robson
DESDEMONA	Mrs Hartley

CHINA HALL, ROTHERHITHE
July 21

OTHELLO	Newton
CASSIO	G. Graham

1777 CHINA HALL, ROTHERHITHE (cont.)
July 21 (cont.)

RODERIGO	Russell
BRABANTIO	Graham
LODOVICO	Vowell
DUKE	Sidney
MONTANO	Trotter
IAGO	Henry
EMILIA	Mrs Graham
DESDEMONA	Miss Powell

1779 DRURY LANE
Oct. 16

OTHELLO	A Gentleman [Henry (Genest, vi. 125); first appearance in London]
RODERIGO	Dodd
CASSIO	[J.] Palmer
BRABANTIO	[J.] Aickin
LODOVICO (1)	Packer
DUKE (2)	Chaplin
MONTANO (2)	Norris
GRATIANO (2)	Wrighten
IAGO	Bensley
EMILIA	Mrs Hopkins
DESDEMONA	Miss Farren

(1) *Nov. 1*

LODOVICO	Davies

(2) *Nov. 10*
    omitted DUKE, MONTANO, GRATIANO

[Both Pb and PA erroneously state that this was Henry's first appearance on the stage. He had, however, been acting in America for about ten years (DAB; MC, Oct. 18, 20, 1779).]

COVENT GARDEN
Mar. 4

OTHELLO	A Gentleman [Daly (MS annotation on JPK); first appearance on the stage]
RODERIGO	Lee Lewes
CASSIO	Whitfield
BRABANTIO	Hull
LODOVICO	Booth
MONTANO	Robson
DUKE	L'Estrange
GRATIANO	Fearon
IAGO	Bensley
EMILIA	Mrs Hopkins
DESDEMONA	Mrs Crawford

OTHELLO

1780 DRURY LANE
Jan. 8; May 11

OTHELLO (1)	Henry
RODERIGO (1)	Dodd
CASSIO	[J.] Palmer
BRABANTIO	[J.] Aickin
LODOVICO	Packer
DUKE	Chaplin
MONTANO	Norris
GRATIANO	Wrighten
IAGO	Bensley
EMILIA	Mrs Hopkins
DESDEMONA (1)	Miss Farren

(1) Nov. 29

OTHELLO	Crawford
RODERIGO	Lamash
DESDEMONA	Mrs Crawford

COVENT GARDEN
Nov. 10

OTHELLO	Wroughton
RODERIGO	Lee Lewes
CASSIO	Whitfield
BRABANTIO	Hull
LODOVICO	Booth
MONTANO	Robson
DUKE	L'Estrange
GRATIANO	Fearon
IAGO	Henderson
EMILIA	Mrs Webb
DESDEMONA	Miss Younge

HAYMARKET
July 24

OTHELLO	Crawford
CASSIO	[J.] Palmer
RODERIGO (1)	Barrett
BRABANTIO	[J.] Aickin
DUKE	Usher
LODOVICO	Egan
MONTANO	Davis
IAGO	Bensley
EMILIA	Miss Sherry
DESDEMONA	Mrs Crawford

(1) Aug. 4

RODERIGO	Lamash

[Both Pb and PA assign RODERIGO to Lamash. But Barrett was the 'substitute for [Lamash], who was suddenly indisposed' (MC, July 26).]

1782 DRURY LANE
Apr. 23

OTHELLO	Farren
RODERIGO	Dodd

(1) Oct. 1

DESDEMONA	Mrs Ward

1782 DRURY LANE (cont.)
Apr. 23 (cont.)

CASSIO	[J.] Palmer
BRABANTIO	[J.] Aickin
LODOVICO	Packer
DUKE	Chaplin
MONTANO	Norris
GRATIANO	Wrighten
IAGO	Bensley
EMILIA	Mrs Hopkins
DESDEMONA (1)	Miss Farren

1783 COVENT GARDEN
Sept. 24, 29

OTHELLO (1)	[S.] Kemble [first appearance, Sept. 24, in London]
RODERIGO	Bonnor
CASSIO	Whitfield
BRABANTIO	Hull
LODOVICO	Davies
MONTANO	Mahon
DUKE	Booth
GRATIANO	Fearon
IAGO	Henderson
EMILIA (1)	Mrs Whitfield
DESDEMONA (1)	Miss Satchell

(1) Dec. 27

OTHELLO	Wroughton
EMILIA	Mrs Bates
DESDEMONA	Mrs [S.] Kemble [i.e. formerly Miss Satchell]

1784 DRURY LANE
May 21

OTHELLO	Farren
RODERIGO	Dodd
CASSIO	[J.] Palmer
BRABANTIO	[J.] Aickin
LODOVICO	Packer
DUKE	Chaplin
MONTANO	R. Palmer
GRATIANO	Wrighten
IAGO	Bensley
DESDEMONA	Mrs Ward
EMILIA	Mrs Hopkins

COVENT GARDEN
Sept. 27

OTHELLO	Farren
RODERIGO	Bonnor

1784 COVENT GARDEN (cont.)
Sept. 27 (cont.)

CASSIO	Davies
BRABANTIO	Hull
LODOVICO	Cubitt
MONTANO	Thompson
DUKE	Booth
GRATIANO	Fearon
IAGO	Henderson
EMILIA	Mrs Bates
DESDEMONA	Miss Ranoe

1785 DRURY LANE
Mar. 8, 12, 29; Apr. 5, 21; Sept. 17; Oct. 10

OTHELLO	Kemble
RODERIGO	Dodd
CASSIO	[J.] Bannister
BRABANTIO	[J.] Aickin
LODOVICO	Packer
DUKE	Chaplin
MONTANO	R. Palmer
GRATIANO	Wrighten
IAGO	Bensley
EMILIA	Mrs Hopkins
DESDEMONA	Mrs Siddons

COVENT GARDEN
Apr. 23; May 16

OTHELLO	Pope
RODERIGO	Bonnor
CASSIO	Davies
BRABANTIO	Hull
LODOVICO	Cubitt
MONTANO	Thompson
DUKE	Booth
GRATIANO	Fearon
IAGO	Henderson
EMILIA	Mrs Bates
DESDEMONA	Miss Younge

HAYMARKET
Sept. 9

OTHELLO	Lacy
CASSIO	[J.] Bannister
BRABANTIO	[J.] Aickin
RODERIGO	R. Palmer

1785 HAYMARKET (cont.)
Sept. 9 (cont.)
- DUKE — Gardner
- LODOVICO — Usher
- MONTANO — Reily
- IAGO — Bensley
- EMILIA — Mrs Bates
- DESDEMONA — Miss Woollery

1786 HAYMARKET
July 14
- OTHELLO — Lacy
- CASSIO — [J.] Bannister
- BRABANTIO — [J.] Aickin
- RODERIGO — R. Palmer
- DUKE — Gardner
- LODOVICO — Usher
- MONTANO — Reily
- IAGO — Bensley
- EMILIA — Mrs Bates
- DESDEMONA — Miss Woollery

1787 DRURY LANE
Jan. 23
- OTHELLO — Kemble
- RODERIGO (1) — Dodd
- CASSIO (1) — [J.] Bannister
- BRABANTIO (1) — Hull
- LODOVICO — Packer
- DUKE — Chaplin
- MONTANO (1) — R. Palmer
- GRATIANO — Fawcett
- IAGO — Bensley
- EMILIA — Mrs Hopkins
- DESDEMONA — Mrs Siddons

(1) *Oct. 27*
- RODERIGO — R. Palmer
- CASSIO — Barrymore
- BRABANTIO — [J.] Aickin
- MONTANO — Benson

COVENT GARDEN
Oct. 12, 15
- OTHELLO — Cambray [first appearance, Oct. 12, in London]
- RODERIGO — Blanchard
- CASSIO — Macready
- BRABANTIO — Hull
- LODOVICO — Davies
- MONTANO — Thompson
- DUKE — Booth
- GRATIANO — Fearon

1787 COVENT GARDEN (cont.)
Oct. 12, 15 (cont.)

IAGO	Ryder
EMILIA	Mrs Morton
DESDEMONA	Mrs Pope

1788 COVENT GARDEN
Apr. 18

OTHELLO	Pope
RODERIGO	Blanchard
CASSIO	Macready
BRABANTIO	Hull
LODOVICO	Davies
MONTANO	Thompson
DUKE	Booth
GRATIANO	Fearon
IAGO	Ryder
EMILIA	Mrs Morton
DESDEMONA	Mrs Pope

1789 DRURY LANE
Nov. 30

OTHELLO	Kemble
RODERIGO	Dodd
CASSIO	Barrymore
BRABANTIO	[J.] Aickin
LODOVICO	Packer
DUKE	Fawcett
MONTANO	Whitfield
GRATIANO	Phillimore
IAGO	Bensley
EMILIA	Mrs Ward
DESDEMONA	Mrs Powell

COVENT GARDEN
Oct. 16, 26

OTHELLO	Fennell
RODERIGO	Blanchard
CASSIO	Macready
BRABANTIO	Hull
LODOVICO	Davies
MONTANO	Thompson
DUKE	Gardner
GRATIANO	Powel
IAGO	Harley
EMILIA	Mrs Bernard
DESDEMONA	Mrs Pope

1790 COVENT GARDEN
May 15; Nov. 8

OTHELLO	Fennell
RODERIGO	Blanchard
CASSIO	Macready
BRABANTIO	Hull
LODOVICO	Davies
MONTANO	Thompson
DUKE	Cubitt
GRATIANO	Powel
IAGO	Harley
EMILIA	Mrs Bernard
DESDEMONA	Mrs Pope

1791 DRURY LANE
Mar. 28

DUKE	Fawcett
BRABANTIO	[J.] Aickin
GRATIANO	Phillimore
LODOVICO	Packer
OTHELLO	Kemble
CASSIO	Barrymore
IAGO	Bensley
RODERIGO	Dodd
MONTANO	Whitfield
DESDEMONA	Mrs Siddons
EMILIA	Mrs Ward

1792 DRURY LANE (company at KING'S, HAYMARKET)

Feb. 14

DUKE (1, 2)	Fawcett
BRABANTIO	[J.] Aickin
GRATIANO	Phillimore
LODOVICO	Packer
OTHELLO	Kemble
CASSIO	Barrymore
IAGO	Bensley
RODERIGO	Dodd
MONTANO	Whitfield
DESDEMONA	Mrs Siddons
EMILIA	Mrs Ward

(1) *Apr. 25*

DUKE	Maddocks

(2) *Dec. 28*

DUKE	Maddocks
added	
JULIO	Benson
ANTONIO	Caulfield
1ST OFFICER	Banks
2ND OFFICER	Lyons
MESSENGER	Bland
SAILOR	Alfred

COVENT GARDEN
Oct. 1

OTHELLO	Pope
RODERIGO	Blanchard

1792 COVENT GARDEN (cont.)

Oct. 1 (cont.)

CASSIO	Macready
BRABANTIO	Hull
LODOVICO	Davies
MONTANO	Marshall
DUKE	Cubitt
GRATIANO	Powel
IAGO	Harley
EMILIA	Mrs Fawcett
DESDEMONA	Mrs Pope

HAYMARKET

Feb. 6

OTHELLO	Baker
DUKE	Miller
BRABANTIO	Sinclair
CASSIO	Wilson
RODERIGO	Mansill
LODOVICO	King
GRATIANO	Hunter
MONTANO	Thompson
1ST OFFICER	[J.] Johnson
2ND OFFICER	Collings
IAGO	Wilkinson
EMILIA	Mrs Murray
DESDEMONA	Mrs Churton

1793 DRURY LANE (company at HAYMARKET)

Apr. 20

DUKE	Maddocks
BRABANTIO	[J.] Aickin
GRATIANO	Benson
LODOVICO	Packer
OTHELLO	Kemble
CASSIO	Barrymore
IAGO	Bensley
RODERIGO	Dodd
MONTANO	Whitfield
JULIO	Webb
ANTONIO	Caulfield
1ST OFFICER	Banks
2ND OFFICER	Lyons
MESSENGER	Bland
SAILOR	Alfred
DESDEMONA	Mrs Siddons
EMILIA	Mrs Ward

OTHELLO

1793 COVENT GARDEN
Sept. 23

OTHELLO	Middleton
RODERIGO	Bernard
CASSIO	Macready
BRABANTIO	Hull
LODOVICO	Davies
MONTANO	Claremont
DUKE	Cubitt
GRATIANO	Powel
IAGO	Harley
EMILIA	Mrs Fawcett
DESDEMONA	Mrs Pope

HAYMARKET
Oct. 21

OTHELLO	Kemble
CASSIO	Barrymore
BRABANTIO	[J.] Aickin
RODERIGO	Bland
LODOVICO	Caulfield
MONTANO	[J.] Palmer Jr.
GRATIANO	Benson
DUKE	Maddocks
1ST OFFICER	[J.] Cooke
2ND OFFICER	Lyons
3RD OFFICER	[G.] Waldron
IAGO	Bensley
EMILIA	Mrs Goodall
DESDEMONA	Mrs Powell

1794 DRURY LANE
Nov. 18

DUKE	Maddocks
BRABANTIO	[J.] Aickin
GRATIANO	Phillimore
LODOVICO	Packer
OTHELLO	Kemble
CASSIO	Barrymore
IAGO	Bensley
RODERIGO	Dodd
MONTANO	Whitfield
1ST OFFICER	Banks
2ND OFFICER	Lyons
JULIO	Benson
ANTONIO	Caulfield
MESSENGER	Bland

521

1794 DRURY LANE (cont.)
Nov. 18 (cont.)

SAILOR	Trueman
DESDEMONA	Mrs Siddons
EMILIA	Mrs Powell

COVENT GARDEN
May 21

OTHELLO	Pope
RODERIGO	Bernard
CASSIO (1)	Richardson
BRABANTIO	Hull
LODOVICO	Davies
MONTANO	Claremont
DUKE (1)	Cubitt
GRATIANO	Powel
IAGO	Harley
EMILIA	Mrs Fawcett
DESDEMONA (1)	Miss Chapman

(1) Sept. 17

CASSIO	Macready
DUKE	Thompson
DESDEMONA	Mrs Pope

1796 COVENT GARDEN
Oct. 24; Dec. 12

OTHELLO	Pope
RODERIGO	Knight
CASSIO	Macready
BRABANTIO	Hull
LODOVICO	Toms
DUKE	Thompson
GRATIANO	Powel
MONTANO	Claremont
IAGO	Murray
EMILIA	Mrs Fawcett
DESDEMONA	Mrs Pope

1797 DRURY LANE
Mar. 20

DUKE	Maddocks
BRABANTIO	[J.] Aickin
GRATIANO (1)	Phillimore
LODOVICO	Packer
OTHELLO	Kemble
CASSIO	C. Kemble
IAGO	[J.] Palmer
RODERIGO	Russell
MONTANO (1)	Campbell
JULIO	Trueman

(1) Nov. 23

GRATIANO	Caulfield
MONTANO	Holland
ANTONIO	Gibbon

[C. Kemble's name is in the bill as CASSIO.]

OTHELLO

1797 DRURY LANE (cont.)
Mar. 20 (cont.)

ANTONIO (I)	Caulfield
DESDEMONA	Mrs Siddons
EMILIA	Mrs Powell

[The bill assigns CASSIO to Barrymore. But O, Mar. 21, has, 'C. Kemble was very much applauded in Cassio'.]

HAYMARKET
Sept. 4

OTHELLO	Elliston
IAGO	[J.] Palmer
CASSIO	C. Kemble
RODERIGO	R. Palmer
BRABANTIO	[J.] Aickin
LODOVICO	Caulfield
MONTANO	[J.] Palmer Jr.
GRATIANO	Abbot
DUKE	Usher
EMILIA	Mrs Harlowe
DESDEMONA	Miss DeCamp

1798 COVENT GARDEN
Oct. 15

OTHELLO	A Young Gentleman [Huddart (EM, Oct. 1798, 258); first appearance in London]
RODERIGO	Knight
CASSIO	Betterton
BRABANTIO	Hull
LODOVICO	Whitfield
DUKE	Waddy
GRATIANO	Powel
MONTANO	Clarke
IAGO	Murray
EMILIA	Mrs Litchfield
DESDEMONA	Mrs [M. A.] Pope

1799 COVENT GARDEN
Oct. 4

OTHELLO	Pope
RODERIGO	Knight
CASSIO	Betterton
BRABANTIO	Hull
LODOVICO	Whitfield
DUKE	Waddy
GRATIANO	Gardner
MONTANO	Claremont

OTHELLO

1799 COVENT GARDEN (*cont.*)
Oct. 4 (cont.)

1ST SENATOR	Davenport
2ND SENATOR	Rees
IAGO	Murray
EMILIA	Mrs Litchfield
DESDEMONA	Mrs [M. A.] Pope

1800 DRURY LANE
June 18

DUKE	Maddocks
BRABANTIO	Packer
GRATIANO	Sparks
LODOVICO	Webb
OTHELLO	Lacy
CASSIO	Holland
IAGO	Cory
RODERIGO	Talbot
MONTANO	DeCamp
1ST GENTLEMAN	Wentworth
2ND GENTLEMAN	Ryder
1ST OFFICER	Evans
2ND OFFICER	Fisher
DESDEMONA	Mrs Powell
EMILIA	Mrs Sparks

COVENT GARDEN
Nov. 28; Dec. 3

OTHELLO (2)	Pope
RODERIGO	Knight
CASSIO	Betterton
BRABANTIO	Hull
LODOVICO	Whitfield
DUKE	Waddy
GRATIANO	Davenport
MONTANO	Claremont
1ST SENATOR (1)	Atkins
2ND SENATOR (1)	Street
IAGO	Cooke
EMILIA	Mrs Litchfield
DESDEMONA	Mrs [M. A.] Pope

(1) *Dec. 11*
omitted SENATORS

(2) *Dec. 20*
OTHELLO A Gentleman [Moisey (MM, Jan. 1801, 55); first appearance on the stage]

PYRAMUS AND THISBE
John Frederick Lampe's alteration of A MIDSUMMER-NIGHT'S DREAM, q.v.

RICHARD III

(1) Altered by Colley Cibber. In five acts.

    n.d. [1700]   B. Lintott.

    For a description of this see my Volume I, 378.

(2) 'As it is acted at the Theatre-Royal in Drury-Lane.'

    1751   J. and R. Tonson [&c.].

    This is identical with (1), but it has occasional minor restorations of the original, notably *IV. iv. 398–411.*

(3) 'As it is acted at the Theatre-Royal in Drury-Lane.'

    1756   W. Feales.

(4) 'As it is now Acted at the Theatres-Royal in Drury-Lane, Covent-Garden, and Smock-Alley [Dublin].'

    1756   Dublin: Brice Edmond.

    Both of these are identical with (1).

(5) 'As it is acted at the Theatre-Royal in Drury-Lane.'

    1769   For the Proprietors.

(6) 'As Performed at the Theatre-Royal, Drury-Lane. Regulated from the Prompt-Book.'

    1773   John Bell.

(7) 'As performed at the Theatres-Royal in Drury-Lane and Covent-Garden.'

    1775   W. Oxlade.

    All these are identical with (2).

(8) 'As it is Acted at the Theatres-Royal in Drury-Lane and Covent-Garden.'

    1778   W. Oxlade.

(9) 'Taken from the Manager's Book, at the Theatre-Royal, Covent-Garden.'

    1787   For the Proprietors.

(10) 'As it is now acted at the Theatres-Royal in Drury-Lane, Covent-Garden, and Crow-Street [Dublin].'

    1790   Dublin: P. Wogan.

(11) 'Marked with the Variations in the Manager's Book, at the Theatre Royal Drury Lane.'

    1793   W. Lowndes and S. Bladon.

(12) 'As performed at the Theatres-Royal. Regulated from the Prompt-Books.'

    n.d. [*c.* 1800]   J. Barker.

    All these are identical with (1).

RICHARD III
[as altered by CIBBER]

1751 DRURY LANE
Feb. 16

RICHARD (2)	Garrick
HENRY	Berry
BUCKINGHAM (2)	Bridges
RICHMOND (2)	Palmer
STANLEY	Winstone
TRESSEL	Blakes
CATESBY	Marr
LIEUTENANT (1)	Ray
PRINCE EDWARD (1)	Miss Minors
DUKE OF YORK	Miss Yates
DUCHESS OF YORK	Mrs Bennet
LADY ANNE (2)	Mrs Mills
QUEEN ELIZABETH	Mrs Pritchard

(1) *May 7*

LIEUTENANT	Mozeen
PRINCE EDWARD	Mrs Green

(2) *Sept. 26, 27; Oct. 1, 5; Nov. 26*

RICHARD	Mossop (on *Sept. 26, 27, Oct. 1, 5* only) [first appearance, Sept. 26, in London]
BUCKINGHAM	Lee
RICHMOND	Havard
LADY ANNE	Mrs Ward

COVENT GARDEN
Nov. 22

RICHARD (1)	Ricard [first appearance in London]
HENRY (1)	Ryan
RICHMOND	Ridout
BUCKINGHAM	Sparks
STANLEY	Redman
CATESBY	Gibson
RATCLIFF	Anderson
TRESSEL	Cushing
NORFOLK	Bransby
LORD MAYOR	Marten
TYRREL	Dunstall
LIEUTENANT	Usher
PRINCE EDWARD	Miss Morrison
DUKE OF YORK	Miss Mullart
LADY ANNE	Mrs Barrington
DUCHESS OF YORK (1)	Miss Pitt
QUEEN ELIZABETH	Mrs Vincent

(1) *Dec. 26*

RICHARD	Ryan
HENRY	Bridgwater
DUCHESS OF YORK	Mrs Bambridge

[The bill states that this was Ricard's first appearance on the stage. This is incorrect: he first appeared in Edinburgh in December 1750 (Dibdin, 69).]

NEW WELLS, GOODMAN'S FIELDS
Aug. 6, 7

RICHARD	Goodfellow

No other parts assigned

RICHARD III [as altered by CIBBER]

1752 DRURY LANE
Jan. 15

RICHARD (1, 3)	Mossop
HENRY (1)	Berry
BUCKINGHAM (3)	Lee
RICHMOND (1)	Havard
STANLEY	Winstone
TRESSEL	Blakes
CATESBY	Marr
LIEUTENANT	Mozeen
PRINCE EDWARD	Miss Minors
DUKE OF YORK	Miss Yates
DUCHESS OF YORK	Mrs Bennet
LADY ANNE (3)	Mrs Ward
QUEEN ELIZABETH	Mrs Pritchard

(1) *Feb. 3*

RICHARD	Garrick
HENRY	Havard
RICHMOND	Palmer

(2) *Apr. 1*
added

SERVANT	Ackman

(3) *Sept. 30; Nov. 24*

RICHARD	Garrick (on *Nov. 24* only)
BUCKINGHAM	Palmer
LADY ANNE	Mrs Davies

COVENT GARDEN
Apr. 18

RICHARD	Ryan
HENRY	Bridgwater
RICHMOND (1)	Ridout
BUCKINGHAM	Sparks
STANLEY	Redman
CATESBY (2)	Gibson
RATCLIFF	Anderson
TRESSEL	Cushing
NORFOLK	Bransby
LORD MAYOR	Marten
TYRREL	Dunstall
LIEUTENANT (2)	Usher
PRINCE EDWARD	Miss Morrison
DUKE OF YORK (2)	Miss Mullart
LADY ANNE	Mrs Barrington
DUCHESS OF YORK	Mrs Bambridge
QUEEN ELIZABETH	Mrs Vincent

(1) *May 5*

RICHMOND	Ricard

(2) *Sept. 22*

CATESBY	Usher
LIEUTENANT	Ricard
DUKE OF YORK	Miss Hallam

NEW WELLS, GOODMAN'S FIELDS
Nov. 23

RICHARD	Goodfellow

No other parts assigned

1753 DRURY LANE
Jan. 18

RICHARD (1, 2, 4)	Mossop
HENRY	Berry
BUCKINGHAM (2, 3, 4)	Burton
RICHMOND (2, 3, 4)	Palmer

(1) *Feb. 23*

RICHARD	Brown [first appearance in London]

(2) *Apr. 7; May 9*

RICHARD	Garrick (on *Apr. 7* only)

RICHARD III [as altered by CIBBER]

1753 DRURY LANE (cont.)

Jan. 18 (cont.)

TRESSEL	Blakes
STANLEY (3, 4)	Winstone
CATESBY	Marr
LIEUTENANT (2, 4)	Mozeen
PRINCE EDWARD	Miss Minors
DUKE OF YORK	Master Simson
DUCHESS OF YORK	Mrs Bennet
LADY ANNE	Mrs Davies
QUEEN ELIZABETH	Mrs Pritchard

(2) Apr. 7; May 9 (cont.)

BUCKINGHAM	Palmer
RICHMOND	Havard

added on *May* 9 only

TYRREL	W. Vaughan

omitted on *May* 9 only

LIEUTENANT

(3) Sept. 25; Oct. 26

BUCKINGHAM	Palmer
RICHMOND	Havard
STANLEY	Bransby

(4) Nov. 28; Dec. 18

RICHARD	Garrick
BUCKINGHAM	Palmer
RICHMOND	Havard
STANLEY	Bransby (on *Nov.* 28 only) / Mozeen (on *Dec.* 18 only)
LIEUTENANT	Jefferson (on *Dec.* 18 only)

COVENT GARDEN

Jan. 6

RICHARD	Ryan
HENRY	Bridgwater
BUCKINGHAM	Sparks
RICHMOND	Joseph Lowe [first appearance on the stage]
LADY ANNE	Mrs Barrington
DUCHESS OF YORK	Mrs Bambridge
QUEEN ELIZABETH	Mrs Vincent

May 18

RICHARD	Ryan
HENRY (1)	Sparks
RICHMOND	Ridout
BUCKINGHAM (1)	Bransby
STANLEY	Redman
CATESBY	Usher
RATCLIFF	Anderson
TRESSEL	Cushing
NORFOLK (1)	Bencraft
LORD MAYOR (1)	Marten
TYRREL	Dunstall
LIEUTENANT (1)	Ricard
PRINCE EDWARD	Miss Morrison
DUKE OF YORK	Miss Hallam
LADY ANNE	Mrs Barrington
DUCHESS OF YORK	Mrs Bambridge
QUEEN ELIZABETH	Mrs Vincent

(1) Sept. 21

HENRY	Bridgwater
BUCKINGHAM	Sparks
NORFOLK	Wignell
LIEUTENANT	White

added

OXFORD	Bencraft

omitted

LORD MAYOR

RICHARD III [as altered by CIBBER]

1753 PHILLIPS'S BOOTH, BOWLING GREEN, SOUTHWARK
Sept. 27. No parts assigned

1754 DRURY LANE
Jan. 9

RICHARD (3)	Mossop
HENRY (1)	Berry
BUCKINGHAM	Palmer
RICHMOND	Havard
STANLEY (1, 2, 3)	Mozeen
TRESSEL	Blakes
CATESBY (1, 3)	Marr
LIEUTENANT (1, 2, 3)	Jefferson
PRINCE EDWARD	Miss Minors
DUKE OF YORK	Master Simson
DUCHESS OF YORK	Mrs Bennet
LADY ANNE	Mrs Davies
QUEEN ELIZABETH	Mrs Pritchard

(1) *May 2*

HENRY	Burton
omitted	
STANLEY, CATESBY, LIEUTENANT	

(2) *Oct. 1*

STANLEY	Bransby
LIEUTENANT	Mozeen

(3) *Oct. 24; Dec. 28*

RICHARD	Garrick (on *Oct. 24* only)
STANLEY	Bransby
CATESBY	Usher
LIEUTENANT	Mozeen

[On *Oct. 24* PA retains Marr as CATESBY.]

COVENT GARDEN
Apr. 2

RICHARD (1)	Shuter
HENRY	Ridout
RICHMOND	Dyer
BUCKINGHAM	Sparks
STANLEY	Redman
CATESBY (1)	Usher
RATCLIFF	Anderson
TRESSEL	Cushing
NORFOLK (1)	Bencraft
OXFORD (1)	Wignell
TYRREL	Dunstall
LIEUTENANT	White
PRINCE EDWARD	Miss Mullart
DUKE OF YORK	Miss Hallam
LADY ANNE	Mrs Barrington
DUCHESS OF YORK	Mrs Bambridge
QUEEN ELIZABETH	Mrs Vincent

(1) *Sept. 20*

RICHARD	Ryan
CATESBY	Gibson
NORFOLK	Wignell
OXFORD	Bencraft
added	
BLUNT	Holtom
LORD MAYOR	Marten

Oct. 26

RICHARD	Sheridan
HENRY	Ryan
RICHMOND	Ridout
BUCKINGHAM	Sparks
STANLEY	Redman
CATESBY	Wignell

(1) *Nov. 14; Dec. 28*

TRESSEL	Cushing
DUCHESS OF YORK	Mrs Pitt
QUEEN ELIZABETH	Mrs Hamilton
added	
OXFORD	Bencraft

RICHARD III [*as altered by* CIBBER]

1754 COVENT GARDEN (*cont.*)
Oct. 26 (cont.)

RATCLIFF	Anderson
TRESSEL (1)	A Gentleman [Hurst (Not. Dram.); first appearance on the stage]
NORFOLK	Gibson
TYRREL	Dunstall
LIEUTENANT	White
BLUNT	Holtom
LORD MAYOR	Marten
PRINCE EDWARD	Miss Mullart
DUKE OF YORK	Miss Hallam
LADY ANNE	Mrs Barrington
DUCHESS OF YORK (1)	Mrs Bambridge
QUEEN ELIZABETH (1)	Mrs Vincent

1755 DRURY LANE
Apr. 26   (1) *Oct. 23; Dec. 8*

RICHARD (1)	Mossop
HENRY (1)	Scrase
BUCKINGHAM (1)	Palmer
RICHMOND	Havard
STANLEY	Bransby
TRESSEL	Blakes
CATESBY	Usher
LIEUTENANT (1)	Mozeen
PRINCE EDWARD (1)	Miss Minors
DUKE OF YORK (1)	Master Simson
DUCHESS OF YORK	Mrs Bennet
LADY ANNE	Mrs Davies
QUEEN ELIZABETH	Mrs Pritchard

RICHARD	Garrick (on *Oct.* 23 only) / Murphy (on *Dec.* 8 only)
HENRY	Berry
BUCKINGHAM	Davies
LIEUTENANT	Jefferson
PRINCE EDWARD	Master Simson
DUKE OF YORK	Master Cautherley

COVENT GARDEN
Apr. 17

RICHARD	Murphy
HENRY	Ryan
RICHMOND	Ridout
BUCKINGHAM	Sparks
STANLEY	Redman
CATESBY	Wignell
RATCLIFF	Anderson
NORFOLK	Gibson
TYRREL	Dunstall
LIEUTENANT	White
PRINCE EDWARD	Miss Mullart

530

RICHARD III [as altered by CIBBER]

1755 COVENT GARDEN (cont.)
Apr. 17 (cont.)

DUKE OF YORK	Miss Hallam
TRESSEL	Cushing
BLUNT	Holtom
OXFORD	Bencraft
LORD MAYOR	Marten
QUEEN ELIZABETH	Mrs Elmy
DUCHESS OF YORK	Mrs Pitt
LADY ANNE	Mrs Woffington

1756 DRURY LANE
Feb. 25

RICHARD (1)	Garrick
HENRY	Berry
BUCKINGHAM	Davies
RICHMOND	Havard
STANLEY	Bransby
TRESSEL	Blakes
CATESBY	Usher
LIEUTENANT	Mozeen
PRINCE EDWARD	Master Simson
DUKE OF YORK	Master Cautherley
DUCHESS OF YORK	Mrs Bennet
LADY ANNE	Mrs Davies
QUEEN ELIZABETH	Mrs Pritchard

(1) Sept. 21; Oct. 22

RICHARD	Mossop

1757 DRURY LANE
Jan. 4; Mar. 5; Sept. 13

RICHARD (2)	Mossop
HENRY (1)	Berry
BUCKINGHAM	Davies
RICHMOND	Havard
STANLEY (2)	Bransby
TRESSEL	Blakes
CATESBY	Usher
LIEUTENANT (2)	Mozeen
PRINCE EDWARD	Master Simson
DUKE OF YORK (1)	Master Cautherley
DUCHESS OF YORK	Mrs Bennet
LADY ANNE	Mrs Davies
QUEEN ELIZABETH	Mrs Pritchard

(1) May 9

HENRY	Scrase
DUKE OF YORK added	Miss Simson
TYRREL	Burton
OXFORD	Ackman

(2) Oct. 28

RICHARD	Garrick
STANLEY	Mozeen
LIEUTENANT	Jefferson

COVENT GARDEN
Jan. 27, 29; Feb. 1, 8, 10

RICHARD (1)	Barry
HENRY	Ryan
RICHMOND	Ridout

(1) Nov. 11

RICHARD	Lee
LADY ANNE	Mrs Vincent
QUEEN ELIZABETH	Mrs Hamilton

RICHARD III [*as altered by* CIBBER]

1757 COVENT GARDEN (*cont.*)
Jan. 27, 29; Feb. 1, 8, 10 (cont.)

STANLEY	Anderson
NORFOLK	Gibson
RATCLIFF	Bennet
CATESBY	White
BUCKINGHAM	Sparks
TRESSEL	Dyer
LORD MAYOR	Marten
LIEUTENANT	Cushing
OXFORD	Bencraft
BLUNT	Redman
PRINCE EDWARD	Miss Mullart
DUKE OF YORK	Miss Hallam
BRANDON	Wignell
TYRREL	Dunstall
FORREST	Holtom
DIGHTON	R. Smith
LADY ANNE (1)	Miss Nossiter
DUCHESS OF YORK	Mrs Elmy
QUEEN ELIZABETH (1)	Mrs Woffington

1758 DRURY LANE
Oct. 12

RICHARD	Mossop
HENRY	Berry
BUCKINGHAM	Davies
RICHMOND	Havard
TRESSEL	Holland
STANLEY	Bransby
NORFOLK	Burton
CATESBY	Packer
LIEUTENANT	Mozeen
PRINCE EDWARD	Master Simson
DUKE OF YORK	Miss Simson
DUCHESS OF YORK	Mrs Bennet
LADY ANNE	Mrs Davies
QUEEN ELIZABETH	Mrs Pritchard

COVENT GARDEN
Mar. 13

RICHARD	Barry
HENRY	Ryan
RICHMOND	Ridout
STANLEY	Anderson
NORFOLK	Gibson
RATCLIFF	Bennet

RICHARD III [as altered by CIBBER]

1758 COVENT GARDEN (cont.)
Mar. 13 (cont.)

CATESBY	White
BUCKINGHAM	Sparks
TRESSEL	Dyer
LORD MAYOR	Marten
LIEUTENANT	Cushing
OXFORD	Bencraft
BLUNT	Redman
PRINCE EDWARD	Miss Mullart
DUKE OF YORK	Miss Hallam
BRANDON	Wignell
TYRREL	Dunstall
FORREST	Holtom
DIGHTON	R. Smith
LADY ANNE	Mrs Vincent
DUCHESS OF YORK	Mrs Elmy
QUEEN ELIZABETH	Mrs Bellamy

1759 DRURY LANE
Feb. 27

RICHARD (1, 2)	Mossop
HENRY (2)	Blakes
BUCKINGHAM (1, 2)	Palmer
RICHMOND (2)	Havard
TRESSEL	Holland
STANLEY	Bransby
NORFOLK	Burton
CATESBY	Packer
LIEUTENANT	Mozeen
PRINCE EDWARD	Master Simson
DUKE OF YORK	Miss Simson
DUCHESS OF YORK	Mrs Bennet
LADY ANNE	Mrs Davies
QUEEN ELIZABETH	Mrs Pritchard

(1) Mar. 8

RICHARD	Garrick
BUCKINGHAM	Davies

(2) Oct. 19

RICHARD	Garrick
HENRY	Havard
BUCKINGHAM	Davies
RICHMOND	Palmer

COVENT GARDEN
May 11

RICHARD	Shuter
HENRY	Ryan
RICHMOND	Anderson
STANLEY	Redman
NORFOLK	Gibson
RATCLIFF	Bennet
CATESBY	Davis
BUCKINGHAM	Sparks
TRESSEL	Dyer

RICHARD III [as altered by CIBBER]

1759 COVENT GARDEN (cont.)
May 11 (cont.)

LORD MAYOR	Marten
LIEUTENANT	R. Smith
OXFORD	Bencraft
BLUNT	Perry
PRINCE EDWARD	Miss Mullart
DUKE OF YORK	Miss Valois
BRANDON	Wignell
TYRREL	Dunstall
FORREST	Holtom
LADY ANNE	Mrs Vincent
DUCHESS OF YORK	Mrs Elmy
QUEEN ELIZABETH	Mrs Hamilton

1760 DRURY LANE
May 1

RICHARD (1, 2)	Holland
HENRY	Havard
BUCKINGHAM	Davies
RICHMOND	Palmer
TRESSEL	Austin
STANLEY (2)	Bransby
NORFOLK (2)	Burton
CATESBY (2)	Packer
LIEUTENANT (2)	Mozeen
PRINCE EDWARD (2)	Miss Simson
DUKE OF YORK	Miss Rogers
DUCHESS OF YORK	Mrs Bennet
LADY ANNE (2)	Mrs Davies
QUEEN ELIZABETH	Mrs Pritchard

(1) *May 22, 31*

RICHARD	Garrick

(2) *Oct. 9, 13; Nov. 19, 21*

RICHARD	Sheridan (on *Oct.* 9, 13, *Nov.* 19 only)
	Garrick (on *Nov.* 21 only)
PRINCE EDWARD	Master Cautherley
LADY ANNE	Miss Pritchard (on *Nov.* 19 only)

omitted
    STANLEY, NORFOLK, CATESBY, LIEUTENANT

1761 DRURY LANE
Apr. 21

RICHARD (1, 2)	Sheridan
HENRY	Havard
PRINCE EDWARD	Master Cautherley
DUKE OF YORK	Miss Rogers
BUCKINGHAM (1, 2)	Bransby
RICHMOND	Palmer
TRESSEL (2)	Austin
LORD MAYOR (1)	Philips
LADY ANNE	Mrs Davies
DUCHESS OF YORK	Mrs Bennet
QUEEN ELIZABETH	Mrs Pritchard

(1) *May 29*

RICHARD	Holland
BUCKINGHAM	Davies
LORD MAYOR	Baddeley

(2) *Sept. 26; Oct. 21*

RICHARD	Holland (on *Sept.* 26 only)
	Garrick (on *Oct.* 21 only)
BUCKINGHAM	Davies
TRESSEL	Kennedy

RICHARD III [as altered by CIBBER]

1761 COVENT GARDEN
Mar. 30

RICHARD	Smith
HENRY	Gibson
RICHMOND (1)	Clarke
BUCKINGHAM	Sparks
TRESSEL (1)	Dyer
PRINCE EDWARD (2)	A Young Gentleman [unidentified]
DUKE OF YORK	Miss Valois
LADY ANNE	Mrs Vincent
DUCHESS OF YORK	Mrs Elmy
QUEEN ELIZABETH	Mrs Hamilton

(1) *May 5, 21*

RICHMOND	Davis (on *May 5* only)
TRESSEL	Perry (on *May 5* only)

added

NORFOLK	Buck
STANLEY	Anderson
LIEUTENANT	R. Smith
RATCLIFF	Bennet
LORD MAYOR	Marten
CATESBY	Holtom
OXFORD	Weller

(2) *Dec. 28*

PRINCE EDWARD	Mrs Evans

added

NORFOLK	Perry
STANLEY	Anderson
LIEUTENANT	R. Smith
RATCLIFF	Bennet
CATESBY	Holtom
LORD MAYOR	Marten
OXFORD	Weller

[Both Pb and PA assign PRINCE EDWARD to Miss Mullart. But earlier this year she had adopted the stage name of Mrs Evans.]

1762 DRURY LANE
Jan. 2

RICHARD	Holland
HENRY (1)	Havard
DUKE OF YORK	Miss Rogers
BUCKINGHAM (2)	Davies
RICHMOND	Palmer
TRESSEL (1, 2)	Kennedy
LORD MAYOR	Philips
LADY ANNE	Mrs Davies
QUEEN ELIZABETH	Mrs Pritchard

(1) *May 6*

HENRY	Moody
TRESSEL	Ackman

added

PRINCE EDWARD	Miss Read
DUCHESS OF YORK	Mrs Bennet

(2) *Oct. 5*

BUCKINGHAM	Lee
TRESSEL	Ackman

added

PRINCE EDWARD	Master Burton
STANLEY	Bransby
DUCHESS OF YORK	Mrs Bennet

Dec. 18

RICHARD	Garrick
HENRY	Havard
PRINCE EDWARD	Master Burton
DUKE OF YORK	Miss Rogers
BUCKINGHAM	Lee
RICHMOND	Palmer
TRESSEL	Ackman
STANLEY	Bransby

(1) *Dec. 23*

NORFOLK	Burton

RICHARD III [as altered by CIBBER]

1762 DRURY LANE (cont.)
Dec. 18 (cont.)

LORD MAYOR	Philips
CATESBY	Packer
NORFOLK (1)	Blakes
RATCLIFF	Castle
LIEUTENANT	Moody
OFFICER	J. Palmer
LADY ANNE	Mrs Davies
DUCHESS OF YORK	Mrs Bennet
QUEEN ELIZABETH	Mrs Pritchard

[The OFFICER is not in the bill. Genest (vii. 342) states that in 1762–3 this part was the 'highest character' acted by J. Palmer, who was then at the commencement of his career.]

COVENT GARDEN
Jan. 5, 8, 11

RICHARD	Smith
HENRY	Gibson
NORFOLK	Perry
STANLEY	Anderson
LIEUTENANT	R. Smith
RATCLIFF	Bennet
CATESBY	Davis
BUCKINGHAM (1, 2, 3, 4)	Sparks
TRESSEL	Dyer
LORD MAYOR (3)	Buck
OXFORD (2, 3, 4)	Weller
PRINCE EDWARD	Mrs Evans
DUKE OF YORK	Miss Valois
RICHMOND	Clarke
BLUNT (2, 3, 4)	Redman
TYRREL (2, 3)	Gardner
LADY ANNE	Mrs Vincent
DUCHESS OF YORK (1, 3, 4)	Mrs Elmy
QUEEN ELIZABETH (3, 4)	Mrs Hamilton

(1) *Jan. 14, 16, 19, 23; Feb. 8, 20; Mar. 6, 16*

BUCKINGHAM	Hull
DUCHESS OF YORK	Mrs Ferguson (on *Feb. 20, Mar. 6* only)

(2) *May 10, 18*

BUCKINGHAM Hull
omitted
    OXFORD, BLUNT, TYRREL

(3) *Oct. 9*

BUCKINGHAM	Hull
LORD MAYOR	Marten
DUCHESS OF YORK	Mrs Ferguson
QUEEN ELIZABETH	Mrs Ward
omitted
    SAME as *May 10*

(4) *Nov. 26*

BUCKINGHAM	Hull
DUCHESS OF YORK	Mrs Ferguson
QUEEN ELIZABETH	Mrs Ward
omitted
    OXFORD, BLUNT

1763 DRURY LANE
Jan. 11

RICHARD (1)	Garrick
HENRY	Havard
PRINCE EDWARD	Master Burton
DUKE OF YORK	Miss Rogers
BUCKINGHAM	Lee

(1) *Oct. 24; Nov. 18*

RICHARD	Holland
QUEEN ELIZABETH	Mrs Pritchard

RICHARD III [*as altered by* CIBBER]

1763 DRURY LANE (*cont.*)
Jan. 11 (cont.)

RICHMOND	Palmer
TRESSEL	Ackman
STANLEY	Bransby
LORD MAYOR	Philips
CATESBY	Packer
NORFOLK	Burton
RATCLIFF	Castle
LIEUTENANT	Moody
LADY ANNE	Mrs Davies
DUCHESS OF YORK	Mrs Bennet
QUEEN ELIZABETH (1)	Mrs Cibber

COVENT GARDEN
Dec. 26

RICHARD	Smith
HENRY	Gibson
RICHMOND	Clarke
BUCKINGHAM	Hull
CATESBY	Davis
NORFOLK	Perry
RATCLIFF	Bennet
STANLEY	Anderson
TRESSEL	Dyer
PRINCE EDWARD	Mrs Evans
DUKE OF YORK	Miss Valois
LORD MAYOR	Buck
LIEUTENANT	R. Smith
LADY ANNE	Mrs Vincent
DUCHESS OF YORK	Mrs Ferguson
QUEEN ELIZABETH	Mrs Ward

1764 DRURY LANE
Feb. 4

RICHARD	Holland
HENRY (1)	Havard
PRINCE EDWARD	Master Burton
DUKE OF YORK	Miss Rogers
BUCKINGHAM	Lee
RICHMOND	Palmer
TRESSEL	Ackman
STANLEY	Bransby
LORD MAYOR (1, 3)	Philips
CATESBY	Packer
NORFOLK	Burton

(1) *May 10*

HENRY	Powell
LORD MAYOR	Baddeley
LIEUTENANT	Mozeen

(2) *Sept. 20*

LADY ANNE	Mrs Palmer

(3) *Nov. 13*

LORD MAYOR	Baddeley
RATCLIFF	Strange
LADY ANNE	Mrs Palmer

537

RICHARD III [as altered by CIBBER]

1764 DRURY LANE (cont.)
Feb. 4 (cont.)

RATCLIFF (3)	Castle
LIEUTENANT (1)	Moody
LADY ANNE (2, 3)	Mrs Davies
DUCHESS OF YORK	Mrs Bennet
QUEEN ELIZABETH	Mrs Pritchard

COVENT GARDEN
Feb. 20

RICHARD	Smith
HENRY (1)	Gibson
RICHMOND (1)	Clarke
BUCKINGHAM	Hull
CATESBY (1)	Davis
NORFOLK	Perry
RATCLIFF	Bennet
STANLEY	Anderson
TRESSEL (1)	Dyer
PRINCE EDWARD	Mrs Evans
DUKE OF YORK (1, 2)	Miss Valois
LORD MAYOR	Buck
LIEUTENANT	R. Smith
LADY ANNE	Mrs Vincent
DUCHESS OF YORK	Mrs Ferguson
QUEEN ELIZABETH	Mrs Ward

(1) *May 15*

HENRY	Hallam
RICHMOND	Davis
CATESBY	Wignell
TRESSEL	White
DUKE OF YORK added	Master Besford
OXFORD	Weller
FORREST	Holtom

(2) *Oct. 8; Nov. 12*

DUKE OF YORK added	Master Besford
SAME as *May 15*	

1765 DRURY LANE
Jan. 4; Mar. 11

RICHARD	Holland
HENRY	Havard
PRINCE EDWARD	Master Burton
DUKE OF YORK	Miss Rogers
BUCKINGHAM	Lee
RICHMOND	Palmer
TRESSEL	Ackman
STANLEY	Bransby
LORD MAYOR (1)	Baddeley
CATESBY	Packer
NORFOLK (2)	Burton
RATCLIFF	Strange
LIEUTENANT	Moody
LADY ANNE	Mrs Palmer
DUCHESS OF YORK	Mrs Bennet
QUEEN ELIZABETH (1)	Mrs Pritchard

(1) *May 8*

LORD MAYOR	Philips
QUEEN ELIZABETH	Mrs Lee

(2) *Oct. 14*
omitted
NORFOLK

RICHARD III [as altered by CIBBER]

1765 COVENT GARDEN

Jan. 1

RICHARD	Smith
HENRY	Gibson
RICHMOND (1, 2)	Clarke
BUCKINGHAM (1)	Hull
CATESBY (2)	Davis
NORFOLK (1, 2)	Wignell
RATCLIFF	Bennet
OXFORD (2)	Weller
FORREST (2)	Holtom
STANLEY	Anderson
TRESSEL	Dyer
PRINCE EDWARD (1)	Miss Valois
DUKE OF YORK	Master Besford
LORD MAYOR (2)	Buck
LIEUTENANT (2)	R. Smith
LADY ANNE (1)	Mrs Vincent
DUCHESS OF YORK	Mrs Ferguson
QUEEN ELIZABETH	Mrs Ward

(1) May 3

RICHMOND	Gardner
BUCKINGHAM	White
NORFOLK	Perry
PRINCE EDWARD	Miss Helme
LADY ANNE	Mrs Stephens

(2) Sept. 30; Nov. 18

RICHMOND	Davis
CATESBY	Wignell
NORFOLK	Perry
LORD MAYOR	[P.] Lewis (on Sept. 30 only)
LIEUTENANT	Gardner (on Nov. 18 only)

omitted
    OXFORD, FORREST
[On Nov. 18 PA assigns the LORD MAYOR to Lewis.]

1766 COVENT GARDEN

Jan. 6; Apr. 21

RICHARD (2)	Smith
HENRY	Gibson
RICHMOND (1, 3, 4)	Davis
BUCKINGHAM	Hull
CATESBY (1, 4)	Wignell
NORFOLK	Perry
RATCLIFF	Bennet
STANLEY	Anderson
TRESSEL	Dyer
PRINCE EDWARD (4)	Miss Valois
DUKE OF YORK (3, 4)	Master Besford
LORD MAYOR	Buck
LIEUTENANT	R. Smith
LADY ANNE	Mrs Vincent
DUCHESS OF YORK	Mrs Ferguson
QUEEN ELIZABETH (4)	Mrs Ward

[PA assigns the LORD MAYOR to Lewis.]

(1) Mar. 10

RICHMOND	Clarke
CATESBY	Davis

(2) Sept. 26

RICHARD	Clarke

(3) Oct. 20, 24, 27

RICHMOND	Gardner
DUKE OF YORK	Miss Besford

(4) Nov. 10; Dec. 26

RICHMOND	Clarke
CATESBY	Davis
PRINCE EDWARD	Master Besford (on Dec. 26 only)
DUKE OF YORK	Miss Besford
QUEEN ELIZABETH	Mrs Bellamy (on Dec. 26 only)

1767 DRURY LANE

Apr. 11

RICHARD	Holland
HENRY (1)	Havard
PRINCE EDWARD	Miss Rogers

(1) May 11

HENRY	Burton
NORFOLK	Hurst

omitted
    RATCLIFF, LIEUTENANT

RICHARD III [as altered by CIBBER]

1767 DRURY LANE (cont.)

Apr. 11 (cont.)

DUKE OF YORK	Miss Collett
BUCKINGHAM (2)	Bensley
RICHMOND	Palmer
TRESSEL	Cautherley
NORFOLK (1)	Burton
STANLEY	Bransby
LORD MAYOR	Baddeley
CATESBY	Packer
RATCLIFF (1)	Strange
LIEUTENANT (1)	Moody
LADY ANNE	Mrs Palmer
DUCHESS OF YORK (2)	Mrs Bennet
QUEEN ELIZABETH	Mrs Pritchard

(2) Sept. 17

BUCKINGHAM	Jefferson
DUCHESS OF YORK	Mrs Johnston

COVENT GARDEN

May 27

RICHARD	Smith
HENRY	Gibson
RICHMOND	Clarke
BUCKINGHAM	Hull
CATESBY	Davis
RATCLIFF	Bennet
STANLEY	Gardner
NORFOLK (1)	Wignell
TRESSEL (1)	Perry
PRINCE EDWARD (1)	Master Besford
DUKE OF YORK	Miss Besford
LORD MAYOR (1)	Buck
LIEUTENANT	R. Smith
LADY ANNE (1)	Mrs Vincent
DUCHESS OF YORK (1)	Mrs Ferguson
QUEEN ELIZABETH (1)	Mrs Bellamy

(1) Nov. 7, 30; Dec. 29

NORFOLK	Perry
TRESSEL	Dyer (on *Nov. 7, Dec. 29* only) / Casey (on *Nov. 30* only)
PRINCE EDWARD	Miss Valois (on *Nov. 7, 30* only) / A Young Gentleman [unidentified; first appearance on the stage] (on *Dec. 29* only)
LORD MAYOR	Wignell
LADY ANNE	Mrs Lessingham
DUCHESS OF YORK	Mrs Vincent
QUEEN ELIZABETH	Mrs Ward

1768 DRURY LANE

Apr. 12

RICHARD (1)	Reddish
HENRY (1)	Burton
RICHMOND (1)	Palmer
PRINCE EDWARD	Miss Rogers
DUKE OF YORK	Miss Collett
BUCKINGHAM (1)	[F.] Aickin
TRESSEL	Cautherley

(1) Sept. 29

RICHARD	Garrick
HENRY	Havard
RICHMOND	[F.] Aickin
BUCKINGHAM	Jefferson
NORFOLK	Burton
LADY ANNE	Mrs W. Barry
QUEEN ELIZABETH	Mrs Hopkins

RICHARD III [as altered by CIBBER]

1768 DRURY LANE (cont.)

Apr. 12 (cont.)

NORFOLK (1)	Hurst
STANLEY	Bransby
LORD MAYOR	Baddeley
CATESBY	Packer
RATCLIFF	Strange
LIEUTENANT	Moody
LADY ANNE (1)	Mrs Reddish
DUCHESS OF YORK	Mrs Johnston
QUEEN ELIZABETH (1)	Mrs Pritchard

COVENT GARDEN

Apr. 11

RICHARD	Smith
HENRY	Gibson
CATESBY	Davis
STANLEY	Gardner
RATCLIFF (1, 2)	Casey
NORFOLK	Perry
RICHMOND	Clarke
BUCKINGHAM	Hull
PRINCE EDWARD	Master Harris
DUKE OF YORK	Miss Besford
TRESSEL (1, 2)	Dyer
LORD MAYOR	Wignell
LIEUTENANT	R. Smith
LADY ANNE (1, 2)	Mrs Vincent
DUCHESS OF YORK (1, 2)	Mrs Ferguson
QUEEN ELIZABETH	Mrs Ward

(1) *May 31*

RATCLIFF	Bennet
TRESSEL	Casey
LADY ANNE	Mrs Lessingham
DUCHESS OF YORK	Mrs Vincent
added	
OXFORD	Redman
TYRREL	[R.] Bates

(2) *Sept. 22; Oct. 19; Nov. 5*

RATCLIFF	[Lee] Lewes
TRESSEL	Wroughton (on Nov. 5 only)
LADY ANNE	Mrs Lessingham
DUCHESS OF YORK	Mrs Vincent

1769 DRURY LANE

Jan. 12

RICHARD (1, 2)	Garrick
HENRY	Reddish
RICHMOND	[F.] Aickin
PRINCE EDWARD	Miss Rogers
DUKE OF YORK (1)	Miss Collett
BUCKINGHAM	Jefferson
TRESSEL	Cautherley
NORFOLK	Burton
STANLEY	Bransby
LORD MAYOR (2)	Baddeley
CATESBY (2)	Packer
RATCLIFF (2)	Strange

(1) *May 16*

RICHARD	Holland
DUKE OF YORK	Master Cape
LADY ANNE	Mrs Stephens
QUEEN ELIZABETH	Mrs Reddish

(2) *Nov. 13*

RICHARD	Holland
LIEUTENANT	Fawcett
LADY ANNE	Miss Younge
added	
OXFORD	Wheeler
OFFICER	Keen
omitted	
LORD MAYOR, CATESBY, RATCLIFF	

541

RICHARD III [as altered by CIBBER]

1769 DRURY LANE (cont.)
Jan. 12 (cont.)

LIEUTENANT (2)	Moody
LADY ANNE (1, 2)	Mrs W. Barry
DUCHESS OF YORK	Mrs Johnston
QUEEN ELIZABETH (1)	Mrs Hopkins

COVENT GARDEN
Mar. 27

RICHARD	Smith
HENRY	Gibson
CATESBY	Davis
RATCLIFF	[Lee] Lewes
STANLEY	Gardner
NORFOLK	Perry
RICHMOND (1, 3)	Clarke
BUCKINGHAM	Hull
PRINCE EDWARD	Master Harris
DUKE OF YORK	Miss Besford
TRESSEL (2)	Dyer
LORD MAYOR (1)	Wignell
LIEUTENANT (1)	R. Smith
LADY ANNE (2, 3)	Mrs Vincent
DUCHESS OF YORK (2, 3)	Mrs Ferguson
QUEEN ELIZABETH	Mrs Ward

(1) *May 18*

RICHMOND	Wroughton
omitted	
LORD MAYOR, LIEUTENANT	

(2) *Oct. 4, 28*

TRESSEL	Wroughton
LADY ANNE	Mrs Lessingham
DUCHESS OF YORK	Mrs Vincent

(3) *Dec. 28*

RICHMOND	Wroughton
LADY ANNE	Mrs Lessingham
DUCHESS OF YORK	Mrs Vincent

HAYMARKET
Aug. 14

RICHARD	Sheridan
HENRY	[C.] Bannister
RICHMOND	[J.] Aickin
BUCKINGHAM	Sowdon
TRESSEL	Wheeler
CATESBY (1)	Strange
LORD MAYOR	[I.] Sparks
OXFORD	Sharpless
STANLEY	Du-Bellamy
RATCLIFF	Jacobs
LIEUTENANT	Kearny
BLUNT	Summers
PRINCE EDWARD	Master Cape
DUKE OF YORK	Miss Rose
LADY ANNE	Mrs Du-Bellam
DUCHESS OF YORK	Mrs Dyer
QUEEN ELIZABETH	Mrs Jefferies

(1) *Sept. 6*

CATESBY	Farrell

RICHARD III [as altered by CIBBER]

1769 HAYMARKET
Sept. 19

RICHARD	F. Gentleman
HENRY	[C.] Bannister
RICHMOND	Davis
BUCKINGHAM	Gardner
PRINCE EDWARD	Master Cape
DUKE OF YORK	Miss Rose
STANLEY	Bailey
CATESBY	Farrell
RATCLIFF	Dancer
LORD MAYOR	Sharpless
LIEUTENANT	Lings
TRESSEL	A Young Gentleman [unidentified; first appearance on the stage]
LADY ANNE	Miss Ogilvie
DUCHESS OF YORK	Mrs Painter
QUEEN ELIZABETH	Mrs Wright

1770 DRURY LANE
Apr. 20

RICHARD	King
HENRY	Reddish
RICHMOND	[F.] Aickin
BUCKINGHAM (1)	Jefferson
TRESSEL (1)	Cautherley
STANLEY (1)	Bransby
NORFOLK (1)	Burton
PRINCE EDWARD	Miss Rogers
DUKE OF YORK	Miss Collett
LIEUTENANT	Fawcett
OXFORD (1)	Wheeler
OFFICER (1)	Keen
CATESBY	Packer
RATCLIFF (1)	Wright
LADY ANNE	Mrs W. Barry
DUCHESS OF YORK	Mrs Johnston
QUEEN ELIZABETH	Mrs Hopkins

(1) *May 16*

BUCKINGHAM	Wright
TRESSEL	Keen
STANLEY	Wrighten
NORFOLK	Hurst
RATCLIFF	[J.] Booth

added
    LORD MAYOR   Hartry
omitted
    OXFORD, OFFICER

COVENT GARDEN
Jan. 26

RICHARD (1)	Smith
HENRY	Gibson
CATESBY (1)	Wignell
RATCLIFF	[Lee] Lewes
STANLEY	Gardner
NORFOLK	Perry
RICHMOND	Clarke

(1) *May 14*

RICHARD	Shuter
CATESBY	Davis
LADY ANNE	Mrs Vincent
DUCHESS OF YORK	Mrs Ferguson

added
    LIEUTENANT   R. Smith
    LORD MAYOR   Wignell

RICHARD III [as altered by CIBBER]

1770 COVENT GARDEN (cont.)

Jan. 26 (cont.)

BUCKINGHAM	Hull
PRINCE EDWARD	Master Harris
DUKE OF YORK	Miss Besford
TRESSEL	Wroughton
LADY ANNE (1)	Mrs Lessingham
DUCHESS OF YORK (1)	Mrs Vincent
QUEEN ELIZABETH	Mrs Ward

[PA assigns RICHMOND to Wroughton.]

Sept. 26

RICHARD	Smith
HENRY	Gibson
CATESBY	Fox
RATCLIFF	[Lee] Lewes
STANLEY	Gardner
NORFOLK (1, 2)	Wignell
RICHMOND	Clarke
BUCKINGHAM	Hull
PRINCE EDWARD	Master Harris
DUKE OF YORK	Miss Cokayne
TRESSEL (2)	Dyer
LIEUTENANT	R. Smith
TYRREL	[R.] Bates
LADY ANNE (1)	Mrs Vincent
DUCHESS OF YORK (1, 2)	Mrs Barrington
QUEEN ELIZABETH	Mrs Ward

(1) Oct. 26

NORFOLK	Perry
LADY ANNE	Mrs Lessingham
DUCHESS OF YORK	Mrs Vincent

(2) Dec. 31

NORFOLK	Perry
TRESSEL	Wroughton
DUCHESS OF YORK	Mrs Ferguson

[PA assigns the DUKE OF YORK to Miss Besford.]

1771 DRURY LANE

Apr. 2

RICHARD	Dodd
HENRY	Reddish
RICHMOND	[F.] Aickin
BUCKINGHAM	Jefferson
TRESSEL	Cautherley
STANLEY	Bransby
NORFOLK	Burton
PRINCE EDWARD	Miss Rogers
DUKE OF YORK	Miss Collett
CATESBY	Packer
RATCLIFF	Wright
LIEUTENANT	Fawcett
LADY ANNE	Mrs W. Barry
DUCHESS OF YORK	Mrs Johnston
QUEEN ELIZABETH	Mrs Hopkins

544

RICHARD III [as altered by CIBBER]

1771 COVENT GARDEN
May 4

RICHARD	Perry
HENRY	Younger
RICHMOND	Clarke
BUCKINGHAM	Hull
CATESBY	Fox
RATCLIFF	[Lee] Lewes
NORFOLK	Wignell
STANLEY	Gardner
PRINCE EDWARD	Master Harris
DUKE OF YORK	Miss Cokayne
TRESSEL	Wroughton
DUCHESS OF YORK	Mrs Ferguson
LADY ANNE	Mrs Vincent
QUEEN ELIZABETH	Mrs Du-Bellamy

Oct. 15

RICHARD	Smith
HENRY	Kniveton
RICHMOND	Clarke
BUCKINGHAM	Hull
CATESBY (1, 2)	Fox
RATCLIFF (1, 2)	Thompson
NORFOLK	Wignell
STANLEY	Gardner
LIEUTENANT	R. Smith
LORD MAYOR	Morris
PRINCE EDWARD	Master Harris
DUKE OF YORK (1)	Miss Cokayne
TRESSEL	Wroughton
LADY ANNE (1)	Mrs Vincent
DUCHESS OF YORK (1)	Mrs Ferguson
QUEEN ELIZABETH	Miss Miller

(1) Nov. 25

CATESBY	Davis
RATCLIFF	[Lee] Lewes
DUKE OF YORK	Master Bates
LADY ANNE	Mrs Lessingham
DUCHESS OF YORK	Mrs Vincent

(2) Dec. 16

CATESBY	Davis
RATCLIFF	[Lee] Lewes

[PA assigns the DUKE OF YORK to Master Bates.]

1772 DRURY LANE
May 30; June 2

RICHARD	Garrick
HENRY	Reddish
RICHMOND	[F.] Aickin
BUCKINGHAM	Jefferson
TRESSEL	Cautherley
STANLEY	Bransby
NORFOLK	Hurst
PRINCE EDWARD	Miss Rogers
DUKE OF YORK	Miss [P.] Hopkins
CATESBY	Packer

RICHARD III [as altered by CIBBER]

1772 DRURY LANE (cont.)
May 30; June 2 (cont.)

RATCLIFF	Wright
LIEUTENANT	Fawcett
LADY ANNE	Miss Younge
DUCHESS OF YORK	Mrs Johnston
QUEEN ELIZABETH	Mrs Hopkins

[In the acting version published by Bell in 1773 the cast is the same as that of these performances (Miss P. Hopkins being specified as the DUKE OF YORK), with the following additions:

OXFORD	Wheeler
BLUNT	Griffith
LORD MAYOR	Baddeley
TYRREL	Wrighten
FORREST	Lings]

COVENT GARDEN
Feb. 3

RICHARD (2)	Smith
HENRY	Kniveton
RICHMOND (4)	Clarke
BUCKINGHAM	Hull
CATESBY	Davis
RATCLIFF	[Lee] Lewes
NORFOLK (2, 3, 4)	Wignell
STANLEY	Gardner
LIEUTENANT	R. Smith
LORD MAYOR (2, 3, 4)	Morris
PRINCE EDWARD	Master Harris
DUKE OF YORK	Master Jones
TRESSEL (4)	Wroughton
DUCHESS OF YORK	Mrs Vincent
LADY ANNE	Mrs Lessingham
QUEEN ELIZABETH	Miss Miller

(1) *Mar. 5.* No parts assigned

[Both Pb and PA announce the first performance of *A Wife in the Right*. But it was postponed because Shuter, who had a principal part, was taken ill at the rehearsal (PA, Mar. 6; Genest, v. 332–4). Egerton 2276 deletes the new comedy, and substitutes *Richard III*. See also Reed, 74: 'Mar. 5. At Covent Garden. Saw *Richard the 3d*'. *A Wife in the Right* was first acted on *Mar. 9.*]

(2) *May 12*

RICHARD	Larken
NORFOLK	Perry
LORD MAYOR	Wignell

(3) *Sept. 28*

NORFOLK	Owenson
LORD MAYOR	Wignell

(4) *Oct. 19; Dec. 30*

RICHMOND	Wroughton
NORFOLK	Owenson
LORD MAYOR	Wignell
TRESSEL	Dyer

HAYMARKET
Sept. 17

RICHARD	A Young Gentleman [Stokes (MC, Sept. 19, 1772; MP, Aug. 26, 1776); first appearance on the stage]
BUCKINGHAM	Fearon
HENRY	Gardner

546

RICHARD III [as altered by CIBBER]

1772 HAYMARKET (cont.)
Sept. 17 (cont.)

RICHMOND	Davis
STANLEY	Lloyd
TRESSEL	Dancer
LORD MAYOR	Francis
CATESBY	Farrell
LIEUTENANT	Vowell
BLUNT	Walters
PRINCE EDWARD	Miss Lings
DUKE OF YORK	Miss [S.] Francis
RATCLIFF	[R.] Smith
TYRREL	Adams
LADY ANNE	Miss Platt
DUCHESS OF YORK	Mrs White
QUEEN ELIZABETH	Mrs Parsons

1773 COVENT GARDEN
May 20

RICHARD	Smith
HENRY	Younger
BUCKINGHAM	Hull
PRINCE EDWARD	Master Harris
DUKE OF YORK	Master Jones
RICHMOND	Davis
TRESSEL	Wroughton
STANLEY	Gardner
LIEUTENANT	R. Smith
NORFOLK	Perry
CATESBY	Fox
RATCLIFF	[Lee] Lewes
LORD MAYOR	Wignell
DUCHESS OF YORK	Mrs Ferguson
LADY ANNE	Miss Ogilvie
QUEEN ELIZABETH	Mrs Vincent

Oct. 4

RICHARD	Smith
HENRY (1)	Kniveton
RICHMOND (1)	Clarke
BUCKINGHAM	Hull
CATESBY	Davis
RATCLIFF (1)	Thompson
PRINCE EDWARD	Miss Besford
DUKE OF YORK	Master Jones
LIEUTENANT (1)	Fox
LORD MAYOR (1)	Wignell
STANLEY	Gardner

(1) Dec. 9, 20

HENRY	Clarke
RICHMOND	Wroughton
RATCLIFF	[Lee] Lewes
TRESSEL	Dyer
DUCHESS OF YORK	Mrs P. Green
LADY ANNE	Mrs Lessingham

omitted
    LIEUTENANT, LORD MAYOR

RICHARD III [*as altered by* CIBBER]

1773 COVENT GARDEN (*cont.*)
Oct. 4 (*cont.*)

TRESSEL (1)	Wroughton
DUCHESS OF YORK (1)	Mrs Ferguson
LADY ANNE (1)	Mrs [T.] Baker
QUEEN ELIZABETH	Miss Miller

1774 DRURY LANE
Sept. 22

RICHARD	Smith
HENRY (1)	[J.] Aickin
RICHMOND	[J.] Palmer
BUCKINGHAM	Jefferson
TRESSEL	Cautherley
STANLEY	Bransby
NORFOLK	Hurst
LORD MAYOR (1)	Ackman
PRINCE EDWARD	Master Blanchard
DUKE OF YORK	Master Pulley
CATESBY	Packer
RATCLIFF	Wright
LIEUTENANT	Fawcett
LADY ANNE (1)	Miss Younge
DUCHESS OF YORK	Mrs Johnston
QUEEN ELIZABETH	Mrs Hopkins

(1) Oct. 29

HENRY	Reddish
LORD MAYOR	Griffiths
LADY ANNE	Mrs Greville

COVENT GARDEN
Jan. 1

RICHARD	Smith
HENRY (1, 2)	Younger
RICHMOND	Wroughton
STANLEY (1)	Gardner
PRINCE EDWARD (1)	Miss Besford
DUKE OF YORK (1)	Master Jones
CATESBY	Davis
BUCKINGHAM	Hull
RATCLIFF (1)	Thompson
NORFOLK (2)	Owenson
TRESSEL (2)	Dyer
DUCHESS OF YORK	Mrs P. Green
LADY ANNE (2)	Mrs Lessingham
QUEEN ELIZABETH (2)	Miss Miller

(1) Jan. 26

HENRY	Clarke
STANLEY	Thompson
RATCLIFF added	[Lee] Lewes
LORD MAYOR	Cushing
LIEUTENANT omitted	R. Smith
PRINCE EDWARD, DUKE OF YORK	

(2) May 10

HENRY	Clarke
NORFOLK	Fox
TRESSEL	Owenson
LADY ANNE	Mrs [T.] Baker
QUEEN ELIZABETH added	Mrs Mattocks
SAME as Jan. 26	

Oct. 22

RICHARD	Lee
HENRY (1, 2)	Hull

(1) Oct. 29; Nov. 7; Dec. 5

HENRY	Clarke
BUCKINGHAM	Hull

548

RICHARD III [as altered by CIBBER]

1774 COVENT GARDEN (cont.)

Oct. 22 (cont.)

RICHMOND	Clinch
BUCKINGHAM (1, 2)	Booth
STANLEY	Fearon
CATESBY	Davis
RATCLIFF (2)	Chaplin
OXFORD (1, 2)	Baker
PRINCE EDWARD	Miss Besford
DUKE OF YORK	Master Jones
TRESSEL	Young
DUCHESS OF YORK	Mrs Hull
LADY ANNE	Miss Macklin
QUEEN ELIZABETH	Mrs Melmoth

(1) *Oct. 29; Nov. 7; Dec. 5 (cont.)*
added
NORFOLK	Whitfield

omitted
OXFORD

(2) *Dec. 31*
HENRY	Clarke
BUCKINGHAM	Hull

omitted
RATCLIFF, OXFORD

HAYMARKET

Sept. 30

RICHARD	Weston
HENRY	Gardner
BUCKINGHAM	[J.] Aickin
STANLEY	Lloyd
TRESSEL	Ward
CATESBY	Everard
LIEUTENANT	Carpenter
NORFOLK	[Lee] Lewes
PRINCE EDWARD	Master Blanchard
DUKE OF YORK	Master Pulley
RICHMOND	Williams
QUEEN ELIZABETH	Mrs Williams
DUCHESS OF YORK	Mrs Mytteer
LADY ANNE	Mrs Jewell

1775 DRURY LANE

Apr. 28

RICHARD	Smith
HENRY (1)	[J.] Aickin
RICHMOND	[J.] Palmer
BUCKINGHAM	Jefferson
TRESSEL (1, 2)	Cautherley
STANLEY	Bransby
NORFOLK	Hurst
LORD MAYOR (1)	Griffiths
PRINCE EDWARD	Master Blanchard
DUKE OF YORK	Master Pulley
CATESBY (2)	Packer
RATCLIFF	Wright
LIEUTENANT	Fawcett

(1) *May 15*
HENRY	Reddish
TRESSEL	Keen
LORD MAYOR	Wrighten

(2) *Oct. 3; Nov. 7; Dec. 12*
TRESSEL	Davies
CATESBY	Whitfield
LADY ANNE	Miss Sherry (on *Nov. 7* only)

RICHARD III [as altered by CIBBER]

1775 DRURY LANE (cont.)
Apr. 28 (cont.)
LADY ANNE (2)	Mrs Greville
DUCHESS OF YORK	Mrs Johnston
QUEEN ELIZABETH	Mrs Hopkins

COVENT GARDEN
Apr. 18
RICHARD (1, 2)	Lee
HENRY	Clarke
RICHMOND	Clinch
BUCKINGHAM	Hull
STANLEY	Fearon
CATESBY	Davis
PRINCE EDWARD (2)	Miss Besford
DUKE OF YORK	Master Jones
TRESSEL	Young
DUCHESS OF YORK	Mrs Hull
LADY ANNE (1, 2)	Mrs [T.] Baker
QUEEN ELIZABETH (1, 2)	Mrs Melmoth

(1) *May 25*
RICHARD	Macklin
LADY ANNE	Miss Macklin
QUEEN ELIZABETH	Mrs Mattocks

(2) *June 1*
RICHARD	Macklin
PRINCE EDWARD	Harris
LADY ANNE	Miss Macklin
QUEEN ELIZABETH	Mrs Hopkins

1776 DRURY LANE
May 27; June 5
RICHARD (2)	Garrick
RICHMOND (1, 2)	[J.] Palmer
BUCKINGHAM	Jefferson
TRESSEL	Davies
STANLEY (2)	Bransby
NORFOLK	Hurst
CATESBY	Packer
PRINCE EDWARD	Miss P. Hopkins
DUKE OF YORK	Master Pulley
LORD MAYOR	Griffiths
RATCLIFF	Wright
LIEUTENANT	Fawcett
HENRY	Reddish
LADY ANNE (2)	Mrs Siddons
DUCHESS OF YORK	Mrs Johnston
QUEEN ELIZABETH	Mrs Hopkins

(1) *June 3*
RICHMOND	Lacy

(2) *Oct. 12; Dec. 6*
RICHARD	Smith
RICHMOND	Brereton (on *Dec. 6* only)
STANLEY	Wrighten (on *Dec. 6* only)
LADY ANNE	Mrs Greville

COVENT GARDEN
Jan. 1
RICHARD (1)	Sheridan
HENRY	Clarke
RICHMOND (1)	Clinch

(1) *Nov. 11*
RICHARD	Macklin
RICHMOND	Wroughton
TRESSEL	Ward

RICHARD III [as altered by CIBBER]

1776 COVENT GARDEN (cont.)

Jan. 1 (cont.)

BUCKINGHAM	Hull
STANLEY	Fearon
TRESSEL (1)	Young
PRINCE EDWARD	Miss Besford
DUKE OF YORK	Master Jones
NORFOLK (1)	Booth
LIEUTENANT	L'Estrange
DUCHESS OF YORK (1)	Mrs Booth
LADY ANNE	Miss Macklin
QUEEN ELIZABETH (1)	Mrs Hunter

(1) Nov. 11 (cont.)

NORFOLK	Whitfield
DUCHESS OF YORK	Mrs Poussin
QUEEN ELIZABETH	Mrs Jackson

CHINA HALL, ROTHERHITHE

Oct. 4

RICHARD	A Gentleman [unidentified; first appearance on the stage]
HENRY	Comerford
BUCKINGHAM	Russell
STANLEY	[P.] Lewis
OXFORD	Thomas
RATCLIFF	[S.] Johnson
CATESBY	[J.] Smith
TRESSEL	The Gentleman who performed King Lear [at this theatre, Sept. 16, q.v.]
LORD MAYOR	Massey
PRINCE EDWARD	Mrs Wilks
DUKE OF YORK	Master Russell
LIEUTENANT	[W.] Smith
TYRREL	Dancer
RICHMOND	West
QUEEN ELIZABETH	Mrs Massey
DUCHESS OF YORK	Mrs Ross
LADY ANNE	Miss Taylor

1777 DRURY LANE

Oct. 7

RICHARD	Henderson
RICHMOND	[J.] Palmer
BUCKINGHAM	Farren
TRESSEL	Davies
STANLEY	Chaplin
NORFOLK	Hurst
CATESBY	Packer
PRINCE EDWARD	Miss Field
DUKE OF YORK	Master Pulley

(1) Oct. 11

HENRY	Bensley

RICHARD III [as altered by CIBBER]

1777 DRURY LANE (cont.)
Oct. 7 (cont.)

LORD MAYOR	Griffiths
RATCLIFF	Wright
LIEUTENANT	R. Palmer
HENRY (I)	[J.] Aickin
LADY ANNE	Mrs Robinson
DUCHESS OF YORK	Mrs Johnston
QUEEN ELIZABETH	Mrs Hopkins

COVENT GARDEN
Nov. 7

RICHARD	A Gentleman [Kirkpatrick (MC, Nov. 8); first appearance in London]
HENRY	Hull
RICHMOND	Wroughton
BUCKINGHAM	Booth
STANLEY	Fearon
TRESSEL	Whitfield
PRINCE EDWARD	Miss [C.] Morris
DUKE OF YORK	Master Jones
NORFOLK	Bowles
LIEUTENANT	L'Estrange
DUCHESS OF YORK	Mrs Poussin
LADY ANNE	Mrs Jackson
QUEEN ELIZABETH	Mrs Hartley

HAYMARKET
Aug. 7, 8, 11

RICHARD	Henderson
HENRY	Younger
CATESBY	T. Davis
RATCLIFF	Egan
LIEUTENANT	R. Palmer
LORD MAYOR	Massey
BUCKINGHAM	[J.] Aickin
TRESSEL	Davies
STANLEY	Fearon
NORFOLK	Griffiths
TYRREL	Kenny
OXFORD	Stevens
PRINCE EDWARD	Miss [S.] Francis
DUKE OF YORK	Master Edwin
RICHMOND	[J.] Palmer
LADY ANNE	Mrs Hunter
DUCHESS OF YORK	Mrs Poussin
QUEEN ELIZABETH	Mrs Massey

RICHARD III [as altered by CIBBER]

1778 DRURY LANE
May 8, 26

RICHARD	Smith
RICHMOND	[J.] Palmer
BUCKINGHAM	[J.] Aickin
TRESSEL	Davies
STANLEY	Chaplin
NORFOLK	Hurst
CATESBY	Packer
PRINCE EDWARD	Miss Field
DUKE OF YORK	Master Pulley
LORD MAYOR (1)	Chambers
RATCLIFF	Wright
LIEUTENANT	R. Palmer
HENRY	Bensley
LADY ANNE	Mrs Robinson
DUCHESS OF YORK	Mrs Johnston
QUEEN ELIZABETH	Mrs Hopkins

(1) *Oct. 26; Nov. 23*
omitted
LORD MAYOR

COVENT GARDEN
Oct. 5

RICHARD	Henderson
HENRY	Clarke
RICHMOND	Wroughton
BUCKINGHAM	Hull
STANLEY	Fearon
TRESSEL (1)	A Gentleman [Burghall (MS annotation on BM bill); first appearance on the stage]
PRINCE EDWARD	Miss [C.] Morris
DUKE OF YORK	Master Pulley
NORFOLK	Booth
LIEUTENANT	L'Estrange
DUCHESS OF YORK	Miss Platt
LADY ANNE	Mrs Jackson
QUEEN ELIZABETH (1)	Mrs Mattocks

(1) *Dec. 7*

TRESSEL	Farren
QUEEN ELIZABETH	Mrs Farren

HAYMARKET
Mar. 24

RICHARD	A Gentleman [unidentified; first appearance on the stage]
HENRY	Lucas
BUCKINGHAM	Thompson

553

RICHARD III [*as altered by* CIBBER]

1778 HAYMARKET (*cont.*)
Mar. 24 (*cont.*)

PRINCE EDWARD	Master Benson [first appearance on the stage]
DUKE OF YORK	Master Kenny
NORFOLK	Massey
OXFORD	Stevens
STANLEY	Painter
BLUNT	Bell
RATCLIFF	Kenny
CATESBY	Bailey
TRESSEL	Mills
LIEUTENANT	Newton
LORD MAYOR	Bowles
TYRREL	Edwards
RICHMOND	A Gentleman [unidentified; first appearance on the stage]
LADY ANNE	Mrs Lefevre
DUCHESS OF YORK	Mrs Leicester
QUEEN ELIZABETH	Mrs [H.] Robinson

[The bill misprints Mrs Leicester's name as 'Leister'.]

CHINA HALL, ROTHERHITHE
June 26

RICHARD	Stokes
HENRY	Newton
PRINCE EDWARD	A Young Gentleman [unidentified; first appearance on the stage]
BUCKINGHAM	Russell
DUKE OF YORK	Master Nelson
STANLEY	Lear
TRESSEL	Cooke
LIEUTENANT	Burnett
CATESBY	Massey
LORD MAYOR	Fildew
BLUNT	Bailey
RICHMOND	West
LADY ANNE	Mrs Bailey
DUCHESS OF YORK	Mrs Newby
QUEEN ELIZABETH	Mrs Russell

1779 DRURY LANE
Jan. 9

RICHARD	Smith
RICHMOND (2)	[J.] Palmer
BUCKINGHAM	[J.] Aickin
TRESSEL	Davies
STANLEY	Chaplin

(1) *May 18*
added
LORD MAYOR	Griffiths

(2) *Sept. 25*
RICHMOND	Brereton
NORFOLK	Fawcett

RICHARD III [as altered by CIBBER]

1779 DRURY LANE (cont.)

Jan. 9 (cont.)

NORFOLK (2)	Hurst
CATESBY	Packer
RATCLIFF	Wright
LIEUTENANT	R. Palmer
PRINCE EDWARD (2)	Miss Field
DUKE OF YORK (2)	Master Pulley
HENRY	Bensley
LADY ANNE	Mrs Robinson
DUCHESS OF YORK (2)	Mrs Johnston
QUEEN ELIZABETH	Mrs Hopkins

(2) Sept. 25 (cont.)

PRINCE EDWARD	Master Pulley
DUCHESS OF YORK added	Mrs Davenett
LORD MAYOR omitted	Phillimore
DUKE OF YORK	

COVENT GARDEN

Nov. 1

RICHARD	Henderson
HENRY	Clarke
RICHMOND	Wroughton
BUCKINGHAM	Hull
STANLEY	Fearon
TRESSEL	Whitfield
PRINCE EDWARD	Miss [C.] Morris
DUKE OF YORK	Miss Langrish
NORFOLK	Booth
LIEUTENANT	L'Estrange
CATESBY	Robson
RATCLIFF	Thompson
DUCHESS OF YORK	Miss Platt
LADY ANNE (1)	Mrs Lewis
QUEEN ELIZABETH (1)	Mrs Jackson

(1) Dec. 6

LADY ANNE	Mrs Jackson
QUEEN ELIZABETH	Mrs Hartley

1780 DRURY LANE

Apr. 10

RICHARD	Smith
RICHMOND (1, 2)	Brereton
BUCKINGHAM	[J.] Aickin
TRESSEL (2)	Davies
STANLEY	Chaplin
NORFOLK (2)	Hurst
CATESBY	Packer
LIEUTENANT (1)	R. Palmer
RATCLIFF	Wright
LORD MAYOR	Phillimore
PRINCE EDWARD	Master Pulley

(1) May 12

RICHMOND	[J.] Palmer
LIEUTENANT	Fawcett

(2) Oct. 23

RICHMOND	[J.] Palmer
TRESSEL	Farren
NORFOLK	Fawcett
LADY ANNE	Mrs Brereton
DUCHESS OF YORK	Mrs Johnston

[PA retains Mrs Davenett as the DUCHESS OF YORK.]

RICHARD III [as altered by CIBBER]

1780 DRURY LANE (cont.)
Apr. 10 (cont.)

DUKE OF YORK	Miss Langrish
HENRY	Bensley
LADY ANNE (2)	Mrs Robinson
DUCHESS OF YORK (2)	Mrs Davenett
QUEEN ELIZABETH	Mrs Hopkins

COVENT GARDEN
Jan. 10

RICHARD	Henderson
HENRY	Clarke
RICHMOND	Wroughton
BUCKINGHAM	Hull
STANLEY	Fearon
TRESSEL	Whitfield
PRINCE EDWARD	Miss [C.] Morris
DUKE OF YORK	Miss Langrish
NORFOLK	Booth
LIEUTENANT	L'Estrange
CATESBY	Robson
RATCLIFF	Thompson
DUCHESS OF YORK	Miss Platt
LADY ANNE (1)	Mrs Jackson
QUEEN ELIZABETH (1)	Mrs Hartley

(1) *Oct. 9; Dec. 26*

LADY ANNE	Mrs Lewis
QUEEN ELIZABETH	Mrs Inchbald
added	
LORD MAYOR	Webb
OXFORD	[R.] Smith

HAYMARKET
July 1

RICHARD	Brunton
HENRY	Bensley
CATESBY	Davis
RATCLIFF	Egan
LIEUTENANT	R. Palmer
LORD MAYOR	Massey
BUCKINGHAM	[J.] Aickin
TRESSEL	[J.] Bannister
STANLEY	Gardner
NORFOLK	Wood
PRINCE EDWARD	Miss [S.] Francis
DUKE OF YORK	Master Edwin
RICHMOND	[J.] Palmer
LADY ANNE	Mrs Cuyler
DUCHESS OF YORK	Mrs Poussin
QUEEN ELIZABETH	Mrs Massey

RICHARD III [as altered by CIBBER]

1780 CROWN INN, ISLINGTON
Mar. 6

RICHARD	Jerrold
HENRY	Leach
PRINCE EDWARD	Miss Painter
DUKE OF YORK	Master Jerrold
BUCKINGHAM	Price
STANLEY	Wilson
TRESSEL	Gardner
CATESBY	Davis
RATCLIFF	Wortley
RICHMOND	Jones
LADY ANNE	Mrs Kingham
DUCHESS OF YORK	Mrs Weeks
QUEEN ELIZABETH	Mrs Jerrold

1781 DRURY LANE
Mar. 8

RICHARD	Smith
RICHMOND	[J.] Palmer
BUCKINGHAM	[J.] Aickin
TRESSEL	Farren
CATESBY	Packer
STANLEY	Chaplin
NORFOLK	Fawcett
LIEUTENANT	R. Palmer
RATCLIFF	Wright
LORD MAYOR	Phillimore
PRINCE EDWARD	Master Pulley
DUKE OF YORK (2)	Miss Langrish
HENRY	Bensley
LADY ANNE	Mrs Sharp
DUCHESS OF YORK (1, 2)	Mrs Johnston
QUEEN ELIZABETH	Mrs Hopkins

(1) *May 18*

DUCHESS OF YORK	Miss Platt

(2) *Sept. 18*

DUKE OF YORK	Master Langrish
DUCHESS OF YORK	Mrs Booth

CROWN INN, ISLINGTON
Mar. 30

STANLEY	Rivers
CATESBY	Jones
RATCLIFF	Farrell
OXFORD	Thompson
BRANDON	Clifford
HENRY	Burnett
DUCHESS OF YORK	Mrs Fowler
LADY ANNE	Mrs Palmer

[The bill has, 'The Parts of RICHARD, BUCKINGHAM, RICHMOND, TRESSEL, PRINCE EDWARD, DUKE OF YORK, LIEUTENANT, LORD MAYOR, NORFOLK, and QUEEN ELIZABETH By Performers from the Theatres Royal, London'.]

RICHARD III [as altered by CIBBER]

1782 COVENT GARDEN
Jan. 7

RICHARD	Henderson
HENRY	Clarke
RICHMOND (1)	Wroughton
BUCKINGHAM	Hull
STANLEY	Fearon
TRESSEL	Whitfield
PRINCE EDWARD (1)	Miss Langrish
DUKE OF YORK (1)	Master Langrish
NORFOLK	Booth
LIEUTENANT (1)	L'Estrange
CATESBY (1)	Robson
RATCLIFF	Thompson
LORD MAYOR (1)	Webb
OXFORD (1)	J. Bates
LADY ANNE (1)	Miss Ambrose
DUCHESS OF YORK	Miss Platt
QUEEN ELIZABETH (1)	Mrs Inchbald

[Pb misprints NORFOLK as OXFORD.]

(1) *Oct. 14; Dec. 16*

RICHMOND	? (on *Dec. 16* only)
PRINCE EDWARD	Miss M. Francis
DUKE OF YORK	Miss Painter
LIEUTENANT	Mahon
CATESBY	Davies
LORD MAYOR	[R.] Bates (on *Dec. 16* only)
OXFORD	W. Bates
LADY ANNE	Mrs Lewis
QUEEN ELIZABETH	Mrs Hunter

[On *Dec. 16* both Pb and PA assign RICHMOND to Wroughton, and the LORD MAYOR to Webb. In the JPK bill both names are deleted. The name of Wroughton's substitute has been cut by the binder; I have been unable to ascertain who acted the part. Bates's name is written above that of Webb.]

HAYMARKET
Mar. 4

RICHARD	Mrs Lefevre
HENRY	Alfred
BUCKINGHAM	Knapp
TRESSEL	Benson
STANLEY	[J.] Johnson
PRINCE EDWARD	Miss Thomas
DUKE OF YORK	Miss Heyborn
NORFOLK	Buxton
LORD MAYOR	Molbery
CATESBY	Essex
RATCLIFF	Daniel
RICHMOND	Holland
LADY ANNE	Miss Shelburne
DUCHESS OF YORK	Mrs Fowler
QUEEN ELIZABETH	Mrs Jackson

[PA assigns STANLEY to Johnston, and LADY ANNE to Miss Shriburne.]

1783 DRURY LANE
Mar. 10; Sept. 23

RICHARD (1, 2)	Smith
RICHMOND	[J.] Palmer
BUCKINGHAM	[J.] Aickin
TRESSEL	Farren

(1) *Nov. 6, 10*

RICHARD	Kemble
LADY ANNE	Mrs Ward

(2) *Dec. 15*

RICHARD	Kemble

RICHARD III [as altered by CIBBER]

1783 DRURY LANE (cont.)

Mar. 10; Sept. 23 (cont.)

STANLEY	Chaplin
NORFOLK	Fawcett
CATESBY	Packer
LIEUTENANT	R. Palmer
RATCLIFF	Wright
LORD MAYOR	Phillimore
PRINCE EDWARD	Miss M. Stageldoir
DUKE OF YORK	Miss Heard
HENRY	Bensley
LADY ANNE (1)	Mrs Brereton
DUCHESS OF YORK	Mrs Hedges
QUEEN ELIZABETH	Mrs Hopkins

(2) Dec. 15 (cont.)

[Genest (vi. 296) erroneously assigns RICHARD to Smith.]

COVENT GARDEN

Oct. 13; Nov. 3

RICHARD	Henderson
HENRY	Clarke
RICHMOND (1)	Wroughton
BUCKINGHAM	Hull
STANLEY	Fearon
TRESSEL	Whitfield
PRINCE EDWARD	Miss [M.] Francis
DUKE OF YORK	Miss Painter
NORFOLK	Booth
LIEUTENANT	Mahon
CATESBY	Davies
RATCLIFF	Thompson
LORD MAYOR	Helme
OXFORD	J. Bates
LADY ANNE (1)	Miss Satchell
DUCHESS OF YORK	Miss Platt
QUEEN ELIZABETH	Mrs Bates

[Miss M. Francis is so specified by PA, but not by Pb.]

(1) Dec. 29

RICHMOND	[S.] Kemble
LADY ANNE	Mrs [S.] Kemble [i.e. formerly Miss Satchell.]

[Both Pb and PA assign RICHMOND to Wroughton. In the JPK bill his name is deleted, and that of Kemble substituted.]

HAYMARKET

Dec. 15

RICHARD	Harricks
HENRY	Hunter
BUCKINGHAM	Thompson
TRESSEL	Cross
STANLEY	Stannard
CATESBY	Powell
LIEUTENANT	Kenrick
NORFOLK	Farrell

RICHARD III [as altered by CIBBER]

1783 HAYMARKET (cont.)
Dec. 15 (cont.)

PRINCE EDWARD	Miss Beaufield
DUKE OF YORK	Miss Barnard
RICHMOND	Brown
LADY ANNE	A Young Lady [unidentified]
DUCHESS OF YORK	Mrs Barnard
QUEEN ELIZABETH	Mrs Lefevre

1784 DRURY LANE
Jan. 12   (1) *Nov. 5*

RICHARD	Smith		TRESSEL	[J.] Bannister
RICHMOND	[J.] Palmer
BUCKINGHAM	[J.] Aickin
TRESSEL (1)	Farren
STANLEY	Chaplin
NORFOLK	Fawcett
CATESBY	Packer
LIEUTENANT	R. Palmer
RATCLIFF	Wright
LORD MAYOR	Phillimore
PRINCE EDWARD	Miss M. Stageldoir
DUKE OF YORK	Miss Heard
HENRY	Bensley
LADY ANNE	Mrs Ward
DUCHESS OF YORK	Mrs Hedges
QUEEN ELIZABETH	Mrs Hopkins

COVENT GARDEN
Oct. 11

RICHARD	Henderson
HENRY	Clarke
BUCKINGHAM	Hull
TRESSEL	Farren
STANLEY	Fearon
CATESBY	Davies
PRINCE EDWARD	Master Farley
DUKE OF YORK	Master Simmons
NORFOLK	Chalmers
LIEUTENANT	Cubitt
RATCLIFF	Thompson
LORD MAYOR	Helme
BLUNT	Jones
OXFORD	Egan
RICHMOND	Wroughton
LADY ANNE	Miss Ranoe
DUCHESS OF YORK	Miss Platt
QUEEN ELIZABETH	Mrs Bates

RICHARD III [as altered by CIBBER]

1784 HAYMARKET
Sept. 17

RICHARD	Calvert
HENRY	Gardner
BUCKINGHAM	Usher
TRESSEL	Reily
STANLEY	[T.] Jackson
RATCLIFF	Frost
NORFOLK	Neale
PRINCE EDWARD	Miss Painter
DUKE OF YORK	Master Simmons
RICHMOND	Stratford
QUEEN ELIZABETH	Mrs Lefevre
DUCHESS OF YORK	Mrs Fowler
LADY ANNE	Mrs Cuyler

1785 DRURY LANE
Nov. 7

RICHARD	Smith
RICHMOND	[J.] Palmer
BUCKINGHAM	[J.] Aickin
TRESSEL	[J.] Bannister
STANLEY	Chaplin
NORFOLK	Fawcett
CATESBY	Packer
LIEUTENANT	R. Palmer
RATCLIFF	Wright
LORD MAYOR	Phillimore
PRINCE EDWARD	Miss [M.] Stageldoir
DUKE OF YORK	Miss Heard
HENRY	Bensley
LADY ANNE	Mrs Brereton
DUCHESS OF YORK	Mrs Hedges
QUEEN ELIZABETH	?

[Both Pb and PA assign QUEEN ELIZABETH to Mrs Hopkins. In the JPK bill her name is deleted, but no substitute name is given.]

COVENT GARDEN
Jan. 12, 17

RICHARD (1)	Holman
HENRY (2)	Clarke
BUCKINGHAM	Hull
TRESSEL	Farren
STANLEY	Fearon
CATESBY	Davies
PRINCE EDWARD	Master Farley
DUKE OF YORK	Master Simmons

(1) *Sept. 21*

RICHARD	Henderson
NORFOLK	Booth
LORD MAYOR	Gardner
OXFORD	Helme

(2) *Dec. 5*

HENRY	[F.] Aickin
NORFOLK	Booth
LORD MAYOR	Gardner
OXFORD	Helme

RICHARD III [as altered by CIBBER]

1785 COVENT GARDEN (cont.)

Jan. 12, 17 (cont.)

NORFOLK (1, 2)	Bonnor
LIEUTENANT	Cubitt
RATCLIFF	Thompson
LORD MAYOR (1, 2)	Helme
OXFORD (1, 2)	Egan
RICHMOND	Wroughton
LADY ANNE (2)	Miss Ranoe
DUCHESS OF YORK	Miss Platt
QUEEN ELIZABETH	Mrs Bates

(2) Dec. 5 (cont.)

LADY ANNE	Mrs Rivers [i.e. formerly Miss Ranoe]

1786 COVENT GARDEN

Sept. 20

RICHARD	Holman
HENRY	[F.] Aickin
BUCKINGHAM	Hull
STANLEY	Fearon
TRESSEL	Farren
PRINCE EDWARD	Master Farley
DUKE OF YORK	Master Simmons
NORFOLK	Macready
LIEUTENANT	Cubitt
CATESBY	Davies
RATCLIFF	Thompson
LORD MAYOR	Gardner
OXFORD	Helme
RICHMOND	Pope
LADY ANNE	Mrs Lewis
DUCHESS OF YORK	Miss Platt
QUEEN ELIZABETH	Mrs Bates

1787 DRURY LANE

Dec. 10, 17

RICHARD	Smith
RICHMOND	Wroughton
BUCKINGHAM	[J.] Aickin
TRESSEL	Whitfield
STANLEY	Staunton
NORFOLK	Fawcett
CATESBY	Packer
LIEUTENANT	Benson
RATCLIFF	Phillimore
LORD MAYOR	Chaplin
PRINCE EDWARD	Miss Heard
DUKE OF YORK	Miss Gaudry
HENRY	Bensley

RICHARD III [as altered by CIBBER]

1787 DRURY LANE (cont.)
Dec. 10, 17 (cont.)
LADY ANNE	Mrs [J.] Kemble
DUCHESS OF YORK	Miss Tidswell
QUEEN ELIZABETH	Mrs [W.] Taylor

1788 DRURY LANE
Jan. 16
RICHARD	Smith
RICHMOND	Wroughton
BUCKINGHAM	[J.] Aickin
TRESSEL	Whitfield
STANLEY (1)	Chaplin
NORFOLK	Fawcett
CATESBY (2)	Packer
LIEUTENANT	Benson
RATCLIFF	Phillimore
PRINCE EDWARD	Miss Heard
DUKE OF YORK	Miss Gaudry
HENRY	Bensley
LADY ANNE	Mrs [J.] Kemble
DUCHESS OF YORK	Miss Tidswell
QUEEN ELIZABETH	Mrs [W.] Taylor

(1) Feb. 18
STANLEY	Staunton
added	
LORD MAYOR	Chaplin

(2) Apr. 17
CATESBY	R. Palmer
added	
LORD MAYOR	Staunton

Oct. 14
RICHARD	Kemble
RICHMOND	[J.] Palmer
BUCKINGHAM	Barrymore
STANLEY (1)	[J.] Aickin
TRESSEL (1, 2)	Seymour
NORFOLK	Williames
CATESBY	Packer
RATCLIFF	Phillimore
PRINCE EDWARD	Miss Heard
DUKE OF YORK	Miss Gaudry
HENRY	Bensley
LADY ANNE (2)	Miss Collins
DUCHESS OF YORK	Mrs Hopkins
QUEEN ELIZABETH	Mrs Ward

(1) Nov. 10
STANLEY	Chaplin
TRESSEL	Whitfield

(2) Dec. 29
TRESSEL	Whitfield
LADY ANNE	Mrs Farmer

1789 DRURY LANE
Jan. 12
RICHARD	Kemble
RICHMOND (1)	[J.] Palmer
BUCKINGHAM	Barrymore
STANLEY	[J.] Aickin
TRESSEL	Whitfield
NORFOLK	Williames

(1) Sept. 12; Nov. 12
RICHMOND	Wroughton
LADY ANNE	Mrs Powell [i.e. formerly Mrs Farmer]

RICHARD III [as altered by CIBBER]

1789 DRURY LANE (cont.)
Jan. 12 (cont.)

CATESBY	Packer
RATCLIFF	Phillimore
PRINCE EDWARD	Miss [M.] Stageldoir
DUKE OF YORK	Miss Gaudry
HENRY	Bensley
LADY ANNE (1)	Mrs Farmer
DUCHESS OF YORK	Mrs Hopkins
QUEEN ELIZABETH	Mrs Ward

COVENT GARDEN
Sept. 25, 28; Oct. 5; Dec. 8   (1) *Oct. 23*

RICHARD	Harley [first appearance, Sept. 25, in London]
HENRY	[F.] Aickin
BUCKINGHAM	Farren
STANLEY	Powel
TRESSEL	Egan [Jr.]
PRINCE EDWARD	Mrs Byrne
DUKE OF YORK	Master Simmons
NORFOLK	Macready
LIEUTENANT	Cubitt
CATESBY	Davies
RATCLIFF	Thompson
LORD MAYOR	Gardner
OXFORD	Evatt
RICHMOND	Holman
LADY ANNE (1)	Miss Brunton
DUCHESS OF YORK	Mrs Platt
QUEEN ELIZABETH	Mrs Pope

(1) LADY ANNE   Mrs Rock [Both Pb and PA retain Miss Brunton as LADY ANNE. But she was indisposed, and Mrs Rock played the part 'at short notice' (MS annotation on BM bill; PA, Oct. 24).]

1790 DRURY LANE
Jan. 4

RICHARD	Kemble
RICHMOND (1)	Wroughton
BUCKINGHAM	Barrymore
STANLEY	[J.] Aickin
TRESSEL	Whitfield
NORFOLK	Williames
CATESBY	Packer
RATCLIFF	Phillimore
PRINCE EDWARD (1)	Miss [M.] Stageldoir
DUKE OF YORK	Miss Gaudry

(1) *Oct. 21, 28*

RICHMOND	[J.] Palmer
PRINCE EDWARD	Miss DeCamp added
OXFORD	Fawcett
BRACKENBURY	Benson
BLUNT	Haymes
TYRREL	Jones
LORD MAYOR	Hollingsworth

RICHARD III [as altered by CIBBER]

1790 DRURY LANE (cont.)

Jan. 4 (cont.)

HENRY	Bensley
LADY ANNE	Mrs Powell
DUCHESS OF YORK	Mrs Hopkins
QUEEN ELIZABETH	Mrs Ward

COVENT GARDEN

Mar. 1

RICHARD (1)	Harley
HENRY	[F.] Aickin
BUCKINGHAM	Farren
STANLEY (2)	Powel
TRESSEL (2)	Egan [Jr.]
NORFOLK (2)	Macready
PRINCE EDWARD (2)	Mrs Byrne
DUKE OF YORK (2)	Master Simmons
LIEUTENANT	Cubitt
CATESBY	Davies
RATCLIFF (1)	Thompson
OXFORD (2)	Evatt
RICHMOND	Holman
LADY ANNE	Miss Brunton
DUCHESS OF YORK	Mrs Platt
QUEEN ELIZABETH	Mrs Pope

(1) *Apr. 6*

RICHARD added	Quick
LORD MAYOR omitted	Reeve
RATCLIFF	

(2) *Oct. 18*

STANLEY	Hull
TRESSEL	Macready
NORFOLK	Evatt
PRINCE EDWARD	Master Simmons
DUKE OF YORK	Miss Standen
OXFORD added	Farley
LORD MAYOR	Powel

1791 DRURY LANE (company at KING'S, HAYMARKET)

Nov. 14

HENRY	Bensley
PRINCE EDWARD	Miss DeCamp
DUKE OF YORK	Miss Standen
RICHARD	Kemble
BUCKINGHAM	Barrymore
RICHMOND	[J.] Palmer
NORFOLK	Dignum
RATCLIFF	Phillimore
CATESBY	Packer
TRESSEL	Whitfield
OXFORD	Fawcett
BRACKENBURY	Benson
STANLEY	[J.] Aickin
BLUNT	Bland
TYRREL	Jones
LORD MAYOR	Hollingsworth
QUEEN ELIZABETH	Mrs Ward
LADY ANNE	Mrs Powell
DUCHESS OF YORK	Mrs Hopkins

[Both Pb and PA omit RICHMOND. The assignment is taken from O, Nov. 14.]

RICHARD III [as altered by CIBBER]

1791 COVENT GARDEN
Oct. 24

RICHARD	Harley
HENRY	[F.] Aickin
BUCKINGHAM	Farren
STANLEY	Hull
TRESSEL	Macready
PRINCE EDWARD	Master Simmons
DUKE OF YORK	Miss Standen
NORFOLK	Evatt
LIEUTENANT	Cubitt
CATESBY	Davies
RATCLIFF	Thompson
LORD MAYOR	Powel
OXFORD	Farley
RICHMOND	Holman
LADY ANNE	Mrs Merry
DUCHESS OF YORK	Mrs Platt
QUEEN ELIZABETH	Mrs Pope

HAYMARKET
Aug. 24

HENRY	Bensley
PRINCE EDWARD	Miss DeCamp
DUKE OF YORK	Miss Standen
RICHARD	[J.] Bannister
RICHMOND	[J.] Palmer
BUCKINGHAM	[J.] Williamson
NORFOLK	Usher
RATCLIFF	Evatt
CATESBY	Davies
TRESSEL	Bland
OXFORD	Farley
LIEUTENANT	Cubitt
STANLEY	[J.] Aickin
BLUNT	Lyons
TYRREL	Rock
LORD MAYOR	Chapman
FORREST	Ledger
QUEEN ELIZABETH	Mrs Whitfield
LADY ANNE	Mrs [S.] Kemble
DUCHESS OF YORK	Mrs [C.] Powell

1792 DRURY LANE (company at KING'S, HAYMARKET)
Feb. 7

HENRY	Bensley			
PRINCE EDWARD (1)	Miss DeCamp			

(1) *Nov. 5, 12*

PRINCE EDWARD	Master DeCamp
DUKE OF YORK	Miss [M.] Menage

RICHARD III [as altered by CIBBER]

1792 DRURY LANE (company at KING'S, HAYMARKET) (cont.)

Feb. 7 (cont.)

DUKE OF YORK (1)	Miss Standen
RICHARD	Kemble
BUCKINGHAM	Barrymore
RICHMOND	[J.] Palmer
NORFOLK	Dignum
RATCLIFF	Phillimore
CATESBY	Packer
TRESSEL	Whitfield
OXFORD (1)	Fawcett
BRACKENBURY	Benson
STANLEY	[J.] Aickin
BLUNT	Bland
TYRREL	Jones
LORD MAYOR	Hollingsworth
QUEEN ELIZABETH (1)	Mrs Siddons
LADY ANNE (1)	Miss Collins
DUCHESS OF YORK (1)	Mrs Ward

(1) Nov. 5, 12 (cont.)

OXFORD	Caulfield
QUEEN ELIZABETH	Mrs Ward
LADY ANNE	Mrs Powell
DUCHESS OF YORK	Miss Tidswell (on Nov. 5 only) / Mrs Hopkins (on Nov. 12 only)

COVENT GARDEN

Oct. 15

RICHARD	Holman
HENRY (1)	[F.] Aickin
BUCKINGHAM	Farren
STANLEY	Hull
TRESSEL	Macready
PRINCE EDWARD	Simmons
DUKE OF YORK	Miss Standen
CATESBY	Davies
LIEUTENANT	Cubitt
NORFOLK	Evatt
RATCLIFF	Thompson
LORD MAYOR	Powel
OXFORD	Farley
RICHMOND	Pope
LADY ANNE	Mrs Wells
DUCHESS OF YORK	Mrs Platt
QUEEN ELIZABETH	Mrs Pope

(1) Dec. 26

HENRY	Harley

[PA retains Aickin as HENRY.]

HAYMARKET

Apr. 16

RICHARD	T. Morris
LIEUTENANT	A. Morris
HENRY	Horwell

567

RICHARD III [as altered by CIBBER]

1792 HAYMARKET (cont.)
Apr. 16 (cont.)

TRESSEL	Birch
RICHMOND	Crewe
CATESBY	Uncle
BUCKINGHAM	Meredith
STANLEY	Webber
PRINCE EDWARD	Miss S. Francis
QUEEN ELIZABETH	Mrs Hunter
LADY ANNE	Mrs Pollard
DUCHESS OF YORK	Mrs McGeorge

[The above cast consisted chiefly of amateurs. With the exception of the DUCHESS OF YORK (which is assigned in DWR, Apr. 17), the assignments are taken from the *St. James's Chronicle*, Apr. 17, and from DWR, Apr. 23. In an obituary notice of Birch in GM, Apr. 1842, 441, he is erroneously assigned to the part of TYRREL.]

1793 COVENT GARDEN
Oct. 14

RICHARD	Holman
HENRY	Harley
BUCKINGHAM	Farren
STANLEY	Hull
TRESSEL	Macready
PRINCE EDWARD	Simmons
DUKE OF YORK	Miss Standen
CATESBY	Davies
LIEUTENANT	Cubitt
NORFOLK	Evatt
RATCLIFF	Thompson
RICHMOND	Pope
LADY ANNE	Miss Chapman
DUCHESS OF YORK	Mrs Platt
QUEEN ELIZABETH	Mrs Pope

HAYMARKET
Aug. 6

RICHARD (2)	Kemble
HENRY	Bensley
PRINCE EDWARD	Master DeCamp
DUKE OF YORK	Miss [M.] Menage
BUCKINGHAM	Benson
RICHMOND	Barrymore
NORFOLK (2)	Usher
RATCLIFF (1, 2)	Evatt
TRESSEL	Bland
CATESBY (1, 2)	Davies
STANLEY	[J.] Aickin

(1) *Sept. 30*

RATCLIFF	Dignum
CATESBY	Caulfield
TYRREL	Jones
LORD MAYOR	Wewitzer
QUEEN ELIZABETH	Mrs Hopkins
LADY ANNE	Mrs Goodall
DUCHESS OF YORK	Mrs Booth

(2) *Dec. 23*

RICHARD	A Gentleman [Holland (Not. Dram.); first appearance in London]
NORFOLK	Dignum

RICHARD III [as altered by CIBBER]

1793 HAYMARKET (cont.)

Aug. 6 (cont.)

BRACKENBURY (2)	[J.] Palmer Jr.
BLUNT	Lyons
TYRREL (1, 2)	Abbot
LORD MAYOR (1, 2)	[J.] Burton
QUEEN ELIZABETH (1, 2)	Mrs Whitfield
LADY ANNE (1, 2)	Mrs [S.] Kemble
DUCHESS OF YORK (1, 2)	Mrs [C.] Powell

(2) Dec. 23 (cont.)

RATCLIFF	Maddocks
CATESBY	Caulfield
BRACKENBURY	[J.] Cooke
TYRREL	Jones
LORD MAYOR	Wewitzer
QUEEN ELIZABETH	Mrs Powell
LADY ANNE	Mrs Goodall
DUCHESS OF YORK	Mrs Hopkins

[A MS annotation on the JPK bill identifies the person who acted RICHARD as Litchfield. But Not. Dram. has, 'A person under the name of Litchfield but as I am informed in reality a Mr Holland Nephew of Mr Holland formerly of Drury Lane appeared 1st time at the HM in Richard III'.]

1794 COVENT GARDEN

Oct. 15

RICHARD	Holman
HENRY	Harley
BUCKINGHAM	Farren
STANLEY	Hull
TRESSEL	Macready
PRINCE EDWARD	Master Curties
DUKE OF YORK	Miss Standen
CATESBY	Davies
LIEUTENANT	Claremont
NORFOLK	Richardson
RATCLIFF	Thompson
RICHMOND	Pope
LADY ANNE	Miss Chapman
DUCHESS OF YORK	Mrs Platt
QUEEN ELIZABETH	Mrs Pope

HAYMARKET

Feb. 25

RICHARD (1)	Pindar [first appearance in London]
HENRY	Bensley
PRINCE EDWARD	Master De Camp
DUKE OF YORK	Miss [M.] Menage
BUCKINGHAM	Benson
RICHMOND (1)	Barrymore
NORFOLK (1)	Dignum

(1) Aug. 27

RICHARD	[J.] Bannister
RICHMOND	[J.] Palmer
NORFOLK	Abbot
RATCLIFF	Pindar
CATESBY	Davies
BRACKENBURY	[J.] Palmer Jr.
QUEEN ELIZABETH	Mrs Harlowe
LADY ANNE	Mrs [S.] Kemble

569

RICHARD III [as altered by CIBBER]

1794 HAYMARKET (cont.)
Feb. 25 (cont.)

RATCLIFF (1)	Maddocks
TRESSEL	Bland
CATESBY (1)	Caulfield
STANLEY	[J.] Aickin
BRACKENBURY (1)	[J.] Cooke
BLUNT	Lyons
TYRREL	[G.] Waldron
LORD MAYOR	[J.] Burton
QUEEN ELIZABETH (1)	Mrs Powell
LADY ANNE (1)	Mrs Goodall
DUCHESS OF YORK	Mrs Hopkins

1795 COVENT GARDEN
Oct. 16

RICHARD	Holman
HENRY	Harley
BUCKINGHAM	Macready
STANLEY	Hull
TRESSEL	Toms
PRINCE EDWARD	Master Curties
DUKE OF YORK	Miss Standen
CATESBY	Claremont
LIEUTENANT	Haymes
NORFOLK	Richardson
RATCLIFF	Thompson
LORD MAYOR	Powel
OXFORD	Farley
TYRREL	Davenport
BLUNT	Cross
FORREST	Rees
SERVANT	Abbot
YEOMAN	Ledger
RICHMOND	Pope
LADY ANNE	Miss Chapman
DUCHESS OF YORK	Mrs Platt
QUEEN ELIZABETH	Mrs Pope

1796 DRURY LANE
Nov. 9

HENRY	Wroughton
PRINCE EDWARD	Miss Granger
DUKE OF YORK	Master Chatterley
RICHARD	Kemble
BUCKINGHAM	Barrymore
RICHMOND	[J.] Palmer

RICHARD III [as altered by CIBBER]

1796 DRURY LANE (cont.)
Nov. 9 (cont.)

NORFOLK	Holland
RATCLIFF	Phillimore
CATESBY	Caulfield
TRESSEL	C. Kemble
OXFORD	Denman
BRACKENBURY	Trueman
STANLEY	Packer
BLUNT	Wentworth
TYRREL	Webb
LORD MAYOR	Maddocks
QUEEN ELIZABETH	Mrs Siddons
LADY ANNE	Miss Miller
DUCHESS OF YORK	Miss Tidswell

COVENT GARDEN
Nov. 5

RICHARD	Holman
HENRY	Murray
BUCKINGHAM	Macready
STANLEY	Hull
TRESSEL	Toms
PRINCE EDWARD	Master Curties
DUKE OF YORK	Miss Standen
CATESBY	Claremont
LIEUTENANT	Haymes
RATCLIFF	Thompson
LORD MAYOR	Powel
RICHMOND	Pope
LADY ANNE	Miss Chapman
DUCHESS OF YORK	Mrs Platt
QUEEN ELIZABETH	Mrs Fawcett

HAYMARKET
Aug. 30

RICHARD	[J.] Palmer
HENRY	[J.] Aickin
RICHMOND	[J.] Palmer Jr.
LADY ANNE	Miss Logan

[The above consisted of parts of I. ii; II. ii; and V only. The entertainment on this evening was called *The School of Shakespeare*, for a description of which see p. 101.]

1797 COVENT GARDEN
June 2

| RICHARD | Holman |
| HENRY | Murray |

571

RICHARD III [*as altered by* CIBBER]

1797 COVENT GARDEN (*cont.*)

June 2 (cont.)

BUCKINGHAM	Macready
STANLEY	Hull
TRESSEL	Toms
PRINCE EDWARD	Curties
DUKE OF YORK	Miss Standen
CATESBY	Claremont
LIEUTENANT	Haymes
RATCLIFF	Thompson
LORD MAYOR	Powel
RICHMOND	Pope
LADY ANNE	Miss Chapman
DUCHESS OF YORK	Mrs Platt
QUEEN ELIZABETH	Miss Morris

Oct. 2

RICHARD	Murray
HENRY	Hull
BUCKINGHAM	Clarke
STANLEY	Thompson
TRESSEL	Wheatley
PRINCE EDWARD	Miss Standen
DUKE OF YORK	Master Standen
LIEUTENANT	Waddy
CATESBY	Claremont
RATCLIFF	Abbot
LORD MAYOR	Powel
OXFORD	Farley
NORFOLK	Davenport
RICHMOND	Pope
LADY ANNE	Mrs Litchfield
DUCHESS OF YORK	Mrs Platt
QUEEN ELIZABETH	Miss Chapman

[Pb assigns RICHARD to Holman, but he was indisposed, and Murray substituted for him (TB, Oct. 3).]

1798 DRURY LANE

Sept. 25; Nov. 19   (1) *Oct. 22*

HENRY	[J.] Aickin	LADY ANNE	Miss Stuart
PRINCE EDWARD	Miss Wentworth		
DUKE OF YORK	Master Chatterley		
RICHARD	Kemble		
BUCKINGHAM	Barrymore		
RICHMOND	C. Kemble		
NORFOLK	Holland		
RATCLIFF	Maddocks		
CATESBY	Caulfield		

572

RICHARD III [as altered by CIBBER]

1798 DRURY LANE (cont.)
Sept. 25; Nov. 19 (cont.)

TRESSEL	Surmont [first appearance, Sept. 25, on the stage]
OXFORD	Sparks
BRACKENBURY	Trueman
STANLEY	Packer
BLUNT	Wentworth
TYRREL	Webb
LORD MAYOR	Hollingsworth
QUEEN ELIZABETH	Mrs Powell
LADY ANNE (1)	Miss Miller
DUCHESS OF YORK	Miss Tidswell

COVENT GARDEN
May 4

RICHARD	Holman
HENRY	Murray
BUCKINGHAM	Clarke
STANLEY	Hull
TRESSEL	Toms
PRINCE EDWARD	Miss Standen
DUKE OF YORK	Master Standen
CATESBY	Claremont
LIEUTENANT	Waddy
RATCLIFF	Thompson
LORD MAYOR	Powel
RICHMOND	Pope
LADY ANNE	Mrs Litchfield
DUCHESS OF YORK	Mrs Platt
QUEEN ELIZABETH	Miss Chapman

HAYMARKET
Apr. 21

RICHARD	A Young Gentleman [unidentified; first appearance on the stage]

No other parts assigned

1799 DRURY LANE
Oct. 7; Nov. 18

HENRY	[J.] Aickin
PRINCE EDWARD	Miss Wentworth
DUKE OF YORK	Master Chatterley
RICHARD	Kemble
BUCKINGHAM	Barrymore
RICHMOND	C. Kemble
NORFOLK	Holland
RATCLIFF	Maddocks

RICHARD III [as altered by CIBBER]

1799 DRURY LANE (cont.)
Oct. 7; Nov. 18 (cont.)

CATESBY	Caulfield
TRESSEL	Surmont
OXFORD	Sparks
BRACKENBURY	Trueman
STANLEY	Packer
BLUNT	Wentworth
TYRREL	Webb
LORD MAYOR	Hollingsworth
QUEEN ELIZABETH	Mrs Powell
LADY ANNE	Miss Biggs
DUCHESS OF YORK	Miss Tidswell

COVENT GARDEN

May 6

RICHARD (1)	A Young Gentleman [Lee (MM, June 1799, 366); first appearance in London]
HENRY	Murray
BUCKINGHAM (1)	Clarke
STANLEY	Hull
TRESSEL	Mansel
PRINCE EDWARD	Miss Sims
DUKE OF YORK	Miss Gilbert
LIEUTENANT	Waddy
CATESBY	Claremont
RATCLIFF	Klanert
LORD MAYOR	Thompson
TYRREL	Abbot
NORFOLK	Davenport
RICHMOND	Pope
LADY ANNE	Mrs Litchfield
DUCHESS OF YORK	Mrs Platt
QUEEN ELIZABETH	Miss Chapman

(1) Sept. 23

RICHARD	Holman
BUCKINGHAM added	Betterton
OXFORD	Atkins

1800 DRURY LANE

Sept. 23

HENRY	Wroughton
PRINCE EDWARD (1)	Master Suett [first appearance on the stage]

(1) Oct. 27

PRINCE EDWARD	Master Chatterley
DUKE OF YORK	Miss Kelly
BUCKINGHAM	Barrymore
STANLEY	Packer
LORD MAYOR	Dowton

574

RICHARD III [as altered by CIBBER]

1800 DRURY LANE (cont.)

Sept. 23 (cont.)

DUKE OF YORK (1)	Miss Jackson [first appearance on the stage]
RICHARD	Kemble
BUCKINGHAM (1)	Raymond
NORFOLK	Holland
RICHMOND	C. Kemble
STANLEY (1)	Sparks
RATCLIFF	Maddocks
CATESBY	Caulfield
BRACKENBURY	Trueman
TYRREL	Webb
LORD MAYOR (1)	Wewitzer
TRESSEL (1)	Surmont
OFFICER (1)	Chippendale
DIGHTON (1)	Evans
FORREST (1)	Fisher
QUEEN ELIZABETH	Mrs Powell
DUCHESS OF YORK	Miss Tidswell
LADY ANNE	Miss Biggs

(1) Oct. 27 (cont.)

omitted
TRESSEL, OFFICER, DIGHTON, FORREST

COVENT GARDEN

Oct. 31; Dec. 29

RICHARD	Cooke
HENRY	Murray
BUCKINGHAM	Whitfield
STANLEY	Davenport
TRESSEL	Betterton
PRINCE EDWARD	Mrs Findlay
DUKE OF YORK	Master Standen
LIEUTENANT	Waddy
CATESBY	Claremont
RATCLIFF	Klanert
LORD MAYOR	Thompson
OXFORD	Atkins
TYRREL (2)	Abbot
NORFOLK (2)	Seaton
RICHMOND	Pope
LADY ANNE	Mrs Litchfield
DUCHESS OF YORK	Miss Leserve
QUEEN ELIZABETH	Miss Chapman

(1) Nov. 5, 17, 24; Dec. 1, 8

added
BLUNT   Curties

(2) Dec. 15

omitted
TYRREL, NORFOLK

ROMEO AND JULIET

(1) 'As it is Performed at the Theatre-Royal in Drury-Lane.'
    1763   J. and R. Tonson. Reprinted 1766.

This adaptation was made by David Garrick. *Act I* is the only Act in which the scenes are rearranged. *The Prologue* is omitted. Scene i is *Act I. i. 1–109*, omitting *11–36a* ('maidenheads'). Lady Montague and Lady Capulet do not appear; Lady Montague's speeches are given to Montague. Scene ii is *I. i. 110–62*, followed by ten new lines: Benvolio promises Montague to question Romeo about his love. Scene iii is *I. ii. 1–23a, 34–37*. Scene iv begins with five new lines: Mercutio sees Romeo approaching. This is followed by *I. i. 165–90, 205–12, 231–43*. Mercutio appears here, and has some of Benvolio's speeches. Then come *I. ii. 87–105*, *I. iv. 50–110a*, and six new lines: Romeo's longing to see Juliet. All references to Rosaline are omitted; Romeo has always been in love with Juliet. Scene v is *I. iii*, omitting *79–95* (Paris likened to a book). Juliet is here referred to as being 18 years old. Scene vi is *I. v. 20–80, 91–107, 115–end*.

From *Act II* are omitted *The Prologue*; *i. 32–38* (the 'poperin pear'); *iii. 66–84* (the Friar's references to Rosaline, for which are substituted eight new lines: Romeo warned against too great recklessness); *iv. 58–110* (the 'single-soled jest').

From *Act III* are omitted *ii. 8–16* ('stainless maidenhoods'); *iii. 117–33, 135–44* (the Friar reasons with Romeo); *v. 76–104* (Juliet pretends to hate Romeo).

From *Act IV* are omitted *i. 24–36* (Juliet and Paris); *v. 49–66a* ('O woeful day'), *68–78* (the Friar consoles Juliet's parents), *96–end* (Peter and the musicians).

Before *Act V. i* is introduced a new scene: the funeral procession of Juliet, and a dirge, written by Garrick. Following *iii. 118* are inserted about 65 new lines by Garrick: Juliet awakens, and she and Romeo take their last farewell of one another. The original is resumed at *121*. Omitted are *123–39* (the Friar and Balthazar), *171b–87* (the Watch), *229–66a, 271–90* (the recapitulation of the story). Six new lines are substituted for the concluding four lines.

Throughout there are minor omissions. For a brief account of the stage history of Garrick's rewriting of the death scene see my Volume I, 405.

(2) 'Printed Exactly agreeable to the Representation [at Drury Lane].'
    n.d. [1763]   Halhed Garland.

(3) 'As it is performed at the Theatre Royal in Drury Lane.'
    n.d. [c. 1769]   The Booksellers.

(4) 'As it is performed at the Theatre-Royal in Drury-Lane.'
    1769   T. Lowndes [&c.].

(5) 'As it is Acted at the Theatres Royal in Drury-Lane, and Covent-Garden.'
    1769   Dublin: Bart. Corcoran.
    All these are identical with (1).

(6) 'As Performed at the Theatre-Royal, Drury-Lane. Regulated from the Prompt-Book.'
    1773   John Bell.

This is identical with (1), except for a few minor restorations from the original, and a few new lines, notably three at the end of Juliet's soliloquy in *Act IV. iii*.

(7) 'As it is now acted at the Theatres Royal, in Drury-Lane and Covent-Garden.'
   1775   W. Oxlade.
This is identical with (1).

(8) 'As it was performed at the Theatre-Royal in Drury-Lane.'
   1775   For the Proprietors.
This is identical with (1), except for *Act V*, which follows the original verbatim.

(9) 'As it is Acted at the Theatres-Royal in Drury-Lane and Covent-Garden.'
   1778   J. Wenman.

(10) 'Marked with the Variations in the Manager's Book, at the Theatre-Royal in Drury-Lane.'
   1784   Lowndes [&c.].
Both of these are identical with (6).

(11) 'Marked with the Variations in the Manager's Books, At the Theatres Drury-Lane and Covent-Garden.'
   n.d. [c. 1785]   For the Proprietors.
This is identical with (1).

(12) 'As it is Acted at the Theatres Royal.'
   1787   G. Lister.

(13) 'Marked with the Variations in the Manager's Books, at the Theatres Royal Drury Lane and Covent Garden.'
   1788   For the Author.

(14) 'Marked with the Variations in the Managers Books, at the Theatres-Royal in Drury-Lane and Covent-Garden.'
   n.d. [1789]   H. Whitworth.
All these are identical with (6).

(15) 'Marked with the Variations in the Manager's Book, at the Theatre-Royal in Drury-Lane.'
   1793   W. Lowndes and S. Bladon.
This is identical with (1).

1751 DRURY LANE

Jan. 31; Feb. 13

ROMEO	Garrick
ESCALUS	Winstone
CAPULET	Berry
PARIS	Scrase
BENVOLIO	Mozeen
TYBALT	Blakes
FRIAR LAURENCE (1)	Burton
OLD CAPULET (1)	Wright
FRIAR JOHN (1)	Paddick

(1) *Sept. 20, 28; Oct. 19; Nov. 18; Dec. 16*

FRIAR LAURENCE   Havard omitted

OLD CAPULET, FRIAR JOHN, GREGORY, SAMPSON, BALTHAZAR, ABRAHAM, APOTHECARY, PETER, OFFICER, PAGE

ROMEO AND JULIET

1751 DRURY LANE (cont.)
Jan. 31; Feb. 13 (cont.)

GREGORY (1)	W. Vaughan
SAMPSON (1)	James
BALTHAZAR (1)	Ackman
ABRAHAM (1)	Marr
MERCUTIO	Woodward
APOTHECARY (1)	Simson
PETER (1)	[H.] Vaughan
OFFICER (1)	Raftor
PAGE (1)	Master Cross
LADY CAPULET	Mrs Bennet
NURSE	Mrs James
JULIET	Miss Bellamy

Mar. 16

ROMEO	Garrick
MERCUTIO	Woodward
JULIET	Miss Bellamy

No other parts assigned

COVENT GARDEN
Jan. 17, 26; Feb. 11

ROMEO (2)	Barry
CAPULET	Sparks
MONTAGUE	Bridgwater
ESCALUS (1, 2)	Bransby
BENVOLIO	Gibson
PARIS (2)	[T.] Lacy
FRIAR LAURENCE	Ridout
GREGORY (1, 2)	Arthur
SAMPSON	Collins
ABRAHAM	Dunstall
BALTHAZAR (1, 2)	Cushing
MERCUTIO	Macklin
TYBALT	Dyer
LADY CAPULET	Mrs Barrington
NURSE	Mrs Macklin
JULIET	Mrs Cibber

(1) *Mar. 18; Apr. 30; May 17, 21*

ESCALUS	Anderson
GREGORY	Cushing
BALTHAZAR	Bransby

(2) *Oct. 7, 15, 23; Nov. 2, 12; Dec. 21, 31*

ROMEO	Dyer (on *Nov. 12* only)
ESCALUS	Anderson
PARIS	Usher
GREGORY	Cushing
BALTHAZAR	Bransby

[On *Oct. 15* JULIET is omitted. On *Nov. 12* Barry's name is in the bill, but he was 'suddenly taken ... ill, and Mr. Dyer, at a very short warning, performed the part' (GA, Nov. 13). It is not stated who acted TYBALT, to which part Dyer is assigned in the bill.]

1752 DRURY LANE
Jan. 27; Feb. 29; May 7; Oct. 13

ROMEO (1)	Garrick
ESCALUS (1)	Winstone
CAPULET	Berry
PARIS (1, 2)	Scrase
BENVOLIO (1, 2)	Mozeen
TYBALT	Blakes
FRIAR LAURENCE	Havard

(1) *Mar. 31*

ROMEO omitted	Ross

ESCALUS, PARIS, BENVOLIO, LADY CAPULET

(2) *Oct. 20*

PARIS	Lacey
BENVOLIO	Scrase

ROMEO AND JULIET

1752 DRURY LANE (cont.)
Jan. 27; Feb. 29; May 7; Oct. 13 (cont.)
- MERCUTIO — Woodward
- LADY CAPULET (1) — Mrs Bennet
- NURSE (3) — Mrs James
- JULIET — Miss Bellamy

(3) Oct. 25; Nov. 10
- NURSE — Mrs Cross

COVENT GARDEN
Jan. 15, 23, 31; Feb. 8, 10; May 11
- ROMEO — Barry
- CAPULET — Sparks
- MONTAGUE — Bridgwater
- ESCALUS (1) — Anderson
- BENVOLIO (1) — Gibson
- PARIS (1) — Usher
- FRIAR LAURENCE — Ridout
- GREGORY (1) — Cushing
- SAMPSON — Collins
- ABRAHAM — Dunstall
- BALTHAZAR (1) — Bransby
- MERCUTIO — Macklin
- TYBALT — Dyer
- LADY CAPULET — Mrs Barrington
- NURSE — Mrs Macklin
- JULIET — Mrs Cibber

(1) Oct. 21, 25; Nov. 13, 18, 24; Dec. 6, 18
- ESCALUS — Bransby
- BENVOLIO — Usher
- PARIS — Anderson
- GREGORY — Paddick (on *Oct. 25* only)
- BALTHAZAR — Ricard

1753 DRURY LANE
Jan. 24
- ROMEO — Garrick
- ESCALUS (1, 2) — Winstone
- CAPULET — Berry
- PARIS (1, 2) — Scrase
- BENVOLIO (1) — Mozeen
- TYBALT (1) — Blakes
- FRIAR LAURENCE (1, 2) — Burton
- MERCUTIO — Woodward
- LADY CAPULET — Mrs Bennet
- NURSE — Mrs James
- JULIET (1, 2) — Miss Haughton

(1) Mar. 29; May 8
- FRIAR LAURENCE — Havard
- JULIET — Miss Bellamy
- omitted on *Mar.* 29 only
- ESCALUS, PARIS, BENVOLIO, TYBALT

(2) Oct. 4, 5, 19
- ESCALUS — Bransby
- PARIS — Lacey
- FRIAR LAURENCE — Havard
- JULIET — Mrs Cibber
- added
- MONTAGUE — Burton

COVENT GARDEN
Jan. 1; Feb. 5; May 4, 19, 26
- ROMEO — Barry
- CAPULET — Sparks
- MONTAGUE — Bridgwater
- ESCALUS (1) — Bransby
- BENVOLIO — Usher

(1) Oct. 10, 11, 12, 13, 15, 18, 23, 25; Nov. 3, 24; Dec. 3, 8, 18
- ESCALUS — Gibson
- GREGORY — Bennet
- BALTHAZAR — White
- MERCUTIO — Dyer
- TYBALT — Cushing

1753 COVENT GARDEN (*cont.*)

Jan. 1; Feb. 5; May 4, 19, 26 (cont.)

PARIS	Anderson
FRIAR LAURENCE	Ridout
GREGORY (1)	Cushing
SAMPSON	Collins
ABRAHAM	Dunstall
BALTHAZAR (1)	Ricard
MERCUTIO (1)	Macklin
TYBALT (1)	Dyer
LADY CAPULET	Mrs Barrington
NURSE (1)	Mrs Macklin
JULIET (1)	Mrs Cibber

(1) *Oct. 10, 11, 12, 13, 15, 18, 23, 25; Nov. 3, 24; Dec. 3, 8, 18 (cont.)*

NURSE	Mrs Pitt
JULIET	A Young Gentlewoman [Miss Nossiter (Genest, iv. 393); first appearance, Oct. 10, on the stage]

[Beginning with *Oct. 23* Miss Nossiter's name is in the bills.]

1754 DRURY LANE

Jan. 15; Feb. 11

ROMEO	Garrick
ESCALUS (1)	Scrase
CAPULET	Berry
PARIS (1)	Lacey
BENVOLIO	Mozeen
MONTAGUE (1)	Burton
TYBALT	Blakes
FRIAR LAURENCE	Havard
MERCUTIO	Woodward
LADY CAPULET	Mrs Bennet
NURSE	Mrs James
JULIET	Mrs Cibber

(1) *Oct. 11, 26*

ESCALUS	Bransby
PARIS	Scrase
MONTAGUE	Simson (on *Oct. 11* only)

COVENT GARDEN

Jan. 5; Mar. 18

ROMEO (2)	Barry
CAPULET	Sparks
MONTAGUE (1, 2)	Bridgwater
ESCALUS (2)	Gibson
BENVOLIO (2)	Usher
PARIS (2)	Anderson
FRIAR LAURENCE	Ridout
GREGORY	Bennet
SAMPSON	Collins
ABRAHAM	Dunstall
BALTHAZAR (2)	White
MERCUTIO	Dyer
TYBALT	Cushing
LADY CAPULET	Mrs Barrington
NURSE	Mrs Pitt
JULIET (2)	Miss Nossiter

(1) *Apr. 15; May 22*

MONTAGUE	Redman

(2) *Nov. 20; Dec. 26, 27*

ROMEO	Sheridan
MONTAGUE	Redman
ESCALUS	Anderson
BENVOLIO	Gibson
PARIS	Hurst (on *Nov. 20* only) / White (on *Dec. 26, 27* only)
BALTHAZAR	Wignell (on *Dec. 26, 27* only)
JULIET	Mrs Bellamy

[PA, Nov. 19: 'Romeo and Juliet is to be performed To-morrow Night ... with several Alterations and Additions; in which, those made by Otway, in his Play of Caius Marius, have been princi-

ROMEO AND JULIET

1754 COVENT GARDEN (cont.)

(2) *Nov. 20; Dec. 26, 27 (cont.)*
pally followed'. This appears to have been the case: the bills for *Dec. 26, 27* have, 'As it is usually Performed'.]

1755 DRURY LANE
Feb. 7; Oct. 8

ROMEO	Garrick
ESCALUS	Bransby
CAPULET	Berry
PARIS	Scrase
BENVOLIO (1)	Mozeen
MONTAGUE	Burton
TYBALT	Blakes
FRIAR LAURENCE	Havard
MERCUTIO	Woodward
NURSE	Mrs Macklin
LADY CAPULET	Mrs Bennet
JULIET	Mrs Cibber

(1) *Nov. 11*

| BENVOLIO | Usher |

[In the acting version published by J. and R. Tonson in 1763 the cast is the same as that of these performances, with the following additions:

OLD CAPULET	Johnston
FRIAR JOHN	Jefferson
BALTHAZAR	Ackman
GREGORY	W. Vaughan
SAMPSON	Clough
ABRAHAM	Marr]

COVENT GARDEN
Apr. 3

ROMEO (1, 3)	Smith
CAPULET	Sparks
MONTAGUE	Redman
ESCALUS	Anderson
BENVOLIO	Gibson
PARIS	White
FRIAR LAURENCE	Ridout
GREGORY (3)	Bennet
SAMPSON	Collins
ABRAHAM	Dunstall
BALTHAZAR	Wignell
MERCUTIO (1)	Dyer
TYBALT	Cushing
LADY CAPULET	Mrs Barrington
NURSE (1, 2, 3)	Mrs Copin
LIET	Mrs Bellamy

(1) *Apr. 11*

ROMEO	Dyer
MERCUTIO	Shuter
NURSE	Mrs Pitt

(2) *May 14; Oct. 20, 29; Nov. 5; Dec. 6*

| NURSE | Mrs Pitt |

(3) *Dec. 27, 29, 30*

ROMEO	Barry
GREGORY	R. Smith (on *Dec. 27, 29* only)
NURSE	Mrs Pitt

581

1755 BOWLING GREEN, SOUTHWARK
Jan. 13, 16. No parts assigned

1756 DRURY LANE
Apr. 1

ROMEO	Garrick
ESCALUS	Bransby
CAPULET	Berry
PARIS (1)	Scrase
BENVOLIO	Usher
MONTAGUE	Burton
TYBALT	Blakes
FRIAR LAURENCE	Havard
MERCUTIO	Woodward
NURSE	Mrs Macklin
LADY CAPULET (1)	Mrs Bennet
JULIET (1)	Mrs Cibber

(1) *Oct. 9, 11, 12, 15, 20, 26; Nov. 16*

PARIS	Jefferson
LADY CAPULET	Mrs Pritchard
JULIET	Miss Pritchard [first appearance, Oct. 9, on the stage]

COVENT GARDEN
Jan. 1; Feb. 14; Mar. 20; Apr. 21; May 12

ROMEO	Barry
CAPULET	Sparks
MONTAGUE	Redman
ESCALUS	Anderson
BENVOLIO	Gibson
PARIS	White
FRIAR LAURENCE	Ridout
GREGORY	Bennet
SAMPSON	Collins
ABRAHAM (2)	Dunstall
BALTHAZAR (2, 3)	Wignell
MERCUTIO	Dyer
TYBALT	Cushing
LADY CAPULET	Mrs Barrington
NURSE (1)	Mrs Pitt
JULIET (2, 3)	Mrs Bellamy

(1) *Feb. 24*

NURSE	Mrs Copin

(2) *Oct. 4, 16*

ABRAHAM	Costollo
BALTHAZAR	R. Smith
JULIET	Miss Nossiter

(3) *Dec. 30*

BALTHAZAR	R. Smith
JULIET	Miss Nossiter

1757 DRURY LANE
Apr. 28

ROMEO (1, 2)	Holland
ESCALUS (1, 2)	Bransby
CAPULET	Berry
PARIS	Jefferson
BENVOLIO	Usher
MONTAGUE	Burton
TYBALT	Blakes
FRIAR LAURENCE	Havard

(1) *Sept. 17*

ROMEO	Garrick
LADY CAPULET	Mrs Bennet

omitted ESCALUS, NURSE

(2) *Oct. 1; Nov. 24*

ROMEO	Garrick
LADY CAPULET	Mrs Bennet
JULIET	Mrs Cibber

1757 DRURY LANE (cont.)
Apr. 28 (cont.)

MERCUTIO	Woodward
LADY CAPULET	
(1, 2)	Mrs Pritchard
NURSE (1)	Mrs Macklin
JULIET (2)	Miss Pritchard

(2) *Oct. 1; Nov. 24 (cont.)*
omitted
ESCALUS

COVENT GARDEN
Jan. 1; May 5, 23

ROMEO	Barry
CAPULET	Sparks
MONTAGUE	Redman
ESCALUS	Anderson
BENVOLIO	Gibson
PARIS	White
FRIAR LAURENCE	Ridout
TYBALT	Cushing
GREGORY	Bennet
SAMPSON	Collins
ABRAHAM	Dunstall
BALTHAZAR	R. Smith
MERCUTIO	Dyer
LADY CAPULET	Mrs Barrington
NURSE (1)	Mrs Pitt
JULIET (2)	Miss Nossiter

(1) *Feb. 12*

NURSE	Mrs Copin

(2) *Dec. 7, 16, 27*

JULIET	Mrs Bellamy

1758 DRURY LANE
Mar. 31

ROMEO	Garrick
CAPULET	Berry
PARIS	Jefferson
BENVOLIO	Usher
MONTAGUE	Burton
TYBALT	Blakes
FRIAR LAURENCE	Havard
MERCUTIO	Woodward
LADY CAPULET	Mrs Bennet
NURSE	Mrs Macklin
JULIET	Mrs Cibber

Sept. 28, 30; Oct. 6

ROMEO	A Young Gentleman [Fleetwood (Genest, iv. 536); first appearance, Sept. 28, on the stage]

(1) *Oct. 13, 28*

JULIET	Mrs Cibber

[Beginning with *Oct. 13* Fleetwood's name is in the bills.]

(2) *Dec. 8*

NURSE	Mrs Cross
JULIET	Mrs Cibber

1758 DRURY LANE (*cont.*)

Sept. 28, 30; Oct. 6 (*cont.*)

CAPULET (3)	Berry
PARIS	Austin
BENVOLIO	Packer
ESCALUS	Bransby
MONTAGUE (3)	Burton
TYBALT	Blakes
FRIAR LAURENCE	Havard
MERCUTIO	Palmer
LADY CAPULET	Mrs Bennet
NURSE (2, 3)	Mrs Macklin
JULIET (1, 2)	Miss Pritchard

(3) *Dec. 26*

CAPULET	Burton
MONTAGUE	Scrase
NURSE	Mrs Cross

COVENT GARDEN

Feb. 14

ROMEO (1, 2)	Barry
CAPULET	Sparks
MONTAGUE	Redman
ESCALUS	Anderson
BENVOLIO	Gibson
PARIS (2)	White
FRIAR LAURENCE	Ridout
TYBALT	Cushing
GREGORY	Bennet
SAMPSON	Collins
ABRAHAM	Dunstall
BALTHAZAR	R. Smith
MERCUTIO (1, 2)	Shuter
LADY CAPULET	Mrs Barrington
NURSE	Mrs Pitt
JULIET	Mrs Bellamy

(1) *Mar. 27*

ROMEO	Smith
MERCUTIO	Dyer

(2) *Nov. 1, 8, 30; Dec. 26*

ROMEO	Ross
PARIS	Perry
MERCUTIO	Dyer

1759 DRURY LANE

Apr. 5

ROMEO (1)	Garrick
MERCUTIO	Palmer
ESCALUS	Bransby
PARIS	Austin
BENVOLIO	Packer
MONTAGUE	Scrase
TYBALT (1)	Blakes
FRIAR LAURENCE	Havard
CAPULET	Burton
LADY CAPULET	Mrs Bennet
NURSE	Mrs Cross
JULIET (2)	Miss Pritchard

(1) *May 10; Sept. 25; Dec. 26*

ROMEO Fleetwood
omitted on *May 10* only
TYBALT

(2) *Oct. 24*

JULIET	Mrs Cibber

1759 COVENT GARDEN
Jan. 6

ROMEO	Ross
CAPULET	Sparks
MONTAGUE (2)	Redman
ESCALUS (2)	Anderson
BENVOLIO (2)	Gibson
PARIS (2)	Perry
FRIAR LAURENCE	Ridout
TYBALT (1, 2)	Cushing
GREGORY (1, 2)	Bennet
SAMPSON (2)	Collins
ABRAHAM (1, 2)	Holtom
BALTHAZAR (2)	R. Smith
MERCUTIO	Dyer
LADY CAPULET (2)	Mrs Barrington
NURSE	Mrs Pitt
JULIET	Mrs Bellamy

(1) *Feb. 26; May 22*

TYBALT	Bennet
GREGORY	Holtom
ABRAHAM	Dunstall

(2) *Apr. 17*
omitted MONTAGUE, ESCALUS, BENVOLIO, PARIS, TYBALT, GREGORY, SAMPSON, ABRAHAM, BALTHAZAR, LADY CAPULET

1760 DRURY LANE
Feb. 7; Apr. 7

ROMEO (1, 3)	Fleetwood
MERCUTIO	Palmer
ESCALUS (2, 3)	Bransby
PARIS (2, 3)	Austin
TYBALT	Blakes
CAPULET	Burton
FRIAR LAURENCE (2)	Havard
BENVOLIO (2, 3)	Packer
MONTAGUE (2, 3)	Scrase
LADY CAPULET	Mrs Bennet
NURSE	Mrs Cross
JULIET (1)	Miss Pritchard

(1) *Mar. 22*

ROMEO	Garrick
JULIET	Mrs Cibber

(2) *May 6*

FRIAR LAURENCE	Clough

omitted ESCALUS, PARIS, BENVOLIO, MONTAGUE

(3) *Sept. 20; Oct. 20; Dec. 26*

ROMEO	Holland

omitted SAME as *May 6*

COVENT GARDEN
Apr. 8; May 20

ROMEO	Ross
CAPULET	Sparks
MONTAGUE	Redman
ESCALUS (2)	Anderson
BENVOLIO (2)	Gibson
PARIS (2)	Perry
FRIAR LAURENCE	Ridout
TYBALT	Bennet
GREGORY (2)	Holtom
SAMPSON (2)	Collins
ABRAHAM (2)	Dunstall

(1) *Apr. 30*

JULIET	Miss Mowat

(2) *Sept. 29; Oct. 3; Nov. 20; Dec. 6*

JULIET	Miss Macklin

omitted GREGORY, SAMPSON, ABRAHAM, BALTHAZAR, and also omitted on *Sept. 29, Oct. 3* ESCALUS, BENVOLIO, PARIS, LADY CAPULET

1760 COVENT GARDEN (cont.)

Apr. 8; May 20 (cont.)

BALTHAZAR (2)	R. Smith
MERCUTIO	Dyer
LADY CAPULET (2)	Mrs Barrington
NURSE	Mrs Pitt
JULIET (1, 2)	Mrs Ward

1761 DRURY LANE

Apr. 6

ROMEO (4)	Holland
CAPULET (1)	Burton
FRIAR LAURENCE	Havard
MERCUTIO (3, 4)	Garrick
NURSE (1)	Mrs Cross
JULIET (2, 3, 4)	Miss Pritchard

(1) *Apr. 13*

CAPULET	Kennedy
NURSE	Mrs Kennedy

(2) *Apr. 20*

JULIET	Mrs Cibber

added

TYBALT	Blakes

(3) *May 5*

MERCUTIO	Palmer
JULIET	Mrs Palmer [i.e. formerly Miss Pritchard]

added

TYBALT	Ackman
BENVOLIO	Phillips [first appearance on the stage]
LADY CAPULET	Mrs Bennet

(4) *Sept. 8; Nov. 7; Dec. 26*

ROMEO	Garrick (on *Nov.* 7 only)
MERCUTIO	Palmer
JULIET	Mrs Cibber

added

TYBALT	Blakes
LADY CAPULET	Mrs Bennet

[On *Dec. 26* PA assigns JULIET to Mrs Palmer.]

COVENT GARDEN

Jan. 13

ROMEO	Ross
CAPULET	Sparks
MONTAGUE	Redman
ESCALUS (1, 2)	Anderson
FRIAR LAURENCE (1, 2)	Ridout
MERCUTIO	Dyer
PARIS (1, 2)	Sutton [first appearance on the stage]

(1) *Mar. 24; Sept. 25; Oct. 28*

FRIAR LAURENCE	Hull
PARIS	Perry
JULIET	Mrs Bellamy (on *Sept.* 25, *Oct.* 28 only)

omitted

ESCALUS, LADY CAPULET

(2) *Apr. 10; May 20*

FRIAR LAURENCE	Hull
PARIS	Perry

ROMEO AND JULIET

1761 COVENT GARDEN (cont.)

Jan. 13 (cont.)

TYBALT	Bennet
BENVOLIO	Gibson
LADY CAPULET (1)	Mrs Barrington
NURSE	Mrs Pitt
JULIET (1, 2)	Miss Macklin

(2) *Apr. 10; May 20 (cont.)*

JULIET { A Young Gentlewoman [Miss Hallam (Genest, iv. 628)] (on *Apr. 10* only) / Mrs Ward (on *May 20* only) }

added on *Apr. 10* only
PETER	Collins
APOTHECARY	Holtom

omitted
ESCALUS

1762 DRURY LANE

Jan. 25

ROMEO	Holland
MERCUTIO	Palmer
TYBALT	Blakes
CAPULET	Burton
FRIAR LAURENCE	Havard
LADY CAPULET	Mrs Bennet
NURSE	Mrs Cross
JULIET (1, 2)	Miss Bride

(1) *May 13*

JULIET added	Mrs Palmer
BENVOLIO	Scrase
ESCALUS	Bransby
MONTAGUE	Moody
PARIS	Kennedy

(2) *Sept. 28; Oct. 27; Dec. 4*

JULIET added	Mrs Cibber
PARIS	Lee

COVENT GARDEN

Feb. 25; Mar. 13

ROMEO	Ross
CAPULET (2)	Gibson
MONTAGUE	Redman
FRIAR LAURENCE	Hull
MERCUTIO	Dyer
PARIS	Perry
TYBALT	Bennet
BENVOLIO	Davis
NURSE	Mrs Pitt
JULIET (1, 2)	Mrs Bellamy

(1) *Apr. 22*

JULIET	Miss Hallam

(2) *Sept. 22; Oct. 18*

CAPULET	Sparks
JULIET added	Miss Macklin
ESCALUS	Anderson

1763 DRURY LANE

Jan. 1; Mar. 5

ROMEO	Holland
MERCUTIO	Palmer
PARIS (2)	Lee
TYBALT (2)	Blakes
CAPULET	Burton
FRIAR LAURENCE	Havard
LADY CAPULET	Mrs Bennet

(1) *Apr. 22*

added
ESCALUS	Bransby
BENVOLIO	Ackman

(2) *Oct. 31; Nov. 25*

PARIS	Jackson
TYBALT	Lee
JULIET	Mrs Palmer

1763 DRURY LANE (cont.)

Jan. 1; Mar. 5 (cont.)

NURSE	Mrs Cross
JULIET (2)	Mrs Cibber

(2) Oct. 31; Nov. 25 (cont.)

added

ESCALUS	Bransby

[In the acting version published by Garland, 1763, ROMEO is assigned to Garrick, and JULIET to Mrs Cibber. The cast is otherwise the same as that of these performances, with the following additions:

MONTAGUE	Moody
BENVOLIO	Packer
OLD CAPULET	Johnston
FRIAR JOHN	Clough
BALTHAZAR	Ackman
GREGORY	Mozeen
SAMPSON	Clough
ABRAHAM	Marr]

[Clough doubled FRIAR JOHN and SAMPSON.]

COVENT GARDEN

Jan. 24; Sept. 21

ROMEO	Ross
CAPULET	Sparks
FRIAR LAURENCE	Hull
MERCUTIO	Woodward
TYBALT	Bennet
ESCALUS	Anderson
BENVOLIO	Davis
PARIS	Perry
MONTAGUE	Redman
NURSE	Mrs Pitt
JULIET (1, 2)	Miss Hallam

(1) May 26

JULIET	Miss Macklin

added

LADY CAPULET	Mrs Barrington

(2) Dec. 29

JULIET	Miss Macklin

[On *Jan. 24* Genest (v. 30) erroneously assigns JULIET to Miss Macklin.]

1764 DRURY LANE

May 21; Sept. 22

ROMEO	Holland
MERCUTIO	Palmer
ESCALUS	Bransby
PARIS	Jackson
TYBALT	Lee
CAPULET	Burton
FRIAR LAURENCE	Havard
LADY CAPULET	Mrs Bennet
NURSE	Mrs Cross
JULIET (1)	Mrs Palmer

(1) Oct. 29

JULIET	Mrs Lessingham

ROMEO AND JULIET

1764 COVENT GARDEN
Apr. 2

ROMEO	Ross
CAPULET	Sparks
FRIAR LAURENCE (1)	Hull
MERCUTIO	Woodward
BENVOLIO	Davis
PARIS	Perry
ESCALUS	Anderson
TYBALT	Bennet
MONTAGUE (2)	Redman
APOTHECARY (2)	Holtom
LADY CAPULET (1, 2)	Mrs Ward
NURSE	Mrs Pitt
JULIET (1, 2)	Miss Ward [first appearance on the stage]

[PA assigns MONTAGUE twice: to Redman and to Lewis. The assignment to Lewis is almost certainly a misprint.]

(1) *May 12*

FRIAR LAURENCE	Gardner
LADY CAPULET	Mrs Barrington
JULIET	Miss Macklin

added
PETER	Weller
PAGE	Master Besford

[PA assigns MONTAGUE twice: to Redman and to Lewis.]

(2) *Sept. 21; Oct. 27*

LADY CAPULET	Mrs Barrington
JULIET	Miss Macklin (on *Sept. 21* only) / Miss Hallam (on *Oct. 27* only)

omitted
MONTAGUE, APOTHECARY

1765 DRURY LANE
Jan. 7

ROMEO	Holland
MERCUTIO	Palmer
ESCALUS (1)	Bransby
PARIS (2)	Jackson
TYBALT (2)	Lee
CAPULET	Burton
FRIAR LAURENCE (2)	Havard
LADY CAPULET	Mrs Bennet
NURSE (1)	Mrs Cross
JULIET	Mrs Palmer

(1) *May 16*

ESCALUS	Adcock
NURSE	Mrs Adcock [first appearance in London]

added
MONTAGUE	Keen

(2) *Sept. 17; Dec. 23*

PARIS	Packer
FRIAR LAURENCE	Love (on *Dec. 23* only)

added
BENVOLIO	Ackman

omitted
TYBALT

COVENT GARDEN
Jan. 21; Oct. 7; Dec. 23

ROMEO	Ross
CAPULET (1, 2)	Gibson
FRIAR LAURENCE	Hull
MERCUTIO (3)	Woodward
TYBALT	Bennet
BENVOLIO	Davis
PARIS	Perry

(1) *Mar. 25*

CAPULET	Sparks

(2) *Apr. 29*

CAPULET	Sparks
NURSE	Mrs Green

(3) *Nov. 25*

MERCUTIO	Dyer

ROMEO AND JULIET

1765 COVENT GARDEN (cont.)
Jan. 21; Oct. 7; Dec. 23 (cont.)

ESCALUS	Anderson
LADY CAPULET	Mrs Barrington
NURSE (2)	Mrs Pitt
JULIET	Mrs Bellamy

1766 DRURY LANE
May 2

ROMEO (1)	Holland
MERCUTIO	Palmer
PARIS (1)	Packer
TYBALT (1)	Lee
ESCALUS	Bransby
BENVOLIO (1)	Ackman
PETER (1)	Master Burton
CAPULET	Burton
FRIAR LAURENCE	Havard
LADY CAPULET	Mrs Bennet
NURSE	Mrs Cross
JULIET (1)	Mrs Palmer

(1) *Sept. 30; Oct. 4; Dec. 26*

ROMEO	Cautherley
PARIS	Fawcett
TYBALT	[F.] Aickin
BENVOLIO	Packer
PETER	Weston
JULIET	Mrs [W.] Barry [first appearance, Sept. 30, in London]

added

APOTHECARY	Castle

[Neither Pb nor PA lists the APOTHECARY. The assignment is taken from a review of the play in PA, Oct. 3.]

COVENT GARDEN
Feb. 20

ROMEO	Ross
CAPULET	Gibson
FRIAR LAURENCE	Hull
MERCUTIO	Woodward
TYBALT	Bennet
BENVOLIO (2)	Davis
PARIS	Perry
ESCALUS	Anderson
LADY CAPULET (1)	Mrs Barrington
NURSE	Mrs Pitt
JULIET (1, 2)	Mrs Bellamy

(1) *Apr. 8, 28; May 19*

LADY CAPULET	Mrs Ward (on *Apr. 8* only)
JULIET	Miss Ward (on *Apr. 8* only)

added

APOTHECARY	Holtom
PETER	Weller (on *Apr. 8, 28* only) / Morgan (on *May 19* only)
BALTHAZAR	R. Smith
MONTAGUE	Redman

(2) *Oct. 21*

BENVOLIO	Baker
JULIET	Miss Macklin

added

SAME as *Apr. 8*

KING'S, HAYMARKET
Aug. 18, 20

ROMEO	Barry
CAPULET	[F.] Aickin
MONTAGUE	Murden
BENVOLIO	Davis

1766 KING'S, HAYMARKET (cont.)

Aug. 18, 20 (cont.)

TYBALT	McGeorge
MERCUTIO	Shuter
ESCALUS	[J.] Palmer
PARIS	Keen
BALTHAZAR	[P.] Lewis
FRIAR LAURENCE	Hurst
PETER	Weston
FRIAR JOHN	Nelson
OLD CAPULET	Pierce
APOTHECARY	Castle
GREGORY	Hamilton
ABRAHAM	Quick
LADY CAPULET	Mrs Burden
NURSE	Mrs Worley
JULIET	Mrs Dancer

1767 DRURY LANE

May 18, 30

ROMEO (1, 2)	Cautherley
MERCUTIO (1)	Dodd
PARIS	Fawcett
TYBALT	[F.] Aickin
ESCALUS	Bransby
BENVOLIO	Packer
PETER	Weston
CAPULET	Burton
FRIAR LAURENCE	Havard
LADY CAPULET (1, 2)	Mrs Bennet
NURSE	Mrs Cross
JULIET (1, 2)	Mrs [W.] Barry

(1) *Sept. 21*

ROMEO	Reddish
MERCUTIO	Palmer
LADY CAPULET	Mrs Johnston
JULIET	Mrs Palmer
added	
MONTAGUE	Hurst

(2) *Dec. 22*

ROMEO	Barry
LADY CAPULET	Mrs Johnston
JULIET	Mrs Dancer
added	
MONTAGUE	Hurst

COVENT GARDEN

Feb. 16

ROMEO (2, 3)	Ross
CAPULET	Gibson
FRIAR LAURENCE	Hull
MERCUTIO (2)	Woodward
BENVOLIO (1, 2, 3)	Baker
PARIS	Perry
TYBALT (3)	Bennet
ESCALUS (2, 3)	Anderson
BALTHAZAR (3)	R. Smith
MONTAGUE (3)	Redman

(1) *Mar. 17*

BENVOLIO	Davis
LADY CAPULET	Mrs Burden

(2) *Apr. 20; May 20*

ROMEO	Dyer (on *Apr. 20* only)
BENVOLIO	Davis
ESCALUS	Gardner
omitted on *Apr. 20* only	
MERCUTIO	

(3) *Sept. 25; Oct. 12; Nov. 16*

ROMEO	Powell

1767 COVENT GARDEN (cont.)

Feb. 16 (cont.)

APOTHECARY (3)	Holtom
PETER (3)	Weller
LADY CAPULET (1)	Mrs Barrington
NURSE	Mrs Pitt
JULIET	Mrs Bellamy

(3) Sept. 25; Oct. 12; Nov. 16 (cont.)

BENVOLIO	Davis
omitted	
TYBALT, ESCALUS, BALTHAZAR, MONTAGUE, APOTHECARY, PETER	

HAYMARKET

June 22

ROMEO	Barry
ESCALUS	[J.] Palmer
PARIS	[R.] Smith
MONTAGUE	Keen
CAPULET	Newton
BENVOLIO	Davis
TYBALT	[C.] Bannister
OLD CAPULET	Pierce
FRIAR LAURENCE	Gardner
MERCUTIO	Shuter
BALTHAZAR	Strange
SAMPSON	Mendez
ABRAHAM	Quick
PETER	Weston
APOTHECARY	Castle
PAGE	Master Palmer
LADY CAPULET	Mrs Burden
NURSE	Mrs Gardner
JULIET	Mrs Dancer

1768 DRURY LANE

Apr. 11

ROMEO (1)	Barry
MERCUTIO	Dodd
PARIS	Fawcett
TYBALT	[F.] Aickin
ESCALUS	Bransby
BENVOLIO	Packer
MONTAGUE	Hurst
PETER (1)	Weston
CAPULET	Burton
FRIAR LAURENCE	Love
LADY CAPULET	Mrs Johnston
NURSE	Mrs Cross
JULIET (1)	Mrs Dancer

(1) May 30

ROMEO	Cautherley
PETER	J. Burton
JULIET	Mrs [W.] Barry

[Genest (v. 169) erroneously assigns JULIET to Mrs [W.] Barry.]

1768 COVENT GARDEN

Jan. 4; Sept. 26

ROMEO	Powell
CAPULET	Gibson
FRIAR LAURENCE	Hull
MERCUTIO	Woodward
TYBALT (2)	Gardner
PARIS	Perry
BENVOLIO	Davis
ESCALUS (2)	Morris
PETER (1)	Morgan
FRIAR JOHN	Wignell
LADY CAPULET	Mrs Barrington
NURSE	Mrs Pitt
JULIET (2)	Mrs Bellamy

(1) *Apr. 29*

PETER added	Quick
APOTHECARY	Holtom
BALTHAZAR	R. Smith

(2) *Nov. 26, 28, 29, 30; Dec. 1, 2*

TYBALT	Mahon
ESCALUS	Gardner
JULIET	A Young Gentlewoman [Miss Morris (Genest, v. 238); first appearance, Nov. 26, on the stage]

1769 DRURY LANE

May 1

ROMEO	Cautherley
MERCUTIO	Dodd
BENVOLIO (1)	Ackman
ESCALUS (1)	Bransby
MONTAGUE (1)	Hurst
CAPULET	Burton
FRIAR LAURENCE	Love
PARIS	Fawcett
PETER (1)	Weston
NURSE (1)	Mrs Bradshaw
LADY CAPULET	Mrs Johnston
JULIET (1)	Mrs [S.] Barry

(1) *Oct. 2*

BENVOLIO	Packer
ESCALUS	Keen
PETER	J. Burton
NURSE	Mrs Cross
JULIET	Miss Younge
added	
TYBALT	J. Aickin
omitted	
MONTAGUE	

COVENT GARDEN

Jan. 6

ROMEO (2)	Powell
CAPULET	Gibson
FRIAR LAURENCE	Hull
MERCUTIO	Woodward
TYBALT (2)	Mahon
BENVOLIO	Davis
PETER (2)	Morgan
PARIS	Perry
ESCALUS (1, 2)	Gardner
FRIAR JOHN	Wignell
LADY CAPULET	Mrs Barrington
NURSE	Mrs Pitt
JULIET (1, 2)	Miss Morris

(1) *Apr. 15; May 9*

ESCALUS	Morris
JULIET	Mrs Bellamy

[On *Apr. 15* PA retains Gardner as ESCALUS.]

(2) *Oct. 6*

ROMEO	Smith
TYBALT	Gardner
PETER	Quick
ESCALUS	Morris
JULIET	Mrs Bellamy

1770 DRURY LANE
May 8

ROMEO (1)	Brereton
MERCUTIO	Dodd
FRIAR LAURENCE	Love
BENVOLIO	Packer
CAPULET (1)	Burton
TYBALT	J. Aickin
ESCALUS	Keen
PARIS	Fawcett
PETER	J. Burton
APOTHECARY (1)	[F.] Waldron
NURSE	Mrs Cross
LADY CAPULET (1)	Mrs [S.] Smith
JULIET (1)	Miss Younge

(1) *Oct. 29; Nov. 1*

ROMEO	Cautherley
CAPULET	Moody (on *Oct. 29* only)
APOTHECARY	Castle
LADY CAPULET	Mrs Johnston
JULIET	A Young Gentlewoman [Mrs Morland (MacMillan, 150); first appearance, Oct. 29, in London]

COVENT GARDEN
Jan. 1

ROMEO	Smith
CAPULET	Gibson
FRIAR LAURENCE	Hull
MERCUTIO	Woodward
TYBALT (1)	Cushing
BENVOLIO (1)	Fox
PARIS	Perry
ESCALUS (1)	Gardner
PETER	Quick
FRIAR JOHN	Wignell
LADY CAPULET	Mrs Barrington
NURSE	Mrs Pitt
JULIET (1)	Mrs Bellamy

(1) *Apr. 28*

TYBALT	Gardner
BENVOLIO	Davis
JULIET	Mrs Lessingham
omitted	
ESCALUS	

[PA retains Cushing as TYBALT.]

1771 DRURY LANE
May 25

ROMEO	Cautherley
MERCUTIO	Dodd
FRIAR LAURENCE	Love
BENVOLIO	Packer
CAPULET (1)	Burton
TYBALT	J. Aickin
ESCALUS	Keen
PARIS	Fawcett
PETER (1)	J. Burton
APOTHECARY (1)	Castle
BALTHAZAR (1)	Lings
NURSE	Mrs Cross

(1) *Oct. 10*

CAPULET	Inchbald
PETER	Weston
APOTHECARY	[F.] Waldron
BALTHAZAR	Wheeler
JULIET	Mrs [S.] Barry

[In the acting version published by Bell in 1773 there are the following additions to the cast:

MONTAGUE	Wright
OLD CAPULET	Johnston
FRIAR JOHN	Keen
GREGORY	Wrighten
SAMPSON	Griffith
ABRAHAM	Marr

1771 DRURY LANE (cont.)

May 25 (cont.)
LADY CAPULET	Mrs Johnston
JULIET (1)	Mrs Morland

(1) *Oct. 10 (cont.)*

The assignments of Keen and Marr are from casts of an earlier year. It is unlikely that Keen doubled ESCALUS and FRIAR JOHN; in Bell ESCALUS is assigned to Bransby. Marr retired from the stage in 1770.]

COVENT GARDEN

Apr. 30; May 28
ROMEO	Smith
CAPULET (1, 2)	Younger
FRIAR LAURENCE	Hull
MERCUTIO (2)	Dyer
TYBALT (2)	Gardner
PARIS (2)	Perry
BENVOLIO (1, 2)	Fox
ESCALUS (1)	Morris
PETER (1)	Quick
APOTHECARY (1, 2)	Holtom
LADY CAPULET	Mrs Barrington
NURSE	Mrs Pitt
JULIET	Miss Miller

(1) *Oct. 25*
CAPULET	Kniveton
omitted	
BENVOLIO, ESCALUS, PETER, APOTHECARY	

(2) *Dec. 17*
CAPULET	Kniveton
MERCUTIO	Woodward
TYBALT	Owenson
PARIS	R. Smith
BENVOLIO	Davis
omitted	
APOTHECARY	

1772 DRURY LANE

Oct. 1, 3
ROMEO	A Young Gentleman [Dimond (Genest, v. 339); first appearance, Oct. 1, on the stage]
MERCUTIO	Dodd
FRIAR LAURENCE	Packer
BENVOLIO	Davies
CAPULET (1)	Inchbald
TYBALT	J. Aickin
ESCALUS	Keen
PARIS	Fawcett
PETER	[J.] Burton
APOTHECARY	Castle
BALTHAZAR	Wheeler
NURSE	Mrs Cross
LADY CAPULET	Mrs Johnston
JULIET	Miss Mansell

(1) *Oct. 10*
CAPULET	Hurst
added	
MONTAGUE	Wright

595

1772 COVENT GARDEN
Feb. 24; Mar. 16

ROMEO (1)	Smith
CAPULET	Kniveton
FRIAR LAURENCE	Hull
MERCUTIO	Woodward
BENVOLIO	Davis
TYBALT	Gardner
PARIS	Perry
ESCALUS	Morris
PETER (2)	Quick
LADY CAPULET	Mrs Barrington
NURSE (1)	Mrs Pitt
JULIET (1)	Miss Miller

(1) *May 2*

ROMEO	A Young Gentleman [unidentified; first appearance on the stage]
NURSE	Mrs Gardner
JULIET	A Young Lady [Miss Dayes (MC, Oct. 28, 1773); first appearance on the stage]

(2) *Nov. 2*
omitted
PETER

[In the acting version published by Bell in 1773 the cast is the same as that of these performances, with the following additions:

MONTAGUE	Redman
FRIAR JOHN	Wignell
BALTHAZAR	R. Smith
APOTHECARY	Holtom]

1773 COVENT GARDEN
Jan. 1

ROMEO	Smith
CAPULET (1)	Kniveton
FRIAR LAURENCE	Hull
MERCUTIO	Woodward
BENVOLIO	Davis
ESCALUS (1, 2)	Morris
PARIS (1, 2)	R. Smith
TYBALT (1, 2)	Gardner
LADY CAPULET (2)	Mrs Barrington
NURSE	Mrs Pitt
JULIET (1, 2)	Miss Miller

(1) *May 17*

CAPULET	Younger
PARIS	Perry
TYBALT	Owenson
JULIET	Mrs Hartley
ESCALUS omitted	

(2) *Oct. 25; Dec. 13*

ESCALUS	Gardner
PARIS	Thompson
TYBALT	Owenson
LADY CAPULET	Miss Pearce
JULIET	Mrs Hartley (on Oct. 25 only)

1774 COVENT GARDEN
Feb. 9

ROMEO	Smith
CAPULET	Kniveton
FRIAR LAURENCE	Hull
MERCUTIO	Lewis
BENVOLIO	Davis
ESCALUS	Gardner
PARIS	Thompson
TYBALT	Owenson
PETER	Quick
APOTHECARY	Holtom

ROMEO AND JULIET

1774 COVENT GARDEN (*cont.*)
Feb. 9 (cont.)
LADY CAPULET	Miss Pearce
NURSE	Mrs Pitt
JULIET	Mrs Hartley

Oct. 13
ROMEO	Lewis
CAPULET	Clarke
FRIAR LAURENCE	Hull
MERCUTIO	Woodward
BENVOLIO	Whitfield
ESCALUS	Fearon
PARIS	Booth
TYBALT	[Lee] Lewes
PETER	Quick
LADY CAPULET	Mrs Hull
NURSE	Mrs Pitt
JULIET	Miss Dayes

1775 COVENT GARDEN
Sept. 25; Oct. 2; Nov. 7
ROMEO	Lewis
CAPULET (2)	Clarke
FRIAR LAURENCE	Hull
MERCUTIO	Woodward
BENVOLIO (2)	Booth
ESCALUS	Fearon
PARIS	Young
TYBALT	L'Estrange
PETER	Quick
LADY CAPULET	Mrs Poussin
NURSE (1)	Mrs Pitt
JULIET	Mrs Jackson [first appearance, Sept. 25, in London]

(1) *Oct. 9*
NURSE	Mrs Bradshaw

(2) *Dec. 27*
CAPULET	Booth
omitted	
BENVOLIO	

1776 DRURY LANE
May 22
ROMEO	Brereton
FRIAR LAURENCE	Packer
BENVOLIO	Davies
CAPULET (1)	Hurst
TYBALT (1)	Farren
ESCALUS	Norris
PARIS (1)	Lamash
PETER	[J.] Burton
APOTHECARY	[F.] Waldron
BALTHAZAR (1)	Everard
MERCUTIO	Dodd

(1) *Dec. 10, 12, 21, 27*
CAPULET	[J.] Aickin
TYBALT	Grist
PARIS	Farren
BALTHAZAR	Chaplin
NURSE	Mrs Love
JULIET	A Young Lady [Mrs Robinson (Genest, v. 548); first appearance, Dec. 10, on the stage]

597

1776 DRURY LANE (*cont.*)

May 22 (cont.)
    NURSE (1)   Mrs Cross
    LADY CAPULET   Mrs Johnston
    JULIET (1)   Miss [E.] Hopkins

COVENT GARDEN

Oct. 7, 14, 21; Nov. 8
    ROMEO   Ward [first appearance, Oct. 7, in London]
    CAPULET   Clarke
    FRIAR LAURENCE Hull
    MERCUTIO   Woodward
    BENVOLIO   Booth
    PARIS   Whitfield
    TYBALT   L'Estrange
    PETER   Jones
    LADY CAPULET   Mrs Poussin
    NURSE   Mrs Pitt
    JULIET   Mrs Jackson

CHINA HALL, ROTHERHITHE

July 15
    CAPULET   Massey
    JULIET   A Young Lady [unidentified]
    No other parts assigned

1777 COVENT GARDEN

Sept. 29
    ROMEO   Wroughton
    CAPULET   Clarke
    FRIAR LAURENCE Hull
    MERCUTIO   Lewis
    BENVOLIO   Booth
    ESCALUS   Fearon
    PARIS   Whitfield
    TYBALT   L'Estrange
    PETER   Jones
    LADY CAPULET   Mrs Poussin
    NURSE   Mrs Pitt
    JULIET   Mrs Jackson

1778 DRURY LANE

May 23
    ROMEO   Brereton
    FRIAR LAURENCE Packer
    CAPULET   [J.] Aickin

ROMEO AND JULIET

1778 DRURY LANE (*cont.*)
May 23 (*cont.*)

BENVOLIO	Davies
ESCALUS	Norris
TYBALT	R. Palmer
PARIS	Phillimore
PETER	[J.] Burton
APOTHECARY	[F.] Waldron
BALTHAZAR	Chaplin
MERCUTIO	Dodd
LADY CAPULET	Mrs Johnston
NURSE	Mrs Bradshaw
JULIET	Mrs Robinson

COVENT GARDEN

Jan. 12

ROMEO	Wroughton
CAPULET (1)	Clarke
FRIAR LAURENCE	Hull
MERCUTIO	Lewis
BENVOLIO (1)	Booth
ESCALUS	Fearon
PARIS (1)	Whitfield
TYBALT	L'Estrange
PETER	Jones
LADY CAPULET	Mrs Poussin
NURSE	Mrs Pitt
JULIET (1, 2)	Mrs O'Keeffe [first appearance in London]

(1) *Feb. 23*

CAPULET	Booth
BENVOLIO	Whitfield
PARIS	Robson
JULIET	Mrs Jackson

[PA retains Mrs O'Keeffe as JULIET.]

(2) *Oct. 26; Dec. 28*

JULIET added	Mrs Jackson
BALTHAZAR	Robson
MONTAGUE	Baker
APOTHECARY	Stevens

[Both Pb and PA misprint Mrs O'Keeffe's name as 'Keeffe'.]

CHINA HALL, ROTHERHITHE

June 10

ROMEO	West
MERCUTIO	Russell
TYBALT	Cooke
CAPULET	Newton
BENVOLIO	Glassington
ESCALUS	Massey
PETER	Bailey
PARIS	Everard
FRIAR LAURENCE	Burnett
LADY CAPULET	Mrs Newby
NURSE	Mrs Russell
JULIET	Miss Glassington

ROMEO AND JULIET

1779 DRURY LANE
Dec. 27

ROMEO	Brereton
FRIAR LAURENCE	Packer
CAPULET	[J.] Aickin
BENVOLIO	Davies
TYBALT	R. Palmer
ESCALUS	Norris
PARIS	Phillimore
PETER	[J.] Burton
APOTHECARY	[F.] Waldron
BALTHAZAR	Chaplin
MERCUTIO	Dodd
LADY CAPULET	Mrs Davenett
NURSE	Mrs Love
JULIET	Mrs Robinson

COVENT GARDEN
Apr. 19

ROMEO	Wroughton
CAPULET	Clarke
FRIAR LAURENCE	Hull
MERCUTIO	Lewis
BENVOLIO	Booth
PARIS (1)	Whitfield
TYBALT	L'Estrange
PETER	Jones
ESCALUS	Fearon
BALTHAZAR (1)	Robson
MONTAGUE	Baker
APOTHECARY (1)	Stevens
LADY CAPULET	Mrs Poussin
NURSE	Mrs Pitt
JULIET (1)	A Young Lady [Mrs Dawes (*Kentish Gazette*, June 19, July 3, 1779; first appearance on the stage]

(1) *Nov. 8*

PARIS	Robson
JULIET	Mrs Jackson

omitted
BALTHAZAR, APOTHECARY

1780 CROWN INN, ISLINGTON
Mar. 13

ROMEO	Wilson
BENVOLIO	Jones
CAPULET	Price
TYBALT	Gardner
PARIS	Wortley
FRIAR LAURENCE	Leach
PETER	Master Jerrold
MERCUTIO	Jerrold
LADY CAPULET	Mrs Jerrold

1780 CROWN INN, ISLINGTON (cont.)
Mar. 13 (cont.)

NURSE	Mrs Weeks
JULIET	Mrs Kingham

1781 DRURY LANE
May 1

ROMEO	Brereton
FRIAR LAURENCE	Packer
CAPULET	[J.] Aickin
BENVOLIO	Williams
TYBALT	R. Palmer
ESCALUS	Norris
PARIS	Phillimore
PETER	[J.] Burton
APOTHECARY	[F.] Waldron
BALTHAZAR	Fawcett
MONTAGUE	Chaplin
MERCUTIO	Dodd
LADY CAPULET	Mrs Johnston
NURSE	Mrs Love
JULIET	Miss Farren

COVENT GARDEN
Sept. 24

ROMEO	A Gentleman [Trew (MS annotation on JPK); second appearance on the stage]
CAPULET	Clarke
FRIAR LAURENCE	Hull
BENVOLIO	Booth
ESCALUS	Fearon
PARIS (2)	J. Bates
TYBALT	L'Estrange
PETER (1, 2)	Jones
APOTHECARY (1, 2)	Stevens
FRIAR JOHN (1, 2)	[R.] Bates
MONTAGUE	Thompson
MERCUTIO	Lewis
LADY CAPULET	Mrs Poussin
NURSE	Mrs Pitt
JULIET	Miss Satchell

[Both Pb and PA omit the APOTHECARY and FRIAR JOHN. The assignments of these two parts are taken from a review of this performance in MC, Sept. 25.]

(1) *Oct. 1, 8*

PETER	Stevens
APOTHECARY omitted	Jones
FRIAR JOHN	

(2) *Oct. 15; Nov. 12*

PETER	Stevens
APOTHECARY omitted	Jones
PARIS, FRIAR JOHN	

[In these four bills the APOTHECARY is listed as above.]

1781 HAYMARKET
Aug. 17

ROMEO	[J.] Bannister
FRIAR LAURENCE	Gardner
CAPULET	Webb
APOTHECARY	Barrett
PARIS	R. Palmer
MONTAGUE	Massey
JULIET	Mrs Cargill

[The above consisted of parts of V. i and iii only. The entertainment on this evening was called *The School of Shakespeare*, for a description of which see p. 73.]

1782 DRURY LANE
Apr. 25

ROMEO	Brereton
FRIAR LAURENCE	Packer
CAPULET	[J.] Aickin
BENVOLIO	Williams
TYBALT	R. Palmer
ESCALUS	Norris
PARIS	Phillimore
PETER	[J.] Burton
APOTHECARY	[F.] Waldron
BALTHAZAR	Fawcett
MONTAGUE	Chaplin
MERCUTIO	Dodd
LADY CAPULET	Mrs Booth
NURSE	Mrs Love
JULIET	Miss Farren

COVENT GARDEN
Oct. 7; Dec. 26

ROMEO	Wroughton
CAPULET	Clarke
FRIAR LAURENCE	Hull
BENVOLIO	Booth
ESCALUS	Fearon
PARIS	Davies
TYBALT	Whitfield
PETER	Stevens
MONTAGUE	Thompson
APOTHECARY	Jones
MERCUTIO	Lewis
LADY CAPULET	Mrs Poussin
NURSE	Mrs Pitt
JULIET	Miss Satchell

1783 COVENT GARDEN
Sept. 22; Oct. 27

ROMEO	Wroughton
CAPULET	Clarke
FRIAR LAURENCE	Hull
BENVOLIO	Whitfield
ESCALUS	Fearon
PARIS	Davies
TYBALT	Booth
MONTAGUE	Thompson
PETER	Stevens
APOTHECARY	Jones
MERCUTIO	Lewis
LADY CAPULET	Mrs Poussin
NURSE	Mrs Pitt
JULIET	Miss Satchell

1784 COVENT GARDEN
Jan. 19; Apr. 12

ROMEO (1)	Wroughton
CAPULET	Clarke
FRIAR LAURENCE	Hull
BENVOLIO (1)	Whitfield
ESCALUS (1)	Fearon
PARIS (1)	Davies
TYBALT (1)	Booth
MONTAGUE (1)	Thompson
PETER	Stevens
APOTHECARY	Jones
MERCUTIO	Lewis
LADY CAPULET	Mrs Poussin
NURSE	Mrs Pitt
JULIET (1)	Mrs [S.] Kemble

(1) *Oct.* 25, 26; *Nov.* 1, 5, 8, 19, 26; *Dec.* 6, 29

ROMEO	A Young Gentleman [Holman (Genest, vi. 354); first appearance, *Oct.* 25, on the stage]
BENVOLIO	Davies
ESCALUS	Thompson (on *Dec.* 29 only)
PARIS	Bonnor
TYBALT	Cubitt
MONTAGUE	Egan (on *Dec.* 29 only)
JULIET	Miss Younge (except on *Nov.* 26)

[Beginning with *Nov.* 5 Holman's name is in the bills. On *Nov.* 26 both Pb and PA retain Miss Younge as JULIET. In the JPK bill her name is deleted, and that of Mrs Kemble substituted.]

1785 COVENT GARDEN
Jan. 31; Mar. 28

ROMEO	Holman
CAPULET	Clarke
FRIAR LAURENCE	Hull
BENVOLIO	Davies
ESCALUS	Fearon
PARIS	Bonnor
TYBALT	Cubitt
PETER	Stevens
MONTAGUE	Thompson
APOTHECARY	Jones

1785 COVENT GARDEN (cont.)
Jan. 31; Mar. 28 (cont.)

MERCUTIO	Lewis
LADY CAPULET	Mrs Poussin
NURSE	Mrs Pitt
JULIET	Miss Younge

[On *Mar. 28* PA assigns ESCALUS to Thompson, and MONTAGUE to Egan.]

Apr. 18

ROMEO	Holman
MERCUTIO	Lewis
JULIET	Miss Younge

No other parts assigned

Nov. 14

ROMEO	Holman
CAPULET	Fearon
FRIAR LAURENCE	Hull
BENVOLIO	Davies
ESCALUS (1)	Gardner
PARIS	[Wm.] Palmer
TYBALT (1, 2)	Cubitt
MONTAGUE	Thompson
MERCUTIO	Lewis
LADY CAPULET	Miss Platt
NURSE	Mrs Pitt
JULIET	Miss Brunton

(1) *Nov. 17, 21, 25, 28*

ESCALUS	Booth
TYBALT	Gardner (on *Nov. 28* only)

added on *Nov. 21, 25, 28* only

APOTHECARY	Swords

(2) *Dec. 19*

TYBALT added	Booth
APOTHECARY	Swords

1786 COVENT GARDEN
Jan. 23; Feb. 20; Apr. 17

ROMEO	Holman
CAPULET	Fearon
FRIAR LAURENCE	Hull
TYBALT (1)	Booth
ESCALUS	Gardner
PARIS (1)	[Wm.] Palmer
MONTAGUE	Thompson
BENVOLIO	Davies
APOTHECARY	Swords
MERCUTIO	Lewis
LADY CAPULET	Miss Platt
NURSE	Mrs Pitt
JULIET	Miss Brunton

(1) *Oct. 23; Dec. 11*

TYBALT	Cubitt
PARIS	Macready

added on *Dec. 11* only

PETER	Stevens

HAMMERSMITH
July 12

ROMEO	Hill
JULIET	Mrs Chambers

No other parts assigned

ROMEO AND JULIET

1787 COVENT GARDEN
Jan. 29

ROMEO (1)	Holman	(1) *Sept. 24; Nov. 12*	
CAPULET	Fearon	ROMEO	Pope
FRIAR LAURENCE	Hull	omitted	
TYBALT	Cubitt	APOTHECARY	
ESCALUS	Gardner		
PARIS	Macready		
MONTAGUE	Thompson		
BENVOLIO	Davies		
APOTHECARY (1)	Swords		
MERCUTIO	Lewis		
LADY CAPULET	Miss Platt		
NURSE	Mrs Pitt		
JULIET	Miss Brunton		

RED LION INN, STOKE NEWINGTON
Mar. 31

ROMEO — Sterne
FRIAR LAURENCE — Young
TYBALT — Simpson
CAPULET — Sidney
PARIS — Wilson
PETER — Russell
MERCUTIO — Marriot
NURSE — Mrs Marriot
LADY CAPULET — Mrs Fowler
JULIET — Mrs Sterne

1788 DRURY LANE
Nov. 17, 18

ROMEO — Kemble
FRIAR LAURENCE — Packer
CAPULET — [J.] Aickin
PARIS — Barrymore
BENVOLIO — Whitfield
TYBALT — Williams
ESCALUS — Phillimore
MONTAGUE — Fawcett
PETER — [J.] Burton
APOTHECARY — [F.] Waldron
BALTHAZAR — Banks
SAMPSON — Hollingsworth
MERCUTIO — Dodd
LADY CAPULET — Mrs Ward
NURSE — Mrs Hopkins
JULIET — A Young Gentlewoman [Mrs Farmer (MS annotation on JPK)]

605

1788 COVENT GARDEN
Jan. 7

ROMEO (1)	Pope
CAPULET	Fearon
BENVOLIO	Davies
FRIAR LAURENCE	Hull
PARIS	Macready
MONTAGUE	Thompson
TYBALT	Cubitt
ESCALUS	Gardner
MERCUTIO	Lewis
LADY CAPULET	Mrs Platt
NURSE	Mrs Pitt
JULIET	Miss Brunton

(1) *Sept. 22, 29; Oct. 6, 13, 20; Nov. 3; Dec. 22*
   ROMEO   Middleton [first appearance, Sept. 22, in London]

1789 DRURY LANE
May 11

ROMEO	Kemble
FRIAR LAURENCE	Packer
CAPULET	[J.] Aickin
PARIS	Barrymore
BENVOLIO	Whitfield
TYBALT	Williames
ESCALUS	Phillimore
MONTAGUE	Fawcett
PETER	[J.] Burton
APOTHECARY	[F.] Waldron
BALTHAZAR	Banks
SAMPSON	Hollingsworth
MERCUTIO	Dodd
LADY CAPULET	Mrs Ward
NURSE	Mrs Hopkins
JULIET	Mrs Siddons

COVENT GARDEN
Sept. 14, 21

ROMEO	Holman
CAPULET	Powel
BENVOLIO	Davies
FRIAR LAURENCE	Hull
PARIS	Macready
TYBALT	Cubitt
ESCALUS	Gardner
PETER	C. Powell
MERCUTIO	Lewis
LADY CAPULET	Mrs Platt
NURSE (1, 2)	Mrs Pitt
JULIET (2, 3)	Mrs Achmet [first appearance, Sept. 14, in London]

(1) *Nov. 9*
   NURSE   Mrs [C.] Powell

(2) *Dec. 7*
   NURSE   Mrs [C.] Powell
   JULIET   Miss Brunton

(3) *Dec. 28*
   JULIET   Miss Brunton

1790 COVENT GARDEN
Sept. 13

ROMEO	Holman	(1) *Oct. 25*	
CAPULET	Powel	ESCALUS	Evatt
BENVOLIO	Davies	PARIS	Macready
FRIAR LAURENCE	Hull		
ESCALUS (1)	Macready		
TYBALT	Cubitt		
PARIS (1)	Evatt		
PETER	C. Powell		
BALTHAZAR	Farley		
MERCUTIO	Lewis		
LADY CAPULET	Mrs Platt		
NURSE	Mrs Pitt		
JULIET	Miss Brunton		

1791 COVENT GARDEN
Sept. 26; Nov. 28

ROMEO	Holman
CAPULET	Powel
BENVOLIO	Davies
FRIAR LAURENCE	Hull
ESCALUS	Macready
TYBALT	Cubitt
PARIS	Bloomfield
PETER	C. Powell
BALTHAZAR	Evatt
MERCUTIO	Lewis
LADY CAPULET	Mrs Platt
NURSE	Mrs Pitt
JULIET	Mrs Merry

1792 COVENT GARDEN
Jan. 16

ROMEO	Holman	(1) *Oct. 8, 22; Nov. 26*	
CAPULET	Powel	PARIS	Marshall
BENVOLIO	Davies	NURSE	Mrs [C.] Powell
FRIAR LAURENCE	Hull	JULIET	Mrs Esten
ESCALUS	Macready	omitted	
TYBALT	Cubitt	PETER	
PARIS (1)	Bloomfield		
PETER (1)	C. Powell		
BALTHAZAR	Evatt		
MERCUTIO	Lewis		
LADY CAPULET	Mrs Platt		
NURSE (1)	Mrs Pitt		
JULIET (1)	Mrs Merry		

1793 COVENT GARDEN
Jan. 7

ROMEO (1)	Holman
CAPULET	Powel
BENVOLIO	Davies
FRIAR LAURENCE	Hull
ESCALUS	Macready
TYBALT	Cubitt
PARIS (1)	Evatt
BALTHAZAR (1)	Ledger
MERCUTIO	Lewis
LADY CAPULET	Mrs Platt
NURSE (1)	Mrs [C.] Powell
JULIET	Mrs Esten

(1) *Oct. 7; Nov. 11*

ROMEO	Middleton
PARIS	Claremont
BALTHAZAR	Evatt
NURSE	Mrs Leicester

1794 COVENT GARDEN
Apr. 30

ROMEO	Holman
CAPULET (1)	Powel
BENVOLIO	Davies
FRIAR LAURENCE	Hull
ESCALUS (1)	Macready
TYBALT (1)	Cubitt
PARIS	Claremont
MERCUTIO	Lewis
LADY CAPULET (1)	Mrs Platt
NURSE (1)	Mrs Leicester
JULIET (1)	Mrs Twistleton

(1) *Oct. 20, 22, 27*

CAPULET	Farren
ESCALUS	Richardson
TYBALT	Macready
LADY CAPULET	Miss Morris
NURSE	Mrs Davenport
JULIET	Miss Wallis
added	
BALTHAZAR	Cross
MONTAGUE	Davenport
PETER	[J.] Burton
FRIAR JOHN	Thompson

1795 COVENT GARDEN
Jan. 5

ROMEO	Holman
CAPULET	Farren
BENVOLIO	Davies
FRIAR LAURENCE	Hull
ESCALUS (1)	Richardson
TYBALT	Macready
PARIS (1)	Claremont
BALTHAZAR (1)	Cross
MONTAGUE (1)	Davenport
PETER (1)	[J.] Burton
FRIAR JOHN (1)	Thompson
MERCUTIO	Lewis
LADY CAPULET	Miss Morris
NURSE (1)	Mrs Davenport
JULIET	Miss Wallis

(1) *Jan. 26*
omitted
  ESCALUS, PARIS, BALTHAZAR, MONTAGUE, PETER, FRIAR JOHN, NURSE

1795 COVENT GARDEN (cont.)

Sept. 21

ROMEO (1)	Toms [first appearance in London]
CAPULET	Powel
BENVOLIO	Macready
FRIAR LAURENCE	Hull
ESCALUS	Richardson
TYBALT	Haymes
PARIS	Claremont
BALTHAZAR	[D.] Williamson
MONTAGUE	Davenport
PETER	Farley
FRIAR JOHN	Thompson
APOTHECARY	Rees
MERCUTIO	Lewis
LADY CAPULET	Miss Morris
NURSE	Mrs Davenport
JULIET	Miss Wallis

(1) *Oct. 12; Nov. 23*

ROMEO	Holman

1796 DRURY LANE

Apr. 25

ESCALUS (2, 3)	Benson
PARIS	C. Kemble
MONTAGUE	Phillimore
CAPULET	[J.] Aickin
ROMEO (1)	Barrymore
MERCUTIO (3)	Dodd
BENVOLIO	Whitfield
TYBALT	Caulfield
FRIAR LAURENCE	Packer
FRIAR JOHN (3)	Maddocks
BALTHAZAR (2, 3)	Banks
SAMPSON (2, 3)	Hollingsworth
GREGORY (2, 3)	Evans
ABRAHAM (2, 3)	Jones
PETER (2, 3)	[J.] Burton
APOTHECARY (3)	[F.] Waldron
WATCH (3)	Webb
PAGE (3)	Miss [M.] Menage
LADY CAPULET	Miss Tidswell
JULIET (3)	Mrs Jordan
NURSE (3)	Mrs Hopkins

(1) *Apr. 28*

ROMEO	Wroughton

(2) *May 20*

ESCALUS	Trueman

omitted
BALTHAZAR, SAMPSON, GREGORY, ABRAHAM, PETER

(3) *Dec. 30*

ESCALUS	Campbell
MERCUTIO	[J.] Palmer
JULIET	Miss Miller
NURSE	Mrs Booth

omitted
FRIAR JOHN, BALTHAZAR, SAMPSON, GREGORY, ABRAHAM, PETER, APOTHECARY, WATCH, PAGE

COVENT GARDEN

May 17

ROMEO (1, 2)	Middleton
CAPULET	Powel

(1) *Sept. 19*

ROMEO	Holman
ESCALUS	Toms

1796 COVENT GARDEN (cont.)
May 17 (cont.)

BENVOLIO	Macready
FRIAR LAURENCE	Hull
ESCALUS (1, 2)	Richardson
TYBALT	Haymes
PARIS	Claremont
BALTHAZAR (1, 2)	[D.] Williamson
MONTAGUE (2)	Davenport
PETER	Farley
FRIAR JOHN (2)	Thompson
APOTHECARY (1, 2)	Rees
MERCUTIO	Lewis
LADY CAPULET	Miss Morris
NURSE	Mrs Davenport
JULIET (2)	Miss Wallis

(1) Sept. 19 (cont.)

BALTHAZAR	Abbot
APOTHECARY	Simmons

(2) Oct. 27

ROMEO	Holman
ESCALUS	Toms
JULIET	A Young Lady [Miss Allingham (Genest, vii. 302); third appearance on the stage]

omitted
BALTHAZAR, MONTAGUE, FRIAR JOHN, APOTHECARY

HAYMARKET
Sept. 7

ROMEO	Elliston
FRIAR LAURENCE	[J.] Aickin
CAPULET	Davies
PARIS	C. Kemble
BENVOLIO	[J.] Palmer Jr.
TYBALT	Caulfield
ESCALUS	Trueman
PETER	Suett
FRIAR JOHN	Abbot
MONTAGUE	Usher
BALTHAZAR	Ledger
SAMPSON	Lyons
APOTHECARY	[F.] Waldron
GREGORY	[G.] Waldron
MERCUTIO	[J.] Bannister
NURSE	Mrs Hopkins
LADY CAPULET	Miss Tidswell
JULIET	Mrs [S.] Kemble

1797 COVENT GARDEN
Nov. 2, 13

ROMEO	[H.] Johnston
CAPULET	Powel
BENVOLIO	Whitfield
FRIAR LAURENCE	Hull
ESCALUS	Clarke
TYBALT	Claremont
PARIS	Toms
MONTAGUE	Davenport

(1) Nov. 6
omitted
FRIAR JOHN, APOTHECARY

(2) Dec. 19
omitted
PETER, FRIAR JOHN, APOTHECARY

ROMEO AND JULIET

1797 COVENT GARDEN (cont.)
Nov. 2, 13 (cont.)

BALTHAZAR	Abbot
PETER (2)	Rees
FRIAR JOHN (1, 2)	Thompson
APOTHECARY (1, 2)	Simmons
MERCUTIO	Lewis
LADY CAPULET	Mrs Platt
NURSE	Mrs Davenport
JULIET	Mrs Spencer

1798 COVENT GARDEN
Jan. 1, 8, 22

ROMEO (2)	[H.] Johnston
CAPULET	Powel
BENVOLIO	Whitfield
FRIAR LAURENCE	Hull
ESCALUS	Clarke
TYBALT	Claremont
PARIS (2)	Toms
MONTAGUE	Davenport
MERCUTIO	Lewis
LADY CAPULET	Mrs Platt
NURSE	Mrs Davenport
JULIET (1, 2)	Mrs Spencer

(1) *Jan. 29; Mar. 12; May 7*

JULIET	Mrs [M.A.] Pope [i.e. formerly Mrs Spencer]

added on *May 7* only

BALTHAZAR	Abbot
PETER	Farley
APOTHECARY	Simmons

(2) *Oct. 8*

ROMEO	Holman
PARIS	Klanert [first appearance in London]
JULIET	Mrs [M.A.] Pope [i.e. formerly Mrs Spencer]

added

BALTHAZAR	Abbot
PETER	Farley
APOTHECARY	Simmons
FRIAR JOHN	Thompson

1799 COVENT GARDEN
May 10

ROMEO (1)	Holman
CAPULET	Waddy
BENVOLIO	Whitfield
FRIAR LAURENCE (1)	Murray
ESCALUS (1)	Clarke
PARIS	Klanert
TYBALT	Claremont
MONTAGUE	Davenport
MERCUTIO	Lewis
LADY CAPULET	Mrs Platt
NURSE	Mrs Davenport
JULIET (1)	Miss Murray

(1) *Oct. 7; Nov. 18; Dec. 9*

ROMEO	C. J. Macartney [first appearance in London] (on *Dec. 9* only)
FRIAR LAURENCE	Hull
ESCALUS	Mansel
JULIET	Mrs [M.A.] Pope (on *Oct. 7, Dec. 9* only) A Young Lady [Mrs Higginson (EM, Nov. 1799, 328); second appearance in London] (on *Nov. 18* only)

added

BALTHAZAR	Abbot
PETER	Farley
APOTHECARY	Simmons

ROMEO AND JULIET

1800 COVENT GARDEN
Oct. 6, 13

ROMEO	Brunton [Jr.]
CAPULET	Waddy
TYBALT	Betterton
ESCALUS	Claremont
BENVOLIO	Whitfield
FRIAR LAURENCE	Hull
PARIS	Klanert
MONTAGUE	Davenport
BALTHAZAR	Abbot
PETER	Farley
APOTHECARY	Simmons
MERCUTIO	Lewis
LADY CAPULET	Miss Leserve
NURSE	Mrs Davenport
JULIET	Mrs [M. A.] Pope

THE SHEEP-SHEARING; OR, FLORIZEL AND PERDITA

McNamara Morgan's alteration of THE WINTER'S TALE, q.v.
[In the bills this is almost invariably announced by its second title]

THE SHEEP SHEARING

George Colman, the elder's, alteration of THE WINTER'S TALE, q.v.

THE SHIPWRECK

An anonymous alteration, for a puppet theatre, of THE TEMPEST, q.v.

THE TAMING OF THE SHREW

(1) Altered as THE COBLER OF PRESTON, by Christopher Bullock. In one act.
   1716   R. Palmer.
For a description of this see my Volume I, 414.

(2) Altered as CATHARINE AND PETRUCHIO, by David Garrick. In three acts. 'As it is perform'd at the Theatre-Royal in Drury-Lane.'
   1756   J. and R. Tonson.
The Induction is omitted.
Act I consists of *Act II*. i. 115–38; I. ii. 77–83, 108–18, 202–14a, 67–76; II. i. 139–311. The whole is linked together with occasional new, brief speeches.

THE TAMING OF THE SHREW

The Act concludes with about 30 new lines: Catharine tells Baptista that she consents to the marriage only because she is dutiful to him, but, in a soliloquy, vows to tame Petruchio. Hortensio's speeches in *II. i* are given to the Music Master (a new character); Hortensio himself is Bianca's husband, not her suitor, and Biondello is servant to Baptista, not to Lucentio.

Act II consists of *Act III. ii. 1–29; II. i. 319–25; III. ii. 30–77, 90–130*, followed by about 20 new lines referring to the marriage and the removal to Petruchio's country house, and by *III. ii. 152–253; IV. i. 1–28, 47b–end*. Tranio's speeches are given to Hortensio and to Pedro (a new character), and Gremio's to Biondello.

Act III consists of *Act IV. iii. 1–38, 52b–152, 171–86; IV. v. 1–49; V. ii. 107–65*. Hortensio's speeches in *IV. iii* and *IV. v* are given to Grumio, and Vincentio's to Baptista. In *V. ii* Lucentio's speeches are given to Hortensio, and the Widow's to Bianca.

Throughout there are minor omissions and additions. Shakespeare's original play was not acted until 1844.

See also Genest, iv. 450–1; Odell, i. 362.

(3) 'Taken from the Manager's Book at the Theatre-Royal, Covent Garden.'
n.d. [*c.* 1780]   J. Wenman.

(4) 'Marked with the Variations in the Manager's Book at the Theatre-Royal in Covent-Garden.'
1787   C. Bathurst [&c.].

(5) 'Taken from the Manager's Book at the Theatre Royal Covent-Garden.'
n.d. [*c.* 1788]   R. Butters.

All these are identical with (2), but have been slightly abridged.

[*as* CATHARINE AND PETRUCHIO]

1754 DRURY LANE
Mar. 18

PETRUCHIO	Woodward
BAPTISTA	Burton
HORTENSIO	Mozeen
BIONDELLO	Blakes
GRUMIO	Yates
CATHARINE	Mrs Pritchard
BIANCA	Mrs Bennet

1756 DRURY LANE
Jan. 21, 23, 24, 26, 27, 28, 29, 31;
Feb. 3, 4, 23; Mar. 13; Apr. 6

PETRUCHIO	Woodward
BAPTISTA	Burton
HORTENSIO	Mozeen
GRUMIO	Yates
MUSIC MASTER	Jefferson

(1) *Apr. 28*

PETRUCHIO	Woodward
GRUMIO	Yates
CATHARINE	Mrs Pritchard

No other parts assigned.

THE TAMING OF THE SHREW [*as* CATHARINE AND PETRUCHIO]

1756 DRURY LANE (*cont.*)
Jan. 21, 23, 24, 26, 27, 28, 29, 31; Feb. 3, 4, 23; Mar. 13; Apr. 6 (cont.)

BIONDELLO	Blakes
PEDRO	Clough
TAILOR	H. Vaughan
NATHANIEL	W. Vaughan
PETER	Ackman
NICHOLAS	Atkins
PHILIP	Marr
JOSEPH	[P.] Lewis
CATHARINE (1)	Mrs Clive
BIANCA	Mrs Bennet
CURTIS	Mrs Bradshaw

[The bill for *Jan. 21* gives neither the parts nor the actors' names. The above assignment is taken from the printed text. Beginning with *Jan. 23* the bills list the names of Woodward, Yates, and Mrs Clive, but assign no parts except on *Apr. 6*, when Mrs Clive is listed as CATHARINE.]

1757 DRURY LANE
Apr. 18

PETRUCHIO	Woodward
CATHARINE (1)	Mrs Pritchard

No other parts assigned

(1) *Apr. 21*

CATHARINE	Mrs Clive
added	
GRUMIO	Yates

COVENT GARDEN
Mar. 26

PETRUCHIO	Shuter
CATHARINE (1, 2)	Mrs Gregory

No other parts assigned

(1) *Apr. 15, 21; Nov. 5*

CATHARINE	Mrs Hamilton

(2) *May 12, 13, 17*

CATHARINE	Mrs Green
added on *May 17* only	
GRUMIO	Costollo

1758 DRURY LANE
Mar. 29

PETRUCHIO	Woodward
GRUMIO	Yates
CATHARINE	Mrs Clive

No other parts assigned

COVENT GARDEN
Jan. 26; Feb. 7; Apr. 17, 29; Oct. 14, 27; Nov. 10; Dec. 14

PETRUCHIO	Shuter
CATHARINE	Mrs Green

No other parts assigned

THE TAMING OF THE SHREW [as CATHARINE AND PETRUCHIO]

1759 COVENT GARDEN
Feb. 3; Oct. 13, 19, 27; Nov. 6, 15; Dec. 3
    PETRUCHIO   Shuter
    CATHARINE (1) Mrs Green
    No other parts assigned

(1) Apr. 17
    CATHARINE   Mrs Vincent

[as THE COBLER OF PRESTON]
COVENT GARDEN
May 23
    TOBY GUZZLE   Shuter
    DAME HACKET Mrs Pitt
    DORCAS   Mrs Baker
    No other parts assigned

[as CATHARINE AND PETRUCHIO]
1760 DRURY LANE
Mar. 29; May 6
    PETRUCHIO   King
    GRUMIO   Yates
    CATHARINE   Mrs Clive
    No other parts assigned

COVENT GARDEN
Jan. 8; Feb. 1; Mar. 25; Apr. 10; May 2; Nov. 25; Dec. 13
    PETRUCHIO   Shuter
    CATHARINE   Mrs Green
    No other parts assigned

1761 COVENT GARDEN
Jan. 9; Mar. 7
    PETRUCHIO   Shuter
    CATHARINE   Mrs Green
    No other parts assigned

1762 DRURY LANE
Jan. 27, 28; Feb. 4, 6; Mar. 29; May 4
    PETRUCHIO   King
    GRUMIO   Yates
    CATHARINE   Mrs Clive
    No other parts assigned

THE TAMING OF THE SHREW [as CATHARINE AND PETRUCHIO]

1762 COVENT GARDEN
Mar. 22
- PETRUCHIO — Shuter
- GRUMIO — Costollo
- BIONDELLO (1) — Bennet
- BIANCA (1) — Mrs Stephens
- CATHARINE — Mrs Green

(1) Apr. 13
omitted
BIONDELLO, BIANCA

1763 DRURY LANE
Jan. 22, 26; Mar. 3, 15; Apr. 20
- PETRUCHIO — King
- BAPTISTA — Burton
- BIONDELLO (1) — Blakes
- GRUMIO — Yates
- CATHARINE — Mrs Clive

(1) Nov. 1
BIONDELLO   Baddeley

COVENT GARDEN
Apr. 30
- PETRUCHIO — Shuter
- GRUMIO — Costollo
- CATHARINE — Mrs Green

No other parts assigned

1764 DRURY LANE
May 9
- PETRUCHIO — King
- BAPTISTA — Burton
- BIONDELLO — Baddeley
- GRUMIO — Yates
- CATHARINE — Mrs Love

1765 COVENT GARDEN
Jan. 10, 14, 26; Apr. 18; May 22; Sept. 25
- PETRUCHIO — Woodward
- GRUMIO — Shuter
- CATHARINE — Mrs Green

No other parts assigned

1766 DRURY LANE
May 2
- PETRUCHIO — King
- BAPTISTA — Burton
- BIONDELLO — Baddeley
- TAILOR (1) — Master Burton
- GRUMIO — Yates
- CATHARINE — Mrs Abington

(1) May 3
TAILOR   [H.] Vaughan

THE TAMING OF THE SHREW [as CATHARINE AND PETRUCHIO]

1766 COVENT GARDEN
Jan. 16; Feb. 7; May 6, 16
- PETRUCHIO — Woodward
- GRUMIO — Shuter
- CATHARINE — Mrs Green

No other parts assigned

(1) *Apr. 25; Nov. 1*
added
- TAILOR — Morgan

(2) *Dec. 12*
added
- TAILOR — Weller

1767 COVENT GARDEN
Jan. 24; May 13
- PETRUCHIO — Woodward
- GRUMIO — Shuter
- TAILOR — Weller
- CATHARINE — Mrs Green

[On *Jan. 24* PA assigns the TAILOR to Morgan.]

1768 DRURY LANE
Mar. 19
- PETRUCHIO — King
- BAPTISTA — Burton
- BIONDELLO — Hartry
- TAILOR — J. Burton
- GRUMIO — Baddeley
- CATHARINE — Miss Pope

(1) *May 23*
added
- MUSIC MASTER — Lings

COVENT GARDEN
Mar. 12, 24; Nov. 3
- PETRUCHIO — Woodward
- GRUMIO — Yates
- CATHARINE — Mrs Green

No other parts assigned

1769 DRURY LANE
Apr. 18
- PETRUCHIO — King
- BAPTISTA — Burton
- BIONDELLO — Hartry
- TAILOR — J. Burton
- HORTENSIO — Keen
- MUSIC MASTER — Fawcett
- GRUMIO — Baddeley
- BIANCA — Mrs [S.] Smith
- CURTIS — Mrs Bradshaw
- CATHARINE (1) — Mrs Jefferies

(1) *May 22*
- CATHARINE — Miss Pope

617

THE TAMING OF THE SHREW [*as* CATHARINE AND PETRUCHIO]

1769 COVENT GARDEN
Mar. 13; Apr. 26   (1) *May 2*
    PETRUCHIO   Woodward   CATHARINE   Mrs Du-Bellamy
    GRUMIO   Yates
    CATHARINE (1)   Mrs Green
    No other parts assigned

1770 COVENT GARDEN
May 22
    PETRUCHIO   Kniveton
    GRUMIO   Hamilton
    TAILOR   Quick
    CATHARINE   Mrs Green

1771 DRURY LANE
Jan. 2
    PETRUCHIO   King
    BAPTISTA   Burton
    BIONDELLO   Hartry
    GRUMIO   Baddeley
    TAILOR   J. Burton
    HORTENSIO   Keen
    MUSIC MASTER   Fawcett
    BIANCA   Mrs [S.] Smith
    CURTIS   Mrs Bradshaw
    CATHARINE   Miss Pope

COVENT GARDEN
Apr. 12; Oct. 4   (1) *Dec. 17*
    PETRUCHIO (1)   Kniveton   PETRUCHIO   Woodward
    GRUMIO   Hamilton
    TAILOR   Quick
    CATHARINE   Mrs Green

HAYMARKET
May 31; June 14
    PETRUCHIO   Woodward
    BAPTISTA   Farrell
    HORTENSIO   Miller
    MUSIC MASTER   Lings
    PEDRO   Vowell
    BIONDELLO   Didier
    TAILOR   Vandermere
    GRUMIO   Hamilton
    BIANCA   Mrs Collet
    CURTIS   Mrs White
    CATHARINE   Mrs Gardner
    [On *June 14* PA assigns BIANCA to Mrs Granger.]

THE TAMING OF THE SHREW [as CATHARINE AND PETRUCHIO]

1772 COVENT GARDEN
May 1
- PETRUCHIO — Woodward
- GRUMIO — Hamilton
- TAILOR — Quick
- CATHARINE — Mrs Green

(1) *May 13*
added
- PEDRO — R. Smith

1773 DRURY LANE
Apr. 1
- PETRUCHIO (1) — Dodd
- GRUMIO — Baddeley
- BAPTISTA — Wright
- BIONDELLO — Hartry
- MUSIC MASTER — Fawcett
- TAILOR — [J.] Burton
- HORTENSIO — J[ames] Bannister
- PEDRO — Griffith
- BIANCA — Miss Platt
- CURTIS — Mrs Bradshaw
- CATHARINE — Miss Pope

(1) *Oct. 11*
- PETRUCHIO — King

COVENT GARDEN
Nov. 16
- PETRUCHIO — Woodward
- GRUMIO (1) — Hamilton
- BAPTISTA — Thompson
- TAILOR (1) — Quick
- CATHARINE — Mrs Green

(1) *Nov. 27*
- GRUMIO — Quick
- TAILOR — Baker

1774 DRURY LANE
Jan. 1
- PETRUCHIO — King
- GRUMIO — Baddeley
- BAPTISTA — Wright
- BIONDELLO (1, 2) — Hartry
- MUSIC MASTER (1, 2) — Fawcett
- TAILOR (1) — [J.] Burton
- HORTENSIO (1, 2) — J[ames] Bannister
- PEDRO (2) — Griffith
- BIANCA (1) — Miss Platt
- CURTIS (1) — Mrs Bradshaw
- CATHARINE — Miss Pope

(1) *Jan. 17*
omitted
  BIONDELLO, MUSIC MASTER, TAILOR, HORTENSIO, BIANCA, CURTIS

(2) *Nov. 30*
- BIONDELLO — Lamash
- HORTENSIO — Wheeler
omitted
  MUSIC MASTER, PEDRO

619

THE TAMING OF THE SHREW [as CATHARINE AND PETRUCHIO]

1774 COVENT GARDEN
Apr. 18

PETRUCHIO	Lewis
GRUMIO	Shuter
CATHARINE	Mrs Green

No other parts assigned

HAYMARKET
Apr. 12

PETRUCHIO	Fearon
GRUMIO	Follett
BIONDELLO	Morris
CATHARINE	Mrs Nost

June 13; July 4, 22; Aug. 5

PETRUCHIO	Fearon
BAPTISTA	Lloyd
BIONDELLO	Follett
PEDRO	Everard
HORTENSIO	Owenson
TAILOR	Jones
MUSIC MASTER	Courtney
GRUMIO	[R.] Wilson
BIANCA	Miss Platt
CURTIS	Mrs Love
CATHARINE	Mrs Gardner

1775 DRURY LANE
Feb. 4

PETRUCHIO	King
GRUMIO	Baddeley
BAPTISTA	Wright
BIONDELLO	Lamash
TAILOR	[J.] Burton
MUSIC MASTER	Fawcett
HORTENSIO	Wheeler
PEDRO (1)	Griffiths
BIANCA	Miss Platt
CURTIS	Mrs Bradshaw
CATHARINE	Miss Pope

(1) *Feb. 18; May 18*

PEDRO	Everard

COVENT GARDEN
Dec. 21

PETRUCHIO	Woodward
BAPTISTA	Thompson
HORTENSIO	Davis
TAILOR	Jones
MUSIC MASTER	Fox

THE TAMING OF THE SHREW [as CATHARINE AND PETRUCHIO]

1775 COVENT GARDEN (cont.)
Dec. 21 (cont.)

BIONDELLO	Cushing
PEDRO	Wewitzer
GRUMIO	Quick
BIANCA	Mrs Poussin
CURTIS	Mrs White
CATHARINE	Mrs Green

HAYMARKET
July 14

PETRUCHIO	Fearon
BAPTISTA	Lloyd
BIONDELLO	L'Estrange
HORTENSIO	Lane
MUSIC MASTER	Jacobs
TAILOR	Jones
GRUMIO	[R.] Wilson
BIANCA	Miss Platt
CATHARINE	Mrs Gardner

1776 COVENT GARDEN
Jan. 3

PETRUCHIO (3)	Woodward
BAPTISTA	Thompson
HORTENSIO (1)	Davis
TAILOR (1, 2)	Baker
MUSIC MASTER	Fox
BIONDELLO	Cushing
PEDRO	Wewitzer
GRUMIO	Quick
BIANCA	Mrs Poussin
CURTIS	Mrs White
CATHARINE	Mrs Green

(1) *Feb. 13, 17; Mar. 14, 23; Apr. 19*

HORTENSIO	Young
TAILOR	Jones

[On *Feb. 13* Pb retains Baker as the TAILOR, and PA retains Davis as HORTENSIO.]

(2) *May 30; Oct. 11*

TAILOR	Jones

(3) *Dec. 12*

PETRUCHIO	Lewis
CATHARINE	Mrs Green

No other parts assigned

HAYMARKET
Apr. 22

PETRUCHIO	A Young Gentleman [unidentified; first appearance in London]
CATHARINE	Mrs Fisher [first appearance in London]

No other parts assigned

July 24; Aug. 21

PETRUCHIO	Fearon
GRUMIO	Baddeley
BAPTISTA	Lloyd
HORTENSIO	R. Palmer
BIONDELLO	Egan

THE TAMING OF THE SHREW [as CATHARINE AND PETRUCHIO]

1776 HAYMARKET (cont.)
July 24; Aug. 21 (cont.)

TAILOR	Jones
PEDRO	Stephens
BIANCA	Mrs W. Palmer
CURTIS	Mrs Love
CATHARINE	Mrs Gardner

1777 COVENT GARDEN
Nov. 19, 24

PETRUCHIO	Lewis
BAPTISTA	Thompson
HORTENSIO	Davis
TAILOR	Jones
MUSIC MASTER	Fox
BIONDELLO	Cushing
PEDRO	Wewitzer
GRUMIO	Quick
BIANCA	Mrs Poussin
CURTIS	Mrs White
CATHARINE	Mrs Green

HAYMARKET
May 1

| PETRUCHIO | West |
| CATHARINE | Mrs West |

No other parts assigned

1778 COVENT GARDEN
Dec. 1

PETRUCHIO	Lewis
HORTENSIO	Robson
TAILOR	Jones
BAPTISTA	Thompson
MUSIC MASTER	Brunsdon
PEDRO	Wewitzer
BIONDELLO	Cushing
GRUMIO	Quick
BIANCA	Mrs Poussin
CURTIS	Mrs White
CATHARINE	Mrs Green

HAYMARKET
Mar. 23

PETRUCHIO	West
GRUMIO	Everard
CATHARINE	Mrs West

No other parts assigned

THE TAMING OF THE SHREW [as CATHARINE AND PETRUCHIO]
1778 CHINA HALL, ROTHERHITHE
May 29

PETRUCHIO	West
BAPTISTA	Bowles
HORTENSIO	Cooke
GRUMIO	Newton
BIONDELLO	Bailey
MUSIC MASTER	Massey
TAILOR	Russell
CATHARINE	Mrs Russell
BIANCA	Mrs Heard

1779 COVENT GARDEN
Feb. 16; Nov. 13

PETRUCHIO	Lewis
HORTENSIO	Robson
TAILOR	Jones
BAPTISTA	Thompson
MUSIC MASTER	Brunsdon
PEDRO	Wewitzer
BIONDELLO	Cushing
GRUMIO	Quick
BIANCA	Mrs Poussin
CURTIS	Mrs White
CATHARINE	Mrs Green

1780 DRURY LANE
Nov. 1

PETRUCHIO	[J.] Palmer
GRUMIO	Baddeley
BAPTISTA	Wright
BIONDELLO (1)	R. Palmer
TAILOR	[J.] Burton
MUSIC MASTER	Fawcett
HORTENSIO	Norris
PEDRO	Griffiths
BIANCA (1)	Miss Kirby
CURTIS	Mrs Love
CATHARINE	Mrs Wrighten

(1) *Nov. 15*

BIONDELLO	Lamash
BIANCA	Miss Simson

[PA assigns BIANCA to Miss Simson.]

COVENT GARDEN
Jan. 19

PETRUCHIO	Lewis
HORTENSIO	Robson
TAILOR	Jones

(1) *Dec. 15*

MUSIC MASTER	Newton
PEDRO	Wewitzer
CATHARINE	Mrs Mattocks

THE TAMING OF THE SHREW [*as* CATHARINE AND PETRUCHIO]

1780 COVENT GARDEN (*cont.*)
Jan. 19 (cont.)

BAPTISTA	Thompson
MUSIC MASTER (1)	Brunsdon
PEDRO (1)	[R.] Smith
BIONDELLO	W. Bates
GRUMIO	Quick
BIANCA	Mrs Poussin
CURTIS	Mrs White
CATHARINE (1)	Mrs Green

[JPK erroneously assigns HORTENSIO to Thompson. A bill in HTC assigns the part to Robson; so does PA.]

1781 DRURY LANE
Jan. 3; Feb. 20; Dec. 11

PETRUCHIO (1, 2)	[J.] Palmer
GRUMIO	Baddeley
BAPTISTA	Wright
BIONDELLO	Lamash
TAILOR	[J.] Burton
MUSIC MASTER (3)	Fawcett
HORTENSIO (3)	Norris
PEDRO (3)	Griffiths
BIANCA (3)	Miss Simson
CURTIS (3)	Mrs Love
CATHARINE (2)	Mrs Wrighten

(1) *Apr. 3*

PETRUCHIO	Dodd

(2) *May 19*

PETRUCHIO	Crawford
CATHARINE	Mrs Crawford

(3) *Oct. 24*
omitted
MUSIC MASTER, HORTENSIO, PEDRO, BIANCA, CURTIS

1782 DRURY LANE
Apr. 23

PETRUCHIO	[J.] Palmer
GRUMIO	Baddeley
BAPTISTA	Wright
BIONDELLO (1, 3)	Lamash
TAILOR	[J.] Burton
MUSIC MASTER	Fawcett
HORTENSIO (2, 3)	Norris
PEDRO (2, 3)	Griffiths
BIANCA	Miss Simson
CURTIS	Mrs Love
CATHARINE	Mrs Wrighten

(1) *May 24*

BIONDELLO	R. Palmer

[PA retains Lamash as BIONDELLO.]

(2) *Sept. 18*
omitted
HORTENSIO, PEDRO

(3) *Oct. 25*

BIONDELLO	R. Palmer

omitted
HORTENSIO, PEDRO

1783 DRURY LANE
Oct. 11

PETRUCHIO	[J.] Palmer
GRUMIO	Baddeley
BAPTISTA	Wright
BIONDELLO	R. Palmer

(1) *Dec. 17*
omitted
HORTENSIO

THE TAMING OF THE SHREW [as CATHARINE AND PETRUCHIO]

1783 DRURY LANE (*cont.*)
Oct. 11 (cont.)

TAILOR	[J.] Burton
MUSIC MASTER	Fawcett
HORTENSIO (1)	[J.] Wilson
BIANCA	Miss Simson
CURTIS	Mrs Love
CATHARINE	Mrs Wrighten

1784 DRURY LANE
Oct. 23

PETRUCHIO	[J.] Palmer
GRUMIO	Baddeley
BAPTISTA	Wright
BIONDELLO	R. Palmer
TAILOR	[J.] Burton
PEDRO	Phillimore
MUSIC MASTER	Fawcett
HORTENSIO	[J.] Wilson
BIANCA	Miss Simson
CURTIS	Mrs Love
CATHARINE	Mrs Wrighten

COVENT GARDEN
Sept. 28

PETRUCHIO	Lewis
BAPTISTA	Thompson
BIONDELLO	Chalmers
MUSIC MASTER	Stevens
HORTENSIO	Helme
TAILOR	Jones
PEDRO	Gaudry
HABERDASHER	Besford
NATHANIEL	Ledger
GRUMIO	Quick
BIANCA	Mrs Poussin
CURTIS	Mrs White
CATHARINE	Mrs Bates

1785 COVENT GARDEN
Oct. 17

PETRUCHIO	Lewis
BAPTISTA	Thompson
BIONDELLO	[T.] Kennedy
MUSIC MASTER	Stevens
HORTENSIO	Helme

THE TAMING OF THE SHREW [as CATHARINE AND PETRUCHIO]

1785 COVENT GARDEN (cont.)

Oct. 17 (cont.)

PEDRO	Swords
TAILOR	Wewitzer
HABERDASHER	Newton
NATHANIEL	Ledger
GRUMIO	Quick
BIANCA	Miss Brangin
CURTIS	Mrs White
CATHARINE	Mrs Bates

1786 DRURY LANE

Apr. 6

PETRUCHIO (1, 2)	Kemble
GRUMIO	Baddeley
BAPTISTA (2)	Wright
BIONDELLO	R. Palmer
TAILOR (2)	[J.] Burton
MUSIC MASTER	Fawcett
PEDRO	Phillimore
HORTENSIO	[J.] Wilson
BIANCA (2)	Miss Simson
CURTIS	Mrs Love
CATHARINE (1)	Mrs Wrighten

(1) *June 2*

PETRUCHIO	[J.] Palmer
CATHARINE	Mrs Bates

(2) *Oct. 3; Dec. 5*

PETRUCHIO	[J.] Palmer
BAPTISTA	Chaplin (on *Dec.* 5 only)
TAILOR	Jones
BIANCA	Mrs A. Palmer

[On *Oct.* 3 PA retains Miss Simson as BIANCA, and on *Dec.* 5 Kemble as PETRUCHIO.]

1788 DRURY LANE

Mar. 13; May 5

PETRUCHIO	Kemble
GRUMIO	Baddeley
BAPTISTA	Packer
BIONDELLO	R. Palmer
TAILOR	[J.] Burton
MUSIC MASTER	Fawcett
PEDRO	Phillimore
HORTENSIO	Benson
BIANCA	Miss Tidswell
CURTIS	Mrs Love
CATHARINE	Mrs Siddons

COVENT GARDEN

Nov. 22

PETRUCHIO	Lewis
BAPTISTA	Thompson
HORTENSIO	Evatt
BIONDELLO	Rock
PEDRO (1)	Helme

(1) *Dec. 15*

PEDRO	Ledger
TAILOR	Milburne

THE TAMING OF THE SHREW [as CATHARINE AND PETRUCHIO]
1788 COVENT GARDEN (cont.)
Nov. 22 (cont.)

TAILOR (1)	Wewitzer
MUSIC MASTER	Stevens
GRUMIO	Quick
BIANCA	Miss Brangin
CURTIS	Mrs White
CATHARINE	Mrs Mattocks

1789 DRURY LANE
Jan. 10; Mar. 30; Apr. 28

PETRUCHIO	Kemble
GRUMIO	Baddeley
BAPTISTA	Packer
BIONDELLO	R. Palmer
TAILOR	[J.] Burton
MUSIC MASTER	Fawcett
PEDRO	Phillimore
HORTENSIO	Benson
BIANCA	Miss Tidswell
CURTIS	Mrs Love
CATHARINE	Mrs Siddons

1790 COVENT GARDEN
Mar. 13; Apr. 6   (1) *May 13*
omitted BIONDELLO, PEDRO, BIANCA, CURTIS

PETRUCHIO	Lewis
BAPTISTA	Thompson
HORTENSIO	Egan [Jr.]
BIONDELLO (1)	Rock
PEDRO (1)	Evatt
TAILOR	Bernard
MUSIC MASTER	C. Powell
GRUMIO	Quick
BIANCA (1)	Miss Brangin
CURTIS (1)	Mrs White
CATHARINE	Mrs Mattocks

HAYMARKET
Aug. 12, 20, 26; Sept. 8

PETRUCHIO	[J.] Palmer
BAPTISTA	Chapman
HORTENSIO	Evatt
GRUMIO	Baddeley
MUSIC MASTER	Barrett
BIONDELLO	R. Palmer
PEDRO	Farley

THE TAMING OF THE SHREW [*as* CATHARINE AND PETRUCHIO]

1790 HAYMARKET (*cont.*)
Aug. 12, 20, 26; Sept. 8 (cont.)

TAILOR	[J.] Burton
NATHANIEL	Lyons
PETER	Abbot
COOK	Ledger
CATHARINE	Mrs Goodall
BIANCA	Miss Palmer
CURTIS	Mrs [C.] Powell

1791 DRURY LANE (company at KING'S, HAYMARKET)
Nov. 30

PETRUCHIO	[J.] Palmer
BAPTISTA	Packer
HORTENSIO	Benson
GRUMIO	Baddeley
MUSIC MASTER	Fawcett
BIONDELLO	R. Palmer
PEDRO	Phillimore
TAILOR	[J.] Burton
NATHANIEL	Lyons
PETER	Alfred
NICHOLAS	Banks
JOSEPH	Webb
CATHARINE	Mrs Goodall
BIANCA	Miss Tidswell
CURTIS	Mrs Booth
HABERDASHER	Miss Palmer

COVENT GARDEN
May 20

PETRUCHIO	Lewis
BAPTISTA	Thompson
HORTENSIO	Evatt
TAILOR	Bernard
MUSIC MASTER	C. Powell
PEDRO	Farley
GRUMIO	Quick
CATHARINE	Mrs Mattocks

HAYMARKET
June 6, 14

PETRUCHIO	[J.] Palmer
BAPTISTA	Chapman
HORTENSIO	Bland
GRUMIO	Baddeley
MUSIC MASTER (2)	Barrett

(1) *Sept. 1, 14*

PEDRO	Evatt
CURTIS	Mrs [C.] Powell

(2) *Sept. 16*
omitted MUSIC MASTER, PEDRO

628

THE TAMING OF THE SHREW [as CATHARINE AND PETRUCHIO]
1791 HAYMARKET (cont.)
June 6, 14 (cont.)

BIONDELLO	R. Palmer
PEDRO (1, 2)	Phillimore
TAILOR	[J.] Burton
GREGORY	Lyons
PETER	Abbot
CATHARINE	Mrs Goodall
BIANCA	Miss Palmer
CURTIS (1)	Miss Hale

1792 DRURY LANE (company at KING'S, HAYMARKET)
Jan. 31

PETRUCHIO (1)	[J.] Palmer
BAPTISTA	Packer
HORTENSIO (3, 4)	Benson
GRUMIO	Baddeley
MUSIC MASTER (1)	Fawcett
BIONDELLO (1, 4)	R. Palmer
PEDRO	Phillimore
TAILOR (1, 2)	[J.] Burton
NATHANIEL (3, 4, 5)	Lyons
PETER (1, 3, 5)	Alfred
NICHOLAS (1, 2, 3, 5)	Banks
JOSEPH	Webb
CATHARINE	Mrs Goodall
BIANCA	Miss Tidswell
CURTIS	Mrs Booth
HABERDASHER	Miss Palmer

(1) *Apr. 24; May 9, 28*

PETRUCHIO	Kemble (on *May 28* only)
MUSIC MASTER	Banks
BIONDELLO	Maddocks (on *Apr. 24* only)
TAILOR	Hollingsworth
omitted	
PETER, NICHOLAS	

[On *May 28* Pb assigns no parts; PA gives the full cast, including Palmer as PETRUCHIO. But 'Mr. Palmer not coming to the Theatre to-night, I acted Petruchio for him' (Kemble Mem.).]

(2) *June 9*

TAILOR	Hollingsworth
omitted	
NICHOLAS	

(3) *Sept. 18*

HORTENSIO	Bland
omitted	
NATHANIEL, PETER, NICHOLAS	

(4) *Nov. 15, 21*

HORTENSIO	Bland
BIONDELLO	Benson
omitted	
NATHANIEL	

(5) *Dec. 1*

omitted
NATHANIEL, PETER, NICHOLAS

COVENT GARDEN
May 15

PETRUCHIO	Lewis
GRUMIO	Quick
TAILOR	Munden
CATHARINE	Miss Chapman

629

THE TAMING OF THE SHREW [as CATHARINE AND PETRUCHIO]

1792 HAYMARKET

Aug. 17

PETRUCHIO	[J.] Palmer
BAPTISTA	[J.] Johnson
HORTENSIO	Bland
GRUMIO	Baddeley
MUSIC MASTER	Edwin [Jr.]
BIONDELLO (1)	R. Palmer
PEDRO (1)	Evatt
TAILOR	Barrett
GREGORY	Lyons
PETER	Abbot
CATHARINE	Mrs Goodall
BIANCA	Miss Palmer
CURTIS	Mrs [C.] Powell

(1) *Sept. 4*

BIONDELLO	Evatt
PEDRO	Ledger

[PA retains R. Palmer as BIONDELLO, and Evatt as PEDRO.]

1793 DRURY LANE (company at KING'S, HAYMARKET)

Jan. 22

PETRUCHIO	[J.] Palmer
BAPTISTA	Packer
HORTENSIO	Benson
GRUMIO	Baddeley
MUSIC MASTER	Fawcett
BIONDELLO	R. Palmer
PEDRO	Phillimore
TAILOR	[J.] Burton
JOSEPH	Webb
CATHARINE	Mrs Goodall
BIANCA	Miss Tidswell
CURTIS	Mrs Booth
HABERDASHER	Miss Palmer

COVENT GARDEN

May 10

PETRUCHIO (1)	Lewis
BAPTISTA	Thompson
HORTENSIO	Evatt
BIONDELLO	Rock
PEDRO	Farley
TAILOR	Munden
MUSIC MASTER	Rees
GRUMIO	Quick
BIANCA	Miss Leserve
CURTIS	Mrs Cross
CATHARINE	Mrs Mattocks

(1) *May 23*

PETRUCHIO	Harley

THE TAMING OF THE SHREW [as CATHARINE AND PETRUCHIO]

1793 HAYMARKET
July 5

PETRUCHIO	Barrymore
BAPTISTA	Usher
HORTENSIO	Bland
GRUMIO	Baddeley
MUSIC MASTER	Evatt
BIONDELLO	Benson
PEDRO	Ledger
TAILOR	[J.] Burton
GREGORY	Lyons
PETER	Abbot
COOK	Alfred
NATHANIEL	[J.] Cooke
CATHARINE	Mrs Goodall
BIANCA	Mrs Jones
CURTIS	Mrs [C.] Powell

1794 DRURY LANE
May 30

PETRUCHIO	[J.] Palmer
BAPTISTA	Packer
HORTENSIO	Bland
GRUMIO	Baddeley
MUSIC MASTER	Banks
BIONDELLO	Benson
PEDRO	Phillimore
TAILOR	[J.] Burton
ADAM	Lyons
PETER	Evans
WALTER	Trueman
GABRIEL	[J.] Cooke
NATHANIEL	Webb
GREGORY	Maddocks
RALPH	Welsh
CATHARINE	Mrs Goodall
BIANCA	Miss Tidswell
CURTIS	Mrs Booth

COVENT GARDEN
Feb. 26

PETRUCHIO	Lewis
BAPTISTA	Thompson
HORTENSIO	Evatt
BIONDELLO	Rock
TAILOR	Bernard
MUSIC MASTER	Rees

THE TAMING OF THE SHREW [*as* CATHARINE AND PETRUCHIO]

1794 COVENT GARDEN (*cont.*)
Feb. 26 (cont.)
GRUMIO	Quick
BIANCA	Miss Leserve
CURTIS	Mrs Platt
CATHARINE	Mrs Mattocks

HAYMARKET
July 10
PETRUCHIO	[J.] Palmer
BAPTISTA	Usher
HORTENSIO	Bland
MUSIC MASTER	Barrett
BIONDELLO	Benson
PEDRO	Ledger
TAILOR	[J.] Burton
GREGORY	Lyons
PETER	Abbot
COOK	[G.] Waldron
NATHANIEL	[J.] Cooke
GRUMIO	Baddeley
BIANCA	Mrs Jones
CURTIS	Mrs Booth
CATHARINE	Mrs Goodall

1795 COVENT GARDEN
Mar. 16
PETRUCHIO	Lewis
BAPTISTA	Thompson
HORTENSIO	Claremont
TAILOR (2)	Bernard
BIONDELLO (1)	Rock
PEDRO	Farley
GRUMIO (2)	Quick
BIANCA (2)	Miss Leserve
CURTIS (2)	Mrs Platt
CATHARINE (1, 2)	Mrs Pope

(1) *Apr. 28*
CATHARINE omitted	Mrs Mattocks
BIONDELLO	

(2) *June 12*
TAILOR	Simmons
GRUMIO	Munden
CATHARINE added	Mrs Mattocks
MUSIC MASTER omitted	Rees
BIANCA, CURTIS	

[The MUSIC MASTER is listed only in an advance bill in MP, June 11.]

1796 DRURY LANE
June 13
PETRUCHIO	[J.] Palmer
BAPTISTA	Packer
HORTENSIO	Trueman
GRUMIO	Hollingsworth
MUSIC MASTER	Banks

632

THE TAMING OF THE SHREW [as CATHARINE AND PETRUCHIO]

1796 DRURY LANE (cont.)
June 13 (cont.)

BIONDELLO	R. Palmer
PEDRO	Phillimore
TAILOR	[J.] Burton
PETER	Evans
GABRIEL	[J.] Cooke
NATHANIEL	Webb
GREGORY	Maddocks
CATHARINE	Mrs Goodall
BIANCA	Miss Tidswell
CURTIS	Mrs Booth

COVENT GARDEN
Mar. 19

PETRUCHIO	Lewis
BAPTISTA	Thompson
TAILOR	Simmons
BIONDELLO (2, 3)	Townsend
GRUMIO (2, 3)	Quick
CATHARINE (2, 3)	Mrs Mattocks

(1) *May 3*
added

HORTENSIO	Claremont
PEDRO	Farley
BIANCA	Miss Leserve
CURTIS	Mrs Platt

(2) *Nov. 21*

BIONDELLO	[H.] Lee
GRUMIO	Munden
CATHARINE	Miss Wallis

added
  SAME as *May 3*

(3) *Dec. 7*

BIONDELLO	Farley
GRUMIO	Munden
CATHARINE	Miss Wallis

added

HORTENSIO	Claremont
PEDRO	Abbot
MUSIC MASTER	[H.] Lee
BIANCA	Miss Leserve
CURTIS	Mrs Platt

HAYMARKET
June 29; July 14, 26

PETRUCHIO	[J.] Palmer
BAPTISTA	Usher
HORTENSIO	Trueman
BIONDELLO	R. Palmer
MUSIC MASTER	[G.] Waldron
TAILOR	[J.] Burton
PEDRO	Ledger
GREGORY	Lyons
NATHANIEL	Abbot
PETER	Chippendale

THE TAMING OF THE SHREW [as CATHARINE AND PETRUCHIO]

1796 HAYMARKET (cont.)
June 29; July 14, 26 (cont.)

GRUMIO	Wathen
BIANCA	Mrs Jones
CURTIS	Mrs Booth
CATHARINE	Mrs Gibbs

1797 DRURY LANE
Apr. 24

PETRUCHIO	[J.] Palmer
BAPTISTA (1)	Packer
HORTENSIO	Trueman
GRUMIO	Suett
MUSIC MASTER (2)	Banks
BIONDELLO	R. Palmer
PEDRO (2)	Phillimore
TAILOR	Hollingsworth
PETER	Evans
CATHARINE	Mrs Goodall
BIANCA	Miss Tidswell
CURTIS (2)	Mrs Booth

(1) *May 2*

BAPTISTA	Maddocks
added	
GABRIEL	[J.] Cooke
NATHANIEL	Webb
ADAM	Fisher

(2) *Dec. 21*

MUSIC MASTER	Sparks
PEDRO	Grimaldi
CURTIS	Mrs Maddocks
added	
ADAM	Fisher
WALTER	Gregson
GABRIEL	Simpson
NATHANIEL	Webb
GREGORY	Maddocks
RALPH	Male
HABERDASHER	Mrs Jones

COVENT GARDEN
Nov. 15

PETRUCHIO	Lewis
BAPTISTA	Thompson
HORTENSIO	Claremont
BIONDELLO	Davenport
PEDRO	Abbot
TAILOR	Simmons
MUSIC MASTER	Rees
GRUMIO	Quick
BIANCA	Miss Leserve
CURTIS	Mrs Platt
CATHARINE	Mrs Mattocks

HAYMARKET
June 13

PETRUCHIO	[J.] Palmer
BAPTISTA	Usher
HORTENSIO	Trueman
BIONDELLO (1)	R. Palmer
MUSIC MASTER (1)	[J.] Palmer Jr.
TAILOR	[G.] Waldron

(1) *June 20*

BIONDELLO	[J.] Palmer Jr.
MUSIC MASTER	Abbot

[Abbot doubled the MUSIC MASTER and NATHANIEL.]

THE TAMING OF THE SHREW [as CATHARINE AND PETRUCHIO]

1797 HAYMARKET (cont.)
June 13 (cont.)

PEDRO	Ledger
GREGORY	Lyons
NATHANIEL	Abbot
PETER	Chippendale
GRUMIO	Wathen
BIANCA	Mrs Jones
CURTIS	Mrs Booth
CATHARINE	Mrs Gibbs

1798 COVENT GARDEN
Apr. 21

(1) *Nov. 19.* No parts assigned

PETRUCHIO	Lewis
BAPTISTA	Thompson
HORTENSIO	Claremont
BIONDELLO	Farley
PEDRO	Abbot
TAILOR	Simmons
MUSIC MASTER	Rees
GRUMIO	Munden
BIANCA	Miss Leserve
CURTIS	Mrs Platt
CATHARINE	Mrs Mattocks

HAYMARKET
Apr. 21. No parts assigned

1799 DRURY LANE
May 3

PETRUCHIO	[J.] Bannister
BAPTISTA	Packer
HORTENSIO (2)	Trueman
GRUMIO (2)	Hollingsworth
BIONDELLO (1, 2)	R. Palmer
MUSIC MASTER	Sparks
TAILOR	Suett
CATHARINE	Miss DeCamp
BIANCA (1)	Mrs Coates
CURTIS (1)	Mrs Maddocks
HABERDASHER (1, 2)	Mrs Jones

June 28

PETRUCHIO	[J.] Powell
CATHARINE	Miss DeCamp

No other parts assigned

(1) *May 20; June 13, 21*

BIONDELLO	Maddocks (on *June 21* only)

added

PEDRO	Grimaldi
ADAM	Fisher

also added on *May 20* only

PETER	Evans
WALTER	Ryder
GABRIEL	Garman
NATHANIEL	Webb
GREGORY	Maddocks
RALPH	Whitmell

omitted on *June 21* only
  BIANCA, CURTIS, HABERDASHER

(2) *Nov. 6*

HORTENSIO	Wentworth
GRUMIO	Wewitzer
BIONDELLO	Maddocks

added

PEDRO	Grimaldi

THE TAMING OF THE SHREW [as CATHARINE AND PETRUCHIO]
1799 DRURY LANE (cont.)

(2) Nov. 6 (cont.)

ADAM	Fisher
PETER	Evans
WALTER	Ryder
GABRIEL	Wells
NATHANIEL	Webb
GREGORY	Chippendale
RALPH	Whitmell
omitted	
HABERDASHER	

COVENT GARDEN
Mar. 16; Sept. 27

PETRUCHIO	Lewis
BAPTISTA	Thompson
HORTENSIO	Claremont
BIONDELLO	Farley
TAILOR	Simmons
MUSIC MASTER	Rees
GRUMIO	Munden
BIANCA	Miss Leserve
CURTIS	Mrs Platt
CATHARINE (1)	Mrs Mattocks

(1) *May 18*

CATHARINE	Mrs Johnson

THE TEMPEST

(1) Altered by John Dryden and Sir William Davenant, and in turn altered by Thomas Shadwell. In five acts.

1674   Henry Herringman.

For a description of this see my Volume I, 422–3.

(2) 'An Opera. As it is Performed at the Theatre-Royal in Drury-Lane.' In three acts.

1756   J. and R. Tonson.

This alteration was made by David Garrick, with music by John Christopher Smith. Act I opens with *I. ii. 196–206*, followed by *I. ii. 1–401*, drastically reduced, by 32 lines from Dryden and Davenant's Act III (Ariel and Ferdinand), and by 54 lines, turned into verse, from their Act II (Stephano, Ventoso, and Mustacho).

Act II opens with *I. ii. 405–end*, considerably reduced. The rest of the Act is from Dryden and Davenant: about 100 lines selected at random from Acts II, III, and IV of their version.

Act III consists of *IV. i. 1–54a*, followed by *V. i*, so much reduced as to be virtually incomprehensible.

Inserted are thirty-two songs by Shakespeare, Dryden, Shadwell, and others.

See also Odell, i. 362–5.

(3) 'As Performed at the Theatre-Royal, Drury-Lane.'

1773   John Bell.

Following are the principal omissions:

Act I. i. 58–end ('We split'), ii. 79–97a (the reasons for Antonio's treachery).

Act II. i. 10–71, 76–112 (Gonzalo mocked by Antonio and Sebastian), 153–73 (Gonzalo's ideal commonwealth), a considerable part of 207–304 (the plot to murder Alonso and Gonzalo).

All of Prospero's asides in Act III. i and iii.

Act IV. i. 60–105, 117–38 (the Masque of Iris, Ceres, and Juno, for which are substituted a new eight-line recitative by Juno, and an eight-line duet, the singers of which are not specified; they were, however, almost certainly Hymen and Ceres).

The Epilogue.

Throughout there are minor omissions.

See also Odell, ii. 28.

(4) Altered as an opera, anonymously. In three acts.

1776   Not published.

This version was acted at CG in 1776, 1777, and 1779. MP, Dec. 28, 1776, refers to it as 'an operatical mutilation', in which 'Miranda and Ferdinand have now each of them two airs . . . and the masque [is] brought from the 4th act into the last scene'. MC, Dec. 28, 1776, notes that the music was selected from Purcell, J. C. Smith, Arne, and Fisher. This does not appear to be the same version as that performed at DL in 1756.

(5) Adapted, probably by Richard Brinsley Sheridan. In five acts.

1777   Not published.

This version was first acted at DL in 1777. The probability that Sheridan was responsible for it is indicated in MP, Jan. 13, 1777. The opening scene was omitted (MP, Jan. 6, 1777), but a representation of the shipwreck was exhibited at the beginning of Act II (MP, Sept. 9, 1777). The music was composed by Thomas Linley, Jr. (Gaz, Jan. 6, 1777). MP, Jan. 7, 1777, notes that Prospero's 'cloud-capp'd towers' was spoken as Shakespeare wrote it, and not, as 'has been customary' in the version that appears on his monument in Westminster Abbey. This consists of Act IV. i. 152–6a, with the following changes: 'capp'd' is 'cupt'; 151 ('baseless fabric') is inserted in place of 155 ('insubstantial pageant'); and 'rack' is 'wreck'.

(6) 'As it is Acted at the Theatres-Royal in Drury-Lane and Covent-Garden.'

1778   J. Wenman.

This is identical with (3).

(7) Altered as THE SHIPWRECK, anonymously. In three acts. 'As performed at the Patagonian Theatre, Exeter-'Change.'

1780   W. Thompson.

This version was made for, and performed at, a puppet theatre; it is chiefly Dryden and Davenant, much reduced. The playbills state that it was accompanied by 'the original music, composed by Smith'. It was performed seventeen times between Dec. 4, 1779 and Apr. 7, 1780.

(8) 'Marked with the Variations in the Manager's Book, at the Theatre-Royal in Drury-Lane.'
    1785   C. Bathurst [&c.].
(9) 'Taken from the Manager's Book, at the Theatre Royal, Drury-Lane.'
    n.d. [c. 1788]   R. Butters.
Both of these are identical with (3).

(10) 'With Additions from Dryden: as Compiled by J. P. Kemble. And First Acted at the Theatre Royal, Drury Lane, October 13th, 1789.'
    1789   J. Debrett.

Act I opens with Dryden and Davenant's [for which read hereafter, D&D] Act I. ii. 1–17 (Prospero and Miranda). This is followed by *I. ii. 20–78a, 108–13, 128–95, 239–374*, all somewhat reduced, and by the concluding dialogue of D&D's Act I (Miranda and Dorinda wonder, never having seen one, what a man is like).

Act II opens with a representation of the shipwreck. Then come *II. ii*, D&D's II. iii (the meeting of Dorinda and Hippolito), D&D's III. i (Prospero warns Dorinda against Hippolito), both of these scenes being considerably reduced, and *I. ii. 375–404a*.

Act III consists of *I. ii. 406–end, III. ii*, D&D's IV. i (Miranda and Ferdinand, and Hippolito's professions of courage), *II. i. 1–9, 72–75, 113–29*, and *III. iii. 18–end*. Everything has been considerably curtailed.

Act IV is *IV. i. 139–42a, 164b–end*, followed by an abridgement of D&D's IV. iii (Hippolito, wounded in the duel with Ferdinand, appears dead; Prospero orders Ferdinand killed; Alonso intercedes for him; Dorinda and Miranda quarrel).

Act V is D&D's V, reduced. It is followed by *V. i. 300–16a, 51b–57*, D&D's Masque of Neptune and Amphitrite, *IV. i. 146–56a*, and *V. i. 88–94*.

See also Genest, vi. 576–8; Odell, ii. 58–60.

[*as* 'a new English Opera']

1756 DRURY LANE
Feb. 11, 13, 18, 20, 26; Mar. 16

ALONSO	Atkins
PROSPERO	Beard
ANTONIO	G. Burton
FERDINAND	Sig. Curioni
GONZALO	?
CALIBAN	Champnes
STEPHANO	Rooker
VENTOSO	Abington
TRINCULO	Beard
MUSTACHO	Champnes

THE TEMPEST [as 'a new English Opera']

1756 DRURY LANE (cont.)
Feb. 11, 13, 18, 20, 26; Mar. 16 (cont.)

ARIEL	Miss [I.] Young
MIRANDA	Mrs Vernon

[The bills give neither the parts nor the actors' names. In the printed text the parts and the actors are listed on the recto and verso of the same leaf respectively, but there is no indication as to who acted which part. Twelve parts are listed, but only nine actors, the reason being that certain parts were doubled. The correct assignment is revealed by comparing the printed text with the musical score, published by I. Walsh. In the text each song is headed by the name of the character who sings it, and in the score by the name of the actor. It will be observed that Beard and Champnes each played two parts. On page 31 of the text is a brief scene in which CALIBAN and MUSTACHO, both acted by Champnes, appear together. In the performance this scene was perhaps omitted or curtailed. ALONSO, ANTONIO, and GONZALO are speaking parts only, and the assignment to Atkins and Burton (the only two names not to appear anywhere in the score) is therefore conjectural. GONZALO cannot be doubled with either of these parts. His speeches, of which he has only two, of two lines each, may have been transferred to ANTONIO, or omitted entirely.]

[The original]

1757 DRURY LANE
Oct. 20, 21, 24, 27

PROSPERO	Mossop
FERDINAND	Holland
ALONSO (1)	Bransby
GONZALO (1)	Burton
ANTONIO (1)	Austin
SEBASTIAN (1)	Mozeen
STEPHANO (1)	Woodward
TRINCULO	Yates
CALIBAN	Berry
BOATSWAIN (1)	Blakes
ARIEL	Miss [I.] Young
HYMEN	Beard
MIRANDA	Miss Pritchard
CERES	Mrs Vernon

(1) *Nov. 7, 9, 11, 14, 16, 21, 23; Dec. 5, 19, 26*

STEPHANO	Vernon

omitted
ALONSO, GONZALO, ANTONIO, SEBASTIAN, STEPHANO, BOATSWAIN

[The bills omit STEPHANO. But C-H, Nov. 7, has, 'Mr Woodward continuing ill (cf. *Measure for Measure* at this theatre, Oct. 31) Vernon did his Part'. On Nov. 19 C-H has, 'Woodward play'd [TOUCHSTONE in *As You Like It*]—1st after his illness'. It is probable, however, that he let Vernon continue as STEPHANO (cf. Feb. 13, 1758). Woodward did not appear again in this part until Dec. 30, 1776 at Covent Garden.]

1758 DRURY LANE
Jan. 21

PROSPERO	Mossop
FERDINAND	Holland
TRINCULO	Yates
CALIBAN (2)	Berry
ARIEL (2)	Miss [I.] Young
HYMEN	Beard
MIRANDA	Miss Pritchard
CERES (1)	Mrs Vernon

(1) *Feb. 13; Mar. 27; Apr. 24*
added
STEPHANO Vernon
omitted on *Apr. 24* only
CERES

(2) *Oct. 24; Nov. 20; Dec. 27*

CALIBAN	Blakes (on *Dec. 27* only)
ARIEL	Miss Eliz. Young (on Oct. 24, Nov. 20 only)

added
STEPHANO [H.] Vaughan

639

1759 DRURY LANE
Mar. 5; Apr. 16

PROSPERO	Mossop
FERDINAND	Holland
STEPHANO	[H.] Vaughan
TRINCULO	Yates
CALIBAN	Blakes
ARIEL	Miss [I.] Young
HYMEN	Beard
MIRANDA	Miss Pritchard
CERES	Mrs Vernon

1760 DRURY LANE
Dec. 11

PROSPERO	Havard
FERDINAND	Holland
STEPHANO	King
TRINCULO	Yates
CALIBAN	Blakes
ARIEL	Miss [I.] Young
HYMEN	Lowe
MIRANDA	Miss Pritchard

(1) *Dec. 27*
added
 CERES Miss [I.] Young
[Miss Young doubled ARIEL and CERES.]

1761 DRURY LANE
Feb. 2; Mar. 24

PROSPERO	Havard
FERDINAND	Holland
STEPHANO	King
TRINCULO	Yates
CALIBAN	Blakes
ARIEL	Miss [I.] Young
HYMEN (1)	Lowe
MIRANDA (1)	Miss Pritchard
CERES	Miss [I.] Young

[Miss Young doubled ARIEL and CERES.]

(1) *May 8*
 MIRANDA Mrs Palmer [i.e. formerly Miss Pritchard]
added
 BOATSWAIN Clough
omitted
 HYMEN

1762 DRURY LANE
Mar. 1; Apr. 12

PROSPERO	Havard
FERDINAND (1)	Holland
STEPHANO	King
TRINCULO	Yates
CALIBAN	Blakes
BOATSWAIN (1)	Clough

(1) *Oct. 30; Nov. 9*
 FERDINAND Vernon
 CERES Mrs Vincent [Jr.]
omitted
 BOATSWAIN

THE TEMPEST

1762 DRURY LANE (cont.)
Mar. 1; Apr. 12 (cont.)

ARIEL	Miss [I.] Young
HYMEN	Lowe
MIRANDA	Mrs Palmer
CERES (1)	Miss [I.] Young

[Miss Young doubled ARIEL and CERES.]

1763 DRURY LANE
Apr. 7

PROSPERO	Havard
FERDINAND	Vernon
STEPHANO (1)	King
TRINCULO	Yates
CALIBAN (1, 2)	Blakes
ARIEL	Miss [I.] Young
HYMEN (2)	Lowe
MIRANDA	Mrs Palmer
CERES (2)	Miss [I.] Young

[Miss Young doubled ARIEL and CERES.]

(1) *May 3*

STEPHANO	Moody
CALIBAN	Ackman

(2) *Nov. 15; Dec. 9*

CALIBAN	Love
HYMEN	W. Palmer [first appearance, Nov. 15, on the stage]
CERES	Mrs Vincent [Jr.]

1765 DRURY LANE
May 1

PROSPERO	Havard
FERDINAND	Vernon
STEPHANO	King
TRINCULO	Yates
CALIBAN	Love
ARIEL	Miss [I.] Young
HYMEN	Kear
CERES	Mrs Vincent [Jr.]
MIRANDA	Mrs Palmer

1766 DRURY LANE
Feb. 3; May 14

PROSPERO	Havard
FERDINAND	Vernon
STEPHANO	King
TRINCULO	Yates
CALIBAN	Love
ARIEL (1)	Miss [I.] Young
HYMEN	Kear
CERES	Mrs Vincent [Jr.]
MIRANDA	Mrs Palmer

(1) *Apr. 30*

ARIEL	Mrs Dorman

THE TEMPEST

1767 DRURY LANE
Apr. 4

PROSPERO	Havard
FERDINAND	Vernon
STEPHANO	King
TRINCULO	Yates
CALIBAN (1)	Love
ARIEL (1)	Mrs Arne
HYMEN	Kear
CERES	Mrs Vincent [Jr.]
MIRANDA	Mrs Palmer

(1) *May 5*

CALIBAN	Champnes
ARIEL	Miss [I.] Young

1768 DRURY LANE
Apr. 22

PROSPERO	Packer
FERDINAND	Vernon
STEPHANO	King
TRINCULO	Baddeley
CALIBAN	Champnes
ARIEL	Miss [I.] Young
HYMEN	Kear
CERES	Mrs Dorman
MIRANDA	Mrs Palmer

1769 DRURY LANE
Mar. 16, 27

PROSPERO	Holland
FERDINAND	Vernon
STEPHANO	King
TRINCULO	Baddeley
CALIBAN	Love
SEBASTIAN	Hurst
ANTONIO (2)	Strange
ALONSO	Bransby
GONZALO	Burton
BOATSWAIN	Clough
ARIEL (1, 2)	Master Brown [first appearance, Mar. 16, on the stage]
HYMEN (1, 2)	Kear
CERES (1, 2)	Mrs Dorman
MIRANDA	Mrs Baddeley

(1) *May 2*

ARIEL omitted	Miss Rogers
HYMEN, CERES	

(2) *May 5*

ARIEL omitted	Mrs Scott
ANTONIO, HYMEN, CERES	

Oct. 9

PROSPERO (1)	Holland
FERDINAND	Vernon

(1) *Nov. 20; Dec. 27*

PROSPERO	Packer (on *Dec. 27* only)

642

THE TEMPEST

1769 DRURY LANE (cont.)

Oct. 9 (cont.)

STEPHANO (1)	King
TRINCULO	Baddeley
CALIBAN (1)	Love
GONZALO	Burton
ALONSO	Bransby
ANTONIO	Hurst
SEBASTIAN	Keen
SHIPMASTER	Ackman
BOATSWAIN	Clough
FRANCISCO (1)	Wright
ARIEL (1)	Miss Rogers
HYMEN	Kear
CERES	Mrs Dorman
MIRANDA	Mrs Baddeley

(1) Nov. 20; Dec. 27 (cont.)

STEPHANO	Love
CALIBAN	[I.] Sparks
ARIEL	Mrs Scott
FRANCISCO omitted	

[On *Dec. 27* PA erroneously retains Holland as PROSPERO. Holland died on Dec. 7.]

1770 DRURY LANE

Apr. 17

PROSPERO	Packer
FERDINAND	Vernon
STEPHANO	Love
TRINCULO (1, 2)	Jefferson
CALIBAN	[I.] Sparks
GONZALO (2)	Burton
ALONSO (1)	Bransby
ANTONIO	Hurst
SEBASTIAN	Keen
FRANCISCO (1)	Wright
SHIPMASTER	Ackman
ARIEL	Mrs Scott
HYMEN	Kear
BOATSWAIN (2)	Clough
CERES	Mrs Dorman
MIRANDA (2)	Miss Younge

(1) May 23

TRINCULO	Parsons
ALONSO	Wrighten
FRANCISCO omitted	

(2) Nov. 19

TRINCULO	Baddeley
GONZALO	J. Aickin
BOATSWAIN	[J.] Booth
MIRANDA	Miss Rogers

1771 DRURY LANE

Apr. 15

PROSPERO	Packer
FERDINAND	Vernon
STEPHANO	Love
TRINCULO	Baddeley
CALIBAN (1, 2)	[I.] Sparks
GONZALO	Burton
ALONSO	Bransby
ANTONIO	Hurst
SEBASTIAN	Keen

(1) May 28

CALIBAN	Ackman
SHIPMASTER	J. Burton

(2) Dec. 2, 21

CALIBAN	Ackman
FRANCISCO	Griffith
SHIPMASTER	Wrighten
BOATSWAIN	Wright

643

THE TEMPEST

1771 DRURY LANE (cont.)
Apr. 15 (cont.)

FRANCISCO (2)	Wright
SHIPMASTER (1, 2)	Ackman
ARIEL	Mrs Scott
HYMEN	Kear
BOATSWAIN (2)	[J.] Booth
CERES	Mrs Dorman
MIRANDA	Miss Rogers

[PA assigns GONZALO to J. Aickin.]

1772 DRURY LANE
May 26

PROSPERO	Packer
FERDINAND	Vernon
STEPHANO	Love
TRINCULO	Baddeley
CALIBAN	Wright
SEBASTIAN	Keen
GONZALO	J. Aickin
ALONSO	Bransby
ANTONIO	Hurst
SHIPMASTER	Wrighten
FRANCISCO	Griffith
ARIEL	Mrs Scott
HYMEN	Fawcett
CERES	Mrs Dorman
MIRANDA	Miss Rogers

1773 DRURY LANE
May 12

PROSPERO	Packer
FERDINAND	Vernon
STEPHANO	George Alexander Stevens
TRINCULO	Baddeley
CALIBAN	Ackman
SEBASTIAN	Keen
GONZALO	J. Aickin
ALONSO	Bransby
ANTONIO	Hurst
SHIPMASTER	Wrighten
FRANCISCO	Griffith
ARIEL	Mrs Scott
HYMEN	Fawcett
CERES	Mrs Wrighten
MIRANDA	Mrs [T.] Smith

1774 DRURY LANE
Apr. 4

PROSPERO	Packer
FERDINAND	Vernon
STEPHANO (1)	King
TRINCULO	Baddeley
CALIBAN (1)	Ackman
GONZALO (1)	J. Aickin
ALONSO	Bransby
SEBASTIAN	Keen
FRANCISCO (1)	Griffith
BOATSWAIN (1)	Wright
SHIPMASTER	Wrighten
ARIEL	Mrs Scott
HYMEN (1)	Fawcett
CERES	Mrs Wrighten
MIRANDA	Mrs [T.] Smith

(1) *Dec. 26*

STEPHANO	Moody
CALIBAN	Wright
GONZALO	Aickin [i.e. J. Aickin]
FRANCISCO	Norris
BOATSWAIN	Griffiths
HYMEN	Kear

1775 DRURY LANE
May 18

PROSPERO	Packer
FERDINAND	Vernon
STEPHANO	Moody
TRINCULO	Baddeley
CALIBAN	Wright
GONZALO	[J.] Aickin
ALONSO	Bransby
SEBASTIAN	Keen
FRANCISCO	Norris
BOATSWAIN	Griffiths
SHIPMASTER	Wrighten
ARIEL	Mrs Scott
HYMEN	Fawcett
CERES	Mrs Wrighten
MIRANDA	Mrs [T.] Smith

1776 DRURY LANE
May 18

PROSPERO	Packer
FERDINAND	Vernon
STEPHANO	Moody
TRINCULO	Baddeley
CALIBAN	Wright
GONZALO	[J.] Aickin
ALONSO	Bransby
ANTONIO	Hurst
SEBASTIAN	Farren

THE TEMPEST

1776 DRURY LANE (cont.)
May 18 (cont.)

FRANCISCO	Norris
BOATSWAIN	Carpenter
SHIPMASTER	Wrighten
ARIEL	Mrs Scott
HYMEN	Fawcett
CERES	Mrs Wrighten
MIRANDA	Mrs [T.] Smith

[as an opera]

COVENT GARDEN
Dec. 27, 31

PROSPERO	Hull
FERDINAND	Mattocks
STEPHANO (1)	[R.] Wilson
TRINCULO	Quick
CALIBAN	Dunstall
GONZALO	Fearon
ALONSO	L'Estrange
SEBASTIAN	Robson
ANTONIO	Booth
SHIPMASTER	Thompson
BOATSWAIN	[R.] Bates
ARIEL	Mrs Farrell
MIRANDA	Miss Brown
JUNO	Miss Dayes
CERES	Miss Valois

(1) *Dec. 30*

STEPHANO	Woodward

[The bills have "In Three Acts".]

[The original]

1777 DRURY LANE
Jan. 4, 6, 10, 13

PROSPERO (3)	Bensley
STEPHANO	Moody
TRINCULO	Baddeley
CALIBAN	[C.] Bannister
GONZALO (1, 2)	[J.] Aickin
ALONSO (2, 3)	Bransby
FERDINAND (2, 3)	Vernon
SEBASTIAN (3)	Farren
FRANCISCO (3)	Norris
BOATSWAIN (1, 2, 3)	Carpenter
ANTONIO (1, 2, 3)	Hurst
SHIPMASTER (1, 2, 3)	Wrighten

(1) *Jan. 18, 23, 25; Feb. 18; Mar. 3*

GONZALO	Wrighten (on *Jan. 18* only)

omitted
BOATSWAIN, ANTONIO, SHIPMASTER

(2) *Jan. 31; Feb. 4; Mar. 15; Apr. 4, 14, 25; May 2, 7, 30*

GONZALO	Grist (on *May 30* only)
ALONSO	Wrighten
FERDINAND	Davies (on *May 2, 7* only)

omitted
SAME as *Jan. 18*
[On *May 30* PA assigns FERDINAND to Davies.]

646

THE TEMPEST

1777 DRURY LANE (cont.)

Jan. 4, 6, 10, 13 (cont.)

ARIEL	A Young Lady [Miss Field (Genest, v. 551); first appearance, Jan. 4, on the stage]
MIRANDA	A Young Lady [Mrs Cuyler (Genest, v. 551); first appearance, Jan. 4, on the stage]

(3) Sept. 20; Nov. 14; Dec. 26

PROSPERO	Packer (on *Sept. 20* only)
ALONSO	Wrighten
FERDINAND	Davies (on *Sept. 20, Nov. 14* only)

omitted SEBASTIAN, FRANCISCO, BOATSWAIN, ANTONIO, SHIPMASTER

[Miss Field's and Mrs Cuyler's names are given in the bills. On Dec. 26 PA assigns FERDINAND to Davies.]

[*as an opera*]

COVENT GARDEN

Jan. 13

PROSPERO	Hull
FERDINAND	Mattocks
TRINCULO	Quick
CALIBAN	Mahon
GONZALO	Fearon
ALONSO	L'Estrange
SEBASTIAN	Robson
ANTONIO	Booth
STEPHANO (1)	Woodward
ARIEL	Mrs Farrell
MIRANDA	Miss Brown
JUNO	Miss Dayes
CERES	Miss Valois

(1) Feb. 13; May 19

STEPHANO	[R.] Wilson

[*The original*]

1778 DRURY LANE

Jan. 6; May 15

PROSPERO (1)	Bensley
STEPHANO	Moody
TRINCULO	Baddeley
CALIBAN	[C.] Bannister
GONZALO	[J.] Aickin
ALONSO	Wrighten
FERDINAND (2)	Vernon
ARIEL	Miss Field
MIRANDA	Mrs Cuyler

(1) Nov. 2

PROSPERO	Packer

(2) Nov. 27

FERDINAND	Davies

647

THE TEMPEST

1779 DRURY LANE
May 8

PROSPERO	Bensley
STEPHANO	Moody
TRINCULO	Baddeley
CALIBAN (1)	[C.] Bannister
GONZALO	[J.] Aickin
ALONSO	Wrighten
FERDINAND (1)	Vernon
ARIEL (1)	Miss Abrams
MIRANDA	Mrs Cuyler

(1) *Nov. 3, 12; Dec. 30*

CALIBAN	Wright (on *Nov. 3* only)
FERDINAND	Davies (on *Nov. 12* only)
ARIEL	Miss Field

added on *Dec.* 30 only

ANTONIO	Hurst
SEBASTIAN	Lamash

[*as an opera*]

COVENT GARDEN
May 13

PROSPERO	A Gentleman [Wright (MS annotation on JPK); second appearance on the stage]
FERDINAND	Mattocks
TRINCULO	Quick
CALIBAN	Mahon
GONZALO	Fearon
ALONSO	L'Estrange
SEBASTIAN	Robson
ANTONIO	Booth
STEPHANO	[R.] Wilson
ARIEL	Mrs Kennedy
MIRANDA	Miss Brown
JUNO	Mrs Morton
CERES	Miss Valois

[*The original*]

1780 DRURY LANE
Mar. 13; Apr. 24

PROSPERO	Bensley
STEPHANO	Moody
TRINCULO	Baddeley
CALIBAN	[C.] Bannister
GONZALO	[J.] Aickin
ALONSO	Wrighten
ANTONIO (1)	Hurst
SEBASTIAN	Lamash
FERDINAND (1)	Vernon
ARIEL	Miss Field
MIRANDA	Mrs Cuyler

(1) *Sept. 23; Dec. 12*

ANTONIO	Phillimore
FERDINAND	Farren

added

FRANCISCO	Norris

648

1781 DRURY LANE
Jan. 3

PROSPERO	Bensley
STEPHANO	Moody
TRINCULO	Baddeley
CALIBAN	[C.] Bannister
GONZALO	[J.] Aickin
ALONSO	Wrighten
ANTONIO	Phillimore
SEBASTIAN	Lamash
FRANCISCO	Norris
FERDINAND	Farren
ARIEL	Miss Field
MIRANDA (1)	Mrs Cuyler

(1) *Nov. 13*

MIRANDA	Miss Phillips

1782 DRURY LANE
Feb. 12

PROSPERO	Bensley
STEPHANO	Moody
TRINCULO	Baddeley
CALIBAN	[C.] Bannister
GONZALO	[J.] Aickin
ALONSO	Wrighten
ANTONIO	Phillimore
SEBASTIAN (1)	Lamash
FRANCISCO	Norris
FERDINAND	Farren
ARIEL	Miss Field
MIRANDA	Miss Phillips

(1) *Apr. 6*

SEBASTIAN	Chaplin

1784 DRURY LANE
Nov. 9, 18

PROSPERO	Bensley
STEPHANO	Moody
TRINCULO	Baddeley
CALIBAN	[C.] Bannister
GONZALO	[J.] Aickin
ALONSO	Wrighten
ANTONIO	Phillimore
SEBASTIAN	Wright
FRANCISCO	[J.] Wilson
FERDINAND	Barrymore
ARIEL	Miss Field
MIRANDA	Miss Phillips

THE TEMPEST

1785 DRURY LANE
Jan. 10

PROSPERO	Bensley
STEPHANO (3)	Moody
TRINCULO	Baddeley
CALIBAN	[C.] Bannister
GONZALO	[J.] Aickin
ALONSO	Wrighten
ANTONIO (1)	Phillimore
SEBASTIAN	Wright
FRANCISCO	[J.] Wilson
FERDINAND	Barrymore
ARIEL	Miss Field
MIRANDA (2, 4)	Miss Phillips

(1) *Jan. 18*

ANTONIO	Chaplin

(2) *Mar. 28*

MIRANDA	Miss Bannister

(3) *Apr. 28*

STEPHANO	Suett

(4) *Oct. 17; Nov. 10, 24*

MIRANDA	Mrs Crouch [i.e. formerly Miss Phillips]

1786 DRURY LANE
Mar. 7

PROSPERO	Bensley
STEPHANO	Moody
TRINCULO	Baddeley
CALIBAN	[C.] Bannister
GONZALO	[J.] Aickin
ALONSO	Wrighten
ANTONIO	Phillimore
SEBASTIAN (1)	Wright
FRANCISCO	[J.] Wilson
FERDINAND	Barrymore
ARIEL	Mrs Forster
MIRANDA	Mrs Crouch

(1) *Dec. 5, 27*

SEBASTIAN	Chaplin

1787 DRURY LANE
Jan. 9

PROSPERO	Bensley
STEPHANO	Moody
TRINCULO	Baddeley
FERDINAND	Barrymore
GONZALO	[J.] Aickin
ALONSO (1)	Wrighten
ANTONIO	Phillimore
SEBASTIAN	Chaplin
FRANCISCO	[J.] Wilson
CALIBAN	[C.] Bannister
ARIEL	Mrs Forster
MIRANDA	Mrs Crouch

(1) *June 4*

ALONSO	Staunton

THE TEMPEST
[as altered by KEMBLE]

1789 DRURY LANE
Oct. 13, 17, 20, 27; Nov. 3, 10, 17; Dec. 21, 30

PROSPERO	Bensley
FERDINAND	Kelly
STEPHANO	Moody
TRINCULO	Baddeley
CALIBAN	Williams
GONZALO	[J.] Aickin
ALONSO	Packer
ANTONIO	Phillimore
ARIEL	Miss Romanzini
HIPPOLITO	Mrs Goodall
NEPTUNE	Sedgwick
MIRANDA	Mrs Crouch
DORINDA	Miss Farren
AMPHITRITE	Mrs Edwards

1790 DRURY LANE
Jan. 11, 18; Feb. 22

PROSPERO	Bensley
FERDINAND	Kelly
STEPHANO	Moody
TRINCULO	Baddeley
CALIBAN	Williams
GONZALO (3, 4)	[J.] Aickin
ALONSO	Packer
ANTONIO	Phillimore
ARIEL (2, 4)	Miss Romanzini
HIPPOLITO (3)	Mrs Goodall
NEPTUNE (1)	Sedgwick
MIRANDA	Mrs Crouch
DORINDA	Miss Farren
AMPHITRITE	Mrs Edwards

(1) *Jan. 25*

NEPTUNE	Shaw

(2) *Apr. 24*

ARIEL	Miss Hagley

(3) *Oct. 11*

GONZALO	Fox
HIPPOLITO	Mrs Williams

(4) *Nov. 24*

GONZALO	Fox
ARIEL	Mrs Bland [i.e. formerly Miss Romanzini]

1791 DRURY LANE
May 5, 30

PROSPERO	Bensley
ALONSO	Packer
ANTONIO	Phillimore
FERDINAND	Kelly
GONZALO (1, 2, 3)	Fox
STEPHANO	Moody
TRINCULO	Baddeley
CALIBAN (1, 2, 3)	Williams

(1) *Nov. 9* (company at KING'S, HAYMARKET)

GONZALO	Maddocks
CALIBAN	Benson

(2) *Nov. 25; Dec. 14* (company at KING'S, HAYMARKET)

GONZALO	Maddocks
CALIBAN	Sedgwick
NEPTUNE	Caulfield

THE TEMPEST [*as altered by* KEMBLE]

1791 DRURY LANE (*cont.*)

May 5, 30 (*cont.*)
ARIEL	Mrs Bland
HIPPOLITO	Mrs Goodall
NEPTUNE (2)	Sedgwick
MIRANDA	Mrs Crouch
DORINDA	Miss Farren
AMPHITRITE	Mrs Edwards

(3) *Dec. 27* (company at KING'S, HAYMARKET)
GONZALO	Maddocks
CALIBAN	[C.] Bannister

1792 DRURY LANE (company at KING'S, HAYMARKET)

Apr. 12
PROSPERO	Bensley
ALONSO	Packer
ANTONIO	Phillimore
FERDINAND	Kelly
GONZALO	Maddocks
STEPHANO	Moody
TRINCULO	Baddeley
CALIBAN (1)	[C.] Bannister
ARIEL	Mrs Bland
HIPPOLITO	Mrs Goodall
NEPTUNE (1)	Sedgwick
MIRANDA (1)	Mrs Crouch
DORINDA (1)	Miss Farren
AMPHITRITE	Mrs Edwards

(1) *May 8; Dec. 13*
CALIBAN	Sedgwick (on *Dec. 13* only)
NEPTUNE	Caulfield
MIRANDA	Miss Collins
DORINDA	Mrs Powell

1793 DRURY LANE (company at KING'S, HAYMARKET)

Jan. 2
PROSPERO	Bensley
ALONSO	Packer
ANTONIO	Phillimore
FERDINAND (1)	Kelly
GONZALO	Maddocks
STEPHANO	Moody
TRINCULO	Baddeley
CALIBAN	[C.] Bannister
ARIEL (1)	Mrs Bland
HIPPOLITO (1)	Mrs Goodall
NEPTUNE	Sedgwick
MIRANDA	Mrs Crouch
DORINDA (1)	Miss Farren
AMPHITRITE	Mrs Edwards

(1) *May 7* (company at HAYMARKET)
FERDINAND	Barrymore
ARIEL	Miss Heard
HIPPOLITO	Miss Collins
DORINDA	Mrs Powell

[In Pb (PA does not advertise the play) ARIEL is assigned to Mrs Bland. But 'Ariel was, on account of the sudden indisposition of Mrs. Bland, read by Miss Heard' (DWR, May 8).]

HAYMARKET

Nov. 19
PROSPERO	Bensley
ALONSO	Usher
ANTONIO	Bland

(1) *Dec. 5*
HIPPOLITO	Miss Heard

(2) *Dec. 26*
NEPTUNE	Caulfield

652

THE TEMPEST [*as altered by* KEMBLE]

1793 HAYMARKET (*cont.*)
Nov. 19 (cont.)

GONZALO	Maddocks
FERDINAND	Barrymore
STEPHANO	Suett
TRINCULO	Baddeley
CALIBAN	[C.] Bannister
ARIEL	Mrs Bland
HIPPOLITO (1)	Mrs Goodall
NEPTUNE (2)	Sedgwick
MIRANDA	Mrs Powell
DORINDA	Mrs Gibbs
AMPHITRITE	Miss Stuart

1794 HAYMARKET
Jan. 4

PROSPERO	Bensley
ALONSO	Usher
ANTONIO	Bland
GONZALO	Maddocks
FERDINAND	Barrymore
STEPHANO	Benson
TRINCULO	Baddeley
CALIBAN	[C.] Bannister
ARIEL	Mrs Bland
HIPPOLITO	Mrs Goodall
NEPTUNE	Caulfield
MIRANDA	Mrs Powell
DORINDA	Mrs Gibbs
AMPHITRITE	Miss Stuart

1797 DRURY LANE
Feb. 22

PROSPERO	[J.] Palmer
ALONSO	Packer
ANTONIO (3)	Denman
FERDINAND	C. Kemble
GONZALO	Maddocks
STEPHANO	[J.] Bannister
TRINCULO (3)	Suett
CALIBAN	[C.] Bannister
ARIEL (2, 3)	Master Welsh
HIPPOLITO (3)	Mrs Powell
NEPTUNE	Sedgwick
MIRANDA (1)	Mrs Crouch
DORINDA (3)	Miss Farren
AMPHITRITE (3)	Miss D'Evelyn

(1) *Feb. 28*

MIRANDA	Miss Miller

(2) *Mar. 18*

ARIEL	Miss Granger

(3) *Dec. 9, 23*

ANTONIO	Gibbon
TRINCULO	Hollingsworth (on *Dec. 23* only)
ARIEL	Miss DeCamp
HIPPOLITO	Mrs Goodall
DORINDA	Miss Miller
AMPHITRITE	Miss Dufour

THE TEMPEST [as altered by KEMBLE]

1798 DRURY LANE
Feb. 24

PROSPERO	[J.] Palmer
ALONSO (I)	Packer
ANTONIO (I)	Gibbon
FERDINAND	C. Kemble
GONZALO	Maddocks
STEPHANO	[J.] Bannister
TRINCULO (I)	Suett
CALIBAN	[C.] Bannister
HIPPOLITO (I)	Mrs Goodall
ARIEL (I)	Miss DeCamp
NEPTUNE	Sedgwick
MIRANDA	Mrs Crouch
DORINDA (I)	Miss Miller
AMPHITRITE	Miss Dufour

(1) *June 5*

TRINCULO	Hollingsworth
HIPPOLITO	Mrs Powell
ARIEL	Mrs Bland
DORINDA	Mrs Jordan
omitted	
ALONSO, ANTONIO	

[MP and O both assign TRINCULO to Hollingsworth.]

1799 DRURY LANE
May 4

PROSPERO	[J.] Powell
ALONSO	Packer
ANTONIO (I)	Sparks
FERDINAND (I)	C. Kemble
GONZALO	Maddocks
STEPHANO	[J.] Bannister
TRINCULO	Suett
CALIBAN	Sedgwick
HIPPOLITO	Miss DeCamp
ARIEL	Mrs Bland
NEPTUNE	Caulfield
MIRANDA	Mrs Crouch
DORINDA (I)	Mrs Jordan
AMPHITRITE (I)	Miss Wentworth

(1) *Nov. 14, 28*

FERDINAND	Holland
DORINDA	Miss Mellon
AMPHITRITE	Miss Leak
omitted	
ANTONIO	

TIMON OF ATHENS

(1) 'As it is acted at the Theatre-Royal on Richmond-Green. Altered [by James Love] from Shakespeare and Shadwell.'

    1768   M. Hingeston.

This version was never performed in London.

(2) 'As it is Acted at the Theatre-Royal in Drury-Lane [altered by Richard Cumberland].'

    1771   T. Becket.

Act I consists of *Act I. i*, omitting *111-52* (the Old Athenian), which is fol-

TIMON OF ATHENS

lowed by 22 new lines: Alcibiades sees and loves Evanthe, Timon's daughter, and by *I. ii. 153–239a*, omitting *190–214a* (Flavius fears that Timon is too generous).

Act II begins with *Act II. i*. This is followed by about 150 new lines: Lucius declares his love for Evanthe; he quarrels with Lucullus, and is taunted for fawning on Timon. Alcibiades makes love to Evanthe. The Act ends with *II. ii*, omitting *46–133* (Apemantus and the Fool).

Act III begins with *Act III. i*. Then come about 145 new lines: Evanthe decides to sell her jewels to aid her father; she is rejected by Lucius when she tells him that Timon is penniless; Alcibiades tells her that he will assist Timon. Next is *III. iv*, followed by 15 new lines: Alcibiades is banished for helping Timon, and by *III. v*.

Act IV opens with about 100 new lines: in return for the Senate's promise to aid Timon, Evanthe consents to dissuade Alcibiades from attacking Athens. Then comes *Act IV. iii*, omitting *74a–95, 130–76* (Timon curses Phrynia and Timandra [who are entirely omitted]), and *278–466* (Timon and Apemantus, and Timon and the thieves). The Act concludes with *IV. iii. 198–277*.

Act V opens with *Act V. ii*. This is followed by *V. iv. 1–64*, in which are interspersed about 20 new lines: Alcibiades threatens vengeance on Athens. The rest of the Act is new: Evanthe decides to leave Alcibiades, and attempt to save her father; Lucius and Caphis quarrel over Timon's supposed treasure; Lucius finds that his house has been plundered; Alcibiades and Evanthe plead in vain with Timon to return to Athens; Timon dies.

Throughout there are minor omissions and transpositions.

See also Genest, v. 317–18; Odell, i. 382–4.

(3) 'As Performed at the Theatre-Royal, Drury-Lane. Regulated from the Prompt-Book.'

1773   John Bell.

This version is verbatim, except for the following omissions: *Act I. i. 111–52* (the Old Athenian); *Act V. ii entire* (the Senators' fear of Alcibiades) and *iii entire* (the Soldier's discovery of Timon's grave); and various minor omissions. Act V begins at *Act IV. iii. 467*.

A revival of the play was perhaps in prospect at about this time, for which this version may have been prepared. But the only eighteenth-century performance of the original play took place at Smock Alley Theatre, Dublin, on June 3, 1761.

(4) 'As it is Acted at the Theatres-Royal in Drury-Lane and Covent-Garden.'

1780   Harrison and Co.

This is a reading edition, verbatim throughout.

(5) Altered by Thomas Hull. In five acts.

1786   Not published.

The dramatis personae indicates that Hull based this alteration on that made by Thomas Shadwell in 1678, for which see my Volume I, 437.

TIMON OF ATHENS
[as altered by CUMBERLAND]

1771 DRURY LANE
Dec. 4, 9, 11, 12, 14, 19, 28

TIMON	Barry
ALCIBIADES	A Young Gentleman [Croft (Genest, v. 316, who misspells the name as 'Crofts'); first appearance, Dec. 4, on the stage]
APEMANTUS	[C.] Bannister
FLAVIUS	Packer
LUCIUS	[J.] Palmer
LUCULLUS	Hurst
1ST SENATOR	J. Aickin
2ND SENATOR	Inchbald
3RD SENATOR	Keen
POET	Jefferson
PAINTER	Davies
JEWELLER	Wright
MERCHANT	Fawcett
FLAMINIUS	Brereton
CAPHIS	Ackman
SOLDIER	Baddeley
SERVILIUS	Wrighten
LUCILIUS	Wheeler
HORTENSIUS	Griffith
TITUS	J. Burton
VARRO	Master Cape
PHILOTUS	Jacobs
1ST MESSENGER	Follett
EVANTHE	Mrs [S.] Barry

[In the printed text, Becket, 1771, the cast is the same as that of these performances, with the following additions:

2ND MESSENGER	Watkins
LUCULLUS'S SERVANT	Lings]

1772 DRURY LANE
Jan. 2, 10, 18   (1) *Feb. 6*

TIMON	Barry	omitted
ALCIBIADES	A Young Gentleman [Croft (see Dec. 4, 1771)]	FLAMINIUS
APEMANTUS	[C.] Bannister	
FLAVIUS	Packer	
LUCIUS	[J.] Palmer	
LUCULLUS	Hurst	
1ST SENATOR	J. Aickin	

656

TIMON OF ATHENS [as altered by CUMBERLAND]

1772 DRURY LANE (cont.)
Jan. 2, 10, 18 (cont.)

2ND SENATOR	Inchbald
3RD SENATOR	Keen
POET	Jefferson
PAINTER	Davies
JEWELLER	Wright
MERCHANT	Fawcett
FLAMINIUS (1)	Brereton
CAPHIS	Ackman
SOLDIER	Baddeley
SERVILIUS	Wrighten
LUCILIUS	Wheeler
HORTENSIUS	Griffith
TITUS	J. Burton
VARRO	Master Cape
PHILOTUS	Jacobs
MESSENGER	Follett
EVANTHE	Mrs [S.] Barry

[as altered by HULL]

1786 COVENT GARDEN
May 13

TIMON	Holman
ALCIBIADES	Farren
LUCULLUS	Quick
LUCIUS	Wewitzer
SEMPRONIUS	Davies
VENTIDIUS	[Wm.] Palmer
OLD ATHENIAN	Fearon
FLAVIUS	Hull
CAPHIS	[T.] Kennedy
PAINTER	Stevens
POET	Booth
JEWELLER	Gardner
APEMANTUS	Wroughton
MELISSA	Mrs Inchbald
PHRYNE	Miss Stuart
EVANDRA	A Young Lady [Mrs Duill (Lysons Coll.); first appearance on the stage]

TWELFTH NIGHT

(1) 'As it is acted at the Theatres-Royal in Drury-Lane and Covent-Garden.' n.d. [c. 1771]   J. Rivington [&c.].
This is a reading edition, verbatim throughout.

TWELFTH NIGHT

(2) 'As Performed at the Theatres-Royal. Regulated from the Prompt-Book.'

    1773   John Bell.

Following are the principal omissions:
Act II. iii. 33b–61a ('O mistress mine!'); iv. 27b–81a ('Come away').
Act III. i. 8–35 ('words are very rascals').
Act V. i. 263b–82a (Sebastian's noble blood).
Throughout there are minor omissions.

(3) 'As it is Acted at the Theatres-Royal in Drury-Lane and Covent-Garden.'

    1779   J. Harrison.

(4) 'Marked with the Variations in the Manager's Book, at the Theatre-Royal in Drury-Lane.'

    1787   C. Bathurst [&c.].

(5) 'Taken from the Manager's Book, at the Theatre-Royal, Drury-Lane.'

    1787   For the Proprietors.

All these are identical with (2).

1751 DRURY LANE

Jan. 7, 11

ORSINO	Sowdon
SEBASTIAN	Palmer
SIR TOBY	Berry
SIR ANDREW	Woodward
CURIO	Paddick
VALENTINE	Mozeen
FABIAN	Winstone
CAPTAIN	Blakes
MALVOLIO	Yates
CLOWN	Shuter
OLIVIA	Mrs Clive
MARIA	Mrs Green
VIOLA	Mrs Pritchard

1752 DRURY LANE

Jan. 6

ORSINO	Sowdon
SEBASTIAN	Havard
SIR TOBY	Berry
SIR ANDREW	Woodward
MALVOLIO	Yates
CLOWN	Shuter
OLIVIA	Mrs Clive
MARIA	Miss Minors
VIOLA	Mrs Pritchard

(1) *Jan. 22*

added

ANTONIO	Burton
FABIAN	Winstone
CAPTAIN	Blakes

TWELFTH NIGHT

1753 DRURY LANE
Jan. 8

ORSINO	Dexter
SEBASTIAN	Palmer
SIR TOBY	Berry
ANTONIO (1)	Burton
SIR ANDREW	Woodward
MALVOLIO	Yates
CLOWN	Shuter
FABIAN (1)	Winstone
CAPTAIN (1)	Blakes
OLIVIA	Mrs Clive
MARIA (1)	Miss Minors
VIOLA	Mrs Pritchard

(1) *Jan. 27*
omitted
 ANTONIO, FABIAN, CAPTAIN, MARIA

1754 DRURY LANE
Jan. 7

SIR ANDREW	Woodward
ORSINO	Havard
MALVOLIO	Yates
SIR TOBY	Berry
SEBASTIAN	Palmer
CLOWN	Blakes
VIOLA	Mrs Cowper
OLIVIA	Mrs Clive

(1) *Jan. 24*
added
 FABIAN   Vernon

(2) *Feb. 12*
added
 MARIA   Miss Minors

1755 DRURY LANE
Jan. 6; Feb. 5

SIR ANDREW	Woodward
ORSINO	Havard
MALVOLIO	Yates
SIR TOBY	Berry
SEBASTIAN	Palmer
CLOWN	Blakes
VIOLA	Mrs Davies
MARIA	Miss Minors
OLIVIA	Mrs Clive

1763 DRURY LANE
Oct. 19, 28

SIR ANDREW	Obrien
ORSINO	Packer
MALVOLIO	Yates
SIR TOBY	Love
SEBASTIAN	Palmer
CLOWN	Vernon

TWELFTH NIGHT

1763 DRURY LANE (cont.)
Oct. 19, 28 (cont.)

ANTONIO	Burton
VALENTINE	Castle
CAPTAIN	Moody
FABIAN	Baddeley
CURIO	Fox
1ST OFFICER	Parsons
2ND OFFICER	Marr
VIOLA	A Young Gentlewoman [Miss Plym (Genest, v. 38); first appearance, Oct. 19, in London]
MARIA	Mrs Lee
OLIVIA	Miss Haughton

[On *Oct. 19* Genest (v. 38) has, 'Mr. Field's bill represents Mrs. Yates and Miss Pope as acting Olivia and Maria—but it is probably wrong'. So it is; there is no evidence that these two actresses ever appeared in these parts.]

1764 DRURY LANE
Jan. 6

SIR ANDREW	Obrien
ORSINO	Packer
MALVOLIO	Yates
SIR TOBY	Love
SEBASTIAN	Palmer
CLOWN	Vernon
ANTONIO	Burton
VALENTINE	Castle
CAPTAIN	Moody
FABIAN	Baddeley
CURIO	Fox
1ST OFFICER	Parsons
2ND OFFICER	Marr
VIOLA	Miss Plym
MARIA	Mrs Lee
OLIVIA	Miss Haughton

1771 DRURY LANE
Dec. 10, 13, 18, 20, 27

MALVOLIO	King
SIR ANDREW	Dodd
ORSINO	Jefferson
SEBASTIAN	Cautherley
SIR TOBY	Love
CLOWN	Vernon
ANTONIO	Davies
FABIAN	[F.] Waldron

TWELFTH NIGHT

1771 DRURY LANE (cont.)
Dec. 10, 13, 18, 20, 27 (cont.)

CAPTAIN	Wright
VALENTINE	Wheeler
PRIEST	Griffith
1ST OFFICER	Wrighten
2ND OFFICER	Follett
VIOLA	Miss Younge
MARIA	Mrs Egerton
OLIVIA	Mrs Abington

1772 DRURY LANE
Jan. 1, 6, 13; Feb. 3, 19; May 29

MALVOLIO	King
SIR ANDREW	Dodd
ORSINO (1, 3)	Jefferson
SEBASTIAN	Cautherley
SIR TOBY (2)	Love
CLOWN	Vernon
ANTONIO	Davies
FABIAN	[F.] Waldron
CAPTAIN (3)	Wright
PRIEST (3)	Griffith
VALENTINE (3)	Wheeler
1ST OFFICER (3)	Wrighten
2ND OFFICER (3)	Follett
VIOLA	Miss Younge
MARIA	Mrs Egerton
OLIVIA	Mrs Abington

(1) *Mar. 3*

ORSINO	Packer

(2) *Apr. 24; May 1*

SIR TOBY	Dunstall

(3) *Oct. 8; Dec. 31*

ORSINO	Brereton (on *Oct. 8* only)

omitted CAPTAIN, PRIEST, VALENTINE, OFFICERS

COVENT GARDEN
Mar. 31

SIR ANDREW	Woodward
MALVOLIO	Yates
ORSINO	Hull
SIR TOBY	Dunstall
SEBASTIAN	Wroughton
CLOWN	Dyer
ANTONIO	Gardner
FABIAN	[Lee] Lewes
OLIVIA	Mrs Mattocks
MARIA (1)	Mrs Gardner
VIOLA	Mrs Yates

(1) *May 5*

MARIA	Mrs Green

[In the acting version published by Bell in 1773 the cast is the same as that of this performance, with the following addition:

CAPTAIN	Fox]

TWELFTH NIGHT

1773 DRURY LANE
Jan. 6; Feb. 16

MALVOLIO	King
SIR ANDREW	Dodd
ORSINO (2)	Jefferson
SEBASTIAN	Cautherley
SIR TOBY (1, 2, 3)	Love
CLOWN	Vernon
ANTONIO (2)	Davies
FABIAN (2)	[F.] Waldron
VIOLA	Miss Younge
MARIA (3)	Mrs Egerton
OLIVIA	Mrs Abington

[In the acting version published by Bell in 1773 the cast is the same as that of these performances, with the following additions:

VALENTINE	Wheeler
CAPTAIN	Wright]

(1) *Apr. 1*

SIR TOBY	[J.] Palmer

(2) *May 15*

ORSINO	Brereton
SIR TOBY	[J.] Palmer
ANTONIO	Fawcett
FABIAN	Hartry

(3) *Dec. 10*

SIR TOBY	[J.] Palmer
MARIA	Mrs Hopkins

1774 DRURY LANE
Apr. 30

MALVOLIO	King
SIR ANDREW	Dodd
ORSINO	Jefferson
SEBASTIAN	Cautherley
SIR TOBY	[J.] Palmer
ANTONIO	Davies
FABIAN	[F.] Waldron
CLOWN	Vernon
VIOLA	Miss Younge
MARIA	Mrs Hopkins
OLIVIA	Mrs Abington

1775 DRURY LANE
Jan. 11

MALVOLIO	King
SIR ANDREW	Dodd
ORSINO (1, 2)	Brereton
SEBASTIAN	Cautherley
SIR TOBY	[J.] Palmer
ANTONIO	Davies
FABIAN	[F.] Waldron
CLOWN	Vernon
OLIVIA (1)	Mrs Baddeley
MARIA	Mrs Hopkins
VIOLA	Miss Younge

(1) *Apr. 4*

ORSINO	Jefferson
OLIVIA	Mrs Abington

(2) *Apr. 26; May 23, 26*

ORSINO	Jefferson

TWELFTH NIGHT

1776 DRURY LANE
Apr. 10

SIR ANDREW	Dodd
SIR TOBY	[J.] Palmer
ORSINO	Jefferson
SEBASTIAN	Davies
ANTONIO	Wrighten
FABIAN (1)	[F.] Waldron
CAPTAIN	Wright
PRIEST	Griffiths
VALENTINE	Norris
OFFICER	Carpenter
CLOWN	Vernon
MALVOLIO (1)	Bensley
VIOLA	Miss Younge
MARIA (1)	Mrs Hopkins
OLIVIA (1)	Mrs Abington

(1) *Sept. 21; Oct. 24*

FABIAN	Lamash
MALVOLIO	Yates
MARIA	Miss P. Hopkins (on *Oct. 24* only)
OLIVIA	Mrs Baddeley
added	
CURIO	Everard

1777 DRURY LANE
Mar. 17

SIR ANDREW	Dodd
SIR TOBY	[J.] Palmer
ORSINO (2)	Jefferson
SEBASTIAN (1)	Davies
FABIAN	Lamash
ANTONIO	Wrighten
CAPTAIN	Wright
OFFICER	Carpenter
PRIEST	Griffiths
VALENTINE	Norris
CURIO (2)	Everard
CLOWN (1)	Vernon
MALVOLIO	Yates
OLIVIA	Mrs Baddeley
MARIA	Miss P. Hopkins
VIOLA	Miss Younge

(1) *Apr. 28*

SEBASTIAN	Farren
CLOWN	Davies

(2) *Oct. 18*

ORSINO	Brereton
omitted	
CURIO	

COVENT GARDEN
Mar. 17

ORSINO	Lewis
SEBASTIAN	Wroughton
SIR TOBY	Dunstall
FABIAN	Whitfield
CAPTAIN	Booth
MALVOLIO	[R.] Wilson
CLOWN	Lee Lewes
SIR ANDREW	Quick

1777 COVENT GARDEN (cont.)
Mar. 17 (cont.)
- OLIVIA — Mrs Hartley
- MARIA — Mrs [S.] Wilson
- VIOLA — Mrs [S.] Barry

1778 DRURY LANE
Jan. 3; Mar. 24
- SIR ANDREW — Dodd
- SIR TOBY — [J.] Palmer
- ORSINO — Brereton
- SEBASTIAN — Davies
- FABIAN — Lamash
- ANTONIO — Wrighten
- CAPTAIN — Wright
- OFFICER — Nash
- PRIEST — Griffiths
- VALENTINE — Norris
- CLOWN — Vernon
- MALVOLIO — Yates
- OLIVIA — Mrs Baddeley
- MARIA (1) — Miss P. Hopkins
- VIOLA — Miss Younge

(1) *Nov. 10*
- MARIA — Mrs Brereton [i.e. formerly Miss P. Hopkins]

1779 DRURY LANE
Jan. 6
- SIR ANDREW — Dodd
- SIR TOBY — [J.] Palmer
- ORSINO — Brereton
- SEBASTIAN — Davies
- FABIAN (1) — Lamash
- ANTONIO — Wrighten
- CAPTAIN (1) — Wright
- OFFICER (1) — Nash
- PRIEST (1) — Griffiths
- VALENTINE (1) — Norris
- CLOWN — Vernon
- MALVOLIO — Yates
- OLIVIA — Mrs Baddeley
- MARIA — Mrs Brereton
- VIOLA (1) — Miss Younge

(1) *Oct. 23; Dec. 21, 31*
- FABIAN — R. Palmer (on *Oct. 23* only)
- VIOLA — Mrs Robinson
- omitted CAPTAIN, OFFICER, PRIEST, VALENTINE

1780 DRURY LANE
Apr. 29
- SIR ANDREW — Dodd
- SIR TOBY — [J.] Palmer
- ORSINO — Brereton

(1) *May 20*
- SEBASTIAN — Davies
- OLIVIA — Miss Farren

1780 DRURY LANE (cont.)
Apr. 29 (cont.)

SEBASTIAN (1)	Norris
FABIAN	Lamash
ANTONIO	Wrighten
CLOWN	Vernon
MALVOLIO	Holcroft
VIOLA	Mrs Robinson
MARIA	Mrs Brereton
OLIVIA (1)	Mrs Baddeley

1782 DRURY LANE
Sept. 21

SIR ANDREW	Dodd
SIR TOBY	[J.] Palmer
ORSINO	Brereton
SEBASTIAN	[J.] Bannister
FABIAN (1)	Lamash
ANTONIO	Wrighten
CLOWN	Parsons
MALVOLIO	Bensley
VIOLA	Mrs Bulkley
MARIA	Mrs Brereton
OLIVIA	Miss Farren

(1) Oct. 19

FABIAN	[F.] Waldron

HAYMARKET
Aug. 15

SIR ANDREW	Edwin
MALVOLIO	Bensley
ORSINO	Staunton
SEBASTIAN	R. Palmer
CLOWN	Parsons
FABIAN	Stevens
SIR TOBY	[J.] Palmer
OLIVIA	Miss Harper
MARIA	Miss Kirby
VIOLA	Mrs Bulkley

(1) Aug. 30
added

ANTONIO	Gardner

1783 DRURY LANE
Jan. 1

SIR ANDREW	Dodd
SIR TOBY	[J.] Palmer
ORSINO	Brereton
SEBASTIAN	[J.] Bannister
FABIAN	[F.] Waldron
ANTONIO	Wrighten

1783 DRURY LANE (cont.)

Jan. 1 (cont.)

CLOWN	Parsons
MALVOLIO	Bensley
VIOLA	Mrs Bulkley
MARIA	Mrs Brereton
OLIVIA	Miss Farren

COVENT GARDEN

May 7

MALVOLIO	Henderson
SEBASTIAN	Wroughton
SIR TOBY (1)	[R.] Wilson
ORSINO	Whitfield
CLOWN	Davies
SIR ANDREW	Edwin
OLIVIA	Mrs Mattocks
MARIA	Mrs [S.] Wilson
VIOLA	Mrs [H.] Robinson

(1) *May 14*

SIR TOBY	Booth
added	
ANTONIO	Fearon
VALENTINE	Thompson
CAPTAIN	Mahon
FABIAN	Stevens

1784 DRURY LANE

May 3

SIR ANDREW	Dodd
SIR TOBY	[J.] Palmer
ORSINO	Brereton
SEBASTIAN	[J.] Bannister
FABIAN	R. Palmer
ANTONIO	Wrighten
CLOWN	Parsons
MALVOLIO	Bensley
VIOLA	Mrs Bulkley
MARIA	Mrs Brereton
OLIVIA	Miss Phillips

1785 DRURY LANE

Nov. 11, 16, 23, 28; Dec. 6, 16

SIR ANDREW	Dodd
SIR TOBY	[J.] Palmer
ORSINO	Staunton
SEBASTIAN	[J.] Bannister
FABIAN	R. Palmer
ANTONIO	Wrighten
CLOWN	Suett
MALVOLIO	Bensley
VIOLA	Mrs Jordan
MARIA	Mrs Brereton
OLIVIA	Mrs Crouch

TWELFTH NIGHT

1786 DRURY LANE
Jan. 3. No parts assigned

[See p. 81. From a review of this performance in MC, Jan. 5, it appears that the cast was probably the same, at least as regards the principal characters, as that of the following performances.]

Mar. 6; Apr. 17; May 1

SIR ANDREW	Dodd
SIR TOBY	[J.] Palmer
ORSINO	Staunton
SEBASTIAN	[J.] Bannister
FABIAN	R. Palmer
ANTONIO (2)	Wrighten
CLOWN (1)	Suett
MALVOLIO	Bensley
VIOLA	Mrs Jordan
MARIA (1)	Mrs Brereton
OLIVIA	Mrs Crouch

(1) *May 9*

CLOWN	Williames
MARIA	Miss Collins

[PA retains Mrs Brereton as MARIA.]

(2) *Oct. 21; Nov. 23*

ANTONIO	Phillimore

1787 DRURY LANE
Jan. 16

SIR ANDREW	Dodd
SIR TOBY	[J.] Palmer
ORSINO (1)	Whitfield
SEBASTIAN	[J.] Bannister
FABIAN	R. Palmer
ANTONIO	Phillimore
CLOWN	Suett
MALVOLIO	Bensley
VIOLA (1)	Mrs Jordan
MARIA	Mrs Brereton
OLIVIA	Mrs Crouch

(1) *May 9*

ORSINO	Staunton
VIOLA added	Mrs T. Kennedy
VALENTINE	[J.] Wilson
CAPTAIN	Chaplin

1788 DRURY LANE
Apr. 8

SIR ANDREW	Dodd
SIR TOBY (1)	Moody
ORSINO	Whitfield
SEBASTIAN	Lamash
FABIAN	R. Palmer
ANTONIO	Phillimore
CLOWN	Suett
MALVOLIO	Bensley
VIOLA	Mrs Jordan
MARIA (1)	Mrs [J.] Kemble
OLIVIA	Mrs Crouch

(1) *Apr. 25; May 27; Oct. 4, 18, 24*

SIR TOBY	[J.] Palmer
MARIA	Miss Collins (on *Oct. 18, 24* only)

TWELFTH NIGHT

1789 DRURY LANE
Mar. 19; May 21

SIR ANDREW	Dodd
SIR TOBY (1)	Moody
ORSINO	Whitfield
SEBASTIAN	Lamash
FABIAN	R. Palmer
ANTONIO	Phillimore
CLOWN	Suett
MALVOLIO	Kemble
OLIVIA	Mrs Crouch
MARIA	Mrs [J.] Kemble
VIOLA (1)	Mrs Jordan

(1) *May 13*

SIR TOBY	[J.] Palmer
VIOLA	Mrs Goodall

1790 DRURY LANE
Feb. 10

ORSINO (1, 3)	Whitfield
SEBASTIAN (1)	Bland [first appearance in London]
ANTONIO	Phillimore
CURIO	Lyons
SIR TOBY (3)	Moody
SIR ANDREW	Dodd
CAPTAIN	Benson
FABIAN	R. Palmer
MALVOLIO	Bensley
CLOWN	Suett
OLIVIA (3)	Mrs Crouch
VIOLA (4)	Mrs Jordan
MARIA (3)	Mrs [J.] Kemble

(1) *Apr. 9, 21*

ORSINO	Barrymore
SEBASTIAN	Whitfield

(2) *Apr. 26.* No parts assigned
[Both Pb and PA give *The Rivals* for this night. See p. 90.]

(3) *Nov. 3*

ORSINO	Barrymore
SIR TOBY	[J.] Palmer
OLIVIA	Mrs Powell
MARIA	Miss Collins

(4) *Dec. 8*

VIOLA	Mrs Goodall

[Both Pb and PA give *Better Late than Never* for this night. See p. 90. Kemble Mem. has, 'Mrs. Jordan being ill, Mrs. Goodall acted Viola'. It is probable that the four characters listed under *Nov. 3* were similarly performed on *Dec. 8*.]

1791 DRURY LANE
Jan. 27

ORSINO	Barrymore
SEBASTIAN	Bland
ANTONIO (1, 2)	Benson
CURIO (1)	Lyons
SIR TOBY	[J.] Palmer
SIR ANDREW	Dodd
CAPTAIN (1, 2)	Haymes
FABIAN	R. Palmer

(1) *Feb. 16, 25*

ANTONIO	Phillimore
CAPTAIN	Benson
MARIA	Miss Collins

omitted on *Feb. 16* only
CURIO

(2) *Nov. 4* (company at KING'S, HAYMARKET)

ANTONIO	Phillimore
CAPTAIN	Benson

668

TWELFTH NIGHT

1791 DRURY LANE (cont.)

Jan. 27 (cont.)

MALVOLIO	Bensley
CLOWN	Suett
OLIVIA	Mrs Powell
VIOLA	Mrs Jordan
MARIA (1)	Mrs [J.] Kemble

(2) Nov. 4 (company at KING'S, HAYMARKET) (cont.)

added

VALENTINE	Caulfield
PRIEST	Maddocks

1792 DRURY LANE (company at KING'S, HAYMARKET)

Feb. 20

ORSINO	Barrymore
SEBASTIAN	Bland
ANTONIO	Phillimore
VALENTINE	Caulfield
CURIO	Lyons
SIR TOBY	[J.] Palmer
SIR ANDREW	Dodd
CAPTAIN	Benson
FABIAN	R. Palmer
MALVOLIO	Bensley
CLOWN	Suett
PRIEST (1)	Maddocks
OLIVIA	Mrs Powell
VIOLA	Mrs Jordan
MARIA (2)	Mrs [J.] Kemble

(1) May 1

omitted
PRIEST

(2) May 31

MARIA	Miss Tidswell

[JPK omits MALVOLIO; the assignment is taken from a BM bill. PA does not advertise the play.]

1793 DRURY LANE (company at KING'S, HAYMARKET)

May 24

ORSINO	Barrymore
SEBASTIAN	Bland
ANTONIO	Benson
VALENTINE	Caulfield
CURIO	Lyons
SIR TOBY	Moody
SIR ANDREW	Dodd
CAPTAIN	Caulfield
FABIAN	R. Palmer
MALVOLIO	Bensley
CLOWN	Suett
OLIVIA	Mrs Powell
VIOLA	Mrs Jordan
MARIA	Mrs [J.] Kemble

[The assignment of Caulfield to the CAPTAIN appears to be a misprint. Doubling this part with that of VALENTINE is not likely. On May 22 PA (which does not advertise the play on May 24) assigns the CAPTAIN to Benson, and ANTONIO to Phillimore.]

TWELFTH NIGHT

1794 DRURY LANE
Nov. 14

ORSINO	Barrymore
SEBASTIAN	Bland
ANTONIO	Phillimore
VALENTINE	Caulfield
SIR TOBY	Moody
SIR ANDREW	Dodd
CAPTAIN	Benson
FABIAN	C. Kemble
MALVOLIO	Bensley
CLOWN	Suett
OLIVIA	Mrs Powell
VIOLA	Mrs Jordan
MARIA	Mrs [J.] Kemble

1795 DRURY LANE
Apr. 22

ORSINO	Barrymore
SEBASTIAN (2)	Bland
ANTONIO	Phillimore
VALENTINE (1)	Caulfield
SIR TOBY	[J.] Palmer
SIR ANDREW	Dodd
CAPTAIN	Benson
FABIAN (2)	R. Palmer
MALVOLIO	Bensley
CLOWN	Suett
OLIVIA (2)	Mrs Powell
VIOLA	Mrs Jordan
MARIA (1)	Mrs [J.] Kemble

(1) *May 30*

MARIA	Miss Collins
omitted	
VALENTINE	

(2) *Nov. 19*

SEBASTIAN	Trueman
FABIAN	C. Kemble
OLIVIA	Miss DeCamp
added	
CURIO	[J.] Cooke
PRIEST	Maddocks

1796 DRURY LANE
Jan. 12

ORSINO	Barrymore
SEBASTIAN	Trueman
ANTONIO	Phillimore
VALENTINE	Caulfield
CURIO	[J.] Cooke
SIR TOBY	[J.] Palmer
SIR ANDREW	Dodd
CAPTAIN	Benson
FABIAN	R. Palmer
MALVOLIO	Bensley
CLOWN	Suett
OLIVIA	Miss DeCamp
VIOLA	Mrs Jordan
MARIA	Miss Mellon

670

1797 DRURY LANE
May 17

ORSINO	Barrymore
SEBASTIAN	Trueman
VALENTINE	Caulfield
SIR TOBY	[J.] Palmer
SIR ANDREW	Suett
CAPTAIN	Holland
FABIAN	R. Palmer
MALVOLIO	[J.] Bannister
CLOWN	Dowton
OLIVIA	Mrs Crouch
VIOLA	Mrs Jordan
MARIA	Miss Mellon

1798 DRURY LANE
Feb. 13

ORSINO	Barrymore
SEBASTIAN	Trueman
ANTONIO	Caulfield
VALENTINE	Gibbon
CURIO	Wentworth
SIR TOBY	Hollingsworth
SIR ANDREW	Suett
CAPTAIN	Holland
FABIAN	R. Palmer
MALVOLIO	Dowton
CLOWN	Russell
PRIEST	Maddocks
1ST OFFICER	Webb
2ND OFFICER	Evans
OLIVIA	Mrs Crouch
VIOLA	Mrs Jordan
MARIA	Miss Mellon

1799 DRURY LANE
Feb. 23

ORSINO	Barrymore
SEBASTIAN	Trueman
ANTONIO	Caulfield
VALENTINE	Surmont
CURIO	Wentworth
SIR TOBY	Hollingsworth
SIR ANDREW	Suett
CAPTAIN	Holland
FABIAN	R. Palmer
MALVOLIO	Dowton

TWELFTH NIGHT

1799 DRURY LANE (*cont.*)
Feb. 23 (*cont.*)
 CLOWN Russell
 OLIVIA Mrs Crouch
 VIOLA Mrs Jordan
 MARIA Miss Mellon

THE TWINS

Thomas Hull's alteration of THE COMEDY OF ERRORS, q.v.

THE TWO GENTLEMEN OF VERONA

(1) 'With Alterations and Additions [by Benjamin Victor]. As it is performed at the Theatre-Royal in Drury-Lane.'
 1763 J. and R. Tonson.

Act I opens with *Act I. i. 1–100*, followed by four new speeches that summarize the rest of the scene. Then come *I. iii*; *I. ii*; about 25 new lines: Lucetta introduces Proteus to Julia; *II. ii* and *II. vii*.

Act II opens with *Act II. i*, followed by about 30 new lines: Thurio's love for Silvia. Then come *II. iv*; *II. iii. 1–36*; *II. v* and *vi*.

Acts III and IV, except for minor deletions, are verbatim. The last scene of Act IV is *V. i*.

Act V opens with *Act V. ii*. Then come *V. iv. 1–18*; about 40 new lines: Launce is captured by the Outlaws; *V. iii*; *V. iv. 19–148*; about 35 new lines: Launce is released; and *IV. iv. 149–end*.

Throughout there are minor omissions and additions.

See also Genest, v. 8–11; Odell, i. 374–5.

(2) 'Taken from the Manager's Book, at the Theatre Royal, Drury-Lane.'
 n.d. [*c*. 1788] R. Butters.

This is identical with (1). But the revival at CG in 1784 'was not Victor's alteration, but the original play with slight alterations' (Genest, vi. 312). It is equally certain that the revival at DL in 1790 was also the original.

[*as altered by* VICTOR]

1762 DRURY LANE
Dec. 22
 PROTEUS Holland
 VALENTINE Obrien
 DUKE Havard
 THURIO Vernon
 EGLAMOUR Packer
 ANTONIO Burton
 HOST Moody

(1) Dec. 28, 30
 added
  4TH OUTLAW Fox

THE TWO GENTLEMEN OF VERONA [as altered by VICTOR]

1762 DRURY LANE (cont.)
Dec. 22 (cont.)

PANTHINO	Stevens
1ST OUTLAW	Ackman
2ND OUTLAW	Marr
3RD OUTLAW	Watkins
SPEED	King
LAUNCE	Yates
SILVIA	Miss Bride
LUCETTA	Miss Pope
JULIA	Mrs Yates

1763 DRURY LANE
Jan. 4, 6; Feb. 2

PROTEUS	Holland
VALENTINE	Obrien
DUKE	Havard
THURIO	Vernon
EGLAMOUR	Packer
ANTONIO	Burton
PANTHINO	Stevens
1ST OUTLAW	Ackman
2ND OUTLAW	Marr
3RD OUTLAW	Watkins
4TH OUTLAW	Fox
SPEED	King
LAUNCE	Yates
SILVIA	Miss Bride
LUCETTA	Miss Pope
JULIA	Mrs Yates

[*The original*]

1784 COVENT GARDEN
Apr. 13

PROTEUS	Wroughton
VALENTINE	Whitfield
DUKE	Hull
THURIO	Chalmers
ANTONIO	Fearon
PANTHINO	Thompson
HOST	Booth
1ST OUTLAW	Stevens
2ND OUTLAW	[R.] Bates
3RD OUTLAW	Helme
SPEED	Edwin
LAUNCE	Quick

THE TWO GENTLEMEN OF VERONA

1784 COVENT GARDEN (*cont.*)
Apr. 13 (cont.)
    SILVIA   Mrs [S.] Kemble
    LUCETTA   Mrs Chalmers
    JULIA   Mrs Mattocks

[Genest (vi. 312) erroneously assigns LUCETTA to Mrs Wilson.]

1790 DRURY LANE

Jan. 15
    PROTEUS   Wroughton
    VALENTINE   Barrymore
    DUKE   [J.] Aickin
    THURIO   Suett
    EGLAMOUR   Benson
    ANTONIO   Maddocks
    HOST   Fawcett
    PANTHINO (2) Haymes
    SPEED   [J.] Bannister
    LAUNCE   Dodd
    SILVIA   Mrs [J.] Kemble
    LUCETTA (1)   Mrs [J.] Wilson
    JULIA   Mrs Goodall

(1) *Jan. 20*
    LUCETTA   Miss Tidswell
(2) *June 3*
    PANTHINO   Lyons
    added
    1ST OUTLAW Phillimore
    2ND OUTLAW [J.] Burton
    3RD OUTLAW Webb
    4TH OUTLAW Jones

THE WINTER'S TALE

As FLORIZEL AND PERDITA, by MacNamara Morgan. In two acts.

(1) 'The Sheep-Shearing: Or, Florizel and Perdita. As it is acted at the Theatre-Royal in Smock-Alley.'
    1755   Dublin: Peter Wilson. Reprinted 1767.

Act I opens with about 25 new lines: Camillo wishes to return to Leontes and comfort him. This is followed by *Act IV. i*, rewritten into 44 lines of verse; by *IV. iii. 1–35a*; and by about 60 new lines: Perdita wishes that Florizel were of humble birth, and Polixenes and Camillo ask Autolycus to direct them to the sheep-shearing.

Act II begins with *Act IV. iii. 55–79a, 103b–47a, 155–463a*, considerably reduced. The rest of the Act consists of about 125 new lines: the Shepherd proves to be Antigonus, disguised under the name of Alcon; Polixenes forgives Florizel and permits him to marry Perdita.

Perdita has one song, and Autolycus has six (two of them new), composed by Thomas Augustine Arne. The playbills almost invariably announce this version under its second title.

See also Genest, iv. 398–9; Odell, i. 357.

(2) 'The Sheep-Shearing: Or, Florizel and Perdita.'
    1762   J. Truman.
This is identical with (1).

THE WINTER'S TALE

(3) In 'Supplement to Bell's British Theatre ... Vol. I.'
    1784   John Bell.

(4) In 'A Collection of the most Esteemed Farces ... Vol. I.'
    1786   Edinburgh: C. Elliot.

Both of these are identical with (1), except that they omit the 25 new lines at the beginning of Act I.

As altered by David Garick. In three acts.

(5) 'Florizel and Perdita [i.e. The Winter's Tale] A Dramatic Pastoral. ... As it is performed at the Theatre Royal in Drury-Lane.'
    1756   J. and R. Tonson. Reprinted 1758.

Act I opens with about 150 new lines: a recital of the events of the story up to the time of Perdita's womanhood. Then come *Act III. iii. 58–123*; about 75 new lines: the return of Leontes to Bohemia; and *IV. ii.*

Act II opens with *Act IV. iii. 1–332*. Then come about 50 new lines: Leontes enters in disguise; *IV. iii. 356–500a*; and about 75 new lines: Leontes promises to stand advocate for Florizel.

Act III consists of *Act IV. iii. 608–34, 705–end*; *V. ii*; about 25 new lines: Leontes grieves for Hermione; and *V. iii. 4–end*.

Throughout there are minor omissions, and occasional new, brief speeches. In *IV. ii. 1–126* the speeches are assigned to Camillo, Paulina, and a Gentleman.

See also Genest, iv. 446–8; Odell, i. 360–1.

(6) 'Marked with the Variations in the Manager's Book, at the Theatre-Royal in Drury-Lane.'
    1785   C. Bathurst [&c.].

This is identical with (5).

As altered by Thomas Hull. In five acts.

(7) 'As Performed at the Theatre-Royal, Covent-Garden. Regulated from the Prompt-Book.'
    1773   John Bell.

Following are the principal omissions:

Act I. ii. 71b–86a (Polixenes' boyhood), *120b–47a* (Leontes questions Mamillius), *190b–209* ('Sir Smile'), *382b–97a* (Camillo refuses to enlighten Polixenes).

Act III. i. entire (the return of Cleomenes and Dion from Delphos); *ii. 184b–200a* (Paulina upbraids Leontes).

Act IV. Chorus. 30–32, for which are substituted nine new lines; *ii. 15–22* ('But shall I go mourn'); *iii. 289–316* ('Get you hence'), *570b–98a* ('unpath'd waters'), *687–704* (Autolycus's reflections on the change of garments).

Act V. ii. 125b–end (the Shepherd and the Clown as 'gentlemen born'); *iii. 136–end* (Leontes gives Paulina to Camillo, for which are substituted 14 new lines: Leontes and Polixenes praise Hermione's innocence).

Throughout there are minor omissions, and in *IV. iii* a few transpositions of

THE WINTER'S TALE

speeches. In *V. ii* Camillo has the 3rd Gentleman's speeches. 'Bohemia' is changed to 'Bithynia'.

(8) 'As it is Acted at the Theatres-Royal in Drury-Lane and Covent-Garden.'
   1779   Harrison and Co.
   This is identical with (7).

As THE SHEEP SHEARING, by George Colman, the elder. In three acts.

(9) 'As it is performed at the Theatre Royal in the Hay-Market.'
   1777   G. Kearsly.
   Act I consists of *Act III. iii. 58–113a*, followed by about 40 lines from Garrick's I. ii: the return of Leontes to Bohemia, and by *IV. ii*.
   Act II consists of *Act IV. iii. 1–494a*, drastically reduced, and of about 20 lines from Garrick's II. i: Leontes promises to stand advocate for Florizel.
   Act III opens with *Act IV. iii. 687–end*, considerably reduced. Then come about 30 lines from Garrick's III. ii: Camillo tells Paulina of the discovery of Perdita; *V. ii. 127–end*; and about 40 lines from Garrick's III. iv: the reconciliation of Leontes and Perdita.
   Throughout there are minor omissions.
   See also Genest, v. 590.

[as FLORIZEL AND PERDITA]

1754 COVENT GARDEN

Mar. 25

FLORIZEL (1)	Barry
POLIXENES	Ridout
ANTIGONUS (1)	Sparks
CAMILLO	Redman
CLOWN	Stevens
AUTOLYCUS	Shuter
DORCAS	Miss [Esther] Young
MOPSA	Mrs Lampe
PERDITA (1)	Miss Nossiter

(1) *Apr. 24*

FLORIZEL	Smith
ANTIGONUS	Anderson
PERDITA	Mrs Elmy

[In these two bills ANTIGONUS is called ALCON.]

[*The original*]
[*as altered by* GARRICK]

1756 DRURY LANE

Jan. 21, 23, 24, 26, 27, 28, 29, 31;
Feb. 3, 4; Mar. 13, 20

LEONTES	Garrick
POLIXENES	Havard
CAMILLO	Davies
SHEPHERD	Berry

(1) *Apr. 28*

PERDITA	Miss Macklin

[The part is not assigned, but Miss Macklin's name is given in place of Mrs Cibber's.]

THE WINTER'S TALE [as altered by GARRICK]

1756 DRURY LANE (cont.)
Jan. 21, 23, 24, 26, 27, 28, 29, 31; Feb. 3, 4; Mar. 13, 20 (cont.)

CLOWN	Woodward
AUTOLYCUS	Yates
CLEOMENES	Jefferson
FLORIZEL	Holland
GENTLEMAN	Blakes
SERVANT	Beard
ROGERO	Walker
PERDITA (1)	Mrs Cibber
PAULINA	Mrs Bennet
DORCAS	Miss Minors
MOPSA	Mrs Bradshaw
HERMIONE	Mrs Pritchard

[The bill for *Jan. 21* gives neither the parts nor the actors' names. Beginning with *Jan. 23* the bills give the actors' names only, but omit Holland (who is listed on *Jan. 24* and thereafter), Jefferson, Walker, Miss Minors, and Mrs Bradshaw. The above assignment is taken from the printed text.]

1757 DRURY LANE
Mar. 24 (1) *May 24*

LEONTES	Garrick	added	
POLIXENES	Havard	CAMILLO	Davies
FLORIZEL	Holland		
CLOWN	Woodward		
AUTOLYCUS	Yates		
SHEPHERD	Berry		
SERVANT	Beard		
DORCAS	Mrs Vernon		
MOPSA	Miss [I.] Young		
HERMIONE	Mrs Pritchard		
PERDITA	Mrs Cibber		

[In the bill the SERVANT is called COUNTRYMAN, and DORCAS and MOPSA are called COUNTRY LASSES.]

1758 DRURY LANE
Mar. 11; Apr. 26

LEONTES	Garrick
POLIXENES	Havard
FLORIZEL	Holland
CAMILLO	Davies
CLOWN	Woodward
AUTOLYCUS	Yates
SHEPHERD	Berry
PAULINA	Mrs Bennet
HERMIONE	Mrs Pritchard
PERDITA	Miss Pritchard

677

THE WINTER'S TALE
[as FLORIZEL AND PERDITA]

1758 COVENT GARDEN
Mar. 13

FLORIZEL (1)	Barry
POLIXENES	Ridout
ANTIGONUS	Sparks
CAMILLO	Redman
CLOWN	Costollo
AUTOLYCUS	Shuter
DORCAS	Miss Mullart
MOPSA	Miss Helme
PERDITA	Mrs Bellamy

(1) *Mar. 14*

FLORIZEL Smith
[In these two bills ANTIGONUS is called ALCON.]

1759 COVENT GARDEN
Mar. 24, 27; Apr. 7, 24; May 2

FLORIZEL	Smith
AUTOLYCUS	Shuter
POLIXENES	Ridout
ANTIGONUS	Sparks
CLOWN	Costollo
DORCAS	Mrs Abegg
MOPSA	Miss [Esther] Young
PERDITA	Mrs Bellamy

[In the bills ANTIGONUS is called the SHEPHERD, and DORCAS and MOPSA are called SHEPHERDESSES.]

1760 COVENT GARDEN
Dec. 22

FLORIZEL	Mattocks
AUTOLYCUS	Shuter
POLIXENES	Ridout
ANTIGONUS	Sparks
PERDITA	Miss Brent

[Genest (iv. 626) says that 'this piece seems to have been turned into an Opera'. Such was probably the case, but no contemporary corroboration has come to light. In the bill POLIXENES is called the KING, and ANTIGONUS is called the SHEPHERD.]

1761 COVENT GARDEN
Jan. 13

FLORIZEL	Mattocks
AUTOLYCUS	Shuter
POLIXENES (1)	Ridout
ANTIGONUS	Sparks
PERDITA	Miss Brent

(1) *Mar. 24; Apr. 16*

POLIXENES Hull

[Everything in the note under *Dec. 22, 1760* is applicable here.]

THE WINTER'S TALE

[*The original*]

[*as altered by* GARRICK]

1762 DRURY LANE
Jan. 27, 28; Feb. 2, 4, 6; Mar. 29

LEONTES	Garrick
POLIXENES	Havard
CAMILLO	Davies
SHEPHERD	Burton
CLOWN	King
AUTOLYCUS	Yates
GENTLEMAN	Blakes
CLEOMENES	Castle
FLORIZEL	Holland
HERMIONE	Mrs Pritchard
PAULINA	Mrs Bennet
PERDITA	Mrs Cibber

[*as* FLORIZEL AND PERDITA]

COVENT GARDEN
Mar. 20, 23; May 3

FLORIZEL	Mattocks
AUTOLYCUS	Shuter
POLIXENES	Hull
ANTIGONUS	Gibson
PERDITA	Miss Brent

[Everything in the note under *Dec. 22, 1760* is applicable here.]

[*The original*]

[*as altered by* GARRICK]

1765 DRURY LANE
Mar. 26 (1) *Apr. 26*

LEONTES	Powell	HERMIONE	Mrs Hopkins
POLIXENES	Havard	PERDITA	Miss Slack
CAMILLO	Lee	added	
SHEPHERD	Burton	CLEOMENES	Parsons
AUTOLYCUS	Yates	SERVANT	Moody
CLOWN	King	DORCAS	Mrs Hippisley
FLORIZEL	Holland	MOPSA	Mrs Bradshaw
HERMIONE (1)	Mrs Pritchard		
PAULINA	Mrs Bennet		
PERDITA (1)	Mrs Yates		

679

THE WINTER'S TALE

[as FLORIZEL AND PERDITA]

1768 DRURY LANE
Mar. 15

FLORIZEL	Cautherley
POLIXENES	Hurst
ANTIGONUS	[F.] Aickin
CAMILLO	Packer
AUTOLYCUS	King
PERDITA	Mrs Dancer

1769 DRURY LANE
Apr. 7

FLORIZEL	Cautherley
POLIXENES	Hurst
ANTIGONUS	[F.] Aickin
CAMILLO	Strange
CLOWN	Moody
AUTOLYCUS	King
PERDITA	Miss Younge

1771 DRURY LANE
Apr. 9

AUTOLYCUS	King
POLIXENES	Hurst
ANTIGONUS	Inchbald
CAMILLO	Wright
CLOWN	Moody
FLORIZEL	Cautherley
PERDITA	Miss Rogers

[*The original*]
[*as altered by* HULL]

COVENT GARDEN
Apr. 24

LEONTES	Smith
POLIXENES	Bensley
ANTIGONUS	Clarke
FLORIZEL	Wroughton
SHEPHERD	Kniveton
AUTOLYCUS	Du-Bellamy
CLOWN	Quick
CAMILLO	Hull
TIME	Hull

THE WINTER'S TALE [as altered by HULL]

1771 COVENT GARDEN (cont.)

Apr. 24 (cont.)

PAULINA	Mrs Hull
PERDITA	Mrs Bulkley
HERMIONE	Mrs Mattocks

[The bill has, 'As originally written by Shakespeare'. Hull doubled CAMILLO and TIME. In the acting version published by Bell in 1773 the cast is the same as that of this performance, with the following additions:

MAMILLIUS	Miss Cokayne
CLEOMENES	R. Smith
DION	[R.] Bates
ARCHIDAMUS	Holtom
MARINER	[R.] Bates
SERVANT	Fox]

[Bates doubled DION and the MARINER.]

1772 COVENT GARDEN

May 4

LEONTES	Smith
POLIXENES	Bensley
ANTIGONUS	Clarke
FLORIZEL	Wroughton
SHEPHERD	Kniveton
ROGERO	Gardner
CLOWN	Quick
AUTOLYCUS	Du-Bellamy
CAMILLO	Hull
TIME	Hull
PAULINA	Mrs Hull
PERDITA	Mrs Bulkley
HERMIONE	Mrs Mattocks

[Hull doubled CAMILLO and TIME.]

[as FLORIZEL AND PERDITA]

1774 DRURY LANE

Apr. 12

AUTOLYCUS	King
POLIXENES	Hurst
ANTIGONUS	J. Aickin
CAMILLO	Wright
CLOWN	Moody
FLORIZEL (1)	Cautherley
PERDITA (1)	Mrs Canning

(1) *May 7*

FLORIZEL	Dimond
PERDITA	Mrs [T.] Smith

681

THE WINTER'S TALE

[*The original*]

[*as altered by* GARRICK]

1774 COVENT GARDEN

Mar. 12

LEONTES (1)	Smith
POLIXENES	Bensley
FLORIZEL	Lewis
CAMILLO (1)	Hull
AUTOLYCUS	Quick
SHEPHERD (1)	Kniveton
CLOWN	Woodward
PERDITA (1)	Miss Dayes
PAULINA (1)	Mrs P. Green
HERMIONE (1)	Mrs Hartley

(1) *Nov. 19, 21*

LEONTES	Melmoth
SHEPHERD	Clarke
PERDITA	The Lady who performed Indiana [in *The Conscious Lovers*, at this theatre, Oct. 7: Mrs Armstead (MS annotation on JPK)]
HERMIONE omitted	Mrs Melmoth
CAMILLO, PAULINA	

[*as* THE SHEEP SHEARING, *by* COLMAN]

1777 HAYMARKET

July 18

AUTOLYCUS	Edwin
CLOWN	[T.] Jackson
FLORIZEL	Du-Bellamy
SHEPHERD	Massey
LEONTES	Fearon
POLIXENES	Egan
CAMILLO	Griffiths
CLEOMENES	T. Davis
GENTLEMAN	Stevens
SERVANT	[C.] Bannister
PERDITA	Mrs Colles
PAULINA	Mrs Poussin
DORCAS	Miss Hale
MOPSA	Mrs Hitchcock

[The bill gives the actors' names only, but omits Stevens. The above assignment is taken from the printed text, which misspells Davis's name as 'Davies'.]

[*The original*]

[*as altered by* GARRICK]

1779 DRURY LANE

Nov. 20, 23, 26; Dec. 3, 11

LEONTES	Smith
POLIXENES	Bensley
FLORIZEL	Brereton
CAMILLO	[J.] Aickin

(1) *Nov. 29; Dec. 1*

HERMIONE	Miss Farren

THE WINTER'S TALE [*as altered by* GARRICK]

1779 DRURY LANE (*cont.*)

Nov. 20, 23, 26; Dec. 3, 11 (cont.)

SHEPHERD	Packer
AUTOLYCUS	Vernon
CLEOMENES	Hurst
GENTLEMAN	Williames
CLOWN	Yates
PERDITA	Mrs Robinson
PAULINA	Mrs Hopkins
HERMIONE (1)	Mrs Hartley

1780 DRURY LANE

Jan. 1, 11, 22; Feb. 10; Mar. 30; (1) *Oct. 19*
Apr. 12; May 18, 24

		PERDITA	Mrs Brereton
LEONTES	Smith	omitted	
POLIXENES	Bensley	CLEOMENES, GENTLEMAN	
FLORIZEL	Brereton		
CAMILLO	[J.] Aickin		
SHEPHERD	Packer		
AUTOLYCUS	Vernon		
CLEOMENES (1)	Hurst		
GENTLEMAN (1)	Williames		
CLOWN	Yates		
PERDITA (1)	Mrs Robinson		
PAULINA	Mrs Hopkins		
HERMIONE	Miss Farren		

1781 DRURY LANE

Jan. 23, 29

LEONTES	Smith
POLIXENES	Bensley
FLORIZEL	Brereton
CAMILLO	[J.] Aickin
SHEPHERD	Packer
AUTOLYCUS	Vernon
CLOWN	Yates
PERDITA	Mrs Brereton
PAULINA	Mrs Hopkins
HERMIONE	Miss Farren

[In the acting version published by Bathurst in 1785 the cast is the same as that of these performances, with the following additions:

CLEOMENES	Chaplin
GENTLEMAN	Phillimore
DORCAS	Miss Simson
MOPSA	Miss Kirby]

THE WINTER'S TALE [*as altered by* GARRICK]

1783 COVENT GARDEN
May 19   (1) *Oct. 9; Dec. 23*

LEONTES	Henderson	SHEPHERD	Clarke
POLIXENES	[F.] Aickin	PERDITA	Mrs [S.] Kemble [i.e. formerly Miss Satchell] (on *Dec. 23* only)
CAMILLO	Hull		
SHEPHERD (1)	Booth		
CLOWN	Quick	PAULINA	Mrs Bates
CLEOMENES	Fearon	HERMIONE	Mrs Inchbald
AUTOLYCUS	Edwin		
FLORIZEL	Lewis		
PERDITA (1)	Miss Satchell		
PAULINA (1)	Mrs Hunter		
MOPSA	Mrs Martyr		
DORCAS	Mrs Morton		
HERMIONE (1)	Mrs Yates		

[*as* THE SHEEP SHEARING, *by* COLMAN]
HAYMARKET
Aug. 20   (1) *Aug. 27*

POLIXENES	Bensley	added	
FLORIZEL	[J.] Bannister	SERVANT	[C.] Bannister
LEONTES	[J.] Williamson	[In the bill the SERVANT is called COUNTRYMAN.]	
CAMILLO	Usher		
SHEPHERD	Massey		
CLOWN	[R.] Wilson		
AUTOLYCUS	Edwin		
PAULINA	Mrs Poussin		
DORCAS	Miss Hale		
MOPSA	Miss [C.] Morris		
PERDITA	Mrs Bannister		

[*The original*]
[*as altered by* GARRICK]

1784 COVENT GARDEN
May 10

LEONTES	Henderson
POLIXENES	[F.] Aickin
CAMILLO	Hull
SHEPHERD	Clarke
CLEOMENES	Fearon
CLOWN	Quick
AUTOLYCUS	Edwin
FLORIZEL	Lewis
PERDITA	Mrs [S.] Kemble
PAULINA	Mrs Bates

684

THE WINTER'S TALE [as altered by GARRICK]

1784 COVENT GARDEN (cont.)

May 10 (cont.)

MOPSA	Mrs Martyr
DORCAS	Mrs Morton
HERMIONE	Mrs Inchbald

[In the acting version published by Bathurst in 1785 the cast is the same as that of this performance (save that CLEOMENES is assigned to Helme), with the following addition:

GENTLEMAN	Thompson]

1785 DRURY LANE

Apr. 18

LEONTES	Smith
POLIXENES	Bensley
FLORIZEL	[J.] Bannister
CAMILLO	[J.] Aickin
SHEPHERD	Packer
CLOWN	Suett
AUTOLYCUS (2)	Dodd
PERDITA (1, 2)	Miss Bannister
PAULINA	Mrs Hopkins
HERMIONE (1)	Miss Farren

(1) *Nov. 18*

PERDITA	Mrs Crouch
HERMIONE	Mrs Ward

(2) *Dec. 29*

AUTOLYCUS	?
PERDITA	Mrs Crouch

[Both Pb and PA retain Dodd as AUTOLYCUS. In the JPK bill his name is deleted, but the substitute name has been cut by the binder.]

COVENT GARDEN

May 7

LEONTES	Henderson
POLIXENES	[F.] Aickin
CAMILLO	Hull
SHEPHERD	Clarke
CLOWN	[R.] Wilson
CLEOMENES	Fearon
AUTOLYCUS	Edwin
FLORIZEL	Lewis
PERDITA	Mrs Bannister
PAULINA	Mrs Bates
MOPSA	Mrs Martyr
DORCAS	Mrs Morton
HERMIONE	Mrs Inchbald

1786 DRURY LANE

Oct. 24

LEONTES	Smith
POLIXENES	Bensley
FLORIZEL	[J.] Bannister
CAMILLO	[J.] Aickin
SHEPHERD	Packer

685

THE WINTER'S TALE [as altered by GARRICK]

1786 DRURY LANE (cont.)
Oct. 24 (cont.)
- CLOWN — Suett
- AUTOLYCUS — Dodd
- PERDITA — Mrs Crouch
- PAULINA — Mrs Hopkins
- HERMIONE — Miss Farren

1787 DRURY LANE
Jan. 15
- LEONTES — Smith
- POLIXENES — Bensley
- FLORIZEL — Barrymore
- CAMILLO — [J.] Aickin
- SHEPHERD — Packer
- CLOWN — Suett
- AUTOLYCUS — Dodd
- PERDITA — Mrs Crouch
- PAULINA — Mrs Hopkins
- HERMIONE — Miss Farren

(1) *May 3*. No parts assigned [See p. 83.]

COVENT GARDEN
May 21
- LEONTES — Pope
- POLIXENES — [F.] Aickin
- CAMILLO — Hull
- CLOWN — Quick
- AUTOLYCUS — Edwin
- SHEPHERD — Booth
- NICHOLAS — Darley
- FLORIZEL — Holman
- PERDITA — Miss Brunton
- PAULINA — Mrs Morton
- DORCAS — Miss Stuart
- HERMIONE — Mrs Pope

1788 DRURY LANE
May 1
- LEONTES — Wroughton
- POLIXENES — Bensley
- FLORIZEL — Barrymore
- CAMILLO — [J.] Aickin
- SHEPHERD — Packer
- CLOWN (2) — Suett
- ROGERO — Williames
- AUTOLYCUS (2) — Dodd

(1) *June 11; Sept. 16*
- PERDITA — Mrs [J.] Kemble
- HERMIONE — Mrs Ward

(2) *Dec. 12*
- CLOWN — Hollingsworth
- AUTOLYCUS — Suett
- PERDITA — Mrs [J.] Kemble
- HERMIONE — Mrs Ward

THE WINTER'S TALE [as altered by GARRICK]

1788 DRURY LANE (cont.)
May 1 (cont.)
PERDITA (1, 2)	Mrs Crouch
PAULINA	Mrs Hopkins
HERMIONE (1, 2)	Miss Farren

COVENT GARDEN
Apr. 11; May 3
FLORIZEL	Mrs Martyr
POLIXENES	[F.] Aickin
CAMILLO	Hull
CLOWN	Quick
AUTOLYCUS	Edwin
SHEPHERD	Booth
NICHOLAS	Darley
LEONTES	Pope
PERDITA	Miss Brunton
PAULINA	Mrs Morton
DORCAS	Miss Stuart
HERMIONE	Mrs Wells

1789 DRURY LANE
June 9
LEONTES	Wroughton
POLIXENES	Williams
FLORIZEL	Barrymore
CAMILLO	[J.] Aickin
SHEPHERD	Packer
CLOWN	Suett
ROGERO	Benson
CLEOMENES	Chaplin
SERVANT	Fawcett
AUTOLYCUS	Dodd
PERDITA	Miss Heard
PAULINA	Mrs Hopkins
MOPSA	Miss Barnes
DORCAS	Miss Cranford
HERMIONE	Mrs Ward

[In the bill the SERVANT is called COUNTRYMAN.]

COVENT GARDEN
May 22
LEONTES	Pope
POLIXENES	[F.] Aickin
CAMILLO	Hull
CLOWN	Bernard

THE WINTER'S TALE [as altered by GARRICK]

1789 COVENT GARDEN (cont.)
May 22 (cont.)
AUTOLYCUS	Edwin
FLORIZEL	Middleton
PERDITA	Miss Brunton
PAULINA	Mrs Bernard
DORCAS	Miss Stuart
MOPSA	Miss Rowson
HERMIONE	Mrs Wells

[as FLORIZEL AND PERDITA]
1790 COVENT GARDEN
Feb. 11
FLORIZEL	Holman
POLIXENES	[F.] Aickin
ANTIGONUS	Hull
CAMILLO	Powel
CLOWN	Cubitt
AUTOLYCUS (1, 2)	King
DORCAS (2)	Miss Rowson
MOPSA	Mrs Byrne
PERDITA	Miss Brunton

(1) *May 28*
AUTOLYCUS	Blanchard

(2) *Nov. 27*
AUTOLYCUS	Blanchard
DORCAS	Mrs Lloyd

[The original]
[as altered by GARRICK]
1792 COVENT GARDEN
May 11
FLORIZEL	Holman
POLIXENES	[F.] Aickin
CAMILLO	Hull
CLEOMENES	Powel
CLOWN	Quick
AUTOLYCUS	Munden
LEONTES	Harley
PERDITA	Mrs Mountain
PAULINA	Mrs Fawcett
DORCAS	Miss Stuart
MOPSA	Mrs Harlowe
HERMIONE	Mrs Pope

1795 COVENT GARDEN
Dec. 22
FLORIZEL	Holman
POLIXENES	Harley

THE WINTER'S TALE [as altered by GARRICK]

1795 COVENT GARDEN (cont.)
Dec. 22 (cont.)

CAMILLO	Davenport
CLEOMENES	Richardson
CLOWN	Quick
AUTOLYCUS	Munden
LEONTES	Pope
PERDITA	Miss Wallis
PAULINA	Mrs Fawcett
DORCAS	Mrs Mountain
MOPSA	Mrs Castelle
HERMIONE	Mrs Pope

[as FLORIZEL AND PERDITA]

1798 COVENT GARDEN
May 12

FLORIZEL	Holman
POLIXENES	Murray
ANTIGONUS	Hull
CAMILLO	Powel
CLOWN	Simmons
AUTOLYCUS	Munden
DORCAS	Mrs Mountain
MOPSA	Mrs Castelle
PERDITA	Miss Murray [first appearance in London]

APPENDIX A
SOURCES

THE first of the two principal sources of which I have availed myself is the great collection of playbills of Drury Lane and Covent Garden theatres formed by John Philip Kemble.[1] The run of Kemble's Drury Lane bills begins with the season of 1751–2, but is occasionally interrupted: the seasons of 1756–7 and 1757–8 are entirely missing, and, *passim*, so are some fifty individual bills.[2] His collections for Covent Garden[1] do not begin until the season of 1758–9; except for the absence of some thirty scattered bills, they are complete. The Kemble bills contain nothing relating to the third Theatre Royal, the Haymarket. Here I have made use of the Beaufoy collection,[3] now at Harvard.

But eighteenth-century playbills do not always give the full complement of parts and actors. In general the reasons for this are two: the occasional printing of the names of the leading actors in such large type that no room remained for the names of the inferior actors, and the descriptions of dances, of pantomimes and other after-pieces that sometimes occupied well over half the playbill. As a consequence the information supplied by the newspaper advertisements of the theatres is of the highest importance. This is, therefore, the second primary source to which I have turned.

The newspaper designated by all the theatres as their official instrument for publishing the correct bill of the play was *The Public Advertiser*, which until December 1, 1752 had been called *The General Advertiser*, and still earlier *The London Daily Post*. The small, more compact print of a newspaper clearly gave room for an almost complete listing of names, and on innumerable occasions the bills inserted in *The Public Advertiser* contain considerably more information than do the actual playhouse bills.[4]

What I have done, in my presentation of the material in Part II, is to make a conflation of these two sources. Usually they are in exact agreement with one another, but not infrequently there are discrepancies of various sorts between them. Noted hereunder are not only all these discrepancies, but also other relevant facts: the occasional unique appearance of bills in newspapers other than *The Public Advertiser*, the whereabouts of bills missing from the Kemble collection, &c. Following the year and the theatre I have listed the actual source or sources. Then come, in alphabetical order, only those plays performed in that year at that theatre whose playhouse bills are not in agreement with *The Public Advertiser* bills, and a record of the discrepancies between them.

To this outline of my sources I have subjoined the sources of the receipts as

[1] See p. ix.
[2] For an account of this collection, and its provenance, see MacMillan, v.
[3] See p. ix.
[4] *The Public Advertiser* was absorbed into another newspaper on Mar. 1, 1794. Thereafter no paper was recognized by the theatres as officially deputed to publish the playbills. I have, however, examined several papers from 1794 to 1800, and from time to time have found information not listed in the playhouse bills. In all instances I have made use of the Burney Collection of newspapers in the British Museum.

APPENDIX A

entered from night to night in the treasurer's account-books at Drury Lane and Covent Garden.

1751 DRURY LANE: GA (Jan. to May); JPK, GA (Sept. to Dec.)
    Merchant *Sept. 10*: JPK missing (no other Pb located).
    Much Ado *Oct. 11; Nov. 1, 27*: Pb omits Dogberry (on Oct. 11 only), Antonio, Friar, Borachio, Verges, Conrade, Town Clerk, Sexton (throughout).
    R & J *Oct. 19; Nov. 18*: Pb also omits Escalus, Paris, Benvolio, Lady Capulet.

    COVENT GARDEN: GA
    J. Caesar *May 1*: Pb is in BPL (Theatre Collection, G. 50. 30).

    HAYMARKET: DA

    NEW WELLS, GOODMAN'S FIELDS: GA

    BOWLING GREEN, SOUTHWARK: GA

1752 DRURY LANE: JPK (for entire year); GA (Jan. to Nov.); PA (Dec.)
    AYLI *Apr. 21*: GA omits Corin.
    Hamlet *Apr. 7*: Pb omits Lucianus, Rosencrantz, Guildenstern, Bernardo, Player King, Player Queen.
    Hen. VIII *Apr. 10*: Pb omits Norfolk, Suffolk, Lord Chamberlain, Cromwell, Patience. *Apr. 29*: Pb also omits Norfolk.
    Lear *Apr. 6*: GA omits Doctor.
    Macbeth *Jan. 29; Dec. 4*: Pb omits Angus, Lennox, Siward, Donalbain.
    Much Ado *Jan. 8; Oct. 19; Nov. 13*: Pb omits Antonio, Borachio, Verges (on Jan. 8 only), Friar, Conrade, Town Clerk, Sexton (throughout).
    Othello *Apr. 14*: Pb omits Montano, Gratiano.
    Rich. III *Jan. 15*: Pb omits Stanley, Tressel, Catesby, Lieutenant.
    Twelfth N. *Jan. 22*: GA omits Captain.

    COVENT GARDEN: GA (Jan. to Nov.); PA (Dec.)
    Hamlet *Apr. 10*: Pb is in Harris.
    Lear *Oct. 16*: Pb is in Harris.

    NEW WELLS, GOODMAN'S FIELDS: GA

1753 DRURY LANE: JPK, PA
    Hamlet *May 1*: Pb omits Rosencrantz, Guildenstern, Player King, Player Queen.
    Hen. VIII *Feb. 5*: Pb omits Norfolk, Surrey, Sands. *May 2*: Pb omits Sands, Gardiner, Cromwell. *Oct. 6, 11*: Pb omits Sands, Suffolk, Surveyor, Cromwell.
    Lear *Nov. 22*: Pb omits Albany, Cornwall, Gentleman Usher, Burgundy.
    Macbeth *Nov. 13*: Pb also omits Angus, Lennox, Siward, Donalbain.
    Merchant *Jan. 11*: Pb omits Morocco, Salarino, Solanio, Gobbo, Tubal, Balthazar, Duke.
    MWW *May 18*: Pb omits Rugby; PA omits Robin.
    Much Ado *Jan. 4*: PA missing from BM file (another copy not located). *Jan. 17*: Pb omits all characters except Benedick, Beatrice. *Mar. 26*: PA omits Don John, Dogberry. *Nov. 21*: Pb omits Friar, Conrade, Margaret, Ursula.

APPENDIX A

1753 DRURY LANE (*cont.*)

Rich. III *Jan. 18*: Pb omits Tressel, Stanley, Catesby, Lieutenant, Duchess of York.
R&J *May 8*: Pb omits Escalus, Paris, Benvolio. *Oct. 19*: Pb omits Escalus, Benvolio, Lady Capulet.
Twelfth N. *Jan. 8*: Pb omits Antonio, Fabian, Captain, Maria.

COVENT GARDEN: PA

AYLI *Oct. 22*: Pb is in FSL.
Hamlet *Apr. 2*: Pb is in Harris.
Merchant *Jan. 4*: PA missing from BM file (another copy not located). *Apr. 23*: Pb is in HTC.
Othello *Apr. 5*: Pb is in Harris. *Oct. 27*: Pb is in FSL.
R&J *May 26*: Pb is in Harris. *Oct. 10*: Pb is in GEC. *Oct. 11, 12, 15, 23*: Pbs are in FSL. *Nov. 24*: Pb is in HTC; it omits Escalus, Benvolio, Paris, Gregory, Sampson, Abraham, Balthazar, Lady Capulet. *Dec. 3, 18*: Pbs are in HTC.

PHILLIPS'S BOOTH, BOWLING GREEN, SOUTHWARK: DA

1754 DRURY LANE: JPK, PA

Coriolanus *Nov. 18, 20, 23, 27, 29*: Pb omits Senator, Aedile, Roman, Lieutenant (throughout), Servants (on Nov. 23, 27, 29 only).
Hen. VIII *May 9*: PA also omits Sands. *Oct. 10*: JPK missing (no other Pb located). *Nov. 1*: Pb omits Sands, Cromwell, Suffolk.
Humourists *July 2*: JPK missing (no other Pb located). This was an extra performance, for Cibber's BT. The season this year had officially closed on May 30.
John *Jan. 31*: Pb omits Prince Henry, Essex, Citizen of Angers, English Herald, R. Falconbridge, Gurney, Austria, Chatillon, French Herald, Lady Falconbridge.
Macbeth *Sept. 24*: JPK missing (no other Pb located).
MWW *Feb. 20*: Pb omits Page, Rugby, Host, Fenton, Mrs Page.
Much Ado *Jan. 12*: Pb omits Dogberry, Antonio, Verges, Borachio. *Nov. 22; Dec. 11*: Pb omits Conrade, Friar, Town Clerk, Sexton.
Rich. III *Jan. 9*: Pb omits Stanley, Tressel, Catesby, Lieutenant.
Twelfth N. *Jan. 24*: PA omits Fabian.

COVENT GARDEN: PA

Coriolanus *Dec. 10, 18*: Pbs are in HTC.
F&P *Mar. 25*: Pb is in HTC. *Apr. 24*: Pb is in GEC.
Hamlet *Mar. 5; Nov. 2*: Pbs are in FSL. *Oct. 24*: Pb is in HTC.
Hen. V *May 8*: Pb is in FSL.
J. Caesar *Mar. 9, 12*: Pbs are in HTC. *Mar. 16*: Pb is in FSL.
MWW *May 7*: Pb is in FSL.
Othello *Jan. 8*: Pb is in Garrick Club. *Apr. 1; Oct. 18*: Pbs are in HTC. *Oct. 19, 21; Nov. 15*: Pbs are in FSL. *Dec. 5*: Pb is in Dyce (3788. 2. K. 21).
Rich. III *Sept. 20; Oct. 26*: Pbs are in FSL.
R&J *Jan. 5; Dec. 26*: Pbs are in FSL. *Apr. 15*: Pb is in BM (1763. a. 5). *May 22*: Pb is in HTC; it omits Escalus, Benvolio, Paris, Gregory, Sampson, Abraham, Balthazar, Lady Capulet. *Nov. 20*: Pb is in HTC.

PHILLIPS'S BOOTH, BOWLING GREEN, SOUTHWARK: DA

692

APPENDIX A

1755 DRURY LANE: JPK, PA
>AYLI *Feb. 18*: Pb omits LeBeau, William, Charles, Audrey.
>Coriolanus *Apr. 22*: Pb omits Lartius, Senator, Aedile, Roman, Lieutenant, Servants.
>Hamlet *Oct. 4*: Pb omits Bernardo.
>Much Ado *Jan. 9, 24; Apr. 12*: Pb omits Conrade, Friar, Town Clerk, Sexton. *Nov. 15*: Pb also omits Antonio, Verges.

>COVENT GARDEN: PA
>>Hamlet *Jan. 16*: Pb is in HTC. *Mar. 3*: Pb is in BM (1763. a. 5). *Apr. 4*: Pb is in Dyce (10, 731. 23. L. 39). *Apr. 25*: Pb is in FSL.
>>1 Hen. IV *Apr. 12; May 3*: Pbs are in FSL. *Oct. 14; Nov. 6*: Pbs are in GEC.
>>Hen. V *Feb. 18*: Pb is in FSL.
>>Macbeth *Nov. 17; Dec. 26*: Pbs are in GEC. *Dec. 8*: Pb is in HTC.
>>Merchant *Dec. 2*: Pb is in HTC.
>>MWW *Dec. 17*: Pb is in GEC.
>>Othello *May 8*: Pb is in FSL.
>>Rich. III *Apr. 17*: Pb is in BM (1763. a. 5).
>>R&J *Apr. 11*: Pb is in BM; it omits Escalus, Benvolio, Paris, Gregory, Sampson, Abraham, Balthazar, Lady Capulet. *May 14*: Pb is in FSL. *Oct. 20, 29; Dec. 30*: Pbs are in GEC. *Dec. 27*: Pb is in HTC.

>HAYMARKET: PA

>BOWLING GREEN, SOUTHWARK: DA
>>Hamlet *Jan. 20*: Bill in PA, not in DA.
>>R&J *Jan. 16*: Bill in DA, Jan. 15.

1756 DRURY LANE: JPK, PA (Jan. to May); PA (Sept. to Dec.)
>Hamlet *Nov. 3; Dec. 13*: Pbs are in HTC.
>Hen. VIII *Jan. 6*: Pb omits Gardiner, Cromwell. *Sept. 25*: Pb is in HTC; it omits Surveyor, Lovell, Guildford, Capucius, Butts, Brandon, Campeius, Old Lady.
>Lear *Oct. 28, 30*: Pbs are in HTC.
>Measure *Dec. 30*: Pb is in HTC; it omits Elbow, Barnardine, Abhorson, Friar Peter.
>Much Ado *Oct. 19; Dec. 4*: Pbs are in HTC.
>Rich. III *Oct. 22*: Pb is in HTC.
>R&J *Apr. 1*: Pb omits all characters except Romeo, Friar Laurence, Mercutio, Juliet. *Oct. 9*: Pb is in Dyce (7556-192). *Oct. 12, 20; Nov. 16*: Pbs are in HTC. *Oct. 15*: Pb is in FSL. *Oct. 26*: Pb is in Garrick Club.

>COVENT GARDEN: PA
>>AYLI *Nov. 22*: Pb is in Harris.
>>Hamlet *Mar. 8*: Pb is in HTC. *Apr. 5*: Pb is in GEC.
>>1 Hen. IV *Jan. 5; May 10*: Pbs are in GEC. *Oct. 8*: Pb is in Garrick Club.
>>Hen. V *May 7*: Pb is in GEC.
>>Lear *Feb. 26; Mar. 6, 9, 13*: Pbs are in GEC. *Feb. 28*: Pb is in Garrick Club. *Mar. 2; Oct. 15*: Pbs are in HTC.
>>Macbeth *Oct. 6; Dec. 28*: Pbs are in Harris. *Nov. 10*: Pb is in HTC.
>>Merchant *Dec. 23*: Pb is in HTC.
>>MWW *Feb. 13; May 5*: Pbs are in GEC.

693

APPENDIX A

1756 COVENT GARDEN (*cont.*)

Othello *Mar. 18; Apr. 26*: Pbs are in HTC. *Oct. 11; Nov. 26*: Pbs are in Harris.

R&J *Jan. 1*: Pb is in GEC; PA missing from BM file (another copy not located). *Feb. 14; Mar. 20*: Pbs are in GEC. *Feb. 24; Apr. 21*: Pbs are in FSL. *Dec. 30*: Pb is in Harris.

HAYMARKET: ? See p. 16.

1757 DRURY LANE: PA

C&P *Apr. 18*: Pb is in HTC. *Apr. 21*: Pb is in FSL.
Hamlet *May 3*: Pb is in HTC.
Hen. VIII *Feb. 17*: Pb is in HTC; it omits Sands, Cromwell, Surveyor, Lovell, Guildford, Capucius, Butts, Brandon, Campeius, Old Lady. *Nov. 28*: Pb is in HTC.
Macbeth *Feb. 24*: Pb is in HTC.
Measure *Jan. 19; May 20*: Pbs are in HTC; they omit Elbow, Barnardine, Abhorson, Friar Peter. *Mar. 1*: Pb is in Harris; it omits same as Jan. 19. *Sept. 22*: Pb is in HTC.
Much Ado *Mar. 19; Apr. 23*: Pbs are in HTC; they omit Antonio, Verges.
Rich. III *Jan. 4*: Pb is in Harris.
R&J *Apr. 28*: Pb is in HTC; it omits Escalus, Paris, Benvolio, Montague, Tybalt.
Wint. T. *Mar. 24*: Pb is in HTC; PA omits Polixenes, Florizel, Autolycus, Shepherd.

COVENT GARDEN: PA

Hamlet *Feb. 16*: Pb is in HTC.
Macbeth and C&P *Mar. 26*: Pb is in HTC.
Othello *Jan. 11*: Pb is in FSL.
Rich. III *Feb. 1*: Pb is in Harris. *Feb. 10*: Pb is in HTC.
R&J *Jan. 1*: Pb is in GEC. *Feb. 12*: Pb is in HTC. *May 23*: Pb is in FSL.

1758 DRURY LANE: PA (Jan. to May); JPK, PA (Sept. to Dec.)

Hamlet *Sept. 26*: Pb omits Polonius, Laertes, Osric, Rosencrantz, Guildenstern, Bernardo, Marcellus, Player King, Player Queen.
R&J *Sept. 28, 30; Oct. 6, 13, 28; Dec. 8*: Pb omits Escalus. *Dec. 26*: Pb omits Paris, Benvolio, Escalus, Montague, Lady Capulet.

COVENT GARDEN: PA (Jan. to May); JPK, PA (Sept. to Dec.)

1759 DRURY LANE: JPK, PA

A&C *May 18*: Pb omits Agrippa, Canidius, Alexas, Menas, Dercetas, Officer.
Much Ado *Mar. 27*: Pb omits Friar, Don John, Verges, Borachio.
R&J *Apr. 5; Dec. 26*: Pb omits Escalus, Paris, Benvolio, Montague (throughout), Tybalt, Lady Capulet (on Apr. 5 only). *May 10*: Pb also omits Escalus.

COVENT GARDEN: JPK, PA

Coriolanus *Feb. 3*: Pb omits 5th Citizen.
Hamlet *Apr. 30*: Pb omits Rosencrantz, Guildenstern, Marcellus, Bernardo, Lucianus, Francisco, Player King, Player Queen.

APPENDIX A

1759 COVENT GARDEN (*cont.*)
    1 Hen. IV *May 1*: Pb omits Prince John, Northumberland, Westmorland, Douglas, Blunt, Peto, Gadshill, Francis, Carriers, Bardolph, Sheriff. *Nov. 28*: PA omits Prince John, Sheriff.
    Hen. V *Apr. 25*: Pb also omits Burgundy, Dauphin. *Dec. 28*: Pb also omits Archbishop of Canterbury, Pistol, Chorus.
    MWW *Dec. 29*: Pb omits all characters except Falstaff, Ford, Page, Evans, Shallow, Mrs Quickly, Mrs Ford.
    Rich. III *May 11*: Pb omits Brandon.
    R&J *May 22*: Pb omits Gregory, Sampson, Abraham, Balthazar.

1760 DRURY LANE: JPK, PA
    Hamlet *Apr. 21*: Pb omits Rosencrantz, Guildenstern, Bernardo, Marcellus, Player King, Player Queen.
    1 Hen. IV *Apr. 28*: Pb omits Prince John, Westmorland, Northumberland, Blunt, Poins, Bardolph, Gadshill, Peto.
    Hen. VIII *Apr. 8; May 26*: Pb omits Sands, Cromwell (throughout), Lord Chamberlain, Suffolk (on Apr. 8 only).
    Much Ado *Sept. 30*: PA omits Balthazar. *Dec. 16*: Pb omits Friar, Verges.
    Rich. III *May 1*: Pb omits Stanley, Norfolk, Catesby, Lieutenant.
    R&J *Feb. 7; Mar. 22; Apr. 7*: Pb omits Escalus, Paris, Benvolio, Montague.

  COVENT GARDEN: JPK, PA
    Coriolanus *Apr. 18*: Pb omits 5th Citizen.
    Hamlet *Mar. 18; Dec. 22*: Pb omits Rosencrantz, Guildenstern, Marcellus, Bernardo, Lucianus, Francisco, Player King, Player Queen (throughout), Osric (on Dec. 22 only).
    1 Hen. IV *Jan. 7; Feb. 9; Dec. 5, 19*: Pb omits Northumberland, Douglas, Westmorland, Blunt, Peto, Gadshill, Francis, Bardolph, Carriers, Sheriff (throughout), Prince John (on Dec. 5, 19 only). *Apr. 9; May 16*: PA omits Prince John.
    Hen. V *May 5*: Pb omits Cambridge, Grey, Jamy, Nym.
    John *Dec. 17, 23*: Pb omits Austria, Chatillon.
    MWW *Jan. 11*: Pb omits all characters except Falstaff, Ford, Page, Evans, Shallow, Mrs Quickly, Mrs Ford.
    R&J *Apr. 8, 30; May 20*: Pb omits Escalus, Benvolio, Paris, Gregory, Sampson, Abraham, Balthazar, Lady Capulet. *Nov. 20; Dec. 6*: Pb also omits Escalus, Paris, Lady Capulet.

1761 DRURY LANE: JPK, PA
    Cymbeline *Dec. 3, 5*: Pb omits Kennedy, Scrase, Castle, Fox, Ackman, Mrs Hippisley.
    Hamlet *Mar. 9*: Pb omits Rosencrantz, Guildenstern, Bernardo, Marcellus, Player King, Player Queen.
    Hen. VIII *June 4*: JPK missing (no other Pb located). *Oct. 6, 23; Nov. 2*: Pb omits Lord Chamberlain, Suffolk, Sands, Cromwell.
    John *Apr. 2*: Pb omits Prince Henry, Essex, Citizen of Angers, English Herald, R. Falconbridge, Gurney, Austria, Chatillon, French Herald, Lady Falconbridge.
    Macbeth *Apr. 29; Nov. 12*: Pb omits Angus, Lennox, Siward (throughout), Donalbain (on Nov. 12 only). *Oct. 31*: PA omits Lady Macduff.
    Much Ado *Feb. 9*: Pb omits Friar, Verges.

APPENDIX A

1761 DRURY LANE (cont.)

Rich. III. *May 29; Sept. 26*: Pb omits Lord Mayor. *Oct. 21*: Pb omits Duchess of York.
R&J *May 5*: Pb omits Lady Capulet.
Tempest *May 8*: Pb also omits Trinculo.

COVENT GARDEN: JPK, PA

Hamlet *Apr. 24*: Pb omits Rosencrantz, Guildenstern, Marcellus, Bernardo, Lucianus, Francisco, Player King, Player Queen.
1 Hen. IV *Jan. 15; Mar. 28*: Pb omits Prince John, Northumberland, Westmorland, Douglas, Blunt, Peto, Gadshill, Francis, Carriers, Bardolph, Sheriff.
2 Hen. IV *Dec. 11, 12, 14, 15, 17, 18, 19, 21, 23, 26, 31*: Pb omits Prince Humphrey, Clarence, Coleville, Gower.
Hen. V *Jan. 1; May 22*: Pb omits Scroop, Bishop of Ely, Bedford, Westmorland, Montjoy, Bardolph (throughout), Dauphin, Hostess (on Jan. 1 only). *Nov. 13, 14, 16*: Pb also omits Hostess.
Merchant *Mar. 12; Apr. 4; May 4; Sept. 21*: Pb omits Salarino, Solanio, Gobbo, Tubal.
MWW *Feb. 12*: Pb omits Pistol, Nym, Bardolph, Host.
Othello *June 23*: JPK missing (no other Pb located). This was an extra performance, for Cooke's BT. The season this year had officially closed on May 25.
Rich. III *May 21; Dec. 28*: Pb omits Norfolk, Stanley, Lieutenant, Ratcliff, Lord Mayor, Catesby, Oxford.
R&J *Jan. 13*: Pb omits Escalus, Lady Capulet. *Apr. 10*: PA also omits Peter, Apothecary. *May 20*: Pb also omits Paris, Lady Capulet. *Oct. 28*: Pb also omits Montague, Paris.

1762 DRURY LANE: JPK, PA

All's Well *Oct. 23*: Pb omits Lords. *Nov. 25*: Pb omits Lords, Gentleman, Widow.
Cymbeline *Jan. 6, 12; Feb. 8, 25*: Pb omits Kennedy, Scrase, Castle, Fox, Ackman, Mrs Hippisley. *Dec. 8*: Pb omits French Gentleman, Philario, Lucius, Queen.
1 Hen. IV *Apr. 30*: PA omits Sheriff. *Sept. 25*: Pb omits Francis; PA omits 2nd Carrier.
2 Hen. IV *Nov. 5*: Pb also omits Hastings, Lord Bardolph, Mowbray, Gower, Coleville, Fang, Servant. *Nov. 11, 15; Dec. 3*: Pb also omits Prince Humphrey, Clarence, Hastings, Lord Bardolph, Mowbray, Gower, Coleville, Bardolph, Feeble, Mouldy, Bullcalf, Davy, Fang, Falstaff's Page.
Lear *Nov. 19*: Pb omits Burgundy.
Much Ado *Jan. 5*: Pb omits Friar, Verges.
R&J *Oct. 27; Dec. 4*: Pb omits Tybalt, Lady Capulet, Nurse.
Tempest *Mar. 1; Apr. 12*: Pb omits Boatswain.
TGV *Dec. 28, 30*: PA omits Host.
Wint. T. *Feb. 2, 4, 6; Mar. 29*: Pb omits Gentleman, Cleomenes (throughout), Paulina (on Mar. 29 only).

COVENT GARDEN: JPK, PA

All's Well *Dec. 2, 6*: Pb omits Lords, Soldier, Widow.
AYLI *Nov. 3*: Pb omits Duke Frederick, Silvius, Charles, Corin, William, LeBeau, Dennis, Jaques de Bois.

APPENDIX A

1762 COVENT GARDEN (*cont.*)

Hamlet *May 7*: Pb omits Lucianus, Francisco, Player King, Player Queen.

1 Hen. IV *May 4*: Pb omits all characters except Falstaff, Henry, Prince of Wales, Worcester, Hotspur, Hostess, Lady Percy.

2 Hen. IV *Jan. 4, 9*: Pb omits Prince Humphrey, Clarence, Colevile, Gower (throughout), Mowbray, Hastings, Lord Bardolph, Westmorland, Poins, Bardolph, Silence, Mouldy, Feeble, Bullcalf (on Jan. 9 only). *Jan. 18, 21, 26; Feb. 10, 27; Mar. 11, 18; May 24*: Pb omits Prince Humphrey, Clarence, Mowbray, Lord Bardolph, Colevile, Gower, Poins, Bardolph, Silence, Mouldy, Feeble, Bullcalf. *Oct. 23; Dec. 31*: Pb also omits Prince Humphrey, Mowbray, Lord Bardolph, Hastings, Poins, Bardolph, Silence, Mouldy, Feeble, Bullcalf (throughout), Westmorland (on Oct. 23 only).

Hen. V *Oct. 16*: Pb omits French Soldier, Montjoy; PA omits Macmorris, Jamy, Bardolph.

John *Jan. 6*: Pb omits Prince Henry, Salisbury, Pembroke, Essex, Chatillon, Austria.

MWW *Jan. 7*: Pb omits Nym, Bardolph. *Apr. 3*: Pb omits all characters except Falstaff, Ford, Page, Evans, Shallow, Mrs Quickly, Mrs Ford. *May 8*: Pb omits Fenton, Rugby, Nym, Bardolph, Simple, Robin. *Nov. 18*: Pb also omits Fenton, Pistol, Host, Simple.

Rich. III *Jan. 5, 8, 11, 14, 16, 19, 23; Feb. 8, 20; Mar. 6, 16*: Pb omits Norfolk, Stanley, Lieutenant, Ratcliff, Catesby, Lord Mayor, Oxford, Blunt, Tyrrel. *May 10, 18*: Pb also omits Norfolk, Lieutenant. *Nov. 26*: Pb also omits Tyrrel.

R&J *Feb. 25; Apr. 22*: Pb omits Montague, Paris. *Mar. 13*: Pb omits Montague. *Sept. 22*: JPK missing (no other Pb located).

1763 DRURY LANE: JPK, PA

Cymbeline *Jan. 15; Apr. 6, 28*: Pb omits French Gentleman, Lucius (throughout), Philario (on Apr. 6, 28 only), Queen (on Apr. 6 only).

Hamlet *Apr. 4, 29*: PA omits Player Queen (throughout), Rosencrantz (on Apr. 29 only).

2 Hen. IV *Jan. 10*: Pb omits Prince Humphrey, Clarence, Hastings, Lord Bardolph, Mowbray, Gower, Colevile, Bardolph, Feeble, Mouldy, Bullcalf, Davy, Fang, Falstaff's Page.

Macbeth *May 2*: Pb omits Angus, Lennox, Siward, Donalbain, Fleance, Doctor.

Much Ado *Mar. 1*: PA omits Ursula.

R&J *Jan. 1*: Pb omits Tybalt, Lady Capulet, Nurse. *Apr. 22*: PA omits Escalus, Benvolio.

Twelfth N. *Oct. 19, 28*: Pb omits Curio, Officers.

TGV *Jan. 4, 6; Feb. 2*: Pb omits Eglamour, Antonio, Panthino, Outlaws.

COVENT GARDEN: JPK, PA

All's Well *Jan. 4; Feb. 5; Mar. 5*: Pb omits Lords, Soldier (throughout), Widow (on Jan. 4, Feb. 5 only). *Apr. 29*: Pb also omits Mariana, Widow.

Hamlet *May 18*: Pb omits Rosencrantz, Guildenstern, Player Queen.

1 Hen. IV *Sept. 26*: Pb omits Prince John, Northumberland, Peto, Gadshill, Bardolph, Sheriff.

MWW *Nov. 10*: Pb omits Pistol, Host, Fenton, Simple.

R&J *May 26; Sept. 21; Dec. 29*: Pb omits Tybalt, Escalus, Benvolio, Paris (throughout), Montague (on Sept. 21, Dec. 29 only).

APPENDIX A

1764 DRURY LANE: JPK, PA

C&P *May 9*: Pb omits Baptista, Biondello.
Fairy T. *Oct. 11; Nov. 14*: Pb has only, 'The Characters as Usual.'
1 Hen. IV *Oct. 17*: Pb omits Messenger, Blunt.
2 Hen. IV *Jan. 18, 21; Feb. 10*: Pb omits Hastings, Mowbray, Feeble, Davy, Shadow, Mouldy; PA omits Falstaff's Page. *Nov. 9; Dec. 21*: Pb also omits Davy, Gower, Lord Bardolph, Mouldy.
MWW *Jan. 4*: PA omits Mrs Page.
Much Ado *Jan. 27; Feb. 7*: Pb omits Friar, Don John, Verges, Borachio, Town Clerk, Sexton, Margaret, Ursula.
Othello *Apr. 14*: Pb omits Messenger.
Twelfth N. *Jan. 6*: Pb omits Curio, Officers.

COVENT GARDEN: JPK, PA

All's Well *May 18*: Pb omits Lords; PA omits Duke.
1 Hen. IV *Jan. 25*: Pb omits all characters except Falstaff, Henry, Prince of Wales, Vernon, Hotspur, Lady Percy.
Hen. V *Feb. 15*: Pb omits Exeter, Westmorland, Gower, Bardolph, Macmorris, Jamy, French Ambassador, Burgundy, Dauphin, Hostess.
Lear *May 7*: Pb omits Albany, Burgundy, Cornwall, Officer, Arante.
Macbeth *May 21*: Pb omits Siward, Fleance.
MWW *Jan. 21*: Pb omits Host, Slender, Anne Page.
Rich. III *May 15*: PA omits Oxford, Forrest. *Oct. 8; Nov. 12*: Pb omits same.
R&J *Apr. 2; May 12*: Pb omits Montague, Apothecary (throughout), Benvolio, Paris, Escalus, Tybalt, Page (on May 12 only).

1765 DRURY LANE: JPK, PA

Fairy T. *Jan. 26, 31*: Pb omits all the actors' names. *Mar. 21*: Pb has only, 'The Characters as Usual.'
1 Hen. IV *May 21*: Pb omits Blunt, Sheriff.
Lear *Feb. 1*: PA omits Cornwall. *Mar. 25; Apr. 17; May 23*: Pb omits Old Man, Arante. *Nov. 23*: Pb also omits Arante.
Macbeth *Apr. 22*: Pb omits Angus, Lennox, Siward, Seyton, Donalbain, Fleance. *Oct. 28*: Pb also omits Seyton.
Othello *Mar. 19; May 10*: Pb omits Messenger (throughout), Montano, Gratiano (on May 10 only).
Wint. T. *Apr. 26*: PA omits Cleomenes, Servant, Dorcas, Mopsa.

COVENT GARDEN: JPK, PA

Hamlet *Nov. 11*: Pb omits Rosencrantz, Guildenstern, Marcellus, Bernardo, Player King, Player Queen.
Lear *May 2*: Pb omits Albany, Cornwall.
Rich. III *Jan. 1; May 3*: Pb omits Oxford, Forrest.
R&J *Jan. 21; Mar. 25; Apr. 29; Nov. 25; Dec. 23*: Pb omits Tybalt, Benvolio, Paris, Escalus.

1766 DRURY LANE: JPK, PA

Cymbeline *Feb. 5*: PA missing from BM file (another copy not located). *Apr. 22*: Pb omits Queen.
Lear *Jan. 11*: Pb omits Arante.
Macbeth *Apr. 2*: Pb omits Sergeant, Doctor, Lennox.
MWW *Jan. 24*: Pb omits Host, Simple, Pistol, Bardolph, Nym, Rugby.

APPENDIX A

1766 DRURY LANE (*cont.*)

    Much Ado *Feb. 11*: PA omits Antonio.
    Othello *Apr. 1; Dec. 6*: Pb omits Messenger.
    R&J *May 2*: PA omits Tybalt. *Sept. 30; Oct. 4; Dec. 26*: Pb omits Peter.

COVENT GARDEN: JPK, PA

    2 Hen. IV *Oct. 6, 7, 9, 13; Dec. 29*: PA omits Bardolph. *Oct. 11*: PA missing from BM file (another copy not located).
    Hen. V *Sept. 22, 24, 29; Oct. 1, 3, 17*: Pb omits English Herald. *Nov. 17*: Pb omits same; PA omits Grey. *Dec. 27*: Pb also omits English Herald.
    J. Caesar *Jan. 31; Feb. 3, 7, 24*: Pb omits Lucilius, Publius (throughout), Pindarus, Soothsayer, Volumnius, Popilius, Lucius, Antony's Servant (on Feb. 24 only).
    R&J *Feb. 20*: Pb omits Tybalt, Benvolio, Paris, Escalus. *Apr. 8*: PA omits Apothecary, Peter, Balthazar, Montague.

KING'S, HAYMARKET: PA

1767 DRURY LANE: JPK, PA

    AYLI *Oct. 22, 27; Nov. 10*: Pb omits LeBeau, Corin, Jaques de Bois, Charles, Silvius, William (throughout); PA omits Audrey (on Oct. 22, 27 only).
    Cymbeline *Oct. 10, 13, 19; Nov. 17*: Pb omits Lucius, Cornelius.
    2 Hen. IV *May 8*: Pb omits Clarence, Lord Chief Justice, Westmorland, Mowbray, Hastings, Lord Bardolph, Feeble, Mouldy.
    John *Feb. 7, 20*: Pb omits Prince Henry, Essex, Citizen of Angers, Austria, French Herald, English Herald.
    Lear *Apr. 23*: PA missing from BM file (another copy not located). *Oct. 21, 24*: Pb omits Burgundy, Arante.
    Macbeth *Mar. 21*: Pb omits Seyton, Siward. *May 13*: Pb also omits Seyton, Angus.
    R&J *May 18*: Pb omits Peter. *May 30*: Pb omits same; PA missing from BM file (another copy not located).

COVENT GARDEN: JPK, PA

    Cymbeline *Dec. 31*: Pb omits Helen.
    Hen. V *Apr. 23*: PA missing from BM file (another copy not located).
    Lear *Jan. 19*: PA omits Burgundy. *May 13*: Pb omits same.
    R&J *Oct. 12; Nov. 16*: Pb also omits Benvolio, Paris.

HAYMARKET: PA

1768 DRURY LANE: JPK, PA

    AYLI *Mar. 26; Apr. 13; Oct. 13*: Pb omits Jaques de Bois, Silvius, William (throughout), Corin (on Mar. 26, Apr. 13 only), LeBeau (on Apr. 13 only), Charles (on Apr. 13, Oct. 13 only).
    Cymbeline *Jan. 18, 29; Apr. 26*: Pb omits Lucius, Cornelius.
    Lear *Apr. 8*: Pb omits Burgundy, Arante.
    Macbeth *Jan. 14*: Pb omits Seyton, Angus, Lennox, Sergeant, Fleance. *Feb. 4, 8; Apr. 25*: Pb also omits Seyton, Angus, Lennox, Sergeant.
    Merchant *Mar. 24; Apr. 16*: Pb omits Gobbo. *Sept. 30*: Pb omits Launcelot. *Nov. 5*: Pb omits Launcelot, Gobbo, Salarino, Solanio, Duke, Balthazar, Tubal. *Dec. 20*: Pb omits Tubal.
    Much Ado *Oct. 20*: Pb omits Conrade, Margaret, Ursula.

APPENDIX A

1768 COVENT GARDEN: JPK, PA
>Cymbeline *Jan. 8*: Pb omits Helen.
>Hen. V *Nov. 4, 22*: Pb omits Boy, French Soldier, Westmorland, Gloucester, Bedford.
>Lear *Mar. 7; Apr. 28*: Pb omits Cornwall, France, Burgundy.
>Merchant *Feb. 29*: Pb omits Solanio, Salarino. *Apr. 6*: PA omits Gratiano.
>MWW *Oct. 13*: Pb omits Pistol, Bardolph, Fenton, Simple, Nym, Robin.
>Rich. III *May 31*: PA omits Tyrrel.
>R&J *Apr. 29*: PA omits Escalus, Balthazar.

1769 DRURY LANE: JPK, PA
>AYLI *May 6*: Pb omits Jaques de Bois, William.
>Cymbeline *Nov. 17*: Pb omits Lucius, Philario, Captain, French Gentleman, Gentlemen. *Dec. 12, 28*: Pb also omits Lucius, Philario, Captain, French Gentleman.
>Hamlet *Oct. 28*: PA omits Player King.
>1 Hen. IV *Oct. 23*: Pb omits Douglas, Northumberland, Westmorland, Bardolph, Carriers, Francis.
>Lear *Oct. 7*: Pb omits Captain, Officers, Old Man.
>Macbeth *Jan. 24*: PA omits Lennox, Sergeant.
>Merchant *Jan. 7, 26; Mar. 30; May 3, 19*: Pb omits Tubal (throughout), Solanio, Balthazar (on May 19 only). *Oct. 5, 26; Dec. 2*: Pb omits Salarino, Solanio, Balthazar, Tubal.
>Much Ado *Nov. 14*: Pb omits Conrade.
>Rich. III *May 16*: Pb omits Norfolk, Stanley, Lord Mayor, Catesby, Ratcliff, Lieutenant. *Nov. 13*: Pb also omits Norfolk, Stanley, Lieutenant, Oxford, Officer.
>R&J *May 1*: Pb omits Escalus, Montague.
>Tempest *Mar. 16, 27*: Pb omits Sebastian, Antonio, Alonso, Gonzalo, Boatswain (throughout), Hymen, Ceres (on Mar. 16 only). *May 2, 5*: Pb also omits Boatswain. *Oct. 9*: Pb omits Shipmaster, Boatswain, Francisco. *Nov. 20; Dec. 27*: Pb also omits Shipmaster, Boatswain.

COVENT GARDEN: JPK, PA
>Cymbeline *Apr. 25*: PA omits Lucius. *May 16*: Pb omits Philario, Lucius.
>Hen. V *Sept. 22*: PA omits Gower.
>Rich. III *Mar. 27; Dec. 28*: Pb omits Lord Mayor, Lieutenant (throughout), Catesby, Ratcliff, Stanley, Norfolk (on Mar. 27 only).
>R&J *Apr. 15; May 9*: Pb omits Peter, Friar John (throughout), Tybalt, Benvolio, Paris, Escalus (on May 9 only).

HAYMARKET: PA
>J. Caesar *Sept. 11*: Pb is in GEC.
>Othello *Aug. 30*: Pb is in HTC.
>Rich. III *Sept. 19*: PA omits Stanley, Catesby, Ratcliff, Lord Mayor, Lieutenant (added by Gaz).

1770 DRURY LANE: JPK, PA
>Cymbeline *Jan. 18; Mar. 12; May 15*: Pb omits Lucius, Philario, French Gentleman (throughout), Captain (on Jan. 18, Mar. 12 only), 1st Gentleman (on May 15 only). *June 1*: JPK missing (no other Pb located). *Dec. 1, 8*: Pb also omits Lucius, Philario, French Gentleman.
>Hamlet *May 2*: Pb omits Rosencrantz, Player King, Guildenstern, Bernardo, Marcellus, Lucianus, Player Queen.

APPENDIX A

1770 DRURY LANE *(cont.)*

 1 Hen. IV *Jan. 9*: Pb omits Douglas, Northumberland, Westmorland, Bardolph, Carriers, Francis. *Feb. 24*: Pb also omits Bardolph, Carriers, Francis.
 2 Hen. IV *Jan. 19; Feb. 2*: Pb omits Hastings, Mowbray, Lord Bardolph, Gower; PA omits Bardolph (on Feb. 2 only).
 Lear *Jan. 15; Feb. 21; Mar. 8, 13*: Pb omits Officer, Messenger, Old Man (throughout), Captain, Arante (on Jan. 15 only). *Oct. 31*: Pb also omits Captain, Officer, Old Man, Curan, Arante.
 Macbeth *Jan. 4; Nov. 14*: Pb omits Angus, Lennox, Seyton, Sergeant (throughout), Doctor (on Nov. 14 only).
 Merchant *May 29*: JPK missing (no other Pb located).
 Much Ado *Nov. 13*: Pb omits Sexton.
 Rich. III *Apr. 20*: Pb omits Lieutenant, Oxford, Officer, Catesby, Ratcliff. *May 16*: Pb also omits Lieutenant, Catesby, Ratcliff.
 R&J *May 8*: PA omits Apothecary.
 Tempest *Apr. 17*: Pb omits Boatswain; PA omits Francisco. *May 23*: Pb also omits Shipmaster, Boatswain. *Nov. 19*: Pb omits Boatswain.

 COVENT GARDEN: JPK, PA

 Cymbeline *Apr. 18*: JPK missing (no other Pb located).
 Hen. V *Dec. 28*: Pb omits Westmorland, French Soldier, Burgundy, Isabel, Hostess.
 Measure *Feb. 12, 15*: Pb omits Friar Thomas.
 Rich. III *Jan. 26*: Pb omits Catesby, Ratcliff, Stanley, Norfolk. *Dec. 31*: Pb omits Lieutenant, Tyrrel.
 R&J *Apr. 28*: Pb also omits Benvolio, Peter, Friar John.

 HAYMARKET: PA

 Othello *Oct. 1*: JPK (the only Haymarket bill in this collection).

1771 DRURY LANE: JPK, PA

 AYLI *Apr. 1*: PA omits Jaques de Bois, William. *May 8*: Pb also omits Charles, Corin.
 C&P *Jan. 2*: Pb omits all characters except Petruchio, Catharine.
 Cymbeline *Jan. 5; Mar 4; Apr. 27; Sept. 26; Dec. 5*: Pb omits Philario, French Gentleman, Lucius, 1st Gentleman, Captain.
 Lear *Nov. 23*: Pb omits Old Man.
 Merchant *Apr. 24*: PA omits Tubal.
 MWW *May 27*: Pb omits Robin.
 Much Ado *May 24*: Pb omits Margaret, Ursula.
 Tempest *Apr. 15; May 28*: Pb omits Boatswain.
 Timon *Dec. 12, 14, 19, 28*: Pb omits Lucilius, Hortensius, Titus, Varro, Philotus, 1st Messenger.
 Twelfth N. *Dec. 13, 18, 20, 27*: Pb omits Officers (throughout), Captain, Valentine, Priest (on Dec. 27 only).

 COVENT GARDEN: JPK, PA

 C&P *Dec. 17*: Pb omits Grumio, Tailor.
 Othello *Dec. 21*: Pb omits Montano, Duke.
 Rich. III *Nov. 25*: Pb omits Norfolk, Stanley, Lieutenant, Lord Mayor, Prince Edward, Duke of York.
 R&J *May 28*: Pb omits Benvolio, Escalus, Peter, Apothecary. *Dec. 17*: Pb also omits Paris, Escalus, Peter.

APPENDIX A

1771 HAYMARKET: PA
    C&P *June 14*: Pb is in FSL.

1772 DRURY LANE: JPK, PA
    AYLI *June 5*: Pb omits Charles, Jaques de Bois, Corin, William. *Nov. 17*: Pb omits Phebe.
    Cymbeline *May 7; Sept. 19*: Pb omits Philario, French Gentleman (throughout), Lucius, Gentleman, Captain (on Sept. 19 only).
    Macbeth *Apr. 25; June 9*: Pb omits Donalbain, Seyton, Lennox, Sergeant, Angus.
    Merchant *Jan. 11; May 2*: Pb omits Tubal.
    Rich. III *June 2*: PA omits Tyrrel.
    R&J *Oct. 10*: Pb omits Montague.
    Timon *Jan. 2, 10, 18; Feb. 6*: Pb omits Lucilius, Hortensius, Titus, Varro, Philotus, 1st Messenger.
    Twelfth N. *Jan. 1, 6, 13; Feb. 3, 19; Mar. 3; Apr. 24; May 1, 29*: Pb omits Captain, Valentine, Priest, Officers.

    COVENT GARDEN: JPK, PA
    C&P *May 1, 13*: Pb omits Tailor (throughout), Pedro (on May 13 only).
    Hen. VIII *Nov. 6, 7, 9, 11, 13, 16, 18, 20; Dec. 21*: Pb omits Capucius, Butts, Surveyor, Brandon, Old Lady (throughout), Norfolk, Suffolk (on Nov. 6, 13, 18, 20 only), Lovell, Campeius (on Nov. 13, 16, 18, 20, Dec. 21 only), Surrey, Lord Chamberlain (on Nov. 18 only), Sands, Guildford (on Nov. 18, 20, Dec. 21 only).
    Rich. III *May 12*: Pb omits Lieutenant, Lord Mayor. *Sept. 28; Oct. 19; Dec. 30*: Pb omits Norfolk, Lieutenant, Lord Mayor.
    R&J *Feb. 24; Mar. 16; May 2*: Pb omits Peter (throughout), Benvolio, Escalus (on May 2 only).

    HAYMARKET: PA

1773 DRURY LANE: JPK, PA
    C&P *Apr. 1*: PA omits Music Master. *Oct. 11*: Pb omits all characters.
    Cymbeline *Feb. 8*: Pb omits Philario, French Gentleman, Lucius, Captain, Gentlemen. *May 31*: Pb omits Captain, 2nd Gentleman; PA omits 1st Gentleman.
    Macbeth *May 10*: PA omits Siward, Doctor, Fleance.
    Merchant *Jan. 4*: Pb omits Solanio, Salarino, Duke.

    COVENT GARDEN: JPK, PA
    Hen. VIII *Jan. 18*: Pb omits Sands, Guildford, Lovell, Campeius, Capucius, Butts, Surveyor, Brandon, Old Lady. *Jan. 29; Feb. 10, 15; Mar. 23*: Pb also omits Guildford, Capucius, Butts, Surveyor, Brandon, Old Lady (throughout), Sands, Campeius (on Jan. 29, Feb. 15, Mar. 23 only), Norfolk, Suffolk (on Feb. 15, Mar. 23 only), Surrey, Lord Chamberlain, Patience (on Mar. 23 only). *Sept. 22*: PA omits Campeius. *Dec. 22*: Pb also omits Norfolk, Suffolk, Surrey, Lord Chamberlain.
    Macbeth *May 10*: Pb omits Duncan, Seyton.
    Merchant *May 24*: PA omits Duke, Solanio, Gobbo.
    Rich. III *May 20*: Pb omits Lieutenant. *Dec. 20*: Pb also omits Catesby, Ratcliff, Prince Edward, Duke of York, Stanley.
    R & J *May 17*: Pb also omits Benvolio.

APPENDIX A

1774 DRURY LANE: JPK, PA

    C&P *Jan. 1*: Pb omits all characters except Petruchio, Grumio, Catharine. *Jan. 17*: Pb also omits Pedro. *Nov. 30*: Pb also omits Baptista, Biondello, Tailor, Hortensio, Bianca, Curtis.

  COVENT GARDEN: JPK, PA

    1 Hen. IV *Mar. 15*: PA omits Prince John, Douglas.
    Hen. VIII *Feb. 14*: Pb omits Norfolk, Suffolk, Surrey, Lord Chamberlain.
    Much Ado *Dec. 10*: Pb omits Don John, Antonio, Borachio, Verges, Conrade, Friar, Margaret, Ursula.
    Rich. III *Jan. 1*: Pb omits Prince Edward, Duke of York; PA omits Norfolk. *May 10*: PA omits Prince Edward, Duke of York. *Dec. 5*: Pb also omits Norfolk, Ratcliff.
    R&J *Feb. 9*: Pb omits Paris, Tybalt, Peter, Apothecary.

  HAYMARKET: PA

    C&P *Apr. 12*: Bill in MC, not in PA. *July 4*: Pb is in HTC.

1775 DRURY LANE: JPK, PA

    AYLI *Sept. 26*: Pb omits LeBeau, Charles, Jaques de Bois, Corin, William.
    Merchant *Dec. 29*: PA omits Gobbo.

  COVENT GARDEN: JPK, PA

    R&J *Nov. 7*: Pb omits Benvolio, Escalus, Paris, Tybalt. *Dec. 27*: Pb also omits Escalus, Paris, Tybalt.

  HAYMARKET: PA

1776 DRURY LANE: JPK, PA

    AYLI *Oct. 9*: Pb also omits Phebe.
    Macbeth *Nov. 25; Dec. 26, 30*: Pb omits Fleance, Seyton.
    Merchant *Jan. 2*: PA omits Gobbo.
    Twelfth N. *Apr. 10*: Pb omits Captain, Priest, Valentine, Officer.

  COVENT GARDEN: JPK, PA

    AYLI *Mar. 19*: Pb omits Phebe, Audrey.
    C&P *Apr. 19*: Pb omits all characters except Petruchio, Baptista, Grumio, Catharine.
    Tempest *Dec. 27, 30, 31*: Pb omits Shipmaster, Boatswain.

  HAYMARKET: PA

  CHINA HALL, ROTHERHITHE: MC

    R&J *July 15*: Reviewed in MC, July 16.

1777 DRURY LANE: JPK, PA

    Cymbeline *Oct. 31*: JPK missing (no other Pb located).
    1 Hen. IV *Oct. 21; Nov. 5, 10, 20; Dec. 10, 30*: Pb omits Sheriff, Gadshill, Peto.
    2 Hen. IV *Dec. 15*: Pb omits Falstaff's Page.
    Macbeth *Apr. 22*: Pb omits Fleance, Seyton.
    Merchant *Oct. 14, 16; Nov. 7*: PA omits Gobbo.
    Tempest *Jan. 4, 6, 10, 13*: Pb omits Sebastian, Francisco, Boatswain, Antonio, Shipmaster. *Jan. 18, 23, 25, 31; Feb. 4, 18; Mar. 3, 15; Apr. 4, 14, 25; May 2, 7, 30*: Pb also omits Sebastian, Francisco.

APPENDIX A

1777 COVENT GARDEN: JPK, PA

    C&P *Nov. 19, 24*: Pb omits all characters except Petruchio, Grumio, Catharine (throughout), Baptista (on Nov. 24 only).

    Lear *Oct. 13; Nov. 10; Dec. 29*: Pb omits Burgundy, Arante.

    Measure *Jan. 8*: Pb omits Friar Peter, Friar Thomas, Elbow, Abhorson, Barnardine.

    Tempest *Feb. 13; May 19*: Pb omits Juno, Ceres.

HAYMARKET: Pbs in BM, PA

    C&P *May 1*: Bill in MC, not in PA.

    Fairy T. *July 18*: Pb also omits 1st Fairy. *July 21, 22, 23, 29; Aug. 25; Sept. 5*: Pb also omits Snout, Starveling, 1st Fairy.

    Hamlet *July 21*: Pb omits Rosencrantz, Guildenstern, Player King, Lucianus, Player Queen. *Sept. 15*: Pb omits Lucianus; PA omits Bernardo.

    1 Hen. IV *Feb. 11*: Bill in MC, not in PA. *July 28, 31; Aug. 2, 13, 21; Sept. 13*: Pb omits Peto, Gadshill (throughout), Westmorland, Blunt (on Aug. 13, Sept. 13 only).

    Hen. VIII *Sept. 5*: Pb omits Lord Chamberlain, Norfolk, Suffolk.

    Merchant *June 18; July 8, 23; Aug. 15*: Pb omits Solanio, Salarino (throughout), Duke (on June 18, July 23 only), Gobbo, Tubal (on July 23 only).

    MWW *Sept. 3, 9*: Pb omits Robin, Simple.

    Rich. III *Aug. 11*: Pb omits Tyrrel, Oxford.

CHINA HALL, ROTHERHITHE: MC

HAMMERSMITH: Gaz, Nov. 8

1778 DRURY LANE: JPK, PA

    AYLI *May 14*: PA omits Jaques de Bois.

    Hamlet *Oct. 16; Dec. 15*: Pb omits Bernardo, Francisco (throughout), Marcellus, Player King, Lucianus, Messenger, Player Queen (on Oct. 16 only).

    1 Hen. IV *Jan. 21; Mar. 21*: Pb omits Sheriff, Gadshill, Peto. *Oct. 30*: Pb also omits Hostess.

    2 Hen. IV *Oct. 24*: Pb omits Mowbray, Hastings, Poins, Bardolph, Davy, Falstaff's Page, Hostess.

    Macbeth *Apr. 30*: PA omits Sergeant. *Nov. 26; Dec. 29*: Pb omits Lennox, Donalbain, Angus, Siward, Doctor, Sergeant, Seyton.

    Measure *Oct. 20*: Pb omits Francisca, Mrs Overdone.

    MWW *Nov. 6*: Pb also omits Rugby, Robin.

    Much Ado *Feb. 17; May 6*: Pb omits Friar, Messenger, Conrade, Sexton, Verges, Watchmen, Margaret, Ursula. *Nov. 4*: Pb also omits Friar, Conrade, Sexton, Verges, Watchmen, Margaret, Ursula.

    Rich. III *Oct. 26*: Pb also omits Ratcliff, Lieutenant. *Nov. 23*: JPK missing (no other Pb located).

    Twelfth N. *Nov. 10*: Pb omits Captain, Officer, Priest, Valentine.

COVENT GARDEN: JPK, PA

    Hen. V *May 11*: PA omits Westmorland. *May 18*: Pb omits Gower, French Soldier, Bishop of Ely, Salisbury, Boy, Montjoy; PA omits Westmorland. *Sept. 21*: Pb also omits Isabel, Hostess.

    Lear *Feb. 5*: Pb omits Burgundy, Arante. *Nov. 9*: Pb omits Arante.

APPENDIX A

1778 COVENT GARDEN (*cont.*)

 Merchant *Jan. 28; Mar. 24; Apr. 24*: Pb omits Solanio, Salarino (throughout), Duke, Tubal (on Jan. 28 only).
 Rich. III *Oct. 5; Dec. 7*: Pb omits Norfolk, Lieutenant.

 HAYMARKET: H–B, PA
  C&P *Mar. 23*: Bill in MC, not in PA.
  Rich. III *Mar. 24*: Bill in MC, not in PA.

 CHINA HALL, ROTHERHITHE: MC

 TEMPORARY BOOTH, CHINA HALL, ROTHERHITHE: MC
  Lear *Aug.?*: Bill not in MC. See p. 67.

1779 DRURY LANE: JPK, PA

 AYLI *Jan. 11*: Pb omits Duke Senior, Duke Frederick, LeBeau, Corin, Jaques de Bois, Silvius, William, Charles.
 Hamlet *Jan. 12; Feb. 6*: Pb omits Rosencrantz, Guildenstern, Marcellus, Player King, Lucianus, Messenger, Bernardo, Francisco, Player Queen. *Oct. 30*: Pb also omits Marcellus, Lucianus, Messenger, Francisco, Bernardo, Player Queen.
 1 Hen. IV *Jan. 22; May 19; Dec. 20*: Pb omits Douglas, Poins, Francis, Bardolph, Hostess.
 2 Hen. IV *June 1*: Pb omits Mowbray, Hastings, Poins, Bardolph, Davy, Falstaff's Page.
 Lear *Apr. 14; May 4*: Pb omits Doctor, Old Man, Cornwall's Servant, Curan (throughout), Captain (on Apr. 14 only).
 Macbeth *Apr. 7*: Pb omits Lennox, Angus, Siward, Doctor, Sergeant, Seyton.
 MWW *Jan. 26; May 3*: Pb omits Rugby, Robin.
 Much Ado *Jan. 5; May 5, 29*: Pb omits Verges, Conrade, Sexton, Friar, Watchmen, Margaret, Ursula.
 Othello *Nov. 1*: Pb omits Duke, Montano, Gratiano.
 Rich. III *Jan. 9; May 18*: Pb omits Ratcliff, Lieutenant (throughout), Duchess of York (on Jan. 9 only).
 Tempest *Dec. 30*: PA omits Antonio, Sebastian.
 Twelfth N. *Jan. 6*: Pb omits Captain, Officer, Priest, Valentine.
 Wint. T. *Nov. 20, 23, 26, 29; Dec. 1, 3, 11*: Pb omits Cleomenes, Gentleman.

 COVENT GARDEN: JPK, PA

  AYLI *Dec. 17*: Pb omits Charles; PA omits William, LeBeau.
  Com. Err. *Jan. 22, 27; Feb. 1, 6, 9, 20; May 4, 21*: Pb omits Balthazar, Officer (throughout), Merchants (on Jan. 27, Feb. 20, May 4, 21 only), Lesbia (on Feb. 1, 9, 20, May 4, 21 only), Angelo, Pinch (on May 4, 21 only).
  Hamlet *Nov. 22*: PA omits Francisco, Player Queen.
  Hen. V *Sept. 20*: PA also omits Bedford.
  Merchant *Dec. 4*: Pb omits Duke, Tubal, Solanio, Salarino.
  MWW *Dec. 22*: Pb omits Simple, Bardolph, Pistol, Robin, Anne Page, Mrs Quickly.
  R&J *Apr. 19*: Pb omits Peter, Balthazar, Montague, Apothecary.

 HAYMARKET: H–B, PA

APPENDIX A

1780 DRURY LANE: JPK, PA

>AYLI *Oct. 5, 20*: Pb omits Corin (throughout), William, Jaques de Bois, Silvius, LeBeau, Charles, Phebe (on Oct. 5 only).
>1 Hen. IV *Jan. 14; Feb. 12; May 23*: Pb omits Hostess (throughout), Douglas, Poins, Francis, Bardolph (on Jan. 14, Feb. 12 only).
>Tempest *Sept. 23*: PA omits Francisco.
>Wint. T. *Jan. 1, 11, 22; Feb. 10; Mar. 30; Apr. 12; May 18, 24*: Pb omits Cleomenes, Gentleman.

>COVENT GARDEN: JPK, PA

>>Hamlet *Apr. 25*: Pb omits Marcellus, Bernardo, Player King, Rosencrantz, Guildenstern, Player Queen.
>>1 Hen. IV *Oct. 2*: Pb omits Westmorland, Blunt, Northumberland, Sheriff, Carriers.
>>Macbeth *Apr. 27*: Pb omits Lennox, Seyton.
>>Much Ado *Jan. 11; Feb. 17; Dec. 30*: Pb omits Borachio, Verges, Conrade, Friar (throughout), Don John, Antonio, Margaret, Ursula (on Dec. 30 only). *Apr. 22*: Pb also omits Margaret, Ursula.

>HAYMARKET: H–B, PA

>CROWN INN, ISLINGTON: Pbs in HTC

1781 DRURY LANE: JPK, PA

>Macbeth *Nov. 5*: Pb omits Donalbain.

>COVENT GARDEN: JPK, PA

>>Com. Err. *Jan. 18*: PA omits Lesbia. *Feb. 8; Mar. 20; May 22*: Pb also omits Pinch.
>>Hamlet *Jan. 1*: Pb omits Player King, Marcellus, Bernardo, Francisco, Rosencrantz, Guildenstern, Player Queen.
>>1 Hen. IV *Dec. 11*: Pb omits Blunt, Northumberland, Sheriff.
>>Macbeth *May 9*: Pb omits Seyton, Siward, Doctor, Gentlewoman.
>>Merchant *Apr. 20*: Pb omits Solanio, Salarino, Duke, Tubal, Gobbo.
>>MWW *Apr. 25*: Pb omits Host, Fenton, Simple, Bardolph, Pistol, Fairy, Anne Page, Mrs Quickly.
>>Much Ado *May 3*: Pb omits Don John, Antonio, Borachio, Conrade, Friar, Verges, Margaret, Ursula.
>>R&J *Oct. 15; Nov. 12*: Pb also omits Tybalt, Peter, Montague.

>HAYMARKET: H–B, PA

>CROWN INN, ISLINGTON: Pb in HTC

1782 DRURY LANE: JPK, PA

>AYLI *Apr. 27*: PA omits Lord. *June 1*: Pb omits Jaques de Bois; PA omits Lord.
>Hamlet *Sept. 24*: Pb also omits Messenger; PA also omits Sailor.
>Macbeth *Feb. 5; May 15*: Pb omits Donalbain.

>COVENT GARDEN: JPK, PA

>>AYLI *Jan. 22*: PA omits William, LeBeau.
>>1 Hen. IV *Jan. 29; May 1*: Pb omits Northumberland, Sheriff (throughout), Blunt, Bardolph, Douglas, Westmorland, Carriers (on May 1 only).
>>Hen. V *May 20*: PA omits Exeter, Burgundy.

706

APPENDIX A

1782 COVENT GARDEN (*cont.*)
    Hen. VIII *Dec. 30*: PA omits Old Lady.
    MWW *May 21*: PA omits Host, Fenton, Simple, Bardolph, Pistol, Fairy.

  HAYMARKET: H–B, PA
    Merchant *Dec. 30*: Pb is in Lysons Coll. and in MC, not in PA.
    Rich. III *Mar. 4*: Bill in PA, not in H–B.
    Twelfth N. *Aug. 15, 30*: PA omits Fabian (throughout), Antonio (on Aug. 30 only).

1783 DRURY LANE: JPK, PA
    Hamlet *Feb. 6; Mar. 24*: PA omits Bernardo. *Oct. 13*: Pb omits Marcellus, Lucianus, Player Queen.
    Merchant *Apr. 26*: Pb omits Gobbo, Tubal.

  COVENT GARDEN: JPK, PA
    1 Hen. IV *Jan. 4; May 29; Oct. 17; Nov. 17*: Pb omits Gadshill, Peto (throughout), Bardolph, Douglas (on Oct. 17, Nov. 17 only).
    Lear *Feb. 24*: Pb omits Arante.
    MWW *Jan. 18*: PA omits Shallow.

  HAYMARKET: H–B, PA
    AYLI *July 4*: PA omits LeBeau.
    Rich. III *Dec. 15*: Bill in MC and in MH, not in PA. MC omits Catesby; MH omits Lieutenant, Norfolk.

1784 DRURY LANE: JPK, PA
    C&P *Oct. 23*: Pb omits Hortensio; PA omits Pedro.
    MWW *Jan. 13*: Pb omits Shallow, Fenton, Simple, Bardolph, Pistol, Nym.
    Rich. III *Jan. 12*: Pb omits Duchess of York.

  COVENT GARDEN: JPK, PA
    1 Hen. IV *Jan. 12*: Pb omits Bardolph, Douglas, Gadshill, Peto.
    John *Jan. 16*: Pb omits Prince Henry, Essex.
    Macbeth *Feb. 9*: Pb omits Lennox, Seyton, Siward, Doctor.
    Merchant *Mar. 18*: Pb omits Duke, Tubal. *June 10*: JPK missing. Pb is in BM. PA omits Lorenzo, Solanio, Salarino.
    MWW *Mar. 23*: Pb omits Pistol, Bardolph.
    Rich. III *Oct. 11*: PA omits Blunt.
    R&J *Apr. 12; Oct. 25, 26; Nov. 1, 5, 8, 19, 26; Dec. 6, 29*: Pb omits Peter, Apothecary (throughout), Tybalt, Montague (on Apr. 12, Oct. 26, Nov. 1, 5, 8, 19 only), Escalus, Paris (on Nov. 5 only).
    TGV *Apr. 13*: Pb omits Outlaws.
    Wint. T. *May 10*: Pb omits Dorcas.

  HAYMARKET: H–B, PA
    Rich. III *Sept. 17*: Bill in PA, not in H–B.

1785 DRURY LANE: JPK, PA
    Othello *Apr. 5*: Pb omits Montano.

  COVENT GARDEN: JPK, PA
    Hamlet *Apr. 22*: Pb omits Player King, Rosencrantz, Guildenstern, Marcellus. *Sept. 23*: PA omits Bernardo.

APPENDIX A

1785 COVENT GARDEN (cont.)
 1 Hen. IV *Oct. 22*: Pb omits Bardolph, Douglas, Gadshill, Peto.
 Hen. VIII *Apr. 8*: Pb omits Lovell.
 MWW *Nov. 1*: Pb omits Simple, Rugby.
 R&J *Jan. 31; Mar. 28; Nov. 21, 25, 28; Dec. 19*: Pb omits Apothecary (throughout), Peter (on Jan. 31, Mar. 28 only).

 HAYMARKET: H–B, PA

1786 DRURY LANE: JPK, PA
 C&P *Apr. 6; June 2; Dec. 5*: PA omits Pedro (throughout), Tailor, Music Master, Hortensio, Bianca, Curtis (on Dec. 5 only).
 Hamlet *May 15*: Pb omits Rosencrantz, Guildenstern, Player King, Marcellus, Lucianus, Player Queen. *Sept. 19*: Pb omits Marcellus; PA omits Bernardo.
 Merchant *Apr. 20, 29; May 13*: PA omits Solanio, Salarino, Tubal, Gobbo.
 Tempest *Dec. 27*: Pb omits Alonso, Antonio, Sebastian, Francisco.

 COVENT GARDEN: JPK, PA
 Lear *Mar. 6*: Pb omits Cornwall, Burgundy.
 Macbeth *Jan. 18*: Pb omits Gentlewoman. *May 29*: PA omits Witches.
 Merchant *Feb. 27*: Pb omits Solanio, Salarino, Duke, Tubal.
 Much Ado *Jan. 24*: Pb omits Balthazar, Don John, Antonio, Borachio, Conrade, Friar, Verges, Margaret, Ursula.
 R&J *Jan. 23; Feb. 20; Apr. 17; Oct. 23*: Pb omits Escalus, Montague, Apothecary (throughout), Tybalt, Paris (on Jan. 23, Feb. 20, Apr. 17 only), Lady Capulet, Nurse (on Jan. 23, Apr. 17 only). *Dec. 11*: Pb omits Escalus, Apothecary; PA omits Peter.
 Timon *May 13*: Pb omits Caphis, Painter; PA omits Phryne.

 HAYMARKET: H–B, PA
 1 Hen. IV *July 21*: PA omits Prince John.

 HAMMERSMITH: Pbs in New York Public Library.

1787 DRURY LANE: JPK, PA
 Cymbeline *Feb. 1, 5, 8; Mar. 20; Nov. 5*: Pb omits Philario, Cornelius (throughout), Lucius, French Gentleman (on Feb. 5, Mar. 20, Nov. 5 only). *May 24*: Pb omits Philario, Cornelius. PA missing from BM file (another copy not located).
 Hamlet *Jan. 11; Dec. 3, 31*: Pb omits Player King, Marcellus, Lucianus (throughout), Rosencrantz, Guildenstern, Player Queen (on Jan. 11 only). *Sept. 18; Oct. 29*: PA omits Osric, Rosencrantz, Guildenstern, Marcellus (throughout), Player King, Lucianus, Bernardo, Gentleman, Francisco, Messenger, Sailor, Player Queen (on Sept. 18 only).
 Macbeth *Nov. 3*: PA omits Lennox.
 Merchant *Nov. 24*: Pb omits Tubal, Gobbo.
 Tempest *Jan. 9*: Pb omits Alonso, Antonio, Sebastian, Francisco.

 COVENT GARDEN: JPK, PA
 Cymbeline *Apr. 27*: PA omits Helen.
 1 Hen. IV *Dec. 31*: Pb omits Gadshill, Peto.
 Much Ado *Apr. 11*: Pb omits Margaret, Ursula.

APPENDIX A

1787 COVENT GARDEN (*cont.*)
    Othello *Oct. 12*: PA missing from BM file (another copy not located).
    R&J *Jan. 29*: Pb omits Escalus, Montague, Apothecary. *Sept. 24; Nov. 12*: Pb also omits Montague.

    HAYMARKET: H–B, PA

    ROYALTY: See p. 140.

    RED LION INN, STOKE NEWINGTON: Pb in BM [Burney Collection]

1788 DRURY LANE: JPK, PA
    AYLI *Oct. 7; Nov. 13*: Pb omits Duke Frederick, William, LeBeau, Silvius, Jaques de Bois, Corin, Charles, Audrey, Phebe. *Dec. 17*: PA also omits Duke Frederick, William, LeBeau.
    Hamlet *June 4*: Pb omits Player King, Marcellus, Lucianus. *Sept. 30*: Pb omits Bernardo.
    Hen. VIII *Nov. 29*: Pb omits Old Lady. *Dec. 2, 6, 13, 20, 27*: Pb omits Guildford, Lovell, Butts, Surveyor, Old Lady (throughout), Gardiner, Campeius (on Dec. 13, 20, 27 only).
    Lear *Mar. 1*: Pb omits Officer.
    MWW *Dec. 11*: Pb omits Nym, Rugby.
    Much Ado *Apr. 30*: PA omits Antonio.
    Rich. III *Jan. 16*: Pb omits Lieutenant. *Apr. 17*: Pb omits Lord Mayor.
    R&J *Nov. 18*: Pb omits Escalus, Montague, Peter, Apothecary, Balthazar, Sampson.
    Wint. T. *May 1; June 11*: PA omits Rogero. *Dec. 12*: PA omits Clown.

    COVENT GARDEN: JPK, PA
    1 Hen. IV *Oct. 8*: Pb omits Gadshill, Peto.
    MWW *Nov. 12*: Pb omits Rugby.
    Much Ado *Apr. 14*: Pb omits Balthazar, Don John, Antonio, Borachio, Conrade, Friar, Verges.
    R&J *Jan. 7; Sept. 22, 29; Oct. 6, 13, 20; Nov. 3; Dec. 22*: Pb omits Montague.

1789 DRURY LANE: JPK, PA
    AYLI *Feb. 20; Mar. 10; June 6*: PA omits Duke Frederick, William, LeBeau, Audrey, Phebe (throughout), Jaques de Bois, Charles (on June 6 only). *June 13*: Bill not in JPK or PA. This was an extra performance, for Palmer's BT. The season this year had officially closed on June 12. Pb is in BM, Burney Collection. *Sept. 22*: Pb omits Jaques de Bois; PA omits Corin.
    Hen. VIII *Jan. 3, 10, 24*: Pb omits Butts, Surveyor, Old Lady (throughout), Guildford, Lovell (on Jan. 10, 24 only), Gardiner, Campeius (on Jan. 24 only). *Feb. 3*: Pb also omits Gardiner, Campeius, Guildford, Lovell, Butts, Old Lady; PA omits Cromwell. *Apr. 29*: Pb also omits Butts, Old Lady.
    Much Ado *Dec. 9, 18, 26*: Pb omits Town Clerk.
    R&J *May 11*: Pb omits Benvolio, Tybalt, Escalus, Montague, Peter, Apothecary, Balthazar, Sampson.
    Tempest *Dec. 21, 30*: Pb omits Alonso, Antonio.
    Twelfth N. *Mar. 19*: JPK missing. Pb is in BM, Burney Collection.
    Wint. T. *June 9*: PA omits Cleomenes, Servant, Mopsa, Dorcas.

APPENDIX A

1789 COVENT GARDEN: JPK, PA

 Com. Err. *Mar. 23*: Pb omits Duke, Angelo, Pinch, Aegeon. *May 29*: PA omits Lesbia.
 R&J *Sept. 14, 21*: PA omits Peter. *Dec. 28*: Pb omits Tybalt, Escalus, Peter.

 HAYMARKET: H–B, PA
 Hamlet *June 1*: Pb omits Francisco, Marcellus.

1790 DRURY LANE: JPK, PA

 AYLI *Feb. 27; Mar. 6; Apr. 28*: PA omits Corin, Silvius, Dennis. *Oct. 27*: PA omits LeBeau.
 Hen. V *May 11*: Bill not in PA. *Oct. 7*: PA omits Hostess.
 Much Ado *Jan. 6; Feb. 3*: Pb omits Town Clerk. *May 12*: Bill not in PA.
 Tempest *Jan. 11, 18, 25*: Pb omits Alonso, Antonio.
 Twelfth N. *Feb. 10*: PA omits Curio, Captain. *Apr. 9*: Bill not in PA.
 TGV *Jan. 20*: Pb omits Host, Panthino. *June 3*: Bill not in PA.

 COVENT GARDEN: JPK, PA
 C&P *Apr. 6; May 13*: Bills not in PA.
 Hamlet *June 2*: Bill not in PA.
 Lear *Jan. 4, 11, 18; Feb. 1*: Pb omits Arante. *Feb. 15*: JPK missing. Pb is in BM; it omits Arante.
 Macbeth *May 3*: Bill not in PA.
 Othello *May 15*: Bill not in PA.
 Rich. III *Mar. 1*: Pb omits Ratcliff, Oxford. *Oct. 18*: PA omits Ratcliff.
 R&J *Sept. 13; Oct. 25*: PA omits Balthazar.

 HAYMARKET: H–B, PA
 C&P *Aug. 12, 20, 26; Sept. 8*: Pb omits Nathaniel, Peter, Cook (throughout), Baptista, Hortensio (on Aug. 20 only), Pedro, Tailor (on Aug. 20, 26, Sept. 8 only).

1791 DRURY LANE [company variously at DL and at KING'S, HAYMARKET]: JPK, PA

 AYLI *Apr. 29; May 28*: Bills not in PA. *Dec. 13*: Pb omits Charles.
 Hen. V *Nov. 28*: Pb omits Bates, Governor of Harfleur, Montjoy, Hostess.
 Tempest *May 5, 30*: Bills not in PA. *Dec. 27*: Pb omits Gonzalo.
 Twelfth N. *Feb. 25*: PA omits Curio.

 COVENT GARDEN: JPK, PA
 C&P *May 20*: Bill not in PA.
 Com. Err. *May 31*: Bill not in PA.
 R&J *Nov. 28*: Pb omits Peter, Balthazar.

 HAYMARKET: H–B, PA
 C&P *Sept. 16*: Bill in MP, not in H–B or PA.

1792 DRURY LANE [company at KING'S, HAYMARKET]: JPK, PA

 AYLI *Apr. 9; June 7*: Bills not in PA.
 C&P *Jan. 31*: Pb omits Baptista. *Apr. 24; May 9*: Pb also omits Nathaniel, Joseph (throughout), Tailor, Haberdasher (on May 9 only). *May 28; Nov. 21*: Pb omits all characters. *June 9*: Pb also omits Joseph; PA also

710

APPENDIX A

1792 DRURY LANE (*cont.*)

omits Peter. *Nov. 15; Dec. 1*: Pb also omits Pedro, Tailor, Joseph (throughout), Peter, Nicholas (on Nov. 15 only), Haberdasher (on Dec. 1 only).

Hen. VIII *Mar. 26*: Pb omits Campeius, Capucius, Surrey, Lord Chamberlain, Gardiner, Sands, Lovell, Butts, Surveyor, Brandon, Sergeant, Door-keeper, Crier. These characters are added by PA in an advance bill on Mar. 24, which omits Old Lady, Patience, Agatha. On Mar. 26 the bill is not in PA. *Apr. 17*: Pb omits Buckingham, Suffolk, Sergeant, Door-keeper, Crier.

Lear *Mar. 6*: PA omits Esquire.

Macbeth *Dec. 26*: Pb omits Sergeant, Murderer, Gentlewoman.

Merchant *Mar. 10*: PA omits Gobbo.

Othello *Dec. 28*: PA omits Julio, Antonio, Officers, Messenger, Sailor.

Rich. III *Feb. 7*: PA omits Richmond.

Tempest *May 8*: PA missing from BM file (another copy not located).

Twelfth N. *Feb. 20; May 31*: Pb omits Valentine, Curio, Priest. *May 1*: Pb also omits Valentine, Curio. *May 31*: Bill not in PA.

COVENT GARDEN: JPK, PA

C&P *May 15*: Bill not in PA.

Com. Err. *May 18*: Pb omits Pinch. Bill not in PA.

Cymbeline *May 19*: Bill not in PA.

Hamlet *Nov. 5; Dec. 27*: Pb omits Bernardo, Lucianus.

Rich. III *Dec. 26*: Pb omits Lord Mayor, Oxford.

R&J *Jan. 16*: Pb omits Peter, Balthazar.

Wint. T. *May 11*: Bill not in PA.

HAYMARKET: H–B, PA

Merchant *Feb. 20*: Bill in Times, not in PA.

Othello *Feb. 6*: Bill in DWR, not in PA.

Rich. III *Apr. 16*: See p. 568.

1793 DRURY LANE [company variously at Hay and at **KING'S, HAYMARKET**]: JPK, PA

AYLI *May 3*: PA omits all characters.

C&P *Jan. 22*: Pb omits Pedro, Tailor, Joseph, Haberdasher.

Hen. VIII *Mar. 9*: Pb omits Door-keeper; PA omits Lord Chancellor, Guildford. *May 14*: PA also omits Lord Chancellor, Guildford.

Lear *Feb. 16*: Pb omits Gentleman; PA omits Esquire.

Macbeth *Apr. 16*: Pb omits Sergeant, Murderer, Gentlewoman. *May 8*: Pb also omits Murderer, Gentlewoman.

Othello *Apr. 20*: PA omits Julio, Antonio, Officers, Messenger, Sailor.

Tempest *May 7*: Bill not in PA.

Twelfth N. *May 24*: Pb omits Valentine, Curio.

COVENT GARDEN: JPK, PA

C&P *May 10, 23*: Bills not in PA.

Com. Err. *June 3*: PA missing from BM file (another copy not located).

Cymbeline *Nov. 22*: PA missing from BM file (another copy not located).

Hamlet *Oct. 9*: PA missing from BM file (another copy not located). *Dec. 16*: PA omits King, Polonius, Osric, Rosencrantz, Guildenstern, Player King, Marcellus, Player Queen.

Hen. VIII *May 24*: Bill not in PA.

APPENDIX A

1793 COVENT GARDEN (*cont.*)

 Macbeth *Oct. 28*: PA omits Fleance. *Dec. 9*: PA omits all characters. *Dec. 27*: PA missing from BM file (another copy not located).
 Rich. III *Oct. 14*: PA missing from BM file (another copy not located).
 R&J *Nov. 11*: Pb omits Paris, Balthazar.

HAYMARKET: H–B, PA

 C&P *July 5*: PA missing from BM file (another copy not located).
 Hen. V *Sept. 24*: PA omits Governor of Harfleur.
 Othello *Oct. 21*: PA omits Officers.
 Rich. III *Dec. 23*: PA omits Prince Edward, Duke of York, Norfolk, Ratcliff, Tressel, Catesby, Brackenbury, Blunt, Tyrrel, Lord Mayor.
 Tempest *Nov. 19; Dec. 5*: PA omits Alonso, Antonio, Gonzalo (throughout), Neptune, Amphitrite (on Dec. 5 only). *Dec. 26*: PA missing from BM file (another copy not located).

1794 DRURY LANE: JPK

COVENT GARDEN: JPK

 Hamlet *Dec. 29*: Pb omits Rosencrantz, Guildenstern, Marcellus (added by MP).

HAYMARKET: H–B

 Rich. III *Aug. 27*: Pb omits Norfolk, Ratcliff, Brackenbury, Blunt, Tyrrel, Lord Mayor (added by O).

1795 DRURY LANE: JPK

 AYLI *Jan. 21*: Pb omits Corin, Silvius, Phebe (added by MP).
 John *Mar. 14*: Pb omits English Herald (added by Powell).
 Macbeth *Apr. 7*: JPK missing. Pb is in FSL; it omits Officer (added by MP). *Nov. 9*: Pb omits Officer, Sergeant (added by O).

COVENT GARDEN: JPK

 C&P *June 12*: Pb also omits Hortensio (retained by MP).
 Hamlet *Jan. 12*: Pb omits King, Rosencrantz, Guildenstern, Marcellus (added by MP).
 R&J *Jan. 5*: Pb omits Escalus, Paris, Balthazar, Montague, Peter, Friar John, Nurse (added by MP). *Nov. 23*: Pb omits Balthazar, Peter, Friar John, Apothecary (added by O).

HAYMARKET: H–B

1796 DRURY LANE: JPK

COVENT GARDEN: JPK

 R&J *May 17*: Pb omits Balthazar, Montague, Peter, Friar John, Apothecary (added by O in advance bill on May 16).

HAYMARKET: H–B

1797 DRURY LANE: JPK

COVENT GARDEN: JPK

 R&J *Nov. 2, 13*: Pb omits Friar John, Apothecary (added by TB).

HAYMARKET: H–B

APPENDIX A

1798 DRURY LANE: JPK

    COVENT GARDEN: JPK
    Hamlet *Apr. 28*: Pb omits Osric, Rosencrantz (added by O).

    HAYMARKET: H–B
    Rich. III. and C&P *Apr. 21*: Bill in TB, not in H–B.

1799 DRURY LANE: JPK

    COVENT GARDEN: JPK

    HAYMARKET: H–B
    Merchant *Apr. 17*: Bill in MP on Apr. 13, not in H–B.

1800 DRURY LANE: JPK

    Hamlet *Jan. 13*: Pb omits Bernardo, Francisco, Player Queen (added by MP). *Sept. 16*: Pb omits 2nd Gravedigger, Sailors, Messenger (added by O).

    COVENT GARDEN: JPK

Here follow the sources of the nightly receipts at the box-office, as recorded in Part I. The only receipts that have come to light are those pertaining to Drury Lane and to Covent Garden. And of these several seasons are missing.[1]

DRURY LANE

1751–May 29, 1758	C–H
Sept. 16, 1758–Mar. 8, 1759	MS annotations on JPK
Mar. 12, 1759–Jan. 5, 1760	C–H[2]
Sept. 20, 1763–May 5, 1764	MS annotations on JPK
Sept. 23, 1766–May 30, 1767	DL Account-Book, FSL
Sept. 26, 1771–1800	DL Account-Books, FSL

COVENT GARDEN

Sept. 23, 1757–May 18, 1758	Egerton 2270
Sept. 26, 1759–May 20, 1760	CG Account-Book, FSL
Sept. 29, 1760–June 23, 1761	Egerton 2271
Sept. 25–Nov. 26, 1761	MS by James Winston, 'Theatrical Records', FSL
Sept. 22, 1766–May 22, 1770	Egerton 2272–5
Sept. 25, 1771–May 10, 1774	Egerton 2276–8
Oct. 7, 1776–May 18, 1778	Egerton 2279–80

[1] One peculiarity of many of the Account-Books is the listing of a relatively small sum called 'after-money'. This is the money received on any given night, usually from latecomers to the theatre, after the usual box-office receipts had already been entered on the books. The after-money was invariably added to the account for the following night's performance. In arriving at the proper figure for each night I have, therefore, subtracted the after-money from its entry on, say, a Tuesday, and applied it to the Monday receipts, on Wednesday to the Tuesday receipts, and so on.

[2] The receipts in this manuscript are nearly always given in round numbers only. Its original compiler, Cross, ceased entering the receipts about a month before his death, which occurred in Feb. 1760. His successor, Hopkins, entered no receipts at all.

APPENDIX A

COVENT GARDEN (*cont.*)

Sept. 20, 1779–May 25, 1784	Egerton 2281–5
Sept. 21, 1785–May 19, 1792	Egerton 2286–92
Oct. 1, 1792–June 5, 1793	MS annotations on Pbs in BM
Sept. 18, 1793–May 21, 1794	CG Account-Book, FSL
Sept. 17, 1794–1800	Egerton 2293–9

APPENDIX B

SHAKESPEARE'S POPULARITY IN THE THEATRE, 1751–1800 [and 1701–1800]

THE records for the major theatres of London for the last fifty years of the eighteenth century may be considered as complete. The same thing cannot be said for the minor theatres. Their financial situation did not permit the expense of advertising every performance in the newspapers. Nor, apparently, was it considered necessary, in view of their fairly small size, to inform the general public of what was in progress at these theatres. Their actual playhouse bills have almost entirely disappeared. The following summary does not, therefore, represent the absolute total of every theatrical performance that took place between 1751 and 1800.

As in Volume I I have arranged the figures in groups of five-year periods; the right-hand column includes both the original plays and their adaptations. Following the figures for 1751–1800 I have noted those for 1701–50 and the grand total for the entire century.

	Total number of plays performed	Number of plays by Shakespeare performed
1751–5	1,832	450
1756–60	1,820	481
1761–5	2,070	488
1766–70	2,173	438
1771–5	2,181	384
1776–80	2,355	471
1781–5	2,385	354
1786–90	2,368	350
1791–5	2,398	287
1796–1800	2,419	285
	22,001	3,988 (of which 70 are double bills)
1701–50	18,663	3,226
	40,664	7,214

Exactly the same ratio of popularity that pertained in the first half of the century was maintained in the second half: approximately one play out of every six that was acted was written by Shakespeare. The largest number of performances in any one year was at Covent Garden in 1761: 73 out of 193; the smallest was at the same theatre in 1763: 14 out of 183.

APPENDIX C

ORDER OF POPULARITY OF SHAKESPEARE'S PLAYS, 1751–1800
[and 1701–1800]

THE most remarkable fact about the theatrical history of Shakespeare in the second half of the eighteenth century is the almost complete disappearance of those drastically rewritten versions of the original texts that are so frequently met with in the first half. Only three such versions were for the first time brought forward: Sheridan's *Coriolanus* in 1754, Hawkins' *Cymbeline* in 1759, and Cumberland's *Timon of Athens* in 1771. None of them was really successful; they were acted sixteen, seven, and eleven times respectively. Tate's re-arrangement of *King Lear* and Cibber's of *Richard III* were perennial favourites, established as such from the beginning of the century. But it will be observed that both Garrick and Colman restored hundreds of lines of the original *Lear*. Cibber, however, remained sacrosanct.

Everything else was what Shakespeare himself wrote. Brief new speeches or scenes were sometimes, although rarely, introduced, but the usual practice was that of pruning and excision, exactly as it is in the theatres of today. Occasionally not much was left: *A Fairy Tale*, for example, consists only of the material relating to the clowns in *A Midsummer-Night's Dream*, and *Florizel and Perdita* only of the sheep-shearing scene in *The Winter's Tale*. The play that was the least tampered with is *Twelfth Night*. In the first fifty years of the century Shakespeare's tragedies were more popular than his comedies or histories. In the succeeding fifty years (in the course of which only four plays, *Hamlet*, *Macbeth*, Cibber's *Richard III*, and *Romeo and Juliet*, were performed uninterruptedly) this situation remained unchanged, and it has remained unchanged ever since.

I have listed the plays in the order of their relative popularity throughout the second half of the century, and noted the various years in which each play or each adaptation of it was acted and the number of performances it received. Following this number is given, in square brackets, the total number of times the play was acted between 1701 and 1800. The number in parentheses indicates the rank held by that play in the total reckoning of popularity for the entire century.

	Times acted 1751–1800	Times acted 1701–1800	Relative popularity 1701–1800
ROMEO AND JULIET (1751–1800)	399[1]	[495]	(4)
HAMLET	343[1]	[601]	(1)
The original (1751–1800): 309			
As altered by Garrick (1772–9): 34			
RICHARD III	323[1]	[523]	(3)
As altered by Cibber (1751–1800)			

[1] Excerpts from this play were acted at Hay in 1781 (or 1782 or 1796). These performances are not included in the enumeration.

APPENDIX C

	Times acted 1751–1800	Times acted 1701–1800	Relative popularity 1701–1800
MACBETH	271	[558]	(2)
As altered by Davenant (1751): 1			
The original (1752–1800): 270			
THE MERCHANT OF VENICE	243[1]	[358]	(9)
The original (1751–61, 1764–5, 1767–90, 1792–3, 1795–1800): 237			
As *The Jew of Venice* (1754): 6			
THE TAMING OF THE SHREW	235	[359]	(8)
As *Catharine and Petruchio* (1754, 1756–86, 1788–99): 234			
As *The Cobler of Preston* (1759): 1			
KING LEAR	186	[372]	(6)
As altered by Tate (1751–8, 1764–7, 1770, 1774, 1776–81, 1783–4, 1786, 1789–91, 1794–7, 1799): 107			
As altered by Garrick (1756–63, 1765–71, 1773–4, 1776, 1779, 1788): 61			
As altered by Colman (1768–73): 15			
As altered by Kemble (1792–3, 1795): 3			
AS YOU LIKE IT (1751–64, 1766–80, 1782–1800)	179[1]	[274]	(12)
OTHELLO (1751–62, 1764–75, 1777, 1779–80, 1782–94, 1796–1800)	176	[441]	(5)
CYMBELINE	175	[200]	(14)
As altered by Hawkins (1759): 7			
The original (1761–80, 1782–7, 1792–5, 1797, 1800): 168			
THE TEMPEST	168[2]	[354]	(10)
As 'A new English Opera', at DL (1756): 6			
The original (1757–63, 1765–82, 1784–7): 114			
As an opera, at CG (1776–7, 1779): 7			
As altered by Kemble (1789–94, 1797–9): 41			
HENRY IV, PART I (1751–3, 1755–66, 1769–70, 1774–92, 1795–9)	149[1]	[363]	(7)
MUCH ADO ABOUT NOTHING (1751–81, 1783–90, 1792–4, 1797–9)	148	[195]	(15)
THE MERRY WIVES OF WINDSOR (1751, 1753–66, 1768–9, 1771–2, 1777–90, 1796–7)	134	[336]	(11)
HENRY VIII (1751–61, 1772–83, 1785, 1787–9, 1792–6, 1799)	126[1]	[262]	(13)

[1] Excerpts from this play were acted at Hay in 1781 (or 1782 or 1796). These performances are not included in the enumeration.

[2] An alteration of this play, designed to be performed by puppets, was produced in 1779–80 at the Patagonian Theatre, Great Room, Exeter 'Change. Its 17 performances are not included in the enumeration. Nor are the 7 performances of a pantomime based on *The Tempest*, entitled *The Duke of Milan*, acted at the Royalty in 1788.

APPENDIX C

	Times acted 1751–1800	Times acted 1701–1800	Relative popularity 1701–1800
TWELFTH NIGHT (1751–5, 1763–4, 1771–80, 1782–99)	113	[131]	(20)
THE WINTER'S TALE	98	[112]	(23)
As *Florizel and Perdita* (1754, 1758–62, 1768–9, 1771, 1774, 1790, 1798): 25			
As altered by Garrick (1756–8, 1762, 1765, 1774, 1779–81, 1783–9, 1792, 1795): 68			
As altered by Hull (1771–2): 2			
As *The Sheep Shearing* (1777, 1783): 3			
HENRY V (1752, 1754–62, 1764, 1766–71, 1773, 1778–9, 1782, 1789–94)	93	[142]	(18)
KING JOHN (1751, 1754, 1758, 1760–2, 1764, 1766–7, 1769–70, 1774–5, 1777–8, 1783–5, 1792–3, 1795, 1800)	70	[113]	(22)
MEASURE FOR MEASURE (1755–9, 1770–2, 1775–8, 1780–5, 1794–9)	64	[133]	(19)
A MIDSUMMER-NIGHT'S DREAM	64	[115]	(21)
As *Pyramus and Thisbe* (1751, 1754): 2			
As *The Fairies* (1755): 11			
The original (1763): 1			
As *A Fairy Tale* (1763–7, 1777): 50			
HENRY IV, PART II	62[1]	[150]	(17)
The original (1751, 1758, 1761–4, 1766–7, 1770, 1773, 1777–9, 1784): 61			
As *The Humourists* (1754): 1			
THE COMEDY OF ERRORS	50	[62]	(25)
As *The Twins* (1762): 1			
As altered by Hull (1779–81, 1785–6, 1788–98): 49			
CORIOLANUS	39	[52]	(26)
The original (1754–5): 9			
As altered by Sheridan (1754–5, 1758–60, 1765, 1768): 16			
As altered by Kemble (1789, 1792–3, 1796–7): 14			
ALL'S WELL THAT ENDS WELL	29	[51]	(27)
The original (1756–8, 1762–4, 1767, 1772, 1774): 26			
As altered by Pilon (1785): 2			
As altered by Kemble (1794): 1			
JULIUS CAESAR (1751, 1753–5, 1758, 1766–7, 1769, 1773, 1780)	23	[186]	(16)
TIMON OF ATHENS	12	[101]	(24)
As altered by Cumberland (1771–2): 11			
As altered by Hull (1786): 1			

[1] Excerpts from this play were acted at Hay in 1781 (or 1782 or 1796). These performances are not included in the enumeration.

APPENDIX C

	Times acted 1751–1800	*Times acted 1701–1800*	*Relative popularity 1701–1800*
THE TWO GENTLEMEN OF VERONA	10	[10]	(31)
As altered by Victor (1762–3): 6			
The original (1784, 1790): 4			
ANTONY AND CLEOPATRA (1759)	6	[6]	(33)
Total	3,988		

Plays acted 1701–50, but not 1751–1800:

HENRY VI, PART I		[1]	(35)
HENRY VI, PART II		[9]	(32)
HENRY VI, PART III		[1]	(36)
PERICLES		[3]	(34)
RICHARD II		[25]	(28)
TITUS ANDRONICUS		[16]	(29)
TROILUS AND CRESSIDA		[10]	(30)
Total		[7,214]	

Play not acted, 1701–1800
LOVE'S LABOUR'S LOST

APPENDIX D

LONDON THEATRES IN USE BETWEEN 1751 AND 1800

THE MAJOR THEATRES

These theatres are listed chronologically, by the date of opening. For fuller descriptions see vol. i, pp. 462–3, and the present volume, p. 1.

DRURY LANE

Opened 1674, demolished 1791. While its new theatre was being built the DL company performed throughout the season of 1791–2 at the King's, Haymarket, and at the same theatre in 1792–3, except in the spring of 1793 when, on Tuesdays and Saturdays, the Theatre Royal, Haymarket, was used. In 1793–4 the company was temporarily disbanded, but most of its members were engaged to play at the last-mentioned theatre. The new Theatre Royal, Drury Lane, was opened for the performance of plays on April 21, 1794. It was burned to the ground on February 24, 1809.

KING'S, HAYMARKET

Opened 1705, burned 1789, reopened March 26, 1791, and again burned 1867. It was the principal opera house of London, but was used for the performance of plays by Spranger Barry's company in the summer of 1766 and, while its new theatre was being erected, by the DL company (see above).

HAYMARKET

Opened 1720, rebuilt 1767, demolished 1820.

COVENT GARDEN

Opened 1732, rebuilt 1792, burned 1808.

THE MINOR THEATRES

These theatres (in most instances 'fit-ups') are listed alphabetically. They do not include places of entertainment not used for plays proper, i.e. Astley's Amphitheatre, the Pantheon, the Royal Circus, Sadler's Wells, and the Sans-Souci.

ASSEMBLY HOUSE, KENTISH TOWN

Fildew's company was acting here in the autumn of 1795. The Assembly House, which was located at the corner of Kentish Town Road and Leighton Road, was demolished in 1852. (Lysons Coll.)

BOWLING GREEN, SOUTHWARK

See vol. i, p. 465. A theatre, possibly only a booth, was in use on this site from 1743 to 1756. It is not to be confused with PHILLIPS'S BOOTH or the TILED BOOTH, qqv. (DA)

APPENDIX D

BROOK GREEN, HAMMERSMITH
A small barn, converted into a theatre, was in use here early in 1799. (MP)

CAMBERWELL
Osborne's company was performing here in the spring of 1799. Reference is made to the 'theatre', which was perhaps the same building referred to in Allport's *History of Camberwell*, 1841, as standing in the High Street. (MM)

CHINA HALL, ROTHERHITHE
This was a proper theatre, situated in the rear of what is now 141, Lower Road. Several eminent actors—Shuter, Charles Bannister, G. F. Cooke, &c.—appeared here. It was erected in 1776 (for use in the summer only), and was opened on May 25 of that year. On June 26, 1778 it was destroyed by fire. For the remainder of that season the company acted in a temporary booth. A new theatre was built, but shortly before it was to be opened it was blown down in a hurricane. No further venture was attempted. (MC)

CROSS KEYS INN, CHELSEA
Linnett's company appeared at this inn in the early 1760's. Its sign, in Lawrence Street, is still in existence. (C. L. Lewes, *Memoirs*, 1805, i. 15)

CROWN INN, HIGHGATE
The location of this inn I have been unable to discover. Plays were performed in it in the spring of 1799 and the autumn of 1800. (HTC)

CROWN INN, ISLINGTON
There are records of plays being acted here in 1780, 1781, and 1783. The inn, which was demolished *c.* 1800, was situated on the south side of Lower Street (now Essex Road), between Popham Street and Britannia Row. (HTC)

DULWICH
Everard acted here with an itinerant company in the autumn of 1778; he does not indicate the location of the playhouse. (E. C. Everard, *Memoirs*, 1818, 84)

GEORGE INN, CHISWICK
The long room in this inn was fitted up as a theatre in April 1784 and in November 1785. The location of the inn I have been unable to trace. (Burney Collection, BM)

HICKFORD'S ROOM, BREWER STREET
This well-known concert-hall was opened in 1739 and closed in 1779. Plays were acted in it in the winter of 1753–4. In the nineteenth century it became part of a private club which was demolished in 1937 to permit enlargement of the Regent Palace Hotel. (DA)

JAMES STREET (now ORANGE STREET), HAYMARKET
See vol. i, p. 463. Opened as a theatre *c.* 1729 and used as such intermittently until the late 1760's. (DA; GA)

APPENDIX D

LION AND LAMB INN, BERMONDSEY

In 1752 what is referred to as a 'playhouse' adjoined this inn. It was situated at Cherry Garden Stairs. (DA)

MILE END ASSEMBLY HOUSE, WHITECHAPEL

This building was located on the south side of Mile End Road, about halfway between Stepney Green and Assembly Passage. Roger Johnston's company was acting in it in the summer of 1778, and an unnamed company in the summer of 1785. (MC; PA)

NEW WELLS, CLERKENWELL

See vol. i, p. 464. It was used for the occasional performance of plays from 1737 to December 1751. On May 17, 1752 it was opened by John Wesley as a Methodist chapel. In 1756 it was demolished. (DA)

NEW WELLS, GOODMAN'S FIELDS

See vol. i, p. 465. Opened 1739, closed November 30, 1752. It was used occasionally thereafter for lectures, pantomimes, &c., and was finally converted into a tobacco warehouse. Its site was on what is now Hooper Street, Leman Street. (DA; PA)

PARSONS GREEN, FULHAM

In the autumn of 1789 a playhouse was opened here in a barn adjoining the White Horse Inn, which was located at the corner of Parsons Green and Ackmar Road. It was again being used, by Duckworth's company, early in 1793. (Lysons Coll.; TM)

PATAGONIAN THEATRE, EXETER 'CHANGE, STRAND

This 'Theatre' was a puppet-show, which enjoyed considerable popularity from 1776 to 1781. It was housed in the Great Room of the 'Change, in which actual plays were also from time to time performed. Exeter 'Change was situated at the corner of the Strand and Burleigh Street; it was erected in 1676 and demolished in 1829. (MP)

PHILLIPS'S BOOTH, BOWLING GREEN, SOUTHWARK

See vol. i, p. 465. This booth, 'facing the Til'd Booth', q.v., was used for the performance of plays from 1741 to 1753. (DA)

RED LION INN, STOKE NEWINGTON

Simpson and Marriot's company was acting here in the spring of 1787. The inn, the sign of which is still in existence, stands at the corner of Stoke Newington Church Street and Lordship Road. (Burney Collection, BM)

ROSE LANE, RATCLIFF

In the summer of 1770 a detachment of actors from the Haymarket performed at a clandestine theatre located here. It was fitted up behind a snuff shop, and the tickets of admission consisted of packets of snuff available at 3s., 2s., and 1s. Rose Lane is no longer in existence; it extended from Cable Street to Branch Road, a little south of Commercial Road. (Faulkner's Dublin Journal)

APPENDIX D

ROYALTY

This theatre was located on the west side of Well Street [not, as all previous historians have stated, Wells Street] (now Ensign Street), a few doors south of Cable Street, Wellclose Square. It was built by John Palmer, and opened on June 20, 1787. But Palmer had no license; the patent theatres therefore brought action and compelled it to close after one performance. It was reopened on July 3, and used thereafter for burlettas and pantomimes. Early in the nineteenth century plays were permitted to be acted. For a brief period, *c.* 1810, it was known as the East London. On April 11, 1826 it was destroyed by fire. (PA)

RUPERT STREET, HAYMARKET

In the late 1760's the upper story of a house in this street was used as a theatre. It was managed by Flockton; there is reason to suppose that it was merely a 'spouting club' for neophyte actors. (Theatrical Inquirer, Feb. 1817)

TENNIS COURT, SOUTHWARK

A temporary theatre was installed here in the winter of 1778-9; its site was probably on what is now Tennis Street, Newcomen Street. (MC)

TILED BOOTH, BOWLING GREEN, SOUTHWARK

See vol. i, p. 464. This booth was in occasional use from 1735 to 1755. (DA)

TOOLEY STREET, BERMONDSEY

Davis and Weston had a temporary theatre in a house (not identified) in this street in the summer of 1770. (WEP)

WHEATLEY'S RIDING SCHOOL, GREENWICH

Humphrey's company was performing here in the spring of 1798 and of 1799. Its location has not been ascertained. (Burney Collection, BM)

WINDSOR CASTLE INN, HAMMERSMITH

Records exist of plays being acted in Hammersmith in 1777, from 1784 to 1786, and in 1794, the playbills for which year alone give the address of the 'theatre'. But it is not unlikely that the Inn in question was used in the earlier years as well. Its sign is still in existence, at 134, King Street. (Gaz; Burney Collection, BM; PA; MC; Lysons Coll.)

INDEX I

ACTORS

All names in this index are those of actors unless the contrary is indicated. Each actor has been indexed according to the parts he performed. Following the names of characters (Antonio, &c.) that are common to more than one play is an abbreviation of the play, or alteration of it, in which the character appears.

It will be noted that nobody is listed as 'flourishing' after 1800. This is, of course, misleading: many of the persons whose names appear below continued to flourish long thereafter. In the interests of consistency, however, I have made 1800 my terminal date.

All names preceded by an asterisk are those of actors, and of persons connected with the theatre in other capacities, who are also listed in the Actor Index to my first volume.

Subjoined is a list of abbreviations used for the alterations of Shakespeare's plays that have titles different from their originals. Complete information regarding these alterations will be found in Part II.

Fairies   The Fairies (MND)
C & P   Catharine and Petruchio (Tam. Shrew)
Cobler   The Cobler of Preston (Tam. Shrew)
F & P   Florizel and Perdita (Wint. T.)

Fairy T.   A Fairy Tale (MND)
Humourists   The Humourists (2 Hen. IV)
P & T   Pyramus and Thisbe (MND)
Sheep S.   The Sheep Shearing (Wint. T.)
Twins   The Twins (Com. Err.)

Abbot [CG stage-door-keeper], fl. 1763: 33.
Abbot, T., fl. 1789–1800: Balthazar (R & J) 610–12; Bernardo 233, 236; Capucius 312; Francisco (Hamlet) 228; Gentleman (Hamlet) 231; Gratiano (Othello) 523; John, Friar 610; Lord (Cymbeline) 186; Messenger (1 Hen. IV) 263; Murderer 395–6, 398; Music Master 634; Nathaniel 633, 635; Norfolk (Rich. III) 569; Northumberland 264; Pedro (C & P) 633–5; Peter (C & P) 628–32; Peto (1 Hen. IV) 262; Ratcliff 572; Servant (Rich. III) 570; Sexton 496; Sheriff (1 Hen. IV) 265–6; Tyrrel 569, 574–5.
Abegg, Mrs, fl. 1759–62: Dorcas (F & P) 678; Jessica 419. Other reference 31.
Abington, James (?), fl. 1756: Ventoso 638.
Abington, Mrs James, Frances, nee Barton, 1737–1815: Beatrice 484–5, 488–92, 495–6; Catharine 616; Desdemona 501; Ford, Mrs 458–9; Olivia 661–3; Ophelia 209–10; Portia (Merchant) 420–4. Other references 19, 54, 84, 86.
Abrams, Miss Harriet, 1760–c. 1825: Ariel 648. Other reference 67.

Achmet, Mrs, stage name of Mrs William Cairns, nee Catherine Ann Egan, 1766–?: Juliet (R & J) 606; Ophelia 228.
*Ackman, Ellis, d. 1774: Alexas 116; Antonio (Much Ado) 480; Balthazar (Merchant) 420–1; Balthazar (R & J) 578, 581, 588; Benvolio 587, 589–90, 593; Borachio 480–3; Caliban 641, 643–5; Caphis 656–7; Captain (Cymbeline) 173–4; Captain (Lear) 346–50; Duke Senior 126; Gentleman (All's Well) 112; Gentleman (Cymbeline) 168–70, 173–7; Guildenstern 192; Hastings 269, 271, 273–4; Herald, French 320–2, 325, 327; LeBeau 118, 120, 125–9; Lennox 365; Lord Mayor 548; Lovell 297–8, 300; Marcellus 197–212; Messenger (Othello) 504–5; Outlaw 673; Oxford 531; Peter (C & P) 614; Pistol (MWW) 447–8, 452–4, 456–9; Roman (Coriolanus) 159–60; Servant (Rich. III) 527; Seyton 373–5, 377–9; Shipmaster 643–4; Snout (Fairy T.) 471–2; Snout (MND) 470; Tressel 535, 537–8; Tybalt 586; Westmorland (1 Hen. IV) 243–50. Other references 7, 11, 17, 26, 32, 34, 38, 45, 47, 53.

725

INDEX I

Adams, stage name of William Woodfall, 1746-1803: Tyrrel 547.
Adcock, William, fl. 1765: Burgundy (Lear) 342; Escalus (R & J) 589; Lennox 373; Mortimer 247. Other reference 36.
Adcock, *Mrs* William, Mary, nee Palmer, d. 1773: Nurse 589.
Aickin, Francis, 1736-1812: Antigonus (F & P) 680; Antonio (Merchant) 437; Banquo 380-1; Belarius 184; Brabantio 506; Buckingham (Rich. III) 540; Capulet 590; Dauphin (John) 325; Douglas 248; Duke Senior 124; Edmund 351-2, 354-5; Falstaff (1 Hen. IV) 260; Ford 457-8; Ghost 213-14, 216-20, 222-4, 227-9; Guiderius 170-3; Henry IV (1 Hen. IV) 259-61; Henry IV (2 Hen. IV) 276; Henry VI (Cibber's Rich. III) 561-2, 564-7; Henry VIII 307; Hubert 327, 330; Jaques 126-8, 132, 138, 141-2, 144-5; John, Don 480; Kent 343, 356-7; Laertes 204-7, 209-10; Leonato 480-3; Macbeth 382; Macduff 378, 388-92; Montano 505-7; Pembroke 324; Polixenes (F & P) 688; Polixenes (Wint. T.) 684-8; Richmond 540-1, 543-5; Rosencrantz 204; Ross 375-7; Sergeant (Macbeth) 374; Tybalt 590-2; Wales, Prince of (2 Hen. IV) 273. Other references 40, 51, 55, 91, 567.
Aickin, James, 1735-1803: Adam (AYLI) 136; Albany 347; Antigonus (F & P) 681; Antonio (Merchant) 432, 435, 437, 441-3; Belarius 174-83, 186; Brabantio 511-23; Buckingham (Rich. III) 549, 552-8, 560-3; Caesar 318; Camillo (Wint. T.) 682-3, 685-7; Capulet 597-8, 600-2, 605-6, 609; Casca 318; Cassio 508; Cominius 163-5; Cranmer 307-11; Duke (TGV) 674; Duke Frederick 126; Duke Senior 134-5, 137-48; Duncan 395-8; Edgar 348; Escalus (Measure) 404-11; Exeter 290-3; Ghost 232-3; Gloucester (Lear) 348-51, 353; Gonzalo 643-51; Henry IV (1 Hen. IV) 262, 264; Henry VI (Cibber's Rich. III) 548-9, 552, 571-3; Horatio 222, 224-5; Hotspur 251, 253; John, Don 481-6, 488, 491-3; Kent 356, 358-9; Laertes 207, 209-13, 215-21; Lafeu 115; Laurence, Friar 610; Leonato 494-6; Lord Chief Justice 274-6; Macduff 383; Montano 507-11; Philip, King 327-9, 331-2; Poins (1 Hen. IV) 249; Richmond 542; Rosencrantz 206, 208-10; Ross 378, 380-5, 387-8; Salarino 421-3; Senator (Timon) 656; Sergeant (Macbeth) 376-7; Siward 393-5; Stanley 563-8, 570; Surrey 304, 306; Tybalt 593-5; Witch 388-92; Worcester 252-4, 261-2, 264. Other references 45, 137, 319, 644.

Aldridge, Robert [dancer], d. 1793: 36, 38, 58, 74.
Alfred, Edward, d. 1793: Abhorson 407-8; Bardolph (1 Hen. IV) 261; Bardolph (Hen. V) 290-2; Charles 140-1; Cook (C & P) 631; Cornelius 184; Crier (Hen. VIII) 309; Dennis 142; Henry VI (Cibber's Rich. III) 558; Leonardo 432; Messenger (Hamlet) 226; Officer, Volscian 164; Peter (C & P) 628-9; Pistol (MWW) 463, 465; Sailor (Othello) 519-20. Other references 87, 165.
Allen, fl. 1753: Nym (MWW) 447.
*Allen, *Miss* Ann (?), fl. 1749-51: Patience 295.
Allingham, *Miss* Maria Caroline, later Mrs Samuel Ricketts, d. 1811: Juliet (R & J) 610.
Ambrose, *Miss* E., fl. 1771-82: Anne, Lady 558; Bullen, Anne 302; Celia 127; Macduff, Lady 379; Nerissa 422-3, 426, 428-9; Page, Mrs 459; Phebe 126; Regan 351-2, 354-5. Other reference 427.
*Anderson, John (?), d. 1767: Albany 336; Antigonus (F & P) 676; Chamberlain, Lord 295; Cornwall 338-9, 341-4; Douglas 239-48; Duke (All's Well) 113; Duke (Com. Err.) 150; Duke (Merchant) 413-20; Duke (Othello) 504-5; Escalus (R & J) 578-91; Gower (Hen. V) 278-84; Hastings 267-8, 270; Host (MWW) 455-6; King (Hamlet) 200; Lodovico 499-503; Lord Chief Justice 270, 272; Malcolm 363, 366-9, 371, 373; Marcellus 190-200, 203; Minucius 160, 162; Oliver 119-22; Paris 579-80; Pembroke 323; Ratcliff 526-30; Richmond 533; Salisbury (John) 321-5; Siward 365; Stanley 532, 535-9; Trebonius 314-17. Other references 3, 16, 23, 25, 39, 202-3, 323.
Andrews, Miles Peter [dramatist], d. 1814: 65.
Ansell [CG box-keeper], fl. 1766-81: 39, 46, 73.
Ansell, Thomas [unidentified], fl. 1774: 57.
Archer, Alexander, 1757-1817: Antonio (Merchant) 442, 444-5; Shylock 441. Other reference 238.
Armstead, *Mrs*, stage name of Elizabeth Bridget Cane, later Mrs Charles James Fox, 1750-1842: Perdita (Wint. T.) 682.
Armstrong, *Miss*, stage name of Kitty Ann Worlock, later Mrs John Moody [the 2nd] [dancer], 1763-1846: 65.
Arne, Michael [composer], c. 1741-86: 38, 150, 469.
Arne, *Mrs* Michael [the 2nd], Elizabeth, nee Wright, d. 1769: Ariel 642; Fairy (Fairy T.) 471-2; Fairy (MND) 471. Other references 34, 40, 45.

726

INDEX I

Arne, *Miss* Sarah, later Mrs Gardiner, d. 1808: Phebe 149.
*Arne, Thomas Augustine [composer], 1710-78: 5, 25, 637, 674.
Arnold, Samuel [composer], 1740-1802: 469.
*Arthur, John, d. 1772: Carrier 239-42; Citizen (J. Caesar) 314-16; Evans 446, 448-50; Fluellen 278-80; Gardiner 295; Gregory (R & J) 578; Hecate 364-9; Launcelot 413-14; Polonius 192-7, 208; Shallow (2 Hen. IV) 267; Shylock 415-16. Other references 3, 7, 10, 15.
*Atkins, fl. 1750-60: Alonso (?) 638; Amiens 123; Balthazar (Much Ado) 477-8; Mecaenas 116; Nicholas (C & P) 614; Peto (1 Hen. IV) 243; Peto (2 Hen. IV) 267. Other reference 470.
Atkins, William, 1763-1831: Oxford 574-5; Philario 186; Senator (Othello) 524.
Atkins, *Mrs* William, Eliza, nee Warrell, fl. 1799: Jessica 444; Patience 312.
*Auguste, *Mme* M. [dancer], fl. 1743-53: 6.
Auretti, *Mme* Anne (?) [dancer], fl. 1751: 2.
Austin, Joseph, 1735-1821: Antonio (Tempest) 639; Buckingham (Hen. VIII) 298-9; Burgundy (Lear) 338-40; Canidius 116; Dauphin (John) 321-2; Douglas 243; Guildenstern 196, 198; Laertes 197-9; Malcolm 369-70; Paris 584-5; Proculeius 116; Silvius 121-3; Tressel 534. Other references 24, 116.
Aylward, Theodore [composer], *c.* 1730-1801: 469.

Baddeley, Robert, 1733-94: Biondello 616; Bottom (Fairy T.) 471-2; Caius 454, 456-61, 463, 465; Chamberlain, Lord 299; Citizen (J. Caesar) 319; Fabian 660; Fluellen 290-3; Flute (Fairy T.) 471; Flute (MND) 470; Gentleman Usher 343; Grumio 617-21, 623-32; Lafeu 114; Lord Mayor 534, 537-8, 540-1, 546; Man, Old (Lear) 342; Menenius 163-4; Pistol (2 Hen. IV) 273, 275-6; Polonius 201-6, 208-13, 215-17, 219-21, 223-7; Roderigo 506; Sands 307-10; Soldier [Interpreter] (?) 112; Soldier (Timon) 656-7; Town Clerk 479-86, 488, 490-2; Trinculo 642-53; Witch 374-85, 387-9. Other references 34, 38, 40, 49, 51, 56, 93, 246, 273, 310, 471.
Baddeley, *Mrs* Robert, Sophia, nee Snow, 1745-86: Celia 125-8, 130, 134; Cordelia 343-4; Desdemona 506; Hero 480-4; Imogen 171-5; Jessica 420-2; Miranda 642-3; Olivia 662-5; Ophelia 202-9, 213, 215-18; Portia (J. Caesar) 319. Other references 38, 40.
Bailey, stage name of William Reilly [who later adopted stage name of O'Reilly], d. 1791: Biondello 623; Blunt (Cibber's Rich. III) 554; Catesby 554; Peter (R & J) 599; Stanley 543.
Bailey, *Mrs*, stage name of Mrs William Reilly, nee Mary Sophia Arnold, fl. 1778: Anne, Lady 554.
Baker, *Mrs*, d. 1760: Dorcas (Cobler) 615; Jessica 415, 418; Ophelia 194, 198; Page, Anne 448-52. Other references 12, 23.
Baker, *Mrs* David Lionel Erskine, Elizabeth, nee Clendon, d. 1778: Countess 112; Elinor 324.
*Baker, Thomas [the elder], fl. 1746-82: Bardolph (1 Hen. IV) 250-1; Bardolph (MWW) 460-2; Bardolph, Lord 272; Benvolio 590-1; Doctor (Lear) 354; Gobbo 430; Humphrey, Prince 267; Montague 599-600; Montjoy 278-83, 285, 288-9; Oxford 549; Tailor 619, 621; Wall (P & T) 469-70. Other reference 621.
Baker, *Mrs* Thomas [the elder], Elizabeth, nee Miller, fl. 1762-75: Anne, Lady 548, 550; Bullen, Anne 301; Celia 127; Jessica 419-25; Nerissa 424; Page, Anne 453-4; Page, Mrs 457; Patience 300-1. Other references 37, 39, 52.
Baker, Thomas [the younger], *c.* 1764-1801: Bassanio 438; Borachio 490; Laertes 226; Othello 520.
Ballard, Jonathan [CG treasurer], fl. 1757-62: 18, 21, 25, 27, 31.
*Bambridge, *Mrs*, fl. 1742-54: Calphurnia 314; Hostess (2 Hen. IV) 267; Isabel 278; Lady, Old 295; Queen, Player 190-3; York, Duchess of 526-30.
Banks, Thomas, 1756-1810: Balthazar (R & J) 605-6, 609; Bates 290-3; Brandon (Hen. VIII) 309-11; Herald (Lear) 359; Le Beau 141, 145; Messenger (1 Hen. IV) 261; Messenger (Macbeth) 391-2, 396-7; Music Master 629, 631-2, 634; Nicholas (C & P) 628-9; Officer (Macbeth) 393, 395; Officer (Othello) 519-21; Verges 496.
*Banks, William [harlequin], d. 1776: 39.
Bannister, Charles, *c.* 1738-1804: Antonio (Merchant) 423; Apemantus 656; Caliban 646-50, 652-4; Casca 317; Hecate 381-5, 387-93, 395-7; Henry IV (1 Hen. IV) 248-9; Henry VI (Cibber's Rich. III) 542-3; Host (MWW) 461; Jaques 130; King (Hamlet) 207; Servant (Sheep S.) 682, 684; Snug (Fairy T.) 473; Tybalt 592. Other references 51, 59, 77, 79, 91, 93, 95, 98-9, 101, 103, 721.
Bannister, James, fl. 1773-4: Burgundy (Lear) 350; Essex 327; Hortensio 619.
Bannister, *Miss* Jane, later Mrs James

727

INDEX I

Swendall, fl. 1785: Miranda 650; Perdita (Wint. T.) 685.

Bannister, John, 1760–1836: Cassio 516–17; Chatillon 331; Clown (All's Well) 115; Florizel (Sheep S.) 684; Florizel (Wint. T.) 685; Francis 261, 264; Gratiano (Merchant) 435; Hamlet 217–20, 231, 233; Launcelot 439; Lucio 408–10; Malvolio 671; Mercutio 610; Orlando 136; Osric 232; Parolles 114; Petruchio 635; Posthumus 181; Richard III 566, 569; Romeo [V. i and iii only] 602; Sebastian (Twelfth N.) 665–7; Shylock 439; Speed 674; Stephano (Tempest) 653–4; Touchstone 140, 142–3, 147–8; Tressel 556, 560–1; Wales, Prince of (1 Hen. IV) 254, 264. Other references 68–9, 71, 73, 75, 80–1, 90, 115.

Bannister, *Mrs* John, Elizabeth, nee Harper, 1757–1849: Olivia 665; Ophelia 218, 223–5; Perdita (Sheep S.) 684; Perdita (Wint. T.) 685. Other references 66, 75, 77.

Barnard, *Miss*, fl. 1783: York, Duke of 560.

Barnard, *Mrs*, fl. 1783: York, Duchess of 560.

Barnes, *Miss*, fl. 1782–91: Juliet (Measure) 407–8; Mopsa (Wint. T.) 687; Phebe 135, 137–43; Ursula 492.

Barnshaw, John, fl. 1769–70: Bardolph (Hen. V) 286–7; Hecate 376.

Barresford, *Mrs* Ebenezer, Mary, nee Wilford, formerly Mrs George Bulkley, d. 1792: Beatrice 484–5, 491; Bullen, Anne 301; Cordelia 343, 346; Ford, Mrs 457; Imogen 173–7, 181–2; Mariana (Measure) 403; Page, Mrs 460–1; Percy, Lady 249; Perdita (Wint. T.) 681; Portia (Merchant) 420, 428–9, 431–2, 435; Queen (Hamlet) 227–8; Rosalind 127, 130, 133, 135; Viola 665–6. Other references 43, 50, 75, 172, 344, 351.

Barrett, Giles Leonard, 1744–1809: Hastings 275; Horatio 215.

Barrett, John, d. 1795: Apothecary 602; Bardolph (Hen. V) 293; Carrier 256; Francis 259, 262; Gobbo 435, 438; Gravedigger 228; Lucianus 218, 225; Music Master 627–8, 632; Roderigo 514; Tailor 630; Verges 491; William 136.

*Barrington, John, d. 1773: Carrier 242; Citizen (Coriolanus) 160–3; Citizen (J. Caesar) 314–17; Launcelot 414; Macmorris 278–80, 283–7; Williams 280–2, 286. Other references 3, 7, 20, 24, 27, 31.

*Barrington, *Mrs* John, Ann, formerly Mrs Sacheverel Hale, fl. 1740–73: Anne, Lady 526–30; Capulet, Lady 578–90, 592–6; Celia 119; Macduff, Lady 364–74; Nerissa 413–15; Page, Mrs 446, 448– 56; Widow 114; York, Duchess of 544. Other references 7, 31.

*Barry, Spranger, 1719–77: Antonio (Merchant) 420; Antony (J. Caesar) 314–16; Bastard (John) 320–1; Florizel (F & P) 676, 678; Hamlet 190–7; Henry V 278–80; Hotspur 239–42, 249; Jaques 129–31; Lear 338–9, 343–51; Macbeth 364, 366–9, 375–7; Othello 498–502, 505–12; Richard III 531–2; Romeo 578–84, 590–2; Timon 656. Other references 3, 10, 18, 20, 40, 42–3, 53, 55, 60, 578, 720.

Barry, *Mrs* Spranger [the 2nd], Anne, nee Street, formerly Mrs William Dancer, later Mrs Thomas Crawford, q.v.

Barry, Thomas, d. 1768: Edgar 345.

Barry, *Mrs* William, Jane, nee Osborne, c. 1739–71: Anne, Lady 540, 542–4; Celia 126; Goneril 344–5; Juliet (R & J) 590–2; Regan 346–7. Other references 42, 592.

Barrymore, stage name of William Blewitt, 1759–1830: Angelo (Measure) 410–11; Arviragus 182; Banquo 387, 397; Bassanio 440–5; Benedick 496; Buckingham (Rich. III) 563–5, 567, 570, 572–4; Cassio 517–21; Claudio (Measure) 408; Claudio (Much Ado) 491–6; Dauphin (Hen. V) 290–3; Dauphin (John) 329, 331–2; Edmund 356, 358–9; Ferdinand 649–50, 652–3; Florizel (Wint. T.) 686–7; Ghost 235–7; Guiderius 182–3; Horatio 234–5; Hubert 333; Laertes 221, 223–7, 232, 234; Macduff 397–8; Malcolm [read by] 387; Orlando 140, 142–9; Orsino 668–71; Osric 220–1; Paris 605–6; Petruchio 631; Richmond 568–9; Romeo 609; Ross 389–96; Salarino 438–9; Sicinius 163–5; Surrey 307–11; Valentine (TGV) 674; Vernon 261, 265. Other references 100, 104, 115, 147, 163, 232, 290, 292, 523.

Barsanti, *Miss* Jane, later (1) Mrs John Richard Kirwan Lyster, but used stage name of Mrs Lisley, q.v.; (2) Mrs Richard Daly.

Barton, *Miss* Frances, later Mrs James Abington, q.v.

Bates, James, d. 1784: Blunt (1 Hen. IV) 256; Borachio 489; Burgundy (Lear) 355; Fenton 463; Francisco (Hamlet) 219, 221; Malcolm 385–6; Oxford 558–9; Paris 601; Rosencrantz 222; Silvius 135.

Bates, *Mrs* James, Patty Ann, nee Scrase, d. 1787: Adriana 152–3; Catharine 625–6; Elizabeth, Queen 559–60, 562; Emilia 515–17; Ford, Mrs 464; Macbeth, Lady 386–8; Nerissa 433; Page, Mrs 465; Paulina (Wint. T.) 684–5; Queen (Hamlet) 223–5.

728

INDEX I

Bates, Robert, d. 1786: Abhorson 403, 405–7; Bardolph (1 Hen. IV) 258; Bardolph (MWW) 462–4; Bernardo 211; Boatswain 646; Carrier 257; Cinna the Conspirator 318; Dion 681; Doctor (Lear) 355; Gravedigger 208; Harfleur, Governor of 288; John, Friar 601; Lord Mayor 558; Mariner (Wint. T.) 681; Outlaw 673; Philario 177; Slender 459; Tubal 424; Tyrrel 541, 544. Other references 44, 48, 54, 459.

Bates, William, d. 1817: Arthur 326; Bardolph (MWW) 465; Biondello 624; Blunt (1 Hen. IV) 255; Borachio 488; Burgundy (Lear) 356; Douglas 257; Elbow 406–7; Falstaff's Page 274; Francis 256; Gentleman Usher 354; Henry, Prince 330; Le Beau 139; Marcellus 218; Officer (Lear) 356; Osric 219–20; Oxford 558; Seyton 385; Simple 460–1; Slender 462–3; Solanio 429; William 133, 135; York, Duke of 545. Other references 257, 489, 545.

Battishill, Jonathan [composer], 1738–1801: 38, 469.

Bayne [unidentified], fl. 1780: 70.

*Beard, John, 1716–91: Amiens 117–18, 120–2; Balthazar (Much Ado) 474–7; Hecate 364–8; Hymen 639–40; Lorenzo 412–17; Prospero 638; Servant (Wint. T.) 677; Theseus (Fairies) 470; Trinculo 638. Other reference 19.

Beaufield, Miss, fl. 1783: Edward, Prince 560.

Belfille, Mrs, stage name of Mrs Arnold, nee Anne Burdett, later Mrs Turner, d. 1789: Rosalind 139.

Bell, Thomas, d. 1815: Blunt (Cibber's Rich. III) 554.

*Bellamy, Mrs George Anne, c. 1727–88 [until 1754 known as Miss Bellamy]: Constance 321, 324–6; Cordelia 335–6, 338–9, 341–4; Desdemona 499–503, 505; Elizabeth, Queen 533, 539–40; Isabella 403; Juliet (R & J) 578–87, 590, 592–4; Katharine (Hen. V) 282–3; Macbeth, Lady 368–9; Percy, Lady 241; Perdita (F & P) 678; Portia (J. Caesar) 317; Veturia 163; Volumnia (Sheridan's Coriolanus) 160–1. Other references 23, 37, 43, 344.

*Bencraft, James, d. 1765: Bernardo 190–200; Burgundy (Lear) 336; Charles 119; Gadshill 239–43; Lepidus (J. Caesar) 314–16; Mouldy 267; Murderer 364, 366–9, 371; Norfolk (Rich. III) 528–9; Oxford 528–9, 531–4; Salisbury (Hen. V) 278–81; Simple 448–9; Witch 364. Other references 3, 5, 10, 12, 21, 23.

*Bennet, Mrs (i.e. Miss) Elizabeth, 1714–91: Bianca (C & P) 613–14; Bullen, Anne 298–9; Capulet, Lady 578–91; Elinor 322–5; Emilia 502; Falconbridge, Lady 320; Goneril 335–44; Macduff, Lady 368, 370–5; Mariana (Measure) 401–3; Nerissa 412–18; Page, Mrs 456; Paulina (Wint. T.) 677, 679; Phebe 118, 120; Queen (Cymbeline) 168–71; Queen, Player 192–205; Valeria 159, 161; York, Duchess of 526–38, 540.

*Bennet, William, d. 1768: Angus 364; Biondello 616; Burgundy (Hen. V) 281–5; Burgundy (Lear) 338–9, 341, 344; Carrier 242–8; Donalbain 363, 366–9, 371, 373; Francis 241; Gloucester (Hen. V) 279–81; Gobbo 415; Gregory (R & J) 579–85; Hastings 272; Launcelot 418; Ratcliff 532–3, 535–41; Roderigo 502; Rosencrantz 194–201, 204–5; Sicinius 160–2; Silvius 119–22; Slender 446, 448–56; Soldier [Interpreter] 112–13; Tybalt 585, 587–91. Other references 18, 25, 27.

Bensley, Robert 1742–1817: Antonio (Merchant) 426, 428–36, 438–9; Banquo 376–9, 387–9, 391–2; Bassanio 420–6, 435, 438; Brutus (J. Caesar) 318; Buckingham (Rich. III) 540; Cassius 318; Duke (Measure) 403–4; Duncan 393–5; Edmund 343–7, 349–50; Ghost 206–8, 210–11, 213, 218, 220–7, 231–2; Guiderius 171–4; Henry IV (1 Hen. IV) 252–4, 258, 261; Henry IV (2 Hen. IV) 274–6; Henry VI (Cibber's Rich. III) 551, 553, 555–7, 559–66, 568–9; Hotspur 262; Hubert 326, 328–32; Iachimo 178; Iago 509–21; Jaques 136; King (All's Well) 115; Leonato 486, 488, 491–3; Malvolio 663, 665–70; Philip, King 325; Polixenes (Sheep S.) 684; Polixenes (Wint. T.) 680–3, 685–6; Posthumus 174–7, 183; Prospero 646–53; Wolsey 300–2, 308–11. Other references 40, 44, 52, 82, 87, 89, 387, 432.

Benson, Robert, 1765–96: Antonio (Twelfth N.) 668–9; Arviragus 183; Bardolph (MWW) 465; Biondello 629, 631–2; Biron 115; Brackenbury 564–5, 567; Buckingham (Rich. III) 568–9; Burgundy (Lear) 356; Caliban 651; Captain (Twelfth N.) 668–70; Chamberlain, Lord 308–9; Chatillon 331–2; Constable 293; Cornwall 356, 358; Cornwall's Servant 359; Cranmer 311; Dauphin (Hen. V) 290, 292; Donalbain 383–4; Duke (Merchant) 440; Edward, Prince 554; Eglamour 674; Escalus (R & J) 609; Froth 409; Gloucester (Hen. V) 290–2; Gower (Hen. V) 290; Gratiano (Othello) 520–1; Hortensio 626–30; Humphrey, Prince 276; Jaques de Bois 142–6; John,

729

INDEX I

Prince (1 Hen. IV) 254–5; Julio 519, 521; King (Hamlet) 231; Le Beau 146; Lennox 389–90, 392; Lieutenant 562–3; Marcellus 226–7, 232; Menenius 165; Montano 517; Officer, Volscian 164; Oliver 141; Peto (1 Hen. IV) 261; Rogero 687; Ross 388–9; Sergeant (Macbeth) 391–2; Seyton 393–5; Sicinius 163; Silvius 139–40, 142; Stephano (Tempest) 653; Surveyor 308–12; Tressel 558; Volusius 164; William 140; Williams 293. Other references 356, 669.

Bernard, John, 1756–1828: Antipholus of Ephesus 153–4; Carrier 260–1; Cloten 185; Clown (Wint. T.) 687; Gentleman Usher 357, 359–60; Gratiano (Merchant) 436–7; Osric 227–8, 230–1; Roderigo 521–2; Tailor 627–8, 631–2; Witch 390–1, 393–5. Other reference 88.

Bernard, *Mrs* John [the 1st], nee Roberts, formerly Mrs Cooper, 1750–92: Adriana 153–4; Emilia 518–19; Page, Mrs 465–7; Paulina (Wint. T.) 688; Queen (Hamlet) 228; Regan 357. Other reference 88.

*Berrisford [DL box-keeper], fl. 1748–76: 14, 19, 58–9.

Berry, C., fl. 1780–1: Gentleman Usher 354; Osric 218–19.

*Berry, Edward, 1706–60 [in my Vol. I, 468, the date of birth of this actor is incorrectly given as 1676]: Antonio (Merchant) 412–16; Brabantio 499–500; Caliban 639; Capulet 577–84; Duncan 365–9; Enobarbus 116; Falstaff (MWW) 447–9; Ghost 190–6; Gloucester (Lear) 335–9; Hecate 364; Henry VI (Cibber's Rich. III) 526–7, 529–32; Henry VIII 295–8; Hubert 320; Jaques 117–22; Lafeu 111; Leonato 474–7; Menenius 159–60; Shepherd (Wint. T.) 676–7; Toby, Sir 658–9. Other reference 22.

Besford, *Miss* Esther, 1757–?: Edward, Prince 547–51; Henry, Prince 328; Humphrey, Prince 274; York, Duke of 539–42, 544. Other references 53–4, 544.

Besford, Joseph, d. 1789: Gadshill 253; Haberdasher 625; Shadow 272.

Besford, Samuel, d. 1791: Edward, Prince 539–40; Falstaff's Page 272; Lucius (J. Caesar) 317; Page (R & J) 589; York, Duke of 538–9.

Betterton, stage name of Thomas Butterton, d. 1834: Buckingham (Rich. III) 574; Cassio 523–4; Cloten 186; Horatio 235; Laertes 238; Macbeth 399; Tressel 575; Tybalt 612. Other reference 105.

Betterton, *Miss*, stage name of Julia Butterton, later Mrs Samuel Glover, 1779–1850: Macbeth, Lady 399; Portia (Merchant) 442–4. Other reference 105.

Biggs, *Miss* Anne, later Mrs Samuel Young, 1775–1825: Anne, Lady 574–5; Beatrice 497; Ophelia 236–8; Rosalind 148–9.

Billington, *Mrs* James, Elizabeth, nee Weichsel, c. 1768–1818: Ophelia 228. Other references 89, 91.

Birch, Samuel, 1757–1841: Tressel 568.

*Blakes, Charles, d. 1763: Biondello 613–14, 616; Boatswain 639; Borachio 474–9; Caius 447–9, 452–3; Caliban 639–41; Captain (Twelfth N.) 658–9; Citizen (Coriolanus) 159; Clown (Twelfth N.) 659; Cornwall 335–41; Duke Senior 117–24; Gentleman (Wint. T.) 677, 679; Gentleman, French 168–9; Gratiano (Merchant) 415; Henry VI (Cibber's Rich. III) 533; Laertes 190–6, 199; Lepidus (A & C) 116; Lodovico 499–500, 502; Malcolm 364–5; Norfolk (Rich. III) 536; Pembroke 320–2; Pistol (2 Hen. IV) 268; Polonius 197–201; Provost 401–2; Salarino 412–14; Silence 269, 271; Soldier [Interpreter] 111–12; Suffolk 295–300; Tressel 526–31; Tybalt 577–87; Vernon 243–4; Witch 365–72. Other references 4, 9, 19, 23, 25, 116, 199, 295.

*Blakey, fl. 1743–60: Feeble (Humourists) 268; Rugby 451–2.

Blanchard, Thomas, 1760–97: Arthur 327; Autolycus (F & P) 688; Carrier 260; Dromio of Syracuse 154; Edward, Prince 548–9; Francis 261; Roderigo 517–19; Witch 390–3.

Blanchard, William, 1769–1835: Witch 400.

Bland, George [the younger] [in 1802 he adopted stage name of Wilson], d. 1806: Antonio (Tempest) 652–3; Blunt (Cibber's Rich. III) 565, 567; Donalbain 391; Froth 408–9; Grey 290–3; Guildford 309–10; Henry, Prince 332; Hortensio 628–32; John, Prince (1 Hen. IV) 261–2; Malcolm 391–2; Messenger (Othello) 519–21; Roderigo 521; Sebastian (Twelfth N.) 668–70; Silvius 143–6; Tourville 115; Tressel 566, 568, 570; Vernon 262.

*Bland, *Mrs* George [the elder], Esther, later (1) Mrs John Hamilton, q.v.; (2) Mrs Sweeny.

Bland, *Mrs* George [the younger], Maria Theresa, nee Romanzini, 1769–1838: Ariel 651–4; Jessica 438, 440–4; Patience 309–12. Other references 93, 439, 652.

Blissett, Francis, 1741–1824: Carrier 253; Chancellor, Lord 304–5; Flute (Fairy T.) 473; Gentleman Usher 353; Gobbo 427, 430; King, Player 218; Lucianus 215; Shallow (MWW) 459; Simple 462.

Bloomfield, fl. 1791–2: Cornwall 357; Paris 607.

730

INDEX I

Blower, *Miss* Elizabeth, 1763–?: Rosalind 135. Other reference 74.

Bludrick, fl. 1780: Lear 354.

Blurton, James, 1756–?: Burgundy (Lear) 357; Traveller (1 Hen. IV) 263. Other reference 65.

Bonnor, Charles, d. *c.* 1829: Chamberlain, Lord 306–7; Gratiano (Merchant) 432–3; Norfolk (Rich. III) 562; Osric 222–3, 225; Paris 603; Poins (2 Hen. IV) 277; Roderigo 515–16.

Booth, Cockran Joseph, d. 1789: Antonio (Tempest) 646–8; Bardolph (1 Hen. IV) 254–6; Benvolio 597–602; Bernardo 214, 217–19, 221; Blunt (1 Hen. IV) 251, 254, 256–7; Buckingham (Rich. III) 549, 552; Burgundy (Lear) 351–2; Captain (Twelfth N.) 663; Capulet 597, 599; Carrier 257–60; Chatillon 330; Cloten 178; Clown (Measure) 406–7; Doctor (Lear) 355; Duke (Othello) 515–18; Duke Senior 136, 141; Escalus (R & J) 604; Fluellen 289; Gravedigger 222, 225; Guildenstern 225; Henry VIII 307; Host (MWW) 460–6; Host (TGV) 673; John, Don 483–5, 487–92; King, Player 222–3, 225; Le Beau 129–30, 133, 135, 137; Lodovico 512–14; Marcellus 219, 222; Norfolk (Rich. III) 551, 553, 555–6, 558–9, 561; Osric 213; Paris 597; Pembroke 328, 330; Philario 180–1; Pinch 153; Poet 657; Rosencrantz 220–2; Sands 307; Shepherd (Wint. T.) 684, 686–7; Solanio 426–36; Suffolk 302, 304–7; Thomas, Friar 405; Toby, Sir 666; Tybalt 603–4; Williams 288–9; Witch 384–9. Other references 58, 71, 76, 81, 84.

Booth, John, d. 1779: Boatswain 643–4; Pistol (MWW) 458; Ratcliff 543.

Booth, *Mrs* John, Ursula Agnes, 1740–1803: Audrey 139–40, 142; Capulet, Lady 602; Curtis 628–35; Elinor 328; Hostess (Hen. V) 290–4; Lady, Old 309–12; Nurse 609; Overdone, Mrs 409–10; Queen, Player 220; Quickly, Mrs (MWW) 465; Widow 115; York, Duchess of 551, 557, 568. Other references 74, 78, 409.

Bowden, Wright, 1752–1823: Hecate 395–6.

Bowles, Robert, d. 1806: Baptista 623; Gower (Hen. V) 288; Lord Mayor 554; Norfolk (Rich. III) 552.

Bowley [DL box-keeper], fl. 1795–9: 98, 105.

Boyce [harlequin], fl. 1790: 91.

Bradney, fl. 1775: Lorenzo 425.

Bradshaw, *Mrs* Mary, d. 1780: Audrey 120–34; Curtis 614, 617–20; Emilia 500; Hostess (1 Hen. IV) 243–50, 252–5; Hostess (2 Hen. IV) 270–6; Lady, Old 297–8, 300; Margaret 478–86; Mopsa (Wint. T.) 677, 679; Nurse 593, 597, 599; Overdone, Mrs 404–6; Quickly, Mrs (MWW) 452–3, 455–60; Tearsheet, Doll (Humourists) 268. Other references 19, 38, 45, 65.

Bramwell, *Mrs* Georgiana [singer], fl. 1796: 100.

Brandon, James William [CG box-book and house-keeper], 1754–1825: 77–8, 81, 96.

Brangin, *Miss*, later Mrs Ralph Wewitzer [the 2nd], fl. 1785–91: Arante 357; Bianca (C & P) 626–7; Margaret 490.

*Bransby, Astley, d. 1789: Alonso 639, 642–6; Austria 320; Balthazar (R & J) 578–9; Buckingham (Rich. III) 528, 534; Capucius 295; Chamberlain, Lord 296–9; Diomedes 116; Duke (Merchant) 415–18, 420–4, 426; Duke (Othello) 502, 504–12; Duke Frederick 118–31; Duncan 364, 370–8, 380–1; Escalus (Measure) 401–2; Escalus (R & J) 578–82, 584–5, 587–93; Ghost 197–206, 208–13, 215; Guildenstern 190–2; Henry VIII 299; Host (MWW) 454, 456–8; John, Don 475–80; Kent 336–51; King, Player 192; Lord (All's Well) 111–12; Lord Chief Justice 268–9, 271–3; Lucius (Cymbeline) 168–79; Marcellus 194–5, 197; Metellus 314; Montano 499; Norfolk (Rich. III) 526–7; Pandulph 321–2, 324–5, 327; Poins (2 Hen. IV) 267; Sicinius 159–60; Siward 363, 365–70; Siward, Young 365; Solanio 413–14; Stanley 528–35, 537–8, 540–1, 543–5, 548–50; Theseus (MND) 470; Williams 278; Worcester 239–40; 243–8, 250. Other references 25, 32, 40.

Branson [unidentified], d. *c.* 1783: 54, 57–8, 76.

Branson, *Mrs* [widow of the preceding], fl. 1783: 76.

Brent, *Miss* Charlotte, later Mrs Thomas Pinto [the 2nd], d. 1802: Ophelia 199; Perdita (F & P) 678–9.

Brereton, William 1751–87: Arviragus 173–7; Claudio (Measure) 405–8; Claudio (Much Ado) 484–6, 488; Dauphin (John) 328–9; Flaminius 656–7; Florizel (Wint. T.) 682–3; Guiderius 178–9; John, Prince (2 Hen. IV) 273; Laertes 208–9; Macduff 382–5, 387; Orlando 126–9, 131–5, 137; Orsino 661–6; Pembroke 327; Posthumus 178–80, 182; Richmond 550, 554–5; Romeo 594, 597–8, 600–2; Wales, Prince of (1 Hen. IV) 254. Other references 47, 67, 129.

Brereton, *Mrs* William, Priscilla, nee Hopkins, later Mrs John Philip Kemble, q.v.

INDEX I

Brett, William, d. 1789: Amiens 136; Balthazar (Much Ado) 489-90.
Brett, *Mrs* William, Hannah, d. 1803: Audrey 136.
Bride, *Miss* Elizabeth, later Mrs Lefevre, d. 1826: Imogen 168-70; John, Prince (1 Hen. IV) 243; Juliet (R & J) 587; Silvia 673. Other reference 29.
Bridges, fl. 1761: Othello 503.
*Bridges, William (?), fl. 1743-51: Buckingham (Rich. III) 526; King (Hamlet) 190.
*Bridgwater, Roger, d. 1754: Adam (AYLI) 119; Caesar 314-15; Constable 278; Cranmer 295; Henry VI (Cibber's Rich. III) 526-8; Hubert 320; Montague 578-80; York, Archbishop of 267.
Broad [DL box-keeper], fl. 1756: 14.
Brown, *Master*, fl. 1769: Ariel 642.
Brown, *Miss* Ann, later Mrs R. Cargill, q.v.
*Brown, Henry, d. 1770: Richard III 527.
Brown, J., d. 1818: Richmond 560; Witch 389.
Brown, *Mrs* J., nee Mills, formerly Mrs Ross, d. 1823: Audrey 139.
Browne, Campbell, fl. 1787: Benedick 490; Hamlet 226.
Brunsdon, John, fl. 1778-80: Dromio of Syracuse 151-2; Gentleman Usher 352, 354; Music Master 622-4; Witch 384.
Brunton, *Miss* Anne, later (1) Mrs Robert Merry, q.v.; (2) Mrs Thomas Wignell; (3) Mrs William Warren [the 2nd].
Brunton, John, Sr., 1741-1822: Hamlet 212; Richard III 556.
Brunton, John, Jr., 1774-1848: Hamlet 238; Romeo 612.
Buck, William, d. 1777: Austria 322-6; Charles 120-3; Gadshill 243-7; Gower (2 Hen. IV) 269-70; Gravedigger 205; Lepidus (J. Caesar) 317; Lord Mayor 536-40; Lucilius (J. Caesar) 316; Mouldy 270, 273; Murderer 373-4; Norfolk (Rich. III) 535; Nym (MWW) 450-6; Pinch 150; Sheriff (1 Hen. IV) 242; Westmorland (Hen. V) 279-82; Williams 282-5. Other references 27, 35.
Bulkley, *Mrs* George, Mary, nee Wilford, later Mrs Ebenezer Barresford, q.v.
Bullbrick, G., fl. 1757: 17.
*Bullock, Christopher [dramatist], c. 1690-1722: 149, 612.
Burden, *Mrs* Kitty, nee White, fl. 1761-7: Capulet, Lady 591-2; Emilia 506-7; Goneril 345; Jessica 419; Macduff, Lady 374; Page, Anne 452-4.
Burghall, J. E., fl. 1778: Tressel 553.
Burk [unidentified], fl. 1752: 4.
Burnet, *Miss*, fl. 1787: Phebe 140.
Burnett, fl. 1778-81: Henry VI (Cibber's Rich. III) 557; Laurence, Friar 599; Lieutenant 554.
Burney, Charles [composer], 1726-1814: 469.
Burroughs [unidentified], fl. 1778: 65.
*Burton, Edmund, d. 1772: Angers, Citizen of 320-2; Antonio (Twelfth N.) 658-60; Antonio (TGV) 672-3; Baptista 613, 616-18; Belarius 170-5; Brabantio 499, 502-9; Brutus (Coriolanus) 159-60; Buckingham (Rich. III) 527; Campeius 296-8; Capulet 584-94; Cornelius 168-9, 171-2; Cranmer 297-300; Duke (All's Well) 111; Duncan 364-5; Egeus (MND) 470; Enobarbus 116; Falstaff (1 Hen. IV) 243; Friar (Much Ado) 474-9, 481; Gloucester (Lear) 341-7; Gonzalo 639, 642-3; Henry VI (Cibber's Rich. III) 529, 539-40; Jaques 123-4; Kent 337; King, Player 190-209; Lafeu 112; Laurence, Friar 577, 579; Menas 116; Montague 579-84; Morocco 412-16; Norfolk (Rich. III) 532-5, 537-8, 540-1, 543-4; Northumberland 245-50; Oliver 117-18, 120-2; Page (MWW) 447-9; Seleucus 116; Shepherd (Wint. T.) 679; Soothsayer (A & C) 116; Steward 111; Tyrrel 531; Westmorland (2 Hen. IV) 269, 271-4; Witch 365-77. Other references 4, 6, 9, 23, 32, 36, 38, 40, 168, 171.
Burton, *Miss* Elizabeth, 1751-71: 47.
Burton, George, fl. 1756: Antonio (Tempest) (?) 638.
Burton, John, d. 1797: Butts 311-12; Carrier 254, 259, 261-2; Citizen (Coriolanus) 163, 165; Citizen (J. Caesar) 319; Clarence 269, 271; Donalbain 372-4; Duke (All's Well) 114; Edward, Prince 535-8; Fleance 372; Gentleman Usher 349-51, 353; Gravedigger 217, 219-24, 226-7, 232; Henry, Prince 325; Humphrey, Prince 273; John, Prince (1 Hen. IV) 244, 250; Launcelot 429; Lord Mayor 569-70; Man, Old (Lear) 356, 358-9; Nym (Hen. V) 290-3; Outlaw 674; Peter (R & J) 590, 592-5, 597, 599-602, 605-6, 608-9; Rosencrantz 225; Shadow 274; Shipmaster 643; Simple 459-60, 463, 465, 467; Tailor 616-20, 623-33; Titus (Timon) 656-7; Verges 484, 488, 491-3; Watchman (Much Ado) 486; William 130-5, 137-46; Witch 389-92. Other references 32, 38, 67, 93, 100, 484.
Burton, *Mrs* Philippina, fl. 1770: Constance 327. Other references 48-9.
Butler, Philip [DL carpenter], d. 1786: 62.
Buxton, fl. 1782: Norfolk (Rich. III) 558.
Byrne, *Mrs*, fl. 1789-90: Edward, Prince 564-5; Mopsa (F & P) 688.

INDEX I

Calvert, Charles, 1754-97: Richard III 561.
Camargo, *Mme* Marie Anne de Cupis de [dancer], 1710-70: 5.
Cambray, stage name of James Fennell, q.v.
Cameron [DL box-keeper], fl. 1778-96: 65, 67, 86, 92, 100.
Campbell, d. 1802: Cornwall 359; Escalus (R & J) 609; John, Don 494; Lennox 397; Lord (Cymbeline) 185; Montano 522; Salarino 440-1.
Canning, *Mrs* George, Mary Anne, nee Costello, later Mrs Richard Hunn, 1747-1827: Hero 483; Perdita (F & P) 681.
Capdeville, *Mlle* [dancer], fl. 1756: 15.
Cape, *Master*, stage name of Edward Cape Everard, q.v.
Capell, Edward [Shakespearean scholar], 1713-81: 115.
Carey, George Saville, 1743-1807: Henry IV (2 Hen. IV) 274.
Cargill, *Mrs* R., Ann, nee Brown, *c*. 1748-84: Juliet (R & J) [V. iii only] 602; Miranda 646-8; Patience 302.
Carleton, Sr. [DL box-lobby door-keeper], fl. 1775-80: 58-9, 62, 67, 70.
Carleton, Jr. [DL box-lobby door-keeper], fl. 1770-86: 47, 49, 52, 58-9, 70, 72, 82.
Carmichael, Thomas [CG prompter], fl. 1758: 21.
Carpenter, Robert, 1748-85: Abhorson 404-6; Boatswain 646; Lieutenant 549; Officer (Twelfth N.) 663; Rugby 459-60; Verges 483-6. Other reference 62.
*Carr, Oliver, fl. 1742-55: Duke (Othello) 501.
Casey, John, d. *c*. 1792: Malcolm 376; Ratcliff 541; Sicinius 163; Tressel 540-1. Other reference 44.
Castelle, *Miss*, fl. 1795-8: Mopsa (F & P) 689; Mopsa (Wint. T.) 689.
Castle, Richard, d. 1779: Apothecary 590-2, 594-5; Captain (Cymbeline) 168-9; Citizen (J. Caesar) 318; Cleomenes (Wint. T.) 679; Corin 124; Denny 300; Doctor (Lear) 343, 345; Falconbridge, Robert 325; Flute (Fairy T.) 471; Gentleman Usher 340-1; Gower (2 Hen. IV) 269, 271; Gravedigger 204-9; Guildenstern 199-202; Mortimer 244-6, 250; Ratcliff 536-8; Rosencrantz 200; Snout (Fairy T.) 472; Starveling (Fairy T.) 472; Steward 112; Valentine (Twelfth N.) 660. Other references 168-9, 471-2.
Caulfield, Thomas, d. 1815: Antonio (Kemble's Othello) 519-21, 523; Antonio (Twelfth N.) 671; Burgundy (Lear) 358; Captain (Twelfth N.) (?) 669; Catesby 568-70, 571-2, 574-5; Conrade 493-4; Douglas 261, 264-5; Duke Frederick 147; Essex 331-2; Gratiano (Othello) 522; Jaquez 115; John, Don 495-6; King (Hamlet) 233-4, 236; Knight (Lear) 359; Lodovico 521, 523; Montjoy 291-4; Neptune 651-4; Officer, Roman 164-5; Oliver 147-9; Oxford 567; Pembroke 332; Pisanio 186; Provost 408-11; Rosencrantz 232, 234-7; Ross 394-5; Sergeant (Macbeth) 393, 395, 397-9; Seyton 392; Solanio 440-4; Suffolk 308-11; Tybalt 609-10; Valentine (Twelfth N.) 669-71; Volusius 165-6. Other reference 669.
Cautherley, Samuel, d. 1805: Bassanio 420-4; Cassio 510-11; Claudio (Much Ado) 480-4; Dauphin (John) 324; Donalbain 370-2; Edward, Prince 534; Florizel (F & P) 680-1; Guiderius 173-8; Hamlet 204, 208-9; Henry, Prince 321-2; Humphrey, Prince 269-70; Malcolm 375-8, 380; Romeo 590-4; Sebastian (Twelfth N.) 660-2; Slender 457-8; Tressel 540-1, 543-5, 548-9; Wales, Prince of (1 Hen. IV) 248-9; Wales, Prince of (2 Hen. IV) 273; York, Duke of 530-1. Other reference 49.
Chalmers, James, d. 1810: Biondello 625; Blunt (1 Hen. IV) 257; Fenton 464; Lovell 306-7; Norfolk (Rich. III) 560; Poins (1 Hen. IV) 257; Silvius 137; Thurio 673.
Chalmers, *Mrs* James, nee Mills, d. 1792: Lucetta 674; Page, Anne 463-4.
Chambers, *Mrs*, d. 1792: Jessica 413-17; Ophelia 193-7. Other references 10, 21.
Chambers, *Mrs*, nee Dyer, d. 1804: Juliet (R & J) 604.
Chambers, A. A., fl. 1777-89: Duncan 382-3; Guildenstern 228; King, Player 216; Lord Mayor 553; Pandulph 328-9; Peter, Friar 406.
*Champnes, Samuel, d. 1803: Caliban 638, 642; Hecate 369-79; Mustacho 638. Other references 19, 40, 42, 49, 53, 470, 639.
Chaplin, Henry, d. 1789: Angus 380-3, 385; Antonio (Tempest) 650; Balthazar (R & J) 597, 599-600; Baptista 626; Bernardo 215; Captain (Lear) 353; Captain (Twelfth N.) 667; Cleomenes (Wint. T.) 683, 687; Cornelius 182-3; Doctor (Lear) 356; Douglas 252-5; Duke (Othello) 513-17; Duke Frederick 131-5, 137-41; Duncan 390; Essex 329, 331; Gentleman, French 180-1; Herald, French 328-9; King, Player 217, 219-21, 223-7; Lord Mayor 562-3; Messenger (Othello) 512; Montague 601-2; Peter, Friar 407-8; Philario 178, 184; Ratcliff 549; Sebastian (Tempest) 649-50; Stanley 551, 553-5, 557, 559-61, 563;

INDEX I

Trebonius 318. Other references 67, 70, 74, 78.
Chapman [unidentified], fl. 1762: 31.
Chapman, *Miss* Charlotte Jane, 1762–1805: Abbess 154–7; Anne, Lady 568–72; Bullen, Anne 310, 312; Catharine 629; Celia 141, 145–6; Desdemona 522; Elizabeth, Queen 572–5; Ford, Mrs 468; Hero 494; Nerissa 437; Percy, Lady 260–1, 263–6; Queen (Hamlet) 235–6, 238. Other reference 94.
Chapman, William (?), fl. 1783–91: Antonio (Much Ado) 490; Baptista 627–8; Lord Mayor 566; Lorenzo 431; Northumberland 262; Rosencrantz 228; Scroop 290–1; Tubal 435, 438. Other references 75, 82.
*Charles, fl. 1744–55: Roderigo 501.
Chatterley, *Miss*, fl. 1792: Nerissa 438.
Chatterley, Robert E., fl. 1799: Lucianus 237.
Chatterley, William Simmonds, 1787–1821: Boy (Hen. V) 293; Crowned Child (Macbeth) 393, 398; Edward, Prince 574; Fleance 397; Goneril's Page 359; Marcius, Young 164–5; York, Duke of 570, 572–3.
Chippendale, William, fl. 1796–1800: Bernardo 237; Gadshill 264; Gravedigger 238; Gregory (C & P) 636; Gurney 333; Messenger (Hamlet) 236; Oatcake 496; Officer (Rich. III) 575; Peter (C & P) 633, 635; William 149.
Chumbley [DL door-keeper], fl. 1799: 105.
Churton, *Mrs*, fl. 1792: Desdemona 520. Other reference 94.
*Cibber, Colley [dramatist], 1671–1757: 525, 716.
*Cibber, Theophilus, 1703–58: Iago 501; Osric 193–4; Pistol (Humourists) 268. Other references 9, 266, 313.
*Cibber, *Mrs* Theophilus [the 2nd], Susannah Maria, nee Arne, 1714–66: Constance 320–1; Cordelia 336–42; Desdemona 499–500, 503; Elizabeth, Queen 537; Isabella 401–2; Juliet (R & J) 578–88; Macbeth, Lady 365; Ophelia 190–203; Perdita (Wint. T.) 677, 679. Other references 5, 9, 32, 337.
Claremont, stage name of William Cleaver, d. 1832: Albany 361; Arviragus 186; Brandon (Hen. VIII) 312; Catesby 570–5; Conrade 493–6; Door-keeper (Hen. VIII) 312; Escalus (R & J) 612; Gentleman, French 185; Guildenstern 231, 233, 235–6, 238; Hortensio 632–6; Lieutenant 569; Lord (Cymbeline) 185; Malcolm 399; Marcellus 230–1; Montano 521–4; Murderer 395–6, 398; Paris 608–10; Poins (1 Hen. IV) 265; Salarino 440;

442–5; Solanio 440; Tybalt 610–11; Westmorland (1 Hen. IV) 263–4, 266.
Clarke, John Woodruffe, fl. 1797–9; Buckingham (Rich. III) 572–4; Chamberlain, Lord 312; Cornwall 360; Duke (Com. Err.) 157; Escalus (R & J) 610–11; Lorenzo 442; Malcolm 398–9; Montano 523; Oliver 148; Page (MWW) 468; Pedro, Don 495; Rosencrantz 235–6; Westmorland (1 Hen. IV) 265–6.
Clarke, Matthew, d. 1786: Angelo (Measure) 403–4, 406–7; Antigonus (Wint. T.) 680–1; Antonio (Merchant) 420–33; Aufidius 162–3; Bassanio 418–20; Belarius 171–8, 180–1, 183; Caesar 316–18; Capulet 597–603; Cassio 506, 509–10; Cloten 168; Constable 281–9; Duke Senior 135, 137; Edmund 341–4; Ghost 208; Henry IV (1 Hen. IV) 250–1, 254–8; Henry VI (Cibber's Rich. III) 547–50, 553, 555–6, 558–61; Henry VIII 300–3, 305–7; Hotspur 242–4; Jaques 127, 131, 133; Kent 345, 347, 349–52, 354–5; King (Hamlet) 210, 213–14, 216–18, 220, 222–5; Lafeu 113–14; Macduff 371, 373–4, 376–87; Philip, King 322–6, 328, 330; Richard III 539; Richmond 535–47; Shepherd (Wint. T.) 682, 684–5; York, Archbishop of 269–70, 272, 274, 276. Other references 24, 27, 31, 44, 46, 52, 56, 81, 163, 433.
Cleland, *Miss*, stage name of Miss Buttery, c. 1762–?: Bullen, Anne 306; Hero 488; Regan 355.
Cleveland, Thomas, fl. 1792: Blunt (1 Hen. IV) 262. Other reference 262.
Clifford, fl. 1781: Brandon (Rich. III) 557.
Clinch, Lawrence, d. 1812: Richmond 549–50; Salisbury (John) 328.
Clingo [CG pit door-keeper], fl. 1763: 33.
*Clive, *Mrs* George, Catherine, nee Raftor, 1711–85: Catharine 614–16; Celia 118, 120–4; Olivia 658–9; Ophelia 190–2; Portia (Merchant) 412–18.
*Clough, Thomas, d. 1770: Bardolph (1 Hen. IV) 243–50; Bardolph (2 Hen. IV) 269, 271, 274; Bardolph (Humourists) 268; Bardolph (MWW) 447, 453–4, 456, 458; Barnardine 401–2; Boatswain 640, 642–3; Citizen (Coriolanus) 159–60; Evans 447; Gardiner 299; John, Friar 588; Laurence, Friar 585; Menas 116; Pedro (C & P) 614; Sampson 581, 588; Sands 297; Sexton 475–6, 479–81; Shallow (MWW) 451; Snug (Fairy T.) 471; Snug (MND) 470. Other references 17, 22, 24, 26, 447.
Coates, *Mrs* Elizabeth, fl. 1799: Bianca (C & P) 635.
Cokayne, *Miss* Mary, fl. 1753–71: John,

734

INDEX I

Prince (1 Hen. IV) 249; Mamillius 681; Page, Anne 452; Phebe 119, 121–2; York, Duke of 544–5.

Colborne, John [CG box-keeper], fl. 1783: 77.

Cole [DL box-keeper], fl. 1796: 100.

Cole, William [Freemason], fl. 1756: 16.

Colles, *Mrs*, née Boyde, fl. 1777–9: Blanch 328–9; Bullen, Anne 303; Humphrey, Prince 275; Juliet (Measure) 405–6; Page, Anne 459–60; Percy, Lady 253–4; Perdita (Sheep S.) 682; Queen, Player 215, 217; Regan 353; Ursula 486. Other references 67, 216, 253, 459.

Collet, *Mrs* John, fl. 1771: Bianca (C & P) 618; Nerissa 422.

Collett, *Miss* Catherine, later Mrs Tetherington, fl. 1767–83: Clarence 275–6; Falstaff's Page 274; Fleance 379; Nerissa 431; Page, Anne 459; Robin 457–8; York, Duke of 540–1, 543–4.

Collings, fl. 1792: Officer (Othello) 520.

Collins, *Miss*, stage name of Clementina Hayward, later Mrs Thomas Woodfall, fl. 1786–95: Agatha 309–10; Anne, Lady 563, 567; Blanch 331–2; Celia 140–1, 143, 145–6; Hippolito 652; Jessica 439; Katharine (Hen. V) 290–2; Maria 667–8, 670; Miranda 652; Nerissa 435, 439; Page, Anne 466; Phebe 142–7. Other references 143, 146.

Collins, John, 1742–1808: Montano 508.

*Collins, William, d. 1763: Citizen (Coriolanus) 160–2; Citizen (J. Caesar) 314–16; Evans 450–3; Feeble 267; Francis 239–45; Gobbo 413–19; Gravedigger 190–1; Launcelot 415; Lucianus 194–7; Peter (R & J) 587; Polonius 197–201; Sampson 578–85; Sands 295; Shallow (2 Hen. IV) 269–70; Shallow (MWW) 446, 448–50; Touchstone 121; William 119–22; Witch 364–72. Other references 6, 18, 23, 27.

Colman, George [the elder] [dramatist], 1732–94: 187, 333, 469, 612, 676, 716–17.

Comerford, Henry, d. 1778: Adam (AYLI) 131; Edgar 352; Ghost 214; Henry VI (Cibber's Rich. III) 551; Norfolk (Hen. VIII) 303; Pisanio 179; Shylock 426; Touchstone 131; Worcester 252.

Condell, John, Sr. [CG box-keeper], d. 1779: 18, 23, 25, 46, 68.

Condell, John, Jr. [CG box-keeper], fl. 1783: 77.

Condill, *Miss* Charlotte, d. 1759: Volumnia (Sheridan's Coriolanus) 161.

Cooke, *Mrs* [unidentified], fl. 1757: 17.

Cooke, George Frederick, 1756–1811: Edgar 353; Hortensio 623; Iago 524; Macbeth 399; Richard III 575; Shylock 445; Tressel 554; Tybalt 599. Other reference 721.

Cooke, James, fl. 1791–1800: Brackenbury 569–70; Charles 149; Curio 670; Francisco (Hamlet) 232, 234; Gabriel 631, 633–4; Gadshill 261; Herald (Lear) 358; Herald, French 333; Leonardo 438–40; Nathaniel 631–2; Officer (Lear) 359; Officer (Othello) 521; Scroop 291–3; Sergeant (Hen. VIII) 311; Sheriff (John) 332. Other references 332, 439.

Cooke, William (?), fl. 1761: Cassio 503. Other reference 27.

Coombs, fl. 1795: Traveller (1 Hen. IV) 263.

Cooper, Thomas Apthorpe, 1776–1849: Hamlet 231; Macbeth 395.

Copin, *Mrs* Roger, Elizabeth, fl. 1755–62: Bridget 151; Nurse 581–3; Quickly, Mrs (MWW) 451.

Cory, Thomas, fl. 1800: Austria 333; Ghost 238; Iago 524.

*Costollo, Patrick, d. 1766: Abraham 582; Carrier 241; Citizen (Coriolanus) 160–3; Citizen (J. Caesar) 316–17; Clown (F & P) 678; Gravedigger 197, 200–1, 203–4; Grumio 614, 616; Nym (Hen. V) 281–2; Polonius 196; Shallow (MWW) 449–55; Silence 269–70; Simple 450; Tubal 413; William 118, 120–1, 123; Witch 367, 370–4. Other references 4, 15, 18, 33, 413, 475.

Courtney, fl. 1761–74: Music Master 620. Other references 26, 29.

Cowper, *Mrs*, fl. 1753–7: Macduff, Lady 366–8; Page, Mrs 449; Regan 336–7; Viola 659.

Cranford, *Miss*, fl. 1789: Dorcas (Wint. T.) 687.

Crawford, Thomas, 1750–94: Othello 514; Petruchio 624; Posthumus 181. Other reference 72.

Crawford, *Mrs* Thomas, Ann, née Street, formerly (1) Mrs William Dancer; (2) Mrs Spranger Barry [the 2nd], 1734–1801: Beatrice 483; Catharine 624; Constance 327–8, 330; Cordelia 344–51; Desdemona 506–14; Evanthe 656–7; Imogen 174–5, 180–1; Juliet (R & J) 591–4; Macbeth, Lady 375–7, 384; Percy, Lady 250; Perdita (F & P) 680; Portia (Merchant) 420, 427–8; Rosalind 124–32, 134; Viola 664. Other references 42, 63, 71.

Crespi, *Signora* [dancer], fl. 1777–80: 62, 70.

Creswick, N., d. 1792: Osric 198–200.

Crewe, fl. 1792: Richmond 568.

Cridland [DL box-keeper], fl. 1767–72: 40, 45, 47, 49, 52.

735

INDEX I

Croft, fl. 1771–2: Alcibiades 656; Posthumus 175. Other reference 51.

Cross, John Cartwright, d. 1809: Balthazar (R & J) 608; Bernardo 231; Blunt (Cibber's Rich. III) 570; Carrier 261; Corin 142, 144–5; Donalbain 390–2; Tressel 559.

Cross, Mrs John Cartwright [the 1st], d. c. 1797: Curtis 630.

*Cross, Richard, Sr., d. 1760: Wales, Prince of (Humourists) 268. Other references 2, 17, 19, 23 n., 713 n.

*Cross, Mrs Richard, Sr., Frances, nee Shireburn, 1707–81: Hostess (Humourists) 268; Nurse 579, 583–95, 598; Queen, Player 191; Regan 335–6; Widow 111–12. Other references 2, 17, 19.

*Cross, Richard, Jr., fl. 1748–54: Donalbain 364; Page (R & J) 578; Poins (Humourists) 268.

Crossman, Mrs, fl. 1797: Helen 186.

Crouch, Mrs Rollings Edward, Anna Maria, nee Phillips, 1763–1805: Miranda 649–54; Olivia 666–8, 671–2; Perdita (Wint. T.) 685–7. Other reference 104.

Crudge, Alexander [CG house-keeper], d. 1759: 12.

Cubitt, William, fl. 1775–94: Bardolph (1 Hen. IV) 262; Burgundy (Lear) 356; Caius 465; Chamberlain, Lord 307, 310; Charles 141–2, 144; Clown (F & P) 688; Conrade 489–92; Cornelius 178; Douglas 257–60; Duke (Othello) 519–22; Fenton 464; Gobbo 437; Hecate 393–4; John, Don 493–4; Lennox 386–8; Lieutenant 560, 562, 564–8; Lodovico 516; Lucianus 227–9; Lucius (Cymbeline) 183–4; Pinch 154–5; Pistol (MWW) 464–5; Rosencrantz 223, 225; Siward 390; Slender 465–7; Tybalt 603–8; Witch 391–2. Other reference 91.

Cumberland, Richard [dramatist], 1732–1811: 654, 716, 718.

Curioni, Signora Rosa, fl. 1755–6: Ferdinand 638. Other reference 470.

Curteen [CG box-keeper], fl. 1779–83: 68, 77.

Curtet, Pierre [dancer], fl. 1765: 37.

Curties, fl. 1794–1800: Abergavenny 312; Balthazar (Merchant) 444–5; Blunt (Cibber's Rich. III) 575; Donalbain 399; Edward, Prince 569–72; Fleance 394–6, 399; Hotspur's Servant 263; John, Prince (1 Hen. IV) 265; Lord (Cymbeline) 186.

*Cushing, John, 1719–90: Antony's Servant 314–16; Balthazar (R & J) 578; Bardolph (Hen. V) 285; Biondello 621–3; Blunt (1 Hen. IV) 239–42; Burgundy (Hen. V) 278–81; Citizen (Coriolanus) 162–3; Constable 284; Francis 247, 250–1, 254; Gentleman Usher 341–5, 347, 349–50; Gower (2 Hen. IV) 272; Gregory (R & J) 578–80; Guildford 295; Lieutenant 532–3; Lord (All's Well) 114; Lord Mayor 548; Lucianus 207; Metellus 316–18; Osric 191–8; Pembroke 321; Pistol (2 Hen. IV) 267; Pistol (MWW) 446, 448–51, 455, 457, 460–2; Poins (1 Hen. IV) 248; Rugby 455; Salisbury (Hen. V) 284, 288; Shallow (MWW) 456; Titus (Sheridan's Coriolanus) 160; Tressel 526–9, 531; Tubal 413–14; Tybalt 579–85, 594; Verges 483–5, 487–8; Westmorland (1 Hen. IV) 249; Witch 364–9, 376. Other references 7, 18, 206, 285, 594.

Cuyler, Mrs Margaret, c. 1758–1814: Anne, Lady 556, 561; Bullen, Anne 305; Diana 114; Falconbridge, Lady 331–2; Goneril 356, 358–9; Miranda 647–9; Percy, Lady 252–5, 259, 262; Queen (Cymbeline) 186.

Dale, W. [DL box-keeper], d. 1807: 93.

Daly, Richard, 1758–1813: Iachimo 181; Othello 513. Other reference 68.

Dancer, John Wimperis, d. 1790: Cassio 508–9; Cornwall 348; Guildenstern 209; Lord (Cymbeline) 179; Lorenzo 422; Pembroke 326; Ratcliff 543; Silvius 131; Tressel 547; Tyrrel 551.

Dancer, Mrs William, Ann, nee Street, later (1) Mrs Spranger Barry [the 2nd]; (2) Mrs Thomas Crawford, q.v.

Dangerfield [DL box-keeper], fl. 1796: 100.

Daniel, fl. 1782: Ratcliff 558.

D'Arcy, stage name of —— Caird, fl. 1798: Balthazar (Much Ado) 496.

D'Arcy, Miss, fl. 1771: Imogen 175. Other reference 50.

Darley, William, c. 1756–1809: Balthazar (Much Ado) 490–2; Charles 137, 139; Hecate 386–9, 391–2; Nicholas (Wint. T.) 686–7. Other reference 91.

*Davenant, Sir William [dramatist], 1606–68: 361–3, 636–8, 717.

Davenett, Mrs, stage name of Harriett Pitt, d. 1814: Audrey 134–6, 138; Capulet, Lady 600; Margaret 489–90; Regan 355; York, Duchess of 555–6. Other reference 555.

Davenport, George Gosling, 1758–1814: Biondello 634; Camillo (Wint. T.) 689; Campeius 312; Doctor (Lear) 360–1; Duke (Merchant) 441–5; Friar (Much Ado) 495–6; Gratiano (Othello) 524; King, Player 236; Lord (Cymbeline) 185; Lucianus 231; Marcellus 233, 235, 238; Montague 608–12; Norfolk (Rich. III) 572, 574; Northumberland 263–6;

INDEX I

Pistol (MWW) 468; Senator (Othello) 524; Siward 394–6, 398–400; Stanley 575; Tyrrel 570.

Davenport, Mrs George Gosling, Mary Ann, nee Harvey, 1759–1843: Hostess (1 Hen. IV) 263–6; Nurse 608–12; Quickly, Mrs (MWW) 468.

Davies, Mrs, fl. 1776: Patience 303.

*Davies, Thomas, c. 1712–85: Adam (AYLI) 119; Antonio (Merchant) 417–18; Bassanio 414; Buckingham (Rich. III) 530–5; Camillo (Wint. T.) 676–7, 679; Chamberlain, Lord 296; Claudio (Measure) 401–2; Cominius 159–60; Cymbeline 168–9; Eros 116; Ford 448; Gloucester (Lear) 340–1; Henry IV (1 Hen. IV) 244; John, Don 475; King (All's Well) 111; King (Hamlet) 191–200; Leonato 476–8; Philip, King 320–2; Ross 364–71; Surrey 296–300. Other reference 475.

Davies, Mrs Thomas, Susanna, nee Yarrow, 1723–1801: Anne, Lady 527–38; Bullen, Anne 300; Cordelia 337; Desdemona 502, 504; Diana 111–12; Hero 475–9; Ophelia 198; Viola 659; Virgilia 159, 161.

Davies, William, 1751–1809: Albany 355–7, 359–60; Amiens 126, 132–3; Antonio (Twelfth N.) 660–2; Arviragus 178–81, 183–4; Banquo 385–6; Bassanio 427; Benvolio 595, 597, 599–600, 603–8; Capulet 610; Cassio 516; Catesby 558–62, 564–9; Chatillon 327–9; Clown (Twelfth N.) 663, 666; Cromwell 305–7, 310; Duke (Com. Err.) 154–6; Fenton 462–3; Ferdinand 646–8; Ford 458; Guildenstern 228–31; Hecate 386; Horatio 215–17, 220, 231, 233, 236; Laertes 222–5, 227–8; Lennox 386, 389; Lodovico 513, 515, 517–22; Lorenzo 433, 437–8, 440–3; Lucius (Cymbeline) 185; Malcolm 380–4, 386–8; Montano 511–12; Mowbray 276; Oliver 129, 137–8, 141–2, 144–5; Painter 656–7; Paris 602–3; Pedro, Don 487–94, 496; Poins (1 Hen. IV) 251, 256–61; Provost 404–7; Rosencrantz 210–13, 215–16; Ross 390–5; Salarino 431–7; Salisbury (John) 330; Sebastian (Twelfth N.) 663–4; Sempronius 657; Sergeant (Macbeth) 378–80; Surrey 303; Tressel 549–55; Vernon 253, 257, 259, 262; Worcester 262, 264. Other references 646–7.

Davies, Mrs William, Elizabeth, d. 1782: Nerissa 424–9; Page, Mrs 459; Phebe 126–32; Tearsheet, Doll 275–6. Other reference 126.

Davis, fl. 1797–8: Abhorson 410–11.

Davis, stage name of Thomas Dibble, d. 1788: Albany 342–4; Antipholus of Ephesus 150; Bardolph (1 Hen. IV) 250–1; Benvolio 587–96; Blunt (1 Hen. IV) 253; Brutus (Coriolanus) 161–3; Cassio 505, 507; Catesby 533, 536–43, 545–50, 552, 556; Chatillon 322–6; Cleomenes (Sheep S.) 682; Conrade 483–4; Cornwall 350, 353; Dauphin (Hen. V) 281–7; Decius 317–18; Edgar 343; Escalus (Measure) 403; Essex 328; Fenton 450–6; France (Lear) 346; Gentleman, French 177–8, 181; Guildenstern 215; Hortensio 620–2; John, Prince (2 Hen. IV) 268, 270, 272, 274; Laertes 200–8, 210–12; Le Beau 122–3, 127; Lord (All's Well) 112–14; Lovell 300–1; Malcolm 374; Marcellus 218; Montano 502–6, 510–12, 514; Norfolk (Hen. VIII) 301–6; Orlando 124; Othello 508–9; Pembroke 326; Peter, Friar 405; Richmond 535, 538–9, 543, 547; Salarino 418–20, 424, 426–8, 430; Sheriff (1 Hen. IV) 244–5; Siward 381; Solanio [IV. i only] 430; Surrey 301; Vernon 248–50; Westmorland (1 Hen. IV) 245–7; Westmorland (2 Hen. IV) [IV. iv and V. ii only] 276. Other references 23, 27, 31, 35, 48–9, 54, 56, 245, 427, 621, 682, 723.

Davis, John, fl. 1780: Catesby 557.

Daw, Miss [dancer], fl. 1765: 37.

Dawes, Mrs, fl. 1779: Juliet (R & J) 600.

Dayes, Miss Mary, later (1) Mrs Morton, q.v.; (2) Mrs John Morgan [the 1st].

Death, Thomas, 1739–1802: Gentleman Usher 352.

DeCamp, Miss Maria Theresa, later Mrs Charles Kemble, 1774–1838: Ariel 653–4; Arthur 331; Bullen, Anne 310, 312; Catharine 635; Desdemona 523; Edward, Prince 564–6; Hero 496; Hippolito 654; John, Prince (1 Hen. IV) 262; Katharine (Hen. V) 294; Nerissa 440, 442–5; Olivia 670; Phebe 146; Portia (Merchant) 442, 444. Other reference 104.

DeCamp, Vincent, 1777–1839: Arthur 331; Boy (Hen. V) 293; Donalbain 391–5; Edward, Prince 566, 568–9; Henry, Prince 332; Montano 524.

D'Egville, Fanny [dancer], fl. 1792: 93.

D'Egville, George [dancer], fl. 1792: 93.

D'Egville, Peter [dancer], fl. 1772: 51.

D'Egville, Sophia [dancer], fl. 1792: 93.

De Henny, Mlle [dancer], fl. 1753: 7.

Delap, John [dramatist], 1725–1812: 72.

Delaval, Edward Thomas, d. 1787: Cassio 498.

Delaval, Francis (later Sir Francis) Blake, 1723–71: Othello 498.

Delaval, John Hussey, later Baron Delaval, 1728–1808: Iago 498.

INDEX I

Delpini, Carlo Antonio [dancer], d. 1828: 70, 82.
Denman, William, 1766–1806: Antonio (Tempest) 653; Lucius (Cymbeline) 186; Oxford 571; Seacoal 494.
*Desse (or De Hesse), Jean Baptiste [dancer], 1705–69: 18.
D'Evelyn, Miss, fl. 1797: Amphitrite 653.
Devisse [dancer], fl. 1753: 6.
Devoto [unidentified], fl. 1778: 65.
Dexter, John, 1726–64: Cranmer 295–6; Orsino 659.
Dibdin, Charles, 1745–1814: Silence 272. Other references 35, 37, 51, 53, 56, 61, 469.
Dibdin, Mrs Thomas John, Ann, nee Hillier, d. 1828: Goneril 361; Queen (Cymbeline) 186.
*Dickinson, John [DL first gallery office-keeper], fl. 1747–74: 7, 11, 19, 34, 40, 56.
Didier, Abraham J., 1739–1823: Biondello 618.
Digges, West Dudley, 1720–86: Falstaff (1 Hen. IV) [II. iv only] 256; Lear 352–3; Macbeth 383; Shylock 430; Wolsey 303–4, 306. Other references 66, 69, 73.
Dignum, Charles, c. 1765–1827: Amiens 142–9; Balthazar (Much Ado) 493–6; Bedford 290–3; Burgundy (Lear) 359; Esquire (Lear) 358; Essex 332; Gentleman (Measure) 408–10; Gower (Hen. V) 293; Lorenzo 438–41, 443, 445; Lovell 310–11; Marcellus 232, 234; Norfolk (Rich. III) 565, 567–9; Pembroke 331–2; Ratcliff 568. Other references 95, 105.
Dimond, William Wyatt, 1750–1812: Dauphin (John) 327; Edgar 353; Florizel (F & P) 681; Romeo 595. Other reference 56.
Dixon, Miss Clara Ann, later Mrs Smith [in 1812 she adopted stage name of Mrs Sterling], fl. 1800: Jessica 445.
Dodd, James William, c. 1740–96: Andrew, Sir 660–70; Autolycus (Wint. T.) 685–7; Balthazar (Much Ado) 480; Cloten 170–84; Elbow 409; Evans 467; Gentleman Usher 342–9; Gratiano (Merchant) 420–5, 427–9, 432, 434–5, 439; Launce 674; Lorenzo 420; Mercutio 591–5, 597, 599–602, 605–6, 609; Osric 204–10; Petruchio 619, 624; Polonius 232; Richard III 544; Roderigo 505–21; Slender 456–8, 460, 463, 466; Touchstone 144; Witch 394–6. Other references 40, 42, 49, 53, 57, 62, 81, 93, 98, 685.
Dorman, Mrs Ridley, Elizabeth, nee Young, d. 1773: Ariel 639, 641; Ceres 642–4. Other references 38, 40.
Dowton, William, 1764–1851: Adam (AYLI) 149; Barnardine 410–11; Carrier 265; Clown (Twelfth N.) 671; Gravedigger 232, 234; Lord Mayor 574; Malvolio 671; Polonius 234–7; Verges 494–5, 497; Witch 397.
*Dryden, John [dramatist], 1631–1700: 636–8.
Du-Bellamy, Charles Clementine, d. 1793: Amiens 124, 131, 134; Autolycus (Wint. T.) 680–1; Balthazar (Much Ado) 483–4; Campeius 301; Capucius 300–1; Duke (All's Well) 114; Duke (Othello) 508; Florizel (Sheep S.) 682; France (Lear) 347; Gower (Hen. V) 285–7; Guiderius 174–5, 178; Horatio 207, 209; Lorenzo 420, 425, 427, 430; Octavius (J. Caesar) 317; Salisbury (John) 326; Stanley 542; Titus (Sheridan's Coriolanus) 163. Other references 46, 60.
Du-Bellamy, Mrs Charles Clementine [the 1st], Frances Maria, d. 1773: Anne, Lady 542; Blanch 326; Calphurnia 318; Catharine 618; Countess 113–14; Elizabeth, Queen 545; Queen (Hamlet) 205, 208; Regan 346–7, 349. Other reference 46.
Duckworth, fl. 1793: 722.
Dufour, Miss Camilla, later Mrs J. H. Sarratt, fl. 1797–8: Amphitrite 653–4.
Duill, Mrs John Lewis, Catherine Mary, nee Satchell, later Mrs John Taylor [the 1st], d. 1789: Evandra 657.
Dumai, D. [dancer], fl. 1767–80: 41, 44, 71.
*Dunstall, John, 1717–78: Abraham 578–85; Bullcalf 267, 269–70, 273–4; Caliban 646; Campeius 295; Carrier 239–51; Citizen (Coriolanus) 160–3; Citizen (J. Caesar) 314–18; Clown (Measure) 403–5; Corin 119–23, 127; Dromio of Syracuse 150; Falstaff (1 Hen. IV) 241; Falstaff (MWW) 448; Gravedigger 190–2, 203–8, 210–14, 216; Host (MWW) 446, 449–50, 454–5, 457; Jamy 278–88; Launcelot 418; Lucianus 197–200; Toby, Sir 661, 663; Tyrrel 526–30, 532–4; Williams 279–80; Witch 364–74, 376–82. Other references 10, 12, 15, 23, 52, 60.
*Dunstall, Mrs John, Mary, d. 1758: Tearsheet, Doll 267. Other references 10, 12.
Duquesney [dancer], fl. 1765–7: 37, 40.
*Dyer, Michael, d. 1774: Chatillon 320; Clown (Twelfth N.) 661; Dauphin (John) 321–3, 326; Edgar 339; Gentleman Usher 336; Gratiano (Merchant) 413–24; Laertes 191–200; Macduff 367, 370, 372; Mercutio 579–87, 589, 595; Mortimer 239; Osric 190–1, 200–8, 210–11; Pisanio (Hawkins' Cymbeline) 168; Pistol (2 Hen. IV) 269–70, 272; Pistol (Hen. V) 278–87; Richmond 529; Roderigo 499–506, 509–10; Romeo 578, 581, 591; Surrey 300–2; Tressel 532–3, 535–42,

INDEX I

544, 546–8; Tybalt 578–80. Other references 10, 12, 15, 20, 24, 41, 44.

Dyer, *Mrs* Michael [the 1st], Harriot, nee Bullock, fl. 1754–70: Desdemona (?) 509; Elinor 327; Katharine (Hen. V) 278–9, 281–2; Percy, Lady 241; Portia (J. Caesar) 318; York, Duchess of 542.

Dyke, John, fl. 1797: Messenger (1 Hen. IV) 265.

Eddis [unidentified], fl. 1769: 46.
Edelston [unidentified], d. *c.* 1778: 59.
Edward, *Mrs*, fl. 1798: Queen, Player 236.
Edwards, *Mrs*, fl. 1789–93: Amphitrite 651–2; Audrey 141, 143–5.
Edwards, John, fl. 1778: Tyrrel 554.
Edwards, John [DL office-keeper], fl. 1796–9: 100, 105.
Edwin, *Mrs*, stage name of Sarah Walmsley, d. 1794: Quickly, Mrs (MWW) 462.
Edwin, John, Sr., 1749–90: Andrew, Sir 665–6; Autolycus (Sheep S.) 682, 684; Autolycus (Wint. T.) 684–8; Cloten 181; Clown (All's Well) 114; Dogberry 487; Dromio of Syracuse 152–4; Evans 460–6; Francis 253–60; Gardiner 306–7; Gravedigger 218; Launcelot 427, 430, 433, 435; Polonius 215, 220, 222, 225, 227–8; Quince (Fairy T.) 473; Speed 673; Touchstone 133, 136; Town Clerk 487–92; Witch 383. Other references 70–1, 73, 76, 83, 90, 114.
Edwin, John, Jr., 1768–1805: Music Master 630; Osric 228; Puck (Fairy T.) 473; Robin 462; York, Duke of 552, 556.
Egan, William, Sr., d. 1785: Balthazar (Com. Err.) 151; Bardolph (1 Hen. IV) 254; Bernardo 221; Biondello 621; Borachio 489; Carrier 256; Chamberlain, Lord 303–6; Charles 136; Essex 330; Fenton 459; Guildenstern 215, 218, 222, 224; Jamy 289; Lennox 383; Lodovico 514; Macmorris 289; Montague 603; Oxford 560, 562; Pistol (MWW) 462–3; Polixenes (Sheep S.) 682; Ratcliff 552, 556; Sheriff (1 Hen. IV) 255; Solanio 427, 430; Westmorland (1 Hen. IV) 253. Other references 71, 76, 215, 604.
Egan, William, Jr., 1762–1822: Donalbain 390; Douglas 260; Hortensio 627; Rosencrantz 227–8; Salarino 437; Tressel 564–5.
Egerton, *Mrs*, stage name of Mrs Kelf, nee Ambrose, fl. 1771–3: Emilia 509; Maria 661–2; Queen (Hamlet) 209–10; Regan 348–9.
Egerton, Daniel, 1772–1835: Horatio 235.
Ellard, Thomas, fl. 1767: Albany 345; Gratiano (Othello) 506.

Elliston, Robert William, 1774–1831: Othello 523; Romeo 610; Shylock 442. Other references 101, 103.

*Elmy, *Mrs* William (?), Mary, nee Morse, 1712–92: Desdemona 499–501; Elinor 320–3; Elizabeth, Queen 531; Perdita (F & P) 676; Portia (J. Caesar) 316; Queen (Hamlet) 190–4, 196–201; Regan 338–9; York, Duchess of 532–6. Other references 10, 12, 15, 18, 20, 23.

*Elrington, Richard, d. 1770: Abergavenny 295; Bernardo 190; Blunt (1 Hen. IV) 239; Colevile 267; Decius 314; Essex 320.

Emery, John, 1777–1822: Butts 312; Carrier 266; Gobbo 445; Gravedigger 238; Witch 398–400.

Errington, d. 1810: Tubal 425.
Essex, fl. 1782: Catesby 558.
Esten, *Mrs* James, Harriet Pye, nee Bennett, later Mrs John Scott-Waring [the 3rd], *c.* 1768–1868: Beatrice 494; Cordelia 359; Juliet (R & J) 607–8; Luciana 155; Ophelia 228–9; Rosalind 143–6.

Evans [CG box-keeper], d. 1780: 12, 23, 68.
Evans, *Master*, fl. 1755: Fairy (Fairies) 470.
Evans, *Mrs*, stage name of Susanna Mullart, 1735–?: Arante 341; Arthur 320–3; Boy (Hen. V) 279–81; Dorcas (F & P) 678; Edward, Prince 529–30, 532–8; Fleance 364, 366–9, 371; Jessica 418; John, Prince (1 Hen. IV) 241–4; Lucius (J. Caesar) 314–15; Phebe 120–2; Robin 446, 448–50; Simple 452, 454; York, Duke of 526–7. Other reference 535.

Evans, Benjamin, fl. 1794–1800: Crier (Hen. VIII) 310–11; Dighton 575; Executioner (John) 332–3; Francisco (Hamlet) 235–7; Gentleman (Hamlet) 232, 234; Gregory (R & J) 609; Leonardo 439, 441, 443–5; Lord (AYLI) 149; Messenger (Hamlet) 238; Messenger (1 Hen. IV) 265; Messenger (Macbeth) 397, 399; Officer (Macbeth) 398; Officer (Othello) 524; Officer (Twelfth N.) 671; Peter (C & P) 631, 633–6; Ruffian (Lear) 359; Stephano (Merchant) 440.

Evans, Thomas [DL sub-treasurer], fl. 1764–9: 34, 36, 38, 45.

Evatt, Robert, fl. 1788–94: Balthazar (R & J) 607–8; Bernardo 227–9; Biondello 630; Cornwall 357; Doctor (Lear) 359; Douglas 262; Escalus (R & J) 607; Hortensio 626–8, 630–1; Lord (Cymbeline) 185; Marcellus 230; Merchant (Com. Err.) 155; Music Master 631; Norfolk (Rich. III) 565–8; Oxford 564–5; Paris 607–8; Pedro (C & P) 627–8, 630; Pistol (MWW) 466–7; Ratcliff 566, 568;

739

INDEX I

Rosencrantz 229; Silvius 141–2, 144–5; Solanio 437–8. Other reference 630.

Everard, Edward Cape, 1755–? [until 1773 he used stage name of Master Cape]: Balthazar (R & J) 597; Catesby 549; Clarence 273; Curio 663; Donalbain 378–81; Edward, Prince 542–3; Grumio 622; Henry, Prince 327; Launcelot 428; Lear 353; Le Beau 128–30, 132; Paris 599; Pedro (C & P) 620; Puck (Fairy T.) 471–2; Puck (MND) 470; Varro (Cumberland's Timon) 656–7; York, Duke of 541. Other references 353, 721.

Farley, Charles, 1771–1859: Balthazar (R & J) 607; Biondello 633, 635–6; Blunt (1 Hen. IV) 262; Borachio 495–6; Douglas 263, 265–6; Edward, Prince 560–2; Francisco (Hamlet) 231; Gentleman, French 185; Gentleman Usher 360–1; Gratiano (Merchant) 440; John, Prince (1 Hen. IV) 259; Lovell 312; Osric 233, 235–6, 238; Oxford 565–7, 570, 572; Pedro (C & P) 627–8, 630, 632–3; Peter (R & J) 609–12; Peto (1 Hen. IV) 262; Rugby 468; Sergeant (Macbeth) 395–6; William 144–5. Other reference 99.

Farmer, *Mrs* Jane, later (1) Mrs William Powell [the younger], q.v.; (2) Mrs John James Renaud.

Farrell, Charles, d. 1794: Baptista 618; Catesby 542–3, 547; Gratiano (Othello) 509; Herald, English (John) 327; King, Player 207, 209; Man, Old (Lear) 348; Norfolk (Rich. III) 559; Popilius 318; Ratcliff 557.

Farrell, *Mrs* Margaret, nee Doyle, later Mrs Morgan Hugh Kennedy, q.v.

Farren, *Mrs*, stage name of Mary Mansell, later (1) Mrs Thomas Orton; (2) Mrs Bell, 1748–1820: Elizabeth, Queen 553; Hero 482; Juliet (R & J) 595.

Farren, *Miss* Elizabeth, later Countess of Derby, c. 1759–1829: Beatrice 490–4; Desdemona 513–15; Dorinda 651–3; Ford, Mrs 462–3, 466; Helena (All's Well) 114; Hermione 682–3, 685–7; Juliet (R & J) 601–2; Olivia 664–6; Portia (Merchant) 430. Other reference 85.

Farren, *Miss* Margaret 'Peggy', later Mrs Thomas Knight, d. 1804: Titania (Fairy T.) 473.

Farren, William, 1754–95: Alcibiades 657; Antonio (Merchant) 434–7; Banquo 384–95; Bassanio 431–2, 437; Belarius 185; Borachio 485; Buckingham (Hen. VIII) 307, 310; Buckingham (Rich. III) 551, 564–9; Capulet 608; Chatillon 329; Claudio (Measure) 404; Claudio (Much Ado) 489–94; Cromwell 304; Fenton 459; Ferdinand 648–9; Ford 464–7; Ghost 213, 229–30; Guiderius 179–80, 182–4; Horatio 215–17, 219–21, 223–4, 227–9; Hotspur 254; Iachimo 184; John, Prince (2 Hen. IV) 276; Lear 355; Le Beau 131; Macduff 380, 382; Octavius (J. Caesar) 318; Othello 514–15; Paris 597; Pembroke 328–9; Salarino 425–6; Sebastian (Tempest) 645–6; Sebastian (Twelfth N.) 663; Sergeant (Macbeth) 380, 382; Solanio 427; Surrey 307; Tressel 553, 555, 557–8, 560–2; Tybalt 597; Vernon 252–4, 258–61; Westmorland (2 Hen. IV) 274–6. Other references 74, 215, 459.

Fawcett, John, Sr., d. 1793: Amiens 126, 130; Angers, Citizen of 329, 331; Antonio (Twelfth N.) 662; Attendant (Lear) 358; Balthazar (Much Ado) 477–8; Balthazar (R & J) 601–2; Bardolph, Lord 273–4; Barnardine 407–8; Blunt (1 Hen. IV) 253–4; Citizen (Coriolanus) 163–5; Constable 290–2; Curan 347–51, 353; Douglas 249–50; Duke (Othello) 518–19; Gentleman (Hamlet) 226; Gentleman (Lear) 356; Gentleman, French 173–9, 182–4; Gratiano (Othello) 517; Guildenstern 204–13, 215–16; Host (TGV) 674; Hymen 644–6; Jaques de Bois 125–30, 135, 137–40, 142; Lennox 375–8, 380; Lieutenant 541, 543–4, 546, 548–50, 555; Lovell 308–9; Merchant (Timon) 656–7; Messenger (Lear) 347; Montague 605–6; Music Master 617–20, 623–30; Norfolk (Rich. III) 554–5, 557, 559–63; Officer (Lear) 346; Oxford 564–5, 567; Paris 590–5; Pembroke 325; Servant (Wint. T.) 687; Siward 391–2; Solanio 420–6, 431–2, 434, 436: Soothsayer (J. Caesar) 319; Westmorland (1 Hen. IV) 261. Other references 29, 45, 53, 59, 70, 93.

Fawcett, John, Jr., 1768–1837: Falstaff (1 Hen. IV) 262–6; Falstaff (MWW) 468; Gratiano (Merchant) 439; Gravedigger 231, 233; Sands 312; Verges 494; Witch 393–5. Other reference 101.

Fawcett, *Mrs* John, Jr. [the 1st], Susan, nee Moore, formerly Mrs John Mills [the 2nd], d. 1797: Adriana 154; Elizabeth, Queen 571; Emilia 520–2; Imogen 182; Luciana 156; Paulina (Wint. T.) 688–9; Queen (Cymbeline) 185–6; Queen (Hamlet) 229; Regan 357, 359–60.

Fearon, James, 1746–89: Angelo (Com. Err.) 151, 153; Antonio (Twelfth N.) 666; Antonio (TGV) 673; Athenian, Old 657; Bassanio 422; Buckingham (Rich. III) 546; Capulet 604–6; Chancellor, Lord 302; Cleomenes (Wint. T.) 684–5;

INDEX I

Cymbeline 183; Doctor (Macbeth) 381, 384–6, 388–9; Duke (Merchant) 425–37; Duke Frederick 129–33, 135–8, 141; Escalus (Measure) 405–7; Escalus (R & J) 597–603; France, King of (Hen. V) 288–9; Friar (Much Ado) 483–5, 487–92; Gonzalo 646–8; Gratiano (Othello) 511–18; Kent 352; King (Hamlet) 215, 217–19, 224; Leontes (Sheep S.) 682; Lucius (Cymbeline) 178, 180–1; Marcellus 214, 217–19, 221–5; Norfolk (Hen. VIII) 306–7; Page (MWW) 459; Pandulph 328, 330; Petruchio 620–1; Philario 184; Shallow (MWW) 462–6; Stanley 549–53, 555–6, 558–62; Steward 114; Suffolk 303; Westmorland (2 Hen. IV) 276; Worcester 251, 253–60. Other references 71, 75, 219, 462–4.

Fennell, James, 1766–1816 [until 1788 he used stage name of Cambray]: Edmund 356–7; Hotspur 260; Laertes 228; Macbeth 389; Othello 517–19. Other references 84, 91.

Ferguson, *Mrs* Jane, fl. 1752–73 [until 1760 known as Miss Ferguson]: Falconbridge, Lady 325–6; Mariana (All's Well) 112–14; Page, Mrs 451; Queen, Player 194–201, 203–5; York, Duchess of 536–45, 547–8. Other references 6, 15.

Field, *Miss* Ann, later Mrs Forster, q.v.

Fielding, *Miss*, fl. 1762: Page, Anne 453. Other reference 31.

Fildew, fl. 1778–95: Lord Mayor 554. Other reference 720.

Findlay, *Mrs* E., fl. 1800: Edward, Prince 575; Fleance 400.

Fishar, James [dancer], fl. 1771: 50.

Fisher, *Mrs*, fl. 1752: Desdemona 500.

Fisher, *Mrs* David, Mary, nee West, 1730–1819: Catharine 621; Portia (Merchant) 426. Other reference 61.

Fisher, John Abraham [composer], 1744–1806: 48, 637.

Fisher, Joshua Bridges, fl. 1797–1800: Adam (C & P) 634–6; Balthazar (Much Ado) 496; Donalbain 397–8; Executioner (John) 333; Forrest 575; Froth 410–11; Officer (Othello) 524; Sailor (Hamlet) 234, 238; Stephano (Merchant) 445; Traveller (1 Hen. IV) 265.

Fitzhenry, *Mrs* Edward, Elizabeth, nee Flanagan, formerly Mrs John Gregory, d. 1790: Catharine 614; Macbeth, Lady 369. Other references 18, 38.

Fleetwood, Charles, Jr., d. 1784: Hamlet 197–8; Octavius (A & C) 116; Romeo 583–5. Other reference 22.

Fleetwood, John Gerrard, d. 1776: Bastard (John) 327.

Flockton, fl. 1767: 723.

*Foley [DL box-lobby door-keeper], fl. 1748–70: 4, 12, 36, 40, 45, 47.

Follett, fl. 1771–4: Biondello 620; Grumio 620; Messenger (Timon) 656–7; Officer (Twelfth N.) 661.

Fontenelle, *Miss* Louisa, later Mrs James Brown Williamson, 1773–99: Nerissa 438.

*Foote, Samuel, 1720–77: Shylock 417. Other references 15, 20, 33.

Ford, *Miss* Harriott Ann, later Mrs Wilkinson, 1754–?: Arthur 326; Titania (Fairy T.) 471–2; Titania (MND) 471.

Forster, *Mrs* Ann, nee Field, d. 1789: Ariel 647–50; Arthur 328–9, 331; Edward, Prince 551, 553, 555; Jessica 434–6; Ophelia 219–27; Page, Anne 463. Other reference 67.

Fosbrook, T. [DL box-book-keeper], fl. 1776–88: 59, 62, 85.

Foster, Emmanuel, fl. 1769: Duke (Othello) 507.

Fotteral, James, fl. 1777: Henry VIII 303.

Fowler, *Mrs* Thomas, fl. 1777–87: Capulet, Lady 605; Hostess (1 Hen. IV) 252; York, Duchess of 557–8, 561.

Fox, Joseph, d. 1791: Angus 370–4; Bardolph (Hen. V) 288; Bardolph (MWW) 457; Benvolio 594–5; Brandon (Hen. VIII) 300–1; Burgundy (Lear) 341, 344–5; Butts 300; Captain (Twelfth N.) 661; Catesby 544–5, 547; Charles 129–30; Colevile 269, 271; Curio 660; Duke Frederick 142–3; Essex 321–2; Fenton 450; Gentleman (Cymbeline) 168–9; Gonzalo 651; Jaques de Bois 125; Lieutenant 547; Lord (All's Well) 112; Lucianus 208; Macmorris 286; Messenger (1 Hen. IV) 246; Montano 504–5; Music Master 620–2; Norfolk (Rich. III) 548; Outlaw 672–3; Rosencrantz 201–3; Scroop 288; Servant (Wint. T.) 681; Sheriff (1 Hen. IV) 244, 247. Other references 48, 178, 370, 372.

Fox, *Mrs* Joseph, Eleanor, formerly Mrs Candler, d. 1798: Celia 139.

Francis, Bodley William, d. 1780: Lord Mayor 547.

Francis, *Miss* Mary, 1770–?: Edward, Prince 558–9; Humphrey, Prince 276.

Francis, *Miss* Sarah, 1765–?: Boy (Hen. V) 288–9; Edward, Prince 552, 556, 568; Henry, Prince 330; John, Prince (2 Hen. IV) [IV. v and V. ii only] 276; York, Duke of 547.

Freeman, fl. 1770: Montano (?) 509.

Frodsham, fl. 1777: Wales, Prince of (1 Hen. IV) 252.

Frodsham, *Miss* Sarah, later (1) Mrs Reily;

INDEX I

(2) Mrs George Inchbald, 1761–?: Rosalind 136.

Frost, fl. 1784: Ratcliff 561.

Gardner, fl. 1780: Tressel 557; Tybalt 600.

Gardner, James, fl. 1799: Gratiano (Othello) 523; Witch 399.

Gardner, William, d. 1790: Antonio (Merchant) [IV. i only] 430; Antonio (Twelfth N.) 661, 665; Brabantio 506, 508–10; Buckingham (Rich. III) 543; Canterbury, Archbishop of 285–7; Casca 318; Charles 141; Cinna the Conspirator 316–17; Colevile 274; Cornwall 344–7, 349–50; Cranmer 300–2, 304; Cymbeline 177–8, 181, 184; Dennis 123; Doctor (Lear) 357; Douglas 249; Duke (Com. Err.) 152–3; Duke (Othello) 517–18; Duke Frederick 127, 136, 141; Duke Senior 138; Duncan 378–9, 383; Edmund 342–3; Escalus (R & J) 591, 593–4, 596, 604–6; Essex 323–4, 326; Friar (Much Ado) 490; Harfleur, Governor of 285; Henry VI (Cibber's Rich. III) 546, 549, 561; Horatio 203; Jeweller 657; Kent 348, 353; King (All's Well) 114; King (Hamlet) 209–12, 218, 220, 222, 224–5, 227; King, Player 225; Laurence, Friar 589, 592, 602; Lieutenant 539; Lodovico 506, 509; Lord (All's Well) 114; Lord Chief Justice [V. ii only] 276; Lord Mayor 561–2, 564; Lucius (Cymbeline) 171–4, 177; Marcellus 201–3; Mouldy 269–70; Northumberland 258; Pembroke 324, 326; Philip, King 327; Provost 403–4; Richmond 539; Rogero 681; Salisbury (Hen. V) 284–5; Seyton 373–4, 376–7; Shylock 422–3, 431; Siward 390; Solanio 420, 424, 433, 437; Stanley 540–8, 556; Suffolk 307; Tybalt 593–6, 604; Tyrrel 536; Volusius 163; Warwick 270, 272; Westmorland (1 Hen. IV) 248; Worcester 250, 259. Other references 35, 46, 53, 56, 75, 285, 593.

Gardner, *Mrs* William, Sarah, nee Cheney, fl. 1766–76: Catharine 618, 620–2; Maria 661; Nurse 592, 596; Portia (Merchant) 422; Regan 345; Tearsheet, Doll 273–4. Other reference 51.

Garland, fl. 1776: Guiderius 179; Surrey 303.

Garman, fl. 1799: Gabriel 635.

Garman, *Miss* Kiza, later Mrs Invill, fl. 1770: Juliet (Measure) 403.

*Garrick, David, 1717–79: Antony (A & C) 116; Bastard (John) 320–2; Benedick 474–84; Ghost 201; Hamlet 190–200, 204–6, 209–13; Henry IV (2 Hen. IV) 268–70, 273; Iago 500; Lear 335–41, 347, 349–51; Leontes (Wint. T.) 676–7, 679; Macbeth 364–6, 368, 370–2, 375; Mercutio 586; Posthumus 168–9; Richard III 526–31, 533–6, 540–1, 545, 550; Romeo 577–86. Other references 2, 4, 8, 11, 14, 21, 38, 67, 115, 149, 167, 186–9, 210 n., 218, 334–5, 362, 366, 468–9, 576, 612, 636, 675, 716–18.

Garton, Jonathan [CG treasurer], fl. 1768–71: 44, 46, 50.

Gaudry, *Miss* Anne, later Mrs John Fawcett, Jr. [the 2nd], 1780–?: York, Duke of 562–4.

Gaudry, Joseph, d. 1782: 65.

Gaudry, Richard, fl. 1784–7: Nym (MWW) 465; Pedro (C & P) 625; Pistol (MWW) 465.

Gaudry, *Mrs* Stephen, Ann, d. 1802: Margaret 491.

Gell, *Master*, fl. 1795–8: Bloody Child (Macbeth) 398; Regan's Page 359.

Gentleman, Francis, 1728–84: Antonio (Merchant) 422; Gloucester (Lear) 348; Hubert 326; Richard III 543.

George [DL box-keeper], fl. 1791–9: 92, 98, 105.

Gibbon, James Deavon, 1778–1852: Antonio (Kemble's Othello) 522; Antonio (Tempest) 653–4; Conrade 495; Gadshill 265; Gentleman (Measure) 410; Lennox 397; Valentine (Twelfth N.) 671.

Gibbs, *Mrs* Maria, nee Logan, 1770–c. 1846: Catharine 634–5; Dorinda 653. Other reference 99.

Gibson [DL box-keeper], fl. 1795: 98.

*Gibson, William, 1713–71: Adam (AYLI) 119–24, 127; Aegeon 150; Antigonus (F & P) 679; Banquo 372; Benvolio 578–85, 587; Brabantio 501, 503–6, 509; Capulet 587, 589–91, 593–4; Casca 316–17; Catesby 526–7, 529; Cominius 162–3; Cymbeline 171–5; Duke Frederick 119; Duncan 363–4, 366–71, 373–4, 376–7; Escalus (R & J) 579–80; Fenton 446, 448–50; France, King of (Hen. V) 278–87; Galesus 160–2; Ghost 199–202, 204–5; Gloucester (Lear) 341–8; Henry IV (1 Hen. IV) 245, 248–9; Henry IV (2 Hen. IV) 267, 270, 272; Henry VI (Cibber's Rich. III) 535–44; Hubert 323, 325–6; King (Hamlet) 206–8; Laertes 190–1; Lafeu 112–13; Lord Chief Justice 269–70; Lucius (Cymbeline) 168; Norfolk (Rich. III) 530, 532–3; Octavius (J. Caesar) 314–16; Pandulph 321–3, 326; Pembroke 320; Solanio 413, 415–19; Vernon 239–47. Other references 48, 245.

*Giffard, William, c. 1712–1807: Lear 336.

Gilbert, *Miss*, fl. 1799: York, Duke of 574.

Giorgi [dancer], d. 1808: 38, 47, 49, 56, 58.

Glassington, *Miss*, fl. 1782: Rosalind 134.

INDEX I

Glassington, *Miss* Elizabeth, later Mrs Charles Charlton, fl. 1778: Juliet (R & J) 599.
Glassington, Joseph, fl. 1778: Benvolio 599.
Glen, *Mrs* Ann, fl. 1758–9: Bullen, Anne 298–9; Macduff, Lady 369–70; Octavia 116.
Godwin, *Mrs*, fl. 1764: Percy, Lady 247.
Gondou, *Mrs* [unidentified], fl. 1751–6: 3, 10, 16.
Goodall, *Mrs* Thomas, Charlotte, nee Stanton, 1765–1830: Anne, Lady 568–70; Catharine 628–34; Emilia 521; Ford, Mrs 467; Hippolito 651–4; Julia 674; Katharine (Hen. V) 293; Mariana (Measure) 409; Nerissa 438–9, 441; Rosalind 140, 146; Viola 668. Other references 87, 91, 93.
*Goodfellow, J., d. 1759: Hamlet 191; Othello 499–500; Richard III 526–7. Other references 4–5.
*Goodwin, Thomas (?) [DL door-keeper], fl. 1748–56: 14.
Gordon, *Mrs*, stage name of Mrs Lloyd, later Mrs Richard Wilson [the 2nd], fl. 1784: Macbeth, Lady 386.
Graham, fl. 1771–7: Brabantio 513; Launcelot 422.
Graham, *Mrs*, fl. 1777: Emilia 513.
Graham, George, fl. 1777: Cassio 512.
Granger, *Miss* Julia, later Mrs Jones, 1782–1806: Ariel 653; Edward, Prince 570; John, Prince (1 Hen. IV) 264.
Granger, Samuel, fl. 1764–5: Carrier 246–7; Davy 271; Witch 373. Other reference 36.
Granger, *Mrs* Samuel, fl. 1771: Jessica 422. Other reference 618.
Gray, fl. 1798: Balthazar (Much Ado) 495.
*Gray, James [DL constable], fl. 1733–58: 19.
Green, *Mrs*, fl. 1781: Adriana 152; Queen (Hamlet) 219.
Green, *Miss*, fl. 1777–80: Arante 352, 354; Francisca 405.
*Green, *Mrs* Henry, Jane, nee Hippisley, 1719–91: Catharine 614–24; Edward, Prince 526; Emilia 500, 503, 509–10; Maria 658, 661; Nurse 589; Tearsheet, Doll 269–70. Other references 23, 37, 39, 46, 52, 56.
Green, Jonathan [CG box-keeper], d. 1794: 18, 25, 39, 46, 73.
Green, *Mrs* P., fl. 1773–4: Paulina (Wint. T.) 682; Queen (Cymbeline) 177–8; York, Duchess of 547–8.
Gregory, *Mrs* John, Elizabeth, nee Flanagan, later Mrs Edward Fitzhenry, q.v.
Gregson, fl. 1789–97: Boy (Hen. V) 290–2;

Donalbain 395–7; Fleance 391, 393–5; John, Prince (1 Hen. IV) 264; Walter 634.
Greville, *Mrs* Susan, d. 1802: Anne, Lady 548, 550.
Griffith, J., d. 1801: Austria 327; Blunt (Cibber's Rich. III) 546; Captain (Lear) 349; Conrade 483; Doctor (Lear) 348; Francisco (Hamlet) 209–10, 212; Francisco (Tempest) 643–5; Gentleman (Cymbeline) 176; Hortensius 656–7; Lodovico 509; Pedro (C & P) 619; Priest (Twelfth N.) 661; Salarino 422; Sampson 594. Other references 65, 67.
Griffith, Richard, d. 1798: Gentleman Usher 342.
Griffith, *Mrs* Richard [but not wife of the preceding], Elizabeth, nee Griffith, 1727–93 [from 1753 to 1762 she used stage name of Miss Kennedy]: Ophelia 193. Other references 10, 36.
Griffiths [DL box-keeper], fl. 1796: 100.
Griffiths, John, d. 1799: Bernardo 212–16; Boatswain 645; Camillo (Sheep S.) 682; Conrade 484–6; Gentleman (Cymbeline) 177–8; King, Player 215; Lord Mayor 548–50, 552, 554; Norfolk (Rich. III) 552; Pedro (C & P) 620, 623–4; Priest (Hamlet) 219–20; Priest (Twelfth N.) 663–4; Seyton 380–3; Sheriff (1 Hen. IV) 252–3; Westmorland (1 Hen. IV) 251. Other reference 49.
Grimaldi, Giuseppe [dancer], *c.* 1713–88: 36, 38, 42, 47, 49, 67.
Grimaldi, Joseph, 1778–1837: Gravedigger 237; Marcius, Young 164; Pedro (C & P) 634–5.
Grist, Thomas, d. 1808: Gonzalo 646; Lennox 380–1; Othello 511; Tybalt 597.
Guadagni, Gaetano, *c.* 1725–92: Lysander (Fairies) 470.
Guard [unidentified], fl. 1782: 75.
Guerin [dancer], fl. 1756: 15.
Gull, fl. 1792: Launcelot 438.

*Hacket, fl. 1744–51: Shadow 267.
Hackett, John, 1734–?: Nym (MWW) 449; Othello 501. Other reference 13.
Hagley, *Miss*, later Mrs Allen, fl. 1790–2: Ariel 651. Other reference 93.
Hale, *Miss* Mary Ann, d. 1805: Audrey 140; Bullen, Anne 304; Curtis 629; Dorcas (Sheep S.) 682, 684.
*Hallam, Adam, d. 1768: Henry VI (Cibber's Rich. III) 538; Herald, English (Hen. V) 284; Man, Old (Lear) 346; Nym (Hen. V) 284–5; Popilius 316. Other reference 35.
Hallam, *Miss* Isabella, later Mrs George Mattocks, q.v.

INDEX I

*Hallam, Lewis, Sr., d. *c.* 1756: Roderigo 499.
Hallam, Lewis, Jr., *c.* 1740–1808: Hamlet 213.
*Hallam, Mrs Lewis, Sr., later Mrs David Douglass [the 1st], d. *c.* 1774: Desdemona 499. Other reference 4.
*Hallam, William, fl. 1735–52: 6.
Hamilton, Mrs, nee Peters, fl. 1800: Portia (Merchant) 445.
Hamilton, *Miss*, fl. 1769: Desdemona 508.
Hamilton, Mrs John, Esther, formerly Mrs George Bland [the elder], later Mrs Sweeny, d. 1787: Catharine 614; Elizabeth, Queen 529, 531, 534–6; Emilia 500–3; Ford, Mrs 448, 450–4; Katharine (Hen. V) 280; Macbeth, Lady 370–2; Portia (J. Caesar) 314–16; Portia (Merchant) 413–15, 417–19; Regan 338–9; Rosalind 119, 121–2; Veturia 161–2. Other references 18, 31.
Hamilton, William, fl. 1766–73: Citizen (J. Caesar) 318; Falconbridge, Robert 327; Francis 249; Gentleman Usher 344, 348; Gregory (R & J) 591; Grumio 618–19; Launcelot 424; Osric 208–9; Pistol (2 Hen. IV) 274; Pistol (Hen. V) 286; Roderigo 506–8; William 124. Other references 48, 54.
Handel, George Frederick [composer], 1685–1759: 469.
Harley, stage name of George Davies, d. 1811: Antipholus of Ephesus 154; Banquo 395; Ghost 229; Guiderius 184; Henry IV (1 Hen. IV) 262–3; Henry VI (Cibber's Rich. III) 567–70; Horatio 230–1; Iago 518–22; Jaques 141, 146; Kent 359–60; Laertes 229; Lear 356–7; Leontes (Wint. T.) 688; Macbeth 390; Norfolk (Hen. VIII) 310; Petruchio 630; Pisanio 185; Polixenes (Wint. T.) 688; Richard III 564–6; Shylock 437, 440. Other references 91, 94–5, 98, 101.
Harlowe, *Master*, fl. 1794: Bloody Child (Macbeth) 393.
Harlowe, *Mrs*, stage name of Mrs Francis Godolphin Waldron, nee Sarah Wilson, 1765–1852: Audrey [III. iii only] 147; Elizabeth, Queen 569; Emilia 523; Mopsa (Wint. T.) 688; Nerissa 442, 444; Queen (Hamlet) 232–3, 236. Other reference 94.
Harper, *Miss* Elizabeth, later Mrs John Bannister, q.v.
Harricks, fl. 1783: Richard III 559. Other reference 77.
Harris, Peter, d. 1789: Abergavenny 301; Edward, Prince 541–2, 544–7, 550; Gloucester (Hen. V) 288; John, Prince (1 Hen. IV) 250; Robin 457. Other reference 71.

Harrison [unidentified], fl. 1776: 61.
Harrison, Samuel, 1760–1812: Fairy (Fairy T.) 473.
Hartley, *Mrs* Elizabeth, nee White, 1750–1824: Abbess 151–2; Cordelia 352; Desdemona 512; Elizabeth, Queen 552, 555–6; Hermione 682–3; Juliet (R & J) 596–7; Katharine, Queen 300–2; Macbeth, Lady 379–81, 384; Olivia 664; Percy, Lady 250–1, 254; Portia (J. Caesar) 318. Other references 54, 56.
Hartry, John, d. 1774: Biondello 617–19; Corin 125–9; Fabian 662; Launcelot 421; Lord Mayor 543; Lucianus 205–9; Man, Old (Lear) 346–9; Shallow (MWW) 457–8; Silence 274; Verges 480–3. Other references 45, 47, 53.
*Haughton, *Miss* Hannah, d. 1771: Beatrice 476; Bullen, Anne 300; Ford, Mrs 447; Goneril 336; Juliet (R & J) 579; Olivia 660; Page, Anne 447; Page, Mrs 452–3, 455; Regan 337–41; Tearsheet, Doll 267. Other references 3, 11.
*Havard, William, 1710–78: Adam (AYLI) 118, 120–5; Angelo (Measure) 401–2; Aufidius 159–60; Bassanio 412–13, 415–18; Belarius 168–71; Cranmer 295–9; Duke (TGV) 672–3; Edgar 335–44; Ford 447–9, 451, 453–4, 456; Henry IV (1 Hen. IV) 243–8; Henry VI (Cibber's Rich. III) 527, 533–40; Horatio 190–202, 204; Hubert 321–2, 324–5; Iago 499, 502–4; King (All's Well) 112; Laurence, Friar 577–91; Leonato 478–80; Macduff 364–75; Orsino 659; Pandulph 320; Pedro, Don 474–9; Polixenes (Wint. T.) 676–7, 679; Pompey 116; Prospero 640–2; Richmond 526–33; Sebastian (Twelfth N.) 658; Wolsey 297–9; York, Archbishop of 268–9, 271–3. Other references 6–7, 14, 19, 22, 29, 32, 38, 42, 170, 504.
*Havard, Mrs William, Elizabeth, formerly Mrs Kilby, d. 1764: Margaret 474–8. Other references 170, 478, 504.
Hawkins, William [dramatist], 1722–1801: 22, 166, 716–17.
Hayes, F., fl. 1764: Evans 455.
Haymes, Thomas, fl. 1789–97: Blunt (Cibber's Rich. III) 564; Captain (Twelfth N.) 668; Conrade 492; Duke (Com. Err.) 156; Lieutenant 570–2; Montjoy 290; Panthino 674; Rosencrantz 233; Sheriff (1 Hen. IV) 263–4; Solanio 440; Tybalt 609–10.
Hayward, *Miss* Clara, fl. 1771–2: Hero 482; Page, Anne 458.
Heard, *Miss* Elizabeth, fl. 1783–1800: Agatha 311–12; Ariel [read by] 652; Arthur 330; Edward, Prince 562–3; Hero 496; Hippolito 652; Jessica 439, 445;

744

INDEX I

Mariana (Measure) 409; Nerissa 445; Page, Anne 467; Perdita (Wint. T.) 687; Phebe 143, 145–9; Ursula 493–7; Valeria 165–6; York, Duke of 559–61. Other references 100, 143.

Heard, *Mrs* William, Ann, nee Madden, 1750–97: Arante 344; Bianca (C & P) 623; Phebe 124. Other reference 290.

Hedges, *Mrs*, d. 1811: Falconbridge, Lady 329, 331; Queen, Player 222–4, 226; York, Duchess of 559–61.

Helme, fl. 1782–8: Antonio's Servant 431; Bardolph (MWW) 465–6; Burgundy (Lear) 355; Essex 330; Francisco (Hamlet) 220–1; Hortensio 625; Lord Mayor 559–60, 562; Outlaw 673; Oxford 561–2; Pedro (C & P) 626; Pistol (MWW) 465; Silvius 136, 139; Siward 386. Other reference 685.

Helme, *Miss* Susannah, d. 1788: Edward, Prince 539; Gentlewoman (Coriolanus) 160; Mopsa (F & P) 678; Queen, Player 202. Other references 15, 21.

Henderson, John, 1747–85: Benedick 485–9; Chorus (Hen. V) 289; Duke (Measure) 406–7; Falstaff (1 Hen. IV) 252–8; Falstaff (2 Hen. IV) 274–5, 277; Falstaff (MWW) 459–64; Hamlet 215–20, 222–3; Iago 514–16; Jaques 133, 135–7; John, King 328–30; Lear 353–5; Leontes (Wint. T.) 684–5; Macbeth 382–7; Malvolio 666; Posthumus 182; Richard III 551–3, 555–6, 558–61; Shylock 426–30; Wolsey 305–7. Other references 64–5, 67, 78, 486.

Henley, *Mrs* [singer], fl. 1798: 104.

Henry, *Mrs*, fl. 1788: Beatrice 491.

Henry, John, 1746–94: Adam (AYLI) 133; Cassius 318; Ghost 218; Iago 507, 513; Othello 513–14; Posthumus 181. Other references 69, 513.

Herrington, stage name of John Heriot, 1760–1833: Orlando 139.

Heyborn, *Miss*, fl. 1782: York, Duke of 558.

Hicks [DL box-keeper], fl. 1780–95: 70, 72, 87, 90, 98.

Higginson, *Mrs*, formerly Mrs Cussans, later Mrs Egerson, fl. 1799: Juliet (R & J) 611.

Hill, fl. 1786: Romeo 604.

Hill, James, d. 1817: Lorenzo 444–5. Other reference 105.

Hilliard, *Miss* P. [dancer], fl. 1758–60: 21, 24.

*Hippisley, *Mrs* Elizabeth (?), fl. 1742–68 [until 1759 usually known as Miss Hippisley] [in my Vol. I, 479, it is incorrectly stated that she later became Mrs Fitzmaurice]: Arante 339–45; Charmian 116; Clarence 267; Dorcas (Wint. T.) 679;

Helen 168–9; Jessica 417–18; John, Prince (1 Hen. IV) 239; Page, Anne 452–3, 455–7; Phebe 119, 121–3; Queen, Player 202–3; Ursula 479–80.

Hitchcock, *Mrs* Robert, Sr., Sarah, fl. 1777–81: Jessica 428, 430; Mopsa (Sheep S.) 682; Ophelia 215; Page, Mrs 462.

Hitchcock, Robert, Jr., 1768–?: Robin 459.

Holcroft, Thomas, 1745–1809: Citizen (J. Caesar) 319; Gadshill 252–3; Malvolio 665; Pistol (MWW) 459–60; Watchman (Much Ado) 486. Other references 67, 69.

Holland, Charles [the elder], 1733–69: Bassanio 420; Bastard (John) 324–5; Buckingham (Hen. VIII) 300; Ferdinand 639–40; Florizel (Wint. T.) 677, 679; Hamlet 194–5, 199–206; Hotspur 243–9; Iachimo 168–73; Iago 505–7; Macbeth 372–5; Orlando 123; Prospero 642; Proteus 672–3; Richard III 534–9, 541; Romeo 582, 585–90; Thyreus 116; Tressel 532–3; Wales, Prince of (2 Hen. IV) 269–72. Other references 14, 25, 29, 36, 38, 116, 643.

Holland, Charles [the younger], 1768–1849: Arviragus 186; Blunt (1 Hen. IV) 265; Captain (Twelfth N.) 671; Cassio 524; Dauphin (John) 333; Ferdinand 654; Horatio 234–7; Jaques de Bois 147–9; John, Prince (1 Hen. IV) 263; Marcellus 232, 234; Montano 522; Norfolk (Rich. III) 571–3, 575; Pedro, Don 495–6; Richard III 568; Ross 397, 399; Salarino 441, 443–5. Other reference 569.

Holland, William (?), fl. 1782: Richmond 558.

Hollingsworth, Thomas, 1748–1814: Bardolph (MWW) 465, 467; Barnardine 410–11; Carrier 265; Citizen (Coriolanus) 165–6; Clown (Wint. T.) 686; Corin 147–9; Elbow 410; Evans 465; Gobbo 436, 440–1, 443–5; Gravedigger 213, 232, 234–5, 237; Grumio 632, 635; Harfleur, Governor of 290–3; Lord Mayor 564–5, 567, 573–4; Lucianus 227, 232; Man, Old (Lear) 358; Sampson 605–6, 609; Sands 310–11; Seacoal 494; Sexton 494–5, 497; Tailor 629, 634; Toby, Sir 671; Trinculo 653–4. Other references 358, 654.

Holloway [dancer], fl. 1780: 71.

Holman, Joseph George, 1764–1817: Antipholus of Ephesus 155–7; Antonio (Merchant) 442–4; Benedick 489–90; Edgar 356–7, 359–61; Florizel (F & P) 688–9; Florizel (Wint. T.) 686, 688; Hamlet 224, 227–30, 232–3, 235; Henry VIII 310, 312; Hotspur 258, 260–1, 263, 265–6; Macbeth 387–8, 390–2, 394–6, 399; Orlando 141–5; Posthumus 183–6; Richard

745

III 561–2, 567–71, 573–4; Richmond 564–6; Romeo 603–11; Timon 657. Other references 80, 100, 189, 572.

*Holtom, Edward, d. 1780: Abraham 585; Apothecary 587, 589–90, 592–3, 595–6; Archidamus 681; Balthazar (Merchant) 424; Bedford 279–82; Blunt (Cibber's Rich. III) 529–31; Caius 449, 452–6; Catesby 535; Colevile 267; Dennis 127; Elbow 403; Falconbridge, Robert 325–6; Feeble 269–70, 273; Forrest 532–4, 538–9; Francisco (Hamlet) 190–201, 211; Gadshill 240; Gentleman Usher 344; Gregory (R & J) 585; Herald (Lear) 346; Jaques de Bois 119–22; Ligarius 314–18; Lovell 295; Macbeth's Servant 371; Merchant (Com. Err.) 150; Messenger (Othello) 510; Murderer 373–4; Nym (MWW) 446, 448–51; Officer (Coriolanus) 160; Simple 450–3; Soldier, French 283–7; Westmorland (1 Hen. IV) 241–5. Other references 15, 21, 27, 35, 41, 48, 54.

Hook, James [composer], 1746–1827: 469.

Hooke, *Miss*, fl. 1783: Celia 136.

Hopkins, *Miss* Elizabeth, later Mrs Michael Sharp, q.v.

Hopkins, *Miss* Priscilla, later (1) Mrs William Brereton; (2) Mrs John Philip Kemble, q.v.

Hopkins, William [DL prompter], d. 1780: 34, 38, 53, 713 n.

Hopkins, Mrs William, Elizabeth, 1731–1801: Elinor 329, 331–2; Elizabeth, Queen 540, 542–4, 546, 548, 550, 552–3, 555–7, 559–60, 568; Emilia 504–17; Falconbridge, Lady 324; Hermione 679; Hippolyta (MND) 471; Hostess (1 Hen. IV) 261, 264; Isabel 293; Macduff, Lady 372; Maria 662–3; Nurse 605–6, 609–10; Ophelia 201–2; Page, Mrs 457; Paulina (Wint. T.) 683, 685–7; Queen (Cymbeline) 171–2, 175–6, 182–4; Queen (Hamlet) 203–4, 206–24, 226–7; Quickly, Mrs (MWW) 463, 466–7; Regan 342–5, 350–1; York, Duchess of 563–5, 567, 569–70. Other references 34, 38, 53, 332, 561.

Horwell, fl. 1792: Henry VI (Cibber's Rich. III) 567.

Howard, Henry, d. 1766: Falstaff (MWW) 451.

Howard, Samuel, 1710–82: Lion (P & T) 469–70. Other references 5, 10, 18.

Huddart, Thomas, d. 1831: Othello 523.

Hudson, fl. 1787: Duke Frederick 139.

Hull, Thomas, 1728–1808: Adam (AYLI) 132–3, 135–8, 141–2, 144–5; Aegeon 151–7; Albany 345–7, 349; Angelo (Measure) 405–7; Antigonus (F & P) 688–9; Antipholus of Syracuse 150; Antonio (Merchant) 420, 427, 433–4; Antony (J. Caesar) 317; Banquo 387; Belarius 173; Brabantio 511–24; Buckingham (Rich. III) 536–42, 544–51, 553, 555–6, 558–62; Burgundy (Hen. V) 282–3; Camillo (Wint. T.) 680–2, 684–8; Canterbury, Archbishop of 288–9, 292; Cassio 503–5; Cassius 318; Chatillon 326, 330; Chorus (Hen. V) 289; Cranmer 302, 304–7, 310; Cromwell 300–2; Dauphin (John) 325–6; Duke (TGV) 673; Duke Senior 127, 129–31; Duncan 380–96, 398–9; Edgar 342; Escalus (Measure) 403–4; Exeter 282, 284–7; Flavius 657; France, King of (Hen. V) 287; Galesius 163; Ghost 220, 224; Gloucester (Lear) 348–52, 354–7, 359–61; Henry IV (1 Hen. IV) 256–8, 260; Henry V 283–4; Henry VI (Cibber's Rich. III) 548, 552, 572; Horatio 200–8, 210–14, 216–20, 222–3; Hubert 328; King (All's Well) 113–14; King (Hamlet) 228–9; Laurence, Friar 586–91, 593–612; Lennox 371, 373–4, 376–9; Leonato 483–95; Lord Chief Justice 276; Macduff 376–7, 379, 385; Octavius (J. Caesar) 316; Orsino 661; Page (MWW) 452–7, 460–7; Pembroke 322–4; Pisanio 171–7, 180–1, 183–4; Polixenes (F & P) 678–9; Prospero 646–7; Salisbury (John) 323; Stanley 565–74; Time (Wint. T.) 680–1; Vernon 250–1, 254; Westmorland (2 Hen. IV) 270, 272, 274; Worcester 244–9, 263, 265–6. Other references 31, 37, 44, 46, 50, 52, 81–2, 92, 96, 149–51, 323, 655, 672, 675, 718.

Hull, Mrs Thomas, Ann Maria, née Morrison, 1727–1805: Boy (Hen. V) 278; Capulet, Lady 597; Countess 114; Donalbain 364; Edward, Prince 526–8; Fleance 363; Henry, Prince 320; Paulina (Wint. T.) 681; Queen (Cymbeline) 178; Queen (Hamlet) 213; York, Duchess of 549–50.

Humphreys [DL door-keeper], fl. 1757: 17.

Humphreys, fl. 1798–9: 723.

Humphries, Mrs (i.e. *Miss*) Eliza, fl. 1800: Falconbridge, Lady 333.

Hunt, Mrs William, Henrietta, née Dunstall, fl. 1774: Shepherdess (AYLI) 129.

Hunter, fl. 1783–92: Gratiano (Othello) 520; Henry VI (Cibber's Rich. III) 559.

Hunter, Mrs, stage name of Mrs Hunt, née Maria Cooper, fl. 1775–92: Anne, Lady 552; Elizabeth, Queen 551, 558, 568; Goneril 351; Nerissa 428; Paulina (Wint. T.) 684; Queen (Hamlet) 213, 215, 220–2.

Hurst, Richard, d. 1805: Adam (AYLI)

INDEX I

124; Aedile 160; Angers, Citizen of 325, 327–9; Antonio (Much Ado) 480–6; Antonio (Tempest) 643–6, 648; Blunt (1 Hen. IV) 252–5; Brabantio 507–11; Capulet 595, 597; Cleomenes (Wint. T.) 683; Cornwall 342–51; Cymbeline 171–81; Doctor (Macbeth) 374; Duke Senior 125–34; Duncan 384; Gratiano (Othello) 505–8; Kent 353; King (Hamlet) 217; King, Player 213, 215–17; Laurence, Friar 591; Leonato 480; Lodovico 505–6; Lucullus 656; Macduff 375; Montague 591–3; Mowbray 273–6; Norfolk (Rich. III) 539, 541, 543, 545, 548–51, 553, 555; Page (MWW) 456; Paris 580; Pisanio 170; Polixenes (F & P) 680–1; Salarino 420–2; Sebastian (Tempest) 642; Sergeant (Macbeth) 375; Siward 379–83; Tressel 530; Vernon 248, 250. Other references 38, 40, 45, 67, 381, 421.

Hussey, John [dancer], fl. 1765: 37.

Hutton, fl. 1774: 57.

Iliff, Edward Henry, fl. 1789–91: Blunt (1 Hen. IV) 262; Laertes 228; Salarino 438.

Inchbald, Joseph, 1735–79: Antigonus (F & P) 680; Capulet 594–5; Friar (Much Ado) 482; Senator (Timon) 656–7.

Inchbald, *Mrs* Joseph, Elizabeth, nee Simpson, 1753–1821: Abbess 152–2; Blanch 330; Bullen, Anne 305–7; Celia 137, 139, 141; Countess 114; Elizabeth, Queen 556, 558; Hermione 684–5; Hero 489–92; Mariana (Measure) 406–7; Melissa 657; Nerissa 433–7; Page, Mrs 464–5; Percy, Lady 256–7, 259–60; Queen (Hamlet) 219, 221–2, 225; Regan 356.

Incledon, Charles Benjamin [singer], 1763–1826: 92, 95, 99, 104.

Irish [DL box-keeper], fl. 1796: 100.

Jackson, *Miss* Anne, later Mrs Charles Mathews [the 2nd], 1782–1869: York, Duke of 575.

Jackson, John, 1730–1806: Cornwall 341–2; Fenton 454; Guiderius 169–70; Malcolm 373; Paris 587–9; Poins (2 Hen. IV) 271; Sergeant (Macbeth) 372–3; Vernon 245–7. Other references 32, 34, 59.

Jackson, *Mrs* John, Hester, nee Sowdon, 1750–1806: Adriana 151–2; Anne, Lady 552–3, 555–6; Cordelia 352, 354; Elizabeth, Queen 551, 555, 558; Isabella 405; Juliet (R & J) 597–600; Katharine, Queen 302; Macbeth, Lady 382–3; Queen (Cymbeline) 180–1; Queen (Hamlet) 214, 216–18.

Jackson, Thomas, 1741–98: Caius 459; Carrier 253; Clown (Sheep S.) 682, Sands 303; Stanley 561.

Jacobs, fl. 1769–75: Bernardo 207; Davy 274; Decius 317; Launcelot 425; Lucianus 209; Music Master 621; Philotus 656–7; Ratcliff 542; Simple 458. Other reference 49.

*James, Harris, d. 1751: Lucianus 190; Sampson 578; Town Clerk 474.

*James, *Mrs* Harris, fl. 1737–54: Audrey 118; Lady, Old 297; Nurse 578–80; Quickly, Mrs (MWW) 447. Other reference 9.

Jansolin, *Mme* [unidentified], fl. 1762: 31.

Jarratt, *Miss*, fl. 1773–6: Blanch 327; Celia 128–9, 131; Jessica 423–6.

Jarvis [unidentified], fl. 1762: 31.

Jefferies, *Mrs*, later Mrs John Lee, fl. 1767–71 [Lee was a provincial actor who died in 1784]: Catharine 617; Cordelia 348; Desdemona 506; Elizabeth, Queen 542; Emilia 508; Nerissa 420–2; Page, Mrs 458; Queen (Hamlet) 209. Other reference 45.

Jefferson, fl. 1774: 57.

Jefferson, Thomas, *c.* 1730–1807: Aedile 159–60; Brandon (Hen. VIII) 297–8; Buckingham (Rich. III) 540–1, 543–5, 548–50; Burgundy (Lear) 336–7; Cleomenes (Wint. T.) 677; Cloten 173; Essex 320; Gratiano (Merchant) 421; Guildenstern 195, 197; Iachimo 176; Jaques 128–31; John, Friar 581; King (Hamlet) 206, 208–13, 215; Leonato 483–4; Lieutenant 528–31; Music Master 613; Orsino 660–3; Paris 582–3; Poet 656–7; Silvius 120–1; Trinculo 643; York, Archbishop of 273. Other reference 47.

Jefferson, *Mrs* Thomas [the 1st], Elizabeth, nee May, d. 1766: Bullen, Anne 296–8; Hippolyta (Fairies) 470; Macduff, Lady 368.

Jefferson, *Mrs* Thomas [the 2nd], nee Bainbridge, fl. 1774: Regan 350.

Jerrold, Robert, 1773–1818 [*c.* 1797 he adopted stage name of Fitzgerald]: Peter (R & J) 600; York, Duke of 557.

Jerrold, Samuel, 1749–1820: Mercutio 600; Richard III 557.

Jerrold, *Mrs* Samuel [the 1st], nee Simpson, d. *c.* 1792: Capulet, Lady 600; Elizabeth, Queen 557.

Jewell, William [Hay treasurer], d. 1828: 64.

Jewell, *Mrs* William, Ann, nee Edwards, d. 1798: Anne, Lady 549; Ophelia 208–9.

Johnson, fl. 1800: Sailor (Hamlet) 238.

Johnson, John, 1759–1819: Baptista 630; Borachio 490; Horatio 226, 228; Lorenzo 435; Northumberland 262; Officer

INDEX I

(Othello) 520; Pedro, Don 490; Stanley 558.
Johnson, *Mrs* John, Elizabeth, nee Ford, 1771–1830: Catharine 636; Macbeth, Lady 398. Other reference 105.
Johnson, Samuel, fl. 1775–7: Albany 352; Chamberlain, Lord 303; Corin 131; Falstaff (1 Hen. IV) 252; Gentleman, French 179; Northumberland 251; Ratcliff 551; Rosencrantz 214; Shylock 425; Solanio 426. Other references 59, 63, 425.
Johnston, stage name of *Peter Bardin, d. 1773: Gloucester (Lear) 343; Oliver 124.
Johnston, Alexander, d. 1775: Capulet, Old 581, 588, 594; Falconbridge, Robert 321–2; Wart (Humourists) 268. Other references 51, 58, 447.
Johnston, Alexander [DL machinist], d. 1810: 93.
Johnston, Henry Erskine, 1777–1845: Buckingham (Hen. VIII) 312; Guiderius 186; Hamlet 235–6; Romeo 610–11. Other reference 104.
Johnston, *Mrs* Henry Erskine, Nannette, nee Parker, 1782–?: Ophelia 235–6, 238.
Johnston, Roger, fl. 1769–78: 45, 722.
Johnston, *Mrs* Roger, Helen, d. 1785: Arante 340; Audrey 126; Capulet, Lady 591–5, 598–9, 601; Emilia 505; Falconbridge, Lady 322–3, 327–9; Francisca 404–6; Goneril 343; Queen (Cymbeline) 171, 176; Queen, Player 205–17; York, Duchess of 540–4, 546, 548, 550, 552–3, 555, 557. Other references 45, 65, 340.
Johnstone, John Henry, 1749–1828: Amiens 137–8, 141–2, 144–5; Lorenzo 433–7, 440.
Jona [King's, Haymarket, prompter], d. 1756: 15.
Jones [violoncellist], fl. 1752: 4.
Jones, fl. 1780–1: Benvolio 600; Catesby 557; Richmond 557.
Jones, d. 1806: Abraham 609; Apothecary 601–3; Armed Head (Macbeth) 393; Bardolph (1 Hen. IV) 256–7; Barnardine 405–7; Blunt (Cibber's Rich. III) 560; Carrier 254–7; Citizen (Coriolanus) 163–5; Crier (Hen. VIII) 309; Doctor (Lear) 358–9; Doctor (Macbeth) 391–4, 396; Door-keeper (Hen. VIII) 309–11; Ely, Bishop of 290–3; Gobbo 431, 435–6, 438; Gravedigger 213–14, 216–19, 221–5; Nym (Hen. V) 288; Officer (Com. Err.) 151; Outlaw 674; Peter (R & J) 598–601; Sailor (Hamlet) 226; Sands 305–6; Tailor 620–3, 625–6; Tyrrel 564–5, 567–9; Verges 482; Witch 387. Other references 223, 225, 254, 395.
Jones, *Master*, fl. 1772–7: York, Duke of 546–52.
Jones, *Miss* Elizabeth, fl. 1793: Imogen 185.

Jones, *Mrs* Esther, nee Young, fl. 1746–73: Dorcas (F & P) 676; Mopsa (F & P) 678. Other references 6, 15, 23, 31, 46, 48, 53–4.
Jones, *Mrs* James, Martha Elizabeth, nee Palmer, fl. 1783–99: Bianca (C & P) 628–32, 634–5; Blanch 329, 331; Haberdasher 628–30, 634–5; Patience 309.
Jordan, *Mrs*, stage name of Dorothy Bland, 1761–1816: Beatrice 495–7; Dorinda 654; Helena (All's Well) 115; Imogen 183; Juliet (R & J) 609; Ophelia 232–5, 237; Rosalind 139–49; Viola 666–72. Other references 83, 86, 100, 668.
Joules, fl. 1781–3: Simple 461–3; Soldier, French 289.

Kaygill [DL pit door-keeper], fl. 1765–78: 36, 43, 45, 49, 52, 58–9, 65.
Kean, Edmund, 1787–1833: Robin 467.
Kear, James Thomas, d. 1796: Bardolph (MWW) 458; Hymen 641–5. Other references 40, 49, 59.
Kearny, fl. 1769: Gratiano (Othello) 508; Guildenstern 208; Lieutenant 542; Metellus 318.
Keen, William, 1740–75: Angus 375, 377–80; Austria 325, 327; Barnardine 404; Burgundy (Lear) 345; Captain (Cymbeline) 173–6, 178; Charles 124–30; Colevile 274; Cornwall's Servant 343, 349; Duke (Othello) 506; Escalus (R & J) 593–5; Gentleman, French 173; Glendower 250; Guiderius 171; Hortensio 617–18; John, Friar 594; King, Player 209–12; Montague 589, 592; Officer (Lear) 346–7; Officer (Rich. III) 541, 543; Paris 591; Salarino 424; Sebastian (Tempest) 643–5; Senator (Timon) 656–7; Tressel 543, 549. Other references 36, 40, 47, 51, 56, 58, 595.
Kelly, *Miss* Frances Maria, 1790–1882: Arthur 333; York, Duke of 574.
Kelly, Michael, *c*. 1762–1826: Ferdinand 651–2.
Kemble, Charles, 1775–1854: Bassanio 441–2; Bastard (John) 333; Cassio 522–3; Claudio (Measure) 410–11; Claudio (Much Ado) 496; Cornwall 359; Cromwell 310–11; Fabian 670; Ferdinand 653–4; Gloucester (Hen. V) 293; Guiderius 186; Henry, Prince 332; Hotspur 264; Jaques de Bois 146–7; Laertes 231–7; Lewis 115; Malcolm 393–8; Orlando 146, 148; Paris 609–10; Richmond 572–3, 575; Salarino 440; Shylock 443; Tressel 571; Wales, Prince of (1 Hen. IV) 264. Other reference 147.
Kemble, *Miss* Elizabeth, later Mrs Charles Edward Whitlock, 1761–1836: Imogen

748

INDEX I

182; Portia (Merchant) 431–2; Rosalind 136–7.
Kemble, *Miss* Frances, later Mrs Francis Twiss, 1759–1822: Beatrice 488.
Kemble, John Philip, 1757–1823: Bassanio 434–5; Benedick 491–6; Bertram 115; Coriolanus 163–5; Cromwell 307–9; Duke (Measure) 408–11; Hamlet 221, 223–7, 232, 234–7; Henry V 290–3; Hotspur 261, 264; Jaques 148–9; John, King 329–32; Lear 356, 358–9; Macbeth 387, 389–95, 397–8; Macduff 387–9; Malvolio 668; Orlando 138–40, 142–3; Othello 516–22; Petruchio 626–7, 629; Posthumus 183, 186; Richard III 558, 563–5, 567–8, 570, 572–3, 575; Romeo 605–6; Shylock 432, 436, 438–41, 443–5; Wolsey 308. Other references 80–1, 85, 87–8, 93, 100, 110, 143, 158–9, 189–90, 226, 277, 319, 335, 363, 394–5, 401, 446, 473, 504, 626, 638, 690, 717–18.
Kemble, *Mrs* John Philip, Priscilla, nee Hopkins, formerly Mrs William Brereton, 1758–1845: Anne, Lady 555, 559, 561, 563; Celia 142–7; Edward, Prince 550; Ford, Mrs 460; Hero 488, 491–3; Maria 663–70; Perdita (Wint. T.) 683, 686; Silvia 674; York, Duke of 545. Other references 67, 85, 146, 667.
Kemble, Stephen George, 1758–1822: King (Hamlet) 226, 228; Leonato 491; Othello 515; Pembroke 330; Richmond 559.
Kemble, *Mrs* Stephen George, Elizabeth, nee Satchell, c. 1763–1841: Anne, Lady 559, 566, 569; Celia 135–6; Cordelia 355; Desdemona 515; Hero 489; Juliet (R & J) 601–3, 610; Ophelia 218–19, 221–2, 227–8, 232–3, 237; Perdita (Wint. T.) 684; Portia (Merchant) 440–1; Silvia 674. Other references 76, 96.
Kennedy, *Miss*, stage name of Mrs Richard Griffith, q.v.
*Kennedy, Lawrence, c. 1729–86: Capulet 586; Chamberlain, Lord 299–300; Douglas 244; Laertes 199–200; Paris 587; Philario 168–9; Tressel 534–5. Other reference 25.
*Kennedy, *Mrs* Lawrence, Elizabeth, nee Orfeur, d. 1774: Emilia 503; Nurse 586. Other reference 25.
Kennedy, *Mrs* Morgan Hugh, Margaret, nee Doyle, formerly Mrs Farrell, d. 1793: Ariel 646–8; Patience 304.
Kennedy, Thomas, d. 1808: Arthur 321, 323; Bernardo 225; Biondello 625; Caphis 657; Carrier 258; Pistol (2 Hen. IV) 277; Poins (1 Hen. IV) 257; Sands 307; Simple 464; Slender 464–5; Verges 489–90; Witch 386–8.
Kennedy, *Mrs* Thomas, nee Holmes, fl. 1785–93: Luciana 152–3; Viola 667. Other reference 155.
Kenny, d. 1784: Amiens 131; Bardolph (MWW) 459; Bernardo 215; Burgundy (Lear) 352; Capucius 305; Guildenstern 214; Lorenzo 426; Northumberland 252; Peto (1 Hen. IV) 253; Ratcliff 554; Snout (Fairy T.) 473; Suffolk 303; Tyrrel 552. Other reference 256.
Kenny, *Master*, fl. 1778: York, Duke of 554.
Kenrick, fl. 1783: Lieutenant 559.
King, fl. 1792: Lodovico 520.
King, George, d. 1805: Balthazar (Much Ado) 490.
King, *Mrs* Henry, Mary, fl. 1775–6: Macbeth, Lady 380; Rosalind 130.
*King, Thomas, 1730–1805: Autolycus (F & P) 680–1, 688; Benedick 488, 490; Cloten 168–71; Clown (Wint. T.) 679; Falstaff (1 Hen. IV) 262; Gentleman Usher 340; Glendower 244; Gravedigger 232, 234–5, 237–8; Iago 504; Lucio 404–6; Malvolio 660–2; Osric 199–200; Parolles 112, 115; Petruchio 615–20; Pistol (2 Hen. IV) 269, 271–3; Richard III 543; Roderigo 504–5; Shylock 420–5, 431, 434–5, 437; Speed 673; Stephano (Tempest) 640–3, 645; Touchstone 125–34, 137–9, 141–9. Other references 23, 36, 38, 40, 42, 57, 81, 90, 100, 115, 199, 504.
*King, *Mrs* Thomas, Mary, nee Baker [dancer], 1730–1813: 42, 47.
Kingham, *Mrs*, fl. 1780: Anne, Lady 557; Juliet (R & J) 601.
Kipling, John, d. 1811: Touchstone 139.
Kirby, *Miss* Susannah (?), fl. 1778–82: Arante 353; Bianca (C & P) 623; Maria 665; Mopsa (Wint. T.) 683; Phebe 132–4. Other reference 67.
Kirkpatrick, fl. 1777: Richard III 552.
Klanert, Charles Moritz, d. 1843: Gentleman (Lear) 361; Gentleman, French 186; Paris 611–12; Ratcliff 574–5; Rosencrantz 238; Sergeant (Macbeth) 398–400; Solanio 444–5.
Knapp, fl. 1782: Buckingham (Rich. III) 558.
Knight, Thomas, d. 1820: Francis 263, 265–6; Gratiano (Merchant) 440, 442–5; Roderigo 522–4; Slender 467–8; Surrey 312.
Kniveton, Thomas, d. 1775: Capulet 595–6; France, King of (Hen. V) 287; Ghost 212; Henry VI (Cibber's Rich. III) 545–7; Petruchio 618; Sands 300–1; Shepherd (Wint. T.) 680–2. Other reference 56.
Kniveton, *Mrs* Thomas, Margaretta Priscilla, nee Ward, later Mrs John Banks,

INDEX I

d. 1793: Cordelia 341; Juliet (R & J) 589–90; Mariana (Measure) 403–4; Page, Anne 457. Other references 50, 56.

Knowles, fl. 1770: Burgundy (Lear) 348; Henry, Prince 326.

Lacey, Charles, d. 1757: Adam (AYLI) 118; Dauphin (John) 320; Gentleman Usher 336–7; Hamlet 191; Macduff 364–5; Malcolm 365; Paris 578–80; Surrey 295–6. Other references 6, 9.

*Lacy, Thomas, fl. 1746–51: Buckingham (Hen. VIII) 295; Caius 446; Dauphin (John) 320; Paris 578.

Lacy, Willoughby, 1749–1831: Hamlet 215, 224–5; Othello 512, 516–17, 524; Richmond 550. Other reference 106.

*Lalauze, Charles [dancer], d. 1775: 3, 23, 33.

Lamash, Philip, d. 1800: Biondello 619–20, 623–4; Borachio 485–6; Conrade 484; Essex 328–9; Fabian 663–5; Fenton 459–60; Gentleman Usher 356; Gratiano (Merchant) 430; Grey 290; Guildenstern 215–17; Guildford 308; Jaques de Bois 132–5; John, Prince (1 Hen. IV) 252–4; John, Prince (2 Hen. IV) 275–6; Le Beau 140; Messenger (Much Ado) 484–5; Osric 217, 219–20; Paris 597; Roderigo 514; Salarino 427; Sebastian (Tempest) 648–9; Sebastian (Twelfth N.) 667–8; Suffolk 304–6. Other references 65, 67, 69, 486, 514, 624.

*Lampe, John Frederick [composer], c. 1703–51: 468, 524.

*Lampe, Mrs John Frederick, Isabella, nee Young, d. 1795: Mopsa (F & P) 676; Thisbe (P & T) 469–70. Other references 6, 20, 24, 27, 31, 46, 48, 53–4.

Lane, William, d. 1795: Hortensio 621.

Langrish, Master, fl. 1781–2: York, Duke of 557–8.

Langrish, Miss Mary, 1769–?: Edward, Prince 558; Fairy (MWW) 461–2; Robin 460; York, Duke of 555–7.

*Lansdowne, George Granville, Baron [dramatist], 1667–1735: 313, 411.

Larken, fl. 1772: Richard III 546.

Lawrance, fl. 1787: Solanio 435.

Lawrence, Herbert (?) [CG box-keeper], fl. 1753–4: 8, 10.

*Layfield, Robert, d. 1761: Charles 118.

Leach, fl. 1780: Henry VI (Cibber's Rich. III) 557; Laurence, Friar 600.

Leak, Miss Elizabeth, c. 1778–?: Amphitrite 654; Hero 495. Other reference 103.

Lear, fl. 1778: Stanley 554.

Lebrun [dancer], fl. 1756: 14.

Ledger, John, 1749–1808: Balthazar (Merchant) 431, 440–3; Balthazar (R & J) 608, 610; Bardolph (1 Hen. IV) 264; Cook (C & P) 628; Forrest 566; Gadshill 256–60, 262; Lord (Cymbeline) 181; Macbeth's Servant 395–6; Nathaniel 625–6; Pedro (C & P) 626, 630–3, 635; Sailor (Hamlet) 231, 236; Seacoal 496; Yeoman (Rich. III) 570.

Lee, fl. 1799: Richard III 574.

Lee, Miss Harriet, 1757–1851: Cordelia 351.

Lee, Henry, 1765–1836: Biondello 633; Music Master 633; Witch 396.

Lee, James Nathaniel, fl. 1796–9: Murderer 396; Sergeant (Hen. VIII) 312.

*Lee, John, 1725–81: Adam (AYLI) 129–31; Belarius 170; Benedick 483–4; Buckingham (Rich. III) 526–7, 535–8; Camillo (Wint. T.) 679; Duke (Measure) 405; Edmund 335–6, 341–3; Glendower 244–7; Hamlet 190; Iago 505; Jaques 124; John, Don 479–80; John, Prince (2 Hen. IV) 269–72; Laertes 200–4; Lear 336, 351; Paris 587; Philip, King 324; Richard III 531, 548, 550; Ross 364, 372–4; Surrey 295; Tybalt 587–90; Vernon 248; Wolsey 302. Other references 2, 4, 32, 34, 36, 60, 170, 361.

Lee, Mrs John, Anna Sophia, d. 1770: Elizabeth, Queen 538; Emilia 505; Falconbridge, Lady 325; Goneril 342; Maria 660; Regan 342–4; Tearsheet, Doll 270–3. Other references 34, 36, 40.

Leeson, Miss Henrietta Amelia, later Mrs William Thomas Lewis, q.v.

Lefevre, Mrs, fl. 1778–90: Anne, Lady 554; Elizabeth, Queen 560–1; Goneril 353; Queen, Player 228; Richard III 558. Other reference 75.

Legg, Jonathan, d. 1778: Hecate 376, 380–1. Other references 12, 18, 25, 27, 46, 48, 53, 58–9, 65.

Legg, Mrs Jonathan, Mary [widow of the preceding], fl. 1779: 67.

Leicester, Mrs Eliza, fl. 1778–94: Nurse 608; York, Duchess of 554.

Leserve, Miss A. M., d. 1831: Arante 357, 359–61; Bianca (C & P) 630, 632–6; Capulet, Lady 612; Gentlewoman (Macbeth) 400; Helen 185; Lesbia 157; Margaret 495–6; Queen, Player 238; York, Duchess of 575.

Lessingham, Mrs, stage name of Mrs John Stott, nee Jane Hemet, 1739–83: Anne, Lady 540–2, 544–8; Desdemona 501, 512; Hero 483–8; Imogen 171, 177–8; Juliet (R & J) 588, 594; Luciana 151–2; Nerissa 420–31; Ophelia 211; Portia (Merchant) 428; Wales, Prince of (2 Hen. IV) 274. Other references 44, 48, 52, 54, 63, 66, 420.

INDEX I

L'Estrange, Joseph, fl. 1774-87: Albany 351-2, 354; Alonso 646-8; Biondello 621; Borachio 485, 487-8; Chatillon 328; Cymbeline 178, 180-1; Douglas 254-6; Duke (Com. Err.) 151-2; Duke (Othello) 511-14; Duke Senior 132-3, 139; Exeter 288-9; Henry IV (1 Hen. IV) 251; King, Player 214, 217-20; Lennox 380-6; Lieutenant 551-3, 555-6, 558; Oliver 130-1; Provost 405-7; Salarino 427, 429-31, 433; Tybalt 597-601. Other reference 75.

*Leviez, Charles [dancer], d. c. 1778: 11, 19.

Lewes, Charles Lee, 1740-1803: Bertram 113-14; Burgundy (Lear) 346-7; Chamberlain, Lord 300-2, 304; Cloten 175, 177, 180-1; Clown (Twelfth N.) 663; Dauphin (Hen. V) 287; Fabian 661; Falstaff (MWW) 463; Fenton 457; Gloucester (Hen. V) 286; Gratiano (Merchant) 424-32, 438; Guildenstern 211; Henry, Prince 326; Lucio 406-8; Montano 509; Mortimer 249; Norfolk (Rich. III) 549; Osric 211-14, 216-18; Poins (1 Hen. IV) 250-1; Ratcliff 541-8; Roderigo 510, 512-14; Touchstone 135; Tybalt 597. Other references 46, 48, 52, 72, 246.

Lewis, Mrs Louisa (?), formerly Mrs Standen, 1739-?: Ford, Mrs 454; Queen (Hamlet) 201-2.

Lewis, Philip, d. 1791: Antonio (Merchant) 425-6; Balthazar (R & J) 591; Bardolph (1 Hen. IV) 245-7; Bardolph (2 Hen. IV) 269-70; Bardolph (Hen. V) 284; Citizen (Coriolanus) 163; Citizen (J. Caesar) 317; Cranmer 303; Duke Senior 131; Evans 452, 454-6; Gloucester (Lear) 352; Gravedigger 204, 214; Joseph 614; King, Player 204; Lord Mayor 539; Lucius (Cymbeline) 179; Man, Old (Lear) 343; Philario 172-3; Shallow (MWW) 457; Silence 272; Stanley 551; Westmorland (Hen. V) 286; Witch 374, 376. Other references 35, 39, 173, 455, 539, 589.

Lewis, William Thomas, c. 1746-1811: Antipholus of Syracuse 151-3; Bastard (John) 328; Benedick 485-6, 490-5; Cassio 511-12; Claudio (Much Ado) 483-4; Cromwell 312; Edgar 350-2, 354-5; Florizel (Wint. T.) 682, 684-5; Hamlet 214; Mercutio 596, 598-612; Orlando 129-33, 135, 137-8, 141; Orsino 663; Petruchio 620-3, 625-36; Posthumus 177-8; Romeo 597; Wales, Prince of (1 Hen. IV) 250-1, 254-61, 263, 265-6. Other references 56, 99-100, 105.

Lewis, Mrs William Thomas, Henrietta Amelia, nee Leeson, 1751-1826: Anne, Lady 555-6, 558, 562; Mariana (Measure) 405, 407; Page, Anne 460-2, 464-7; Percy, Lady 255-8.

Lings, Miss, fl. 1772: Edward, Prince 547.

Lings, John, fl. 1768-72: Balthazar (R & J) 594; Bernardo 207, 209; Forrest 546; Lepidus (J. Caesar) 317; Lieutenant 543; Lucullus's Servant 656; Music Master 617-18; Officer (Othello) 508; Servant (Lear) 348. Other references 43, 49, 508.

Linley, Thomas, Jr. [composer], 1756-78: 637.

*Linnett, fl. 1740-60: 721.

Linton, Charles [musician in CG band], d. 1784: 78.

Linton, Mrs Charles, Mary [widow of the preceding], fl. 1784: 78.

Lisley, Mrs, stage name of Mrs John Richard Kirwan Lyster, nee Jane Barsanti, later Mrs Richard Daly, d. 1795: Ford, Mrs 459; Portia (Merchant) 428. Other reference 54.

Litchfield, John, d. 1858: 569.

Litchfield, Mrs John, Harriett Sylvester, nee Hay, 1777-1854: Anne, Lady 572-5; Emilia 523-4; Macbeth, Lady 400; Nerissa 445; Regan 361.

Lloyd, fl. 1789: Hamlet 228.

Lloyd, Mrs, fl. 1790: Dorcas (F & P) 688.

Lloyd, Edward (?), fl. 1770-6: Baptista 620-1; Bardolph (1 Hen. IV) 252; Brabantio 508; Duke (Merchant) 422; Iago (?) 509; Stanley 547, 549.

Logan, Miss, fl. 1795-6: Anne, Lady 571; Nerissa 440-1; Percy, Lady 264.

Longley, fl. 1797: Falstaff (1 Hen. IV) 265.

Louisa Anne, Princess [sister of George III], 1749-68: 43.

*Love, stage name of James Dance, 1722-74: Brabantio 505; Caliban 641-3; Cymbeline 169-71; Falstaff (1 Hen. IV) 244-8, 250; Falstaff (2 Hen. IV) 270-4; Falstaff (MWW) 454, 456-8; Jaques 125-8; King (Hamlet) 202-6; Laurence, Friar 589, 592-4; Polonius 208; Quince (Fairy T.) 471; Quince (MND) 470; Stephano (Tempest) 643-4; Toby, Sir 659-62; Touchstone 126; Witch 372-5. Other references 32, 37-8, 49, 201, 654.

Love, Mrs, stage name of Mrs James Dance, nee Hooper, d. 1807: Audrey 126, 141; Catharine 616; Curtis 620, 622-7; Hostess (1 Hen. IV) 252-4, 256, 259; Lady, Old 308; Nurse 597, 600-2; Quickly, Mrs (MWW) 459. Other reference 65.

Lowe, Joseph, fl. 1753: Richmond 528. Other reference 7.

*Lowe, Thomas, d. 1783: Amiens 119-23; Balthazar (Much Ado) 478; Cadwal 168;

INDEX I

Hymen 640–1; Lorenzo 413–18; Pyramus (P & T) 469–70. Other references 3, 7, 18, 24.

Lucas, fl. 1775–8: Gobbo 425; Henry VI (Cibber's Rich. III) 553.

Lyons, John, d. 1824: Adam (C & P) 631; Blunt (Cibber's Rich. III) 566, 569–70; Cambridge 292; Conrade 490; Curio 668–9; Gregory (C & P) 629–33, 635; Gurney 331–2; Jaques de Bois 141; Leonardo 440–3; Marcellus 233, 236; Nathaniel 628–9; Officer (Othello) 519–21; Panthino 674; Peto (1 Hen. IV) 264; Sampson 610; Scroop 290; Sergeant (Hen. VIII) 309–10; Traveller (1 Hen. IV) 261.

Macartney, fl. 1799: Cornwall 361.

Macartney, Charles Justin, 1760–?: Romeo 611.

McGeorge, Horatio Thomas, fl. 1766–70: Captain (Lear) 348; Le Beau 124; Messenger (Othello) 506; Officer (Lear) 343; Tybalt 591.

McGeorge, *Mrs* Horatio Thomas, fl. 1766–92: Celia 124; Regan 344; York, Duchess of 568.

Machin, O'Brien, fl. 1778: Shylock 428.

*Macklin, Charles, *c.* 1700–97: Fluellen 278; Iago 499–500, 506, 512; Macbeth 379–81; Mercutio 578–80; Polonius 190–1; Richard III 550; Shylock 413–14, 417–22, 424–37. Other references 43, 55, 58, 63, 66, 70–1, 76, 88, 437.

*Macklin, *Mrs* Charles [the 1st], Anne, nee Purvor, formerly Mrs Grace, d. 1758: Emilia 499–500; Hostess (1 Hen. IV) 239–40; Hostess (2 Hen. IV) 267–8; Hostess (Hen. V) 278; Nurse 578–84; Quickly, Mrs (MWW) 447–9.

*Macklin, *Miss* Maria, *c.* 1732–81: Anne, Lady 549–51; Beatrice 477; Desdemona 504; Helena (All's Well) 111–14; Juliet (R & J) 585, 587–90; Ophelia 193–7, 199, 201–7, 209–11; Perdita (Wint. T.) 676; Portia (Merchant) 419–27; Rosalind 120–4, 127; Volumnia (Sheridan's Coriolanus) 163. Other references 22, 35, 37, 41, 43, 48, 50, 54, 58, 60, 63, 588.

Macready, William, 1755–1829: Antipholus of Syracuse 154; Antonio (Merchant) 440; Banquo 396; Benvolio 609–10; Blunt (1 Hen. IV) 258–61; Borachio 490–4; Buckingham (Rich. III) 570–2; Cassio 517–22; Cornwall 357, 359–60; Edmund 357; Escalus (R & J) 607–8; Fenton 464–7; Gentleman, French 184; Gratiano (Merchant) 434–5; Guiderius 185; Guildenstern 227–8; Horatio 233; Laertes 229; Le Beau 141–2, 144–5;

Malcolm 389–95; Norfolk (Rich. III) 562, 564–5; Page (MWW) 467–8; Paris 604–7; Poins (1 Hen. IV) 263; Rosencrantz 228–31; Ross 395; Surrey 307, 310; Tressel 565–9; Tybalt 608. Other references 91, 96.

Madden, *Miss* Ann, later Mrs William Heard, q.v.

Maddocks, Walter, fl. 1789–1800: Angiers, Citizen of 333; Antonio (TGV) 674; Balthazar (Merchant) 438–9; Baptista 634; Biondello 629, 635; Canterbury, Archbishop of 290–3; Captain (Lear) 358; Chancellor, Lord 309–11; Citizen (Coriolanus) 164–6; Doctor (Macbeth) 392, 395, 397, 399; Duke (Othello) 519–22, 524; Duke Frederick 140–1, 147–9; Friar (Much Ado) 494–5, 497; Gonzalo 651–4; Gregory (C & P) 631, 633–5; John, Friar 609; King, Player 232, 234, 236, 238; Knight (Lear) 359; Lord Mayor 571; Philario 186; Priest (Twelfth N.) 669–71; Ratcliff 569–70, 572–3, 575; Sheriff (1 Hen. IV) 261, 265; Thomas, Friar 409–11; Tubal 440–1, 443–5. Other reference 392.

Maddocks, *Mrs* Walter, fl. 1795–9: Curtis 634–5; Overdone, Mrs 409–11; Regan 359.

Maguire, fl. 1761–2: Poins (2 Hen. IV) 269–70.

Mahon, Robert, 1734–99: Austria 328, 330; Caliban 647–8; Captain (Twelfth N.) 666; Conrade 488–9; Cornwall 346; Dennis 124; Douglas 256–7; Essex 326; King, Player 220–2; Lennox 386; Lieutenant 558–9; Lucius (Cymbeline) 173; Macmorris 288–9; Montano 515; Tybalt 593; Wales, Prince of (1 Hen. IV) 257.

Male, George, d. 1815: Ralph 634.

Mallet, David [dramatist], *c.* 1705–65: 32.

Manesière, *Signora* Louisa, later Mrs James Fishar [dancer], d. 1775: 37, 50.

Mansel, *Miss* Elizabeth, later Mrs Frederick Reynolds, d. 1851: Goneril 361; Nerissa 440, 442–3; Page, Anne 468.

Mansel, Robert, d. 1824: Blunt (1 Hen. IV) 266; Escalus (R & J) 611; Lucius (Cymbeline) 186; Malcolm 399; Tressel 574.

Mansell, *Miss* Mary, later (1) Mrs Thomas Orton; (2) Mrs Bell [in 1778 she adopted stage name of Mrs Farren, q.v.].

Mansill, fl. 1792: Roderigo 520.

Marklew, *Mrs* [unidentified], fl. 1776: 61.

*Marr, Harry, d. 1783: Abraham 578, 581, 588, 594; Bernardo 190–1, 194–5, 197–208; Burgundy (Lear) 335–6; Catesby 526–9; Davy 270–1; Gadshill 243; Guildford 297–8, 300; Officer (Twelfth N.) 660; Outlaw 673; Philip (C & P) 614;

752

Rugby 447, 453, 455–6, 458; Servant (2 Hen. IV) 269; Siward, Young 364. Other references 19, 529, 595.

Marriot, F., fl. 1787: Mercutio 605; Silvius 139. Other reference 722.

Marriot, Mrs F., fl. 1787: Nurse 605.

*Marshall, James (?), fl. 1731–55: Brabantio 501.

Marshall, Thomas, d. 1816: Caius 467; Cloten 184; Douglas 261; Montano 520; Osric 229; Paris 607; Suffolk 310. Other reference 94.

*Marten, John, d. 1764: Austria 321; Bardolph (1 Hen. IV) 239–40; Bardolph (2 Hen. IV) 267; Bardolph (Hen. V) 278–84; Bardolph (MWW) 446; Chancellor, Lord 295; Duke (Merchant) 413, 415; Duke (Othello) 499–503; Host (MWW) 448–55; Lord Mayor 526–36; Murderer 364–9, 371; Soothsayer (J. Caesar) 315–16. Other references 6, 10, 23, 25.

Martial, fl. 1769: Brabantio 507.

Martyr, Mrs Margaret, nee Thornton, d. 1807: Florizel (Wint. T.) 687; Mopsa (Wint. T.) 684–5. Other references 74, 78, 86.

Massey (of CH), fl. 1776–8: Capulet 598; Catesby 554; Cymbeline 179; Duke (Merchant) 426; Duke Frederick 131; Escalus (R & J) 599; Gardiner 303; Kent 352; Lord Mayor 551; Music Master 623; Polonius 214.

Massey (of Hay), d. 1784: Bardolph (1 Hen. IV) 253, 256; Bardolph (MWW) 462; Corin 136; Doctor (Macbeth) 383; Gravedigger 215, 218, 222; Host (MWW) 459; Lord Mayor 552, 556; Montague [V. iii only] 602; Norfolk (Rich. III) 554; Sands 304; Shepherd (Sheep S.) 682, 684; Tubal 427.

Massey, Mrs E., fl. 1776–81: Cordelia 353; Elizabeth, Queen 551–2, 556; Imogen 179; Katharine, Queen 303–5; Macbeth, Lady 383; Portia (Merchant) [IV. i only] 430. Other reference 61.

Massingham [DL door-keeper], fl. 1799: 105.

Masters, Mrs, nee Lalauze, 1753–?: Arante 351.

Mathews, fl. 1766: Ruffian (Lear) 344.

*Mattocks, George, 1735–1804: Amiens 123–4, 127, 129–33, 135–6; Balthazar (Much Ado) 485–9; Donalbain 364; Ferdinand 646–8; Florizel (F & P) 678–9; Lorenzo 419–33. Other references 21, 23, 46, 68, 70, 420.

Mattocks, Mrs George, Isabella, nee Hallam, 1746–1826: Adriana 155–7; Boy (Hen. V) 281; Catharine 623, 627–8, 630, 632–6; Celia 129–32; Cordelia 341;

Diana 112–14; Elizabeth, Queen 548, 550, 553; Emilia 511–12; Ford, Mrs 461–4; Hermione 681; Jessica 420; Julia 674; Juliet (R & J) 587–9; Katharine (Hen. V) 283–9; Olivia 661, 666; Ophelia 207, 210–19; Page, Mrs 468; Robin 451; York, Duke of 527–33. Other references 43, 46, 52, 461.

Meadows, William, fl. 1786–7: Balthazar (Much Ado) 490; Osric 226. Other reference 82.

Mellon, Miss Harriot, later (1) Mrs Thomas Coutts [the 2nd]; (2) Duchess of St. Albans, 1777–1837: Blanch 332; Celia 148–9; Dorinda 654; Hero 494–5, 497; Maria 670–2.

Melmoth, Courtney, stage name of Samuel Jackson Pratt, 1749–1814: Hamlet 213; Leontes (Wint. T.) 682. Other reference 58.

Melmoth, Mrs Courtney, stage name of Mrs Samuel Jackson Pratt, nee Charlotte ——, 1749–1823: Elizabeth, Queen 549–50; Hermione 682; Macbeth, Lady 381; Queen (Hamlet) 213. Other reference 58.

Menage, Miss Arabella 'Bella', later Mrs Michael William Sharp, d. 1817: Blanch 333.

Menage, Frederick, 1788–1822: Fleance 395, 397.

Menage, Miss Mary, 1778–1830: Fleance 391–2; Page (R & J) 609; York, Duke of 566, 568–9.

Mendez, fl. 1767: Sampson 592.

Meredith, d. 1810: Buckingham (Rich. III) 568.

Merrifield, John [dancer], fl. 1770: 48.

Merry, Mrs Robert, Anne, nee Brunton, later (1) Mrs Thomas Wignell; (2) Mrs William Warren [the 2nd], 1769–1808: Anne, Lady 564–6; Beatrice 490; Cordelia 356–7; Juliet (R & J) 604–7; Perdita (F & P) 688; Perdita (Wint. T.) 686–8. Other references 84, 564.

Messink, James, 1721–89: Bullcalf 274; Carrier 254–5; Gravedigger 205, 208; Tubal 420–6; William 125–30, 132. Other references 47, 49, 56.

Metteer, fl. 1755: Lodovico 501.

Mexborough, Sarah, Countess of, nee Delaval, 1742–1821: 498.

Middleton, stage name of James Magan, c. 1769–99: Arviragus 185; Edmund 359–60; Florizel (Wint. T.) 688; Laertes 230–1, 233; Macduff 395; Malcolm 395–6; Othello 521; Romeo 606, 608–9; Vernon 263. Other reference 101.

Milburne, fl. 1788–91: Gravedigger 227–9; Simple 466–7; Tailor 626.

INDEX I

*Miles, Francis [dancer], d. 1771: 3, 12, 23, 37, 39, 50.
Miles, *Mrs* Francis, Mary [widow of the preceding], fl. 1771: 50.
Miles, William Augustus [dramatist], c. 1753–1817: 70.
Miller, *Mrs* [unidentified], fl. 1758: 19.
Miller, *Miss*, fl. 1770–4: Cordelia 347, 349–50; Countess 113; Desdemona 509–10; Elizabeth, Queen 545–6, 548; Juliet (R & J) 595–6; Queen (Hamlet) 210–12. Other reference 50.
Miller, Alexander, d. 1796: Antony (J. Caesar) 317; Duke (Othello) 520; Hortensio 618.
Miller, *Miss* Anne, d. 1805: Anne, Lady 571, 573; Diana 115; Dorinda 653–4; Juliet (R & J) 609; Miranda 653.
Miller, *Miss* Elizabeth, later Mrs Thomas Baker [the elder], q.v.
Millidge, *Mrs* Josiah, Elizabeth, nee Matthews, d. 1800: Ursula 481–5.
Mills, fl. 1778: Tressel 554.
Mills, *Mrs*, fl. 1782: Portia (Merchant) [IV. i only] 431.
Mills, *Miss*, fl. 1800: Helen 186.
Mills, Henry, 1776–?: Burgundy (Lear) 361; Donalbain 399.
Mills, John, d. 1787: Verges 488.
Mills, *Mrs* John [the 2nd], Susan, nee Moore, later Mrs John Fawcett, Jr. [the 1st], q.v.
Mills, *Miss* Theodosia, fl. 1759–70: Francisca 403; Helen 171–2; Iras 116.
*Mills, *Mrs* William [the 2nd], Elizabeth, nee Holliday, fl. 1728–55: Anne, Lady 526; Bullen, Anne 295–6; Elinor 321; Hero 474; Macduff, Lady 364–6; Page, Mrs 447–8. Other reference 4.
*Minors, *Miss* Sybilla, later Mrs John Walker, 1723-1802: Arante 337–8; Blanch 321; Dorcas (Wint. T.) 677; Edward, Prince 526–30; Jessica 412–16; Maria 658–9; Page, Anne 447–9; Tearsheet, Doll 268; Ursula 474–6. Other references 9, 19.
Mitchell, Colin, d. 1789: Gloucester (Lear) 353.
Moisey, fl. 1800: Othello 524.
Molbery, fl. 1782: Lord Mayor 558.
Monet [unidentified], fl. 1751: 2.
Montgomery, Robert, 1725–53: Iago 499.
Moody, John, c. 1727–1812: Adam (AYLI) 125–30, 132–5, 137–47; Captain (Twelfth N.) 660; Capulet 594; Carrier 244–50, 252–5, 261; Charles 125; Clown (F & P) 680–1; Dogberry 486, 492–3; Henry VI (Cibber's Rich. III) 535; Henry VIII 298–9, 301–2; Herald, English (John) 321–2, 324–5; Host (MWW) 459–60,
463, 465, 467; Host (TGV) 672; King, Player 202; Lieutenant 536–8, 540–2; Lorenzo 417–18; Montague 587–8; Mouldy 269, 271, 273–4; Quince (Fairy T.) 471–2; Servant (Wint. T.) 679; Siward 370–5; Stephano (Tempest) 641, 645–52; Thyreus 116; Toby, Sir 667–70; Witch 376–85, 387–93, 395–6. Other references 29, 32, 34, 38, 42, 116, 299, 324, 471.
Moore, *Master*, fl. 1755–6: Puck (Fairies) 470. Other reference 14.
Moore, *Mrs* Mark (?), d. c. 1787: Jessica 425.
Morgan, James, fl. 1762–9: Bardolph (Hen. V) 286; Citizen (J. Caesar) 317; Fleance 373; Francis 248; Lucianus 206; Peter (R & J) 590, 593; Simple 453–7; Tailor 617; Witch 376. Other reference 617
Morgan, McNamara [dramatist], d. 1762: 187, 612, 674.
Morland, *Mrs*, nee Western, fl. 1770–1: Hero 481; Juliet (R & J) 594–5; Ophelia 209.
Morris, *Miss*, d. 1769: Cordelia 347; Juliet (R & J) 593. Other reference 46.
Morris, *Miss*, later Mrs Pierce, fl. 1794–7: Capulet, Lady 608–10; Elizabeth, Queen 572; Goneril 360; Lesbia 156–7; Queen (Hamlet) 230, 232, 234.
Morris, A., fl. 1792: Lieutenant 567.
Morris, *Miss* Catherine, later Mrs George Colman, Jr., 1766–1836: Edward, Prince 552–3, 555–6; Mopsa (Sheep S.) 684; Oberon (Fairy T.) 473; Page, Anne 461–3; Phebe 136.
Morris, David, d. 1777: Austria 326; Biondello 620; Campeius 300–1; Charles 127; Cymbeline 175–7; Duke (Merchant) 420–2, 424; Duke (Othello) 506, 509–10; Escalus (R & J) 593, 595–6; Glendower 249; Kent 343; Lepidus (J. Caesar) 316; Lodovico 505; Lord Mayor 545–6; Mowbray 272; Philario 171–4; Westmorland (Hen. V) 284–5; Williams 285–7. Other references 39, 46, 48, 50, 52.
Morris, Edward [dramatist], d. 1815: 89.
Morris, James [dancer], d. 1767: 14, 19.
Morris, Thomas, fl. 1792: Richard III 567.
*Morrison, *Miss* Ann Maria, later Mrs Thomas Hull, q.v.
Mortimer [unidentified], fl. 1764–80: 34, 38, 43, 49, 58–9, 62, 67, 70.
Morton, *Mrs* Mary, nee Dayes, later Mrs John Morgan [the 1st], 1756–1800: Arante 351; Blanch 328; Bullen, Anne 304; Celia 133; Dorcas (Wint. T.) 684–5; Emilia 518; Jessica 425–36; Juliet (R & J) 596–7; Juno 646–8; Patience 302; Paulina (Wint. T.) 686–7; Perdita (Wint.

INDEX I

T.) 682; Phebe 129–32. Other reference 68.
Moss, William Henry, 1751–1817: Dogberry 490; Gravedigger 226; Launcelot 438; Montano 508; Polonius 226, 228.
Mossop, Henry, 1729–74: Coriolanus 159–60; Duke (Measure) 401–2; Hamlet 196–7; John, King 320; Macbeth 364–70; Othello 499–500; Prospero 639–40; Richard III 526–7, 529–33; Wolsey 295–8. Other references 4, 6, 19, 366.
Mountain, *Mrs* John, Rosemond, nee Wilkinson, *c.* 1770–1841: Celia 142, 144; Dorcas (F & P) 689; Dorcas (Wint. T.) 689; Hero 495–6; Jessica 436–7, 441–3, 445; Luciana 153–7; Ophelia 230–1, 233, 235–6; Perdita (Wint. T.) 688. Other references 86, 91, 94.
Mowat, *Miss*, fl. 1760–1: Desdemona 503; Juliet (R & J) 585. Other references 24, 26.
*Mozeen, Thomas, d. 1768: Albany 335–7; Austria 320–2; Bardolph, Lord 269, 271–2; Benvolio 577–81; Blunt (1 Hen. IV) 243–4; Citizen (Coriolanus) 159–60; Conrade 474–6; Cromwell 295–300; Dolabella 116; Duke Frederick 121; Gratiano (Merchant) 413; Gratiano (Othello) 506; Gregory (R & J) 588; Hortensio 613; Lieutenant 526–34, 537; Lord (All's Well) 112; Montano 499, 504; Pedro, Don 474–5; Sebastian (Tempest) 639; Silvius 118; Stanley 528–9, 531; Valentine (Twelfth N.) 658. Other reference 19.
*Mullart, *Miss* Susanna [in 1761 she adopted stage name of Mrs Evans, q.v.].
Munden, Joseph Shepherd, 1758–1832: Autolycus (F & P) 689; Autolycus (Wint. T.) 688–9; Carrier 261, 263, 265; Dogberry 495–6; Dromio of Syracuse 155–7; Gardiner 312; Gentleman Usher 357; Grumio 632–3, 635–6; Launcelot 443–5; Polonius 229–31, 233, 235–6, 238; Tailor 629–30; Town Clerk 494; Witch 391–6, 398–9. Other reference 100.
Murden, fl. 1765–7: Burgundy (Lear) 343; Clarence 272; Donalbain 374; Gloucester (Hen. V) 284–5; Gratiano (Othello) 506; Lucilius (J. Caesar) 316; Montague 590.
Murphy, Arthur, 1727–1805: Hamlet 194; Macbeth 366; Othello 500–1; Richard III 530. Other reference 12.
Murray, *Mrs*, stage name of Mrs Francis Molloy, nee Eliza Wheeler, later Mrs Cotter, d. 1794: Emilia 520.
Murray, Charles, 1754–1821: Antonio (Merchant) 445; Banquo 398–9; Belarius 186; Caius 468; Cranmer 312; Ghost 235, 238; Henry IV (1 Hen. IV) 264–6;

Henry VI (Cibber's Rich. III) 571, 573–5; Iago 522–4; Laurence, Friar 611; Lear 360; Polixenes (F & P) 689; Richard III 572; Shylock 440, 442–3. Other references 104–5.
Murray, *Miss* Harriot, later Mrs Henry Siddons, 1783–1844: Juliet (R & J) 611; Perdita (F & P) 689; Portia (Merchant) 445.
Mytteer, *Mrs*, d. 1814: York, Duchess of 549.

Nash, Joseph, d. 1793: Nym (MWW) 459; Officer (Twelfth N.) 664; Peto (1 Hen. IV) 252–3.
Naylor, *Mrs* [unidentified] fl. 1767–71: 41, 50.
Neale, fl. 1784: Norfolk (Rich. III) 561.
Nelson, fl. 1766: John, Friar 591.
Nelson, *Master*, fl. 1778: York, Duke of 554.
Newby, *Mrs*, fl. 1778: Capulet, Lady 599; York, Duchess of 554.
Newton, fl. 1767–86: Adam (AYLI) 131; Belarius 179; Capulet 592, 599; Gobbo 426; Gravedigger 214; Grumio 623; Haberdasher 626; Henry VI (Cibber's Rich. III) 554; Lieutenant 554; Music Master 623; Othello 512. Other reference 82.
Nix, Samuel [DL box-keeper], fl. 1784–96: 78, 93, 100.
*Norris, *Miss* Elizabeth, later Mrs Chitty, fl. 1750–2: Patience 296.
Norris, William, d. 1816: Balthazar (Merchant) 432; Burgundy (Lear) 350–1, 353; Captain (Cymbeline) 178; Cinna the Conspirator 319; Escalus (R & J) 597, 599–602; Francisco (Hamlet) 212–17, 219–20; Francisco (Tempest) 645–6, 648–9; Gower (Hen. V) 289; Hortensio 623–4; Lennox 382–3, 385; Lord (AYLI) 135; Messenger (John) 328–9; Montano 513–15; Sebastian (Twelfth N.) 665; Valentine (Twelfth N.) 663–4. Other references 65, 69, 74.
Nossiter, *Miss* Maria Isabella, *c.* 1735–59: Anne, Lady 532; Cordelia 338–9; Desdemona 501–2; Juliet (R & J) 580, 582–3; Perdita (F & P) 676. Other reference 10.
Nost, *Mrs*, fl. 1774–8: Catharine 620; Jessica 428.
Noverre, Jean Georges [dancer], 1727–1810: 29.

Obrien, William, d. 1815: Andrew, Sir 659–60; Benedick 479; Guiderius 168–9; Laertes 197; Lucio 402–3; Slender 452–4; Valentine (TGV) 672–3; Wales, Prince of (1 Hen. IV) 245.

INDEX I

Ogilvie, *Miss* Ann, fl. 1767–74: Anne, Lady 543, 547; Arante 345; Bullen, Anne 300–2; Juliet (Measure) 403; Mariana (Measure) 403. Other reference 46.

O'Keeffe, John [dramatist], 1747–1833: 66, 84, 90.

O'Keeffe, *Mrs* John, Mary, nee Heaphy, 1757–1813: Juliet (R & J) 599.

Osborne, *Mrs*, fl. 1761: Desdemona 504.

Osborne, David, fl. 1799: 721.

*Otway, Thomas [dramatist], 1652–85: 580.

Owenson, Robert, 1744–1812: Albany 348–50; Douglas 250; Duke (All's Well) 113; Hortensio 620; Lodovico 509–10; Malcolm 379; Norfolk (Rich. III) 546, 548; Solanio 423–4; Suffolk 300–2; Tressel 548; Tybalt 595–6.

Packer, John Hayman, 1730–1806: Adam (AYLI) 147–9; Agrippa 116; Albany 339–51, 353; Alonso 651–4; Antonio (Much Ado) 491–6; Banquo 375–8, 380–4, 390, 393–7, 399; Baptista 626–32, 634–5; Benvolio 584–5, 588, 590–4; Brabantio 524; Caesar 318; Camillo (F & P) 680; Campeius 300, 307–11; Catesby 532–4, 536–8, 540–1, 543–5, 548–51, 553, 555, 557, 559–65, 567; Cymbeline 186; Doctor (Macbeth) 393–4; Duke (Merchant) 427–9, 431–2, 434, 436, 438–42, 444–5; Duke Frederick 143–7; Duncan 384–5, 387–9, 391–2; Eglamour 672–3; Flavius 656; France, King of (Hen. V) 290–3; Gloucester (Lear) 356, 358–9; Horatio 200, 202–6, 208–13, 215; King (Hamlet) 200–1, 215–17, 219–21, 223–7, 232, 234–7; Laurence, Friar 595, 597–8, 600–2, 605–6, 609; Lodovico 504–22; Malcolm 370–5; Northumberland 252–4, 261, 264; Oliver 123–6, 128–30, 132–5, 137–41; Orsino 659–61; Page (MWW) 452–4, 457–60, 463, 465, 467; Pandulph 329, 331–3; Paris 589–90; Pedro, Don 478–86, 488; Peter, Friar 408–11; Pisanio 168–84; Poins (1 Hen. IV) 243–8, 250; Poins (2 Hen. IV) 269, 271–4; Prospero 642–5, 647; Rosencrantz 196–200; Salisbury (John) 321–2, 324–5, 327–9; Shepherd (Wint. T.) 683, 685–7; Siward 395, 397; Stanley 571, 573–4; Steward 115; Surveyor 300; York, Archbishop of 275–6. Other references 393–4.

*Paddick, fl. 1744–52: Curio 658; Gregory (R & J) 579; John, Friar 577; Scroop 278; Seyton 365. Other reference 6.

Painter, Joshua, d. 1790: Attendant (2 Hen. IV) 276; Campeius 305; Leonardo 431; Peto (1 Hen. IV) [II. iv only] 256; Stanley 554.

Painter, *Mrs* Joshua, Elizabeth, fl. 1769: York, Duchess of 543.

Painter, *Miss* Sarah Lenox, 1768–?: Edward, Prince 557, 561; Humphrey, Prince 276; Nerissa [IV. i only] 431; York, Duke of 558–9.

Palmer, *Master*, fl. 1798: Donalbain 397.

Palmer, *Mrs* Alicia (?), fl. 1786: Bianca (C & P) 626.

*Palmer, John [the elder], 1728–68: Arviragus 168–71; Banquo 366, 368–75; Bertram 111–12; Buckingham (Rich. III) 527–30, 533; Cassio 499–500, 502–6; Claudio (Much Ado) 474–80; Edmund 336–41; Gratiano (Merchant) 412–18, 420; Horatio 190–1; Mercutio 584–91; Norfolk (Hen. VIII) 295–300; Orlando 117–25; Osric 194–5, 197–203; Richmond 526–7, 533–5, 537–8, 540; Salisbury (John) 320; Sebastian (Twelfth N.) 658–60; Siward, Young 364; Wales, Prince of (1 Hen. IV) 243–4, 246–8; Wales, Prince of (2 Hen. IV) 268. Other references 23, 32, 36, 38, 40, 42.

Palmer, *Mrs* John [the elder], Hannah Mary, nee Pritchard, later Mrs Morrice Lloyd, d. 1781: Anne, Lady 534, 537–8, 540; Beatrice 476–9; Cordelia 342, 344; Desdemona 504; Helena (All's Well) 112; Imogen 170; Isabella 402–3; Juliet (R & J) 582–91; Macbeth, Lady 373; Miranda 639–42; Percy, Lady 243–8; Perdita (Wint. T.) 677. Other references 16, 32, 586.

Palmer, John [the younger], 1744–98: Albany 343; Angelo (Measure) 404–10; Arviragus 171–3; Banquo 383; Bassanio 427–30; Bastard (John) 327, 331–2; Blunt (1 Hen. IV) 245, 249–50; Brutus (J. Caesar) 319; Buckingham (Hen. VIII) 303–4; Burgundy (Lear) 344; Cassio 507–15; Duke Frederick 124; Edmund 344–51, 353; Escalus (R & J) 591–2; Falstaff (1 Hen. IV) 254–5, 261–2; Falstaff (MWW) 466–7; Ford 459, 462; Ghost 215–17, 219–20, 232; Gratiano (Merchant) 428, 431–2; Hamlet 232; Henry VIII 307–11; Iachimo 173–7, 182, 186; Iago 508, 510–11, 522–3; Jaques 131–9, 142–7; John, Prince (2 Hen. IV) 273; Kent 345; Lucius (Timon) 656; Macbeth 393–4, 396–7; Macduff 393–5, 397; Mercutio 609; Montano 506–7; Officer (Rich. III) 536; Osric 206; Petruchio 623–34; Prospero 653–4; Richard III [I. ii, II. ii, V only] 571; Richmond 548–58, 560–1, 563–7, 569–70; Shylock 441; Toby, Sir 662–71; Touchstone 140–1, 147–8; Wales, Prince of (1 Hen. IV) 252–4, 256, 259; Wales,

INDEX I

Prince of (2 Hen. IV) 274–6; Wolsey [III. ii only] 312. Other references 40, 56–7, 59, 61, 87, 101, 394, 536, 629, 723.

Palmer, John, Jr., 1776–1809: Benvolio 610; Blondello 634; Brackenbury 569; Gloucester (Hen. V) 292; Guildenstern 233, 236; Laertes 237; Malcolm 391; Montano 521, 523; Music Master 634; Richmond 571; Vernon 264; Wales, Prince of (1 Hen. IV) 261, 264.

Palmer, *Miss* Martha Elizabeth, later Mrs James Jones, q.v.

Palmer, Robert, Sr. [DL pit door-keeper], 1699–1787: 14, 34, 38, 43, 45, 49, 52, 54, 72.

Palmer, Robert, Jr., 1754–1817: Arviragus 182–4; Barnardine 409–10; Biondello 623–30, 633–5; Catesby 563; Chamberlain, Lord 307–9; Cloten 182, 184, 186; Cornwall's Servant 353; Cromwell 303–4, 306, 308; Donalbain 380–2; Fabian 664, 666–71; Fenton 459; Gentleman Usher 358; Gower (Hen. V) 291–3; Gratiano (Merchant) 434–6, 438, 440–5; Guiderius 181; Henry VIII [III. ii only] 312; Henry, Prince 328–9; Hortensio 621; Laertes 222; Le Beau 141–7; Lieutenant 552–3, 555–7, 559–61; Lucio 410–11; Malcolm 383–5, 387–9; Menenius 165; Montano 515–17; Mustardseed 471; Osric 215, 218, 221, 223–7, 232–7; Page (R & J) 592; Paris [V. iii only] 602; Pindarus 319; Pistol (MWW) 467; Poins (1 Hen. IV) 252–6, 259, 261–2, 264; Poins (2 Hen. IV) 275–6; Roderigo 516–17, 523; Rosencrantz 216–17, 219–21; Sebastian (Twelfth N.) 665; Silvius 130, 132–8; Slender 459, 462; Soldier [Interpreter] 114–15; Tybalt 599–602; Vernon 251; Westmorland (Hen. V) 290; Witch 395, 397–9. Other references 78, 82, 93, 100, 104, 387, 459, 471, 630.

Palmer, William, d. 1797: Amiens 139; Antipholus of Ephesus 152–3; Blunt (1 Hen. IV) 258; Borachio 489–90; Edmund 356; Gratiano (Merchant) 434; Le Beau 139; Osric 225; Paris 604; Ventidius (Timon) 657. Other reference 82.

Palmer, Wingfield, d. 1776 [throughout season of 1767–8 he used stage name of Wingfield]: Cassio 507; Demetrius (MND) 470; Falconbridge, Robert 327; Hymen 641; Launcelot 420–4; Simple 457–9.

Palmer, *Mrs* Wingfield, Hannah, d. 1813: Anne, Lady 557; Bianca (C & P) 622; Phebe 125–6.

Panchaud [DL box-keeper], fl. 1796: 100.

Parker, George, 1732–1800: Duke (Othello) 509; Montano 501.

Parsons, William, 1736–95: Bardolph, Lord 271; Borachio 479; Bottom (Fairy T.) 473; Carrier 248–50, 252–5, 259, 262; Cleomenes (Wint. T.) 679; Clown (Measure) 404–8; Clown (Twelfth N.) 665–6; Cornwall 342; Davy 269; Dogberry 480–6, 488, 491; Douglas 244–7; Elbow 408–9; Evans 456–60, 463, 465; Gardiner 303–4; Gobbo 420–4; Gratiano (Othello) 504–5; Gravedigger 205–10, 215, 217, 219–27; Kent 338; Launcelot 424, 426–9, 431–2, 434; Lennox 372–4; Lucianus 212–14; Officer (Twelfth N.) 660; Philario 169–70, 173–5; Polonius 201; Rosencrantz 200–1; Shadow 269, 271; Shallow (2 Hen. IV) 274; Shallow (MWW) 456; Silence 275–6; Starveling (Fairy T.) 471–2; Starveling (MND) 470; Trinculo 643; Verges 479; Witch 373, 377–85, 387–8. Other references 16, 45, 202, 213, 222, 338, 342, 486.

Parsons, *Mrs* William [the 1st], formerly Mrs Price, d. 1787: Elizabeth, Queen 547; Emilia 501.

Passerini, *Signora* Giuseppe, fl. 1755: Hermia (Fairies) 470.

Pearce, *Miss* J., fl. 1771–4: Capulet, Lady 596–7; Francisca 403; Goneril 351; Helen 177; Phebe 127; Queen, Player 211; Regan 348–50; Widow 114.

Pearce, William (?), fl. 1770: Servant (Lear) 348.

Peile, fl. 1777–81: Banquo 384–5; Constable 289; Ford 461; Hotspur 254; Macduff 385; Norfolk (Hen. VIII) 304–5; Othello 512; Pedro, Don 487. Other references 70, 73.

Peirce, fl. 1777: Starveling (Fairy T.) 473.

Percey [DL box-keeper], fl. 1771–99: 49, 52, 58, 65, 67, 86, 92, 98, 105.

Perry, James, d. 1783: Angelo (Com. Err.) 150; Angus 369–70; Antony's Servant 317; Arviragus 171–7; Blunt (1 Hen. IV) 242–8; Blunt (Cibber's Rich. III) 534; Burgundy (Hen. V) 285–8; Cassio 505; Claudio (Measure) 403; Dercetas 116; Edmund 344; Escalus (Measure) 403; Gentleman Usher 340; Guildenstern 201–7; Humphrey, Prince 268, 270; Jaques de Bois 123; Laertes 204, 208, 210; Lennox 376–7, 379; Malcolm 376–9; Mardian 116; Minucius 163; Norfolk (Hen. VIII) 300–1; Norfolk (Rich. III) 535–44, 546–7; Oliver 127; Osric 198, 201; Paris 584–91, 593–6; Pisanio 173; Poins (1 Hen. IV) 249; Poins (2 Hen. IV) 272; Richard III 545; Salisbury (John) 326; Scroop 284–5; Trebonius 317–18; Tressel 535, 540. Other references 27, 31, 35, 37, 41, 50, 52.

757

INDEX I

Philipps, Thomas, 1774–1841: Burgundy (Lear) 360.

Philips, Thomas, d. 1768: Bullcalf 269, 271; Carrier 243; Corin 121–3; Elbow 401–2; Gravedigger 200; Host (MWW) 452–3; Lord Mayor 534–8; Polonius 195; Sands 296–300; Servant (Coriolanus) 159, 161; Verges 475–9. Other references 25, 32, 34, 36.

Phillimore, John, d. 1799: Abhorson 409–10; Antonio (Tempest) 648–52; Antonio (Twelfth N.) 667–70; Antony's Servant 319; Austria 331–2; Bardolph (Hen. V) 293; Bedford 289; Bernardo 216–17, 219–21, 232; Borachio 492–4; Burgundy (Hen. V) 290–2; Captain (Lear) 356; Capucius 308–11; Charles 139–40, 142–4, 146; Escalus (R & J) 605–6; Fenton 463, 465; Francisco (Hamlet) 215; Gentleman (Lear) 358; Gentleman (Wint. T.) 683; Gratiano (Othello) 518–19, 521–2; Guildenstern 220; Knight (Lear) 359; Le Beau 132–5, 137–8; Lennox 389; Lord Mayor 555, 557, 559–61; Lucius (Cymbeline) 182–4; Montague 609; Murderer 393; Officer (Coriolanus) 165; Officer, Roman 163; Officer, Volscian 165; Outlaw 674; Paris 599–602; Pedro (C & P) 625–31, 633–4; Ratcliff 562–5, 567, 571; Rosencrantz 221, 223–7, 234; Salarino 431–2, 434, 436; Seyton 391–2; Soldier (All's Well) 115. Other references 78, 93, 115, 669.

Phillips, fl. 1761: Benvolio 586.

Phillips, fl. 1769: Othello 507. Other reference 46.

Phillips, *Miss* Anna Maria, later Mrs Rollings Edward Crouch, q.v.

*Phillips, William, 1699–c. 1775: Falstaff (Humourists) 268. Other references 4, 13.

Pierce, fl. 1766–7: Capulet, Old 591–2.

Pilon, Frederick [dramatist], 1750–88: 110, 718.

Pindar, John, d. 1812: Ratcliff 569; Richard III 569.

Pine, Simon, d. 1772: Brabantio 498; Lodovico 498.

*Pitt, *Mrs* Ann, 1720–99 [until 1753 usually known as Miss Pitt]: Audrey 119–22, 127, 129–33; Hacket, Dame 615; Hostess (1 Hen. IV) 241–51, 254–61; Hostess (2 Hen. IV) 269–70, 273–4, 277; Hostess (Hen. V) 278–89; Lady, Old 300–1, 306–7; Margaret 474; Nurse 580–90, 592–607; Quickly, Mrs (MWW) 448–57, 460–7; Witch 376–81, 384–9; York, Duchess of 526, 529, 531. Other references 10, 12, 21, 23, 33, 39, 50, 58.

Platt, *Mrs* S. J., d. 1800 [until 1787 known as Miss Platt]: Anne, Lady 547; Arante 347, 349–51; Bianca (C & P) 619–21; Capulet, Lady 604–8, 611; Curtis 632–6; Elinor 330; Gentlewoman (Macbeth) 388–9, 393, 395–6, 398–9; Goneril 352, 354–7, 359; Hostess (1 Hen. IV) 264; Juliet (Measure) 404–5; Lesbia 151–3, 155; Macduff, Lady 382; Margaret 487; Page, Anne 458–9; Phebe 126; Queen (Cymbeline) 183–4; Queen, Player 229–31, 233, 235–6; Tearsheet, Doll 274, 277; Ursula 489–90, 495–6; York, Duchess of 553, 555–60, 562, 564–74.

Plummer [CG box-keeper], fl. 1753: 8.

Plym, *Miss*, fl. 1763–7: Blanch 324–5; Hero 479–80; Humphrey, Prince 271–2; Imogen 170–1; Viola 660. Other reference 36.

Poitier, Jr. [dancer], fl. 1757–60: 18, 24.

Poitier, *Miss* Jane, later (1) Mrs Joseph Vernon [the 1st]; (2) Mrs Thompson, q.v.

*Poitier, Michael [dancer], d. 1774: 20.

Pollard, *Mrs*, fl. 1792: Anne, Lady 568.

Poole, *Miss* Martha Frances Caroline, later Mrs Peter Dickons, c. 1770–1833: Ophelia 230. Other references 96, 155.

Pope, Alexander, 1763–1835: Antipholus of Syracuse 155–7; Bassanio 434–7, 440, 443–5; Ford 467–8; Hamlet 229–30; Hotspur 259–60; Iachimo 184–6; Lear 359–61; Leontes (Wint. T.) 686–7, 689; Macduff 392, 394–6, 398–9; Othello 516, 518–19, 522–4; Richmond 562, 567–75; Romeo 605–6; Wolsey 307, 310, 312. Other references 81, 84, 86, 98.

Pope, *Mrs* Alexander [the 1st], Elizabeth, nee Younge, 1740–97: Anne, Lady 541, 546, 548; Beatrice 487–9; Catharine 632; Cordelia 349–55; Desdemona 509, 511–12, 514, 516, 518–22; Elizabeth, Queen 564–70; Ford, Mrs 460–2, 465–8; Hermione 686, 688–9; Imogen 172–80, 183–4; Juliet (R & J) 593–4, 603–4; Katharine, Queen 304–7, 310; Macbeth, Lady 379, 382, 387, 389–96; Miranda 643; Perdita (F & P) 680; Portia (Merchant) 427–37, 441; Queen (Hamlet) 228, 230–1, 233; Rosalind 127–8, 130–3, 135–7, 141; Viola 661–4. Other references 45, 74, 84, 99–100, 461–2, 603.

Pope, *Mrs* Alexander [the 2nd], Maria Anne, nee Campion, formerly known by stage name of Mrs Spencer, 1775–1803: Cordelia 361; Desdemona 523–4; Imogen 186; Juliet (R & J) 611–12; Katharine, Queen 312. Other references 105–6.

Pope, *Miss* Jane, 1742–1818: Audrey 146–9; Beatrice 478–84, 486; Catharine 617–20; Lucetta 673; Page, Mrs 460, 463, 466–7. Other references 29, 102, 660.

758

INDEX I

Portal, Abraham [DL box-keeper], fl. 1789–99: 87, 90, 98, 105.
Potter [CG box-keeper], fl. 1769: 46.
Poussin, *Mrs* Joseph, Isabella, fl. 1775–87: Bianca (C & P) 621–5; Capulet, Lady 597–604; Falconbridge, Lady 328, 330; Francisca 406–7; Gentlewoman (Macbeth) 383–8; Goneril 352; Helen 182–3; Isabel 289; Paulina (Sheep S.) 682, 684; Queen, Player 214–15, 217–19, 221–5; Ursula 487–9, 491; Widow 114; York, Duchess of 551–2, 556.
Powel, Sparks, d. 1798: Angelo (Com. Err.) 154–7; Camillo (F & P) 688–9; Capulet 606–11; Carrier 262–3, 266; Cleomenes (Wint. T.) 688; Cymbeline 184–5; Doctor (Macbeth) 390–6; Duke (Merchant) 437; Duke Senior 141–2, 144–5; Friar (Much Ado) 494; Gobbo 440, 442–3; Gratiano (Othello) 518–23; Gravedigger 228, 235; King (Hamlet) 230, 233; Lord Mayor 565–7, 570–3; Marcellus 227–9; Philario 185; Priest (Hamlet) 231; Shallow (MWW) 466–8; Stanley 564–5; Town Clerk 495–6; Worcester 260–1. Other references 99, 104, 357.
Powell, *Miss* Ann, later (1) Mrs Thomas Warren; (2) Mrs John Martindale, d. 1821: Desdemona 513.
Powell, Charles Stuart, d. 1810: Caius 466; Music Master 627–8; Peter (R & J) 606–7; William 141–2, 144. Other reference 145.
Powell, *Mrs* Charles Stuart [the 1st], Mary Ann, nee Masterman, formerly Mrs William Skinn, fl. 1789–93: Curtis 628, 630–1; Nurse 606–8; York, Duchess of 566, 569.
Powell, John, *c.* 1755–1836: Benedick 496; Catesby 559; Duke Senior 149; Pandulph 333; Petruchio 635; Prospero 654. Other reference 105.
Powell, Thomas, 1740–98: Ruffian (Lear) 344.
Powell, William [the elder], 1735–69: Chorus (Hen. V) 285; Edmund 338; Ford 457; Ghost 202; Hamlet 206–7; Henry IV (2 Hen. IV) 271–3; Henry VI (Cibber's Rich. III) 537; John, King 324–6; Lear 342–6; Leontes (Wint. T.) 679; Macbeth 376; Othello 504–6; Posthumus 169–73; Romeo 591, 593. Other references 34, 36, 43, 46.
Powell, *Mrs* William [the younger], Jane, formerly Mrs Farmer, later Mrs John James Renaud, d. 1831: Anne, Lady 563–5, 567; Bullen, Anne 308–11; Constance 333; Countess 115; Desdemona 518, 521, 524; Dorinda 652; Elizabeth, Queen 569–70, 573–5; Emilia 522–3; Hamlet 232, 234; Hippolito 653–4; Isabel 294; Juliet (R & J) 605; Macbeth, Lady 397; Mariana (Measure) 409–11; Miranda 653; Olivia 668–70; Percy, Lady 261, 265; Portia (Merchant) 444–5; Queen (Hamlet) 232–5, 237–8; Virgilia 164–6. Other references 93, 95, 100, 102, 106, 115.
Preston, fl. 1765: 36.
Price, fl. 1780: Buckingham (Rich. III) 557; Capulet 600.
Price, *Mrs*, later Mrs William Parsons [the 1st], q.v.
Pritchard, *Miss* Hannah Mary, later (1) Mrs John Palmer [the elder], q.v.; (2) Mrs Morrice Lloyd.
*Pritchard, William [DL treasurer], d. 1763: 9, 14, 19, 22, 26.
*Pritchard, *Mrs* William, Hannah, nee Vaughan, 1711–68: Beatrice 474–6; Capulet, Lady 582–3; Catharine 613–14; Countess 111–12; Elizabeth, Queen 526–36, 538, 540–1; Emilia 499–500, 503; Ford, Mrs 447–9, 452–3, 455–7; Hermione 677, 679; Isabella 401; Katharine, Queen 296–300; Macbeth, Lady 364–75; Queen (Hamlet) 190–206; Rosalind 118; Viola 658–9; Volumnia 159, 161. Other references 9, 19, 40, 42.
Pulley, John Griffin, d. 1788: Arthur 329; Donalbain 384–5; Edward, Prince 555, 557; Falstaff's Page 275–6; Fleance 380–2; Lucius (J. Caesar) 319; Robin 459–60; Simple 459; York, Duke of 548–51, 553, 555.
*Purcell, Henry [composer], c. 1658–95: 637.
Purser, William [DL box-keeper], d. 1790: 90.

Quarme, *Mrs*, nee Roche, d. 1759: Desdemona 498.
Quelch, William, fl. 1755: Cassio 501.
Quick, John, 1748–1831: Abraham 591–2; Andrew, Sir 663; Autolycus (Wint. T.) 682; Burgundy (Lear) 343; Caius 457, 467; Carrier 249–51, 263–5; Citizen (Coriolanus) 163; Citizen (J. Caesar) 318; Cloten 182–4; Clown (All's Well) 113; Clown (Wint. T.) 680–1, 684, 686–9; Dogberry 485, 487–92, 494; Dromio of Ephesus 151–7; Elbow 403; Gardiner 310; Gentleman Usher 350–2; Gravedigger 208, 210, 217–19, 221–3, 225, 227–31, 233, 236; Grumio 619, 621–30, 632–4; Launce 673; Launcelot 423, 425–37, 440, 442; Lucullus 657; Peter (R & J) 593–7; Pistol (Hen. V) 288–9; Polonius 213–14, 216, 219, 222; Richard III 565; Sands 301–2, 304; Silence 277; Silvius

759

INDEX I

124; Slender 460–4; Tailor 618–19; Touchstone 132–3, 135–7, 139, 141–5; Town Clerk 483–4; Trinculo 646–8; William 127; Witch 376–82, 384. Other references 48, 52, 54, 68, 78, 90, 99, 151, 223, 225.

*Quin, James, 1693–1766: Brutus (J Caesar) 314; Falstaff (1 Hen. IV) 239–40; Falstaff (2 Hen. IV) 267; Falstaff (MWW) 446; Henry VIII 295; Iago 498; John, King 320; Macbeth 363; Othello 498. Other reference 3.

Radley, *Miss* Eleanor, later Mrs William Fitzgerald, d. 1772: Jessica 421; Ophelia 208. Other reference 45.

*Raftor, James, d. 1790: Abergavenny 300; Francisco (Hamlet) 191–2; Officer (R & J) 578. Other references 4, 11, 14, 17, 22, 24, 45, 47.

Ranoe, *Miss*, later (1) Mrs Rivers, q.v.; (2) Mrs Giles Leonard Barrett.

Raworth, *Master*, fl. 1763–5: Fairy (Fairy T.) 471–2; Fairy (MND) 471.

*Ray, John, d. 1752: Gobbo 412; Gravedigger 190; Lieutenant 526; Sexton 474–5.

Raymond, stage name of James Grant, 1768–1817: Buckingham (Rich. III) 575; Salisbury (John) 333.

Read, *Mrs*, fl. 1770: Emilia (?) 509.

Read, *Miss* Grace, later (1) Mrs John Arthur [the 2nd]; (2) Mrs Daniel Williams, fl. 1760–2: Blanch 322–3; Edward, Prince 535. Other references 26, 29.

Reddish, Samuel, 1735–85: Antonio (Merchant) 420–5; Claudio (Measure) 404; Edgar 344–51; Ghost 215; Hamlet 216; Henry VI (Cibber's Rich. III) 541, 543–5, 548–50; Iago 507–10, 512; John, King 327; Macbeth 378; Macduff 375–7, 380–1; Orlando 125–6, 128–31; Posthumus 171–9, 181; Richard III 540; Romeo 591. Other references 42, 68, 180.

Reddish, *Mrs* Samuel, Polly, nee Hart, d. 1799: Anne, Lady 541; Elizabeth, Queen 541; Goneril 347–8; Macduff, Lady 375–8; Queen (Cymbeline) 171–6; Queen, Player 210; Regan 347.

*Redman, Samuel, d. 1776: Blunt (Cibber's Rich. III) 532–3, 536; Butts 295; Camillo (F & P) 676, 678; Cinna the Conspirator 314–16; Cornelius 177; Doctor (Lear) 346; Duke Frederick 119–22; Erpingham 279–81; Essex 320–4, 326; Fang 273; Gratiano (Othello) 499–505, 510; Grey 278, 282, 284–5, 288; Harfleur, Governor of 284; King, Player 190–201, 203–7; Lennox 365; Montague 580–91, 596; Mowbray 267; Murderer 374; Northumberland 239–47, 249; Oxford 541; Senator (Coriolanus) 160; Seyton 366–9, 371; Soothsayer (J. Caesar) 316; Stanley 526–30, 533; Thomas, Friar 403. Other references 7, 41, 44, 50, 285.

Rees, *Master*, fl. 1798–9: Fleance 398–9.

Rees, Thomas David, fl. 1792–9: Apothecary 609–10; Bardolph (MWW) 467; Carrier 265–6; Corin 145; Dromio of Ephesus 157; Forrest 570; Gravedigger 229–31, 233, 235–6; Man, Old (Lear) 361; Murderer 395; Music Master 630–2, 634–6; Peter (R & J) 611; Peto (1 Hen. IV) 263; Porter (Hen. VIII) 312; Senator (Othello) 524; Shylock 444; Witch 398–9. Other references 104–5, 157.

Reeve, William, 1757–1815: Lord Mayor 565; Marcellus 228; Witch 390–1.

Reily, d. *c.* 1791: Blunt (1 Hen. IV) 259; Le Beau 136; Marcellus 224; Montano 517; Osric 222; Tressel 561.

Reinhold, Frederick Charles, 1737–1815: Balthazar (Much Ado) 487; Dercetas 116; Hecate 376–82, 384–7; Oberon (Fairies) 470. Other references 54, 56, 73.

Reinhold, *Mrs* Thomas [widow of the singer], fl. 1754: 9.

Reynolds, *Miss* Ann, later (1) Mrs Saunders; (2) Mrs Young, fl. 1767: Phebe 125.

Reynolds, *Miss* C., fl. 1776: Lady of the Bedchamber (Hen. VIII) 303.

Reynolds, *Miss* Lucy, fl. 1776: Katharine, Queen 303; Rosalind 131. Other reference 61.

Ricard, fl. 1751–3: Balthazar (R & J) 579–80; Lieutenant 527–8; Pindarus 314; Richard III 526; Richmond 527; Siward, Young 364; Westmorland (1 Hen. IV) 240; Westmorland (Hen. V) 278. Other references 6, 526.

Richardson, stage name of John Richards, d. 1811: Albany 360; Blunt (1 Hen. IV) 263; Cassio 522; Cleomenes (Wint. T.) 689; Cymbeline 185; Duke (Com. Err.) 156; Escalus (R & J) 608–10; Hecate 394–5; John, Don 494; King (Hamlet) 231; Norfolk (Rich. III) 569–70.

*Ridout, Isaac, d. 1761: Casca 314–16; Cassio 499–503; Cominius 159, 161–2; Cromwell 295; Duke Senior 119–22; Edmund 336; Exeter 278–82; Glendower 239; Gloucester (Lear) 338–9; Henry VI (Cibber's Rich. III) 529; Horatio 190–9; Hubert 321–3; John, Prince (2 Hen. IV) 267; Laurence, Friar 578–86; Lennox 364, 366–70; Page (MWW) 446, 448–52; Philario (Hawkins' Cymbeline) 168; Polixenes (F & P) 676, 678; Richmond 526–32; Ross 365;

INDEX I

Salarino 413, 415-17; Salisbury (John) 320; Worcester 241-4. Other references 3, 5, 414.

*Ridout, Mrs Isaac, Mary, nee Woodman, d. 1756: Jessica 413; Regan 336.

Rivers, fl. 1781: Stanley 557.

Rivers, Mrs, nee Ranoe, later Mrs Giles Leonard Barrett, d. 1832: Anne, Lady 560, 562; Desdemona 516; Portia (Merchant) 432.

*Roberts, fl. 1750-1: Publius 314.

Roberts [DL box-lobby door-keeper], fl. 1764-73: 34, 38, 43, 45, 49, 52, 54.

Roberts, Miss, fl. 1770: Emilia 509.

Roberts, David Benjamin, fl. 1782: Duke (Merchant) 431.

*Roberts, Ellis, fl. 1734-62: Moonshine (P & T) 469-70. Other references 21, 31.

Robinson, Mrs Hannah Henrietta, nee Pritchard, later (1) Mrs William Perkins Taylor, q.v.; (2) Mrs Benjamin Wrench.

Robinson, Mrs Thomas, Mary, nee Darby, 1758-1800: Anne, Lady 552-3, 555-6; Cordelia 353; Imogen 181; Juliet (R & J) 597, 599-600; Macbeth, Lady 382; Ophelia 215-17; Perdita (Wint. T.) 683; Rosalind 134; Viola 664-5. Other references 65, 67, 69.

Robinson, William [DL upper gallery doorkeeper], d. 1778: 36, 40, 45, 47, 49, 52, 58.

Robinson, Mrs William [widow of the preceding], fl. 1778: 65.

Robson, Thomas, 1737-1813: Balthazar (R & J) 599-600; Burgundy (Hen. V) 288-9; Burgundy (Lear) 352, 354; Catesby 555-6, 558; Chamberlain, Lord 305; Conrade 485, 487-8; Dauphin (John) 327; Edmund 348; Fenton 460-2; Hortensio 622-3; Merchant (Com. Err.) 151; Montano 512-14; Paris 599-600; Poins (1 Hen. IV) 254-6; Rosencrantz 214, 217-19, 221; Sebastian (Tempest) 646-8; Silvius 133; Siward 384-6.

Roche, Miss Elizabeth, later Lady [Sir Henry] Echlin, fl. 1751: 498.

Rock, Edward Anthony, d. 1815: Bardolph (1 Hen. IV) 259-62; Bardolph (MWW) 466-7; Biondello 626-7, 630-2; Doctor (Lear) 357; Philario 185; Simple 465-6; Tyrrel 566. Other reference 99.

Rock, Mrs Edward Anthony, nee Essex, fl. 1789-93: Anne, Lady 564; Audrey 141, 143-6.

Roffe [unidentified], fl. 1771: 50.

Roger [dancer], fl. 1754-7: 9, 17.

Rogers, fl. 1770: Brabantio (?) 509.

Rogers, Miss, fl. 1760-72: Ariel 642-3; Arthur 324-5; Celia 126, 128; Edward, Prince 539-41, 543-5; Falstaff's Page 270-3; Fleance 372-5; Humphrey, Prince 273; Jessica 422-3; Miranda 653-4; Oberon (Fairy T.) 471-2; Oberon (MND) 470; Perdita (F & P) 680; Robin 454, 456; York, Duke of 534-8. Other references 38, 45, 49.

Rolt, Richard [dramatist], c. 1725-70: 38.

Romanzini, Miss Maria Theresa, later Mrs George Bland [the younger], q.v.

Rooker, Edward, 1724-74: Silence 268, 271-3; Stephano (Tempest) 638. Other references 19, 23, 32, 38, 40, 45, 56.

Roope, Mrs, nee Russell, fl. 1781: Cordelia 354.

Rose, Miss, stage name of Rose (?) De Franchetti, fl. 1769: York, Duke of 542-3.

Ross, Mrs, fl. 1776: Lady, Old 303; York, Duchess of 551.

Ross, David, 1728-90: Antonio (Merchant) 420; Antony (J. Caesar) 316; Banquo 364-8; Bertram 112-13; Buckingham (Hen. VIII) 295-7; Edgar 337; Ford 452-6; Hamlet 196-205; John, King 323-4, 326; Lear 341-4, 347-50, 352; Leonatus 168; Macbeth 370-4; Macduff 366; Othello 501-5, 509-10, 512; Romeo 578, 584-91; Wales, Prince of (1 Hen. IV) 242-8; Wales, Prince of (2 Hen. IV) 268, 270, 272. Other references 4, 14, 24, 27, 31, 37, 317.

Rowson, Miss Elizabeth, d. 1790: Arante 357; Dorcas (F & P) 688; Luciana 153; Mopsa (Wint. T.) 688; Page, Anne 465.

Rowson, William, d. 1842: Charles 145-6.

Rundell, Francis, d. 1791: Lear 352.

Russell, Samuel, 1747-1808: Buckingham (Rich. III) 551, 554; Cloten 179; Gentleman Usher 352; Gratiano (Merchant) 425-6; Laertes 214; Mercutio 599; Roderigo 513; Tailor 623; William 131.

Russell, Mrs Samuel, fl. 1776-8: Audrey 131; Catharine 623; Elizabeth, Queen 554; Nurse 599.

Russell, Samuel Thomas, 1769-1845: Clown (Twelfth N.) 671-2; Froth 410; Gentleman Usher 359; Gratiano (Merchant) 441; Guildford 311; Le Beau 148; Osric 234; Peter (R & J) 605; Poins (1 Hen. IV) 265; Roderigo 522; Slender 467; York, Duke of 551. Other references 100, 104.

*Ryan, Lacy, 1694-1760: Aufidius 160-2; Bassanio 413-16, 418; Cassius 314-16; Chorus (Hen. V) 278-81; Cymbeline 168; Edgar 336, 338-9; Ford 446, 448-52; Ghost 190-9; Henry VI (Cibber's Rich. III) 526, 529-33; Iago 498, 500-2; Macduff 363-4, 366-9; Philip, King 320-1; Richard III 526-9; Wales, Prince of (1 Hen. IV) 239-42; Wales, Prince of

INDEX I

(2 Hen. IV) 267; Wolsey 295. Other references 5, 7, 10.

Ryder, Corbet, d. 1839: Gentleman (Othello) 524; Lucianus 236; Walter 635–6.

Ryder, *Miss* Mary, d. 1791: Portia (Merchant) 438.

Ryder, Thomas, 1735–91: Falstaff (1 Hen. IV) 258–60; Falstaff (MWW) 464–7; Iago 518; Shylock 437.

Sage, Mrs L. A., nee Hoare, d. 1803: Macbeth, Lady 384.

Sarjant, Charles, Sr. [CG box-book and house-keeper], d. 1770: 37.

Sarjant, Charles, Jr. [CG box-book and house-keeper], d. 1787: 50, 54, 63, 66.

Satchell, *Miss* Elizabeth, later Mrs Stephen George Kemble, q.v.

Saul, fl. 1775: Duke (Merchant) 425.

Saunders, fl. 1770–3: Citizen (J. Caesar) 318; Gobbo 424; Gravedigger 208; Herald, French 327; Porter (Hen. VIII) 301; Witch 378.

Saunders, *Master*, fl. 1770: Arthur 327.

Saunderson [DL machinist], fl. 1755–66: 11, 14, 32, 37.

Schuchart, Mrs [unidentified], fl. 1766: 39.

Scott, the Hon. *Mrs* John, Isabella, nee Young, 1741–91 [she was married in 1757, but on the stage continued to use her maiden name until 1768]: Ariel 639–46; Ceres 640–1; Hermia (MND) 471; Mopsa (Wint. T.) 677; Patience 297–300; Titania (Fairies) 470. Other references 11, 36, 40, 42, 49, 53.

*Scrase, Henry, 1717–1807: Benvolio 578, 587; Capucius 297–8, 300; Chatillon 321–2; Cromwell 296; Escalus (R & J) 580; Fenton 447–9, 452–3; Gentleman, French 168–9; Guildenstern 190–5, 197–200; Henry VI (Cibber's Rich. III) 530–1; Herald, English (John) 320; Le Beau 118; Lennox 364–71; Lieutenant (Coriolanus) 159–60; Malcolm 365; Montague 584–5; Northumberland 243–4; Officer (A & C) 116; Oliver 118; Paris 577–82; Solanio 412–14. Other references 4, 9, 11, 17, 26, 29, 168, 370, 372.

Seaton, fl. 1800: Norfolk (Rich. III) 575.

Sedgwick, Thomas, d. 1803: Caliban 651–2, 654; Hecate 397, 399; Neptune 651–4; Westmorland (Hen. V) 291–3. Other references 100, 105.

Serres, *Mrs* Dominic Michael, Lucretia, nee Maddan, fl. 1796: 101.

Sestini, *Signora* Giovanna [singer], fl. 1783: 76.

Settree, Joseph [dancer], d. 1783: 26.

Seymour, stage name of Edward Hickey, 1755–1819: Hamlet 227; Macbeth 389; Malcolm 389; Tressel 563.

Shade, John [DL box-keeper], fl. 1786–95: 82, 98.

Shade, Thomas [DL box-keeper], fl. 1779–96: 67, 87, 90, 100.

*Shadwell, Thomas [dramatist], c. 1642–92: 636, 655.

Sharp, *Mrs* Michael, Elizabeth, nee Hopkins, 1756–1821: Anne, Lady 557; Celia 128, 132–4; Hero 482, 484–6; Juliet (R & J) 598; Macduff, Lady 384–5; Mariana (Measure) 404–6; Percy, Lady 252. Other reference 67.

Sharpe, *Miss* Ann, later Mrs William Palmer, d. 1785: 59.

Sharpless, fl. 1769: Artemidorus 318; Lord Mayor 543; Oxford 542; Priest (Hamlet) 208; Senator (Othello) 508.

Shatford, James, 1764–1809: Oliver 139. Other reference 140.

Shaw, fl. 1790: Neptune 651.

Shaw, *Mrs*, fl. 1792–3: Margaret 493. Other reference 493.

*Shawford, Joseline [dancer], d. 1763: 9, 22.

Shelburne, *Miss*, fl. 1782: Anne, Lady 558.

Sheridan, Richard Brinsley [dramatist], 1751–1816: 70, 637.

*Sheridan, Thomas, 1719–88: Brutus (J. Caesar) 315, 317; Coriolanus 159, 161; Hamlet 193–4, 198–200, 207, 209, 213; John, King 321–2, 326, 328; Macbeth 366, 370; Othello 503, 508; Richard III 529, 534, 542, 550; Romeo 580; Shylock 415. Other references 46, 157, 159, 716, 718.

Sherry, *Miss* Katherine, 1745–82: Anne, Lady 549; Calphurnia 319; Elinor 327–9; Emilia 514; Goneril 349–51, 353; Macbeth, Lady 378, 382, 384–5; Macduff, Lady 380–4; Queen (Cymbeline) 177–82; Queen (Hamlet) 218, 220. Other references 62, 69.

Shriburne, *Miss*, fl. 1782: 558.

*Shuter, Edward, c. 1728–76: Adam (AYLI) 117; Autolycus (F & P) 676, 678–9; Clown (All's Well) 112–14; Clown (Twelfth N.) 658–9; Dogberry 483–4; Dromio of Ephesus 150; Falstaff (1 Hen. IV) 241–51; Falstaff (2 Hen. IV) 269–70, 272, 274; Falstaff (MWW) 448–57; Fluellen 278, 281–7; Gardiner 300–2; Gentleman Usher 335–6, 338–9, 341; Gravedigger 192–202; Grumio 616–17, 620; Guzzle, Toby 615; Launcelot 412–17, 419–22, 424–6; Lucianus 190–1; Menenius 159, 161–3; Mercutio 581, 584, 591–2; Osric 190–2; Petruchio 614–16; Polonius 202–8, 210–13; Richard III

529, 533, 543; Sands 295-6; Shallow (Humourists) 268; Shylock 417-18, 424; Touchstone 119-24, 127, 129-31; Verges 474-5; Witch 364-5, 376. Other references 10, 12, 52, 54, 56, 58, 61, 210, 448, 546, 721.

Siddons, *Mrs* William, Sarah, nee Kemble, 1755-1831: Anne, Lady 550; Catharine 626-7; Constance 329, 331-3; Cordelia 356, 358, 360; Desdemona 516-17, 519-20, 522-3; Elizabeth, Queen 567, 571; Imogen 184; Isabella 407-11; Juliet (R & J) 606; Katharine, Queen 308-12; Macbeth, Lady 387-92, 394-9; Ophelia 226; Portia (Merchant) 425-6, 434-6, 438-41, 443, 445; Queen (Hamlet) 232; Rosalind 138-9; Volumnia 164-6. Other references 79-80, 82-3, 85, 87, 93, 115, 397.

Sidney, Laurence, fl. 1777-87: Capulet 605; Duke (Othello) 513.

Simmons, *Mrs*, fl. 1775: Nerissa 425.

Simmons, Samuel, *c.* 1777-1819: Apothecary 610-12; Clown (F & P) 689; Donalbain 393-6, 398-9; Edward, Prince 565-8; Francis 265; Gentleman Usher 360; Gravedigger 238; Simple 467-8; Tailor 632-6; Verges 495-6; Witch 400; York, Duke of 560-2, 564-5.

Simpson, fl. 1787-97: Gabriel 634; Peto (1 Hen. IV) 265; Sailor (Hamlet) 234; Tybalt 605. Other reference 722.

Simpson [harlequin], fl. 1798: 104.

Sims, *Miss* Sarah, later Mrs William Penson, fl. 1799: Edward, Prince 574; Nerissa 444. Other reference 105.

*Simson, d. 1758: Angus 364-7; Antonio (Much Ado) 474-6; Apothecary 578; Balthazar (Merchant) 412-14; Doctor (Lear) 336; Duke Frederick 118; Falconbridge, Robert 320; Fenton 447; Gratiano (Othello) 499; Jaques de Bois 118; Lartius 159-60; Montague 580; Rosencrantz 190-4; Ross 365; Steward 111; Surrey 295; Surveyor 295-8. Other references 4, 7, 9.

Simson, *Miss*, fl. 1780-6: Bianca (C & P) 623-6; Dorcas (Wint. T.) 683; Francisca 407. Other references 623, 626.

Simson, *Miss*, later (1) Mrs Charles Fleetwood, Jr.; (2) Mrs White, *c.* 1752-1807: Edward, Prince 534; Phebe 125; York, Duke of 531-3. Other references 22, 24.

*Simson, *Mrs* Elizabeth, fl. 1749-70: Gentlewoman (Macbeth) 365; Quickly, Mrs (MWW) 447; Widow (?) 112. Other references 7, 9, 22, 24, 34, 45, 47.

Simson, John, d. *c.* 1770: Arthur 320; Donalbain 366-70; Edward, Prince 530-3; Marcius, Young 161; Page, William 447; Robin 447-9; York, Duke of 528-30. Other references 7, 9. 22.

Sinclair, fl. 1792: Brabantio 520.

Slack, *Miss*, later Mrs Brown, fl. 1765: Perdita (Wint. T.) 679. Other reference 36.

Sledge, *Miss*, fl. 1764: 35.

Slim, fl. 1754: Shadow (Humourists) 268.

Slingsby, Simon [dancer], d. 1811: 36.

Sloper [CG machinist], fl. 1795: 99.

Smith, fl. 1769: Gratiano (Othello) 507.

Smith, *Mrs*, fl. 1769-76: Desdemona 508; Phebe 131; Queen (Cymbeline) 179; Queen (Hamlet) 215; Regan 352.

Smith, Charles, *c.* 1703-75: Rugby 448-53, 455-7.

Smith, J., fl. 1776: Catesby 551; Edmund 352; Horatio 214; Lord (Cymbeline) 179; Oliver 131; Salarino 426.

Smith, John Christopher [composer], 1712-95: 11, 469, 636-8.

Smith, Richard, fl. 1753-81: Abergavenny 304; Arviragus 173-4, 176-8; Balthazar (R & J) 582-6, 590-1, 593, 596; Bedford 284-6; Bernardo 194, 196, 204; Blunt (1 Hen. IV) 249-50; Cleomenes (Wint. T.) 681; Colevile 269-70, 272; Dighton 532-3; Francisco (Hamlet) 217-19; Gregory (R & J) 581; Guildford 300-1; Henry, Prince 321-4, 326; Lieutenant 534-48; Merchant (Com. Err.) 150; Officer (Hamlet) 201; Oxford 556; Paris 592, 595-6; Pedro (C & P) 619, 624; Peter, Friar 403; Peto (1 Hen. IV) 241-7; Pindarus 315-16, 318; Pistol (MWW) 451-6; Publius 314; Ratcliff 547; Rosencrantz 206-7, 210-11; Rugby 449; Salarino 423; Scroop 279-82; Silvius 119, 123, 127; Siward 371, 373; Westmorland (Hen. V) 287-9. Other references 23, 25, 46, 53, 57, 304.

Smith, *Mrs* Sarah, d. 1812: Bianca (C & P) 617-18; Capulet, Lady 594; Emilia 504; Mariana (All's Well) 112.

Smith, Theodore [composer], fl. 1777: 469.

Smith, *Mrs* Theodore, Maria, nee Harris, fl. 1772-6: Helen 176; Miranda 644-6; Ophelia 210-14; Perdita (F & P) 681. Other reference 57.

Smith, Thomas, fl. 1768-9: Cornwall's Servant 346; Gadshill 249.

Smith, Walter, 1752-1809: Hotspur 253.

Smith, William, fl. 1776: Cornwall 352; Cromwell 303; Lieutenant 551; Philario 179.

Smith, William, *c.* 1730-1819: Antony (J. Caesar) 315, 318; Bastard (John) 322-6, 328-9, 331; Cassius 316-17; Coriolanus 161-3; Duke (Measure) 404-8; Edgar 341-50; Edmund 338-9; Florizel (F &

INDEX I

P) 676, 678; Ford 459–60, 463, 465; Hamlet 196, 199, 207–8, 210–13, 215–17, 219–21; Henry V 279–89; Hotspur 241-2, 245–50, 252–4; Iachimo 171–84; Iago 505; Leontes (Wint. T.) 680–3, 685–6; Macbeth 376–85, 387–9; Orlando 119–24, 127; Palador 168; Richard III 535–50, 553–5, 557–8, 560–3; Romeo 581, 584, 593–6. Other references 12, 18, 20, 23–4, 27, 31, 43, 57, 79, 83, 85, 212, 559.
Smyth, fl. 1770: Albany 348; Chatillon 327; Rosencrantz 209.
*Sowdon, John, d. 1789: Banquo 364; Buckingham (Rich. III) 542; Cassius 318; Edmund 336, 345; Ghost 207, 209; Henry VIII 295; Iago 506, 508; Orsino 658. Other reference 4.
Sparks, Hugh, 1752–1816: Antonio (Tempest) 654; Gratiano (Othello) 524; Gravedigger 236; Jailer (Merchant) 445; Lord (AYLI) 149; Lucianus 237–8; Music Master 634–5; Oxford 573–4; Seacoal 495, 497; Siward 397, 399; Stanley 575.
Sparks, Mrs Hugh, Sarah, nee Mills, 1754–1837: Elinor 333; Emilia 524.
*Sparks, Isaac, 1719–76: Caliban 643; Citizen (J. Caesar) 318; Gravedigger 207; Lord Mayor 542.
*Sparks, Luke 1711–68: Antigonus (F & P) 676, 678; Antonio (Merchant) 413–19; Banquo 363, 365–71, 373–4; Belarius 168; Brabantio 499–502; Brutus (J. Caesar) 314–16; Buckingham (Rich. III) 526–30, 532–3, 535–6; Caesar 314–15; Canterbury, Archbishop of 278–84; Capulet 578–89; Gloucester (Lear) 336; Henry IV (1 Hen. IV) 239–47; Henry IV (2 Hen. IV) 268, 270; Henry VI (Cibber's Rich. III) 528; Hubert 323–4; Iago 503–4; Jaques 119–24; John, King 321–3; Kent 338–9, 341; King (Hamlet) 190–200, 202; Lord Chief Justice 267; Norfolk (Hen. VIII) 295; Pandulph 320; Volusius 160–2. Other reference 31.
Sparrow, fl. 1776: Campeius 303.
Spencer, Mrs, stage name of Maria Anne Campion, later Mrs Alexander Pope [the 2nd], q.v.
Spencer, William Barber, 1757–1803: Antonio's Servant 432; Francisco (Hamlet) 226; Rugby 465. Other reference 70.
Stacy, fl. 1776: Buckingham (Hen. VIII) 303.
Stageldoir, Miss Martha, fl. 1783–90: Edward, Prince 559–61, 564.
Stamper, Francis, d. 1766: Francis 246; Polonius 202.
Standen, Master, fl. 1797–1800: York, Duke of 572–3, 575.

Standen, Miss, fl. 1790–8: Edward, Prince 572–3; Fleance 392–3; York, Duke of 565–72.
Stannard, fl. 1783: Stanley 559.
Staunton, Richard Collet, fl. 1781–8: Alonso 650; Bassanio [IV. i only] 430; Cornwall 356; Cymbeline 184; Duke Senior 137; Ghost [III. iv only] 220; Horatio 223–6; Lord Mayor 563; Orsino 665–7; Page (MWW) 462; Pisanio 181; Salisbury (John) 329, 331; Stanley 562–3. Other references 220, 356, 430, 462.
*Stede, John [CG prompter], 1687–1768: 18, 23, 33, 39.
Stede, Miss Mary [dancer], fl. 1774: 57.
Stephens, Mrs, fl. 1755–70: Anne, Lady 539, 541; Bianca (C & P) 616; Emilia 507; Goneril 338–9, 341–4, 346–7; Isabel 279–85; Lesbia 151; Page, Anne 455; Page, Mrs 458; Percy, Lady 242, 248–9; Tearsheet, Doll 270; Widow 112–13. Other references 15, 21, 286.
Stephens, George, fl. 1776: Gadshill 252; Pedro (C & P) 622.
Sterne, Everard, stage name of John Knight, fl. 1787: Romeo 605.
Sterne, Mrs Everard, stage name of Mrs John Knight, fl. 1787: Juliet (R & J) 605.
Stevens, stage name of William Castevens, d. 1790: Apothecary 599–601; Carrier 256; Fabian 665–6; Gentleman (Sheep S.) 682; Lord (Cymbeline) 181; Lovell 304–5; Lucianus 225; Music Master 625, 627; Outlaw 673; Oxford 552, 554; Painter 657; Peter (R & J) 601–4; Peto (1 Hen. IV) 256–60; Pistol (MWW) 459; Rosencrantz 215, 218, 222, 224; Rugby 464–6; Slender 463; Tubal 430; Witch 382, 386. Other references 76, 387.
Stevens, Captain, fl. 1751: Roderigo 498.
Stevens, Mrs (Captain), fl. 1751: Emilia 498.
*Stevens, George Alexander, 1710–84: Brutus (Coriolanus) 160–1; Charles 119; Clown (F & P) 676; Cornelius 169; Doctor (Macbeth) 370–3; Falstaff (MWW) 453; Glendower 244; Metellus 315; Mowbray 269, 271; Panthino 673; Sheriff (1 Hen. IV) 245; Stephano (Tempest) 644; Touchstone 127. Other references 10, 29.
Stevenson [DL box-keeper], fl. 1795–9: 98, 105.
Stewart, James, d. 1804: 57.
Stokes, fl. 1772–8: King (Hamlet) 214; Orlando 131; Posthumus 179; Richard III 546, 548; Wolsey 303.
Stone, George Winchester, Jr. [theatrical historian], 1907– : 188.
*Stoppelaer, Michael, fl. 1730–74: Bar-

764

INDEX I

dolph (1 Hen. IV) 241–4; Barnardine 403; Butts 300–1; Caius 448–53; Citizen (Coriolanus) 160–3; Citizen (J. Caesar) 314–16; Duke (Othello) 502, 504; Gravedigger 190–200, 202, 206–8, 210–12; Murderer 365; Nym (Hen. V) 278–81, 288; Nym (MWW) 457; Silence (2 Hen. IV) 267, 274; Silence (Humourists) 268; Tubal 413–19. Other references 6, 10, 23, 31, 33, 35.

*Storer, Charles, d. c. 1765: Iago 503; Shylock 419; Westmorland (2 Hen. IV) 269–70.

Stott, Mrs John, Jane, nee Hemet [in 1762 she adopted stage name of Mrs Lessingham, q.v.].

Strange, fl. 1764–9: Antonio (Tempest) 642; Balthazar (R & J) 592; Bernardo 202; Blunt (1 Hen. IV) 246–8; Camillo (F & P) 680; Catesby 542; Conrade 480–1; Essex 325; Fenton 456–7; Gower (2 Hen. IV) 271; Guildenstern 202–4; Lodovico 507; Messenger (Othello) 505; Ratcliff 537–8, 540–1; Rosencrantz 202, 204–7; Silvius 125–6; Snug (Fairy T.) 471–2. Other reference 45.

Stratford, fl. 1784: Richmond 561.

Street, James, fl. 1797–1800: Bardolph (MWW) 468; Crier (Hen. VIII) 312; Peto (1 Hen. IV) 265–6; Senator (Othello) 524.

Stuart, Miss Ann, d. 1809: Amphitrite 653; Anne, Lady 572; Arante 354–6; Dorcas (Wint. T.) 686–8; Helen 184; Juliet (Measure) 407; Phebe 135–7, 139, 141, 143–6; Phryne 657; Queen, Player 222–3, 225.

Sturt, fl. 1757: 17.

Suett, Master, fl. 1800: Edward, Prince 574.

Suett, Richard, 1755–1805: Andrew, Sir 671; Autolycus (Wint. T.) 686; Carrier 264; Citizen (Coriolanus) 163–6; Clown (Measure) 409–11; Clown (Twelfth N.) 666–70; Clown (Wint. T.) 685–7; Dogberry 494–7; Francis 261, 265; Gardiner 307–11; Gobbo 439; Gravedigger 222, 224, 226–7, 236–7; Grumio 634; Launcelot 431, 434, 436, 438, 440–5; Peter (R & J) 610; Pistol (Hen. V) 290–3; Polonius 231–4; Slender 465; Stephano (Tempest) 650, 653; Tailor 635; Thurio 674; Touchstone 140–1; Trinculo 653–4; Witch 391, 394–9. Other references 75, 78, 82, 93, 102.

Sumbel, Mrs Joseph, Mary Stephens, nee Davies, formerly Mrs Ezra Wells, 1762–1829: Anne, Lady 567; Audrey 136; Hermione 687–8; Imogen 182–3; Page, Mrs 465; Percy, Lady 258; Portia (Merchant) 434, 444; Rosalind 139.

Summers, Robert, fl. 1769: Blunt (Cibber's Rich. III) 542; Cinna the Conspirator 317; Lucianus 208; Senator (Othello) 508.

Surmont, fl. 1798–1800: Balthazar (Merchant) 445; Conrade 495–6; Gentleman (Measure) 410–11; Herald, English (John) 333; LeBeau 148–9; Lennox 399; Marcellus 235–7; Tressel 573–5; Valentine (Twelfth N.) 671.

Sutton, fl. 1761: Paris 586.

Sutton, Mrs, nee Froment [dancer], 1756–97: 57.

Swendall, James, fl. 1787: Adam (AYLI) 139.

Swords, William, fl. 1782–7: Apothecary 604–5; Bardolph (1 Hen. IV) 258; Bardolph (MWW) 464–5; Clown (All's Well) 114; Cornelius 181; Gobbo 434–5; Marcellus 225; Pedro (C & P) 626; Salarino 435.

Talbot, Montague, 1744–1831: Roderigo 524.

Tanner, fl. 1792: Lorenzo 438.

Tassoni [dancer], fl. 1767: 40.

*Taswell, James, d. 1759: Corin 118, 120–1; Dogberry 474–7; Elbow 401–2; Gardiner 295–8; Polonius 190–6; Servant (Coriolanus) 159–60; Shallow (MWW) 447–9; Tubal 412–14.

*Tate, Nahum [dramatist], 1652–1715: 333–5, 716–17.

Taylor, fl. 1778: Albany 353.

Taylor, Miss, fl. 1776–8: Anne, Lady 551; Arante 352; Nerissa 426; Ophelia 215; Portia (Merchant) 428.

Taylor, Mrs Mary, nee Valentine, 1753–1834: Jessica 438.

Taylor, Mrs William Perkins, Hannah Henrietta, nee Pritchard, formerly Mrs Robinson, later Mrs Benjamin Wrench, fl. 1778–88: Cordelia 355; Elizabeth, Queen 554, 563; Imogen 184; Viola 666. Other reference 85.

Thomas, fl. 1776: Oxford 551.

Thomas, Miss [singer], fl. 1754–5: 9, 11.

Thomas, Miss Elizabeth, fl. 1782: Edward, Prince 558.

Thompson, fl. 1767: Gloucester (Lear) 345.

Thompson [unidentified], fl. 1776: 61.

Thompson, fl. 1792: Montano 520.

Thompson, Miss, fl. 1782: 431.

Thompson, Edward (?), fl. 1778–83: Buckingham (Rich. III) 553, 559; Oxford 557.

Thompson, James, fl. 1771–1800: Angers, Citizen of 328, 330; Antonio (Much Ado) 483–5, 487–96; Baptista 619–28, 630–6; Bardolph (1 Hen. IV) 263, 265–6; Burgundy (Lear) 351; Corin 129–30, 133,

INDEX I

135–7, 139, 141; Cornelius 178, 184–6; Cornwall 351–2, 354–6; Cornwall's Servant 360–1; Duke (Merchant) 423–4; Duke (Othello) 510, 522; Duke Frederick 142, 144–6; Duncan 385; Ely, Bishop of 288–9; Escalus (R & J) 603; Gentleman (Wint. T.) 685; Guildenstern 210, 214, 217–19, 221–3, 225; Host (MWW) 464–8; John, Friar 608–11; King, Player 227–31, 233, 235–6, 238; Lord Mayor 574–5; Marcellus 211, 217; Merchant (Com. Err.) 151, 155; Montague 601–6; Montano 516–19; Panthino 673; Paris 596; Peter, Friar 406–7; Philario 183; Pistol (MWW) 463–6; Ratcliff 545, 547–8, 555–6, 558–60, 562, 564–73; Salarino 424; Seyton 378–82, 384–6, 388–96, 398–400; Shipmaster 646; Soldier [Interpreter] 113–14; Stanley 548, 572; Surveyor 300–1, 312; Tubal 425–37, 440, 442–5; Valentine (Twelfth N.) 666; Westmorland (1 Hen. IV) 250–1, 254–6, 258. Other references 75, 91, 604, 624.

Thompson, *Mrs* Jane, nee Poitier, formerly Mrs Joseph Vernon [the 1st], fl. 1755–70: Ceres 639–40; Dorcas (Wint. T.) 677; Helena (Fairies) 470; Miranda 639; Patience 298. Other references 43, 48, 470.

Thompson, John [DL gallery door-keeper], fl. 1784: 78.

Thompson, *Miss* Mary Anne, later Mrs Joseph Clarke, 1776–1852: Portia (Merchant) [probably] 438.

Thomson, *Miss*, fl. 1769: Emilia 508.

Thomson, James [dramatist], 1700–48: 157–60.

Tidswell, *Miss* Charlotte, 1760–1846: Arante 356, 360; Bianca (C & P) 626–31, 633–4; Capulet, Lady 609–10; Elinor 333; Francisca 409–11; Gentlewoman (Coriolanus) 164–6; Gentlewoman (Macbeth) 391–6, 394–9; Lucetta 674; Margaret 492–5, 497; Maria 669; Mariana (All's Well) 115; Queen, Player 225–7, 232–4, 236–8; York, Duchess of 563, 567, 571, 573–5. Other references 93, 100, 115.

Tindal, Charles, fl. 1761–5: Balthazar (Com. Err.) 150; Duke Frederick 123; Exeter 282–3; Lodovico 504–5; Macduff 374; Mowbray 268, 270; Pandulph 323–4. Other reference 37.

Tomlinson [unidentified], fl. 1752–80: 4, 17, 34, 38, 43, 49, 58–9, 62, 67, 70.

Toms, fl. 1795–8: Albany 360; Blunt (1 Hen. IV) 264–6; Claudio (Much Ado) 495; Escalus (R & J) 609–10; Fenton 467–8; Ghost 231, 233; Horatio 235; Lodovico 522; Paris 610–11; Romeo 609; Ross 396; Solanio 442–3; Tressel 570–3.

Toogood, *Mrs* Sarah, d. 1755: Henry, Prince 320.

Townsend, Edward Evans, 1766–1809: Arviragus 185; Balthazar (Much Ado) 494–5; Biondello 633; Evans 467–8; Hecate 398–400; Lorenzo 440, 443; Westmorland (1 Hen. IV) 265; Witch 395–6. Other reference 105.

Townsend, *Mrs* Edward Evans, Elizabeth, fl. 1796: Nerissa 441.

Trew, fl. 1781: Romeo 601.

Trott, John [CG lobby door-keeper], d. c. 1766: 33.

Trotter, fl. 1777: Montano 513.

Trowell, *Miss*, fl. 1770: Arante 348; Blanch 327.

Trueman, Thomas (?), fl. 1794–1800: Balthazar (Merchant) 440; Blunt (1 Hen. IV) 264; Borachio 495–6; Brackenbury 571, 573–5; Burgundy (Hen. V) 293; Captain (Lear) 359; Chamberlain, Lord 310–11; Chatillon 333; Escalus (R & J) 609–10; Fenton 467; Gentleman (Measure) 408–11; Guildenstern 232, 234–7; Herald, English (John) 332; Hortensio 632–5; Julio 522; Lennox 394; Lorenzo 444; Officer (Coriolanus) 165–6; Rosencrantz 233, 236; Sailor (Othello) 522; Salarino 441–3; Sebastian (Twelfth N.) 670–1; Sergeant (Macbeth) 394, 396, Seyton 395, 397, 399; Silvius 148–9; Solanio 441, 443, 445; Walter 631; Westmorland (1 Hen. IV) 265.

Turner, fl. 1761–78: Burgundy (Lear) 353; Montano 504.

Turner, fl. 1798: Macbeth 398.

Twist, *Miss*, fl. 1777–9: Fairy (Fairy T.) 473; Patience 303–5.

Twist, Miss S., fl. 1773–4: Patience 301–2.

Twistleton, the Hon. *Mrs* Thomas James, Charlotte Anne Frances, nee Wattell, later Mrs Thomas Sandon [c. 1800 she adopted stage name of Mrs Stanley], d. 1815: Cordelia 359; Juliet (R & J) 608. Other reference 97.

Uncle, fl. 1792: Catesby 568.

*Usher, Howard, d. 1802 [in my Vol. I, 492, the initials of this actor are incorrectly given as 'N. L.']: Albany 337–8; Alonso 652–3; Antonio (Merchant) [IV. i only] 431; Antonio (Much Ado) 496; Baptista 631–4; Benvolio 579–83; Borachio 483–5; Buckingham (Rich III) 561; Camillo (Sheep S.) 684; Catesby 527–31; Cornwall 336; Cromwell 297–8; Dauphin (Hen. V) 278; Decius 314; Duke (Merchant) 430, 435, 438, 441; Duke (Othello) 514, 523; Duke Senior 136; Duncan 380; France, King of

INDEX I

(Hen. V) 293; Guildenstern 195; Henry VIII 304-6; John, Don 490; John, Prince (2 Hen. IV) 268; King, Player 213-14, 224-5, 228, 233; Lieutenant 526-7; Ligarius 314; Lodovico 517; Lucius (Cymbeline) 177, 181; Malcolm 364-9; Montague 610; Norfolk (Hen. VIII) 297; Norfolk (Rich. III) 566, 568; Octavius (J. Caesar) 314-15; Paris 578-9; Peter, Friar 404; Priest (Hamlet) 236; Rosencrantz 190-3, 195, 197; Salarino 414; Sergeant (Macbeth) 380-1; Seyton 364; Suffolk 295; Vernon 240; Westmorland (1 Hen. IV) 239-40, 259, 262, 264; Westmorland (2 Hen. IV) 267.

Valois, *Miss* Catherine, fl. 1758-79: Arthur 324; Boy (Hen. V) 284-6, 288; Ceres 646-8; Edward, Prince 539-40; Jessica 424; John, Prince (1 Hen. IV) 246-7; Margaret 483-4; Robin 450-4; York, Duke of 534-8.
Vandermere, John Byron, 1743-86: Gratiano (Merchant) 422; Gravedigger 209; King, Player 208; Lodovico 508; Pindarus 317; Polonius 207; Roderigo 508-9; Tailor 618.
Varney [DL house-keeper], fl 1753-8: 7, 19.
*Vaughan, Henry, 1713-79: Abhorson 401-2; Butts 297-8; Carrier 244; Citizen (Coriolanus) 159-60; Davy (Humourists) 268; Feeble 269, 271; Francis 243-8; Gravedigger 191-204; Launcelot 417-18; Peter (R & J) 578; Roderigo 503; Simple 447, 452-4, 456; Slender 449; Stephano (Tempest) 639-40; Tailor 614, 616; William 118, 120. Other reference 9.
*Vaughan, M. [CG box-keeper], fl. 1726-60: 8, 10, 18, 25.
Vaughan, R., fl. 1751-2: Town Clerk 474-5.
*Vaughan, William, fl. 1750-8: Citizen (Coriolanus) 159-60; Gobbo 413-14; Gravedigger 190; Gregory (R & J) 578, 581; Gurney 320; Host (MWW) 447-9; Mouldy (Humourists) 268; Nathaniel 614; Town Clerk 475-6; Tyrrel 528; Witch 364-5. Other references 7, 475.
Veal [DL first gallery door-keeper], d. c. 1772: 12, 17.
Vernon, Joseph, c. 1738-82: Amiens 121, 124-6, 128-34; Autolycus (Wint. T.) 683; Balthazar (Much Ado) 479-86; Bernardo 192; Chatillon 320, 324-5; Clown (Twelfth N.) 659-65; Demetrius (Fairies) 470; Denny 297; Donalbain 365-6; Fabian 659; Ferdinand 640-8; Gentleman Usher 337-8; Hecate 372; Launcelot 415; Lorenzo 420-5, 427-9; Lysander (MND) 470; Roderigo 504, 507; Sands 296; Servant (Coriolanus) 159, 161; Stephano (Tempest) 639; Thurio 672-3; Verges 475. Other references 34, 38, 42, 45, 55, 62, 65, 486.
Vernon, *Mrs* Joseph [the 1st], Jane, nee Poitier, later Mrs Thompson, q.v.
Victor, Benjamin [dramatist], d. 1778: 32, 672, 719.
Vidini, *Signora* Victoria [dancer], fl. 1772: 51.
Vincent, *Miss*, fl. 1764-7: Blanch 324-6; Page, Anne 455-6.
*Vincent, *Mrs* Richard, Sr., Elizabeth, nee Bincks, fl. 1732-73: Adriana 151; Anne, Lady 531, 533-45; Blanch 320-3; Bullen, Anne 295; Calphurnia 315-18; Catharine 615; Celia 119-24; Cordelia 336; Elinor 325-6; Elizabeth, Queen 526-30, 547; Goneril 345, 347, 349-50; Imogen 168; Isabel 286-8; Katharine (Hen. V) 278; Nerissa 413-21, 424; Ophelia 190, 192-3, 197-201; Percy, Lady 239-48; Portia (Merchant) 413-15; Queen (Cymbeline) 171-7; Regan 341-4; Rosalind 119; Volumnia (Sheridan's Coriolanus) 161-2; York, Duchess of 540-2, 544-6. Other references 3, 5, 18, 21, 23, 27, 50, 194.
Vincent, *Mrs* Richard, Jr., Isabella, nee Burchell, later Mrs John Mills, 1735-1802: Ceres 640-2; Helena (MND) 471; Ophelia 199. Other references 25, 34.
Viviez, *Mrs* [dancer], fl. 1765-7: 37, 41.
Vowell, fl. 1771-7: Lieutenant 547; Lodovico 513; Pedro (C & P) 618; Solanio 422.

Waddy, John, 1751-1814: Capulet 611-12; Cymbeline 186; Doctor (Macbeth) 398-400; Duke (Othello) 523-4; John, Don 495; Kent 360-1; King (Hamlet) 235, 238; Lieutenant 572-5; Suffolk 312; Vernon 265-6.
Walcot, *Mrs*, later Mrs Chambers, fl. 1797: Hostess (1 Hen. IV) 265.
Waldron, Francis Godolphin, 1744-1818: Apothecary 594, 597, 599-602, 605-6, 609-10; Butts 308-11; Carrier 252; Citizen (J. Caesar) 319; Corin 128, 130, 132-5, 137-40, 142-6, 149; Davy 275-6; Dogberry 484; Elbow 290; Erpingham 290-3; Fabian 660-3, 665; Falconbridge, Robert 328-9, 331-3; Feeble 274; Francis 249-50, 252-5; Gobbo 424, 426; Gravedigger 208-10; Lucianus 213, 215-17, 219-21, 223-4, 226-7, 233; Man, Old (Lear) 351, 353; Sands 311; Sexton 481, 483; Shallow (MWW) 459-60, 462-3, 465, 467; Shylock 434; Tubal 427, 431-2, 434, 436, 438-9, 441-3, 445; Verges 496. Other references 56, 67, 221.

767

INDEX I

Waldron, George, fl. 1793–8: Bates 293; Conrade 496; Cook (C & P) 632; Francis 264; Gobbo 442–3; Gravedigger 232–3, 236; Gregory (R & J) 610; Music Master 633; Officer (Othello) 521; Tailor 634; Tyrrel 570.

Walker [DL door-keeper], fl. 1759–84: 22, 24, 45, 47, 74, 78.

Walker, John, 1732–1807: Angus 368–9; Antonio (Much Ado) 476; Banquo 374; Brutus (J. Caesar) 316–17; Canterbury, Archbishop of 284–5; Duke Senior 123–4; Ghost 203; Kent 342–4; King (All's Well) 112–13; King (Hamlet) 201, 203–5; Lord (All's Well) 111; Pandulph 325–6; Peter, Friar 401–2; Rogero 677; Senator (Coriolanus) 159–60; Volusius 163. Other references 35, 41.

Wallis, *Miss* Tryphosa Jane, later Mrs James Elijah Campbell, 1774–1848: Adriana 156; Beatrice 494; Catharine 633; Cordelia 360; Imogen 185–6; Juliet (R & J) 608–10; Perdita (Wint. T.) 689; Rosalind 141. Other references 88, 102.

Walpole, *Miss* Charlotte, later Mrs Edward Atkyns, *c.* 1758–1836: Jessica 427, 429.

Walters, fl. 1772: Blunt (Cibber's Rich. III) 547.

Walton [unidentified], fl. 1775–7: 58–9, 62.

Warboys, Thomas, 1748–85: Posthumus 174.

Ward, fl. 1776: Butts 303.

*Ward, *Mrs* Henry, Sarah, *c.* 1727–71: Abbess 151; Anne, Lady 526–7; Capulet, Lady 589–90; Constance 322–4; Cordelia 336; Countess 112–13; Desdemona 502–3; Elizabeth, Queen 536–42, 544; Emilia 504–6; Ford, Mrs 452, 454–6; Hero 474; Juliet (R & J) 586–7; Macbeth, Lady 373–4; Portia (Merchant) 419; Queen (Hamlet) 203–5, 207, 209. Other references 4, 35, 39, 50, 296.

Ward, *Miss* Margaretta Priscilla, later (1) Mrs Thomas Kniveton, q.v.; (2) Mrs John Banks.

Ward, Thomas Achurch, 1747–1835: Malcolm 381; Romeo 598; Slender 463; Surrey 302; Tressel 549 50.

Ward, *Mrs* Thomas Achurch, Sarah, nee Hoare, 1756–1838: Anne, Lady 558, 560; Capulet, Lady 605–6; Desdemona 514–15; Elinor 332; Elizabeth, Queen 563–5, 567; Emilia 518–20; Hermione 685–7; Isabel 290–2; Mariana (Measure) 407–8; Queen (Cymbeline) 184; Queen (Hamlet) 226; Regan 356, 358; Valeria 164–5; York, Duchess of 567. Other references 115, 184.

Ware, fl. 1776: Sands 303.

Warrell, *Mrs*, fl. 1790: 91.

Wathen, George, 1762–1849: Carrier 264; Citizen (Coriolanus) 165–6; Gobbo 439, 441; Gravedigger 236; Grumio 634–5; Lucianus 234; Osric 231. Other reference 104.

Watkins, fl. 1760–72: Dennis 127; Fang 270–1; Flute (Fairy T.) 471–2; Gurney 321–2, 325, 327; Messenger (Timon) 656; Nym (MWW) 453–4, 456, 458–9; Outlaw 673; Peto (1 Hen. IV) 250. Other references 24, 34.

Watson [unidentified], fl. 1766–81: 38, 43, 45, 49, 52, 54, 65, 70, 72.

Watts, *Mrs* John [the 2nd], Louisa, nee Cranfield, fl. 1792–3: Helen 184–5.

Webb, Alexander, d. 1823: Bardolph (1 Hen. IV) 265; Bernardo 232, 234; Cambridge 290–3; Citizen (Coriolanus) 164; Dennis 143; Herald, English (John) 332; Joseph 628–30; Julio 520; Lodovico 524; Lord (AYLI) 149; Murderer 391–3, 397–9; Nathaniel 631, 633–6; Nym (MWW) 467; Officer (Coriolanus) 165–6; Officer (Twelfth N.) 671; Officer, Volscian 164; Outlaw 674; Pietro 440, 445; Priest (Hamlet) 234–7; Ruffian (Lear) 359; Sexton 497; Surveyor 308–9, 311; Tyrrel 571, 573–5; Watch (R & J) 609.

Webb, Richard (?), d. 1784: Capulet [V. iii only] 602; Charles 135–6; Lord Mayor 556, 558; Northumberland 255–6; Philario 181; Seyton 383; Witch 384–6. Other reference 558.

Webb, *Mrs* Richard (?), nee Child, formerly Mrs Day, 1737–93: Emilia 514; Falstaff (1 Hen. IV) 258; Hecate 388; Hostess (1 Hen. IV) 262; Queen (Hamlet) 218. Other references 81, 83.

Webber, fl. 1792: Stanley 568.

Webster, Anthony, d. *c.* 1785: Edgar 351, 353. Other reference 60.

Weeks, *Mrs*, fl. 1780: Nurse 601; York, Duchess of 557.

Weller, fl. 1760–7: Bernardo 199, 201, 203; Falconbridge, Robert 326; Herald, English (Hen. V) 284–5; Lucianus 201, 203; Oxford 535–6, 538–9; Peter (R & J) 589–90, 592; Tailor 617; Volumnius 316. Other reference 35.

Wells, fl. 1796–9: Gabriel 636; Marcius, Young 165–6.

Wells, *Mrs* Ezra, Mary Stephens, nee Davies, later Mrs Joseph Sumbel, q.v.

Welsh, James, fl. 1794–5: Gurney 332; Knight (Lear) 359; Ralph 631.

Welsh, Thomas, 1781–1848: Ariel 653; Arthur 332.

Wentworth, fl. 1796–1800: Abhorson 410–11; Bernardo 234–7; Blunt (Cibber's Rich. III) 571, 573–4; Curio 671; Gentle-

INDEX I

man (Othello) 524; Hortensio 635; Murderer 397–9; Officer (Coriolanus) 165.

Wentworth, *Miss* S., fl. 1798–9: Amphitrite 654; Edward, Prince 572–3; Ursula 496–7.

Wesley, John [preacher], 1703–91: 722.

West [unidentified], fl. 1764–6: 34, 38.

West, Thomas Wade, fl. 1775–8: Bassanio 425–6; Edmund 353; Hamlet 214; Hotspur 252; Jaques 131; Petruchio 622–3; Richmond 551, 554; Romeo 599. Other references 63, 66.

West, *Mrs* Thomas Wade [the 1st], fl. 1776–8: Bullen, Anne 303; Catharine 622; Helen 179; Percy, Lady 252; Regan 353. Other reference 252.

Weston, *Mrs*, stage name used previous to 1775 by Mrs Wilson (Sarah Maria Adcock), q.v.

Weston, Thomas, 1737–76: Carrier 244–5; Davy 271; Feeble 273; Gentleman Usher 345; Lucianus 205–6; Peter (R & J) 590–4; Polonius 199, 209; Porter (Hen. VIII) 300; Richard III 549; Roderigo 507; Sexton 480; Shallow (2 Hen. IV) 273; Shallow (MWW) 453–4. Other references 29, 34, 46, 199, 206, 723.

Wetherhead, fl. 1782: Gratiano (Merchant) [IV. i only] 431.

Wewitzer, *Miss*, fl. 1781: Page, Anne 462.

Wewitzer, Ralph, 1748–1825: Bardolph (1 Hen. IV) 259; Caius 460–7; Carrier 254, 257–60, 262; Chamberlain, Lord 306; Elbow 405, 409–11; Francis 258; Francisco (Hamlet) 214; Gardiner 307; Gentleman Usher 355–6; Gobbo 436–7, 445; Gravedigger 224–5, 235, 237; Grumio 635; Lord Mayor 568–9, 575; Lucianus 232, 234; Lucius (Timon) 657; Oatcake 494; Osric 220–2; Pedro (C & I) 621 3, Pinch 151–3; Sands 302, 307; Seacoal 495; Soldier, French 288–9; Tailor 626–7; Town Clerk 485, 487, 489; Verges 489–92; William 129–30, 136–7, 139, 141; Witch 395, 397–9. Other references 88, 236–7.

Wheatley, Frederick, d. 1836: Laertes 235; Tressel 572.

Wheatly, *Mrs*, fl. 1783: Queen (Hamlet) 223.

Wheeler, *Miss* Frances, later Mrs Richard Reyner, 1754–?: Celia 134–6; Jessica 431–3; Ophelia 220–1, 223; Page, Anne 463.

Wheeler, John, d. 1804: Balthazar (R & J) 594–5; Fenton 457–8; Gentleman (Cymbeline) 175–6; Hortensio 619–20; Lucilius (Timon) 656–7; Marcellus 207, 209; Messenger (Othello) 510–11; Montano 508; Oxford 541, 543, 546; Pandulph 327; Rosencrantz 207; Silvius 125–9; Trebonius 317; Tressel 542; Valentine (Twelfth N.) 661–2.

White, *Mrs*, fl. 1769–90: Curtis 618, 621–7; Falconbridge, Lady 327; Overdone, Mrs 403; Queen, Player 208–9; York, Duchess of 547.

White, Edward, d. 1766: Albany 338–9, 341–2; Ambassador, French 283–4; Balthazar (R & J) 579–80; Brutus (Coriolanus) 161; Buckingham (Rich. III) 539; Catesby 532–3; Chatillon 321; Dauphin (Hen. V) 279–81; Dauphin (John) 324; Decius 314–16; Fenton 450; Guildenstern 192–7; Herald (Coriolanus) 160; Le Beau 119–22; Lieutenant 528–30; Lord (All's Well) 112–13; Montano 500–2; Oliver 123–4; Paris 580–4; Poins (1 Hen. IV) 245–7; Poins (2 Hen. IV) 270; Rosencrantz 200–3; Salarino 416; Siward 366–9; Titus (Sheridan's Coriolanus) 163; Tressel 538; Westmorland (Hen. V) 284. Other references 18, 284.

*White, James [CG treasurer], fl. 1741–56: 7, 12, 16.

Whitfield, John, 1752–1814: Albany 350, 356, 358–9; Angus 380–1; Antipholus of Ephesus 151–2; Arviragus 178, 180–1; Banquo 385–6; Bassanio 430, 442; Benvolio 597, 599, 603, 605–6, 609–12; Blunt (1 Hen. IV) 254, 261; Borachio 483; Brutus (Coriolanus) 163–6; Buckingham (Rich. III) 575; Caius 460–2; Captain (Lear) 351; Cassio 512–15; Catesby 549; Claudio (Much Ado) 485, 487–9; Cromwell 302; Dauphin (Hen. V) 288–9; Dauphin (John) 330; Dumain 115; Edmund 360–1; Fabian 663; Fenton 460; Ford 468; Gratiano (Merchant) 432–3; Guiderius 179; Horatio 222, 226–7, 232, 234, 238; Hotspur 251; Laertes 214, 216–20, 222, 235; Lennox 391–6, 398–400; Lodovico 511–12, 523–4; Macduff 386, 389; Malcolm 382–5, 389–90; Messenger (Othello) 511; Montano 518–21; Norfolk (Hen. VIII) 307–12; Norfolk (Rich. III) 549, 551; Oliver 132–3, 135–6, 142–7; Orlando 141; Orsino 666–8; Paris 598–600; Pedro, Don 491–4; Pisanio 186; Poins (1 Hen. IV) 265–6; Salisbury (John) 331–2; Sebastian (Twelfth N.) 668; Silvius 129–30; Solanio 438–41; Surrey 305–6; Tressel 552, 555–6, 558–9, 562–5, 567; Tybalt 602; Valentine (TGV) 673; Vernon 255–7; Williams 290–3. Other references 58–9, 68, 90.

Whitfield, *Mrs* John, Mary, nee Lane, d. 1795: Blanch 330; Elizabeth, Queen 566, 569; Emilia 515; Juliet (Measure) 405–6; Katharine (Hen. V) 289; Luciana 151–2;

INDEX I

Margaret 487–8; Page, Mrs 461, 463; Percy, Lady 257; Phebe 133; Regan 351, 355; Ursula 483. Other reference 407.

Whitmell, fl. 1799: Ralph 635–6.

Whitmore, James, fl. 1799: Chancellor, Lord 312.

*Wignell, John, d. 1774: Angers, Citizen of 325–6; Balthazar (R & J) 580–2; Bardolph (1 Hen. IV) 242, 244–5, 249; Bardolph (2 Hen. IV) 273–4; Bardolph (Hen. V) 288; Bardolph (MWW) 448–57; Bardolph, Lord 269–70; Bernardo 193; Brabantio 503; Brandon (Rich. III) 532–4; Cambridge 282, 284–5, 288; Captain (Lear) 346; Catesby 529–30, 538–9, 543; Doctor (Macbeth) 366–9; Duke (Othello) 500; Duke Frederick 120; Ely, Bishop of 279–82; Guildenstern 197–201, 204; Hecate 370–4; Iago 500; John, Friar 593–4, 596; King, Player 202, 211; Lodovico 502; Lord Mayor 540–3, 546–7; Norfolk (Rich. III) 528–9, 539–40, 544–6; Officer (Com. Err.) 150; Officer (Lear) 341; Oxford 529; Publius 317–18; Rosencrantz 193–4; Senator (Coriolanus) 160; Sheriff (1 Hen. IV) 241–7; Steward 113–14. Other references 16, 23, 31, 33, 35, 39, 54.

Wignell, Thomas, c. 1753–1803: Arthur 325–6.

Wild, James, 1749–1801: Bedford 288; Peto (1 Hen. IV) 249. Other references 50, 54, 66, 76, 78, 84.

Wilde, Miss, fl. 1774–5: 56, 58.

Wilde, William, d. 1810: Caius 468; Gadshill 265–6; Gobbo 444; Lucianus 233, 235–6, 238; Pinch 157; Porter's Man (Hen. VIII) 312; Traveller (1 Hen. IV) 263.

*Wilder, James, 1724–?: Amiens 118; Balthazar (Much Ado) 474; Brandon (Hen. VIII) 297; Charles 118, 120; Egeus (Fairies) 470. Other references 4, 6.

Wilford, Edward [CG pit door-keeper], d. 1789: 33.

Wilford, Miss Mary, later (1) Mrs George Bulkley; (2) Mrs Ebenezer Barresford, q.v.

Wilkinson, fl. 1792: Iago 520; Shylock 438. Other reference 94.

Wilkinson, Tate, 1739–1803: Othello 502. Other references 22, 116, 196.

Wilks, Mrs, fl. 1776: Celia 131; Edward, Prince 551; Goneril 352; Jessica 426; Queen, Player 215.

Williames, Matthew, d. 1801: Amiens 134–5, 137–41; Balthazar (Much Ado) 488, 491–2; Benvolio 601–2; Caliban 651; Clown (Twelfth N.) 667; Fluellen 290; Gentleman (Wint. T.) 683; Gower (Hen. V) 290; Guildenstern 217, 219–21, 223–7; Hecate 389–90; Lorenzo 431–2, 434, 436; Metellus 318; Norfolk (Rich. III) 563–4; Pembroke 329, 331; Polixenes (Wint. T.) 687; Rogero 686; Ross 388; Suffolk 307–8; Tybalt 605–6; Vernon 254; Volusius 164. Other references 82, 90.

Williames, Mrs Matthew, Elizabeth, nee Smedley, formerly Mrs James Wilson, d. 1791: Audrey 142–3; Celia 137–40, 142; Hippolito 651; Lucetta 674; Nerissa 432, 434, 436. Other references 83, 85, 90.

Williams, fl. 1762–83: Evans 453; Richmond 549. Other reference 77.

Williams, Mrs Mary, fl. 1774–5: Elizabeth, Queen 549; Ursula 484. Other reference 57.

Williamson, David, d. 1810: Balthazar (Much Ado) 493; Balthazar (R & J) 609–10; Charles 143; Gadshill 263; Marcellus 231; Pistol (MWW) 467; Salarino 440.

Williamson, James Brown, d. 1802: Bertram 114; Buckingham (Rich. III) 566; Claudio (Much Ado) 490; Ghost 226, 228; Hamlet 222; Henry IV (1 Hen. IV) 261; Leontes (Sheep S.) 684; Oliver 136; Othello 510; Shylock 435; Wales, Prince of (1 Hen. IV) 262. Other references 85, 223, 510.

*Willoughby, Mrs, d. 1768: Hero 474–5.

Wilson [DL box-keeper], fl. 1778–96: 65, 70, 72, 78, 82, 92, 100.

Wilson, fl. 1787–92: Cassio 520; Paris 605.

Wilson, Mrs, stage name of Sarah Maria Adcock, 1752–86 [from 1772–5 she used stage name of Mrs Weston; from 1775–86 that of Mrs Wilson]: Audrey 137; Beatrice 487; Jessica 429; Maria 664, 666; Nerissa 430–4; Page, Mrs 460–4. Other references 57, 76, 78, 461, 674.

Wilson, James, d. 1789: Bernardo 219, 225–7; Francisco (Tempest) 649–50; Hortensio 625–6; Lucianus 221; Marcellus 226–7; Nym (MWW) 463, 465; Romeo 600; Scroop 290; Sheriff (1 Hen. IV) 255–6; Stanley 557; Valentine (Twelfth N.) 667. Other reference 221.

Wilson, Mrs James, Elizabeth, nee Smedley, later Mrs Matthew Williames, q.v.

Wilson, Richard, 1744–96: Carrier 257; Clown (Sheep S.) 684; Clown (Wint. T.) 685; Evans 467; Falstaff (1 Hen. IV) 261; Fluellen 288–9; Gardiner 302, 304–6; Grumio 620–1; Malvolio 663; Polonius 217–25, 228–9; Shallow (2 Hen. IV) 277; Shallow (MWW) 460–4; Stephano (Tempest) 646–8; Toby, Sir 666. Other references 73, 81, 229, 463–4.

770

INDEX I

Wingfield, stage name of Wingfield Palmer, q.v.

*Winstone, Richard, 1699–1787: Chamberlain, Lord 295–6; Duke (Merchant) 412–14; Duke (Othello) 499; Duke Frederick 117–18; Escalus (R & J) 577–9; Fabian 658–9; Hecate 364–5; John, Don 474–5; Kent 335–6; King (Hamlet) 190–1; Page (MWW) 447; Siward 364; Stanley 526–8. Other references 4, 6.

*Woffington, Mrs (i.e. Miss) Margaret, c. 1714–60: Anne, Lady 531; Constance 320; Elizabeth, Queen 532; Ford, Mrs 447, 449–50; Katharine, Queen 295; Macbeth, Lady 364, 366–8; Portia (J. Caesar) 314; Portia (Merchant) 413, 415–16; Queen (Hamlet) 190, 194–6; Rosalind 120–1; Veturia 160–1. Other reference 196.

Wood [DL box-keeper], fl. 1775–96: 58, 65, 67, 86, 92, 100.

Wood, Miss, fl. 1781: Clarence 276.

Wood, Charles, fl. 1780–2: Arviragus 181; Fenton 462; Horatio 218; Norfolk (Rich. III) 556.

Wood, John [DL sub-treasurer], d. 1763: 9, 14, 17, 24.

*Woodward, Henry, 1714–77: Andrew, Sir 658–9, 661; Clown (Wint. T.) 677, 682; Falstaff (2 Hen. IV) 268; Launcelot 415; Lucio 401–3, 405; Mercutio 578–83, 588–91, 593–8; Osric 190–4; Parolles 111–14; Petruchio 613–14, 616–21; Polonius 193–4; Roderigo 511; Shallow (2 Hen. IV) 272, 274; Slender 447–8, 457; Stephano (Tempest) 639, 646–7; Touchstone 118–21, 131. Other references 2, 11, 16, 19, 46, 48, 56, 60, 402, 639.

Wooldridge [DL box-keeper], fl. 1796: 100.

Woollams, Thomas [DL box-keeper], fl. 1779–99: 67, 70, 92, 100, 105.

Wooller, fl. 1769–71: Gobbo 422; Lodovico 507.

Woollery, Miss Frances Barnet, later Mrs James Henry Cottingham, d. 1810: Desdemona 517; Hero 491. Other reference 83.

Worley, Mrs, fl. 1766: Audrey 124; Goneril 344; Nurse 591.

*Worsdale, James [dramatist], c. 1692–1767: 4.

Worthington, Mrs, nee Jessup, fl. 1797: Imogen 186.

Wortley, fl. 1780: Paris 600; Ratcliff 557.

*Wright, fl. 1741–51: Capulet, Old 577.

Wright, fl. 1779: Prospero 648.

Wright, Mrs, fl. 1769: Elizabeth, Queen 543.

Wright, Miss Charlotte, later Mrs Thomas Blanchard, fl. 1782: Phebe 135. Other reference 69.

Wright, Miss Elizabeth, later Mrs Michael Arne [the 2nd], q.v.

Wright, Roger, d. 1786: Baptista 619–20, 623–6; Bardolph (1 Hen. IV) 252–5; Bardolph (2 Hen. IV) 275–6; Bardolph (MWW) 459–60, 463; Bernardo 209; Blunt (1 Hen. IV) 251; Boatswain 643, 645; Buckingham (Rich. III) 543; Caliban 644–5, 648; Camillo (F & P) 680–1; Captain (Twelfth N.) 661–4; Doctor (Lear) 349, 353; Doctor (Macbeth) 377, 379–83; Duke (Merchant) 421–2, 424; Elbow 404–8; Francisco (Tempest) 643–4; Friar (Much Ado) 482–6; Gentleman (Cymbeline) 173–4; Gower (2 Hen. IV) 274; Herald, English (John) 327–9; Jeweller 656–7; Launcelot 434; Le Beau 126; Messenger (Hamlet) 212–17, 219–20; Montague 494–5; Philario 175–83; Ratcliff 543–4, 546, 548–50, 552–3, 555, 557, 559–61; Sailor (Hamlet) 220; Sebastian (Tempest) 649–50. Other references 47, 51, 56, 62.

Wrighten, James, 1745–93: Alonso 643, 646–50; Antonio (Much Ado) 488; Antonio (Twelfth N.) 663–7; Austria 328–9, 331; Barnardine 404–6; Bernardo 210, 212; Borachio 486; Burgundy (Lear) 347; Charles 129, 132–5, 137–8; Cornelius 176, 178; Cornwall 353; Cymbeline 178, 182–3; Decius 318; Duke Senior 126; Gadshill 250; Gobbo 427, 431–2, 434; Gonzalo 646; Gratiano (Othello) 510–16; Gregory (R & J) 594; Hastings 275–6; Lord Mayor 549; Lucius (Cymbeline) 174, 180–1; Marcellus 212–17, 219–21, 223–4, 226; Officer (Twelfth N.) 661; Peto (2 Hen. IV) 274; Provost 407–8; Sergeant (Macbeth) 382–3; Servilius 656–7; Sexton 484–6; Shipmaster 643–6; Stanley 543, 550; Tyrrel 546; Verges 484; Westmorland (1 Hen. IV) 252–5. Other references 91, 381, 486.

Wrighten, Mrs James, Mary Ann, nee Matthews, later Mrs A. M. Pownall, 1751–96: Audrey 134–5, 137–8; Catharine 623–6; Ceres 644–6. Other references 49, 57.

Wroughton, stage name of Richard Rotton, 1748–1822: Antonio (Merchant) 440–1, 445; Apemantus 657; Aufidius 164–5; Banquo 382–4, 393–5, 397; Bassanio 422, 424–36, 438–9; Bastard (John) 330; Buckingham (Hen. VIII) 300–3, 305–11; Claudio (Measure) 403–10; Dauphin (John) 328; Edgar 356, 358–9; Florizel (Wint. T.) 680–1; Ford 460–5, 467;

INDEX I

Ghost 232, 234–5, 237; Guiderius 174–8, 180–1; Hamlet 226, 232; Henry IV (1 Hen. IV) 264; Henry V 288–9; Henry VI (Cibber's Rich. III) 570, 574; Hotspur 251, 254–7; Iachimo 183; Jaques 139–41, 145–8; Laertes 213; Lear 354; Leontes (Wint. T.) 686–7; Macduff 389–97; Malcolm 376–80; Octavius (J. Caesar) 318; Oliver 129–31; Othello 514–15; Pedro, Don 483–5, 487; Philip, King 333; Pisanio 175, 178; Poins (2 Hen. IV) 274; Proteus 673–4; Richmond 542, 546–8, 550, 552–3, 555–6, 558–60, 562–4; Romeo 598–600, 602–3, 609; Sebastian (Twelfth N.) 661, 663, 666; Tressel 541–2, 544–8; Wales, Prince of (1 Hen. IV) 249, 261; Wales, Prince of (2 Hen. IV) 276. Other references 54, 151, 394, 544, 558–9.

Yates, fl. 1773: Burgundy (Lear) 349.

*Yates, *Miss*, fl. 1744–52: York, Duke of 526–7.

*Yates, Richard, *c.* 1706–96: Autolycus (Wint. T.) 677, 679; Bottom (Fairy T.) 471; Bottom (MND) 470; Carrier 243; Citizen (Coriolanus) 159–60; Cloten 171–6; Clown (All's Well) 111–12; Clown (Measure) 401–3; Clown (Wint. T.) 683; Dogberry 475–80; Evans 447–9, 451, 454, 456–7; Falstaff (1 Hen. IV) 244; Gardiner 300; Gentleman Usher 337, 339; Gravedigger 190–205; Grumio 613–18; Launce 673; Lucio 402–4; Malvolio 658–61, 663–4; Roderigo 499–500, 502–3; Shallow (2 Hen. IV) 268–9, 271–3, 275–6; Shylock 412–17, 421–2; Touchstone 118, 121–4; Trinculo 639–42; Witch 364–74. Other references 9, 14, 34, 36, 48, 296, 423, 471, 477.

*Yates, *Mrs* Richard [the 1st], Elizabeth Mary, d. 1753: Margaret 474; Queen, Player 190–1.

Yates, *Mrs* Richard [the 2nd], Mary Ann, nee Graham, 1728–87: Bullen, Anne 300; Cleopatra 116; Constance 322–5, 328–30; Cordelia 342–3, 346; Desdemona 504–6; Hermione 684; Imogen 170–4, 176; Isabella 403–7; Julia 673; Macbeth, Lady 376–8, 380–1, 383–6; Perdita (Wint. T.) 679; Portia (Merchant) 421, 429–31; Queen (Hamlet) 206; Rosalind 123–4; Viola 661. Other references 25, 34, 46, 660.

York, Edward Augustus, Duke of [brother of George III], 1739–67: 41.

Young, *Miss* Elizabeth, later Mrs Ridley Dorman, q.v.

*Young, *Miss* Esther, later Mrs Jones, q.v.

Young, *Miss* Isabella, later the Hon. Mrs John Scott, q.v.

Young, Thomas, fl. 1761–87: Borachio 484; Burgundy (Lear) 351; Clarence 268, 270; Cromwell 302; Henry, Prince 328; Hortensio 621; John, Prince (1 Hen. IV) 245; Laertes 202; Laurence, Friar 605; Paris 597; Tressel 549–51. Other reference 33.

Younge, *Miss* Elizabeth, later Mrs Alexander Pope [the 1st], q.v.

Younger, *Master*, fl. 1761–2: Simple 452–3.

Younger, Joseph, 1734–84: Antonio (Merchant) 427; Aufidius 163; Capulet 595–6; Cranmer 303; Duncan 377; Exeter 284, 287; Henry IV (1 Hen. IV) 253; Henry VI (Cibber's Rich. III) 545, 547–8, 552; King (Hamlet) 210, 215; Lord Chief Justice 274. Other references 27, 35, 37, 39, 163, 250, 400.

INDEX II

CHARACTERS

THIS index lists all the characters that appear in the playbills. Under each character will be found the names of all the performers who undertook that particular part. In many instances actresses appeared in the same part both before and after their marriage. In such instances I have given both their maiden and married names. If, however, an actress appeared in a part only under her maiden name or only under her married name, that name alone is listed.

For the abbreviations of the adaptations of Shakespeare's plays as given here, see the foreword to Index I.

Abbess (Com. Err.) *See* Miss Chapman, Mrs Hartley, Mrs Inchbald, Mrs H. Ward.
Abergavenny (Hen. VIII). *See* Curties, Elrington, Harris, Raftor, R. Smith.
Abhorson (Measure) *See* Alfred, R. Bates, Carpenter, Davis (fl. 1797–8), Phillimore, H. Vaughan, Wentworth.
Abraham (R & J). *See* Costollo, Dunstall, Holtom, Jones (d. 1806), Marr, Quick.
Adam (AYLI). *See* J. Aickin, Bridgwater, Comerford, T. Davies, Dowton, Gibson, Havard, Henry, Hull, Hurst, Lacey, J. Lee, Moody, Newton, Packer, Shuter, Swendall.
Adam (Tam. Shrew) In Garrick's alteration (C & P), *see* Fisher, Lyons.
Adriana (Com. Err.). *See* Mrs Bates, Mrs Bernard, Mrs Fawcett, Mrs Green (fl. 1781), Mrs Jackson, Mrs Mattocks, Mrs R. Vincent Sr., Miss Wallis.
Aedile (Coriolanus). *See* Hurst, Jefferson.
Aegeon (Com. Err.). *See* Gibson, Hull.
Agatha (Hen. VIII). In Kemble's adaptation the name given to one of the Queen's attendants in IV. ii. *See* Miss Collins, Miss Heard.
Agrippa (A & C). *See* Packer.
Albany (Lear). *See* J. Aickin, Anderson, Claremont, W. Davies, T. Davis, Ellard, Hull, S. Johnson, L'Estrange, Mozeen, Owenson, Packer, J. Palmer the younger, Richardson, Smyth, Taylor, Toms, Usher, White, Whitfield.
Alcibiades (Timon). *See* Croft, Farren.
Alcon. In Morgan's alteration of Wint. T. (F & P) the name given to the disguised Antigonus, q.v., and thus occasionally printed in the bills.
Alexas (A & C). *See* Ackman.
Alonso (Tempest). *See* Atkins (fl. 1751–

60) (?), Bransby, L'Estrange, Packer, Staunton, Usher, Wrighten.
Ambassador, French (Hen. V). *See* White.
Amiens (AYLI). *See* Atkins (fl. 1751–60), Beard, Brett, W. Davies, Dignum, Du-Bellamy, J. Fawcett Sr., Johnstone, Kenny, T. Lowe, Mattocks, Wm. Palmer, Vernon, Wilder, Williames.
Amphitrite (Kemble's Tempest). A character not in the original play (introduced by Kemble from Dryden and Davenant's version). *See* Miss D'Evelyn, Miss Dufour, Mrs Edwards, Miss Leak, Miss Stuart, Miss Wentworth.
Andrew, Sir (Twelfth N.). *See* Dodd, J. Edwin Sr., Obrien, Quick, Suett, Woodward.
Angelo (Com. Err.). *See* Fearon, Perry, Powel.
Angelo (Measure). *See* Barrymore, M. Clarke, Havard, Hull, J. Palmer the younger.
Angers, Citizen of (John). *See* E. Burton, J. Fawcett Sr., Hurst, Maddocks, J. Thompson, J. Wignell.
Angus (Macbeth). *See* Bennet, Chaplin, Fox, Keen, Perry, Simson (d. 1758), Walker, Whitfield.
Anne, Lady (Rich. III). *See* Miss Ambrose, Mrs Bailey, Mrs T. Baker, Mrs Barrington, Mrs W. Barry, Miss Biggs, Mrs Brereton [i.e. later Mrs J. P. Kemble], Miss Brunton [i.e. later Mrs Merry], Miss Chapman, Miss Collins, Mrs Cuyler, Mrs T. Davies, Mrs Du-Bellamy, Mrs Farmer [i.e. later Mrs W. Powell], Mrs Goodall, Mrs Greville, Mrs Hunter, Mrs Jackson, Miss Jewell, Mrs J. P. Kemble, Mrs S. G. Kemble, Mrs Kingham, Mrs Lefevre, Mrs Lessingham, Mrs W. T. Lewis, Mrs Litchfield, Miss

773

INDEX II

Logan, Miss Macklin, Mrs Merry, Miss A. Miller, Mrs W. Mills, Miss Nossiter, Miss Ogilvie, Mrs J. Palmer the elder, Mrs W. Palmer, Mrs Platt, Mrs Pollard, Mrs W. Powell, Miss Pritchard [i.e. later Mrs J. Palmer the elder], Miss Ranoe [i.e. later Mrs Rivers], Mrs Reddish, Mrs Rivers, Mrs T. Robinson, Mrs Rock, Miss Satchell [i.e. later Mrs S. G. Kemble], Mrs Sharp, Miss Shelburne, Miss Sherry, Mrs Siddons, Mrs Stephens, Miss Stuart, Miss Taylor, Mrs R. Vincent Sr., Mrs H. Ward, Mrs T. A. Ward, Mrs Wells, Mrs Woffington, Miss Younge.

Antigonus [see also Alcon] (Wint. T.). See M. Clarke. In Morgan's alteration (F & P), see F. Aickin, J. Aickin, Anderson, Gibson, Hull, Inchbald, L. Sparks.

Antipholus of Ephesus (Com. Err.). See Bernard, T. Davis, Harley, Holman, Wm. Palmer, Whitfield.

Antipholus of Syracuse (Com. Err.). See Hull, W. T. Lewis, Macready, Pope.

Antonio (Merchant). See F. Aickin, J. Aickin, Archer, C. Bannister, S. Barry, Bensley, E. Berry, M. Clarke, T. Davies, Farren, W. Gardner [IV. i only], F. Gentleman, Holman, Hull, P. Lewis, Macready, Murray, Reddish, Ross, L. Sparks, Usher [IV. i only], Wroughton, Younger.

Antonio (Much Ado). See Ackman, Chapman, Hurst, Packer, Simson (d. 1758), J. Thompson, Usher, Walker, Wrighten.

Antonio (Tempest). See Austin, Bland, C. J. Booth, G. Burton (?), Chaplin, Denman, Gibbon, Hurst, Phillimore, H. Sparks, Strange.

Antonio (Twelfth N.). See Benson, E. Burton, Caulfield, W. Davies, J. Fawsett Sr., Fearon, W. Gardner, Phillimore, Wrighten.

Antonio (TGV). See E. Burton, Fearon, Maddocks.

Antonio. In Kemble's adaptation of Othello the name given to the Messenger, q.v.

Antonio's Servant (Merchant). See Helme, Spencer.

Antony (A & C). See Garrick.

Antony (J. Caesar). See S. Barry, Hull, Miller, Ross, Wm. Smith (d. 1819).

Antony's Servant (J. Caesar). See Cushing, Perry, Phillimore.

Apemantus (Timon). See C. Bannister, Wroughton.

Apothecary (R & J). See J. Barrett, Castle, Holtom, Jones (d. 1806), Rees, Simmons, Simson (d. 1758), W. Stevens, Swords, F. G. Waldron.

Arante (Tate's Lear). A character not in the original play. See Miss Brangin, Miss Dayes, Mrs Evans, Miss Green, Mrs Hippisley, Mrs R. Johnston, Miss Kirby, Miss Leserve, Miss Madden, Mrs Masters, Miss Minors, Miss Ogilvie, Mrs Platt, Miss Rowson, Miss Stuart, Miss Taylor, Miss Tidswell, Miss Trowell.

Archidamus (Wint. T.). See Holtom.

Ariel (Tempest). See Miss Abrams, Mrs Arne, Mrs Bland the younger, Master Brown, Miss DeCamp, Mrs Dorman, Mrs Farrell [i.e. later Mrs M. H. Kennedy], Miss Field [i.e. later Mrs Forster], Mrs Forster, Miss Granger, Miss Hagley, Miss Heard [read by], Mrs M. H. Kennedy, Miss Rogers, Miss Romanzini [i.e. later Mrs Bland the younger], Mrs Scott, T. Welsh, Miss Eliz. Young [i.e. later Mrs Dorman], Miss I. Young [i.e. later Mrs Scott].

Armed Head (Macbeth). See Jones (d. 1806).

Artemidorus (J. Caesar). See Sharpless.

Arthur (John). See W. Bates, T. Blanchard, DeCamp, Miss DeCamp, Mrs Evans, Miss Field, Miss Ford, Miss Heard, Miss Kelly, T. Kennedy, Miss Mullart [i.e. later Mrs Evans], Pulley, Miss Rogers, Master Saunders, J. Simson, Miss Valois, T. Welsh, T. Wignell.

Arviragus (Cymbeline). See Barrymore, Benson, Brereton, Claremont, W. Davies, C. Holland the younger, Middleton, J. Palmer the elder, J. Palmer the younger, R. Palmer, Perry, R. Smith, Townsend, Whitfield, Wood. In Hawkins's alteration this character named Cadwal. See T. Lowe.

Astringer (All's Well). In Kemble's alteration this character named Tourville. See Bland.

Athenian, Old (Timon). See Fearon.

Attendant (2 Hen. IV). See Painter.

Attendant (Lear). See J. Fawcett Sr.

Audrey (AYLI). See Mrs Booth, Mrs Bradshaw, Mrs Brett, Mrs Brown, Mrs Davenett, Mrs Edwards, Miss Hale, Mrs Harlowe [III. iii only], Mrs James, Mrs R. Johnston, Mrs Love, Mrs Pitt, Miss Pope, Mrs Rock, Mrs Russell, Mrs Wells, Mrs Williames, Mrs S. M. Wilson, Mrs Worley, Mrs Wrighten.

Aufidius (Coriolanus). See M. Clarke, Havard, Ryan, Wroughton, Younger.

Austria (John). See Bransby, Buck, Cory, J. Griffith, Keen, Mahon, Marten, D. Morris, Mozeen, Phillimore, Wrighten.

Autolycus (Wint. T.). See Dodd, Du-

INDEX II

Bellamy, J. Edwin Sr., Munden, Quick, Suett, Vernon, R. Yates. In Morgan's alteration (F & P), *see* T. Blanchard, T. King, Munden, Shuter. In Colman's alteration (Sheep S.), *see* J. Edwin Sr.

Balthazar (Merchant). *See* Ackman, Curties, Holtom, Ledger, Maddocks, Norris, Simson (d. 1758), Surmont, Trueman.

Balthazar (Much Ado). *See* Atkins (fl. 1751–60), Beard, Brett, D'Arcy, Darley, Dignum, Dodd, Du-Bellamy, J. Fawcett Sr., Fisher, Gray, G. King, T. Lowe, Mattocks, Meadows, Reinhold, Townsend, Vernon, Wilder, Williams, D. Williamson.

Balthazar (R & J). *See* Abbot, Ackman, Banks, Bransby, Chaplin, J. C. Cross, Cushing, Evatt, Everard, Farley, J. Fawcett Sr., Ledger, P. Lewis, Lings, Ricard, Robson, R. Smith, Strange, Wheeler, White, J. Wignell, D. Williamson.

Banquo (Macbeth). *See* F. Aickin, Barrymore, Bensley, W. Davies, Farren, Gibson, Harley, Hull, Macready, Murray, Packer, J. Palmer the elder, J. Palmer the younger, Peile, Ross, Sowdon, L. Sparks, Walker, Whitfield, Wroughton.

Baptista (Tam. Shrew). In Garrick's alteration (C & P), *see* Bowles, E. Burton, Chaplin, Chapman, Farrell, J. Johnson, E. (?) Lloyd, Maddocks, Packer, J. Thompson, Usher, R. Wright.

Bardolph (1 Hen. IV). *See* Alfred, T. Baker the elder, R. Bates, C. J. Booth, Clough, Cubitt, T. Davis, W. Egan Sr., Jones (d. 1806), Ledger, P. Lewis, E. (?) Lloyd, Marten, Massey (of Hay), Rock, Stoppelaer, Swords, J. Thompson, A. Webb, Wewitzer, J. Wignell, R. Wright.

Bardolph (2 Hen. IV). *See* Clough, P. Lewis, Marten, J. Wignell, R. Wright. In the anonymous alteration (Humourists), *see* Clough.

Bardolph (Hen. V). *See* Alfred, Barnshaw, J. Barrett, Cushing, Fox, P. Lewis, Marten, Morgan, Phillimore, J. Wignell.

Bardolph (MWW). *See* T. Baker the elder, R. Bates, W. Bates, Benson, Clough, Fox, Helme, Hollingsworth, Kear, Kenny, Marten, Massey (of Hay), Rees, Rock, Street, Swords, J. Wignell, R. Wright.

Bardolph, Lord (2 Hen. IV). *See* T. Baker the elder, J. Fawcett Sr., Mozeen, Parsons, J. Wignell.

Barnardine (Measure). *See* Clough, Dowton, J. Fawcett Sr., Hollingsworth, Jones (d. 1806), Keen, R. Palmer, Stoppelaer, Wrighten.

Bassanio (Merchant). *See* T. Baker the younger, Barrymore, Bensley, Cautherley, M. Clarke, T. Davies, W. Davies, Farren, Fearon, Havard, C. Holland the elder, C. Kemble, J. P. Kemble, J. Palmer the younger, Pope, Ryan, Staunton [IV. i only], West, Whitfield, Wroughton.

Bastard (John). *See* S. Barry, J. G. Fleetwood, Garrick, C. Holland the elder, C. Kemble, W. T. Lewis, J. Palmer the younger, Wm. Smith (d. 1819), Wroughton.

Bates (Hen. V). *See* Banks, G. Waldron.

Beatrice (Much Ado). *See* Mrs Abington, Mrs S. Barry, Miss Biggs, Miss Brunton, Mrs Bulkley, Mrs Esten, Miss E. Farren, Miss Haughton, Mrs Henry, Mrs Jordan, Miss F. Kemble, Miss Macklin, Mrs J. Palmer the elder, Miss Pope, Mrs Pritchard, Miss Pritchard [i.e. later Mrs J. Palmer the elder], Miss Wallis, Mrs S. M. Wilson, Miss Younge.

Bedford (Hen. V). *See* Dignum, Holtom, Phillimore, R. Smith, Wild.

Belarius (Cymbeline). *See* F. Aickin, J. Aickin, E. Burton, M. Clarke, Farren, Havard, Hull, J. Lee, Murray, Newton, L. Sparks.

Benedick (Much Ado). *See* Barrymore, Browne, Garrick, Henderson, Holman, J. P. Kemble, T. King, J. Lee, W. T. Lewis, Obrien, J. Powell.

Benvolio (R & J). *See* Ackman, T. Baker the elder, C. J. Booth, W. Davies, T. Davis, Fox, Gibson, Glassington, Jones (fl. 1780–1), Macready, Mozeen, Packer, J. Palmer Jr., Phillips (fl. 1761), Scrase, Usher, Whitfield, Williames.

Bernardo (Hamlet). *See* Abbot, R. Bates, Bencraft, C. J. Booth, Chaplin, Chippendale, J. C. Cross, W. Egan Sr., Elrington, Evatt, Griffiths, Jacobs, T. Kennedy, Kenny, Lings, Marr, Phillimore, R. Smith, Strange, Vernon, A. Webb, Weller, Wentworth, J. Wignell, J. Wilson, R. Wright, Wrighten.

Bertram (All's Well). *See* J. P. Kemble, Lewes, J. Palmer the elder, Ross, J. B. Williamson.

Bianca (Tam. Shrew). In Garrick's alteration (C & P), *see* Mrs Bennet, Miss Brangin, Mrs Coates, Mrs Collet, Mrs Heard, Mrs James Jones, Miss Kirby, Miss Leserve, Miss Palmer [i.e. later Mrs James Jones], Mrs A. Palmer, Mrs W. Palmer, Mrs Platt, Mrs Poussin, Miss Simson (fl. 1780–6), Mrs S. Smith, Mrs Stephens, Miss Tidswell.

Biondello (Tam. Shrew). In Garrick's

INDEX II

alteration (C & P), see Baddeley, Bailey, W. Bates, Bennet, Benson, Blakes, Chalmers, Cushing, Davenport, Didier, W. Egan Sr., Evatt, Farley, Follett, Hartry, T. Kennedy, Lamash, H. Lee, L'Estrange, Maddocks, D. Morris, J. Palmer Jr., R. Palmer, Rock, Townsend.

Biron. In Kemble's alteration of All's Well the name given to the 1st Gentleman, q.v.

Blanch (John). See Mrs Colles, Miss Collins, Miss Dayes, Mrs Du-Bellamy, Mrs Inchbald, Miss Jarratt, Miss Mellon, Miss A. Menage, Miss Minors, Miss Palmer, Miss Plym, Miss Read, Miss Trowell, Miss Vincent, Mrs R. Vincent Sr., Mrs Whitfield.

Bloody Child (Macbeth). See Master Gell, Master Harlowe.

Blunt (1 Hen. IV). See J. Bates, W. Bates, C. J. Booth, Chalmers, Cleveland, Cushing, T. Davis, Elrington, Farley, J. Fawcett Sr., C. Holland the younger, Hurst, Iliff, Macready, Mansel, Mozeen, J. Palmer the younger, Wm. Palmer, Perry, Reily, Richardson, R. Smith, Strange, Toms, Trueman, Whitfield, R. Wright.

Blunt (Cibber's Rich. III). See Bailey, Bell, Bland, J. C. Cross, Curties, J. Griffith, Haymes, Holtom, Jones (d. 1806), Lyons, Perry, Redman, Summers, Walters, Wentworth.

Boatswain (Tempest). See R. Bates, Blakes, J. Booth, Carpenter, Clough, Griffiths, R. Wright.

Borachio (Much Ado). See Ackman, T. Baker the younger, J. Bates, W. Bates, Blakes, W. Egan Sr., Farley, Farren, J. Johnson, Lamash, L'Estrange, Macready, Wm. Palmer, Parsons, Phillimore, Trueman, Usher, Whitfield, Wrighten, Young.

Bottom (MND). See R. Yates. In Colman's alteration (Fairy T.), see Baddeley, Parsons, R. Yates.

Boy (Hen. V). See W. S. Chatterley, De Camp, Miss S. Francis, Gregson, Miss Hallam, Miss Morrison, Miss Mullart, Miss Valois.

Brabantio (Othello). See F Aickin, J. Aickin, E. Berry, E. Burton, W. Gardner, Gibson, Graham (fl. 1771–7), Hull, Hurst, E. (?) Lloyd, Love, J. (?) Marshall, Martial, Packer, Pine, Rogers (?), Sinclair, L. Sparks, J. Wignell.

Brackenbury [see also Lieutenant] (Rich. III). See Benson, J. Cooke, J. Palmer Jr., Trueman.

Brandon (Hen. VIII). See Banks, Claremont, Fox, Jefferson, Wilder.

Brandon (Rich. III). See Clifford, J. Wignell.

Bridget. In Hull's alteration of Com. Err. (Twins) the name given to Luce, q.v.

Brutus (Coriolanus). See E. Burton, T. Davis, G. A. Stevens, White, Whitfield.

Brutus (J. Caesar). See Bensley, J. Palmer the younger, Quin, Sheridan, L. Sparks, Walker.

Buckingham (Hen. VIII). See Austin, Farren, C. Holland the elder, H. E. Johnston, T. Lacy, J. Palmer the younger, Ross, Stacy, Wroughton.

Buckingham (Rich. III). See F. Aickin, J. Aickin, Barrymore, Bensley, Benson, Betterton, C. J. Booth, Bransby, W. Bridges, E. Burton, J. W. Clarke, T. Davies, Farren, Fearon, W. Gardner, Hull, Jefferson, Knapp, J. Lee, Macready, Meredith, J. Palmer the elder, Price, Raymond, S. Russell, Sowdon, L. Sparks, E. (?) Thompson, Usher, White, Whitfield, J. B. Williamson, R. Wright.

Bullcalf (2 Hen. IV). See Dunstall, Messink, Philips.

Bullen, Anne (Hen. VIII). See Miss Ambrose, Mrs T. Baker, Mrs Bennet, Mrs Bulkley, Miss Chapman, Miss Cleland, Mrs Colles, Mrs Cuyler, Mrs T. Davies, Miss DeCamp, Mrs Farmer [i.e. later Mrs W. Powell], Mrs Glen, Miss Hale, Miss Haughton, Mrs Inchbald, Mrs T. Jefferson the 1st, Mrs W. Mills, Mrs Morton, Miss Ogilvie, Mrs W. Powell, Mrs R. Vincent Sr., Mrs West, Mrs R. Yates the 2nd.

Burgundy (Hen. V). See Bennet, Cushing, Hull, Perry, Phillimore, Robson, Trueman.

Burgundy (Lear). See Adcock, Austin, James Bannister, J. Bates, W. Bates, Bencraft, Bennet, Benson, Blurton, C. J. Booth, Caulfield, Cubitt, Dignum, Fox, Helme, Jefferson, Keen, Kenny, Knowles, Lewes, Marr, H. Mills, Murden, Norris, J. Palmer the younger, Philipps, Quick, Robson, J. Thompson, Turner (fl. 1761–78), Wrighten, Yates (fl. 1773), Young.

Butts (Hen. VIII). See J. Burton, Emery, Fox, Redman, Stoppelaer, H. Vaughan, F. G. Waldron, Ward (fl. 1776).

Cadwal. In Hawkins' alteration of Cymbeline the name given to Arviragus, q.v.

Caesar (J. Caesar). See J. Aickin, Bridgwater, M. Clarke, Packer, L. Sparks.

Caius (MWW). See Baddeley, Blakes, Cubitt, Holtom, T. Jackson, T. Lacy, T. Marshall, Murray, C. S. Powell, Quick, Stoppelaer, Wewitzer, Whitfield, Wilde.

INDEX II

Caliban (Tempest). See Ackman, C. Bannister, Benson, E. Berry, Blakes, Champnes, Dunstall, Love, Mahon, Sedgwick, I. Sparks, Williames, R. Wright.

Calphurnia (J. Caesar). See Mrs Bambridge, Mrs Du-Bellamy, Miss Sherry, Mrs R. Vincent Sr.

Cambridge (Hen. V). See Lyons, A. Webb, J. Wignell.

Camillo (Wint. T.). See J. Aickin, Davenport, T. Davies, Hull, J. Lee. In Morgan's alteration (F & P), see Packer, Powel, Redman, Strange, R. Wright. In Colman's alteration (Sheep S.), see Griffiths, Usher.

Campeius (Hen. VIII). See E. Burton, Davenport, Du-Bellamy, Dunstall, D. Morris, Packer, Painter, Sparrow.

Canidius (A & C). See Austin.

Canterbury, Archbishop of (Hen. V). See W. Gardner, Hull, Maddocks, L. Sparks, Walker.

Caphis (Timon). See Ackman, T. Kennedy

Captain (Cymbeline). See Ackman, Castle, Keen, Norris.

Captain (Lear). See Ackman, Chaplin, J. Griffith, McGeorge, Maddocks, Phillimore, Trueman, Whitfield, J. Wignell.

Captain (Twelfth N.). See Benson, Blakes, C. J. Booth, Caulfield, Chaplin, Fox, Haymes, C. Holland the younger, Mahon, Moody, R. Wright.

Capucius (Hen. VIII). See Abbot, Bransby, Du-Bellamy, Kenny, Phillimore, Scrase.

Capulet (R & J). See F. Aickin, J. Aickin, E. Berry, C. J. Booth, E. Burton, M. Clarke, W. Davies, Farren, Fearon, Gibson, Hurst, Inchbald, L. Kennedy, Kniveton, Massey (of CH), Moody, Newton, Powel, Price, Sidney, L. Sparks, Waddy, R. Webb [V. iii only], Younger.

Capulet, Lady (R & J). See Mrs Barrington, Mrs Bennet, Mrs Booth, Mrs Burden, Mrs Davenett, Mrs Fowler, Mrs Hull, Mrs Jerrold, Mrs R. Johnston, Miss Leserve, Miss Morris (fl. 1794-7), Mrs Newby, Miss Pearce, Mrs Platt, Mrs Poussin, Mrs Pritchard, Mrs S. Smith, Miss Tidswell, Mrs H. Ward, Mrs T. A. Ward.

Capulet, Old (R & J). See A. Johnston, Pierce, Wright (fl. 1751).

Carrier (1 Hen. IV). See Arthur, J. Barrett, Barrington, R. Bates, Bennet, Bernard, T. Blanchard, Blissett, C. J. Booth, J. Burton, Costollo, J. C. Cross, Dowton, Dunstall, W. Egan Sr., Emery, Granger, Hollingsworth, T. Jackson, Jones (d. 1806), T. Kennedy, Messink, Moody, Munden, Parsons, Philips, Powel, Quick, Rees, W. Stevens, Suett, H. Vaughan, F. G. Waldron, Wathen, Weston, Wewitzer, R. Wilson, R. Yates.

Casca (J. Caesar). See J. Aickin, C. Bannister, W. Gardner, Gibson, Ridout.

Cassio (Othello). See J. Aickin, John Bannister, Barrymore, Betterton, Cautherley, M. Clarke, W. (?) Cooke, Dancer, W. Davies, T. Davis, E. T. Delaval, G. Graham, C. Holland the younger, Hull, C. Kemble, W. T. Lewis, Macready, J. Palmer the elder, J. Palmer the younger, Wingfield Palmer, Perry, Quelch, Richardson, Ridout, Whitfield, Wilson (fl. 1787-92).

Cassius (J. Caesar). See Bensley, Henry, Hull, Ryan, Wm. Smith (d. 1819), Sowdon.

Catesby (Rich. III). See Bailey, Caulfield, Claremont, W. Davies, J. Davis, T. Davis, Essex, Everard, Farrell, Fox, Gibson, Holtom, Jones (fl. 1780-1), Marr, Massey (of CH), Packer, R. Palmer, J. Powell, Robson, J. Smith, Strange, Uncle, Usher, White, Whitfield, J. Wignell.

Catharine. In Garrick's alteration of Tam. Shrew (C & P) the name given to Katharina, q.v.

Celia (AYLI). See Miss Ambrose, Mrs Baddeley, Mrs T. Baker, Mrs Barrington, Mrs W. Barry, Miss Chapman, Mrs Clive, Miss Collins, Mrs Fox, Miss Hooke, Miss E. Hopkins [i.e. later Mrs Sharp], Mrs Inchbald, Miss Jarratt, Mrs J. P. Kemble, Mrs McGeorge, Mrs Mattocks, Miss Mellon, Mrs Morton, Mrs Mountain, Miss Rogers, Miss Satchell, Mrs Sharp, Mrs R. Vincent Sr., Miss Wheeler, Mrs Wilks, Mrs J. Wilson.

Ceres (Tempest). See Miss Dorman, Miss Valois, Mrs Vernon, Mrs R. Vincent Jr., Mrs Wrighten, Miss I. Young.

Chamberlain, Lord (Hen. VIII). See Anderson, Baddeley, Benson, Bonnor, Bransby, J. W. Clarke, Cubitt, T. Davies, W. Egan Sr., S. Johnson, L. Kennedy, Lewes, R. Palmer, Robson, Trueman, Wewitzer, Winstone.

Chancellor, Lord (Hen. VIII). See Blissett, Fearon, Maddocks, Marten, Whitmore.

Charles (AYLI). See Alfred, Bencraft, Buck, J. Cooke, Cubitt, Darley, W. Egan Sr., Fox, W. Gardner, Keen, Layfield, Moody, D. Morris, Phillimore, Rowson, G. A. Stevens, R. Webb, Wilder, D. Williamson, Wrighten.

Charmian (A & C). See Mrs Hippisley.

Chatillon (John). See John Bannister, Benson, C. J. Booth, W. Davies, T. Davis,

INDEX II

Dyer, Farren, Hull, L'Estrange, Scrase, Smyth, Trueman, Vernon, White.

Chorus (Hen. V). *See* Henderson, Hull, W. Powell, Ryan.

Cinna [the Conspirator] (J. Caesar). *See* R. Bates, W. Gardner, Norris, Redman, Summers.

Citizen (Coriolanus). *See* Barrington, Blakes, J. Burton, Clough, W. Collins, Costollo, Cushing, Dunstall, J. Fawcett Sr., Hollingsworth, Jones (d. 1806), P. Lewis, Maddocks, Mozeen, Quick, Stoppelaer, Suett, H. Vaughan, W. Vaughan, Wathen, A. Webb, R. Yates.

Citizen (J. Caesar). *See* Arthur, Baddeley, Barrington, J. Burton, Castle, W. Collins, Costollo, Dunstall, Hamilton, Holcroft, P. Lewis, Morgan, Quick, Saunders, I. Sparks, Stoppelaer, F. G. Waldron.

Clarence (2 Hen. IV). *See* J. Burton, Master Cape, Miss Collett, Mrs Hippisley, Murden, Miss Wood, Young.

Claudio (Measure). *See* Barrymore, Brereton, T. Davies, Farren, C. Kemble, Perry, Reddish, Wroughton.

Claudio (Much Ado). *See* Barrymore, Brereton, Cautherley, Farren, C. Kemble, W. T. Lewis, J. Palmer the elder, Toms, Whitfield, J. B. Williamson.

Claudio. In Garrick's alteration of Cymbeline the name occasionally used in the bills for the Gentleman, q.v.

Cleomenes (Wint. T.). *See* Castle, Chaplin, Fearon, Hurst, Jefferson, Parsons, Powel, Richardson, R. Smith. In Colman's alteration (Sheep S.), *see* T. Davis.

Cleopatra (A & C). *See* Mrs R. Yates the 2nd.

Cloten (Cymbeline). *See* Bernard, Betterton, C. J. Booth, M. Clarke, Dodd, J. Edwin Sr., Jefferson, T. King, Lewes, T. Marshall, R. Palmer, Quick, S. Russell, R. Yates.

Clown (All's Well). *See* John Bannister, J. Edwin Sr., Quick, Shuter, Swords, R. Yates.

Clown (Measure). *See* C. J. Booth, Dunstall, Parsons, Suett, R. Yates.

Clown (Twelfth N.). *See* Blakes, W. Davies, Dowton, Dyer, Lewes, Parsons, S. T. Russell, Shuter, Suett, Vernon, Williams.

Clown (Wint. T.). *See* Bernard, Hollingsworth, T. King, Quick, Suett, R. Wilson, Woodward, R. Yates. In Morgan's alteration (F & P), *see* Costollo, Cubitt, Moody, Simmons, G. A. Stevens. In Colman's alteration (Sheep S.), *see* T. Jackson, R. Wilson.

Colevile (2 Hen. IV). *See* Elrington, Fox, W. Gardner, Holtom, Keen, R. Smith.

Cominius (Coriolanus). *See* J. Aickin, T. Davies, Gibson, Ridout.

Conrade (Much Ado). *See* Caulfield, Claremont, Cubitt, T. Davis, Gibbon, J. Griffith, Griffiths, Haymes, Lamash, Lyons, Mahon, Mozeen, Robson, Strange, Surmont, G. Waldron.

Constable (Hen. V). *See* Benson, Bridgwater, M. Clarke, Cushing, J. Fawcett Sr., Peile.

Constance (John). *See* Mrs S. Barry [i.e. later Mrs Crawford], Mrs Bellamy, Mrs Burton, Mrs Cibber, Mrs Crawford, Mrs W. Powell, Mrs Siddons, Mrs H. Ward, Mrs Woffington, Mrs R. Yates the 2nd.

Cook (Tam. Shrew). In Garrick's alteration (C & P), *see* Alfred, Ledger, G. Waldron.

Cordelia (Lear). *See* Mrs Baddeley, Mrs S. Barry, Mrs Bellamy, Miss Brunton [i.e. later Mrs Merry], Mrs Bulkley, Mrs Cibber, Mrs Dancer [i.e. later Mrs S. Barry], Mrs T. Davies, Mrs Esten, Miss Hallam, Mrs Hartley, Mrs Jackson, Mrs Jefferies, Mrs S. G. Kemble, Mrs Massey, Mrs Merry, Miss Miller (fl. 1770-4), Miss Morris (d. 1769), Miss Nossiter, Mrs J. Palmer the elder, Mrs A. Pope the 2nd, Mrs. H. H. Robinson, Mrs T. Robinson, Mrs Roope, Miss Satchell [i.e. later Mrs S. G. Kemble], Mrs Siddons, Mrs Spencer [i.e. later Mrs A. Pope the 2nd], Mrs Twistleton, Mrs R. Vincent Sr., Miss Wallis, Miss Ward, Mrs H. Ward, Miss Wilford [i.e. later Mrs Bulkley], Mrs R. Yates the 2nd, Miss Younge.

Corin (AYLI). *See* Castle, J. C. Cross, Dunstall, Hartry, Hollingsworth, S. Johnson, Massey (of Hay), Philips, Rees, Taswell, J. Thompson, F. G. Waldron.

Coriolanus (Coriolanus). *See* J. P. Kemble, Mossop, Sheridan, Wm. Smith (d. 1819).

Cornelius (Cymbeline). *See* Alfred, E. Burton, Chaplin, Cubitt, Redman, G. A. Stevens, Swords, J. Thompson, Wrighten.

Cornwall (Lear). *See* Anderson, Benson, Blakes, Bloomfield, Campbell, J. W. Clarke, Dancer, T. Davis, Evatt, W. Gardner, Hurst, J. Jackson, C. Kemble, Macartney (fl. 1799), Macready, Mahon, Parsons, Wm. Smith (fl. 1776), Staunton, J. Thompson, Usher, Wrighten.

Cornwall's Servant (Lear). *See* Benson, Keen, R. Palmer, T. Smith, J. Thompson.

Countess (All's Well). *See* Mrs D. L. E. Baker, Mrs Du-Bellamy, Mrs Hull, Mrs

778

INDEX II

Inchbald, Miss Miller (fl. 1770–4), Mrs W. Powell, Mrs Pritchard, Mrs H. Ward.

Courtezan (Com. Err.). In Hull's two alterations this character named Lesbia. See Miss Leserve, Miss Morris (fl. 1794–7), Mrs Platt, Mrs Stephens.

Cranmer (Hen. VIII). See J. Aickin, Benson, Bridgwater, E. Burton, Dexter, W. Gardner, Havard, Hull, P. Lewis, Murray, Younger.

Crier (Hen. VIII). See Alfred, Evans, Jones (d. 1806), Street.

Cromwell (Hen. VIII). See W. Davies, Farren, Hull, C. Kemble, J. P. Kemble, W. T. Lewis, Mozeen, R. Palmer, Ridout, Scrase, Wm. Smith (fl. 1776), Usher, Whitfield, Young.

Crowned Child (Macbeth). See W. S. Chatterley.

Curan (Lear). See J. Fawcett Sr.

Curio (Twelfth N.). See J. Cooke, Everard, Fox, Lyons, Paddick, Wentworth.

Curtis (Tam. Shrew). In Garrick's alteration (C & P), see Mrs Booth, Mrs Bradshaw, Mrs J. C. Cross, Miss Hale, Mrs Love, Mrs Maddocks, Mrs Platt, Mrs C. S. Powell, Mrs White.

Cymbeline (Cymbeline). See T. Davies, Fearon, W. Gardner, Gibson, Hurst, L'Estrange, Love, Massey (of CH), D. Morris, Packer, Powel, Richardson, Ryan, Staunton, Waddy, Wrighten.

Dauphin (Hen. V). See Barrymore, Benson, T. Davis, Lewes, Usher, White, Whitfield.

Dauphin (John). See F. Aickin, Austin, Barrymore, Brereton, Cautherley, Dimond, Dyer, C. Holland the younger, Hull, Lacey, T. Lacy, Robson, White, Whitfield, Wroughton.

Davy (2 Hen. IV). See Granger, Jacobs, Marr, Parsons, F. G. Waldron, Weston. In the anonymous alteration (Humourists), see H. Vaughan.

Decius (J. Caesar). See T. Davis, Elrington, Jacobs, Usher, White, Wrighten.

Demetrius (MND). See Wingfield Palmer. In Garrick's alteration (Fairies), see Vernon.

Dennis (AYLI). See Alfred, W. Gardner, Holtom, Mahon, Watkins, A. Webb.

Denny (Hen. VIII). See Castle, Vernon.

Dercetas (A & C). See Perry, Reinhold.

Desdemona (Othello). See Mrs Baddeley, Mrs S. Barry [i.e. later Mrs Crawford], Miss Barton, Mrs Bellamy, Mrs Chapman, Mrs Churton, Mrs Cibber, Mrs Crawford, Mrs Dancer [i.e. later (1) Mrs S. Barry, (2) Mrs Crawford], Mrs T. Davies, Miss DeCamp, Mrs Dyer (?), Mrs Elmy, Miss E. Farren, Mrs Fisher (fl. 1752), Mrs Hallam, Miss Hamilton, Mrs Hartley, Mrs Jefferies, Mrs S. G. Kemble, Mrs Lessingham, Miss Macklin, Miss Miller (fl. 1770–4), Miss Mowat, Miss Nossiter, Mrs Osborne, Mrs J. Palmer the elder, Mrs A. Pope the 1st, Mrs A. Pope the 2nd, Miss Powell, Mrs W. Powell, Mrs Quarme, Miss Ranoe, Miss Satchell [i.e. later Mrs S. G. Kemble], Mrs Siddons, Mrs Smith (fl. 1769–76), Mrs Stott [i.e. later Mrs Lessingham], Mrs H. Ward, Mrs T. A. Ward, Miss Woollery, Mrs R. Yates the 2nd, Miss Younge [i.e. later Mrs A. Pope the 1st].

Diana (All's Well). See Mrs Cuyler, Mrs T. Davies, Miss Hallam [i.e. later Mrs Mattocks], Mrs Mattocks, Miss A. Miller.

Dighton (Cibber's Rich. III). A character not in the original play. See Evans, R. Smith.

Diomedes (A & C). See Bransby.

Dion (Wint. T.). See R. Bates.

Doctor (Lear). See T. Baker the elder, R. Bates, C. J. Booth, Castle, Chaplin, Davenport, Evatt, W. Gardner, J. Griffith, Jones (d. 1806), Redman, Rock, Simson (d. 1758), R. Wright.

Doctor (Macbeth). See Fearon, Hurst, Jones (d. 1806), Maddocks, Massey (of Hay), Packer, Powel, G. A. Stevens, Waddy, J. Wignell, R. Wright.

Dogberry [see also Town Clerk] (Much Ado). See J. Edwin Sr., Moody, Moss, Munden, Parsons, Quick, Shuter, Suett, Taswell, F. G. Waldron, R. Yates.

Dollabella (A & C). See Mozeen.

Donalbain (Macbeth). See Bennet, Benson, Bland, J. Burton, Master Cape [i.e. Everard], Cautherley, J. C. Cross, R. Cross Jr., Curties, DeCamp, W. Egan Jr., Everard, Fisher, Gregson, Mattocks, H. Mills, Miss Morrison, Murden, Master Palmer, R. Palmer, Pulley, Simmons, J. Simson, Vernon.

Door-keeper (Hen. VIII). See Claremont, Jones (d. 1806).

Dorcas (Wint. T.). See Miss Cranford, Mrs Hippisley, Miss Minors, Mrs Morton, Mrs Mountain, Miss Simson (fl. 1780–6), Miss Stuart, Mrs Vernon. In Morgan's alteration (F & P), see Mrs Abegg, Mrs Lloyd, Mrs Mountain, Miss Mullart, Miss Rowson, Mrs Esther Young. In Colman's alteration (Sheep S.), see Miss Hale.

Dorcas (Cobler). A character not in the original play. See Mrs Baker (d. 1760).

INDEX II

Dorinda (Kemble's Tempest). A character not in the original play (introduced by Kemble from Dryden and Davenant's version). *See* Miss E. Farren, Mrs Gibbs, Mrs Jordan, Miss Mellon, Miss A. Miller, Mrs W Powell.

Douglas (1 Hen. IV). *See* F. Aickin, Anderson, Austin, W. Bates, Caulfield, Chaplin, Cubitt, W. Egan Jr., Evatt, Farley, J. Fawcett Sr., W. Gardner, L. Kennedy, L'Estrange, Mahon, T. Marshall, Owenson, Parsons.

Dromio of Ephesus (Com. Err.). *See* Quick, Rees, Shuter.

Dromio of Syracuse (Com. Err.). *See* T. Blanchard, Brunsdon, Dunstall, J. Edwin Sr., Munden.

Duke (All's Well). *See* Anderson, E. Burton, J. Burton, Du-Bellamy, Owenson.

Duke (Com. Err.). *See* Anderson, J. W. Clarke, W. Davies, W. Gardner, Haymes, L'Estrange, Richardson.

Duke (Measure). *See* Bensley, Henderson, J. P. Kemble, J. Lee, Mossop, Wm. Smith (d. 1819).

Duke (Merchant). *See* Anderson, Benson, Bransby, Davenport, Fearon, E. (?) Lloyd, Marten, Massey (of CH), D. Morris, Packer, Powel, D. B. Roberts, Saul, J. Thompson, Usher, Winstone, R. Wright.

Duke (Othello). *See* Anderson, C. J. Booth, Bransby, Carr, Chaplin, Cubitt, Du-Bellamy, J. Fawcett Sr., Foster, W. Gardner, Keen, L'Estrange, Maddocks, Marten, Miller, D. Morris, Parker, Sidney, Stoppelaer, J. Thompson, Usher, Waddy, J. Wignell, Winstone.

Duke (TGV). *See* J. Aickin, Havard, Hull.

Duke Frederick (AYLI). *See* J. Aickin, Bransby, Caulfield, Chaplin, Fearon, Fox, W. Gardner, Gibson, Hudson, Maddocks, Massey (of CH), Mozeen, Packer, J. Palmer the younger, Redman, Simson (d. 1758), J. Thompson, Tindal, J. Wignell, Winstone.

Duke Senior (AYLI). *See* Ackman, F. Aickin, J. Aickin, Blakes, C. J. Booth, M. Clarke, W. Gardner, Hull, Hurst, L'Estrange, P. Lewis, Powel, J. Powell, Ridout, Staunton, Usher, Walker, Wrighten.

Dumain. In Kemble's alteration of All's Well the name given to the 1st Lord, q.v.

Duncan (Macbeth). *See* J. Aickin, Bensley, E. Berry, Bransby, E. Burton, Chambers, Chaplin, W. Gardner, Gibson, Hull, Hurst, Packer, J. Thompson, Usher, Younger.

Edgar (Lear). *See* J. Aickin, T. Barry, Comerford, G. F. Cooke, T. Davis, Dimond, Dyer, Havard, Holman, Hull, W. T. Lewis, Reddish, Ross, Ryan, Wm. Smith (d. 1819), Webster, Wroughton.

Edmund (Lear). *See* F. Aickin, Barrymore, Bensley, M. Clarke, Fennell, W. Gardner, J. Lee, Macready, Middleton, J. Palmer the elder, J. Palmer the younger, Wm. Palmer, Perry, W. Powell, Ridout, Robson, J. Smith, Wm. Smith (d. 1819), Sowdon, West, Whitfield.

Edward, Prince (Rich. III). *See* Miss Beaufield, Benson, Miss Besford, S. Besford, T. Blanchard, J. Burton, Mrs Byrne, Master Cape, Cautherley, W. S. Chatterley, Curties, Miss DeCamp, DeCamp, Mrs Evans, Farley, Miss Field, Mrs Findlay, Miss M. Francis, Miss S. Francis, Miss Granger, Mrs H. Green, Harris, Miss Heard, Miss Helme, Miss P. Hopkins, Miss Langrish, Miss Lings, Miss Minors, Miss C. Morris, Miss Morrison, Miss Mullart [i.e. later Mrs Evans], Miss Painter, Pulley, Miss Read, Miss Rogers, Simmons, Miss Sims, Miss Simson (d. 1807), J. Simson, Miss Stageldoir, Miss Standen, Master Suett, Miss Thomas, Miss Valois, Miss Wentworth, Mrs Wilks.

Egeus (MND). *See* E. Burton. In Garrick's alteration (Fairies), *see* Wilder.

Eglamour (TGV). *See* Benson, Packer.

Elbow (Measure). *See* W. Bates, Dodd, Hollingsworth, Holtom, Parsons, Philips, Quick, Taswell, F. G. Waldron, Wewitzer, R. Wright.

Elinor (John). *See* Mrs D. L. E. Baker, Mrs Bennet, Mrs Booth, Mrs Dyer, Mrs Elmy, Mrs Hopkins, Mrs W. Mills, Mrs Platt, Miss Sherry, Mrs Sparks, Miss Tidswell, Mrs R. Vincent Sr., Mrs T. A. Ward.

Elizabeth, Queen (Rich. III). *See* Mrs Bates, Mrs Bellamy, Miss Chapman, Mrs Cibber, Mrs Du-Bellamy, Mrs Elmy, Mrs Farren, Mrs Fawcett, Mrs J. Hamilton, Mrs Harlowe, Mrs Hartley, Mrs Hopkins, Mrs Hunter, Mrs Inchbald, Mrs Jackson, Mrs Jefferies, Mrs Jerrold, Mrs Lee, Mrs Lefevre, Mrs Massey, Mrs Mattocks, Mrs Melmoth, Miss Miller (fl. 1770-4), Miss Morris (fl. 1794-7), Mrs Parsons, Mrs A. Pope the 1st, Mrs W. Powell, Mrs Pritchard, Mrs Reddish, Mrs H. H. Robinson [i.e. later Mrs W. P. Taylor], Mrs Russell, Mrs Siddons, Mrs W. P. Taylor, Mrs R. Vincent Sr., Mrs H. Ward, Mrs T. A. Ward, Mrs Whitfield,

INDEX II

Mrs Williams, Mrs Woffington, Mrs Wright.

Ely, Bishop of (Hen. V). *See* Jones (d. 1806), J. Thompson, J. Wignell.

Emilia (Othello). *See* Mrs Bates, Mrs Bennet, Mrs Bernard, Mrs Bland the elder [i.e. later Mrs J. Hamilton], Mrs Bradshaw, Mrs Burden, Mrs Egerton, Mrs Fawcett, Mrs Goodall, Mrs Graham, Mrs H. Green, Mrs J. Hamilton, Mrs Harlowe, Mrs Hopkins, Mrs Jefferies, Mrs R. Johnston, Mrs L. Kennedy, Mrs Lee, Mrs Litchfield, Miss Macklin, Mrs Mattocks, Mrs Morton, Mrs Murray, Mrs W. Powell, Mrs Price, Mrs Pritchard, Mrs Read (?), Miss Roberts, Miss Sherry, Mrs S. Smith, Mrs Sparks, Mrs Stephens, Mrs Stevens, Miss Thomson, Mrs H. Ward, Mrs T. A. Ward, Mrs Webb, Mrs Whitfield.

Enobarbus (A & C). *See* E. Berry, E. Burton.

Eros (A & C). *See* T. Davies.

Erpingham (Hen. V). *See* Redman, F. G. Waldron.

Escalus (Measure). *See* J. Aickin, Bransby, T. Davis, Fearon, Hull, Perry.

Escalus (R & J). *See* Adcock, Anderson, Benson, C. J. Booth, Bransby, Campbell, Claremont, J. W. Clarke, Evatt, Fearon, W. Gardner, Gibson, Keen, Macready, Mansel, Massey (of CH), D. Morris, Norris, J. Palmer the younger, Phillimore, Richardson, Scrase, J. Thompson, Toms, Trueman, Winstone.

Esquire (Lear). *See* Dignum.

Essex (John). *See* James Bannister, Caulfield, Chaplin, T. Davis, Dignum, W. Egan Sr., Elrington, Fox, W. Gardner, Helme, Jefferson, Lamash, Mahon, Redman, Strange.

Evandra (Hull's Timon). A character not in the original play (introduced by Hull from Shadwell's version). *See* Mrs Duill.

Evans (MWW). *See* Arthur, Clough, W. Collins, Dodd, J. Edwin Sr., Hayes, Hollingsworth, P. Lewis, Parsons, Townsend, Williams, R. Wilson, R. Yates.

Evanthe (Cumberland's Timon). A character not in the original play. *See* Mrs S. Barry.

Executioner (John). *See* Evans, Fisher.

Exeter (Hen. V). *See* J. Aickin, Hull, L'Estrange, Ridout, Tindal, Younger.

Fabian (Twelfth N.). *See* Baddeley, Hartry, C. Kemble, Lamash, Lewes, R. Palmer, W. Stevens, Vernon, F. G. Waldron, Whitfield, Winstone.

Fairy (MWW). *See* Miss Langrish.

Fairy (MND). *See* Master Raworth, Miss E. Wright. In Garrick's alteration (Fairies), *see* Master Evans. In Colman's alteration (Fairy T.), *see* Mrs Arne, Harrison, Master Raworth, Miss Twist (fl. 1777–9), Miss E. Wright [i.e. later Mrs Arne].

Falconbridge, Lady (John). *See* Mrs Bennet, Mrs Cuyler, Mrs Ferguson, Mrs Hedges, Mrs Hopkins, Mrs Humphries, Mrs R. Johnston, Mrs Lee, Mrs Poussin, Mrs White.

Falconbridge, Robert (John). *See* Castle, Hamilton, Holtom, A. Johnston, Wingfield Palmer, Simson (d. 1758), F. G. Waldron, Weller.

Falstaff (1 Hen. IV). *See* F. Aickin, E. Burton, Digges [II. iv only], Dunstall, J. Fawcett Jr., Henderson, S. Johnson, T. King, Longley, Love, J. Palmer the younger, Quin, T. Ryder, Shuter, Mrs Webb, R. Wilson, R. Yates.

Falstaff (2 Hen. IV). *See* Henderson, Love, Quin, Shuter, Woodward. In the anonymous alteration (Humourists), *see* W. Phillips.

Falstaff (MWW). *See* E. Berry, Dunstall, J. Fawcett Jr., Henderson, H. Howard, Lewes, Love, J. Palmer the younger, Quin, T. Ryder, Shuter, G. A. Stevens.

Falstaff's Page (2 Hen. IV). *See* W. Bates, S. Besford, Miss Collett, Pulley, Miss Rogers.

Fang (2 Hen. IV). *See* Redman, Watkins.

Feeble (2 Hen. IV). *See* W. Collins, Holtom, H. Vaughan, F. G. Waldron, Weston. In the anonymous alteration (Humourists), *see* Blakey.

Fenton (MWW). *See* J. Bates, Chalmers, Cubitt, W. Davies, T. Davis, W. Egan Sr., Farren, Fox, Gibson, J. Jackson, Lamash, Lewes, Macready, R. Palmer, Phillimore, Robson, Scrase, Simson (d. 1758), Strange, Toms, Trueman, Wheeler, White, Whitfield, Wood.

Ferdinand (Tempest). *See* Barrymore, Sig. Curioni, W. Davies, Farren, C. Holland the elder, C. Holland the younger, Kelly, C. Kemble, Mattocks, Vernon.

Flaminius (Timon). *See* Brereton.

Flavius (Timon). *See* Hull, Packer.

Fleance (Macbeth). *See* J. Burton, W. S. Chatterley, Miss Collett, Curties, Mrs Evans, Mrs Findlay, Gregson, Menage, Miss M. Menage, Morgan, Miss Morrison, Miss Mullart [i.e. later Mrs Evans], Pulley, Master Rees, Miss Rogers, Miss Standen.

Florizel (Wint. T.). *See* John Bannister, Barrymore, Brereton, C. Holland the

INDEX II

elder, Holman, W. T. Lewis, Mrs Martyr, Middleton, Wroughton. In Morgan's alteration (F & P), see S. Barry, Cautherley, Dimond, Holman, Mattocks, Wm. Smith (d. 1819). In Colman's alteration (Sheep S.), see John Bannister, Du-Bellamy.

Fluellen (Hen. V). See Arthur, Baddeley, C. J. Booth, Macklin, Shuter, Williams, R. Wilson.

Flute (MND). See Baddeley. In Colman's alteration (Fairy T.), see Baddeley, Blissett, Castle, Watkins.

Ford (MWW). See F. Aickin, T. Davies, W. Davies, Farren, Havard, J. Palmer the younger, Peile, Pope, W. Powell, Ross, Ryan, Wm. Smith (d. 1819), Whitfield, Wroughton.

Ford, Mrs (MWW). See Mrs Abington, Mrs Bates, Mrs Bland the elder [i.e. later Mrs J. Hamilton], Mrs Brereton, Mrs Bulkley, Miss Chapman, Miss E. Farren, Mrs Goodall, Mrs J. Hamilton, Miss Haughton, Mrs L. Lewis, Mrs Lisley, Mrs Mattocks, Mrs A. Pope the 1st, Mrs Pritchard, Mrs H. Ward, Mrs Woffington, Miss Younge [i.e. later Mrs A. Pope the 1st].

Forrest (Cibber's Rich. III). A character not in the original play. See Fisher, Holtom, Ledger, Lings, Rees.

France, King of (Hen. V). See Fearon, Gibson, Hull, Kniveton, Packer, Usher.

France, King of (Lear). See T. Davis, Du-Bellamy.

Francis (1 Hen. IV). See John Bannister, J. Barrett, W. Bates, Bennet, T. Blanchard, W. Collins, Cushing, J. Edwin Sr., Hamilton, Knight, Morgan, Simmons, Stamper, Suett, H. Vaughan, F. G. Waldron, G. Waldron, Wewitzer.

Francisca (Measure). See Miss Green, Mrs R. Johnston, Miss T. Mills, Miss Pearce, Mrs Poussin, Miss Simson (fl. 1780–6), Miss Tidswell.

Francisco (Hamlet). See Abbot, J. Bates, J. Cooke, Evans, Farley, J. Griffith, Helme, Holtom, Norris, Phillimore, Raftor, R. Smith, Spencer, Wewitzer.

Francisco (Tempest). See J. Griffith, Norris, J. Wilson, R. Wright.

Friar (Much Ado). See E. Burton, Davenport, Fearon, W. Gardner, Inchbald, Maddocks, Powel, R. Wright.

Froth (Measure). See Benson, Bland, Fisher, S. T. Russell.

Gabriel (Tam. Shrew). In Garrick's alteration (C & P), see J. Cooke, Garman, Simpson, Wells.

Gadshill (1 Hen. IV). See Bencraft, J. Besford, Buck, Chippendale, J. Cooke, Gibbon, Holcroft, Holtom, Ledger, Marr, T. Smith, Stephens, Wilde, D. Williamson, Wrighten.

Galesus (Sheridan's Coriolanus). A character not in the original play. See Gibson, Hull.

Gardiner (Hen. VIII). See Arthur, Clough, J. Edwin Sr., Massey (of CH), Munden, Parsons, Quick, Shuter, Suett, Taswell, Wewitzer, R. Wilson, R. Yates.

Gentleman (All's Well). See Ackman. In Kemble's alteration the 1st Gentleman is named Biron: see Benson; the 2nd is named Jaquez: see Caulfield.

Gentleman [see also Claudio] (Cymbeline). See Ackman, Fox, J. Griffith, Griffiths, Wheeler, R. Wright.

Gentleman (Hamlet). See Abbot, Evans, J. Fawcett Sr.

Gentleman (Lear). See J. Fawcett Sr., Klanert, Phillimore.

Gentleman (Measure). See Dignum, Gibbon, Surmont, Trueman.

Gentleman (Othello). See C. Ryder, Wentworth. In Kemble's adaptation the 2nd Gentleman is named Julio. See Benson, Trueman, A. Webb.

Gentleman (Wint. T.). See Blakes, Phillimore, J. Thompson, Williames. At CG in 1787 and 1788 this character named Nicholas. See Darley. In Colman's alteration (Sheep S.), see W. Stevens.

Gentleman, French (Cymbeline). See Blakes, Chaplin, Claremont, T. Davis, Farley, J. Fawcett Sr., S. Johnson, Keen, Klanert, Macready, Scrase.

Gentleman Usher. In all alterations of Lear the name given to Oswald, q.v.

Gentlewoman (Coriolanus). See Miss Helme, Miss Tidswell.

Gentlewoman (Macbeth). See Miss Leserve, Mrs Platt, Mrs Poussin, Mrs Simson, Miss Tidswell.

Ghost (Hamlet). See F. Aickin, J. Aickin, Barrymore, Bensley, E. Berry, Bransby, M. Clarke, Comerford, Cory, Farren, Garrick, Gibson, Harley, Henry, Hull, Kniveton, Murray, J. Palmer the younger, W. Powell, Reddish, Ryan, Sowdon, Staunton [III. iv only], Toms, Walker, J. B. Williamson, Wroughton.

Glendower (1 Hen. IV). See Keen, T. King, J. Lee, D. Morris, Ridout, G. A. Stevens.

Gloucester (Hen. V). See Bennet, Benson, Harris, C. Kemble, Lewes, Murden, J. Palmer Jr.

Gloucester (Lear). See J. Aickin, E. Berry,

782

INDEX II

E. Burton, T. Davies, F. Gentleman, Gibson, Hull, Johnston [i.e. Bardin], P. Lewis, Mitchell, Packer, Ridout, L. Sparks, Thompson (fl. 1767).

Gobbo (Merchant). See T. Baker the elder, J. Barrett, Bennet, Blissett, W. Collins, Cubitt, Emery, Hollingsworth, Jones (d. 1806), Lucas, Newton, Parsons, Powel, Ray, Saunders, Suett, Swords, W. Vaughan, F. G. Waldron, G. Waldron, Wathen, Wewitzer, Wilde, Wooller, Wrighten.

Goneril (Lear). See Mrs W. Barry, Mrs Bennet, Mrs Burden, Mrs Cuyler, Mrs Dibdin, Miss Haughton, Mrs Hunter, Mrs R. Johnston, Mrs Lee, Mrs Lefevre, Miss Mansel, Miss Morris (fl. 1794–7), Miss Pearce, Mrs Platt, Mrs Poussin, Mrs Reddish, Miss Sherry, Mrs Stephens, Mrs R. Vincent Sr., Mrs Wilks, Mrs Worley.

Goneril's Page (Lear). See W. S. Chatterley.

Gonzalo (Tempest). See J. Aickin, E. Burton, Fearon, Fox, Grist, Maddocks, Wrighten.

Gower (2 Hen. IV). See Buck, Castle, Cushing, Strange, R. Wright.

Gower (Hen. V). See Anderson, Benson, Bowles, Dignum, Du-Bellamy, Norris, R. Palmer, Williams.

Gratiano (Merchant). See John Bannister, Bernard, Blakes, Bonnor, Dodd, Dyer, Farley, J. Fawcett Jr., Jefferson, Knight, Lamash, Lewes, Macready, Mozeen, J. Palmer the elder, J. Palmer the younger, R. Palmer, Wm. Palmer, S. Russell, S. T. Russell, Vandermere, Wetherhead [IV. i only], Whitfield.

Gratiano (Othello). See Abbot, Benson, Caulfield, Davenport, Ellard, Farrell, J. Fawcett Sr., Fearon, J. Gardner, Hunter, Hurst, Kearny, Mozeen, Murden, Parsons, Phillimore, Powel, Redman, Simson (d. 1758), Smith (fl. 1769), H. Sparks, Wrighten.

Gravedigger (Hamlet). See J. Barrett, R. Bates, C. J. Booth, Buck, J. Burton, Castle, Chippendale, W. Collins, Costollo, Dowton, Dunstall, J. Edwin Sr., Emery, J. Fawcett Jr., Grimaldi, Hollingsworth, Jones (d. 1806), T. King, P. Lewis, Massey (of Hay), Messink, Milburne, Moss, Newton, Parsons, Philips, Powel, Quick, Ray, Rees, Saunders, Shuter, Simmons, H. Sparks, I. Sparks, Stoppelaer, Suett, Vandermere, H. Vaughan, W. Vaughan, F. G. Waldron, G. Waldron, Wathen, Wewitzer, R. Yates.

Gregory (R & J). See Arthur, Bennet, Cushing, Evans, Hamilton, Holtom, Mozeen, Paddick, R. Smith, W. Vaughan, G. Waldron, Wrighten.

Gregory (Tam. Shrew). In Garrick's alteration (C & P), see Chippendale, Lyons, Maddocks.

Grey (Hen. V). See Bland, Lamash, Redman.

Grumio (Tam. Shrew). In Garrick's alteration (C & P), see Baddeley, Costollo, Everard, Follett, Hamilton, Hollingsworth, Munden, Newton, Quick, Shuter, Suett, Wathen, Wewitzer, R. Wilson, R. Yates.

Guiderius (Cymbeline). See F. Aickin, Barrymore, Bensley, Brereton, Cautherley, Du-Bellamy, Farren, Garland, Harley, J. Jackson, H. E. Johnston, Keen, C. Kemble, Macready, Obrien, R. Palmer, Whitfield, Wroughton. In Hawkins' alteration this character named Palador. See Wm. Smith (d. 1819).

Guildenstern (Hamlet). See Ackman, Austin, C. J. Booth, Bransby, Castle, Chambers, Claremont, Dancer, W. Davies, T. Davis, W. Egan Sr., J. Fawcett Sr., Jefferson, Kearny, Kenny, Lamash, Lewes, Macready, J. Palmer Jr., Perry, Phillimore, Scrase, Strange, J. Thompson, Trueman, Usher, White, J. Wignell, Williames.

Guildford (Hen. VIII). See Bland, Cushing, Lamash, Marr, S. T. Russell, R. Smith.

Gurney (John). See Chippendale, Lyons, W. Vaughan, Watkins, J. Welsh.

Guzzle, Toby. In Bullock's alteration of the Induction to Tam. Shrew (Cobler) the name given to Christopher Sly, q.v.

Haberdasher (Tam. Shrew). In Garrick's alteration (C & P), see J. Besford, Mrs James Jones, Newton, Miss Palmer [i.e. later Mrs James Jones].

Hacket, Dame. In Bullock's alteration of the Induction to Tam. Shrew (Cobler) the name given to the Hostess, q.v.

Hamlet (Hamlet). See John Bannister, S. Barry, Browne, J. Brunton Sr., J. Brunton Jr., Cautherley, Cooper, C. Fleetwood, Garrick, Goodfellow, L. Hallam Jr., Henderson, C. Holland the elder, Holman, H. E. Johnston, J. P. Kemble, Lacey, W. Lacy, J. Lee, W. T. Lewis, Lloyd (fl. 1789), Melmoth, Mossop, Murphy, J. Palmer the younger, Pope, W. Powell, Mrs W. Powell, Reddish, Ross, Seymour, Sheridan, Wm. Smith (d. 1819), West, J. B. Williamson, Wroughton.

INDEX II

Harfleur, Governor of (Hen. V). *See* R. Bates, W. Gardner, Hollingsworth, Redman.

Hastings (2 Hen. IV). *See* Ackman, Anderson, G. L. Barrett, Bennet, Wrighten.

Hecate (Macbeth). *See* Arthur, C. Bannister, Barnshaw, Beard, E. Berry, Bowden, Champnes, Cubitt, Darley, W. Davies, Legg, Reinhold, Richardson, Sedgwick, Townsend, Vernon, Mrs Webb, J. Wignell, Williames, Winstone.

Helen (Cymbeline). *See* Mrs Crossman, Mrs Hippisley, Miss Leserve, Miss Mills (fl. 1800), Miss T. Mills, Miss Pearce, Mrs Poussin, Mrs T. Smith, Miss Stuart, Mrs Watts, Mrs West.

Helena (All's Well). *See* Miss E. Farren, Mrs Jordan, Miss Macklin, Mrs J. Palmer the elder.

Helena (MND). *See* Mrs R. Vincent Jr. In Garrick's alteration (Fairies), *see* Miss Poitier.

Henry IV (1 Hen. IV). *See* F. Aickin, J Aickin, C. Bannister, Bensley, M. Clarke, T. Davies, Gibson, Harley, Havard, Hull, L'Estrange, Murray, L. Sparks, J. B. Williamson, Wroughton, Younger.

Henry IV (2 Hen. IV). *See* F. Aickin, Bensley, Carey, Garrick, Gibson, W. Powell, L. Sparks.

Henry V (Hen. V). *See* S. Barry, Hull, J. P. Kemble, Wm. Smith (d. 1819), Wroughton.

Henry VI (Cibber's Rich. III). A character not in the original play. *See* F. Aickin, J Aickin, Alfred, C. Bannister, Bensley, E. Berry, Blakes, Bridgwater, Burnett, E. Burton, M. Clarke, Comerford, W. Gardner, Gibson, A. Hallam, Harley, Havard, Horwell, Hull, Hunter, Kniveton, Leach, Lucas, Moody, Murray, Newton, W. Powell, Reddish, Ridout, Ryan, Scrase, L. Sparks, Wroughton, Younger.

Henry VIII (Hen. VIII). *See* F. Aickin, E. Berry, C. J. Booth, Bransby, M. Clarke, Fotteral, Holman, Moody, J. Palmer the younger, R. Palmer [III. ii only], Quin, Sowdon, Usher.

Henry, Prince (John). *See* W. Bates, Miss Besford, Bland, J. Burton, Cautherley, DeCamp, Everard, Miss S. Francis, C. Kemble, Knowles, Lewes, Miss Morrison, R. Palmer, R. Smith, Mrs Toogood, Young.

Herald (Coriolanus). *See* White.

Herald (Lear). *See* Banks, J. Cooke, Holtom.

Herald, English (Hen. V). *See* A. Hallam, Weller.

Herald, English (John). *See* Farrell, Moody, Scrase, Surmont, Trueman, A. Webb, R. Wright.

Herald, French (John). *See* Ackman, Chaplin, J. Cooke, Saunders.

Hermia (MND). *See* Miss I. Young. In Garrick's alteration (Fairies), *see* Sig. Passerini.

Hermione (Wint. T.). *See* Miss E. Farren, Mrs Hartley, Mrs Hopkins, Mrs Inchbald, Mrs Mattocks, Mrs Melmoth, Mrs A. Pope the 1st, Mrs Pritchard, Mrs T. A. Ward, Mrs Wells, Mrs R. Yates the 2nd.

Hero (Much Ado). *See* Mrs Baddeley, Mrs Brereton [i.e. later Mrs J. P. Kemble], Mrs Canning, Miss Chapman, Miss Cleland, Mrs T. Davies, Miss DeCamp, Miss Hayward, Miss Heard, Miss E. Hopkins [i.e. later Mrs Sharp], Mrs Inchbald, Mrs J. P. Kemble, Mrs S. G. Kemble, Miss Leak, Mrs Lessingham, Miss Mansell, Miss Mellon, Mrs W. Mills, Mrs Morland, Mrs Mountain, Miss Plym, Mrs Sharp, Mrs H. Ward, Mrs Willoughby, Miss Woollery.

Hippolito (Kemble's Tempest). A character not in the original play (introduced by Kemble from Dryden and Davenant's version). *See* Miss Collins, Miss De Camp, Mrs Goodall, Miss Heard, Mrs W. Powell, Mrs Williames.

Hippolyta (MND). *See* Mrs Hopkins. In Garrick's alteration (Fairies), *see* Mrs T. Jefferson the 1st.

Horatio (Hamlet). *See* J. Aickin, G. L. Barrett, Barrymore, Betterton, W. Davies, Du-Bellamy, Egerton, Farren, W. Gardner, Harley, Havard, C. Holland the younger, Hull, J. Johnson, Macready, Packer, J. Palmer the elder, Ridout, J. Smith, Staunton, Toms, Whitfield, Wood.

Hortensio [*see also* Music Master] (Tam. Shrew). In Garrick's alteration (C & P), *see* James Bannister, Benson, Bland, Claremont, G. F. Cooke, T. Davis, W. Egan Jr., Evatt, Helme, Keen, Lanc, Miller, Mozeen, Norris, Owenson, R. Palmer, Robson, Trueman, Wentworth, Wheeler, J. Wilson, Young.

Hortensius (Timon). *See* J. Griffith.

Host (MWW). *See* Anderson, C. Bannister, C. J. Booth, Bransby, Dunstall, Marten, Massey (of Hay), Moody, Philips, J. Thompson, W. Vaughan.

Host (TGV). *See* C. J. Booth, J. Fawcett Sr., Moody.

Hostess (1 Hen. IV). *See* Mrs Bradshaw, Mrs Davenport, Mrs Fowler, Mrs

784

INDEX II

Hopkins, Mrs Love, Mrs Macklin, Mrs Pitt, Mrs Platt, Mrs Walcot, Mrs Webb.
Hostess (2 Hen. IV). *See* Mrs Bambridge, Mrs Bradshaw, Mrs Macklin, Mrs Pitt. In the anonymous alteration (Humourists), *see* Mrs R. Cross.
Hostess (Hen. V). *See* Mrs Booth, Mrs Macklin, Mrs Pitt.
Hostess (Tam. Shrew). In Bullock's alteration of the Induction (Cobler) this character named Dame Hacket. *See* Mrs Pitt.
Hotspur (1 Hen. IV). *See* J. Aickin, S. Barry, Bensley, M. Clarke, Farren, Fennell, C. Holland the elder, Holman, C. Kemble, J. P. Kemble, Peile, Pope, Walter Smith, Wm. Smith (d. 1819), West, Whitfield, Wroughton.
Hotspur's Servant (1 Hen. IV). *See* Curties
Hubert (John). *See* F. Aickin, Barrymore, Bensley, E. Berry, Bridgwater, F. Gentleman, Gibson, Havard, Hull, Ridout, L. Sparks.
Humphrey, Prince (2 Hen. IV). *See* T. Baker the elder, Benson, Miss Besford, J. Burton, Cautherley, Mrs Colles, Miss M. Francis, Miss Painter, Perry, Miss Plym, Miss Rogers.
Hymen (Tempest). A character not in the original play (at DL from 1757–63 and 1765–76 included in a revised version of the Masque in IV. i). *See* Beard, J. Fawcett Sr., Kear, T. Lowe, Wingfield Palmer.

Iachimo (Cymbeline). *See* Bensley, Daly, Farren, C. Holland the elder, Jefferson, J. Palmer the younger, Pope, Wm. Smith (d. 1819), Wroughton. In Hawkins' alteration this character named Pisanio. *See* Dyer.
Iago (Othello). *See* Bensley, Cibber, G. F. Cooke, Cory, J. H. Delaval, Garrick, Harley, Havard, Henderson, Henry, C. Holland the elder, T. King, J. Lee, E. (?) Lloyd (?), Macklin, Montgomery, Murray, J. Palmer the younger, Quin, Reddish, Ryan, T. Ryder, Wm. Smith (d. 1819), Sowdon, L. Sparks, Storer, J. Wignell, Wilkinson (fl. 1792).
Imogen (Cymbeline). *See* Mrs Baddeley, Mrs S. Barry [i.e. later Mrs Crawford], Miss Bride, Mrs Bulkley, Mrs Crawford, Miss D'Arcy, Miss Jones, Mrs Jordan, Miss E. Kemble, Mrs Lessingham, Mrs Massey, Mrs J. Mills, Mrs J. Palmer the elder, Miss Plym, Mrs A. Pope the 1st, Mrs A. Pope the 2nd, Mrs T. Robinson, Mrs Siddons, Mrs W. P. Taylor, Mrs R. Vincent Sr., Miss Wallis, Mrs Wells,

Mrs Worthington, Mrs R. Yates the 2nd, Miss Younge [i.e. later Mrs A. Pope the 1st].
Iras (A & C). *See* Miss T. Mills.
Isabel (Hen. V). *See* Mrs Bambridge, Mrs Hopkins, Mrs Poussin, Mrs W. Powell, Mrs Stephens, Mrs R. Vincent Sr., Mrs T. A. Ward.
Isabella (Measure). *See* Mrs Bellamy, Mrs Cibber, Mrs Jackson, Mrs Pritchard, Miss Pritchard, Mrs Siddons, Mrs R. Yates the 2nd.

Jailer (Merchant). *See* H. Sparks.
Jamy (Hen. V). *See* Dunstall, W. Egan Sr.
Jaques (AYLI). *See* F. Aickin, C. Bannister, S. Barry, Bensley, E. Berry, E. Burton, M. Clarke, Harley, Henderson, Jefferson, J. P. Kemble, J. Lee, Love, J. Palmer the younger, L. Sparks, West, Wroughton.
Jaques de Bois (AYLI). *See* Benson, J. Fawcett Sr., Fox, C. Holland the younger, Holtom, C. Kemble, Lamash, Lyons, Perry, Simson (d. 1758).
Jaquez. In Kemble's alteration of All's Well the name given to the 2nd Gentleman, q.v.
Jessica (Merchant). *See* Mrs Abegg, Mrs Atkins, Mrs Baddeley, Mrs Baker (d. 1760), Mrs T. Baker, Mrs Bland the younger, Mrs Burden, Mrs Chambers (d. 1792), Miss Collins, Miss Dayes [i.e. later Mrs Morton], Miss Dixon, Mrs Forster, Mrs Granger, Miss Heard, Mrs Hippisley, Mrs Hitchcock, Miss Jarratt, Mrs Mattocks, Miss E. Miller [i.e. later Mrs T. Baker], Miss Minors, Mrs Moore, Mrs Morton, Mrs Mountain, Miss Mullart, Mrs Nost, Miss Radley, Mrs Ridout, Miss Rogers, Mrs M. Taylor, Miss Valois, Miss Walpole, Miss Wheeler, Mrs Wilks, Mrs S. M. Wilson.
Jeweller (Timon). *See* W. Gardner, R. Wright.
John, Don (Much Ado). *See* F. Aickin, J. Aickin, C. J. Booth, Bransby, Campbell, Caulfield, Cubitt, T. Davies, J. Lee, Richardson, Usher, Waddy, Winstone.
John, Friar (R & J). *See* Abbot, R. Bates, Clough, Jefferson, Keen, Maddocks, Nelson, Paddick, J. Thompson, J. Wignell.
John, King (John). *See* Henderson, J. P. Kemble, Mossop, W. Powell, Quin, Reddish, Ross, Sheridan, L. Sparks.
John, Prince (1 Hen. IV). *See* Benson, Bland, Miss Bride, J. Burton, Miss Cokayne, Curties, Miss DeCamp, Farley, Miss Granger, Gregson, Harris, Mrs

INDEX II

Hippisley, C. Holland the younger, Lamash, Miss Mullart, Miss Valois, Young.

John, Prince (2 Hen. IV). *See* Brereton, T. Davis, Farren, Miss S. Francis [IV. v and V. ii only], Lamash, J. Lee, J. Palmer the younger, Ridout, Usher.

Joseph (Tam. Shrew). In Garrick's alteration (C & P), *see* P. Lewis, A. Webb.

Julia (TGV). *See* Mrs Goodall, Mrs Mattocks, Mrs R. Yates the 2nd.

Juliet (Measure). *See* Miss Barnes, Mrs Colles, Miss Garman, Miss Ogilvie, Mrs Platt, Miss Stuart, Mrs Whitfield.

Juliet (R & J). *See* Mrs Achmet, Miss Allingham, Mrs S. Barry, Mrs W. Barry, Mrs Bellamy, Miss Bride, Miss Brunton [i.e. later Mrs Merry], Mrs Cargill [V. iii only], Mrs Chambers (d. 1804), Mrs Cibber, Mrs Dancer [i.e. later Mrs S. Barry], Mrs Dawes, Miss Dayes, Mrs Esten, Mrs Farmer, Miss E. Farren, Miss E. Glassington, Miss Hallam, Mrs Hartley, Miss Haughton, Mrs Higginson, Miss E. Hopkins, Mrs Jackson, Mrs Jordan, Mrs S. G. Kemble, Mrs Kingham, Mrs Lessingham, Miss Macklin, Miss Mansell, Mrs Merry, Miss Miller (fl. 1770–4), Miss A. Miller, Mrs Morland, Miss Morris (d. 1769), Miss Mowat, Miss Murray, Miss Nossiter, Mrs O'Keeffe, Mrs J. Palmer the elder, Mrs A. Pope the 2nd, Miss Pritchard [i.e. later Mrs J. Palmer the elder], Mrs T. Robinson, Miss Satchell [i.e. later Mrs S. G. Kemble], Mrs Siddons, Mrs Spencer [i.e. later Mrs A. Pope the 2nd], Mrs Sterne, Mrs Twistleton, Miss Wallis, Miss Ward, Mrs H. Ward, Miss Younge.

Julio. In Kemble's adaptation of Othello the name given to the 2nd Gentleman, q.v.

Juno (Tempest). *See* Miss Dayes [i.e. later Mrs Morton], Mrs Morton.

Katharina (Tam. Shrew). In Garrick's alteration (C & P) this character named Catharine. *See* Mrs Abington, Mrs Bates, Miss Chapman, Mrs Clive, Mrs Crawford, Miss DeCamp, Mrs DuBellamy, Mrs D. Fisher, Mrs Gardner, Mrs Gibbs, Mrs Goodall, Mrs H. Green, Mrs Gregory, Mrs J. Hamilton, Mrs Jefferies, Mrs Johnson, Mrs Love, Mrs Mattocks, Mrs Nost, Miss Pope, Mrs A. Pope the 1st, Mrs Pritchard, Mrs Russell, Mrs Siddons, Mrs R. Vincent Sr., Miss Wallis, Mrs West, Mrs Wrighten.

Katharine (Hen. V). *See* Mrs Bellamy, Miss Collins, Miss DeCamp, Mrs Dyer, Mrs Goodall, Miss Hallam [i.e. later Mrs Mattocks], Mrs J. Hamilton, Mrs Mattocks, Mrs R. Vincent Sr., Mrs Whitfield.

Katharine, Queen (Hen. VIII). *See* Mrs Hartley, Mrs Jackson, Mrs Massey, Mrs A. Pope the 1st, Mrs A. Pope the 2nd, Mrs Pritchard, Miss L. Reynolds, Mrs Siddons, Mrs Woffington, Miss Younge [i.e. later Mrs A. Pope the 1st].

Kent (Lear). *See* F. Aickin, J. Aickin, Bransby, E. Burton, M. Clarke, Fearon, W. Gardner, Harley, Hurst, Massey (of CH), D. Morris, J. Palmer the younger, Parsons, L. Sparks, Waddy, Walker, Winstone.

King (All's Well). *See* Bensley, T. Davies, W. Gardner, Havard, Hull, Walker.

King (Hamlet). *See* Anderson, C. Bannister, Benson, W. Bridges, Caulfield, M. Clarke, T. Davies, Fearon, W. Gardner, Gibson, Hull, Hurst, Jefferson, S. G. Kemble, Love, Packer, Powel, Richardson, L. Sparks, Stokes, Waddy, Walker, Winstone, Younger.

King, Player (Hamlet). *See* Blissett, C. J. Booth, Bransby, E. Burton, Chambers, Chaplin, Davenport, Farrell, W. Gardner, Griffiths, Hurst, Keen, L'Estrange, P. Lewis, Maddocks, Mahon, Moody, Redman, J. Thompson, Usher, Vandermere, J. Wignell.

Knight (Lear). *See* Caulfield, Maddocks, Phillimore, J. Welsh.

Lady, Old (Hen. VIII). *See* Mrs Bambridge, Mrs Booth, Mrs Bradshaw, Mrs James, Mrs Love, Mrs Pitt, Mrs Ross.

Lady of the Bedchamber (Hen. VIII). *See* Miss C. Reynolds.

Laertes (Hamlet). *See* F. Aickin, J. Aickin, Austin, T. Baker the younger, Barrymore, Betterton, Blakes, Brereton, W. Davies, T. Davis, Dyer, Fennell, Gibson, Harley, Iliff, C. Kemble, L. Kennedy, J. Lee, Macready, Middleton, Obrien, J. Palmer Jr., R. Palmer, Perry, S. Russell, Wheatley, Whitfield, Wroughton, Young.

Lafeu (All's Well). *See* J. Aickin, Baddeley, E. Berry, E. Burton, M. Clarke, Gibson.

Lartius (Coriolanus). *See* Simson (d. 1758).

Launce (TGV). *See* Dodd, Quick, R. Yates.

Launcelot (Merchant). *See* Arthur, John Bannister, Barrington, Bennet, J. Burton, W. Collins, Dunstall, J. Edwin Sr., Everard, Graham (fl. 1771–7), Gull, Hamilton, Hartry, Jacobs, Moss, Munden, Wingfield Palmer, Parsons, Quick,

INDEX II

Shuter, Suett, H. Vaughan, Vernon, Wingfield [i.e. Wingfield Palmer], Woodward, R. Wright.

Laurence, Friar (R & J). *See* J. Aickin, Burnett, E. Burton, Clough, W. Gardner, Havard, Hull, Hurst, Leach, Love, Murray, Packer, Ridout, Young.

Lear (Lear). *See* S. Barry, Bludrick, Digges, Everard, Farren, Garrick, Giffard, Harley, Henderson, J. P. Kemble, J. Lee, Murray, Pope, W. Powell, Ross, Rundell, Wroughton.

Le Beau (AYLI). *See* Ackman, Banks, W. Bates, Benson, C. J. Booth, T. Davis, Everard, Farren, Lamash, McGeorge, Macready, R. Palmer, Wm. Palmer, Phillimore, Reily, S. T. Russell, Scrase, Surmont, White, R. Wright.

Lennox (Macbeth). *See* Ackman, Adcock, Benson, Campbell, Cubitt, W. Davies, W. Egan Sr., J. Fawcett Sr., Gibbon, Grist, Hull, L'Estrange, Mahon, Norris, Parsons, Perry, Phillimore, Redman, Ridout, Scrase, Surmont, Trueman, Whitfield.

Leonardo (Merchant). *See* Alfred, J. Cooke, Evans, Lyons, Painter.

Leonato (Much Ado). *See* F. Aickin, J. Aickin, Bensley, E. Berry, T. Davies, Havard, Hull, Hurst, Jefferson, S. G. Kemble.

Leonatus. In Hawkins' alteration of Cymbeline the name given to Posthumus, q.v.

Leontes (Wint. T.). *See* Garrick, Harley, Henderson, Melmoth, Pope, W. Powell, Wm. Smith (d. 1819), Wroughton. In Colman's alteration (Sheep S.), *see* Fearon, J. B. Williamson.

Lepidus (A & C). *See* Blakes.

Lepidus (J. Caesar). *See* Bencraft, Buck, Lings, D. Morris.

Lesbia. In Hull's two alterations of Com. Err. the name given to the Courtezan, q.v.

Lewis. In Kemble's alteration of All's Well the name given to the 2nd Lord, q.v.

Lieutenant (Coriolanus). *See* Scrase.

Lieutenant [of the Tower] (Cibber's Rich. III). *See* Benson, Burnett, Carpenter, Claremont, Cubitt, Cushing, J. Fawcett Sr., Fox, W. Gardner, Haymes, Jefferson, Kearny, Kenrick, L'Estrange, Lings, Mahon, Moody, A. Morris, Mozeen, Newton, R. Palmer, Ray, Ricard, R. Smith, Wm. Smith (fl. 1776), Usher, Vowell, Waddy, White. At DL 1790–1800 and at Hay 1793–4 this character named, as in the original, Brackenbury, q.v.

Ligarius (J. Caesar). *See* Holtom, Usher.

Lion (MND). In Lampe's alteration (P & T), *see* S. Howard.

Lodovico (Othello). *See* Anderson, Blakes, C. J. Booth, Caulfield, Cubitt, W. Davies, W. Egan Sr., W. Gardner, J. Griffith, Hurst, King (fl. 1792), Metteer, D. Morris, Owenson, Packer, Pine, Strange, Tindal, Toms, Usher, Vandermere, Vowell, A. Webb, Whitfield, J. Wignell, Wooller.

Lord (All's Well). *See* Bransby, Cushing, T. Davis, Fox, W. Gardner, Mozeen, Walker, White. In Kemble's alteration the 1st Lord is named Dumain: *see* Whitfield; the 2nd is named Lewis: *see* C. Kemble.

Lord (AYLI). *See* Evans, Norris, H. Sparks, A. Webb.

Lord (Cymbeline). *See* Abbot, Campbell, Claremont, Curties, Dancer, Davenport, Evatt, Ledger, J. Smith, W. Stevens.

Lord Chief Justice (2 Hen. IV). *See* J. Aickin, Anderson, Bransby, W. Gardner [V. ii only], Gibson, Hull, L. Sparks, Younger.

Lord Mayor (Rich. III). *See* Ackman, Baddeley, R. Bates, Bowles, Buck, J. Burton, Chambers, Chaplin, Chapman, Cushing, Dowton, Fildew, Francis, W. Gardner, Griffiths, Hartry, Helme, Hollingsworth, P. Lewis, Maddocks, Marten, Massey (of CH), Massey (of Hay), Molbery, D. Morris, Philips, Phillimore, Powel, Reeve, Sharpless, I. Sparks, Staunton, J. Thompson, R. Webb, Wewitzer, J. Wignell, Wrighten.

Lorenzo (Merchant). *See* Beard, Bradney, Chapman, J. W. Clarke, Dancer, W. Davies, Dignum, Dodd, Du-Bellamy, J. Hill, J. Johnson, Johnstone, Kenny, T. Lowe, Mattocks, Moody, Tanner, Townsend, Trueman, Vernon, Williames.

Lovell (Hen. VIII). *See* Ackman, Chalmers, T. Davis, Dignum, Farley, J. Fawcett Sr., Holtom, W. Stevens.

Luce (Com. Err.). In Hull's alteration (Twins) this character named Bridget. *See* Mrs Copin.

Lucetta (TGV). *See* Mrs Chalmers, Miss Pope, Miss Tidswell, Mrs J. Wilson.

Luciana (Com. Err.). *See* Mrs Esten, Mrs Fawcett, Mrs T. Kennedy, Mrs Lessingham, Mrs Mountain, Miss Rowson, Mrs Whitfield.

Lucianus (Hamlet). *See* J. Barrett, Blissett, R. E. Chatterley, W. Collins, Cubitt, Cushing, Davenport, Dunstall, Fox, Hartry, Hollingsworth, Jacobs, James, Morgan, Parsons, C. Ryder, Shuter,

INDEX II

H. Sparks, W. Stevens, Summers, F. G. Waldron, Wathen, Weller, Weston, Wewitzer, Wilde, J. Wilson.

Lucilius (J. Caesar). *See* Buck, Murden.

Lucilius (Timon). *See* Wheeler.

Lucio (Measure). *See* John Bannister, T. King, Lewes, Obrien, R. Palmer, Woodward, R. Yates.

Lucius (Cymbeline). *See* Bransby, Cubitt, W. Davies, Denman, Fearon, W. Gardner, Gibson, P. Lewis, Mahon, Mansel, Phillimore, Usher, Wrighten.

Lucius (J. Caesar). *See* S. Besford, Miss Mullart, Pulley.

Lucius (Timon). *See* J. Palmer the younger, Wewitzer.

Lucullus (Timon). *See* Hurst, Quick.

Lucullus's Servant (Timon). *See* Lings.

Lysander (MND). *See* Vernon. In Garrick's alteration (Fairies), *see* Guadagni.

Macbeth (Macbeth). *See* F. Aickin, S. Barry, Betterton, Cambray, G. F. Cooke, Cooper, Digges, Garrick, Harley, Henderson, C. Holland the elder, Holman, J. P. Kemble, Macklin, Mossop, Murphy, J. Palmer the younger, W. Powell, Quin, Reddish, Ross, Seymour, Sheridan, Wm. Smith (d. 1819), Turner (fl. 1798).

Macbeth, Lady (Macbeth). *See* Mrs S. Barry [i.e. later Mrs Crawford], Mrs Bates, Mrs Bellamy, Miss Betterton, Mrs Cibber, Mrs Crawford, Mrs Dancer [i.e. later (1) Mrs S. Barry, (2) Mrs Crawford], Mrs Gordon, Mrs Gregory, Mrs J. Hamilton, Mrs Hartley, Mrs Jackson, Mrs Johnson, Mrs King, Mrs Litchfield, Mrs Massey, Mrs Melmoth, Mrs J. Palmer the elder, Mrs A. Pope the 1st, Mrs W. Powell, Mrs Pritchard, Mrs T. Robinson, Mrs Sage, Miss Sherry, Mrs Siddons, Mrs H. Ward, Mrs Woffington, Mrs R. Yates the 2nd, Miss Younge [i.e. later Mrs A. Pope the 1st].

Macbeth's Servant (Macbeth). *See* Holtom, Ledger.

Macduff (Macbeth). *See* F. Aickin, J. Aickin, Barrymore, Brereton, M. Clarke, Dyer, Farren, Havard, Hull, Hurst, J. P. Kemble, Lacey, Middleton, J. Palmer the younger, Peile, Pope, Reddish, Ross, Ryan, Tindal, Whitfield, Wroughton.

Macduff, Lady (Macbeth). *See* Miss Ambrose, Mrs Barrington, Mrs Bennet, Mrs Burden, Mrs Cowper, Mrs Glen, Mrs Hopkins, Mrs T. Jefferson the 1st, Mrs W. Mills, Mrs Platt, Mrs Reddish, Mrs Sharp, Miss Sherry.

Macmorris (Hen. V). *See* Barrington, W. Egan Sr., Fox, Mahon.

Malcolm (Macbeth). *See* Anderson, Austin, Barrymore [read by], J. Bates, Blakes, Bland, Casey, Cautherley, Claremont, J. W Clarke, W. Davies, T. Davis, J. Jackson, C. Kemble, Lacey, Macready, Mansel, Middleton, Owenson, Packer, J. Palmer Jr., R. Palmer, Perry, Scrase, Seymour, Usher, T. A. Ward, Whitfield, Wroughton.

Malvolio (Twelfth N.). *See* John Bannister, Bensley, Dowton, Henderson, Holcroft, J. P. Kemble, T. King, R. Wilson, R. Yates.

Mamillius (Wint. T.). *See* Miss Cokayne.

Man, Old (Lear). *See* Baddeley, J. Burton, Farrell, A. Hallam, Hartry, Hollingsworth, P. Lewis, Rees, F. G. Waldron.

Marcellus (Hamlet). *See* Ackman, Anderson, W. Bates, Benson, C. J. Booth, Bransby, Claremont, Davenport, T. Davis, Dignum, Evatt, Fearon, W. Gardner, C. Holland the younger, Lyons, Powel, Reeve, Reily, Surmont, Swords, J. Thompson, Wheeler, D. Williamson, J. Wilson, Wrighten.

Marcius, Young (Coriolanus). *See* W. S. Chatterley, Grimaldi, J. Simson, Wells.

Mardian (A & C). *See* Perry.

Margaret (Much Ado). *See* Mrs Bradshaw, Miss Brangin, Mrs Davenett, Mrs Gaudry, Mrs Havard, Miss Leserve, Mrs Pitt, Mrs Platt, Mrs Shaw, Miss Tidswell, Miss Valois, Mrs Whitfield, Mrs R. Yates the 1st.

Maria (Twelfth N.). *See* Mrs Brereton [i.e. later Mrs J. P. Kemble], Miss Collins, Mrs Egerton, Mrs Gardner, Mrs H. Green, Mrs Hopkins, Miss P. Hopkins [i.e. later (1) Mrs Brereton, (2) Mrs J. P. Kemble], Mrs J. P. Kemble, Miss Kirby, Mrs Lee, Miss Mellon, Miss Minors, Miss Tidswell, Mrs S. M. Wilson.

Mariana (All's Well). *See* Mrs Ferguson, Mrs S. Smith, Miss Tidswell.

Mariana (Measure). *See* Mrs Bennet, Mrs Bulkley, Mrs Goodall, Miss Heard, Miss E. Hopkins [i.e. later Mrs Sharp], Mrs Inchbald, Mrs Kniveton, Miss Leeson [i.e. later Mrs W. T. Lewis], Mrs W. T. Lewis, Miss Ogilvie, Mrs W. Powell, Mrs Sharp, Mrs T. A. Ward.

Mariner (Wint. T.). *See* R. Bates.

Mecaenas (A & C). *See* Atkins (fl. 1751–60).

Melissa (Hull's Timon). A character not in the original play (introduced by Hull from Shadwell's version). *See* Mrs Inchbald.

Menas (A & C). *See* E. Burton, Clough.

Menenius (Coriolanus). *See* Baddeley, Benson, E. Berry, R. Palmer, Shuter.

INDEX II

Merchant (Com. Err.). *See* Evatt, Holtom, Robson, R. Smith, J. Thompson.

Merchant (Timon). *See* J. Fawcett Sr.

Mercutio (R & J). *See* John Bannister, Dodd, Dyer, Garrick, S. Jerrold, W. T. Lewis, Macklin, Marriot, J. Palmer the elder, J. Palmer the younger, S. Russell, Shuter, Woodward.

Messenger (Hamlet). *See* Alfred, Chippendale, Evans, R. Wright.

Messenger (1 Hen. IV). *See* Abbot, Banks, Dyke, Evans, Fox.

Messenger (John). *See* Norris.

Messenger (Lear). *See* J. Fawcett Sr.

Messenger (Macbeth). *See* Banks, Evans.

Messenger (Much Ado). *See* Lamash.

Messenger (Othello). *See* Ackman, Bland, Chaplin, Holtom, McGeorge, Strange, Wheeler, Whitfield. In Kemble's adaptation this character named Antonio. *See* Caulfield, Gibbon.

Messenger (Timon). *See* Follett, Watkins.

Metellus (J. Caesar). *See* Bransby, Cushing, Kearny, G. A. Stevens, Williames.

Minucius (Sheridan's Coriolanus). A character not in the original play. *See* Anderson, Perry.

Miranda (Tempest). *See* Mrs Baddeley, Miss Bannister, Miss Brown, Miss Collins, Mrs Crouch, Mrs Cuyler, Miss A. Miller, Mrs J. Palmer the elder, Miss Phillips [i.e. later Mrs Crouch], Mrs W. Powell, Miss Pritchard [i.e. later Mrs J. Palmer the elder], Miss Rogers, Mrs T. Smith, Mrs Vernon, Miss Younge.

Montague (R & J). *See* T. Baker the elder, Bridgwater, E. Burton, Chaplin, Davenport, W. Egan Sr., J. Fawcett Sr., Hurst, Keen, Massey (of Hay) [V. iii only], Moody, Murden, Phillimore, Redman, Scrase, Simson (d. 1758), J. Thompson, Usher, R. Wright.

Montano (Othello). *See* F. Aickin, J. Aickin, Benson, Bransby, Campbell, Claremont, J. W. Clarke, J. Collins, W. Davies, T. Davis, DeCamp, Fox, Freeman (?), C. Holland the younger, Lewes, Mahon, T. Marshall, Moss, Mozeen, Norris, J. Palmer the younger, J. Palmer Jr., R. Palmer, Parker, Reily, Robson, E. (?) Thompson, J. Thompson, Trotter, Turner (fl. 1761-78), Wheeler, White, Whitfield.

Montjoy (Hen. V). *See* T. Baker the elder, Caulfield, Haymes.

Moonshine (MND). In Lampe's alteration (P & T), *see* E. Roberts.

Mopsa (Wint. T.). *See* Miss Barnes, Mrs Bradshaw, Mrs Castelle, Mrs Harlowe, Miss Kirby, Mrs Martyr, Miss Rowson,

Miss I. Young. In Morgan's alteration (F & P), *see* Mrs Byrne, Mrs Castelle, Miss Helme, Mrs Lampe, Miss Esther Young. In Colman's alteration (Sheep S.), *see* Mrs Hitchcock, Miss C. Morris.

Morocco (Merchant). *See* E. Burton.

Mortimer (1 Hen. IV). *See* Adcock, Castle, Dyer, Lewes.

Mouldy (2 Hen. IV). *See* Bencraft, Buck, W. Gardner, Moody. In the anonymous alteration (Humourists), *see* W. Vaughan.

Mowbray (2 Hen. IV). *See* W. Davies, Hurst, D. Morris, Redman, G. A. Stevens, Tindal.

Murderer (Macbeth). *See* Abbot, Bencraft, Buck, Claremont, Holtom, J. N. Lee, Marten, Phillimore, Redman, Rees, Stoppelaer, A. Webb, Wentworth.

Music Master. In Garrick's alteration of Tam. Shrew (C & P) a new character; in II. i. 144-60 he has Hortensio's speeches. *See* Abbot, Banks, J. Barrett, Brundson, Courtney, J. Edwin Jr., Evatt, J. Fawcett Sr., Fox, Jacobs, Jefferson, H. Lee, Lings, Massey (of CH), Newton, J. Palmer Jr., C. S. Powell, Rees, H. Sparks, W. Stevens, G. Waldron.

Mustacho (Garrick's Tempest). A character not in the original play (introduced by Garrick from Dryden and Davenant's version). *See* Champnes.

Mustardseed (MND). *See* R. Palmer.

Nathaniel (Tam. Shrew). In Garrick's alteration (C & P), *see* Abbot, J. Cooke, Ledger, Lyons, W. Vaughan, A. Webb.

Neptune (Kemble's Tempest). A character not in the original play (introduced by Kemble from Dryden and Davenant's version). *See* Caulfield, Sedgwick, Shaw.

Nerissa (Merchant). *See* Miss Ambrose, Mrs T. Baker, Mrs Barrington, Mrs Bates, Mrs Bennet, Miss Chapman, Miss Chatterley, Mrs Collet, Miss Collett, Miss Collins, Mrs W. Davies, Miss De Camp, Miss Fontenelle, Mrs Goodall, Mrs Harlowe, Miss Heard, Mrs Hunter, Mrs Inchbald, Mrs Jefferies, Mrs Lessingham, Mrs Litchfield, Miss Logan, Miss Mansel, Miss Painter [IV. i only], Mrs Simmons, Miss Sims, Miss Taylor, Mrs Townsend, Mrs R. Vincent Sr., Mrs J. Wilson, Mrs S. M. Wilson.

Nicholas (Tam. Shrew). In Garrick's alteration (C & P), *see* Atkins (fl. 1751-60), Banks.

Nicholas (Wint. T.). At CG in 1787 and 1788 the name given to the Gentleman, q.v.

Norfolk (Hen. VIII). *See* Comerford,

INDEX II

T. Davis, Fearon, Harley, J. Palmer the elder, Peile, Perry, L. Sparks, Usher, Whitfield.

Norfolk (Rich. III). *See* Abbot, Bencraft, Blakes, Bonnor, C. J. Booth, Bowles, Bransby, Buck, E. Burton, Buxton, Chalmers, Davenport, Dignum, Evatt, Farrell, J. Fawcett Sr., Fox, Gibson, Griffiths, C. Holland the younger, Hurst, Lewes, Macready, Massey (of Hay), Neale, Owenson, Perry, Richardson, Seaton, Usher, Whitfield, J. Wignell, Williames, Wood.

Northumberland (1 Hen. IV). *See* Abbot, E. Burton, Chapman, Davenport, W. Gardner, J. Johnson, S. Johnson, Kenny, Packer, Redman, Scrase, R. Webb.

Nurse (R & J). *See* Mrs Adcock, Mrs Booth, Mrs Bradshaw, Mrs Copin, Mrs R. Cross, Mrs Davenport, Mrs Gardner, Mrs H. Green, Mrs Hopkins, Mrs James, Mrs L. Kennedy, Mrs Leicester, Mrs Love, Mrs Macklin, Mrs Marriot, Mrs Pitt, Mrs C. S. Powell, Mrs Russell, Mrs Weeks, Mrs Worley.

Nym (Hen. V). *See* J. Burton, Costollo, A. Hallam, Jones (d. 1806), Stoppelaer.

Nym (MWW). *See* Allen, Buck, Gaudry, Hackett, Holtom, Nash, Stoppelaer, Watkins, A. Webb, J. Wilson.

Oatcake [i.e. a Watchman] (Much Ado). *See* Chippendale, Wewitzer.

Oberon (MND). *See* Miss Rogers. In Garrick's alteration (Fairies), *see* Reinhold. In Colman's alteration (Fairy T.), *see* Miss C. Morris, Miss Rogers.

Octavia (A & C). *See* Mrs Glen.

Octavius (A & C). *See* C. Fleetwood.

Octavius (J. Caesar). *See* Du-Bellamy, Farren, Gibson, Hull, Usher, Wroughton.

Officer (A & C). *See* Scrase.

Officer (Com. Err.). *See* Jones (d. 1806), J. Wignell.

Officer (Coriolanus). *See* Holtom, Phillimore, Trueman, A. Webb, Wentworth.

Officer (Hamlet). *See* R. Smith.

Officer (Lear). *See* W. Bates, J. Cooke, J. Fawcett Sr., Keen, McGeorge, J. Wignell.

Officer (Macbeth). *See* Banks, Evans.

Officer (Othello). *See* Banks, Collings, J. Cooke, Evans, Fisher, J. Johnson, Lings, Lyons, G. Waldron.

Officer (Rich. III). *See* Chippendale, Keen, J. Palmer the younger.

Officer (R & J). *See* Raftor.

Officer (Twelfth N.). *See* Carpenter, Evans, Follett, Marr, Nash, Parsons, A. Webb, Wrighten.

Officer, Roman (Coriolanus). *See* Caulfield, Phillimore.

Officer, Volscian (Coriolanus). *See* Alfred, Benson, Phillimore, A. Webb.

Oliver (AYLI). *See* Anderson, Benson, E. Burton, Caulfield, J. W. Clarke, W. Davies, Johnston [i.e. Bardin], L'Estrange, Packer, Perry, Scrase, Shatford, J. Smith, White, Whitfield, J. B. Williamson, Wroughton.

Olivia (Twelfth N.). *See* Mrs Abington, Mrs Baddeley, Mrs Clive, Mrs Crouch, Miss DeCamp, Miss E. Farren, Miss Harper, Mrs Hartley, Miss Haughton, Mrs Mattocks, Miss Phillips [i.e. later Mrs Crouch], Mrs W. Powell.

Ophelia (Hamlet). *See* Mrs Abington, Mrs Achmet, Mrs Baddeley, Mrs Baker (d. 1760), Mrs Bannister, Miss Biggs, Mrs Billington, Miss Brent, Mrs Chambers (d. 1792), Mrs Cibber, Mrs Clive, Mrs T. Davies, Mrs Esten, Miss Field [i.e. later Mrs Forster], Mrs Forster, Miss Harper [i.e. later Mrs Bannister], Mrs Hitchcock, Mrs Hopkins, Mrs Jewell, Mrs H. E. Johnston, Mrs Jordan, Mrs S. G. Kemble, Miss Kennedy, Mrs Lessingham, Miss Macklin, Mrs Mattocks, Mrs Morland, Mrs Mountain, Miss Poole, Miss Radley, Mrs T. Robinson, Miss Satchell [i.e. later Mrs S. G. Kemble], Mrs Siddons, Mrs T. Smith, Miss Taylor, Mrs R. Vincent Sr., Mrs R. Vincent Jr., Miss Wheeler.

Orlando (AYLI). *See* John Bannister, Barrymore, Brereton, T. Davis, Herrington, C. Holland the elder, Holman, C. Kemble, J. P. Kemble, W. T. Lewis, J. Palmer the elder, Reddish, Wm. Smith (d. 1819), Stokes, Whitfield.

Orsino (Twelfth N.). *See* Barrymore, Brereton, Dexter, Havard, Hull, Jefferson, W. T. Lewis, Packer, Sowdon, Staunton, Whitfield.

Osric (Hamlet). *See* John Bannister, Barrymore, W. Bates, Bernard, C. Berry, Bonnor, C. J. Booth, Cibber, Creswick, Cushing, Dodd, Dyer, J. Edwin Jr., Farley, Hamilton, T. King, Lamash, Lewes, T. Marshall, Meadows, J. Palmer the elder, J. Palmer the younger, R. Palmer, Wm. Palmer, Perry, Reily, S. T. Russell, Shuter, Wathen, Wewitzer, Woodward.

Oswald (Lear). In all alterations this character named Gentleman Usher. *See* Baddeley, W. Bates, Bernard, C. Berry, Blissett, Brunsdon, J. Burton, Castle, Cushing, Death, Dodd, Dyer, Farley, R. Griffith, Hamilton, Holtom, T. King,

Lacey, Lamash, Munden, R. Palmer, Perry, Quick, S. Russell, S. T. Russell, Shuter, Simmons, Vernon, Weston, Wewitzer, R. Yates.

Othello (Othello). *See* T. Baker the younger, S. Barry, Bridges (fl. 1761), Cambray [i.e. Fennell], Crawford, Daly, T. Davis, F. B. Delaval, Elliston, Farren, Fennell, Goodfellow, Grist, Hackett, Henry, Huddart, J. P. Kemble, S. G. Kemble, W. Lacy, Middleton, Moisey, Mossop, Murphy, Newton, Peile, Phillips (fl. 1769), Pope, W. Powell, Quin, Ross, Sheridan, T. Wilkinson, J. B. Williamson, Wroughton.

Outlaw (TGV). *See* Ackman, R. Bates, J. Burton, Fox, Helme, Jones (d. 1806), Marr, Phillimore, W. Stevens, Watkins, A. Webb.

Overdone, Mrs (Measure). *See* Mrs Booth, Mrs Bradshaw, Mrs Maddocks, Mrs White.

Oxford (Rich. III). *See* Ackman, W. Atkins, T. Baker the elder, J. Bates, W. Bates, Bencraft, Caulfield, Denman, W. Egan Sr., Evatt, Farley, J. Fawcett Sr., Helme, Redman, Sharpless, R. Smith, H. Sparks, W. Stevens, Thomas, E. (?) Thompson, Weller, Wheeler, J. Wignell.

Page (MWW). *See* E. Burton, J. W. Clarke, Fearon, Hull, Hurst, Macready, Packer, Ridout, Staunton, Winstone.

Page (R & J). *See* S. Besford, R. Cross Jr., Miss M. Menage, R. Palmer.

Page, Anne (MWW). *See* Mrs Baker (d. 1760), Mrs Burden, Mrs Chalmers, Miss Cokayne, Mrs Colles, Miss Collett, Miss Collins, Miss Field, Miss Fielding, Miss Haughton, Miss Hayward, Miss Heard, Mrs Hippisley, Mrs W. T. Lewis, Miss Mansel, Miss E. Miller, Miss Minors, Miss C. Morris, Mrs Platt, Miss Rowson, Mrs Stephens, Miss Vincent, Miss Ward, Miss Wewitzer, Miss Wheeler.

Page, Mrs (MWW). *See* Miss Ambrose, Mrs T. Baker, Mrs Barrington, Mrs Bates, Mrs Bennet, Mrs Bernard, Mrs Bulkley, Mrs Cowper, Mrs W. Davies, Mrs Ferguson, Miss Haughton, Mrs Hitchcock, Mrs Hopkins, Mrs Inchbald, Mrs Jefferies, Mrs Mattocks, Mrs W. Mills, Miss Pope, Mrs Stephens, Mrs Wells, Mrs Whitfield, Mrs S. M. Wilson.

Page, William (MWW). *See* J. Simson.

Painter (Timon). *See* W. Davies, W. Stevens.

Palador. In Hawkins' alteration of Cymbeline the name given to Guiderius, q.v.

Pandulph (John). *See* Bransby, Chambers,

Fearon, Gibson, Havard, Packer, J. Powell, L. Sparks, Tindal, Walker, Wheeler.

Panthino (TGV). *See* Haymes, Lyons, G. A. Stevens, J. Thompson.

Paris (R & J). *See* Anderson, Austin, Barrymore, J. Bates, Bloomfield, Bonnor, C. J. Booth, Claremont, W. Davies, Evatt, Everard, Farren, J. Fawcett Sr., Hurst, J. Jackson, Jefferson, Keen, C. Kemble, L. Kennedy, Klanert, Lacey, T. Lacy, Lamash, J. Lee, Macready, T. Marshall, Packer, R. Palmer [V. iii only], Wm. Palmer, Perry, Phillimore, Robson, Scrase, R. Smith, Sutton, J. Thompson, Toms, Usher, White, Whitfield, Wilson [fl. 1787–92], Wortley, Young.

Parolles (All's Well). *See* John Bannister, T. King, Woodward.

Patience (Hen. VIII). *See* Miss Allen, Mrs Atkins, Mrs T. Baker, Mrs Bland the younger, Miss Brown, Mrs Davies (fl. 1776), Miss Dayes, Mrs Farrell, Mrs James Jones, Miss Norris, Miss Twist (fl. 1777–9), Miss S. Twist, Mrs Vernon, Miss I. Young.

Paulina (Wint. T.). *See* Mrs Bates, Mrs Bennet, Mrs Bernard, Mrs Fawcett, Mrs P. Green, Mrs Hopkins, Mrs Hull, Mrs Hunter, Mrs Morton. In Colman's alteration (Sheep S.), *see* Mrs Poussin.

Pedro. In Garrick's alteration of Tam. Shrew (C & P) a new character; in III. ii. 152–69 he has Tranio's speeches. *See* Abbot, Clough, Evatt, Everard, Farley, Gaudry, J. Griffith, Griffiths, Grimaldi, Helme, Ledger, Phillimore, R. Smith, Stephens, Swords, Vowell, Wewitzer.

Pedro, Don (Much Ado). *See* J. W. Clarke, W. Davies, Havard, C. Holland the younger, J. Johnson, Mozeen, Packer, Peile, Whitfield, Wroughton.

Pembroke (John). *See* F. Aickin, Anderson, Blakes, C. J. Booth, Brereton, Caulfield, Cushing, Dancer, T. Davis, Dignum, Farren, J. Fawcett Sr., W. Gardner, Gibson, Hull, S. G. Kemble, Williams.

Percy, Lady (1 Hen. IV). *See* Mrs S. Barry, Mrs Bellamy, Mrs Bulkley, Miss Chapman, Mrs Colles, Mrs Cuyler, Mrs Dyer, Mrs Godwin, Mrs Hartley, Miss E. Hopkins, Mrs Inchbald, Mrs W. T. Lewis, Miss Logan, Mrs J. Palmer the elder, Mrs W. Powell, Miss Pritchard [i.e. later Mrs J. Palmer the elder], Mrs Stephens, Mrs R. Vincent Sr., Mrs Wells, Mrs West, Mrs Whitfield.

Perdita (Wint. T.). *See* Mrs Armstead, Mrs Bannister, Miss Bannister, Mrs Brereton

INDEX II

[i.e. later Mrs J. P. Kemble], Miss Brunton, Mrs Bulkley, Mrs Cibber, Mrs Crouch, Miss Dayes, Miss Heard, Mrs J. P. Kemble, Mrs S. G. Kemble, Miss Macklin, Mrs Mountain, Miss Pritchard, Mrs T. Robinson, Miss Satchell [i.e. later Mrs S. G. Kemble], Miss Slack, Miss Wallis, Mrs R. Yates the 2nd. In Morgan's alteration (F & P), see Mrs Bellamy, Miss Brent, Miss Brunton, Mrs Canning, Mrs Dancer, Mrs Elmy, Miss Murray, Miss Nossiter, Miss Rogers, Mrs T. Smith, Miss Younge. In Colman's alteration (Sheep S.), see Mrs Bannister, Mrs Colles.

Peter (R & J). See Bailey, J. Burton, W. Collins, Farley, R. Jerrold, Jones (d. 1806), Morgan, C. S. Powell, Quick, Rees, S. T. Russell, W. Stevens, Suett, H. Vaughan, Weller, Weston.

Peter (Tam. Shrew). In Garrick's alteration (C & P), see Abbot, Ackman, Alfred, Chippendale, Evans.

Peter, Friar (Measure). See Chambers, Chaplin, T. Davis, Packer, R. Smith, J. Thompson, Usher, Walker.

Peto (1 Hen. IV). See Abbot, Atkins (fl. 1751–60), Benson, Farley, Kenny, Lyons, Nash, Painter [II. iv only], Rees, Simpson, R. Smith, W. Stevens, Street, Watkins, Wild.

Peto (2 Hen. IV). See Atkins (fl. 1751–60), Wrighten.

Petruchio (Tam. Shrew). In Garrick's alteration (C & P), see John Bannister, Barrymore, Crawford, Dodd, Fearon, Harley, J. P. Kemble, T. King, Kniveton, W. T. Lewis, J. Palmer the younger, J. Powell, Shuter, West, Woodward.

Phebe (AYLI). See Miss Ambrose, Miss Arne, Miss Barnes, Mrs Bennet, Miss Burnet, Miss Cokayne, Miss Collins, Mrs W Davies, Miss Dayes, Miss De Camp, Miss Heard, Mrs Hippisley, Miss Kirby, Miss Madden, Miss C. Morris, Miss Mullart, Mrs W. Palmer, Miss Pearce, Mrs Platt, Miss L. Reynolds, Miss Simson (d. 1807), Mrs Smith (fl. 1769–76), Miss Stuart, Mrs Whitfield, Miss C. Wright.

Philario (Cymbeline). See W. Atkins, R. Bates, C. J. Booth, Chaplin, Fearon, L. Kennedy, P. Lewis, Maddocks, D. Morris, Parsons, Powel, Rock, Wm. Smith (fl. 1776), J. Thompson, R. Webb, R. Wright.

Philario. In Hawkins' alteration of Cymbeline the name given to Pisanio, q.v.

Philip (Tam. Shrew). In Garrick's alteration (C & P), see Marr.

Philip, King (John). See J. Aickin, Bensley, M. Clarke, T. Davies, W. Gardner, J. Lee, Ryan, Wroughton.

Philotus (Timon). See Jacobs.

Phryne. In Hull's Timon the name given to Phrynia, q.v.

Phrynia (Timon). In Hull's alteration this character named Phryne. See Miss Stuart.

Pietro. In Kemble's adaptation of Merchant the name given to the Servant in III. i. See A. Webb.

Pinch (Com. Err.). See C. J. Booth, Buck, Cubitt, Wewitzer, Wilde.

Pindarus (J. Caesar). See R. Palmer, Ricard, R. Smith, Vandermere.

Pisanio (Cymbeline). See Caulfield, Comerford, Harley, Hull, Hurst, Packer, Perry, Staunton, Whitfield, Wroughton. In Hawkins' alteration this character named Philario. See Ridout.

Pisanio. In Hawkins' alteration of Cymbeline the name given to Iachimo, q.v.

Pistol (2 Hen. IV). See Baddeley, Blakes, Cushing, Dyer, Hamilton, T. Kennedy, T. King. In the anonymous alteration (Humourists), see Cibber.

Pistol (Hen. V). See Dyer, Hamilton, Quick, Suett.

Pistol (MWW). See Ackman, Alfred, J. Booth, Cubitt, Cushing, Davenport, W. Egan Sr., Evatt, Gaudry, Helme, Holcroft, R. Palmer, R. Smith, W. Stevens, J. Thompson, D. Williamson.

Poet (Timon). See C. J. Booth, Jefferson.

Poins (1 Hen. IV). See J. Aickin, Chalmers, Claremont, Cushing, W. Davies, T. Kennedy, Lewes, Macready, Packer, R. Palmer, Perry, Robson, S. T. Russell, White, Whitfield.

Poins (2 Hen. IV). See Bonnor, Bransby, J. Jackson, Maguire, Packer, R. Palmer, Perry, White, Wroughton. In the anonymous alteration (Humourists), see R. Cross Jr.

Polixenes (Wint. T.). See F. Aickin, Bensley, Harley, Havard, Williams. In Morgan's alteration (F & P), see F. Aickin, Hull, Hurst, Murray, Ridout. In Colman's alteration (Sheep S.), see Bensley, W. Egan Sr.

Polonius (Hamlet). See Arthur, Baddeley, Blakes, W. Collins, Costollo, Dodd, Dowton, J. Edwin Sr., Love, Macklin, Massey (of CH), Moss, Munden, Parsons, Philips, Quick, Shuter, Stamper, Suett, Taswell, Vandermere, Weston, R. Wilson, Woodward.

Pompey (A & C). See Havard.

Popilius (J. Caesar). See Farrell, A. Hallam.

Porter (Hen. VIII). *See* Rees, Saunders, Weston.

Porter's Man (Hen. VIII). *See* Wilde.

Portia (J. Caesar). *See* Mrs Baddeley, Mrs Bellamy, Mrs Bland the elder [i.e. later Mrs J. Hamilton], Mrs Dyer, Mrs Elmy, Mrs J. Hamilton, Mrs Hartley, Mrs Woffington.

Portia (Merchant). *See* Mrs Abington, Mrs S. Barry, Miss Barsanti, Miss Betterton, Mrs Bland the elder [i.e. later Mrs J. Hamilton], Mrs Bulkley, Mrs Clive, Mrs Dancer [i.e. later Mrs S. Barry], Miss DeCamp, Miss E. Farren, Mrs D. Fisher, Mrs Gardner, Mrs Hamilton (fl. 1800), Mrs J. Hamilton, Miss E. Kemble, Mrs S. G. Kemble, Mrs Lessingham, Miss Macklin, Mrs Massey [IV. i only], Mrs Mills (fl. 1782) [IV. i only], Miss Murray, Mrs A. Pope the 1st, Mrs W. Powell, Miss Ranoe, Miss Ryder, Mrs Siddons, Mrs Sumbel, Miss Taylor, Miss Thompson [probably], Mrs R. Vincent Sr., Mrs H. Ward, Mrs Wells [i.e. later Mrs Sumbel], Mrs Woffington, Mrs R. Yates the 2nd, Miss Younge [i.e. later Mrs A. Pope the 1st].

Posthumus (Cymbeline). *See* John Bannister, Bensley, Brereton, Crawford, Croft, Garrick, Henderson, Henry, Holman, J. P. Kemble, W. T. Lewis, W. Powell, Reddish, Stokes, Warboys. In Hawkins' alteration this character named Leonatus. *See* Ross.

Priest (Hamlet). *See* Griffiths, Powel, Sharpless, Usher, A. Webb.

Priest (Twelfth N.). *See* J. Griffith, Griffiths, Maddocks.

Proculeius (A & C). *See* Austin.

Prospero (Tempest). *See* Beard, Bensley, Havard, C. Holland the elder, Hull, Mossop, Packer, J. Palmer the younger, J. Powell, Wright (fl. 1779).

Proteus (TGV). *See* C. Holland the elder, Wroughton.

Provost (Measure). *See* Blakes, Caulfield, W. Davies, W. Gardner, L'Estrange, Wrighten.

Publius (J. Caesar). *See* Roberts (fl. 1751), R. Smith, J. Wignell.

Puck (MND). *See* Master Cape. In Garrick's alteration (Fairies), *see* Master Moore. In Colman's alteration (Fairy T.), *see* Master Cape, J. Edwin Jr.

Pyramus (MND). In Lampe's alteration (P & T), *see* T. Lowe.

Queen (Cymbeline). *See* Mrs Bennet, Mrs Cuyler, Mrs Dibdin, Mrs Fawcett, Mrs P. Green, Mrs Hopkins, Mrs Hull, Mrs Jackson, Mrs R. Johnston, Mrs Platt, Mrs Reddish, Miss Sherry, Mrs Smith (fl. 1769–76), Mrs R. Vincent Sr., Mrs T. A. Ward.

Queen (Hamlet). *See* Mrs Barresford, Mrs Bates, Mrs Bernard, Mrs Bulkley [i.e. later Mrs Barresford], Miss Chapman, Mrs Du-Bellamy, Mrs Egerton, Mrs Elmy, Mrs Fawcett, Mrs Green (fl. 1781), Mrs Harlowe, Mrs Hopkins, Mrs Hull, Mrs Hunter, Mrs Inchbald, Mrs Jackson, Mrs Jefferies, Mrs L. Lewis, Mrs Melmoth, Miss Miller (fl. 1770–4), Miss Morris (fl. 1794–7), Mrs A. Pope the 1st, Mrs W. Powell, Mrs Pritchard, Miss Sherry, Mrs Siddons, Mrs Smith (fl. 1769–76), Mrs H. Ward, Mrs T. A. Ward, Mrs Webb, Mrs Wheatly, Mrs Woffington, Mrs R. Yates the 2nd.

Queen, Player (Hamlet). *See* Mrs Bambridge, Mrs Bennet, Mrs Booth, Mrs Colles, Mrs R. Cross, Mrs Edward, Mrs Ferguson, Mrs Hedges, Miss Helme, Mrs Hippisley, Mrs R. Johnston, Mrs Lefevre, Miss Leserve, Miss Pearce, Mrs Platt, Mrs Poussin, Mrs Reddish, Miss Stuart, Miss Tidswell, Mrs White, Mrs Wilks, Mrs R. Yates the 1st.

Quickly, Mrs (MWW). *See* Mrs Booth, Mrs Bradshaw, Mrs Copin, Mrs Davenport, Mrs Edwin, Mrs Hopkins, Mrs James, Mrs Love, Mrs Macklin, Mrs Pitt, Mrs Simson.

Quince (MND). *See* Love. In Colman's alteration (Fairy T.), *see* J. Edwin Sr., Love, Moody.

Ralph (Tam. Shrew). In Garrick's alteration (C & P), *see* Male, J. Welsh, Whitmell.

Ratcliff (Rich. III). *See* Abbot, Anderson, Bennet, J. Booth, Casey, Castle, Chaplin, Dancer, Daniel, Dignum, W. Egan Sr., Evatt, Farrell, Frost, Jacobs, S. Johnson, Kenny, Klanert, Lewes, Maddocks, Phillimore, Pindar, R. Smith, Strange, J. Thompson, Wortley, R. Wright.

Regan (Lear). *See* Miss Ambrose, Mrs W. Barry, Mrs Bernard, Miss Cleland, Mrs Colles, Mrs Cowper, Mrs R. Cross, Mrs Davenett, Mrs Du-Bellamy, Mrs Egerton, Mrs Elmy, Mrs Fawcett, Mrs Gardner, Mrs J. Hamilton, Miss Haughton, Mrs Hopkins, Mrs Inchbald, Mrs T. Jefferson the 2nd, Mrs Lee, Mrs Litchfield, Mrs McGeorge, Mrs Maddocks, Miss Pearce, Mrs Reddish, Mrs Ridout, Mrs Smith (fl. 1769–76), Mrs R. Vincent Sr., Mrs T. A. Ward, Mrs West, Mrs Whitfield.

INDEX II

Regan's Page (Lear). *See* Master Gell.
Richard III (Rich. III). *See* John Bannister, S. Barry, H. Brown, J. Brunton Sr., Calvert, M. Clarke, G. F. Cooke, Dodd, Garrick, F. Gentleman, Goodfellow, Harley, Harricks, Henderson, C. Holland the elder, C. Holland the younger, Holman, S. Jerrold, J. P. Kemble, T. King, Kirkpatrick, Larken, Lee (fl. 1799), J. Lee, Mrs Lefevre, Macklin, T. Morris, Mossop, Murphy, Murray, J. Palmer the younger [I. ii, II. ii, V only], Perry, Pindar, Quick, Reddish, Ricard, Ryan, Sheridan, Shuter, Wm. Smith (d. 1819), Stokes, Weston.
Richmond (Rich. III). *See* F. Aickin, J. Aickin, Anderson, Barrymore, Brereton, J. Brown, M. Clarke, Clinch, Crewe, T. Davis, Dyer, W. Gardner, Havard, W. (?) Holland, Holman, Jones (fl. 1780–1), C. Kemble, S. G. Kemble, W. Lacy, J. Lowe, J. Palmer the elder, J. Palmer the younger, J. Palmer Jr., Pope, Ricard, Ridout, Stratford, West, Williams, Wroughton.
Robin (MWW). *See* Miss Collett, J. Edwin Jr., Miss Hallam, Harris, Hitchcock, Kean, Miss Langrish, Miss Mullart, Pulley, Miss Rogers, J. Simson, Miss Valois.
Roderigo (Othello). *See* Baddeley, J. Barrett, Bennet, Bernard, T. Blanchard, Bland, Bonnor, Charles, Dodd, Dyer, L. Hallam Sr., Hamilton, T. King, Knight, Lamash, Lewes, Mansill, R. Palmer, S. Russell, S. T. Russell, Capt. Stevens, Talbot, Vandermere, H. Vaughan, Vernon, Weston, Woodward, R. Yates.
Rogero (Wint. T.). *See* Benson, W. Gardner, Walker, Williams.
Roman (Coriolanus). *See* Ackman.
Romeo (R & J). *See* John Bannister [V. i and iii only], S. Barry, Barrymore, Brereton, J. Brunton Jr., Cautherley, Dimond, Dyer, Elliston, C. Fleetwood, Garrick, Hill (fl. 1786), C. Holland the elder, Holman, H. E. Johnston, J. P. Kemble, W. T. Lewis, C. J. Macartney, Middleton, Pope, W. Powell, Reddish, Ross, Sheridan, Wm. Smith (d. 1819), Sterne, Toms, Trew, T. A. Ward, West, J. Wilson, Wroughton.
Rosalind (AYLI). *See* Mrs S. Barry [i.e. later Mrs Crawford], Mrs Belfille, Miss Biggs, Mrs Bland the elder [i.e. later Mrs J. Hamilton], Miss Blower, Mrs Bulkley, Mrs Crawford, Mrs Dancer [i.e. later (1) Mrs S. Barry, (2) Mrs Crawford], Mrs Esten, Miss Frodsham, Miss Glassington (fl. 1782), Mrs Goodall, Mrs J. Hamilton, Mrs Jordan, Miss E. Kemble, Mrs King, Miss Macklin, Mrs A. Pope the 1st, Mrs Pritchard, Miss L. Reynolds, Mrs T. Robinson, Mrs Siddons, Mrs R. Vincent Sr., Miss Wallis, Mrs Wells, Mrs Woffington, Mrs R. Yates the 2nd, Miss Younge [i.e. later Mrs A. Pope the 1st].
Rosencrantz (Hamlet). *See* F. Aickin, J. Aickin, J. Bates, Bennet, C. J. Booth, J. Burton, Castle, Caulfield, Chapman, J. W. Clarke, Cubitt, W. Davies, W. Egan Jr., Evatt, Fox, Haymes, S. Johnson, Klanert, Macready, Packer, R. Palmer, Parsons, Phillimore, Robson, Simson (d. 1758), R. Smith, Smyth, W. Stevens, Strange, Trueman, Usher, Wheeler, White, J. Wignell.
Ross (Macbeth). *See* F. Aickin, J. Aickin, Barrymore, Benson, Caulfield, T. Davies, W. Davies, C. Holland the younger, J. Lee, Macready, Ridout, Simson (d. 1758), Toms, Williames.
Ruffian (Tate's Lear). A character not in the original play. *See* Evans, Mathews, T. Powell, A. Webb.
Rugby (MWW). *See* Blakey, Carpenter, Cushing, Farley, Marr, C. Smith, R. Smith, Spencer, W. Stevens.

Sailor (Hamlet). *See* Fisher, Johnson (fl. 1800), Jones (d. 1806), Ledger, Simpson, R. Wright.
Sailor (Othello). *See* Alfred, Trueman.
Salarino (Merchant). *See* J. Aickin, Barrymore, Blakes, Campbell, Claremont, W. Davies, T. Davis, W. Egan Jr., Farren, J. Griffith, C. Holland the younger, Hurst, Iliff, Keen, C. Kemble, Lamash, L'Estrange, Phillimore, Ridout, J. Smith, R. Smith, Swords, J. Thompson, Trueman, Usher, White, D. Williamson.
Salisbury (Hen. V). *See* Bencraft, Cushing, W. Gardner.
Salisbury (John). *See* Anderson, Clinch, W. Davies, Du-Bellamy, Hull, Packer, J. Palmer the elder, Perry, Raymond, Ridout, Staunton, Whitfield.
Sampson (R & J). *See* W. Collins, Clough, J. Griffith, Hollingsworth, James, Lyons, Mendez.
Sands (Hen. VIII). *See* Baddeley, C. J. Booth, Clough, W. Collins, J. Fawcett Jr., Hollingsworth, T. Jackson, Jones (d. 1806), T. Kennedy, Kniveton, Massey (of Hay), Philips, Quick, Shuter, Vernon, Ware, F. G. Waldron, Wewitzer.
Scroop (Hen. V). *See* Chapman, J. Cooke, Fox, Lyons, Paddick, Perry, R. Smith, J. Wilson.

794

INDEX II

Seacoal [i.e. a Watchman] (Much Ado). *See* Denman, Hollingsworth, Ledger, H. Sparks, Wewitzer.

Sebastian (Tempest). *See* Chaplin, Farren, Hurst, Keen, Lamash, Mozeen, Robson, R. Wright.

Sebastian (Twelfth N.). *See* John Bannister, Bland, Cautherley, W. Davies, Farren, Havard, Lamash, Norris, J. Palmer the elder, R. Palmer, Trueman, Whitfield, Wroughton.

Seleucus (A & C). *See* E. Burton.

Sempronius (Timon). *See* W. Davies.

Senator (Coriolanus). *See* Redman, Walker, J. Wignell.

Senator (Othello). *See* W. Atkins, Davenport, Rees, Sharpless, Street, Summers.

Senator (Timon). *See* J. Aickin, Inchbald, Keen.

Sergeant (Hen. VIII). *See* J. Cooke, J. N. Lee, Lyons.

Sergeant (Macbeth). *See* F. Aickin, J. Aickin, Benson, Caulfield, W. Davies, Farley, Farren, Hurst, J. Jackson, Klanert, Trueman, Usher, Wrighten.

Servant (Coriolanus). *See* Philips, Taswell, Vernon.

Servant (2 Hen. IV). *See* Marr.

Servant (Lear). *See* Lings, Pearce.

Servant (Rich. III). *See* Abbot, Ackman.

Servant (Wint. T.). *See* Beard, J. Fawcett Sr., Fox, Moody. In Column's alteration (Sheep S.), *see* C. Bannister.

Servilius (Timon). *See* Wrighten.

Sexton (Much Ado). *See* Abbot, Clough, Hollingsworth, Ray, F. G. Waldron, A. Webb, Weston, Wrighten.

Seyton (Macbeth). *See* Ackman, W. Bates, Benson, Caulfield, W. Gardner, Griffiths, Paddick, Phillimore, Redman, J. Thompson, Trueman, Usher, R. Webb.

Shadow (2 Hen. IV). *See* J. Besford, J. Burton, Hacket, Parsons. In the anonymous alteration (Humourists), *see* Slim.

Shallow (2 Hen. IV). *See* Arthur, W. Collins, Parsons, Weston, R. Wilson, Woodward, R. Yates. In the anonymous alteration (Humourists), *see* Shuter.

Shallow (MWW). *See* Blissett, Clough, W. Collins, Costollo, Cushing, Fearon, Hartry, P. Lewis, Parsons, Powel, Taswell, F. G. Waldron, Weston, R. Wilson.

Shepherd (Wint. T.). *See* E. Barry, C. J. Booth, E. Burton, M. Clarke, Kniveton, Packer. In Colman's alteration (Sheep S), *see* Massey (of Hay).

Shepherdess (AYLI). *See* Mrs Hunt.

Sheriff (1 Hen. IV). *See* Abbot, Buck, T. Davis, W. Egan Sr., Fox, Griffiths, Haymes, Maddocks, G. A. Stevens, J. Wignell, J. Wilson.

Sheriff (John). *See* J. Cooke.

Shipmaster (Tempest). *See* Ackman, J. Burton, J. Thompson, Wrighten.

Shylock (Merchant). *See* Archer, Arthur, John Bannister, Comerford, G. F. Cooke, Digges, Elliston, Foote, W. Gardner, Harley, Henderson, S. Johnson, C. Kemble, J. P. Kemble, T. King, Machin, Macklin, Murray, J. Palmer the younger, Rees, T. Ryder, Sheridan, Shuter, Storer, F. G. Waldron, Wilkinson (fl. 1792), J. B. Williamson, R. Yates.

Sicinius (Coriolanus). *See* Barrymore, Bennet, Benson, Bransby, Casey.

Silence (2 Hen. IV). *See* Blakes, Costollo, Dibdin, Hartry, P. Lewis, Parsons, Quick, Rooker, Stoppelaer. In the anonymous alteration (Humourists), *see* Stoppelaer.

Silvia (TGV). *See* Miss Bride, Mrs J. P. Kemble, Mrs S. G. Kemble.

Silvius (AYLI). *See* Austin, J. Bates, Bennet, Benson, Bland, Chalmers, Dancer, Evatt, Helme, Jefferson, Marriot, Mozeen, R. Palmer, Quick, Robson, R. Smith, Strange, Trueman, Wheeler, Whitfield.

Simple (MWW). *See* W. Bates, Bencraft, Blissett, J. Burton, Costollo, Mrs Evans, Holtom, Jacobs, Joules, T. Kennedy, Milburne, Morgan, Miss Mullart [i.e. later Mrs Evans], Wingfield Palmer, Pulley, Rock, Simmons, H. Vaughan, Wingfield [i.e. Wingfield Palmer], Master Younger.

Siward (Macbeth). *See* J. Aickin, Anderson, Bransby, Cubitt, Davenport, T. Davis, J. Fawcett Sr., W. Gardner, Helme, Hurst, Moody, Packer, Robson, R. Smith, H. Sparks, White, Winstone.

Siward, Young (Macbeth). *See* Bransby, Marr, J. Palmer the elder, Ricard.

Slender (MWW). *See* R. Bates, W. Bates, Bennet, Cautherley, Cubitt, Dodd, T. Kennedy, Knight, Obrien, R. Palmer, Quick, S. T. Russell, W. Stevens, Suett, H. Vaughan, T. A. Ward, Woodward.

Sly, Christopher (Tam. Shrew). In Bullock's alteration of the Induction (Cobler) this character named Toby Guzzle. *See* Shuter.

Snout (MND). *See* Ackman. In Colman's alteration (Fairy T.), *see* Ackman, Castle, Kenny.

Snug (MND). *See* Clough. In Colman's alteration (Fairy T.), *see* C. Bannister, Clough, Strange.

Solanio (Merchant). *See* W. Bates, C. J. Booth, Bransby, Caulfield, Claremont,

795

INDEX II

T. Davis [IV. i only], W. Egan Sr., Evatt, Farren, J. Fawcett Sr., W. Gardner, Gibson, Haymes, S. Johnson, Klanert, Lawrance, Owenson, Scrase, Toms, Trueman, Vowell, Whitfield.

Soldier (All's Well). *See* Phillimore.

Soldier (Timon). *See* Baddeley.

Soldier, French (Hen. V). *See* Holtom, Joules, Wewitzer.

Soldier [Interpreter] (All's Well). *See* Baddeley (?), Bennet, Blakes, R. Palmer, J. Thompson.

Soothsayer (A & C). *See* E. Burton.

Soothsayer (J. Caesar). *See* J. Fawcett Sr., Marten, Redman.

Speed (TGV). *See* John Bannister, J. Edwin Sr., T. King.

Stanley (Rich. III). *See* J. Aickin, Anderson, Bailey, Bransby, Chaplin, Davenport, Du-Bellamy, Fearon, W. Gardner, Hull, T. Jackson, J. Johnson, Lear, P. Lewis, E. (?) Lloyd, Mozeen, Packer, Painter, Powel, Redman, Rivers, H. Sparks, Stannard, Staunton, J. Thompson, Webber, J. Wilson, Winstone, Wrighten.

Starveling (MND). *See* Parsons. In Colman's alteration (Fairy T.), *see* Castle, Parsons, Peirce.

Stephano (Merchant). *See* Evans, Fisher.

Stephano (Tempest). *See* John Bannister, Benson, T. King, Love, Moody, Rooker, G. A. Stevens, Suett, H. Vaughan, Vernon, R. Wilson, Woodward.

Steward (All's Well). *See* E. Burton, Castle, Fearon, Packer, Simson (d. 1758), J. Wignell.

Suffolk (Hen. VIII). *See* Blakes, C. J. Booth, Caulfield, Fearon, W. Gardner, Kenny, Lamash, T. Marshall, Owenson, Usher, Waddy, Williams.

Surrey (Hen. VIII). *See* J. Aickin, Barrymore, T. Davies, W. Davies, T. Davis, Dyer, Farren, Garland, Knight, Lacey, J. Lee, Macready, Simson (d. 1758), T. A. Ward, Whitfield.

Surveyor (Hen. VIII). *See* Benson, Packer, Simson (d. 1758), J. Thompson, A. Webb.

Tailor (Tam. Shrew). In Garrick's alteration (C & P), *see* T. Baker the elder, J. Barrett, Bernard, J. Burton, Hollingsworth, Jones (d. 1806), Milburne, Morgan, Munden, Quick, S. Russell, Simmons, Suett, Vandermere, H. Vaughan, G. Waldron, Weller, Wewitzer.

Tearsheet, Doll (2 Hen. IV). *See* Mrs W. Davies, Mrs Dunstall, Mrs Gardner, Mrs H. Green, Miss Haughton, Mrs Lee, Miss Minors, Mrs Platt, Mrs Stephens. In the anonymous alteration (Humourists), *see* Mrs Bradshaw.

Theseus (MND). *See* Bransby. In Garrick's alteration (Fairies), *see* Beard.

Thisbe (MND). In Lampe's alteration (P & T), *see* Mrs Lampe.

Thomas, Friar (Measure) *See* C. J. Booth, Maddocks, Redman.

Thurio (TGV). *See* Chalmers, Suett, Vernon.

Thyreus (A & C). *See* C. Holland the elder, Moody.

Time (Wint. T.). *See* Hull.

Timon (Timon). *See* S. Barry, Holman.

Titania (MND). *See* Miss Ford. In Garrick's alteration (Faires), *see* Miss I. Young. In Colman's alteration (Fairy T.), *see* Miss M. Farren, Miss Ford.

Titus (Sheridan's Coriolanus). A character not in the original play. *See* Cushing, Du-Bellamy, White.

Titus (Timon). *See* J. Burton.

Toby, Sir (Twelfth N.). *See* E. Berry, C. J. Booth, Dunstall, Hollingsworth, Love, Moody, J. Palmer the younger, R. Wilson.

Touchstone (AYLI). *See* John Bannister, W. Collins, Comerford, Dodd, J. Edwin Sr., T. King, Kipling, Lewes, Love, J. Palmer the younger, Quick, Shuter, G. A. Stevens, Suett, Woodward, R. Yates.

Tourville. In Kemble's alteration of All's Well the name given to the Astringer, q.v.

Town Clerk (Much Ado). A character not in the original play; in IV. ii he has most of Dogberry's speeches. *See* Baddeley, J. Edwin Sr., James, Munden, Powel, Quick, R. Vaughan, W. Vaughan, Wewitzer.

Traveller (1 Hen. IV). *See* Blurton, Coombs, Fisher, Lyons, Wilde.

Trebonius (J. Caesar). *See* Anderson, Chaplin, Perry, Wheeler.

Tressel (Cibber's Rich. III). A character not in the original play. *See* Ackman, Austin, John Bannister, Benson, Betterton, Birch, Blakes, Bland, Burghall, Casey, Cautherley, G. F. Cooke, J. C. Cross, Cushing, Dancer, W. Davies, Dyer, W. Egan Jr., Farren, Gardner (fl. 1780), C. Holland the elder, Hurst, Keen, C. Kemble, L. Kennedy, Macready, Mansel, Mills (fl. 1778), Owenson, Perry, Reily, Seymour, Surmont, Toms, T. A. Ward, Wheatley, Wheeler, White, Whitfield, Wroughton, Young.

Trinculo (Tempest). *See* Baddeley, Beard, Hollingsworth, Jefferson, Parsons, Quick, Suett, R. Yates.

796

INDEX II

Tubal (Merchant). *See* R. Bates, Chapman, Costollo, Cushing, Errington, Maddocks, Massey (of Hay), Messink, W. Stevens, Stoppelaer, Taswell, J. Thompson, F. G. Waldron.

Tybalt (R & J). *See* Ackman, F. Aickin, J. Aickin, C. Bannister, Bennet, Betterton, Blakes, C. J. Booth, Caulfield, Claremont, G. F. Cooke, Cubitt, Cushing, Dyer, Farren, Gardner (fl. 1780), W. Gardner, Grist, Haymes, J. Lee, L'Estrange, Lewes, McGeorge, Macready, Mahon, Owenson, R. Palmer, Simpson, Whitfield, Williams.

Tyrrel (Rich. III). *See* Abbot, Adams, R. Bates, E. Burton, Dancer, Davenport, Dunstall, Edwards, W. Gardner, Jones (d. 1806), Kenny, Rock, W. Vaughan, G. Waldron, A. Webb, Wrighten.

Ursula (Much Ado). *See* Miss Barnes, Mrs Colles, Miss Heard, Mrs Hippisley, Mrs Millidge, Miss Minors, Mrs Platt, Mrs Poussin, Miss Wentworth, Mrs Whitfield, Mrs Williams.

Valentine (Twelfth N.). *See* Castle, Caulfield, Gibbon, Mozeen, Norris, Surmont, J. Thompson, Wheeler, J. Wilson.

Valentine (TGV). *See* Barrymore, Obrien, Whitfield.

Valeria (Coriolanus). *See* Mrs Bennet, Miss Heard, Mrs T. A. Ward.

Varro's Servant (Timon). In Cumberland's alteration this character named Varro. *See* Master Cape.

Ventidius (Timon). *See* Wm. Palmer.

Ventoso (Garrick's Tempest). A character not in the original play (introduced by Garrick from Dryden and Davenant's version). *See* Abington.

Verges (Much Ado). *See* Banks, J. Barrett, J. Burton, Carpenter, Cushing, Dowton, J. Fawcett Jr., Hartry, Jones (d. 1806), T. Kennedy, J. Mills, Parsons, Philips, Shuter, Simmons, Vernon, F. G. Waldron, Wewitzer, Wrighten.

Vernon (1 Hen. IV). *See* Barrymore, Blakes, Bland, W. Davies, T. Davis, Farren, Gibson, Hull, Hurst, J. Jackson, J. Lee, Middleton, J. Palmer Jr., R. Palmer, Usher, Waddy, Whitfield, Williames.

Veturia. In Sheridan's alteration of Coriolanus the name given to Volumnia, q.v.

Viola (Twelfth N.). *See* Mrs S. Barry, Mrs Bulkley, Mrs Cowper, Mrs T. Davies, Mrs Goodall, Mrs Jordan, Mrs T. Kennedy, Miss Plym, Mrs Pritchard, Mrs H. H. Robinson, Mrs T. Robinson, Mrs R. Yates the 2nd, Miss Younge.

Virgilia (Coriolanus). *See* Mrs T. Davies, Mrs Farmer [i.e. later Mrs W. Powell], Mrs W. Powell. In Sheridan's alteration this character named Volumnia. *See* Mrs Bellamy, Miss Condill, Miss Macklin, Mrs R. Vincent Sr.

Volumnia (Coriolanus). *See* Mrs Pritchard, Mrs Siddons. In Sheridan's alteration this character named Veturia. *See* Mrs Bellamy, Mrs J. Hamilton, Mrs Woffington.

Volumnia. In Sheridan's alteration of Coriolanus the name given to Virgilia, q.v.

Volumnius (J. Caesar). *See* Weller.

Volusius (Sheridan's Coriolanus). A character not in the original play; also retained in Kemble's alteration. *See* Benson, Caulfield, W. Gardner, L. Sparks, Walker, Williams.

Wales, Prince of (1 Hen. IV). *See* John Bannister, Brereton, Cautherley, Frodsham, C. Kemble, W. T. Lewis, Mahon, Obrien, J. Palmer the elder, J. Palmer the younger, J. Palmer Jr., Ross, Ryan, J. B. Williamson, Wroughton.

Wales, Prince of (2 Hen. IV). *See* F. Aickin, Cautherley, C. Holland the elder, Mrs Lessingham, J. Palmer the elder, J. Palmer the younger, Ross, Ryan, Wroughton. In the anonymous alteration (Humourists), *see* R. Cross Sr.

Wall (MND). In Lampe's alteration (P & T), *see* T. Baker the elder.

Walter (Tam. Shrew). In Garrick's alteration (C & P), *see* Gregson, C. Ryder, Trueman.

Wart (2 Hen. IV). In the anonymous alteration (Humourists), *see* A. Johnston.

Warwick (2 Hen. IV). *See* W. Gardner.

Watch (R & J). *See* A. Webb.

Watchman [*see also* Oatcake, Seacoal] (Much Ado). *See* J. Burton, Holcroft.

Westmorland (1 Hen. IV). *See* Ackman, Claremont, J. W. Clarke, Cushing, T. Davis, W. Egan Sr., J. Fawcett Sr., W. Gardner, Griffiths, Holtom, Ricard, J. Thompson, Townsend, Trueman, Usher, Wrighten.

Westmorland (2 Hen. IV). *See* E. Burton, T. Davis [IV. iv and V. ii only], Farren, Fearon, Hull, Storer, Usher.

Westmorland (Hen. V). *See* Buck, P. Lewis, D. Morris, R. Palmer, Ricard, Sedgwick, R. Smith, White.

Widow (All's Well). *See* Mrs Barrington,

797

Mrs Booth, Mrs R. Cross, Miss Pearce, Mrs Poussin, Mrs Simson (?), Mrs Stephens.

William (AYLI). *See* J. Barrett, W. Bates, Benson, J. Burton, Chippendale, W. Collins, Costollo, Farley, Hamilton, Messink, C. S. Powell, Quick, S. Russell, H. Vaughan, Wewitzer.

Williams (Hen. V). *See* Barrington, Benson, C. J. Booth, Bransby, Buck, Dunstall, D. Morris, Whitfield.

Witch (Macbeth). *See* J. Aickin, Baddeley, Bencraft, Bernard, Blakes, T. Blanchard, W. Blanchard, C. J. Booth, J. Brown, Brunsdon, E. Burton, J. Burton, W. Collins, Costollo, Cubitt, Cushing, Dodd, Dowton, Dunstall, J. Edwin Sr., Emery, J. Fawcett Jr., J. Gardner, Granger, Jones (d. 1806), T. Kennedy, H. Lee, P. Lewis, Love, Moody, Morgan, Munden, R. Palmer, Parsons, Mrs Pitt, Quick, Rees, Reeve, Saunders, Shuter, Simmons, W. Stevens, Suett, Townsend, W. Vaughan, R. Webb, Wewitzer, R. Yates.

Wolsey (Hen. VIII). *See* Bensley, Digges, Havard, Henderson, J. P. Kemble, J. Lee, Mossop, J. Palmer the younger [III. i only], Pope, Ryan, Stokes.

Worcester (1 Hen. IV). *See* J. Aickin, Bransby, Comerford, W. Davies, Fearon, W. Gardner, Hull, Powel, Ridout.

Yeoman (Rich. III). *See* Ledger.

York, Archbishop of (2 Hen. IV). *See* Bridgwater, M. Clarke, Havard, Jefferson, Packer.

York, Duchess of (Rich. III). *See* Mrs Bambridge, Mrs Barnard, Mrs Barrington, Mrs Bennet, Mrs Booth, Mrs Davenett, Mrs Dyer, Mrs Elmy, Mrs Ferguson, Mrs Fowler, Mrs P. Green, Mrs Hedges, Mrs Hopkins, Mrs Hull, Mrs R. Johnston, Mrs Leicester, Miss Leserve, Mrs McGeorge, Mrs Mitteer, Mrs Newby, Mrs Painter, Mrs Pitt, Mrs Platt, Mrs Poussin, Mrs C. S. Powell, Mrs Ross, Miss Tidswell, Mrs R. Vincent Sr., Mrs T. A. Ward, Mrs Weeks, Mrs White.

York, Duke of (Rich. III). *See* Miss Barnard, W. Bates, Miss Besford, S. Besford, Master Cape, Cautherley, W. S. Chatterley, Miss Cokayne, Miss Collett, J. Edwin Jr., Miss S. Francis, Miss Gaudry, Miss Gilbert, Miss Hallam, Miss Heard, Miss Heyborn, Miss P. Hopkins, Miss Jackson, R. Jerrold, Jones (d. 1806), Miss Kelly, Master Kenny, Master Langrish, Miss Langrish, Miss M. Menage, Miss Mullart, Master Nelson, Miss Painter, Pulley, Miss Rogers, Miss Rose, S. T. Russell, Simmons, Miss Simson (d. 1807), J. Simson, Master Standen, Miss Standen, Miss Valois, Miss Yates.

PRINTED IN
GREAT BRITAIN
AT THE
UNIVERSITY PRESS
OXFORD
BY
CHARLES BATEY
PRINTER
TO THE
UNIVERSITY